Brief Contents

Contents

PART THREE Sensory and Motor Systems

Preface

Welcome to the Tenth Edition of *Biopsychology*! The Tenth Edition of *Biopsychology* is a clear, engaging introduction to current biopsychological theory and research. It is intended for use as a primary text in one- or two-semester courses in biopsychology—variously titled Biopsychology, Physiological Psychology, Brain and Behavior, Psychobiology, Behavioral Neuroscience, or Behavioral Neurobiology.

The defining feature of *Biopsychology* is its unique combination of biopsychological science and personal, reader-oriented discourse. It is a text that is "untextlike." Instead of presenting the concepts of biopsychology in the usual textbook fashion, it addresses students directly and interweaves the fundamentals of the field with clinical case studies, social issues, personal implications, useful metaphors, and memorable anecdotes.

Key Features Maintained in the Tenth Edition

The following are features that have characterized recent editions of *Biopsychology* and have been maintained or expanded in this edition.

EMPHASIS ON BROAD THEMES The emphasis of *Biopsychology* is "the big picture." Four broad themes are highlighted throughout the text by distinctive tabs: (1) thinking creatively, (2) clinical implications, (3) evolutionary perspective, and (4) neuroplasticity. A Themes Revisited section at the end of each chapter briefly summarizes how each theme was developed in that chapter. The four major themes provide excellent topics for essay assignments and exam questions.

EFFECTIVE USE OF CASE STUDIES *Biopsychology* features many carefully selected case studies, which are highlighted in the text. These provocative cases stimulate interest, promote retention of the materials, and allow students to learn how biopsychological principles apply to the diagnosis and treatment of brain disorders.

REMARKABLE ILLUSTRATIONS The illustrations in *Biopsychology* are special. Each one was conceptualized and meticulously designed to clarify and reinforce the text by uniquely qualified scientists. John Pinel and his artist/designer wife, Maggie Edwards, created many of the original illustrations from previous editions.

FOCUS ON BEHAVIOR In some biopsychological textbooks, the coverage of neurophysiology, neurochemistry, and neuroanatomy subverts the coverage of behavioral research. *Biopsychology* gives top billing to behavior: It stresses that neuroscience is a team effort and that the unique contribution made by biopsychologists to this effort is their behavioral expertise.

EMPHASIS ON THE SCIENTIFIC METHOD *Biopsychology* emphasizes the scientific method. It portrays the scientific method as a means of answering questions that is as applicable in daily life as in the laboratory. And *Biopsychology* emphasizes that being a scientist is fun.

DISCUSSION OF PERSONAL AND SOCIAL IMPLICATIONS Several chapters of *Biopsychology*—particularly those on eating, sleeping, sex, and drug addiction—carry strong personal and social messages. In these chapters, students are encouraged to consider the relevance of biopsychological research to their lives outside the classroom.

ENGAGING, INSPIRING VOICE Arguably the strongest pedagogical feature of *Biopsychology* is its personal tone. In previous editions, Pinel had addressed students directly and talked to them with warmth, enthusiasm, and good humor about recent advances in biopsychological science. This edition has not changed in this respect, except the addition of Barnes as coauthor has added another friendly voice as well as making possible some new approaches to teaching.

Additions to the Tenth Edition

Three new features are available in the Tenth Edition of *Biopsychology*.

NEW! INTEGRATED WRITING OPPORTUNITIES Questions for review and reflection are integrated into the text, giving students an opportunity to stop and think about the content presented and to respond in a written format. There are writing prompts tied to the major themes of this book throughout each chapter for individual student response.

NEW! BUILT-IN END-OF-MODULE AND END-OF-CHAPTER QUIZZES This edition includes both end-of-module and end-of-chapter formative review questions and the Test Bank.

NEW! EXPANDED AND COMPREHENSIVE LEARNING OBJECTIVES This edition has expanded the use of learning objectives, written by Pinel and Barnes. Additional learning objectives were added in as a means of better specifying to students what the major points are in each portion of the text.

New, Expanded, or Updated Coverage in the Tenth Edition

Biopsychology remains one of the most rapidly progressing scientific fields. Like previous editions, the Tenth Edition of *Biopsychology* has meticulously incorporated recent developments in the field—it contains more than 1,265 citations of articles or books that did not appear in the preceding edition. These recent developments have dictated changes to many parts of the text. The following list presents some of the content changes to this edition, organized by chapter.

CHAPTER 1: BIOPSYCHOLOGY AS A NEUROSCIENCE

- Nobel Prize–winning work on grid cells and place cells by John O'Keefe, May-Britt Moser, and Edvard Moser
- Coverage of the topic of translational research
- 21 new citations

CHAPTER 2: EVOLUTION, GENETICS, AND EXPERIENCE

- Updated coverage of the emergence of humankind
- Discussion of the evidence of mating between *Homo sapiens* and *Homo neanderthalensis*
- Coverage of the use of ancient DNA
- Summary of the human proteome project
- Expanded coverage of the topic of epigenetics, including coverage of the topic of transgenerational epigenetics
- 90 new citations

CHAPTER 3: ANATOMY OF THE NERVOUS SYSTEM

- Updated coverage of cerebrospinal fluid production and absorption
- Summary of the issues associated with the classification of neurons
- Updated coverage of glial cells
- 38 new citations

CHAPTER 4: NEURAL CONDUCTION AND SYNAPTIC TRANSMISSION

- 36 new citations

CHAPTER 5: THE RESEARCH METHODS OF BIOPSYCHOLOGY

- Updated coverage of positron emission tomography (PET)

- Coverage of combined use of PET and functional magnetic resonance imaging (fMRI)
- Coverage of the use of fMRI to communicate with patients who are in a "vegetative state" (patients who appear to lack consciousness)
- Introduction of the Human Connectome Project and related projects in other species
- Expanded coverage of transcranial stimulation techniques, including the addition of transcranial direct current stimulation (tDCS)
- Better explanation of how the skin conductance response (SCR) works
- Coverage of the new field of optogenetics
- 38 new citations

CHAPTER 6: THE VISUAL SYSTEM

- Explanation of the number of different sorts of retinal ganglion cells
- Coverage of retinal implants
- Expanded coverage of the dorsal versus ventral streams
- Better definition of prosopagnosia that distinguishes between developmental prosopagnosia versus acquired prosopagnosia
- Expanded coverage of prosopagnosia
- 46 new citations

CHAPTER 7: MECHANISMS OF PERCEPTION: HEARING, TOUCH, SMELL, TASTE, AND ATTENTION

- Updated coverage of the study of the auditory cortex
- Statement of the role of skin cells in somatosensation
- Two new key terms: *merkel's disks, ruffini endings*
- Improved definition of anosagnosia
- Updated coverage of the rubber-hand illusion
- Updated coverage of the cortical representation of pain
- Updated coverage of the gustatory system
- 79 new citations

CHAPTER 8: THE SENSORIMOTOR SYSTEM

- Recent research on the posterior parietal association cortex
- Updated coverage of contralateral neglect
- Updated discussion of the current view of the function of the primary motor cortex
- Coverage of the control of robotic limbs by patients with electrode arrays implanted in their primary motor cortex

- Coverage of the idea of an *action map* in the primary motor cortex
- 59 new citations

CHAPTER 9: DEVELOPMENT OF THE NERVOUS SYSTEM

- New figure on stem cells
- Updated coverage of neural tube defects
- Updated coverage of the development of the neural crest
- Updated coverage of the topographic gradient hypothesis
- Expanded and updated coverage of adult neurogenesis
- Substantial changes to the coverage of autism spectrum disorders—to account for changes in the diagnostic criteria in the DSM-5
- Updated coverage of savantism
- Updated coverage of the genetic basis of autism spectrum disorders
- Coverage of the potential role of glial cells in the etiology of autism spectrum disorders
- Updated coverage of Williams syndrome, including expanded coverage of its neural correlates and its genetic basis
- Coverage of the role of microglia in synapse rearrangement
- 106 new citations

CHAPTER 10: BRAIN DAMAGE AND NEUROPLASTICITY

- Updated coverage of drug treatments for acute stroke
- Coverage of chronic traumatic encephalopathy
- New case study: Junior Seau, Football Player
- Introduction of the term *focal seizures*
- Coverage of transcranial magnetic stimulation and the ketogenic diet as treatments for epilepsy
- Updated coverage of Parkinson's disease
- Role of protein aggregation in Huntington's disease
- Updated coverage of the pathology, risk factors, and drug treatments associated with multiple sclerosis
- Updated coverage of the genetics of Alzheimer's disease
- Coverage of the role of apoliprotein E (APOE) in Alzheimer's disease
- Improved discussion of the amyloid hypothesis of Alzheimer's disease

- Further coverage of treatments for Alzheimer's disease (e.g., tissue plasminogen activator)
- Discussion of how the study of Down syndrome has informed our understanding of the neural mechanisms of Alzheimer's disease
- Coverage of the role of the tau protein in the neurofibrillary tangles of Alzheimer's disease
- Discussion of the role of glial scarring in inhibiting axonal regrowth following axonal damage
- 123 new citations

CHAPTER 11: LEARNING, MEMORY, AND AMNESIA

- Updated coverage of H.M.
- Updated coverage of reconsolidation
- Updated coverage of place cells and grid cells, and their relationship
- Introduction of the concept of "time cells" in the hippocampus
- Coverage of roles of the hippocampus in nonspatial forms of memory
- Updated coverage of Jennifer Aniston neurons (concept cells)
- New section on "engram cells"
- Updated coverage of the relationship between LTP and learning and memory
- Introduction of new key term: *metaplasticity*
- 81 new citations

CHAPTER 12: HUNGER, EATING, AND HEALTH

- Introduction of research on the gut microbiome
- New section on modern research on the role of hypothalamic nuclei in hunger and satiety
- Updated coverage of the obesity epidemic
- New section on the role of alterations to the gut microbiome in the obesity epidemic
- Updated coverage of treatments for obesity
- 78 new citations

CHAPTER 13: HORMONES AND SEX

- Updated coverage of the X- and Y-chromosomes
- Updated coverage of the role of progesterone in men
- Introduction of new key terms: *intersexed person, gay, asexual*
- Updated coverage of the role of alpha fetoprotein in humans
- Updated coverage of the development of sex differences in the behavior of humans

- Updated coverage of female sexual behavior and gonadal hormones
- New section on gender identity
- 42 new citations

CHAPTER 14: SLEEP, DREAMING, AND CIRCADIAN RHYTHMS

- Updated the sleep stages to be consistent with the guidelines set forth by the American Academy of Sleep Medicine
- New table to summarize the various sleep stages and their naming
- Updated coverage of recuperation theories of sleep
- Updated coverage of experimental studies of sleep deprivation in humans
- Improved figure of the carousel apparatus (used for sleep deprivation studies in rodents)
- Updated coverage of the role of sleep in memory
- Updated coverage of drugs that affect sleep
- Updated coverage of narcolepsy
- Introduction of new key term: *REM-sleep-behavior disorder*
- Updated coverage of the effects of shorter sleep times on health
- 85 new citations

CHAPTER 15: DRUG USE, DRUG ADDICTION, AND THE BRAIN'S REWARD CIRCUITS

- Increased coverage of marijuana
- Introduction of new key term: drug-addicted individual
- Updated coverage of the effects of marijuana on brain function
- Updated coverage of treatments for heroin addiction
- 81 new citations

CHAPTER 16: LATERALIZATION, LANGUAGE, AND THE SPLIT BRAIN

- Updated coverage of what abilities or cognitive processes are lateralized
- Updated coverage of brain differences between sinestrals and dextrals
- Updated coverage of anatomical asymmetries in the brain
- Updated coverage of the evolution of cerebral lateralization
- Improved coverage of the motor theory of speech perception

- Expanded coverage of developmental dyslexia
- 59 new citations

CHAPTER 17: BIOPSYCHOLOGY OF EMOTION, STRESS, AND HEALTH

- Updated coverage of the James-Lange and Cannon-Bard theories
- Updated coverage of the guilty knowledge technique
- Expanded coverage of current perspectives on facial expressions
- Updated coverage of aggression and testosterone
- Updated coverage of the role of the medial prefrontal lobes in human emotion
- Expanded coverage of psychoneuroimmuonology
- 76 new citations

CHAPTER 18: BIOPSYCHOLOGY OF PSYCHIATRIC DISORDERS

- Introduction of the category label *schizophrenia spectrum disorders* to reflect the associated change in the DSM-5
- Expanded coverage of causal factors in schizophrenia
- Introduction of new key terms: *antipsychotic drug typical antipsychotics*
- Updated coverage of the dopamine theory of schizophrenia
- Expanded coverage of current research on and treatments for schizophrenia
- Updated coverage of genetics of schizophrenia
- Updated coverage of brain differences associated with schizophrenia
- New and separate modules for depressive disorders and bipolar disorders to reflect the new categories in the DSM-5
- Expanded coverage of depressive disorders
- Expanded coverage of causal factors in major depressive disorder
- Introduction of new key term *peripartum depression*
- Expanded coverage of antidepressant drugs
- Expanded coverage of the brain differences associated with depressive disorders
- Expanded coverage of theories of depression
- New section on treatment of depression with brain stimulation
- Expanded coverage of bipolar disorders
- Introduction of two new key terms *bipolar disorder type II* and *bipolar disorder type I*

- New expanded three-part version of the case of S.B.
- Expanded coverage of causal factors in bipolar disorders
- Expanded coverage of mood stabilizers
- Expanded coverage of brain differences associated with bipolar disorder
- Expanded coverage of theories of bipolar disorders
- Updated module on anxiety disorders to reflect the changes made to the category in the DSM-5
- Updated section on the use of antidepressant drugs for the treatment of anxiety disorders
- Update of name of Tourette syndrome to Tourette's disorder to reflect the name change in the DSM-5
- Updated coverage of Tourette's disorder
- Expanded coverage of the neural bases and treatment of Tourette's disorder
- 127 new citations

Pedagogical Learning Aids

Biopsychology has several features expressly designed to help students learn and remember the material:

- **Scan Your Brain** study exercises appear within chapters at key transition points, where students can benefit most from pausing to consolidate material before continuing.
- **Check It Out** demonstrations apply biopsychological phenomena and concepts for students to experience themselves.
- **Themes Revisited** section at the end of each chapter summarizes the ways in which the book's four major themes relate to that chapter's subject matter.
- **Key Terms** appear in **boldface**, and other important terms of lesser significance appear in *italics*.
- **Appendixes** serve as convenient sources of additional information for students who want to expand their knowledge of selected biopsychology topics.

Ancillary Materials Available with *Biopsychology*

FOR INSTRUCTORS Pearson Education is pleased to offer the following supplements to qualified adopters.

Test Bank The test bank for the Tenth Edition of *Biopsychology* comprises more than 2,000 multiple-choice questions, including questions about accompanying brain images. The difficulty of each item is rated—easy (1), moderate (2), or difficult (3)—to assist instructors with test construction. Each item is also labeled with a topic and a page reference so that instructors can easily select appropriate questions for their tests. Textbook authors rarely prepare their own test banks; the fact that Pinel and Barnes insisted on preparing the *Biopsychology* test bank attests to its consistency with the text—and their commitment to helping students learn.

Instructor's Manual The instructor's manual contains helpful teaching tools, including at-a-glance grids, activities and demonstrations for the classroom, handouts, lecture notes, chapter outlines, and other valuable course organization material for new and experienced instructors.

Video Embedded PowerPoint Slides These slides, available in the Instructor's Resource Center, bring highlights of this edition of *Biopsychology* right into the classroom, drawing students into the lecture and providing engaging visuals, and videos.

Standard Lecture PowerPoint Slides These slides have a more traditional format, with excerpts of the text material and artwork, and are available online at www.pearsonglobaleditions.com/pinel.

MyPsychLab MyPsychLab is an online homework, tutorial, and assessment program that truly engages students in learning. It helps students better prepare for class, quizzes, and exams—resulting in better performance in the course. It provides educators a dynamic set of tools for gauging individual and class performance.

Acknowledgments

Four people deserve special credit for helping us create this edition of *Biopsychology*: Maggie Edwards, Linnea Ritland, Chandra Jade, and Olivia Sorley. Maggie is an artist/designer/writer/personal trainer who is John's partner in life. She is responsible for the original designs of most of the illustrations in this book. Linnea, Chandra, and Olivia are three remarkable students at the University of British Columbia; Linnea helped with the drawing, editing, and voiceovers for the Chalk It Up Animations, Chandra helped with the editing of some of the Chalk It Up Animations, and Olivia helped with the drawing of some of the Chalk It Up Animations.

Pearson Education did a remarkable job of producing the original textbook. They shared the dream of a textbook that meets the highest standards of pedagogy but is also personal, attractive, and enjoyable. Now they have stepped up to support the conversion of *Biopsychology* to electronic format. Thank you to Bill Barke, Stephen Frail, Susan Hartman, and other executives for having faith in *Biopsychology* and providing the financial and personal support necessary for it to stay at the forefront of its field. Special thanks also go to Amber Chow and Thomas Finn at Pearson and Ron Watson at Integra for coordinating the production—an excruciatingly difficult and often thankless job.

We thank the following instructors for providing us with reviews of various editions of *Biopsychology*. Their comments have contributed substantially to the evolution of this edition:

L. Joseph Acher, Baylor University
Nelson Adams, Winston-Salem State University
Marwa Azab, Golden West College
Michael Babcock, Montana State University–Bozeman
Ronald Baenninger, College of St. Benedict
Mark Basham, Regis University
Carol Batt, Sacred Heart University
Noel Jay Bean, Vassar College
Patricia Bellas, Irvine Valley College
Danny Benbasset, George Washington University
Thomas Bennett, Colorado State University
Linda Brannon, McNeese State University
Peter Brunjes, University of Virginia
John Bryant, Bowie State University
Michelle Butler, United States Air Force Academy
Donald Peter Cain, University of Western Ontario
Deborah A. Carroll, Southern Connecticut State University
John Conklin, Camosun College
Sherry Dingman, Marist College
Michael A. Dowdle, Mt. San Antonio College
Doug Engwall, Central Connecticut State University
Gregory Ervin, Brigham Young University
Robert B. Fischer, Ball State University
Allison Fox, University of Wollongong
Michael Foy, Loyola Marymount University
Ed Fox, Purdue University
Thomas Goettsche, SAS Institute, Inc.
Arnold M. Golub, California State University–Sacramento
Nakia Gordon, Marquette University
Mary Gotch, Solano College
Jeffrey Grimm, Western Washington University
Kenneth Guttman, Citrus College
Melody Smith Harrington, St. Gregory's University
Theresa D. Hernandez, University of Colorado
Cindy Ellen Herzog, Frostburg State University
Peter Hickmott, University of California–Riverside
Michael Jarvinen, Emmanuel College
Tony Jelsma, Atlantic Baptist University

Roger Johnson, Ramapo College
John Jonides, University of Michigan
Jon Kahane, Springfield College
Craig Kinsley, University of Richmond
Ora Kofman, Ben-Gurion University of the Negev
Louis Koppel, Utah State University
Maria J. Lavooy, University of Central Florida
Victoria Littlefield, Augsburg College
Eric Littman, University of Cincinnati
Linda Lockwood, Metropolitan State College of Denver
Charles Malsbury, Memorial University
Michael R. Markham, Florida International University
Vincent Markowski, State University of New York–Geneseo
Michael P. Matthews, Drury College
Lin Meyers, California State University–Stanislaus
Maura Mitrushina, California State University, Northridge
Russ Morgan, Western Illinois University
Henry Morlock, SUNY–Plattsburgh
Caroline Olko, Nassau Community College
Lauretta Park, Clemson University
Ted Parsons, University of Wisconsin–Platteville
Jim H. Patton, Baylor University
Edison Perdorno, Minnesota State University
Michael Peters, University of Guelph
Michelle Pilati, Rio Hondo College
Joseph H. Porter, Virginia Commonwealth University
David Robbins, Ohio Wesleyan University
Dennis Rodriguez, Indiana University–South Bend
Margaret G. Ruddy, College of New Jersey
Jeanne P. Ryan, SUNY–Plattsburgh
Jerome Siegel, David Geffen School of Medicine, UCLA
Angela Sikorski, Texas A&M University–Texarkana
Patti Simone, Santa Clara University
Ken Sobel, University of Central Arkansas
David Soderquist, University of North Carolina at Greensboro
Michael Stoloff, James Madison University
Stuart Tousman, Rockford College
Dallas Treit, University of Alberta
Margaret Upchurch, Transylvania University
Dennis Vincenzi, University of Central Florida
Ashkat Vyas, Hunter College
Charles Weaver, Baylor University
Linda Walsh, University of Northern Iowa
David Widman, Juniata College
Jon Williams, Kenyon College
David Yager, University of Maryland
H.P. Ziegler, Hunter College

To the Student

We have tried to make *Biopsychology* a different kind of text, a text that includes clear, concise, and well-organized explanations of the key points but is still interesting to read—a text from which you might suggest suitable sections to an interested friend or relative. To accomplish this goal, we thought about what kind of textbook we would have liked when we were students, and we decided to avoid the stern formality and ponderous style of conventional textbook writing and to focus on ideas of relevance to your personal life.

We want *Biopsychology* to have a relaxed and personal style. In order to accomplish this, we imagined that we were chatting with you as we wrote and that we were telling you—usually over a glass of something—about the interesting things that go on in the field of biopsychology. Imagining these chats kept our writing from drifting back into conventional "textbookese," and it never let us forget that we were writing this book for you.

As we write these words, we have finished work on this new edition, and now we are waiting with great excitement for the text to be released. There is more excitement around this edition than there has been since the first edition appeared in 1990—this time the excitement is about the conversion of *Biopsychology* to an electronic format and all the opportunities that it creates for effective teaching. We really hope that you will find this new format to be easy to use, interesting, and, most importantly, an effective learning tool—we already know that you will be pleased with the reduced price and the savings of natural resources.

We hope that *Biopsychology* teaches you much of relevance to your personal life and that reading it generates in you the same positive feelings that writing it did in us.

About the Authors

JOHN PINEL obtained his Ph.D. from McGill University in Montreal and worked briefly at the Massachusetts Institute of Technology before taking a faculty position at the University of British Columbia in Vancouver, where he is currently Professor Emeritus. Professor Pinel is an award-winning teacher and the author of more than 200 scientific papers. However, he feels that *Biopsychology* is his major career-related accomplishment: "It ties together everything I love about my job: students, teaching, writing, and research."

STEVEN BARNES obtained his Ph.D. from the University of British Columba. He then worked as a postdoctoral fellow—first in the Department of Epileptology at the University of Bonn and then in the School of Interactive Arts and Technology at Simon Fraser University. He is currently a faculty member in the Department of Psychology at the University of British Columbia, where he has won multiple departmental and institutional awards for his teaching and educational leadership. His current research is focused on bipolar disorders: He is a core member and the co-deputy director of the Collaborative RESearch Team to study psychosocial issues in Bipolar Disorder (CREST. BD)—a multidisciplinary international collaborative network of researchers, healthcare providers, people living with bipolar disorder, and their family members and supporters. When he isn't teaching, writing, or doing research, he engages in the production of traditional pieces of visual art as well as interactive electronic artworks—some of which have been exhibited at prominent international venues. He sees his involvement in the creation of this new edition of *Biopsychology* as a complement to everything he loves to do: teaching, writing, visual and interactive art, and research.

Global Edition Acknowledgments

For their contribution to the Global Edition, Pearson wishes to acknowledge and thank the following people:

Contributors

Shweta Sharma Sehgal, Emory University

Pooja Thakur (writer)

Reviewers

Ashum Gupta (writer)

Albert Lee Kai Chung, Nanyang Technological University

Pooja Thakur (writer)

Manchong Limlunthang Zou, North Eastern Police Academy (NEPA), Government of India

Chapter 1
Biopsychology as a Neuroscience

What Is Biopsychology, Anyway?

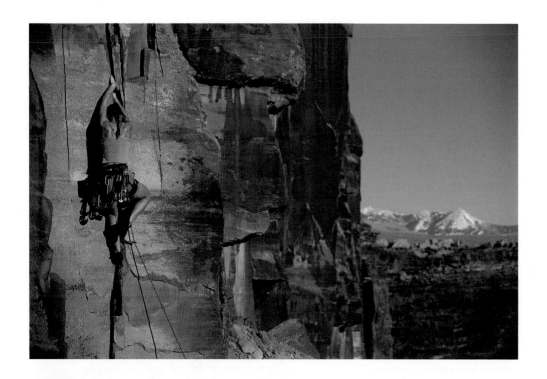

Chapter Overview and Learning Objectives (LOs)

What Is Biopsychology?	**LO 1.1**	Define and discuss what is meant by *biopsychology*.
	LO 1.2	Discuss the origins of the field of biopsychology.
	LO 1.3	List the six fields of neuroscience that are particularly relevant to biopsychological inquiry.
What Types of Research Characterize the Biopsychological Approach?	**LO 1.4**	Compare the advantages and disadvantages of humans and nonhumans as subjects in biopsychological research.
	LO 1.5	Compare experiments, quasiexperimental studies, and case studies, emphasizing the study of causal effects.
	LO 1.6	Compare pure and applied research.
What Are the Divisions of Biopsychology?	**LO 1.7**	Describe the division of biopsychology known as physiological psychology.

The appearance of the human brain is far from impressive (see Figure 1.1). The human brain is a squishy, wrinkled, walnut-shaped hunk of tissue weighing about 1.3 kilograms. It looks more like something you might find washed up on a beach than like one of the wonders of the world—which it surely is. Despite its disagreeable external appearance, the human brain is an amazingly intricate network of **neurons** (cells that receive and transmit electrochemical signals). Contemplate for a moment the complexity of your own brain's neural circuits. Consider the 90 billion neurons in complex array (see Lent et al., 2012; Walløe, Pakkenberg & Fabricius, 2014), the estimated 100 trillion connections among them, and the almost infinite number of paths that neural signals can follow through this morass (see Zimmer, 2011). The complexity of the human brain is hardly surprising, considering what it can do. An organ capable of creating a *Mona Lisa*, an artificial limb, and a supersonic aircraft; of traveling to the moon and to the depths of the sea; and of experiencing the wonders of an alpine sunset, a newborn infant, and a reverse slam dunk *must* be complex. Paradoxically, **neuroscience** (the scientific study of the nervous system) may prove to be the brain's ultimate challenge: Does the brain have the capacity to understand something as complex as itself (see Gazzaniga, 2010)?

Neuroscience comprises several related disciplines. The primary purpose of this chapter is to introduce you to one

Figure 1.1 The Human Brain.

of them: biopsychology. Each of this chapter's five modules characterizes the neuroscience of biopsychology in a different way.

Before you proceed to the body of this chapter, we would like to tell you about two things: (1) the case of Jimmie G. (Sacks, 1986), which will give you a taste of the interesting things that lie ahead, and (2) the major themes of this text.

The Case of Jimmie G., the Man Frozen in Time

Jimmie G. was a good-looking, friendly 49-year-old. He liked to talk about his school days and his experiences in the navy, which he was able to describe in detail. Jimmie was an intelligent man with superior abilities in math and science. In fact, it was not readily apparent why he was a resident of a neurological ward.

When Jimmie talked about his past, there was a hint of his problem. When he talked about his school days, he used the past tense; when he recounted his early experiences in the navy, however, he switched to the present tense. More worrisome was that he never talked about anything that happened to him after his time in the navy.

Jimmie G. was tested by eminent neurologist Oliver Sacks, and a few simple questions revealed a curious fact: The 49-year-old patient believed that he was 19. When he was asked to describe what he saw in a mirror, Jimmie became so frantic and confused that Dr. Sacks immediately took the mirror out of the room.

Returning a few minutes later, Dr. Sacks was greeted by a once-again cheerful Jimmie, who acted as if he had never seen Sacks before. Indeed, even when Sacks suggested that they had met recently, Jimmie was certain that they had not.

Then Dr. Sacks asked where Jimmie thought he was. Jimmie replied that all the beds and patients made him think that the place was a hospital. But he couldn't understand why he would be in a hospital. He was afraid that he might have been admitted because he was sick but didn't know it.

Further testing confirmed what Dr. Sacks feared. Although Jimmie had good sensory, motor, and cognitive abilities, he had one terrible problem: He forgot everything that was said or shown to him within a few seconds. Basically, Jimmie could not remember anything that had happened to him since his early 20s, and he was not going to remember anything that happened to him for the rest of his life. Sacks was stunned by the implications of Jimmie's condition.

Jimmie G.'s situation was heart-wrenching. Unable to form new lasting memories, he was, in effect, a man frozen in time, a man without a recent past and no prospects for a future, stuck in a continuous present, lacking any context or meaning.

Remember Jimmie G.; you will encounter him again later in this chapter.

Four Major Themes of This Text

You will learn many new facts in this text—new findings, concepts, terms, and the like. But more importantly, many years from now, long after you have forgotten most of those facts, you will still be carrying with you productive new ways of thinking. We have selected four of these for special emphasis: Thinking Creatively, Clinical Implications, Evolutionary Perspective, and Neuroplasticity.

To help give these themes the special attention they deserve and to help you follow their development as you progress through the text, we have marked relevant passages with tabs denoting each of the four major themes, which we describe in more detail here.

Watch this video on MyPsychLab CHALK IT UP!: FOUR THEMES OF THE TEXT

THINKING CREATIVELY ABOUT BIOPSYCHOLOGY. We are all fed a steady diet of biopsychological information, misinformation, and opinion—by television, newspapers, the Internet, friends, relatives, teachers, and so on. As a result, you likely already hold strong views about many of the topics you will encounter in this text. Because these preconceptions are shared by many biopsychological researchers, they have often impeded scientific progress, and some of the most important advances in biopsychological science have been made by researchers who have managed to overcome the restrictive effects of conventional thinking and have taken creative new approaches. Indeed, **thinking creatively** (thinking in productive, unconventional ways) is the cornerstone of any science. The thinking creatively tab marks points in the text where **Thinking Creatively** we describe research that involves thinking "outside the box," where we have tried to be creative in the analysis of the research that we are presenting, or where we encourage you to base your thinking on the evidence rather than on widely accepted views.

CLINICAL IMPLICATIONS. Clinical (pertaining to illness or treatment) considerations are woven through the fabric of biopsychology. There are two aspects to clinical implications: Much of what biopsychologists learn about the functioning of the normal brain comes from studying the diseased or damaged brain; and, conversely, much of what biopsychologists discover has relevance for the treatment of brain disorders.

This text focuses on the interplay between brain dysfunction and biopsychological research, and each major **Clinical Implications** example is highlighted by a clinical implications tab.

THE EVOLUTIONARY PERSPECTIVE. Although the events that led to the evolution of the human species can never be determined with certainty, thinking of the environmental pressures that likely led to the evolution of our brains and behavior often leads to important biopsychological insights. This approach is called the evolutionary perspective. An important component of the **evolutionary perspective** is the comparative approach **Evolutionary Perspective** (trying to understand biological phenomena by comparing them in different species). You will learn throughout the text that we humans have learned much about ourselves by studying species that are related to us through evolution. The evolutionary approach has proven to be one of the cornerstones of modern biopsychological inquiry. Each discussion that relates to the evolutionary perspective is marked by an evolutionary perspective tab.

NEUROPLASTICITY. Until the early 1990s, most neuroscientists thought of the brain as a three-dimensional array of neural elements "wired" together in a massive network of circuits. The complexity of this "wiring diagram" of the brain was staggering, but it failed to capture one of the brain's most important features. In the past two decades, research has clearly demonstrated that the adult brain is not a static network of neurons: It is a plastic (changeable) organ that continuously grows and changes in response to the individual's genes and experiences. The discovery of neuroplasticity, arguably **Neuroplasticity** the single most influential discovery in modern neuroscience, is currently influencing many areas of biopsychological research. A neuroplasticity tab marks each discussion or study of neuroplasticity.

What Is Biopsychology?

This module introduces you to the discipline of biopsychology. We begin by exploring the definition and origins of biopsychology. Next, we examine how biopsychology is related to the various disciplines of neuroscience.

Defining Biopsychology

LO 1.1 **Define and discuss what is meant by** *biopsychology.*

Biopsychology is the scientific study of the biology of behavior—see Dewsbury (1991). Some refer to this field as *psychobiology, behavioral biology,* or *behavioral neuroscience;* but we prefer the term *biopsychology* because it denotes a biological approach to the study of psychology rather than a psychological approach to the study of biology: Psychology commands center stage in this text. *Psychology* is the scientific study of behavior—the scientific study of all overt activities of the organism as well as all the internal processes that are presumed to underlie them (e.g., learning, memory, motivation, perception, emotion).

What Are the Origins of Biopsychology?

LO 1.2 **Discuss the origins of the field of biopsychology.**

The study of the biology of behavior has a long history, but biopsychology did not develop into a major neuroscientific discipline until the 20th century. Although it is not possible to specify the exact date of biopsychology's birth, the publication of *The Organization of Behavior* in 1949 by D. O. Hebb played a key role in its emergence (see Brown & Milner, 2003; Cooper, 2005; Milner, 1993). In his book, Hebb developed the first comprehensive theory of how complex psychological phenomena, such as perceptions, emotions, thoughts, and memories, might be produced by brain activity. Hebb's theory did much to discredit the view that psychological functioning is too complex to have its roots in the physiology and chemistry of the brain. Hebb based his theory on experiments involving both humans and laboratory animals, on clinical case studies, and on logical arguments developed from his own insightful observations of daily life. This eclectic approach has become a hallmark of biopsychological inquiry.

In comparison to physics, chemistry, and biology, biopsychology is an infant—a healthy, rapidly growing infant, but an infant nonetheless. In this text, you will reap the benefits of biopsychology's youth. Because biopsychology does not have a long and complex history, you will be able to move quickly to the excitement of current research.

How Is Biopsychology Related to the Other Disciplines of Neuroscience?

LO 1.3 **List six fields of neuroscience that are particularly relevant to biopsychological inquiry.**

Neuroscience is a team effort, and biopsychologists are important members of the team (see Albright, Kandel, & Posner, 2000; Kandel & Squire, 2000). Biopsychology can be further defined by its relation to other neuroscientific disciplines.

Biopsychologists are neuroscientists who bring to their research a knowledge of behavior and of the methods of behavioral research. It is their behavioral orientation and expertise that make their contribution to neuroscience unique (see Cacioppo & Decety, 2009). You will be able to better appreciate the importance of this contribution if you consider that the ultimate purpose of the nervous system is to produce and control behavior (see Grillner & Dickinson, 2002).

Biopsychology is an integrative discipline. Biopsychologists draw together knowledge from the other neuroscientific disciplines and apply it to the study of behavior. The following are a few of the disciplines of neuroscience that are particularly relevant to biopsychology (see Figure 1.2):

Neuroanatomy. The study of the structure of the nervous system (see Chapter 3).

Neurochemistry. The study of the chemical bases of neural activity (see Chapter 4).

Neuroendocrinology. The study of interactions between the nervous system and the endocrine system (see Chapters 13 and 17).

Neuropathology. The study of nervous system disorders (see Chapters 10 and 18).

Neuropharmacology. The study of the effects of drugs on neural activity (see Chapters 4, 15, and 18).

Neurophysiology. The study of the functions and activities of the nervous system (see Chapter 4).

Figure 1.2 Biopsychology and a few of the disciplines of neuroscience that are particularly relevant to it.

What Types of Research Characterize the Biopsychological Approach?

Although biopsychology is only one of many disciplines that contribute to neuroscience, it is broad and diverse. Biopsychologists study many different phenomena, and they approach their research in many different ways. In order to characterize biopsychological research, this module discusses three major dimensions along which approaches to biopsychological research vary. Biopsychological research can involve either human or nonhuman subjects, it can take the form of either formal experiments or nonexperimental studies, and it can be either pure or applied.

Human and Nonhuman Subjects

LO 1.4 Compare the advantages and disadvantages of humans and nonhumans as subjects in biopsychological research.

Both human and nonhuman animals are the subject of biopsychological research. Of the nonhumans, mice and rats are the most common subjects; however, cats, dogs, and nonhuman primates are also commonly studied.

Humans have several advantages over other animals as experimental subjects of biopsychological research: They can follow instructions, they can report their subjective experiences, and their cages are easier to clean. Of course, we are joking about the cages, but the joke does serve to draw attention to one advantage humans have over other species of experimental subjects: Humans are often cheaper. Because only the highest standards of animal care are acceptable, the cost of maintaining an animal laboratory can be prohibitive for all but the most well-funded researchers.

Of course, the greatest advantage humans have as subjects in a field aimed at understanding the intricacies of human brain function is that they have human brains. In fact, you might wonder why biopsychologists would **Evolutionary Perspective** bother studying nonhuman subjects at all. The answer lies in the evolutionary continuity of the brain. The brains of humans differ from the brains of other mammals primarily in their overall size and the extent of their cortical development. In other words, the differences between the brains of humans and those of related species are more quantitative than qualitative, and thus many of the principles of human brain function can be clarified by the study of nonhumans (see Hofman, 2014; Katzner & Weigelt, 2013; Krubitzer & Stolzenberg, 2014).

> **Evolutionary Perspective** What ethical considerations should guide biopsychological research on nonhuman animals?

Conversely, nonhuman animals have three advantages over humans as subjects in biopsychological research. The first is that the brains and behavior of nonhuman subjects are simpler than those of human subjects. Hence, the study of nonhuman species is more likely to reveal fundamental brain–behavior interactions. The second advantage is that insights frequently arise from the **comparative approach**, the study of biological processes by comparing different species. For example, comparing the behavior of species that do not have a cerebral cortex with the behavior of species that do can provide valuable clues about cortical function. The third advantage is that it is possible to conduct research on laboratory animals that, for ethical reasons, is not possible with human participants. This is not to say that the study of nonhuman animals is not governed by a strict code of ethics (Blakemore et al., 2012)—it is. However, there are fewer ethical constraints on the study of laboratory species than on the study of humans.

In our experience, most biopsychologists display considerable concern for their subjects, whether they are of their own species or not; however, ethical issues are not left to the discretion of the individual researcher. All biopsychological research, whether it involves human or nonhuman subjects, is regulated by independent committees according to strict ethical guidelines: "Researchers cannot escape the logic that if the animals we observe are reasonable models of our own most intricate actions, then they must be respected as we would respect our own sensibilities" (Ulrich, 1991, p. 197).

Watch this video on MyPsychLab ETHICS OF ANIMAL RESEARCH

Experiments and Nonexperiments

LO 1.5 **Compare experiments, quasiexperimental studies, and case studies, emphasizing the study of causal effects.**

Biopsychological research involves both experiments and nonexperimental studies. Two common types of nonexperimental studies are quasiexperimental studies and case studies.

EXPERIMENTS. The experiment is the method used by scientists to study causation, that is, to find out what causes what. As such, it has been almost single-handedly responsible for the knowledge that is the basis for our modern way of life. It is paradoxical that a method capable of such complex feats is so simple. To conduct an experiment involving living subjects, the experimenter first designs two or more conditions under which the subjects will be tested. Usually, a different group of subjects is tested under each condition (**between-subjects design**), but sometimes it is possible to test the same group of subjects under each condition (**within-subjects design**). The experimenter assigns the subjects to conditions, administers the treatments, and measures the outcome in such a way that there is only one relevant difference between the conditions being compared. This difference between the conditions is called the **independent variable**. The variable measured by the experimenter to assess the effect of the independent variable is called the **dependent variable**. If the experiment is done correctly, any differences in the dependent variable between the conditions must have been caused by the independent variable.

Why is it critical that there be no differences between conditions other than the independent variable? The reason is that when there is more than one difference that

Watch this video on MyPsychLab THE BASICS:
SCIENTIFIC RESEARCH METHODS

Independent variable: hours of sleep per night

Dependent variable: performance on a standardized test

could affect the dependent variable, it is difficult to determine whether it was the independent variable or the unintended difference—called a **confounded variable**—that led to the observed effects on the dependent variable. Although the experimental method is conceptually simple, eliminating all confounded variables can be quite difficult. Readers of research papers must be constantly on the alert for confounded variables that have gone unnoticed by the experimenters.

An experiment by Lester and Gorzalka (1988) illustrates the prevention of confounded variables with good experimental design. The experiment was a demonstration of the **Coolidge effect** (see Lucio et al., 2014; Tlachi-López et al., 2012). The Coolidge effect is the fact that a copulating male who becomes incapable of continuing to copulate with one sex partner can often recommence copulating with a new sex partner (see Figure 1.3). Before your imagination starts running wild, we should mention that the subjects in Lester and Gorzalka's experiment were hamsters, not university students.

Lester and Gorzalka argued that the Coolidge effect had not been demonstrated in females because it is more difficult to conduct well-controlled Coolidge-effect experiments with females—not because females do not display a Coolidge effect. The confusion, according to Lester and Gorzalka, stemmed from the fact that the males of most mammalian species become sexually fatigued more readily than the females. As a result, attempts to demonstrate the Coolidge effect in females are almost always confounded by the fatigue of the males. When, in the midst of copulation, a female is provided with a new sex partner, the increase in her sexual receptivity could be either a legitimate Coolidge effect or a reaction to the greater vigor of the new male. Because female mammals usually display little sexual fatigue, this confounded variable is not a serious problem in demonstrations of the Coolidge effect in males.

Figure 1.3 President Calvin Coolidge and Mrs. Grace Coolidge. Many students think the Coolidge effect is named after a biopsychologist named Coolidge. In fact, it is named after President Calvin Coolidge, of whom the following story is told. (If the story isn't true, it should be.) During a tour of a poultry farm, Mrs. Coolidge inquired of the farmer how his farm managed to produce so many eggs with such a small number of roosters. The farmer proudly explained that his roosters performed their duty dozens of times each day.

"Perhaps you could point that out to Mr. Coolidge," replied the First Lady in a pointedly loud voice.

The President, overhearing the remark, asked the farmer, "Does each rooster service the same hen each time?"

"No," replied the farmer, "there are many hens for each rooster."

"Perhaps you could point that out to Mrs. Coolidge," replied the President.

Lester and Gorzalka devised a clever procedure to control for this confounded variable. At the same time a female subject was copulating with one male (the familiar male), the other male to be used in the test (the unfamiliar male) was copulating with another female. Then both males were given a rest while the female was copulating with a third male. Finally, the female subject was tested with either the familiar male or the unfamiliar male. The dependent variable was the amount of time that the female displayed **lordosis** (the arched-back, rump-up, tail-diverted posture of female

Thinking Creatively

Figure 1.4 The experimental design and results of Lester and Gorzalka (1988). On the third test, the female hamsters were more sexually receptive to an unfamiliar male than they were to the male with which they had copulated on the first test.

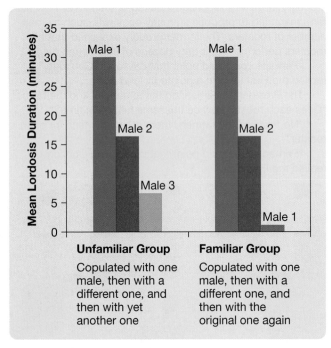

rodent sexual receptivity) during each sex test. As Figure 1.4 illustrates, the females responded more vigorously to the unfamiliar males than they did to the familiar males during the third test, despite the fact that both the unfamiliar and familiar males were equally fatigued and both mounted the females with equal vigor. The purpose of this example—in case you have forgotten—is to illustrate the critical role played by good experimental design in eliminating confounded variables.

QUASIEXPERIMENTAL STUDIES. It is not possible for biopsychologists to bring the experimental method to bear on all problems of interest to them. Physical or ethical impediments frequently make it impossible to assign subjects to particular conditions or to administer the conditions once the subjects have been assigned to them. For example, experiments on the causes of brain damage in human alcoholics are not feasible because it would not be ethical to assign a subject to a condition that involves years of alcohol consumption. (Some of you may be more concerned about the ethics of assigning subjects to a control condition that involves years of sobriety.) In such prohibitive situations, biopsychologists sometimes conduct **quasiexperimental studies**—studies of groups of subjects who have been exposed to the conditions of interest in the real world. These studies have the appearance of experiments, but they are not true experiments because potential confounded variables have not been controlled—for example, by the random assignment of subjects to conditions.

In one quasiexperimental study, a team of researchers compared 100 detoxified male alcoholics from an alcoholism treatment unit with 50 male nondrinkers obtained from various sources (Acker et al., 1984). The alcoholics as a group performed more poorly on various tests of perceptual, motor, and cognitive ability, and their brain scans revealed extensive brain damage. Although this quasiexperimental study seems like an experiment, it is not. Because the participants themselves decided which group they would be in—by drinking alcohol or not—the researchers had no means of ensuring that exposure to alcohol was the only variable that distinguished the two groups. Can you think of differences other than exposure to alcohol that could reasonably be expected to exist between a group of alcoholics and a group of abstainers—differences that could have contributed to the neuroanatomical or intellectual differences that were observed between them? There are several. For example, alcoholics as a group tend to be more poorly educated, more prone to accidental head injury, more likely to use other drugs, and more likely to have poor diets. Accordingly, quasiexperimental studies have revealed that alcoholics tend to have more brain damage than nonalcoholics, but such studies have not indicated why.

Have you forgotten Jimmie G.? His condition was a product of long-term alcohol consumption.

CASE STUDIES. Studies that focus on a single case or subject are called **case studies**. Because they focus on a single case, they often provide a more in-depth picture than that provided by an experiment or a quasiexperimental study, and they are an excellent source of testable hypotheses. However, there is a major problem with all case studies: their **generalizability**—the degree to which their results can be applied to other cases. Because humans differ from one another in both brain function and behavior, it is important to be skeptical of any biopsychological theory based entirely on a few case studies.

Pure and Applied Research

LO 1.6 Compare pure and applied research.

Biopsychological research can be either pure or applied. Pure research and applied research differ in a number of respects, but they are distinguished less by their own attributes than by the motives of the individuals involved in their pursuit. **Pure research** is motivated primarily by the curiosity of the researcher—it is done solely for the purpose of acquiring knowledge. In contrast, **applied research** is intended to bring about some direct benefit to humankind.

Many scientists believe that pure research will ultimately prove to be of more practical benefit than applied research. Their view is that applications flow readily from an understanding of basic principles and that attempts to move directly to application without first gaining a basic

Table 1.1 Nobel prizes specifically related to the nervous system or behavior.

Nobel Winner(s)	Date	Accomplishment
Ivan Pavlov	1904	Research on the physiology of digestion
Camillo Golgi and Santiago Romón y Cajal	1906	Research on the structure of the nervous system
Charles Sherrington and Edgar Adrian	1932	Discoveries about the functions of neurons
Henry Dale and Otto Loewi	1936	Discoveries about the transmission of nerve impulses
Joseph Erlanger and Herbert Gasser	1944	Research on the functions of single nerve fibers
Walter Hess	1949	Research on the role of the brain in behavior
Egas Moniz	1949	Development of the prefrontal lobotomy
Georg von Békésy	1961	Research on the auditory system
John Eccles, Alan Hodgkin, and Andrew Huxley	1963	Research on the ionic basis of neural transmission
Ragnor Granit, Haldan Hartline, and George Wald	1967	Research on the chemistry and physiology of vision
Bernard Katz, Ulf von Euler, and Julius Axelrod	1970	Discoveries related to synaptic transmission
Karl Von Frisch, Konrad Lorenz, and Nikolass Tinbergen	1973	Studies of animal behavior
Roger Guillemin and Andrew Schally	1977	Discoveries related to hormone production by the brain
Herbert Simon	1979	Research on human cognition
Roger Sperry	1981	Research on separation of the cerebral hemispheres
David Hubel and Torsten Wiesel	1981	Research on neurons of the visual system
Rita Levi-Montalcini and Stanley Cohen	1986	Discovery and study of nerve growth factors
Erwin Neher and Bert Sakmann	1991	Research on ion channels
Alfred Gilman and Martin Rodbell	1994	Discovery of G-protein–coupled receptors
Arvid Carlsson, Paul Greengard, and Eric Kandel	2000	Discoveries related to synaptic transmission
Linda Buck and Richard Axel	2004	Research on the olfactory system
John O'Keefe, May-Britt Moser, and Edvard Moser	2014	Research on the brain's system for recognizing locations

understanding are shortsighted. Of course, it is not necessary for a research project to be completely pure or completely applied; many research programs have elements of both approaches. Moreover, pure research often becomes the topic of **translational research**: research that aims to translate the findings of pure research into useful applications for humankind (see Howells, Sena, & Macleod, 2014; Woolf, 2008).

One important difference between pure and applied research is that pure research is more vulnerable to the vagaries of political regulation because politicians and the voting public have difficulty understanding why research of no immediate practical benefit should be supported. If the decision were yours, would you be willing to grant hundreds of thousands of dollars to support the study of squid *motor neurons* (neurons that control muscles), learning in recently hatched geese, the activity of single nerve cells in the visual systems of monkeys, the hormones released by the *hypothalamus* (a small neural structure at the base of the brain) of pigs and sheep, or the function of the *corpus callosum* (the large neural pathway that connects the left and right halves of the brain)? Which, if any, of these projects would you consider worthy of support? Each of these seemingly esoteric projects was supported, and each earned a Nobel Prize.

Table 1.1 provides a timeline of some of the Nobel Prizes awarded for research related to the brain and behavior. The purpose of this table is to give you a general sense of the official recognition that behavioral and brain research has received, not to have you memorize the list. You will learn later in the chapter that, when it comes to evaluating science, the Nobel Committee has not been infallible.

What Are the Divisions of Biopsychology?

As you have just learned, biopsychologists conduct their research in a variety of fundamentally different ways. Biopsychologists who take the same approaches to their research tend to publish their research in the same journals, attend the same scientific meetings, and belong to the same professional societies. The particular approaches to biopsychology that have flourished and grown have gained wide recognition as separate divisions of biopsychological research. The purpose of this module of the chapter is to give you a clearer sense of biopsychology and its diversity by describing six of its major divisions (see Figure 1.5): (1) physiological psychology, (2) psychopharmacology, (3) neuropsychology, (4) psychophysiology, (5) cognitive neuroscience, and (6) comparative psychology. For simplicity,

Figure 1.5 The six major divisions of biopsychology.

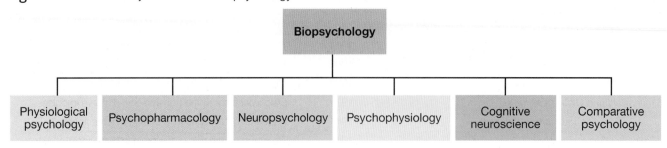

they are presented as distinct approaches, but there is much overlap among them, and many biopsychologists regularly follow more than one approach.

Physiological Psychology

LO 1.7 Describe the division of biopsychology known as physiological psychology.

Physiological psychology is the division of biopsychology that studies the neural mechanisms of behavior through the direct manipulation and recording of the brain in controlled experiments—surgical and electrical methods are most common. The subjects of physiological psychology research are almost always laboratory animals because the focus on direct brain manipulation and controlled experiments precludes the use of human participants in most instances. There is also a tradition of pure research in physiological psychology; the emphasis is usually on research that contributes to the development of theories of the neural control of behavior rather than on research of immediate practical benefit.

Psychopharmacology

LO 1.8 Describe the division of biopsychology known as psychopharmacology.

Psychopharmacology is similar to physiological psychology except that it focuses on the manipulation of neural activity and behavior with drugs. In fact, many of the early psychopharmacologists were simply physiological psychologists who moved into drug research, and many of today's biopsychologists identify closely with both approaches. However, the study of the effects of drugs on the brain and behavior has become so specialized that psychopharmacology is regarded as a separate discipline. A substantial portion of psychopharmacological research is applied. Although drugs are sometimes used by psychopharmacologists to study the basic principles of brain–behavior interaction, the purpose of many psychopharmacological experiments is to develop therapeutic drugs (see Chapter 18) or to reduce drug abuse (see Chapter 15). Psychopharmacologists study the effects of drugs on laboratory species—and on humans, if the ethics of the situation permits it.

Neuropsychology

LO 1.9 Describe the division of biopsychology known as neuropsychology.

Neuropsychology is the study of the psychological effects of brain damage in human patients. Because human volunteers cannot ethically be exposed to experimental treatments that endanger normal brain function, neuropsychology deals almost exclusively with case studies and quasiexperimental studies of patients with brain damage resulting from disease, accident, or neurosurgery. The outer layer of the cerebral hemispheres—the **cerebral cortex**—is most likely to be damaged by accident or surgery; this is one reason why neuropsychology has focused on this important part of the human brain.

Neuropsychology is the most applied of the biopsychological subdisciplines; the neuropsychological assessment of human patients, even when part of a program of pure research, is always done with an eye toward benefiting them in some way. Neuropsychological tests facilitate diagnosis and thus help the attending physician prescribe effective treatment (see Benton, 1994). They can also be an important basis for patient care and counseling; Kolb and Whishaw (1990) described such an application.

The Case of Mr. R., the Brain-Damaged Student Who Switched to Architecture

Mr. R. was a 21-year-old honor student at a university. One day he was involved in a car accident in which he struck his head against the dashboard. Following the accident, Mr. R's grades began to decline; his once exceptional academic performance was now only average. He seemed to have particular trouble completing his term papers. Finally, after a year of struggling academically, he went for a neuropsychological assessment. The findings were striking.

Figure 1.6 Visual tracking of a pendulum by a normal control participant (top) and people with schizophrenia (adapted from Iacono & Koenig, 1983.)

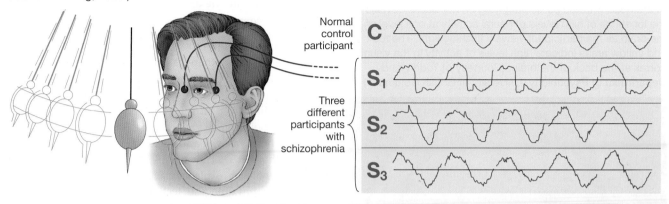

Normal control participant

Three different participants with schizophrenia

C

S₁

S₂

S₃

Mr. R. turned out to be one of roughly one-third of left-handers whose language functions are represented in the right hemisphere of their brain, rather than in their left hemisphere. Furthermore, although Mr. R. had a superior IQ score, his verbal memory and reading speed were low-average—something that is quite unusual for a person with such a good education and of such high intelligence.

The neuropsychologists concluded that he may have suffered some damage to his right temporal lobe during the car accident, which would help explain his diminished language skills. The neuropsychologists also recommended that Mr. R pursue a field that didn't require superior verbal memory skills. Following his exam and based on the recommendation of his neuropsychologists, Mr. R. switched majors and began studying architecture.

Psychophysiology

LO 1.10 Describe the division of biopsychology known as psychophysiology.

Psychophysiology is the division of biopsychology that studies the relation between physiological activity and psychological processes in human subjects. Because the subjects of psychophysiological research are human, psychophysiological recording procedures are typically noninvasive; that is, the physiological activity is recorded from the surface of the body. The usual measure of brain activity is the scalp **electroencephalogram (EEG)** (see Chapter 5). Other common psychophysiological measures are muscle tension, eye movement, and several indicators of autonomic nervous system activity (e.g., heart rate, blood pressure, pupil dilation, and electrical conductance of the skin). The **autonomic nervous system (ANS)** is the division of the nervous system that regulates the body's inner environment (see Chapter 3).

Most psychophysiological research focuses on understanding the physiology of psychological processes, such as attention, emotion, and information processing, but there have been some interesting clinical applications of the psychophysiological

method. For example, psychophysiological experiments have indicated that persons with schizophrenia have difficulty smoothly tracking a moving object such as a pendulum (see Meyhöfer et al., 2014)—see Figure 1.6.

 Clinical Implications If people with schizophrenia have difficulty smoothly tracking moving objects, what clinical implications do you think this might have? (For a description of the symptoms of schizophrenia, see Chapter 18.)

Cognitive Neuroscience

LO 1.11 Describe the division of biopsychology known as cognitive neuroscience.

Cognitive neuroscience is the youngest division of biopsychology. Cognitive neuroscientists study the neural bases of **cognition**, a term that generally refers to higher intellectual processes such as thought, memory, attention, and complex perceptual processes (see Gutchess, 2014; Raichle, 2008). Because of its focus on cognition, most cognitive neuroscience research involves human participants, and because of its focus on human participants, its methods tend to be noninvasive, rather than involving penetration or direct manipulation of the brain.

The major method of cognitive neuroscience is *functional brain imaging*: recording images of the activity of the living human brain (see Chapter 5) while a participant is engaged in a particular cognitive activity. For example, Figure 1.7 shows that the visual areas of the left and right cerebral cortex at the back of the brain became active when the participant viewed a flashing light.

Because the theory and methods of cognitive neuroscience are so complex and pertinent to so many fields, most cognitive neuroscientific publications result from interdisciplinary collaboration among many individuals with

Figure 1.7 Functional brain imaging is the major method of cognitive neuroscience. This image—taken from the top of the head with the participant lying on her back—reveals the locations of high levels of neural activity at one level of the brain as the participant views a flashing light. The red and yellow areas indicate high levels of activity in the visual cortex at the back of the brain. (Courtesy of Todd Handy, Department of Psychology, University of British Columbia.)

different types of training. For example, biopsychologists, cognitive psychologists, social psychologists, economists, computing and mathematics experts, and various types of neuroscientists commonly contribute to the field. Cognitive neuroscience research sometimes involves noninvasive electrophysiological recording, and it sometimes focuses on patients with brain pathology; in these cases, the boundaries between cognitive neuroscience and psychophysiology and neuropsychology, respectively, are blurred.

Comparative Psychology

LO 1.12 Describe the division of biopsychology known as comparative psychology.

Although most biopsychologists study the neural mechanisms of behavior, there is more to biopsychology than this. As Dewsbury (1991) asserted:

> The "biology" in "psychobiology" should include the whole-animal approaches of ethology, ecology, evolution…as well as the latest in physiological methods and thought…. The "compleat psychobiologist" should use whatever explanatory power can be found with modern physiological techniques, but never lose sight of the problems that got us going in the first place: the integrated behavior of whole, functioning, adapted organisms. (p. 122)

The division of biopsychology that deals generally with the biology of behavior, rather than specifically with the neural mechanisms of behavior, is **comparative psychology**. Comparative psychologists compare the behavior of different species in order to understand the evolution, genetics, and adaptiveness of behavior. Some comparative psychologists study behavior in the laboratory; others engage in **ethological research**—the study of animal behavior in its natural environment.

Because two important areas of biopsychological research often employ comparative analysis, we have included them as part of comparative psychology. One of these is *evolutionary psychology* (a subfield that focuses on understanding behavior by considering its likely evolutionary origins)—see Burke (2014), Caporael, (2001), Duchaine, Cosmides, and Tooby (2001), Kenrick (2001). The other is *behavioral genetics* (the study of genetic influences on behavior)—see Carson and Rothstein (1999), Jaffee, Price and Reyes (2013), Plomin et al. (2002).

In case you have forgotten, the purpose of this module has been to demonstrate the diversity of biopsychology by describing six of its major divisions; these are summarized for you in Table 1.2. You will learn much about these divisions in subsequent chapters.

Table 1.2 The six major divisions of biopsychology with examples of how they have approached the study of memory

The Six Divisions of Biopsychology	Examples of How the Six Approaches Have Pursued the Study of Memory
Physiological psychology: study of the neural mechanisms of behavior by manipulating the nervous systems of nonhuman animals in controlled experiments	Physiological psychologists have studied the contributions of the hippocampus to memory by surgically removing the hippocampus in rats and assessing their ability to perform various memory tasks.
Psychopharmacology: study of the effects of drugs on the brain and behavior	Psychopharmacologists have tried to improve the memory of Alzheimer's patients by administering drugs that increase the levels of the neurotransmitter acetylcholine.
Neuropsychology: study of the psychological effects of brain damage in human patients	Neuropsychologists have shown that patients with alcohol-produced brain damage have particular difficulty in remembering recent events.

Table 1.2 Continued

The Six Divisions of Biopsychology	Examples of How the Six Approaches Have Pursued the Study of Memory
Psychophysiology: study of the relation between physiological activity and psychological processes in human volunteers by noninvasive physiological recording	Psychophysiologists have shown that familiar faces elicit the usual changes in autonomic nervous system activity even when patients with brain damage report that they do not recognize a face.
Cognitive neuroscience: study of the neural mechanisms of human cognition, largely through the use of functional brain imaging	Cognitive neuroscientists have used brain-imaging technology to observe the changes that occur in various parts of the brain while human volunteers perform memory tasks.
Comparative psychology: study of the evolution, genetics, and adaptiveness of behavior, largely through the use of the comparative method	Comparative psychologists have shown that species of birds that cache their seeds tend to have big hippocampi, confirming that the hippocampus is involved in memory for location.

Scan Your Brain

To see if you are ready to proceed to the next module of the chapter, scan your brain by filling in each of the following blanks with one of the six divisions of biopsychology. The correct answers are provided at the end of the exercise. Before proceeding, review material related to your errors and omissions.

1. Brain is a _____ organ that keeps growing as a result of genes and human experience.

2. Biopsychologists apply the knowledge of _____ disciplines to study human behavior.

3. The main difference between the brains of humans and other mammals is in the overall size and the extent of _____ development.

4. A _____ design allows the experimenter to study the same group of subjects under two or more conditions.

5. _____ of subjects is not possible in quasi experimental studies.

6. Research that aims to bring about some benefit to mankind is _____ in nature.

Scan Your Brain answers: (1) plastic, (2) neuroscientific, (3) cortical, (4) within-subject, (5) Random assignment, (6) applied

How Do Biopsychologists Conduct Their Work?

Converging Operations: How Do Biopsychologists Work Together?

LO 1.13 Explain how converging operations has contributed to the study of Korsakoff's syndrome.

Because none of the six biopsychological approaches to research is without its shortcomings and because of the complexity of the brain and its role in psychological processes, major biopsychological issues are rarely resolved by a single experiment or even by a single series of experiments taking the same general approach. Progress is most likely when different approaches are focused on a single problem in such a way that the strengths of one approach compensate for the weaknesses of the others; this combined approach is called **converging operations** (see Thompson, 2005).

Consider, for example, the relative strengths and weaknesses of neuropsychology and physiological psychology in the study of the psychological effects of damage to the human cerebral cortex. In this instance, the strength of the neuropsychological approach is that it deals directly with human patients; its weakness is that its focus on human patients precludes experiments. In contrast, the strength of the physiological psychology approach is that it can bring the power of the experimental method and neuroscientific technology to bear through research on nonhuman animals; its weakness is that the relevance of research on laboratory animals to human neuropsychological deficits is always open to question (see Couzin-Frankel, 2013; Reardon, 2016). Clearly these two approaches complement each other well; together they can answer questions that neither can answer individually.

To examine converging operations in action, let's return to the case of Jimmie G. The neuropsychological disorder from which Jimmie G. suffered was first described in the late 19th century by S. S. Korsakoff, a Russian physician, and subsequently became known as **Korsakoff's syndrome**. The primary symptom of Korsakoff's syndrome is severe memory loss, which is made all the more heartbreaking—as you have seen in Jimmie G.'s case—by the fact that its sufferers are often otherwise quite capable. Because Korsakoff's syndrome commonly occurs in alcoholics, it was initially believed to be a direct consequence of the toxic effects of alcohol on the brain. This conclusion proved to be a good illustration of the inadvisability of basing causal conclusions on quasiexperimental research. Subsequent research showed that Korsakoff's syndrome is largely caused by the brain damage associated with *thiamine* (vitamin B$_1$) deficiency.

> **Clinical Implications** Korsakoff's syndrome accounts for approximately 10 percent of adult dementias in the United States. Despite its relatively high prevalence, few people have heard of it. Why do you think this is the case?

The first support for the thiamine-deficiency interpretation of Korsakoff's syndrome came from the discovery of the syndrome in malnourished persons who consumed little or no alcohol. Additional support came from experiments in which thiamine-deficient rats were compared with otherwise identical groups of control rats. The thiamine-deficient rats displayed memory deficits and patterns of brain damage similar to those observed in human alcoholics (see Mumby, Cameli, & Glenn, 1999). Alcoholics often develop Korsakoff's syndrome because most of their caloric intake comes in the form of alcohol, which lacks vitamins, and because alcohol interferes with the metabolism of what little thiamine they do consume. However, alcohol has been shown to accelerate the development of brain damage in thiamine-deficient rats, so it may have a direct toxic effect on the brain as well (see Ridley, Draper, & Withall, 2013).

The point of this discussion of Korsakoff's syndrome is to show you that progress in biopsychology typically comes from converging operations—in this case, from the convergence of neuropsychological case studies (case studies of Korsakoff patients), quasiexperiments with human participants (comparisons of alcoholics with people who do not drink alcohol), and controlled experiments on laboratory animals (comparison of thiamine-deficient and control rats). The strength of biopsychology lies in the diversity of its methods and approaches. This means that, in evaluating biopsychological claims, it is rarely sufficient to consider the results of one study or even of one line of experiments using the same method or approach.

So what has all the research on Korsakoff's syndrome done for Jimmie G. and others like him? Today, alcoholics are counseled to stop drinking and are treated with massive doses of thiamine. The thiamine limits the development of further brain damage and often leads to a slight improvement in the patient's condition; unfortunately, the brain damage that has already occurred is mostly irreversible.

Scientific Inference: How Do Biopsychologists Study the Unobservable Workings of the Brain?

LO 1.14 Explain scientific inference with reference to research on eye movement and the visual perception of motion.

Scientific inference is the fundamental method of biopsychology and of most other sciences—it is what makes being a scientist fun. This section provides further insight into the nature of biopsychology by defining, illustrating, and discussing scientific inference.

The scientific method is a system for finding things out by careful observation, but many of the processes studied by scientists cannot be observed. For example, scientists use empirical (observational) methods to study ice ages, gravity, evaporation, electricity, and nuclear fission—none of which can be directly observed; their effects can be observed, but the processes themselves cannot. Biopsychology is no different from other sciences in this respect. One of its main goals is to characterize, through empirical methods, the unobservable processes by which the nervous system controls behavior.

The empirical method that biopsychologists and other scientists use to study the unobservable is called **scientific inference**. Scientists carefully measure key events they can observe and then use these measures as a basis for logically inferring the nature of events they cannot observe. Like a detective carefully gathering clues from which to re-create an unwitnessed crime, a biopsychologist carefully gathers relevant measures of behavior and neural activity from which to infer the nature of the neural processes that regulate behavior. The fact that the neural mechanisms of behavior cannot be directly observed and must be studied through scientific inference is what makes biopsychological research such a challenge—and, as we said before, so much fun.

To illustrate scientific inference, we have selected a research project in which you can participate. By making a few simple observations about your own visual abilities under different conditions, you will be able to discover the principle by which your brain translates the movement of images on your retinas into perceptions of movement (see Figure 1.8). One feature of the mechanism is immediately obvious. Hold your hand in front of your face, and then move its image across your retinas by moving your eyes, by moving your hand, or by moving both at once. You will notice that only those movements of the retinal image produced by the movement of your hand

Figure 1.8 The perception of motion under four different conditions.

1 Eye is stationary, and object is stationary; therefore, retinal image is stationary. No movement is seen.

2 Eye actively rotates upward, and object is stationary; therefore, retinal image moves up. No movement is seen.

3 Eye is stationary, and object moves down; therefore, retinal image moves up. Object is seen to move down.

4 Eye is passively rotated upward by finger, and object is stationary; therefore, retinal image moves up. Object is seen to move down.

Conclusion
Therefore, the brain sees as movement the total movement of an object's image on the retina minus that portion produced by active movement of the eyes: It does not subtract passive movement of the eyes.

are translated into the perception of motion; movements of the retinal image produced by your own eye movements are not. Obviously, there must be a part of your brain that monitors the movements of your retinal image and subtracts from the total those image movements produced by your own eye movements, leaving the remainder to be perceived as motion.

Now, let's try to characterize the nature of the information about your eye movements used by your brain in its perception of motion. Try the following. Shut one eye, then rotate your other eye slightly upward by gently pressing on your lower eyelid with your fingertip. What do you see? You see all of the objects in your visual field moving downward. Why? It seems that the brain mechanism responsible for the perception of motion does not consider eye movement per se. It considers only those eye movements that are actively produced by neural signals from the brain to the eye muscles, not those that are passively produced by external means (e.g., by your finger). Thus, when your eye was moved passively, your brain assumed it had remained still and attributed the movement of your retinal image to the movement of objects in your visual field.

It is possible to trick the visual system in the opposite way; instead of the eyes being moved when no active signals have been sent to the eye muscles, the eyes can be held stationary despite the brain's attempts to move them. Because this experiment involves paralyzing the eye muscles, you cannot participate. Hammond, Merton, and Sutton (1956) injected a *paralytic* (movement-inhibiting) substance into the eye muscles of their participant—who was Merton himself. This paralytic substance was the active ingredient of *curare*, with which some Indigenous people of South America coat their blow darts. What do you think Merton saw when he then tried to move his eyes? He saw the stationary visual world moving in the same direction as his attempted eye movements. If a visual object is focused on part of your retina, and it stays focused there despite the fact that you have moved your eyes to the right, it too must have moved to the right. Consequently, when Merton sent signals to his eye muscles to move his eyes to the right, his brain assumed the movement had been carried out, and it perceived stationary objects as moving to the right.

The point of the eye-movement example is that biopsychologists can learn much about the activities of the brain through scientific inference without directly observing them—and so can you. By the way, neuroscientists are still interested in the kind of feedback mechanisms inferred from the demonstrations of Hammond and colleagues, and they are finding a lot of direct evidence for such mechanisms using modern neural recording techniques (e.g., Joiner et al., 2013; Wurtz et al., 2011).

Critical Thinking about Biopsychological Claims

We have all heard or read that we use only a small portion of our brains, it is important to eat three meals a day, intelligence is inherited, everybody needs at least 8 hours of sleep per night, there is a gene for schizophrenia, heroin is a particularly dangerous (hard) drug, neurological diseases can now be cured by genetic engineering, and homosexuality is caused by inappropriate upbringing—to note just a few claims about biopsychological phenomena that have been widely disseminated (see Howard-Jones, 2014). You may believe some of these claims. But are they true? How does one find out? And if they are not true, why do so many people believe them?

As you have already learned, one of the major goals of this text is to teach you how to think creatively (to think in productive, unconventional ways) about biopsychological information. Often, the first step in creative thinking is spotting the weaknesses of existing ideas and the evidence on which they are based—the process by which these weaknesses are recognized is called **critical thinking**. The identification of weaknesses in existing beliefs is one of the major stimuli for scientists to adopt creative new approaches.

> **Thinking Creatively** Creative thinking is as important in the life of biopsychology students as it is in biopsychological laboratories. Discuss.

The purpose of this final module of the chapter is to develop your own critical thinking abilities by describing two claims that played major roles in the history of biopsychology. In both cases, the evidence proved to be grossly flawed. Notice that if you keep your wits about you, you do not have to be an expert to spot the weaknesses.

The first step in judging the validity of any scientific claim is to determine whether the claim and the research on which it is based were published in a reputable scientific journal (Rensberger, 2000). The reason is that, in order to be published in a reputable scientific journal, an article must first be reviewed by experts in the field—usually three or four of them—and judged to be of good quality. Indeed, the best scientific journals publish only a small proportion of the manuscripts submitted to them. You should be particularly skeptical of scientific claims that have not gone through this review process.

The first case that follows deals with an unpublished claim that was largely dispensed through the news media. The second deals with a claim that was initially supported by published research. Because both of these cases are part of the history of biopsychology, we have the advantage of 20/20 hindsight in evaluating their claims.

Case 1: José and the Bull

LO 1.15 Discuss Delgado's bull-ring demonstration, emphasizing its flawed interpretation.

José Delgado, a particularly charismatic neuroscientist, demonstrated to a group of newspaper reporters a remarkable new procedure for controlling aggression (see Horgan, 2005). Delgado strode into a Spanish bull ring carrying only a red cape and a small radio transmitter. With the transmitter, he could activate a battery-powered stimulator that had previously been mounted on the horns of the other inhabitant of the ring. As the raging bull charged, Delgado calmly activated the stimulator and sent a weak electrical current from the stimulator through an electrode that had been implanted in the caudate nucleus (see Chapter 3), a structure deep in the bull's brain. The bull immediately veered from its charge. After a few such interrupted charges, the bull stood tamely as Delgado swaggered about the ring. According to Delgado, this demonstration marked a significant scientific breakthrough—the discovery of a caudate taming center and the fact that stimulation of this structure could eliminate aggressive behavior, even in bulls specially bred for their ferocity.

To those present at this carefully orchestrated event and to most of the millions who subsequently read about it, Delgado's conclusion was compelling. Surely, if caudate stimulation could stop the charge of a raging bull, the caudate must be a taming center. It was even suggested that caudate stimulation through implanted electrodes might be an effective treatment for human psychopaths. What do you think?

Analysis of Case 1 Delgado's demonstration provided little or no support for his conclusion. It should have been obvious to anyone who did not get caught up in the provocative nature of Delgado's media event that brain stimulation can abort a bull's charge in numerous ways, most of which are simpler or more direct, and thus more probable, than the one suggested by Delgado. For example, the stimulation may have simply rendered the bull confused, dizzy, nauseous, sleepy, or temporarily blind rather than nonaggressive; or the stimulation could have been painful. Clearly, any observation that can be interpreted in so many different ways provides little support for any one interpretation. When there are several possible interpretations for a behavioral observation, the rule is to give precedence to the simplest one; this rule is called **Morgan's Canon**. The following comments of Valenstein (1973) provide a reasoned view of Delgado's demonstration:

> Actually there is no good reason for believing that the stimulation had any direct effect on the bull's aggressive tendencies. An examination of the film record makes it apparent that the charging bull was stopped because as long as the stimulation was on it was forced to turn around in the same direction continuously. After examining the film, any scientist with knowledge in this field could conclude only that the stimulation had been activating a neural pathway controlling movement. (p. 122)...he [Delgado] seems to capitalize on every individual effect

his electrodes happen to produce and presents little, if any, experimental evidence that his impression of the underlying cause is correct. (p. 127)…his propensity for dramatic, albeit ambiguous, demonstrations has been a constant source of material for those whose purposes are served by exaggerating the omnipotence of brain stimulation. (p. 123)

Case 2: Becky, Moniz, and the Prefrontal Lobotomy

LO 1.16 Describe the rise and fall of prefrontal lobotomy.

In 1949, Dr. Egas Moniz was awarded the Nobel Prize in Physiology and Medicine for the development of **prefrontal lobotomy**—a surgical procedure in which the connections between the prefrontal lobes and the rest of the brain are cut as a treatment for mental illness. The **prefrontal lobes** are the large areas, left and right, at the very front of the brain (see Figure 1.9). Moniz's discovery was based on the report that Becky, a chimpanzee that frequently became upset when she made errors during the performance of a food-rewarded task, did not do so following the creation of a large bilateral lesion (an area of damage to both sides of the brain) of her prefrontal lobes. After hearing about this observation at a scientific meeting in 1935, Moniz convinced neurosurgeon Almeida Lima to operate on a series of psychiatric patients (see Heller et al., 2006). Lima cut out six large cores of prefrontal tissue with a surgical device called a **leucotome** (see Figure 1.10).

Following Moniz's claims that prefrontal surgery was therapeutically useful, there was a rapid proliferation of various forms of prefrontal psychosurgery. One such variation was **transorbital lobotomy**, which was developed in Italy and then popularized in the United States by Walter Freeman in the late 1940s. It involved inserting an ice pick–like device under the eyelid, driving it through the orbit (the eye socket) with a few taps of a mallet, and pushing it into the frontal lobes, where it was waved back and forth to sever the connections between the prefrontal lobes and the rest of the brain (see Figure 1.11). This operation was frequently performed in the surgeon's office.

Analysis of Case 2 Incredible as it may seem, Moniz's program of **psychosurgery** (any brain surgery, such as prefrontal lobotomy, performed for the treatment of a psychological problem) was largely based on the observation of a single chimpanzee in a single situation. Thus, Moniz displayed a lack of appreciation for the diversity of brain and behavior, both within and between species. No program of

Figure 1.10 The prefrontal lobotomy procedure developed by Moniz and Lima.

The leucotome was inserted six times into the patient's brain with the cutting wire retracted.

After each insertion, the cutting wire was extruded and the leucotome rotated to cut out a core of tissue.

Figure 1.9 The right and left prefrontal lobes, whose connections to the rest of the brain are disrupted by prefrontal lobotomy.

Right prefrontal lobe

Left prefrontal lobe

Figure 1.11 The transorbital procedure for performing prefrontal lobotomy.

psychosurgery should ever be initiated without a thorough assessment of the effects of the surgery on a large sample of subjects from various nonhuman mammalian species. To do so is not only unwise, it is unethical.

A second major weakness in the scientific case for prefrontal lobotomy was the failure of Moniz and others to carefully evaluate the consequences of the surgery in the first patients to undergo the operation (see Mashour, Walker, & Martuza, 2005; Singh, Hallmayer, & Illes, 2007). The early reports that the operation was therapeutically effective were based on the impressions of the individuals who were the least objective—the physicians who had prescribed the surgery and their colleagues. Patients were frequently judged as improved if they were more manageable, and little effort was made to evaluate more important aspects of their psychological adjustment or to document the existence of adverse side effects.

Eventually, it became clear that prefrontal lobotomies are of little therapeutic benefit and that they can produce a wide range of undesirable side effects, such as amorality, lack of foresight, emotional unresponsiveness, epilepsy, and urinary incontinence. This led to the abandonment of prefrontal lobotomy in many parts of the world—but not before more than 40,000 patients had been lobotomized in the United States alone. And prefrontal lobotomies still continue to be performed in some countries.

A particularly troubling aspect of the use of prefrontal lobotomy is that not only informed, consenting adults received this "treatment." In his memoir, Howard Dully described how he had been lobotomized at the age of 12 (Dully & Fleming, 2007). The lobotomy was arranged by Dully's stepmother, agreed to by his father, and performed in 10 minutes by Walter Freeman. Dully spent most of the rest of his life in asylums, jails, and halfway houses, wondering what he had done to deserve the lobotomy and how much it had been responsible for his troubled life. Investigation of the medical documents and interviews with some of those involved in the case have indicated that Dully was a normal child whose stepmother was obsessed by her hatred for him. Tragically, neither his father nor the medical profession intervened to protect him from Freeman's ice pick.

Some regard sound scientific methods as unnecessary obstacles in the paths of patients seeking treatment and therapists striving to provide it. However, the unforeseen consequences of prefrontal lobotomy should caution us against abandoning science for expediency. Only by observing the rules of science can scientists protect the public from bogus claims.

You are about to enter a world of amazing discovery and intriguing ideas: the world of biopsychology. We hope your brain enjoys learning about itself.

Themes Revisited

The seeds of three of the major themes of this text were planted in this chapter, but the thinking creatively theme predominated. First, you saw the creative approach that Lester and Gorzalka took in their research on the Coolidge effect in females. Then, you learned three important new ideas that will help you think about biopsychological claims: (1) the experimental method, (2) converging operations, and (3) scientific inference. Finally, you were introduced to two biopsychological claims that were once widely believed and saw how critical thinking identified their weaknesses and replaced them with creative new interpretations.

You also learned that two of the other major themes of the text—clinical implications and the evolutionary perspective—tend to be associated with particular divisions of biopsychology. Clinical implications most commonly emerge from **Clinical Implications** neuropsychological, psychopharmacological, and psychophysiological research; the evolutionary perspective is a defining feature of comparative psychology. **Evolutionary Perspective**

Key Terms

Chapter 2
Evolution, Genetics, and Experience

Thinking about the Biology of Behavior

Chapter Overview and Learning Objectives (LOs)

Thinking about the Biology of Behavior: From Dichotomies to Interactions	**LO 2.1**	Explain the origins of dichotomous thinking.
	LO 2.2	Explain why thinking about the biology of behavior in terms of traditional physiological–psychological and nature–nurture dichotomies is flawed.
Human Evolution	**LO 2.3**	Describe the origins of evolutionary theory.
	LO 2.4	Explain the evolutionary significance of social dominance and courtship displays.
	LO 2.5	Summarize the pathway of evolution from single-cell organisms to humans.
	LO 2.6	Describe nine commonly misunderstood points about evolution.
	LO 2.7	Describe how research on the evolution of the human brain has changed over time.

LO 2.8 Discuss the field of evolutionary psychology and the study of mate bonding.

Fundamental Genetics

LO 2.9 Describe what Mendel's work with pea plants tells us about the mechanisms of inheritance.

LO 2.10 Understand the structure and function of chromosomes.

LO 2.11 Outline the mechanisms of gene expression.

LO 2.12 Discuss several ways in which modern advances have changed our understanding of genetic processes.

LO 2.13 Define epigenetics, and explain how it is transforming our understanding of genetics.

Epigenetics of Behavioral Development: Interaction of Genetic Factors and Experience

LO 2.14 Discuss what insights into the genetics of behavior was gained from early research on selective breeding.

LO 2.15 Explain how classic research on phenylketonuria (PKU) has informed our understanding of the genetics of behavior.

LO 2.16 Describe how research on the ontogenetic development of birdsong has provided insight into the development of human language.

Genetics of Human Psychological Differences

LO 2.17 Explain why it is important to distinguish between the development of individuals and the development of individual differences.

LO 2.18 Explain heritability estimates and how they are commonly misinterpreted.

LO 2.19 Describe two ways that twin studies can be used to study the interaction of genes and experience (i.e., nature and nurture).

We all tend to think about things in ways that have been ingrained in us by our **zeitgeist** (pronounced "ZYTE-gyste"), the general intellectual climate of our culture. That is why this is a particularly important chapter for you. You see, you are the intellectual product of a zeitgeist that promotes ways of thinking about the biological bases of behavior that are inconsistent with the facts. The primary purpose of this chapter is to help you bring your thinking about the biology of behavior in line with modern biopsychological science.

Thinking about the Biology of Behavior: From Dichotomies to Interactions

We tend to ignore the subtleties, inconsistencies, and complexities of our existence and to think in terms of simple, mutually exclusive dichotomies: right–wrong, good–bad, attractive–unattractive, and so on. The allure of this way of thinking is its simplicity.

The Origins of Dichotomous Thinking

LO 2.1 Explain the origins of dichotomous thinking.

The tendency to think about behavior in terms of dichotomies is illustrated by two kinds of questions commonly asked about behavior: (1) Is it physiological, or is it psychological? (2) Is it inherited, or is it learned? Both questions have proved to be misguided, yet they are among the most common kinds of questions asked in biopsychology classrooms. That is why we are dwelling on them here.

IS IT PHYSIOLOGICAL, OR IS IT PSYCHOLOGICAL? The idea that human processes fall into one of two categories, physiological or psychological, has a long history in many cultures. In Western cultures, it rose to prominence following the Dark Ages in response to a 17th-century conflict between science and the Roman Church. For much of the history of Western civilization, truth was whatever was decreed to be true by the Church.

Then, in about 1400, things started to change. The famines, plagues, and marauding armies that had repeatedly swept Europe during the Dark Ages subsided, and interest turned to art, commerce, and scholarship—this was the period of the Renaissance, or rebirth (1400–1700). Some Renaissance scholars were not content to follow the dictates of the Church; instead, they started to study things directly by observing them—and so it was that modern science was born.

Much of the scientific knowledge that accumulated during the Renaissance was at odds with Church dictates. However, the conflict was resolved by the prominent French philosopher René Descartes (pronounced "day-CART"). Descartes (1596–1650) advocated a philosophy that, in a sense, gave one part of the universe to science and the other part to the Church. He argued that the universe is composed of two elements: (1) physical matter, which behaves according to the laws of nature and is thus a suitable object of scientific investigation—the human body, including the brain, was assumed to be entirely physical, and so were nonhuman animals; and (2) the human mind (soul, self, or spirit), which lacks physical substance, controls human behavior, obeys no natural laws, and is thus the appropriate purview of the Church.

Cartesian dualism, as Descartes's philosophy became known, was sanctioned by the Roman Church, and so the idea that the human brain and the mind are separate entities became even more widely accepted. It has survived to this day, despite the intervening centuries of scientific progress. Most people now understand that human behavior has a physiological basis, but many still cling to the dualistic assumption that there is a category of human activity that somehow transcends the human brain (Riekki, Lindeman, & Lipsanen, 2013).

IS IT INHERITED, OR IS IT LEARNED? The tendency to think in terms of dichotomies extends to the way people think about the development of behavioral capacities. For centuries, scholars have debated whether humans and other animals inherit their behavioral capacities or acquire them through learning. This debate is commonly referred to as the **nature–nurture issue**.

Most of the early North American experimental psychologists were totally committed to the nurture (learning) side of the nature–nurture issue (de Waal, 1999). The degree of this commitment is illustrated by the oft-cited words of John B. Watson, the father of *behaviorism*:

We have no real evidence of the inheritance of [behavioral] traits. I would feel perfectly confident in the ultimately favorable outcome of careful upbringing of a healthy, well-formed baby born of a long line of crooks, murderers and thieves, and prostitutes. Who has any evidence to the contrary?

…Give me a dozen healthy infants, well-formed, and my own specified world to bring them up in and I'll guarantee to take any one at random and train him to become any type of specialist I might select—doctor, lawyer, artist, merchant-chief and, yes even beggar-man and thief. (Watson, 1930, pp. 103–104)

At the same time experimental psychology was taking root in North America, **ethology** (the study of animal behavior in the wild) was becoming the dominant approach to the study of behavior in Europe. European ethology, in contrast to North American experimental psychology, focused on the study of **instinctive behaviors** (behaviors that occur in all like members of a species, even when there seems to have been no opportunity for them to have been learned), and it emphasized the role of nature, or inherited factors, in behavioral development. Because instinctive behaviors are not learned, the early ethologists assumed they are entirely inherited. They were wrong, but then so were the early experimental psychologists.

Problems with Thinking about the Biology of Behavior in Terms of Traditional Dichotomies

LO 2.2 Explain why thinking about the biology of behavior in terms of traditional physiological–psychological and nature–nurture dichotomies is flawed.

The physiological-or-psychological debate and the nature-or-nurture debate are based on incorrect ways of thinking about the biology of behavior, and a new generation of questions is directing the current boom in biopsychological research (Churchland, 2002). What is wrong with these old ways of thinking about the biology of behavior, and what are the new ways?

PHYSIOLOGICAL-OR-PSYCHOLOGICAL THINKING RUNS INTO DIFFICULTY. Not long after Descartes's mind–brain dualism was officially sanctioned by the Roman Church, it started to come under public attack.

In 1747, Julien Offroy de la Mettrie anonymously published a pamphlet that scandalized Europe.…La Mettrie fled to Berlin, where he was forced to live in exile for the rest of his life. His crime? He had argued that thought was produced by the brain—a dangerous assault, in the eyes of his contemporaries. (Corsi, 1991, cover)

There are two lines of evidence against *physiological-or-psychological thinking* (the assumption that some aspects of human psychological functioning are so complex that they could not possibly be the product of a physical brain). The first line is composed of the many demonstrations that even the most complex psychological changes (e.g., changes in self-awareness, memory, or emotion) can be produced by damage to, or stimulation of, parts of the brain (see Farah & Murphy, 2009). The second line of evidence is composed of demonstrations that some nonhuman species, particularly *primate* species, possess some abilities that were once assumed to be purely psychological and thus purely human (see Bartal, Decety, & Mason, 2011; Hauser, 2009; Kornell, 2009). The following two cases illustrate these two kinds of evidence. Both cases deal with self-awareness, which is widely regarded as one hallmark of the human mind (see Apps & Tsakiris, 2014).

The first case is Oliver Sacks's (1985) account of "the man who fell out of bed." This patient was suffering from **asomatognosia**, a deficiency in the awareness of parts of one's own body. Asomatognosia typically involves the left side of the body and usually results from damage to the *right parietal lobe* (see Figure 2.1).

Clinical Implications The point here is that although the changes in self-awareness displayed by the patient were very complex, they were clearly the result of brain damage: Indeed, the full range of human experience can be produced by manipulations of the brain.

Figure 2.1 Asomatognosia typically involves damage to the right parietal lobe.

Right parietal lobe

The Case of the Man Who Fell Out of Bed

When he awoke, Dr. Sacks's patient felt fine—that is, until he touched the thing in bed next to him. It was a severed human leg, all hairy and still warm! At first, the patient was confused. Then he figured it out. One of the nurses must have taken it from the autopsy department and put it in his bed as a joke. Some joke; it was disgusting. So, he threw the leg out of the bed, but somehow he landed on the floor with it attached to him.

The patient became agitated and desperate, and Dr. Sacks tried to comfort him and help him back into the bed. Making one last effort to reduce the patient's confusion, Sacks asked him where his left leg was, if the one attached to him wasn't it. Turning pale and looking like he was about to pass out, the patient replied that he had no idea where his own leg was—it had disappeared.

The second case describes G. G. Gallup's research on self-awareness in chimpanzees (see Gallup, 1983; Parker, Mitchell, & Boccia, 1994). The point of this case is that even nonhumans, which are assumed to have no mind, are capable of considerable psychological complexity—in this case, self-awareness. Although their brains are less complex than the brains of humans, some species are capable of high levels of psychological complexity (see Gomez-Marin & Mainen, 2016).

Case of the Chimps with Mirrors*

One way of assessing an organism's self-awareness is to confront it with a mirror. Invariably, the first reaction of a chimpanzee to a mirror is to respond as if it were seeing another chimpanzee. However, after a day or two, it starts to act as if it were self-aware. It starts to use the mirror to groom, to inspect parts of its body, and to experiment with its reflection by making faces and assuming unusual postures while monitoring the results in the mirror.

In an attempt to provide even more convincing evidence of self-awareness, Gallup (1983) devised a clever test. Each chimpanzee was anesthetized, and its eyebrow was painted with a red, odorless, dye. Following recovery from anesthesia, the mirror was reintroduced. Upon seeing its painted eyebrow in the mirror, each chimpanzee repeatedly touched the marked area on its eyebrow while watching the image. [See Figure 2.2.] Moreover, there was over a threefold increase in the time that the chimps spent looking in the mirror, and several kept touching their eyebrows and smelling their fingers. We suspect that you would respond pretty much the same way if you saw yourself in the mirror with a red spot on your face.

(continued)

* "Toward a Comparative Psychology of Mind" by G. G. Gallup, Jr., *American Journal of Primatology* 2:237–248, 1983. Copyright © 1983 John Wiley & Sons, Inc.

Figure 2.2 The reactions of chimpanzees to their *own* images suggest that they are self-aware. In this photo, the chimpanzee is reacting to the bright red, odorless dye that was painted on its eyebrow ridge while it was anesthetized. (Photograph by Donna Bierschwale, courtesy of the New Iberia Research Center.)

Watch this video on MyPsychLab

SELF AWARENESS IN TODDLERS

NATURE-OR-NURTURE THINKING RUNS INTO DIFFICULTY. The history of nature-or-nurture thinking can be summed up by paraphrasing Mark Twain: "Reports of its death have been greatly exaggerated." Each time it has been discredited, it has resurfaced in a slightly modified form. First, factors other than genetics and learning were shown to influence behavioral development; factors such as the fetal environment, nutrition, stress, and sensory stimulation all proved to be influential. This led to a broadening of the concept of nurture to include a variety of experiential factors in addition to learning. In effect, it changed the nature-or-nurture dichotomy from "genetic factors or learning" to "genetic factors or experience."

Next, it was argued convincingly that behavior always develops under the combined control of both nature and nurture (see Johnston, 1987; Rutter, 1997), not under the control of one or the other. Faced with this point, many people merely substituted one kind of nature-or-nurture thinking for another. They stopped asking, "Is it genetic, or is it the result of experience?" and started asking, "How much of it is genetic, and how much of it is the result of experience?"

Like earlier versions of the nature-or-nurture question, the how-much-of-it-is-genetic-and-how-much-of-it-is-the-result-of-experience version is fundamentally flawed. The problem is that it is based on the premise that genetic factors and experiential factors combine in an additive fashion—that a behavioral capacity, such as intelligence, is created through the combination or mixture of so many parts of genetics and so many parts of experience rather than through the interaction of genetics and experience. Once you learn more about how genetic factors and experience interact, you will better appreciate the folly of this assumption. For the time being, however, let us illustrate its weakness with a metaphor embedded in an anecdote.

The Case of the Thinking Student

One of my students told me (JP) she had read that intelligence was one-third genetic and two-thirds experience, and she wondered whether this was true. I responded by asking her the following question: "If I wanted to get a better understanding of music, would it be reasonable for me to begin by asking how much of it came from the musician and how much of it came from the instrument?"

"That would be dumb," she said. "The music comes from both; it makes no sense to ask how much comes from the musician and how much comes from the instrument. Somehow the music results from the interaction of the two together. You would have to ask about the interaction."

"That's exactly right," I said. "Now, do you see why…"

"Don't say any more," she interrupted. "I see what you're getting at. Intelligence is the product of the interaction of genes and experience, and it is dumb to try to find how much comes from genes and how much comes from experience."

"Yes!" I thought.

The point of this metaphor, in case you have forgotten, is to illustrate why it is nonsensical to try to understand interactions between two factors by asking how much each factor contributes. We would not ask how much a musician and how much her instrument contributes to producing music; we would not ask how much the water and how much the temperature contributes to evaporation; and we would not ask how much a male and how much a female contributes to reproduction. Similarly, we shouldn't ask how much genetic and how much experiential factors contribute to behavioral development. The answers to all these questions lie in understanding the nature of the interactions (see Sung et al., 2014; Uher, 2014). The importance of thinking about development in terms of interactions will become even more apparent later in this chapter.

A MODEL OF THE BIOLOGY OF BEHAVIOR.
So far in this module, you have learned why people tend to think about the biology of behavior in terms of dichotomies, and you have learned some of the reasons why this way of thinking is inappropriate. Now, let's look at the way of thinking about the biology of behavior that has been adopted by many biopsychologists (see Kimble, 1989). It is illustrated in Figure 2.3. Like other powerful ideas, it is simple and logical. This model boils down to the single premise that all behavior is the product of interactions among three factors: (1) the organism's genetic endowment, which is a product of its evolution; (2) its experience; and (3) its perception of the current situation. Please examine the model carefully, and consider its implications.

Thinking Creatively Imagine you are a biopsychology instructor. One of your students asks you whether depression is physiological or psychological. What would you say?

The next three modules of this chapter deal with three elements of this model of behavior: evolution, genetics, and the interaction of genetics and experience in behavioral development. The final module of the chapter deals with the genetics of human psychological differences.

Human Evolution

Darwin's Theory of Evolution

LO 2.3   Describe the origins of evolutionary theory.

Modern biology began in 1859 with the publication of Charles Darwin's *On the Origin of Species*. In this monumental work, Darwin described his theory of evolution—the single most influential theory in the biological sciences. Darwin

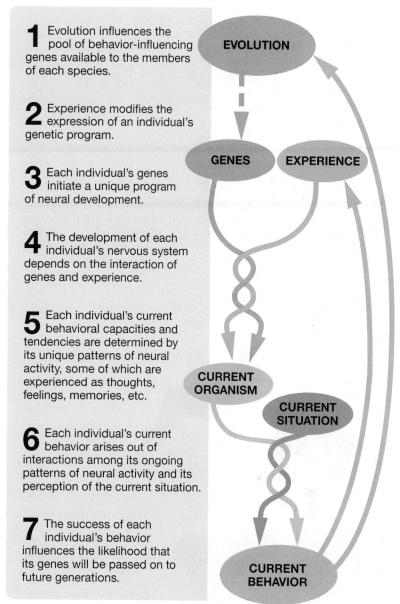

Figure 2.3 A schematic illustration of the way in which many biopsychologists think about the biology of behavior.

1 Evolution influences the pool of behavior-influencing genes available to the members of each species.

2 Experience modifies the expression of an individual's genetic program.

3 Each individual's genes initiate a unique program of neural development.

4 The development of each individual's nervous system depends on the interaction of genes and experience.

5 Each individual's current behavioral capacities and tendencies are determined by its unique patterns of neural activity, some of which are experienced as thoughts, feelings, memories, etc.

6 Each individual's current behavior arises out of interactions among its ongoing patterns of neural activity and its perception of the current situation.

7 The success of each individual's behavior influences the likelihood that its genes will be passed on to future generations.

was not the first to suggest that species **evolve** (undergo gradual orderly change) from preexisting species, but he was the first to amass a large body of supporting evidence and the first to suggest how evolution occurs (see Bowler, 2009).

Darwin presented three kinds of evidence to support his assertion that species evolve: (1) He documented the evolution of fossil records through progressively more recent geological layers. (2) He described striking structural similarities among living species (e.g., a human's hand, a bird's wing, and a cat's paw), which suggested that they had evolved from common ancestors. (3) He pointed to the major changes that had been brought about in domestic plants and animals by programs of selective breeding. However, the most convincing evidence of evolution comes from direct observations of rapid

Figure 2.4 Four kinds of evidence supporting the theory that species evolve.

Fossil records change systematically through geological layers. Illustrated here is the evolution of the hominid skull.

There are striking structural similarities among diverse living species (e.g., between a human arm and a bat's wing).

Major changes have been created in domestic plants and animals by programs of selective breeding.

Evolution has been observed in progress. For example, an 18-month drought on one of the Galápagos Islands left only large, difficult-to-eat seeds and increased the beak size in one species of finch.

when repeated for generation after generation, leads to the evolution of species that are better adapted to surviving and reproducing in their particular environmental niche. Darwin called this process *natural selection* to emphasize its similarity to the artificial selective breeding practices employed by breeders of domestic animals. Just as horse breeders create faster horses by selectively breeding the fastest of their existing stock, nature creates fitter animals by selectively breeding the fittest. **Fitness**, in the Darwinian sense, is the ability of an organism to survive and contribute its genes to the next generation.

The theory of evolution was at odds with the various dogmatic views embedded in the 19th-century zeitgeist, so it met with initial resistance. Although resistance still exists, virtually none comes from people who understand the evidence (see Curry, 2009; Short & Hawley, 2015).

> Evolution is both a beautiful concept and an important one, more crucial nowadays to human welfare, to medical science, and to our understanding of the world than ever before [see Mindell, 2009]. It's also deeply persuasive—a theory you can take to the bank...the supporting evidence is abundant, various, ever increasing, and easily available in museums, popular books, textbooks, and a mountainous accumulation of scientific studies. No one needs to, and no one should, accept evolution merely as a matter of faith. (Quammen, 2004, p. 8)

Evolution and Behavior

LO 2.4 **Explain the evolutionary significance of social dominance and courtship displays.**

Some behaviors play an obvious role in evolution. For example, the ability to find food, avoid predation, or defend one's young obviously increases an animal's ability to pass on its genes to future generations. Other behaviors play a role that is less obvious but no less important—for example, social dominance and courtship displays, which are discussed in the following two sections.

SOCIAL DOMINANCE. The males of many species establish a stable *hierarchy of social dominance* through combative encounters with other males (see Clutton-Brock & Huchard, 2013). In some species, these encounters often

evolution in progress (see Barrick & Lenski, 2013). For example, Grant (1991) observed evolution of the finches of the Galápagos Islands—a population studied by Darwin himself (see Lamichhaney et al., 2015)—after only a single season of drought. Figure 2.4 illustrates these four kinds of evidence.

Darwin argued that evolution occurs through **natural selection** (see Pritchard, 2010). He pointed out that the members of each species vary greatly in their structure, physiology, and behavior and that the heritable traits associated with high rates of survival and reproduction are the most likely ones to be passed on to future generations (see Kingsley, 2009). He argued that natural selection,

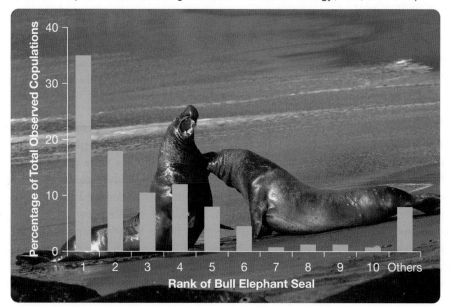

Figure 2.5 Two massive bull elephant seals challenge one another. Dominant bull elephant seals copulate more frequently than those lower in the dominance hierarchy. (Based on McCann, T. S. (1981). Aggression and sexual activity of male southern elephant seals, *Mirounga leonina. Journal of Zoology*, *195*, 295–310.)

(Chart axes: y-axis "Percentage of Total Observed Copulations" 0–40; x-axis "Rank of Bull Elephant Seal" 1 2 3 4 5 6 7 8 9 10 Others)

and that these offspring were more likely to survive to sexual maturity. They attributed these advantages to the fact that high-ranking female chimpanzees are more likely to maintain access to productive food foraging areas (see Pusey & Schroepfer-Walker, 2013).

COURTSHIP DISPLAY. An intricate series of courtship displays precedes copulation in many species. The male approaches the female and signals his interest. His signal (which may be olfactory, visual, auditory, or tactual) may elicit a signal in the female, which may elicit another response in the male, and so on, until copulation ensues. But copulation is unlikely to occur if one of the pair fails to react appropriately to the signals of the other.

Courtship displays are thought to promote the evolution of new species. Let us explain. A **species** is a group of organisms reproductively isolated from other organisms; that is, the members of a species can produce fertile offspring only by mating with members of the same species (see Mallet, 2010; de Knijff, 2014). A new species begins to branch off from an existing species when some barrier discourages breeding between a subpopulation of the existing species and the remainder of the species. Once such a reproductive barrier forms, the subpopulation evolves independently of the remainder of the species until cross-fertilization becomes impossible (see Arnegard et al., 2014; Roesti & Salzburger, 2014).

The reproductive barrier may be geographic; for example, a few birds may fly together to an isolated island, where many generations of their offspring breed among themselves and evolve into a separate species. Alternatively—to get back to the main point—the reproductive barrier may be behavioral. A few members of a species may develop different courtship displays, and these may form a reproductive barrier between themselves and the rest of their **conspecifics** (members of the same species): Only the suitable exchange of displays between a courting couple will lead to reproduction.

involve physical damage; in others, they involve mainly posturing and threatening until one of the two combatants backs down. The dominant male usually wins encounters with all other males of the group; the number two male usually wins encounters with all males except the dominant male; and so on down the line. Once a hierarchy is established, hostilities diminish because the low-ranking males learn to avoid or quickly submit to the dominant males. Because most of the fighting goes on between males competing for positions high in the social hierarchy, low-ranking males fight little and the lower levels of the hierarchy tend to be only vaguely recognizable.

Why is social dominance an important factor in evolution? One reason is that in some species, dominant males copulate more than nondominant males and thus are more effective in passing on their characteristics to future generations. McCann (1981) studied the effect of social dominance on the rate of copulation in 10 bull elephant seals that cohabited the same breeding beach. These massive animals challenge each other by raising themselves to full height and pushing chest to chest. Usually, the smaller of the two backs down; if it does not, a vicious neck-biting battle ensues (see Figure 2.5). McCann found that the dominant male accounted for about 37 percent of the copulations during the study, whereas poor number 10 accounted for only about 1 percent (see Figure 2.5).

Another reason why social dominance is an important factor in evolution is that in some species, dominant females are more likely to produce more and healthier offspring. For example, Pusey, Williams, and Goodall (1997) found that high-ranking female chimpanzees produced more offspring

Course of Human Evolution

LO 2.5   **Summarize the pathway of evolution from single-cell organisms to humans.**

By studying fossil records and comparing current species, we humans have looked back in time and pieced together the evolutionary history of our species (e.g., Hublin,

Neubauer, & Gunz, 2015)—although some of the details are still controversial. The course of human evolution, as it is currently understood, is summarized in this section.

EVOLUTION OF VERTEBRATES. Complex multicellular water-dwelling organisms first appeared on earth about 600 million years ago (Bottjer, 2005). About 150 million years later, the first chordates evolved. **Chordates** (pronounced "KOR-dates") are animals with dorsal nerve cords (large nerves that run along the center of the back, or *dorsum*); they are 1 of the 20 or so large categories, or *phyla* (pronounced "FY-la"), into which zoologists group animal species. The first chordates with spinal bones to protect their dorsal nerve cords evolved about 25 million years later. The spinal bones are called *vertebrae* (pronounced "VERT-eh-bray"), and the chordates that possess them are called **vertebrates**. The first vertebrates were primitive bony fishes. Today, there are seven classes of vertebrates: three classes of fishes, plus amphibians, reptiles, birds, and mammals.

Recently, an important fossil was discovered in northern Canada (Pierce, Clack, & Hutchinson, 2012; Pierce, Hutchinson, & Clack, 2013). The fossil is about 375 million years old, from a time when some fish were starting to evolve into four-legged land vertebrates. This fossilized creature had been a little of each: Along with the scales, teeth, and gills of a fish, it had several anatomical features found only in land animals (such as primitive wrists and finger bones). In short, this is just the type of link between fish and land vertebrates predicted by the theory of evolution. See Figure 2.6.

EVOLUTION OF AMPHIBIANS. About 410 million years ago, the first bony fishes started to venture out of the water.

Fishes that could survive on land for brief periods of time had two great advantages: They could escape from stagnant pools to nearby fresh water, and they could take advantage of terrestrial food sources. The advantages of life on land were so great that natural selection transformed the fins and gills of bony fishes to legs and lungs, respectively—and so it was that the first **amphibians** evolved about 400 million years ago. Amphibians (e.g., frogs, toads, and salamanders) in their larval form must live in the water; only adult amphibians can survive on land.

EVOLUTION OF REPTILES. About 300 million years ago, reptiles (e.g., lizards, snakes, and turtles) evolved from a branch of amphibians. Reptiles were the first vertebrates to lay shell-covered eggs and to be covered by dry scales. Both of these adaptations reduced the reliance of reptiles on watery habitats. A reptile does not have to spend the first stage of its life in the watery environment of a pond or lake; instead, it spends the first stage of its life in the watery environment of a shell-covered egg. And once hatched, a reptile can live far from water because its dry scales greatly reduce water loss through its water-permeable skin.

EVOLUTION OF MAMMALS. About 180 million years ago, during the height of the age of dinosaurs, a new class of vertebrates evolved from one line of small reptiles. The females of this new class fed their young with secretions from special glands called *mammary glands*, and the members of the class are called **mammals** after these glands. Eventually, mammals stopped laying eggs; instead, the females nurtured their young in the watery environment of their bodies until the young were mature enough to be born. The duck-billed platypus is one surviving mammalian species that lays eggs.

Spending the first stage of life inside one's mother proved to have considerable survival value; it provided the long-term security and environmental stability necessary for complex programs of development to unfold. Today, most classification systems recognize about 20 different orders of mammals (see Helgen, 2011; Meredith et al., 2011). The order to which we belong is the order **primates**. We humans—in our usual humble way—named our order using the Latin term *primus*, which means "first" or "foremost."

Primates have proven particularly difficult to categorize because there is no single characteristic possessed by all primates but no other animals. Still, most experts agree there are about 16 families of primates. Members of four of them appear in Figure 2.7.

Figure 2.6 A recently discovered fossil of a missing evolutionary link is shown on the right, and a reconstruction of the creature is shown on the left. It had scales, teeth, and gills like a fish and primitive wrist and finger bones similar to those of land animals.

Apes (gibbons, orangutans, gorillas, and chimpanzees) are thought to have evolved from a line of Old World monkeys. Like Old World monkeys, apes have long arms and grasping hind feet that are specialized for arboreal (treetop) travel, and they have opposable thumbs that are not long enough to be of much use for precise manipulation (see Figure 2.8). Unlike Old World monkeys, though, apes have no tails and can walk upright for short distances. Chimpanzees are the closest living relatives of humans; almost 99 percent of genes are identical in the two species (see Rogers & Gibbs, 2014)—but see Cohen (2007); however, the actual ape ancestor of humans is likely long extinct (Jaeger & Marivaux, 2005).

EMERGENCE OF HUMANKIND. Primates of the tribe that includes humans are the **Hominini** (see Figure 2.9). This tribe is composed of at least six *genera* (the plural of *genus*): *Australopithecus, Paranthropus, Sahelanthropus, Orrorin, Pan,* and *Homo. Homo* is thought to be composed of at least eight species (see Wiedemann, 2014; Gibbons, 2015a); seven of those *Homo* species are now extinct, whereas *Homo sapiens* (humans) are not.

It is difficult to reconstruct the events of human evolution because the evidence is so sparse. Only a few partial hominin fossils dating from the critical period have been discovered. However, three important hominin fossil discoveries have recently been made (see Harmon, 2013):

- An uncommonly complete fossil of a 3-year-old early *Australopithecus* girl in Ethiopia (see Figure 2.10; Gibbons, 2009; Suwa et al., 2009; White et al., 2009).

- Fossils indicating that a population of tiny hominins inhabited the Indonesian island of Flores as recently as 18,000 years ago (see Callaway, 2014; Stringer, 2014).

- Several early Australopithecine fossils with combinations of human and nonhuman characteristics in a pit in South Africa (Pickering et al., 2011; Wong, 2012).

Many experts believe that the australopithecines evolved about 4 million years ago in Africa (see Krubitzer & Stolzenberg, 2014; Skinner et al., 2015; Wood, 2010) from a line of apes (*australo* means "southern," and *pithecus* means "ape"). Several species of Australopithecus are thought to have roamed the African plains for about 2 million years before becoming extinct. Australopithecines were only about 1.3 meters (4 feet) tall, and they had small brains, but analysis of their pelvis and leg bones indicates that their posture was upright. Any doubts about their upright posture were erased by the discovery of the fossilized footprints pictured in Figure 2.11 (see Raichlen et al., 2010).

The first *Homo* species are thought to have evolved from one species of *Australopithecus* about 2 to 2.8 million years ago (see Antón, Potts, & Aiello, 2014; Dimaggio et al., 2015; Schroeder et al., 2014; Villmoore et al., 2015), although there are alternative views of the origins of the *Homo* genus (see Wiedemann, 2014; Wood, 2014). One distinctive feature of the early *Homo* species was the large size of their brain cavity, larger than that of *Australopithecus* but smaller than that of modern humans. The early *Homo* species used fire and tools (see Orban & Caruana, 2014;

Figure 2.7 Examples of four different families of primates.

HOMINID
Silver-Backed Lowland Gorilla

HOMINID
Human

OLD-WORLD MONKEY
Hussar Monkey

CEBID
Squirrel Monkey

TARSIER
Tarsier Monkey

Figure 2.8 A comparison of the feet and hands of a human and a chimpanzee.

Human   Chimpanzee

Figure 2.9 A taxonomy of the human species.

KINGDOM Animal

PHYLUM   Chordate

CLASS   Mammal

ORDER   Primate

FAMILY   Hominid

TRIBE   Hominini

GENUS   Homo

SPECIES   Sapiens

Figure 2.10 The remarkably complete skull of a 3-year-old *Australopithecus* girl; the fossil is 3.3 million years old.

Schwartz & Tattersall, 2015) and coexisted in Africa with various species of *Australopithecus* for about a half-million years, until the australopithecines died out. Early *Homo* species also existed outside of Africa for about 1.85 million years (see Lordkipanidze et al., 2013; Wood, 2011).

About 275,000 years ago (see Adler et al., 2014), early *Homo* species were gradually replaced in the African fossil record by modern humans (*Homo sapiens*). Then, about 130,000 years ago, modern humans began to migrate out of Africa (see Gibbons, 2015b; Reyes-Centeno et al., 2014).

Paradoxically, although the big three human attributes—large brain, upright posture, and free hands with an opposable thumb—have been evident for hundreds of thousands of years, most human accomplishments are of recent origin. Artistic products (e.g., wall paintings and carvings) did not appear until about 40,000 years ago (see Krubitzer & Stolzenberg, 2014; Pringle, 2013), ranching and farming were not established until about 10,000 years ago (see Larson et al., 2014), and writing was not invented until about 7,500 years ago.

Thinking about Human Evolution

LO 2.6 Describe nine commonly misunderstood points about evolution.

Figure 2.12 illustrates the main branches of vertebrate evolution. As you examine it, consider the following commonly misunderstood points about evolution. They should provide you with a new perspective from which to consider your own origins.

Thinking Creatively

- Evolution does not proceed in a single line. Although it is common to think of an evolutionary ladder or scale, a far better metaphor for evolution is a dense bush.

- We humans have little reason to claim evolutionary supremacy. We are the last surviving species of a

Figure 2.11 Fossilized footprints of Australopithecus hominins who strode across African volcanic ash about 3.6 million years ago, leaving a 70-meter trail. There were two adults and a child; the child often walked in the footsteps of the adults.

family (i.e., hominins) that has existed for only a blip of evolutionary time.

- Evolution does not always proceed slowly and gradually. Rapid evolutionary changes (i.e., in a few generations) can be triggered by sudden changes in the environment or by adaptive genetic mutations. Whether human evolution occurred gradually or suddenly is still a matter of intense debate among *paleontologists* (those who scientifically study fossils). About the time hominins evolved, there was a cooling of the earth, leading to a decrease in African forests and an increase in African grasslands (see Behrensmeyer, 2006). This may have accelerated human evolution.

- Few products of evolution have survived to the present day—only the tips of the branches of the evolutionary bush have survived. Fewer than 1 percent of all known species are still in existence.

- Evolution does not progress to preordained perfection—evolution is a tinkerer, not an architect. Increases in adaptation occur through changes to existing programs of development; and, although the results are improvements in their particular environmental context, they are never perfect designs. For example, the fact that mammalian sperm do not develop effectively at body temperature led to the evolution of the scrotum—hardly a perfect solution to any design problem (see Shubin, 2009).

- Not all existing behaviors or structures are adaptive. Evolution often occurs through changes in developmental programs that lead to several related characteristics, only one of which might be adaptive—the incidental nonadaptive evolutionary by-products are called **spandrels**. The human belly button is a spandrel; it serves no adaptive function and is merely the by-product of the umbilical cord. Also, behaviors or structures that were once adaptive might become nonadaptive, or even maladaptive, if the environment changes.

> **Evolutionary Perspective** Can you think of an example of a behavior or structure that is currently adaptive but that might become nonadaptive, or even maladaptive, if the environment were to change?

- Not all existing adaptive characteristics evolved to perform their current function. Some characteristics, called **exaptations**, evolved to serve one function and were later co-opted to serve another. For example, bird wings are exaptations—they are limbs that initially evolved for the purpose of walking.

- Similarities among species do not necessarily mean that the species have common evolutionary origins. Structures that are similar because they have a common evolutionary origin are termed **homologous**; structures that are similar but do not have a common evolutionary origin are termed **analogous**. The similarities between analogous structures result from **convergent evolution**, the evolution in unrelated species of similar solutions to the same environmental demands (see Stern, 2013). Deciding whether a structural similarity is analogous or homologous requires careful analysis of the similarity. For example, a bird's wing and a human's arm have a basic underlying commonality of skeletal structure that suggests a common ancestor; in contrast, a bird's wing and a bee's wing have few structural similarities, although they do serve the same function.

- There is now considerable evidence that *Homo sapiens* mated with the other *Homo* species (e.g., *Homo neanderthalensis*) they encountered both within Africa and

Figure 2.12 Vertebrate evolution.

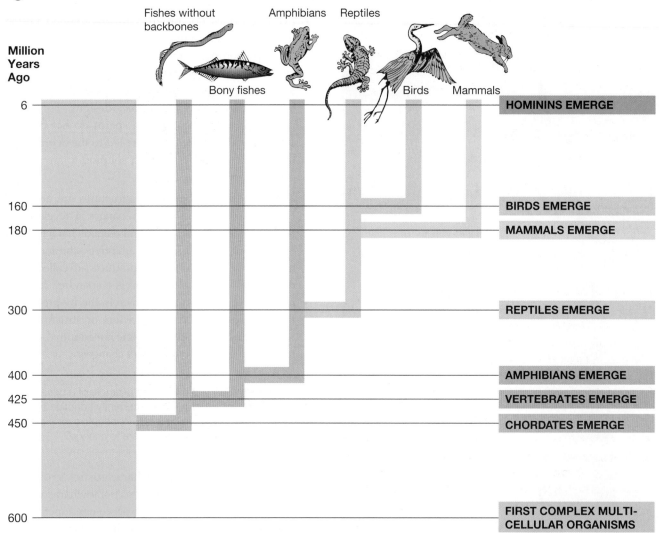

as they migrated out of Africa (see Gibbons, 2014; Hammer, 2013; Wong, 2015). These findings change the way we see our origins: We are not the product of a single ancestral population originating in Africa; rather, we are the offspring of many *Homo* populations that once coexisted.

Evolution of the Human Brain

LO 2.7   Describe how research on the evolution of the human brain has changed over time.

Early research on the evolution of the human brain focused on size. This research was stimulated by the assumption that brain size and intellectual capacity are closely related—an assumption that quickly ran into two problems. First, it was shown that modern humans, whom modern humans believe to be the most intelligent of all creatures, do not have the biggest brains. With brains weighing about 1,350 grams, humans rank far behind whales and elephants, whose brains weigh between 5,000 and 8,000 grams (Manger, 2013; Patzke et al., 2014). Second, the sizes

of the brains of acclaimed intellectuals (e.g., Einstein) were found to be unremarkable, certainly no match for their gigantic intellects. It is now clear that, although healthy adult human brains vary greatly in size—between about 1,000 and 2,000 grams—there is no clear relationship between overall human brain size and intelligence.

One obvious problem in relating brain size to intelligence is the fact that larger animals tend to have larger brains, presumably because larger bodies require more brain tissue to control and regulate them. Thus, the facts that large men tend to have larger brains than small men, that men tend to have larger brains than women, and that elephants have larger brains than humans do not suggest anything about the relative intelligence of these populations. This problem led to the proposal that brain weight expressed as a percentage of total body weight might be a better measure of intellectual capacity. This measure allows humans (2.33 percent) to take their rightful place ahead of elephants (0.20 percent), but it also allows both humans and elephants to be surpassed by that intellectual giant of the animal kingdom, the shrew (3.33 percent).

A more reasonable approach to the study of brain evolution has been to compare the evolution of different brain regions. For example, it has been informative to consider the evolution of the **brain stem** separately from the evolution of the **cerebrum** (cerebral hemispheres). In general, the brain stem regulates reflex activities that are critical for survival (e.g., heart rate, respiration, and blood glucose level), whereas the cerebrum is involved in more complex adaptive processes such as learning, perception, and motivation.

Figure 2.13 is a schematic representation of the relative size of the brain stems and cerebrums of several species that are living descendants of species from which humans evolved. This figure makes three important points about the evolution of the human brain:

- The brain has increased in size during evolution.
- Most of the increase in size has occurred in the cerebrum.
- An increase in the number of **convolutions**—folds on the cerebral surface—has greatly increased the surface area of the *cerebral cortex*, the outermost layer of cerebral tissue (see Geschwind & Rakic, 2013; Zilles, Palermo-Gallagher, & Amunts, 2013).

Although the brains of related species differ, there are fundamental similarities: All brains are constructed of neurons, and the neural structures in the brains of one species can usually be found in the same locations in the brains of related species (e.g., Goulas et al., 2014). For example, the brains of humans, monkeys, rats, and mice contain the same major structures connected in similar ways, and similar structures tend to perform similar functions (see Cole et al., 2009). The human brain appears to have evolved from the brains of our closest primate relatives (see Hofman, 2014; Matsuzawa, 2013).

Evolutionary Psychology: Understanding Mate Bonding

LO 2.8 **Discuss the field of evolutionary psychology and the study of mate bonding.**

The evolutionary approach has been embraced by many psychologists. Indeed, a field of psychology, termed *evolutionary psychology*, has coalesced around it. Evolutionary psychologists try to understand human behaviors through a consideration of the pressures that led to their evolution (see Burke, 2014). Some of the most interesting and controversial work in this field has focused on questions of sex differences in mate bonding, questions you may be dealing with in your own life.

Evolutionary Perspective

In most vertebrate species, mating is totally promiscuous—*promiscuity* is a mating arrangement in which the members of both sexes indiscriminately copulate with many different partners during each mating period.

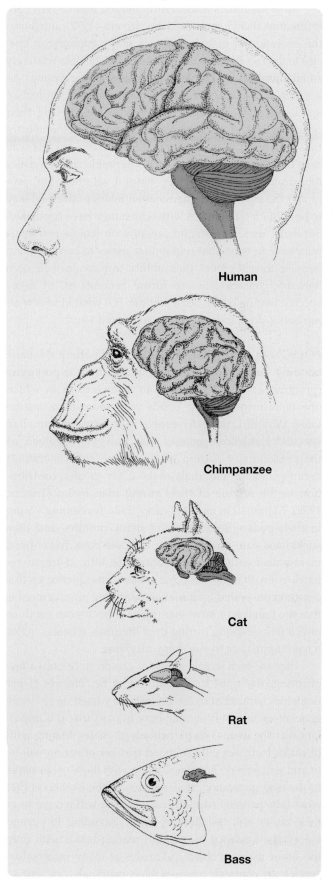

Figure 2.13 The brains of animals of different evolutionary ages—cerebrums are shown in pink; brain stems are shown in orange.

Human

Chimpanzee

Cat

Rat

Bass

However, the males and females of some species form *mating bonds* (enduring mating relationships) with particular members of the other sex.

Most mammals tend to form mating bonds. Why? An influential theory, proposed by Trivers (1972), attributes the evolution of mate bonding in many mammalian species to the fact that female mammals give birth to relatively small numbers of helpless, slow-developing young. As a result, it is adaptive for the males of many mammalian species to stay with the females who are carrying their offspring and to promote the successful development of those offspring. A male mammal that behaves in this way may be more likely to pass on his heritable characteristics to future generations. Thus, natural selection has promoted the evolution in mammalian males of the tendency to bond with the females with which they have copulated. Similarly, there is selection pressure on female mammals to behave in ways that will induce males to bond to them because this improves their ability to pass on their own heritable characteristics to future generations. In many species, mating bonds last a lifetime. But what kind of mating bonds do mammals tend to form, and why?

POLYGYNY AND POLYANDRY. The pattern of mate bonding that is most prevalent in mammals is **polygyny** (pronounced "pol-IG-in-ee"), an arrangement in which one male forms mating bonds with more than one female. Why did polygyny evolve in so many mammalian species? Evidence suggests that polygyny evolved as the predominant pattern of mate bonding in mammals because female mammals make a far greater contribution to the rearing of their young than males (Trivers, 1972). Mammalian mothers carry their developing young in their bodies, sometimes for many months, and then suckle and care for them after they are born. In contrast, mammalian fathers often contribute little more to reproduction than sperm. One major consequence of this common one-sided mammalian parenting arrangement is that the females of most mammalian species can produce only a few offspring during their lifetimes, whereas males have the capacity to sire many offspring.

Because each female mammal can produce only a few offspring, she must make the best of her chances if her heritable characteristics are going to be passed on to future generations in significant numbers. In particular, it is important that she mate with particularly fit males. Mating with fit males increases the likelihood that her offspring will be fit and will pass on her genes, along with those of her mate, to the next generation; it also increases the likelihood that what little parental support her offspring will receive from their father will be effective. Thus, according to current theory, the tendency to establish mating bonds with only the fittest males evolved in females of many mammalian species. In contrast, because male mammals can sire so

Figure 2.14 Horses, like most mammals, are polygynous. The stallion breeds with all the mares in the herd by virtue of his victories over other males.

many offspring, there has been little evolutionary pressure on them to become selective in their bonding—the males of most mammalian species will form mating bonds with as many females as possible. The inevitable consequence of the selective bonding of female mammals and the nonselective bonding of male mammals is polygyny—see Figure 2.14.

The strongest evidence in support of the theory that polygyny evolves when females make a far greater contribution to reproduction and parenting than males do comes from studies of **polyandry** (pronounced "pol-ee-AN-dree")—see Parker and Birkhead (2013). Polyandry is a mating arrangement in which one female forms mating bonds with more than one male. Polyandry does not occur in mammals; it occurs only in species in which the contributions of the males to reproduction are greater than those of the females. For example, in one polyandrous species, the seahorse, the female deposits her eggs in the male's pouch, and he fertilizes them and carries them until they are mature enough to venture out on their own.

The current thinking is that both large body size and the tendency to engage in aggression evolved in male mammals because female mammals tend to be more selective in their reproductive bonding. Because of the selectivity of the females, the competition among the males for reproductive partners becomes fierce, with only the successful competitors passing on their genes. In contrast, mammalian females rarely have difficulty finding reproductive partners.

MONOGAMY. Although most mammals are polygynous, about 9 percent of mammalian species are primarily monogamous (see Kappeler, 2013; Lukas & Clutton-Brock, 2013). **Monogamy** is a mate-bonding pattern in which enduring bonds are formed between one male and one female. Monogamy is thought to have evolved in those mammalian species in which each female could raise more young, or more fit young, if she had undivided help (see Dewsbury, 1988). In such species, any change in the behavior of a female that would encourage a male to bond exclusively with her would increase the likelihood that her heritable characteristics would be passed on to future generations. One such behavioral change is for each female to drive other females of reproductive age away from her mate. This strategy is particularly effective if a female will not copulate with a male until he has stayed with her for a period of time. Once this pattern of behavior evolved in the females of a particular species, the optimal mating strategy for males would change. It would become difficult for each male to bond with many females, and a male's best chance of producing many fit offspring would be for him to bond with a fit female and to put most of his reproductive effort into her and their offspring.

Western cultures promote monogamy, but are humans monogamous? Many of our students believed so until they were asked to consider the following three points; then they were not so sure:

- Many human cultures do not practice monogamy.
- Even in Western cultures most people bond with more than one partner during their lives.
- Infidelity is common.

When it comes to living up to the ideal of monogamy, we humans cannot compete with many other species.

Geese, for example, once bonded, will never mate with another partner.

Think about how the information presented in this section on the evolution of mate bonding might relate to events that you have experienced or observed in your daily life. Has your newly acquired evolutionary perspective enabled you to think about these events in new ways? **Thinking Creatively**

THINKING ABOUT EVOLUTIONARY PSYCHOLOGY. It is easy to speculate about how particular human behaviors evolved without ever having one's theories disproved because it is not possible to know for sure how an existing behavior evolved. Good theories of behavioral evolution have predictions about current behaviors built into them so that the predictions—and thus the theory—can be tested. Theories that cannot be tested have little use.

The foregoing evolutionary theory of mate bonding has led to several predictions about current aspects of human mate selection. Buss* (1992) confirmed several of them, for example:

- Men in most cultures value youth and attractiveness (both indicators of fertility) in their mates more than women do; in contrast, women value power and earning capacity more than men do.

*Based on Buss, D. M. (1992). Mate preference mechanisms: Consequences for partner choice and intrasexual competition. In J. M. Barkow, L. Cosmides, & J. Tooby (Eds.), *The adapted mind* (pp. 249–265). New York: Oxford University Press.

Scan Your Brain

This is a good place for you to pause to scan your brain to see if you are ready to proceed: Do you remember what you have read about misleading dichotomies and evolution? Fill in the following blanks with the most appropriate terms from the first two modules of the chapter. The correct answers are provided at the end of the exercise. Before proceeding, review material related to your errors and omissions.

1. Cartesian dualism proposed that the universe is made up of two components: physical matter and _____.
2. Asomatognosia is a condition that usually affects the left side of the body and is a result of damage to the_____.
3. Dominant males are likely to pass on their characteristics to future generations because they _____ more than nondominant males.
4. A _____ is a group of reproductively isolated organisms.
5. Mammals are thought to have evolved from _____ about 180 million years ago.

6. The first *Homo* species are believed to have evolved from a species of _____.
7. The best metaphor for evolution is not a ladder; it is a dense _____.
8. Research evidence indicates that *Homo Sapiens* mated with other *Homo* species like the _____.
9. In order to study how the brain evolved, it is important to _____ the evolution of different brain regions.
10. Structures or behaviors that evolved to perform one function but were later co-opted to perform another are called _____.
11. Structures that are similar because they have a common evolutionary origin are called _____ structures.
12. _____structures are similar because of convergent evolution.

Scan Your Brain answers: (1) the human mind, (2) right parietal lobe, (3) copulate, (4) species, (5) reptiles, (6) *Australopithecus*, (7) bush, (8) *Homo neanderthalensis*, (9) compare, (10) exaptations, (11) homologous, (12) Analogous.

- Physical attractiveness best predicts which women will bond with men of high occupational status.
- The major mate-attraction strategy of women is increasing their physical attractiveness; in men, it is displaying their power and resources.
- Men are more likely than women to commit adultery.

Fundamental Genetics

Darwin did not understand two of the key facts on which his theory of evolution was based. He did not understand why conspecifics differ from one another, and he did not understand how anatomical, physiological, and behavioral characteristics are passed from parent to offspring. While Darwin puzzled over these questions, an unread manuscript in his files contained the answers. It had been sent to him by an unknown Augustinian monk, Gregor Mendel. Unfortunately for Darwin (1809–1882) and for Mendel (1822–1884), the significance of Mendel's research was not recognized until the early part of the 20th century, well after both of their deaths.

Mendelian Genetics

LO 2.9   Describe what Mendel's work with pea plants tells us about the mechanisms of inheritance.

Mendel studied inheritance in pea plants. In designing his experiments, he made two wise decisions. He decided to study dichotomous traits, and he decided to begin his experiments by crossing the offspring of true-breeding lines. **Dichotomous traits** occur in one form or the other, never in combination. For example, seed color is a dichotomous pea plant trait: Every pea plant has either brown seeds or white seeds. **True-breeding lines** are breeding lines in which interbred members always produce offspring with the same trait (e.g., brown seeds), generation after generation.

In one of his early experiments, Mendel studied the inheritance of seed color: brown or white. He began by crossbreeding the offspring of a line of pea plants that had bred true for brown seeds with the offspring of a line of pea plants that had bred true for white seeds. The offspring of this cross all had brown seeds. Then, Mendel bred these first-generation offspring with one another, and he found that about three-quarters of the resulting second-generation offspring had brown seeds and about one-quarter had white seeds. Mendel repeated this experiment many times with various pairs of dichotomous pea plant traits, and each time the result was the same. One trait, which Mendel called the **dominant trait**, appeared in all of the first-generation offspring; the other trait, which he called the **recessive trait**, appeared in about one-quarter of the second-generation offspring. Mendel

would have obtained a similar result if he had conducted an experiment with true-breeding lines of brown-eyed (dominant) and blue-eyed (recessive) humans.

The results of Mendel's experiment challenged the central premise on which all previous ideas about inheritance had rested: that offspring inherit the traits of their parents. Somehow, the recessive trait (white seeds) was passed on to one-quarter of the second-generation pea plants by first-generation pea plants that did not themselves possess it. An organism's observable traits are referred to as its **phenotype**; the traits that it can pass on to its offspring through its genetic material are referred to as its **genotype**.

Mendel devised a theory to explain his results. It comprised four ideas. First, Mendel proposed that there are two kinds of inherited factors for each dichotomous trait—for example, that a brown-seed factor and a white-seed factor control seed color. Today, we call each inherited factor a **gene**. Second, Mendel proposed that each organism possesses two genes for each of its dichotomous traits; for example, each pea plant possesses either two brown-seed genes, two white-seed genes, or one of each. The two genes that control the same trait are called **alleles** (pronounced "a-LEELZ"). Organisms that possess two identical genes for a trait are said to be **homozygous** for that trait; those that possess two different genes for a trait are said to be **heterozygous** for that trait. Third, Mendel proposed that one of the two kinds of genes for each dichotomous trait dominates the other in heterozygous organisms. For example, pea plants with a brown-seed gene and a white-seed gene always have brown seeds because the brown-seed gene always dominates the white-seed gene. And fourth, Mendel proposed that for each dichotomous trait, each organism randomly inherits one of its "father's" two factors and one of its "mother's" two factors. Figure 2.15 illustrates how Mendel's theory accounts for the result of his experiment on the inheritance of seed color in pea plants.

Chromosomes

LO 2.10 Understand the structure and function of chromosomes.

REPRODUCTION AND RECOMBINATION. It was not until the early 20th century that genes were found to be located on **chromosomes**—the threadlike structures in the nucleus of each cell (see Brenner, 2012). Chromosomes occur in matched pairs, and each species has a characteristic number of pairs in each of its body cells; humans have 23 pairs. The two genes (alleles) that control each trait are situated at the same location, one on each chromosome of a particular pair.

The process of cell division that produces **gametes** (egg cells and sperm cells) is called **meiosis** (pronounced "my-OH-sis")—see Sluder and McCollum (2000). In meiosis, the chromosomes divide, and one chromosome of each

Figure 2.15 How Mendel's theory accounts for the results of his experiment on the inheritance of seed color in pea plants.

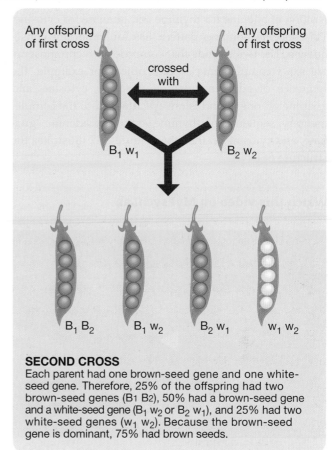

FIRST CROSS
One parent had two dominant brown-seed genes (B₁ B₂); the other had two recessive white-seed genes (w₁ w₂). Therefore, all offspring had one brown-seed gene and one white-seed gene (B₁ w₁, B₁ w₂, B₂ w₁, or B₂ w₂). Because the brown-seed gene is dominant, all had brown seeds.

SECOND CROSS
Each parent had one brown-seed gene and one white-seed gene. Therefore, 25% of the offspring had two brown-seed genes (B1 B2), 50% had a brown-seed gene and a white-seed gene (B₁ w₂ or B₂ w₁), and 25% had two white-seed genes (w₁ w₂). Because the brown-seed gene is dominant, 75% had brown seeds.

pair goes to each of the two gametes that results from the cell division. As a result, each gamete has only half the usual number of chromosomes (23 in humans); and when a sperm cell and an egg cell combine during fertilization (see Figure 2.16), a **zygote** (a fertilized egg cell) with the full complement of chromosomes is produced.

Figure 2.16 During fertilization, sperm cells attach themselves to the surface of an egg cell; one will enter the egg cell and fertilize it.

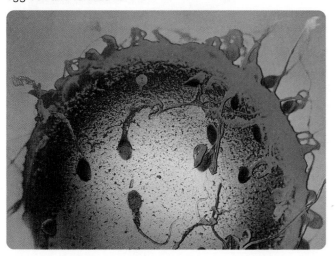

The random division of the pairs of chromosomes into two gametes is not the only way meiosis contributes to genetic diversity. Let us explain. During the first stage of meiosis, the chromosomes line up in their pairs. Then, the members of each pair cross over one another at random points, break apart at the points of contact, and exchange sections. As a result of this **genetic recombination**, each of the gametes that formed the zygote that developed into you contained chromosomes that were unique, spliced-together recombinations of chromosomes from your mother and father.

In contrast to the meiotic creation of the gametes, all other cell division in the body occurs by **mitosis** (pronounced "my-TOE-sis"). Just prior to mitotic division, the number of chromosomes doubles so that, when the cell divides, both daughter cells end up with the full complement of chromosomes.

STRUCTURE AND REPLICATION. Each chromosome is a double-stranded molecule of **deoxyribonucleic acid (DNA)**. Each strand is a sequence of **nucleotide bases** attached to a chain of *phosphate* and *deoxyribose*; there are four nucleotide bases: *adenine, thymine, guanine,* and *cytosine*. It is the sequence of these bases on each chromosome that constitutes the genetic code—just as sequences of letters constitute the code of our language.

The two strands that compose each chromosome are coiled around each other and bonded together by the attraction of adenine for thymine and guanine for cytosine. This specific bonding pattern has an important consequence: The two strands that compose each chromosome are exact complements of each other. For example, the sequence of adenine, guanine, thymine, cytosine, and guanine on one strand is always attached to the complementary sequence of thymine, cytosine, adenine, guanine, and cytosine on the other. Figure 2.17 illustrates the structure of DNA.

Watch this video on MyPsychLab

MEIOSIS

Watch this video on MyPsychLab

MITOSIS

Replication is a critical process of the DNA molecule. Without it, mitotic cell division would not be possible. Figure 2.18 illustrates how DNA replication is thought to work. The two strands of DNA start to unwind. Then the exposed nucleotide bases on each of the two strands attract their complementary bases, which are floating in the fluid of the nucleus. Thus, when the unwinding is complete, two double-stranded DNA molecules, both of which are identical to the original, have been created.

Chromosome replication does not always go according to plan; there may be errors. Sometimes, these errors are gross errors. For example, in *Down syndrome*, which you will learn about in Chapter 10, there is an extra chromosome in each cell. But more commonly, errors in duplication take the form of **mutations**—accidental alterations in individual genes. In most cases, mutations disappear from the gene pool within a few generations because the organisms that inherit them are less fit. However, in rare instances, mutations increase fitness and in so doing contribute to rapid evolution.

Figure 2.17 A schematic illustration of the structure of a DNA molecule. Notice the complementary pairings of nucleotide bases: thymine with adenine and guanine with cytosine.

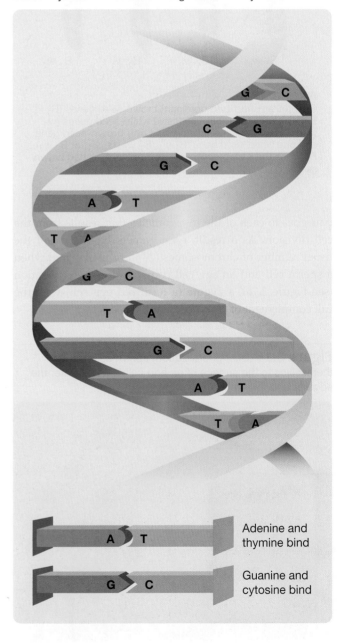

Figure 2.18 DNA replication. As the two strands of the original DNA molecule unwind, the nucleotide bases on each strand attract free-floating complementary bases. Once the unwinding is complete, two DNA molecules, each identical to the first, will have been created.

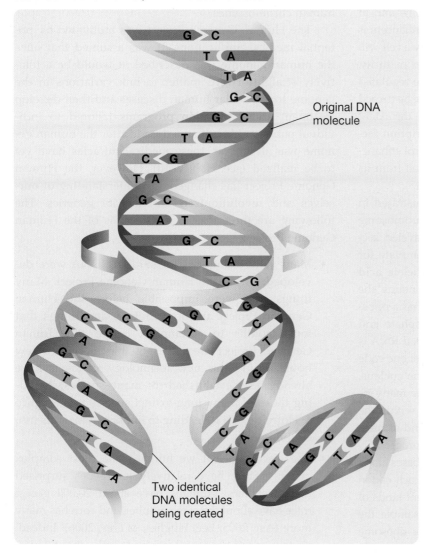

Original DNA molecule

Two identical DNA molecules being created

Watch this video on MyPsychLab

DNA REPLICATON

Video

SEX CHROMOSOMES AND SEX-LINKED TRAITS. There is one exception to the rule that chromosomes always come in matched pairs. The typical chromosomes, which come in matched pairs, are called **autosomal chromosomes**; the one exception is the pair of **sex chromosomes**—the pair of chromosomes that determines an individual's sex. There are two types of sex chromosomes, X and Y, and the two look different and carry different genes. Female mammals have two X chromosomes, and male mammals have one X chromosome and one Y chromosome. Traits influenced by genes on the sex chromosomes are referred to as **sex-linked traits**. Virtually all sex-linked traits are controlled by genes on the X chromosome because the Y chromosome is small and carries few genes (see Maekawa et al., 2014).

Traits controlled by genes on the X chromosome occur more frequently in one sex than the other. If the trait is dominant, it occurs more frequently in females. Females have twice the chance of inheriting the dominant gene because they have twice the number of X chromosomes. In contrast, recessive sex-linked traits occur more frequently in males. The reason is that recessive sex-linked traits are manifested only in females who possess two of the recessive genes—one on each of their X chromosomes—whereas the traits are manifested in all males who possess the gene because they have only one X chromosome. The classic example of a recessive sex-linked trait is color blindness. Because the color-blindness gene is quite rare, females almost never inherit two of them and thus almost never possess the disorder; in contrast, every male who possesses one color-blindness gene is color blind.

Genetic Code and Gene Expression

LO 2.11 Outline the mechanisms of gene expression.

Structural genes contain the information necessary for the synthesis of proteins. **Proteins** are long chains of **amino acids**; they control the physiological activities of cells and are important components of cellular structure. All the cells in the body (e.g., brain cells, hair cells, and bone cells) contain exactly the same genes. How then do different kinds of cells develop? The answer lies in stretches of DNA that lack structural genes—indeed, although all genes were once assumed to be structural genes, those genes comprise only a small portion of each chromosome.

The stretches of DNA that lack structural genes are not well understood, but it is clear that they include portions called *enhancers* (or *promoters*). **Enhancers** are stretches of DNA whose function is to determine whether particular structural genes initiate the synthesis of proteins and at what rate. The control of **gene expression** by enhancers is an important process because it determines how a cell will develop and how it will function once it reaches maturity. Enhancers are like switches because they can be regulated in two ways: They can be turned up, or they can be turned down. Proteins that bind to DNA and influence the extent to which genes are expressed are called **transcription factors**. Many of the transcription factors that control enhancers are influenced by signals received by the cell from its environment (see Shibata, Gulden, & Sestan, 2015).

The expression of a structural gene is illustrated in Figure 2.19. First, the small section of the chromosome that contains the gene unravels, and the unraveled section of one of the DNA strands serves as a template for the transcription of a short strand of **ribonucleic acid (RNA)**. RNA is like DNA except that it contains the nucleotide base uracil instead of thymine and has a phosphate and ribose backbone instead of a phosphate and deoxyribose backbone. The strand of transcribed RNA is called **messenger RNA** because it carries the genetic code out of the nucleus of the cell. Once it has left the nucleus, the messenger RNA attaches itself to one of the many **ribosomes** in the cell's *cytoplasm* (the clear fluid within the cell). The ribosome then moves along the strand of messenger RNA, translating the genetic code as it proceeds.

Each group of three consecutive nucleotide bases along the messenger RNA strand is called a **codon**. Each codon instructs the ribosome to add 1 of the 20 different kinds of amino acids to the protein it is constructing; for example, the sequence guanine-guanine-adenine instructs the ribosome to add the amino acid glycine. Each kind of amino acid is carried to the ribosome by molecules of **transfer RNA**; as the ribosome reads a codon, it attracts a transfer RNA molecule that is attached to the appropriate amino acid. The ribosome reads codon after codon and adds amino acid after amino acid until it reaches a codon that tells it the protein is complete, whereupon the completed protein is released into the cytoplasm. Thus, the process of gene expression involves two phases: the *transcription* of the DNA base-sequence code to an RNA base-sequence code and the *translation* of the RNA base-sequence code into a sequence of amino acids.

Human Genome Project

LO 2.12 Discuss several ways in which modern advances have changed our understanding of genetic processes.

One of the most ambitious scientific projects of all time began in 1990. Known as the **Human Genome Project**, it was a loosely knit collaboration of major research institutions and individual research teams in several countries. The purpose of this collaboration was to compile a map of the sequence of all 3 billion bases that compose human chromosomes.

The Human Genome Project was motivated by potential medical applications. It was assumed that once the human genome was described, it would be a relatively straightforward matter to link variations in the genome to particular human diseases and then develop treatment and prevention programs tailored to individual patients. More than a decade after the human genome was described, these medical miracles have yet to be realized (see Hall, 2010). However, the Human Genome Project has changed our understanding of ourselves and revolutionized the field of genetics. The following are three major contributions of the Human Genome Project:

- Many new techniques for studying DNA were developed during the Human Genome Project. Many things that were impossible before the Human Genome Project are now routine, and things that took months to accomplish before the Human Genome Project are now possible in only a few hours. Using this new technology, genomes have already been established for many species, including those of many long-extinct species (see Shapiro & Hofreiter, 2014), leading to important insights into evolution.

- The discovery that we humans, the most complex of all species, have relatively few genes surprised many scholars. Humans have about 20,000 genes; mice have about the same number, and corn has many more (Ast, 2005; Lee, Hughes, & Frey, 2006). Indeed, protein-encoding genes constitute only about 1 percent of human DNA. Researchers have now generated a nearly complete map of the entire set of proteins encoded for by our genes: the **human proteome** (Kim et al., 2014).

- Many variations in the human genome related to particular diseases have been identified. However, this has proven to be less useful than anticipated: So many genes have been linked to each disease that it has proven difficult to sort out the interactions among the numerous genes and experience (Hall, 2010). Compounding the problem is that even when many genes have been linked to a disease, all of them together often account for only a small portion of its heritability (Manolio et al., 2009). For example, 18 different gene variants have been linked to adult-onset diabetes, but these 18 variants account for only 6 percent of the heritability of the disease (see Stumvoll, Goldstein, & Haeften, 2005).

Figure 2.19 Gene expression. Transcription of a section of DNA into a complementary strand of messenger RNA is followed by the translation of the messenger RNA strand into a protein.

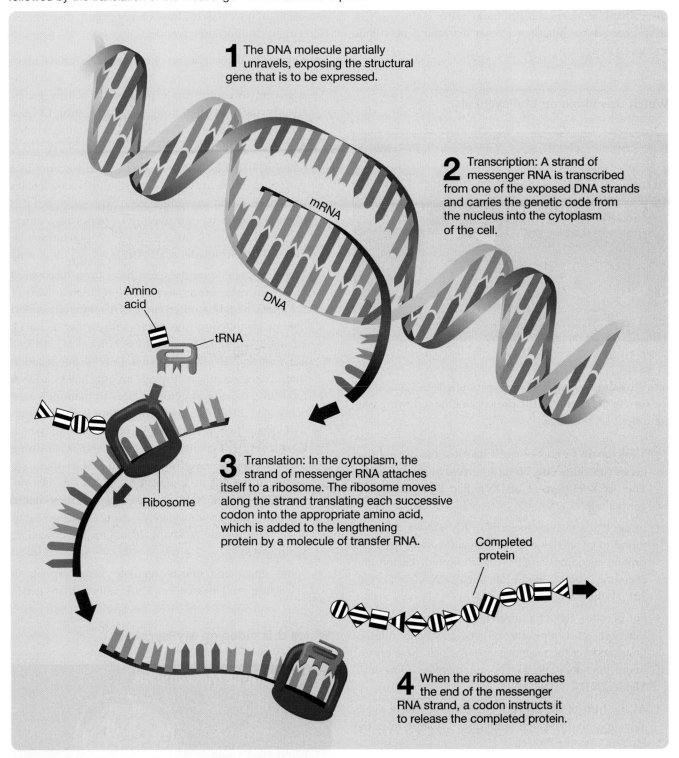

1 The DNA molecule partially unravels, exposing the structural gene that is to be expressed.

2 Transcription: A strand of messenger RNA is transcribed from one of the exposed DNA strands and carries the genetic code from the nucleus into the cytoplasm of the cell.

mRNA

Amino acid

tRNA

DNA

3 Translation: In the cytoplasm, the strand of messenger RNA attaches itself to a ribosome. The ribosome moves along the strand translating each successive codon into the appropriate amino acid, which is added to the lengthening protein by a molecule of transfer RNA.

Ribosome

Completed protein

4 When the ribosome reaches the end of the messenger RNA strand, a codon instructs it to release the completed protein.

Modern Genetics: Growth of Epigenetics

LO 2.13 Define epigenetics, and explain how it is transforming our understanding of genetics.

Around the turn of the century, the field of genetics changed. Interest shifted away from protein-encoding genes and their expression to other possible mechanisms of inheritance. In particular, interest shifted to the mechanisms by which experience exerts its effects on development. This led to an explosion of interest in an area of genetics research that had been lingering in the background since 1942: epigenetics.

Epigenetics is often defined by what it is not: It is not what genetics had been prior to epigenetics' rise to prominence. Since the discovery of genes in the 1960s, the structure and expression of genes had been the focus of genetics research and thinking (see Franklin & Mansuy, 2010; Zhang & Meaner, 2010). **Epigenetics** is the study of all mechanisms of inheritance other than the genetic code and its expression.

Watch this video on MyPsychLab
EPIGENETICS

Why did epigenetics rise to prominence so quickly at the turn of the century? The presence of the following four conditions set the stage:

- The Human Genome Project had just discovered that genes constitute only about 1 percent of human DNA. The other 99 percent of DNA had been widely regarded as *junk DNA.*

- In the 1990s, the vast majority of RNA molecules were found to be small—only 1.2 percent were of the large protein-encoding variety. This indicated that protein encoding is only a minor function of RNA (see Dolgin, 2015; Wilusz & Sharp, 2013).

- For decades, there had been a general consensus that inheritance was a product of gene-experience interactions, and yet the mechanisms by which these critical interactions took place were unknown (see Oureshi & Mehler, 2012).

- At the turn of the century, there was a newly available arsenal of research techniques resulting from the Human Genome Project.

Stimulated by these four factors, it was not long before the wave of research into epigenetics began to produce important discoveries, which further fanned the flames of enthusiasm for epigenetic research. Genetics had just spent half a century focused exclusively on the genetic code as the mechanism of inheritance, and the new

epigenetic research led to discoveries that challenged this narrow view.

Despite its youth, epigenetic research has already amassed an impressive array of important discoveries. Here are five important advances:

- Epigenetic investigations of nongene DNA have identified many active areas. Many of these active areas seem to control the expression of nearby genes. Clearly, the belief that nongene DNA is junk DNA is no longer tenable (see Pennisi, 2014; Tragante, Moore, & Asselbergs, 2014).

- Small RNA molecules have been found to come in a variety of different types. Some small RNA molecules have been found to regulate gene expression, but it is likely that each type of small RNA performs a different function (see Gorman & Maron, 2014; Hoffman & Pilpel, 2015; Schmiedel et al., 2015).

- Many epigenetic mechanisms have been discovered by which gene expression can be regulated. Two of the most widely studied are DNA methylation and histone remodeling (see Baker-Andresen et al., 2013; LaSalle, Powell, & Yasui, 2013; Schultz et al., 2015)— see Figure 2.20. **DNA methylation** is the reaction that occurs when a methyl group attaches to a DNA molecule, usually at cytosine sites in mammals (see Schübeler, 2012). **Histone remodeling** is the reaction that occurs when **histones** (proteins around which DNA is coiled) change their shape and in so doing influence the shape of the adjacent DNA—there are several different mechanisms by which this can occur. Both DNA methylation and histone remodeling can either decrease or increase expression (see Bintu et al., 2016; Keung & Khalil, 2016; LaSalle, Powell, & Yasui, 2013).

- Some epigenetic effects regulate gene expression by acting on messenger RNA rather than genes

Watch this video on MyPsychLab
CHALK IT UP! EPIGENETIC MECHANISMS

Figure 2.20 Two epigenetic mechanisms. Histone remodeling involves modifications to a histone protein (around which DNA is coiled). DNA methylation involves the attachment of a methyl group to DNA. Both DNA methylation and histone remodeling can either decrease or increase gene expression.

Epigenetic mechanisms are known to produce enduring changes in an individual. But can those experience-induced changes be passed on to future generations? That is, can the experiences of your mother and father be passed on to you and on to your children? Biologists first observed such transgenerational epigenetic effects in plants, but such effects have now been observed in mammals as well. **Transgenerational epigenetics** is a subfield of epigenetics that examines the transmission of experiences via epigenetic mechanisms across generations (see Hughes, 2014). For example, it has been shown that when mice experience an odor associated with a painful shock, the memory of that experience is passed on to subsequent generations through epigenetic mechanisms (see Dias et al., 2015; Dias & Ressler, 2014; Szyf, 2014; Welberg, 2014). There is some suggestive evidence that inheritance via transgenerational epigenetic mechanisms can also occur in humans (e.g., Marczylo et al., 2012).

Before leaving this subsection on epigenetics, pause to consider the important implications of what you have just learned. It now seems likely that each person's genetic material changes through life as experiences accumulate, and there is evidence that these experience-induced changes can be passed on to future generations. These findings are revolutionizing the field of genetics, and they have major implications for how we humans think about ourselves, our ancestors, and our descendants.

(see Izaurralde, 2015 Mattick, Mehler, 2008); this is called **RNA editing**. Small RNA molecules and other proteins have been shown to cleave messenger RNA apart at precise points and sometimes to splice sections of new RNA to create a new sequence of bases.

- Remarkably, epigenetic changes such as DNA methylation and histone remodeling can be induced by particular experiences (e.g., neural activity, hormonal state, changes to the environment) that can last a lifetime (Handel & Ramagoplan, 2010; Nadeau, 2009; Nelson & Nadeau, 2010; Riccio, 2010; Sweatt, 2013).

Thinking Creatively What implications does the study of epigenetics have for researchers who are trying to determine the genetic bases of a particular disorder, like schizophrenia?

Scan Your Brain

Do you remember what you have just read about genetics so that you can move on to the next module with confidence? To find out, fill in the following blanks with the most appropriate terms. The correct answers are provided at the end of the exercise. Before proceeding, review material related to your errors and omissions.

1. In his groundbreaking experiments, Mendel studied _____ traits in true-breeding lines of pea plants.
2. The double strands of a chromosome are held together by the attraction of adenine for thymine and guanine for _____.
3. The chances of inheriting the _____ gene are double in females because they have two X chromosomes.
4. _____ are found in the stretches of DNA that lack structural genes.
5. Egg cells and sperm cells are _____.
6. All body cells except sperm cells and egg cells are created by _____.

7. The _____ gives complete information about the sets of proteins present in genes.
8. Each strand of DNA is a sequence of _____ bases.
9. Because organisms that inherit them are less fit, _____ usually disappear from the gene pool within a few generations.
10. The subject of _____ is the transmission of experiences across generations through epigenetic mechanisms.
11. Genes can be turned off or on by transcription factors acting on _____.
12. The massive international research effort that mapped the sequence of bases in human chromosomes was the _____ Project.
13. _____ is the study of mechanisms of inheritance other than modifications to the genetic code.

Scan Your Brain answers: (1) dichotomous, (2) cytosine, (3) dominant, (4) Enhancers, (5) gametes, (6) mitosis, (7) human proteome, (8) nucleotide, (9) mutations, (10) transgenerational epigenetics, (11) enhancers, (12) Human Genome, (13) Epigenetics.

Epigenetics of Behavioral Development: Interaction of Genetic Factors and Experience

This module comprises three classic examples of how genetic factors and experience interact to direct behavioral ontogeny. (**Ontogeny** is the development of individuals over their life span; **phylogeny**, in contrast, is the evolutionary development of species through the ages.) In each example, you will see that development is a product of the interaction of genetic and experiential factors, which we now know is likely mediated by epigenetic mechanisms (see Sweatt, 2013).

Selective Breeding of "Maze-Bright" and "Maze-Dull" Rats

LO 2.14 Discuss what insight into the genetics of behavior was gained from early research on selective breeding.

You have already learned in this chapter that most early psychologists assumed that behavior develops largely through learning. Tryon (1934) undermined this assumption by showing that behavioral traits can be selectively bred.

Tryon focused his selective-breeding experiments on the behavior that had been the focus of early psychologists in their investigations of learning: the maze running of laboratory rats. Tryon began by training a large heterogeneous group of laboratory rats to run a complex maze; the rats received a food reward when they reached the goal box. Tryon then mated the females and males that least frequently entered incorrect alleys during training—he referred to these rats as *maze-bright*. And he bred the females and males that most frequently entered incorrect alleys during training—he referred to these rats as *maze-dull*.

When the offspring of both the maze-bright and the maze-dull rats matured, their maze-learning performance was assessed. Then, the brightest of the maze-bright offspring were mated with one another, as were the dullest of the maze-dull offspring. This selective breeding procedure was continued for 21 generations (and the descendants of Tryon's original strains are still available today). By the eighth generation, there was almost no overlap in the maze-learning performance of the two strains. With a few exceptions, the worst of the maze-bright strain made fewer errors than the best of the maze-dull strain (see Figure 2.21).

To control for the possibility that good maze-running performance was somehow being passed from parent to offspring through learning, Tryon used a *cross-fostering control procedure*: He tested maze-bright offspring that had been reared by maze-dull parents and maze-dull offspring that had been reared by maze-bright parents. However, the offspring of maze-bright rats made few errors even when

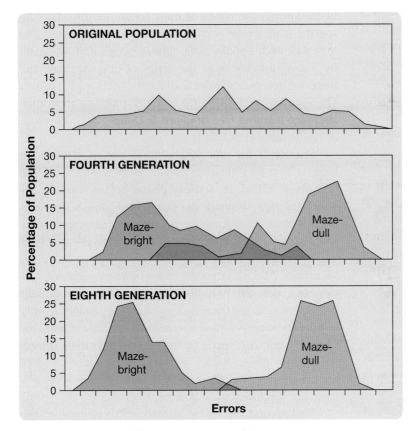

Figure 2.21 Selective breeding of maze-bright and maze-dull strains of rats by Tryon (1934). (Data from Cooper, R. M., & Zubek, J. P. (1958). Effects of enriched and restricted early environments on the learning ability of bright and dull rats. *Canadian Journal of Psychology, 12,* 159–164.)

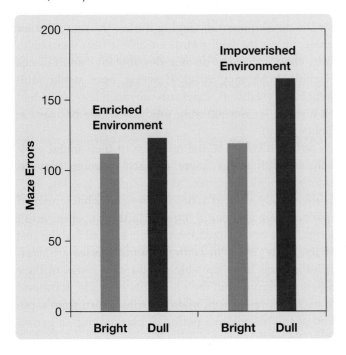

Figure 2.22 Maze-dull rats did not make significantly more errors than maze-bright rats when both groups were reared in an enriched environment. (Adapted from Cooper & Zubek, 1958.)

they were reared by maze-dull rats, and the off-spring of maze-dull rats made many errors even when they were reared by maze-bright rats.

Since Tryon's seminal selective-breeding experiments, many behavioral traits have been selectively bred. Indeed, it appears that any measurable behavioral trait that varies among members of a species can be selectively bred.

An important general point made by studies of selective breeding is that selective breeding based on one behavioral trait usually brings a host of other behavioral traits along with it. This indicates that the behavioral trait used as the criterion for selective breeding is not the only behavioral trait influenced by the genes segregated by the breeding. Indeed, Searle (1949) compared maze-dull and maze-bright rats on 30 different behavioral tests and found that they differed on many of them. The pattern of differences suggested that the maze-bright rats were superior maze learners not because they were more intelligent but because they were less fearful—a trait that is not adaptive in many natural environments.

Selective-breeding studies have proved that genes influence the development of behavior. This conclusion in no way implies that experience does not. This point was driven home by Cooper and Zubek (1958) in a classic study of maze-bright and maze-dull rats. The researchers reared maze-bright and maze-dull rats in one of two environments: (1) an impoverished environment (a barren wire-mesh group cage) or (2) an enriched environment (a wire-mesh group cage that contained tunnels, ramps, visual displays, and other objects designed to stimulate interest). When the maze-dull rats reached maturity, they made significantly more errors than the maze-bright rats only if they had been reared in the impoverished environment (see Figure 2.22).

Phenylketonuria: A Single-Gene Metabolic Disorder

LO 2.15 Explain how classic research on phenylketonuria (PKU) has informed our understanding of the genetics of behavior.

It is often easier to understand the genetics of a behavioral disorder than it is to understand the genetics of normal behavior. The reason is that many genes influence the development of a normal behavioral trait, but it sometimes takes only one abnormal gene to screw it up. A good example of this point is the neurological disorder **phenylketonuria (PKU)**.

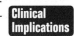

PKU was discovered in 1934 when a Norwegian dentist, Asbjörn Fölling, noticed a peculiar odor in the urine of his two intellectually disabled children. He correctly assumed that the odor was related to their disorder, and he had their urine analyzed. High levels of **phenylpyruvic acid** were found in both samples. Spurred on by his discovery, Fölling identified other intellectually disabled children who had abnormally high levels of urinary phenylpyruvic acid, and he concluded that this subpopulation of intellectually disabled children was suffering from the same disorder. In addition to intellectually disability, the symptoms of PKU include vomiting, seizures, hyperactivity, irritability, and brain damage (Strisciuglio & Concolino, 2014).

The pattern of transmission of PKU through the family trees of afflicted individuals indicates that it is transmitted by a single gene mutation. About 1 in 100 people of European descent carry the PKU gene; but because the gene is recessive, PKU develops only in homozygous individuals (those who inherit a PKU gene from both their mother and their father). In the United States, about 1 in 10,000 Caucasian infants is born with PKU; the incidence is much lower among infants of African Americans.

The biochemistry of PKU turned out to be reasonably straightforward. PKU homozygotes lack *phenylalanine hydroxylase*, an enzyme required for the conversion of the amino acid *phenylalanine* to *tyrosine*. As a result, phenylalanine accumulates in the body; and levels of *dopamine*, a neurotransmitter normally synthesized from tyrosine, are low. The consequence is abnormal brain development.

Like other behavioral traits, the behavioral symptoms of PKU result from an interaction between genetic and environmental factors: between the PKU gene and diet (see Rohde et al., 2014). Accordingly, in most modern hospitals, the blood of newborn infants is routinely screened for high phenylalanine levels (see Casey, 2013). If the level is high, the infant is immediately placed on a special phenylalanine-restricted diet; this diet reduces both the amount of phenylalanine in the blood and the development of intellectual disability—however, it does not prevent the development of subtle cognitive deficits (Moyle et al., 2007; Simon et al., 2008). The timing of this treatment is extremely important. The phenylalanine-restricted diet does not significantly reduce the development of intellectual disability in PKU homozygotes unless it is initiated within the first few weeks of life; conversely, the restriction of phenylalanine in the diet is usually relaxed in late childhood, with few obvious adverse consequences to the patient. The period, usually early in life, during which a particular experience must occur to have a major effect on the development of a trait is the **sensitive period** for that trait.

Development of Birdsong

LO 2.16 Describe how research on the ontogenetic development of birdsong has provided insight into the development of human language.

In the spring, the songs of male songbirds threaten conspecific male trespassers and attract potential mates. The males of each species sing similar songs that are readily distinguishable from the songs of other species, and there are recognizable local dialects within each species. The learning of birdsong has many parallels to human language learning (see Brainard & Doupe, 2013; Elemans, 2014; Pfenning et al., 2014).

Studies of the ontogenetic development of birdsong suggest that this behavior develops in two phases. The first phase, called the **sensory phase**, begins several days after hatching. Although the young birds do not sing during this phase, they form memories of the adult songs they hear—usually sung by their own male relatives—that later guide the development of their own singing (see Bolhuis & Moorman, 2015). The young males of many songbird species are genetically prepared to acquire the songs of their own species during the sensory phase. They cannot readily acquire the songs of other species, nor can they acquire the songs of their own species if they do not hear them during the sensory phase. Males who do not hear the songs of their own species early in their lives may later develop a song, but it is likely to be abnormal.

The second phase of birdsong development, the **sensorimotor phase**, begins when the juvenile males begin to twitter *subsongs* (the immature songs of young birds), usually when they are several months old. During this phase, the rambling vocalizations of subsongs are gradually refined until they resemble the songs of the birds' earlier adult tutors. Auditory feedback is necessary for the development of singing during the sensorimotor phase; unless the young birds are able to hear themselves sing, their subsongs do not develop into adult songs (Tschida & Mooney, 2012). However, once stable adult song has crystallized, songbirds are much less dependent on hearing for normal song production (see Brainard & Doupe, 2013).

When it comes to the retention of their initial crystallized adult songs, there are two common patterns among songbird species. Most songbird species, such as the widely studied zebra finches and white-crowned sparrows, are *age-limited learners*; in these species, adult songs, once crystallized, remain unchanged for the rest of the birds' lives. In contrast, some species are *open-ended learners*; they are able to add new songs to their repertoire throughout their lives. For example, at the end of each mating season, male canaries return from a period of stable song to a period of plastic song—a period during which they can add new songs for the next mating season. Male zebra finches (age-limited learners) and male canaries (open-ended learners) are shown in Figure 2.23.

Figure 2.24 is a simplified version of the neural circuit that controls birdsong in the canary (see Hahnloser & Kotowicz, 2010). It has two major components: the descending motor pathway and the anterior forebrain pathway. The *descending motor pathway* descends from the high vocal center on each side of the brain to the syrinx (voice box) on the same side; it mediates song production. The *anterior forebrain pathway* mediates song learning (see Prather, 2013).

The canary song neural circuit is remarkable in three respects. First, the left descending motor pathway plays a more important role in singing than the right descending motor pathway (which duplicates the left-hemisphere dominance for language in humans). Second,

Neuroplasticity the high vocal center is four times larger in male canaries than in females. Third, each spring, as the male canary prepares its new repertoire of songs for the summer seduction, the song-control structures of its brain double in size, only to shrink back in the fall. This springtime burst of brain growth and singing is triggered by elevated levels of the hormone testosterone that result from the increasing daylight (see De Groof et al., 2013).

> **Neuroplasticity** In what way is this an example of neuroplasticity? And why do you think the song-control structures wouldn't just stay consistently enlarged, rather than demonstrate seasonal variation in their size?

Figure 2.23 Male zebra finches (age-limited song learners) and male canaries (open-ended song learners) are common subjects of research on birdsong development. (Illustration kindly provided by Trends in Neuroscience; original photograph by Arturo Alvarez-Buylla.)

Figure 2.24 The neural pathways responsible for the production and learning of song in the male canary.

○ Descending motor pathway
○ Anterior forebrain pathway   To syrinx

Syrinx

Genetics of Human Psychological Differences

This chapter has focused on three topics: human evolution, genetics, and the interaction of genetics and experience through epigenetic mechanisms. All three topics converge on one fundamental question: Why are we the way we are?

You have learned that each of us is a product of gene–experience interactions and that the effects of genes and experience on individual development are inseparable. This final module of the chapter continues to look at the effects of gene–experience interactions, but it focuses on a developmental issue that is fundamentally different from the ones we have been discussing: the development of individual differences rather than the development of individuals.

Development of Individuals versus Development of Differences among Individuals

LO 2.17 **Explain why it is important to distinguish between the development of individuals and the development of individual differences.**

So far, this chapter has focused on the development of individuals. The remainder of the chapter deals with the development of differences among individuals. In the development of individuals, the effects of genes and experience are inseparable. In the development of differences among individuals, they are separable. This distinction is extremely important, but it confuses many people. Let's return to the musician metaphor to explain it.

The music of an individual musician is the product of the interaction of the musician and the instrument, and it doesn't make sense to ask what proportion of the music is produced by the musician and what proportion by the instrument. However, if we evaluated the playing of a large sample of musicians, each playing a different instrument, we could statistically estimate the degree to which the differences in the quality of the music they produced resulted from differences in the musicians themselves as opposed to differences in their instruments. For example, if we selected 100 people at random and had each one play a different professional-quality guitar, we would likely find that most of the variation in the quality of the music resulted from differences in the subjects, some being experienced players and some never having played before. In the same way, researchers can select a group of volunteers and ask what proportion of the variation among them in some attribute (e.g., intelligence) results from genetic differences as opposed to experiential differences.

To assess the relative contributions of genes and experience to the development of differences in psychological attributes, behavioral geneticists study individuals of known genetic similarity. For example, they often compare **monozygotic twins**, who developed from the same zygote and thus are genetically similar, with **dizygotic twins**, who developed from two zygotes and thus are no more similar than any pair of *siblings* (brothers and sisters). Studies of pairs of monozygotic and dizygotic twins who have been separated at infancy by adoption are particularly informative about the relative contributions of genetics and experience to differences in human psychological development. The most extensive of such adoption studies is the Minnesota Study of Twins Reared Apart (see Bouchard & Pedersen, 1998).

Watch this video on MyPsychLab
TWINS AND PERSONALITY

Heritability Estimates: Minnesota Study of Twins Reared Apart

LO 2.18 **Explain heritability estimates and how they are commonly misinterpreted.**

The Minnesota Study of Twins Reared Apart involved 59 pairs of monozygotic twins and 47 pairs of dizygotic twins who had been reared apart as well as many pairs of monozygotic and dizygotic twins who had been reared together. Their ages ranged from 19 to 68. Each twin was brought to the University of Minnesota for approximately 50 hours of testing, which focused on the assessment of intelligence and personality. Would the adult monozygotic twins reared apart prove to be similar because they were genetically similar, or would they prove to be different because they had been brought up in different environments?

The results of the Minnesota Study of Twins Reared Apart proved to be remarkably consistent—both internally, between the various cognitive and personality dimensions that were studied, and externally, with the findings of other studies. In general, adult monozygotic twins were substantially more similar to one another on all psychological dimensions than were adult dizygotic twins, whether or not both twins of a pair were raised in the same family environment (see Turkheimer, 2000).

In order to quantify the contributions of genetic variations in a particular study, researchers calculate heritability estimates. A **heritability estimate** is not about individual development; it is a numerical estimate of the proportion of variability that occurred in a particular trait in a particular study as a result of the genetic variation in that study (see Turkheimer, Pettersson, & Horn, 2014). Heritability estimates tell us about the contribution of genetic differences to phenotypic differences among the participants in a study; they have nothing to say about the relative contributions of genes and experience to the development of individuals.

The concept of heritability estimates can be quite confusing. We suggest that you pause here and carefully think

Thinking Creatively about the definition before proceeding. The musician metaphor may help you.

The magnitude of a study's heritability estimate depends on the amount of genetic and environmental variation from which it was calculated, and it cannot be applied to other kinds of situations. For example, in the Minnesota study, there was relatively little environmental variation. All participants were raised in industrialized countries (Great Britain, Canada, and the United States) by parents who met the strict standards required for adoption. Accordingly, most of the variation in the subjects' intelligence and personality resulted from genetic variation. If the twins had been separately adopted by European royalty, Los Angeles rap stars, London advertising executives, and Inuit, the resulting heritability estimates for IQ and personality would likely have been much lower.

Now that you understand the meaning of heritability estimates, let us tell you how big they tend to be for a variety of complex human traits and behaviors: for example, for intelligence, personality traits, aggression, divorce, religious beliefs, sports participation, psychiatric disorders, and television watching. The answer is simple because heritability estimates tend to be about the same regardless of the particular trait or behavior under consideration and regardless of the particular basis used to calculate them (i.e., twin, adoption, or family-tree studies). In the representative Western samples that have been studied, all complex traits and behaviors have substantial heritability estimates—most between 40 and 80 percent.

The discovery that genetic variability contributes substantially to individual differences in virtually all human traits and behaviors has led several eminent geneticists to argue that no more heritability estimate studies should be conducted (e.g., Johnson et al., 2009; Petronis, 2010). What could more heritability estimate studies possibly add? These geneticists are, however, excited about the potential of two other types of twin studies that have recently been reported. The chapter ends with them.

A Look into the Future: Two Kinds of Twin Studies

LO 2.19 Describe two ways that twin studies can be used to study the interaction of genes and experience (i.e., nature and nurture).

Two lines of research on twins have recently created considerable excitement among geneticists and other scholars. We hope you share their enthusiasm.

TWIN STUDIES OF EPIGENETIC EFFECTS. Most studies of epigenetic effects have focused on nonhuman species. In plants and nonhuman animals, it is quite clear that epigenetic changes can be triggered by experience, can last a lifetime, and can be passed on to future generations (see Szyf, 2014). To what extent do these amazing results apply to humans? Twin studies may provide a route to the answers (see Aguilera et al., 2010; Feil & Fraga, 2012).

The study of epigenetic effects in humans is difficult because experimental manipulation of human genetic material is not ethical. Monozygotic twins, however, provide a method of circumventing this difficulty. At conception monozygotic twins are genetically identical, and by repeatedly assessing their DNA one can document the development and survival of the many epigenetic differences that develop between them (see Bell & Saffery, 2012; Bell & Spector, 2011; Chatterjee & Morison, 2011; Silva et al., 2011). Moreover, by comparing monozygotic and dizygotic twins, it is possible to get a sense of the degree to which changes are caused by experiential as opposed to genetic factors—if epigenetic changes developed under genetic control, one would expect that the pattern of epigenetic changes would be more similar in monozygotic than dizygotic pairs.

The first systematic demonstration of epigenetic differences in human twins was published by Fraga and colleagues (2005). They took tissue samples (blood, skin, muscle) from 40 pairs of monozygotic twins, ranging in age from 3 to 74. Then, they screened the tissues for DNA methylation and histone modifications. They found that the twins were epigenetically indistinguishable early in life, but differences accumulated as they aged, each type of tissue displaying a different epigenetic profile (see Zong et al., 2012). As a result, the former assumption that monozygotic twins are genetically identical was disproven, and the common practice of referring to monozygotic twins as *identical twins* should be curtailed.

In another study of epigenetic changes in twins, Wong and colleagues (2010) examined DNA methylation in *buccal cells* (cells of the lining of the mouth) scraped from 46 pairs of monozygotic twins and 45 pairs of dizygotic twins. They took samples from the twins at age 5 and again from the same twins at age 10. Then they assessed DNA methylation. Wong and colleagues found DNA methylation to be prominent in both groups of twins at both ages. Because the concordance rates of DNA methylation were the same between monozygotic and between dizygotic twins, they concluded that differences in DNA methylation are mainly a consequence of experiential factors.

The discovery of epigenetic differences in monozygotic twins raises the possibility that epigenetic differences may explain why one twin develops a disease and the other doesn't

Figure 2.25 Epigenetic research suggests that the common practice of referring to monozygotic twins as 'identical twins' should be curtailed.

(Bell & Spector, 2011; Haque, Gottesman, & Wong, 2009). Once

Clinical Implications identified, such epigenetic differences would provide important clues to the cause and mechanisms of the disease. Bell and Spector (2011) suggest that *disease-discordant monozygotic twin studies* are a particularly powerful approach (see also Czyz et al., 2012). This kind of study begins with the identification of monozygotic twins who are discordant for the disease of interest. Then one searches each pair for epigenetic differences focusing on those areas of DNA that are thought to be involved in the disorder. Large-scale studies in monozygotic twins across different ages, tissues, and epigenetic effects could greatly improve our understanding of human disease (see Bell & Spector, 2011; Tan et al., 2014).

TWIN STUDIES OF THE EFFECTS OF EXPERIENCE ON HERITABILITY. In thinking about heritability estimates, it is paramount to remember that heritability estimates depend on the particular conditions and subjects of a particular study. This point was driven home by the influential study of Turkheimer and colleagues (2003). Before the Turkheimer et al. study, all published studies of the heritability of intelligence were conducted on middle- to upper-class families, and the heritability estimates for intelligence tended to be about 75 percent.

Turkheimer and colleagues assessed heritability of intelligence in two samples of 7-year-old twins: those from families of low socioeconomic status (SES) and those from families of middle to high SES. The heritability estimates for intelligence in the middle- to high-SES twins was, as expected, about 70 percent. However, the heritability estimate for intelligence in the twins from low-SES families was only 10 percent. This effect was subsequently replicated and extended to other age groups: babies (Tucker-Drob et al., 2010) and adolescents (Harden, Turkheimer, & Loehlin, 2007).

One major implication of this finding is that it forces one to think of intelligence as developing from the interaction of genes and experience, not from one or the other. It seems that one can inherit the **Thinking Creatively** potential to be of superior intelligence, but this potential is rarely realized in a poverty-stricken environment (see Loehllin, Harden, & Turkheimer, 2009; Nisbett et al., 2012).

This finding also has important implications for the development of programs to help the poor. Many politicians have argued against special programs for the poor because most heritability estimates of intelligence are high. They incorrectly argue that because intelligence is inherited, special programs for the poor are a waste of money. However, the findings of Turkheimer and colleagues suggest otherwise: Reducing poverty would permit many of the poor to develop their genetic **Thinking Creatively** potential.

Thinking Creatively	Do you think that reducing poverty would improve educational achievements? Why or why not?

Themes Revisited

This chapter introduced the topics of evolution, genetics, and development, but its unifying focus was thinking creatively about the biology of behavior. Not surprisingly, then, of this text's four major themes, the thinking creatively theme received the most attention. This chapter **Thinking Creatively** challenged you to think about important biopsychological phenomena in new ways. Thinking creatively tabs marked points in the chapter where you were encouraged to sharpen your thinking about the nature–nurture issue, the physiological-or-psychological dichotomy, human evolution, the biopsychological implications of the Human Genome Project, the implications of epigenetics, the genetics of human psychological differences, the meaning of heritability estimates, and the important study of Turkheimer and colleagues.

The other three themes also received coverage in this chapter, and each case was marked by the appropriate tab. The evolutionary perspective was illustrated by comparative research on self-awareness in chimps, by consideration of the evolutionary significance of social dominance and courtship displays, and by efforts to understand mate bonding.

The clinical implications theme was illustrated by the case of the man who fell out of bed, the discussion of phenylketonuria (PKU), and the discussion of disease-discordant twin studies. 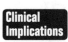 The neuroplasticity theme arose when you learned that brain growth occurs in male songbirds prior to each breeding season.

Key Terms

Chapter 3
Anatomy of the Nervous System

Systems, Structures, and Cells That Make Up Your Nervous System

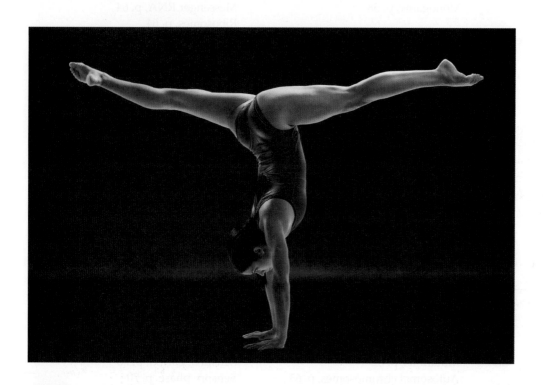

⌄ Chapter Overview and Learning Objectives (LOs)

General Layout of the Nervous System

LO 3.1 List and describe the major divisions of the nervous system.

LO 3.2 Describe the three meninges and explain their functional role.

LO 3.3 Explain where cerebrospinal fluid is produced and where it flows.

LO 3.4 Explain what the blood–brain barrier is and what functional role it serves.

Cells of the Nervous System

LO 3.5 Draw, label, and define the major features of a multipolar neuron.

In order to understand what the brain does, it is first necessary to understand what it is—to know the names and locations of its major parts and how they are connected to one another. This chapter introduces you to these fundamentals of brain anatomy.

Before you begin this chapter, we want to apologize for the lack of foresight displayed by early neuroanatomists in their choice of names for neuroanatomical structures—but how could they have anticipated that Latin and Greek, universal languages of the educated in their day, would not be compulsory university fare in our time? To help you, we have provided the literal English meanings of many of the neuroanatomical terms, and we have kept this chapter as brief, clear, and to the point as possible, covering only the most important structures. The payoff for your effort will be a fundamental understanding of the structure of the human brain and a new vocabulary to discuss it.

General Layout of the Nervous System

Divisions of the Nervous System

LO 3.1 List and describe the major divisions of the nervous system.

The vertebrate nervous system is composed of two divisions: the central nervous system and the peripheral nervous system (see Figure 3.1). Roughly speaking, the **central nervous system (CNS)** is the division of the nervous system located within the skull and spine, and the

Figure 3.1 The human central nervous system (CNS) and peripheral nervous system (PNS). The CNS is represented in red; the PNS in orange. Notice that even those portions of nerves that are within the spinal cord are considered to be part of the PNS.

Central nervous
system

Peripheral nervous
system

peripheral nervous system (PNS) is the division located outside the skull and spine.

Watch this video on MyPsychLab
DIVISIONS OF THE NERVOUS SYSTEM

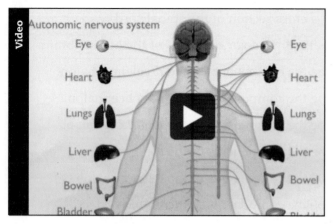

The central nervous system is composed of two divisions: the brain and the spinal cord. The *brain* is the part of the CNS located in the skull; the *spinal cord* is the part located in the spine.

The peripheral nervous system is also composed of two divisions: the somatic nervous system and the autonomic nervous system. The **somatic nervous system (SNS)** is the part of the PNS that interacts with the external environment. It is composed of **afferent nerves** that carry sensory signals from the skin, skeletal muscles, joints, eyes, ears, and so on, to the central nervous system and **efferent nerves** that carry motor signals from the central nervous system to the skeletal muscles. The **autonomic nervous system (ANS)** is the part of the peripheral nervous system that regulates the body's internal environment. It is composed of afferent nerves that carry sensory signals from internal organs to the CNS and efferent nerves that carry motor signals from the CNS to internal organs. You will not confuse the terms *afferent* and *efferent* if you remember that many words that involve the idea of going toward something—in this case, going toward the CNS—begin with an *a* (e.g., *advance, approach, arrive*) and that many words that involve the idea of going away from something begin with an *e* (e.g., *exit, embark, escape*).

The autonomic nervous system has two kinds of efferent nerves: sympathetic nerves and parasympathetic nerves. The **sympathetic nerves** are autonomic motor nerves that project from the CNS in the *lumbar* (small of the back) and *thoracic* (chest area) regions of the spinal cord. The **parasympathetic nerves** are those autonomic motor nerves that project from the brain and *sacral* (lower back) region of the spinal cord. See Appendix I. (Ask your instructor to specify the degree to which you are responsible for material in the appendices.) All sympathetic and parasympathetic nerves are two-stage neural paths: The

sympathetic and parasympathetic neurons project from the CNS and go only part of the way to the target organs before they *synapse on* other neurons (second-stage neurons) that carry the signals the rest of the way. However, the sympathetic and parasympathetic systems differ in that the sympathetic neurons that project from the CNS synapse on second-stage neurons at a substantial distance from their target organs, whereas the parasympathetic neurons that project from the CNS synapse near their target organs on very short second-stage neurons (see Appendix I).

The conventional view of the respective functions of the sympathetic and parasympathetic systems stresses three important principles: (1) sympathetic nerves stimulate, organize, and mobilize energy resources in threatening situations, whereas parasympathetic nerves act to conserve energy; (2) each autonomic target organ receives opposing sympathetic and parasympathetic input, and its activity is thus controlled by relative levels of sympathetic and parasympathetic activity; and (3) sympathetic changes are indicative of psychological arousal, whereas parasympathetic changes are indicative of psychological relaxation. Although these principles are generally correct, there are significant qualifications and exceptions to each of them (see Guyenet, 2006)—see Appendix II.

Most of the nerves of the peripheral nervous system project from the spinal cord, but there are 12 pairs of exceptions: the 12 pairs of **cranial nerves**, which project from the brain. They are numbered in sequence from front to back. The cranial nerves include purely sensory nerves such as the olfactory nerves (I) and the optic nerves (II), but most contain both sensory and motor fibers. The longest cranial nerves are the vagus nerves (X), which contain motor and sensory fibers traveling to and from the gut. The 12 pairs of cranial nerves and their targets are illustrated in Appendix III; the functions of these nerves are listed in Appendix IV. The autonomic motor fibers of cranial nerves are parasympathetic.

The functions of the various cranial nerves are commonly assessed by neurologists as a basis for diagnosis. Because the functions and locations of the cranial nerves are specific, disruptions **Clinical Implications** of particular cranial nerve functions provide excellent clues about the location and extent of tumors and other kinds of brain pathology.

Figure 3.2 summarizes the major divisions of the nervous system. Notice that the nervous system is a "system of twos."

Meninges

LO 3.2 Describe the three meninges and explain their functional role.

The brain and spinal cord (the CNS) are the most protected organs in the body. They are encased in bone and

Figure 3.2 The major divisions of the nervous system.

covered by three protective membranes, the three **meninges** (pronounced "men-IN-gees"). The outer *meninx* (which, believe it or not, is the singular of *meninges*) is a tough membrane called the **dura mater** (tough mother). Immediately inside the dura mater is the fine **arachnoid membrane** (spider-web-like membrane). Beneath the arachnoid membrane is a space called the **subarachnoid space**, which contains many large blood vessels and cerebrospinal fluid; then comes the innermost meninx, the delicate **pia mater** (pious mother), which adheres to the surface of the CNS.

Ventricles and Cerebrospinal Fluid

LO 3.3   Explain where cerebrospinal fluid is produced and where it flows.

Also protecting the CNS is the **cerebrospinal fluid (CSF)**, which fills the subarachnoid space, the central canal of the spinal cord, and the cerebral ventricles of the brain. The **central canal** is a small central channel that runs the length of the spinal cord; the **cerebral ventricles** are the four large internal chambers of the brain: the two lateral ventricles, the third ventricle, and the fourth ventricle (see Figure 3.3). The subarachnoid space, central canal, and cerebral ventricles are interconnected by a series of openings and thus form a single reservoir.

The cerebrospinal fluid supports and cushions the brain. Patients who have had some of their cerebrospinal fluid drained away often suffer raging headaches and experience stabbing pain each time they jerk their heads.

According to the traditional view, cerebrospinal fluid is produced by the **choroid plexuses** (networks of *capillaries*, or small blood vessels that protrude into the ventricles from the pia mater), and the excess cerebrospinal fluid is continuously absorbed from the subarachnoid space into large blood-filled spaces, or *dural sinuses*, which run through the dura mater and drain into the large jugular veins of the neck. However, there is growing appreciation that cerebrospinal fluid production and absorption are more complex than was originally thought (see Brinker et al., 2014). Figure 3.4 illustrates the absorption of cerebrospinal fluid from the subarachnoid space into the large sinus that runs along the top of the brain between the two cerebral hemispheres.

Occasionally, the flow of cerebrospinal fluid is blocked by a tumor near one of the narrow channels that link the ventricles—for example, near the *cerebral aqueduct*, which connects the third and fourth ventricles. **Clinical Implications** The resulting buildup of fluid in the ventricles causes the walls of the ventricles, and thus the entire brain, to expand, producing a condition called *hydrocephalus* (water head). Hydrocephalus is treated by draining the excess fluid from the ventricles and trying to remove the obstruction.

 Clinical Implications   Hydrocephalus is often congenital (present from birth). What do you think might be some of the long-term effects of being born with hydrocephalus?

Figure 3.3 The cerebral ventricles and central canal.

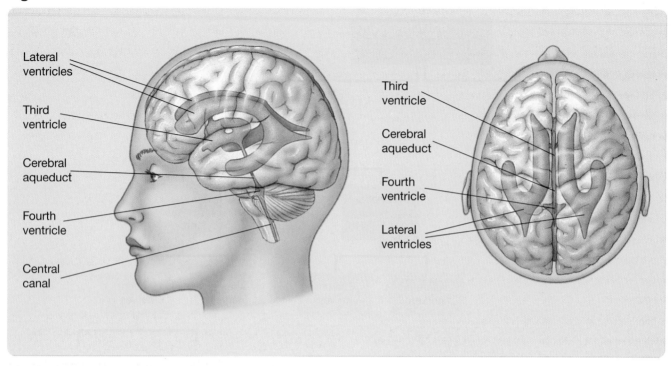

Figure 3.4 The absorption of cerebrospinal fluid (CSF) from the subarachnoid space (blue) into a major sinus. Note the three meninges.

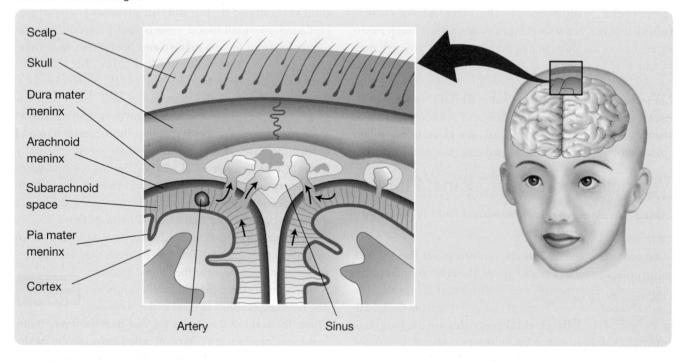

Blood–Brain Barrier

LO 3.4 **Explain what the blood–brain barrier is and what functional role it serves.**

The brain is a finely tuned electrochemical organ whose function can be severely disturbed by the introduction of certain kinds of chemicals. Fortunately, a mechanism impedes the passage of many toxic substances from the blood into the brain: the **blood–brain barrier**. This barrier is a consequence of the special structure of cerebral blood vessels. In the rest of the body, the cells that compose the walls of blood vessels are loosely packed; as a result, most molecules pass readily through them into surrounding tissue. In the brain, however, the cells of the blood vessel walls are tightly packed, thus forming a barrier to the passage of many molecules—particularly proteins and other large molecules (see Chow & Gu, 2015). The degree to which therapeutic or recreational drugs can influence brain activity depends on the ease with which they penetrate the blood–brain barrier (see Interlandi, 2013; Siegenthaler, Sohet, & Daneman, 2013).

The blood–brain barrier does not impede the passage of all large molecules. Some large molecules that are critical for normal brain function (e.g., glucose) are actively transported through cerebral blood vessel walls. Also, the blood vessel walls in some areas of the brain allow certain large molecules to pass through them unimpeded. Many CNS disorders are associated with impairment of the blood-brain barrier (see Bentivoglio & Kristensson, 2014).

Scan Your Brain

This is a good place for you to scan your brain: Are you ready to learn about the cells of the nervous system? Test your grasp of the first module of this chapter by filling in the following blanks with the most appropriate terms. The correct answers are provided at the end of the exercise. Before proceeding, review material related to your errors and omissions.

1. The peripheral nervous system is located outside the _____.
2. The part of the peripheral nervous system that regulates the body's internal environment is the _____ system.
3. Nerves that carry sensory messages from the skin, joints, eyes, and ears to the central nervous system are called _____ nerves.
4. Sympathetic nerves are a part of the _____ nervous system.
5. _____ nerves stimulate, organize, and mobilize energy resources in threatening situations.
6. The vagus nerves are the longest _____.
7. The olfactory nerves and optic nerves are the only two purely sensory _____.
8. The innermost meninx is the _____.
9. The _____ space, made up of large blood vessels and cerebrospinal fluid, lies between the arachnoid membrane and the pia matter.
10. The traditional view on cerebrospinal fluid production says that it is made by small blood vessels called the _____.
11. A tumor near the _____ can produce hydrocephalus.
12. The cells in the brain are tightly packed and act as a _____ to any protein or large molecules.

Scan Your Brain answers: (1) skull and spine, (2) autonomic nervous, (3) afferent, (4) autonomic, (5) Sympathetic, (6) cranial nerves, (7) cranial nerves, (8) pia mater, (9) subarachnoid, (10) choroid plexus, (11) cerebral aqueduct, (12) barrier.

Cells of the Nervous System

Most of the cells of the nervous system are of two fundamentally different types: neurons and glial cells. Their anatomy is discussed in the following two sections.

Anatomy of Neurons

LO 3.5 Draw, label, and define the major features of a multipolar neuron.

As you learned in Chapter 1, **neurons** are cells that are specialized for the reception, conduction, and transmission of electrochemical signals. They come in an incredible variety of shapes and sizes (see Sharpee, 2014; Shen, 2015; Underwood, 2015); however, many are similar to the one illustrated in Figures 3.5 and 3.6.

EXTERNAL ANATOMY OF NEURONS. Figure 3.5 is an illustration of the major external features of one type of neuron. For your convenience, the definition of each feature is included in the illustration.

INTERNAL ANATOMY OF NEURONS. Figure 3.6 is an illustration of the major internal features of one type of neuron. Again, the definition of each feature is included in the illustration.

NEURON CELL MEMBRANE. The neuron cell membrane is composed of a *lipid bilayer*, or two layers of fat molecules (see Figure 3.7). Embedded in the lipid bilayer are numerous protein molecules that are the basis of many of the cell membrane's functional properties. Some membrane proteins are *channel proteins*, through which certain molecules can pass; others are *signal proteins*, which transfer a signal to the inside of the neuron when particular molecules bind to them on the outside of the membrane.

Figure 3.5 The major external features of a neuron.

Cell membrane. The semipermeable membrane that encloses the neuron.

Dendrites. The short processes emanating from the cell body, which receive most of the synaptic contacts from other neurons.

Axon hillock. The cone-shaped region at the junction between the axon and the cell body.

Axon. The long, narrow process that projects from the cell body.

Cell body. The metabolic center of the neuron; also called the *soma*.

Myelin. The fatty insulation around many axons.

Nodes of Ranvier (pronounced "RAHN-vee-yay"). The gaps between sections of myelin.

Buttons. The buttonlike endings of the axon branches, which release chemicals into synapses.

Synapses. The gaps between adjacent neurons across which chemical signals are transmitted.

CLASSES OF NEURONS. Figure 3.8 illustrates a way of classifying neurons based on the number of processes (projections) emanating from their cell bodies. A neuron with more than two processes extending from its cell body is classified as a **multipolar neuron**; most neurons are multipolar. A neuron with one process extending from its cell body is classified as a **unipolar neuron**, and a neuron with two processes extending from its cell body is classified as a **bipolar neuron**. Neurons with a short axon or no axon at all are called **interneurons**; their function is to integrate neural activity within a single brain structure, not to conduct signals from one structure to another. Classifying neurons is a complex task, and neuroscientists still don't agree on the

Figure 3.6 The major internal features of a neuron.

Endoplasmic reticulum. A system of folded membranes in the cell body; rough portions (those with ribosomes) play a role in the synthesis of proteins; smooth portions (those without ribosomes) play a role in the synthesis of fats.

Cytoplasm. The clear internal fluid of the cell.

Ribosomes. Internal cellular structures on which proteins are synthesized; they are located on the endoplasmic reticulum.

Golgi complex. A connected system of membranes that packages molecules in vesicles.

Nucleus. The spherical DNA-containing structure of the cell body.

Mitochondria. Sites of aerobic (oxygen-consuming) energy release.

Microtubules. Tubules responsible for the rapid transport of material throughout neurons.

Synaptic vesicles. Spherical membrane packages that store neurotransmitter molecules ready for release near synapses.

Neurotransmitters. Molecules that are released from active neurons and influence the activity of other cells.

Figure 3.7 The cell membrane is a lipid bilayer with signal proteins and channel proteins embedded in it.

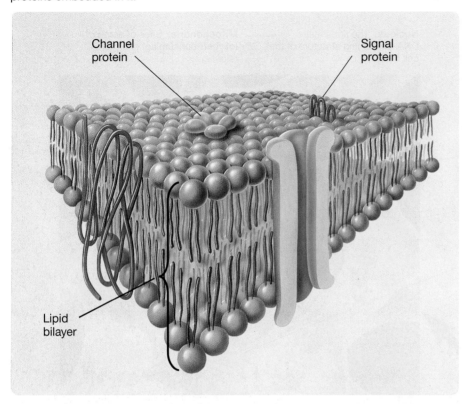

best method of classification (see Wichterle, Gifford, & Mazzoni, 2013).

NEURONS AND NEURO-ANATOMICAL STRUCTURE. In general, there are two kinds of gross neural structures in the nervous system: those composed primarily of cell bodies and those composed primarily of axons. In the central nervous system, clusters of cell bodies are called **nuclei** (singular *nucleus*); in the peripheral nervous system, they are called **ganglia** (singular *ganglion*). (Note that the word *nucleus* has two different neuroanatomical meanings; it is a structure in the neuron cell body and a cluster of cell bodies in the CNS.) In the central nervous system, bundles of axons are called **tracts**; in the peripheral nervous system, they are called **nerves**.

Glia: The Forgotten Cells

LO 3.6 Briefly describe four kinds of glial cells.

Neurons are not the only cells in the nervous system; there are about as many **glial cells**, or *glia* (pronounced "GLEE-a"). It has been reported that there are 10 times as many glia as neurons, but this is incorrect (see Lent et al., 2012): In the human brain, there are roughly equal numbers of neurons and glia (see Nimmerjahn & Bergles, 2015).

There are several kinds of glia (see Freeman, 2010). **Oligodendrocytes**, for example, are glial cells with extensions that wrap around the axons of some neurons of the central nervous system. These extensions are rich in **myelin**, a fatty insulating substance, and the **myelin sheaths** they form increase the speed and efficiency of axonal conduction (see Long & Corfas, 2014;

Figure 3.8 A unipolar neuron, a bipolar neuron, a multipolar neuron, and an interneuron.

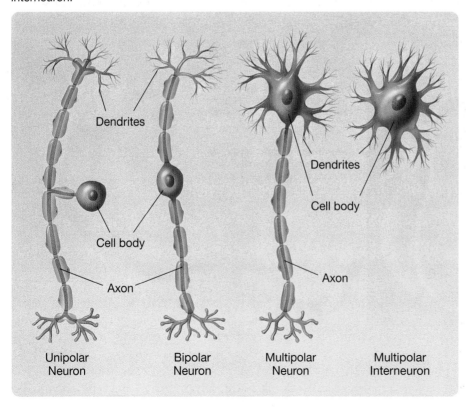

Figure 3.9 The myelination of CNS axons by an oligodendrocyte and the myelination of PNS axons by Schwann cells.

Myelination in the Central Nervous System

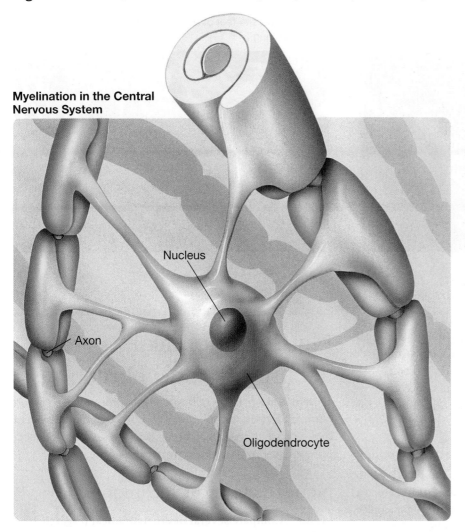

Nucleus

Axon

Oligodendrocyte

Myelination in the Peripheral Nervous System

Axon

Nucleus

Schwann cell

McKenzie et al., 2014). A similar function is performed in the peripheral nervous system by **Schwann cells**, a second class of glia. Oligodendrocytes and Schwann cells are illustrated in Figure 3.9. Notice that each Schwann cell constitutes one myelin segment, whereas each oligodendrocyte provides several myelin segments, often on more than one axon. Another important difference between Schwann cells and oligodendrocytes is that only Schwann cells can guide axonal *regeneration* (regrowth) after damage. That is why effective axonal regeneration in the mammalian nervous system is restricted to the PNS.

 Why is axonal regeneration an example of neuroplasticity?

Microglia make up a third class of glia. Microglia are smaller than other glial cells—thus their name. They respond to injury or disease by multiplying, engulfing cellular debris or even entire cells (see Brown & Neher,

2014), and triggering inflammatory responses (see Smith & Dragunow, 2014).

Astrocytes constitute a fourth class of glia. They are the largest glial cells, and they are so named because they are star-shaped (*astron* means "star"). The extensions of some astrocytes cover the outer surfaces of blood vessels that course through the brain; they also make contact with neurons (see Figure 3.10). These particular astrocytes appear to play a role in allowing the passage of some chemicals from the blood into CNS neurons and in blocking other chemicals (see Paixão & Klein, 2010), and they have the ability to contract or relax blood vessels based on the blood flow demands of particular brain regions (see Howarth, 2014; Muoio, Persson, & Sendeski, 2014).

For decades, it was assumed that the function of glia was mainly to provide support for neurons—providing them with nutrition, clearing waste, and forming a physical matrix to hold neural circuits together (*glia* means "glue"). But this limited view of the role of glial cells has changed, thanks to a series of remarkable

Figure 3.10 Astrocytes have an affinity for blood vessels, and they also make contact with neurons. The photograph on the left is of a slice of brain tissue stained with a glial stain; the unstained channels are blood vessels. The illustration on the right is a three-dimensional representation of the image on the left showing how the feet of astrocytes cover blood vessels and contact neurons. Compare the two panels. (Photograph courtesy of T. Chan-Ling.)

findings. For example, astrocytes, the most studied of the glial cells, have been shown to exchange chemical signals with neurons and other astrocytes (see Araque et al., 2014; Montero & Orellana, 2015; Yoon & Lee, 2014), to control the establishment and maintenance of synapses between neurons (Jourdain et al., 2007), to modulate neural activity (see Bouzier-Sore & Pellerin, 2013), to form functional networks with neurons and other astrocytes (see Gittis & Brasier, 2015; Lee et al., 2014; Perea, Sur, & Araque, 2014), to control the blood–brain barrier (see Alvarez, Katayama, & Prat, 2013; Cabezas et al., 2014), and to respond to brain injury (see Khakh & Sofroniew, 2015). Microglia have also been shown to play more than just a supportive role; for example, they have recently been shown to play a role in the regulation of cell death (see Wake et al., 2012), synapse formation (see Parkhurst et al., 2013; Welberg, 2014), and synapse elimination (see Wake et al., 2012).

Research on the function of glia, although still in its early stages, is creating considerable excitement. There is now substantial evidence that the physiological effects of glia are numerous, but the exact nature of their functions is still largely a matter of conjecture (e.g., Bergles, Jabs, & Steinhäuser, 2010; Reichenbach, Derouiche, & Kirchhoff, 2010); for example, some have suggested that glial networks may be the dwelling places of thoughts (Verkhratsky, Parpura, & Rodríguez, 2010). Arguably, the most important discovery about glial cells is that they are a lot more varied than implied by the four different types that we have just described: oligodendrocytes, Schwann cells, microglia, and astrocytes. For example, at least nine different kinds of astrocytes have been identified, each with its own structure and physiology (Matyash & Kettenmann, 2010). Sorting out the functions of each type is not going to be easy.

Neuroanatomical Techniques and Directions

This module first describes a few of the most common neuroanatomical techniques. Then, it explains the system of directions that neuroanatomists use to describe the location of structures in vertebrate nervous systems.

Neuroanatomical Techniques

LO 3.7 Compare several neuroanatomical research techniques.

The major problem in visualizing neurons is not their minuteness. The major problem is that neurons are so tightly packed and their axons and dendrites so intricately intertwined that looking through a microscope at unprepared neural tissue reveals almost nothing about them. The key to the study of neuroanatomy lies in preparing neural tissue in a variety of ways, each of which permits a clear view of a different aspect of neuronal structure, and then combining the knowledge obtained from each of the preparations. This point is illustrated by the following widely used neuroanatomical techniques.

GOLGI STAIN. The greatest blessing to befall neuroscience in its early years was the accidental discovery of the **Golgi stain** by Camillo Golgi (pronounced "GOLE-jee"), an Italian physician, in the early 1870s—see Rapport (2005). Golgi was trying to stain the meninges, by exposing a block of neural tissue to potassium dichromate and silver nitrate, when he noticed an amazing thing. For some unknown reason, the silver chromate created by the chemical reaction of the two substances Golgi was using invaded a few neurons

Figure 3.11 Neural tissue that has been stained by the Golgi method. Because only a few neurons take up the stain, their silhouettes are revealed in great detail, but their internal details are invisible. (Ed Reschke © Peter Arnold, Inc.)

Figure 3.12 The Nissl stain. Presented here is a Nissl-stained section through the rat hippocampus, at two levels of magnification to illustrate two uses of Nissl stains. Under low magnification (top panel), Nissl stains provide a gross indication of brain structure by selectively staining groups of neural cell bodies—in this case, the layers of the hippocampus. Under higher magnification (bottom panel), one can distinguish individual neural cell bodies and thus count the number of neurons in various areas. (Courtesy of our good friends Carl Ernst and Brian Christie, Department of Psychology, University of British Columbia.)

in each slice of tissue and stained each invaded neuron entirely black. This discovery made it possible to see individual neurons for the first time, although only in silhouette (see Figure 3.11). Golgi stains are commonly used when the overall shape of neurons is of interest.

NISSL STAIN. Although the Golgi stain permits an excellent view of the silhouettes of the few neurons that take up the stain, it provides no indication of the number of neurons in an area. The first neural staining procedure to overcome this shortcoming was the **Nissl stain**, which was developed by Franz Nissl, a German psychiatrist, in the 1880s. The most common dye used in the Nissl method is cresyl violet. Cresyl violet and other Nissl dyes penetrate all cells on a slide, but they bind effectively only to structures in neuron cell bodies. Thus, they often are used to estimate the number of cell bodies in an area, by counting the number of Nissl-stained dots. Figure 3.12 is a photograph of a slice of brain tissue stained with cresyl violet. Notice that only the layers composed mainly of neuron cell bodies are densely stained.

ELECTRON MICROSCOPY. A neuroanatomical technique that provides information about the details of neuronal structure is **electron microscopy** (pronounced "my-CROSS-cuh-pee"). Because of the nature of light, the limit of magnification in light microscopy is about 1,500 times, a level of magnification insufficient to reveal the fine anatomical details of neurons. Greater detail can be obtained by first coating thin slices of neural tissue with an electron-absorbing substance that is taken up by different parts of neurons to different degrees, then passing a beam of electrons through the tissue onto a photographic film. The result is an *electron micrograph*, which captures neuronal structure in exquisite detail. A *scanning electron microscope* provides spectacular electron micrographs in three dimensions (see Figure 3.13),

Figure 3.13 A color-enhanced scanning electron micrograph of a neuron cell body (grey) studded with terminal buttons (gold). Each neuron receives numerous synaptic contacts.

but it is not capable of as much magnification as conventional electron microscopy. The strength of electron microscopy is also a weakness: Because the images are so detailed, they can make it difficult to visualize general aspects of neuroanatomical structure.

NEUROANATOMICAL TRACING TECHNIQUES. Neuroanatomical tracing techniques are of two types: anterograde (forward) tracing methods and retrograde (backward) tracing methods. *Anterograde tracing methods* are used when an investigator wants to trace the paths of axons projecting away from cell bodies located in a particular area. The investigator injects into the area one of several chemicals commonly used for anterograde tracing— chemicals that are taken up by cell bodies and then transported forward along their axons to their terminal buttons. After a few days, the brain is removed and sliced; the slices are then treated to reveal the locations of the injected chemical. *Retrograde tracing methods* work in reverse; they are used when an investigator wants to trace the paths of axons projecting into a particular area. The investigator injects into the area one of several chemicals commonly used for retrograde tracing—chemicals that are taken up by terminal buttons and then transported backward along their axons to their cell bodies. After a few days, the brain is removed and sliced; the slices are then treated to reveal the locations of the injected chemical.

Directions in the Vertebrate Nervous System

LO 3.8 Illustrate the neuroanatomical directions.

It would be difficult for you to develop an understanding of the layout of an unfamiliar city without a system of directional coordinates: north–south, east–west. The same goes for the nervous system. Thus, before introducing you to the locations of major nervous system structures, we

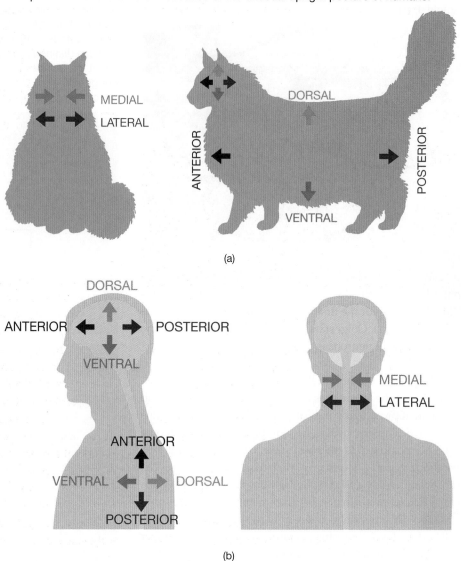

Figure 3.14 (a) Anatomical directions in representative vertebrates, my (JP) cats Sambala and Rastaman. (b) Anatomical directions in a human. Notice that the directions in the cerebral hemispheres are rotated by 90° in comparison to those in the spinal cord and brain stem because of the unusual upright posture of humans.

will describe the three-dimensional system of directional coordinates used by neuroanatomists.

Directions in the vertebrate nervous system are described in relation to the orientation of the spinal cord. This system is straightforward for most vertebrates, as Figure 3.14a indicates. The vertebrate nervous system has three axes: anterior–posterior, dorsal–ventral, and medial–lateral. First, **anterior** means toward the nose end (the anterior end), and **posterior** means toward the tail end (the posterior end); these same directions are sometimes referred to as *rostral* and *caudal*, respectively. Second, **dorsal** means toward the surface of the back or the top of the head (the dorsal surface), and **ventral** means toward the surface of the chest or the bottom of the head (the ventral surface). Third, **medial** means toward the midline of the body, and **lateral** means away from the midline toward the body's lateral surfaces.

We humans complicate this simple three-axis (anterior–posterior, ventral–dorsal, medial–lateral) system of neuroanatomical directions by insisting on walking around on our hind legs. This changes the orientation of our cerebral hemispheres in relation to our spines and brain stems.

Watch this video on MyPsychLab

CHALK-IT-UP! DIRECTIONS AND AXES IN THE VERTEBRATE NERVOUS SYSTEM

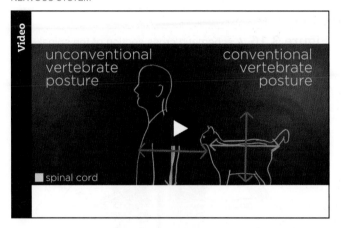

You can save yourself a lot of confusion if you remember that the system of vertebrate neuroanatomical directions was adapted for use in humans in such a way that the terms used to describe the positions of various body surfaces are the same in humans as they are in more typical, non-upright vertebrates. Specifically, notice that the top of the human head and the back of the human body are both referred to as *dorsal* even though they are in different directions, and the bottom of the human head and the front of the human body are both referred to as *ventral* even though they are in different directions (see Figure 3.14b). To circumvent this complication, the terms

Figure 3.15 Horizontal, frontal (coronal), and sagittal planes in the human brain and a cross section of the human spinal cord.

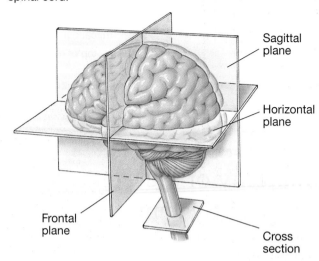

superior and **inferior** are often used to refer to the top and bottom of the primate head, respectively.

Proximal and *distal* are two other common directional terms. In general, **proximal** means "close," and **distal** means "far." Specifically, with regard to the peripheral nervous system, *proximal* means closer to the CNS, and *distal* means farther from the CNS. Your shoulders are proximal to your elbows, and your elbows are proximal to your fingers.

In the next module, you will be seeing drawings of sections (slices) of the brain cut in one of three different planes: **horizontal sections**, **frontal sections** (also termed *coronal sections*), and **sagittal sections**. These three planes are illustrated in Figure 3.15. A section cut down the center of the brain, between the two hemispheres, is called a *midsagittal section*. A section cut at a right angle to any long, narrow structure, such as the spinal cord or a nerve, is called a **cross section**.

Scan Your Brain

This is a good place for you to pause to scan your brain. Are you ready to proceed to the structures of the brain and spinal cord? Test your grasp of the preceding modules of this chapter by drawing a line between each term in the left column and the appropriate word or phrase in the right column. The correct answers are provided at the end of the exercise. Before proceeding, review material related to your errors and omissions.

1. myelin
2. soma
3. axon hillock
4. Golgi complex
5. ribosomes
6. synapses
7. glial cells
8. synaptic vesicles

a. gaps
b. cone-shaped region
c. packaging membranes
d. fatty substance
e. neurotransmitter storage
f. cell body
g. PNS clusters of cell bodies
h. protein synthesis

9. astrocytes
10. ganglia
11. oligodendrocytes
12. Golgi stain
13. dorsal
14. posterior

   i. the forgotten cells
   j. CNS myelinators
   k. black
   l. largest glial cells
   m. caudal
   n. top of head

Scan Your Brain answers: (1) d, (2) f, (3) b, (4) c, (5) h, (6) a, (7) i, (8) e, (9) l, (10) g, (11) j, (12) k, (13) n, (14) m.

Anatomy of the Central Nervous System

In the first three modules of this chapter, you learned about the divisions of the nervous system, the cells that compose it, and some of the neuroanatomical techniques used to study it. This final module focuses exclusively on the anatomy of the CNS. Your ascent through the CNS will begin with a focus on the spinal cord, and then you will move up to the brain.

Spinal Cord

LO 3.9 Draw and label a cross section of the spinal cord.

In cross section, it is apparent that the spinal cord comprises two different areas (see Figure 3.16): an inner H-shaped core of gray matter and a surrounding area of white matter. **Gray matter** is composed largely of cell bodies and unmyelinated interneurons, whereas **white matter** is composed largely of myelinated axons. (It is the myelin that gives the white matter its glossy white sheen.) The two dorsal arms of the spinal gray matter are called the **dorsal horns**, and the two ventral arms are called the **ventral horns**.

Pairs of *spinal nerves* are attached to the spinal cord—one on the left and one on the right—at 31 different levels of the spine. Each of these 62 spinal nerves divides as it nears the cord (see Figure 3.16), and its axons are joined to the cord via one of two roots: the *dorsal root* or the *ventral root*.

All dorsal root axons, whether somatic or autonomic, are sensory (afferent) unipolar neurons with their cell bodies grouped together just outside the cord to form the **dorsal root ganglia** (see Figure 3.16). Many of their synaptic terminals are in the dorsal horns of the spinal gray matter (see Figure 3.16). In contrast, the neurons of the ventral root are motor (efferent) multipolar neurons with their cell bodies in the ventral horns. Those that are part of the somatic nervous system project to skeletal muscles; those that are part of the autonomic nervous system project to ganglia, where they synapse on neurons that in turn project to internal organs (heart, stomach, liver, etc.). See Appendix I.

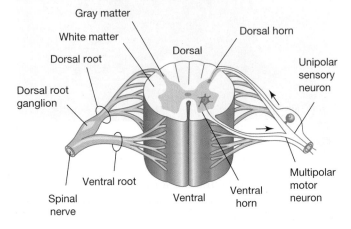

Figure 3.16 A schematic cross section of the spinal cord, and the dorsal and ventral roots.

Five Major Divisions of the Brain

LO 3.10 List and discuss the five major divisions of the human brain.

A necessary step in learning to live in an unfamiliar city is learning the names and locations of its major neighborhoods or districts. Those who possess this information can easily communicate the general location of any destination in the city. This section of the chapter introduces you to the five "neighborhoods," or divisions, of the brain—for much the same reason.

To understand why the brain is considered to be composed of five divisions, it is necessary to understand its early development (see Holland, 2009). In the vertebrate embryo, the tissue that eventually develops into the CNS is recognizable as a fluid-filled tube (see Figure 3.17). The first indications of the developing brain are three swellings that occur at the anterior end of this tube. These three swellings eventually develop into the adult *forebrain, midbrain*, and *hindbrain*.

Before birth, the initial three swellings in the neural tube become five (see Figure 3.17). This occurs because the forebrain swelling grows into two different swellings, and so does the hindbrain swelling. From anterior to posterior, the five swellings that compose the developing brain at birth are the *telencephalon*, the *diencephalon*, the *mesencephalon* (or midbrain), the *metencephalon*, and the *myelencephalon*

Figure 3.17 The early development of the mammalian brain illustrated in schematic horizontal sections. Compare with the adult human brain in Figure 3.18.

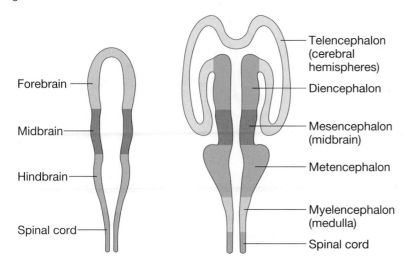

(*encephalon* means "within the head"). These swellings ultimately develop into the five divisions of the adult brain. As students, we memorized their order by remembering that the telencephalon is on the top and the other four divisions are arrayed below it in alphabetical order.

Figure 3.18 illustrates the locations of the telencephalon, diencephalon, mesencephalon, metencephalon, and myelencephalon in the adult human brain. Notice that in humans, as in other higher vertebrates, the telencephalon (the left and right *cerebral hemispheres*) undergoes the greatest growth during development. The other four divisions of the brain are often referred to collectively as the **brain stem**—the stem on which the cerebral hemispheres sit. The myelencephalon is often referred to as the *medulla*.

Now that you have learned the five major divisions of the brain, it is time to introduce you to their major structures. We begin our survey of brain structures in the myelencephalon, then ascend through the other divisions to

the telencephalon. The brain structures introduced and defined in the remainder of this module are boldfaced but are not included in the key terms list at the end of the chapter. Rather, they are arranged according to their locations in the brain in Figure 3.28.

Myelencephalon

LO 3.11   List and describe the components of the myelencephalon.

Not surprisingly, the **myelencephalon (or medulla)**, the most posterior division of the brain, is composed largely of tracts carrying signals between the rest of the brain and the body. An interesting part of the myelencephalon from a psychological perspective is the **reticular formation** (see Figure 3.19). It is a complex network of about 100 tiny nuclei that occupies the central core of the brain stem from the posterior boundary of the myelencephalon to the anterior boundary of the midbrain. It is so named because of its netlike appearance (*reticulum* means "little net"). Sometimes, the reticular formation is referred to as the *reticular activating system* because parts of it seem to play a role in arousal. However, the various nuclei of the reticular formation are involved in a variety of functions—including sleep, attention, movement, the maintenance of muscle tone, and various cardiac, circulatory, and respiratory reflexes. Accordingly, referring to this collection of nuclei as a *system* can be misleading.

Metencephalon

LO 3.12 List and describe the components of the metencephalon.

The **metencephalon**, like the myelencephalon, houses many ascending and descending tracts and part of the

Figure 3.18 The five divisions of the adult human brain.

Figure 3.19 Structures of the human myelencephalon (medulla) and metencephalon.

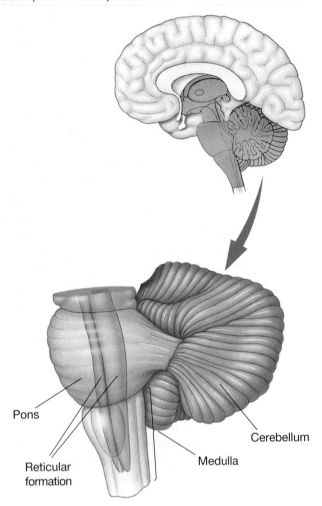

Pons

Reticular formation

Medulla

Cerebellum

Figure 3.20 The human mesencephalon (midbrain).

Superior colliculus

Periaqueductal gray

Mesencephalic reticular formation

Cerebral aqueduct

Red nucleus

Substantia nigra

Dorsal

Ventral

Superior colliculus

Inferior colliculus

Tectum

Tegmentum

reticular formation. These structures create a bulge, called the **pons**, on the brain stem's ventral surface. The pons is one major division of the metencephalon; the other is the cerebellum (little brain)—see Figure 3.20. The **cerebellum** is the large, convoluted structure on the brain stem's dorsal surface. It is an important sensorimotor structure; cerebellar damage eliminates the ability to precisely control one's movements and to adapt them to changing conditions. However, the fact that cerebellar damage also produces a variety of cognitive deficits (e.g., deficits in decision making and in the use of language) suggests that the functions of the cerebellum are not restricted to sensorimotor control.

Mesencephalon

LO 3.13 List and describe the components of the mesencephalon.

The **mesencephalon**, like the metencephalon, has two divisions. The two divisions of the mesencephalon are the tectum and the tegmentum (see Figure 3.20). The **tectum** (roof) is the dorsal surface of the midbrain. In mammals, the tectum is composed of two pairs of bumps, the *colliculi* (little hills). The posterior pair, called the **inferior colliculi**, have an auditory function. The anterior pair, called the **superior colliculi**, have a visual-motor function, specifically to direct the body's orientation toward or away from particular visual stimuli (see Gandhi & Katnani, 2011). In lower vertebrates, the function of the tectum is entirely visual-motor, and it is sometimes referred to as the *optic tectum*.

The **tegmentum** is the division of the mesencephalon ventral to the tectum. In addition to the reticular formation and tracts of passage, the tegmentum contains three colorful structures of particular interest to biopsychologists: the periaqueductal gray, the substantia nigra, and the red nucleus (see Figure 3.20). The **periaqueductal gray** is the gray matter situated around the **cerebral aqueduct**, the duct connecting the third and fourth ventricles; it is of special interest because of its role in mediating the analgesic (pain-reducing) effects of opioid drugs. The **substantia nigra** (black substance) and the **red nucleus** are both important components of the sensorimotor system.

Diencephalon

LO 3.14 List and describe the components of the diencephalon.

The **diencephalon** is composed of two structures: the thalamus and the hypothalamus (see Figure 3.21). The **thalamus** is the large, two-lobed structure that constitutes the top of the brain stem. One lobe sits on each side of the third ventricle, and the two lobes are joined by the **massa intermedia**, which runs through the ventricle. Visible on the surface of the thalamus are white *lamina* (layers) that are composed of myelinated axons.

The thalamus comprises many different pairs of nuclei, most of which project to the cortex. The general organization of the thalamus is illustrated in Appendix V.

The most well-understood thalamic nuclei are the **sensory relay nuclei**—nuclei that receive signals from sensory receptors, process them, and then transmit them to the appropriate areas of sensory cortex. For example, the **lateral geniculate nuclei**, the **medial geniculate nuclei**, and the **ventral posterior nuclei** are important relay stations in the visual, auditory, and somatosensory systems, respectively.

Sensory relay nuclei are not one-way streets; they all receive feedback signals from the very areas of cortex to which they project (e.g., Zembrzycki et al., 2013). Although less is known about the other thalamic nuclei, the majority of them receive input from areas of the cortex and project to other areas of the cortex (see Sherman, 2007).

The **hypothalamus** is located just below the anterior thalamus (*hypo* means "below")—see Figure 3.22. It plays an important role in the regulation of several motivated behaviors (e.g., eating, sleep, and sexual behavior). It exerts its effects in part by regulating the release of hormones from the **pituitary gland**, which dangles from it on the ventral surface of the brain. The literal meaning of *pituitary gland* is "snot gland"; it was discovered in a gelatinous state behind the nose of an unembalmed cadaver and was incorrectly assumed to be the main source of nasal mucus.

In addition to the pituitary gland, two other structures appear on the inferior surface of the hypothalamus: the optic chiasm and the mammillary bodies (see Figure 3.22). The **optic chiasm** is the point at which the *optic nerves* from

Figure 3.22 The human hypothalamus (in color) in relation to the optic chiasm and the pituitary gland.

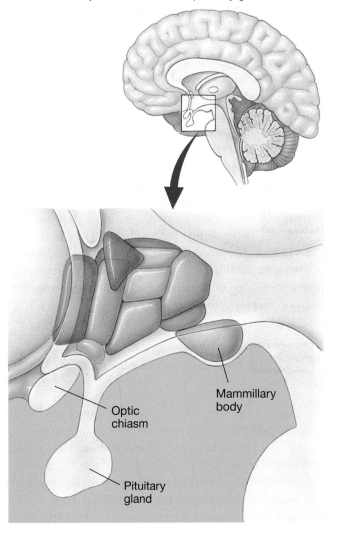

Figure 3.21 The human diencephalon.

each eye come together. The X shape is created because some of the axons of the optic nerve **decussate** (cross over to the other side of the brain) via the optic chiasm. The decussating fibers are said to be **contralateral** (projecting from one side of the body to the other), and the nondecussating fibers are said to be **ipsilateral** (staying on the same side of the body). The **mammillary bodies**, which are often considered to be part of the hypothalamus, are a pair of spherical nuclei located on the inferior surface of the hypothalamus, just behind the pituitary. The mammillary bodies and the other nuclei of the hypothalamus are illustrated in Appendix VI.

Telencephalon

LO 3.15 List and describe the components of the telencephalon.

The **telencephalon**, the largest division of the human brain, mediates the brain's most complex functions. It initiates voluntary movement, interprets sensory input, and mediates complex cognitive processes such as learning, speaking, and problem solving.

CEREBRAL CORTEX.   The cerebral hemispheres are covered by a layer of tissue called the **cerebral cortex** (cerebral bark). Because the cerebral cortex is mainly composed of small, unmyelinated neurons, it is gray and is often referred to as the *gray matter*. In contrast, the layer beneath the cortex is mainly composed of large myelinated axons, which are white and often referred to as the *white matter*.

In humans, the cerebral cortex is deeply convoluted (furrowed)—see Figure 3.23. The *convolutions* have the effect of increasing the amount of cerebral cortex without increasing the overall volume of the brain. Not all mammals have convoluted cortexes; most mammals are *lissencephalic* (smooth-brained). It was once believed that the number and size of cortical convolutions determined a species' intellectual capacities; however, the number and size of cortical convolutions appear to be related more to body size. Every large mammal has an extremely convoluted cortex.

> **Evolutionary Perspective**   Why do you think only large mammals have extremely convoluted cortices?

The large furrows in a convoluted cortex are called **fissures**, and the small ones are called **sulci** (singular *sulcus*). The ridges between fissures and sulci are called **gyri** (singular *gyrus*). It is apparent in Figure 3.23 that the cerebral hemispheres are almost completely separated by the largest of the fissures: the **longitudinal fissure**. The cerebral hemispheres are directly connected by a few tracts

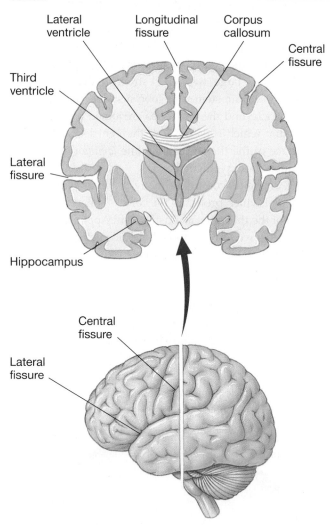

Figure 3.23 The major fissures of the human cerebral cortex.

spanning the longitudinal fissure; these hemisphere-connecting tracts are called **cerebral commissures**. The largest cerebral commissure, the **corpus callosum**, is clearly visible in Figure 3.23.

As Figures 3.23 and 3.24 indicate, the two major landmarks on the lateral surface of each hemisphere are the **central fissure** and the **lateral fissure**. These fissures partially divide each hemisphere into four lobes: the **frontal lobe**, the **parietal lobe** (pronounced "pa-RYE-e-tal"), the **temporal lobe**, and the **occipital lobe** (pronounced "ok-SIP-i-tal"). Among the largest gyri are the **precentral gyri**, the **postcentral gyri**, and the **superior temporal gyri** in the frontal, parietal, and temporal lobes, respectively.

It is important to understand that the cerebral lobes are not functional units. It is best to think of the cerebral cortex as a flat sheet of cells that just happens to be divided into lobes because pressure causes it to be folded in on itself at certain places during development. Thus, it is incorrect to think that a lobe is a functional unit, having one set of functions. Still, it is useful at this early stage of your

Figure 3.24 The lobes of the cerebral hemisphere.

Longitudinal fissure

Precentral gyrus Central fissure Postcentral gyrus

Lateral fissure

Superior temporal gyrus

Cerebellum

Frontal lobe   Parietal lobe   Temporal lobe   Occipital lobe

the posterior parts of the parietal lobes play roles in perceiving the location of both objects and our own bodies and in directing our attention. The cortex of each temporal lobe has three general functional areas: The superior temporal gyrus is involved in hearing and language, the inferior temporal cortex identifies complex visual patterns, and the medial portion of temporal cortex (which is not visible from the usual side view) is important for certain kinds of memory. Lastly, each frontal lobe has two distinct functional areas: The precentral gyrus and adjacent frontal cortex have a motor function, whereas the frontal cortex anterior to motor cortex performs complex cognitive functions, such as planning response sequences, evaluating the outcomes of potential patterns of behavior, and assessing the significance of the behavior of others (see Euston, Gruber, & McNaughton, 2012; Isoda & Noritake, 2013; Pezzulo et al., 2014).

About 90 percent of human cerebral cortex is **neocortex** (new cortex); that is, it is six-layered cortex of relatively recent evolution (see Rakic, 2009). By convention, the layers of neocortex are numbered I through VI, starting at the surface. Figure 3.25 illustrates two adjacent sections of neocortex. One has been stained with a Nissl stain to reveal the number and shape of its cell bodies; the other has been stained with a Golgi stain to reveal the silhouettes of a small proportion of its neurons.

Evolutionary Perspective

Three important characteristics of neocortical anatomy are apparent from the sections in Figure 3.25. First, it is apparent that many cortical neurons fall into one of two different categories: pyramidal (pyramid-shaped) cells and stellate (star-shaped) cells. **Pyramidal cells** are large multipolar neurons with pyramid-shaped cell bodies, a large dendrite called an *apical dendrite* that extends from the apex of the pyramid straight toward the cortex surface, and a very long axon (see Lodato, Shetty, & Arlotta, 2015). In contrast, **stellate cells** are small star-shaped interneurons (neurons with a short axon or no axon). Second, it is apparent that the six layers of neocortex differ from one another in terms of the size and density of their cell bodies and the relative proportion of pyramidal and stellate cell bodies that they contain. Third, it is apparent that many long axons and dendrites course vertically (i.e., at right angles to the cortical layers) through the neocortex. This vertical flow of information is the basis of the neocortex's **columnar organization**: neurons in a given vertical column of neocortex often form a mini-circuit that performs a single function (see Rowland & Moser, 2014).

A fourth important characteristic of neocortical anatomy is not apparent in Figure 3.25: Although neocortex is six-layered, there are variations in the thickness of the respective layers from area to area (see Zilles & Amunts, 2010). For example, because the stellate cells of layer IV

biopsychological education to get a general idea of various functions of areas within each lobe. More thorough discussions of the cerebral localization of brain functions are presented in later chapters.

The main function of the occipital lobes is quite straightforward: We humans rely heavily on the analysis of visual input to guide our behavior, and the occipital cortex and large areas of adjacent cortex perform this function. There are two large functional areas in each parietal lobe: The postcentral gyrus analyzes sensations from the body (e.g., touch), whereas the remaining areas of cortex in

Figure 3.25 The six layers of neocortex. The thickness of layer IV indicates that this is sensory neocortex. (Based on Rakic, P. (1979). Genetic and epigenetic determinants of local neuronal circuits in the mammalian central nervous system. In F. O. Schmitt & F. G. Worden (Eds.), *The neurosciences: Fourth study program.* Cambridge, MA: MIT Press.)

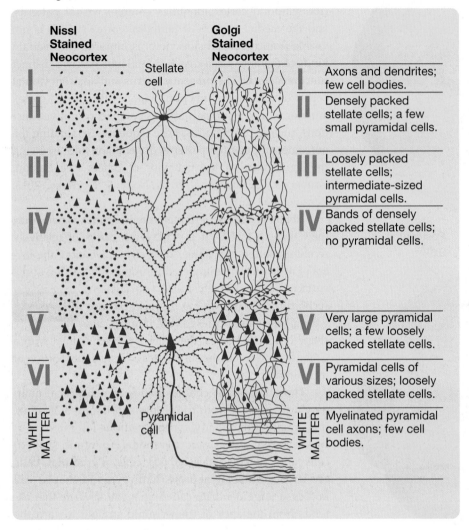

Limbic System and the Basal Ganglia

LO 3.16   List and describe the components of the limbic system and of the basal ganglia.

Although much of the subcortical portion of the telencephalon is taken up by axons projecting to and from the neocortex, there are several large subcortical nuclear groups. Some of them are considered part of either the *limbic system* or the *basal ganglia system*. Don't be misled by the word *system* in these contexts; it implies a level of certainty that is unwarranted. It is not entirely clear exactly what these hypothetical systems do, exactly which structures should be included in them, or even whether it is appropriate to view them as unitary systems. Nevertheless, if not taken too literally, the concepts of *limbic system* and *basal ganglia system* provide a useful means of conceptualizing the organization of several subcortical structures.

The **limbic system** is a circuit of midline structures that circle the thalamus (*limbic* means "ring"). The limbic system is involved in the regulation of motivated behaviors—including the four F's of motivation: fleeing, feeding, fighting, and sexual behavior. (This joke is as old as biopsychology itself, but it is a good one.) In addition to the structures about which you have already read (the mammillary bodies and the hippocampus), major structures of the limbic system include the amygdala, the fornix, the cingulate cortex, and the septum.

Let's begin tracing the limbic circuit (see Figure 3.26) at the **amygdala**—the almond-shaped nucleus in the anterior temporal lobe (*amygdala* means "almond" and is pronounced "a-MIG-dah-lah"). Posterior to the amygdala is the hippocampus, which runs beneath the thalamus in the medial temporal lobe. Next in the ring are the cingulate cortex and the fornix. The **cingulate cortex** is the large strip of cortex in the **cingulate gyrus** on the medial surface of the cerebral hemispheres, just superior to the corpus callosum; it encircles the dorsal thalamus (*cingulate* means "encircling"). The **fornix**, the major tract of the limbic system, also

are specialized for receiving sensory signals from the thalamus, layer IV is extremely thick in areas of sensory cortex. Conversely, because the pyramidal cells of layer V conduct signals from the neocortex to the brain stem and spinal cord, layer V is extremely thick in areas of motor cortex.

The **hippocampus** is one important area of cortex that is not neocortex—it has only three major layers (see Schultz & Engelhardt, 2014). The hippocampus is located at the medial edge of the cerebral cortex as it folds back on itself in the medial temporal lobe (see Figure 3.23). This folding produces a shape that is, in cross section, somewhat reminiscent of a seahorse (*hippocampus* means "sea horse"). The hippocampus plays a major role in some kinds of memory, particularly memory for spatial location (see Chapter 11).

Figure 3.26 The major structures of the limbic system: amygdala, hippocampus, cingulate cortex, fornix, septum, and mammillary body.

Figure 3.27 The basal ganglia: amygdala, striatum (caudate plus putamen), and globus pallidus. Notice that, in this view, the right globus pallidus is largely hidden behind the right thalamus and the left globus pallidus is totally hidden behind the left putamen. Although the globus pallidus is usually considered to be a telencephalic structure, it actually originates from diencephalic tissue that migrates into its telencephalic location during the course of prenatal development.

encircles the dorsal thalamus; it leaves the dorsal end of the hippocampus and sweeps forward in an arc coursing along the superior surface of the third ventricle and terminating in the septum and the mammillary bodies (*fornix* means "arc"). The **septum** is a midline nucleus located at the anterior tip of the cingulate cortex. Several tracts connect the septum and mammillary bodies with the amygdala and hippocampus, thereby completing the limbic ring.

The functions of the hippocampus, the hypothalamus and the amygdala have been investigated more than those of the other limbic structures. As stated previously, the hippocampus plays a role in certain forms of memory, and the hypothalamus is involved in a variety of motivated behaviors such as eating, sleep, and sexual behavior. The amygdala, on the other hand, is involved in emotion, particularly fear—you will learn much more about these structures in Chapters 11, 12, 13, 14, and 17.

The **basal ganglia** are illustrated in Figure 3.27. As we did with the limbic system, let's begin our examination of the basal ganglia with the amygdala, which is

considered part of both systems. Sweeping out of each amygdala, first in a posterior direction and then in an anterior direction, is the long tail-like **caudate** (*caudate* means "tail-like"). Each caudate forms an almost complete circle; in its center, connected to it by a series of fiber bridges, is the **putamen** (pronounced "pew-TAY-men"). Together, the caudate and the putamen, which both have a striped appearance, are known as the **striatum** (striped structure). The remaining structure of the basal ganglia is the pale circular structure known as the **globus pallidus** (pale globe). The globus pallidus is located medial to the putamen between the putamen and the thalamus.

The basal ganglia play a role in the performance of voluntary motor responses and decision making

Figure 3.28 Summary of major brain structures.

Telencephalon	Cerebral cortex	Neocortex Hippocampus
	Major fissures	Central fissure Lateral fissure Longitudinal fissure
	Major gyri	Precentral gyrus Postcentral gyrus Superior temporal gyrus Cingulate gyrus
	Four lobes	Frontal lobe Temporal lobe Parietal lobe Occipital lobe
	Limbic system	Amygdala Hippocampus Fornix Cingulate cortex Septum Mammillary bodies
	Basal ganglia	Amygdala Caudate } Putamen } Striatum Globus pallidus
	Cerebral commissures	Corpus callosum
Diencephalon	Thalamus	Massa intermedia Lateral geniculate nuclei Medial geniculate nuclei Ventral posterior nuclei
	Hypothalamus	Mammillary bodies
	Optic chiasm	
	Pituitary gland	
Mesencephalon	Tectum	Superior colliculi Inferior colliculi
	Tegmentum	Reticular formation Cerebral aqueduct Periaqueductal gray Substantia nigra Red nucleus
Metencephalon	Reticular formation Pons Cerebellum	
Myelencephalon or Medulla	Reticular formation	

(see Hikosaka et al., 2014). Of particular interest is a pathway that projects to the striatum from the substantia nigra of the midbrain: *Parkinson's disease*, a disorder characterized by rigidity, tremors, and poverty of voluntary movement, is associated with the deterioration of this pathway. Another part of the basal ganglia that is of particular interest to biopsychologists is the *nucleus accumbens*, which is in the medial portion of the ventral striatum (see Figure 3.27). The nucleus accumbens is thought to play a role in the rewarding effects of addictive drugs and other reinforcers.

Clinical Implications

Figure 3.28 summarizes the major brain divisions and structures whose names have appeared in boldface in this section.

Figure 3.29 concludes this chapter, for reasons that too often get lost in the shuffle of neuroanatomical terms and technology. We have included it here to illustrate the beauty of the brain and the art of those who study its structure. We hope you are inspired by it. We wonder what thoughts its neural circuits once contained.

Scan Your Brain

If you have not previously studied the gross anatomy of the brain, your own brain is probably straining under the burden of new terms. To determine whether you are ready to proceed, scan your brain by labeling the following midsagittal view of a real human brain. You may find it challenging to switch from color-coded diagrams to a photograph of a real brain.

The correct answers are provided at the end of the exercise. Before proceeding, review material related to your errors and omissions. Notice that Figure 3.28 includes all the brain anatomy terms that have appeared in bold type in this module and thus is an excellent review tool.

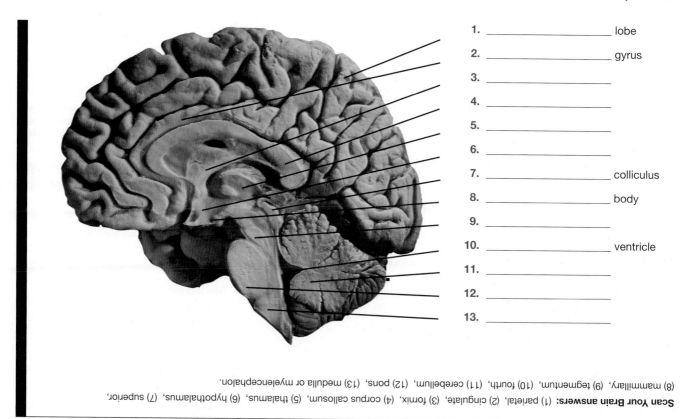

1. _____ lobe
2. _____ gyrus
3. _____
4. _____
5. _____
6. _____
7. _____ colliculus
8. _____ body
9. _____
10. _____ ventricle
11. _____
12. _____
13. _____

Scan Your Brain answers: (1) parietal, (2) cingulate, (3) fornix, (4) corpus callosum, (5) thalamus, (6) hypothalamus, (7) superior, (8) mammillary, (9) tegmentum, (10) fourth, (11) cerebellum, (12) pons, (13) medulla or myelencephalon.

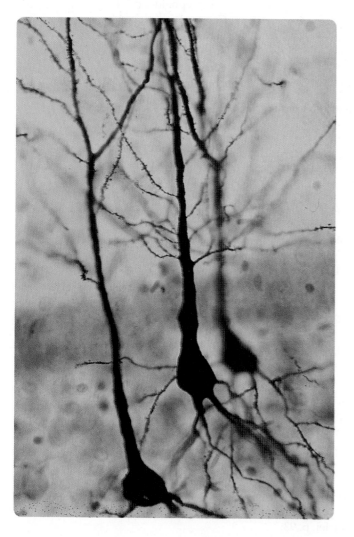

Figure 3.29 The art of neuroanatomical staining. This slide was stained with both a Golgi stain and a Nissl stain. Clearly visible on the Golgi-stained pyramidal neurons are the pyramid-shaped cell bodies, the large apical dendrites, and numerous dendritic spines. Less obvious here is the long, narrow axon that projects from each pyramidal cell body off the bottom of this slide. (Courtesy of Miles Herkenham, Unit of Functional Neuroanatomy, National Institute of Mental Health, Bethesda, MD.)

Themes Revisited

This chapter contributed relatively little to the development of the text's themes; that development was temporarily slowed while you were being introduced to the key areas and structures of the human brain. A knowledge of 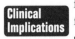 fundamental neuroanatomy will serve as the foundation of discussions of brain function in subsequent chapters. However, the clinical implications theme did arise three times: in discussions of the importance of the cranial nerves in neurological

diagnosis, the role of blockage of cerebral aqueducts in hydrocephalus, and the involvement of damage to the pathway from the substantia nigra to the striatum in Parkinson's disease. Also, the evolutionary perspective was evident when the text discussed neocortex and described interspecies differences in cortical convolutions, and the neuroplasticity theme arose during the discussion of axonal regeneration.

Key Terms

Chapter 4

Neural Conduction and Synaptic Transmission

How Neurons Send and Receive Signals

LO 4.7 Describe how action potentials are conducted along axons—both myelinated and unmyelinated.

LO 4.8 Explain the shortcomings of the Hodgkin-Huxley model when applied to neurons in the mammalian brain.

Synaptic Transmission: Chemical Transmission of Signals among Neurons

LO 4.9 Describe the structure of different types of synapses.

LO 4.10 Describe how neurotransmitter molecules are synthesized and packaged in vesicles.

LO 4.11 Explain the process of neurotransmitter exocytosis.

LO 4.12 Describe the differences between ionotropic and metabotropic receptors.

LO 4.13 Explain how neurotransmitters are removed from a synapse.

LO 4.14 Describe the roles of glia and gap junctions in synaptic transmission.

Neurotransmitters

LO 4.15 Name the classes of neurotransmitters.

LO 4.16 Name and compare the different neurotransmitters.

Pharmacology of Synaptic Transmission and Behavior

LO 4.17 Provide a general overview of how drugs influence synaptic transmission.

LO 4.18 Describe three examples of how drugs have been used to influence neurotransmission.

Chapter 3 introduced you to the anatomy of neurons. This chapter introduces you to their function—how neurons conduct and transmit electrochemical signals through your nervous system. It begins with a description of how signals are generated in resting neurons; then it follows the signals as they are conducted through neurons and transmitted across synapses to other neurons. It concludes with a discussion of how drugs are used to study the relation between synaptic transmission and behavior. The following case study of a patient with Parkinson's disease will help you appreciate why a knowledge of neural conduction and synaptic transmission is an integral part of biopsychology (Klawans, 1990).

The Lizard, a Case of Parkinson's Disease*

"I have become a lizard," he began. "A great lizard frozen in a dark, cold, strange world."

His name was Roberto Garcia d'Orta. He was a tall thin man in his sixties, but like most patients with Parkinson's disease, he appeared to be much older than his actual age. Not many years before, he had been an active, vigorous businessman. Then it happened—not all at once, not suddenly, but slowly, subtly, insidiously. Now he turned like a piece of granite, walked in slow shuffling steps, and spoke in a monotonous whisper.

What had been his first symptom?

A tremor.

Had his tremor been disabling?

"No," he said. "My hands shake worse when they are doing nothing at all"—a symptom called *tremor-at-rest*.

The other symptoms of Parkinson's disease are not quite so benign. They can change a vigorous man into a lizard. These include rigid muscles, a marked poverty of spontaneous movements, difficulty in starting to move, and slowness in executing voluntary movements once they have been initiated.

The term *reptilian stare* is often used to describe the characteristic lack of blinking and the widely opened eyes gazing out of a motionless face, a set of features that seems more reptilian than human. Truly a lizard in the eyes of the world.

What was happening in Mr. d'Orta's brain? A small group of nerve cells called the *substantia nigra* (black substance) were unaccountably dying. These neurons make a particular chemical called dopamine, which they deliver to another part of the brain, known as the *striatum*. As the cells of the substantia nigra die, the amount of dopamine they can deliver goes down. The striatum helps control movement, and to do that normally, it needs dopamine.

*Based on NEWTON'S MADNESS by Harold Klawans (Harper & Row 1990). Reprinted by permission of Jet Literary Associates, Inc.

Although dopamine levels are low in Parkinson's disease, dopamine is not an effective treatment because it does not readily penetrate the blood–brain barrier. However, knowledge of dopaminergic transmission has led to the development of an effective treatment: L-dopa, the chemical precursor of dopamine, which readily penetrates the blood–brain barrier and is converted to dopamine once inside the brain.

Mr. d'Orta's neurologist prescribed L-dopa, and it worked. He still had a bit of tremor, but his voice became stronger, his feet no longer shuffled, his reptilian stare faded away, and he was once again able to perform with ease many of the activities of daily life (e.g., eating, bathing, writing, speaking, and even making love with his wife). Mr. d'Orta had been destined to spend the rest of his life trapped inside a body that was becoming increasingly difficult to control, but his life sentence was repealed—at least temporarily.

Mr. d'Orta's story does not end here. You will learn what ultimately happened to him in Chapter 10. Meanwhile, keep him in mind while you read this chapter: His case illustrates why knowledge of the fundamentals of neural conduction and synaptic transmission is a must for any biopsychologist.

Resting Membrane Potential

As you are about to learn, the key to understanding how neurons work—and how they malfunction—is the membrane potential. The **membrane potential** is the difference in electrical charge between the inside and the outside of a cell.

Recording the Membrane Potential

LO 4.1 **Describe how the membrane potential is recorded.**

To record a neuron's membrane potential, it is necessary to position the tip of one electrode inside the neuron and the tip of another electrode outside the neuron in the extracellular fluid. Although the size of the extracellular electrode is not critical, it is paramount that the tip of the intracellular electrode be fine enough to pierce the neural membrane without severely damaging it. The intracellular electrodes are called **microelectrodes**; their tips are less than one-thousandth of a millimeter in diameter—much too small to be seen by the naked eye.

When both electrode tips are in the extracellular fluid, the voltage difference between them is zero. However, when the tip of the intracellular electrode is inserted into a neuron, a steady potential of about −70 millivolts (mV) is recorded. This indicates that the potential inside the resting neuron is about 70 mV less than that outside the neuron. This steady membrane potential of about −70 mV is called the neuron's **resting potential**. In its resting state, with the −70 mV charge built up across its membrane, a neuron is said to be *polarized*.

Ionic Basis of the Resting Potential

LO 4.2 **Describe the resting membrane potential and its ionic basis, and describe the three factors that influence the distribution of Na^+ and K^+ ions across the neural membrane.**

Like all salts in solution, the salts in neural tissue separate into positively and negatively charged particles called **ions**. There are many different kinds of ions in neurons, but this discussion focuses on only two of them: sodium ions and potassium ions. The abbreviations for sodium ions (Na^+) and potassium ions (K^+) are derived from their Latin names: *natrium* (Na) and *kalium* (K). The plus signs indicate that each Na^+ and K^+ ion carries a single positive charge.

In resting neurons, there are more Na^+ ions outside the cell than inside and more K^+ ions inside than outside. These unequal distributions of Na^+ and K^+ ions are maintained even though there are specialized pores, called **ion channels**, in neural membranes through which ions can pass. Each type of ion channel is specialized for the passage of particular ions (e.g., Na^+ or K^+).

There is substantial pressure on Na^+ ions to enter the resting neurons. This pressure is of two types. First is the *electrostatic pressure* from the resting membrane potential: Because opposite charges attract, the -70 mV charge attracts the positively charged Na^+ ions into resting neurons. Second is the pressure from *random motion* for Na^+ ions to move down their *concentration gradient*. Let us explain. Like all ions in solution, the ions in neural tissue are in constant random motion, and particles in random motion tend to become evenly distributed because they are more likely to move down their *concentration gradients* than up them; that is, they are more likely to move from areas of high concentration to areas of low concentration than vice versa.

So, why then do Na^+ ions under electrostatic pressure and pressure from random movement not come rushing into neurons, thus reducing the resting membrane potential? The answer is simple: The sodium ion channels in resting neurons are closed, thus greatly reducing the flow of Na^+ ions into the neuron. In contrast, the potassium channels are open in resting neurons, but only a few K^+ ions exit because they are largely held inside by the negative resting membrane potential.

In the 1950s, Alan Hodgkin and Andrew Huxley became interested in the stability of the resting membrane potential. Some Na^+ ions do manage to enter resting neurons despite the closed sodium channels and some K^+ ions do exit; then why does the resting membrane potential stay fixed? In a series of clever experiments, for which they were awarded Nobel Prizes, Hodgkin and Huxley discovered the answer. At the same rate that Na^+ ions leaked into resting neurons, other Na^+ ions were actively transported out; and at the same rate that K^+ ions leaked out of resting neurons, other K^+ ions were actively transported in. Such ion transport is performed by mechanisms in the cell membrane that continually exchange three Na^+ ions inside the neuron for two K^+ ions outside. These transporters are commonly referred to as **sodium–potassium pumps**.

Since the discovery of sodium–potassium pumps, several other classes of **transporters** (mechanisms in the membrane of a cell that actively transport ions or molecules across the membrane) have been discovered (see Kaila et al., 2014). You will encounter more of them later in this chapter.

Watch this video on MyPsychLab

THE RESTING MEMBRANE POTENTIAL

Figure 4.1 summarizes the status of Na^+ and K^+ ions in resting neurons. Now that you understand the basic properties of resting neurons, you are prepared to consider how neurons respond to input.

Figure 4.1 Three factors that influence the distribution of Na^+ and K^+ ions across the neural membrane.

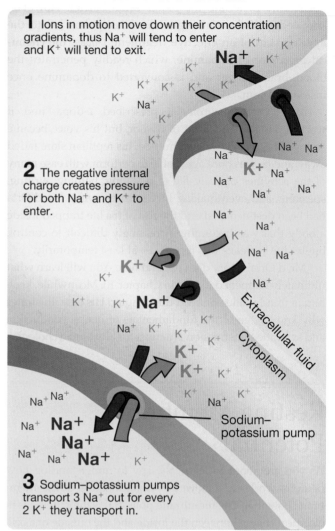

1 Ions in motion move down their concentration gradients, thus Na^+ will tend to enter and K^+ will tend to exit.

2 The negative internal charge creates pressure for both Na^+ and K^+ to enter.

Extracellular fluid

Cytoplasm

Sodium–potassium pump

3 Sodium–potassium pumps transport 3 Na^+ out for every 2 K^+ they transport in.

Generation, Conduction, and Integration of Postsynaptic Potentials

Generation and Conduction of Postsynaptic Potentials

LO 4.3 **Know the types of postsynaptic potentials and how they are conducted.**

When neurons fire, they release from their terminal buttons chemicals called *neurotransmitters*, which diffuse across the synaptic clefts and interact with specialized receptor molecules on the receptive membranes of the next neurons in the circuit. When neurotransmitter molecules bind to postsynaptic receptors, they typically have one of two effects, depending on the neurotransmitter, receptor, and postsynaptic neuron in question. They may **depolarize** the receptive membrane (decrease the resting membrane potential, from −70 to −67 mV, for example), or they may **hyperpolarize** it (increase the resting membrane potential, from −70 to −72 mV, for example). The ionic mechanisms mediating postsynaptic potentials are different in different kinds of neurons, so we will not discuss them here.

Postsynaptic depolarizations are called **excitatory postsynaptic potentials (EPSPs)** because, as you will soon learn, they increase the likelihood that the neuron will fire. Postsynaptic hyperpolarizations are called **inhibitory postsynaptic potentials (IPSPs)** because they decrease the likelihood that the neuron will fire. Both EPSPs and IPSPs are **graded responses**. This means that the amplitudes of EPSPs and IPSPs are proportional to the intensity of the signals that elicit them: Weak signals elicit small postsynaptic potentials, and strong signals elicit large ones.

EPSPs and IPSPs travel passively from their sites of generation at synapses, usually on the dendrites or cell body, in much the same way that electrical signals travel through a cable. Accordingly, the transmission of postsynaptic potentials has two important characteristics. First, it is rapid—so rapid that it can be assumed to be instantaneous for most purposes. It is important not to confuse the duration of EPSPs and IPSPs with their rate of transmission; although the duration of EPSPs and IPSPs varies considerably, all postsynaptic potentials, whether brief or enduring, are transmitted at great speed. Second, the transmission of EPSPs and IPSPs is *decremental*: EPSPs and IPSPs decrease in amplitude as they travel through the neuron, just as a sound wave loses amplitude (the sound grows fainter) as it travels through air. Most EPSPs and IPSPs do not travel more than a couple of millimeters from their site of generation before they fade out; thus, few travel very far along an axon.

Watch this video on MyPsychLab

POSTSYNAPTIC POTENTIALS

Integration of Postsynaptic Potentials and Generation of Action Potentials

LO 4.4   Describe how postsynaptic potentials summate, and how action potentials are generated.

The postsynaptic potentials created at a single synapse typically have little effect on the firing of the postsynaptic neuron. The receptive areas of most neurons are covered with thousands of synapses, and whether a neuron fires is determined by the net effect of their activity. More specifically, whether a neuron fires depends on the balance between the excitatory and inhibitory signals reaching its axon. It was once believed that action potentials were generated at the **axon hillock** (the conical structure at the junction between the cell body and the axon), but they are actually generated in the adjacent section of the axon, called the **axon initial segment** (see Kuba, Adachi, & Ohmori, 2014; Tian et al., 2014).

The graded EPSPs and IPSPs created by the action of neurotransmitters at particular receptive sites

on a neuron's membrane are conducted instantly and decrementally to the axon initial segment. If the sum of the depolarizations and hyperpolarizations reaching the axon initial segment at any time is sufficient to depolarize the membrane to a level referred to as its **threshold of excitation**—usually about –65 mV—an action potential is generated. The **action potential (AP)** is a massive but momentary—lasting for 1 millisecond—reversal of the membrane potential from about –70 to about +50 mV. Unlike postsynaptic potentials, action potentials are not graded responses; their magnitude is not related in any way to the intensity of the stimuli that elicit them. To the contrary, they are **all-or-none responses**; that is, they either occur to their full extent or do not occur at all. See Figure 4.2

Figure 4.2 An EPSP, an IPSP, and an EPSP followed by a typical action potential.

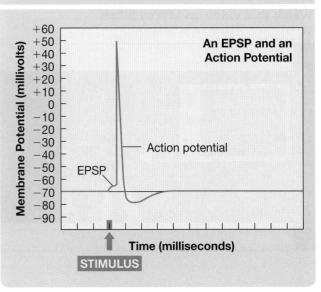

for an illustration of an EPSP, an IPSP, and an AP. Although many neurons display APs of the type illustrated in Figure 4.2, others do not—for example, some neurons display APs that are longer, that have lower amplitude, or that involve multiple spikes.

In effect, each multipolar neuron adds together all the graded excitatory and inhibitory postsynaptic potentials reaching its axon and decides to fire or not to fire on the basis of their sum. Adding or combining a number of individual signals into one overall signal is called **integration**. Neurons integrate incoming signals in two ways: over space and over time.

Figure 4.3 shows the three possible combinations of **spatial summation**. It shows how local EPSPs that are produced simultaneously on different parts of the receptive membrane sum to form a greater EPSP, how simultaneous IPSPs sum to form a greater IPSP, and how simultaneous EPSPs and IPSPs sum to cancel each other out.

Figure 4.4 illustrates **temporal summation**. It shows how postsynaptic potentials produced in rapid succession at the same synapse sum to form a greater signal. The reason that stimulations of a neuron can add together over time is that the postsynaptic potentials they produce often outlast them. Thus, if a particular synapse is activated and then activated again before the original postsynaptic potential has completely dissipated, the effect of the second stimulus will be superimposed on the lingering postsynaptic potential produced by the first. Accordingly, it is possible for a brief

Figure 4.3 The three possible combinations of spatial summation.

Two simultaneous EPSPs sum to produce a greater EPSP

Two simultaneous IPSPs sum to produce a greater IPSP

A simultaneous IPSP and EPSP cancel each other out

Membrane potential (millivolts)

Watch this video on MyPsychLab
SUMMATION OF POSTSYNAPTIC POTENTIALS

subthreshold excitatory stimulus to fire a neuron if it is administered twice in rapid succession. In the same way, an inhibitory synapse activated twice in rapid succession can produce a greater IPSP than that produced by a single stimulation.

Each neuron continuously integrates signals over both time and space as it is continually bombarded with stimuli through the thousands of synapses covering its dendrites and cell body. Although schematic diagrams of neural circuitry rarely show neurons with more than a few representative synaptic contacts, most neurons receive thousands of such contacts.

The location of a synapse on a neuron's receptive membrane had long been assumed to be an important factor in determining its potential to influence the neuron's firing. Because EPSPs and IPSPs are transmitted

Figure 4.4 The two possible combinations of temporal summation.

decrementally, synapses near the axon trigger zone had been assumed to have the most influence on the firing of the neuron. However, it has been demonstrated that some neurons have a mechanism for amplifying dendritic signals that originate far from their axon initial segments (see Adrian et al., 2014; Araya, 2014).

In some ways, the firing of a neuron is like the firing of a gun. Both reactions are triggered by graded responses. As a trigger is squeezed, it gradually moves back until it causes the gun to fire; as a neuron is stimulated, it becomes less polarized until the threshold of excitation is reached and firing occurs. Furthermore, the firing of a gun and neural firing are both all-or-none events. Just as squeezing a trigger harder does not make the bullet travel faster or farther, stimulating a neuron more intensely does not increase the speed or amplitude of the resulting action potential.

Thinking Creatively Try to think of another metaphor for the firing of a neuron.

Scan Your Brain

Before you learn how action potentials are conducted along the axon, pause here to make sure you understand how action potentials are created. Fill in each blank with the most appropriate term. The correct answers are provided at the end of the exercise. Before proceeding, review material related to your errors and omissions.

1. Roberto Garcia d'Orta referred to himself as "a great lizard frozen in a dark, cold, strange world." He suffered from _____.
2. *Substantia nigra* produces a chemical called _____.
3. The difference in electrical charge between the inside and the outside of a cell is called the _____.
4. The _____ is about –70 mV.

5. _____ are the positively and negatively charged particles of salts inside the neuron.
6. Two factors pressure Na⁺ ions to enter resting neurons: random _____ and electrostatic pressure.
7. When a neuron is in a resting state, there is a greater concentration of _____ ions outside the neuron.
8. The _____ channels are open in a resting neuron.
9. Ions pass through neural membranes via specialized pores called _____.
10. The firing of neurons releases chemicals at their button terminals called _____.
11. Neurotransmitters typically have one of two effects on postsynaptic neurons: They either depolarize them or _____ them.

12. When neurons add or combine a number of individual signals into one overall signal, this is called _____.

13. _____ is the sum of the postsynaptic potentials produced in rapid succession at the same synapse to form a greater signal.

14. An action potential is elicited when the depolarization of the neuron reaches the _____.

15. Unlike postsynaptic potentials, which are graded, action potentials are _____ responses.

16. Neurons integrate postsynaptic potentials in two ways: through spatial summation and through _____ summation.

Scan Your Brain answers: (1) Parkinson's disease, (2) dopamine, (3) membrane potential, (4) resting potential, (5) ions, (6) motion, (7) sodium, (8) potassium, (9) ion channels, (10) neurotransmitters, (11) hyperpolarize, (12) integration, (13) Temporal summation, (14) threshold of excitation, (15) all-or-none, (16) temporal.

Conduction of Action Potentials

How are action potentials produced, and how are they conducted along the axon? The answer to both questions is basically the same: through the action of **voltage-activated ion channels**—ion channels that open or close in response to changes in the level of the membrane potential (see Moran et al., 2015).

Ionic Basis of Action Potentials

LO 4.5   Explain the ionic basis of an action potential.

Recall that the membrane potential of a neuron at rest is relatively constant despite the high pressure acting to drive Na$^+$ ions into the cell. This is because the resting membrane is relatively impermeable to Na$^+$ ions and because those few that do pass in are pumped out. But things suddenly change when the membrane potential of the axon is depolarized to the threshold of excitation by an EPSP. The voltage-activated sodium channels in the axon membrane open wide, and Na$^+$ ions rush in, suddenly driving the membrane potential from about −70 to about +50 mV. The rapid change in the membrane potential associated with the *influx* of Na$^+$ ions then triggers the opening of voltage-activated potassium channels. At this point, K$^+$ ions near the membrane are driven out of the cell through these channels—first by their relatively high internal concentration and then, when the action potential is near its peak, by the positive internal charge. After about 1 millisecond, the sodium channels close. This marks the end of the *rising phase* of the action potential and the beginning of *repolarization* by the continued efflux of K$^+$ ions. Once repolarization has been achieved, the potassium channels gradually close. Because they close gradually, too many K$^+$ ions flow out of the neuron, and it is left *hyperpolarized* for a brief period of time. Figure 4.5 illustrates the timing of the opening and closing of the sodium and potassium channels during an action potential.

The number of ions that flow through the membrane during an action potential is extremely small in relation to the total number inside and around the neuron. The action potential involves only those ions right next to the membrane. Therefore, a single action potential has little effect on the relative concentrations of various ions inside and outside the neuron, and the resting ion concentrations next to the membrane are rapidly reestablished by the random movement of ions. The sodium–potassium pumps play only a minor role in the reestablishment of the resting potential.

Watch this video on MyPsychLab
ACTION POTENTIALS

Refractory Periods

LO 4.6   Explain how the refractory period is responsible for two important characteristics of neural activity.

There is a brief period of about 1 to 2 milliseconds after the initiation of an action potential during which it is impossible to elicit a second one. This period is called the **absolute refractory period**. The absolute refractory period is followed by the **relative refractory period**—the period during which it is possible to fire the neuron again but only by applying higher-than-normal levels of stimulation. The end of the relative refractory period is the point at which the amount of stimulation necessary to fire a neuron returns to baseline.

The refractory period is responsible for two important characteristics of neural activity. First, it is responsible for the fact that action potentials normally travel along axons in only one direction. Because the portions of an axon over which an action potential has just traveled are left momentarily refractory, an action potential cannot

Figure 4.5 The three phases of an action potential. The opening and closing of voltage-activated sodium and potassium channels during the three phases of the action potential: rising phase, repolarization, and hyperpolarization.

reverse direction. Second, the refractory period is responsible for the fact that the rate of neural firing is related to the intensity of the stimulation. If a neuron is subjected to a high level of continual stimulation, it fires and then fires again as soon as its absolute refractory period is over—a maximum of about 1,000 times per second. However, if the level of stimulation is of an intensity just sufficient to fire the neuron when it is at rest, the neuron does not fire again until both the absolute and the relative refractory periods have run their course. Intermediate levels of stimulation produce intermediate rates of neural firing.

Axonal Conduction of Action Potentials

LO 4.7 **Describe how action potentials are conducted along axons—both myelinated and unmyelinated.**

The conduction of action potentials along an axon differs from the conduction of EPSPs and IPSPs in two important ways. First, the conduction of action potentials along an axon is *nondecremental*; action potentials do not grow weaker as they travel along the axonal membrane. Second, action potentials are conducted more slowly than postsynaptic potentials.

The reason for these two differences is that the conduction of EPSPs and IPSPs is passive, whereas the axonal conduction of action potentials is largely active. Once an action potential has been generated, it travels passively along the axonal membrane to the adjacent voltage-activated sodium channels, which have yet to open. The arrival of

the electrical signal opens these channels, thereby allowing Na^+ ions to rush into the neuron and generate a full-blown action potential on this portion of the membrane. This signal is then conducted passively to the next sodium channels, where another action potential is actively triggered. These events are repeated again and again until a full-blown action potential is triggered in all the terminal buttons. However, because there are so many ion channels on the axonal membrane and they are so close together, it is usual to think of axonal conduction as a single wave of excitation spreading actively at a constant speed along the axon, rather than as a series of discrete events.

The wave of excitation triggered by the generation of an action potential near the axon hillock always spreads passively back through the cell body and dendrites of the neuron. Although little is yet known about the functions of these backward propagating action potentials, they are currently the subject of intensive investigation.

The following analogy may help you appreciate the major characteristics of axonal conduction. Consider a row of mouse traps on a wobbly shelf, all of them set and ready to be triggered. Each trap stores energy by holding back its striker against the pressure of the spring, in the same way that each sodium channel stores energy by holding back Na^+ ions, which are under pressure to move down their concentration and electrostatic gradients into the neuron. When the first trap in the row is triggered, the vibration is transmitted passively through the shelf, and the next trap is sprung—and so on down the line.

Thinking Creatively

The nondecremental nature of action potential conduction is readily apparent from this analogy; the last trap on the shelf strikes with no less intensity than did the first. This analogy also illustrates the refractory period: A trap cannot respond again until it has been reset, just as a section of axon cannot fire again until it has been repolarized. Furthermore, the row of traps can transmit in either direction, just like an axon. If electrical stimulation of sufficient intensity is applied to the terminal end of an axon, an action potential will be generated and will travel along the axon back to the cell body; this is called **antidromic conduction**. Axonal conduction in the natural direction—from cell body to terminal buttons—is called **orthodromic conduction**. The elicitation of an action potential and the direction of orthodromic conduction are summarized in Figure 4.6.

CONDUCTION IN MYELINATED AXONS. In Chapter 3, you learned that the axons of many neurons are insulated from the extracellular fluid by segments of fatty tissue called *myelin*. In myelinated axons, ions can pass through the axonal membrane only at the **nodes of Ranvier**—the gaps between adjacent myelin segments. Indeed, in myelinated axons, axonal sodium channels are concentrated at the nodes of Ranvier (see Normand & Rasband, 2015). How, then, are action potentials transmitted in myelinated axons?

When an action potential is generated in a myelinated axon, the signal is conducted passively—that is, instantly and decrementally—along the first segment of myelin to the next node of Ranvier. Although the signal is somewhat diminished by the time it reaches that node, it is still strong enough to open the voltage-activated sodium channels at the node and to generate another full-blown action potential. This action potential is then conducted passively along the axon to the next node, where another full-blown action potential is elicited, and so on.

Myelination increases the speed of axonal conduction. Because conduction along the myelinated segments

Figure 4.6 The direction of signals conducted orthodromically through a multipolar neuron.

1 Postsynaptic potentials (PSPs) are elicited on the cell body and dendrites.

2 PSPs are conducted decrementally to the axon.

3 When the summated PSPs exceed the threshold of excitation at the axon initial segment, an action potential (AP) is triggered.

4 The AP is conducted nondecrementally down the axon to the terminal button.

5 Arrival of the AP at the terminal button triggers exocytosis.

of the axon is passive, it occurs instantly, and the signal thus "jumps" along the axon from node to node. There is, of course, a slight delay at each node of Ranvier while the action potential is actively generated, but conduction is still much faster in myelinated axons than in unmyelinated axons, in which passive conduction plays a less prominent role. The transmission of action potentials in myelinated axons is called **saltatory conduction** (*saltare* means "to skip or jump")—see Nave and Werner (2014). Given the important role of myelin in neural conduction, it is hardly surprising that diseases that damage the nervous system by attacking myelin have devastating effects on neural activity and behavior—see the discussion of multiple sclerosis in Chapter 10.

THE VELOCITY OF AXONAL CONDUCTION. At what speed are action potentials conducted along an axon? The answer to this question depends on two properties of the axon. Conduction is faster in large-diameter axons, and—as you have just learned—it is faster in those that are myelinated. Mammalian *motor neurons* (neurons that synapse on skeletal muscles) are large and myelinated; thus, some can conduct at speeds of 100 meters per second (about 224 miles per hour). In contrast, small, unmyelinated axons conduct action potentials at about 1 meter per second.

There is a misconception about the velocity of motor neuron action potentials in humans. The maximum velocity of motor neuron action potentials was found to be about 100 meters per second in cats and was then assumed to be the same in humans. It is not. The maximum velocity of conduction in human motor neurons is about 60 meters per second.

CONDUCTION IN NEURONS WITHOUT AXONS. Action potentials are the means by which axons conduct all-or-none signals nondecrementally over relatively long distances. Thus, to keep what you have just learned about action potentials in perspective, it is important for you to remember that many neurons in mammalian brains either do not have axons or have very short ones, and many of these neurons do not normally display action potentials. Conduction in these *interneurons* is typically passive and decremental.

The Hodgkin-Huxley Model in Perspective

LO 4.8 Explain the shortcomings of the Hodgkin-Huxley model when applied to neurons in the mammalian brain.

The preceding account of neural conduction is based heavily on the *Hodgkin-Huxley model*, the theory first proposed by Hodgkin and Huxley in the early 1950s (see Catterall et al., 2012). Perhaps you have previously encountered some of this information about neural conduction in introductory biology and psychology courses, where it is often presented as

Watch this video on MyPsychLab
STUDYING SQUID

a factual account of neural conduction and its mechanisms rather than as a theory. The Hodgkin-Huxley model was a major advance in our understanding of neural conduction (Catterall et al., 2012). Fully deserving of the 1963 Nobel Prize, the model provided a simple, effective introduction to what we now understand about the general ways in which neurons conduct signals. The problem is that the simple neurons and mechanisms of the Hodgkin-Huxley model are not representative of the variety, complexity, and plasticity of many of the neurons in the mammalian brain.

The Hodgkin-Huxley model was based on the study of squid motor neurons. Motor neurons are simple, large, and readily accessible in the PNS—squid motor neurons are particularly large. The simplicity, size, and accessibility of squid motor neurons contributed to the initial success of Hodgkin and Huxley's research, but these same properties make it difficult to apply the model directly to the mammalian brain. Hundreds of different kinds of neurons are found in the mammalian brain, and many of these have actions not found in motor neurons (see Nusser, 2009). Thus, the Hodgkin-Huxley model must be applied to cerebral neurons with caution. The following are some properties of cerebral neurons that are not shared by motor neurons:

- Many cerebral neurons fire continually even when they receive no input (Lisman, Raghavachari, & Tsien, 2007; Schultz, 2007).
- Axons of some cerebral neurons can actively conduct both graded signals and action potentials (Debanne, Bialowas, & Rama, 2013).
- Action potentials of different classes of cerebral neurons vary greatly in duration, amplitude, and frequency (Bean, 2007).
- Many cerebral neurons do not display action potentials.
- The dendrites of some cerebral neurons can actively conduct action potentials (Urban & Castro, 2010).

Clearly, cerebral neurons are far more varied and complex than motor neurons, which have traditionally been the focus of neurophysiological research. Accordingly, results of studies of motor neurons should be applied to the brain with caution.

Synaptic Transmission: Chemical Transmission of Signals among Neurons

You have learned in this chapter how postsynaptic potentials are generated on the receptive membrane of a resting neuron, how these graded potentials are conducted passively to the axon, how the sum of these graded potentials can trigger action potentials, and how these all-or-none potentials are actively conducted down the axon to the terminal buttons. In the remaining modules of this chapter, you will learn how action potentials arriving at terminal buttons trigger the release of neurotransmitters into synapses and how neurotransmitters carry signals to other cells. This module provides an overview of five aspects of synaptic transmission: (1) the structure of synapses; (2) the synthesis, packaging, and transport of neurotransmitter molecules; (3) the release of neurotransmitter molecules; (4) the activation of receptors by neurotransmitter molecules; and (5) the reuptake, enzymatic degradation, and recycling of neurotransmitter molecules.

Structure of Synapses

LO 4.9   Describe the structure of different types of synapses.

Some communication among neurons occurs across synapses such as the one illustrated in Figure 4.7. At such synapses, neurotransmitter molecules are released from specialized sites on buttons into synaptic clefts, where they induce EPSPs or IPSPs in other neurons by binding to receptors on their postsynaptic membranes. The synapses featured in Figure 4.7 are *axodendritic synapses*—synapses of axon terminal buttons on dendrites. Notice that many axodendritic synapses terminate on **dendritic spines** (nodules of various shapes that are located on the surfaces of many dendrites)—see Figure 3.29. Also common are *axosomatic synapses*—synapses of axon terminal buttons on *somas* (cell bodies).

Although axodendritic and axosomatic synapses are the most common synaptic arrangements, there are many others (see Matthews & Fuchs, 2010). For example, there are *dendrodendritic synapses*, which are interesting because they are often capable of transmission in either direction (see Urban & Castro, 2010). In addition, *axoaxonic synapses* are particularly important because they can mediate *presynaptic facilitation and inhibition*. As illustrated in Figure 4.8, an axoaxonic synapse on, or near, a terminal button can selectively facilitate or inhibit the effects of that button on the postsynaptic neuron. The advantage of presynaptic facilitation and inhibition (compared to EPSPs and IPSPs, which you have already learned about)

Figure 4.7 The anatomy of a typical synapse.

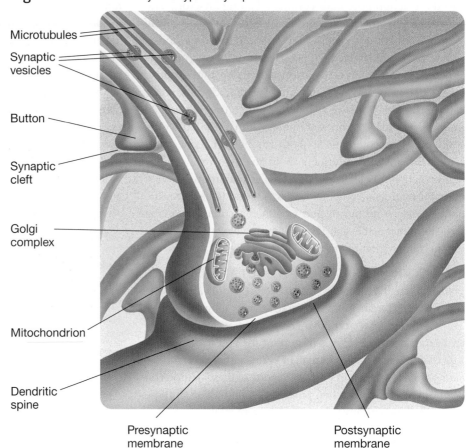

Microtubules
Synaptic vesicles
Button
Synaptic cleft
Golgi complex
Mitochondrion
Dendritic spine
Presynaptic membrane
Postsynaptic membrane

is that they can selectively influence one particular synapse rather than the entire presynaptic neuron.

The synapses depicted in Figures 4.7 and 4.8 are **directed synapses**—synapses at which the site of neurotransmitter release and the site of neurotransmitter reception are in close proximity. This is a common arrangement, but there are also many nondirected synapses in the mammalian nervous system. **Nondirected synapses** are synapses at which the site of release is at some distance from the site of reception. One type of nondirected synapse is depicted in Figure 4.9. In this type of arrangement, neurotransmitter molecules are released from a series of *varicosities* (bulges or swellings) along the axon and its branches and thus are widely dispersed to surrounding targets. Because of their appearance, these synapses are often referred to as *string-of-beads synapses*.

Synthesis, Packaging, and Transport of Neurotransmitter Molecules

LO 4.10 Describe how neurotransmitter molecules are synthesized and packaged in vesicles.

There are two basic categories of neurotransmitter molecules: small and large. The small neurotransmitters are

Figure 4.8 Presynaptic facilitation and inhibition.

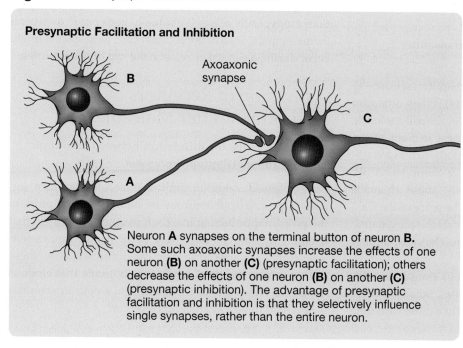

Presynaptic Facilitation and Inhibition

Axoaxonic synapse

B

A

C

Neuron **A** synapses on the terminal button of neuron **B**. Some such axoaxonic synapses increase the effects of one neuron **(B)** on another **(C)** (presynaptic facilitation); others decrease the effects of one neuron **(B)** on another **(C)** (presynaptic inhibition). The advantage of presynaptic facilitation and inhibition is that they selectively influence single synapses, rather than the entire neuron.

Figure 4.9 Nondirected neurotransmitter release. Some neurons release neurotransmitter molecules diffusely from varicosities along the axon and its branches.

Varicosity

Neurotransmitter molecules

of several types; large neurotransmitters are all neuropeptides. **Neuropeptides** are short amino acid chains composed of between 3 and 36 amino acids; in effect, they are short proteins.

Small-molecule neurotransmitters are typically synthesized in the cytoplasm of the terminal button and packaged in **synaptic vesicles** by the button's **Golgi complex**. (This may be a good point at which to review the internal structures of neurons in Figure 3.6.) Once filled with neurotransmitter, the vesicles are stored in clusters next to the presynaptic membrane. In contrast, neuropeptides, like other proteins, are assembled in the cytoplasm of the cell body on *ribosomes*; they are then packaged in vesicles by the cell body's Golgi complex and transported by *microtubules* to the terminal buttons at a rate of about 40 centimeters per day. The vesicles that contain neuropeptides are usually larger than those that contain small-molecule neurotransmitters, and they do not usually congregate as closely to the presynaptic membrane as the other vesicles do.

It was once believed that each neuron synthesizes and releases only one neurotransmitter, but it has been clear for some time that many neurons contain two neurotransmitters—a situation generally referred to as **coexistence**. It may have escaped your notice that the button illustrated in Figure 4.7 contains synaptic vesicles of two sizes. This suggests that it contains two neurotransmitters: a neuropeptide in the larger vesicles and a small-molecule neurotransmitter in the smaller vesicles. So far, most documented cases of coexistence have involved one small-molecule neurotransmitter and one neuropeptide, although coexistence of small-molecule neurotransmitters has also been noted (see Tritsch, Granger, & Sabatini, 2016).

Release of Neurotransmitter Molecules

LO 4.11 Explain the process of neurotransmitter exocytosis.

Exocytosis—the process of neurotransmitter release—is illustrated in Figure 4.10 (see Shin, 2014). When a neuron is at rest, synaptic vesicles that contain small-molecule neurotransmitters tend to congregate near sections of the presynaptic membrane that are particularly rich in *voltage-activated calcium channels* (see Simms & Zamponi, 2014). When stimulated by action potentials, these channels open, and Ca^{2+} ions enter the button. The entry of the Ca^{2+} ions causes synaptic vesicles to fuse with the presynaptic membrane and empty their contents into the synaptic cleft (see Marx, 2014; Südhof, 2013).

The exocytosis of small-molecule neurotransmitters differs from the exocytosis of neuropeptides. Small-molecule neurotransmitters are typically released in a pulse each time an action potential triggers a momentary influx of Ca^{2+} ions through the presynaptic membrane; in contrast, neuropeptides are typically released gradually in response to general increases in the level of intracellular Ca^{2+} ions, such as might occur during a general increase in the rate of neuron firing.

Activation of Receptors by Neurotransmitter Molecules

LO 4.12 Describe the differences between ionotropic and metabotropic receptors.

Once released, neurotransmitter molecules produce signals in postsynaptic neurons by binding to **receptors** in the postsynaptic membrane. Each receptor is a protein that contains binding sites for only particular neurotransmitters; thus, a neurotransmitter can influence only those cells that have receptors for it. Any molecule that binds to another is referred to as its **ligand**, and a neurotransmitter is thus said to be a ligand of its receptor.

Figure 4.10 Schematic illustration of exocytosis.

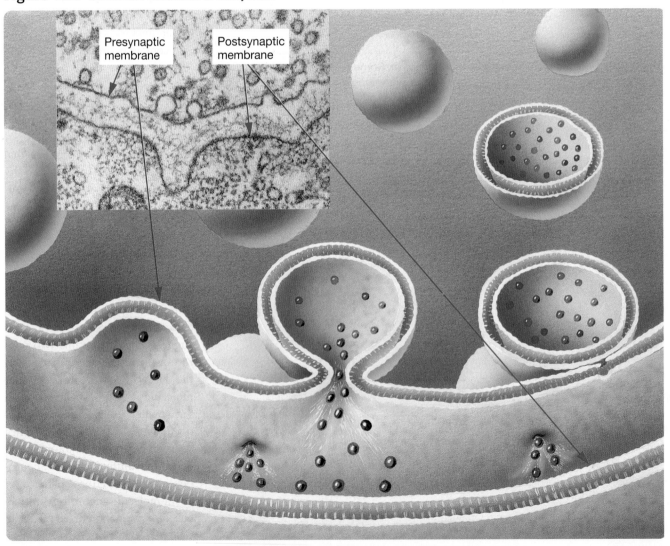

It was initially assumed that there is only one type of receptor for each neurotransmitter, but this has not proved to be the case. As more receptors have been identified, it has become clear that most neurotransmitters bind to several different types of receptors. The different types of receptors to which a particular neurotransmitter can bind are called the **receptor subtypes** for that neurotransmitter. The various receptor subtypes for a neurotransmitter are typically located in different brain areas, and they typically respond to the neurotransmitter in different ways. Thus, one advantage of receptor subtypes is that they enable one neurotransmitter to transmit different kinds of messages to different parts of the brain.

The binding of a neurotransmitter to one of its receptor subtypes can influence a postsynaptic neuron in one of two fundamentally different ways, depending on whether the receptor is ionotropic or metabotropic. **Ionotropic receptors** are associated with ligand-activated ion channels; **metabotropic receptors** are associated with signal proteins and **G proteins** (*guanosine-triphosphate–sensitive proteins*); see Figure 4.11.

When a neurotransmitter molecule binds to an ionotropic receptor, the associated ion channel usually opens or closes immediately, thereby inducing an immediate postsynaptic potential. For example, in some neurons, EPSPs (depolarizations) occur because the neurotransmitter opens sodium channels, thereby increasing the flow of Na^+ ions into the neuron. In contrast, IPSPs (hyperpolarizations) often occur because the neurotransmitter opens potassium channels or chloride channels, thereby increasing the flow of K^+ ions out of the neuron or the flow of Cl^- ions into it, respectively.

Metabotropic receptors are more prevalent than ionotropic receptors, and their effects are slower to develop, longer-lasting, more diffuse, and more varied. There are many different kinds of metabotropic receptors, but each is attached to a serpentine signal protein that winds its way back and forth through the cell membrane seven times. The metabotropic receptor is attached to a portion of the signal protein outside the neuron; the G protein is attached to a portion of the signal protein inside the neuron.

When a neurotransmitter binds to a metabotropic receptor, a subunit of the associated G protein breaks

Figure 4.11 Ionotropic and metabotropic receptors.

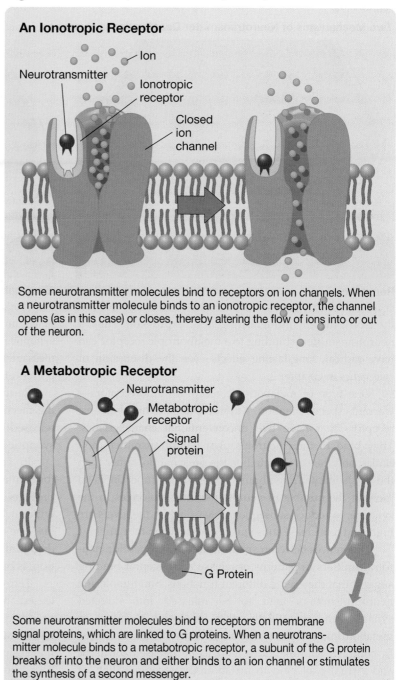

An Ionotropic Receptor

Some neurotransmitter molecules bind to receptors on ion channels. When a neurotransmitter molecule binds to an ionotropic receptor, the channel opens (as in this case) or closes, thereby altering the flow of ions into or out of the neuron.

A Metabotropic Receptor

Some neurotransmitter molecules bind to receptors on membrane signal proteins, which are linked to G proteins. When a neurotransmitter molecule binds to a metabotropic receptor, a subunit of the G protein breaks off into the neuron and either binds to an ion channel or stimulates the synthesis of a second messenger.

away. Then, one of two things happens, depending on the particular G protein. The subunit may move along the inside surface of the membrane and bind to a nearby ion channel, thereby inducing an EPSP or IPSP; or it may trigger the synthesis of a chemical called a **second messenger** (neurotransmitters are considered to be the *first messengers*). Once created, a second messenger diffuses through the cytoplasm and may influence the activities of the neuron in a variety of ways (Lyon, Taylor, & Tesmer, 2014)—for example, it may enter the nucleus and bind to

Figure 4.12 The two mechanisms for terminating neurotransmitter action in the synapse: reuptake and enzymatic degradation.

Two Mechanisms of Neurotransmitter Deactivation in Synapses

Reuptake

Enzymatic Degradation

the DNA, thereby influencing genetic expression. Thus, a neurotransmitter's binding to a metabotropic receptor can have radical, long-lasting effects—see the discussion of *epigenetics* in Chapter 2.

One type of metabotropic receptor—autoreceptors—warrants special mention. **Autoreceptors** are metabotropic receptors that have two unconventional characteristics: They bind to their neuron's own neurotransmitter molecules, and they are located on the presynaptic, rather than the postsynaptic, membrane. Their usual function is to monitor the number of neurotransmitter molecules in the synapse, to reduce subsequent release when the levels are high, and to increase subsequent release when they are low.

Differences between small-molecule and peptide neurotransmitters in patterns of release and receptor binding suggest that they serve different functions. Small-molecule neurotransmitters tend to be released into directed synapses and to activate either ionotropic receptors or metabotropic receptors that act directly on ion channels. In contrast, neuropeptides tend to be released diffusely, and virtually all bind to metabotropic receptors that act through second messengers. Consequently, the function of small-molecule neurotransmitters appears to be the transmission of rapid, brief excitatory or inhibitory signals to adjacent cells; and the function of neuropeptides appears to be the transmission of slow, diffuse, long-lasting signals.

Reuptake, Enzymatic Degradation, and Recycling

LO 4.13 Explain how neurotransmitters are removed from a synapse.

If nothing intervened, a neurotransmitter molecule would remain active in the synapse, in effect clogging that channel

of communication. However, two mechanisms terminate synaptic messages and keep that from happening. These two message-terminating mechanisms are **reuptake** by transporters and **enzymatic degradation** (see Figure 4.12).

Reuptake is the more common of the two deactivating mechanisms. The majority of neurotransmitters, once released, are almost immediately drawn back into the presynaptic buttons by transporter mechanisms.

In contrast, other neurotransmitters are degraded (broken apart) in the synapse by the action of **enzymes**—proteins that stimulate or inhibit biochemical reactions without being affected by them. For example, *acetylcholine*, one of the few neurotransmitters for which enzymatic degradation is the main mechanism of synaptic deactivation, is broken down by the enzyme **acetylcholinesterase**.

Terminal buttons are models of efficiency. Once released, neurotransmitter molecules or their breakdown products are drawn back into the button and recycled, regardless of the mechanism of their deactivation. Even the vesicles, once they have done their job, are drawn back into the neuron from the presynaptic membrane and are used to create new vesicles (see Alabi & Tsien, 2012; Kononenko & Haucke, 2015).

Glia, Gap Junctions, and Synaptic Transmission

LO 4.14 Describe the roles of glia and gap junctions in synaptic transmission.

You learned in Chapter 3 that glial cells, once overlooked as playing merely supportive roles in the nervous system, have been thrust to center stage by a wave of remarkable findings. For example, astrocytes have been shown to release chemical transmitters, to contain receptors for neurotransmitters, to conduct signals, and to influence synaptic transmission between neurons (see Bazargani & Attwell, 2015; Martín et al., 2015; Pannasch & Rouach, 2013; Rusakov et al., 2014; but see Sloan & Barres, 2014). Indeed, it is now inappropriate to think of brain function solely in terms of neuron–neuron connections. Neurons are only part of the story. The importance of glial cells in brain function is suggested by the greater prevalence of these cells in humans and other intelligent organisms. Will *neuroscience* prove to be a misnomer? Anybody for "gliascience"?

Evolutionary Perspective Why do you think there is a greater prevalence of glial cells in humans and other intelligent organisms?

The explosion of interest in the role of glial cells in brain function has gone hand in hand with an increased interest in the role of gap junctions. **Gap junctions** are narrow spaces between adjacent cells that are bridged by fine, tubular, cytoplasm-filled protein channels, called *connexins*. Consequently, gap junctions connect the cytoplasm of two adjacent cells, allowing electrical signals and small molecules (e.g., second messengers) to pass from one cell to the next (see Figure 4.13). Gap junctions are sometimes called *electrical synapses*. Gap junctions transmit signals more rapidly than chemical synapses.

The presence of gap junctions between adjacent neurons was first reported in the 1950s, but because the first studies were limited to invertebrates and simple vertebrates, gap junction–mediated communication between neurons was assumed to be of little significance in the mammalian brain. Even after the presence of gap junctions was established in mammalian (i.e., rodent) brains in the early 1970s, the idea that gap junctions could play a major role in human brain function was not widely entertained. Then in the 1990s, stimulated by several important technical developments and the identification of the gap junction gene, gap junctions became the focus of neuroscientific research (see McCracken & Roberts, 2006).

We wish we could tell you that the recent focus of neuroscientific research on glial cells and gap junctions has clarified their role in neural transmission and behavior, but we can't. However, recent research has clearly established that glial cells (particularly astrocytes) and gap junctions

Figure 4.13 Gap junctions connect the cytoplasm of two adjacent cells. In the mammalian brain, there are many gap junctions between glial cells, between neurons, and between neurons and glia cells.

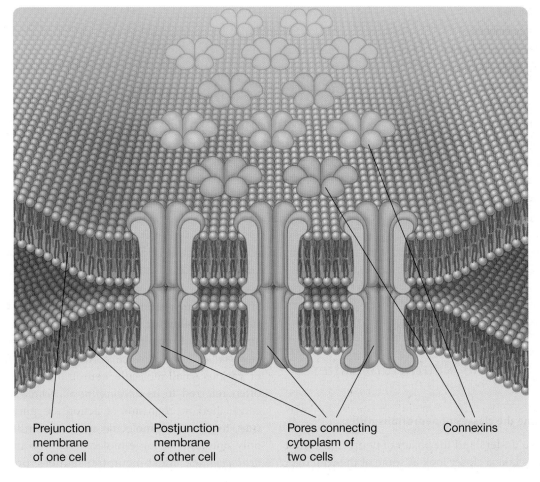

Prejunction membrane of one cell — Postjunction membrane of other cell — Pores connecting cytoplasm of two cells — Connexins

play major roles in brain function (see O'Brien, 2014; Perea, Sur, & Araque, 2014; Pereda, 2014; Rusakov et al., 2014).

The principles according to which astrocytes and gap junctions are distributed in the mammalian brain provide some of the best clues about their function. First, let's consider cerebral gap junctions. Cerebral gap junctions occur between all classes of cerebral cells; however, the majority of them seem to occur between cells of like kind. For example, many gap junctions link astrocytes together into glial networks. Also, gap junctions between neurons are particularly prevalent between inhibitory interneurons of the same type (e.g., Lee et al., 2014). Accordingly, one function of gap junctions appears to be to synchronize the activities of like cells in a particular area.

One aspect of astrocytic organization suggests that they too play a role of synchronizing activities of like cells in a particular area. Unlike neurons, astrocytes are distributed evenly throughout a particular area, with only one astrocyte per location and little overlap between the projections of adjacent astrocytes. This suggests that each astrocyte coordinates the activity of neurons in its domain, and with as many as 40,000 processes, each astrocyte has a great potential to coordinate activity (see Panasch & Rouach, 2013). Gap junctions on astrocytes tend to occur at the end of each process, where it comes in contact with processes from adjacent astrocytes.

What could astrocytes be coordinating? The fact that many astrocytic processes wrap around synapses and are connected to both presynaptic and postsynaptic neurons by gap junctions suggests that each astrocyte may coordinate the activity of synapses in its domain. The hypothesis that synaptic transmission depends on communication among three cells (presynaptic neuron, postsynaptic neuron, and astrocyte) is referred to as the *tripartite synapse* (see Grosche & Reichenbach, 2013; Navarrete & Araque, 2014; Sun et al., 2013).

Scan Your Brain

Before moving on to the discussion of specific neurotransmitters, review the general principles of axon conduction and synaptic transmission. Draw a line to connect each term in the left column with the appropriate word or phrase in the right column. The correct answers are provided at the end of the exercise. Before proceeding, review material related to your errors and omissions.

1. fatty
2. sclerosis
3. cell bodies
4. nondecremental
5. presynaptic facilitation
6. nondirected synapses
7. synaptic vesicles
8. from cell body to terminal buttons
9. acetylcholinesterase
10. short amino acid chains
11. saltatory
12. metabotropic receptors
13. electrical synapses
14. spines

a. axonal conduction of action potentials
b. orthodromic
c. myelin
d. nodes of Ranvier
e. multiple
f. dendritic
g. somas
h. axoaxonic synapses
i. string-of-beads
j. neuropeptides
k. store neurotransmitters
l. G proteins
m. enzymatic degradation
n. gap junctions

Scan Your Brain answers: (1) c, (2) e, (3) g, (4) a, (5) h, (6) i, (7) k, (8) b, (9) m, (10) j, (11) d, (12) l, (13) n, (14) f.

Neurotransmitters

Overview of the Neurotransmitter Classes

LO 4.15 Name the classes of neurotransmitters.

Now that you understand the basics of neurotransmitter function, let's take a closer look at some of the well over 100 neurotransmitter substances that have been identified. The following are three classes of conventional small-molecule neurotransmitters: the *amino acids*, the *monoamines*, and *acetylcholine*. Also, there is a fourth group of various small-molecule neurotransmitters, which are often referred to as *unconventional neurotransmitters* because their mechanisms of action are unusual. In contrast to the small-molecule neurotransmitters, there is only one class of large-molecule neurotransmitters: the *neuropeptides*. Most neurotransmitters produce either excitation or inhibition, not both, but a few produce excitation under some circumstances and inhibition under others. All of the neurotransmitter classes and individual neurotransmitters that appear in this module in boldface type are presented in Figure 4.16 at the end of this module.

The Roles and Functions of Neurotransmitters

LO 4.16 Name and compare different neurotransmitters.

AMINO ACID NEUROTRANSMITTERS. The neurotransmitters in the vast majority of fast-acting, directed synapses in the central nervous system are amino acids—the molecular building blocks of proteins. The four most widely studied **amino acid neurotransmitters** are **glutamate**, **aspartate**, **glycine**, and **gamma-aminobutyric acid (GABA)**. The first three are common in the proteins we consume, whereas GABA is synthesized by a simple modification of the structure of glutamate. Glutamate is the most prevalent excitatory neurotransmitter in the mammalian central nervous system. GABA is the most prevalent inhibitory neurotransmitter (see Valeeva, Valiullina, & Khazipov, 2013); however, it has excitatory effects at some synapses (see Watanabe, Fukuda, & Nabekura, 2014).

MONOAMINENEUROTRANSMITTERS. Monoamines are another class of small-molecule neurotransmitters. Each is synthesized from a single amino acid—hence the name *monoamine* (one amine). **Monoamine neurotransmitters** are slightly larger than amino acid neurotransmitters, and their effects tend to be more diffuse. The monoamines are present in small groups of neurons whose cell bodies are, for the most part, located in the brain stem. These neurons often have highly branched axons with many varicosities (string-of-beads synapses), from which monoamine neurotransmitters are diffusely released into the extracellular fluid (see Figures 4.9 and 4.14).

There are four monoamine neurotransmitters: **dopamine**, **epinephrine**, **norepinephrine**, and **serotonin**. They are subdivided into two groups, **catecholamines** and **indolamines**, on the basis of their structures. Dopamine, norepinephrine, and epinephrine are catecholamines. Each is synthesized from the amino acid *tyrosine*. Tyrosine is converted to L-dopa, which in turn is converted to dopamine. Neurons that release norepinephrine have an extra enzyme (one that is not present in dopaminergic neurons), which converts the dopamine

Figure 4.14 String-of-beads noradrenergic nerve fibers. The bright, beaded structures represent sites in these multiple-branched axons where the monoamine neurotransmitter norepinephrine is stored in high concentration and released into the surrounding extracellular fluid.

in them to norepinephrine. Similarly, neurons that release epinephrine have all the enzymes present in neurons that release norepinephrine, along with an extra enzyme that converts norepinephrine to epinephrine (see Figure 4.15). In contrast to the other monoamines, serotonin (also called *5-hydroxytryptamine*, or *5-HT*) is synthesized from the amino acid *tryptophan* and is classified as an indolamine.

Neurons that release norepinephrine are called *noradrenergic*; those that release epinephrine are called *adrenergic*. There are two reasons for this naming. One is that

Figure 4.15 The steps in the synthesis of catecholamines from tyrosine.

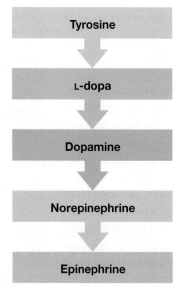

epinephrine and norepinephrine used to be called *adrenaline* and *noradrenaline*, respectively, by many scientists, until a drug company registered *Adrenalin* as a brand name. The other reason will become apparent to you if you try to say *norepinephrinergic*.

ACETYLCHOLINE. Acetylcholine (abbreviated Ach) is a small-molecule neurotransmitter that is in one major respect like a professor who is late for a lecture: It is in a class by itself. It is created by adding an *acetyl* group to a *choline* molecule. Acetylcholine is the neurotransmitter at neuromuscular junctions, at many of the synapses in the autonomic nervous system, and at synapses in several parts of the central nervous system. As you learned in the previous module, acetylcholine is broken down in the synapse by the enzyme *acetylcholinesterase*. Neurons that release acetylcholine are said to be *cholinergic*.

UNCONVENTIONAL NEUROTRANSMITTERS. The unconventional neurotransmitters act in ways that are different from those that neuroscientists have come to think of as typical for such substances. One class of unconventional neurotransmitters, the **soluble-gas neurotransmitters**, includes **nitric oxide** and **carbon monoxide**. These neurotransmitters are produced in the neural cytoplasm and immediately diffuse through the cell membrane into the extracellular fluid and then into nearby cells. They easily pass through cell membranes because they are soluble in lipids. Once inside another cell, they stimulate the production of a second messenger and in a few seconds are deactivated by being converted to other molecules. They are difficult to study because they exist for only a few seconds.

Soluble-gas neurotransmitters have been shown to be involved in *retrograde transmission*. At some synapses, they transmit feedback signals from the postsynaptic neuron back to the presynaptic neuron. The function of retrograde transmission seems to be to regulate the activity of presynaptic neurons (see Iremonger, Wamsteeker Cusulin, & Bains, 2013).

Another class of unconventional neurotransmitters is the endocannabinoids. **Endocannabinoids** are neurotransmitters that are similar to *delta-9-tetrahydrocannabinol* (THC), the main *psychoactive* (producing psychological effects) constituent of marijuana (see Chapter 15). So far, two endocannabinoids have been discovered (see Di Marzo, Stella, & Zimmer, 2015; Mechoulam et al., 2014). The most widely studied is **anandamide** (from the Sanskrit word *ananda*, which means "eternal bliss"). Like the soluble gases, the endocannabinoids are produced immediately before they are released. Endocannabinoids are synthesized from fatty compounds in the cell membrane; they tend to be released from the dendrites and cell body; and they tend to have most of their effects on presynaptic neurons, inhibiting subsequent synaptic transmission (see Katona & Freund, 2012; Ohno-Shosaku & Kano, 2014; Younts & Castillo, 2014).

NEUROPEPTIDES. About 100 neuropeptides have been identified. The actions of each neuropeptide depend on its amino acid sequence.

It is usual to loosely group **neuropeptide transmitters** into five categories. Three of these categories acknowledge that neuropeptides often function in multiple capacities, not just as neurotransmitters: One category (**pituitary peptides**) contains neuropeptides that were first identified as hormones released by the pituitary, a second category (**hypothalamic peptides**) contains neuropeptides that were first identified as hormones released by the hypothalamus;

Figure 4.16 Classes of neurotransmitters and the particular neurotransmitters that were discussed (and appeared in boldface) in this module.

Small-Molecule Neurotransmitters

		Glutamate
Amino acids		Glutamate Aspartate Glycine GABA
Monoamines	Catecholamines	Dopamine Epinephrine Norepinephrine
	Indolamines	Serotonin
Acetylcholine		Acetylcholine
Unconventional neurotransmitters	Soluble gases	Nitric oxide Carbon monoxide
	Endocannabinoids	Anandamide

Large-Molecule Neurotransmitters

Neuropeptides	Pituitary peptides Hypothalamic peptides Brain–gut peptides Opioid peptides Miscellaneous peptides

and a third category (**brain–gut peptides**) contains neuropeptides that were first discovered in the gut. The fourth category (**opioid peptides**) contains neuropeptides that are similar in structure to the active ingredients of opium, and the fifth (**miscellaneous peptides**) is a catch-all category that contains all of the neuropeptide transmitters that do not fit into one of the other four categories.

Figure 4.16 summarizes all the neurotransmitters that were introduced in this module. If it has not already occurred to you, this table should be very useful for reviewing the material in this module.

Pharmacology of Synaptic Transmission and Behavior

In case you have forgotten, the reason we have asked you to invest so much effort in learning about the neurotransmitters is that they play a key role in how the brain works. This chapter began on a behavioral note by considering the pathological behavior of Roberto Garcia d'Orta, which resulted from a Parkinson's disease–related disruption of his dopamine function. Now, let's return to behavior.

Most of the methods that biopsychologists use to study the behavioral effects of neurotransmitters are *pharmacological* (involving drugs). To study neurotransmitters and behavior, researchers administer to human or nonhuman subjects drugs that have particular effects on particular neurotransmitters and then assess the effects of the drugs on behavior.

Drugs have two fundamentally different kinds of effects on synaptic transmission: They facilitate it or they inhibit it. Drugs that facilitate the effects of a particular neurotransmitter are said to be **agonists** of that neurotransmitter. Drugs that inhibit the effects of a particular neurotransmitter are said to be its **antagonists**.

Watch this video on MyPsychLab

AGONIST AND ANTAGONIST

How Drugs Influence Synaptic Transmission

LO 4.17 Provide a general overview of how drugs influence synaptic transmission.

Although synthesis, release, and action vary from neurotransmitter to neurotransmitter, the following seven general steps are common to most neurotransmitters: (1) synthesis of the neurotransmitter, (2) storage in vesicles, (3) breakdown in the cytoplasm of any neurotransmitter that leaks from the vesicles, (4) exocytosis, (5) inhibitory feedback via autoreceptors, (6) activation of postsynaptic receptors, and (7) deactivation. Figure 4.17 illustrates these seven steps, and Figure 4.18 illustrates some ways that agonistic and antagonistic drugs influence them. For example, some agonists of a particular neurotransmitter bind to postsynaptic receptors and activate them, whereas some antagonistic drugs, called **receptor blockers**, bind to postsynaptic receptors without activating them and, in so doing, block the access of the usual neurotransmitter.

Behavioral Pharmacology: Three Influential Lines of Research

LO 4.18 Describe three examples of how drugs have been used to influence neurotransmission.

You will encounter discussions of the *putative* (hypothetical) behavioral functions of various neurotransmitters in subsequent chapters. However, this chapter ends with descriptions of three particularly influential lines of research on neurotransmitters and behavior. Each line of research led to the discovery of an important principle of neurotransmitter function, and each illustrates how drugs are used to study the nervous system and behavior.

WRINKLES AND DARTS: DISCOVERY OF RECEPTOR SUBTYPES. It was originally assumed that there was one kind of receptor for each neurotransmitter, but this notion was dispelled by research on acetylcholine receptors (see Changeux, 2013; Papke, 2014). Some acetylcholine receptors bind to *nicotine* (a CNS stimulant and the major psychoactive ingredient of tobacco), whereas other acetylcholine receptors bind to *muscarine* (a poisonous substance found in some mushrooms). These two kinds of acetylcholine receptors thus became known as *nicotinic receptors* and *muscarinic receptors*.

Next, it was discovered that nicotinic and muscarinic receptors are distributed differently in the nervous system, have different modes of action, and consequently have different behavioral effects. Both nicotinic and muscarinic

Figure 4.17 Seven steps in neurotransmitter action: (1) synthesis, (2) storage in vesicles, (3) breakdown of any neurotransmitter leaking from the vesicles, (4) exocytosis, (5) inhibitory feedback via autoreceptors, (6) activation of postsynaptic receptors, and (7) deactivation.

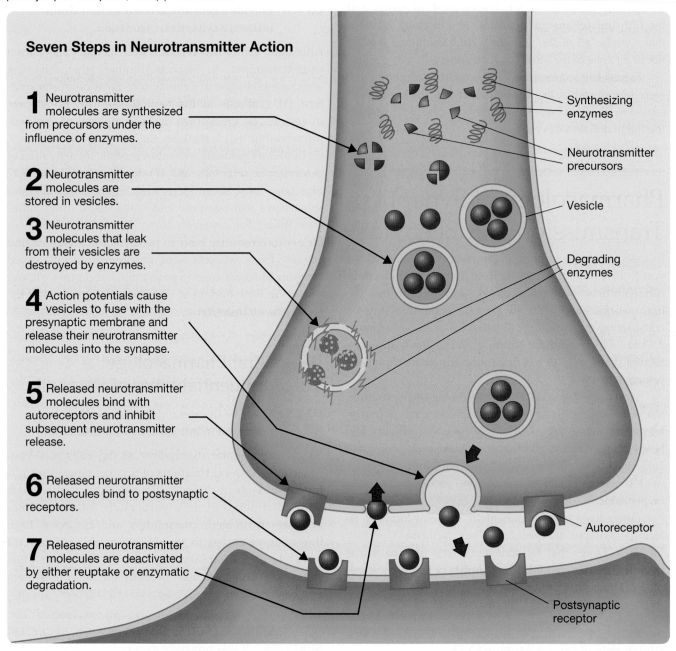

Seven Steps in Neurotransmitter Action

1 Neurotransmitter molecules are synthesized from precursors under the influence of enzymes.

2 Neurotransmitter molecules are stored in vesicles.

3 Neurotransmitter molecules that leak from their vesicles are destroyed by enzymes.

4 Action potentials cause vesicles to fuse with the presynaptic membrane and release their neurotransmitter molecules into the synapse.

5 Released neurotransmitter molecules bind with autoreceptors and inhibit subsequent neurotransmitter release.

6 Released neurotransmitter molecules bind to postsynaptic receptors.

7 Released neurotransmitter molecules are deactivated by either reuptake or enzymatic degradation.

Synthesizing enzymes

Neurotransmitter precursors

Vesicle

Degrading enzymes

Autoreceptor

Postsynaptic receptor

receptors are found in the CNS and the PNS. In the PNS, many nicotinic receptors occur at the junctions between motor neurons and muscle fibers, whereas many muscarinic receptors are located in the autonomic nervous system (ANS). Nicotinic and muscarinic receptors are ionotropic and metabotropic, respectively.

Many of the drugs used in research and medicine are extracts of plants that have long been used for medicinal and recreational purposes. The cholinergic agonists and antagonists illustrate this point well. For example, the ancient Greeks consumed extracts of the belladonna plant to treat stomach ailments and to make themselves more attractive. Greek women believed that the pupil-dilating effects of these extracts enhanced their beauty (*belladonna* means "beautiful lady"). **Atropine**, which is the main active ingredient of belladonna, is a receptor blocker that exerts its antagonist effect by binding to muscarinic receptors, thereby blocking the effects of acetylcholine on them. The pupil-dilating effects of atropine are mediated by its antagonist actions on muscarinic receptors in the ANS. In

Figure 4.18 Some mechanisms of agonistic and antagonistic drug effects.

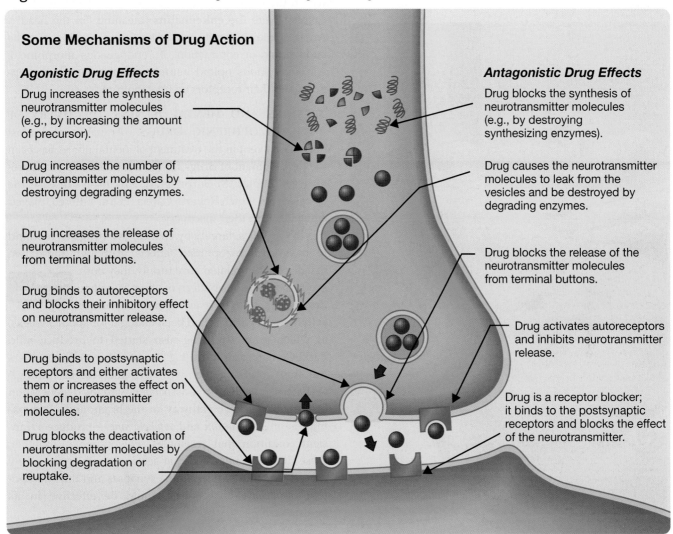

Some Mechanisms of Drug Action

Agonistic Drug Effects

Drug increases the synthesis of neurotransmitter molecules (e.g., by increasing the amount of precursor).

Drug increases the number of neurotransmitter molecules by destroying degrading enzymes.

Drug increases the release of neurotransmitter molecules from terminal buttons.

Drug binds to autoreceptors and blocks their inhibitory effect on neurotransmitter release.

Drug binds to postsynaptic receptors and either activates them or increases the effect on them of neurotransmitter molecules.

Drug blocks the deactivation of neurotransmitter molecules by blocking degradation or reuptake.

Antagonistic Drug Effects

Drug blocks the synthesis of neurotransmitter molecules (e.g., by destroying synthesizing enzymes).

Drug causes the neurotransmitter molecules to leak from the vesicles and be destroyed by degrading enzymes.

Drug blocks the release of the neurotransmitter molecules from terminal buttons.

Drug activates autoreceptors and inhibits neurotransmitter release.

Drug is a receptor blocker; it binds to the postsynaptic receptors and blocks the effect of the neurotransmitter.

contrast, the disruptive effects of large doses of atropine on memory are mediated by its antagonistic effect on muscarinic receptors in the CNS. The disruptive effect of high doses of atropine on memory was one of the earliest clues that cholinergic mechanisms may play a role in memory (see Chapter 11).

South American natives have long used *curare*—an extract of a certain class of woody vines—on the tips of darts they use to kill their game. Like atropine, curare is a receptor blocker at cholinergic synapses, but it acts at nicotinic receptors. By binding to nicotinic receptors, curare blocks transmission at neuromuscular junctions, thus paralyzing its recipients and killing them by blocking their respiration. You may be surprised, then, to learn that the active ingredient of curare is sometimes administered to human patients during surgery to ensure that their muscles do not contract during an incision. When curare is used for

Clinical Implications

this purpose, the patient's breathing must be artificially maintained by a respirator.

Botox (short for *Botulinium toxin*), a neurotoxin released by a bacterium often found in spoiled food, is another nicotinic antagonist, but its mechanism of action is different: It blocks the release of acetylcholine at neuromuscular junctions and is thus a deadly poison. However, injected in minute doses at specific sites, it has applications in medicine (e.g., reduction of tremors) and cosmetics (e.g., reduction of wrinkles; see Figure 4.19).

PLEASURE AND PAIN: DISCOVERY OF ENDOGENOUS OPIOIDS. Opium, the sticky resin obtained from the seed pods of the opium poppy, has been used by humans since prehistoric times for its pleasurable effects. Morphine, its major psychoactive ingredient, is addictive. But morphine also has its good side: It is an effective *analgesic* (painkiller)—see Chapters 7 and 15.

Figure 4.19 A woman receiving cosmetic Botox injections.

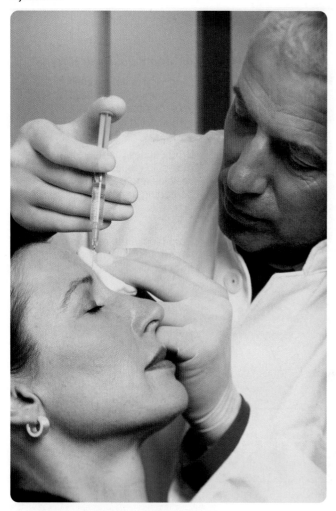

In the 1970s, it was discovered that opioid drugs such as morphine bind effectively to receptors in the brain. These receptors were generally found in the hypothalamus and other limbic areas, but they were most concentrated in the area of the brain stem around the cerebral aqueduct, which connects the third and fourth ventricles; this part of the brain stem is called the **periaqueductal gray (PAG)**. Microinjection of morphine into the PAG, or even electrical stimulation of the PAG, produces strong analgesia.

The existence of selective opioid receptors in the brain raised an interesting question: Why are they there? They are certainly not there so that once humans discovered opium, opioids would have a place to bind. The existence of opioid receptors suggested that *opioid* chemicals occur naturally in the brain, and that possibility triggered an intensive search for them.

Several families of **endogenous** (occurring naturally within the body) opioids have been discovered. First discovered were the **enkephalins** (meaning "in the head"). Another major family of endogenous opioids are the **endorphins** (a contraction of "endogenous morphine"). All endogenous opioid neurotransmitters are neuropeptides, and their receptors are metabotropic.

TREMORS AND MENTAL ILLNESS: DISCOVERY OF ANTISCHIZOPHRENIC DRUGS. Arguably, the most important event in the treatment of mental illness has been the development of drugs for the treatment of schizophrenia (see Chapter 18). Surprisingly, Parkinson's disease, the disease from which Roberto Garcia d'Orta suffered, played a major role in their discovery.

In the 1950s, largely by chance, two drugs were found to have antischizophrenic effects. Although these two drugs were not related structurally, they both produced a curious pattern of effects: Neither drug appeared to have any antischizophrenic activity until patients had been taking it for about 3 weeks, at which point the drug also started to produce mild Parkinsonian symptoms (e.g., tremor-at-rest). Researchers put this result together with two then-recent findings: (1) Parkinson's disease is associated with the degeneration of a main *dopamine* pathway in the brain, and (2) dopamine agonists—*cocaine* and *amphetamines*—produce a transient condition that resembles schizophrenia. Together, these findings suggested that schizophrenia is caused by excessive activity at dopamine synapses and thus that potent dopamine antagonists would be effective in its treatment.

> **Clinical Implications** Why is it important for biopsychologists to understand neural conduction and synaptic transmission? Is it important for all psychologists to have such knowledge? Discuss.

It was ultimately discovered that one particular dopamine receptor, the D_2 receptor, plays a key role in schizophrenia and that drugs that most effectively block it are the most effective antischizophrenic drugs.

It would be a mistake to think that antischizophrenic drugs cure schizophrenia or that they help in every case. However, they help many patients, and the help is sometimes enough to allow them to live at home. You will learn much more about this important line of research in Chapter 18.

Themes Revisited

The function of the nervous system, like the function of any circuit, depends on how signals travel through it. The primary purpose of this chapter was to introduce you to neural conduction and synaptic transmission. This introduction touched on three of the text's four main themes.

The clinical implications theme was illustrated by the opening case of the Lizard, Roberto Garcia d'Orta. Then this **Clinical Implications** theme was picked up again at the end of the chapter during discussions of curare, Botox, endogenous opioids, and antischizophrenic drugs.

The evolutionary perspective theme **Evolutionary Perspective** was implicit throughout the entire chapter because almost all neurophysiological research is conducted on the neurons and synapses of nonhuman subjects.

The thinking creatively theme arose in **Thinking Creatively** two metaphors: the firing-gun metaphor of action potentials and the mouse-traps-on-a-wobbly-shelf metaphor of axonal conduction. Metaphors are useful in teaching, and scientists find them useful for thinking about the phenomena they study.

Key Terms

Resting Membrane Potential

Membrane potential, p. 103
Microelectrodes, p. 103
Resting potential, p. 103
Ions, p. 103
Ion channels, p. 103
Sodium–potassium pumps, p. 104
Transporters, p. 104

Generation, Conduction, and Integration of Postsynaptic Potentials

Depolarize, p. 104
Hyperpolarize, p. 104
Excitatory postsynaptic potentials (EPSPs), p. 104
Inhibitory postsynaptic potentials (IPSPs), p. 104
Graded responses, p. 104
Axon hillock, p. 105
Axon initial segment, p. 105
Threshold of excitation, p. 105
Action potential (AP), p. 105
All-or-none responses, p. 105
Integration, p. 106
Spatial summation, p. 106
Temporal summation, p. 106

Conduction of Action Potentials

Voltage-activated ion channels, p. 108
Absolute refractory period, p. 108
Relative refractory period, p. 108
Antidromic conduction, p. 110
Orthodromic conduction, p. 110

Nodes of Ranvier, p. 110
Saltatory conduction, p. 110

Synaptic Transmission: Chemical Transmission of Signals among Neurons

Dendritic spines, p. 112
Directed synapses, p. 112
Nondirected synapses, p. 112
Neuropeptides, p. 113
Synaptic vesicles, p. 113
Golgi complex, p. 113
Coexistence, p. 113
Exocytosis, p. 114
Receptors, p. 114
Ligand, p. 115
Receptor subtypes, p. 115
Ionotropic receptors, p. 115
Metabotropic receptors, p. 115
G proteins, p. 115
Second messenger, p. 115
Autoreceptors, p. 116
Reuptake, p. 116
Enzymatic degradation, p. 116
Enzymes, p. 116
Acetylcholinesterase, p. 116
Gap junctions, p. 117

Neurotransmitters

Amino acid neurotransmitters, p. 119
Glutamate, p. 119
Aspartate, p. 119
Glycine, p. 119

Gamma-aminobutyric acid (GABA), p. 119
Monoamine neurotransmitters, p. 119
Dopamine, p. 119
Epinephrine, p. 119
Norepinephrine, p. 119
Serotonin, p. 119
Catecholamines, p. 119
Indolamines, p. 119
Acetylcholine, p. 120
Soluble-gas neurotransmitters, p. 120
Nitric oxide, p. 120
Carbon monoxide, p. 120
Endocannabinoids, p. 120
Anandamide, p. 120
Neuropeptide transmitters, p. 120
Pituitary peptides, p. 120
Hypothalamic peptides, p. 120
Brain–gut peptides, p. 121
Opioid peptides, p. 121
Miscellaneous peptides, p. 121

Pharmacology of Synaptic Transmission and Behavior

Agonists, p. 121
Antagonists, p. 121
Receptor blockers, p. 121
Atropine, p. 122
Botox, p. 123
Periaqueductal gray (PAG), p. 124
Endogenous, p. 124
Enkephalins, p. 124
Endorphins, p. 124

Chapter 5
The Research Methods of Biopsychology

Understanding What Biopsychologists Do

 Chapter Overview and Learning Objectives (LOs)

PART ONE Methods of Studying the Nervous System

Methods of Visualizing and Stimulating the Living Human Brain	**LO 5.1**	Describe two x-ray-based techniques for visualizing the living human brain.
	LO 5.2	Describe the positron emission tomography (PET) technique.
	LO 5.3	Describe three magnetic-field-based techniques for imaging the living human brain.
	LO 5.4	Describe two transcranial stimulation techniques.
Recording Human Psychophysiological Activity	**LO 5.5**	Describe two psychophysiological measures of brain activity.
	LO 5.6	Describe two sorts of psychophysiological measures of somatic nervous system activity.
	LO 5.7	Describe two psychophysiological measures of autonomic nervous system activity.

Invasive Physiological Research Methods	**LO 5.8**	Describe the process of stereotaxic surgery.
	LO 5.9	Describe four types of lesion methods, and explain why it is important to be cautious when interpreting the effects of lesions.
	LO 5.10	Describe the technique of electrical brain stimulation.
	LO 5.11	Describe four invasive electrophysiological recording methods.
Pharmacological Research Methods	**LO 5.12**	Describe the various methods of drug administration.
	LO 5.13	Describe the method of selective neurotoxic lesions.
	LO 5.14	Describe two techniques for measuring chemical activity in the brain.
	LO 5.15	Describe two techniques for locating particular neurotransmitters or receptors in the brain.
Genetic Engineering	**LO 5.16**	Describe gene knockout and gene replacement techniques, and explain what is meant by the term *transgenic*.
	LO 5.17	Explain how green fluorescent protein has been used as a research tool in the neurosciences.
	LO 5.18	Explain how opsins have been used as a research tool in the neurosciences.

PART TWO Behavioral Research Methods of Biopsychology

Neuropsychological Testing	**LO 5.19**	Describe three approaches to neuropsychological testing.
	LO 5.20	Describe those tests that are often administered as part of an initial common neuropsychological test battery.
	LO 5.21	Describe tests that might be used by a neuropsychologist to investigate in more depth general problems revealed by a common neuropsychological test battery.
	LO 5.22	Describe the Wisconsin Card Sorting Test.
Behavioral Methods of Cognitive Neuroscience	**LO 5.23**	Describe the paired-image subtraction technique.
	LO 5.24	Understand the default mode network, and know the structures that are part of that network.
	LO 5.25	Explain what a mean difference image is.
Paradigms for Assessment of Species-Common Behaviors	**LO 5.26**	Describe three behavioral paradigms used to study species-common behaviors.
	LO 5.27	Describe the Pavlovian conditioning paradigm and the operant conditioning paradigm.
	LO 5.28	Describe four seminatural animal learning paradigms.

Chapters 1 and 2 introduced you to the general interests, ideas, and approaches that characterize biopsychology. In Chapters 3 and 4, your introduction to biopsychology was temporarily curtailed while background material in neuroanatomy, neurophysiology, and neurochemistry was presented. This chapter gets down to the nitty-gritty of biopsychology; it describes the specific day-to-day activities of the biopsychology laboratory. It is intended to prepare you for later chapters and to sharpen your understanding of biopsychology by describing how biopsychologists do their research.

The organization of this chapter reflects biopsychology's intrinsic duality. The chapter has two major parts: One deals with methods of studying the nervous system, and the other deals with methods of studying behavior.

As you read through this chapter, you should keep in mind that most of the methods used to study the human brain are also used for clinical purposes, for either diagnosis or treatment. The case of Professor P. makes this point.

The Ironic Case of Professor P.

Two weeks before his brain surgery, Professor P. reported to the hospital for a series of tests. What amazed Professor P.

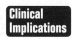

most about these tests was how familiar they seemed. No, Professor P. was not a psychic; he was a biopsychologist, and he was struck by how similar the tests performed on him were to the tests he had seen in his department.

Professor P. had a brain tumor on his right auditory-vestibular cranial nerve (cranial nerve VIII; see Appendices III and IV), and he had to have it *excised* (cut out). First, Professor P.'s auditory abilities were assessed by measuring his ability to detect sounds of various volumes and pitches and then by measuring the magnitude of the EEG signals evoked in his auditory cortex by clicks in his right ear.

Next, Professor P.'s vestibular function (balance) was tested by injecting cold water into his ear.

"Do you feel anything, Professor P.?"

"Well, a cold ear."

"Nothing else?"

"No."

So colder and colder water was tried with no effect until the final, coldest test was conducted. "Ah, that feels weird," said Professor P. "It's kind of like the bed is tipping."

The results of the tests were bad, or good, depending on your perspective. Professor P.'s hearing in his right ear was poor, and his right vestibular nerve was barely functioning. "At the temperatures we flushed down there, most people would have been on their hands and knees puking their guts out," said the medical technician. Professor P. smiled at the technical terminology.

Of course, he was upset that his brain had deteriorated so badly, but he sensed that his neurosurgeon was secretly pleased: "We won't have to try to save the nerve; we'll just cut it."

There was one last test. The skin of his right cheek was lightly pricked while the EEG responses of his somatosensory

cortex were recorded from his scalp. "This is just to establish a baseline for the surgery," it was explained. "One main risk of removing tumors on the auditory-vestibular cranial nerve (VIII) is damaging the facial cranial nerve (VII), and that would make the right side of your face sag. So during the surgery, electrodes will be inserted in your cheek, and your cheek will be repeatedly stimulated with tiny electrical pulses. The cortical responses will be recorded and fed into a loudspeaker so that the surgeon can immediately hear changes in the activity if his scalpel starts to stray into the area."

As Professor P. was driving home, his mind wandered from his own plight to his day at the hospital. "Quite interesting," he thought to himself. There were biopsychologists everywhere, doing biopsychological things. In all three labs he had visited, there were people who began their training as biopsychologists.

Two weeks later, Professor P. was rolled into the preparation room. "Sorry to do this, Professor P., you were one of my favorite instructors," the nurse said, as she inserted a large needle into Professor P.'s face and left it there.

Professor P. didn't mind; he was barely conscious. He did not know that he wouldn't regain consciousness for several days—at which point he would be incapable of talking, eating, or even breathing.

Don't forget Professor P.; you will learn more about him in Chapter 10. This case demonstrates that many of the research methods of biopsychology are also used in clinical settings. Let's move on to the methods themselves.

PART ONE Methods of Studying the Nervous System

Methods of Visualizing or Stimulating the Living Human Brain

This module presents three different sorts of methods for visualizing the living human brain: x-ray-based techniques, a radioactivity-based technique, and magnetic-field-based techniques. It also presents two techniques for noninvasively stimulating the living human brain.

X-Ray-Based Techniques

LO 5.1   Describe two x-ray-based techniques for visualizing the living human brain.

Prior to the early 1970s, biopsychological research was impeded by the inability to obtain images of the organ of primary interest: the living human brain. Conventional x-ray photography is next to useless for this purpose. When an

Figure 5.1 A cerebral angiogram of a healthy human subject.

x-ray photograph is taken, an x-ray beam is passed through an object and then onto a photographic plate. Each of the molecules through which the beam passes absorbs some of the radiation; thus, only the unabsorbed portions of the beam reach the photographic plate. X-ray photography is therefore effective in characterizing internal structures that differ substantially from their surroundings in the degree to which they absorb x-rays—for example, a revolver in a suitcase full of clothes or a bone in flesh. However, by the time an x-ray beam has passed through the numerous overlapping structures of the brain, which differ only slightly from one another in their ability to absorb x-rays, it carries little information about the structures through which it has passed.

CONTRAST X-RAYS. Although conventional x-ray photography is not useful for visualizing the brain, contrast x-ray techniques are. **Contrast x-ray techniques** involve injecting into one compartment of the body a substance that absorbs x-rays either less than or more than the surrounding tissue. The injected substance then heightens the contrast between the compartment and the surrounding tissue during x-ray photography.

One contrast x-ray technique, **cerebral angiography**, uses the infusion of a radio-opaque dye into a cerebral artery to visualize the cerebral circulatory system during x-ray photography (see Figure 5.1). Cerebral angiograms are most useful for localizing vascular damage, but the displacement of blood vessels from their normal position also can indicate the location of a tumor.

 Clinical Implications

Clinical Implications Egas Moniz, the inventor of the lobotomy (see Chapter 1), was also the pioneer of cerebral angiography. Some have argued that Moniz's Nobel Prize for the lobotomy should have been revoked. However, others have argued that he would have won it anyway for his important work on cerebral angiography. Do you think Moniz deserved to win the Nobel Prize? Why or why not?

COMPUTED TOMOGRAPHY. In the early 1970s, the study of the living human brain was revolutionized by the introduction of computed tomography. **Computed tomography (CT)** is a computer-assisted x-ray procedure that can be used to visualize the brain and other internal structures of the living body. During cerebral computed tomography, the neurological patient lies with his or her head positioned in the center of a large cylinder, as depicted in Figure 5.2. On one side of the cylinder is an x-ray

Figure 5.2 Computed tomography (CT) uses x-rays to create a CT scan of the brain.

tube that projects an x-ray beam through the head to an x-ray detector mounted on the other side. The x-ray tube and detector automatically rotate around the head of the patient at one level of the brain, taking many individual x-ray photographs as they rotate. The meager information in each x-ray photograph is combined by a computer to generate a CT scan of one horizontal section of the brain. Then the x-ray tube and detector are moved along the axis of the patient's body to another level of the brain, and the process is repeated. Scans of eight or nine horizontal brain sections are typically obtained from a patient; when combined, they can provide three-dimensional representations of the brain.

Radioactivity-Based Techniques

LO 5.2 **Describe the positron emission tomography (PET) technique.**

POSITRON EMISSION TOMOGRAPHY. **Positron emission tomography (PET)** was the first brain-imaging technique to provide images of brain activity (*functional brain images*) rather than images of brain structure (*structural brain images*). In one common version of PET, radioactive **fluorodeoxyglucose (FDG)** is injected into the patient's *carotid artery* (an artery of the neck that feeds the ipsilateral cerebral hemisphere). Because of its similarity to glucose, the primary metabolic fuel of the brain, fluorodeoxyglucose is rapidly taken up by active (energy-consuming) cells. However, unlike glucose, fluorodeoxyglucose cannot be metabolized; it therefore accumulates in active neurons— or in associated astrocytes—until it is gradually broken down (see Nasrallah & Dubroff, 2013). Each PET scan is an image of the levels of radioactivity (indicated by color coding) in various parts of one horizontal level of the brain. Thus, if a PET scan is taken of a patient who engages in an activity such as reading for about 30 seconds after the FDG injection, the resulting scan will indicate the areas of the target brain level that were most active during the 30 seconds (see Figure 5.3).

Notice from Figure 5.3 that PET scans are not really images of the brain. Each PET scan is merely a colored map of the amount of radioactivity in each of the tiny cubic voxels (volume pixels) that compose the scan. Exactly how each voxel maps onto a particular brain structure can be estimated only by superimposing the scan

on a brain image. This shortcoming of PET has recently been addressed by combining PET with MRI (see Wehrl et al., 2013).

The most significant current application of PET technology is its use in identifying the distribution in the brain of molecules of interest (e.g., particular neurotransmitters, receptors, or transporters)—see Camardese et al. (2014). This is readily accomplished by injecting volunteers with radioactively labeled **ligands** (ions or molecules that bind to other molecules under investigation). Then, PET technology can be used to document the distribution of radioactivity in the brain.

Magnetic-Field-Based Techniques

LO 5.3 **Describe three magnetic-field-based techniques for imaging the living human brain.**

MAGNETIC RESONANCE IMAGING. Magnetic **resonance imaging (MRI)** is a structural brain-imaging procedure in which high-resolution images are constructed from the measurement of radio-frequency waves that hydrogen atoms emit as they align with a powerful magnetic field. MRI provides clearer images of the brain than does CT. A two-dimensional MRI scan of the midsagittal plane of the brain is presented in Figure 5.4.

In addition to providing relatively high **spatial resolution** (the ability to detect and represent differences in spatial location), MRI can produce images in three dimensions. Figure 5.5 is a three-dimensional

Figure 5.3 A series of two PET scans. A scan was done when the volunteer's eyes were either open (left) or closed (right). Areas of high activity are indicated by reds and yellows. For example, notice the high level of activity in the visual cortex of the occipital lobe when the volunteer's eyes were open.

Occipital lobe

Figure 5.4 A color-enhanced midsagittal MRI scan.

MRI scan. Figure 5.6 shows a three-dimensional MRI scan of a patient with a growing tumor.

FUNCTIONAL MRI. MRI technology has been used to produce functional images of the brain. Indeed, functional MRI has become the most influential tool of cognitive neuroscience and is now widely used for medical diagnosis. It has even been used to communicate with patients in a "vegetative state" (patients who appear to lack consciousness)—see Owen (2014).

Functional MRI (fMRI) produces images representing the increase in oxygen flow in the blood to active areas of the brain. Functional MRI is possible because of two attributes of oxygenated blood. First, active areas of the brain take up more oxygenated blood than they need for their energy requirements, and thus oxygenated blood accumulates in active areas of the brain (see Hillman, 2014). Second, oxygenated blood has magnetic properties that influence the radio-frequency waves emitted by hydrogen atoms in an MRI. The signal recorded by fMRI is called the **BOLD signal** (the blood-oxygen-level-dependent signal).

Watch this video on MyPsychLab
BRAIN IMAGING

Figure 5.5 Structural MRI can be used to provide three-dimensional images of the entire brain.

Figure 5.6 MRI of a growing tumor. The tumor is colored red.

Figure 5.7 Functional magnetic resonance image (fMRI). This image illustrates the areas of cortex that became more active when the volunteers observed strings of letters and were asked to specify which strings were words; in the control condition, volunteers viewed strings of asterisks (Kiehl et al., 1999). This fMRI illustrates surface activity; but images of sections through the brain can also be displayed. (Courtesy of Kent Kiehl and Peter Liddle, Department of Psychiatry, University of British Columbia.)

Functional MRI has four advantages over PET: (1) Nothing has to be injected into the volunteer; (2) it provides both structural and functional information in the same image; (3) its spatial resolution is better; and (4) it can be used to produce three-dimensional images of activity over the entire brain. A functional MRI is shown in Figure 5.7.

It is important not to be unduly swayed by the impressiveness of fMRI images and technology. The images are often presented—particularly in the popular press or general textbooks—as if they are pictures of human neural activity. They aren't: They are images of the BOLD signal, and the relation between the BOLD signal and neural activity is proving to be complex (see Hillman, 2014). Furthermore, fMRI technology has poor **temporal resolution**, that is, it is poor at specifying the timing of neural events. Indeed, it takes 2 or 3 seconds to measure the BOLD signal, and many neural responses, such as action potentials, occur in the millisecond range.

DIFFUSION TENSOR IMAGING. Many variations of MRI have been developed (Pan et al., 2011). Arguably, the most influential of these new MRI techniques has been diffusion tensor imaging. **Diffusion tensor imaging** is a method of identifying those pathways along which water molecules rapidly diffuse (see Jbadi et al., 2015). Because *tracts* (bundles of axons) are the major routes of rapid water diffusion in the brain, diffusion tensor imaging provides an image of major tracts—see Figure 5.8.

Figure 5.8 Diffusion tensor image. This three-dimensional image shows the major tracts of the brain.

Most brain research focuses on the structures of the brain. However, in order to understand how the brain works, it is also important to understand the connections among those structures—the so-called *connectome* (see Calhoun et al., 2014; Lichtman, Pfister, & Shavit, 2014; Mitra, 2014; Park & Friston, 2013; Smith et al., 2013; van den Heuvel, 2013). This is why diffusion tensor images have become a major focus of neuroscientific research (see Cavaliere et al., 2015; Wandell & Yeatman, 2013; Zhang, Aggarwal, & Mori, 2012). The so-called *Human Connectome Project* is nearing completion (see Dance, 2015; Poldrack & Farah, 2015), and there are already complete connectomes for other organisms, including the nematode *C. elegans* and the mouse (see Oh et al., 2014).

Transcranial Stimulation

LO 5.4 **Describe two transcranial stimulation techniques.**

PET and fMRI have allowed cognitive neuroscientists to create images of brain activity while volunteers are engaging in particular cognitive activities. Although technically impressive, these kinds of studies of brain activity and cognition all have the same shortcoming: They can be used to show a correlation between brain activity and cognitive activity, but they can't prove that the brain activity caused the cognitive activity (Sack, 2006). For example, a brain-imaging technique may show that the cingulate cortex becomes active when volunteers view disturbing photographs, but it can't prove that the cingulate activity causes the emotional experience—there are many other explanations. There are two obvious ways of supporting the hypothesis that the cingulate cortex is an area for emotional experience. (1) One way would be to assess emotional experience in people lacking a functional cingulate cortex. This can be accomplished by studying patients with cingulate damage or by "turning off" the cingulate cortex of healthy patients—transcranial magnetic stimulation is a way of turning off particular areas of cortex. (2) A second way would be to assess emotional experiences of volunteers after "turning on" their cingulate cortex—transcranial direct current stimulation is a way of turning on areas of cortex.

Let us briefly introduce you to transcranial magnetic stimulation and transcranial direct current stimulation, which are currently playing a major role in establishing the causal effects of human cortical activity on cognition and behavior. **Transcranial magnetic stimulation (TMS)** is a technique that can be used to turn off an area of human cortex by creating a magnetic field under a coil positioned next to the skull (e.g., Candidi et al., 2015). The magnetic stimulation temporarily turns off part of the brain while the effects of the disruption on cognition and behavior are assessed. Although there are still fundamental questions about safety, depth of effect, and mechanisms of neural disruption (see Rossini et al., 2015), TMS is often employed to circumvent the difficulty that brain-imaging studies have in determining causation. Using different stimulation parameters, TMS can also be used to "turn on" an area of cortex (see Rossini et al., 2015).

Transcranial direct current stimulation (tDCS) is a technique that can be used to stimulate ("turn on") an area of the cortex by applying an electrical current through two electrodes placed directly on the scalp. The electrical stimulation temporarily increases activity in part of the brain while the effects of the stimulation on cognition and behavior are assessed (see Brunoni et al., 2012).

Recording Human Psychophysiological Activity

The preceding module introduced you to structural and functional brain imaging. This module deals with *psychophysiological recording methods* (methods of recording physiological activity from the surface of the human body). Six of the most widely studied psychophysiological measures are described: two measures of brain activity (the scalp EEG and magnetoencephalography), two measures of somatic nervous system activity (muscle tension and eye movement), and two measures of autonomic nervous system activity (skin conductance and cardiovascular activity).

Psychophysiological Measures of Brain Activity

LO 5.5 Describe two psychophysiological measures of brain activity.

SCALP ELECTROENCEPHALOGRAPHY. The *electroencephalogram (EEG)* is a measure of the gross electrical activity of the brain. It is recorded through large electrodes by a device called an *electroencephalograph (EEG machine)*, and the technique is called **electroencephalography**. In EEG studies of human subjects, each channel of EEG activity is usually recorded from disk-shaped electrodes, about half the size of a dime, which are attached to the scalp.

The scalp EEG signal reflects the sum of electrical events throughout the head. These events include action potentials and postsynaptic potentials as well as electrical signals from the skin, muscles, blood, and eyes.

Thus, the utility of the scalp EEG does not lie in its ability to provide an unclouded view of neural activity. Its value as a research and diagnostic tool rests on the fact that some EEG wave forms are associated with particular states of consciousness or particular types of cerebral pathology (e.g., epilepsy). For example, **alpha waves** are regular, 8- to 12-per-second, high-amplitude waves that are associated with relaxed wakefulness. A few examples of EEG wave forms and their psychological correlates are presented in Figure 5.9.

Because EEG signals decrease in amplitude as they spread from their source, a comparison of signals recorded

Figure 5.9 Some typical electroencephalograms and their psychological correlates.

from various sites on the scalp can sometimes indicate the origin of particular waves. This is why it is usual to record EEG activity from many sites simultaneously.

Psychophysiologists are often more interested in the EEG waves that accompany certain psychological events than in the background EEG signal. These accompanying EEG waves are generally referred to as **event-related potentials (ERPs)**. One commonly studied type of event-related potential is the **sensory evoked potential**—the change in the cortical EEG signal elicited by the momentary presentation of a sensory stimulus. As Figure 5.10 illustrates, the cortical EEG that follows a sensory stimulus has two components: the response to the stimulus (the signal) and the ongoing background EEG activity (the noise). The *signal* is the part of any recording that is of interest; the *noise* is the part that isn't. The problem in recording sensory evoked potentials is that the noise of the background EEG is often so great that the sensory evoked potential is masked. Measuring a sensory evoked potential can be like detecting a whisper at a rock concert. A method used to reduce the noise of the background EEG is **signal averaging**. First, a subject's response to a stimulus, such as a click, is recorded many—let's say 1,000—times. Then, a computer identifies the millivolt value of each of the 1,000 traces at its starting point (i.e., at the click) and calculates the mean of these 1,000 scores. Next, it considers the value of each of the 1,000 traces 1 millisecond (msec) from its start, for example, and calculates the mean of these values. It repeats this process at the 2-msec mark, the 3-msec mark, and so on. When these averages are plotted, the average response evoked by the click is more apparent because the random background EEG is canceled out by the averaging. See Figure 5.10, which illustrates the averaging of an auditory evoked potential.

The analysis of *average evoked potentials* (*AEPs*) focuses on the various waves in the averaged signal. Each wave is characterized by its direction, positive or negative, and by its latency. For example, the **P300 wave** illustrated in Figure 5.11 is the positive wave that occurs about 300 milliseconds after a momentary stimulus that has meaning for the subject (e.g., a stimulus to which the subject must respond)—see Chen et al. (2014). In contrast, the portions of an evoked potential recorded in the first few milliseconds

after a stimulus are not influenced by the meaning of the stimulus for the subject. These small waves are called **far-field potentials** because, although they are recorded from the scalp, they originate far away in the sensory nuclei of the brain stem.

Figure 5.10 Signal averaging: averaging of auditory evoked potentials. Averaging increases the signal-to-noise ratio.

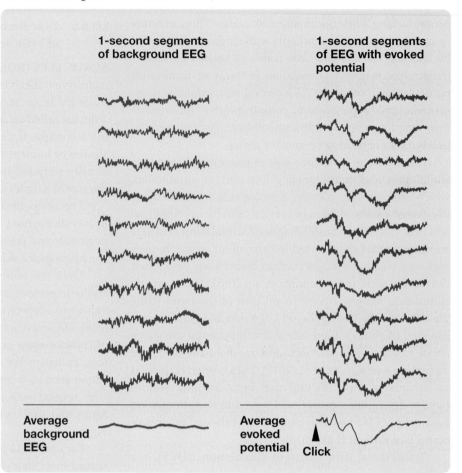

1-second segments of background EEG

1-second segments of EEG with evoked potential

Average background EEG

Average evoked potential   Click

Figure 5.11 An average auditory evoked potential. Notice the P300 wave. This wave occurs only if the stimulus has meaning for the subject; in this case, the click signals the imminent delivery of a reward. By convention, positive EEG waves are always shown as downward deflections.

Far-field potentials

Meaningful click   200   400   600
P300

Time (milliseconds)

MAGNETOENCEPHALOGRAPHY. Another technique used to monitor brain activity from the scalp of human subjects is **magnetoencephalography (MEG)**. MEG measures changes in magnetic fields on the surface of the scalp that are produced by changes in underlying patterns of neural activity. Because the magnetic signals induced by neural activity are so small, only those induced near the surface of the brain can be recorded from the scalp (see Hari & Parkkonen, 2015).

Psychophysiological Measures of Somatic Nervous System Activity

LO 5.6 Describe two psychophysiological measures of somatic nervous system activity.

MUSCLE TENSION. Each skeletal muscle is composed of millions of threadlike muscle fibers. Each muscle fiber contracts in an all-or-none fashion when activated by the motor neuron that innervates it. At any given time, a few fibers in each resting muscle are likely to be contracting, thus maintaining the overall tone (tension) of the muscle. Movement results when a large number of fibers contract at the same time.

In everyday language, anxious people are commonly referred to as "tense." This usage acknowledges the fact that anxious or otherwise aroused individuals typically display high resting levels of tension in their muscles. This is why psychophysiologists are interested in this measure; they use it as an indicator of psychological arousal.

Electromyography is the usual procedure for measuring muscle tension. The resulting record is called an *electromyogram* (*EMG*). EMG activity is usually recorded between two electrodes taped to the surface of the skin over the muscle of interest. An EMG record is presented in Figure 5.12. You will notice from this figure that the main correlate of an increase in muscle contraction is an increase in the amplitude of the raw EMG signal, which reflects the number of muscle fibers contracting at any one time.

Most psychophysiologists do not work with raw EMG signals; they convert them to a more workable form. The raw signal is fed into a computer that calculates the total amount of EMG spiking per unit of time—in consecutive 0.1-second intervals, for example. The integrated signal (i.e., the total EMG activity per unit of time) is then plotted. The result is a smooth curve, the amplitude of which is a simple, continuous measure of the level of muscle tension (see Figure 5.12).

EYE MOVEMENT. The electrophysiological technique for recording eye movements is called **electrooculography**, and the resulting record is called an *electrooculogram* (*EOG*). Electrooculography is based on the fact that a steady potential difference exists between the front

Figure 5.12 The relation between a raw EMG signal and its integrated version. The volunteer tensed her muscle beneath the electrodes and then gradually relaxed it.

(positive) and back (negative) of the eyeball. Because of this steady potential, when the eye moves, a change in the electrical potential between electrodes placed around the eye can be recorded. It is usual to record EOG activity between two electrodes placed on each side of the eye to measure its horizontal movements and between two electrodes placed above and below the eye to measure its vertical movements (see Figure 5.13).

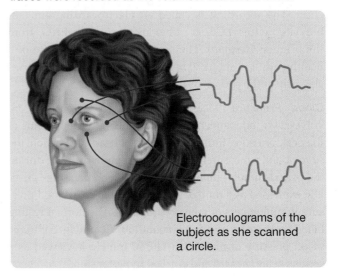

Figure 5.13 The typical placement of electrodes around the eye for electrooculography. The two electrooculogram traces were recorded as the volunteer scanned a circle.

Electrooculograms of the subject as she scanned a circle.

Psychophysiological Measures of Autonomic Nervous System Activity

LO 5.7 **Describe two sorts of psychophysiological measures of autonomic nervous system activity.**

SKIN CONDUCTANCE. Emotional thoughts and experiences are associated with increases in the ability of the skin to conduct electricity. The two most commonly employed indexes of *electrodermal activity* are the **skin conductance level (SCL)** and the **skin conductance response (SCR)**. The SCL is a measure of the background level of skin conductance that is associated with a particular situation, whereas the SCR is a measure of the transient changes in skin conductance that are associated with discrete experiences.

The physiological bases of skin conductance changes are not fully understood, but there is considerable evidence implicating the sweat glands. Although the main function of sweat glands is to cool the body, these glands tend to become active in emotional situations, causing the release of sweat that in turn increases the electrical conductivity of the skin (see Green et al., 2014). Sweat glands are distributed over most of the body surface; but, as you are almost certainly aware, those of the hands, feet, armpits, and forehead are particularly responsive to emotional stimuli.

CARDIOVASCULAR ACTIVITY. The presence in our language of phrases such as *chicken-hearted, white with fear*, and *blushing bride* indicates that modern psychophysiologists were not the first to recognize the relationship between *cardiovascular activity* and emotion. The cardiovascular system has two parts: the blood vessels and the heart. It is a system for distributing oxygen and nutrients to the tissues of the body, removing metabolic wastes, and transmitting chemical messages. Three different measures of cardiovascular activity are frequently employed in psychophysiological research: heart rate, arterial blood pressure, and local blood volume.

Heart Rate The electrical signal associated with each heartbeat can be recorded through electrodes placed on the chest. The recording is called an **electrocardiogram** (abbreviated either **ECG**, for obvious reasons, or **EKG**, from the original German). The average resting heart rate of a healthy adult is about 70 beats per minute, but it increases abruptly at the sound, or thought, of a dental drill.

Blood Pressure Measuring arterial blood pressure involves two independent measurements: a measurement of the peak pressure during the periods of heart contraction, the *systoles*, and a measurement of the minimum pressure during the periods of relaxation, the *diastoles*. Blood pressure is usually expressed as a ratio of systolic over diastolic blood pressure in millimeters of mercury (mmHg). The normal resting blood pressure for an adult is about 130/70 mmHg. A chronic blood pressure of more than 140/90 mmHg is viewed as a serious health hazard and is called **hypertension**.

You have likely had your blood pressure measured with a *sphygmomanometer*—a crude device composed of a hollow cuff, a rubber bulb for inflating it, and a pressure gauge for measuring the pressure in the cuff (*sphygmos* means "pulse"). More reliable, fully automated methods are used in research.

Blood Volume Changes in the volume of blood in particular parts of the body are associated with psychological events. The best-known example of such a change is the engorgement of the genitals associated with sexual arousal in both males and females. **Plethysmography** refers to the various techniques for measuring changes in the volume of blood in a particular part of the body (*plethysmos* means "an enlargement").

One method of measuring these changes is to record the volume of the target tissue by wrapping a strain gauge around it. Although this method has utility in measuring blood flow in fingers or similarly shaped organs, the possibilities for employing it are somewhat limited. Another plethysmographic method is to shine a light through the tissue under investigation and to measure the amount of light absorbed by it. The more blood there is in a structure, the more light it will absorb.

Invasive Physiological Research Methods

We turn now from a consideration of the noninvasive techniques employed in research on living human brains to a consideration of more direct techniques, which are commonly employed in biopsychological studies of laboratory animals. Most physiological techniques used in biopsychological research on laboratory animals fall into one of three categories: lesion methods, electrical stimulation methods, and invasive recording methods. Each of these three methods is discussed in this module, but we begin with a description of *stereotaxic surgery* because each of these methods involves the use of stereotaxic surgery.

Stereotaxic Surgery

LO 5.8 **Describe the process of stereotaxic surgery.**

Stereotaxic surgery is the first step in many biopsychological experiments. *Stereotaxic surgery* is the means by which experimental devices are precisely positioned in the depths of the brain. Two things are required in stereotaxic surgery: an atlas to provide directions to the target site and an instrument for getting there.

The **stereotaxic atlas** is used to locate brain structures in much the same way that a geographic atlas is used to locate geographic landmarks. There is, however, one important difference. In contrast to the surface of the earth, which has only two dimensions, the brain has three. Accordingly, the brain is represented in a stereotaxic atlas by a series of individual maps, one per page, each representing the structure of a single, two-dimensional frontal brain slice. In stereotaxic atlases, all distances are given in millimeters from a designated reference point. In some rat atlases, the reference point is **bregma**—the point on the top of the skull where two of the major *sutures* (seams in the skull) intersect.

The **stereotaxic instrument** has two parts: a *head holder*, which firmly holds each subject's brain in the prescribed position and orientation; and an *electrode holder*, which holds the device to be inserted. A system of precision gears allows the electrode holder to be moved in three dimensions: anterior–posterior, dorsal–ventral, and lateral–medial. The implantation by stereotaxic surgery of an electrode in the amygdala of a rat is illustrated in Figure 5.14.

Lesion Methods

LO 5.9 **Describe four types of lesion methods, and explain why it is important to be cautious when interpreting the effects of lesions.**

Those of you with an unrelenting drive to dismantle objects to see how they work will appreciate the lesion methods. In those methods, a part of the brain is damaged, destroyed, or inactivated; then the behavior of the subject is carefully assessed in an effort to determine the functions of the lesioned structure. Four types of lesions are discussed here: aspiration lesions, radio-frequency lesions, knife cuts, and reversible lesions.

ASPIRATION LESIONS. When a lesion is to be made in an area of cortical tissue that is accessible to the eyes and instruments of the surgeon, **aspiration** is frequently the method of choice. The cortical tissue is drawn off by suction through a fine-tipped handheld glass pipette. Because the underlying white matter is slightly more resistant to suction than the cortical tissue itself, a skilled surgeon can delicately peel off the layers of cortical tissue from the surface of the brain, leaving the underlying white matter and major blood vessels undamaged.

RADIO-FREQUENCY LESIONS. Small subcortical lesions are commonly made by passing *radio-frequency current* (high-frequency current) through the target tissue from the tip of a stereotaxically positioned electrode. The heat from the current

destroys the tissue. The size and shape of the lesion are determined by the duration and intensity of the current and the configuration of the electrode tip.

KNIFE CUTS. *Sectioning* (cutting) is used to eliminate conduction in a nerve or tract. A tiny, well-placed cut can unambiguously accomplish this task without producing extensive damage to surrounding tissue. How does one insert a knife into the brain to make a cut without severely damaging the overlying tissue? One method is depicted in Figure 5.15.

REVERSIBLE LESIONS. Reversible lesions are useful alternatives to *destructive lesions*. **Reversible lesions** are methods for temporarily eliminating the activity in a particular area of the brain while tests are being conducted. The advantage of reversible lesions is that the same subjects can be repeatedly tested in both the lesion and control conditions. Reversible lesions can be produced by cooling the target structure or by injecting an anesthetic (e.g., *lidocaine*) into it.

Figure 5.14 Stereotaxic surgery: implanting an electrode in the rat amygdala.

1 The atlas indicates that the amygdala target site is 2.8 mm posterior to bregma, 4.5 mm lateral, and 8.5 mm ventral.

2 A hole is drilled 2.8 mm posterior to bregma and 4.5 mm lateral to it. Then, the electrode holder is positioned over the hole, and the electrode is lowered 8.5 mm through the hole.

3 The electrode is anchored to the skull with several stainless steel screws and dental acrylic that is allowed to harden around the electrode connector.

Figure 5.15 A device for performing subcortical knife cuts. The device is stereotaxically positioned in the brain; then the blade swings out to make the cut. Here, the anterior commissure is being sectioned.

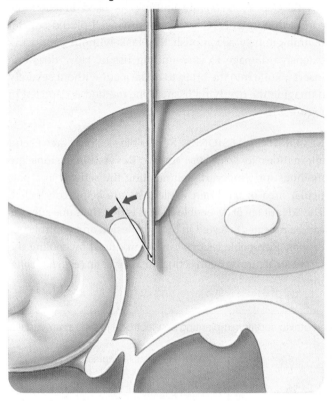

INTERPRETING LESION EFFECTS. Before you leave this section on lesions, a word of caution is in order. Lesion effects are deceptively difficult to interpret. Because the structures of the brain are small, convoluted, and tightly packed together, even a highly skilled surgeon cannot completely destroy a structure without producing significant damage to adjacent structures. There is, however, an unfortunate tendency to lose sight of this fact. For example, a lesion that leaves major portions of the amygdala intact and damages an assortment of neighboring structures comes to be thought of simplistically as an *amygdala lesion*. Such an apparently harmless abstraction can be misleading in two ways. If you believe that all lesions referred to as "amygdala lesions" include damage to no other brain structure, you may incorrectly attribute all of their behavioral effects to amygdala damage; conversely, if you believe that all lesions referred to as "amygdala lesions" include the entire amygdala, you may incorrectly conclude that the amygdala does not participate in behaviors uninfluenced by the lesion.

BILATERAL AND UNILATERAL LESIONS. As a general principle—but one with several notable exceptions—the behavioral effects of *unilateral lesions* (lesions restricted to one half of the brain) are much milder than those of symmetrical *bilateral lesions* (lesions involving both sides of the brain), particularly in nonhuman species. Indeed, behavioral effects of unilateral lesions to some brain structures can be difficult to detect. As a result, most experimental studies of lesion effects are studies of bilateral, rather than unilateral, lesions.

Electrical Stimulation

LO 5.10 Describe the technique of electrical brain stimulation.

Clues about the function of a neural structure can be obtained by stimulating it electrically. Electrical brain stimulation is usually delivered across the two tips of a *bipolar electrode*—two insulated wires wound tightly together and cut at the end. Weak pulses of current produce an immediate increase in the firing of neurons near the tip of the electrode.

Electrical stimulation of the brain is an important biopsychological research tool because it often has behavioral effects, usually opposite to those produced by a lesion to the same site. It can elicit a number of behavioral sequences, including eating, drinking, attacking, copulating, and sleeping. The particular behavioral response elicited depends on the location of the electrode tip, the parameters of the current, and the test environment in which the stimulation is administered.

Because electrical stimulation of the brain is an invasive procedure, its use is usually limited to nonhumans. However, there are situations in which it is administered to conscious human patients (e.g., Jonas et al., 2014).

Invasive Electrophysiological Recording Methods

LO 5.11 Describe four invasive electrophysiological recording methods.

This section describes four invasive electrophysiological recording methods: intracellular unit recording, extracellular unit recording, multiple-unit recording, and invasive EEG recording. See Figure 5.16 for an example of each method.

INTRACELLULAR UNIT RECORDING. This method, whose findings were discussed at length in Chapter 4, provides a moment-by-moment record of the graded fluctuations in one neuron's membrane potential. Most experiments using this recording procedure are performed on chemically immobilized animals because it is difficult to keep the tip of a microelectrode positioned inside a neuron of a freely moving animal (see Long & Lee, 2012).

EXTRACELLULAR UNIT RECORDING. It is possible to record the action potentials of a neuron through a

Figure 5.16 Four methods of recording electrical activity of the nervous system.

An Intracellular Unit Recording
An intracellular microelectrode records the membrane potential from one neuron as it fires.

A Multiple-Unit Recording
A small electrode records the action potentials of many nearby neurons. These are added up and plotted. In this example, firing in the area of the electrode tip gradually declined and then suddenly increased.

An Extracellular Unit Recording
An extracellular microelectrode records the electrical disturbance that is created each time an adjacent neuron fires. In this example, each vertical line represents an action potential.

An Invasive EEG Recording
A large implanted electrode picks up general changes in electrical brain activity. The EEG signal is not related to neural firing in any obvious way.

microelectrode whose tip is positioned in the extracellular fluid next to it—each time the neuron fires, there is an electrical disturbance and a blip is recorded at the electrode tip. Accordingly, *extracellular unit recording* provides a record of the firing of a neuron but no information about the neuron's membrane potential. It is difficult to record extracellularly from a single neuron in a freely moving animal without the electrode tip shifting away from the neuron, but it can be accomplished with special flexible microelectrodes that can shift slightly with the brain. Initially, extracellular unit recording involved recording from one neuron at a time, each at the tip of a separately implanted electrode. However, it is now possible to simultaneously record extracellular signals from up to about 100 neurons by analyzing the correlations among the signals picked up through several different electrodes implanted in the same general area (see Tsien et al., 2013).

MULTIPLE-UNIT RECORDING. In *multiple-unit recording*, the electrode tip is much larger than that of a microelectrode; thus, it picks up signals from many neurons, and slight shifts in its position due to movement of the subject

have little effect on the overall signal. The many action potentials picked up by the electrode are fed into an integrating circuit, which adds them together. A multiple-unit recording is a graph of the total number of recorded action potentials per unit of time (e.g., per 0.1 second).

INVASIVE EEG RECORDING. In laboratory animals, EEG signals are recorded through large implanted electrodes rather than through scalp electrodes. Cortical EEG signals are frequently recorded through stainless steel skull screws, whereas subcortical EEG signals are typically recorded through stereotaxically implanted wire electrodes.

Pharmacological Research Methods

In the preceding module, you learned how physiological psychologists study the brain by manipulating it and recording from it using surgical and electrical methods.

In this module, you will learn how psychopharmacologists manipulate the brain and record from it using chemical methods.

The major research strategy of psychopharmacology is to administer drugs that either increase or decrease the effects of particular neurotransmitters and to observe the behavioral consequences. You learned in Chapter 4 how agonists and antagonists affect neurotransmitter systems. Described here are routes of drug administration, methods of using chemicals to make selective brain lesions, methods of measuring the chemical activity of the brain that are particularly useful in biopsychological research, and methods for locating neurotransmitter systems.

Routes of Drug Administration

LO 5.12 Describe the various methods of drug administration.

In most psychopharmacological experiments, drugs are administered in one of the following ways: (1) they are fed to the subject; (2) they are injected through a tube into the stomach (*intragastrically*); or (3) they are injected hypodermically into the peritoneal cavity of the abdomen (*intraperitoneally, IP*), into a large muscle (*intramuscularly, IM*), into the fatty tissue beneath the skin (*subcutaneously, SC*), or into a large surface vein (*intravenously, IV*). A problem with these peripheral routes of administration is that many drugs do not readily pass through the blood–brain barrier (see Chapter 3). To overcome this problem, drugs can be administered in small amounts through a fine, hollow tube, called a **cannula**, that has been stereotaxically implanted in the brain.

Selective Chemical Lesions

LO 5.13 Describe the method of selective neurotoxic lesions.

The effects of surgical, radio-frequency, and reversible lesions are frequently difficult to interpret because they affect all neurons in the target area. In some cases, it is possible to make more selective lesions by injecting **neurotoxins** (neural poisons) that have an affinity for certain components of the nervous system. There are many selective neurotoxins. For example, when either *kainic acid* or *ibotenic acid* is administered by microinjection, it is preferentially taken up by cell bodies at the tip of the cannula and destroys those neurons, while leaving neurons with axons passing through the area largely unscathed.

Another selective neurotoxin that has been widely used is *6-hydroxydopamine* (*6-OHDA*). It is taken up by only those neurons that release the neurotransmitter *norepinephrine* or *dopamine*, and it leaves other neurons at the injection site undamaged.

Measuring Chemical Activity of the Brain

LO 5.14 Describe two techniques for measuring chemical activity in the brain.

There are many procedures for measuring the chemical activity of the brains of laboratory animals. Two techniques that have proved particularly useful in biopsychological research are the 2-deoxyglucose technique and cerebral dialysis.

2-DEOXYGLUCOSE TECHNIQUE. The *2-deoxyglucose* (*2-DG*) *technique* entails placing an animal that has been injected with radioactive 2-DG in a test situation in which it engages in an activity of interest. Because 2-DG is similar in structure to glucose—the brain's main source of energy— neurons active during the test absorb it at a high rate but do not metabolize it. Then the subject is killed, and its brain is removed and sliced. The slices are then subjected to **autoradiography**: they are coated with a photographic emulsion, stored in the dark for a few days, and then developed much like film. Areas of the brain that absorbed high levels of radioactive 2-DG during the test appear as black spots on the slides. The density of the spots in various regions of the brain can then be color-coded (see Figure 5.17).

CEREBRAL DIALYSIS. **Cerebral dialysis** is a method of measuring the extracellular concentration of specific neurochemicals in behaving animals (e.g., Amato, 2015)—most other techniques for measuring neurochemicals require that the subjects be killed so that tissue can be extracted. Cerebral dialysis involves the implantation in the brain of a fine tube with a short semipermeable section. The semipermeable section is positioned in the brain structure of interest so that extracellular chemicals from the structure will diffuse into the tube. Once in the tube, they can be collected for freezing, storage, and later analysis; or they can be carried in solution directly to a *chromatograph* (a device for measuring the chemical constituents of liquids or gases).

Locating Neurotransmitters and Receptors in the Brain

LO 5.15 Describe two techniques for locating particular neurotransmitters or receptors in the brain.

A key step in trying to understand the psychological function of a particular neurotransmitter or receptor is finding out where it is located in the brain. Two of the techniques available for this purpose are immunocytochemistry and in situ hybridization. Each involves exposing brain slices to a labeled *ligand* of the molecule under investigation (the ligand of a molecule is another molecule that binds to it).

IMMUNOCYTOCHEMISTRY. When a foreign protein (an *antigen*) is injected into an animal, the animal's body

Figure 5.17 The 2-deoxyglucose technique. The accumulation of radioactivity is shown in three frontal sections taken from the brain of a Richardson's ground squirrel. The subject was injected with radioactive 2-deoxyglucose; then, for 45 minutes, it viewed brightly illuminated black and white stripes through its left eye while its right eye was covered. Because the ground squirrel visual system is largely crossed, most of the radioactivity accumulated in the visual structures of the right hemisphere. (Courtesy of Rod Cooper, Department of Psychology, University of Calgary.)

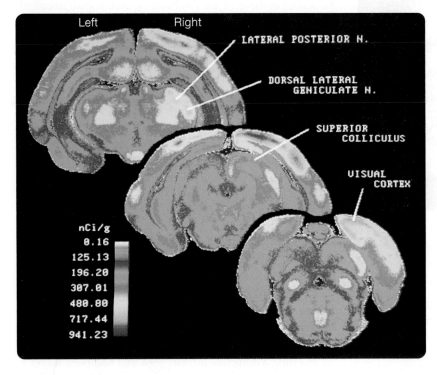

Figure 5.18 immunocytochemistry. This section through a rat's pons reveals noradrenergic neurons that have attracted the antibody for dopamine-beta-hydroxylase, the enzyme that converts dopamine to norepinephrine. (Courtesy of Richard Mooney, Dept. of Neurosciences, University of Toledo College of Medicine.)

creates *antibodies* that bind to it and help the body remove or destroy it; this is known as the body's *immune reaction*. Neurochemists have created stocks of antibodies for the brain's peptide neurotransmitters (neuropeptides; see Chapter 4) and their receptors. **Immunocytochemistry** is a procedure for locating particular neuroproteins in the brain by labeling their antibodies with a dye or radioactive element and then exposing slices of brain tissue to the labeled antibodies. Regions of dye or radioactivity accumulation in the brain slices mark the locations of the target neuroprotein.

Because all enzymes are proteins and because only those neurons that release a particular neurotransmitter are likely to contain all the enzymes required for its synthesis, immunocytochemistry can be used to locate neurotransmitters by binding to their enzymes. This is done by exposing brain slices to labeled antibodies that bind to enzymes located in only those neurons that contain the neurotransmitter of interest (see Figure 5.18).

IN SITU HYBRIDIZATION. Another technique for locating peptides and other proteins in the brain is **in situ hybridization**. This technique takes advantage of the fact that all peptides and proteins are transcribed from sequences of nucleotide bases on strands of messenger RNA (mRNA; see Chapter 2). The nucleotide base sequences that direct the synthesis of many neuroproteins have been identified, and hybrid strands of mRNA with the complementary base sequences have been artificially created. In situ hybridization (see Figure 5.19) involves the following steps. First, hybrid RNA strands with the base sequence complementary to that of the mRNA that directs the synthesis of the target neuroprotein are obtained. Next, the hybrid RNA strands are labeled with a dye or radioactive element. Finally, the brain slices are exposed to the labeled hybrid RNA strands; they bind to the complementary mRNA strands, marking the location of neurons that release the target neuroprotein.

Figure 5.19 In situ hybridization. This color-coded frontal section through a rat brain reveals high concentrations of mRNA expression for an endorphin in the striatum (in red and yellow). (Courtesy of Ningning Guo and Chris Fibiger, Department of Psychiatry, University of British Columbia.)

Genetic Engineering

Genetics is a science that has made amazing progress in the past two decades, and biopsychologists are reaping the benefits. Modern genetic methods are now widely used in biopsychological research, which just a few decades ago would have seemed like science fiction.

Gene Knockout and Gene Replacement Techniques

LO 5.16 Describe gene knockout and gene replacement techniques, and explain what is meant by the term *transgenic*.

Two of the most fundamental approaches in genetic engineering to better understand the impact of genes entail creating organisms that lack certain genes or replacing genes that are present in an organism. These two approaches are, respectively, gene knockout techniques and gene replacement techniques.

GENE KNOCKOUT TECHNIQUES. Gene knockout techniques are procedures for creating organisms that lack a particular gene under investigation (e.g., Gingras et al., 2014). Mice (the favored mammalian subjects of genetic research) that are the products of gene knockout techniques are referred to as *knockout mice*. (This term often makes us smile, as images of little mice with boxing gloves flit through our minds.)

Many gene knockout studies have been conducted to clarify the neural mechanisms of behavior. For example, Ruby and colleagues (2002) and Hattar and colleagues (2003)

used *melanopsin knockout mice* (mice in whom the gene for the synthesis of melanopsin has been deleted) to study the role of melanopsin in regulating the light–dark cycles that control circadian (about 24 hours) rhythms of bodily function—for example, daily cycles of sleep, eating, and body temperature. *Melanopsin* is a protein found in some neurons in the mammalian *retina* (the receptive layer of the eye), and it had been implicated in the control of circadian rhythms by light. Knockout of the gene for synthesizing melanopsin impaired, but did not eliminate, the ability of mice to adjust their circadian rhythms in response to changes in the light–dark cycle. Thus, melanopsin appears to contribute to the control of circadian rhythms by light, but it is not the only factor.

This type of result is typical of gene knockout studies of behavior: Many genes have been discovered that contribute to particular behaviors, but invariably other mechanisms are involved. It may be tempting to think that each behavior is controlled by a single gene, but the reality is much more complex. Each behavior is controlled by many genes interacting with one another, and with experience through epigenetic mechanisms.

Thinking Creatively

GENE REPLACEMENT TECHNIQUES. It is now possible to replace one gene with another. **Gene replacement techniques** have created interesting possibilities for research and therapy. Pathological genes from human cells can be inserted in other animals such as mice—mice that contain the genetic material of another species are called **transgenic mice**. For example, Shen and colleagues (2008) created transgenic mice by inserting a defective human gene that had been found to be associated with schizophrenia in a Scottish family with a particularly high incidence of the condition. The transgenic mice displayed a variety of cerebral abnormalities (e.g., reduced cerebral cortex and enlarged ventricles) and atypical behaviors reminiscent of human schizophrenia. Treating neurological disease by replacing faulty genes in patients suffering from genetic disorders is an exciting, but as yet unrealized, goal.

Clinical Implications

In another gene replacement technique, a gene is replaced with one that is identical except for the addition of a few bases that can act as a switch, turning the gene off or on in response to particular chemicals (Deisseroth, 2010; Dieterich, 2010; Rana & Dolmetsch, 2010). As a result, the gene can be activated or suppressed at a particular point in development.

Fantastic Fluorescence and the Brainbow

LO 5.17 Explain how green fluorescent protein has been used as a research tool in the neurosciences.

Green fluorescent protein (GFP) is a protein that exhibits bright green fluorescence when exposed to blue light. First isolated by Shimomura, Johnson, and Saiga (1962), from a species of jellyfish found off the west coast of North America, GFP is currently stimulating advances in many fields of biological research. Martin Chalfie, Osamu Shimomura, and Roger Tsien were awarded the 2008 Nobel Prize in chemistry for its discovery and study.

The utility of GFP as a research tool in the biological sciences could not be realized until its gene was identified and cloned in the early 1990s. The general strategy is to activate the GFP gene in only the particular cells under investigation so that they can be readily visualized. This can be accomplished in two ways: by inserting the GFP gene in only the target cells or by introducing the GFP gene in all cells of the subject but expressing the gene in only the target cells. Chalfie and colleagues (1994) were the first to use GFP to visualize neurons. They introduced the GFP gene into a small transparent roundworm, *Caenorhabditis elegans*, in an area of its chromosomes that controls the development of touch receptor neurons. Figure 5.20 shows the glowing touch receptor neurons. The GFP gene has now been expressed in the cells of many plant and animal species, including humans.

Livet and colleagues (2007) took the very useful GFP technique one step further—one big step. First, Tsien (1998) found that making minor alterations to the GFP gene resulted in the synthesis of proteins that fluoresced in different colors. Livet and colleagues (2007) then introduced the mutated genes for cyan, yellow, and blue fluorescent proteins into the

Figure 5.20 Touch receptor neurons of the transparent *Caenorhabditis elegans* labeled by green fluorescent protein.

genomes of developing mice in such a way that they were expressed in developing neurons. Each neuron produced different amounts of the three proteins, giving it a distinctive color—in the same way that a color printer can make any color by mixing only three colored inks in differing proportions. Because each neuron was labeled with its own distinctive color, the pathways of neural axons could be traced to their destinations through the cellular morass. This technique has been dubbed **brainbow** for obvious reasons—see Figure 5.21.

Thinking Creatively

Figure 5.21 With the research technique called *brainbow*, each neuron is labeled with a different color, facilitating the tracing of neural axons.

Optogenetics: A Neural Light Switch

LO 5.18 Explain how opsins have been used as a research tool in the neurosciences.

Opsins are light-sensitive ion channels that are found in the cell membranes of certain bacteria and algae (see Boyden, 2014). When opsins are illuminated with light, they open and allow ions to enter the cell. Depending on the particular opsin, light can either hyperpolarize or depolarize the cell membrane they are embedded in. The use of opsins is currently revolutionizing how neuroscientists study the brain (see Boyden, 2015; Deisseroth, 2015).

The utility of opsins for neuroscience research couldn't be realized until their gene was identified and rendered into a form that was expressible within a mammalian cell—a feat that was first accomplished in 2003 (see Boyden, 2014).

Soon thereafter, neuroscientists started to use genetic engineering techniques to insert the opsin gene, or variants of the opsin gene, into particular types of neurons. In effect, by inserting an opsin gene into a particular type of neuron, a neuroscientist could use light to hyperpolarize or depolarize neurons. This novel method is known as **optogenetics** (see Goshen, 2014; Yuste & Church, 2014), and it is increasingly being used by many neuroscientists (see Berndt & Deisseroth, 2015). For example, it can be used in living animals by injecting the animal with a virus carrying an opsin gene that targets a particular type of neuron (e.g., dopaminergic neurons; see Chang et al., 2016). An optical fiber can then be implanted in the animal and light can be shone through the fiber to activate the opsin ion channels—causing the activity of specific neurons to either be increased or suppressed (see Steinberg et al., 2015).

Scan Your Brain

The research methods of biopsychology illustrate a psychological disorder suffered by many scientists. We call it "unabbreviaphobia"— the fear of leaving any term unabbreviated. To determine whether you have mastered Part One of this chapter and are ready for Part Two, supply the full term for each of the following abbreviations. The correct answers are provided at the end of the exercise. Before proceeding, review material related to your incorrect answers and omissions.

1. CT: _____
2. MRI: _____
3. PET: _____
4. 2-DG: _____
5. fMRI: _____
6. MEG: _____
7. TMS: _____
8. EEG: _____
9. ERP: _____
10. AEP: _____
11. EMG: _____

12. EOG: _____
13. SCL: _____
14. SCR: _____
15. ECG: _____
16. EKG: _____
17. IP: _____
18. IM: _____
19. IV: _____
20. SC: _____
21. 6-OHDA: _____
22. GFP: _____

Scan Your Brain answers: (1) computed tomography, (2) magnetic resonance imaging, (3) positron emission tomography, (4) 2-deoxyglucose, (5) functional MRI, (6) magnetoencephalography, (7) transcranial magnetic stimulation, (8) electroencephalogram, (9) event-related potential, (10) average evoked potential, (11) electromyogram, (12) electrooculogram, (13) skin conductance level, (14) skin conductance response, (15) electrocardiogram, (16) electrocardiogram, (17) intraperitoneal, (18) intramuscular, (19) intravenous, (20) subcutaneous, (21) 6-hydroxydopamine, (22) green fluorescent protein.

PART TWO Behavioral Research Methods of Biopsychology

We turn now from methods used by biopsychologists to study the nervous system to those that deal with the behavioral side of biopsychology. Because of the inherent invisibility of

neural activity, the primary objective of the methods used in its investigation is to render the unobservable observable. In contrast, the major objectives of behavioral research methods are to control, to simplify, and to objectify.

A single set of procedures developed for the investigation of a particular behavioral phenomenon is commonly referred to as a **behavioral paradigm**. Each behavioral paradigm normally comprises a method for producing the behavioral phenomenon under investigation and a method for objectively measuring it.

Neuropsychological Testing

A patient suspected of suffering from some sort of nervous system dysfunction is usually referred to a *neurologist*, who assesses simple sensory and motor functions. More subtle changes in perceptual, emotional, motivational, or cognitive functions are the domain of the *neuropsychologist*.

Because neuropsychological testing is so time consuming, it is typically prescribed for only a small portion of brain-damaged patients. This is unfortunate; the results of neuropsychological testing can help brain-damaged patients in three important ways: (1) by assisting in the diagnosis of neural disorders, particularly in cases in which brain imaging, EEG, and neurological testing have proved equivocal; (2) by serving as a basis for counseling and caring for the patients; and (3) by providing a basis for objectively evaluating the effectiveness of a treatment or the seriousness of its side effects.

Modern Approach to Neuropsychological Testing

LO 5.19 Describe three approaches to neuropsychological testing.

The nature of neuropsychological testing has changed radically since the 1950s. Indeed, the dominant approach to psychological testing has evolved through three distinct phases: the *single-test approach*, the *standardized-test-battery approach*, and the modern *customized-test-battery approach*.

THE SINGLE-TEST APPROACH. Before the 1950s, the few existing neuropsychological tests were designed to detect the presence of brain damage; in particular, the goal of these early tests was to discriminate between patients with psychological problems resulting from structural brain damage and those with psychological problems resulting from functional, rather than structural, changes to the brain. This approach proved unsuccessful, in large part because no single test could be developed that would be sensitive to all the varied and complex psychological symptoms that could potentially occur in a brain-damaged patient.

THE STANDARDIZED-TEST-BATTERY APPROACH. The standardized-test-battery approach to neuropsychological testing grew out of the failures of the single-test approach, and by the 1960s, it was predominant. The objective stayed the same—to identify brain-damaged patients—but the testing involved *standardized batteries* (sets) of tests rather than a single test. The most widely used standardized test battery has been the *Halstead-Reitan Neuropsychological Test Battery*. The Halstead-Reitan is a set of tests that tend to be performed poorly by brain-damaged patients in relation to other patients or healthy controls; the scores on each test are added together to form a single aggregate score. An aggregate score below the designated cutoff leads to a diagnosis of brain damage. The standardized-test-battery approach proved only marginally successful; standardized test batteries discriminate effectively between neurological patients and healthy individuals, but they are not so good at discriminating between neurological patients and psychiatric patients.

THE CUSTOMIZED-TEST-BATTERY APPROACH. The customized-test-battery approach began to be used routinely in a few elite neuropsychological research institutions in the 1960s. This approach proved highly successful in research, and it soon spread to clinical practice. It now predominates in both the research laboratory and the neurological ward.

The objective of current neuropsychological testing is not merely to identify patients with brain damage; the objective is to characterize the nature of the psychological deficits of each brain-damaged patient. So how does the customized-test-battery approach to neuropsychological testing work? It usually begins in the same way for all patients: with a common battery of tests selected by the neuropsychologist to provide an indication of the general nature of the neuropsychological symptoms. Then, depending on the results of the common test battery, the neuropsychologist selects a series of tests customized to each patient in an effort to characterize in more detail the general symptoms revealed by the common battery. For example, if the results of the test battery indicated that a patient had a memory problem, subsequent tests would include those designed to reveal the specific nature of the memory problem.

The tests used in the customized-test-battery approach differ in three respects from earlier approaches. First, the newer tests are specifically designed to measure aspects of psychological function that have been spotlighted by modern theories and data. For example, modern theories, and the evidence on which they are based, suggest that the mechanisms of short-term and long-term memory are totally different; thus, the testing of patients with memory problems virtually always involves specific tests of both short-term and long-term memory. Second, the interpretation of the test results often does not rest entirely on how well the patient does; unlike early neuropsychological tests, currently used tests often require the neuropsychologist to assess the cognitive strategy that the patient employs in performing the test. Third, the customized-test-battery approach requires more skill and knowledge on the part of the neuropsychologist to select just the right battery of tests to expose a particular patient's deficits and to identify qualitative differences in cognitive strategy.

Because the customized-test-battery approach to neuro-psychological testing typically involves two phases—a battery of general tests given to all patients followed by a series of specific tests customized to each patient—the following examples of neuropsychological tests are presented in two sections. First are some tests that are often administered as part of the initial common test battery, and second are some tests that might be used by a neuropsychologist to investigate in more depth particular problems revealed by the common battery.

Clinical Implications

Tests of the Common Neuropsychological Test Battery

LO 5.20 Describe those tests that are often administered as part of an initial common neuropsychological test battery.

INTELLIGENCE. Although the overall *intelligence quotient* (*IQ*) is a notoriously poor measure of brain damage, a test of general intelligence is nearly always included in the battery of neuropsychological tests routinely given to all patients. Many neuropsychological assessments begin with the **Wechsler Adult Intelligence Scale (WAIS)**, first published in 1955 and standardized in 1981 on a sample of 1,880 U.S. citizens between 16 and 71. The WAIS is often the first test because knowing a patient's IQ can help a neuropsychologist interpret the results of subsequent tests. Also, a skilled neuropsychologist can sometimes draw inferences about a patient's neuropsychological dysfunction from the pattern of deficits on the 15 subtests of the WAIS (see Table 5.1). For example, low scores on subtests of verbal comprehension tend to be associated with left hemisphere damage.

MEMORY. One weakness of the WAIS is that it often fails to detect memory deficits, despite including subtests specifically designed to test memory function. For example, the information subtest of the WAIS assesses memory for general knowledge (e.g., "Who is Queen Elizabeth?"), and the **digit span** subtest (the most widely used test of short-term memory) identifies the longest sequence of random digits that a patient can repeat correctly 50 percent of the time; most people have a digit span of 7. However, these

---

Table 5.1 The 15 Subtests of the Wechsler Adult Intelligence Scale (WAIS).

Verbal Comprehension Subtests

Information   The patient is asked 29 questions of general information—for example "Who is the president of the United States?"

Vocabulary   The patient is asked to define 35 words that range in difficulty.

Comprehension   The patient is asked 16 questions that test the ability to understand general principles—for example "Why should people vote?"

Similarities   The patient is presented with pairs of items and is asked to explain how the items in each pair are similar.

Perceptual Reasoning Subtests

Picture Completion   The patient must identify the important part missing from 20 drawings—for example, a squirrel with no tail.

Matrix Reasoning   The patient is presented with an incomplete matrix made up of pictures and designs and is asked to complete the matrix by selecting the missing item from a set of items.

Block Design   The patient is presented with nine blocks that are red on two sides, white on two sides, and half red and half white on the other two. Then, the patient is shown several patterns and is asked to duplicate them by arranging the blocks appropriately.

Figure Weights   The patient is presented with drawings of balance scales that are missing weights and must select the weights needed to keep the scale balanced.

Visual Puzzles   The patient is shown a picture of a completed puzzle and then must select three shapes, from a set of six shapes, to complete the puzzle.

Working Memory Subtests

Digit Span   Digits are read at 1-second intervals and the patient tries to repeat them in the same order. Two trials are given at three digits, four digits, five digits, and so on, until the patient fails both trials at one level.

Arithmetic   The patient must answer 14 arithmetic questions without benefit of pencil and paper.

Letter-Number Sequencing   The patient listens to sequences of letters and numbers and after each sequence must recall the numbers of each sequence in ascending order and the letters in alphabetical order.

Processing Speed Subtests

Symbol Search   The patient is shown a target symbol and then must identify it from a list. How many symbols can be located within the time limit?

Coding   The patient must use a code key to look up and copy the symbols that are paired with particular geometric shapes or numbers. How many symbols can be copied within the time limit?

Cancellation   The patient is shown an arrangement of different-colored items and must identify the target items within the time limit.

two forms of memory are among the least likely to be disrupted by brain damage—patients with seriously disturbed memories often show no deficits on either the information or the digit span subtest. Be that as it may, memory problems rarely escape unnoticed because they are usually reported by the patient or the family of the patient.

LANGUAGE. If a neuropsychological patient has taken the WAIS, deficits in the use of language can be inferred from a low aggregate score on the verbal subtests. A patient who has not taken the WAIS can be quickly screened for language-related deficits with the **token test**. Twenty tokens of two different shapes (squares and circles), two different sizes (large and small), and five different colors (white, black, yellow, green, and red) are placed on a table in front of the patient. The test begins with the examiner reading simple instructions—for example, "Touch a red square"—and the patient trying to follow them. Then the test progresses to more difficult instructions, such as "Touch the small, red circle and then the large, green square." Finally, the patient is asked to read the instructions aloud and follow them.

LANGUAGE LATERALIZATION. It is usual for one hemisphere to participate more than the other in language-related activities. In most people, the left hemisphere is dominant for language, but in some, the right hemisphere is dominant (see Chapter 16). A test of language lateralization is often included in the common test battery because knowing which hemisphere is dominant for language is often useful in interpreting the results of other tests. Furthermore, a test of language lateralization is virtually always given to patients before any surgery that might encroach on the cortical language areas. The results are used to plan the surgery, trying to avoid the language areas if possible.

There are two widely used tests of language lateralization. The sodium amytal test (Wada, 1949) is one, and the dichotic listening test (Kimura, 1973) is the other.

The **sodium amytal test** involves injecting the anesthetic *sodium amytal* into either the left or right carotid artery in the neck. This temporarily anesthetizes the *ipsilateral* (same-side) hemisphere while leaving the *contralateral* (opposite-side) hemisphere largely unaffected. Several tests of language function are quickly administered while the ipsilateral hemisphere is anesthetized. Later, the process is repeated for the other side of the brain. When the injection is on the side dominant for language, the patient is completely mute for about 2 minutes. When the injection is on the nondominant side, there are only a few minor speech problems. Because the sodium amytal test is invasive, it can be administered only for medical reasons—usually to determine the dominant language hemisphere prior to brain surgery.

In the standard version of the **dichotic listening test**, sequences of spoken digits are presented to volunteers through stereo headphones. Three digits are presented

to one ear at the same time that three different digits are presented to the other ear. Then, they are asked to report as many of the six digits as they can. Kimura (1973) found that patients correctly report more of the digits heard by the ear contralateral to their dominant hemisphere for language, as determined by the sodium amytal test.

Tests of Specific Neuropsychological Function

LO 5.21 Describe tests that might be used by a neuropsychologist to investigate in more depth general problems revealed by a common neuropsychological test battery.

Following analysis of the results of a neuropsychological patient's performance on a common test battery, the neuropsychologist selects a series of specific tests to clarify the nature of the general problems exposed by the common battery. There are thousands of tests that might be selected from. This section 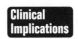 describes a few of them and mentions some of the considerations that might influence their selection.

> **Clinical Implications** What are some of the clinical implications of this two-stage approach to neuropsychological testing?

MEMORY. Following the discovery of memory impairment by the common test battery, at least four fundamental questions about the memory impairment must be answered (see Chapter 11): (1) Does the memory impairment involve *short-term memory, long-term memory,* or both? (2) Are any deficits in long-term memory *anterograde* (affecting the retention of things learned after the damage), *retrograde* (affecting the retention of things learned before the damage), or both? (3) Do any deficits in long-term memory involve *semantic memory* (memory for knowledge of the world) or *episodic memory* (memory for personal experiences)? (4) Are any deficits in long-term memory deficits of *explicit memory* (memories of which the patient is aware and can thus express verbally), *implicit memory* (memories demonstrated by the improved performance of the patient without the patient being conscious of them), or both?

Many amnesic patients display severe deficits in explicit memory with no deficits at all in implicit memory (see Squire & Dede, 2015). **Repetition priming tests** have proven instrumental in the assessment and study of this pattern. Patients are first shown a list of words and asked to study them; they are not asked to remember them. Then, at a later time, they are asked to complete a list of word fragments, many of which are fragments of words from the initial list. For example, if "purple" had been in the initial test, "pu_p_ _" could be one of the test word fragments. Amnesic patients often complete the fragments as accurately as healthy control subjects. But—and this is the really important part—they often have no conscious memory of any of the words in the initial list or even of ever having seen the list. In other words, they display good implicit memory of experiences without explicit memories of them.

LANGUAGE. If a neuropsychological patient turns out to have language-related deficits on the common test battery, a complex series of tests is administered to clarify the nature of the problem (see Chapter 16). For example, if a patient has a speech problem, it may be one of three fundamentally different problems: problems of *phonology* (the rules governing the sounds of the language), problems of *syntax* (the grammar of the language), or problems of *semantics* (the meaning of the language). Because brain-damaged patients may have one of these problems but not the others, it is imperative that the testing of all neuropsychological patients with speech problems include tests of each of these three capacities.

Reading aloud can be disrupted in different ways by brain damage, and follow-up tests must be employed that can differentiate between the different patterns of disruption. Some *dyslexic* patients (those with reading problems) remember the rules of pronunciation but have difficulties pronouncing words that do not follow these rules, words such as *come* and *tongue*, whose pronunciation must be remembered. Other dyslexic patients pronounce simple familiar words based on memory but have lost the ability to apply the rules of pronunciation—they cannot pronounce nonwords such as *trapple* or *fleeming*.

Frontal-Lobe Function

LO 5.22 Describe the Wisconsin Card Sorting Test.

Injuries to the frontal lobes are common, and the **Wisconsin Card Sorting Test** (see Figure 5.22) is a component of many customized test batteries because performance on it is sensitive to frontal-lobe damage (see Eling, Derckx, & Maes, 2008). On each Wisconsin card is either one symbol or two, three, or four identical symbols. The symbols are all either triangles, stars, circles, or crosses; and they are all either red, green, yellow, or blue. At the beginning of the test, the patient is confronted with four stimulus cards that differ from one another in the form, color, and number of symbols they display. The task is to correctly sort cards from a deck into piles in front of the stimulus cards. However, the patient does not know whether to sort by form, by color, or by number. The patient begins by guessing and is told after each card has been sorted whether it was sorted correctly or incorrectly. At first, the task is to learn to sort by color. But as soon as the patient makes several consecutive

Figure 5.22 The Wisconsin Card Sorting Test. This woman is just starting the test. If she places the first card in front of the stimulus card with the three green circles, she is sorting on the basis of color. She must guess until she can learn which principle—color, shape, or number—should guide her sorting. After she has placed a card, she is told whether her placement is correct.

correct responses, the sorting principle is changed to shape or number without any indication other than the fact that responses based on color become incorrect. Thereafter, each time the patient learns a new sorting principle, the principle is changed.

Patients with damage to their frontal lobes often continue to sort on the basis of one sorting principle for 100 or more trials after it has become incorrect. They seem to have great difficulty learning and remembering that previously appropriate guidelines for effective behavior are no longer appropriate, a problem called *perseveration*.

Behavioral Methods of Cognitive Neuroscience

Cognitive neuroscience is predicated on two related assumptions. The first premise is that each complex cognitive process results from the combined activity of simple cognitive processes called **constituent cognitive processes**.

The second premise is that each constituent cognitive process is mediated by neural activity in a particular area of the brain. One of the main goals of cognitive neuroscience is to identify the parts of the brain that mediate various constituent cognitive processes.

Paired-Image Subtraction Technique

LO 5.23 Describe the paired-image subtraction technique.

With the central role played by PET and fMRI in cognitive neuroscience research, the **paired-image subtraction technique** has become one of the key behavioral research methods in such research (see Kriegeskorte, 2010; Posner & Raichle, 1994). Let us illustrate this technique with the classic PET study of single-word processing by Petersen and colleagues (1988). Petersen and his colleagues were interested in locating the parts of the brain that enable a person to make a word association (to respond to a printed word by saying a related word). You might think this would be an easy task to accomplish by having a volunteer perform a word-association task while a PET image of the volunteer's brain is recorded. The problem with this approach is that many parts of the brain that would be active during the test period would have nothing to do with the constituent cognitive process of forming a word association; much of the activity recorded would be associated with other processes such as seeing the words, reading the words, and speaking. The paired-image subtraction technique was developed to deal with this problem.

The paired-image subtraction technique involves obtaining functional brain images during several different cognitive tasks. Ideally, the tasks are designed so that pairs of them differ from each other in terms of only a single constituent cognitive process. Then the brain activity associated with that process can be estimated by subtracting the activity in the image associated with one of the two tasks from the activity in the image associated with the other. For example, in one of the tasks in the study by Petersen and colleagues, volunteers spent a minute reading aloud printed nouns as they appeared on a screen; in another, they observed the same nouns on the screen but responded to each of them by saying aloud an associated verb (e.g., *truck—drive*). Then Petersen and his colleagues subtracted the activity in the images they recorded during the two tasks to obtain a *difference image*. The difference image illustrated the areas of the brain specifically involved in the constituent cognitive process of forming the word association; the activity associated with fixating on the screen, seeing the nouns, saying the words, and so on, was eliminated by the subtraction.

Watch this video on MyPsychLab

CHALK IT UP! FUNCTIONAL BRAIN SCANS AND THE PAIRED-IMAGE SUBTRACTION TECHNIQUE

Default Mode Network

LO 5.24 Understand the default mode network, and know the structures that are part of that network.

Interpretation of difference images is complicated by the fact that there is substantial brain activity when humans sit quietly and let their minds wander—this level of activity has been termed the brain's **default mode** (Raichle, 2010). Brain structures typically active in the default mode and less active during cognitive or behavioral tasks are collectively referred to as the **default mode network**. The default mode network comprises many structures (see Fox et al., 2015) including the following four cortical areas: medial parietal cortex, lateral parietal cortex, medial prefrontal cortex, and lateral temporal cortex. See Figure 5.23.

Mean Difference Images

LO 5.25 Explain what a mean difference image is.

Another difficulty in using PET and fMRI to locate constituent cognitive processes results from the *noise* associated with random cerebral events that occur during the test—for example, thinking about a sudden pang of hunger, noticing a fly on the screen, or wondering whether the test will last much longer (see Mason et al., 2007). The noise created by such events can be significantly reduced with a technique discussed earlier in this chapter: *signal averaging*. By averaging the difference images obtained from repetitions of the same tests, the researchers can greatly increase the *signal-to-noise ratio*. It is standard practice to average the images obtained from several volunteers; the resulting **mean** (averaged) **difference image** emphasizes areas of activity that are common to many volunteers and de-emphasizes areas of activity that are peculiar to a few of them. However, this averaging

Thinking Creatively

Figure 5.23 The default mode network: areas of the brain in which activity is commonly recorded by functional brain-imaging techniques when the mind wanders, but not when it is actively engaged.

Midsagittal view of right hemisphere

Lateral view of right hemisphere

procedure can lead to a serious problem: If two volunteers had specific but different patterns of cortical activity, the average image derived from the two would reveal little about either. Because people differ substantially from one another in the cortical localization of cognitive abilities, this is a serious problem (see Braver, Cole, & Yarkoni, 2010; Kanai & Rees, 2011; Lichtman & Denk, 2011). Moreover, the area of cortex that controls a particular ability can change in an individual as a result of experience.

Neuroplasticity If an area of cortex that controls a particular ability can change in an individual based on their experiences, what implications, if any, does this neuroplasticity have for the reliability and validity of mean difference images?

Biopsychological Paradigms of Animal Behavior

Noteworthy examples of the behavioral paradigms used to study the biopsychology of laboratory species are provided here under three headings: (1) paradigms for the assessment of species-common behaviors, (2) traditional conditioning paradigms, and (3) seminatural animal learning paradigms. In each case, the focus is on methods used to study the behavior of the laboratory rat, one of the most common subjects of biopsychological research.

Paradigms for the Assessment of Species-Common Behaviors

LO 5.26 Describe three behavioral paradigms used to study species-common behaviors.

Many of the behavioral paradigms used in biopsychological research are used to study species-common behaviors. **Species-common behaviors** are those displayed by virtually all members of a species, or at least by all those of the same age and sex. Commonly studied species-common behaviors include grooming, swimming, eating, drinking, copulating, fighting, and nest building. Described here are the open-field test, tests of aggressive and defensive behavior, and tests of sexual behavior.

OPEN-FIELD TEST. In the **open-field test**, the subject is placed in a large, barren chamber, and its activity is recorded (see Brooks & Dunnett, 2009). It is also common in the open-field test to count the number of *boluses* (pieces of excrement) that were dropped by an animal during the test. Low activity scores and high bolus counts are frequently used as indicators of fearfulness. Fearful rats are also highly **thigmotaxic**; that is, they rarely venture away from the walls of the test chamber and rarely engage in such activities as rearing and grooming. Rats are often fearful when they are first placed in a strange open field, but this fearfulness usually declines with repeated exposure to the same open field.

TESTS OF AGGRESSIVE AND DEFENSIVE BEHAVIOR.
Typical patterns of aggressive and defensive behavior can be observed and measured during combative encounters between the dominant male rat of an established colony and a smaller male intruder (see Blanchard & Blanchard, 1988). This is called the **colony-intruder paradigm**. The behaviors of the dominant male are considered to be aggressive and those of the hapless intruder defensive. The dominant male of the colony (the *alpha male*) moves sideways toward the intruder, with its hair erect. When it nears the intruder, it tries to push the intruder off balance and to deliver bites to its back and flanks. The defender tries to protect its back and flanks by rearing up on its hind legs and pushing the attacker away with its forepaws or by rolling onto its back. Thus, piloerection, lateral approach, and flank- and back-biting indicate conspecific aggression in the rat; freezing, boxing (rearing and pushing away), and rolling over indicate defensiveness.

Some tests of rat defensive behavior assess reactivity to the experimenter rather than to another rat. For example, it is common to rate the resistance of a rat to being picked up—no resistance being the lowest category and biting the highest—and to use the score as one measure of defensiveness.

The **elevated plus maze**, a four-armed, plus-sign-shaped maze typically mounted 50 centimeters above the floor, is a test of defensiveness commonly used to study the *anxiolytic* (anxiety-reducing) effects of drugs. Two of the arms of the maze have sides, and two do not. The measure of defensiveness, or anxiety, is the proportion of time the rats spend in the protected closed arms rather than on the exposed arms. Many established anxiolytic drugs significantly increase the proportion of time that rats spend on the open arms, and new drugs that prove to be effective in reducing rats' defensiveness on the maze often turn out to be effective in the treatment of human anxiety.

TESTS OF SEXUAL BEHAVIOR. Most attempts to study the physiological bases of rat sexual behavior have focused on the copulatory act itself. The male mounts the female from behind and clasps her hindquarters. If the female is receptive, she responds by assuming the posture called **lordosis**; that is, she sticks her hindquarters in the air, she bends her back in a U, and she deflects her tail to the side. During some mounts, the male inserts his penis into the female's vagina; this act is called **intromission**. After intromission, the male dismounts by jumping backward. He then returns a few seconds later to mount and intromit once again. Following about 10 such cycles of mounting, intromitting, and dismounting, the male mounts, intromits, and **ejaculates** (ejects his sperm).

Three common measures of male rat sexual behavior are the number of mounts required to achieve intromission, the number of intromissions required to achieve ejaculation, and the interval between ejaculation and the reinitiation of mounting. The most common measure of female rat sexual behavior is the **lordosis quotient** (the proportion of mounts that elicit lordosis).

Traditional Conditioning Paradigms

LO 5.27 Describe the Pavlovian conditioning paradigm and the operant conditioning paradigm.

Learning paradigms play a major role in biopsychological research for three reasons. The first is that learning is a phenomenon of primary interest to psychologists. The second is that learning paradigms provide an effective technology for producing and controlling animal behavior. Because animals cannot follow instructions from the experimenter, it is often necessary to train them to behave in a fashion consistent with the goals of the experiment. The third reason is that it is possible to infer much about the sensory, motor, motivational, and cognitive state of an animal from its ability to learn and perform various responses.

If you have taken a previous course in psychology, you will likely be familiar with the Pavlovian and operant conditioning paradigms. In the **Pavlovian conditioning paradigm**, the experimenter pairs an initially neutral stimulus called a *conditional stimulus* (e.g., a tone or a light) with an *unconditional stimulus* (e.g., meat powder)—a stimulus that elicits an *unconditional* (reflexive) *response* (e.g., salivation). As a result of these pairings, the conditional stimulus eventually acquires the capacity, when administered alone, to elicit a *conditional response* (e.g., salivation)—a response that is often, but not always, similar to the unconditional response.

In the **operant conditioning paradigm**, the rate at which a particular voluntary response (such as a lever press) is emitted is increased by *reinforcement* or decreased by *punishment*. One widely used operant conditioning paradigm in biopsychology is the self-stimulation paradigm. In the **self-stimulation paradigm**, animals press a lever to deliver electrical stimulation to particular sites in their own brains; those structures in the brain that support self-stimulation have often been called *pleasure centers*.

Seminatural Animal Learning Paradigms

LO 5.28 Describe four seminatural animal learning paradigms.

In addition to Pavlovian and operant conditioning paradigms, biopsychologists use animal learning paradigms that have been specifically designed to mimic situations that an animal might encounter in its natural environment. Development of these paradigms stemmed in part from the reasonable assumption that forms of learning tending to benefit an animal's survival in the wild are likely to be more highly developed and more directly related to innate neural mechanisms. The following are four common seminatural learning paradigms: conditioned taste aversion, radial arm maze, Morris water maze, and conditioned defensive burying.

CONDITIONED TASTE AVERSION. A **conditioned taste aversion** is the avoidance response that develops to tastes of food whose consumption has been followed by illness (see Garcia & Koelling, 1966; Lin, Arthurs, & Reilly, 2014). In the standard conditioned taste aversion experiment, rats receive an *emetic* (a nausea-inducing drug) after they consume a food with an unfamiliar taste. On the basis of this single conditioning trial, the rats learn to avoid the taste.

The ability of rats to readily learn the relationship between a particular taste and subsequent illness unquestionably increases their chances of survival in their natural environment, where potentially edible substances are not routinely screened by government agencies. Rats and many other animals are *neophobic* (afraid of new things); thus, when they first encounter a new food, they consume it in only small quantities. If they subsequently become ill, they will not consume it again. Conditioned aversions also develop to familiar tastes, but these typically require more than a single trial to be learned.

Humans also develop conditioned taste aversions. Cancer patients have been reported to develop aversions to foods consumed before nausea-inducing chemotherapy (Bernstein & Webster, 1980). Many of you will be able to testify on the basis of personal experience about the effectiveness of conditioned taste aversions. I (JP) still have vivid memories of a batch of red laboratory punch that I overzealously consumed after eating two pieces of blueberry pie. But that is another story—albeit a particularly colorful one.

The discovery of conditioned taste aversion challenged three widely accepted principles of learning (see Revusky & Garcia, 1970) that had grown out of research on traditional operant and Pavlovian conditioning paradigms. First, it challenged the view that animal conditioning is always a gradual step-by-step process; robust taste aversions can be established in only a single trial. Second, it showed that *temporal contiguity* is not essential for conditioning; rats acquire taste aversions even when they do not become ill until several hours after eating. Third, it challenged the *principle of equipotentiality*—the view that conditioning proceeds in basically the same manner regardless of the particular stimuli and responses under investigation. Rats appear to have evolved to readily learn associations between tastes and illness; it is only with great difficulty that they learn relations between the color of food and nausea or between taste and footshock.

RADIAL ARM MAZE. The radial arm maze taps the well-developed spatial abilities of rodents. The survival of rats in the wild depends on their ability to navigate quickly and accurately through their environment and to learn which locations in it are likely to contain food and water. This task is much more complex for a rodent than it is for us. Most of us obtain food from locations where the supply is continually replenished; we go to the market confident that we will find enough food to satisfy our needs. In contrast, the foraging rat must learn and retain a complex pattern of spatially coded details. It must not only learn where morsels of food are likely to be found but must also remember which of these sites it has recently stripped of their booty so as not to revisit them too soon. Designed by Olton and Samuelson (1976) to study these spatial abilities, the **radial arm maze** (see Figure 5.24) is an array of arms—usually eight or more—radiating from a central starting area. At the end of each arm is a food cup, which may or may not be baited, depending on the purpose of the experiment.

In one version of the radial arm maze paradigm, rats are placed each day in a maze that has the same arms baited each day. After a few days of experience, rats rarely visit unbaited arms at all, and they rarely visit baited arms more than once in the same day—even when control procedures make it impossible for them to recognize odors left during previous visits to an arm or to make their visits in a systematic sequence. Because the arms are identical, rats must orient themselves in the maze with reference to external room cues; thus, their performance can be disrupted by rotation of the maze or by changes in the appearance of the room.

MORRIS WATER MAZE. Another seminatural learning paradigm that has been designed to study the spatial abilities of rats is the **Morris water maze** (Morris, 1981). The rats are placed in a circular, featureless pool of cool milky water in which they must swim until they discover the escape platform—which is invisible just beneath the surface of the water. The rats are allowed to rest on the platform before being returned to the water for another trial. Despite the fact that the starting point is varied from

Figure 5.24 A radial arm maze.

trial to trial, the rats learn after only a few trials to swim directly to the platform, presumably by using spatial cues from the room as a reference. The Morris water maze is useful for assessing the navigational skills of brain-lesioned or drugged animals.

CONDITIONED DEFENSIVE BURYING. Yet another seminatural learning paradigm useful in biopsychological research is conditioned defensive burying (e.g., Pinel & Mana, 1989; Pinel & Treit, 1978). In studies of **conditioned defensive burying**, rats receive a single aversive stimulus (e.g., a shock, air blast, or noxious odor) from an object mounted on the wall of the chamber just above the floor, which is littered with bedding material. After a single trial, almost every rat learns that the test object is a threat and responds by flinging bedding material at the test object with its head and forepaws (see Figure 5.25). Antianxiety drugs reduce the amount of conditioned defensive burying, and thus the paradigm is used to study the neurochemistry of anxiety (see Steimer, 2011).

Before moving on to the next chapter, you need to appreciate that to be effective, the research methods you have encountered in this chapter must be used together; seldom, if ever, is an important biopsychological issue resolved by use of a single method. The reason for this is that neither the methods used to manipulate the brain nor the methods used to assess the behavioral consequences of these manipulations are totally selective; there are no methods of manipulating the brain that change only a single aspect of brain function, and there are no measures of behavior that reflect only a single psychological process. Accordingly, lines of research that use a single method can usually be interpreted in more than one way and thus cannot provide unequivocal evidence for any one interpretation. Typically, important research questions are resolved only when several methods are brought to bear on a single problem. This general approach, as you learned in Chapter 1, is called *converging operations*.

Thinking Creatively

Thinking Creatively Think of a research question that would require converging operations (i.e., using several methods to address a single problem) among two or more of the research methods described in this chapter.

Figure 5.25 These photos show a rat burying a test object from which it has just received a single mild shock.

Themes Revisited

This chapter introduced you to the two kinds of research methods used by biopsychologists: methods of studying the brain and methods of studying behavior. In the descriptions of these methods, all four of the main themes of the text were apparent.

The chapter-opening case of Professor P. alerted you to the fact that many of the methods used by biopsychologists to study the human brain are also used clinically, in either diagnosis or treatment. The clinical implications theme came up again during discussions of brain imaging, genetic engineering, neuropsychological testing, and use of the elevated plus maze to test anxiolytic drugs.

The neuroplasticity theme arose during the discussion of the methods of cognitive neuroscience. Experience can produce changes in brain organization that can complicate the interpretation of functional brain images.

The evolutionary perspective theme arose in the discussion of green fluorescent protein, first isolated from jellyfish, and again during the discussion of the rationale for using seminatural animal learning paradigms, which assess animal behavior in environments similar to those in which it evolved.

The thinking creatively theme came up several times. The development of new research methods often requires considerable creativity, and understanding the particular weaknesses and strengths of each research method is the foundation on which creative scientific thinking often rests.

Key Terms

Chapter 6
The Visual System

How We See

⌄ Chapter Overview and Learning Objectives (LOs)

Light Enters the Eye and Reaches the Retina

LO 6.1 Explain how the pupil and the lens can affect the image that falls on the retina.

LO 6.2 Explain why some vertebrates have one eye on each side of their head whereas other vertebrates have their eyes mounted side by side on the front of their heads. Also, explain the importance of binocular disparity.

The Retina and Translation of Light into Neural Signals

LO 6.3 Describe the structure of the retina, and name the cell types that make up the retina.

LO 6.4 Describe the duplexity theory of vision, and explain the differences between the photopic and scotopic systems.

LO 6.5 Explain the difference between the photopic and scotopic spectral sensitivity curves, and explain how that difference can account for the Purkinje effect.

LO 6.6 Describe the three types of involuntary fixational eye movements, and explain what happens when all eye movements are blocked.

LO 6.7 Describe the process of visual transduction.

From Retina to Primary Visual Cortex

LO 6.8 Describe the components and layout of the retina-geniculate-striate system.

LO 6.9 In the context of the retina-geniculate-striate system, explain what is meant by *retinotopic*.

LO 6.10 Describe the M and P channels.

Seeing Edges

LO 6.11 Explain the neural basis of contrast enhancement.

LO 6.12 Describe the methods used by David Hubel and Torsten Wiesel to map the receptive fields of visual system neurons, and define the term *receptive field*.

LO 6.13 Describe the characteristics of the receptive fields of retinal ganglion cells, lateral geniculate neurons, and striate neurons of lower layer IV.

LO 6.14 Describe the characteristics of the receptive fields of simple and complex cells.

LO 6.15 Describe the organization of the primary visual cortex.

LO 6.16 Describe the changing view of visual system receptive fields.

Seeing Color

LO 6.17 Describe the component and opponent-process theories of color vision.

LO 6.18 Describe Land's demonstration of color constancy, and explain his retinex theory.

Cortical Mechanisms of Vision and Conscious Awareness

LO 6.19 Describe the three classes of visual cortex, and identify their locations in the brain.

LO 6.20 Explain what happens when an area of primary visual cortex is damaged.

LO 6.21 Describe the areas of secondary visual cortex and association cortex involved in vision.

LO 6.22 Explain the difference between the dorsal and ventral streams and the functions that have been attributed to each stream by different theories.

LO 6.23 Describe the phenomenon of prosopagnosia and discuss the associated theoretical issues.

LO 6.24 Describe the phenomenon of akinetopsia and discuss the associated theoretical issues.

This chapter is about your visual system. Most people think their visual system has evolved to respond as accurately as possible to the patterns of light that enter their eyes. They recognize the obvious limitations in the accuracy of their visual system, of course; and they appreciate those curious instances, termed *visual illusions*, in which it is "tricked" into seeing things the way they aren't. But such shortcomings are generally regarded as minor imperfections in a system that responds as faithfully as possible to the external world.

But, despite the intuitive appeal of thinking about it in this way, this is not how the visual system works. The visual system does not produce an accurate internal copy of the external world. It does much more. From the tiny, distorted, upside-down, two-dimensional retinal images projected on the visual receptors that line the backs of the eyes, the visual system creates an accurate, richly detailed, three-dimensional perception that is—and this is the really important part—in some respects even better than the external reality from which it was created. Our primary goal in this chapter is to help you appreciate the inherent creativity of your own visual system.

You will learn in this chapter that understanding the visual system requires the integration of two types of research: (1) research that probes the visual system with sophisticated neuroanatomical, neurochemical, and neurophysiological techniques; and (2) research that focuses on the assessment of what we see. Both types of research receive substantial coverage in this chapter, but it is the second type that provides you with a unique educational opportunity: the opportunity to participate in the very research you are studying. Throughout this chapter, you will be encouraged to participate in a series of Check It Out demonstrations designed to illustrate the relevance of what you are learning in this text to life outside its pages.

This chapter is composed of six modules. The first three modules take you on a journey from the external visual world to the visual receptors of the retina and from there over the major visual pathway to the primary visual cortex. The next two modules describe how the neurons of this visual pathway mediate the perception of two particularly important features of the visual world: edges and color. The final module deals with the flow of visual signals from the primary visual cortex to other parts of the cortex that participate in the complex process of vision.

Before you begin the first module of the chapter, we'd like you to consider an interesting clinical case. Have you ever wondered whether one person's subjective experiences are like those of others? This case provides evidence that at least some of them are. It was reported by Whitman Richards (1971), and his subject was his wife. Mrs. Richards suffered from migraine headaches (see Goadsby, 2015), and like 20 percent of migraine sufferers, she often experienced visual displays,

Clinical Implications

called *fortification illusions*, prior to her attacks (see Charles & Baca, 2013; Thissen et al., 2014).

The Case of Mrs. Richards: Fortification Illusions and the Astronomer

Each fortification illusion began with a gray area of blindness near the center of her visual field—see Figure 6.1. During the next few minutes, the gray area would begin to expand into a horseshoe shape, with a zigzag pattern of flickering lines at its advancing edge (this pattern reminded people of the plans for a fortification, hence the name of the illusions).

It normally took about 20 minutes for the lines and the trailing area of blindness to reach the periphery of her visual field. At this point, her headache would usually begin.

Because the illusion expanded so slowly, Mrs. Richards was able to stare at a point on the center of a blank sheet of paper and periodically trace on the sheet the details of her illusion. This method made it apparent that the lines became thicker and the expansion of the area of blindness occurred faster as the illusion spread into the periphery.

Interestingly, Dr. Richards discovered that a similar set of drawings was published in 1870 by the famous British astronomer George Biddell Airy. They were virtually identical to those done by Mrs. Richards.

Figure 6.1 The fortification illusions associated with migraine headaches.

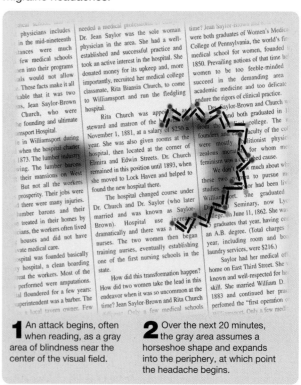

1 An attack begins, often when reading, as a gray area of blindness near the center of the visual field.

2 Over the next 20 minutes, the gray area assumes a horseshoe shape and expands into the periphery, at which point the headache begins.

We will return to fortification illusions after you have learned a bit about the visual system. At that point, you will be better able to appreciate their significance.

Light Enters the Eye and Reaches the Retina

Everybody knows that cats, owls, and other nocturnal animals can see in the dark. Right? Wrong! Some animals have special adaptations that allow them to see under very dim illumination, but no animal can see in complete darkness. The light reflected into your eyes from the objects around you is the basis for your ability to see them; if there is no light, there is no vision.

You may recall from high-school physics that light can be thought of in two different ways: as discrete particles of energy, called photons, traveling through space at about 300,000 kilometers (186,000 miles) per second, or as waves of energy. Both theories are useful; in some ways, light behaves like particles; and in others, it behaves like waves. Physicists have learned to live with this nagging inconsistency, and we must do the same.

Light is sometimes defined as waves of electromagnetic energy between 380 and 760 *nanometers* (billionths of a meter) in length (see Figure 6.2). There is nothing special about these wavelengths except that the human visual system responds to them. In fact, some animals **[Evolutionary Perspective]** can see wavelengths that we cannot (see Gehring, 2014). For example, rattlesnakes can see *infrared waves*, which are too long for humans to see; as a result, they can see warm-blooded prey in what for us would be complete darkness. So, if we were writing this text for rattlesnakes, we would be forced to provide a different definition of light for them.

Wavelength and intensity are two properties of light that are of particular interest—wavelength because it plays an important role in the perception of color, and intensity because it plays an important role in the perception of brightness. In everyday language, the concepts of *wavelength* and *color* are often used interchangeably and so are *intensity* and *brightness*. For example, we commonly refer to an intense light with a wavelength of 700 nanometers as being a bright red light (see Figure 6.2), when in fact it is our perception of the light, not the light itself, that is bright and red. We know that these distinctions may seem trivial to you now, but by the end of the chapter you will appreciate their importance.

Figure 6.2 The electromagnetic spectrum and the colors associated with wavelengths visible to humans.

Watch this video on MyPsychLab

THE VISUAL SPECTRUM AND PROPERTIES OF LIGHT

Pupil and Lens

LO 6.1 Explain how the pupil and the lens can affect the image that falls on the retina.

The amount of light reaching the *retinas* is regulated by the donut-shaped bands of contractile tissue, the *irises*, which give our eyes their characteristic color (see Figure 6.3). Light enters the eye through the *pupil*, the hole in the iris. The adjustment of pupil size in response to changes in illumination represents a compromise between **sensitivity** (the ability to detect the presence of dimly lit objects) and **acuity** (the ability to see the details of objects).

Figure 6.3 The human eye. Light enters the eye through the pupil, whose size is regulated by the iris. The iris gives the eye its characteristic color—blue, brown, or other.

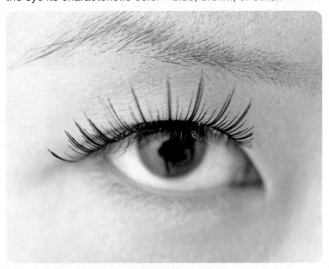

When the level of illumination is high and sensitivity is thus not important, the visual system takes advantage of the situation by constricting the pupils. When the pupils are constricted, the image falling on each retina is sharper and there is a greater *depth of focus*; that is, a greater range of depths is simultaneously kept in focus on the retinas. However, when the level of illumination is too low to adequately activate the receptors, the pupils dilate to let in more light, thereby sacrificing acuity and depth of focus.

Behind each pupil is a *lens*, which focuses incoming light on the retina (see Figure 6.4). When we direct our gaze at something near, the tension on the ligaments holding each lens in place is adjusted by the **ciliary muscles**, and the lens assumes its natural cylindrical shape. This increases the ability of the lens to *refract* (bend) light and thus brings close objects into sharp focus. When we focus on a distant object, the lens is flattened. The process of adjusting the configuration of the lenses to bring images into focus on the retina is called **accommodation**.

Eye Position and Binocular Disparity

LO 6.2 Explain why some vertebrates have one eye on each side of their head whereas other vertebrates have their eyes mounted side-by-side on the front of their heads. Also, explain the importance of binocular disparity.

No description of the eyes of vertebrates would be complete without a discussion of their most obvious feature: the fact that they

Figure 6.4 The human eye, a product of approximately 600 million years of evolution (Based on Lamb, Collin, & Pugh, 2007).

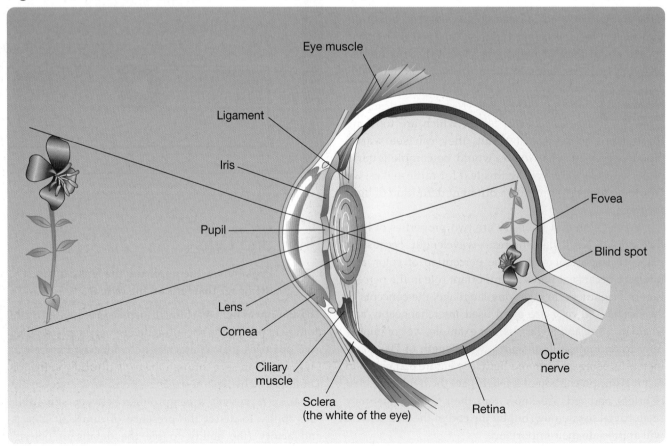

come in pairs. One reason vertebrates have two eyes is that vertebrates have two sides: left and right. By having one eye on each side, which is by far the most common arrangement, vertebrates can see in almost every direction without moving their heads. But then why do some vertebrates, including humans, have their eyes mounted side by side on the front of their heads? (See the Check It Out demonstration at the bottom.) This arrangement sacrifices the ability to see behind so that what is in front can be viewed through both eyes simultaneously—an arrangement that is an important basis for our visual system's ability to create three-dimensional perceptions (to see depth) from two-dimensional retinal images.

Evolutionary Perspective Why do you think the two-eyes-on-the-front arrangement has evolved in some species but not in others? (After you've written your answer, see the following Check It Out demonstration below for more on this issue.)

The movements of your eyes are coordinated so that each point in your visual world is projected to corresponding points on your two retinas. To accomplish this, your eyes must *converge* (turn slightly inward); convergence is greatest when you are inspecting things that are close. But the positions of the images on your two retinas can never correspond exactly because your two eyes do not

Check It Out
The Position of Eyes

Here you see three animals whose eyes are on the front of their heads (a human, an owl, and a lion) and three whose eyes are on the sides of their heads (an antelope, a canary, and a squirrel). Why do a few vertebrate species have their eyes side by side on the front of the head while most species have one eye on each side?

In general, predators tend to have the front-facing eyes because this enables them to accurately perceive how far away prey animals are; prey animals tend to have side-facing eyes because this gives them a larger field of vision and the ability to see predators approaching from most directions.

Check It Out
Binocular Disparity and the Mysterious Cocktail Sausage

If you compare the views from each eye (by quickly closing one eye and then the other) of objects at various distances in front of you—for example, your finger held at different distances—you will notice that the disparity between the two views is greater for closer objects. Now try the mysterious demonstration of the cocktail sausage. Face the farthest wall in the room (or some other distant object) and bring the tips of your two pointing fingers together at

arm's length in front of you—with the backs of your fingers away from you (unless you prefer sausages with fingernails). Now, with both eyes open, look through the notch between your touching fingertips, but focus on the wall. Do you see the cocktail sausage between your fingertips? Where did it come from? To prove to yourself that the sausage is a product of binocularity, make it disappear by shutting one eye. Warning: Do not eat this sausage.

view the world from exactly the same position. **Binocular disparity**—the difference in the position of the same image on the two retinas—is greater for close objects than for distant objects; therefore, your visual system can use the degree of binocular disparity to construct one three-dimensional perception from two two-dimensional retinal images (see Lappin, 2014; Westheimer, 2009). (Look at the Check It Out demonstration at the bottom of the previous page.)

The Retina and Translation of Light into Neural Signals

After light passes through the pupil and the lens, it reaches the retina. The retina converts light to neural signals, conducts them toward the CNS, and participates in the processing of the signals (Hoon et al., 2014; Seung & Sümbül, 2014).

Structure of the Retina

LO 6.3   Describe the structure of the retina, and name the cell types that make up the retina.

Figure 6.5 illustrates the fundamental cellular structure of the retina. The retina is composed of five different types of neurons: **receptors**, **horizontal cells**, **bipolar cells**, **amacrine cells**, and **retinal ganglion cells**. Each of these five types of retinal neurons comes in a variety of subtypes: More than 60 different kinds of retinal neurons have been identified (see Cepko, 2015; Seung & Sümbül, 2014), including about 30 different retinal ganglion cells (see Baden et al., 2016). Notice that the amacrine cells and the horizontal cells are specialized for *lateral communication* (communication across the major channels of sensory input). Retinal neurons communicate both chemically via synapses and electrically via gap junctions (see Pereda, 2014).

Also notice in Figure 6.5 that the retina is in a sense inside-out: Light reaches the receptor layer only after passing through the other four layers. Then, once the receptors have been activated, the neural message is transmitted back out through the retinal layers to the retinal ganglion cells, whose axons project across the outside of the retina before gathering together in a bundle and exiting the eyeball. This inside-out arrangement creates two visual problems: One is that the incoming light is distorted by the retinal tissue through which it must pass before reaching the receptors. The other is that for the bundle of retinal ganglion cell axons to leave the eye, there must be a gap in the receptor layer; this gap is called the **blind spot**.

Figure 6.5 The cellular structure of the mammalian retina.

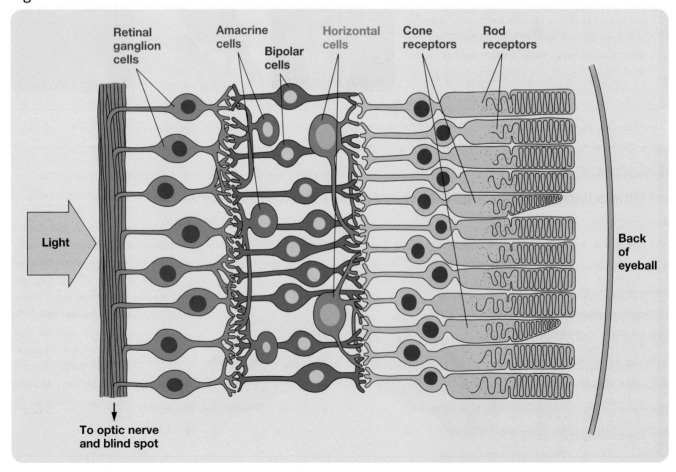

Figure 6.6 A section of the retina. The fovea is the indentation at the center of the retina; it is specialized for high-acuity vision.

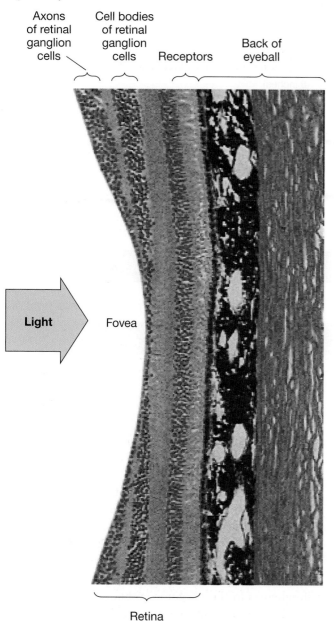

Axons of retinal ganglion cells   Cell bodies of retinal ganglion cells   Receptors   Back of eyeball

Light   Fovea

Retina

in the gaps in your retinal images. When the visual system detects a straight bar going into one side of the blind spot and another straight bar leaving the other side, it fills in the missing bit for you; and what you see is a continuous straight bar, regardless of what is actually there. The completion phenomenon is one of the most compelling demonstrations that the visual system does much more than make a faithful copy of the external world.

It is a mistake to think that completion is merely a response to blind spots. Indeed, completion plays an important role in normal vision (see Murray & Herrmann, 2013; Weil & Rees, 2011). When you look at an object, your visual system does not conduct an image of that object from your retina to your cortex. Instead, it extracts key information about the object—primarily information about its edges and their location—and conducts that information to the cortex, where a perception of the entire object is created from that partial information. For example, the color and brightness of large unpatterned surfaces are not perceived directly but are filled in (completed) by a completion process called **surface interpolation** (the process by which we perceive surfaces; the visual system extracts information about edges and from it infers the appearance of large surfaces). The central role of surface interpolation in vision is an extremely important but counterintuitive concept. We suggest you read this paragraph again and think about it. Are your creative thinking skills developed enough to feel comfortable with this new way of thinking about your own visual system?

Thinking Creatively

Thinking Creatively Try to give a specific example of a situation where surface interpolation would occur.

Cone and Rod Vision

LO 6.4 Describe the duplexity theory of vision, and explain the differences between the photopic and scotopic systems.

You likely noticed in Figure 6.5 that there are two different types of receptors in the human retina: cone-shaped receptors called **cones** and rod-shaped receptors called **rods** (see Figure 6.7). The existence of these two types of receptors puzzled researchers until 1866, when it was first noticed that species active only in the day tend to have cone-only retinas, and species active only at night tend to have rod-only retinas.

From this observation emerged the **duplexity theory** of vision—the theory that cones and rods mediate different kinds of vision. **Photopic vision** (cone-mediated vision) predominates in good lighting and provides high-acuity (finely detailed) colored perceptions of the world. In dim illumination, there is not enough light to reliably

The first of these two problems is minimized by the fovea (see Figure 6.6). The **fovea** is an indentation, about 0.33 centimeter in diameter, at the center of the retina; it is the area of the retina that is specialized for high-acuity vision (for seeing fine details). The thinning of the retinal ganglion cell layer at the fovea reduces the distortion of incoming light. The blind spot, the second of the two visual problems created by the inside-out structure of the retina, requires a more creative solution—which is illustrated in the Check It Out demonstration on the next page.

In the Check It Out demonstration, you will experience **completion** (or *filling in*). The visual system uses information provided by the receptors around the blind spot to fill

Check It Out
Your Blind Spot and Completion

First, prove to yourself that you do have areas of blindness that correspond to your retinal blind spots. Close your left eye and stare directly at the A below, trying as hard as you can to not shift your gaze. While keeping the gaze of your right eye fixed on the A, hold the text at different distances from you until the black dot to the right of the A becomes focused on your blind spot and disappears at about 20 centimeters (8 inches).

If each eye has a blind spot, why is there not a black hole in your perception of the world when you look at it with one eye? You will discover the answer by focusing on B with your right eye while holding the text at the same distance as before. Suddenly, the broken line to the right of B will become whole. Now focus on C at the same distance with your right eye. What do you see?

Figure 6.7 Cones and rods. The red colored cells are cones; the blue colored cells are rods.

excite the cones, and the more sensitive **scotopic vision** (rod-mediated vision) predominates. However, the sensitivity of scotopic vision is not achieved without cost: Scotopic vision lacks both the detail and the color of photopic vision.

The differences between photopic and scotopic vision result in part from a difference in the way the two systems are "wired." As Figure 6.8 illustrates, there is a large difference in convergence between the two systems. In the scotopic system, the output of several hundred rods converges on a single retinal ganglion cell, whereas in the photopic system, only a few cones converge on each retinal ganglion cell. As a result, the effects of dim light simultaneously stimulating many rods can summate (add) to influence the firing of the retinal ganglion cell onto which the output of the stimulated rods converges, whereas the effects of the same dim light applied to a sheet of cones cannot summate to the same degree, and the retinal ganglion cells may not respond at all to the light.

The convergent scotopic system pays for its high degree of sensitivity with a low level of acuity. When a retinal ganglion cell that receives input from hundreds of rods changes its firing, the brain has no way of knowing which portion of the rods contributed to the change. Although a more intense light is required to change the firing of a retinal ganglion cell that receives signals from cones, when such a retinal ganglion cell

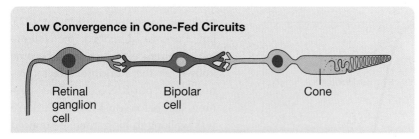

Figure 6.8 A schematic representation of the convergence of cones and rods on retinal ganglion cells. There is a low degree of convergence in cone-fed pathways and a high degree of convergence in rod-fed pathways.

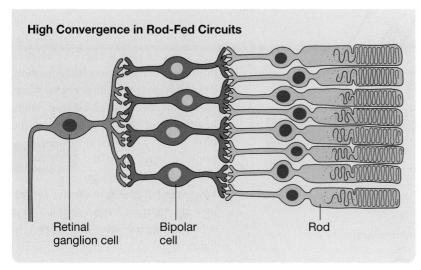

Figure 6.9 The distribution of cones and rods over the human retina. The figure illustrates the number of cones and rods per square millimeter as a function of distance from the center of the fovea. (Based on Lindsay & Norman, 1977.)

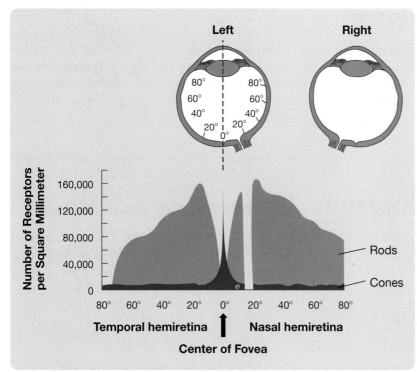

does react, there is less ambiguity about the location of the stimulus that triggered the reaction.

Cones and rods differ in their distribution on the retina. As Figure 6.9 illustrates, there are no rods at all in the fovea, only cones. At the boundaries of the foveal indentation, the proportion of cones declines markedly, and there is an increase in the number of rods. The density of rods reaches a maximum at 20 degrees from the center of the fovea. Notice that there are more rods in the *nasal hemiretina* (the half of each retina next to the nose) than in the *temporal hemiretina* (the half of each retina next to the temples).

Spectral Sensitivity

LO 6.5 **Explain the difference between the photopic and scotopic spectral sensitivity curves, and explain how that difference can account for the Purkinje effect.**

Generally speaking, more intense lights appear brighter. However, wavelength also has a substantial effect on the perception of brightness. Because our visual systems are not equally sensitive to all wavelengths in the visible spectrum, lights of the same intensity but of different wavelengths can differ markedly in brightness. A graph of the relative brightness of lights of the same intensity presented at different wavelengths is called a *spectral sensitivity curve*.

By far the most important thing to remember about spectral sensitivity curves is that humans and other animals with both cones and rods have two of them: a **photopic spectral sensitivity curve** and a **scotopic spectral sensitivity curve**. The photopic spectral sensitivity of humans can be determined by having subjects judge the relative brightness of different wavelengths of light shone on the fovea. Their scotopic spectral sensitivity can be determined by asking subjects to judge the relative brightness of different wavelengths of light shone on the periphery of the retina at an intensity too low to activate the few peripheral cones located there.

The photopic and scotopic spectral sensitivity curves of human subjects are

Figure 6.10 Human photopic (cone) and scotopic (rod) spectral sensitivity curves. The peak of each curve has been arbitrarily set at 100 percent.

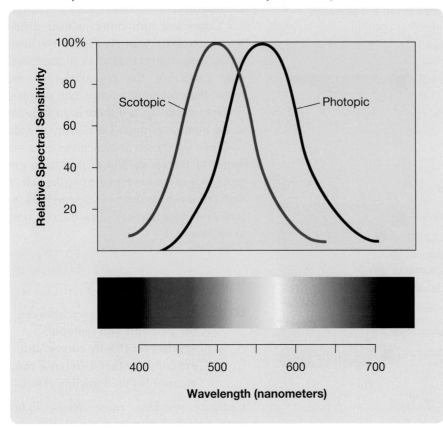

Because of the difference in photopic and scotopic spectral sensitivity, an interesting visual effect can be observed during the transition from photopic to scotopic vision. In 1825, Jan Purkinje described the following occurrence, which has become known as the **Purkinje effect** (pronounced "pur-KIN-jee"). One evening, just before dusk, while Purkinje was walking in his garden, he noticed how bright most of his yellow and red flowers appeared in relation to his blue ones. What amazed him was that just a few minutes later the relative brightness of his flowers had somehow been reversed; the entire scene, when viewed at night, appeared completely in shades of gray, but most of the blue flowers appeared as brighter grays than the yellow and red ones. Can you explain this shift in relative brightness by referring to the photopic and scotopic spectral sensitivity curves in Figure 6.10?

Thinking Creatively

plotted in Figure 6.10. Under photopic conditions, notice that the visual system is maximally sensitive to wavelengths of about 560 nanometers; thus, under photopic conditions, a light at 500 nanometers would have to be much more intense than one at 560 nanometers to be seen as equally bright. In contrast, under scotopic conditions, the visual system is maximally sensitive to wavelengths of about 500 nanometers; thus, under scotopic conditions, a light of 560 nanometers would have to be much more intense than one at 500 nanometers to be seen as equally bright.

Eye Movement

LO 6.6 Describe the three types of involuntary fixational eye movements, and explain what happens when all eye movements are blocked.

If cones are responsible for mediating high-acuity color vision under photopic conditions, how can they accomplish their task when most of them are crammed into the fovea? (See Figure 6.9) Look around you. What you see is not a few colored details at the center of a grayish scene. You seem to see an expansive, richly detailed,

Check It Out
Periphery of Your Retina Does Not Mediate the Perception of Detail or Color

Close your left eye, and with your right eye stare at the fixation point (+) at a distance of about 12 centimeters (4.75 inches) from the page. Be very careful that your gaze does not shift. You will notice when your gaze is totally fixed that it is difficult to see

detail and color at 20 degrees or more from the fixation point because there are so few cones there. Now look at the page again with your right eye, but this time without fixing your gaze. Notice the difference that eye movement makes to your vision.

W	**F**	**D**	**M**	**E**	**A**	**✛**
50°	40°	30°	20°	10°	5°	0°

lavishly colored world. How can such a perception be the product of a photopic system that, for the most part, is restricted to a few degrees in the center of your *visual field* (the entire area that you can see at a particular moment)? The Check It Out demonstration on the previous page provides a clue. It shows that what we see is determined not just by what is projected on the retina at that instant. Although we are not aware of it, the eyes continually scan the visual field, and our visual perception at any instant is a summation of recent visual information. It is because of this *temporal integration* that the world does not vanish momentarily each time we blink.

Our eyes continuously move even when we try to keep them still (i.e., fixated). Involuntary **fixational eye movements** are of three kinds: tremor, drifts, and **saccades** (small jerky movements, or flicks; pronounced "sah-KAHDS"). Although we are normally unaware of fixational eye movements, they have a critical visual function (see Ibbotson & Krekelberg, 2011; Spering & Carrasco, 2015; Zirnsak & Moore, 2014). When eye movements or their main effect (movement of images on the retina) are blocked, visual objects begin to fade and disappear. This happens because most visual neurons respond only to changing images; if retinal images are artificially stabilized (kept from moving on the retina), the images start to disappear and reappear. Thus, eye movements enable us to see during fixation by keeping the images moving on the retina.

Visual Transduction: The Conversion of Light to Neural Signals

LO 6.7   Describe the process of visual transduction.

Transduction is the conversion of one form of energy to another. *Visual transduction* is the conversion of light to neural signals by the visual receptors. A breakthrough in the study of visual transduction came in 1876 when a red *pigment* (a pigment is any substance that absorbs light) was extracted from rods. This pigment had a curious property. When the pigment—which became known as **rhodopsin**—was exposed to continuous intense light, it was *bleached* (lost its color) and lost its ability to absorb light, but when it was returned to the dark, it regained both its redness and its light-absorbing capacity.

It is now clear that rhodopsin's absorption of light (and the accompanying bleaching) is the first step in rod-mediated vision. Evidence comes from demonstrations that the degree to which rhodopsin absorbs light in various situations predicts how humans see under the very same conditions. For example, it has been shown that the degree to which rhodopsin absorbs lights of different wavelengths is related to the ability of humans and other animals with rods to detect the presence of different wavelengths of light under scotopic conditions. Figure 6.11 illustrates the relationship between the **absorption spectrum** of rhodopsin and the human scotopic spectral sensitivity curve. The goodness of the fit leaves little doubt that, in dim light, our sensitivity to various wavelengths is a direct consequence of rhodopsin's ability to absorb them.

Rhodopsin is a G-protein–coupled receptor (see Chapter 4) that responds to light rather than to neurotransmitter molecules (see Krishnan & Schiöth, 2015; Manglik & Kobilka, 2014). Rhodopsin receptors, like other G-protein–coupled receptors, initiate a cascade of intracellular chemical events when they are activated (see Figure 6.12). When

Figure 6.11 The absorption spectrum of rhodopsin compared with the human scotopic spectral sensitivity curve.

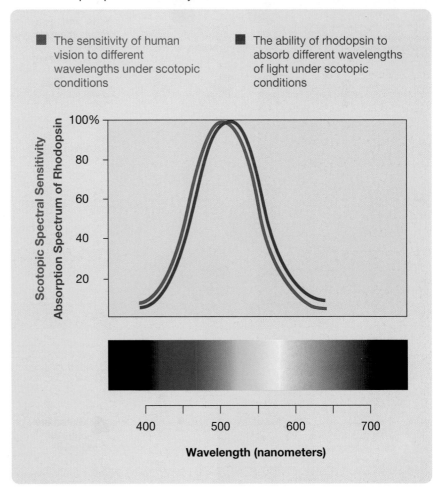

rods are in darkness, their sodium channels are partially open, thus keeping the rods slightly depolarized and allowing a steady flow of excitatory glutamate neurotransmitter molecules to emanate from them. However, when rhodopsin receptors are bleached by light, the resulting cascade of intracellular chemical events closes the sodium channels, hyperpolarizes the rods, and reduces the release of glutamate (see Oesch, Kothmann, & Diamond, 2011). The transduction of light by rods exemplifies an important point: Signals are often transmitted through neural systems by inhibition.

Figure 6.12 The inhibitory response of rods to light. When light bleaches rhodopsin molecules, the rods' sodium channels close; as a result, the rods become hyperpolarized and release less glutamate.

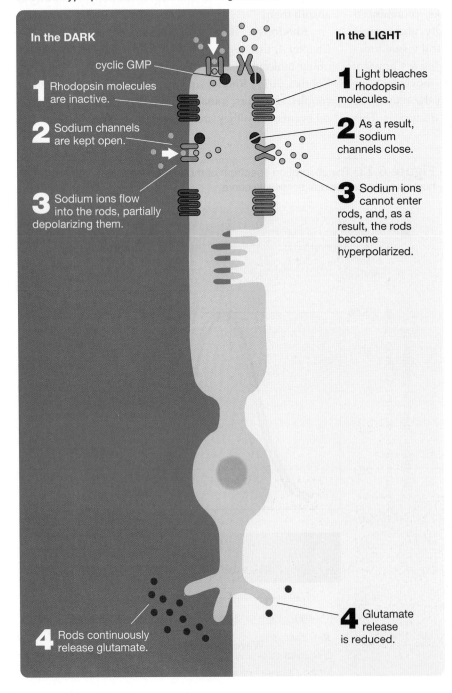

From Retina to Primary Visual Cortex

Many pathways in the brain carry visual information. By far the largest and most thoroughly studied visual pathways are the **retina-geniculate-striate pathways**, which conduct signals from each retina to the **primary visual cortex**, or striate cortex, via the **lateral geniculate nuclei** of the thalamus.

Retina-Geniculate-Striate System

LO 6.8   Describe the components and layout of the retina-geniculate-striate system.

About 90 percent of axons of retinal ganglion cells become part of the retina-geniculate-striate pathways (see Tong, 2003). No other sensory system has such a predominant pair (left and right) of pathways to the cortex. The organization of these visual pathways is illustrated in Figure 6.13. Examine it carefully.

The main idea to take away from Figure 6.13 is that all signals from the left visual field reach the right primary visual cortex, either ipsilaterally from the *temporal hemiretina* of the right eye or contralaterally (via the *optic chiasm*) from the *nasal hemiretina* of the left eye—and that the opposite is true of all signals from the right visual field. Each lateral geniculate nucleus has six layers, and each layer of each nucleus receives input from all parts of the contralateral visual field of one eye. In other words, each lateral geniculate nucleus receives visual input only from the contralateral visual field; three layers receive input from one eye, and three from the other. Most of the lateral geniculate neurons that project to the primary visual cortex terminate in the lower part of cortical layer IV (see Muckli & Petro, 2013), producing a characteristic stripe, or striation, when viewed in cross section—hence, primary visual cortex is often referred to as *striate cortex*.

Figure 6.13 The retina-geniculate-striate system: the neural projections from the retinas through the lateral geniculate nuclei to the left and right primary visual cortex (striate cortex). The colors indicate the flow of information from various parts of the receptive fields of each eye to various parts of the visual system.

Watch this video on MyPsychLab

CHALK IT UP! MAPPING THE ROUTES FROM EYES TO VISUAL CORTEX

Retinotopic Organization

LO 6.9 In the context of the retina-geniculate-striate system, explain what is meant by retinotopic.

The retina-geniculate-striate system is **retinotopic**; each level of the system is organized like a map of the retina. This means two stimuli presented to adjacent areas of the retina excite adjacent neurons at all levels of the system. The retinotopic layout of the primary visual cortex has a disproportionate representation of the fovea; although the fovea is only a small part of the retina, a relatively large proportion of the primary visual cortex (about 25 percent) is dedicated to the analysis of its input.

A dramatic demonstration of the retinotopic organization of the primary visual cortex was provided by Dobelle, Mladejovsky, and Girvin (1974). They implanted an array of electrodes in the primary visual cortex of patients who were blind because of damage to their eyes. If electrical current was administered simultaneously through an array of electrodes forming a shape, such as a cross, on the surface of a patient's cortex, the patient reported "seeing" a glowing image of that shape. This finding, and related work on retinal implants (see Chuang, Margo, & Greenberg, 2014), could be the basis for the development of visual prostheses that could benefit many blind people (see Shepherd et al., 2013).

Clinical Implications Briefly explain why this prosthesis is a demonstration of the retinotopic organization of the primary visual cortex.

The M and P Channels

LO 6.10 Describe the M and P channels.

Not apparent in Figure 6.13 is the fact that at least two parallel channels of communication flow through each lateral geniculate nucleus. One channel runs through the top four layers. These layers are called the **parvocellular layers** (or

P layers) because they are composed of neurons with small cell bodies (*parvo* means "small"). The other channel runs through the bottom two layers, which are called the **magnocellular layers** (or *M layers*) because they are composed of neurons with large cell bodies (*magno* means "large").

The parvocellular neurons are particularly responsive to color, fine pattern details, and stationary or slowly moving objects. In contrast, the magnocellular neurons are particularly responsive to movement. Cones provide the majority of the input to the P layers, whereas rods provide the majority of the input to the M layers.

The parvocellular and magnocellular neurons project to different areas in the lower part of layer IV of the striate cortex. In turn, these M and P areas of lower layer IV project to different areas of visual cortex.

Watch this video on MyPsychLab
PROCESSING IN THE RETINA

Scan Your Brain

This is a good place to pause to scan your brain. Are you ready to proceed to the next two modules of the chapter, which describe how the visual system mediates the perception of edges and color? Find out by filling in the blanks in the following statements. The correct answers are provided at the end of the exercise. Before proceeding, review material related to your errors and omissions.

1. The _____ are donut-shaped bands of contractile tissue that regulate the amount of light that reaches the retina.

2. Prey animals have _____ eyes, which allow them to see the predators approaching from most directions due to a larger field of vision.

3. _____ is the difference in the position of the same image on two retinas.

4. Amacrine cells and horizontal cells are responsible for _____ communication.

5. _____ is the process of perceiving large surfaces by extracting information about the edges and making inferences about the shape from it.

6. In scotopic vision, hundreds of _____ converge on a single retinal ganglion cell.

7. The majority of the visual neurons respond only to _____ images.

8. Rhodopsin is a _____ receptor that does not respond to neurotransmitter molecules.

9. The path that all the signals take to reach the right primary visual cortex from the left visual field is either _____ or contralateral.

Scan Your Brain answers: (1) irises, (2) side-facing, (3) Binocular disparity, (4) lateral, (5) Surface interpolation, (6) rods, (7) changing, (8) G-protein-coupled, (9) ipsilateral.

Seeing Edges

Edge perception (seeing edges) does not sound like a particularly important topic, but it is. Edges are the most informative features of any visual display because they define the extent and position of the various objects in it. Given the importance of perceiving visual edges and the unrelenting pressure of natural selection, it is not surprising that the visual systems of many species are particularly good at edge perception.

Before considering the visual mechanisms underlying edge perception, it is important to appreciate exactly what a visual edge is. In a sense, a visual edge is nothing: It is merely the place where two different areas of a visual image meet.

Accordingly, the perception of an edge is really the perception of a contrast between two adjacent areas of the visual field. This module reviews the perception of edges (the perception of contrast) between areas that differ from one another in brightness (i.e., that show brightness contrast).

Lateral Inhibition and Contrast Enhancement

LO 6.11 Explain the neural basis of contrast enhancement.

Carefully examine the stripes in Figure 6.14. The intensity graph in the figure indicates what is there—a series of

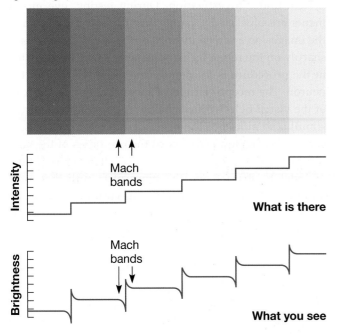

In order to understand the physiological basis of contrast enhancement in the horseshoe crab, you must know two things. The first is that if a single ommatidium is illuminated, it fires at a rate that is proportional to the intensity of the light striking it; more intense lights produce more firing. The second is that when a receptor fires, it inhibits its neighbors via the lateral neural network; this inhibition is called **lateral inhibition** because it spreads laterally across the array of receptors. The amount of lateral inhibition produced by a receptor is greatest when the receptor is most intensely illuminated, and the inhibition has its greatest effect on the receptor's immediate neighbors.

The neural basis of contrast enhancement can be understood in terms of the firing rates of the receptors on each side of an edge, as indicated in Figure 6.15. Notice that the receptor adjacent to the edge on the more intense side (receptor D) fires more than the other intensely illuminated receptors (A, B, C), while the receptor adjacent to the edge on the less well-illuminated side (receptor E) fires less than the other receptors on that side (F, G, H). Lateral inhibition accounts for these differences. Receptors A, B, and C all fire at the same rate because they are all receiving the same high level of stimulation and the same high degree of lateral inhibition from all their highly stimulated neighbors. Receptor D fires more than A, B, and C because it receives as much stimulation as they do but less inhibition from its neighbors, many of which are on the dimmer side of

homogeneous stripes of different intensity. But this is not exactly what you see, is it? What you see is indicated in the brightness graph. Adjacent to each edge, the brighter stripe looks brighter than it really is and the darker stripe looks darker than it really is. The nonexistent stripes of brightness and darkness running adjacent to the edges are called *Mach bands*; they enhance the contrast at each edge and make the edge easier to see.

It is important to appreciate that **contrast enhancement** is not something that occurs just in books. Although we are normally unaware of it, every edge we look at is highlighted for us by the contrast-enhancing mechanisms of our nervous systems. In effect, our perception of edges is better than the real thing (as determined by measurements of the physical properties of the light entering our eyes).

The classic studies of the physiological basis of contrast enhancement were conducted on the eyes of an unlikely subject: the *horseshoe crab* (e.g., Ratliff, 1972). The lateral eyes of the horseshoe crab are ideal for certain types of neurophysiological research. Unlike mammalian eyes, they are composed of very large receptors, called *ommatidia*, each with its own large axon. The axons of the ommatidia are interconnected by a lateral neural network.

Evolutionary Perspective

Figure 6.15 How lateral inhibition produces contrast enhancement. (Based on Ratliff, 1972.)

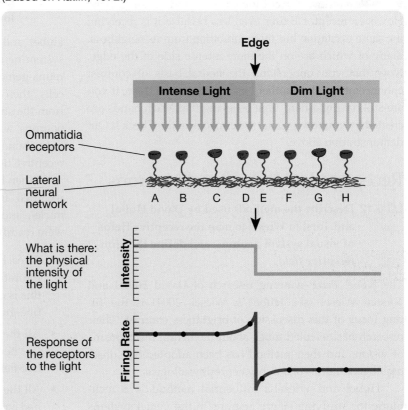

Check It Out

Contrast Enhancement and Mach Bands

The Mach band demonstration is so compelling, you may be confused by it. You may think the Mach bands below have been created by the printers of the text rather than by your own visual system. To prove to yourself that the Mach bands are a creation of your visual system, view each stripe individually by covering the adjacent ones with two pieces of paper. You will see at once that each stripe is completely homogeneous. Then take the paper away, and the Mach bands will suddenly reappear along the edges of the stripe.

the edge. Now consider the receptors on the dimmer side. Receptors F, G, and H fire at the same rate because they are all stimulated by the same low level of light and receiving the same low level of inhibition from their neighbors. However, receptor E fires even less because it is receiving the same excitation but more inhibition from its neighbors, many of which are on the more intense side of the edge. Now that you understand the neural basis of contrast enhancement, take another look at Figure 6.14. Also, if you are still having a hard time believing that Mach bands are created by your own visual system, look at the Check It Out demonstration above.

Receptive Fields of Visual Neurons

LO 6.12 Describe the methods used by David Hubel and Torsten Wiesel to map the receptive fields of visual system neurons, and define the term *receptive field*.

The Nobel Prize–winning research of David Hubel and Torsten Wiesel (see Hubel & Wiesel, 2004) is the fitting focus of this discussion of brightness contrast. Their research has revealed much about the neural mechanisms of vision, and their method has been adopted by subsequent generations of sensory neurophysiologists.

Hubel and Wiesel's influential method is a technique for studying single neurons in the visual systems of laboratory animals—their research subjects were cats and monkeys. First, the tip of a microelectrode is positioned near a single neuron in the part of the visual system under investigation. During testing, eye movements are blocked by paralyzing the eye muscles, and the images on a screen in front of the subject are focused sharply on the retina by an adjustable lens. The next step in the procedure is to identify the receptive field of the neuron. The **receptive field** of a visual neuron is the area of the visual field within which it is possible for a visual stimulus to influence the firing of that neuron. The final step in the method is to record the responses of the neuron to various simple stimuli within its receptive field in order to characterize the types of stimuli that most influence its activity. Then the electrode is advanced slightly, and the entire process of identifying and characterizing the receptive field properties is repeated for another neuron, and then for another, and another, and so on. The general strategy is to begin by studying neurons near the receptors and gradually work up through "higher" and "higher" levels of the system in an effort to understand the increasing complexity of the neural responses at each level.

Receptive Fields: Neurons of the Retina-Geniculate-Striate System

LO 6.13 Describe the characteristics of the receptive fields of retinal ganglion cells, lateral geniculate neurons, and striate neurons of lower layer IV.

Hubel and Wiesel (1979) began their studies of visual system neurons by recording from the three levels of the retina-geniculate-striate system: first from retinal ganglion cells, then from lateral geniculate neurons, and finally from the striate neurons of lower layer IV. They tested the neurons with stationary spots of *achromatic* (uncolored) light shone on the retina. They found little change in the receptive fields as they worked through the levels.

When Hubel and Wiesel compared the receptive fields recorded from retinal ganglion cells, lateral geniculate nuclei, and lower layer IV neurons, four commonalties were readily apparent:

- At each level, the receptive fields in the foveal area of the retina were smaller than those at the periphery; this is consistent with the fact that the fovea mediates fine-grained (high-acuity) vision.

- All the neurons (retinal ganglion cells, lateral geniculate neurons, and lower layer IV neurons) had receptive fields that were circular.

- All the neurons were **monocular**; that is, each neuron had a receptive field in one eye but not the other.

Figure 6.16 The receptive fields of an on-center cell and an off-center cell.

Responses of an on-center cell

There is an "on" response when a spot of light is shone anywhere in the center of the field.

OFF / ON

LIGHT ON

There is an "off" response when a spot of light is shone anywhere in the periphery of the field.

OFF / ON

LIGHT ON

Responses of an off-center cell

There is an "off" response when a spot of light is shone anywhere in the center of the field.

ON / OFF

LIGHT ON

There is an "on" response when a spot of light is shone anywhere in the periphery of the field.

ON / OFF

LIGHT ON

- Many neurons at each of the three levels of the retina-geniculate-striate system had receptive fields that comprised an excitatory area and an inhibitory area separated by a circular boundary.

Let us explain this last point—it is important. When Hubel and Wiesel shone a spot of achromatic light onto the various parts of the receptive fields of a neuron in the retina-geniculate-striate pathway, they discovered two different responses. The neuron responded with either "on" firing or "off" firing, depending on the location of the spot of light in the receptive field. That is, the neuron either displayed a burst of firing when the light was turned on ("*on*" *firing*), or it displayed an inhibition of firing when the light was turned on and a burst of firing when it was turned off ("*off*" *firing*).

For most of the neurons in the retina-geniculate-striate system, the reaction—"on" firing or "off" firing—to a light in a particular part of the receptive field was quite predictable. It depended on whether they were on-center cells or off-center cells, as illustrated in Figure 6.16.

On-center cells respond to lights shone in the central region of their receptive fields with "on" firing and to

lights shone in the periphery of their receptive fields with inhibition, followed by "off" firing when the light is turned off. **Off-center cells** display the opposite pattern: They respond with inhibition and "off" firing in response to lights in the center of their receptive fields and with "on" firing to lights in the periphery of their receptive fields.

In effect, on-center and off-center cells respond best to contrast. Figure 6.17 illustrates this point. The most effective way to influence the firing rate of an on-center or off-center cell is to maximize the contrast between the center and the periphery of its receptive field by illuminating either the entire center or the entire surround (periphery) while leaving the other region completely dark. Diffusely illuminating the entire receptive field has little effect on firing. Hubel and Wiesel thus concluded that one function of many of the neurons in the retina-geniculate-striate system is to respond to the degree of brightness contrast between the two areas of their receptive fields (see Livingstone & Hubel, 1988).

Before moving on, notice one important thing from Figures 6.16 and 6.17 about visual system neurons: Most are continually active, even when there is no visual input (see Lee et al., 2013). Indeed, spontaneous activity is a characteristic of most cerebral neurons, and

Figure 6.17 The responses of an on-center cell to contrast.

The most effective way of maximizing the firing of an on-center or off-center cell is to completely illuminate either the "on area" or the "off area" of its receptive field.

If both areas of a cell's receptive field are illuminated together, there is little reaction from the cell.

responses to external stimuli consume only a small portion of the energy required by ongoing brain activity (see Zhang & Raichle, 2010).

Receptive Fields

LO 6.14 **Describe the characteristics of the receptive fields of simple and complex cells.**

The striate cortex neurons you just read about—that is, the neurons of lower layer IV—are exceptions. Their receptive fields are unlike those of the vast majority of striate neurons. The receptive fields of most primary visual cortex neurons fall into one of two classes: simple or complex. Neither of these classes includes the neurons of lower layer IV.

SIMPLE CORTICAL CELLS. Simple cells, like lower layer IV neurons, have receptive fields that can be divided into antagonistic "on" and "off" regions and are thus unresponsive to diffuse light. And like lower layer IV neurons, they are all monocular. The main difference is that the borders between the "on" and "off" regions of the cortical receptive fields of simple cells are straight lines rather than circles. Several examples of receptive fields of simple cortical cells are presented in Figure 6.18. Notice that simple cells respond best to bars of light in a dark field, dark bars in a light field, or single straight edges between dark and light areas; that each simple cell responds maximally only when its preferred straight-edge stimulus is in a particular position and in a particular orientation (see Vidyasagar & Eysel, 2015); and that the receptive fields of simple cortical cells are rectangular rather than circular.

COMPLEX CORTICAL CELLS. Complex cells are more numerous than simple cells. Like simple cells, complex cells have rectangular receptive fields, respond best to straight-line stimuli in a specific orientation, and are unresponsive to diffuse light. However, complex cells differ from simple cells in three important ways. First, they have larger receptive fields. Second, it is not possible to divide the receptive fields of complex cells into static "on" and "off" regions: A complex cell responds to a particular straight-edge stimulus of a particular orientation regardless of its position within the receptive field of that cell. Thus, if a stimulus (e.g., a 45-degree bar of light) that produces "on" firing in a particular complex cell is swept across that cell's receptive field, the cell will respond continuously to it as it moves across the field. Many complex cells respond more robustly to the movement of a straight line across their receptive fields in a particular direction. Third, unlike simple cortical cells, which are all monocular (respond to stimulation of only one of the eyes), many complex cells are

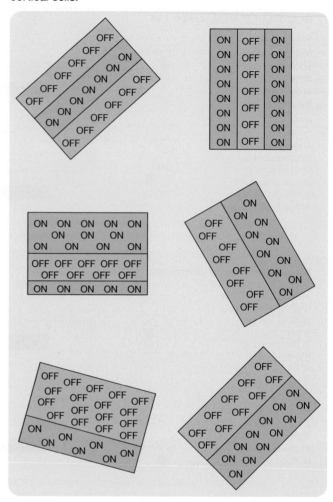

Figure 6.18 Examples of visual fields of simple cortical cells.

binocular (respond to stimulation of either eye). Indeed, in monkeys, more than half the complex cortical cells are binocular.

If the receptive field of a binocular complex cell is measured through one eye and then through the other, the receptive fields in each eye turn out to have almost exactly the same position in the visual field as well as the same orientation preference. In other words, what you learn about the cell by stimulating one eye is confirmed by stimulating the other. What is more, if the appropriate stimulation is applied through both eyes simultaneously, a binocular cell usually fires more robustly than if only one eye is stimulated.

Most of the binocular cells in the primary visual cortex of monkeys display some degree of *ocular dominance*; that is, they respond more robustly to stimulation of one eye than they do to the same stimulation of the other. In addition, some binocular cells fire best when the preferred stimulus is presented to both eyes at the same time but in slightly different positions on the two retinas (e.g., Ohzawa, 1998). In other words, these cells respond best to *retinal disparity* and thus are likely to play a role in depth perception (e.g., Livingstone & Tsao, 1999).

Watch this video on MyPsychLab

MONOCULAR CUES

Organization of Primary Visual Cortex

LO 6.15 Describe the organization of the primary visual cortex.

After describing the receptive fields of visual cortex neurons, Hubel and Wiesel focused their analyses on how neurons with different receptive fields are organized in the primary visual cortex. They reached three important conclusions about the organization of primate visual cortex:

- They concluded that the primary visual cortex was organized into functional *vertical* (in this context, *vertical* means at right angles to the cortical layers) columns: All of the neurons in the same vertical column respond to stimuli applied to the same area of the retina, are dominated by the same eye (if they display dominance or monocularity), and "prefer" the same straight-line angles (if they display a preference for straight-line stimuli).

- They found that the location of various functional columns in primary visual cortex is influenced by the location on the retina of the column's visual fields, by the dominant eye of the column, and by the column's preferred straight-line angle. Hubel and Wiesel concluded that all of the functional columns in the primary visual cortex that analyze input from one area of the retina are clustered together, that half of a cluster receives input from the left eye and the other half receives input from the right eye, and that each cluster includes neurons with preferences for straight-line stimuli of various orientations.

- As Hubel and Wiesel's studies progressed from retina, to thalamus, to lower layer IV of visual cortex, to simple cortical cells, to complex cortical cells, the "preferences" of the neurons became more complex. Hubel and Wiesel concluded that this occurred because neurons with simpler preferences converged on neurons with more complex preferences.

Now that you know a bit about how the visual cortex is organized, you are in a better position to think constructively about Mrs. Richards's fortification illusions.

The Case of Mrs. Richards, Revisited

There was obviously a disturbance in Mrs. Richards's visual system. But where? And what kind of disturbance? And why the straight lines? A simple test located the disturbance. Mrs. Richards was asked to shut one eye and then the other and to report what happened to her illusion when she changed eyes. The answer was "Nothing." This suggested that the disturbance was cortical because the visual cortex is the first part of the retina-geniculate-striate system that contains neurons that receive input from both eyes.

Clinical Implications

This hypothesis was confirmed by a few simple calculations: The gradual acceleration of the illusion as it spread out to the periphery is consistent with a wave of disturbance expanding from the "foveal area" of the primary visual cortex to its boundaries at a constant rate of about 3 millimeters per minute—the illusion accelerated because proportionally less visual cortex is dedicated to receiving signals from the periphery of the visual field.

And why the lines? Would you expect anything else from an area of the cortex whose elements appear to have a preference for straight-line stimuli?

Watch this video on MyPsychLab

VISUAL PROCESSING IN THE STRIATE CORTEX

Changing Concept of Visual Receptive Fields: Contextual Influences in Visual Processing

LO 6.16 Describe the changing view of visual system receptive fields.

Most investigations of the responsiveness of visual system neurons are based on two implicit assumptions. The first is that the mechanisms of visual processing can be best identified by studies using simplified, controllable, artificial stimuli (Einhäuser & König, 2010). The second is that the receptive field properties of each neuron are static, unchanging properties of that neuron. Research that has employed video clips of real scenes involving natural movement suggests that neither of these assumptions is correct (see Felsen & Dan, 2005; Haslinger et al., 2012).

Thinking Creatively

Studies of the responses of visual cortex to natural scenes—just the type of scenes the visual system has evolved to perceive—indicate that the response of a visual cortex neuron depends not only on the stimuli in its receptive field but on the larger scene in which these stimuli are embedded (see Coen-Cagli, Kohn, & Schwartz, 2015). The influences on a visual neuron's activity that are caused by stimuli outside the neuron's receptive field are generally referred to as *contextual influences* (see Gilbert & Li, 2013). Contextual influences can take many forms depending on the exact timing, location, and shape of the visual stimuli under investigation and on the ambient light levels (e.g., Cai, Lu, & Li, 2012; Haslinger et al., 2012; Ishikawa et al., 2010; Osaki et al., 2011; Roth et al., 2016; Tikidji-Hamburyan et al., 2015). Think for a moment about the implications that the discovery of contextual influences has for understanding how visual receptive fields function. A visual neuron's receptive field was initially assumed to be a property of the neuron resulting from the hard-wired convergence of neural circuits; now, a neurons's receptive field is viewed as a plastic property of the neuron that is continually fine-tuned on the basis of changing signals from the context.

Neuroplasticity

> **Neuroplasticity** Why should natural scenes be used to study visual system neurons?

Seeing Color

Color is one of the most obvious qualities of human visual experience. So far in this chapter, we have largely limited our discussion of vision to black, white, and gray. Black is experienced when there is an absence of light; the perception of white is produced by an intense mixture of a wide range of wavelengths in roughly equal proportions; and the perception of gray is produced by the same mixture at lower intensities. In this module, we deal with the perception of colors such as blue, green, and yellow. The correct term for colors is *hues*, but in everyday language they are referred to as colors; and for the sake of simplicity, we will do the same.

What is there about a visual stimulus that determines the color we perceive? To a large degree, the perception of an object's color depends on the wavelengths of light that it reflects into the eye. Figure 6.2 is an illustration of the colors associated with individual wavelengths; however, outside the laboratory, one never encounters objects that reflect single wavelengths. Sunlight and most sources of artificial light contain complex mixtures of most visible wavelengths. Most objects absorb the different wavelengths of light that strike them to varying degrees and reflect the rest. The mixture of wavelengths that objects reflect influences our perception of their color, but it is not the entire story—as you are about to learn.

Component and Opponent Processing

LO 6.17 Describe the component and opponent-process theories of color vision.

The **component theory** (*trichromatic theory*) of color vision was proposed by Thomas Young in 1802 and refined by Hermann von Helmholtz in 1852. According to this theory, there are three different kinds of color receptors (cones), each with a different spectral sensitivity, and the color of a particular stimulus is presumed to be encoded by the ratio of activity in the three kinds of receptors. Young and Helmholtz derived their theory from the observation that any color of the visible spectrum can be matched by a mixing together of three different wavelengths of light in different proportions. This can be accomplished with any three wavelengths, provided that the color of any one of them cannot be matched by a mixing of the other two. The fact that three is normally the minimum number of different wavelengths necessary to match every color suggested that there were three types of receptors.

Another theory of color vision, the **opponent-process theory** of color vision, was proposed by Ewald Hering in 1878. He suggested that there are two different classes of cells in the visual system for encoding color and another class for encoding brightness. Hering hypothesized that each of the three classes of cells encoded two complementary color perceptions. One class of color-coding cells signaled red by changing its activity in one direction (e.g., hyperpolarization) and signaled red's complementary color, green, by changing its activity in the other direction (e.g., depolarization). Another class of color-coding cells was hypothesized to signal blue and its complement, yellow, in the same opponent fashion; and a class of brightness-coding cells was hypothesized to similarly signal both black and white. **Complementary colors** are pairs of colors (e.g., green light and red light) that produce white or gray when combined in equal measure.

Hering based his opponent-process theory of color vision on several behavioral observations. One was that complementary colors cannot exist together: There is no such thing as bluish yellow or reddish green (see Billock & Tsou, 2010). Another was that the afterimage produced by staring at red is green and vice versa, and the afterimage produced by staring at yellow is blue and vice versa (try the Check It Out demonstration).

A somewhat misguided debate raged for many years between supporters of the component and opponent theories of color vision. We say "misguided" because it was fueled more by the adversarial predisposition of scientists than by the incompatibility of the two theories. In fact, research subsequently proved that both color-coding mechanisms coexist in our visual systems (see DeValois et al., 2000).

Watch this video on MyPsychLab

NEGATIVE AFTERIMAGES

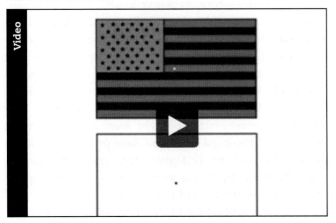

It was the development in the early 1960s of a technique for measuring the absorption spectrum of the photopigment contained in a single cone that allowed researchers (e.g., Wald, 1964) to confirm the conclusion that Young had reached more than a century and a half before. They found that there are indeed three different kinds of cones in the retinas of those vertebrates with good color vision, and they found that each of the three has a different photopigment with its own characteristic absorption spectrum. As Figure 6.19 illustrates, some cones are most sensitive to short wavelengths, some

Check It Out
Complementary Afterimages

Have you ever noticed complementary afterimages? To see them, stare at the fixation point (x) in the left panel for 1 minute without moving your eyes, then quickly shift your gaze to the fixation point in the right panel. In the right panel, you will see four squares whose colors are complementary to those in the left panel.

are most sensitive to medium wavelengths, and some are most sensitive to long wavelengths (see Shevell & Kingdom, 2008), but they all respond to most of the wavelengths of the visible spectrum.

Although the coding of color by cones seems to operate on a purely component basis (see Jameson, Highnote, & Wasserman, 2001), there is evidence of opponent processing of color at all subsequent levels of the retina-geniculate-striate system. That is, at all subsequent levels, there are cells that respond in one direction (e.g., increased firing) to one color and in the opposite direction (e.g., decreased firing) to its complementary color (see Chatterjee & Callaway, 2003; Gegenfurtner & Kiper, 2003).

Most primates are *trichromats* (possessing three color vision photopigments)—see Jacobs & Nathans (2009). Most other mammals are *dichromats* (possessing two color vision photopigments)—they lack the photopigment sensitive to long wavelengths and thus have difficulty seeing light at the red end of the visible spectrum (see Figure 6.2). In contrast, some birds, fish, and reptiles have four photopigments; the fourth allows them to detect ultraviolet light, which is invisible to humans.

In a remarkable study, Jacobs and colleagues (2007) introduced into mice the gene for the long-wavelength photopigment, thus converting them from dichromats to trichromats. Behavioral tests indicated that the transgenic mice had acquired the ability to perceive long wavelengths and to make color discriminations between lights at that end of the spectrum.

Figure 6.19 The absorption spectra of the three classes of cones.

Although the phenomenon of color constancy is counterintuitive, its advantage is obvious. Color constancy improves our ability to tell objects apart in a memorable way so that we can respond appropriately to them; our ability to recognize objects would be greatly lessened if their color changed every time there was a change in illumination (see Foster, 2011). In essence, if it were not for color constancy, color vision would have little survival value.

> **Evolutionary Perspective** Think of and explain a specific example where color constancy would be adaptive.

Color Constancy and the Retinex Theory

LO 6.18 Describe Land's demonstration of color constancy, and explain his retinex theory.

Neither component nor opponent processing can account for the single most important characteristic of color vision: color constancy. **Color constancy** refers to the fact that the perceived color of an object is not a simple function of the wavelengths reflected by it.

Color constancy is an important—but much misunderstood—concept. Let us explain it with an example. As I (SB) write this at 6:15 on a January morning, it is dark outside, and I am working in my office by the light of a tiny incandescent desk lamp. Later in the morning, when students **Thinking Creatively** start to arrive, I will turn on my nasty fluorescent office lights; and then, in the afternoon, when the sun is brighter on my side of the building, I will turn off the lights and work by natural light. The point is that because these light sources differ markedly in the wavelengths they emit, the wavelengths reflected by various objects in my office—my blue shirt, for example—change substantially during the course of the day. However, although the wavelengths reflected by my shirt change markedly, its color does not—my shirt will be just as blue in midmorning and in late afternoon as it is now. Color constancy is the tendency for an object to stay the same color despite major changes in the wavelengths of light that it reflects.

Although color constancy is an important feature of our vision, we are normally unaware of it. Under everyday conditions, we have no way of appreciating just how much the wavelengths reflected by an object can change without the object changing its color. It is only in the controlled environment of the laboratory that one can fully appreciate that color constancy is more than an important factor in color vision: It is the essence of color vision.

Edwin Land (1977) developed several dramatic laboratory demonstrations of color constancy. In these demonstrations, Land used three adjustable projectors. Each projector emitted only one wavelength of light: one a short-wavelength light, one a medium-wavelength light, and one a long-wavelength light. Thus, it was clear that only three wavelengths of light were involved in the demonstrations. Land shone the three projectors on a test display like the one in Figure 6.20. (These displays are called *Mondrians* because they resemble the paintings of the Dutch artist Piet Mondrian.)

Land found that adjusting the amount of light emitted from each projector—and thus the amount of light of each wavelength being reflected by the Mondrian—had no effect at all on the perception of its colors. For example, in one demonstration Land used a photometer to measure the amounts of the three wavelengths reflected by a rectangle judged to be pure blue by his participants. He then adjusted the emittance of the projectors, and he measured the wavelengths reflected by a red rectangle on a different Mondrian, until the wavelengths were exactly the same as those that had been reflected by the blue rectangle on the original. When he showed this new Mondrian to his participants, the red rectangle looked—you guessed it—red, even though it reflected exactly the

Figure 6.20 The method of Land's (1977) color-vision experiments. Subjects viewed Mondrians illuminated by various proportions of three different wavelengths: a short wavelength, a middle wavelength, and a long wavelength.

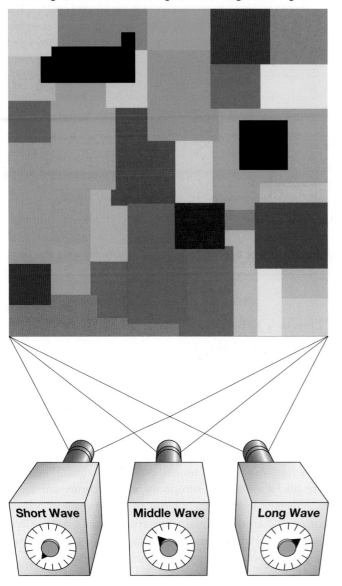

same wavelengths as had the blue rectangle on the original Mondrian.

The point of Land's demonstration is that blue objects stay blue, green objects stay green, and so forth, regardless of the wavelengths they reflect. This color constancy occurs as long as the object is illuminated with light that contains some short, medium, and long wavelengths (such as daylight, firelight, and virtually all manufactured lighting) and as long as the object is viewed as part of a scene, not in isolation.

According to Land's **retinex theory** of color vision, the color of an object is determined by its *reflectance*—the proportion of light of different wavelengths that a surface reflects. Although the wavelengths of light reflected by a surface change dramatically with changes in illumination, the efficiency with which a surface absorbs each wavelength and reflects the unabsorbed portion does not change. According to the retinex theory, the visual system calculates the reflectance of surfaces, and thus perceives their colors, by comparing the light reflected by adjacent surfaces in at least three different wavelength bands (short, medium, and long). You learned in the previous module that the context plays an important role in the processing of spatial contrast (i.e., edges) and the retinex theory suggests that the context plays a similarly important role in processing color (Shevell & Kingdom, 2008).

Why is Land's research so critical for neuroscientists trying to discover the neural mechanisms of color vision? It is important because it suggests how some of the neurons involved in color vision must work (see Shapely & Hawken, 2002): If the perception of color depends on the analysis of contrast **Evolutionary Perspective** between adjacent areas of the visual field, then some color neurons must be responsive to color contrast (see Hurlbert, 2003). And they are. For example, **dual-opponent color cells** in the monkey visual cortex respond with vigorous "on" firing when the center of their circular receptive field is illuminated with one wavelength, such as green, and the surround (periphery) is simultaneously illuminated with another wavelength, such as red. And the same cells display vigorous "off" firing when the pattern of illumination is reversed—for example, red in the center and green in the surround. In essence, dual-opponent color cells respond to the contrast between wavelengths reflected by adjacent areas of their receptive field.

A major breakthrough in the understanding of the organization of the primary visual cortex came with the discovery that dual-opponent color cells are not distributed evenly throughout the primary visual cortex of monkeys (see Zeki, 1993a). Livingstone and Hubel (1984) found that these neurons are concentrated in the primary visual cortex in peglike columns that penetrate the layers of the monkey primary visual cortex, with the exception of lower layer IV. Many neurons in these peglike columns are particularly rich in the mitochondrial enzyme **cytochrome oxidase**; thus, their distribution in the primary visual cortex can be visualized if one stains slices of tissue with stains that have an affinity for this enzyme.

When a section of monkey striate tissue is cut parallel to the cortical layers and stained in this way, the pegs are seen as "blobs" of stain scattered over the cortex (unless the section is cut from lower layer IV). To the relief of instructors and students alike, the term "**blobs**" has become the accepted scientific label for peglike, cytochrome oxidase–rich, dual-opponent color columns. The blobs were found to be located in the midst of ocular dominance columns. Functional MRI studies have provided evidence of dual-opponent color cells in the human visual cortex (Engel, 1999).

Scan Your Brain

The striate cortex is the main entrance point of visual signals to the cortex. In the upcoming module, we will follow visual signals to other parts of the cortex. This is a good point to pause and review what you have learned. Draw a line to connect each term in the first column with the closely related word or phrase in the second column. Each term should be linked to only one item in the second column. The correct answers are provided at the end of this exercise. Before proceeding, review material related to your errors and omissions.

1. Ommatidia
2. Color constancy
3. Simple cortical cells
4. Striate cortex
5. Perception of edges
6. Trichromatic
7. Stimulation outside receptor field
8. Off-center cells
9. Cytochrome oxidase

a. neurons of lower layer IV
b. mitochondrial enzyme
c. large receptors
d. contextual influences
e. component theory
f. Firing on periphery of receptive field
g. contrast-enhancement
h. Unresponsive to diffuse light
i. Mondrians

Scan Your Brain answers: (1) c, (2) i, (3) h, (4) a, (5) g, (6) e, (7) d, (8) f, (9) b.

Cortical Mechanisms of Vision and Conscious Awareness

So far, you have followed the major visual pathways from the eyes to the primary visual cortex, but there is much more to the human visual system—we are visual animals. The entire occipital cortex as well as large areas of temporal cortex and parietal cortex are involved in vision (see Figure 6.21).

Figure 6.21 The visual areas of the human cerebral cortex.

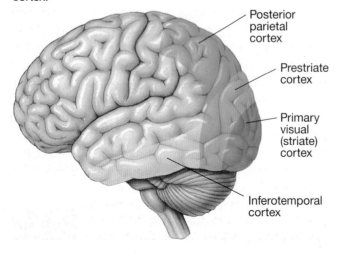

Posterior parietal cortex

Prestriate cortex

Primary visual (striate) cortex

Inferotemporal cortex

Three Different Classes of Visual Cortex

LO 6.19 Describe the three classes of visual cortex, and identify their locations in the brain.

Visual cortex is often considered to be of three different classes. *Primary visual cortex*, as you have learned, is that area of cortex that receives most of its input from the visual relay nuclei of the thalamus (i.e., from the lateral geniculate nuclei). Areas of **secondary visual cortex** are those that receive most of their input from the primary visual cortex, and areas of **visual association cortex** are those that receive input from areas of secondary visual cortex as well as from the secondary areas of other sensory systems.

The primary visual cortex is located in the posterior region of the occipital lobes, much of it hidden from view in the longitudinal fissure. Most areas of secondary visual cortex are located in two general regions: in the prestriate cortex and in the inferotemporal cortex. The **prestriate cortex** is the band of tissue in the occipital lobe that surrounds the primary visual cortex. The **inferotemporal cortex** is the cortex of the inferior temporal lobe. Areas of association cortex that receive visual input are located in several parts of the cerebral cortex, but the largest single area is in the **posterior parietal cortex**.

The major flow of visual information in the cortex is from primary visual cortex to the various areas of secondary visual cortex to the areas of association cortex. As one moves up this visual hierarchy, the neurons have larger receptive fields and the stimuli to which the neurons respond are more specific and more complex.

Damage to Primary Visual Cortex: Scotomas and Completion

LO 6.20 Explain what happens when an area of primary visual cortex is damaged.

Damage to an area of the primary visual cortex produces a **scotoma**—an area of blindness—in the corresponding area of the contralateral visual field of both eyes (see Figure 6.13). Neurological patients with suspected damage to the primary visual cortex are usually given a **perimetry test**. While the patient's head is held motionless on a chin rest, the patient stares with one eye at a fixation point on a screen. A small dot of light is then flashed on various parts of the screen, and the patient presses a button to record when the dot is seen. Then, the entire process is repeated for the other eye. The result is a map of the right and left visual field of each eye, which indicates any areas of blindness. Figure 6.22 illustrates the perimetric maps of each eye of a man with a bullet wound in his left primary visual cortex. Notice the massive scotoma in the right visual field of each eye.

Many patients with scotomas are not consciously aware of their deficits. One factor that contributes to this lack of awareness is completion. A patient with a scotoma who looks at a complex figure, part of which lies in the scotoma, often reports seeing a complete image (see Silvanto, 2014). In some cases, this completion may depend on residual visual capacities in the scotoma; however, completion also occurs in cases in which this explanation can be ruled out. For example, patients who are **hemianopsic** (having a scotoma covering half of the visual field) may see an entire face when they focus on a person's nose, even when the side of the face in the scotoma has been covered by a blank card.

Consider the completion phenomenon experienced by the esteemed physiological psychologist Karl Lashley (1941). He often developed a large scotoma next to his fovea during migraine attacks (see Figure 6.23).

The Case of the Physiological Psychologist Who Made Faces Disappear

Talking with a friend, I glanced just to the right of his face wherein his head disappeared. His shoulders and necktie were still visible but the vertical stripes on the wallpaper behind him seemed to extend down to the necktie. It was impossible to see this as a blank area when projected on the striped wallpaper of uniformly patterned surface, although any intervening object failed to be seen. (Lashley, 1941, p. 338)

Figure 6.22 The perimetric maps of a subject with a bullet wound in his left primary visual cortex. The scotomas (areas of blindness) are indicated in gray. (Based on Teuber, Battersby, & Bender, 1960.)

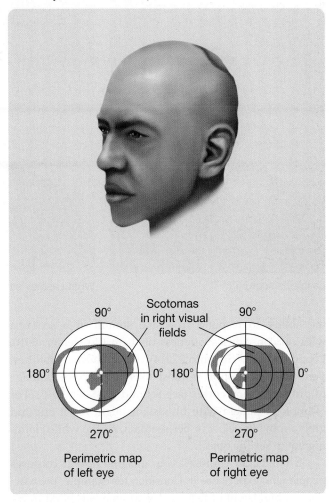

Clinical Implications Earlier you learned about surface interpolation. How is surface interpolation at work in this case study? (Hint: Take a close look at Figure 6.23.)

You probably equate perception with **conscious awareness**; that is, you assume that if a person sees something, he or she will be consciously aware of seeing it. In everyday thinking, perceiving and being aware are inseparable processes: We assume that someone who has seen something will be able to acknowledge that he or she has seen it and be able to describe it. In the following pages, you will encounter examples of phenomena for which this is not the case: people who see things but have no conscious awareness of them. Blindsight is the first example.

Blindsight is sometimes displayed by patients with scotomas resulting from damage to primary visual cortex. **Blindsight** is

Figure 6.23 The completion of a migraine-induced scotoma, as described by Karl Lashley (1941).

Lashley's scotoma

What Lashley saw

the ability to respond to visual stimuli in a scotoma with no conscious awareness of them (de Gelder, 2010; Leopold, 2012; Silvanto, 2014). Of all visual abilities, perception of motion is most likely to survive damage to primary visual cortex (see Schmid & Maier, 2015). For example, a patient with blindsight might reach out and grab a moving object in her scotoma, all the while claiming not to see the object.

If blindsight confuses you, imagine how it confuses people who experience it. Consider, for example, the reactions to blindsight of D.B., a patient who was blind in his left visual field following surgical removal of his right occipital lobe (Weiskrantz et al., 1974).

The Case of D.B., the Man Confused by His Own Blindsight

D.B. had no awareness of "seeing" in his blind, left field. Despite this apparent left-field blindness, he could accurately reach for visual stimuli in his left field and could accurately differentiate between a horizontal or diagonal line in his left field if forced to "guess." When he was questioned about his vision in his left field, his most usual response was that he saw nothing. When he was shown a video of his accurate left-field performance through his good, right field, he was astonished and insisted he was just guessing.

Two neurological interpretations of blindsight have been proposed. One is that the striate cortex is not completely destroyed and the remaining islands of functional cells are capable of mediating some visual abilities in the absence of conscious awareness (see Wüst, Kasten, & Sabel, 2002). The other is that those visual pathways that ascend directly to the secondary visual cortex from subcortical visual structures without passing through the primary visual cortex are capable of maintaining some visual abilities in the absence of cognitive awareness (see Schmid & Maier, 2015). There is some support for both theories, but it is far from conclusive in either case (see Gross, Moore, & Rodman, 2004; Rosa, Tweedale, & Elston, 2000; Schärli, Harman, & Hogben, 1999a, 1999b). Indeed, it is possible that both mechanisms contribute to the phenomenon.

Functional Areas of Secondary and Association Visual Cortex

LO 6.21 Describe the areas of secondary visual cortex and association cortex involved in vision.

Secondary visual cortex and the portions of association cortex involved in visual analysis are both composed of many different areas, each specialized for a particular type of visual analysis. For example, in the macaque monkey, whose visual cortex has been most thoroughly mapped, there are more than 30 different functional areas of visual cortex; in addition to primary visual cortex, 24 areas of secondary visual cortex and 7 areas of association visual cortex have been identified. The neurons in each functional area respond most vigorously to different aspects of visual stimuli (e.g., to their color, movement, or shape); selective lesions to the different areas produce different visual losses; and there are anatomical and organizational differences among the areas (see Patel et al., 2014).

The various functional areas of secondary and association visual cortex in the macaque are prodigiously interconnected. Anterograde and retrograde tracing studies have identified more than 300 interconnecting pathways (see Markov & Kennedy, 2013). Connections between areas are virtually always reciprocal (see Gilbert & Li, 2013).

PET, fMRI, and evoked potentials (see Chapter 5) have been used to identify various areas of visual cortex in humans. The activity of volunteers' brains has been

Figure 6.24 Some of the visual areas that have been identified in the human brain.

- V3A
- V3
- V2
- V1/Primary
- V4
- MT/V5

monitored while they inspect various types of visual stimuli. By identifying the areas of activation associated with various visual properties (e.g., movement or color), researchers have so far delineated about a dozen different functional areas of human visual cortex (see Grill-Spector & Mallach, 2004). A map of some of these areas is shown in Figure 6.24. Most are similar in terms of location, anatomical characteristics, and function to areas already identified in the macaque.

Dorsal and Ventral Streams

LO 6.22 **Explain the difference between the dorsal and ventral streams, and the functions that have been attributed to each stream by different theories.**

As you have already learned, most visual information enters the primary visual cortex via the lateral geniculate nuclei. The information from the two lateral geniculate nuclei is received in the primary visual cortex, combined, and then segregated into multiple pathways that project separately to the various functional areas of secondary, and then association, visual cortex (see Horton & Sincich, 2004).

Many pathways that conduct information from the primary visual cortex through various specialized areas of secondary and association cortex can be thought of as components of two major streams: the dorsal stream and the ventral stream (Ungerleider & Mishkin, 1982). The **dorsal stream** flows from the primary visual cortex to the dorsal prestriate cortex to the posterior parietal cortex, and the **ventral stream** flows from the primary visual cortex to the ventral prestriate cortex to the inferotemporal cortex—see Figure 6.25.

Most visual cortex neurons in the dorsal stream respond most robustly to spatial stimuli, such as those indicating the location of objects or their direction of movement. In contrast, most neurons in the ventral stream respond to the characteristics of objects, such as color and shape (see Tompa & Sáry, 2010). Indeed, there are clusters of visual neurons in the ventral stream, and each cluster responds specifically to a particular class of objects—for example, most neurons in a particular cluster may respond to faces, whereas most neurons in another cluster might respond to animals (Haxby, 2006; Reddy & Kanwisher, 2006). Accordingly, Ungerleider and Mishkin (1982) proposed that the dorsal and ventral visual streams perform different visual functions. They suggested that the dorsal stream is involved in the perception of "where" objects are and the ventral stream is involved in the perception of "what" objects are.

Figure 6.25 Information about particular aspects of a visual display flow out of the primary visual cortex over many pathways. The pathways can be grouped into two general streams: dorsal and ventral.

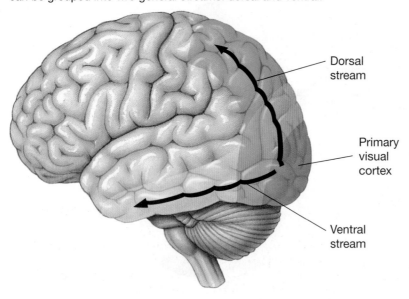

Dorsal stream

Primary visual cortex

Ventral stream

A major implication of the **"where" versus "what" theory** of vision is that damage to some areas of cortex may abolish certain aspects of vision while leaving others unaffected. Indeed, the most convincing support for the influential "where" versus "what" theory has come from the comparison of the specific effects of damage to the dorsal and ventral streams (see Ungerleider & Haxby, 1994). Patients with damage to the posterior parietal cortex often have difficulty reaching accurately for objects they have no difficulty describing; conversely, patients with damage to the inferotemporal cortex often have no difficulty reaching accurately for objects they have difficulty describing.

Although the "where" versus "what" theory is widely accepted, there is an alternative interpretation for the same evidence (de Haan & Cowet, 2011; Goodale, 2004; O'Reilly, 2010). Goodale and Milner (1992) argued that the primary difference between the dorsal and ventral streams is not the kinds of information they carry but the use to which that information is put. They suggested that the primary function of the dorsal stream is to direct behavioral interactions with objects, whereas the primary function of the ventral stream is to mediate the conscious perception of objects. Goodale and Milner's assertion has been termed the **"control of behavior" versus "conscious perception" theory** (see Logothetis & Sheinberg, 1996). One of the most interesting **Evolutionary Perspective** aspects of this theory is its evolutionary implication: Goodale (2004) suggested that the conscious awareness mediated by the ventral stream is one thing that distinguishes humans and their close relatives from their evolutionary ancestors.

The "control of behavior" versus "conscious perception" theory can readily explain the two major neuropsychological

findings that are the foundation of the "where" versus "what" theory. Namely, the "control of behavior" versus "conscious perception" theory suggests that patients with dorsal stream damage may do poorly on tests of location and movement because most tests of location and movement involve performance measures, and that patients with ventral stream damage may do poorly on tests of visual recognition because most tests of visual recognition involve verbal responses, and thus, conscious awareness.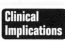

The major support for the "control of behavior" versus "conscious perception" theory is the confirmation of its two primary predictions: (1) that some patients with bilateral lesions to the ventral stream may have no conscious experience of seeing and yet be able to interact with objects under visual guidance, and (2) that some patients with bilateral lesions to the dorsal stream may consciously see objects but be unable to interact with them under visual guidance (see Figure 6.26). Following are two such cases.

The Case of D.F., the Woman Who Could Grasp Objects She Did Not Consciously See

D.F. has bilateral damage to her ventral prestriate cortex, thus interrupting the flow of the ventral stream; her case is described by Goodale and Milner (2004). Amazingly, she can respond accurately to visual stimuli that she does not consciously see.

Despite her inability to consciously recognize the size, shape and orientation of visual objects, D.F. displayed accurate hand movements directed at the same objects. For example, when she was asked to indicate the width of blocks with her index finger and thumb, her matches were variable and unrelated to the actual size of the blocks. However, when she was asked to pick up blocks of different sizes, the distance between her index finger and thumb changed appropriately with the size of the object. In other words, D.F. adjusted her hand to the size of objects she was about to pick up, even though she did not consciously perceive their size.

A similar dissociation occurred in her responses to the orientation of stimuli. When presented with a large slanted slot, she could not indicate the orientation of the slot either verbally or manually. However, she was as good as healthy volunteers at quickly placing a card in the slot, orienting her hand appropriately from the start of the movement.

Figure 6.26 The "where" versus "what" and the "control of behavior" versus "conscious perception" theories make different predictions.

Dorsal and Ventral Streams: Two Theories and What They Predict

"Where" vs. "What" Theory

Dorsal stream specializes in visual spatial perception
Ventral stream specializes in visual pattern recognition

Predicts
• Damage to **dorsal stream** disrupts visual spatial perception
• Damage to **ventral stream** disrupts visual pattern recognition

"Control of Behavior" vs. "Conscious Perception" Theory

Dorsal stream specializes in visually guided behavior
Ventral stream specializes in conscious visual perception

Predicts
• Damage to **dorsal stream** disrupts visually guided behavior but not conscious visual perception
• Damage to **ventral stream** disrupts conscious visual perception but not visually guided behavior

The Case of A.T., the Woman Who Could Not Accurately Grasp Unfamiliar Objects That She Saw

The case of A.T. is in major respects complementary to that of D.F. A.T. is a woman with a lesion of the occipitoparietal region, which likely interrupts her dorsal route (Jeannerod et al., 1995).

A.T. was able to recognize objects and demonstrate their size with her fingers. In contrast, the preshape of her hand during object-directed movements was incorrect. As a consequence, she could not pick up objects between her fingertips—instead, the patient made awkward palmar grasps. Although A.T. could not preshape her hand to pick up neutral objects like blocks, when presented with a familiar object of standard size, like a lipstick, she grasped it with reasonable accuracy.

The characterization of functional differences between the dorsal and ventral streams is far from complete. For example, the streams certainly do not function in isolation from one another (e.g., Theys et al., 2015; Zachariou, Klatzky, & Behrmann, 2014), but little attention has been paid to when and how they might interact. Also, it has been suggested that the two streams are composed of substreams (see Kravitz et al., 2011).

The remainder of the chapter deals with two areas of secondary visual cortex: the *fusiform face area* in the ventral stream, and the *MT (middle temporal) area* in the

dorsal stream. The focus is on the two neuropsychological disorders that have been linked to damage to them: *prosopagnosia* and *akinetopsia*, respectively.

Watch this video on MyPsychLab
RECOGNIZING FACES

Prosopagnosia

LO 6.23 Describe the phenomenon of prosopagnosia and discuss the associated theoretical issues.

Prosopagnosia, briefly put, is a visual agnosia for faces (see DeGutis et al., 2014) that can be acquired either during development (*developmental prosopagnosia*) or as a result of brain injury (*acquired prosopagnosia*; see Susilo & Duchaine, 2013). Let us explain. **Agnosia** is a failure of recognition (*gnosis* means "to know") that is not attributable to a sensory deficit or to verbal or intellectual impairment; **visual agnosia** is a specific

Clinical Implications

agnosia for visual stimuli. In other words, visual agnosics can see things, but they don't know what they are.

Visual agnosias are often specific to a particular aspect of visual input and are named accordingly; for example, *movement agnosia*, *object agnosia*, and *color agnosia* are difficulties in recognizing movement, objects, and color, respectively.

Prosopagnosics are visual agnosics with a specific difficulty in recognizing faces. They can recognize a face as a face, but they have problems recognizing whose face it is. They often report seeing a jumble of individual facial parts (e.g., eyes, nose, chin, cheeks) that for some reason are never fused into an easy-to-recognize whole (see Stephan & Caine, 2009). In extreme cases, prosopagnosics cannot recognize themselves: Imagine what it would be like to stare in the mirror every morning and not recognize the face that is looking back.

IS PROSOPAGNOSIA SPECIFIC TO FACES?

The belief that prosopagnosia is a deficit specific to the recognition of faces has been challenged. To understand this challenge, you need to know that the diagnosis of prosopagnosia is typically applied to neuropsychological patients who have difficulty recognizing particular faces but can readily identify other test objects (e.g., a chair, a dog, or a tree). Surely, this is powerful evidence that prosopagnosics have recognition difficulties specific to faces. Not so. Pause for a moment, and think about this evidence: It is seriously flawed.

Because prosopagnosics have no difficulty recognizing faces as faces, the fact that they can recognize chairs as chairs, pencils as pencils, and doors as doors is not relevant. The critical question is whether they can recognize which chair, which pencil, and which door. Careful testing of this sort usually reveals that their recognition deficits are not restricted to faces: For example, a farmer lost his ability to recognize particular cows when he lost his ability to recognize faces. This suggests that some prosopagnosic patients have a general problem recognizing specific objects that belong to complex classes of objects (e.g., particular automobiles or particular houses), not a specific problem recognizing faces (see Behrmann et al., 2005)—although in daily life the facial-recognition problems are likely to be the most problematic. Still, it is difficult to rule out the possibility that at least a few prosopagnosic patients have recognition deficits limited to faces. Indeed, several thorough case studies of prosopagnosia have failed to detect recognition deficits unrelated to faces (De Renzi, 1997; Duchaine & Nakayama, 2005; Farah, 1990). It seems likely that prosopagnosia is not a unitary disorder (Duchaine & Nakayama, 2006), and it appears that only some patients with this diagnosis have pattern-recognition deficits restricted to facial recognition.

R.P., a Typical Prosopagnosic

With routine testing, R.P. displayed a severe deficit in recognizing faces and in identifying facial expressions (Laeng & Caviness, 2001) but no other obvious recognition problems. If testing had stopped there, as it often does, it would have been concluded that R.P. is an agnosic with recognition problems specific to human faces. However, more thorough testing indicated that R.P. is deficient in recognizing all objects with complex curved surfaces, not just faces.

WHAT BRAIN PATHOLOGY IS ASSOCIATED WITH PROSOPAGNOSIA?

The diagnosis of *acquired prosopagnosia* is often associated with damage to the ventral surface of the brain at the boundary between the occipital and temporal lobes. This area of human cortex has become known as the **fusiform face area** (see Figure 6.27) because parts of it are selectively activated by human faces (see Collins & Olson, 2014; van den Hurk et al., 2015) and because electrical stimulation of this brain area in humans can metamorphose a viewed face into a completely different face (see Rangarajan et al., 2014). Similar face-specific areas have been found in the ventral streams of macaque monkeys (Freiwald & Tsao, 2010; McMahon et al., 2015; Meyers et al., 2015). It makes sense that specialized mechanisms to perceive faces have evolved in the human brain because face perception plays such a major role in human social behavior (Pascalis & Kelly, 2009; Tsao & Livingstone, 2008). The extent to which the development of the fusiform face area depends on a person's early experience with faces is still unclear (see McKone et al., 2012).

CAN PROSOPAGNOSICS PERCEIVE FACES IN THE ABSENCE OF CONSCIOUS AWARENESS?

The fact that prosopagnosia results from bilateral damage to the ventral stream suggests that dorsal-stream function may be intact. For example the "control of behavior" versus "conscious perception theory" suggests that prosopagnosics may be able to unconsciously recognize faces they cannot recognize consciously. This is, indeed, the case.

Tranel and Damasio (1985) were the first to demonstrate that prosopagnosics can recognize faces in the absence of conscious awareness. They presented a series of photographs to several patients, some familiar to the patients, some not. The patients claimed not to recognize any of the faces. However, when familiar faces were presented, the subjects displayed a large skin conductance response, which did not occur with unfamiliar faces, thus indicating that the faces were being unconsciously recognized by undamaged portions of the brain.

Akinetopsia

LO 6.24 Describe the phenomenon of akinetopsia and discuss the associated theoretical issues.

Akinetopsia is a deficiency in the ability to see movement progress in a normal smooth fashion. Akinetopsia can be triggered by high doses of certain antidepressants, as the following two cases illustrate (Horton, 2009).

Clinical Implications

Two Cases of Drug-Induced Akinetopsia

A 47-year-old depressed male receiving 100 mg of nefazodone twice daily reported a bizarre derangement of motion perception. Each moving object was followed by a trail of multiple freeze-frame images, which disappeared once the motion ceased. A 48-year-old female receiving 400 mg of nefazodone once daily at bedtime reported similar symptoms, with persistent multiple strobelike trails following moving objects. In both cases, stationary elements were perceived normally, indicating a selective impairment of the visual perception of motion. Vision returned to normal in both patients once the dosage was reduced.

Akinetopsia is often associated with damage to the **MT area** (middle temporal area) of the cortex. The location of MT—near the junction of the temporal, parietal, and occipital lobes—is illustrated in Figure 6.27.

Sometimes MT is called V5, or MT/V5. This is because researchers studying the visual system in different primate species have used different systems of neuroanatomical classification. All three terms appear to refer to comparable areas.

The function of MT appears to be the perception of motion. Given the importance of the perception of motion in primate survival, it is reasonable that an area of the visual system is dedicated to it. Some neurons at lower levels of the visual hierarchy (e.g., in the primary visual cortex) respond to movement as well as color and shape; however, they provide little information about the direction of movement because their receptive fields are so small. In contrast, 95 percent of the neurons of MT respond to specific directions of movement and little else. Also, each MT neuron has a large binocular receptive field, allowing it to track movement over a wide range.

The following four lines of research implicate MT in the visual perception of motion and damage to MT as a cause of akinetopsia:

- Patients with akinetopsia tend to have unilateral or bilateral damage to MT (Cooper et al., 2012).
- As measured by fMRI, activity in MT increases when humans view movement (see Zeki, 2015).
- Blocking activity in MT with transcranial magnetic stimulation (TMS) produces motion blindness (see Vetter, Grosbras, & Muckli, 2015).
- Electrical stimulation of MT in human patients induces the visual perception of motion (Blanke et al., 2002).

Conclusion

A key goal of this chapter was to help you understand that vision is a creative process. Your visual system does not transmit complete and intact visual images of the world to the cortex. It carries information about a few critical features of the visual field—for example, information about location, movement, brightness contrast, and color contrast—and from these bits of information, it creates a perception far better than the retinal image in all respects and better than the external reality in some. Another main point is that your visual system can perceive things without your conscious awareness of them.

The Check It Out demonstrations in this chapter offered you many opportunities to experience firsthand important aspects of the visual process. We hope you checked them out and your experience made you more aware of the amazing abilities of your own visual system and the relevance of what you have learned in this chapter to your everyday life.

Figure 6.27 The location of the fusiform face area and the MT area: Damage to the fusiform face area is associated with prosopagnosia, damage to the MT area is associated with akinetopsia.

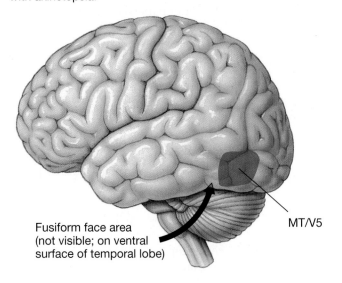

Fusiform face area
(not visible; on ventral
surface of temporal lobe)

MT/V5

Themes Revisited

This chapter developed all four of the text's major themes. First, the evolutionary perspective theme was emphasized, largely because the majority of research on the neural mechanisms of human vision has been comparative and because thinking about the adaptiveness of various aspects of vision (e.g., color vision) has led to important insights.

Second, the thinking creatively theme was emphasized because the main point of the chapter was that we tend to think about our own visual systems in a way that is fundamentally incorrect: The visual system does not passively provide images of the external world; it extracts some features of the external world, and from these it creates our visual perceptions. Once you learn to think in this unconventional way, you will be able to better appreciate the amazingness of your own visual system.

Third, the clinical implications theme was developed through a series of clinical case studies: Mrs. Richards, who experienced fortification illusions before her migraine attacks; Karl Lashley, the physiological psychologist who used his scotoma to turn a friend's head into a wallpaper pattern; D.B., the man with blind- sight; D.F., who showed by her accurate reaching that she detected the size, shape, and orientation of objects that she could not describe; A.T., who could describe the size and shape of objects she could not accurately reach for; R.P., a typical prosopagnosic; and two patients with akinetopsia induced by a particular antidepressant.

Fourth, this chapter touched on the neuroplasticity theme. The study of the visual system has focused on the receptive field properties of neurons in response to simple stimuli, and receptive fields have been assumed to be static. However, when natural visual scenes have been used in such studies, it has become apparent that each neuron's receptive field changes depending on the visual context.

Key Terms

Light Enters the Eye and Reaches the Retina

Sensitivity, p. 159
Acuity, p. 159
Ciliary muscles, p. 160
Accommodation, p. 160
Binocular disparity, p. 162

The Retina and Translation of Light into Neural Signals

Receptors, p. 162
Horizontal cells, p. 162
Bipolar cells, p. 162
Amacrine cells, p. 162
Retinal ganglion cells, p. 162
Blind spot, p. 162
Fovea, p. 163
Completion, p. 163
Surface interpolation, p. 163
Cones, p. 163
Rods, p. 163
Duplexity theory, p. 163
Photopic vision, p. 163
Scotopic vision, p. 164
Photopic spectral sensitivity
    curve, p. 165
Scotopic spectral sensitivity
    curve, p. 165
Purkinje effect, p. 166
Fixational eye movements, p. 167

Saccades, p. 167
Transduction, p. 167
Rhodopsin, p. 167
Absorption spectrum, p. 167

From Retina to Primary Visual Cortex

Retina-geniculate-striate
    pathways, p. 168
Primary visual cortex, p. 168
Lateral geniculate nuclei, p. 168
Retinotopic, p. 169
Parvocellular layers, p. 169
Magnocellular layers, p. 170

Seeing Edges

Contrast enhancement, p. 171
Lateral inhibition, p. 171
Receptive field, p. 172
Monocular, p. 172
On-center cells, p. 173
Off-center cells, p. 173
Simple cells, p. 174
Complex cells, p. 174
Binocular, p. 174

Seeing Color

Component theory, p. 176
Opponent-process theory, p. 176
Complementary colors, p. 177

Color constancy, p. 178
Retinex theory, p. 179
Dual-opponent color
    cells, p. 179
Cytochrome oxidase, p. 179
Blobs, p. 179

Cortical Mechanisms of Vision and Conscious Awareness

Secondary visual cortex, p. 180
Visual association cortex, p. 180
Prestriate cortex, p. 180
Inferotemporal cortex, p. 180
Posterior parietal cortex, p. 180
Scotoma, p. 181
Perimetry test, p. 181
Hemianopsic, p. 181
Conscious awareness, p. 181
Blindsight, p. 181
Dorsal stream, p. 183
Ventral stream, p. 183
"Where" versus "what" theory, p. 184
"Control of behavior" versus
    "conscious perception" theory, p. 184
Prosopagnosia, p. 185
Agnosia, p. 185
Visual agnosia, p. 185
Fusiform face area, p. 186
Akinetopsia, p. 187
MT area, p. 187

Chapter 7
Mechanisms of Perception: Hearing, Touch, Smell, Taste, and Attention

How You Know the World

Chapter Overview and Learning Objectives (LOs)

Principles of Sensory System Organization	**LO 7.1** Name and define the three types of sensory cortex.
	LO 7.2 In the context of sensory system organization, explain what is meant by each of the following terms: *hierarchical organization*, *functional segregation*, and *parallel processing*. Summarize the current model of sensory system organization.
Auditory System	**LO 7.3** Explain the relationship between the physical and perceptual dimensions of sound.
	LO 7.4 Describe the components of the human ear, and explain how sound is processed within its various structures.

LO 7.5   Describe the major pathways that lead from the ear to the primary auditory cortex.

LO 7.6   Describe the neural mechanisms underlying sound localization.

LO 7.7   Describe the organization of auditory cortex.

LO 7.8   Describe the effects of damage to the auditory system.

Somatosensory System: Touch and Pain

LO 7.9   Name some of the cutaneous receptors, and explain the functional significance of fast versus slow receptor adaptation.

LO 7.10   Describe the two major somatosensory pathways.

LO 7.11   Describe the cortical somatosensory areas and their somatotopic layout.

LO 7.12   Name the areas of association cortex that somatosensory signals are sent to, and describe the functional properties of one of those areas.

LO 7.13   Describe the two major types of somatosensory agnosia.

LO 7.14   Describe the rubber-hand illusion and its neural mechanisms.

LO 7.15   Explain why the perception of pain is said to be paradoxical.

LO 7.16   Define neuropathic pain and describe some of its putative neural mechanisms.

Chemical Senses: Smell and Taste

LO 7.17   Describe two adaptive roles for the chemical senses.

LO 7.18   Describe the olfactory system.

LO 7.19   Describe the gustatory system.

LO 7.20   In the context of the gustatory system, explain what is meant by broad versus narrow tuning.

LO 7.21   Explain the potential effects of brain damage on the chemical senses.

Selective Attention

LO 7.22   Describe the two characteristics of selective attention, and explain what is meant by exogenous versus endogenous attention.

LO 7.23   Describe the phenomenon of change blindness.

LO 7.24   Describe the neural mechanisms of attention.

LO 7.25   Describe the disorder of attention known as simultanagnosia.

Two chapters in this text focus primarily on sensory systems—Chapter 6 and this one. Chapter 6 introduced the visual system; this chapter focuses on the remaining four of the five **exteroceptive sensory systems**: the *auditory* (hearing), *somatosensory* (touch), *olfactory* (smell), and *gustatory* (taste) systems. In addition, this chapter describes the mechanisms of attention: how our brains manage to attend to a small number of sensory stimuli despite being continuously bombarded by thousands of them. Before you begin the first module of this chapter, consider the following case (Williams, 1970). As you read the chapter, think about this patient, the nature of his deficit, and the likely location of his brain damage. By the time you have reached the final section of this chapter, you will better understand this patient's problem.

The Case of the Man Who Could See Only One Thing at a Time

A 68-year-old patient was referred because he had difficulty finding his way around—even around his own home. The patient attributed his problems to his "inability to see properly." It was found that if two objects (e.g., two pencils) were held in front of him at the same time, he could see only one of them, whether they were held side by side, one above the other, or even one partially behind the other. Pictures of single objects or faces could be identified, even when quite complex; but if a picture included two objects, only one object could be identified at one time, though that one would sometimes fade, whereupon the other would enter the patient's perception. If a sentence were presented in a line, only the rightmost word could be read, but if one word were presented spread over the entire area previously covered by the sentence, the word could be read in its entirety. If the patient was shown overlapping drawings (i.e., one drawn on top of another), he would see one but deny the existence of the other.

Principles of Sensory System Organization

The visual system, which you learned about in Chapter 6, is by far the most thoroughly studied sensory system and, as a result, the most well understood. However, as more has been discovered about the other sensory systems, it has become apparent that each is organized like the visual system in fundamental ways.

Watch this video on MyPsychLab
CHALK IT UP! THINKING ABOUT SENSORY SYSTEMS

Types of Sensory Areas of Cortex

LO 7.1 Name and define the three types of sensory cortex.

The sensory areas of the cortex are, by convention, considered to be of three fundamentally different types: primary, secondary, and association. The **primary sensory cortex** of a system is the area of sensory cortex that receives most of its input directly from the thalamic relay nuclei of that system. For example, as you learned in Chapter 6, the primary visual cortex is the area of the cerebral cortex that receives most of its input from the lateral geniculate nucleus of the thalamus. The **secondary sensory cortex** of a system comprises the areas of the sensory cortex that receive most of their input from the primary sensory cortex of that system or from other areas of secondary sensory cortex of the same system. **Association cortex** is any area of cortex that receives input from more than one sensory system. Most input to areas of association cortex comes via areas of secondary sensory cortex.

The interactions among these three types of sensory cortex and among other sensory structures are characterized by three major principles: hierarchical organization, functional segregation, and parallel processing.

Features of Sensory System Organization

LO 7.2 In the context of sensory system organization, explain what is meant by each of the following terms: *hierarchical organization*, *functional segregation*, and *parallel processing*. Summarize the current model of sensory system organization.

HIERARCHICAL ORGANIZATION.   Sensory systems are characterized by **hierarchical organization**. A hierarchy is a system whose members can be assigned to specific levels or ranks in relation to one another. For example, an army is a hierarchical system because all soldiers are ranked with respect to their authority. In the same way, sensory structures are organized in a hierarchy on the basis of the specificity and complexity of their function. As one moves through a sensory system from receptors, to thalamic nuclei, to primary sensory cortex, to secondary sensory cortex, to association cortex, one finds neurons that respond optimally to stimuli of greater and greater specificity and complexity. Each level of a sensory hierarchy receives most of its input from lower levels and adds another layer of analysis before passing it on up the hierarchy (see Rees, Kreiman, & Koch, 2002).

The hierarchical organization of sensory systems is apparent from a comparison of the effects of damage to various levels: The higher the level of damage, the more specific and complex the deficit. For example, destruction of a sensory system's receptors produces a complete loss of ability to perceive in that sensory modality (e.g., total blindness or deafness); in contrast, destruction of an area of association or secondary sensory cortex typically produces complex and specific sensory deficits, while leaving fundamental sensory abilities intact. Dr. P., the man who mistook his wife for a hat (Sacks, 1985), displayed such a pattern of deficits.

Case of the Man Who Mistook His Wife for a Hat*

Dr. P. was a highly respected musician and teacher—a charming and intelligent man. He had been referred to the eminent

Clinical Implications neurologist Oliver Sacks for help with a vision problem. At least, as Dr. P. explained to the neurologist, other people seemed to think that he had a vision problem, and he did admit that he sometimes made odd errors.

Dr. Sacks tested Dr. P.'s vision and found his visual acuity to be excellent—Dr. P. could easily spot a pin on the floor. The first sign of a problem appeared when Dr. P. needed to put his shoe back on following a standard reflex test. Gazing at his foot, he asked Sacks if it was his shoe.

Continuing the examination, Dr. Sacks showed Dr. P. a glove and asked him what it was. Taking the glove and puzzling over it, Dr. P. could only guess that it was a container divided into five compartments for some reason. Even when Sacks asked whether the glove might fit on some part of the body, Dr. P. displayed no signs of recognition.

At that point, Dr. P. seemed to conclude that the examination was over and, from the expression on his face, that he had done rather well. Preparing to leave, he turned and grasped his wife's head and tried to put it on his own. Apparently, he thought it was his hat.

Mrs. P. showed little surprise. That kind of thing happened a lot.

In recognition of the hierarchical organization of sensory systems, psychologists sometimes divide the general process of perceiving into two general phases: sensation and perception. **Sensation** is the process of detecting the presence of stimuli, and **perception** is the higher-order process of integrating, recognizing, and interpreting complete patterns of sensations. Dr. P.'s problem was clearly one of visual perception, not visual sensation.

FUNCTIONAL SEGREGATION. It was once assumed that the primary, secondary, and association areas of a sensory system were each *functionally homogeneous*. That is, it was assumed that all areas of cortex at any given level of a sensory hierarchy acted together to perform the same function.

However, research has shown that **functional segregation**, rather than functional homogeneity, characterizes the organization of sensory systems. It is now clear that each of the three levels of cerebral cortex—primary, secondary, and association—in each sensory system contains functionally distinct areas that specialize in different kinds of analysis.

PARALLEL PROCESSING. It was once believed that the different levels of a sensory hierarchy were connected in a serial fashion. In a *serial system*, information flows among the components over just one pathway, like a string through a strand of beads. However, evidence now suggests that sensory systems are *parallel systems* in which information flows through the components over multiple pathways. Parallel systems feature **parallel processing**—the simultaneous analysis of a signal in different ways by the multiple parallel pathways of a neural network.

There appear to be two fundamentally different kinds of parallel streams of analysis in our sensory systems: one capable of influencing our behavior without our conscious awareness and one that influences our behavior by engaging our conscious awareness.

SUMMARY MODEL OF SENSORY SYSTEM ORGANIZATION. Figure 7.1 summarizes the information in this module of the chapter by illustrating how thinking about the organization of sensory systems has changed. In the 1960s, sensory systems were believed to be hierarchical, functionally homogeneous, and serial. However, subsequent research has established that sensory systems are hierarchical, functionally segregated, and parallel (see Rauschecker, 2015).

Sensory systems are characterized by a division of labor: Multiple specialized areas, at multiple levels, are interconnected by multiple parallel pathways. For example, each area of the visual system is specialized for perceiving specific aspects of visual scenes (e.g., shape, color, movement). Yet, complex stimuli are normally perceived as integrated wholes, not as combinations of independent attributes. How does the brain combine individual sensory attributes to produce integrated perceptions? This is called the *binding problem* (see Feldman, 2013; but see Di Lollo, 2012).

One possible solution to the binding problem is that there is a single area of the cortex at the top of the sensory hierarchy that receives signals from all other areas of the various sensory systems and puts them together to form perceptions. One area of the brain that has received recent attention as the potential location for the binding of sensory information is the *claustrum*, a structure that is made up of a fine sheet of neurons located just underneath the neocortex towards the middle of the brain (see Goll, Atlan, & Citri, 2015).

Not shown in Figure 7.1 are the many neurons that descend through the sensory hierarchies. Although most

---

*Based on *The Man Who Mistook His Wife for a Hat and Other Clinical Tales* by Oliver Sacks. Copyright © 1970, 1981, 1983, 1984, 1986 by Oliver Sacks.

Figure 7.1 Two models of sensory system organization: The former model was hierarchical, functionally homogeneous, and serial; the current model, which is more consistent with the evidence, is hierarchical, functionally segregated, and parallel. Not shown in the current model are the many descending pathways that are the means by which higher levels of sensory systems can influence sensory input.

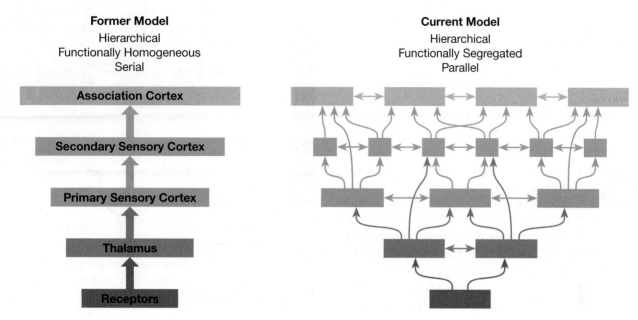

sensory neurons carry information from lower to higher levels of their respective sensory hierarchies, some conduct in the opposite direction (from higher to lower levels). These are said to carry *top-down signals* (see Bressler & Richter, 2015; Ruff, 2013).

Now that you have an understanding of the general principles of sensory system organization, let's take a look at the auditory system, the somatosensory system, and the chemical sensory systems (smell and taste).

Auditory System

The function of the auditory system is the perception of sound. Sounds are vibrations of air molecules that stimulate the auditory system; humans hear only those molecular vibrations between about 20 and 20,000 hertz (cycles per second).

Physical and Perceptual Dimensions of Sound

LO 7.3   Explain the relationship between the physical and perceptual dimensions of sound.

Figure 7.2 illustrates how sounds are commonly recorded in the form of waves and the relation between the physical

Figure 7.2 The relation between the physical and perceptual dimensions of sound.

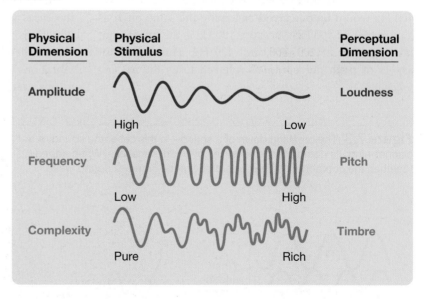

dimensions of sound vibrations and our perceptions of them. The *amplitude, frequency,* and *complexity* of the molecular vibrations are most closely linked to perceptions of *loudness, pitch,* and *timbre,* respectively.

Pure tones (sine wave vibrations) exist only in laboratories and sound recording studios; in real life, sound is always associated with complex patterns of vibrations. For example, Figure 7.3 illustrates the complex sound wave associated with one note of a clarinet. The figure also illustrates that any complex sound wave can be broken down mathematically into a series of sine waves of various frequencies and amplitudes; these component sine waves produce the original sound when they are added together. **Fourier analysis** is the mathematical procedure for breaking down complex waves into their component sine waves. One theory of audition is that the auditory system performs a Fourier-like analysis of complex sounds in terms of their component sine waves.

For any pure tone, there is a close relationship between the frequency of the tone and its perceived pitch; however, the relation between the frequencies that make up natural sounds (which are always composed of a mixture of frequencies) and their perceived pitch is complex (see Bidelman & Grall, 2014): The pitch of such sounds is related to their *fundamental frequency* (the highest frequency of which the various component frequencies of a sound are multiples). For example, a sound that is a mixture of 100, 200, and 300 Hz frequencies normally has a pitch related to 100 Hz because 100 Hz is the highest frequency of which the three components are multiples. An extremely important characteristic of pitch perception is the fact that the pitch of a complex sound may not be directly related to the frequency of any of the sound's components (see Lau & Werner, 2014). For example, a mixture of pure tones with frequencies of 200, 300, and 400 Hz would be perceived as having the same pitch as a pure tone of 100 Hz—because 100 Hz is the fundamental frequency of 200, 300, and 400 Hz. This important aspect of pitch perception is referred to as the *missing fundamental*.

Watch this video on MyPsychLab
AUDITION

The Ear

LO 7.4 Describe the components of the human ear, and explain how sound is processed within its various structures.

The ear is illustrated in Figure 7.4. Sound waves travel from the outer ear down the auditory canal and cause the **tympanic membrane** (the eardrum) to vibrate. These vibrations are then transferred to the three **ossicles**—the small bones of the middle ear: the *malleus* (the hammer), the *incus* (the anvil), and the *stapes* (the stirrup). The vibrations of the stapes trigger vibrations of the membrane called the **oval window**, which in turn transfers the vibrations to the fluid of the snail-shaped **cochlea** (*kokhlos* means "land snail"). The cochlea is a long, coiled tube with an internal structure running almost to its tip. This internal structure is the auditory receptor organ, the **organ of Corti**.

Each pressure change at the oval window travels along the organ of Corti as a wave. The organ of Corti is composed of several membranes; we will focus on two of them: the basilar membrane and the tectorial membrane. The auditory receptors, the **hair cells**, are mounted in the **basilar membrane**, and the **tectorial membrane** rests on the hair cells (see Hudspeth, 2014). Accordingly, a deflection of the organ of Corti at any point along its length produces a shearing force on the hair cells at the same point. This force stimulates the hair cells, which in turn increase firing in axons of the **auditory nerve**—a branch of cranial nerve VIII (the *auditory-vestibular nerve*). The vibrations of the cochlear fluid are ultimately dissipated by the *round window*, an elastic membrane in the cochlea wall.

Figure 7.3 The breaking down of a sound—in this case, the sound of a clarinet—into its component sine waves by Fourier analysis. When added together, the component sine waves produce the complex sound wave.

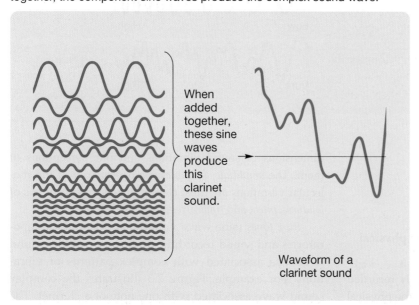

When added together, these sine waves produce this clarinet sound.

Waveform of a clarinet sound

Figure 7.4 Anatomy of the ear.

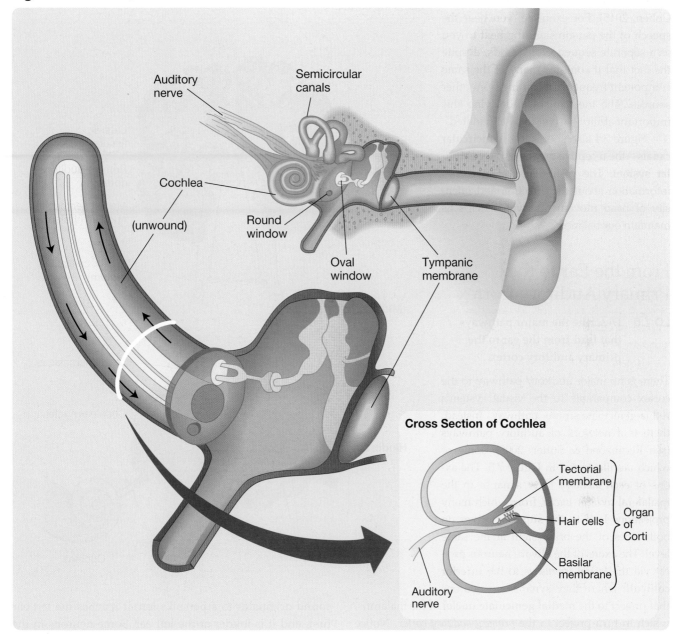

The cochlea is remarkably sensitive (see Hudspeth, 2014). Humans can hear differences in pure tones that differ in frequency by only 0.2 percent. The major principle of cochlear coding is that different frequencies produce maximal stimulation of hair cells at different points along the basilar membrane—with higher frequencies producing greater activation closer to the windows and lower frequencies producing greater activation at the tip of the basilar membrane. Thus, the many component frequencies that compose each complex sound activate hair cells at many different points along the basilar membrane, and the many signals created by a single complex sound are carried out of the ear by many different auditory neurons. Like the cochlea, most other structures of the auditory system are arrayed according to frequency. Thus, in the same way that the organization of the visual system is largely **retinotopic**, the organization of the auditory system is largely **tonotopic** (see Schreiner & Polley, 2014).

This brings us to the major unsolved mystery of auditory processing. Imagine yourself in a complex acoustic environment such as a party. The music is playing; people are dancing, eating, and drinking; and numerous conversations are going on around you. Because the component frequencies in each individual sound activate many sites along your basilar membrane, the number of sites simultaneously activated at any one time by the party noises is enormous. But somehow your auditory system manages to sort these individual frequency messages into separate categories and combine them so that you hear each source of complex sounds independently (see Bremen &

Middlebrooks, 2013; Christison-Lagay & Cohen, 2014; Christison-Lagay, Gifford, & Cohen, 2015). For example, you hear the speech of the person standing next to you as a separate sequence of sounds, despite the fact that it contains many of the same component frequencies coming from other sources. The mechanism underlying this important ability has yet to be elucidated.

Figure 7.4 also shows the **semicircular canals**—the receptive organs of the **vestibular system**. The vestibular system carries information about the direction and intensity of head movements, which helps us maintain our balance.

From the Ear to the Primary Auditory Cortex

LO 7.5   Describe the major pathways that lead from the ear to the primary auditory cortex.

There is no major auditory pathway to the cortex comparable to the visual system's retina-geniculate-striate pathway. Instead, there is a network of auditory pathways (see Recanzone & Sutter, 2008), some of which are illustrated in Figure 7.5. The axons of each *auditory nerve* synapse in the ipsilateral *cochlear nuclei*, from which many projections lead to the **superior olives** on both sides of the brain stem at the same level. The axons of the olivary neurons project via the *lateral lemniscus* to the **inferior colliculi**, where they synapse on neurons that project to the **medial geniculate nuclei** of the thalamus, which in turn project to the *primary auditory cortex*. Notice that signals from each ear are combined at a very low level (in the superior olives) and are transmitted to both ipsilateral and contralateral auditory cortex.

Because of the complexity of the subcortical auditory pathways, an analysis of their functions has been difficult. However, one function of the subcortical auditory system is well understood: the localization of sounds in space.

Subcortical Mechanisms of Sound Localization

LO 7.6   Describe the neural mechanisms underlying sound localization.

Localization of sounds in space is mediated by the lateral and medial superior olives, but in different ways. When a

Figure 7.5 Some of the pathways of the auditory system that lead from one ear to the cortex.

sound originates to a person's left, it reaches the left ear first, and it is louder at the left ear. Some neurons in the *medial superior olives* respond to slight differences in the time of arrival of signals from the two ears (see Phillips, Quinlan, & Dingle, 2012; Vonderschen & Wagner, 2014), whereas some neurons in the *lateral superior olives* respond to slight differences in the amplitude of sounds from the two ears (see Park et al., 2008; Pollack, 2012).

The medial and lateral superior olives project to the *superior colliculus* (not shown in Figure 7.5), as well as to the inferior colliculus. In contrast to the general tonotopic organization of the auditory system, the deep layers of the superior colliculi, which receive auditory input, are laid out according to a map of auditory space (see Ghose & Wallace, 2014). The superficial layers of the superior colliculi, which receive visual input, are organized retinotopically. Thus, it appears that the general function of the superior colliculi is locating sources of sensory input in space.

Many researchers interested in sound localization have studied barn owls because these owls can locate sources of sounds better than any other animal whose hearing has been tested (see Pena & Gutfreund, 2014). They are nocturnal hunters and must be able to locate field mice solely by the rustling sounds the mice make in the dark. Not surprisingly, the auditory neurons of the barn owl's superior colliculus region are very finely tuned; that is, each neuron responds to sounds from only a particular location in the range of the owl's hearing (see Mysore & Knudsen, 2014).

Auditory Cortex

LO 7.7   Describe the organization of auditory cortex.

Recent progress in the study of human auditory cortex has resulted from the convergence of functional brain-imaging studies in humans and invasive neural recording studies in monkeys (see Saenz & Langers, 2014). Still, primate auditory cortex is far from being well understood—for example, our understanding of it lags far behind our current understanding of visual cortex.

In primates, the primary auditory cortex, which receives the majority of its input from the medial geniculate nucleus, is located in the temporal lobe, hidden from view within the lateral fissure (see Figure 7.6). Primate primary auditory cortex comprises three adjacent areas (see Moerel, De Martino, & Formisano, 2014): Together these three areas are referred to as the *core region*. Surrounding the core region is a band—often called the *belt*—of areas of secondary auditory cortex. Areas of secondary auditory cortex outside the belt are called *parabelt areas*. There seem to be about 20 separate areas of auditory cortex in primates (see Bendor & Wang, 2006).

ORGANIZATION OF PRIMATE AUDITORY CORTEX. Two important principles of organization of primary auditory cortex have been identified. First, like the primary visual cortex, the primary auditory cortex is organized in functional columns (see Mizrahi, Shalev, & Nelken, 2014): All of the neurons encountered during a vertical microelectrode penetration of primary auditory cortex (i.e., a penetration at right angles to the cortical layers) tend to respond optimally to sounds in the same frequency range. Second, like the cochlea, auditory cortex is organized tonotopically (see Schreiner & Polley, 2014): Each area of primary and secondary auditory cortex appears to be organized on the basis of frequency.

WHAT SOUNDS SHOULD BE USED TO STUDY AUDITORY CORTEX? Why has research on auditory cortex lagged behind research on visual cortex? There are several reasons,. but a major one is a lack of clear understanding of the dimensions along which auditory cortex evaluates sound (Sharpee, Atencio, & Schreiner, 2011). You may recall from Chapter 6 that research on the visual cortex did not start to progress rapidly until Hubel and Weisel discovered that most visual neurons respond to contrast. There is clear evidence of a hierarchical organization in auditory cortex—the neural responses of secondary auditory cortex tend to be more complex and varied than those of primary auditory cortex (see Scott, 2005).

Many neurons in auditory cortex respond only weakly to simple stimuli such as pure tones, which have been widely employed in electrophysiological studies of auditory cortex. This practice is changing, however, partly in response to the discovery that many auditory cortex neurons in the belt and parabelt areas of monkeys respond robustly to monkey calls (see Romanski & Averbeck, 2009). Indeed, it has become apparent that natural sounds, in general, are better at eliciting responses from neurons in mammalian auditory cortex (see Mizrahi, Shalev, & Nelken, 2014; Theunissen & Elie, 2014). Be that as it may, we still have no idea what analysis the auditory cortex performs, which makes it difficult to ask the right research questions and to probe the system with appropriate acoustic stimuli (Hromádka & Zador, 2009).

TWO STREAMS OF AUDITORY CORTEX. Thinking about the general organization of auditory cortex has been inspired by research on visual cortex. Researchers have proposed that, just as there are two main cortical streams of visual analysis (dorsal and ventral), there are two main cortical streams of auditory analysis. Auditory signals are ultimately conducted to two large areas of association cortex: prefrontal cortex and posterior parietal cortex. It has been hypothesized that the

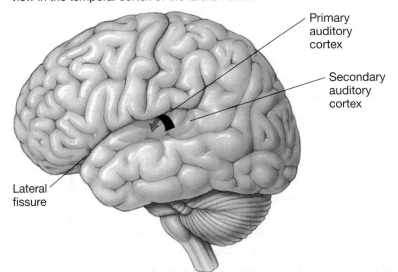

Figure 7.6 General location of the primary auditory cortex and areas of secondary auditory cortex. Most auditory cortex is hidden from view in the temporal cortex of the lateral fissure.

Primary auditory cortex

Secondary auditory cortex

Lateral fissure

Figure 7.7 The hypothesized anterior and posterior auditory pathways.

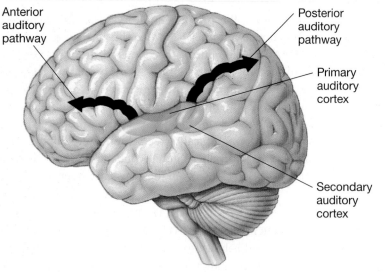

anterior auditory pathway is more involved in identifying sounds (what), whereas the *posterior auditory pathway* is more involved in locating sounds (where)—see Cloutman (2013) and Du et al. (2015). These pathways are illustrated in Figure 7.7. Some authors have suggested that the primary function of the auditory posterior pathway is the preparation for action (Arnott & Alain, 2011).

AUDITORY-VISUAL INTERACTIONS. Sensory systems have traditionally been assumed to interact in association cortex. Indeed, as you have already learned, association cortex is usually defined as areas of cortex where such interactions, or associations, take place. Much of the research on sensory system interactions has focused on interactions between the auditory and visual systems, particularly on those that occur in the posterior parietal cortex (see Brang et al., 2013; Cohen, 2009). In one study of monkeys (Mulette-Gillman, Cohen, & Groh, 2005), some posterior parietal neurons were found to have visual receptive fields, some were found to have auditory receptive fields, and some were found to have both. Those that had both visual and auditory receptive fields had both fields covering the same location of the monkey's immediate environment.

Functional brain imaging is widely used to investigate sensory system interactions. One advantage of functional brain imaging is that it does not focus on any one part of the brain; it records activity throughout the brain. Functional brain-imaging studies have confirmed that sensory interactions do occur in association cortex, but more importantly, they have repeatedly found evidence of sensory interactions at the lowest level of the sensory cortex hierarchy, in areas of primary sensory cortex (see Man et al., 2013; Smith & Goodale, 2015). This discovery is changing how we think about the interaction of sensory systems: Sensory system interaction is not merely tagged on after *unimodal* (involving one system) analyses are

complete; sensory system interaction seems to be an early and integral part of sensory processing.

WHERE DOES THE PERCEPTION OF PITCH OCCUR? Recent research has answered one fundamental question about auditory cortex: Where does the perception of pitch likely occur? This seemed like a simple question to answer because most areas of auditory cortex have a clear tonotopic organization. However, when experimenters used sound stimuli in which frequency and pitch were different—for example, by using the missing fundamental technique—most auditory neurons responded to changes in frequency rather than pitch. This information led Bendor and Wang (2005) to probe primary and secondary areas of monkey auditory cortex with microelectrodes to assess the responses of individual neurons to missing fundamental stimuli. They discovered one small area just anterior to primary auditory cortex that contained many neurons that responded to pitch rather than frequency, regardless of the quality of the sound. The same small area also contained neurons that responded to frequency, and Bendor and Wang suggested that this area was likely the place where frequencies of sound were converted to the perception of pitch. A comparable pitch area has been identified by fMRI studies in a similar location in the human brain.

Effects of Damage to the Auditory System

LO 7.8 Describe the effects of damage to the auditory system.

The study of damage to the auditory system is important for two reasons. First, it provides information about how the auditory system works. Second, it can serve as a source of information about the causes and treatment of clinical deafness.

Clinical Implications

AUDITORY CORTEX DAMAGE. Efforts to characterize the effects of damage to human auditory cortex have been complicated by the fact that most human auditory cortex is in the lateral fissure. Consequently, it is rarely destroyed in its entirety; and if it is, there is almost always extensive damage to surrounding tissue. As a result, efforts to understand the effects of auditory cortex damage have relied largely on the study of surgically placed lesions in nonhumans.

Most studies of the effects of auditory cortex lesions have assessed the effects of large lesions that involve the core region and most of the belt and parabelt areas. Given the large size of the lesions in most studies, the lack of severe permanent deficits is surprising, suggesting that the subcortical circuits serve more complex and important auditory functions than was once assumed.

Figure 7.8 Cochlear implant: The surgical implantation is shown on the left, and a child with an implant is shown on the right.

Although the effects of auditory cortex lesions depend somewhat on the species, the effects in humans and monkeys appear to be quite similar (see Heffner & Heffner, 2003). Following bilateral lesions, there is often a complete

Evolutionary Perspective

loss of hearing, which presumably results from the shock of the lesion because hearing recovers in the ensuing weeks. The major permanent effects are loss of the ability to localize sounds and impairment of the ability to discriminate frequencies (see Heffner & Heffner, 2003).

The effects of unilateral auditory cortex lesions suggest that the system is partially contralateral. A unilateral lesion disrupts the ability to localize sounds in space contralateral, but not ipsilateral, to the lesion. However, other auditory deficits produced by unilateral auditory cortex lesions tend to be only slightly greater for contralateral sounds.

DEAFNESS IN HUMANS. Deafness is one of the most prevalent human disabilities: An estimated 360 million people currently suffer from disabling hearing impairments (World Health Organization, 2015). Total deafness is rare, occurring in only 1 percent of hearing-impaired individuals.

Severe hearing problems typically result from damage to the inner ear or the middle ear or to the nerves leading from them rather than from more central damage. There are two common classes of hearing impairments: those associated with damage to the ossicles (*conductive deafness*) and

those associated with damage to the cochlea or auditory nerve (*nerve deafness*). The major cause of nerve deafness is a loss of hair cell receptors (see Wong & Ryan, 2015).

If only part of the cochlea is damaged, individuals may have nerve deafness for some frequencies but not others. For example, age-related hearing loss features a specific deficit in hearing high frequencies. That is why elderly people often have difficulty distinguishing "s," "f," and "t" sounds: They can hear people speaking to them but often have difficulty understanding what people are saying. Often, relatives and friends do not realize that much of the confusion displayed by the elderly stems from difficulty discriminating sounds (see Wingfield, Tun, & McCoy, 2005).

Hearing loss is sometimes associated with **tinnitus** (ringing of the ears). When only one ear is damaged, the ringing is perceived as coming from that ear; however, cutting the nerve from the ringing ear has no effect on the ringing. This suggests that changes to the central auditory system that were caused **Neuroplasticity** by the deafness are the cause of tinnitus (see Eggermont & Tass, 2015; Elgoyhen et al., 2015; Noreña & Farley, 2013).

Neuroplasticity Why do you think tinnitus is associated with deafness? [Hint: Do sensory neurons stop firing in the absence of sensory input?]

Some people with nerve deafness benefit from cochlear implants (see Figure 7.8). *Cochlear implants* bypass damage to the auditory hair cells by converting sounds picked up by a microphone on the patient's ear to electrical signals, which are then carried into the cochlea by a bundle of electrodes.

These signals excite the auditory nerve. Although cochlear implants can provide major benefits, they do not restore normal hearing. The sooner a person receives a cochlear implant after becoming deaf, the more likely he or she is to benefit, because disuse leads to alterations of the auditory neural pathways (see Kral & Sharma, 2012).

Scan Your Brain

Before we go on to discuss the other sensory systems, pause and test your knowledge of what you have learned in this chapter so far. The correct answers are provided at the end of the exercise. Before proceeding, review material related to your errors and omissions.

1. The _____ is the area of the sensory cortex that receives most of its input directly from the thalamic relay nuclei of the system.
2. _____ is the process of detecting the presence of stimuli.
3. Simultaneous analysis of a signal in different ways by the multiple pathways of a neural network is referred to as _____.
4. _____ is the mathematical procedure for breaking down complex waves into their component sine waves.
5. _____ are also called sine wave vibrations.
6. The three _____ are malleus, incus, and the stapes.

7. The layout of the auditory system tends to be _____.
8. The axons of the auditory nerves synapse in the ipsilateral _____ nuclei.
9. One function of the superior olives is sound _____.
10. The _____ is made up of a fine sheet of neurons located just underneath the neocortex, toward the middle of the brain.
11. The _____ is the membrane that transfers vibrations from the ossicles to the fluid of the cochlea.
12. Many studies of auditory-visual interactions have focused on association cortex in the posterior _____ cortex.

Scan Your Brain answers: (1) primary sensory cortex, (2) Sensation, (3) parallel processing, (4) Fourier analysis, (5) Pure tones, (6) ossicles, (7) tonotopic, (8) cochlear, (9) localization, (10) claustrum, (11) oval window, (12) parietal.

Somatosensory System: Touch and Pain

Sensations from your body are referred to as *somatosensations*. The system that mediates these bodily sensations—the *somatosensory system*—is three separate but interacting systems: (1) an *exteroceptive system*, which senses external stimuli that are applied to the skin; (2) a *proprioceptive system*, which monitors information about the position of the body that comes from receptors in the muscles, joints, and organs of balance; and (3) an *interoceptive system*, which provides general information about conditions within the body (e.g., temperature and blood pressure). This module deals almost exclusively with the exteroceptive system, which itself comprises three somewhat distinct divisions: a division for perceiving *mechanical stimuli* (touch), one for *thermal stimuli* (temperature), and one for *nociceptive stimuli* (pain).

Cutaneous Receptors

LO 7.9 Name some of the cutaneous receptors, and explain the functional significance of fast versus slow receptor adaptation.

There are many kinds of receptors in the skin (see Owens & Lumpkin, 2014; Zimmerman, Bai, & Ginty, 2014). Figure 7.9

Figure 7.9 Four cutaneous receptors that occur in human skin.

Ruffini ending   Merkel's disks   Free nerve ending   Pacinian corpuscles

Artery   Vein   Sweat gland   Fat

illustrates four of them. The simplest cutaneous receptors are the **free nerve endings** (neuron endings with no specialized structures on them), which are particularly sensitive to temperature change and pain. The largest and deepest cutaneous receptors are the onionlike **Pacinian corpuscles**; because they adapt rapidly, they respond to sudden displacements of the skin but not to constant pressure. In contrast, **Merkel's disks** and **Ruffini endings** both adapt slowly and respond to gradual skin indentation and skin stretch, respectively.

To appreciate the functional significance of fast and slow receptor adaptation, consider what happens when a constant pressure is applied to the skin. The pressure evokes a burst of firing in all receptors, which corresponds to the sensation of being touched; however, after a few hundred milliseconds, only the slowly adapting receptors remain active, and the quality of the sensation changes. In fact, you are often totally unaware of constant skin pressure; for example, you are usually unaware of the feeling of your clothes against your body until you focus attention on it. As a consequence, when you try to identify objects by touch, you manipulate them in your hands so that the pattern of stimulation continually changes. (The identification of objects by touch is called **stereognosis**.) Having some receptors that adapt quickly and some that adapt slowly provides information about both the dynamic and static qualities of tactual stimuli.

The structure and physiology of each type of somatosensory receptor seems to be specialized for a different function. However, in general, the various receptors tend to function in the same way: Stimuli applied to the skin deform or change the chemistry of the receptor, and this in turn changes the permeability of the receptor cell membrane to various ions (see Delmas, Hao, & Rodat-Despoix, 2011; Tsunozaki & Bautista, 2009). The result is a neural signal.

Initially, it was assumed that each type of receptor located in the skin (see Figure 7.9) mediates a different tactile sensation (e.g., touch, pain, heat), but this has not proven to be the case. Each tactile sensation appears to be produced by the interaction of multiple receptor mechanisms, and each receptor mechanism appears to contribute to multiple sensations (see Hollins, 2010; Lumpkin & Caterina, 2007; McGlone & Reilly, 2009). In addition, skin cells that surround particular receptors also seem to play a role in the quality of the sensations produced by that receptor (see Zimmerman, Bai, & Ginty, 2014). Indeed, new forms of tactile sensation are still being discovered (see McGlone, Wessberg, & Olausson, 2014).

DERMATOMES. The neural fibers that carry information from cutaneous receptors and other somatosensory receptors gather together in nerves and enter the spinal

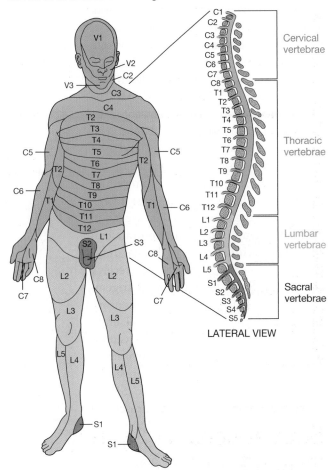

Figure 7.10 The dermatomes of the human body. S, L, T, and C refer respectively to the sacral, lumbar, thoracic, and cervical regions of the spinal cord. V1, V2, and V3 stand for the three branches of the trigeminal nerve.

cord via the *dorsal roots*. The area of the body that is innervated by the left and right dorsal roots of a given segment of the spinal cord is called a **dermatome**. Figure 7.10 is a dermatomal map of the human body. Because there is considerable overlap between adjacent dermatomes, destruction of a single dorsal root typically produces little somatosensory loss.

Two Major Somatosensory Pathways

LO 7.10 Describe the two major somatosensory pathways.

Somatosensory information ascends from each side of the body to the human cortex over several pathways, but there are two major ones: the dorsal-column medial-lemniscus system and the anterolateral system. The **dorsal-column medial-lemniscus system** tends to carry information about touch and proprioception, and the **anterolateral system** tends to carry information about pain and temperature. The key words in the preceding sentence are "tends to": The separation of function in the two pathways is far from complete. Accordingly, lesions of the dorsal-column medial-lemniscus system do not eliminate touch perception or proprioception, and lesions of the anterolateral system do not eliminate perception of pain or temperature.

The dorsal-column medial-lemniscus system is illustrated in Figure 7.11. The sensory neurons of this system enter the spinal cord via a dorsal root, ascend ipsilaterally in the **dorsal columns**, and synapse in the *dorsal column nuclei* of the medulla. The axons of dorsal column nuclei neurons *decussate* (cross over to the other side of the brain) and then ascend in the **medial lemniscus** to the contralateral **ventral posterior nucleus** of the thalamus. The ventral posterior nuclei also receive input via the three branches of the trigeminal nerve, which carry somatosensory information from the contralateral areas of the face. Most neurons of the ventral posterior nucleus project to the *primary somatosensory cortex (SI)*; others project to the *secondary somatosensory cortex (SII)* or the posterior parietal cortex. Neuroscience trivia buffs will almost certainly want to add to their collection the fact that the dorsal column neurons that originate in the toes are the longest neurons in the human body.

The anterolateral system is illustrated in Figure 7.12. Most dorsal root neurons of the anterolateral system synapse as soon as they enter the spinal cord. The axons of most of the second-order neurons decussate but then ascend to the brain in the contralateral anterolateral portion of the spinal cord; however, some do not decussate but ascend ipsilaterally. The anterolateral system comprises three different tracts: the *spinothalamic tract*, the *spinoreticular tract*, and the *spinotectal tract*. The three branches of the trigeminal nerve carry pain and temperature information from the face to the same thalamic sites. The pain and temperature information that reaches the thalamus is then distributed to somatosensory cortex and other parts of the brain.

If both ascending somatosensory paths are completely transected by a spinal injury, the patient can feel no body sensation from below the level of the cut. 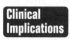 Clearly, when it comes to spinal injuries, lower is better.

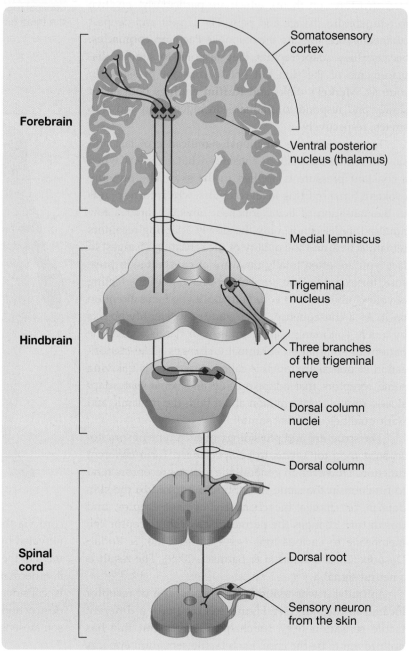

Figure 7.11 The dorsal-column medial-lemniscus system. The pathways from only one side of the body are shown.

Cortical Areas of Somatosensation

LO 7.11 Describe the cortical somatosensory areas and their somatotopic layout.

In 1937, Penfield and his colleagues mapped the primary somatosensory cortex of patients during neurosurgery (see Figure 7.13). Penfield applied electrical stimulation to various sites on the cortical surface, and the patients, who were fully conscious under a local anesthetic, described what they felt. When stimulation was applied to the *postcentral gyrus*, the patients reported somatosensory sensations in

Figure 7.12 The anterolateral system. The pathways from only one side of the body are shown.

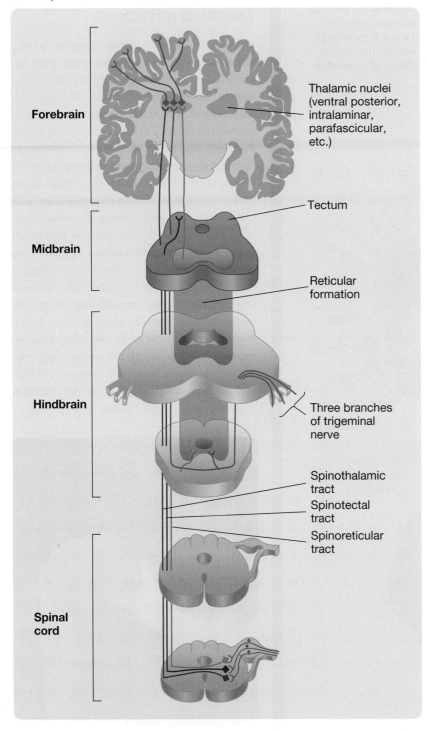

Forebrain

Thalamic nuclei (ventral posterior, intralaminar, parafascicular, etc.)

Midbrain

Tectum

Reticular formation

Hindbrain

Three branches of trigeminal nerve

Spinothalamic tract

Spinotectal tract

Spinoreticular tract

Spinal cord

Notice in Figure 7.13 that the somatosensory homunculus is distorted; the greatest proportion of SI is dedicated to receiving input from the parts of the body we use to make tactile discriminations (e.g., hands, lips, and tongue). In contrast, only small areas of SI receive input from large areas of the body, such as the back, that are not usually used to make somatosensory discriminations. The Check It Out demonstration on page 180 allows you to experience the impact this organization has on your ability to perceive touches.

A second somatotopically organized area, SII, lies just ventral to SI in the postcentral gyrus, and much of it extends into the lateral fissure. SII receives most of its input from SI and is thus regarded as secondary somatosensory cortex. In contrast to SI, whose input is largely contralateral, SII receives substantial input from both sides of the body. Much of the output of SI and SII goes to the association cortex of the *posterior parietal lobe* (see McGlone & Reilly, 2010).

Studies of the responses of single neurons in primary somatosensory cortex found evidence for columnar organization—similar to what you have already seen in visual and auditory cortex. Each neuron in a particular column of primary somatosensory cortex had a receptive field on the same part of the body and responded most robustly to the same type of tactile stimuli (e.g., light touch or heat). Moreover, single-neuron recordings suggested that primary somatosensory cortex is composed of four functional strips, each with a similar, but separate, somatotopic organization. Each strip of primary somatosensory cortex is most sensitive to a different kind of somatosensory input (e.g., to light touch or pressure). Thus, if one were to record from neurons across the four strips, one would find neurons that "preferred" four different kinds of tactile stimulation, all to the same part of the body.

Reminiscent of the developments in the study of visual and auditory cortex, it has been proposed that two streams of analysis proceed from SI: a dorsal stream that projects to posterior parietal cortex and participates in multisensory integration and direction of attention and a ventral stream that projects to SII and

various parts of their bodies. When Penfield mapped the relation between each site of stimulation and the part of the body in which the sensation was felt, he discovered that the human primary somatosensory cortex (SI) is **somatotopic**—organized according to a map of the body surface (see Chen et al., 2015). This somatotopic map is commonly referred to as the **somatosensory homunculus** (*homunculus* means "little man").

Figure 7.13 The locations of human primary somatosensory cortex (SI) and one area of secondary somatosensory cortex (SII) with the conventional portrayal of the somatosensory homunculus. Something has always confused us about this portrayal of the somatosensory homunculus: The body is upside down, while the face is right side up. It now appears that this conventional portrayal is wrong. The results of an fMRI study suggest that the face representation is also inverted. (Based on Servos et al., 1999.)

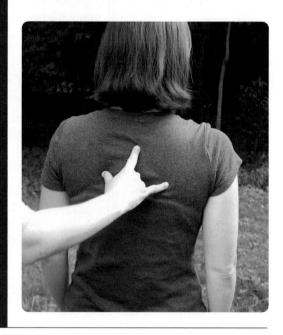

Check It Out
Touching a Back

Because only a small portion of human primary somatosensory cortex receives input from the entire back, people have difficulty recognizing objects that touch their backs. You may not have noticed this tactile deficiency—unless, of course, you often try to identify objects by feeling them with your back. You will need one thing to demonstrate the recognition deficiencies of the human back: a friend. Touch your friend on the back with one, two, or three fingers, and ask your friend how many fingers he or she feels. When using two or three fingers, be sure they touch the back simultaneously because temporal cues invalidate this test of tactile discrimination. Repeat the test many times, adjusting the distance between the touches on each trial. Record the results. What you should begin to notice is that the back is incapable of discriminating between separate touches unless the distance between the touches is considerable. In contrast, fingertips can distinguish the number of simultaneous touches even when the touches are very close.

participates in the perception of objects' shapes (Yau, Connor, & Hsiao, 2013).

EFFECTS OF DAMAGE TO THE PRIMARY SOMATO-SENSORY CORTEX. Like the effects of damage to the primary auditory cortex, the effects of damage to the primary somatosensory cortex are often remarkably mild—presumably because, like the auditory system, the somatosensory system features numerous parallel pathways. Corkin, Milner, and Rasmussen (1970) assessed the somatosensory abilities of epileptic patients before and after a unilateral excision that included SI. Following the surgery, the patients displayed two minor contralateral deficits: a reduced ability to detect light touch and a reduced ability to identify objects by touch (i.e., a deficit in stereognosis). These deficits were bilateral only in those cases in which the unilateral lesion encroached on SII.

Somatosensory System and Association Cortex

LO 7.12 Name the areas of association cortex that somatosensory signals are sent to, and describe the functional properties of one of those areas.

Somatosensory signals are ultimately conducted to the highest level of the sensory hierarchy, to areas of association cortex in prefrontal and posterior parietal cortex.

Posterior parietal cortex contains *bimodal neurons* (neurons that respond to activation of two different sensory systems) that respond to both somatosensory and visual stimuli (see Rosenblum, 2013). The visual and somatosensory receptive fields of each neuron are spatially related; for example, if a neuron has a somatosensory receptive field centered in the left hand, its visual field is adjacent to the left hand. Remarkably, as the left hand moves, the visual receptive field of the neuron moves with it. The existence of these bimodal neurons motivated the following interesting case study by Schendel and Robertson (2004).

The Case of W.M., Who Reduced His Scotoma with His Hand

W.M. suffered a stroke in his right posterior cerebral artery. The stroke affected a large area of his right occipital and parietal lobes and left him with severe left *hemianopsia* (a condition in which a scotoma covers half the visual field). When tested with his left hand in his lap, W.M. detected 97.8 percent of the stimuli presented in his right visual field and only 13.6 percent of those presented in his left visual field. However, when he was tested with his left hand extended into his left visual field, his ability to detect stimuli in his left visual field improved significantly. Further analysis showed that this general improvement resulted from W.M.'s greatly improved ability to see those objects in the left visual field that were near his left hand. Remarkably, this area of improved performance around his left hand was expanded even further when he held a tennis racket in his extended left hand.

Somatosensory Agnosias

LO 7.13 Describe the two major types of somatosensory agnosia.

There are two major types of somatosensory agnosia. One is **astereognosia**—the inability to recognize objects by touch. Cases of pure astereognosia—those that occur in the absence of simple sensory deficits—are rare (Corkin, Milner, & Rasmussen, 1970). The other type of somatosensory agnosia is **asomatognosia**—the failure to recognize parts of one's own body. Asomatognosia is usually unilateral, affecting only the left side of the body, and it is usually associated with extensive damage to the right temporal and posterior parietal lobe (Feinberg et al., 2010). The case of Aunt Betty (Klawans, 1990) is an example.

The Case of Aunt Betty, Who Lost Half of Her Body*

Aunt Betty was my patient. She wasn't really my aunt, she was my mother's best friend.

As we walked to her hospital room, one of the medical students described the case. "Left hemiplegia [left-side paralysis], following a right-hemisphere stroke." I was told.

Aunt Betty was lying on her back with her head and eyes turned to the right. "Betty," I called out.

I approached her bed from the left, but Aunt Betty did not turn her head or even her eyes to look toward me.

"Hal," she called out. "Where are you?"

I turned her head gently toward me, and we talked. It was clear that she had no speech problems, no memory loss, and no confusion. She was as sharp as ever. But her eyes still looked to the right, as if the left side of her world did not exist.

I held her right hand in front of her eyes. "What's this?" I asked.

"My hand, of course," she said with an intonation that suggested what she thought of my question.

"Well then, what's this?" I said, as I held up her limp left hand where she could see it.

"A hand."

"Whose hand?"

"Your hand, I guess," she replied. She seemed puzzled. I placed her hand back on the bed.

"Why have you come to the hospital?" I asked.

"To see you," she replied hesitantly. I could tell that she didn't know why.

Aunt Betty was in trouble.

As in the case of Aunt Betty, asomatognosia is often accompanied by **anosognosia**—the failure of neuropsychological patients to recognize their own symptoms. Indeed, anosognosia is a common, but curious, symptom of many neurological disorders—many neurological patients with severe behavioral problems think that they are doing quite well.

Asomatognosia is commonly a component of **contralateral neglect**—the tendency not to respond to stimuli that are contralateral to a right-hemisphere injury. You will learn more about contralateral neglect in Chapter 8.

Rubber-Hand Illusion

LO 7.14 Describe the rubber-hand illusion and its neural mechanisms.

We perceive ownership of our own body parts. Somesthetic sensation is so fundamental that it is taken for granted.

*Based on NEWTON'S MADNESS by Harold Klawans (Harper & Row 1990).

This is why exceptions to it, such as asomatognosia, are so remarkable. In the past decade, another exception—one that is in some respects the opposite of asomatognosia—has been a focus of research. This exception is the **rubber-hand illusion** (the feeling that an extraneous object, in this case a rubber hand, is actually part of one's own body).

The rubber-hand illusion can be generated in a variety of ways, but it is usually induced in the following manner (see Kilteni et al., 2015; Moseley, Gallace, & Spence, 2012). A healthy volunteer's hand is hidden from view by a screen, and a rubber hand is placed next to the hidden hand but in clear sight. Then the experimenter repeatedly strokes the hidden hand and the rubber hand synchronously—see Figure 7.14. In less than a minute, many volunteers begin to feel that the rubber hand is part of their own body (see Blanke, Slater, & Serino, 2015). Interestingly, when this happens, the temperature in the hidden hand drops (Moseley et al., 2008).

Although the neural mechanisms for the rubber-hand illusion are unknown, functional imaging studies have suggested that association cortex in the posterior parietal and frontal lobes plays a role in its induction (see Limanowski & Blankenburg, 2015; Tsakiris et al., 2007). It has been suggested that those frontal and parietal *bimodal neurons* with both visual and somatosensory fields play a critical role (see Kilteni et al., 2015).

Schaefer and colleagues (Schaefer et al., 2007; Schaefer, Heinze, & Rotte, 2009) adapted the rubber-hand technique to induce two particularly interesting somatosensory illusions. In one, volunteers felt that one

of their arms had been stretched, and in the other they felt that they had three arms.

Perception of Pain

LO 7.15 Explain why the perception of pain is said to be paradoxical.

A paradox is a logical contradiction. The perception of pain is paradoxical in three important respects, which are explained in the following three subsections.

ADAPTIVENESS OF PAIN.   One paradox of pain is that an experience that seems in every respect to be so bad is in fact extremely important for our survival. There is no special stimulus for pain; it is a response to potentially harmful stimulation of any type. It **Evolutionary Perspective** warns us to stop engaging in potentially harmful activities or to seek treatment (see Navratilova & Porreca, 2014).

The value of pain is best illustrated by the cases of people, like Miss C., who experience no pain (Melzack & Wall, 1982).

The Case of Miss C., the Woman Who Felt No Pain

Miss C., a university student, was very intelligent, and she was normal in every way except that she never felt pain. Her condition is now referred to as *congenital insensitivity to pain*.

She felt no pain when subjected to strong electric shock, burning hot water, or an ice bath. Equally astonishing was the fact that she showed no changes in blood pressure, heart rate, or respiration when these stimuli were **Clinical Implications** presented. Furthermore, she did not sneeze, cough, or display corneal reflexes (blinking to protect the eyes). As a child, she had bitten off the tip of her tongue while chewing food and had suffered severe burns after kneeling on a radiator.

Miss C. exhibited pathological changes in her knees, hip, and spine because of the lack of protection to joints provided by pain sensation. She apparently failed to shift her weight when standing, to turn over in her sleep, or to avoid harmful postures.

Miss C. died at the age of 29 of massive infections and extensive skin and bone trauma.

Clinical Implications   Cases of congenital insensitivity to pain illustrate something important about the adaptive value of pain. Based on this case study, can you specify what that adaptive value might be?

Cox and colleagues (2006) studied six cases of congenital insensitivity to pain among members of a family from Pakistan. They were able to identify the gene abnormality underlying the disorder in these **Clinical Implications** six individuals: a gene that influences the synthesis of sodium ion channels. Indeed, knockout mice that

Figure 7.14 Induction method for the rubber-hand illusion. The participant's hand is hidden from view by a screen, and a rubber hand is placed next to their hidden hand but in clear sight. Then the experimenter repeatedly strokes the hidden hand and the rubber hand synchronously.

Rubber left hand   Real left hand

are missing this sodium ion channel gene show a comparable indifference to pain (Gingras et al., 2014). Other genetic disorders of painlessness have been identified—each involve a different genetic alteration (see Nahorski, Chen, & Woods, 2015).

LACK OF CLEAR CORTICAL REPRESENTATION OF PAIN. The second paradox of pain is that it has no obvious cortical representation (Rainville, 2002). Painful stimuli activate many areas of cortex including the thalamus, SI and SII, the insula, and the anterior cingulate cortex (see Figure 7.15)—see Navratilova and Porreca (2014). However, none of those areas seems necessary for the perception of pain. For example, painful stimuli usually elicit responses in SI and SII (see Zhuo, 2008). However, removal of SI and SII in humans is not associated with any change in the threshold for pain. Indeed, *hemispherectomized* patients (those with one cerebral hemisphere removed) can still perceive pain from both sides of their bodies.

The cortical area that has been most frequently linked to pain is the **anterior cingulate cortex** (see Figure 7.15). However, the anterior cingulate cortex appears to be involved in the expectation of pain, the emotional reaction to pain, and adaptive responses to minimize pain—rather than to the perception of pain itself (Shackman et al., 2011).

DESCENDING PAIN CONTROL. The third paradox of pain is that this most compelling of all sensory experiences

Thinking Creatively

can be so effectively suppressed by cognitive and emotional factors (see Bushnell, Čeko, & Low, 2013; Senkowski, Höfle, & Engel, 2014). For example, men participating in a certain religious

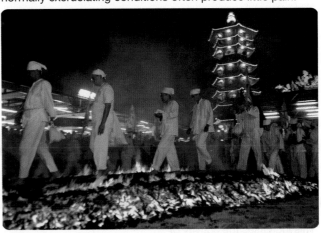

Figure 7.16 When experienced as part of a ritual, normally excruciating conditions often produce little pain.

ceremony suspend objects from hooks embedded in their backs with little evidence of pain (see Figure 7.16); severe wounds suffered by soldiers in battle are often associated with little pain; and people injured in life-threatening situations frequently feel no pain until the threat is over.

Three discoveries led to the identification of a descending pain-control circuit. First was the discovery that electrical stimulation of the **periaqueductal gray (PAG)** has analgesic (pain-blocking) effects: Reynolds (1969) was able to perform surgery on rats with no analgesia other than that provided by PAG stimulation. Second was the discovery that the PAG and other areas of the brain contain specialized receptors for opioid analgesic drugs such as morphine. And third was the isolation of several endogenous (internally produced) opioid analgesics, the **endorphins**, which you learned about in Chapter 4. These three findings together suggested that analgesic drugs and psychological factors might block pain through an endorphin-sensitive circuit that descends from the PAG.

Figure 7.17 illustrates the descending analgesia circuit first hypothesized by Basbaum and Fields (1978). They proposed that the output of the PAG excites the serotonergic neurons of the *raphé nuclei* (a cluster of serotonergic nuclei in the core of the medulla), which in turn project down the dorsal columns of the spinal cord and excite interneurons that block incoming pain signals in the dorsal horn.

Descending analgesia pathways have been the subject of intensive investigation since the first model was proposed by Basbaum and Fields in 1978. In order to incorporate the mass of accumulated data, models of the descending analgesia circuits have grown much more complex (see Lau & Vaughan, 2014). Still, a descending component involving endogenous opioid activity in the PAG and serotonergic activity in the raphé nuclei remains a key part of most models (see Mason, 2012).

Figure 7.15 Location of the anterior cingulate cortex in the cingulate gyrus.

Anterior cingulate cortex

Cingulate gyrus

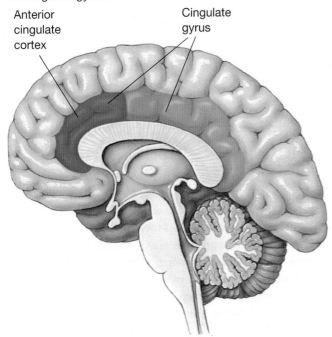

Figure 7.17 Basbaum and Field's (1978) model of the descending analgesia circuit.

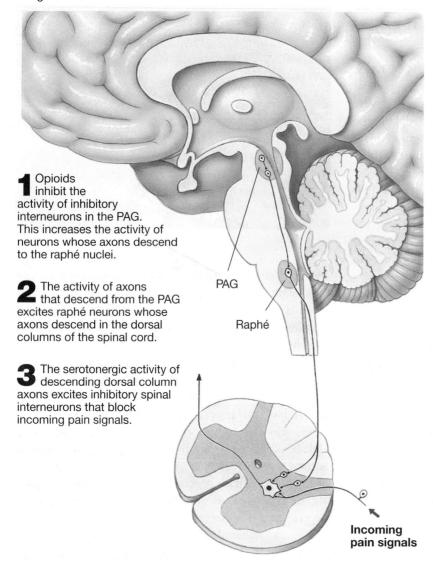

1 Opioids inhibit the activity of inhibitory interneurons in the PAG. This increases the activity of neurons whose axons descend to the raphé nuclei.

2 The activity of axons that descend from the PAG excites raphé neurons whose axons descend in the dorsal columns of the spinal cord.

3 The serotonergic activity of descending dorsal column axons excites inhibitory spinal interneurons that block incoming pain signals.

PAG

Raphé

Incoming pain signals

Watch this video on MyPsychLab

MANAGING PAIN

Neuropathic Pain

LO 7.16 Define neuropathic pain and describe some of its putative neural mechanisms.

In most cases, plasticity of the human nervous system helps it function more effectively. In the case of neuropathic pain, just the opposite is true (see Luo, Kuner, & Kuner, 2014). **Neuropathic pain** is severe chronic pain in the absence of a recognizable pain stimulus. A typical case of neuropathic pain develops after an injury: The injury heals and there seems to be no reason for further pain, but the patient experiences chronic excruciating pain. In many cases, neuropathic pain can be triggered by an innocuous stimulus, such as a gentle touch.

Although the exact mechanisms of neuropathic pain are unknown, it is somehow caused by pathological changes in the nervous system induced by the original injury (see Elman & Borsook, 2016). Recent research has implicated signals from aberrant microglia in neuropathic pain; these signals are thought to trigger hyperactivity in neural pain pathways (Beggs & Salter, 2010; Tsuda et al., 2013).

Although the neuropathic pain may be perceived to be in a limb—even in an amputated limb (see Chapter 10)—it is caused by abnormal activity in the CNS. Thus, cutting nerves from the perceived location of the pain often brings little or no comfort. And, unfortunately, medications that have been developed to treat the pain associated with injury are usually ineffective against neuropathic pain.

Neuroplasticity

Chemical Senses: Smell and Taste

Olfaction (smell) and *gustation* (taste) are referred to as the chemical senses because their function is to monitor the chemical content of the environment. Smell is the response of the olfactory system to airborne chemicals that are drawn by inhalation over receptors in the nasal passages, and taste is the response of the gustatory system to chemicals in solution in the oral cavity.

Adaptive Roles of the Chemical Senses

LO 7.17 Describe two adaptive roles for the chemical senses.

When we are eating, smell and taste act in concert. Molecules of food excite both smell and taste receptors and produce an integrated sensory impression termed **flavor**. The contribution of olfaction to flavor is often underestimated, but you won't make this mistake if you remember that people with no sense of smell have difficulty distinguishing the flavors of apples and onions. Flavor is also influenced by a number of other factors such as the temperature, texture, and appearance of the food and a person's level of satiety (see Chaudhauri & Roper, 2010; Rolls et al., 2010).

In humans, the main adaptive role of the chemical senses is the evaluation of potential foods (i.e., encouraging the consumption of sources of energy and nutrients while avoiding toxins) in natural environments, where potential foods do not come with labels (see Yarmolinksy, Zuker, & Ryba, 2009). However, in many other species, the chemical senses also play a major role in regulating social interactions (e.g., Roberts et al., 2012). The members of many species release **pheromones**—chemicals that influence the physiology and behavior of *conspecifics* (members of the same species)—see Stowers and Kuo (2015). For example, Murphy and Schneider (1970) showed that the sexual and aggressive behavior of hamsters is under pheromonal control. Normal male hamsters attack and kill unfamiliar males that are placed in their colonies, whereas they mount and impregnate unfamiliar sexually receptive females. However, male hamsters that are unable to smell the intruders engage in neither aggressive nor sexual behavior. Murphy and Schneider confirmed the olfactory basis of hamsters' aggressive and sexual behavior in a particularly devious fashion. They swabbed a male intruder with the vaginal secretions of a sexually receptive female before placing it in an unfamiliar colony; in so doing, they converted it from an object of hamster assassination to an object of hamster lust.

Evolutionary Perspective Many mammals release pheromones that serve as sexual attractants. However, as you will read in this section, there is no direct evidence that humans do so. Why do you think this difference exists?

The possibility that humans may release sexual pheromones has received considerable attention because of its financial and recreational potential. There have been many suggestive findings. For example, (1) the olfactory sensitivity of women is greatest when they are ovulating or pregnant, (2) the menstrual cycles of women living together tend to become synchronized, (3) humans—particularly women—can predict the sex of a person from their breath or their underarm odor, and (4) men can judge the stage of a woman's menstrual cycle on the basis of her vaginal odor. However, there is still no direct evidence that human odors can serve as sex attractants—most volunteers do not find the aforementioned body odors to be particularly attractive.

Olfactory System

LO 7.18 Describe the olfactory system.

The olfactory system is illustrated in Figure 7.18. The olfactory receptor cells are located in the upper part of the nose, embedded in a layer of mucus-covered tissue called the **olfactory mucosa**. Their dendrites are located in the nasal passages, and their axons pass through a porous portion of the skull (the *cribriform plate*) and enter the **olfactory bulbs**, where they synapse on neurons that project via the *olfactory* tracts to the brain.

For decades, it was assumed that there were only a few types of olfactory receptors. Different profiles of activity in a small number of receptor types were thought to lead to the perception of various smells—in the same way that the profiles of activity in three types of cones were once thought to lead to the perception of colors. Then, at the turn of the 21st century, it was discovered that rats and mice have about 1,000 different kinds of receptor proteins and that humans have about 300 (see Uchida, Poo, & Haddad, 2014).

In mammals, each olfactory receptor cell contains only one type of receptor protein molecule (see Giessel & Datta, 2014; Uchida, Poo, & Haddad, 2014). Olfactory receptor proteins are in the membranes of the dendrites of the olfactory receptor cells, where they can be stimulated by circulating airborne chemicals in the nasal passages. Researchers have attempted to discover the functional principle by which the various receptors are distributed through the olfactory mucosa. If there is such a principle, it has not yet been discovered: All of the types of receptor appear to be scattered throughout the mucosa, providing no clue about the organization of the system. Because each type of receptor responds in varying degrees to a wide variety of odors, each odor seems to be encoded by component processing—that is, by the pattern of activity across receptor types (see Giessel & Datta, 2014).

The axons of olfactory receptors terminate in discrete clusters of neurons that lie near the surface of the olfactory bulbs—these clusters are called the **olfactory glomeruli**. Each glomerulus receives input from several thousand

Figure 7.18 The human olfactory system.

- The layout of the glomeruli is similar in related species (i.e., rats and mice).

Although it is clear that the olfactory bulbs are organized topographically, the topographic principle according to which the glomeruli are arrayed has yet to be discovered (see Murthy, 2011; Schoppa, 2009). The poorly understood topographic organization of the olfactory bulbs has been termed a **chemotopic** map (see Falasconi et al., 2012).

New olfactory receptor cells are created throughout each individual's life to replace those that have deteriorated. Once created, the new receptor cells develop axons, which grow until they reach the appropriate target sites in the olfactory bulb. Each new olfactory receptor cell survives only a few weeks before being replaced. How the axons from newly formed receptors scattered about the nasal mucosa find their target glomeruli in the olfactory bulb remains a mystery (see Mori & Sakano, 2011).

Each olfactory bulb projects axons to several structures of the medial temporal lobes, including the amygdala and the **piriform cortex**—an area of medial temporal cortex adjacent to the amygdala (see Bekkers & Suzuki, 2013). The piriform cortex is considered to be primary olfactory cortex, but this designation is somewhat arbitrary (see Gottfried, 2010). The olfactory system is the only sensory system whose major sensory pathway reaches the cerebral cortex without first passing through the thalamus.

Two major olfactory pathways leave the amygdala-piriform area. One projects diffusely to the limbic system, and the other projects via the **medial dorsal nuclei** of the thalamus to the **orbitofrontal cortex**—the area of cortex on the inferior surface of the frontal lobes next to the *orbits* (eye sockets)—see Mainland et al. (2014). The limbic pathway is thought to mediate the emotional response to odors; the thalamic-orbitofrontal pathway is thought to mediate the conscious perception of odors.

olfactory receptor cells, all with the same receptor protein (see Giessel & Datta, 2014; Gupta, Albeanu, & Bhalla, 2015). In mice, there are one or two glomeruli in each olfactory bulb for each receptor protein (see Schoppa, 2009).

Because systematic topographic organization is apparent in other sensory systems (e.g., *retinotopic* and *tonotopic* layouts), researchers have been trying to discover whether glomeruli sensitive to particular odors are arrayed systematically on the surfaces of the olfactory bulbs. Indeed, the evidence indicates that there is a systematic layout (see Cheetham & Belluscio, 2014; Soucy et al., 2009; Tsai & Barnea, 2014):

- There is mirror symmetry between the left and right olfactory bulbs—glomeruli sensitive to particular odors tend to be located at the same sites on the two bulbs.

- The glomeruli sensitive to particular odors are arrayed on the olfactory bulbs in the same way in different members of the same species (i.e., mice).

Watch this video on MyPsychLab

SMELL

Gustatory System

LO 7.19 Describe the gustatory system.

Taste receptor cells are found on the tongue and in parts of the oral cavity; they typically occur in clusters of 50 to 100 called **taste buds** (see Barretto et al., 2015). On the tongue, taste buds are often located around small protuberances called *papillae* (singular *papilla*). The relation between taste receptors, taste buds, and papillae is illustrated in Figure 7.19.

The 50 to 100 receptor cells that compose each taste bud come in several types and subtypes, the functional significance of which is unknown (see Chaudhari & Roper, 2010; Yarmolinsky et al., 2010). In each taste bud, only one of the receptor cells, the *presynaptic cell*, synapses onto the neuron carrying signals away from the bud; communication among the other cells of a taste bud appears to occur via gap junctions (see Dando & Roper, 2009). Like olfactory receptor cells, gustatory receptor cells survive only a few weeks before being replaced by new cells.

How is taste encoded by the taste buds? It was once assumed that there are five different kinds of taste receptor cells, one for each primary taste, and that all tastes would be encoded by the pattern of activity in the five types. The primary tastes are assumed

to be sweet, sour, bitter, salty, and *umami* (savory), but a case can be made for others (see Liman, Zhang, & Montell, 2014). One serious problem with this theory is that many tastes cannot be created by a combination of these five primaries.

A major advance in the study of taste *transduction* occurred with the discovery of various *g-protein-linked* receptor proteins embedded in the membranes of taste receptor cells. One receptor protein responded to umami, 2 to sweet, and 30 to bitter (see Dalton & Lomvardas, 2015; Trivedi, 2012). There does not appear to be a *g-protein-linked* receptor protein for salty: Salts influence receptor cells by entering them through a specific type of sodium ion channel. The receptor mechanism for sour is currently unclear (see Dalton & Lomvardas, 2015). The mechanisms by which the responses of particular receptor proteins

Figure 7.19 Taste receptors, taste buds, and papillae on the surface of the tongue. Two sizes of papillae are visible in the photograph; only the larger papillae contain taste buds and receptors.

Surface of Tongue

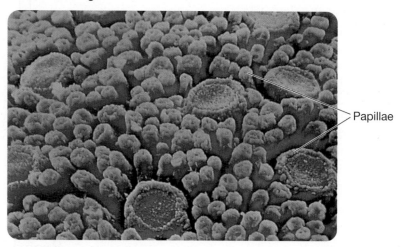

Cross Section of a Papilla

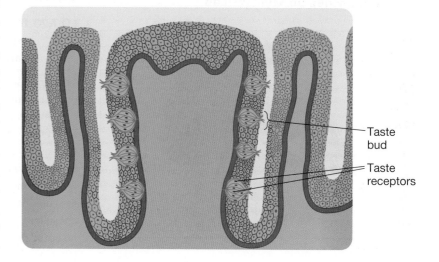

are translated into particular tastes are not well understood (see Liman, Zhang, & Montell, 2014).

Once many receptor proteins were identified, two important features of the gustatory system became apparent. First, there appears to be only one receptor protein per taste receptor cell. Second, taste receptor proteins are not restricted to the oral cavity; many are found in the throat, esophagus, and lungs (see Kinnamon, 2012).

The major pathways over which gustatory signals are conducted to the cortex are illustrated in Figure 7.20. Gustatory afferent neurons leave the mouth as part of the *facial* (VII), *glossopharyngeal* (IX), and *vagus* (X) *cranial nerves*, which carry information from the front of the tongue, the back of the tongue, and the back of the oral cavity, respectively. These fibers all terminate in the **solitary nucleus** of the medulla, where they synapse on neurons that project to the *ventral posterior nucleus* of the thalamus. The gustatory axons of the ventral posterior nucleus project to the *primary gustatory cortex*, which is in the *insula*, an area of cortex hidden in the lateral fissure (see Linster & Fontanini, 2014). A different area of primary gustatory cortex represents each taste (see Peng et al., 2015). Secondary gustatory cortex is in orbitofrontal cortex (see Figure 7.20). Unlike the projections of other sensory systems, the projections of the gustatory system are primarily ipsilateral.

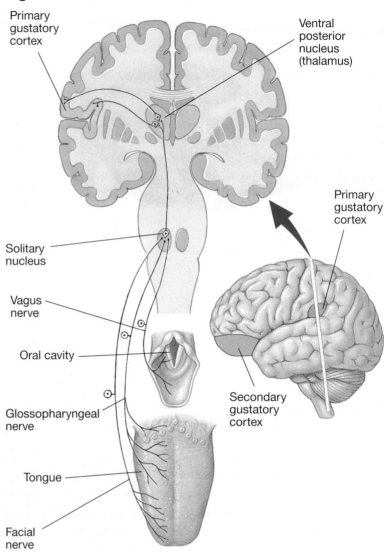

Figure 7.20 The human gustatory system.

Watch this video on MyPsychLab

TASTE

Video

Broad Tuning Versus Narrow Tuning

LO 7.20 In the context of the gustatory system, explain what is meant by broad versus narrow tuning.

The archaic five-primary component processing theory of taste implied that each gustatory receptor and neuron is *broadly tuned* (responds to a wide range of tastes). However, the rapidly accumulating list of receptor molecules and mechanisms suggests that each gustatory receptor is *narrowly tuned* (responds to only one taste, or at least to very few of them). Indeed, the majority of receptor cells have been found to be narrowly tuned, which is consistent with the fact that each cell has only one type of receptor protein molecule.

There is one exception to narrow tuning in the taste bud: the presynaptic cell. Each presynaptic cell seems to integrate the signals from all the receptive cells in its taste bud, and as a result the majority of presynaptic cells are broadly tuned (see Maffei et al., 2012). In the cortex, coding is even more broad because many neurons there respond to the odor, texture, and temperature of food (see de Araujo & Simon, 2010). In secondary gustatory cortex, many neurons seem to signal the pleasantness of food; they do not fire at all if the subject is *satiated* (fully fed)—see Rolls et al. (2010).

Some evidence suggests that the primary gustatory cortex is chemotopically organized. Schoenfeld et al. (2004) measured fMRI responses to the five primary tastes and found that each primary taste produced activity in a different area of primary gustatory cortex. The chemotopic map was different in each volunteer, and there was considerable overlap of the five areas, but the map in each volunteer was stable over time. A similar finding has been reported in mice (Chen et al., 2011).

Brain Damage and the Chemical Senses

LO 7.21 Explain the potential effects of brain damage on the chemical senses.

The inability to smell is called **anosmia**; the inability to taste is called **ageusia**. The most common neurological cause of anosmia is a blow to the head that causes a displacement of the brain within the skull and shears the olfactory nerves where they pass through the cribriform plate. Less complete deficits in olfaction have been linked to a wide variety of neurological disorders including Alzheimer's disease, Down syndrome, epilepsy, multiple sclerosis, Korsakoff's syndrome, and Parkinson's disease (see Godoy et al., 2015).

Ageusia is rare, presumably because sensory signals from the mouth are carried via three separate pathways. However, partial ageusia, limited to the anterior two-thirds of the tongue on one side, is sometimes observed after damage to the ear on the same side of the body. This is because the branch of the facial nerve (VII) that carries gustatory information from the anterior two-thirds of the tongue passes through the middle ear.

Scan Your Brain

Now that you have reached the threshold of this chapter's final module, a module that focuses on attention, you should scan your brain to test your knowledge of the sensory systems covered in the preceding modules. Complete each sentence with the name of the appropriate system. The correct answers are provided at the end of the exercise. Before proceeding, review material related to your incorrect answers and omissions.

1. The primary _____ cortex is organized tonotopically.
2. The inferior colliculi and medial geniculate nuclei are components of the _____ system.
3. The dorsal-column medial-lemniscus system and the anterolateral system are pathways of the _____ system.
4. The ventral posterior nuclei, the intralaminar nuclei, and the parafascicular nuclei are all thalamic nuclei of the _____ system.
5. The periaqueductal gray and the raphé nuclei are involved in blocking the perception of _____.
6. One pathway of the _____ system projects from the amygdala and piriform cortex to the orbitofrontal cortex.
7. Parts of the ventral posterior nuclei are thalamic relay nuclei of both the somatosensory system and the _____ system.
8. Unlike the neuronal projections of all other sensory systems, those of the _____ system are primarily ipsilateral.
9. Anosmia is caused by damage to the _____ system.
10. Ageusia is caused by damage to the _____ system.

Scan Your Brain answers: (1) auditory, (2) auditory, (3) somatosensory, (4) somatosensory, (5) pain, (6) olfactory, (7) gustatory, (8) gustatory, (9) olfactory, (10) gustatory.

Selective Attention

We consciously perceive only a small subset of the many stimuli that excite our sensory organs at any one time and largely ignore the rest (see Peelen & Kastner, 2014; Squire et al., 2013). The process by which this occurs is selective attention.

Characteristics of Selective Attention

LO 7.22 Describe the two characteristics of selective attention, and explain what is meant by exogenous versus endogenous attention.

Selective attention has two characteristics: It improves the perception of the stimuli that are its focus, and it interferes with the perception of the stimuli that are not its focus (see Sprague, Saproo, & Serences, 2015). For example, if you focus your attention on a potentially important announcement in a noisy airport, your chances of understanding it increase, but your chances of understanding a simultaneous comment from a traveling companion decrease.

Attention can be focused in two different ways: by internal cognitive processes (*endogenous attention*) or by external events (*exogenous attention*)—see Chica, Bartolomeo, and Lupiáñez (2013), but see Macaluso and Doricchi (2013). For example, your attention can be focused on a tabletop because you are searching for your keys (endogenous attention), or it can be drawn there because your cat tipped over a lamp (exogenous attention). Endogenous attention is thought to be mediated by **top-down** (from higher to lower levels) neural mechanisms, whereas exogenous attention is thought to be mediated by **bottom-up** (from lower to higher levels) neural mechanisms (see Miller & Buschman, 2013).

Eye movements often play an important role in visual attention, but it is important to realize that visual attention can be shifted without shifting the direction of visual focus (see Krauzlis, Lovejoy, & Zénon, 2013). To prove this to yourself, look at the next Check It Out demonstration.

One other important characteristic of selective attention is the cocktail-party phenomenon (see Du et al., 2011).

Check It Out
Shifting Visual Attention Without Shifting Visual Focus

Fix your gaze on the +; concentrate on it. Next, shift your attention to one of the letters without shifting your gaze from +. Now, shift your attention to other letters, again without shifting your gaze from the +. You have experienced *covert attention*—a shift of visual attention without any corresponding eye movement. A change in visual attention that involves a shift in gaze is called *overt attention*.

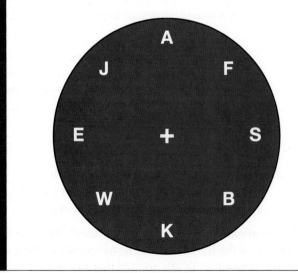

The **cocktail-party phenomenon** is the fact that even when you are focusing so intently on one conversation that you are totally unaware of the content of other conversations going on around you, the mention of your name in one of the other conversations will immediately gain access to your consciousness. This phenomenon suggests that your brain can block from conscious awareness all stimuli except those of a particular kind while still unconsciously monitoring the blocked-out stimuli just in case something comes up that requires your attention.

Change Blindness

LO 7.23 Describe the phenomenon of change blindness.

There is no better illustration of the importance of attention than the phenomenon of change blindness (Land, 2014; Simons & Rensink, 2005). To study **change blindness**, a volunteer is shown a photographic image on a computer screen and is asked to report any change in the image as soon as it is noticed. In fact, the image is composed of two images that alternate with a delay of less than 0.1 second between them. The two photographic images are identical except for one gross feature. For example, the two images in Figure 7.21 are identical except that the picture in the center of the wall is missing from one. You might think that any person would immediately notice the picture disappearing and reappearing. But this is not what happens. Most volunteers spend many seconds staring at the image—searching, as instructed, for some change—before they notice the disappearing and reappearing picture. When they finally notice it, they wonder in amazement why it took them so long.

Why does change blindness occur? It occurs because, contrary to our impression, when we view a scene, we have absolutely no memory for parts of the scene that are not the focus of our attention. When viewing the scene in Figure 7.21, most volunteers attend to the two people and do not notice when the picture disappears from the wall between them. Because they have no memory of the parts of the image to which they did not attend, they are not aware when those parts change.

The change blindness phenomenon does not occur without the brief (i.e., less than 0.1 second) intervals between images, although they barely produce a flicker. Without the intervals, no memory is required and the changes are perceived immediately.

This is one demonstration you should not miss. It is truly amazing.

Neural Mechanisms of Attention

LO 7.24 Describe the neural mechanisms of attention.

Where do top-down attentional influences on sensory systems originate? There is a general consensus that both

Figure 7.21 The change blindness phenomenon. These two illustrations were continually alternated, with a brief (less than 0.1 second) interval between each presentation, and the subjects were asked to report any changes they noticed. Amazingly, it took most of them many seconds to notice the disappearing and reappearing picture in the center of the wall.

< 0.1 second

prefrontal cortex and posterior parietal cortex play major roles in directing top-down attention (see Baluch & Itti, 2011; Noudoost et al., 2010).

Moran and Desimone (1985) were the first to demonstrate the effects of attention on neural activity. They trained monkeys to stare at a fixation point on a screen while they recorded the activity of neurons in a prestriate area that was part of the ventral stream and particularly sensitive to color. In one experiment, they recorded from individual neurons that responded to either red or green bars of light in their receptive fields. When the monkey was trained to perform a task that required attention to the red cue, the response to the red cue was increased, and the response to the green cue was reduced. The opposite happened when the monkey attended to green.

Experiments paralleling those in monkeys have been conducted in humans using functional brain-imaging techniques. For example, Corbetta and colleagues (1990) presented a collection of moving, colored stimuli of various shapes and asked volunteers to discriminate among the stimuli based on their movement, color, or shape. Attention to shape or color produced increased activity in areas of the ventral stream; attention to movement produced increased activity in an area of the dorsal stream (see Chapter 6).

In another study of attention in human volunteers, Ungerleider and Haxby (1994) showed volunteers a series of faces. The volunteers were asked whether the faces belonged to the same person or whether they were located in the same position relative to the frame. When they were attending to identity, regions of the ventral stream were more active; when they were attending to position, regions of the dorsal stream were more active.

The preceding studies indicate the principle by which the neural mechanisms of selective attention work.

Selective attention works by strengthening the neural responses to attended-to aspects and by weakening the responses to others (see Buschman, 2015; Luo & Maunsell, 2015). This dual mechanism has been termed a *push-pull mechanism* (see Stevens & Bavelier, 2012).

Some neural mechanisms of attention involve a surprising degree of neural plasticity. For example, the location of the receptive fields of visual neurons, which had been assumed to be a static property of visual neurons, can be shifted by spatial attention (see **Neuroplasticity** Anton-Erxleben & Carrasco, 2013). Recording from neurons in an area of monkey secondary visual cortex in the dorsal stream, Wommelsdorf and colleagues (2006) found that the receptive fields of many of the neurons shifted toward points in the visual field to which the subjects were attending. Similarly, Rolls (2008) found that visual receptive fields of inferotemporal cortex neurons shrink to become little more than the size of objects on which they are focusing.

| **Neuroplasticity** | Provide a brief explanation as to why this is an example of neuroplasticity. |

If you concluded from the foregoing studies that most of the research on the neural mechanisms of selective attention has focused on visual attention, you would be correct (see Chelazzi et al., 2010; Petersen & Posner, 2012). However, there are also studies of attention to auditory (e.g., Saupe et al., 2009; Shamma, Elhilali, & Michey, 2011), somesthetic (e.g., Fujiwara et al., 2002), gustatory (e.g., Stevenson, 2012; Veldhuizen, Gitelman, & Small, 2012), and olfactory (Veldhuizen & Small, 2011) stimuli. Fortunately, regardless of the particular stimuli that have been used to study the neural bases of attention, the mechanisms have been the same: Attention is activated by circuits in prefrontal (see Bichot et al., 2015; Moore & Zirnsak, 2015) and parietal cortex (see Amso & Scerif, 2015) that enhance activity in task-relevant sensory circuits and suppress activity in irrelevant sensory circuits.

Simultanagnosia

LO 7.25 Describe the disorder of attention known as simultanagnosia.

We have not forgotten that we asked you to think about the patient whose case opened this chapter. He could identify objects in any part of his visual field if they were presented individually; thus, he was not suffering from blindness or other visual field defects. His was a disorder of attention called **simultanagnosia**. Specifically, he suffered from *visual simultanagnosia*—a difficulty in attending visually to more than one object at a time. Because the dorsal stream of the posterior parietal cortex is responsible for visually localizing objects in space, you may have hypothesized that the patient's problem was associated with damage to this area. If you did, you were correct. Simultanagnosia is usually associated with bilateral damage to the posterior parietal cortex.

Themes Revisited

The clinical implications theme was prominent in this chapter, but you saw it in a different light. Previous chapters discussed how biopsychological research is leading to the development of new treatments; this chapter focused exclusively on what particular clinical cases have revealed about the organization of healthy sensory systems. The following cases played a key role in this chapter: the patient with visual simultanagnosia; Dr. P., the visual agnosic who mistook his wife for a hat; Aunt Betty, the asomatognosic who lost the left side of her body; Miss C., the student who felt no pain and died as a result; and W.M., the man who reduced his scotoma with his hand.

Two of the other major themes were also developed in this chapter: the neuroplasticity theme and the evolutionary perspective theme. Although this chapter did not systematically discuss the plasticity of sensory systems—upcoming chapters focus on this topic—three important examples of sensory system plasticity were mentioned: the effects of tinnitus on the auditory system, partial recovery of vision in a scotoma by placing a hand in the scotoma, and the movement of the receptive fields of visual neurons toward a location that is the focus of attention. The value of the evolutionary perspective was illustrated by comparative studies of some species that have proven particularly informative because of their evolutionary specializations (e.g., the auditory localization abilities of the barn owl and the tendency of the secondary auditory cortex of monkeys to respond to monkey calls).

The thinking creatively theme came up once. The case of Miss C. taught us that pain is a positive sensation that we can't live without.

Key Terms

Chapter 8
The Sensorimotor System

How You Move

Chapter Overview and Learning Objectives (LOs)

Three Principles of
Sensorimotor Function

LO 8.1 In the context of the sensorimotor system, explain what *hierarchically organized* means.

LO 8.2 Explain the important role of sensory input for motor output.

LO 8.3 Describe how learning changes the nature and locus of sensorimotor control.

LO 8.4 Describe and/or draw the general model of sensorimotor function.

Sensorimotor Association
Cortex

LO 8.5 Explain the role of the posterior parietal cortex in sensorimotor function, and describe what happens when it is damaged or stimulated.

LO 8.6 Explain the role of the dorsolateral prefrontal association cortex in sensorimotor function, and describe the response properties of neurons in this region of cortex.

The evening before we started to write this chapter, I (JP) was standing in a checkout line at the local market. As I waited, I scanned the headlines on the prominently displayed magazines—WOMAN GIVES BIRTH TO CAT; FLYING SAUCER LANDS IN CLEVELAND SHOPPING MALL; HOW TO LOSE 20 POUNDS IN 2 DAYS. Then, my mind began to wander, and

I started to think about beginning to write this chapter. That is when I began to watch Rhonelle's movements, and to wonder about the neural system that controlled them. Rhonelle is a cashier—the best in the place.

The Case of Rhonelle, the Dexterous Cashier

I was struck by the complexity of even Rhonelle's simplest movements. As she deftly transferred a bag of tomatoes to the scale, there was a coordinated adjustment in almost every part of her body. In addition to her obvious finger, hand, arm, and shoulder movements, coordinated movements of her head and eyes tracked her hand to the tomatoes; and there were adjustments in the muscles of her feet, legs, trunk, and other arm, which kept her from lurching forward. The accuracy of these responses suggested that they were guided in part by the patterns of visual, somatosensory, and vestibular changes they produced. The term *sensorimotor* in the title of this chapter formally recognizes the critical contribution of sensory input to guiding motor output.

As my purchases flowed through her left hand, Rhonelle registered the prices with her right hand and bantered with Rick, the bagger. I was intrigued by how little of what Rhonelle was doing appeared to be under her conscious control. She made general decisions about which items to pick up and where to put them, but she seemed to give no thought to the exact means by which these decisions were carried out. Each of her responses could have been made with an infinite number of different combinations of finger, wrist, elbow, shoulder, and body adjustments; but somehow she unconsciously picked one. The higher parts of her sensorimotor system—perhaps her cortex—seemed to issue conscious general commands to other parts of the system, which unconsciously produced a specific pattern of muscular responses that carried them out.

The automaticity of Rhonelle's performance was a far cry from the slow, effortful responses that had characterized her first days at the market. Somehow, experience had integrated her individual movements into smooth sequences, and it seemed to have transferred the movements' control from a mode that involved conscious effort to one that did not.

I was suddenly jarred from my contemplations by a voice. "Sir, excuse me, sir, that will be $18.65," Rhonelle said, with just a hint of delight at catching me in mid-daydream. I hastily paid my bill, muttered "thank you," and scurried out of the market.

As we write this, I am smiling both at my own embarrassment and at the thought that Rhonelle has unknowingly introduced you to three principles of sensorimotor control that are the foundations of this chapter: (1) The sensorimotor system is hierarchically organized. (2) Motor output is guided by sensory input. (3) Learning can change the nature and the locus of sensorimotor control.

Three Principles of Sensorimotor Function

Before getting into the details of the sensorimotor system, let's take a closer look at the three principles of sensorimotor function introduced by Rhonelle. You will better appreciate these principles if you recognize that they also govern the operation of any large, efficient company—perhaps because that is another system for controlling output that has evolved in a competitive environment. You may find this metaphor useful in helping you understand the principles of sensorimotor system organization—many scientists find that metaphors help them think creatively about their subject matter.

The Sensorimotor System Is Hierarchically Organized

LO 8.1 In the context of the sensorimotor system, explain what *hierarchically organized* means.

The operation of both the sensorimotor system and a large, efficient company is directed by commands that cascade down through the levels of a hierarchy (see Graziano, 2009)—from the association cortex or the company president (the highest levels) to the muscles or the workers (the lowest levels). Like the orders issued from the office of a company president, the commands that emerge from the association cortex specify general goals rather than specific plans of action. Neither the association cortex nor the company president routinely gets involved in the details. The main advantage of this *hierarchical organization* is that the higher levels of the hierarchy are left free to perform more complex functions.

Both the sensorimotor system and a large, efficient company are parallel hierarchical systems; that is, they are hierarchical systems in which signals flow between levels over multiple paths (see Cisek & Kalaska, 2010). This parallel structure enables the association cortex or company president to exert control over the lower levels of the hierarchy in more than one way. For example, the association cortex can directly inhibit an eye blink reflex to allow the insertion of a contact lens, just as a company president can personally organize a delivery to an important customer.

The sensorimotor and company hierarchies are also characterized by *functional segregation*. That is, each level of the sensorimotor and company hierarchies tends to be composed of different units (neural structures or departments), each of which performs a different function.

Thinking Creatively Can you think of another analogy for the sensorimotor system?

In summary, the sensorimotor system—like the sensory systems you read about in Chapter 7—is a parallel, functionally segregated, hierarchical system. The main difference between the sensory systems and the sensorimotor system is the primary direction of information flow. In sensory systems, information mainly flows up through the hierarchy; in the sensorimotor system, information mainly flows down.

Motor Output Is Guided by Sensory Input

LO 8.2 **Explain the important role of sensory input for motor output.**

Efficient companies are flexible. They continuously monitor the effects of their own activities, and they use this information to fine-tune their activities. The sensorimotor system does the same (see Azim, Fink, & Jessell, 2014; Danna & Velay, 2015). The eyes, the organs of balance, and the receptors in skin, muscles, and joints all monitor the body's responses, and they feed their information back into sensorimotor circuits. In most instances, this **sensory feedback** plays an important role in directing the continuation of the responses that produced it. The only responses that are not normally influenced by sensory feedback are *ballistic movements*—brief, all-or-none, high-speed movements, such as swatting a fly.

Behavior in the absence of just one kind of sensory feedback—the feedback carried by the somatosensory nerves of the arms—was studied in G.O., a former darts champion (Rothwell et al., 1982).

The Case of G.O., the Man with Too Little Feedback

An infection had selectively destroyed the somatosensory nerves of G.O.'s arms. He had great difficulty performing intricate responses such as doing up his buttons or picking up coins, even under visual guidance. Other difficulties resulted from his inability to adjust his motor output in light of unanticipated external disturbances; for example, he could not keep from spilling a cup of coffee if somebody brushed against him. However, G.O.'s greatest problem was his inability to maintain a constant level of muscle contraction.

The result of his infection was that even simple tasks requiring a constant motor output to the hand required continual visual monitoring. For example, when carrying a suitcase, he had to watch it to reassure himself that he had not dropped it. However, even visual feedback was of little use to him in tasks requiring a constant force, tasks such as grasping a pen while writing or holding a cup. In these cases, he had no indication of the pressure that he was exerting on the object; all he saw was the pen or cup slipping from his grasp.

Many adjustments in motor output that occur in response to sensory feedback are controlled unconsciously by the lower levels of the sensorimotor hierarchy without the involvement of the higher levels (see Deliagina, Zelenin, & Orlovsky, 2012). In the same way, large companies run more efficiently if the clerks do not check with the company president each time they encounter a minor problem.

Learning Changes the Nature and Locus of Sensorimotor Control

LO 8.3 **Describe how learning changes the nature and locus of sensorimotor control.**

When a company is just starting up, each individual decision is made by the company president after careful consideration. However, as the company develops, many individual actions are coordinated into sequences of prescribed procedures routinely carried out by personnel at lower levels of the hierarchy.

Similar changes occur during sensorimotor learning (see Bassett et al., 2015). During the initial stages of motor learning, each individual response is performed under conscious control; then, after much practice, individual responses become organized into continuous integrated sequences of action that flow smoothly and are adjusted by sensory feedback without conscious regulation. If you think for a moment about the sensorimotor skills you have acquired (e.g., typing, swimming, knitting, basketball playing, dancing, piano playing), you will appreciate that the organization of individual responses into continuous motor programs and the transfer of their control to lower levels of the CNS characterize most sensorimotor learning.

General Model of Sensorimotor System Function

LO 8.4 **Describe and/or draw the general model of sensorimotor function.**

Figure 8.1 is a model that illustrates several principles of sensorimotor system organization; it is the framework of this chapter. Notice its hierarchical structure, the functional segregation of the levels (e.g., of secondary motor cortex), the parallel connections between levels, and the numerous feedback pathways.

This chapter focuses on the neural structures that play important roles in the control of voluntary behavior (e.g., picking up an apple). It begins at the level of association cortex and traces major motor signals as they descend the sensorimotor hierarchy to the skeletal muscles that ultimately perform the movements.

Figure 8.1 A general model of the sensorimotor system. Notice its hierarchical structure, functional segregation, parallel descending pathways, and feedback circuits.

Sensorimotor Association Cortex

Association cortex is at the top of your sensorimotor hierarchy. There are two major areas of sensorimotor association cortex: the posterior parietal association cortex and the dorsolateral prefrontal association cortex. Posterior parietal cortex and the dorsolateral prefrontal cortex are each composed of several different areas, each with different functions (see Davare et al., 2011; Wilson et al., 2010). However, there is no general consensus on how best to divide either of them for analysis or even how comparable the areas are in humans, monkeys, and rats (see D'Esposito & Postle, 2015; Teixeira et al., 2014; Turella & Lingnau, 2014).

Posterior Parietal Association Cortex

LO 8.5 **Explain the role of the posterior parietal cortex in sensorimotor function, and describe what happens when it is damaged or stimulated.**

Before an effective movement can be initiated, certain information is required. The nervous system must know the original positions of the parts of the body that are to be moved, and it must know the positions of any external objects with which the body is going to interact. The **posterior parietal association cortex** (the portion of parietal neocortex posterior to the primary somatosensory cortex) plays an important role in integrating these two kinds of information, in directing behavior by providing spatial information, and in directing attention (Hutchinson et al., 2014; Kuang, Morel, & Gail, 2015; WIlber et al., 2014).

You learned in Chapter 7 that the posterior parietal cortex is classified as *association cortex* because it receives input from more than one sensory system. It receives information from the three sensory systems that play roles in the localization of the body and external objects in space: the visual system, the auditory system, and the somatosensory system (see Figure 8.2)—see Sereno and Huang (2014). In turn, much of the output of the posterior parietal cortex goes to areas of motor cortex, which are located in the frontal cortex: to the *dorsolateral prefrontal association cortex*, to the various areas of *secondary motor cortex*, and to the **frontal eye field**—a small area of prefrontal cortex that controls eye movements (see Figure 8.2). Electrophysiological studies in macaque monkeys and functional magnetic resonance imaging (fMRI) and transcranial magnetic stimulation (TMS) studies in humans indicate that the posterior parietal cortex contains a mosaic of small areas, each specialized for guiding particular movements of eyes, head, arms, or hands (Man et al., 2015; Wang et al., 2015).

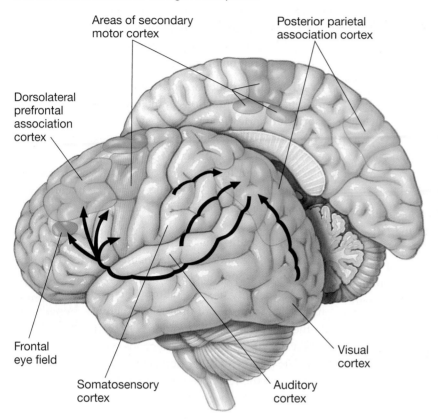

Figure 8.2 The major cortical input and output pathways of the posterior parietal association cortex. Shown are the lateral surface of the left hemisphere and the medial surface of the right hemisphere.

Labels: Areas of secondary motor cortex; Posterior parietal association cortex; Dorsolateral prefrontal association cortex; Frontal eye field; Somatosensory cortex; Auditory cortex; Visual cortex

Desmurget and colleagues (2009) applied electrical stimulation to the inferior portions of the posterior parietal cortexes of conscious neurosurgical patients. At low current levels, the patients experienced an intention to perform a particular action, and, at high levels, they felt that they had actually performed it. However, in neither case did the action actually occur (see Desmurget & Sirigu, 2012).

Aflalo and colleagues (2015) recorded the neural population activity within the posterior parietal cortex of a *tetraplegic* person (a person suffering from paralysis of all four limbs) using a large multi-electrode array. They found that the patient could control the activity of particular neurons by imagining particular actions. A computer was then trained to decode the firing patterns of the neurons in this patient into motor imagery; such motor imagery included certain imagined goals, certain imagined trajectories of limb movements, and the imagination of different types of movements.

Damage to the posterior parietal cortex can produce a variety of deficits, including deficits in the perception and memory of spatial relationships, in accurate reaching and grasping, in the control of eye movement, and in attention (see Andersen et al., 2014; Turella & Lingnau, 2014). However, apraxia and contralateral neglect are the two most striking consequences of posterior parietal cortex damage.

Apraxia is a disorder of voluntary movement that is not attributable to a simple motor deficit (e.g., not to paralysis or weakness) or to any deficit in comprehension or motivation (see Neissen, Fink, & Weiss, 2014). Remarkably, apraxic patients have difficulty making specific movements when they are requested to do so, particularly when the movements are out of context; however, they can often readily perform the very same movements under natural conditions when they are not thinking about what they are doing. For example, an apraxic carpenter who has no difficulty at all hammering a nail during the course of her work might not be able to demonstrate hammering movements when requested to make them, particularly in the absence of a hammer. Although its symptoms are bilateral, apraxia is often caused by unilateral damage to the left posterior parietal cortex or its connections (Hoeren et al., 2014; Neissen, Fink, & Weiss, 2014).

Contralateral neglect, the other striking consequence of posterior parietal cortex damage, is a disturbance of a patient's ability to respond to stimuli on the side of the body opposite (contralateral) to the side of a brain lesion in the absence of simple sensory or motor deficits. Most patients with contralateral neglect often behave as if the left side of their world does not exist, and they often fail to appreciate that they have a problem (see Li & Malhotra, 2015). The disturbance is often associated with large lesions of the right posterior parietal cortex (see Mort et al., 2003; Van Vleet & Robertson, 2006), though damage to other brain regions has also been implicated (see Karnath & Otto, 2012). Mrs. S. suffered from contralateral neglect after a massive stroke to the posterior portions of her right hemisphere (Sacks, 1970).

The Case of Mrs. S., the Woman Who Turned in Circles

After her stroke, Mrs. S. could not respond to things on her left—including objects and parts of her own body. For example, she often put makeup on the right side of her face but ignored the left.

Mrs. S.'s left-side contralateral neglect created many problems for her, but a particularly bothersome one was that she had difficulty getting enough to eat. When a plate of food was put in front of her, she could see only the food on the right half of the plate and ate only that half, even if she was very hungry. However, Mrs. S. developed an effective way of getting more food. If she was still hungry after completing a meal, she turned her wheelchair to the right in a full circle until she saw the remaining half of her meal. Then, she ate that food, or more precisely, she ate the right half of that food. If she was still hungry after that, she turned once again to the right until she discovered the remaining quarter of her meal and ate half of that…and so on.

Clinical Implications Speculate as to why contralateral neglect is most commonly associated with damage to the right hemisphere (rather than the left).

Most patients with contralateral neglect have difficulty responding to things to the left. But to the left of what? For most patients with contralateral neglect, the deficits in responding occur for stimuli to the left of their own bodies, referred to as *egocentric left* (see Karnath, 2015). Egocentric left is partially defined by gravitational coordinates: When patients tilt their heads, their field of neglect is not normally tilted with it.

In addition to failing to respond to objects on their egocentric left, many patients tend not to respond to the left sides of objects, regardless of where the objects are in their visual fields (see Karnath, 2015). Some of these patients, who are said to suffer from *object-based contralateral neglect*, fail to respond to the left side of objects (e.g., the left hand of a statue) even when the objects are presented horizontally or upside down.

You have learned in the preceding chapters that failure to perceive an object consciously does not necessarily mean the object is not perceived. Indeed, two types of evidence suggest that information about objects that are not noticed by patients with contralateral neglect may be unconsciously perceived (see Jerath & Crawford, 2014). First, when objects were repeatedly presented at the same spot to the left of patients with contralateral neglect, they tended to look to the same spot on future trials, although they were unaware of the objects (Geng & Behrmann, 2002). Second, patients could more readily identify fragmented (partial) drawings viewed to their right if complete versions of the drawings had previously been presented to the left, where they were not consciously perceived (Vuilleumier et al., 2002).

Dorsolateral Prefrontal Association Cortex

LO 8.6 Explain the role of the dorsolateral prefrontal association cortex in sensorimotor function, and describe the response properties of neurons in this region of cortex.

The other large area of association cortex that has important sensorimotor functions is the **dorsolateral prefrontal association cortex** (see Kaller et al., 2011). It receives projections from the posterior parietal cortex, and it sends projections to areas of *secondary motor cortex*, to *primary motor cortex*, and to the *frontal eye field*. These projections are shown in Figure 8.3. Not shown are the major projections back from dorsolateral prefrontal cortex to posterior parietal cortex.

Several studies have characterized the activity of monkey dorsolateral prefrontal neurons as the monkeys identify and respond to objects (e.g., Rao, Rainer, & Miller, 1997). The activity of some neurons depends on the characteristics of objects; the activity of others depends on the locations of objects; **Evolutionary Perspective** and the activity of still others depends on a combination of both. The activity of other dorsolateral prefrontal neurons is related to the response rather than to the object. These neurons typically begin to fire before the response and

Figure 8.3 The major cortical input and output pathways of the dorsolateral prefrontal association cortex. Shown are the lateral surface of the left hemisphere and the medial surface of the right hemisphere.

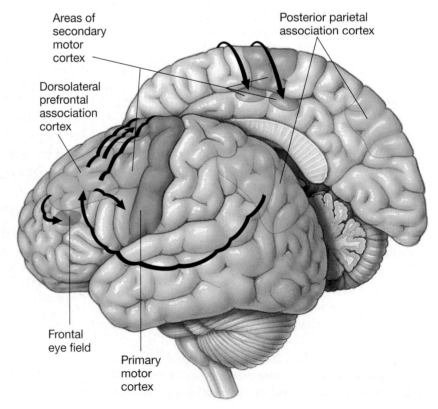

Areas of secondary motor cortex

Posterior parietal association cortex

Dorsolateral prefrontal association cortex

Frontal eye field

Primary motor cortex

continue to fire until the response is complete. Neurons in many cortical motor areas begin to fire in anticipation of a motor activity (see Rigato, Murakami, & Mainen, 2014; Siegel, Buschman, & Miller, 2015), but those in the dorsolateral prefrontal association cortex tend to fire first.

The response properties of dorsolateral prefrontal neurons suggest that decisions to initiate voluntary movements may be made in this area of cortex (Rowe et al., 2000; Tanji & Hoshi, 2001), but these decisions depend on critical interactions with posterior parietal cortex and other areas of frontal cortex (Lee, Seo, & Jung, 2012).

Secondary Motor Cortex

Areas of **secondary motor cortex** are those that receive much of their input from association cortex (i.e., posterior parietal cortex and dorsolateral prefrontal cortex) and send much of their output to primary motor cortex (see Figure 8.4). For many years, only two areas of secondary motor cortex were known: the supplementary motor area and the premotor cortex. Both of these large areas are clearly visible on the lateral surface of the

Figure 8.4 Three sorts of secondary motor cortex—supplementary motor area, premotor cortex, and cingulate motor areas—and their output to the primary motor cortex. Shown are the lateral surface of the left hemisphere and the medial surface of the right hemisphere.

frontal lobe, just anterior to the *primary motor cortex*. The **supplementary motor area** wraps over the top of the frontal lobe and extends down its medial surface into the longitudinal fissure, and the **premotor cortex** runs in a strip from the supplementary motor area to the lateral fissure.

Identifying the Areas of Secondary Motor Cortex

LO 8.7 Explain the general role of areas of secondary motor cortex.

The simple two-area conception of secondary motor cortex has become more complex. Neuroanatomical and neurophysiological research with monkeys has made a case for at least eight areas of secondary motor cortex in each hemisphere, each with its own subdivisions (see Nachev, Kennard, & Husain, 2008): three different supplementary motor areas (SMA, preSMA, and supplementary eye field), two premotor areas (dorsal and ventral), and three small areas—the **cingulate motor areas**—in the cortex of the cingulate gyrus. Although most of the research on secondary motor cortex has been done in monkeys, functional brain-imaging studies have suggested that human secondary motor cortex is similarly organized (see Caminiti, Innocenti, & Battaglia-Mayer, 2015).

To qualify as secondary motor cortex, an area must be appropriately connected with association and secondary motor areas (see Figure 8.4). Electrical stimulation of an area of secondary motor cortex typically elicits complex movements, often involving both sides of the body. Neurons in an area of secondary motor cortex often become more active just prior to the initiation of a voluntary movement and continue to be active throughout the movement.

In general, areas of secondary motor cortex are thought to be involved in the programming of specific patterns of movements after taking general instructions from dorsolateral prefrontal cortex (see Pearce & Moran, 2012). Evidence of such a function comes from brain-imaging studies in which the patterns of activity in the brain have been measured while a volunteer is either imagining his or her own performance of a particular series of movements or planning the performance of the same movements (see Olshansky et al., 2015; Park et al., 2015).

Despite evidence of similarities among areas of secondary motor cortex, substantial effort has been put into discovering their differences. Until recently, this research has focused on differences between the supplementary motor area and the premotor cortex as originally defined. Although several theories have been proposed to explain functional differences between these areas (e.g., Hoshi & Tanji, 2007), none has received consistent support. As the boundaries between various areas of secondary motor cortex become more accurately characterized, the task of determining the function of each area should become easier.

Mirror Neurons

LO 8.8 Describe the major features of mirror neurons and explain why they have received so much attention from neuroscientists.

Few discoveries have captured the interest of neuroscientists as much as the discovery of mirror neurons (see Rizzolatti & Fogassi, 2014). **Mirror neurons** are neurons that fire when an individual performs a particular goal-directed hand movement or when they observe the same goal-directed movement performed by another.

Mirror neurons were discovered in the early 1990s in the laboratory of Giacomo Rizzolatti (see Ferrari & Rizzolatti, 2014). Rizzolatti and his colleagues had been studying a class of macaque monkey ventral premotor area neurons that seemed to encode particular goal objects; that is, these neurons fired when the monkey reached for one object (e.g., a toy) but not when the monkey reached for another object. Then, the researchers noticed something strange: Some of these neurons, later termed

mirror neurons, fired just as robustly when the monkey watched the experimenter pick up the same object but not any other—see Figure 8.5.

Why did the discovery of mirror neurons in the ventral premotor area create such a stir? The reason is that they provide a possible mechanism for *social cognition* (knowledge of the perceptions, ideas, and intentions of others). Mapping the actions of others onto one's own action repertoire would facilitate social understanding, cooperation, and imitation (see Bernhardt & Singer, 2012; Cook et al., 2014; Heyes, 2010; Ocampo & Kritikos, 2011; Rizzolatti & Sinigaglia, 2010).

Figure 8.5 Responses of a mirror neuron of a monkey.

Time
Pickup
A mirror neuron in the premotor cortex of a monkey fires when the monkey picks up the ball.

Time
Pickup
The same monkey mirror neuron fires when the experimenter picks up the ball.

Time
Pickup
The same monkey mirror neuron does not fire when the monkey picks up an object other than the ball.

Time
Pickup
The same monkey mirror neuron does not fire when the experimenter picks up an object other than the ball.

Support for the idea that mirror neurons might play a role in social cognition has come from demonstrations that these neurons respond to the *understanding* of the purpose of an action, not to some superficial characteristic of the action itself (Rizzolatti & Sinigaglia, 2010; but see Churchland, 2014). For example, mirror neurons that reacted to the sight of an action that made a sound (e.g., cracking a peanut) were found to respond just as robustly to the sound alone—in other words, they responded fully to the particular action and its goal regardless of how it was detected. Indeed, many ventral premotor mirror neurons fire even when a monkey does not perceive the key action but just creates a mental representation of it.

Mirror neurons have been found in several areas of the macaque monkey frontal and parietal cortex (see Bonini & Ferrari, 2011; Giese & Rizzolatti, 2015). However, despite more than 300 published studies of "mirror systems" in humans, descriptions of individual mirror neurons in humans are rare (see Molenberghs, Cunnington, & Mattingley, 2012). Indeed, as we write this, we know of only one: Mukamel and colleagues (2010). There are few opportunities to record the firing of individual neurons in humans while conducting the required behavioral tests.

Most of the research on human mirror neuron mechanisms have been functional MRI studies. Many of these studies have found areas of human motor cortex that are active when a person performs, watches, or imagines a particular action (e.g., Rizzolatti & Fabbri-Destro, 2008; Rodriguez et al., 2008). There is no direct evidence that mirror neurons are responsible for these human findings—it is possible that different neurons in the same cortical areas contribute to the functional MRI activity in these different conditions. However, the mirror mechanisms identified by functional MRI in humans tend to be in the same areas of cortex as those identified by single cell recording in macaques (Molenerghs et al., 2012).

Primary Motor Cortex

The **primary motor cortex** is located in the *precentral gyrus* of the frontal lobe (see Figures 8.3, 8.4 and 8.6). It is the major point of convergence of cortical sensorimotor signals, and it is the major, but not the only, point of departure of sensorimotor signals from the cerebral cortex. Understanding of the function of primary motor cortex has undergone radical changes over the past two decades—see Graziano (2015). The following two sections describe these changes.

Figure 8.6 The motor homunculus: the somatotopic map of the human primary motor cortex. Electrical stimulation of various sites in the primary motor cortex elicits simple movements in the indicated parts of the body. (Based on Penfield & Rasmussen, 1950.)

Conventional View of Primary Motor Cortex Function

LO 8.9 Describe the conventional view of primary motor cortex function and the evidence upon which it was based.

In 1937, Penfield and Boldrey mapped the primary motor cortex of conscious human patients during neurosurgery by applying brief, low-intensity electrical stimulations to various points on the cortical surface and noting which part of the body moved in response to each stimulation. They found that the stimulation of each particular cortical site activated a particular contralateral muscle and produced a simple movement. When they mapped out the relation between each cortical site and the muscle that was activated by its stimulation, they found that the primary motor cortex is organized somatotopically—that is, according to a map of the body. The **somatotopic** layout of the human primary motor cortex is commonly referred to as the **motor homunculus** (see Figure 8.6). Notice that most of the primary motor cortex is dedicated to controlling parts of the body that are capable of intricate movements, such as the hands and mouth.

It is important to appreciate that each site in the primary motor cortex receives sensory feedback from receptors in the muscles and joints that the site influences. One interesting exception to this general pattern of feedback has been described in monkeys: Monkeys have at least two different hand areas in the primary motor cortex of each hemisphere, and one receives input from receptors in the skin rather than from receptors in the muscles and joints. Presumably, this latter adaptation facilitates **stereognosis**— the process of identifying objects by touch. Close your eyes and explore an object with your hands; notice how stereognosis depends on a complex interplay between motor responses and the somatosensory stimulation produced by them (see Kappers, 2011).

What is the function of each primary motor cortex neuron? Until recently, each neuron was thought to encode the direction of movement. The main evidence for this was the finding that each neuron in the arm area of the primary motor cortex fires maximally when the arm reaches in a particular direction, and that each neuron has a different preferred direction.

Current View of Primary Motor Cortex Function

LO 8.10 Describe the current view of primary motor cortex function and the evidence upon which it is based.

Recent efforts to map the primary motor cortex have used a new stimulation technique—see Graziano (2015). Rather than stimulating with brief pulses of current that are just above the threshold to produce a reaction, investigators have used longer bursts of current (e.g., 0.5 to 1 seconds; see Van Acker et al., 2014), which are more similar to the duration of a motor response. The results were amazing: Rather than eliciting the contractions of individual muscles, these currents elicited complex natural-looking response sequences. For example, stimulation at one site reliably produced a feeding response: The arm reached forward, the hand closed as if clasping some food, the closed hand was brought to the mouth, and finally the mouth opened. These recent studies have revealed a crude somatotopic organization—that is, stimulation in the face area tended to elicit face movements. However, the elicited responses were complex species-typical movements that often involved several parts of the body (e.g., hand, shoulder, and mouth), rather than individual muscle contractions (see Ejaz, Hamada, & Diedrichson, 2015). Also,

sites that moved a particular body part overlapped greatly with sites that moved other body parts (Sanes et al., 1995). Presumably that is why small lesions in the hand area of the primary motor cortex of humans (Scheiber, 1999) or monkeys (Scheiber & Poliakov, 1998) do not selectively disrupt the activity of a single finger.

Watch this video on MyPsychLab
CHALK IT UP! CODING IN THE PRIMARY MOTOR CORTEX

The conventional view that many primary motor cortex neurons are tuned to movement in a particular direction has also been challenged. In the many studies that have supported this conventional view, the monkey subjects were trained to make arm movements from a central starting point so that the relation between neural firing and the direction of movement could be precisely assessed. In each case, each neuron fired only when the movements were made at a particular angle. However, an alternative to the idea that motor neurons are coded to particular angles of movement has come from the findings of studies in which the activity of individual primary motor cortex neurons is recorded as monkeys moved about freely (see Graziano, 2015; Harrison & Murphy, 2014)—rather than as they performed simple, learned arm movements from a set starting point. The firing of many primary motor cortex neurons in freely moving monkeys was often related to the particular end point of a movement, not to the direction of the movement. That is, if a monkey reached toward a particular location, primary motor cortex neurons sensitive to that target location tended to become active regardless of the direction of the movement that was needed to get to the target.

The importance of the target of a movement, rather than the direction of a movement, for the function of primary motor cortex was also apparent in stimulation studies (see Graziano, 2015; Harrison & Murphy, 2014). For example, if stimulation of a particular motor cortex site caused a straight left arm to bend at the elbow to a 90-degree angle, the same stimulation of the same site caused a tightly bent arm to straighten to 90 degrees. In other words, the same stimulation of motor cortex can produce opposite movements depending on the starting position, but the end position of the movements remains the same. Stop for a moment and consider the implications of this finding—they are as important as they are counterintuitive. First, the finding means that the signals from every site in the primary motor cortex diverge greatly, so each particular site has the ability to get a body part (e.g., an arm) to a target location regardless of the starting position. Second, it

Neuroplasticity means that the sensorimotor system is inherently plastic. Apparently, each location in the primary motor cortex can produce innumerable patterns of muscle contraction required to get a body part from any starting point to a target location (Davidson et al., 2007). Accordingly, it has been suggested that the primary motor cortex contains an **action map** (see Graziano, 2015) in addition to its topographic map.

The neurons of the primary motor cortex play a major role in initiating body movements. With an appropriate interface, could they control the movements of a machine (see Georgopoulos & Carpenter, 2015)? Belle says, "Yes."

Belle: The Monkey That Controlled a Robot with Her Mind

In the laboratory of Miguel Nicolesis and John Chapin, a tiny owl monkey called Belle watched a series of lights on a control panel. Belle had learned that if she moved the joystick in her right hand in the direction of a light, she would be rewarded with a drop of fruit juice. On this particular day, as a light flashed on the panel, 100 microelectrodes recorded extracellular unit activity from neurons in Belle's primary motor cortex. This activity moved Belle's arm toward the light, but at the same time, the signals were analyzed by a computer, which fed the output to a laboratory several hundred kilometers away, at the Massachusetts Institute of Technology. At MIT, the signals from Belle's brain entered the circuits of a robotic arm. On each trial, the activity of Belle's primary motor cortex moved her arm toward the test light, and it moved the robotic arm in the same direction. Belle's neural signals were directing the activity of a robot.

Belle's remarkable feat raised a possibility that is already starting to be realized. Perhaps someday injured people will routinely control wheelchairs, prosthetic limbs, or even their own paralyzed limbs through the power of

Clinical Implications their thoughts (see Bensmaia & Miller, 2014; Wander & Rao, 2014). For example, paralyzed patients have learned to control robotic arms with neural signals collected via multi-electrode arrays implanted in the primary motor cortex (Collinger et al., 2013; Golub et al., 2016; Pruszynski & Diedrichsen, 2015).

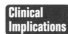 **Clinical Implications** There has recently been a flurry of technological advances involving brain–computer interfaces (i.e., direct communication between a computer and the brain—usually via an array of electrodes placed in the brain), such as those described here. What sorts of brain–computer interfaces do you envision for the future?

EFFECTS OF PRIMARY MOTOR CORTEX LESIONS. Extensive damage to the human primary motor cortex has less effect than you might expect, given that this cortex is the major point of departure of motor fibers from the cerebral cortex. Large lesions to 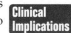 **Clinical Implications** the primary motor cortex may disrupt a patient's ability to move one body part (e.g., one finger) independently of others, may produce **astereognosia** (deficits in stereognosis), and may reduce the speed, accuracy, and force of a patient's movements. Such lesions do not, however, eliminate voluntary movement, presumably because there are parallel pathways that descend directly from secondary and association motor areas to subcortical motor circuits without passing through primary motor cortex.

Cerebellum and Basal Ganglia

The cerebellum and the basal ganglia (see Figures 3.19 and 3.27) are both important sensorimotor structures, but neither is a major part of the pathway by which signals descend through the sensorimotor hierarchy. Instead, both the cerebellum and the basal ganglia interact with different levels of the sensorimotor hierarchy and, in so doing, coordinate and modulate its activities.

Watch this video on MyPsychLab
SUBCORTICAL REGIONS

Inhibitory neurons in a patient with Huntington's Disease

Cerebellum

LO 8.11 Describe the structure and connectivity of the cerebellum, and explain the current view of cerebellar function.

The functional complexity of the cerebellum is suggested by its structure and complex connectivity with other brain structures (see Apps & Hawkes, 2009; Buckner, 2013). Although it constitutes only 10 percent of the mass of the brain, the cerebellum contains more than half of the brain's neurons (Azevedo et al., 2009).

The cerebellum receives information from primary and secondary motor cortex, information about descending motor signals from brain-stem motor nuclei, and feedback from motor responses via the somatosensory and vestibular systems. The cerebellum is thought to compare these three sources of input and correct ongoing movements that deviate from their intended course (see Bastian, 2006; Bell, Han, & Sawtell, 2008; Herzfeld & Shadmehr, 2014). By performing this function, it is believed to play a major role in motor learning, particularly in the learning of sequences of movements in which timing is a critical factor (see Pritchett & Carey, 2014).

The effects of diffuse cerebellar damage on motor function are devastating. The patient loses the ability to control precisely the direction, force, velocity, and amplitude of movements and the ability to adapt patterns of motor output to changing conditions. It is difficult to maintain steady postures (e.g., standing), and attempts to do so frequently lead to tremor. There are also severe disturbances in balance, gait, speech, and the control of eye movement. Learning new motor sequences is particularly difficult (Thach & Bastian, 2004).

The functions of the cerebellum were once thought to be entirely sensorimotor, but this conventional view is no longer tenable (see Buckner, 2013; Koziol et al., 2014). Patients with cerebellar damage often display diverse 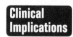 sensory, cognitive, and emotional deficits. Also, healthy volunteers often display cerebellar activity during sensory, cognitive, or emotional activities (see Bastien, 2011; Murdoch, 2009). There are currently no widely accepted theories of cerebellar function that account for this diversity (see Koziol et al., 2014).

The cerebellum has more computing power than the cerebral hemispheres: What in the world does it do with it?

Basal Ganglia

LO 8.12 Describe the anatomy of the basal ganglia, and explain the current view of their function.

The basal ganglia do not contain as many neurons as the cerebellum, but in one sense they are more complex. Unlike the cerebellum, which is organized systematically in lobes, columns, and layers, the basal ganglia are a complex heterogeneous collection of interconnected nuclei.

The anatomy of the basal ganglia suggests that, like the cerebellum, they perform a modulatory function (see Nelson & Kreitzer, 2014). They contribute few fibers to descending motor pathways; instead, they are part of neural loops that receive cortical input from various cortical areas and transmit it back to the cortex via the thalamus (see Nelson & Kreitzer, 2014; Oldenburg & Sabatini, 2015). Many of these loops carry signals to and from the motor areas of the cortex (see Nambu, 2008).

Theories of basal ganglia function have changed in much the same way that theories of cerebellar function have changed. The traditional view of the basal ganglia was that they, like the cerebellum, play a role in the modulation of motor output. Now, the basal ganglia are thought to also be involved in a variety of cognitive functions (see Gittis et al., 2014; Hikosaka et al., 2014; Lim, Fiez, & Holt, 2014; Rektor et al., 2015). This expanded view of the function of the basal ganglia is consistent with the fact that they project to cortical areas known to have cognitive functions (e.g., prefrontal lobes).

The basal ganglia have been shown to participate in habit learning, a type of motor learning that is usually acquired gradually, trial by trial (see Ashby, Turner, & Horovitz, 2010; Joshua, Adler, & Bergman, 2009; Surmeier, Plotkin, & Shen, 2009). However, the basal ganglia's functions do not appear to be limited to habit learning (e.g., Shohamy, 2011; Turner & Desmurget, 2010).

Scan Your Brain

Are you ready to continue your descent into the sensorimotor circuits of the spinal cord? This is a good place for you to pause to scan your brain to evaluate your knowledge of the sensorimotor circuits of the cortex, cerebellum, and basal ganglia by completing the following statements. The correct answers are provided at the end of the exercise. Before proceeding, review material related to your incorrect answers and omissions.

1. Sensory signals that are produced by a response and are often used to guide the continuation of the response are referred to as _____.

2. _____ is the disturbance of a patient's ability to respond to a stimulus on the side of the body opposite to the side of a brain lesion.

3. _____ is a disorder in which patients have great difficulty performing movements when asked to do so out of

context but can readily perform them spontaneously in natural situations.

4. _____ fire when individuals perform a particular goal-directed hand movement or when they observe the same goal-directed movement performed by another.

5. _____ refers to the process of identifying objects by touch.

6. The _____ cortex is the main point of departure of motor signals from the cerebral cortex to lower levels of the sensorimotor hierarchy.

7. The foot area of the motor homunculus is in the _____ fissure.

8. Although the _____ constitutes only 10 percent of the mass of the brain, it contains more than half of the brain's neurons.

9. The _____ are part of neural loops that receive input from various cortical areas and transmit it back to the cortex via the thalamus.

10. Although both are considered to be motor structures, damage to the _____ or the _____ also produce cognitive changes.

Descending Motor Pathways

Neural signals are conducted from the primary motor cortex to the motor neurons of the spinal cord over four different pathways. Two pathways descend in the *dorsolateral* region of the spinal cord—collectively known as the dorsolateral motor pathways, and two descend in the *ventromedial* region of the spinal cord—collectively known as the ventromedial motor pathways. Signals conducted over these pathways act together in the control of voluntary movement (see Iwaniuk & Whishaw, 2000). Like a large company, the sensorimotor system does not work well unless there are good lines of communication from the executive level (the cortex) to the office personnel (the spinal motor circuits) and workers (the muscles).

Dorsolateral Corticospinal Tract and Dorsolateral Corticorubrospinal Tract

LO 8.13 Describe the two descending dorsolateral motor pathways of the spinal cord.

One group of axons that descends from the primary motor cortex does so through the *medullary pyramids*—two bulges on the ventral surface of the medulla—then decussates and continues to descend in the contralateral dorsolateral spinal white matter. This group of axons constitutes the **dorsolateral corticospinal tract**. Most notable among its neurons are the **Betz cells**—extremely large pyramidal neurons of the primary motor cortex.

Most axons of the dorsolateral corticospinal tract synapse on small interneurons of the spinal gray matter, which synapse on the motor neurons of distal muscles of the wrist, hands, fingers, and toes. Primates and the few other mammals (e.g., hamsters and raccoons) that are capable of moving their digits independently have dorsolateral corticospinal tract neurons that

synapse directly on digit motor neurons (see Porter & Lemon, 1993).

A second group of axons that descends from the primary motor cortex synapses in the *red nucleus* of the midbrain. The axons of neurons in the red nucleus then decussate and descend through the medulla, where some of them terminate in the nuclei of the cranial nerves that control the muscles of the face. The rest continue to descend in the dorsolateral portion of the spinal cord. This pathway is called the **dorsolateral corticorubrospinal tract** (*rubro* refers to the red nucleus). The axons of the dorsolateral corticorubrospinal tract synapse on interneurons that in turn synapse on motor neurons that project to the distal muscles of the arms and legs.

The two divisions of the dorsolateral motor pathway—the direct dorsolateral corticospinal tract and the indirect dorsolateral corticorubrospinal tract—are illustrated schematically in Figure 8.7.

Ventromedial Corticospinal Tract and Ventromedial Cortico-brainstem-spinal Tract

LO 8.14 Describe the two descending ventromedial motor pathways of the spinal cord.

Just as there are two major divisions of the dorsolateral motor pathway, one direct (the corticospinal tract) and one indirect (the corticorubrospinal tract), there are two major divisions of the ventromedial motor pathway, one direct and one indirect. The direct ventromedial pathway is the **ventromedial corticospinal tract**, and the indirect one—as you might infer from its cumbersome but descriptive name—is the **ventromedial cortico-brainstem-spinal tract**.

The long axons of the ventromedial corticospinal tract descend ipsilaterally from the primary motor cortex directly into the ventromedial areas of the spinal white matter. As each axon of the ventromedial corticospinal tract descends, it branches diffusely and innervates the interneuron circuits in several different spinal segments on both sides of the spinal gray matter.

The ventromedial cortico-brainstem-spinal tract comprises motor cortex axons that feed into a complex network of brain stem structures. The axons of some of the neurons in this complex brain stem motor network then descend bilaterally in the ventromedial portion of the spinal cord. Each side carries signals from both hemispheres, and each neuron synapses on the interneurons of several different spinal cord segments that control the proximal muscles of the trunk and limbs.

Which brain stem structures interact with the ventromedial cortico-brainstem-spinal tract? There are four major ones: (1) the **tectum**, which receives auditory and visual information about spatial location; (2) the **vestibular nucleus**, which receives information about balance from receptors in the semicircular canals of the inner ear; (3) the **reticular formation**, which, among other things, contains motor programs that regulate complex species-typical movements such as walking, swimming, and jumping; and (4) the motor nuclei of the cranial nerves that control the muscles of the face.

The two divisions of the descending ventromedial pathway—the direct ventromedial corticospinal tract and the indirect ventromedial cortico-brainstem-spinal tract—are illustrated in Figure 8.8.

Comparison of the Two Dorsolateral Motor Pathways and the Two Ventromedial Motor Pathways

LO 8.15 Compare and contrast the two dorsolateral motor pathways and the two ventromedial motor pathways.

The descending dorsolateral and ventromedial motor pathways are similar in that each is composed of two major tracts, one whose axons descend directly to the spinal cord and another whose axons synapse in the brain stem on neurons that in turn descend to the spinal cord. However,

Figure 8.7 The two divisions of the dorsolateral motor pathway: the dorsolateral corticospinal tract and the dorsolateral corticorubrospinal tract. The projections from only one hemisphere are shown.

the two dorsolateral tracts differ from the two ventromedial tracts in two major respects:

- The two ventromedial tracts are much more diffuse. Many of their axons innervate interneurons on both sides of the spinal gray matter and in several different segments, whereas the axons of the two dorsolateral tracts terminate in the contralateral half of one spinal cord segment, sometimes directly on a motor neuron.

- The motor neurons activated by the two ventromedial tracts project to proximal muscles of the trunk and limbs (e.g., shoulder muscles), whereas the motor neurons activated by the two dorsolateral tracts project to distal muscles (e.g., finger muscles).

Because all four of the descending motor tracts originate in the cerebral cortex, all are presumed to mediate voluntary movement; however, major differences in their routes and destinations suggest that they have different functions. This difference was first **Evolutionary Perspective** demonstrated in two experiments on monkeys that were reported by Lawrence and Kuypers in 1968.

Figure 8.8 The two divisions of the ventromedial motor pathway: the ventromedial corticospinal tract and the ventromedial cortico-brainstem-spinal tract. The projections from only one hemisphere are shown.

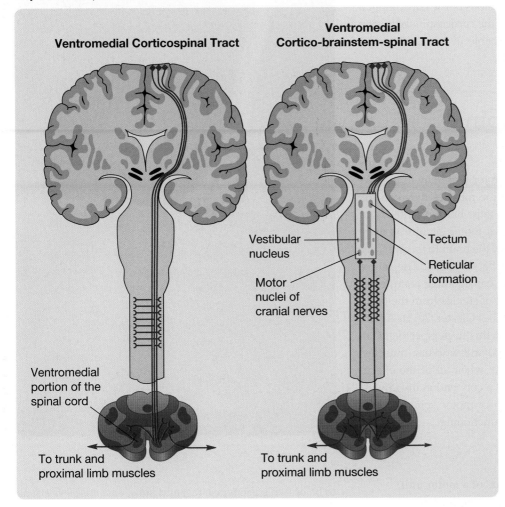

climbing. This point is important because it shows that the same response performed in different contexts can be controlled by different parts of the central nervous system. The point is underlined by the finding that some patients can stretch otherwise paralyzed limbs when they yawn (see Kang & Dhand, 2015).

In their second experiment, Lawrence and Kuypers (1968b) made additional transections in the monkeys whose dorsolateral corticospinal tracts had already been transected in the first experiment. The dorsolateral corticorubrospinal tract was transected in one group of these monkeys. The monkeys could stand, walk, and climb after this second transection, but when they were sitting, their arms hung limply by their sides (remember that monkeys normally use their arms for standing and walking). In those few instances in which the monkeys did use an arm for reaching, they used it like a rubber-handled rake—throwing it out from the shoulder and using it to draw small objects of interest back along the floor.

In their first experiment, Lawrence and Kuypers (1968a) transected (cut through) the left and right dorsolateral corticospinal tracts of their subjects in the medullary pyramids, just above the decussation of the tracts. Following surgery, these monkeys could stand, walk, and climb quite normally; however, their ability to use their limbs for other activities was impaired. For example, their reaching movements were weak and poorly directed, particularly in the first few days following the surgery. Although there was substantial improvement in the monkeys' reaching ability over the ensuing weeks, two other deficits remained unabated. First, the monkeys never regained the ability to move their fingers independently of one another; when they picked up pieces of food, they did so by using all of their fingers as a unit, as if they were glued together. And second, they never regained the ability to release objects from their grasp; as a result, once they picked up a piece of food, they often had to root for it in their hand like a pig rooting for truffles in the ground. In view of this latter problem, it is remarkable that they had no difficulty releasing their grasp on the bars of their cage when they were

The other group of monkeys in the second experiment had both of their ventromedial tracts transected. In contrast to the first group, these subjects had severe postural abnormalities: They had great difficulty walking or sitting. If they did manage to sit or stand without clinging to the bars of their cages, the slightest disturbance, such as a loud noise, frequently made them fall. Although they had some use of their arms, the additional transection of the two ventromedial tracts eliminated their ability to control their shoulders. When they fed, they did so with elbow and whole-hand movements while their upper arms hung limply by their sides.

What do these experiments tell us about the roles of the various descending sensorimotor tracts in the control of primate movement? They suggest that the two ventromedial tracts are involved in the control of posture and whole-body movements (e.g., walking and climbing) and that they can exert control over the limb movements involved in such activities. In contrast, both dorsolateral tracts—the corticospinal tract and the corticorubrospinal tract—control the movements of the limbs. This redundancy was presumably the basis for the good recovery of limb movement after the initial lesions of the corticospinal dorsolateral tract. However, only the corticospinal division of the dorsolateral system is capable of mediating independent movements of the digits.

Sensorimotor Spinal Circuits

We have descended the sensorimotor hierarchy to its lowest level: the spinal circuits and the muscles they control. Psychologists, including us, tend to be brain-oriented, and they often think of the spinal cord motor circuits as mere cables that carry instructions from the brain to the muscles. If you think this way, you will be surprised: The motor circuits of the spinal cord show considerable complexity in their functioning, independent of signals from the brain (see Levine, Lewallen, & Pfaff, 2012; Giszter, 2015). Again, the business metaphor helps put this in perspective: Can the office workers (spinal circuits) and workers (muscles) of a company function effectively when all of the executives and branch managers are at a convention in Hawaii? Of course they can—and the sensorimotor spinal circuits are also capable of independent functioning.

Muscles

LO 8.16 Describe the components of a motor unit, and also distinguish between the different types of muscles.

Motor units are the smallest units of motor activity. Each motor unit comprises a single motor neuron and all of the individual skeletal muscle fibers that it innervates (see Figure 8.9). When the motor neuron fires, all the muscle fibers of its unit contract together. Motor units differ appreciably in the number of muscle fibers they contain; the units with the fewest fibers—those of the fingers and face—permit the highest degree of selective motor control.

A skeletal muscle comprises hundreds of thousands of threadlike muscle fibers bound together in a tough membrane and attached to a bone by a *tendon. Acetylcholine,* which is released by motor neurons at *neuromuscular junctions,* activates the **motor end-plate** on each muscle fiber and causes the fiber to contract. Contraction is the only method that muscles have for generating force, thus any muscle can generate force in only one direction. All of the motor neurons that innervate the fibers of a single muscle are called its **motor pool**.

Although it is an oversimplification (see Gollnick & Hodgson, 1986), skeletal muscle fibers are often considered

Figure 8.9 An electron micrograph of a motor unit: a motor neuron (pink) and the muscle fibers it innervates.

to be of two basic types: fast and slow. *Fast muscle fibers*, as you might guess, are those that contract and relax quickly. Although they are capable of generating great force, they fatigue quickly because they are *poorly vascularized* (have few blood vessels, which gives them a pale color). In contrast, *slow muscle fibers*, although slower and weaker, are capable of more sustained contraction because they are more richly vascularized (and hence much redder). Each muscle has both fast and slow fibers—the fast muscle fibers participate in quick movements such as jumping, whereas the slow muscle fibers participate in gradual movements such as walking. Because each muscle can apply force in only one direction, joints that move in more than one direction must be controlled by more than one muscle. Many skeletal muscles belong unambiguously to one of two categories: flexors or extensors. **Flexors** act to bend or flex a joint, and **extensors** act to straighten or extend it. Figure 8.10 illustrates the *biceps* and *triceps*—the flexor and extensor, respectively, of the elbow joint. Any two muscles whose contraction produces the same movement, be it flexion or extension, are said to be **synergistic muscles**; those that act in opposition, like the biceps and the triceps, are said to be **antagonistic muscles**.

Figure 8.10 The biceps and triceps, which are the flexor and extensor muscles, respectively, of the elbow joint.

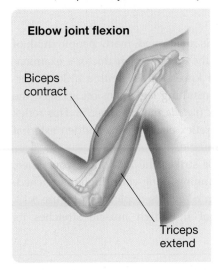

Elbow joint flexion

Biceps contract

Triceps extend

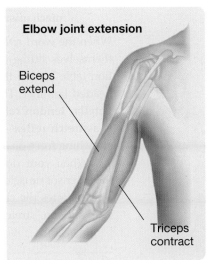

Elbow joint extension

Biceps extend

Triceps contract

To understand how muscles work, it is important to realize that they are elastic, rather than inflexible and cablelike. If you think of an increase in muscle tension as analogous to an increase in the tension of an elastic band joining two bones, you will appreciate that muscle contraction can be of two types. Activation of a muscle can increase the tension that it exerts on two bones without shortening and pulling them together; this is termed **isometric contraction**. Or it can shorten and pull them together; this is termed **dynamic contraction**. The tension in a muscle can be increased by increasing the number of neurons in its motor pool that are firing, by increasing the firing rates of those already firing, or more commonly by a combination of these two changes.

Receptor Organs of Tendons and Muscles

LO 8.17 Describe the receptor organs of tendons and muscles.

The activity of skeletal muscles is monitored by two kinds of receptors: Golgi tendon organs and muscle spindles. **Golgi tendon organs** are embedded in the *tendons*, which connect each skeletal muscle to bone; **muscle spindles** are embedded in the muscle tissue itself. Because of their different locations, Golgi tendon organs and muscle spindles respond to different aspects of muscle contraction. Golgi tendon organs respond to increases in muscle tension (i.e., to the pull of the muscle on the tendon), but they are completely insensitive to changes in muscle length. In contrast, muscle spindles respond to changes in muscle length, but they do not respond to changes in muscle tension.

Under normal conditions, the function of Golgi tendon organs is to provide the central nervous system with information about muscle tension, but they also serve a protective function. When the contraction of a muscle is so extreme that there is a risk of damage, the Golgi tendon organs excite inhibitory interneurons in the spinal cord that cause the muscle to relax.

Figure 8.11 is a schematic diagram of the *muscle-spindle feedback circuit*. Examine it carefully. Notice that each

Figure 8.11 The muscle-spindle feedback circuit. There are many muscle spindles in each muscle; for clarity, only one much-enlarged muscle spindle is illustrated here.

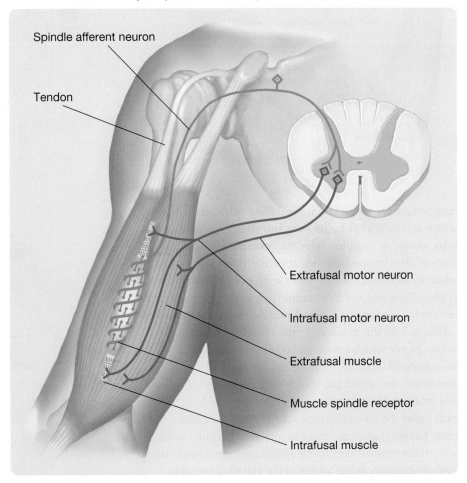

Spindle afferent neuron

Tendon

Extrafusal motor neuron

Intrafusal motor neuron

Extrafusal muscle

Muscle spindle receptor

Intrafusal muscle

Figure 8.12 The function of intrafusal motor neurons.

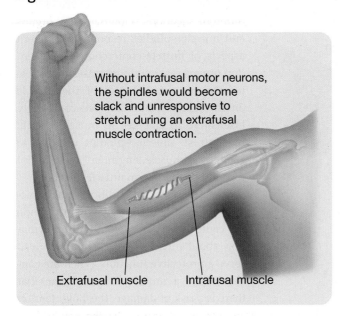

Without intrafusal motor neurons, the spindles would become slack and unresponsive to stretch during an extrafusal muscle contraction.

Extrafusal muscle   Intrafusal muscle

The function of intrafusal motor neurons is to adjust the length of intrafusal muscles, thus maintaining an appropriate degree of tension on muscle spindles, regardless of the length of the extrafusal muscle.

Intrafusal motor neuron

muscle spindle has its own threadlike **intrafusal muscle**, which is innervated by its own **intrafusal motor neuron**. Why would a receptor have its own muscle and motor neuron? The reason becomes apparent when you consider what would happen to a muscle spindle without them. Without its intrafusal motor input, a muscle spindle would fall slack each time its **skeletal muscle (extrafusal muscle)** contracted. In this slack state, the muscle spindle could not do its job, which is to respond to slight changes in extrafusal muscle length. As Figure 8.12 illustrates, the intrafusal motor neuron solves this problem by shortening the intrafusal muscle each time the extrafusal muscle becomes shorter, thus keeping enough tension on the middle, stretch-sensitive portion of the muscle spindle to keep it responsive to slight changes in the length of the extrafusal muscle.

Stretch Reflex

LO 8.18 Describe the stretch reflex, and explain its mechanism.

When the word *reflex* is mentioned, many people think of themselves sitting on the edge of their doctor's examination table having their knees rapped with a little rubber-headed hammer. The resulting leg extension is called the **patellar tendon reflex** (*patella* means "knee"). This reflex is a **stretch reflex**—a reflex elicited by a sudden external stretching force on a muscle.

When your doctor strikes the tendon of your knee, the extensor muscle running along your thigh is stretched. This initiates the chain of events depicted in Figure 8.13. The sudden stretch of the thigh muscle stretches its

Figure 8.13 The elicitation of a stretch reflex. All of the muscle spindles in a muscle are activated during a stretch reflex, but only a single muscle spindle is depicted here.

Rap occurs here

The rap on the knee tendon stretches the spindles of the thigh muscle and elicits a burst of firing in their afferent neurons.

Rap occurs here

The burst of firing in the spindle afferent neurons triggers a burst of firing in the thigh muscle motor neurons, which causes the thigh muscle to contract.

Figure 8.14 The automatic maintenance of limb position by the muscle-spindle feedback system.

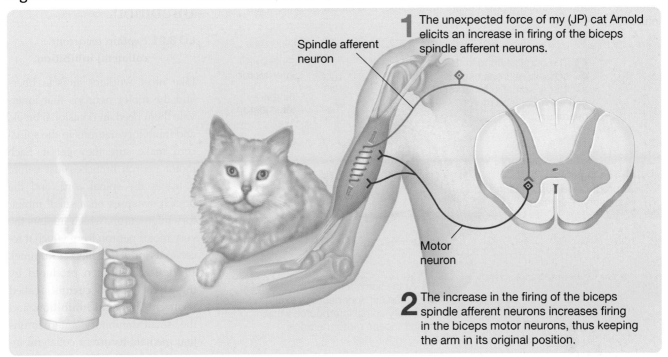

1 The unexpected force of my (JP) cat Arnold elicits an increase in firing of the biceps spindle afferent neurons.

Spindle afferent neuron

Motor neuron

2 The increase in the firing of the biceps spindle afferent neurons increases firing in the biceps motor neurons, thus keeping the arm in its original position.

muscle-spindle stretch receptors, which in turn initiate a volley of action potentials carried from the stretch receptors into the spinal cord by **spindle afferent neurons** via the *dorsal root*. This volley of action potentials excites motor neurons in the *ventral horn* of the spinal cord, which respond by sending action potentials back to the muscle whose stretch originally excited them (see Illert & Kummel, 1999). The arrival of these impulses back at the starting point results in a compensatory muscle contraction and a sudden leg extension.

The method by which the patellar tendon reflex is typically elicited in a doctor's office—that is, by a sharp blow to the tendon of a completely relaxed muscle—is designed to make the reflex readily observable. However, it does little to communicate its functional significance. In real-life situations, the function of the stretch reflex is to keep external forces from altering the intended position of the body. When an external force, such as a push on your arm while you are holding a cup of coffee, causes an unanticipated extrafusal muscle stretch, the muscle-spindle feedback circuit produces an immediate compensatory contraction of the muscle that counteracts the force and keeps you from spilling the coffee—unless, of course, you are wearing your best clothes.

The mechanism by which the stretch reflex maintains limb stability is illustrated in Figure 8.14. Examine it carefully because it illustrates two of the principles of sensorimotor system function that are the focus of this chapter: the important role played by sensory feedback in the regulation of motor output and the ability

of lower circuits in the motor hierarchy to take care of "business details" without the involvement of higher levels.

Withdrawal Reflex

LO 8.19 Describe the withdrawal reflex, and explain its mechanism.

We are sure that, at one time or another, you have touched something painful—a hot pot, for example—and suddenly pulled back your hand. This is a **withdrawal reflex**. Unlike the stretch reflex, the withdrawal reflex is *not monosynaptic*. When a painful stimulus is applied to the hand, the first responses are recorded in the motor neurons of the arm flexor muscles about 1.6 milliseconds later, about the time it takes a neural signal to cross two synapses. Thus, the shortest route in the withdrawal-reflex circuit involves one interneuron. Other responses are recorded in the motor neurons of the arm flexor muscles after the initial volley; these responses are triggered by signals that have traveled over multisynaptic pathways—some involving the cortex. See Figure 8.15.

Reciprocal Innervation

LO 8.20 Explain what is meant by *reciprocal innervation*.

Reciprocal innervation is an important principle of spinal cord circuitry. It refers to the fact that antagonistic

Figure 8.15 The reciprocal innervation of antagonistic muscles in the arm. During a withdrawal reflex, elbow flexors are excited, and elbow extensors are inhibited.

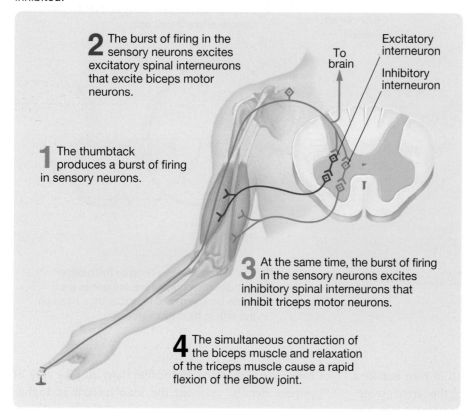

2 The burst of firing in the sensory neurons excites excitatory spinal interneurons that excite biceps motor neurons.

To brain

Excitatory interneuron

Inhibitory interneuron

1 The thumbtack produces a burst of firing in sensory neurons.

3 At the same time, the burst of firing in the sensory neurons excites inhibitory spinal interneurons that inhibit triceps motor neurons.

4 The simultaneous contraction of the biceps muscle and relaxation of the triceps muscle cause a rapid flexion of the elbow joint.

muscles are innervated in a way that permits a smooth, unimpeded motor response: When one is contracted, the other relaxes. Figure 8.15 illustrates the role of reciprocal innervation in the withdrawal reflex. "Bad news" of a sudden painful event in the hand arrives in the dorsal horn of the spinal cord and has two effects: The signals excite both excitatory and inhibitory interneurons. The excitatory interneurons excite the motor neurons of the elbow flexor; the inhibitory interneurons inhibit the motor neurons of the elbow extensor. Thus, a single sensory input produces a coordinated pattern of motor output; the activities of agonists and antagonists are automatically coordinated by the internal circuitry of the spinal cord.

Movements are quickest when there is simultaneous excitation of all agonists and complete inhibition of all antagonists; however, this is not the way voluntary movement is normally produced. Most muscles are always contracted to some degree, and movements are produced by adjustment in the level of relative cocontraction between antagonists. Movements produced by **cocontraction** are smooth, and they can be stopped with precision by a slight increase in the contraction of the antagonistic muscles. Moreover, cocontraction insulates us from the effects of unexpected external forces.

Recurrent Collateral Inhibition

LO 8.21 Explain recurrent collateral inhibition.

Like most workers, muscle fibers and the motor neurons that innervate them need an occasional break, and inhibitory neurons in the spinal cord make sure they get it. Each motor neuron branches just before it leaves the spinal cord, and the branch synapses on a small inhibitory interneuron, which inhibits the very motor neuron from which it receives its input (see Illert & Kummel, 1999). The inhibition produced by these local feedback circuits is called **recurrent collateral inhibition**, and the small inhibitory interneurons that mediate recurrent collateral inhibition are called *Renshaw cells*. As a consequence of recurrent collateral inhibition, each time a motor neuron fires, it momentarily inhibits itself and shifts the responsibility for the contraction of a particular muscle to other members of the muscle's motor pool.

Figure 8.16 provides a summary; it illustrates recurrent collateral inhibition and other factors that directly excite or inhibit motor neurons.

Walking: A Complex Sensorimotor Reflex

LO 8.22 Describe the phenomenon of walking and the degree to which it is controlled by spinal circuits.

Most reflexes are much more complex than withdrawal and stretch reflexes. Think for a moment about the complexity of the program of reflexes that is needed to control an activity such as walking. Such a program must integrate visual information from the eyes; somatosensory information from the feet, knees, hips, arms, and so on; and information about balance from the semicircular canals of the inner ears. And it must produce, on the basis of this information, an integrated series of movements that involves the muscles of the trunk, legs, feet, and upper arms. This program of reflexes must also be **Neuroplasticity** incredibly plastic; it must be able to adjust its output immediately to changes in the slope of the terrain, to instructions from the brain, or to sudden external forces.

Figure 8.16 The excitatory and inhibitory signals that directly influence the activity of a motor neuron.

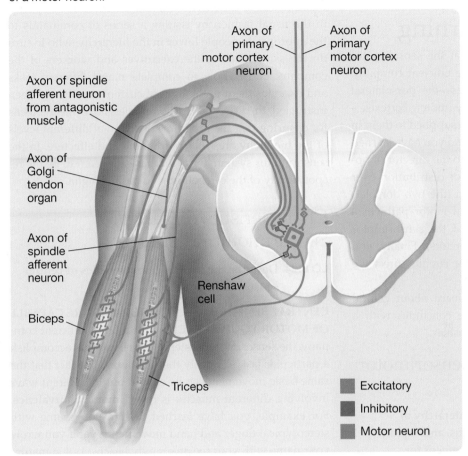

Axon of primary motor cortex neuron

Axon of primary motor cortex neuron

Axon of spindle afferent neuron from antagonistic muscle

Axon of Golgi tendon organ

Axon of spindle afferent neuron

Biceps

Renshaw cell

Triceps

■ Excitatory
■ Inhibitory
■ Motor neuron

Remarkably, similar patterns of neural activity control walking in humans, other mammals, and birds (see Dominici et al., 2011; Grillner, 2011).

Grillner (1985) showed that the spinal cord, with no contribution whatsoever from the brain, can control walking. Grillner's subjects were cats whose spinal cords had been separated from their brains by transection. He suspended the cats in a sling over a treadmill; amazingly, when the treadmill was started so that the cats received sensory feedback of the sort that normally accompanies walking, they began to walk. Similar results have been observed in other species (see Kiehn, 2016).

Evolutionary Perspective Why might walking have evolved in such a way that it can be controlled independent of input from the brain?

Scan Your Brain

Before beginning the important module on central sensorimotor programs, test your knowledge of descending sensorimotor pathways and spinal circuits. Before each item on the left, write the letter for the most related item on the right. The correct answers are provided at the end of the exercise. Before proceeding, review material related to your incorrect answers and omissions.

1. _____ cocontraction
2. _____ medullary pyramids
3. _____ ventromedial tracts
4. _____ recurrent collateral inhibition
5. _____ dorsolateral tracts
6. _____ triceps
7. _____ motor units
8. _____ flexors
9. _____ muscle length
10. _____ reciprocal innervation
11. _____ patellar tendon reflex
12. _____ withdrawal reflex
13. _____ Renshaw cells
14. _____ walking

a. axons innervate neurons
b. control movements of limbs
c. smallest units of motor activity
d. act to bend
e. smooth unimpeded motor response
f. contraction of antagonistic muscles
g. local feedback circuits
h. two synapses
i. complex reflex
j. small inhibitory interneurons
k. bulges
l. stretch reflex
m. muscle spindles
n. extensor

Scan Your Brain answers: (1) f, (2) k, (3) a, (4) g, (5) b, (6) n, (7) c, (8) d, (9) m, (10) e, (11) l, (12) h, (13) j, (14) i.

Central Sensorimotor Programs and Learning

In this chapter, you have learned that the sensorimotor system is like the hierarchy of a large efficient company. You have learned how the executives—the dorsolateral prefrontal cortex and the secondary motor cortexes—issue commands based on information supplied to them in part by the posterior parietal cortex. And you have learned how these commands are forwarded to the director of operations (the primary motor cortex) for distribution over four main channels of communication (the two dorsolateral and the two ventromedial spinal motor pathways) to the metaphoric office managers of the sensorimotor hierarchy (the spinal sensorimotor circuits). Finally, you have learned how spinal sensorimotor circuits direct the activities of the workers (the muscles).

In this final module, you will learn about central sensorimotor programs. The module concludes with a revisiting of the case of Rhonelle the cashier.

A Hierarchy of Central Sensorimotor Programs

LO 8.23 Explain what is meant by a hierarchy of central sensorimotor programs, and explain the importance of this arrangement for sensorimotor functioning.

One view of sensorimotor function is that the sensorimotor system comprises a hierarchy of **central sensorimotor programs** (see Brooks, 1986; Georgopoulos, 1991). According to this view, all but the highest levels of the sensorimotor system have certain patterns of activity programmed into them, and complex movements are produced by activating the appropriate combinations of these programs (see Swinnen, 2002; Tresch et al., 2002). For example, if you want to look at a magazine, your association cortex will activate high-level cortical programs that in turn will activate lower-level programs—perhaps in your brain stem—for walking, bending over, picking up, and thumbing through. These programs in turn will activate spinal programs that control the various elements of the sequences and cause your muscles to complete the objective (Grillner & Jessell, 2009).

Once activated, each level of the sensorimotor system is capable of operating on the basis of current sensory feedback without the direct control of higher levels. Thus, although the highest levels of your sensorimotor system retain the option of directly controlling your activities, most of the individual responses that you make are performed without direct cortical involvement, and you are often barely aware of them (see Custers & Aarts, 2010).

In much the same way, a company president who wishes to open a new branch office simply issues the command to one of the executives, and the executive responds in the usual fashion by issuing a series of commands to the appropriate people lower in the hierarchy, who in turn do the same. Each of the executives and workers of the company knows how to complete many different tasks and executes them in the light of current conditions when instructed to do so. Good companies have mechanisms for ensuring that the programs of action at different levels of the hierarchy are well coordinated and effective. In the sensorimotor system, these mechanisms seem to be the responsibility of the cerebellum and basal ganglia.

Characteristics of Central Sensorimotor Programs

LO 8.24 Describe the various characteristics of central sensorimotor programs.

CENTRAL SENSORIMOTOR PROGRAMS ARE CAPABLE OF MOTOR EQUIVALENCE.   Like a large, efficient company, the sensorimotor system does not always accomplish a particular task in exactly the same way. The fact that the same basic movement can be carried out in different ways involving different muscles is called **motor equivalence**. For example, you have learned to sign your name with stereotypical finger and hand movements, yet if you wrote your name with your toe on a sandy beach, your signature would still retain many of its typical characteristics.

Motor equivalence illustrates the inherent plasticity of the sensorimotor system. It suggests that specific central sensorimotor programs for signing your name are not stored in the neural circuits that directly control your preferred hand; general programs are stored higher in your sensorimotor hierarchy and then are adapted to the situation as required. In an fMRI study, Rijntjes and others (1999) showed that the central sensorimotor programs for signing one's name seem to be stored in areas of secondary motor cortex that control the preferred hand. Remarkably, these same hand areas were also activated when the signature was made with a toe.

SENSORY INFORMATION THAT CONTROLS CENTRAL SENSORIMOTOR PROGRAMS IS NOT NECESSARILY CONSCIOUS.   In Chapter 6, you learned that the neural mechanisms of conscious visual perception (ventral stream) are not necessarily the same as those that mediate the visual control of behavior (dorsal stream). Initial evidence for this theory came from neuropsychological patients who could respond to visual stimuli of which they had little conscious awareness and from others who could not effectively interact with objects that they consciously perceived.

Is there evidence for the separation of conscious perception and sensory control of behavior in intact humans?

Haffenden and Goodale (1998) supplied such evidence (see also Ganel, Tanzer, & Goodale, 2008; Goodale & Westwood, 2004). They showed healthy volunteers a three-dimensional version of the visual illusion in Figure 8.17—notice that the two central disks appear to be different sizes, even though they are identical. Remarkably, when the volunteers were asked to indicate the size of each central disk with their right thumb and pointing finger, they judged the disk on the left to be bigger than the one on the right; however, when they were asked to reach out and pick up the disks with the same two digits, the preparatory gap between the digits was a function of the actual size of each disk rather than its perceived size.

CENTRAL SENSORIMOTOR PROGRAMS CAN DEVELOP WITHOUT PRACTICE. Although central sensorimotor programs for some behaviors can be established by practicing the behaviors, the central sensorimotor programs for many species-typical behaviors are established without explicit practice of the behaviors. This point was made clear by the classic study of Fentress (1973). Fentress

showed that adult mice raised from birth without forelimbs still made the patterns of shoulder movements typical of grooming in their species—and that these movements were well coordinated with normal tongue, head, and eye movements. For example, the mice blinked each time they made the shoulder movements that would have swept their forepaws across their eyes. Fentress's study also demonstrated the importance of sensory feedback in the operation of central sensorimotor programs. The forelimbless mice, deprived of normal tongue–forepaw contact during face grooming, would often interrupt ostensible grooming sequences to lick a cage-mate or even the floor.

Evolutionary Perspective

PRACTICE CAN CREATE CENTRAL SENSORIMOTOR PROGRAMS. Although central sensorimotor programs for many species-typical behaviors develop without practice, practice can generate or modify them (Sanes, 2003). Theories of sensorimotor learning emphasize two kinds of processes that influence the learning of central sensorimotor programs: response chunking and shifting control to lower levels of the sensorimotor system.

Response Chunking According to the **response-chunking hypothesis**, practice combines the central sensorimotor programs that control individual responses into programs that control sequences (chunks) of behavior. In a novice typist, each response necessary to type a word is individually triggered and controlled; in a skilled typist, sequences of letters are activated as a unit, with a marked increase in speed and continuity.

An important principle of chunking is that chunks can themselves be combined into higher-order chunks. For example, the responses needed to type the individual letters and digits of one's address may be chunked into longer sequences necessary to produce the individual words and numbers, and these chunks may in turn be combined so that the entire address can be typed as a unit.

Shifting Control to Lower Levels In the process of learning a central sensorimotor program, control is shifted from higher levels of the sensorimotor hierarchy to lower levels (see Bassett et al., 2015; Huber al., 2012; Kawai et al., 2015). Shifting the level of control to lower levels of the sensorimotor system during training has two advantages. One is that it frees up the higher levels of the system to deal with more esoteric aspects of performance. For example, skilled pianists can concentrate on interpreting a piece of music because they do not have to consciously focus on pressing the right keys. The other advantage of shifting the level of control is that it permits great speed because different circuits at the lower levels of the hierarchy can act simultaneously, without interfering with one another. It is possible to

Figure 8.17 The Ebbinghaus illusion. Notice that the central disk on the left appears larger than the one on the right. Haffenden and Goodale (1998) found that when volunteers reached out to pick up either of the central disks, the position of their fingers as they approached the disks indicated that their responses were being controlled by the actual sizes of the disks, not their consciously perceived sizes.

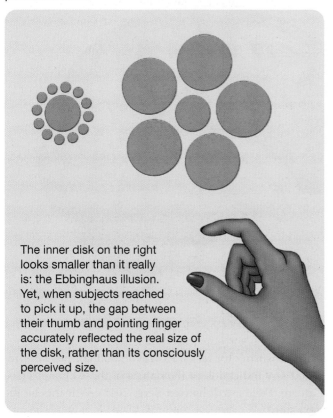

The inner disk on the right looks smaller than it really is: the Ebbinghaus illusion. Yet, when subjects reached to pick it up, the gap between their thumb and pointing finger accurately reflected the real size of the disk, rather than its consciously perceived size.

type 120 words per minute only because the circuits responsible for activating each individual key press can become active before the preceding response has been completed.

Functional Brain Imaging of Sensorimotor Learning

LO 8.25 Explain how the classic Jenkins and colleagues PET study of simple motor learning summarizes the main points of this chapter.

Functional brain-imaging techniques have provided opportunities for studying gross neural correlates of sensorimotor learning. By recording the brain activity of human volunteers as they learn to perform new motor sequences, researchers can develop hypotheses about the roles of various structures in sensorimotor learning. One of the first studies of this type was the PET study of Jenkins and colleagues (1994). These researchers recorded PET activity from human volunteers who performed two different sequences of key presses. There were four different keys, and each sequence was four presses long. The presses were performed with the right hand, one every 3 seconds, and tones indicated when to press and whether or not a press was correct. There were three conditions: (1) a rest control condition, (2) a condition in which the subjects performed a newly learned sequence, and (3) a condition in which they performed a well-practiced sequence.

The results of Jenkins and colleagues are summarized in Figure 8.18. Notice two things. First, notice the involvement of the cortical sensorimotor areas that you were introduced to in this chapter. Second, notice how the involvement of association areas and the cerebellum diminished when sequences were well practiced.

Let's put things in perspective. The Jenkins and colleagues brain-imaging study of sensorimotor learning and the subsequent studies like it (e.g., Bassett et al., 2015; Ostry & Gribble, 2015) have made important contributions by identifying where changes occur in the brain while volunteers

Figure 8.18 The activity recorded by PET scans during the performance of newly learned and well-practiced sequences of finger movements. (Based on Jenkins et al., 1994.)

Sensorimotor areas activated by performing a newly learned sequence of finger movements

Supplementary motor area

Primary motor and somatosensory cortexes

Premotor cortex

Posterior parietal cortex

Dorsolateral prefrontal cortex

Active

Very active

Cerebellum

Sensorimotor areas activated by performing a well-practiced sequence of finger movements

learn sensorimotor tasks. However, nobody has yet provided any indication of the nature of these changes (see Zatorre, Fields, & Johansen-Berg, 2012). Will this be the next step?

The Case of Rhonelle, Revisited

A few days after we finished writing this chapter, I (JP) stopped off to pick up a few fresh vegetables and some fish for dinner, and I once again found myself waiting in Rhonelle's line. It was the longest line, but I am a creature of habit. This time, I felt rather smug as I watched her. All of the reading and thinking that had gone into the preparation of this chapter had provided me with some new insights into what she was doing and how she was doing it. I wondered whether she appreciated her own finely tuned sensorimotor system as much as I did. Then I hatched my plot—a little test of Rhonelle's muscle-spindle feedback system. How would Rhonelle's finely tuned sensorimotor system react to a bag that looked heavy but was in fact extremely light? Next time, I would get one of those paper bags at the mushroom counter, blow it up, drop one mushroom in it, and then fold the top so it looked completely full. I smiled at the thought. But I wasn't the only one smiling. My daydreaming ended abruptly, and the smile melted from my face as I noticed Rhonelle's extended hand and her amused grin. Will I never learn?

Themes Revisited

All four of this text's major themes were addressed in this chapter. Most prominent was the clinical implications theme.

 You learned how research with neuropsychological patients with sensorimotor deficits, as well as with normal human volunteers, has contributed to current theories of sensorimotor functioning.

The evolutionary perspective theme was evident in the discussion of several comparative experiments on the sensorimotor system, largely in nonhuman primates. An important point to keep in mind is that although the senso-

 rimotor functions of nonhuman primates are similar to those of humans, they are not identical (e.g., monkeys walk on both hands and feet). Remarkably, programs for walking tend to be similar in humans, other mammals, and birds.

You learned how metaphors can be used to think productively about science—in particular, how a large, efficient company can serve as a useful metaphor for the sensorimotor system. You also leaned how recent analyses have suggested that primary motor cortex encodes the end point of movements rather than the movements themselves.

Finally, you learned that the sensorimotor system is fundamentally plastic. General commands to act are issued by cortical circuits, but exactly how an act is actually completed depends on the current situation (e.g., body position). Moreover, the sensorimotor system **Neuroplasticity** maintains the ability to change itself in response to practice.

Key Terms

Central Sensorimotor Programs and Learning

Chapter 9
Development of the Nervous System

From Fertilized Egg to You

Chapter Overview and Learning Objectives (LOs)

Five Phases of
Neurodevelopment

LO 9.1 Describe the development of the neural plate into the neural tube, and explain the term *stem cell*.

LO 9.2 Describe the process of neural proliferation, and identify the two organizer areas.

LO 9.3 Describe the processes of migration and aggregation.

LO 9.4 Describe the processes of axon growth and synapse formation. Also, explain the chemoaffinity hypothesis and the topographic gradient hypothesis.

LO 9.5 Describe the processes of neuron death and synapse rearrangement. Why is apoptosis safer than necrosis?

Most of us tend to think of the brain as a three-dimensional array of neural elements "wired" together in a massive network of circuits. However, the brain is not a static network of interconnected elements. It is a *plastic* (change-able), living organ that continuously changes in response to its genetic programs and environment.

This chapter focuses on the incredible process of *neurodevelopment* (neural development), which begins with a single fertilized egg cell and ends with a functional adult brain. Three general ideas are emphasized: (1) the amazing nature of neurodevelopment, (2) the important role of experience in neurodevelopment, and (3) the dire consequences of neurodevelopmental errors. The chapter culminates in a discussion of two disorders of human neurodevelopment: autism spectrum disorders and Williams disorder.

But first, a case study. Many of us are reared in similar circumstances—we live in warm, safe, stimulating environments with supportive families and communities and plenty to eat and drink. Because there is so little variation in most people's early experience, the critical role of experience in human cerebral and psychological development is not always obvious. In order to appreciate the critical role played by experience in neurodevelopment, it is important to consider cases in which children have been reared in grossly abnormal environments. Genie is such a case (Curtiss, 1977; Rymer, 1993).

Thinking Creatively

The Case of Genie

When Genie was admitted to the hospital at the age of 13, she was only 1.35 meters (4 feet, 5 inches) tall and weighed only 28.1 kilograms (62 pounds). She could not stand erect, chew solid food, or control her bladder or bowels. Since the age of 20 months, Genie had spent most days tied to a potty in a small, dark, closed room. Her only clothing was a cloth harness, which kept her from moving anything other than her feet and hands. In the evening, Genie was transferred to a covered crib and a straitjacket. Her father was intolerant of noise, and he beat Genie if she made any sound whatsoever. According to her mother, who was almost totally blind, Genie's father and brother rarely spoke to Genie, although they sometimes barked at her like dogs. The mother was permitted only a few minutes with Genie each day, during which time she fed Genie cereal or baby food—Genie was allowed no solid food. Genie's severe childhood deprivation left her seriously scarred. When she was admitted to the hospital, she made almost no sounds and was totally incapable of speech.

After Genie was discovered a major effort was made to get her development back on track and to document her problems and improvements; however, after a few years, Genie "disappeared" in a series of legal proceedings, foster homes, and institutions.

Genie received special care and training after her rescue, but her behavior never became typical. The following were a few of her continuing problems: She did not react to extremes of warmth and cold; she tended to have silent tantrums during which she would flail, spit, scratch, urinate, and rub her own "snot" on herself; she was easily terrified (e.g., of dogs and men wearing khaki); she could not chew; she could speak only short, poorly pronounced phrases. Genie is currently living in a home for intellectually disabled adults. Clearly, experience played a major role in the processes of Genie's neurodevelopment, processes to which you are about to be introduced.

Five Phases of Neurodevelopment

In the beginning, there is a *zygote*, a single cell formed by the amalgamation of an *ovum* and a *sperm*. The zygote divides to form two daughter cells. These two divide to form four, the four divide to form eight, and so on, until a mature organism is produced. Of course, there must be more to development than this; if there were not, each of us would have ended up like a bowl of rice pudding: an amorphous mass of homogeneous cells.

To save us from this fate, three things other than cell multiplication must occur. First, cells must *differentiate*; some must become muscle cells, some must become multipolar neurons, some must become glial cells, and so on. Second, cells must make their way to appropriate sites and align themselves with the cells around them to form particular structures. And third, cells must establish appropriate functional relations with other cells. This module describes how developing neurons accomplish these three things in five phases: (1) induction of the neural plate, (2) neural proliferation, (3) migration and aggregation, (4) axon growth and synapse formation, and (5) neuron death and synapse rearrangement.

A fertilized egg is **totipotent**, that is, the cell has the ability to develop into any class of cell in the body (e.g., bone, skin, neuron, or heart cells). However, soon after, generations of new cells start to be created by cell division; these newly created cells tend to be specialized and are no longer totipotent (see Boroviak & Nichols, 2014; Kohwi & Doe, 2013). At this stage, developing cells have the ability to develop into many, but not all, classes of body cells and are said to be **pluripotent**. As the embryo develops, new cells become more and more specialized. Eventually, new cells can develop into different cells of only one class (e.g., different kinds of blood cells). These new cells are said to be **multipotent**. Most developing cells will eventually become **unipotent**: they can develop into only one type of cell (e.g., bipolar neurons).

Induction of the Neural Plate

LO 9.1 Describe the development of the neural plate into the neural tube, and explain the term *stem cell*.

Three weeks after conception, the tissue that is destined to develop into the human nervous system becomes recognizable as the **neural plate**—a small patch of ectodermal tissue on the dorsal surface of the developing embryo. The ectoderm is the outermost of the three layers of embryonic cells: *ectoderm, mesoderm,* and *endoderm*. The development of the neural plate is the first major stage of neurodevelopment in all vertebrates.

Neuroplasticity

Watch this video on MyPsychLab
DEVELOPMENT OF NERVOUS SYSTEM

The development of the neural plate is *induced* by chemical signals from an area of the underlying **mesoderm layer**—an area consequently referred to as an *organizer* (see Araya et al., 2014; Kiecker & Lumsden, 2012). Tissue taken from the dorsal mesoderm of one embryo (i.e., the *donor*) and implanted beneath the ventral ectoderm of another embryo (i.e., the *host*) induces the development of an extra neural plate on the ventral surface of the host.

The cells of the neural plate are often referred to as embryonic stem cells. **Stem cells** are cells that meet

Figure 9.1 Stem cells.

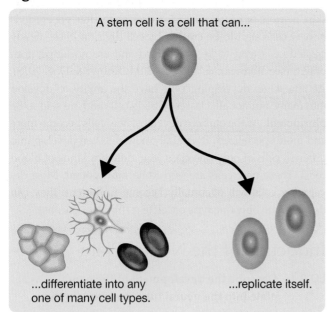

two specific criteria (see Morey, Santanach, & Di Croce, 2015): (1) They have an almost unlimited capacity for self-renewal if maintained in an appropriate cell culture, and (2) they have the ability to develop into many different kinds of cells—they are either totipotent, pluripotent, or multipotent (see Figure 9.1). In general, as the neural plate develops into the neural tube, the fates of its new cells become more specified.

It was once assumed that neuronal and glial lineages were separately specified during the development of the neural tube. Each new cell was thought to be destined to become either a mature neuron or a mature glial cell, the exact type to be determined later in development (see Doetsch, 2003). However, this simplistic view was shot down in flames by the discovery that many neurons develop from glial cells (see Kriegstein & Alvarez-Buylla, 2009).

Why do stem cells have an almost unlimited capacity for self-renewal? This capacity results from the fact that when a stem cell divides, two different daughter cells are created: one that eventually develops into some type of body cell and one that develops into another stem cell (see Figure 9.1)—see Ito and Suda (2014). In theory, when stem cells are maintained in a cell culture, they can keep dividing forever, but eventually errors accumulate, which disrupt the process. That is why stem-cell cultures do not last forever.

Because of the ability of embryonic stem cells to develop into different types of mature cells, their therapeutic potential is under intensive investigation. Will embryonic stem cells injected into a damaged part of a mature brain develop into the appropriate brain structure and improve function? You will learn about the potential of stem-cell therapy in Chapter 10.

As Figure 9.2 illustrates, the growing neural plate folds to form the *neural groove*, and then the lips of the neural groove fuse to form the **neural tube**— *neural tube defects,* which develop into severe **Clinical Implications** birth defects of the CNS, can result from errors in this folding process (see Green & Copp, 2014). The inside of the neural tube eventually becomes the *cerebral ventricles* and *spinal canal*. By 40 days after conception, three swellings are visible at the anterior end of the human neural tube; these swellings ultimately develop into the *forebrain, midbrain*, and *hindbrain* (see Figure 3.18).

Neural Proliferation

LO 9.2   Describe the process of neural proliferation, and identify the two organizer areas.

Once the lips of the neural groove have fused to create the neural tube, the cells of the tube begin to *proliferate* (increase greatly in number). This **neural proliferation** does not occur simultaneously or equally in all parts of the tube. Most cell division in the **Neuroplasticity** neural tube occurs in the **ventricular zone**— the region adjacent to the *ventricle* (the fluid-filled center of the tube). In each species, the cells in different parts of the neural tube proliferate in a particular sequence that is responsible for the pattern of swelling and folding that gives the brain of each member of that species its characteristic shape. The complex pattern of proliferation is in part controlled by chemical signals from two organizer areas in the neural tube: the *floor plate*, which runs along the midline of the ventral surface of the tube, and the *roof plate*, which runs along the midline of the dorsal surface of the tube (see Kanold & Luhmann, 2010).

Migration and Aggregation

LO 9.3   Describe the processes of migration and aggregation.

MIGRATION.   Once cells have been created through cell division in the ventricular zone of the neural tube, they migrate to the appropriate target location. During this period of **migration**, the cells are still in an immature form, lacking the processes (i.e., axons and dendrites) that characterize mature neurons. Two **Neuroplasticity** major factors govern migration in the developing neural tube: time and location. In a given region of the tube, subtypes of neurons arise on a precise and predictable schedule and then migrate together to their prescribed destinations (see Itoh, Tyssowski, & Gotoh, 2013; Kohwi & Doe, 2013).

Cell migration in the developing neural tube is considered to be of two kinds (see Figure 9.3): **Radial migration** proceeds from the ventricular zone in a straight line outward toward the outer wall of the tube; **tangential migration**

Figure 9.2 How the neural plate develops into the neural tube during the third and fourth weeks of human embryological development. (Based on Cowan, 1979.)

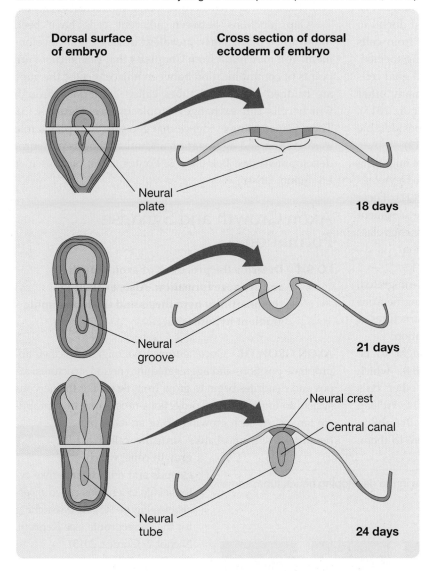

Dorsal surface of embryo

Cross section of dorsal ectoderm of embryo

Neural plate

18 days

Neural groove

21 days

Neural crest

Central canal

Neural tube

24 days

cells, appears in the developing neural tube. At this point, many cells engaging in radial migration do so by moving along the radial glial network (see Ohshima, 2015).

Providing a matrix for radial migration was assumed to be the only function of radial glial cells until the early years of this century (see Dimou & Götz, 2014; Gage & Temple, 2013). However, it is now clear that many radial glial cells eventually develop into neurons. As we mentioned previously, the discovery that many neurons develop from glial cells has led to a major revision in thinking about neural development. It has also focused attention on the roles of radial glial cells in neurodevelopment: Some radial glial cells are pluripotent (see Franco & Müller, 2013; Borrell & Götz, 2014), whereas others are committed to specific neural fates (Franco et al., 2012).

Most research on migration in the developing neural tube has focused on the cortex. This research has revealed orderly waves of migrating cells, progressing from deeper to more superficial layers. Because each wave of cortical cells migrates through the already formed lower layers of cortex before reaching its destination, this radial pattern of cortical development is referred to as an **inside-out pattern** (see Greig et al., 2013). Cortical migration patterns are more complex than was first thought: Many cortical cells engage in long tangential migrations to reach their final

occurs at a right angle to radial migration—that is, parallel to the tube's walls. Many cells engage in both radial and tangential migration to get from their point of origin in the ventricular zone to their target destination (see Budday, Steinmann, & Kuhl, 2015; Evsyukova, Plestant, & Anton, 2013).

There are two methods by which developing cells migrate (see Figure 9.4). One is somal translocation. In **somal translocation**, an extension grows from the developing cell in the direction of the migration; the extension seems to explore the immediate environment for attractive and repulsive cues as it grows. Then, the cell body itself moves into and along the extending process, and trailing processes are retracted (see Cooper, 2013).

The second method of migration is **glia-mediated migration** (see Figure 9.4). Once the period of neural proliferation is under way and the walls of the neural tube are thickening, a network of glial cells, called **radial glial**

Figure 9.3 Two types of neural migration: radial migration and tangential migration.

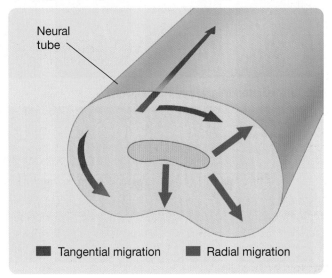

Neural tube

■ Tangential migration   ■ Radial migration

destinations, and the patterns of proliferation and migration are different for different areas of the cortex (see Anderson & Vanderhaeghen, 2014; Sun & Hevner, 2014).

The **neural crest** is a structure situated just dorsal to the neural tube (see Figure 9.2). It is formed from cells that break off from the neural tube as it is being formed. Neural crest cells develop into the neurons and glial cells of the peripheral nervous system as well as many other cell types in the body (see Buitrago-Delgado et al., 2015), and thus many of them must migrate over considerable distances (see Takahashi, Sipp, & Enomoto, 2013).

Numerous chemicals guide various classes of migrating neurons by either attracting or repelling them (see Devreotes & Horwitz, 2015; Maeda, 2015; Mirakaj et al., 2011). These guidance molecules play a critical role in neurodevelopment because the brain cannot function normally unless each class of developing neurons arrives at the correct location.

AGGREGATION. Once developing neurons have migrated, they must align themselves with other developing neurons that have migrated to the same area to form the structures of the nervous system. This process is called **aggregation**.

Both migration and aggregation are thought to be mediated by **cell-adhesion molecules (CAMs)**, which are located on the surfaces of neurons and other cells (see Famulski & Solecki, 2012; Mori et al., 2014; Weledji & Assob, 2014). Cell-adhesion molecules have the ability to recognize molecules on other cells and adhere to them.

Elimination of just one type of CAM in a *knockout mouse* (see Chapter 5) has been shown to have a devastating effect on brain development (DiCicco-Bloom, 2006; Lien et al., 2006).

Gap junctions between adjacent cells have been found to be particularly prevalent during brain development. You may recall from Chapter 4 that *gap junctions* are points of communication between adjacent cells; the gaps are bridged by narrow tubes called *connexins*, through which cells can exchange cytoplasm (see Figure 4.13). There is increasing evidence that gap junctions play a role in migration and aggregation and other aspects of neurodevelopment (see Belousov & Fontes, 2013; Niculescu & Lohmann, 2014).

Axon Growth and Synapse Formation

LO 9.4 Describe the processes of axon growth and synapse formation. Also, explain the chemoaffinity hypothesis and the topographic gradient hypothesis.

AXON GROWTH. Once neurons have migrated to their appropriate positions and aggregated into neural structures, axons and dendrites begin to grow from them. For the nervous system to function, these projections must grow to appropriate targets. At each growing tip of an axon or dendrite is an amoebalike structure called a **Neuroplasticity** **growth cone**, which extends and retracts fingerlike cytoplasmic extensions called *filopodia* (see Figure 9.5), as if searching for the correct route (see Kerstein, Nichol, & Gomez, 2015).

Remarkably, most growth cones reach their correct targets. A series of studies of neural regeneration by Roger Sperry in the early 1940s first demonstrated that axons are capable of precise growth and suggested how it occurs.

In one study, Sperry cut the optic nerves of frogs, rotated their eyeballs 180 degrees, and waited for the axons of the **retinal ganglion cells**, which compose the optic nerve, to *regenerate* (grow again). (Frogs, unlike mammals, have retinal ganglion cells that regenerate.) Once regeneration was complete, Sperry used a convenient behavioral **Evolutionary Perspective** test to assess the

Figure 9.4 Two methods by which cells migrate in the developing neural tube: somal translocation and glia-mediated migration.

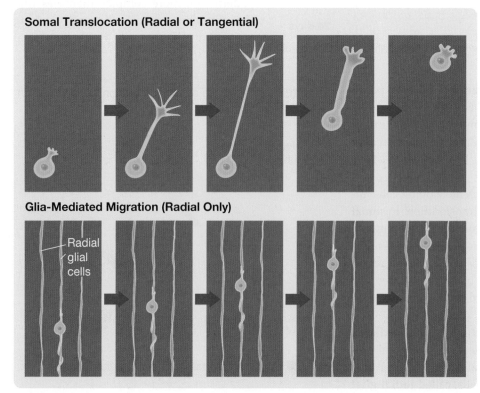

Somal Translocation (Radial or Tangential)

Glia-Mediated Migration (Radial Only)

Radial glial cells

Figure 9.5 Growth cones. The cytoplasmic fingers (the filopodia) of growth cones seem to grope for the correct route. (Courtesy of Naweed I. Syed, Ph.D., Departments of Anatomy and Medical Physiology, the University of Calgary.)

frogs' visual capacities (see Figure 9.6). When he dangled a lure behind the frogs, they struck forward, thus indicating that their visual world, like their eyes, had been rotated 180 degrees. Frogs whose eyes had been rotated, but whose optic nerves had not been cut, responded in exactly the same way. This was strong behavioral evidence that each retinal ganglion cell had grown back to the same point of the **optic tectum** (called the *superior colliculus* in mammals) to which it had originally been connected. Neuroanatomical investigations have confirmed that this is exactly what happens (see Guo & Udin, 2000).

On the basis of his studies of regeneration, Sperry proposed the **chemoaffinity hypothesis** of axonal development (see Sperry, 1963). He hypothesized that each postsynaptic surface in the nervous system releases a specific chemical label and that each growing axon is attracted by the label

Watch this video on MyPsychLab

CHALK IT UP! FROGS, TONGUES, AND AXON REGENERATION

to its postsynaptic target during both neural development and regeneration. Indeed, it is difficult to imagine another mechanism by which an axon growing out from a rotated eyeball could find its precise target on the optic tectum. Many guidance molecules for axon growth have been identified (see Dudanova & Klein, 2013; Onishi, Hollis, & Zou, 2014).

The chemoaffinity hypothesis fails to account for the discovery that some growing axons follow the same circuitous route to reach their target in every member of a species rather than growing directly to it. This discovery led to a revised notion of how growing axons reach their specific targets. According to this revised hypothesis, a growing axon is not attracted to its target by a single specific attractant released by the target, as Sperry thought. Instead, growth cones seem to be influenced by a series of chemical and physical signals along the route

Figure 9.6 Sperry's classic study of eye rotation and regeneration.

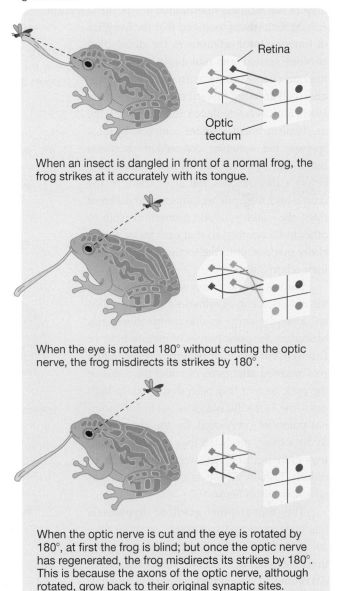

When an insect is dangled in front of a normal frog, the frog strikes at it accurately with its tongue.

When the eye is rotated 180° without cutting the optic nerve, the frog misdirects its strikes by 180°.

When the optic nerve is cut and the eye is rotated by 180°, at first the frog is blind; but once the optic nerve has regenerated, the frog misdirects its strikes by 180°. This is because the axons of the optic nerve, although rotated, grow back to their original synaptic sites.

(see Goodhill, 2016; Squarzoni, Thion, & Garel, 2015; Tamariz & Varela-Echavarría, 2015). These axonal guideposts are similar to those that guide neural migration in the sense that some attract and others repel the growing axons. Other signals that guide growing axons come from adjacent growing axons (see Wang & Marquardt, 2013).

Pioneer growth cones—the first growth cones to travel along a particular route in a developing nervous system—are presumed to follow the correct trail by interacting with guidance molecules along the route. Then, subsequent growth cones embarking on the same journey follow the routes blazed by the pioneers. The tendency of developing axons to grow along the paths established by preceding axons is called **fasciculation**.

Much of the axonal development in complex nervous systems involves growth from one topographic array of neurons to another. The neurons on one array project to another, maintaining the same topographic relation they had on the first array; for example, the topographic map of the retina is maintained on the optic tectum.

At first, it was assumed that the integrity of topographical relations in the developing nervous system was maintained by a point-to-point chemoaffinity, with each retinal ganglion cell growing toward a specific chemical label. However, evidence indicates that the mechanism must be more complex. In most species, the synaptic connections between retina and optic tectum are established long before either reaches full size. Then, as the retinas and the optic tectum grow at different rates, the initial synaptic connections shift to other tectal neurons so that each retina is precisely mapped onto the tectum, regardless of their relative sizes.

Studies of the regeneration (rather than the development) of retinal-tectum projections tell a similar story. In one informative series of studies, the optic nerves of mature frogs or fish were cut and their pattern of regeneration was assessed after parts of either the retina or the optic tectum had been destroyed. In both cases, the axons did not grow out to their original points of connection (as the chemoaffinity hypothesis predicted they would); instead, they grew out to fill the available space in an orderly fashion. These results are illustrated schematically in Figure 9.7.

The **topographic gradient hypothesis** has been proposed to explain accurate axonal growth involving topographic mapping in the developing brain (see Weth et al., 2014). According to this hypothesis, axons growing from one topographic surface (e.g., the retina)

to another (e.g., the optic tectum) are guided to specific targets that are arranged on the terminal surface in the same way as the axons' cell bodies are arranged on the original surface (see Cang & Feldheim, 2013; Klein & Kania, 2014; Triplett, 2014). The key part of this hypothesis is that the growing axons are guided to their destinations by two intersecting signal gradients (e.g., an anterior–posterior gradient and a medial–lateral gradient). However, other mechanisms have also been shown to contribute to topographic mapping, such as spontaneous neural activity (see Ackman & Crair, 2014) and neuron–astrocyte interactions (see López-Hidalgo & Schummers, 2014).

SYNAPSE FORMATION. Once axons have reached their intended sites, they must establish an appropriate pattern of synapses. A single neuron can grow an axon on its own, but it takes coordinated activity in at least two neurons to create a synapse between them (see Andreae & Burrone, 2014). This is one reason why our understanding of how axons connect to their targets has lagged behind our

Figure 9.7 The regeneration of the optic nerve of the frog after portions of either the retina or the optic tectum have been destroyed. These phenomena support the topographic gradient hypothesis.

Axons normally grow from the frog retina and terminate on the optic tectum in an orderly fashion. The assumption that this orderliness results from point-to-point chemoaffinity is challenged by the following two observations.

1 When half the retina was destroyed and the optic nerve cut, the retinal ganglion cells from the remaining half retina projected systematically over the entire optic tectum.

2 When half the optic tectum was destroyed and the optic nerve cut, the retinal ganglion cells from the retina projected systematically over the remaining half of the optic tectum.

understanding of how they reach them. Still, some exciting breakthroughs have been made—for example, some of the chemical signals that play a role in the location and formation of synapses have been identified (see Christensen, Shao, & Colón-Ramos, 2013; Inestrosa & Arenas, 2010; Koropouli & Kolodkin, 2014; Krueger et al., 2012).

Perhaps the most exciting recent discovery about **synaptogenesis** (the formation of new synapses) is that it depends on the presence of glial cells, particularly astrocytes (see Allen, 2013; Tsai et al., 2012). Retinal ganglion cells maintained in culture formed seven times more synapses when astrocytes were present. Moreover, synapses formed in the presence of astrocytes were quickly lost when the astrocytes were removed. Early theories about the contribution of astrocytes to synaptogenesis emphasized a nutritional role: Developing neurons need high levels of cholesterol during synapse formation, and the extra cholesterol is supplied by astrocytes. However, current evidence suggests that astrocytes play a much more extensive role in synaptogenesis by processing, transferring, and storing information supplied by neurons (see Clarke & Barres, 2013).

Most current research on synaptogenesis is focusing on elucidating the chemical signals that must be exchanged between presynaptic and postsynaptic neurons for a synapse to be created (see Ou & Shen, 2010; Sheffler-Collins & Dalva, 2012). One complication researchers face is the promiscuity that developing neurons display when it comes to synaptogenesis. Although the brain must be "wired" according to a specific plan in order to function, in vitro studies suggest that any type of neuron will form synapses with any other type. However, once established, synapses that do not function appropriately tend to be eliminated.

Neuron Death and Synapse Rearrangement

LO 9.5 Describe the processes of neuron death and synapse rearrangement. Why is apoptosis safer than necrosis?

NEURON DEATH. Neuron death is a normal and important part of neurodevelopment. Many more neurons—about 50 percent more—are produced than required, and large-scale neuron death occurs in waves in various parts of the brain throughout development.

Neuroplasticity

> **Neuroplasticity** Why do you think the developing nervous system would produce 50 percent more neurons than are required?

Neuron death during development was initially assumed to be a passive process. It was assumed that

developing neurons died when they failed to get adequate nutrition. However, it is now clear that cell death during development is usually active. Genetic programs inside neurons are triggered and cause them to actively complete suicide. Passive cell death is called **necrosis** ("ne-KROE-sis"); active cell death is called **apoptosis** ("A-poe-toe-sis").

Watch this video on MyPsychLab
APOPTOSIS

Apoptosis is safer than necrosis. Necrotic cells break apart and spill their contents into extracellular fluid, and the consequence is potentially harmful inflammation. In contrast, in apoptotic cell death, DNA and other internal structures are cleaved apart and packaged in membranes before the cell breaks apart. These membranes contain molecules that attract scavenger microglia and other molecules that prevent inflammation. Apoptosis removes excess neurons in a safe, neat, and orderly way. But apoptosis has a dark side as well. If genetic programs for apoptotic cell death are blocked, the consequence can be cancer; if the programs are inappropriately activated, the consequence can be neurodegenerative disease.

What triggers the genetic programs that cause apoptosis in developing neurons? There appear to be two kinds of triggers (Miguel-Aliaga & Thor, 2009). First, some developing neurons appear to be genetically programmed for an early death—once they have fulfilled their functions, groups of neurons die together in the absence of any obvious external stimulus (see Dekkers & Barde, 2013; Underwood, 2013). Second, some developing neurons seem to die because they fail to obtain the life-preserving chemicals that are supplied by their targets (see Deppmann et al., 2008). Evidence that life-preserving chemicals are supplied to developing neurons by their postsynaptic targets comes from two kinds of observations: Grafting an extra target structure (e.g., an extra limb) to an embryo before the period of synaptogenesis reduces the death of neurons growing into the area, and destroying some of the neurons growing into an area before the period of cell death increases the survival rate of the remaining neurons.

Several life-preserving chemicals that are supplied to developing neurons by their targets have been identified. The most prominent class of these chemicals is the

Figure 9.8 The effect of synapse rearrangement on the selectivity of synaptic transmission. The synaptic contacts of each axon become focused on a smaller number of cells.

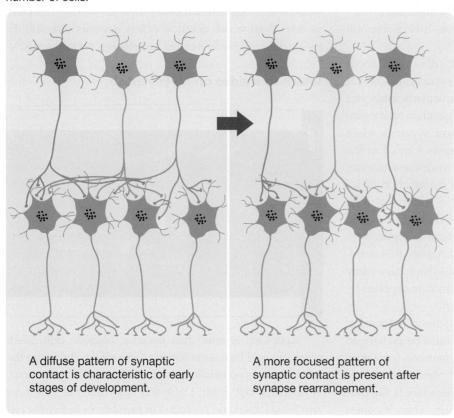

A diffuse pattern of synaptic contact is characteristic of early stages of development.

A more focused pattern of synaptic contact is present after synapse rearrangement.

neurotrophins. Nerve growth factor (NGF) was the first neurotrophin to be isolated (see Levi-Montalcini, 1952, 1975). The neurotrophins promote the growth and survival of neurons, function as axon guidance molecules, and stimulate synaptogenesis (Park & Poo, 2013).

SYNAPSE REARRANGEMENT. During the period of cell death, neurons that have established incorrect connections are particularly likely to die. As they die, the space they leave vacant on postsynaptic membranes is filled by the sprouting axon terminals of surviving neurons. Thus, cell death results in a massive rearrangement of synaptic connections. This phase of synapse rearrangement also tends to focus the output of each neuron on a smaller number of postsynaptic cells, thus increasing the selectivity of transmission (see Figure 9.8). There is evidence that microglia play a role in synapse rearrangement (see Ueno & Yamashita, 2014).

Scan Your Brain

Are you ready to focus on the continuing development of the human brain after birth? To find out if you are prepared to proceed, scan your brain by filling in the blanks in the following *chronological list of stages of neurodevelopment.* The correct answers are provided at the end of the exercise. Before proceeding, review material related to your errors and omissions.

1. Induction of the neural ____
2. Formation of the ____ tube
3. Neural ____
4. Neural ____
5. ____ aggregation
6. Growth of neural ____
7. Formation of ____
8. Neuron ____ and synapse ____

Scan Your Brain answers: (1) plate, (2) neural, (3) proliferation, (4) migration, (5) Neural, (6) processes (axons and dendrites), (7) synapses, (8) death; rearrangement.

Postnatal Cerebral Development in Human Infants

Most of our knowledge of the development of the human brain comes from the study of nonhuman species. This fact emphasizes the value of the evolutionary perspective. There is, however, one way in which the development of the human brain is unique: The human brain develops more slowly than those of other species, not achieving full maturity until late adolescence or early adulthood (see Crone & Dahl, 2012; Fuhrmann, Knoll, & Blakemore, 2015).

Evolutionary Perspective

Much of our knowledge about human neurodevelopment is inferred from studies of nonhuman animals. Given that the human brain is unique in that it develops more slowly, what implications does this have for the validity of our knowledge of human neurodevelopment?

This module deals with the part of cerebral development that occurs after birth. It focuses on the development of the *prefrontal cortex* (see Figure 1.9) because the prefrontal cortex is the last part of the human brain to reach maturity (see Giedd, 2015).

Postnatal Growth of the Human Brain

LO 9.6 Describe the postnatal growth of the human brain. What sorts of growth account for its substantial increase in volume?

The human brain grows substantially after birth: Its volume quadruples between birth and adulthood, with much of the growth occurring in the first year (Gilmore et al., 2012; Li et al., 2015) and continuing into the third year (see Silbereis et al., 2016). This increase in size does not, however, result from the development of additional neurons. The postnatal growth of the human brain seems to result from three other kinds of growth: synaptogenesis, myelination of axons, and increased branching of dendrites.

There has been particular interest in the postnatal formation of synapses because the number of connections between neurons in a particular region of the brain is assumed to be an indicator of its analytic ability. There is a general increase in *synaptogenesis* in the human cortex shortly after birth, but there are differences among the cortical regions. For example, in the primary visual and auditory cortexes, there is a major burst of synaptogenesis in the fourth postnatal month, and maximum synapse density (150 percent of adult levels) is achieved in the seventh or eighth postnatal month; in contrast, synaptogenesis in the prefrontal cortex occurs at a relatively steady rate, reaching maximum synapse density in the second year.

Myelination increases the speed of axonal conduction, and the myelination of various areas of the human brain during development roughly parallels their functional development (see Purger, Gibson, & Monje, 2015). Myelination of sensory areas occurs in the first few months after birth, and myelination of the motor areas follows soon after that, whereas myelination of the prefrontal cortex continues into adulthood (Yap et al., 2013). It has been suggested that some of the growth in myelinated tracts revealed by diffusion tensor MRI (see Chapter 5) may reflect growth and reorganization of axons in addition to myelination, but this still remains a matter of conjecture (see Paus, 2010; Schmithorst & Yuan, 2010).

In general, the pattern of *dendritic branching* in the cortex duplicates the original pattern of neural migration in the sense that dendritic branching progresses from deeper to more superficial layers. Technical advances in imaging live neurons in culture are leading to insights into how dendrites can reconfigure themselves. Most surprising is the speed with which even mature dendrites can change their shape—some changes can be observed in a few seconds (see Bourne & Harris, 2012; Koleske, 2013).

Postnatal human brain development is not a one-way street; there are regressive changes as well as growth (see Jernigan et al., 2011). For example, once maximum synaptic density and gray matter volume have been achieved, there are periods of decline. Like periods of synaptogenesis, periods of synaptic and gray matter loss occur at different times in different parts of the brain. For example, cortical thinning occurs first in primary sensory and motor areas, progresses to secondary areas, and culminates in association areas (see Jernigan et al., 2011). The achievement of the adult level of gray matter in a particular cortical area is correlated with that area's reaching functional maturity—sensory and motor areas reach functional maturity before association areas (see Purger, Gibson, & Monje, 2015).

Development of the Prefrontal Cortex

LO 9.7 Describe the functions of the prefrontal cortex and what sorts of behaviors infants display prior to its development.

As you have just learned, the prefrontal cortex displays the most prolonged period of development of any brain region. Its development is believed to be largely responsible for the course of human cognitive development, which occurs over the same period (see Giedd, 2015).

Given the size, complexity, and heterogeneity of the prefrontal cortex, it is hardly surprising that no single theory can explain its function. Nevertheless, four types of cognitive functions have often been linked to this area in studies of adults with extensive prefrontal damage. Various parts of the adult prefrontal cortex seem to play roles in (1) *working memory*, that is, keeping relevant information accessible for short periods of time while a task is being completed; (2) planning and carrying out sequences of actions; (3) inhibiting responses that are inappropriate in the current context but not in others; and (4) following rules for social behavior (see Fareri & Delgado, 2014; Watanabe & Yamamoto, 2015). Young humans do not begin to demonstrate these cognitive functions until prefrontal development has progressed.

One interesting line of research on prefrontal cortex development is based on Piaget's classic studies of psychological development in human babies. In his studies of 7-month-old children, Piaget noticed an intriguing error. A small toy was shown to an infant; then, as the child watched, it was placed behind one of two screens, left or right. After a brief delay, the infant was allowed to reach for the toy. Piaget found that almost all 7-month-old infants reached for the screen behind which they had seen the toy being placed. However, if, after being placed behind the same screen on several consecutive trials, the toy was placed behind the other screen (as the infant watched), most of the 7-month-old infants kept reaching for the previously correct screen rather than the screen that currently hid the toy. Children tend to make this *perseverative error* between about 7 and 12 months, but not thereafter (Diamond, 1985). **Perseveration** is the tendency to continue making a formerly correct response when it is currently incorrect.

Diamond (1991) hypothesized that this perseverative error occurred in infants between 7 and 12 months because the neural circuitry of the prefrontal cortex is not yet developed during that period. Synapse numbers in the prefrontal cortex are not maximal until the second year, and correct performance of the task involved two of the major functions of this brain area: holding information in working memory and suppressing previously correct, but currently incorrect, responses.

Effects of Experience on Postnatal Development of Neural Circuits

Because the human brain develops so slowly, as you learned in the previous module, there are many opportunities for experience to influence its development. The effects of experience on brain development are many and varied, but they are considered to be of two general types: permissive or instructive. **Permissive experiences** are those that permit the information in genetic programs of brain development to be expressed and maintained. **Instructive experiences** are those that contribute to the information in genetic programs and influence the course of development (see Assali, Gaspar, & Rebsam, 2014).

Critical Periods vs. Sensitive Periods

LO 9.8 **Explain the difference between a "critical period" and a "sensitive period" of development.**

An important feature of the effects of experience on development is that they are time-dependent: The effect of a given experience on development depends on when it occurs during development (see Makinodan et al., 2012). In most cases,

there is a window of opportunity in which a particular experience can influence development. If it is absolutely essential (i.e., critical) for an experience to occur within a particular interval to influence development, the interval is called a **critical period**. If an experience has a great effect on development when it occurs during a particular interval but can still have weak effects outside the interval, the interval is called a **sensitive period**. Although the term *critical period* is widely used, the vast majority of experiential effects on development have been shown to be sensitive periods.

Early Studies of Experience and Neurodevelopment: Deprivation and Enrichment

LO 9.9 **Explain the different effects of deprivation vs. enrichment on neurodevelopment.**

Most research on the effects of experience on the development of the brain has focused on sensory and motor systems—which lend themselves to **Neuroplasticity** experiential manipulation. Much of the early research focused on two general manipulations of experience: sensory deprivation and enrichment.

The first studies of sensory deprivation assessed the effects of rearing animals in the dark. Rats reared from birth in the dark were found to have fewer synapses and fewer dendritic spines in their primary visual cortexes, and as adults they were found to have deficits in depth and pattern vision. In contrast, the first studies of early exposure to enriched environments found that enrichment had beneficial effects. For example, rats that were raised in enriched (complex) group cages rather than by themselves in barren cages were found to have thicker cortexes with more dendritic spines and more synapses per neuron (see Berardi, Sale, & Maffei, 2015).

The early studies of sensory restriction in rats have been extended to human babies born with cataracts in both eyes, which render them nearly blind (Lewis & Maurer, 2005). When the cataracts were removed, between 1 and 9 months after birth, their vision was comparable to that of a newborn. Thereafter, some aspects of vision improved quickly, but visual deficits were still present 2 years later (Maurer, Ellenberg, & Lewis, 2006).

Competitive Nature of Experience and Neurodevelopment: Ocular Dominance Columns

LO 9.10 **Describe the effects of monocular deprivation on the development of ocular dominance columns.**

Research on the effects of experience on brain development has progressed beyond simply assessing general sensory deprivation or enrichment. Manipulations of early experience have become more selective. Many of these selective manipulations of early experience have revealed a competitive aspect to the effects of experience on neurodevelopment. This competitive aspect is clearly illustrated by the disruptive effects of monocular deprivation on ocular dominance columns in primary visual cortex (see Chapter 6).

Depriving one eye of input for a few days early in life has a lasting adverse effect on vision in the deprived eye, but this does not happen if the other eye is also blindfolded. When only one eye is blindfolded, the ability of that eye to activate the visual cortex is reduced, whereas the ability of the other eye is increased. Both of these effects occur because early monocular deprivation changes the pattern of synaptic input into layer IV of the primary visual cortex.

In many species, ocular dominance columns in layer IV of the primary visual cortex are largely developed at birth. However, blindfolding one eye for several days during the first few months of life reorganizes the system: The width of the columns of input from the deprived eye is decreased, and the width of the columns of input from the nondeprived eye is increased (Hata & Stryker, 1994; Hubel, Wiesel, & LeVay, 1977). The exact timing of the sensitive period for this effect is specific to each species, with modest effects occurring even in adulthood (see Levelt & Hübener, 2012).

Because the adverse effects of early monocular deprivation manifest themselves so quickly (i.e., in a few days), it was believed that they could not be mediated by structural changes. However, Antonini and Stryker (1993) found that a few days of monocular deprivation produce a massive decrease in the axonal branching of the lateral geniculate nucleus neurons that normally carry signals from the deprived eye to layer IV of the primary visual cortex (see Figure 9.9).

Effects of Experience on Topographic Sensory Cortex Maps

LO 9.11 Describe three examples of the effects of experience on topographic sensory maps.

Neuroplasticity Some of the most remarkable demonstrations of the effects of experience on the organization of the nervous system come from research on sensory topographic maps. The following are three such demonstrations:

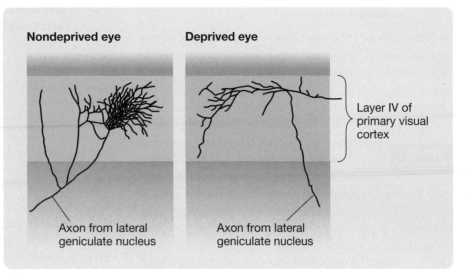

Figure 9.9 The effect of a few days of early monocular deprivation on the structure of axons projecting from the lateral geniculate nucleus into layer IV of the primary visual cortex. Axons carrying information from the deprived eye displayed substantially less branching. (Based on Antonini & Stryker, 1993.)

- Roe and colleagues (1990) surgically altered the course of developing axons of ferrets' retinal ganglion cells so that the axons synapsed in the medial geniculate nucleus of the auditory system instead of in the lateral geniculate nucleus of the visual system. Remarkably, the experience of visual input caused the auditory cortex of the ferrets to become organized retinotopically (laid out like a map of the retina). Typically, surgically attaching the inputs of one sensory system to cortex that would normally develop into the primary cortex of another system leads that cortex to develop many, but not all, characteristics typical of the newly attached system (see Majewska & Sur, 2006).

- Knudsen and Brainard (1991) raised barn owls with vision-displacing prisms over their eyes. This led to a corresponding change in the auditory spatial map in the tectum. For example, **Evolutionary Perspective** an owl that was raised wearing prisms that shifted its visual world 23 degrees to the right had an auditory map that was also shifted 23 degrees to the right, so that objects were heard to be where they were seen to be.

- Several studies have shown that early music training influences the organization of human cortex (see Miendlarzewska & Trost, 2014). For example, early musical training expands the area of auditory cortex that responds to complex musical tones.

Experience Fine-Tunes Neurodevelopment

LO 9.12   Explain the role of spontaneous neural firing on neurodevelopment.

Don't be misled by the way studies of the effects of experience on neurodevelopment are normally conducted. In their studies, biopsychologists often alter the typical course of neurodevelopment by exposing their subjects to pathological early experiences such as blindness or isolation. Consequently, you may come to think of the role of experience in neurodevelopment as pathological rather than typical. The truth is that long before the nervous system is fully developed, neurons begin to fire spontaneously (Blankenship & Feller, 2010) and begin to interact with the environment. The resulting patterns of neural activity fine-tune subsequent stages of neurodevelopment as the animal grows (see Borodinsky, Belgacem, & Swapna, 2012; Froemke & Jones, 2011; Ruthazer & Aizenman, 2010). This fine-tuning constitutes the critical, final phase of typical development.

Thinking Creatively

Experience clearly has major effects on the development and maintenance of neural circuits, but the mechanisms through which experience exerts these effects are not well understood. The problem is not the lack of possible mechanisms, but rather that there are so many. For example, we now know that experience influences genes and gene expression (see Fagiolini, Jensen, & Champagne, 2009; Vo, Cambronne, & Goodman, 2010) and that neurotransmitters influence brain development (see Daubert & Condron, 2010; Platel et al., 2010).

Neuroplasticity

Neuroplasticity Why do you think this discussion of the effects of experience has a neuroplasticity icon associated with it?

Neuroplasticity in Adults

If this text were a road trip we were taking together, at this point, we would spot the following highway sign: SLOW, IMPORTANT VIEWPOINT AHEAD. You see, you are about to encounter an idea that has changed how neuroscientists think about the human brain.

Neuroplasticity was once thought to be restricted to the developmental period. Mature brains were considered to be set in their ways, incapable of substantial reorganization. Now, the accumulation of evidence has made clear that mature brains are continually changing and adapting. Many lines of research are contributing to this changing view. For now, consider the following two. You will encounter many more in the next two chapters.

Neurogenesis in Adult Mammals

LO 9.13   Describe the evolution in our thinking about the birth of new neurons in the adult mammalian brain. Also, explain the possible function(s) of adult-born hippocampal neurons.

When I (SB) was a student, I learned two important principles of brain development. The first I learned through experience: The human brain starts to function in the womb and never stops working until one stands up to speak in public. The second I learned in a course on brain development: **Neurogenesis** (the growth of new neurons) does not occur in adults. The first principle appears to be fundamentally correct, at least when applied to me, but the second has been proven wrong.

Prior to the early 1980s, brain development after the early developmental period was seen as a downhill slope: Neurons continually die throughout a person's life, and it was assumed that the lost cells are never replaced by new ones. Although researchers began to chip away at this misconception in the early 1980s, it persisted until the turn of the century as one of the central principles of neurodevelopment.

The first serious challenge to the assumption that neurogenesis is restricted to early stages of development came with the discovery of the growth of new neurons in the brains of adult birds. Nottebohm and colleagues (e.g., Goldman & Nottebohm, 1983) found that brain structures involved in singing begin to grow in songbirds just before each mating season and that this growth results from an increase in the number of neurons.

Evolutionary Perspective

Evolutionary Perspective As you will learn in this module, even the adult brain displays significant plasticity. What do you think is the evolutionary significance of this adult plasticity?

Then, in the 1990s, researchers, armed with newly developed immunohistochemical markers that have a selective affinity for recently created neurons, showed that adult neurogenesis occurs in the rat hippocampus (Cameron et al., 1993)—see Figure 9.10. And shortly thereafter, it was discovered that new neurons are also continually added to adult rat olfactory bulbs.

Neuroplasticity

At first, reports of adult neurogenesis were not embraced by a generation of neuroscientists who had been trained to think of the adult brain as fixed, but acceptance grew as confirmatory reports accumulated. Particularly influential were reports that new neurons are added to the hippocampuses of primates (e.g., Kornack & Rakic, 1999), including humans (Erikkson et al., 1998), and that

Figure 9.10 Adult neurogenesis. The top panel shows new cells in the dentate gyrus of the hippocampus—the cell bodies of neurons are stained blue, mature glial cells are stained green, and new cells are stained red. The bottom panel shows the new cells from the top panel under higher magnification, which makes it apparent that the new cells have taken up both blue and red stain and are thus new neurons. (Courtesy of Carl Ernst and Brian Christie, Department of Psychology, University of British Columbia.)

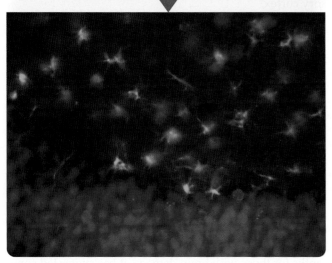

the number of new neurons added to the adult human hippocampus is substantial, an estimated 700 per day per hippocampus (Kempermann, 2013; Kheirbek & Hen, 2013; Spalding et al., 2013).

In most nonhuman adult mammals, substantial neurogenesis seems to be restricted to the olfactory bulb and hippocampus—although low levels have been observed in the hypothalamus (see Sousa-Ferreira, de Almeida, & Cavadas, 2014) and in the cortex (under certain conditions; see Feliciano & Bordey, 2012). In adult humans, neurogenesis has been observed in the striatum (Ernst et al., 2014; Inta, Cameron, & Gass, 2015; Welberg, 2014a) and in the hippocampus, but not in the olfactory bulbs (see Bergmann & Frisén, 2013).

Where do the neurons created during adult neurogenesis come from? New olfactory bulb and striatal neurons are created from *adult neural stem cells* at certain sites in the *subventricular zone of the lateral ventricles* and then migrate to the olfactory bulbs or striatum in nonhuman mammals and humans, respectively. In contrast, new hippocampal cells are created near their final location in the dentate gyrus of the hippocampus.

From a biopsychological perspective, evidence that experience can influence adult neurogenesis is particularly exciting. One line of research on adult neurogenesis began with a study of the effects on adult rodents living in *enriched environments* (variable environments, with toys, running wheels, and other rats). It turned out that adult rats living in enriched environments produced 60 percent more new hippocampal neurons than did adult rats living in nonenriched environments (Kempermann & Gage, 1999). However, before you start enriching your home, you should be aware that the observed positive effect on neurogenesis in the adult rat hippocampus depends largely on the increases in exercise that typically occur in enriched environments (Farmer et al., 2004; Van Praag et al., 1999). This finding has a provocative implication: Since the hippocampus is involved in some kinds of memory, exercise may reduce or delay memory problems (Hertzog et al., 2008).

Clinical Implications

What are the functions of neurons that are the products of adult neurogenesis? It is now established that neurons generated during adulthood survive, become integrated into neural circuits, and begin to conduct neural signals (see Doetsch & Hen, 2005; Kelsch, Sim, & Lois, 2010; Toni et al., 2008). Adult-generated olfactory bulb and striatal neurons become *interneurons* (see Brann & Firestein, 2014; Ernst et al., 2014; Sakamoto, Kageyama, & Imayoshi, 2015); and adult-generated hippocampal

Figure 9.11 Studies of adult neurogenesis suggest that exercise may reduce or delay memory problems.

neurons become *granule cells* in the *dentate gyrus*—see Figure 9.10. Although there has been some progress in understanding the anatomy and physiology of adult-generated neurons, understanding their function has proven more difficult.

Most research on the function of adult-generated neurons has focused on the hippocampus. Based on that research, a number of theories have been proposed over the past two decades. Some researchers have proposed a role for these new hippocampal neurons in memory function (see Kropf, Yang, & Schinder, 2015; Stuchlik, 2014)—including forgetting (see Akers et al., 2014; Mongiat & Schinder, 2014; Welberg, 2014b). One currently popular theory is that adult hippocampal neurogenesis is important for pattern separation: **Pattern separation** refers to our ability to separate distinct percepts into individual memories for storage (see Aimone et al., 2014; Bergmann & Frisén, 2013). Other researchers have proposed that adult hippocampal neurogenesis serves a role in mood and anxiety regulation (see Cameron & Glover, 2015; Christian, Song, & Ming, 2014; Miller & Hen, 2015).

Freund et al. (2013) took a naturalistic approach to studying the role of adult hippocampal neurogenesis: They monitored the exploratory behavior of a large number of genetically identical mice in a complex enriched environment over the course of a 3-month period. They found that variation in individual behavior increased over time. As mentioned previously, physical activity promotes neurogenesis, so, as expected, those animals that were more active had greater amounts of hippocampal neurogenesis. However, Freund and colleagues also found that exploration had an even greater influence on adult hippocampal neurogenesis than physical activity; that is, those animals that explored over larger areas, and consequently were exposed to more cognitive challenges, showed the greatest amounts of newly born hippocampal neurons (see Bergmann & Frisén, 2013; Freund et al., 2013). Accordingly, one role of adult hippocampal neurogenesis might be to allow us to adapt to complex environments.

Effects of Experience on the Reorganization of the Adult Cortex

LO 9.14 Describe four examples of experience affecting the organization of the adult cortex.

We said we would consider two lines of current research on adult neuroplasticity, and you have just learned about one: adult neurogenesis. The second deals with the effects of experience on the reorganization of adult cortex.

Experience in adulthood can lead to reorganization of sensory and motor cortical maps. For example, Mühlnickel and colleagues (1998) found that *tinnitus* (ringing in the ears) produces a major reorganization of primary auditory cortex; Elbert and colleagues (1995) showed that adult musicians who play stringed instruments that are fingered with the left hand (e.g., the violin) have an enlarged hand-representation area in their right somatosensory cortex; and Rossini and colleagues (1994) showed that anesthetizing particular fingers reduced their representation in contralateral somatosensory cortex.

One study of adult neuroplasticity warrants special attention because it demonstrates an important aspect of this plasticity. Hofer and colleagues (2005) showed that elimination of visual input to one eye of adult mice reduced the size of the ocular dominance columns for that eye in layer IV of primary visual cortex. More importantly, they showed that the reductions in size of the ocular dominance columns occurred more quickly and were more enduring if the adult mice had previously experienced visual deprivation in the same eye. Thus, once the brain has adapted to abnormal environmental conditions, it acquires the ability to adapt more effectively if it encounters the same conditions again.

The discovery of adult neuroplasticity is changing the way that we humans think about ourselves. More importantly, for those with brain damage, it has suggested some promising new treatment options. You will learn about these in Chapter 10.

Scan Your Brain

Before you delve into the last module of the chapter on disorders of neurodevelopment, review what you have learned since the first module. Fill in each of the blanks with the most appropriate term. The correct answers are provided at the end of the exercise. Before proceeding, review material related to your errors and omissions.

1. _____ increases the speed of axonal conduction.
2. Lack of, or incomplete, schema of object performance is referred to as a _____.
3. Various parts of the _____ play various roles, working memory being one of them.
4. Experiences that contribute to the information in genetic programs are called _____ experiences.
5. The two important periods of development are the critical and the _____ period.
6. An experimental technique used by neuroscientists to study central nervous system plasticity is called _____.

7. Roe and colleagues performed a study involving surgically altering the _____ of ferrets.

8. Before the nervous system is fully developed, _____ begin to fire and begin to interact with environment.

9. The output in the _____ goes primarily to the amygdala and piriform cortex.

10. Adult-generated olfactory bulbs and striatal neurons become interneurons, and adult-generated hippocampal neurons become _____.

11. _____ refers to the ability to separate distinct percepts into individual memories for storage.

12. Experience in adulthood can lead to reorganization of sensory and _____ maps.

Disorders of Neurodevelopment: Autism Spectrum Disorder and Williams Syndrome

Like all complex processes, neurodevelopment is easily thrown off track, and, unfortunately, one tiny misstep can have far-reaching consequences because it can disrupt subsequent stages. Ironically, much of what we have learned about typical development has come from studying developmental disorders—as you have already seen with the case of Genie. This final module of the chapter focuses on two disorders of neurodevelopment: autism spectrum disorder and Williams syndrome. It is informative to consider these two disorders together because, as you will soon learn, they are similar in some respects and opposite in others.

Autism Spectrum Disorder

LO 9.15 Describe autism spectrum disorder and attempts to identify its neural mechanisms.

Autism spectrum disorder (ASD) is a complex neurodevelopmental disorder. It is a difficult disorder to define because cases differ so greatly. Be that as it may, ASD is almost always apparent before the age of 3 and typically does not increase in severity after that age, and two symptoms are considered to be *core symptoms* because they are required for a diagnosis: (1) a reduced capacity for social interaction and communication and (2) restricted and repetitive patterns of behavior, interests, or activities (American Psychiatric Association, 2013; Volkmar & McPartland, 2014). Also, there are other characteristics that tend to be associated with the disorder—about 75 percent of those with ASD are male (see Tordjman et al., 2014), many suffer from either an intellectual or learning disability, and they are more likely to suffer from epilepsy (see Lee, Smith, & Paciorkowski, 2015). Older mothers are more likely to give birth to a child with ASD, but the probability of a young mother (under 30) giving

birth to a child with ASD increases if the father is over 40 (Shelton, Tancredi, & Hertz-Picciotto, 2010).

Alex suffers from a relatively severe form of ASD.

The Case of Alex: Are You Ready to Rock?

Alex cried so hard when he was a baby that he would sometimes vomit. It was the first sign of his autism. Alex is now 7, and he spends much of each day scampering around the house.

When Alex sees the delivery boy, he yells, "Are you ready to rock?" because the delivery boy once said that in passing to him. Alex is obsessed by spaghetti, chocolate ice cream, and trucks. He can spot trucks in a magazine that are so small that most people would not immediately recognize them, and he has all his toy trucks lined up in the main hallway of his house.

Despite his severe intellectual disability, Alex has little difficulty with computers. He recently went on the Internet and ordered a video.

Alex has echolalia; that is, he repeats almost everything that he hears. He recently told his mother that he loves her, but she doubts very much that he understands what this means—he is just repeating what she has said to him. He loves music and knows the words to many popular songs.

Watch this video on MyPsychLab
PROFILES OF ASD

ASD is common enough that everybody should be alert for its main early warning sign: a delay in the development of social interaction. For example, the following specific signs would be cause for concern: a decline in eye contact between 2 and 6 months (see Jones & Klin, 2014; Yoon & Vouloumanos, 2014), no smiles or happy expressions by 9 months, and no communicative gestures such as pointing or waving by 12 months.

ASD is the most prevalent neurodevelopmental disorder. Until the early 1990s, most epidemiological studies (studies of the incidence and distribution of disease in the general population) reported that ASD in the United States occurred in fewer than 1 in 1,000 births; however, the Centers for Disease Control and Prevention now estimate the incidence to be 1 in 68 births (see Biyani et al., 2015). This large increase in the incidence of ASD is cause for concern—although it may, in part, reflect recent broadening of the diagnostic criteria, increasing public awareness of the disorder, and improved methods of identifying cases (see Kim & Leventhal, 2015).

ASD is a difficult disorder to treat (see Walsh et al., 2011). Intensive behavioral therapy can improve the lives of some individuals (see Lange & McDougle, 2013), but it is often difficult for a person with ASD to live independently.

ASD IS A HETEROGENEOUS DISORDER. ASD is *heterogeneous* in the sense that affected individuals may be severely impaired in some respects but may be typical, or even superior, in others. For example, ASD patients who suffer from an intellectual disability often perform well on tests involving rote memory, jigsaw puzzles, music, and art.

ASD SAVANTS. Perhaps the single most remarkable aspect of ASD is the tendency for some persons with ASD to be savants. **Savants** are persons with developmental disabilities who nevertheless display amazing and specific cognitive or artistic abilities (see Treffert, 2014a). Between 10 and 30 percent of individuals with ASD display some savant abilities (see Dubischar-Krivec et al., 2014); conversely, about 50 percent of savants are diagnosed with ASD. Savant abilities can take many forms: feats of memory, naming the day of the week for any future or past date, identifying prime numbers (any number divisible only by itself and 1), drawing, and playing musical instruments (see Bonnel

et al., 2003). Consider the following savants (Ramachandran & Blakeslee, 1998; Sacks, 1985).

Savant abilities remain a mystery. These abilities do not appear to develop through learning or practice; they seem to emerge spontaneously. Even ASD savants with good language abilities cannot explain their own feats. They seem to recognize patterns and relations that escape others. Several investigators have speculated that somehow atypical development of certain parts of their brains has led to compensatory responses in other parts. Indeed, savant abilities can emerge in otherwise healthy people following brain damage or transcranial magnetic stimulation (see Chapter 5) to the left anterior temporal lobe (see Treffert, 2014b).

GENETIC BASIS OF ASD. Genetic factors influence the development of ASD (see Bourgeron, 2015). Siblings of people with ASD have about a 20 percent chance of being diagnosed with the disorder (see Gliga et al., 2014). This is well above the rate in the general population, but well below the 50 percent chance that would be expected if ASD were caused solely by a single dominant gene. Also, if one monozygotic twin is diagnosed with ASD, the other has a 60 percent chance of receiving the same diagnosis. These findings suggest that ASD is triggered by several genes interacting with the environment (see State & Levitt, 2011). Several dozen genes have already been implicated, and in less than 5 percent of ASD cases there is a single gene mutation that can account for the disorder (see Mullins, Fishell, & Tsien, 2016; Lange & McDougle, 2013; Willsey & State, 2015).

NEURAL MECHANISMS OF ASD. The heterogeneity of the symptoms of ASD—that is, deficits in some behavioral functions but not others—suggests underlying alterations to some neural structures but not others. In addition, marked differences in the symptoms displayed by various ASD patients suggest similar variability from case to case in the underlying neural correlates. Given this complex situation, it is clear that large, systematic studies will be required to identify the neural correlates of the various symptoms of ASD. Unfortunately, such studies have not been conducted (see Philip et al., 2012).

There have been numerous postmortem and structural MRI studies that involve only a few individuals with ASD and focus on particular parts of the brain. These studies suggest differences in the cerebellum (Wang, Kloth, & Badura, 2014), amygdala (see Nomi & Uddin, 2015), and frontal cortex (Bachevalier & Loveland, 2006), but there is little agreement on the nature of the differences (Amaral et al., 2008) or how they develop.

One line of research on the neural mechanisms of ASD has focused on the atypical reaction of individuals with ASD to faces: They spend less time than typical looking at faces, particularly at the eyes, and they remember faces less well (see Weigelt, Koldewyn, & Kanwisher, 2012; but

Cases of Amazing Savant Abilities

- One savant could tell the time of day to the exact second without ever referring to his watch. Even when he was asleep, he would mumble the correct time.

- Tom was blind and could not tie his own shoes. He had never had any musical training, but he could play the most difficult piano piece after hearing it just once, even if he was playing with his back to the piano.

- One pair of ASD twins had difficulty doing simple addition and subtraction and could not even comprehend multiplication and division. Yet, if given any date in the last or next 40,000 years, they could specify the day of week that it fell on.

see Guillon et al., 2014). Subsequently, the *fusiform face area* (see Chapter 6) of ASD individuals was found to display less fMRI activity than typical in response to the presentation of faces (see Nomi & Uddin, 2015).

It should be emphasized that the underlying mechanism of ASD may not be entirely neural. Indeed, there is substantial interest in the role of glial activity in the development of ASD (see Welberg, 2014c; Zeidán-Chuliá et al., 2014).

Williams Syndrome

LO 9.16 Describe Williams syndrome and attempts to identify its neural mechanisms.

Williams syndrome, like ASD, is a neurodevelopmental disorder associated with intellectual disability and with a heterogeneous pattern of abilities and disabilities (see Van Herwegen, 2015). However, in contrast to the socially withdrawn individuals who have ASD, people with Williams syndrome are sociable, empathetic, and talkative. In many respects, ASD and Williams syndrome are opposites, which is why they can be fruitfully studied together.

> **Clinical Implications** Autism spectrum disorder and Williams syndrome are similar, but they are also opposites in several ways. Thus, the study of their neural mechanisms can be complimentary. Discuss.

Williams syndrome occurs in approximately 1 in 7,500 births (see Martens, 2013; Van Herwegen, 2015). Anne Louise McGarrah has Williams syndrome (Finn, 1991).

The Case of Anne Louise McGarrah: Uneven Abilities

Anne Louise McGarrah, 42, can't add 13 and 18. Yet, she is an enthusiastic reader. "I love to read," she says. "Biographies, fiction, novels, just about anything…"

McGarrah has difficulty telling left from right, and if asked to get several items, she often comes back with only one. But she plays the piano and loves classical music: "I love listening to music. I like Beethoven, but I love Mozart and Chopin and Bach. I like the way they develop their music—it's very light, very airy, and very cheerful…"

She's aware of her own condition. "One time I had a very weird experience. I was in the store, shopping, minding my own business. A woman came up to me and was staring. I felt really, really bewildered by it. I wanted to talk to her and ask her if she understood that I have a disability."

It is the language abilities of Williams syndrome patients that have attracted the most attention. Although they display a delay in language development and language deficits in adulthood (see Martens, 2013), their language skills are remarkable considering their characteristically low IQs—which average around 55. For example, in one test, children with Williams syndrome were asked to name as many animals as they could in 60 seconds. Answers included koala, yak, ibex, condor, Chihuahua, brontosaurus, and hippopotamus. When asked to look at a picture and tell a story about it, children with Williams syndrome often produced an animated narrative. As they told the story, the children altered the pitch, volume, rhythm, and vocabulary of their speech to engage the audience. Sadly, the verbal and social skills of these children often lead teachers to overestimate their cognitive abilities, and they do not always receive the extra academic support they need.

The cognitive strengths of persons with Williams syndrome are not limited to language: They are often musically gifted (Lennoff et al., 1997). Although most cannot learn to read music, some have perfect or near-perfect pitch and an uncanny sense of rhythm. Many retain melodies for years, and some are professional musicians. As a group, people with Williams syndrome show more interest in, and emotional reaction to, music (see Järvinen et al., 2015) than does the general population. Another cognitive strength of individuals with Williams syndrome is their near-typical ability to recognize faces—although whether they process faces in a typical manner is still a matter of debate (see D'Souza et al., 2015).

On the other hand, persons with Williams syndrome display several serious cognitive deficits. For example, they have severe attentional problems (see Lense, Key, & Dykens, 2011). Also, their spatial abilities are even worse than those of people with comparable IQs: They have difficulty remembering the locations of a few blocks placed on a test board, their space-related speech is poor, and their ability to draw objects is almost nonexistent (see Nagai, Inui, & Iwata, 2010; Rhodes et al., 2011).

Williams syndrome is also associated with a variety of health problems, including several involving the heart. One heart disorder was found to result from a mutation in a gene on chromosome 7 that controls the synthesis of *elastin*, a protein that imparts elasticity to many organs and tissues, including the heart. Aware that the same cardiac problem is prevalent in people with Williams syndrome, investigators assessed the status of this gene in that group. They found that the gene was absent from one of the two copies of chromosome 7 in 95 percent of individuals with Williams syndrome (see Howald et al., 2006). It was missing through an accident of reproduction that deleted an entire segment of chromosome 7, a segment that included the elastin gene and about 25 others (see Järvinen, Korenberg, & Bellugi, 2013). Once the functions

Figure 9.12 Two areas of reduced cortical volume and one area of increased cortical volume observed in people with Williams syndrome. (See Meyer-Lindenberg et al., 2006; Toga & Thompson, 2005.)

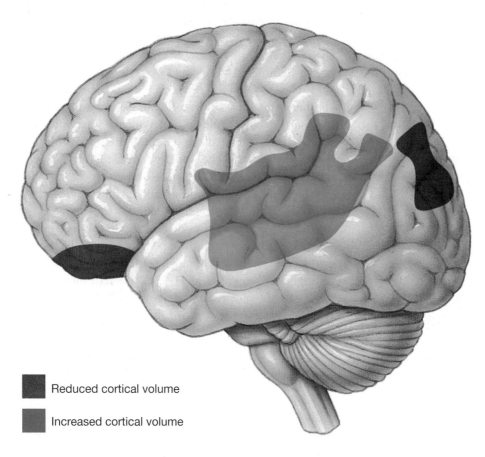

■ Reduced cortical volume

■ Increased cortical volume

of the other genes in this region have been determined, researchers should have a much fuller understanding of the etiology of Williams syndrome.

Several brain differences have been reported in people with Williams syndrome (e.g., a decrease in basal ganglia volume; see Dennis & Thompson, 2013); however, most research on the neural correlates of Williams syndrome has focused on the cortex. Williams syndrome is associated with a general thinning of the cortex and underlying white matter (Meyer-Lindenberg, Mervis, & Berman, 2006; Toga, Thompson, & Sowell, 2006). The cortical thinning is greatest in two areas: at the boundary of the parietal and occipital lobes and in the **orbitofrontal cortex** (the inferior area of frontal cortex near the orbits, or eye sockets)—see Figure 9.12. Reduced

cortical development in these two areas may be related to two of the major symptoms of Williams syndrome: profound impairment of spatial cognition and remarkable hypersociability, respectively. Conversely, the thickness of the cortex in one area in people with Williams syndrome is often typical: the **superior temporal gyrus**, which includes primary and secondary auditory cortex (refer to Figure 9.12). The typical nature of this area may be related to the relatively high levels of language and music processing in those with Williams syndrome.

Many cultures feature tales involving magical little people (pixies, elves, leprechauns, etc.). Descriptions of these creatures portray them as virtually identical to persons with Williams syndrome: short with small upturned noses, oval ears, broad mouths, full lips, puffy eyes, and small chins. Even the typical behavioral characteristics of elves—engaging storytellers, talented musicians, loving, trusting, and sensitive to the feelings of others—match those of individuals with Williams syndrome. These similarities suggest that folktales about elves may have originally been based on persons with Williams syndrome.

EPILOGUE. As a student, I (SB) was amazed to learn that—starting as one cell—my brain had constructed itself through the interaction of its genetic programs and experience. Later, I was astounded to learn that my adult brain is still plastic. We hope that this chapter has helped your brain appreciate its own development. Also, we hope that the case of Genie, which began the chapter, and the cases about people with ASD and Williams syndrome, which completed it, have helped you appreciate the consequences when complex programs of neurodevelopment go wrong.

Themes Revisited

This chapter was all about neurodevelopment, with a particular emphasis on how the brain continues to develop throughout an individual's life span. We hope you now fully appreciate that your own brain is constantly changing in response to interactions between your genetic programs and experience.

The clinical implications and evolutionary perspective themes were also emphasized in this chapter. One of the best ways to understand the principles of typical neurodevelopment is to consider what happens when it goes wrong: Accordingly, the chapter began with the tragic case of Genie and ended with a discussion of ASD and Williams syndrome. The evolutionary perspective theme was emphasized because much of the information that we have about typical human neurodevelopment has come from studying other species.

The thinking creatively tab appeared infrequently in this chapter, but the theme was pervasive. Thinking creatively tabs highlighted discussions that made two general points. First, neurodevelopment always proceeds from gene–experience interactions rather than from either genetics or environment alone. Second, it is important to realize that "normal" experience plays an important role in fine-tuning the development of neural function.

Key Terms

Five Phases of Neurodevelopment

Totipotent, p. 247
Pluripotent, p. 247
Multipotent, p. 247
Unipotent, p. 247
Neural plate, p. 247
Mesoderm layer, p. 247
Stem cells, p. 247
Neural tube, p. 248
Neural proliferation, p. 248
Ventricular zone, p. 248
Migration, p. 248
Radial migration, p. 248
Tangential migration, p. 248
Somal translocation, p. 249
Glia-mediated migration, p. 249
Radial glial cells, p. 249
Inside-out pattern, p. 249
Neural crest, p. 250
Aggregation, p. 250

Cell-adhesion molecules (CAMs), p. 250
Growth cone, p. 250
Retinal ganglion cells, p. 250
Optic tectum, p. 251
Chemoaffinity hypothesis, p. 251
Pioneer growth cones, p. 252
Fasciculation, p. 252
Topographic gradient hypothesis, p. 252
Synaptogenesis, p. 253
Necrosis, p. 253
Apoptosis, p. 253
Neurotrophins, p. 254
Nerve growth factor (NGF), p. 254

Postnatal Cerebral Development in Human Infants

Perseveration, p. 256

Effects of Experience on Postnatal Development of Neural Circuits

Permissive experiences, p. 256
Instructive experiences, p. 256
Critical period, p. 256
Sensitive period, p. 256

Neuroplasticity in Adults

Neurogenesis, p. 258
Pattern separation, p. 260

Disorders of Neurodevelopment: Autism Spectrum Disorder and Williams Syndrome

Autism spectrum disorder (ASD), p. 261
Savants, p. 262
Williams syndrome, p. 263
Orbitofrontal cortex, p. 264
Superior temporal gyrus, p. 264

Chapter 10
Brain Damage and Neuroplasticity

Can the Brain Recover from Damage?

Chapter Overview and Learning Objectives (LOs)

Causes of Brain Damage

LO 10.1 Describe different types of brain tumors, and explain the difference between an encapsulated and an infiltrating brain tumor.

LO 10.2 Describe differences between the two types of stroke: cerebral hemorrhage and cerebral ischemia.

LO 10.3 Explain the difference between a contusion and a concussion, and define a contrecoup injury.

LO 10.4 Describe two different types of infections of the brain.

LO 10.5 Describe three different types of neurotoxins.

LO 10.6 Discuss the symptoms of Down syndrome and what causes this disorder.

LO 10.7 Explain the difference between apoptosis and necrosis.

Neurological Diseases	**LO 10.8** Define epilepsy. Also, describe four categories of epileptic disorders and some treatments for epilepsy.
	LO 10.9 Describe the symptoms of Parkinson's disease and some treatments for this disorder.
	LO 10.10 Describe the symptoms of Huntington's disease, and explain its genetic basis.
	LO 10.11 Describe the symptoms of multiple sclerosis and its risk factors.
	LO 10.12 Describe the symptoms of Alzheimer's disease, and evaluate the amyloid hypothesis.
Animal Models of Human Neurological Diseases	**LO 10.13** Describe the kindling model of epilepsy, and explain the ways in which it models human epilepsy.
	LO 10.14 Describe the transgenic mouse models of Alzheimer's disease, and evaluate their efficacy.
	LO 10.15 Describe the events that led to the discovery of the MPTP model of Parkinson's disease, and evaluate the utility of this animal model.
Responses to Nervous System Damage: Degeneration, Regeneration, Reorganization, and Recovery	**LO 10.16** Explain the various types of neural degeneration that ensue following axotomy.
	LO 10.17 Compare neural regeneration within the CNS vs. the PNS.
	LO 10.18 Describe three examples of cortical reorganization following damage to the brain, and discuss the mechanisms that might underlie such reorganization.
	LO 10.19 Describe the concept of "cognitive reserve," and discuss the potential role of adult neurogenesis in recovery following CNS damage.
Neuroplasticity and the Treatment of CNS Damage	**LO 10.20** Discuss early work on neurotransplantation for the treatment of CNS damage.
	LO 10.21 Discuss the methods and findings of modern research on neurotransplantation.
	LO 10.22 Discuss methods of promoting recovery from CNS damage through rehabilitative treatment.

The study of human brain damage serves two purposes: It increases our understanding of the healthy brain, and it serves as a basis for the development of new treatments. The first three modules of this chapter focus on brain damage itself. The last two modules continue the neuroplasticity theme that was the focus of Chapter 9: The fourth module focuses on the recovery and reorganization of the brain after damage, and the fifth discusses exciting new treatments that promote neuroplasticity. But first, the continuation of the ironic case of Professor P.,

which you first encountered in Chapter 5, provides a personal view of brain damage.

The Ironic Case of Professor P.

One night Professor P. sat at his desk staring at a drawing of the cranial nerves, much like the one in Appendix III of this book. As he mulled over the location and function of each cranial nerve (see Appendix IV), the painful truth became impossible for him to deny. The irony of the situation was that Professor P. was a neuroscientist, all too familiar with what he was experiencing.

His symptoms started subtly, with slight deficits in balance. Professor P. chalked up his occasional lurches to aging—after all, he thought to himself, he was past his prime. Similarly, his doctor didn't seem to think that it was a problem, but Professor P. monitored his symptoms nevertheless. Three years later, his balance problems unabated, Professor P. started to worry. He was trying to talk on the phone but was having trouble hearing until he changed the phone to his left ear. Professor P. was going deaf in his right ear.

Professor P. made an appointment with his doctor, who referred him to a specialist. After a cursory and poorly controlled hearing test, the specialist gave him good news. "You're fine, Professor P.; lots of people experience a little hearing loss when they reach middle age; don't worry about it." To this day, Professor P. regrets that he did not insist on a second opinion.

It was about a year later that Professor P. sat staring at the illustration of the cranial nerves. By then, he had begun to experience numbness on the right side of his mouth, he was having problems swallowing, and his right tear ducts were not releasing enough tears. He stared at the point where the auditory and vestibular nerves come together to form cranial nerve VIII (the auditory-vestibular nerve). He knew it was there, and he knew that it was large enough to be affecting cranial nerves V through X as well. It was something slow-growing, perhaps a tumor? Was he going to die? Was his death going to be terrible and lingering?

He didn't see his doctor right away. A friend of his was conducting a brain MRI study, and Professor P. volunteered to be a control subject, knowing that his problem would show up on the scan. It did: a large tumor sitting, as predicted, on the right cranial nerve VIII.

Then, MRI in hand, Professor P. went back to his doctor, who referred him to a neurologist, who in turn referred him to a neurosurgeon. Several stressful weeks later, Professor P. found himself on life support in the intensive care unit of his local hospital, tubes emanating seemingly from every part of his body. During the 6-hour surgery, Professor P. had stopped breathing.

In the intensive care unit, near death and hallucinating from the morphine, Professor P. thought he heard his wife, Maggie, calling for help, and he tried to go to her assistance. But one gentle morphine-steeped professor was no match for five nurses intent on saving his life. They quickly turned up his medication, and the next time he regained consciousness, he was tied to the bed.

Professor P.'s auditory-vestibular nerve was transected during his surgery, which has left him permanently deaf and without vestibular function on the right side. He was also left with partial hemifacial paralysis, including serious blinking and tearing problems.

Professor P. is still alive and much improved. Indeed, at the very moment that these words are being written, Professor P. is working on the forthcoming edition of our text . . . If it has not yet occurred to you, I (JP) am Professor P. This chapter has come to have special meaning for me.

Causes of Brain Damage

This module provides an introduction to six causes of brain damage: brain tumors, cerebrovascular disorders, closed-head injuries, infections of the brain, neurotoxins, and genetic factors. It concludes with a discussion of programmed cell death, which mediates many forms of brain damage.

Brain Tumors

LO 10.1 Describe different types of brain tumors, and explain the difference between an encapsulated and an infiltrating brain tumor.

A **tumor**, or **neoplasm** (literally, "new growth"), is a mass of cells that grows independently of the rest of the body. About 20 percent of tumors found in the human brain are **meningiomas** (see Figure 10.1)—tumors that grow between the *meninges*, the three membranes that cover the central nervous system. All meningiomas are **encapsulated tumors**—tumors that grow within their own membrane. As a result, they are particularly easy to identify on a CT scan, they can influence the function of the brain only by the pressure they exert on surrounding tissue, and they are almost always **benign tumors**—tumors that are surgically removable with little risk of further growth in the body.

 Were you surprised that one of the authors of your textbook suffered significant brain damage? Why or why not?

Figure 10.1 A meningioma.

Unfortunately, encapsulation is the exception rather than the rule when it comes to brain tumors. Aside from meningiomas, most brain tumors are infiltrating. **Infiltrating tumors** are those that grow diffusely through surrounding tissue. As a result, they are usually **malignant tumors**; that is, it is difficult to remove or destroy them completely, and any cancerous tissue that remains after surgery continues to grow. **Gliomas** (brain tumors that develop from glial cells) are infiltrating, rapidly growing, and unfortunately common (see Vigneswaran, Neill, & Hadjipanayis, 2015; Wang et al., 2015; Wen & Reardon, 2016).

About 10 percent of brain tumors do not originate in the brain. They grow from infiltrating cells that are carried to the brain by the bloodstream from some other part of the body. These tumors are called **metastatic tumors** (*metastasis* refers to the transmission of disease from one organ to another)—see Cheung and Ewald (2016); Di Giacoma and Margolin (2015); Kaiser (2016). Many metastatic brain tumors originate as cancers of the lungs. Figure 10.2 illustrates the ravages of metastasis. Currently, the chance of recovering from a cancer that has already attacked two or more separate sites is slim.

Fortunately, my (JP) tumor was encapsulated. Encapsulated tumors that grow on cranial nerve VIII are

Figure 10.3 An MRI of Professor P.'s acoustic neuroma. The arrow indicates the tumor.

Figure 10.2 Multiple metastatic brain tumors. The colored areas indicate the location of the larger metastatic brain tumors in this patient.

referred to as *acoustic neuromas* (neuromas are tumors that grow on nerves or tracts). Figure 10.3 is an MRI scan of my acoustic neuroma, the same scan that I took to my doctor.

Cerebrovascular Disorders: Strokes

LO 10.2 Describe differences between the two types of stroke: cerebral hemorrhage and cerebral ischemia.

Strokes are sudden-onset cerebrovascular disorders that cause brain damage. In the United States, stroke is the fifth leading cause of death, the major cause of neurological dysfunction, and a leading cause of adult disability (see Prabhakaran, Ruff, & Bernstein, 2015). The symptoms of a stroke depend on the area of the brain affected, but common consequences of stroke are amnesia, aphasia (language difficulties), paralysis, and coma.

The area of dead or dying tissue produced by a stroke is called an *infarct*. Surrounding the infarct is a dysfunctional area called the **penumbra**. The tissue in the penumbra may recover or die in the ensuing days, depending on a variety of factors. The primary goal of treatment following stroke is to save the penumbra (see Prabhakaran, Ruff, & Bernstein, 2015).

There are two major types of strokes: those resulting from cerebral hemorrhage and those resulting from cerebral ischemia (pronounced "iss-KEEM-ee-a").

CEREBRAL HEMORRHAGE. Cerebral hemorrhage (bleeding in the brain) occurs when a cerebral blood vessel ruptures and blood seeps into the surrounding neural tissue and damages it. Bursting aneurysms are a common cause of intracerebral hemorrhage. An **aneurysm** is a pathological balloonlike dilation that forms in the wall of an artery at a point where the elasticity of the artery wall is defective (see Etminan & Rinkel, 2015). Although aneurysms of the brain are particularly problematic, aneurysms can occur in any part of the body. Aneurysms can be **congenital** (present at birth) or can result from exposure to vascular poisons or infection (see Caranci et al., 2013). Individuals at risk for aneurysms should make every effort to avoid cigarette smoking, alcohol consumption, and hypertension (see Brown & Broderick, 2014).

CEREBRAL ISCHEMIA. Cerebral ischemia is a disruption of the blood supply to an area of the brain. The three main causes of cerebral ischemia are thrombosis, embolism, and arteriosclerosis. In **thrombosis**, a plug called a *thrombus* is formed and blocks blood flow at the site of its formation. A thrombus may be composed of a blood clot, fat, oil, an air bubble, tumor cells, or any combination thereof. **Embolism** is similar, except that the plug, called an *embolus* in this case, is carried by the blood from a larger vessel, where it was formed, to a smaller one, where it becomes lodged; in essence, an embolus is just a thrombus that has taken a trip. In **arteriosclerosis**, the walls of blood vessels thicken and the channels narrow, usually as the result of fat deposits; this narrowing can eventually lead to complete blockage of the blood vessels. The *angiogram* in Figure 10.4 illustrates partial blockage of one carotid artery.

Ischemia-induced brain damage has two important properties. First, it takes a while to develop. Soon after a temporary cerebral ischemic episode, there usually is little or no evidence of brain damage; however, substantial neuron loss can often be detected a day or two later. Second, ischemia-induced brain damage does not occur equally in all parts of the brain—particularly susceptible are neurons in certain areas of the hippocampus (see Schmidt-Kastner, 2015).

Paradoxically, **glutamate**, the brain's most prevalent excitatory neurotransmitter, plays a major role in ischemia-induced brain damage (see Chisholm & Sohrabji, 2015; Parsons & Raymond, 2014). Here is how this mechanism is thought to work (see Lai, Zhang, & Wang, 2014; Leng et al., 2014). After a blood vessel becomes blocked, many of the blood-deprived neurons become overactive and release excessive quantities of glutamate. The glutamate in turn overactivates glutamate receptors in the membranes

Figure 10.4 An angiogram that illustrates narrowing of the carotid artery (see arrow), the main pathway of blood to the brain.

of postsynaptic neurons; the glutamate receptors most involved in this reaction are the **NMDA (N-methyl-D-aspartate) receptors**. As a result, large numbers of Na+ and Ca2+ ions enter the postsynaptic neurons. The excessive internal concentrations of Na+ and Ca2+ ions in postsynaptic neurons affect them in two ways: They trigger the release of excessive amounts of glutamate from the neurons, thus spreading the toxic cascade to yet other neurons; and they trigger a sequence of internal reactions that ultimately kill the postsynaptic neurons. See Figure 10.5.

An implication of the discovery that excessive glutamate release causes much of the brain damage associated with stroke is the possibility of preventing stroke-related brain damage by blocking the glutaminergic cascade. Some clinical trials have shown that NMDA-receptor antagonists are clinically effective following acute ischemic stroke, but to be effective they need to be administered almost immediately after the stroke. This makes them impractical in most human clinical situations (see Leng et al., 2014). Accordingly, the search is still on for a drug treatment that is both effective and practical (see Tymianski, 2014). That said, there is mounting evidence that the administration of *tissue plasminogen activator* (a drug that breaks down blood clots) soon after the onset of ischemic stroke (i.e., within 3 to 4 hours) can lead to better recovery (see Law & Levine, 2016; Romano & Sacco, 2015).

Figure 10.5 The cascade of events by which the ischemia-induced release of glutamate kills neurons.

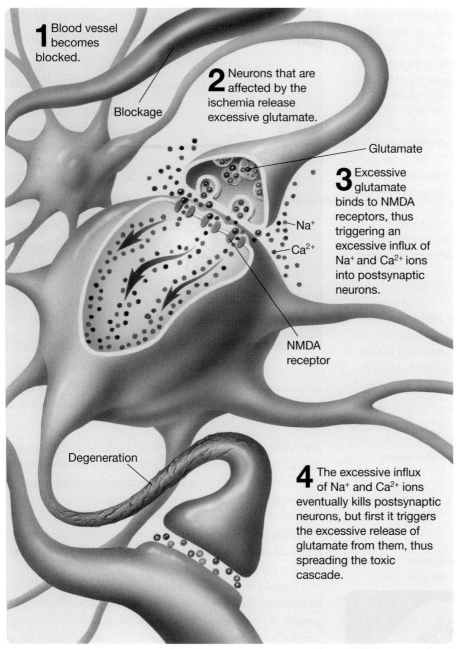

1 Blood vessel becomes blocked.

Blockage

2 Neurons that are affected by the ischemia release excessive glutamate.

Glutamate

3 Excessive glutamate binds to NMDA receptors, thus triggering an excessive influx of Na⁺ and Ca²⁺ ions into postsynaptic neurons.

Na⁺

Ca²⁺

NMDA receptor

Degeneration

4 The excessive influx of Na⁺ and Ca²⁺ ions eventually kills postsynaptic neurons, but first it triggers the excessive release of glutamate from them, thus spreading the toxic cascade.

Closed-Head Injuries

LO 10.3 Explain the difference between a contusion and a concussion, and define a contrecoup injury.

For the brain to be seriously damaged, it is not necessary for the skull to be penetrated. In fact, any blow to the head 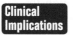 should be treated with extreme caution, particularly when confusion, sensorimotor disturbances, or loss of consciousness ensues. Brain injuries produced by blows that do not penetrate the skull are called *closed-head injuries*.

Contusions are closed-head injuries that involve damage to the cerebral circulatory system. Such damage produces internal hemorrhaging, which results in a hematoma. A **hematoma** is a localized collection of clotted blood in an organ or tissue—in other words, a bruise.

It is paradoxical that the very hardness of the skull, which protects the brain from penetrating injuries, is the major factor in the development of contusions. Contusions from closed-head injuries occur when the brain slams against the inside of the skull. As Figure 10.6 illustrates, blood from such injuries can accumulate in the *subdural space*—the space between the dura mater and arachnoid membrane—and severely distort the surrounding neural tissue.

It may surprise you to learn that contusions frequently occur on the side of the brain opposite the side struck by a blow. The reason for such so-called **contrecoup injuries** is that the blow causes the brain to strike the inside of the skull on the other side of the head.

When there is a disturbance of consciousness following a blow to the head and there is no evidence of a contusion or other structural damage, the diagnosis is **concussion**. It was once assumed that a concussion entails a temporary disruption of normal cerebral function with no long-term damage. However, there is now substantial evidence that the effects of concussion can last many years and that the effects of repeated concussions can accumulate (see Carman et al., 2015). **Chronic traumatic encephalopathy (CTE)** is the **dementia** (general intellectual deterioration) and cerebral scarring observed in boxers, rugby players, American football players (see Figure 10.7), and other individuals who have experienced repeated concussive, or even subconcussive, blows to the head (see Azad et al., 2016; Maroon et al., 2015; Underwood, 2015a). For example, one study found that 34 of 35 former American football players met the diagnostic criteria for chronic traumatic encephalopathy (see Riley et al., 2015). The case of Junior Seau is particularly tragic (Azad et al., 2015).

The Case of Junior Seau

Junior Seau was an all-star linebacker in the National Football League (NFL) for 20 years. He was known for his hard-hitting aggressive play. Although Seau never complained about head injuries to his coaches or medical staff, his family members reported that he had suffered many concussions. When he came home from games, he often experienced severe head-aches and would go straight to his darkened bedroom. But, according to his ex-wife, "he always bounced back and kept on playing." He was a warrior.

After Seau's retirement from the NFL in 2010, his fam-ily and friends noticed several disturbing behavioral changes: heavy consumption of alcohol, reckless business and financial decisions, and gambling. Most disturbing were his frequent violent outbursts that were completely out of character for him and were often directed at friends and family—the very people who were trying to help him. He was even arrested for a violent incident involving his girlfriend.

On May 2, 2012, at the age of 43, Junior Seau shot him-self. He left no note—no explanation.

Seau's family donated his brain to the American National Institutes for Health (NIH) for study. A detailed autopsy of Seau's brain revealed a proliferation of neurofibrillary tangles, a defining characteristic of chronic traumatic encephalopathy.

Infections of the Brain

LO 10.4 Describe two different types of infections of the brain.

Clinical Implications An invasion of the brain by microorganisms is a *brain infection*, and the resulting inflammation

Figure 10.6 A CT scan of a subdural hematoma. Notice that the hematoma has displaced the left lateral ventricle.

Hematoma

Left lateral ventricle

Figure 10.7 The NFL has recently acknowledged that there is a connection between playing football and CTE.

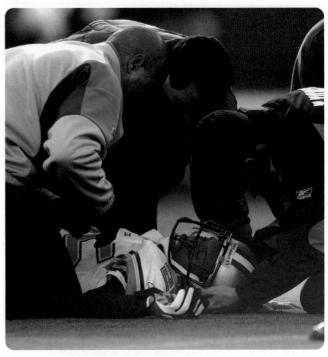

is called **encephalitis** (see Bentivoglio, Mariotti, & Bertini, 2011; Kristensson, 2011). There are two common types of brain infections: bacterial infections and viral infections.

BACTERIAL INFECTIONS.   When bacteria infect the brain, they often lead to the formation of *cerebral abscesses*—pockets of pus in the brain. Bacteria are also the major cause of **meningitis** (inflammation of the meninges), which is fatal in 30 percent of adults (see Castelblanco, Lee, & Hasbun, 2014). Penicillin and other antibiotics sometimes eliminate bacterial infections of the brain, but they cannot reverse brain damage that has already been produced.

Syphilis is one bacterial brain infection you have likely heard about (see Berger & Dean, 2014). Syphilis bacteria are passed from infected to noninfected individuals through contact with genital sores. The infecting bacteria then go into a dormant stage for several years before they become virulent and attack many parts of the body, including the brain. The syndrome of mental illness and dementia that results from a syphilitic infection is called **general paresis**.

VIRAL INFECTIONS.   There are two types of viral infec-tions of the nervous system: those that have a particular affinity for neural tissue and those that attack neural tissue but have no greater affinity for it than for other tissues.

Rabies, which is usually transmitted through the bite of a rabid animal, is a well-known example of a virus that has a particular affinity for the nervous system. The fits of rage caused by the virus's effects on the brain increase the probability that rabid animals that normally attack by bit-ing (e.g., dogs, cats, raccoons, bats, and mice) will spread the disorder. Although the effects of the rabies virus on the brain are almost always lethal (see Schnell et al., 2010), the virus does have one redeeming feature: It does not usually attack the brain for at least a month after it has been contracted, thus allowing time for preventive vaccination.

The *mumps* and *herpes* viruses are common examples of viruses that can attack the nervous system but have no special affinity for it. Although these viruses sometimes spread into the brain, they typically attack other tissues of the body.

Viruses may play a far greater role in neuropsychological disorders than is currently thought (see van den Pol, 2009). Their involvement in the *etiology* (cause) of disorders is often difficult to recognize because they can lie dormant for many years before producing symptoms.

Neurotoxins

LO 10.5 Describe three different types of neurotoxins.

The nervous system can be damaged by exposure to any one of a variety of toxic chemicals, which can enter general circulation from the gastrointestinal tract, from the lungs, or through the skin (see Block & Calderón-Garcidueñas, 2009). For example, heavy metals such as mercury and lead (see Chen, 2013a; Hare et al., 2015; Tshala-Katumbay et al., 2015) can accumulate in the brain and permanently damage it, producing a **toxic psychosis** (chronic mental illness produced by a neurotoxin). Have you ever wondered why *Alice in Wonderland*'s Mad Hatter was a "mad hatter" and not a "mad" something else? In 18th- and 19th-century England, hat makers commonly developed toxic psychosis from the mercury employed in the preparation of the felt used to make hats. In a similar vein, the word *crackpot* originally referred to the toxic psychosis observed in some people in England—primarily the poor—who steeped their tea in cracked ceramic pots with lead cores.

Sometimes, the very drugs used to treat neurological or psychiatric disorders prove to be toxic. For example, some of the antipsychotic drugs introduced in the early 1950s produced effects of distressing scope. By the late 1950s, millions of patients with schizophrenia were being maintained on these drugs. However, after several years of treatment, many of the patients developed a motor disorder termed **tardive dyskinesia (TD)**—see Cloud, Zutshi, and Factor (2014). Its primary symptoms are involuntary smacking and sucking movements of the lips, thrusting and rolling of the tongue, lateral jaw movements, and puffing of the cheeks.

Some neurotoxins are *endogenous* (produced by the patient's own body). For example, the body can produce antibodies that attack particular components of the nervous system (see Melzer, Meuth, & Wiendl, 2012). Also, you have just learned from the discussion of glutamate and ischemic stroke that excessive release of neurotransmitters can damage the brain.

Genetic Factors

LO 10.6 Discuss the symptoms of Down syndrome and what causes this disorder.

Some neuropsychological diseases of genetic origin are caused by abnormal recessive genes that are passed from parent to offspring. (In Chapter 2, you learned about one such disorder, *phenylketonuria*, or *PKU*.) Inherited neuropsychological disorders are rarely associated with dominant genes because dominant genes that disturb neuropsychological function tend to be eliminated from the gene pool—individuals who carry one usually have major survival and reproductive disadvantages. In contrast, individuals who inherit one abnormal recessive gene do not develop the disorder, and the gene is passed on to future generations.

Genetic accident is another major cause of neuropsychological disorders of genetic origin. **Down syndrome**, which occurs in about 0.15 percent of births, is such a disorder. The genetic accident associated with Down syndrome occurs in the mother during ovulation, when an extra chromosome 21 is created in the egg. Thus, when the egg is fertilized, there are three chromosome 21s, rather than two, in the zygote (see Dekker et al., 2015). The consequences tend to be characteristic disfigurement, intellectual impairment, and troublesome medical complications. The probability of giving birth to a child with Down syndrome increases markedly with advancing maternal age: For example, the probability goes from 1 in 1,667 at maternal age 20 to 1 in 11 at maternal age 49 (Egan, 2004).

Watch this video on MyPsychLab
DOWN SYNDROME

There was great optimism among professionals who study and treat neuropsychological disorders when the human genome was documented at the beginning of this century. Inherited factors play major roles in virtually all neuropsychological disorders, and it seemed that the offending genes would soon be identified and effective treatments developed to target them. This has not happened, for two reasons (see Hall, 2012; Maurano et al., 2012). First, numerous loci on human chromosomes have been associated with each disorder—not just one or two. Second, about 90 percent of the chromosomal loci involved in neuropsychological disorders were not conventional protein-coding genes—the loci were in poorly understood sections of the DNA.

Programmed Cell Death

LO 10.7 Explain the difference between apoptosis and necrosis.

You learned in Chapter 9 that neurons and other cells have genetic programs for destroying themselves by a process called **apoptosis** (pronounced "A-poe-toe-sis"). Apoptosis **Clinical Implications** plays a critical role in early development by eliminating extra neurons. It also plays a role in brain damage. Indeed, all of the six causes of brain damage that have been discussed in this chapter (tumors, cerebrovascular disorders, closed-head injuries, infections, toxins, and genetic factors) produce neural damage, in part, by activating apoptotic programs of self-destruction (see Viscomi & **Neuroplasticity** Molinari, 2014).

It was once assumed that the death of neurons following brain damage was totally necrotic—*necrosis* is passive cell death resulting from injury. It now seems that if cells are not damaged too severely, they will attempt to marshal enough resources to "complete suicide." However, cell death is not an either-or situation: Some dying cells display signs of both necrosis and apoptosis (see Zhou & Yuan, 2014).

It is easy to understand why apoptotic mechanisms have evolved: Apoptosis is clearly more adaptive than **Evolutionary Perspective** necrosis. In necrosis, the damaged neuron swells and breaks apart, beginning in the axons and dendrites and ending in the cell body. This fragmentation leads to inflammation, which can damage other cells in the vicinity. Necrotic cell death is quick—it is typically complete in a few hours. In contrast, apoptotic cell death is slow, typically requiring a day or two. Apoptosis of a neuron proceeds gradually, starting with shrinkage of the cell body. Then, as parts of the neuron die, the resulting debris is packaged in vesicles. As a result, there is no inflammation, and damage to nearby cells is kept to a minimum.

Neurological Diseases

The preceding module focused on the causes of human brain damage. This module considers five diseases associated with brain damage: epilepsy, Parkinson's disease, Huntington's disease, multiple sclerosis, and Alzheimer's disease.

Epilepsy

LO 10.8 Define epilepsy. Also, describe four categories of epileptic disorders and some treatments for epilepsy.

The primary symptom of **epilepsy** is the epileptic *seizure*, but not all persons who suffer seizures are considered to have epilepsy. Sometimes, an otherwise healthy person may have one seizure and never have another (see Haut & Shinnar, 2008)—such a 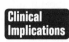 one-time seizure could be triggered by exposure to a convulsive toxin or by a high fever. The diagnosis of *epilepsy* is applied to only those patients whose seizures are repeatedly generated by their own chronic brain dysfunction. About 3.8 percent of the population are diagnosed as epileptic at some point in their lives (see Jensen, 2014).

Because epilepsy is characterized by epileptic seizures—or, more accurately, by spontaneously recurring epileptic seizures—you might think that the task of diagnosing epilepsy would be an easy one. But you would be wrong. The task is made difficult by the diversity and complexity of epileptic seizures. You are probably familiar with seizures that take the form of **convulsions** (motor seizures); these often involve tremors (*clonus*), rigidity (*tonus*), and loss of both balance and consciousness. But most seizures do not take this form; instead, they involve subtle changes of thought, mood, or behavior that are not easily distinguishable from normal ongoing activity.

There are many causes of epilepsy. Indeed, all of the causes of brain damage that have been described in this chapter—including viruses, neurotoxins, tumors, and blows to the head—can cause epilepsy, and more than 100 different faulty genes have been linked to it (see Jensen, 2014; Noebels, 2015; Thomas & Berkovic, 2014). Many cases of epilepsy appear to be associated with faults at inhibitory synapses (e.g., GABAergic synapses) that cause many neurons in a particular area to fire in synchronous bursts (see Hirose, 2014; Kaila et al., 2014), a pattern of firing that is rare in the normal brain (Ecker et al., 2010). In other cases of epilepsy, inflammatory processes seem to be responsible for seizure activity (see Marchi, Granata, & Janigro, 2014).

The diagnosis of epilepsy rests heavily on evidence from electroencephalography (EEG). The value of scalp electroencephalography in confirming suspected cases of epilepsy stems from the fact that epileptic seizures are associated with bursts of high-amplitude EEG spikes, which are often apparent in the scalp EEG during a seizure (see Figure 10.8), and from the fact that individual spikes often punctuate the scalp EEGs of epileptics between seizures (see Bragatti et al., 2014).

Some epileptics experience peculiar psychological changes just before a seizure. These changes, called **epileptic auras**, may take many different forms—for example, a bad smell, a specific thought, a vague feeling of familiarity, a hallucination, or a tightness of the chest.

Figure 10.8 Cortical EEG recorded during epileptic seizures. Notice that each trace is characterized by epileptic spikes (sudden, high amplitude EEG signals that accompany epileptic seizures).

EEG during an absence seizure

EEG at the onset of a tonic-clonic seizure

EEG during the clonic phase of a tonic-clonic seizure

primarily sensory or motor or both; they are sometimes called *Jacksonian seizures* after the famous 19th-century neurologist Hughlings Jackson. As the epileptic discharges spread through the sensory or motor areas of the brain, the symptoms spread systematically through the body.

In contrast, **complex partial seizures** are often restricted to the temporal lobes, and those who experience them are often said to have *temporal lobe epilepsy*. During a complex partial seizure, the patient engages in compulsive, repetitive, simple behaviors commonly referred to as *automatisms* (e.g., doing and undoing a button) and in more complex behaviors that appear almost normal. The diversity of complex partial seizures is illustrated by the following two cases (Lennox, 1960).

Epileptic auras are important for two reasons. First, the nature of the auras provides clues concerning the location of the epileptic focus. Second, epileptic auras can warn the patient of an impending convulsion (see Lohse et al., 2015).

Once an individual has been diagnosed with epilepsy, it is common to assign the type of seizures they experience to one of two general categories—*focal seizures* or *generalized seizures*—and then to one of their respective subcategories (see Berg & Millichap, 2013). The various seizure types are so different from one another that epilepsy is best viewed not as a single disease but as a number of different, but related, diseases.

FOCAL SEIZURES. A **focal seizure** is a seizure that does not involve the entire brain. The epileptic neurons at a focus begin to discharge together in bursts, and it is this synchronous bursting of neurons (see Figure 10.9) that produces epileptic spiking in the EEG. The synchronous activity tends to spread to other areas of the brain—but, in the case of focal seizures, not to the entire brain. The specific behavioral symptoms of a focal epileptic seizure depend on where the disruptive discharges begin and into what structures they spread. Because focal seizures do not involve the entire brain, they are not usually accompanied by a total loss of consciousness or equilibrium.

There are two major categories of focal seizures: simple partial seizures and complex partial seizures. **Simple partial seizures** are focal seizures whose symptoms are

The Subtlety of Complex Partial Seizures: Two Cases

A doctor received a call from his hospital informing him that he was needed to perform an emergency operation. A few hours after the surgery, he returned home feeling dazed and confused. He had performed the operation, a very difficult one, with his usual competence, but afterward he had said and done things that seemed peculiar to his colleagues. The next day he had no memory of the surgery or the related events.

A young music teacher while attending a concert suddenly jumped up from his seat, walked down the aisle onto the stage, circled the piano twice, jumped to the floor, and hopped up the aisle out of the exit. He did not regain his senses until he was on his way home. This was not the first time that he had had such a seizure: He often found himself on a bus with no idea where he was going or how he got there.

Although patients appear to be conscious throughout their complex partial seizures, they usually have little or no subsequent recollection of them (see Farzampour & Huguenard, 2015). About half of all cases of epilepsy in adults are of the complex partial variety—the temporal lobes are particularly susceptible to epileptic discharges (see Bertram, 2014).

GENERALIZED SEIZURES. **Generalized seizures** involve the entire brain. Some begin as focal discharges that gradually spread through the entire brain. In other cases, the discharges seem to begin almost simultaneously in all parts of the brain. Such sudden-onset generalized seizures may result from diffuse pathology or may begin focally in a structure, such as the thalamus, that projects to many parts of the brain.

Figure 10.9 The bursting of an epileptic neuron, recorded by extracellular unit recording.

Like focal seizures, generalized seizures occur in many forms. One is the **tonic-clonic seizure**. The primary symptoms of a tonic-clonic seizure are loss of consciousness, loss of equilibrium, and a violent *tonic-clonic convulsion*—a convulsion involving both tonus and clonus. Tongue biting, urinary incontinence, and *cyanosis* (turning blue from excessive extraction of oxygen from the blood during the convulsion) are common manifestations of tonic-clonic convulsions. The **hypoxia** (shortage of oxygen supply to a tissue, for example, to the brain) that accompanies a tonic-clonic seizure can itself cause brain damage.

A second type of generalized seizure is the **absence seizure**. Absence seizures are not associated with convulsions; their primary behavioral symptom is a disruption of consciousness associated with a cessation of ongoing behavior, a vacant look, and sometimes fluttering eyelids. The EEG of an absence seizure is different from that of other seizures; it is a bilaterally symmetrical **3-per-second spike-and-wave discharge** (see Figure 10.10). Absence seizures are most common in children, and they frequently cease at puberty.

Although there is no cure for epilepsy, the frequency and severity of seizures can often be reduced by antiepileptic medication (see Iyer & Marson, 2014; Rheims & Ryvlin, 2014). Unfortunately, these drugs often have adverse side effects, and they don't work for everyone (see Devinsky et al., 2013; Lowenstein, 2015). Other treatment options include stimulation of the vagus nerve (see Dugan & Devinsky, 2013; Vonck et al., 2014), transcranial magnetic stimulation (see Chapter 5; Manganotti & Del Felice, 2013), and the so-called *ketogenic diet* (a diet consisting of high levels of fat, moderate levels of protein, and low levels of carbohydrates)—see Klein, Tyrlikova, and Mathews (2014); Scharfman (2015). Brain surgery is sometimes used, but only when other treatment options have been exhausted.

Figure 10.10 The bilaterally symmetrical, 3-per-second spike-and-wave EEG discharge associated with absence seizures.

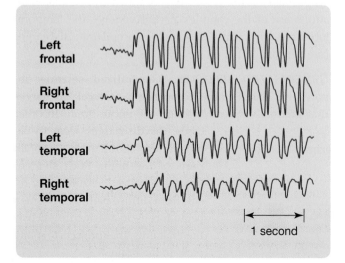

Left frontal

Right frontal

Left temporal

Right temporal

1 second

Parkinson's Disease

LO 10.9 Describe the symptoms of Parkinson's disease and some treatments for this disorder.

Parkinson's disease is a movement disorder of middle and old age that affects 1 percent of the population over the age of 55 (see Goetz & Pal, 2014; Suchowersky, 2015). It is slightly more prevalent in males than in females (see Pringsheim et al., 2014).

Clinical Implications

The initial symptoms of Parkinson's disease are mild—perhaps no more than a slight stiffness or tremor of the fingers—but they inevitably increase in severity with advancing years. The most common symptoms of the full-blown disorder are a tremor that is pronounced during inactivity but not during voluntary movement or sleep, muscular rigidity, difficulty initiating movement, slowness of movement, and a masklike face. Pain and depression often develop before the motor symptoms become severe (see Chaudhuri & Sauerbier, 2016; Klingelhoefer & Reichmann, 2015).

Although Parkinson's patients often display cognitive deficits, dementia is not always associated with the disorder (see Gratwicke, Jahanshahi, & Foltynie, 2015; Irwin, Lee, & Trojanowski, 2013). In essence, many Parkinson's disease victims are thinking people trapped inside bodies they cannot control. Do you remember the case of "The Lizard"—Roberto Garcia d'Orta—from Chapter 4?

Like epilepsy, Parkinson's disease seems to have no single cause; faulty DNA, brain infections, strokes, tumors, traumatic brain injury, and neurotoxins have all been implicated in specific cases (see Haelterman et al., 2014; Klingelhoefer & Reichmann, 2015). However, in the majority of cases, no cause is obvious, and there is no family history of the disorder (see Haelterman et al., 2014). Numerous genes have been linked to Parkinson's disease (see Verstraetan, Theuns, & Van Broeckhoven, 2015).

Parkinson's disease is associated with widespread degeneration, but it is particularly severe in the **substantia nigra**—the midbrain nucleus whose neurons project via the **nigrostriatal pathway** to the **striatum** of the basal ganglia (see Gittis & Kreitzer, 2012; Surmeier, Graves, & Shen, 2014). Although *dopamine* is normally the major neurotransmitter released by most neurons of the substantia nigra, there is little dopamine in the substantia nigra and striatum of long-term Parkinson's patients. Autopsy often reveals clumps of proteins in the surviving dopaminergic neurons of the substantia nigra—the clumps are called **Lewy bodies**, after the German pathologist who first reported them in 1912 (see Lashuel et al., 2013).

As you saw in the case of d'Orta, the symptoms of Parkinson's disease can be alleviated by injections of L-**dopa**—the chemical from which the body synthesizes dopamine. However, L-dopa is not a permanent solution; it typically becomes less

Neuroplasticity

and less effective with continued use, until its side effects (e.g., involuntary movements) outweigh its benefits (see Amanzio et al., 2010; Lieu & Subramanian, 2012). This is what happened to d'Orta. L-Dopa therapy gave him a 3-year respite from his disease, but ultimately it became ineffective. His prescription was then changed to another dopamine agonist, and again his condition improved—but again the improvement was only temporary. There is currently no drug that will permanently block the progressive development of Parkinson's disease or permanently reduce the severity of its symptoms (see Brichta, Greengard, & Flajolet, 2013; Worth, 2013). Indeed, current evidence suggests that by the time the motor symptoms of Parkinson's disease become apparent, and a diagnosis is made, irreversible damage has already occurred (see Tison & Meissner, 2014). We will return to d'Orta's roller-coaster case later in this chapter.

One of the more controversial treatments for Parkinson's disease (others will be encountered later in the chapter) is **deep brain stimulation** (see Underwood, 2015b), a treatment in which low-intensity electrical stimulation is continually applied to an area of the brain through a stereotaxically implanted electrode (see Shen, 2014) (see Figure 10.11). The treatment of Parkinson's disease by this method usually involves chronic bilateral electrical

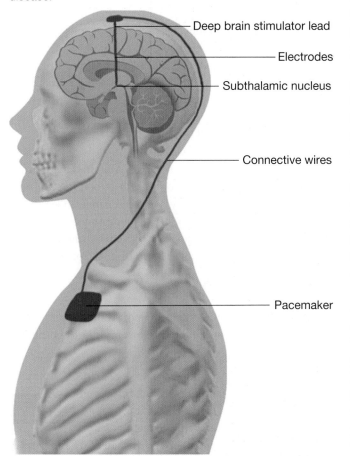

Figure 10.11 Deep brain stimulation for Parkinson's disease.

- Deep brain stimulator lead
- Electrodes
- Subthalamic nucleus
- Connective wires
- Pacemaker

stimulation of a nucleus that lies just beneath the thalamus and is connected to the basal ganglia: the **subthalamic nucleus** (see de Hemptinne et al., 2015; Fasano et al., 2015; Williams, 2015). High-frequency electrical stimulation is employed, which blocks the function of the target structure, much as a lesion would. Once the current is turned on, symptoms are sometimes alleviated within seconds, but the effectiveness of deep brain stimulation slowly declines over the ensuing months. However, if the stimulation is turned off, the therapeutic improvements dissipate very quickly. Unfortunately, deep brain stimulation can cause side effects such as cognitive, speech, and gait problems (see Deuschl & Agid, 2013; Moldovan et al., 2015).

Huntington's Disease

LO 10.10 Describe the symptoms of Huntington's disease, and explain its genetic basis.

Like Parkinson's disease, **Huntington's disease** is a progressive motor disorder, but, unlike Parkinson's disease, it is rare (1 in 10,000), it has a simple genetic basis, and it is always associated with severe dementia. **Clinical Implications**

The first clinical sign of Huntington's disease is often increased fidgetiness. As the disorder develops, rapid, complex, jerky movements of entire limbs (rather than individual muscles) begin to predominate. Eventually, motor and intellectual deterioration become so severe that sufferers are incapable of feeding themselves, controlling their bowels, or recognizing their own children. There is no cure; death typically occurs about 15 years after the appearance of the first symptoms.

Huntington's disease is passed from generation to generation by a single mutated dominant gene, called **huntingtin** (see Milnerwood & Raymond, 2010). The protein it codes for is known as the **huntingtin protein**. Because the gene is dominant, all individuals carrying the gene develop the disorder, as do about half their offspring. The huntingtin gene is often passed from parent to child because the first symptoms of the disease do not appear until after the peak reproductive years (at about age 40). We still do not know exactly how changes to the huntingtin protein damage the brain, but they may do so by increasing protein aggregation—leading to the accumulation of abnormal clumps of protein within cells (see Martin et al., 2015; Whalley, 2014).

If one of your parents were to develop Huntington's disease, the chance would be 50/50 that you too would develop it. If you were in such a situation, would you want to know whether you would suffer the same fate? Medical geneticists have developed a test that can tell relatives of Huntington's patients whether they are carrying the gene. Some choose to take the test, and some do not. One advantage of the test is that it permits the relatives of Huntington's patients who have not inherited the gene to have children without the fear of passing the disorder on to them.

Watch this video on MyPsychLab

GENETIC COUNSELING

Multiple Sclerosis

LO 10.11 Describe the symptoms of multiple sclerosis and its risk factors.

Multiple sclerosis (MS) is a progressive disease that attacks the myelin of axons in the CNS. It is particularly disturbing

because it typically attacks people in their early adulthood. First, there are microscopic areas of degeneration on myelin sheaths (see Lucchinetti et al., 2011); but eventually damage to the myelin is so severe that the associated axons become dysfunctional and degenerate (see Nave, 2010; Siffrin et al., 2010). Ultimately, many areas of hard scar tissue develop in the CNS (*sclerosis* means "hardening"). Figure 10.12 illustrates degeneration of the white matter of a patient with multiple sclerosis (see Nikić et al., 2011).

Multiple sclerosis is often considered to be an *autoimmune disorder*—a disorder in which the body's immune system attacks part of the body as if it were a foreign substance. In multiple sclerosis, myelin is the focus of the faulty immune reaction. Indeed, an animal model of multiple sclerosis, termed *experimental autoimmune encephalomyelitis* (see Deshmukh et al., 2013), can be induced by injecting laboratory animals with

myelin and a preparation that stimulates the immune system. However, it should be noted that in multiple sclerosis, damage to axons and neurons occurs even without demyelination (see Friese, Schattling, & Fugger, 2014).

Diagnosing multiple sclerosis is difficult because the nature and severity of the disorder depend on a variety of factors, including the number, size, and position of the sclerotic lesions. Furthermore, in some cases, there are periods of remission (up to 2 years) during which the patient seems almost normal; however, these are usually just oases in the progression of the disorder, which eventually becomes continuous and severe. Common symptoms of advanced multiple sclerosis are visual disturbances, muscular weakness, numbness, tremor, and **ataxia** (loss of motor coordination). In addition, cognitive deficits and emotional changes occur in some patients (see Ransohoff, Hafler, & Lucchinetti, 2015).

Epidemiological studies have revealed several puzzling features of multiple sclerosis (see Ascherio & Munger, 2008; Ramagopalan, Dyment, & Ebers, 2008). **Epidemiology** is the study of the various factors such as diet, geographic location, age, gender, and race that influence the distribution of a disease in the general population. Genetic factors seem to play less of a causal role in multiple sclerosis than they do in other neurological disorders: The concordance rate is only 25 percent in monozygotic twins, compared with 5 percent in dizygotic twins. Also, the incidence of multiple sclerosis is substantially higher in females than in males (see Friese, Schattling, & Fugger, 2014; Ransohoff, Hafler, & Lucchinetti, 2015) and in Caucasians (0.15 percent) than in other ethnic groups. Also, the incidence is higher in people who have lived in colder climates, particularly during their childhoods.

Several established risk factors exist for multiple sclerosis. The most well-established ones include vitamin D deficiency, exposure to the *Epstein-Barr virus* (the most common cause of mononucleosis), and cigarette smoking (see Hauser, Chan, & Oksenberg, 2013).

In the 1990s, *immunomodulatory drugs* were approved for the treatment of multiple sclerosis. Although these drugs are still widely prescribed for MS, their benefits are only marginal, and they help only some MS patients (see Aktas, Kieseier, & Hartung, 2009). Still, this modest success has stimulated the current search for more effective drug treatments (e.g., Ledford, 2015; Matthews, 2015; Oh & O'Connor, 2015).

Alzheimer's Disease

LO 10.12 Describe the symptoms of Alzheimer's disease, and evaluate the amyloid hypothesis.

Alzheimer's disease is the most common cause of *dementia* in the elderly (see Andrade-Moraes et al., 2013; Kunz et al., 2015). It sometimes appears in individuals as young as 40, but the likelihood of its development becomes greater with advancing years. About 10 percent of people over the age of 65 suffer from the disease (see Mielke, Vemuri, & Rocca, 2014).

Figure 10.12 Areas of sclerosis (see arrows) in the white matter of a patient with MS.

Clinical Implications Total dementia often creates less suffering than partial dementia (for the individual with the dementia). Why do you think that is the case?

Alzheimer's disease is progressive. Its early stages are often characterized by a selective decline in memory, deficits in attention, and personality changes; its intermediate stages are marked by confusion, irritability, anxiety, and deterioration of speech; and in its advanced stages, the patient deteriorates to the point that even simple responses such as swallowing and bladder control are difficult. Alzheimer's disease is terminal.

Watch this video on MyPsychLab
A CLOSER LOOK AT ALZHEIMER'S DISEASE

Because Alzheimer's disease is not the only cause of dementia, it cannot be diagnosed with certainty on the basis of its behavioral symptoms. Definitive diagnosis of Alzheimer's disease must await autopsy; however, recent cerebrospinal fluid and brain-imaging tests have greatly improved early diagnosis (see Chen, 2013b; De Deyn, 2015; Jack & Holtzman, 2013; Nordberg, 2015).

The three defining characteristics of the disease are neurofibrillary tangles, amyloid plaques, and neuron loss. *Neurofibrillary tangles* are threadlike tangles of protein in the neural cytoplasm, and *amyloid plaques* are clumps of scar tissue composed of degenerating neurons and aggregates of a protein called **beta-amyloid** which is present in normal brains in only small amounts. The presence of amyloid plaques in the brain of a patient who died of Alzheimer's disease is illustrated in Figure 10.13.

Recently, small dot-like lesions have been noticed in the brains of some Alzheimer's patients. These appear to result from microhemorrhages and have been termed **microbleeds** (see Scheltens & Goos, 2012). As a result of this discovery, many researchers are exploring the role of neurovascular factors in Alzheimer's disease (see Zlokovic, 2011).

Although neurofibrillary tangles, amyloid plaques, and neuron loss tend to occur throughout the brains of Alzheimer's patients, they are more prevalent in some areas than in others (see Figure 10.14). For example, they are

Figure 10.13 Amyloid plaques (stained blue) in the brain of a deceased patient who had Alzheimer's disease.

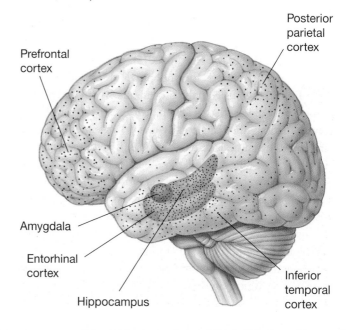

particularly prevalent in medial temporal lobe structures such as the *entorhinal cortex, amygdala,* and *hippocampus*—all structures involved in various aspects of memory (see Ewers et al., 2011: Gallagher & Koh, 2011). They are also

Figure 10.14 The typical distribution of neurofibrillary tangles and amyloid plaques in the brains of patients with advanced Alzheimer's disease. (Based on Goedert, 1993 and Selkoe, 1991.)

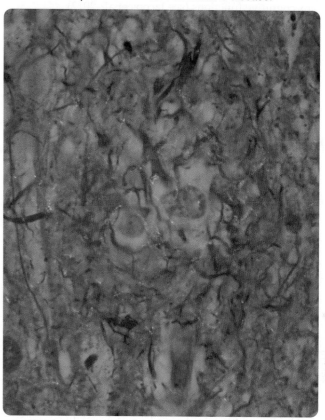

prevalent in the inferior temporal cortex, posterior parietal cortex, and prefrontal cortex—all areas that mediate complex cognitive functions (see Jacobs et al., 2012).

Alzheimer's disease has a major genetic component. People with an Alzheimer's victim in their immediate family are twice as likely to be stricken by the disease if they survive to old age (see Chouraki & Seshadri, 2014).

Early attempts to identify the genes involved in Alzheimer's disease focused on a rare, early-onset form of the disorder that runs in a few families—one Bolivian family has been widely studied. Mutations to three different genes were shown to contribute to the early-onset, familial form; however, these three gene mutations seem to contribute to only 1 percent of the more common, late-onset form (see Kanekiyo, Xu, & Bu, 2014).

Subsequent research on the late-onset form of Alzheimer's disease has implicated another 15 genes (see Tanzi, 2012). Recently, attention has focused on one particular gene, the *gene* on chromosome 19 that codes for the protein *apolipoprotein E (APOE)*. Notably, a particular allele of the APOE gene, APOE4, has been shown to increase susceptibility to the late-onset form of Alzheimer's disease by approximately 50 percent (see Yu, Tan, & Hardy, 2014; Karch, Cruchaga, & Goate, 2014). The exact cellular functions of APOE are not yet known (see Spinney, 2014), but we do know that APOE binds to beta-amyloid, and that such binding reduces beta-amyloid clearance, and increases beta-amyloid aggregation (see Karch, Cruchaga, & Goate, 2014)—leading to the development of amyloid plaques.

There is currently no cure for Alzheimer's disease. One factor complicating the search for a treatment or cure for

Thinking Creatively

Alzheimer's disease is that it is not clear which symptom is primary (see O'Brien & Wang, 2011; Spires-Jones & Hyman, 2014). This is a key issue because an effective treatment will most likely be developed only by research focusing on the primary symptom. The *amyloid hypothesis* is currently the dominant view. It proposes that amyloid plaques are the primary symptom of the disorder and cause all the other symptoms (Musiek & Holtzman, 2015; but see Herrup, 2015).

The main support for the amyloid hypothesis has come from the genetic analysis of families with early-onset Alzheimer's disease (see Herrup, 2015). All three different gene mutations that cause early-onset Alzheimer's disease influence the synthesis of beta-amyloid. One of the main arguments against the amyloid hypothesis is the fact that many people without observable dementia carry significant loads of amyloid plaques. These individuals are known as *high-plaque normals* (see Herrup, 2015; Spires-Jones & Hyman, 2014). However, recent evidence from longitudinal studies suggests that high-plaque normals are at increased risk for cognitive decline and that some go on to develop Alzheimer's disease (see Sperling, Mormino, & Johnson, 2014).

The first efforts to develop treatments for Alzheimer's disease focused on the fact that declines in acetylcholine levels were among the earliest neurochemical changes to be detected in patients. Cholinergic agonists are still sometimes prescribed, but, except for a few minor benefits early in the disorder, they have proven ineffective (see Craig, Hong, & MacDonald, 2011).

In the past decade, researchers trying to develop a cure for Alzheimer's disease by reducing the amyloid deposits have been taken on a roller-coaster ride: One treatment after another was found to be promising in animal models of the disease only to be found ineffective when applied to human patients (see Busche et al., 2015). These failures have led some researchers to challenge the amyloid hypothesis (see Herrup, 2015; Karran, Mercken, & de Strooper, 2011), but others believe that in order to be effective, treatments must be administered before disease onset or at least in its early stages (see Huang & Mucke, 2012; Zahs & Ashe, 2010). The problem is that when patients first seek help for Alzheimer's symptoms, they typically already have extensive brain pathology (see Selkoe, 2012). That is why recent advances in early diagnosis may prove to be critical in the development of effective treatments (Miller, 2012). In any case, two recent clinical trials have shown that the administration of antibodies for beta-amyloid can slow the progression of Alzheimer's disease (see Reardon, 2015; Underwood, 2015c).

Recently, attention has focused on Down syndrome as a potential provider of insights into the neural mechanisms of Alzheimer's disease. This link stems from the fact that, by age 40, almost all patients with Down syndrome have developed numerous amyloid plaques and neurofibrillary tangles, the core symptoms of Alzheimer's disease (see Marshall, 2014); and that, by age 60, two-thirds of individuals with Down syndrome will have developed dementia (see Wiseman et al., 2015). As you learned earlier, people with Down syndrome have three copies of chromosome 21, instead of the normal two. The gene that codes for beta-amyloid resides on chromosome 21. Accordingly, scientists have hypothesized that the presence of an extra chromosome 21 leads to greater production of beta-amyloid in persons with Down syndrome (see Wiseman et al., 2015). Interestingly, recent research has shown that approximately 15 percent of the neurons in the brains of Alzheimer's patients contain an extra copy of chromosome 21 (see Marshall, 2014).

In the past 5 years, increasing attention has been paid to a new hypothesis known as the *pathogenic spread hypothesis.* The pathogenic spread hypothesis proposes that many common neurodegenerative diseases (e.g., Alzheimer's disease, Parkinson's disease) result from the presence of misfolded proteins that initiate a chain reaction wherein they cause other proteins to misfold. For example, according to this hypothesis, in Alzheimer's disease a misfolded beta-amyloid protein acts as a "seed" that leads to the misfolding of other beta-amyloid proteins; these misfolded beta-amyloid proteins subsequently spread to other neurons (through as yet unknown mechanisms; see Brettschenider et al., 2015) and also aggregate into the amyloid plaques that are characteristic of Alzheimer's disease (see Goedert, 2015; Walker & Jucker, 2013; Walsh & Selkoe, 2016).

Scan Your Brain

This is a good place for you to pause to scan your brain. Are you ready to progress to the following module, which discusses animal models of some of the disorders that you have just learned about? Fill in the following blanks. The correct answers are provided at the end of the exercise. Before proceeding, review material related to your errors and omissions.

1. A _____ is a mass of cells that grows independently of the rest of the body.
2. Brain tumors that develop from glial cells are called _____.
3. _____ are sudden-onset cerebrovascular disorders that cause brain damage.
4. _____ is a disruption of the blood supply to an area of the brain.
5. _____ is the brain's most prevalent excitatory neurotransmitter.
6. The dysfunction area surrounding the infract is called _____.
7. When there is no evidence of a contusion or other structural damage but there is disturbance of consciousness, the diagnosis is _____.
8. _____ is usually defined as general intellectual deterioration.
9. Patients whose seizures are repeatedly generated by their own chronic brain dysfunction are diagnosed as _____.
10. Shortage of oxygen supply to a tissue is called _____.
11. _____, or loss of motor coordination, is a common symptom of multiple sclerosis.

Scan Your Brain answers: (1) tumor, (2) gliomas, (3) Strokes, (4) Cerebral ischemia, (5) Glutamate, (6) penumbra, (7) concussion, (8) Dementia, (9) epileptic, (10) hypoxia, (11) Ataxia.

Animal Models of Human Neurological Diseases

The first two modules of this chapter focused on neuropsychological diseases and their causes, but they also provided some glimpses into the ways in which researchers attempt to solve the puzzles of neurological dysfunction. This module focuses on one of these ways: the experimental investigation of animal models.

Because identifying the neuropathological bases of human neuropsychological diseases is seldom possible based on research on the patients themselves, research on **Evolutionary Perspective** animal models of the diseases often plays an important role. Unfortunately, using and interpreting animal models is far from straightforward: Even the best animal models of neuropsychological diseases display only some of the features of the diseases they are modeling (see Wekerle et al., 2012), though researchers often treat animal models as if they duplicate in every respect the human conditions that they are claimed to model. That is why we have included **Thinking Creatively** this module on animal models in this chapter: We do not want you to fall into the trap of thinking about them in this way. This module discusses three widely used animal models: the kindling model of epilepsy, the transgenic mouse model of Alzheimer's disease, and the MPTP model of Parkinson's disease.

Kindling Model of Epilepsy

LO 10.13 Describe the kindling model of epilepsy, and explain the ways in which it models human epilepsy.

In the late 1960s, Goddard, McIntyre, and Leech (1969) delivered one mild electrical stimulation per day to rats through an implanted amygdalar electrode. There was no behavioral response to the first few stimulations, but soon each stimulation began to elicit a convulsive response. The first convulsions were mild, involving only a slight tremor of the face. However, with each subsequent stimulation, the elicited convulsions became more generalized, until each convulsion involved the entire body. The progressive development and intensification of convulsions elicited by a series of periodic brain stimulations became known as the **kindling phenomenon**, one of the first neuroplastic phenomena to be widely studied.

Although kindling is most frequently studied in rats subjected to repeated amygdalar stimulation, it is a remarkably general phenomenon. For example, kindling has been reported in mice, rabbits, cats, **Evolutionary Perspective** dogs, and various primates. Moreover, kindling can be produced by the repeated stimulation of many brain sites other than the amygdala, and it can be produced by the repeated application of initially subconvulsive doses of convulsive chemicals.

There are many interesting features of kindling, but two warrant emphasis. The first is that the neuroplastic changes underlying kindling are **Neuroplasticity** permanent. A subject that has been kindled and then left unstimulated for several months still responds to each low-intensity stimulation with a generalized convulsion. The second is that kindling is produced by distributed, as opposed to massed, stimulations. If the intervals between successive stimulations are shorter than an hour or two, many more stimulations are usually required to kindle a subject, and under normal circumstances, no kindling at all occurs at intervals of less than about 20 minutes.

 Why is the fact that kindling is produced by distributed, as opposed to massed, stimulations an example of neuroplasticity? (Hint: Think about the effects of distributed vs. massed study sessions on human learning.)

Much of the interest in kindling stems from the fact that it models epilepsy in two ways (see Morimoto, Fahnestock, & Racine, 2004). First, the convulsions elicited in kindled animals are similar in many respects to those observed in some types of human epilepsy. Second, the kindling phenomenon itself is comparable to the **epileptogenesis** (the development, or genesis, of epilepsy) that can follow a head injury (see Goldberg & Coulter, 2013): Some individuals who at first appear to have escaped serious injury after a blow to the head begin to experience convulsions a few weeks later, and these convulsions sometimes begin to recur more and more frequently and with greater and greater intensity.

It must be stressed that the kindling model as it is applied in most laboratories does not model epilepsy in one important respect. You will recall from earlier in this chapter that epilepsy is a disease in which seizures recur spontaneously; in contrast, kindled convulsions are elicited. However, a model that overcomes this shortcoming has been developed in several species. If subjects are kindled for a very long time—about 300 stimulations in rats—a syndrome can be induced that is much more like epilepsy, in the sense that the subjects begin to display spontaneous seizures and continue to display them even after the regimen of stimulation is curtailed (see Grone & Baraban, 2015).

Transgenic Mouse Models of Alzheimer's Disease

LO 10.14 Describe the transgenic mouse models of Alzheimer's disease, and evaluate their efficacy.

Perhaps the most promising step forward in the study of Alzheimer's disease has been the development of several transgenic models of the disorder. **Transgenic** refers to animals into which genes of another species have been introduced (see Braidy et al., 2015).

In transgenic mouse models of Alzheimer's disease, gene mutations that promote the accumulation of human beta-amyloid are injected into newly fertilized mouse eggs, which are then injected into a foster mother to develop. When the transgenic mice mature, their brains contain many amyloid plaques like those of human Alzheimer's patients. Moreover, the distribution of the amyloid plaques is comparable to that observed in human Alzheimer's patients, with the highest concentrations occurring in structures of the medial temporal lobes. These mice also display neural loss and memory disturbances (see LaFerla & Green, 2012; Wirths & Bayer, 2010).

Although transgenic mouse models are arguably the best current animal models of Alzheimer's disease, they are not without problems (see Elder, Gama Sosa, & De Gasperi, 2010). For example, most of these models do not display neurofibrillary tangles, which is a serious problem if neurofibrillary tangles prove to be the primary symptom of Alzheimer's disease. However, this problem has been resolved by injecting into the transgenic mice human gene mutations that promote accumulation of the protein *tau* (a protein implicated in the production of neurofibrillary tangles)—see Giacobini and Gold (2013); Iqbal, Liu, & Gong (2016)..

MPTP Model of Parkinson's Disease

LO 10.15 Describe the events that led to the discovery of the MPTP model of Parkinson's disease, and evaluate the utility of this animal model.

The preeminent animal model of Parkinson's disease grew out of an unfortunate accident, which resulted in the following cases (Langston, 1985).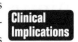

The Cases of the Frozen Addicts

Parkinson's disease rarely occurs before the age of 50. Thus, it was surprising when a group of young drug-addicted individuals developed severe parkinsonism. The one link among these patients was their recent use of a new "synthetic heroin." They exhibited all of the typical symptoms of Parkinson's disease, including bradykinesia (slowness of movement), tremor, and muscle rigidity. Even subtle Parkinson's symptoms, such as seborrhea (oiliness of the skin) and micrographia (small handwriting), were present. After obtaining samples of the synthetic heroin, the offending agent was tentatively identified as 1-methyl-4-phenyl-1,2,3,6-tetrahydropyridine or **MPTP**. None of the patients recovered.

Researchers immediately turned the misfortune of these few to the advantage of many by developing a much-needed animal model of Parkinson's disease. It was quickly established that nonhuman primates respond to MPTP the same way humans do. They display Parkinsonian motor symptoms, cell loss in the substantia nigra, and a major reduction in brain dopamine. For unknown reasons, rats are resistant to MPTP, and mice vary greatly from strain to strain in their response to it (see Blesa et al., 2012).

Although the MPTP model does not model all aspects of Parkinson's disease, particularly its causation, the model has proven extremely useful (see Porras, Le, & Bezard, 2011). It has been instrumental in the development of many of the treatments, mainly dopaminergic drugs, that are currently in use (see Fox & Brotchie, 2010).

Responses to Nervous System Damage: Degeneration, Regeneration, Reorganization, and Recovery

In the first three modules of this chapter, you have learned about three things: (1) causes of brain damage, (2) neurological diseases associated with brain damage, and (3) animal models of neurological diseases. This module focuses on four neuroplastic responses of the brain to damage: degeneration, regeneration, reorganization, and recovery of function.

Neural Degeneration

LO 10.16 Explain the various types of neural degeneration that ensue following axotomy.

Neural degeneration (neural deterioration and death) is a component of both brain development and disease. Neural degeneration, as it typically occurs, is a complex process: It is greatly influenced by nearby glial cells (see Burda & Sofroniew, 2014; Gao et al., 2013; Tsude & Inoue, 2015), by the activity of the degenerating neurons (see Bell & Hardingham, 2011), and by the particular cause of the degeneration (see Conforti, Adalbert, & Coleman, 2007). In the laboratory, however, neural degeneration is often induced in a simple, controlled way: By cutting axons (i.e., by *axotomy*). Two kinds of neural degeneration ensue: anterograde degeneration and retrograde degeneration. **Anterograde degeneration** is the degeneration of the **distal segment**—the segment of a cut axon from the cut to the synaptic terminals (see Neukomm & Freeman, 2014). **Retrograde degeneration** is the degeneration of the **proximal segment**—the segment of a cut axon from the cut back to the cell body.

Anterograde degeneration occurs quickly following axotomy because the cut separates the distal segment of the axon from the cell body, which is the metabolic center of the neuron. The entire distal segment becomes badly swollen within a few hours, and it breaks into fragments within a few days.

The course of retrograde degeneration is different; it progresses gradually back from the cut to the cell body. In about 2 or 3 days, major changes become apparent in the cell bodies of most axotomized neurons. These early cell body changes are either degenerative or regenerative in nature. Early degenerative changes to the cell body (e.g., a decrease in size) suggest that the neuron will ultimately die—usually by apoptosis but sometimes by necrosis or a combination of both. Early regenerative changes (e.g., an increase in size) indicate that the cell body is involved in a massive synthesis of the proteins that will be used to replace the degenerated axon. But early regenerative changes in the cell body do not guarantee the long-term survival of the neuron; if the regenerating axon does not manage to make synaptic contact with an appropriate target, the neuron eventually dies.

Sometimes, degeneration spreads from damaged neurons to neurons that are linked to them by synapses; this is called **transneuronal degeneration**. In some cases, transneuronal degeneration spreads from damaged neurons to the neurons on which they synapse; this is called *anterograde transneuronal degeneration*. And in some cases, it spreads from damaged neurons to the neurons that synapse on them; this is called *retrograde transneuronal degeneration*. Neural and transneuronal degeneration are illustrated in Figure 10.15.

Neural Regeneration

LO 10.17 Compare neural regeneration within the CNS vs. the PNS.

Neural regeneration—the regrowth of damaged neurons—does not proceed as successfully in mammals and other higher vertebrates as it does in most invertebrates and lower vertebrates. For example, in Chapter 9, you learned about accurate regeneration in the frog visual system as demonstrated by Sperry's eye-rotation experiments. The capacity for accurate axonal growth, which higher vertebrates possess during their development, is lost once they reach maturity. Regeneration is virtually nonexistent in the CNS of adult mammals and is at best a hit-or-miss affair in the PNS.

In the mammalian PNS, regrowth from the proximal stump of a damaged nerve usually begins 2 or 3 days after axonal damage, once new growth cones have formed (see Bradke, Fawcett, & Spira, 2012). What happens next depends on the nature of the injury; there are three possibilities. First, if the original Schwann cell myelin sheaths remain intact, the regenerating peripheral axons grow

Figure 10.15 Neural and transneuronal degeneration following axotomy.

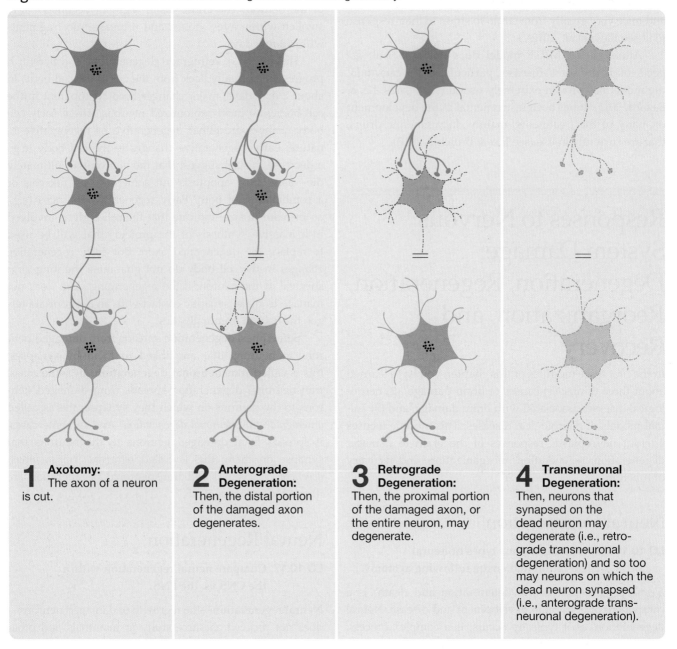

1 Axotomy:
The axon of a neuron is cut.

2 Anterograde Degeneration:
Then, the distal portion of the damaged axon degenerates.

3 Retrograde Degeneration:
Then, the proximal portion of the damaged axon, or the entire neuron, may degenerate.

4 Transneuronal Degeneration:
Then, neurons that synapsed on the dead neuron may degenerate (i.e., retrograde transneuronal degeneration) and so too may neurons on which the dead neuron synapsed (i.e., anterograde transneuronal degeneration).

through them to their original targets at a rate of a few millimeters per day. Second, if the peripheral nerve is severed and the cut ends become separated by a few millimeters, regenerating axon tips often grow into incorrect sheaths and are guided by them to incorrect destinations; that is why it is often difficult to regain the coordinated use of a limb affected by nerve damage even if there has been substantial regeneration. And third, if the cut ends of a severed mammalian peripheral nerve become widely separated or if a lengthy section of the nerve is damaged, there may be no meaningful regeneration at all; regenerating axon tips grow in a tangled mass around the proximal stump, and the neurons ultimately die. These three patterns of mammalian peripheral nerve regeneration are illustrated in Figure 10.16.

Why do mammalian PNS neurons regenerate but mammalian CNS neurons normally do not? The obvious answer is that adult PNS neurons are inherently capable of regeneration whereas adult CNS neurons are not (see Liu et al., 2011; Sun & He, 2010). However, this answer has proved to be only partially correct. Some CNS neurons are capable of regeneration if they are transplanted to the PNS, whereas some PNS neurons are not capable of regeneration if they are transplanted to the CNS. Clearly, something about the environment of the PNS promotes regeneration and something about the environment of the CNS does not. Schwann cells seem to be one factor (see Fontana et al., 2012).

Schwann cells, which myelinate PNS axons, clear the debris and scar tissue resulting from neural degeneration and promote regeneration in the mammalian PNS by producing both neurotrophic factors and cell-adhesion molecules (CAMs). The neurotrophic factors released by Schwann cells stimulate the growth of growth cones and new axons, and the cell-adhesion molecules on the cell membranes of Schwann cells mark the paths along which regenerating PNS axons grow. In contrast, **oligodendroglia**, which myelinate CNS axons, do not clear debris or stimulate or guide regeneration; indeed, they release factors that actively block regeneration (see Geoffroy & Zheng, 2014). Moreover, in the CNS, astrocytes form a *glial scar* after injury that presents a physical barrier to axonal regrowth and also actively releases inhibitors of axonal growth (see Chen & Zheng, 2014; but see Anderson et al., 2016).

When an axon degenerates, axon branches grow out from adjacent healthy axons and synapse at the sites vacated by the degenerating axon; this is called **collateral sprouting**. Collateral sprouts may grow out from the axon terminal branches or the nodes of Ranvier on adjacent neurons. Collateral sprouting is illustrated in Figure 10.17.

Evolutionary Perspective The accuracy of regeneration in invertebrates and lower vertebrates offers hope of a medical breakthrough. If the factors that promote accurate

Figure 10.16 Three patterns of axonal regeneration in mammalian peripheral nerves.

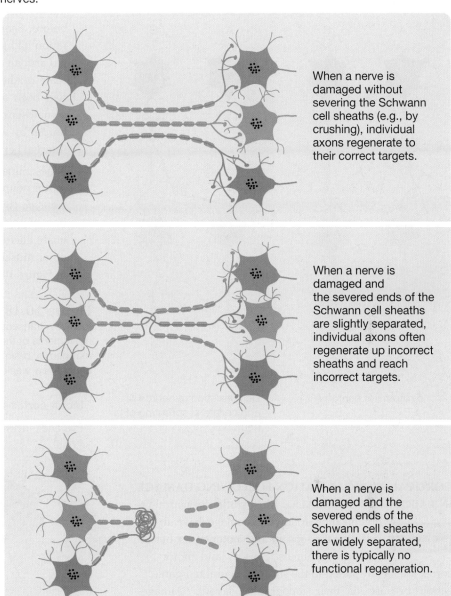

When a nerve is damaged without severing the Schwann cell sheaths (e.g., by crushing), individual axons regenerate to their correct targets.

When a nerve is damaged and the severed ends of the Schwann cell sheaths are slightly separated, individual axons often regenerate up incorrect sheaths and reach incorrect targets.

When a nerve is damaged and the severed ends of the Schwann cell sheaths are widely separated, there is typically no functional regeneration.

regeneration can be identified and applied to the human brain, it might be possible to repair human brain damage.

Neural Reorganization

LO 10.18 Describe three examples of cortical reorganization following damage to the brain, and discuss the mechanisms that might underlie such reorganization.

You learned in Chapter 9 that adult mammalian brains have the ability to reorganize **Neuroplasticity** themselves in response to experience. You will learn in this section that they can also reorganize themselves in response to damage.

Watch this video on MyPsychLab

CHALK IT UP! HUMANS: THE NEURAL REGENERATION STORY

Figure 10.17 Collateral sprouting after neural degeneration.

Axotomy of neuron A

Degeneration of neuron A and collateral sprouting of neuron B

CORTICAL REORGANIZATION FOLLOWING DAMAGE IN LABORATORY ANIMALS.

Evolutionary Perspective

Most studies of neural reorganization following damage have focused on the sensory and motor cortex of laboratory animals. Sensory and motor cortex are ideally suited to the study of neural reorganization because of their topographic layout. Damage-induced reorganization of the primary sensory and motor cortices has been studied under two conditions: following damage to peripheral nerves and following damage to the cortical areas themselves.

Demonstrations of cortical reorganization following neural damage in laboratory animals started to be reported in substantial numbers in the early 1990s. The following three studies were particularly influential:

- Kaas and colleagues (1990) assessed the effect of making a small lesion in one retina and removing the other. Several months after the retinal lesion was made, primary visual cortex neurons that originally had receptive fields in the lesioned area of the retina were found to have receptive fields in the area of the retina next to the lesion; remarkably, this change began within minutes of the lesion (Gilbert & Wiesel, 1992).

- Pons and colleagues (1991) mapped the primary somatosensory cortex of monkeys whose contralateral arm sensory neurons had been cut 10 years before. They found that the cortical face representation had systematically expanded into the original arm area. This study created a stir because the scale of the reorganization was far greater than had been assumed to be possible: The primary somatosensory cortex face area had expanded its border by well over a centimeter over the 10-year interval between surgery and testing.

- Sanes, Suner, and Donoghue (1990) transected the motor neurons that controlled the muscles of rats' *vibrissae* (whiskers). A few weeks later, stimulation of the area of motor cortex that had previously elicited vibrissae movement now activated other muscles of the face. This result is illustrated in Figure 10.18.

Figure 10.18 Reorganization of the rat motor cortex following transection of the motor neurons that control movements of the vibrissae. The motor cortex was mapped by brain stimulation before transection and then again a few weeks after. (Based on Sanes et al., 1990.)

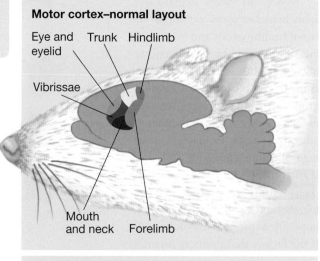

Motor cortex–normal layout

Eye and eyelid   Trunk   Hindlimb

Vibrissae

Mouth and neck   Forelimb

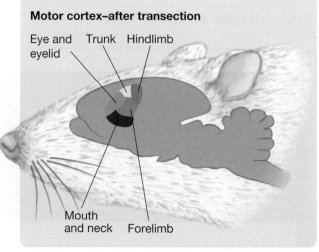

Motor cortex–after transection

Eye and eyelid   Trunk   Hindlimb

Mouth and neck   Forelimb

CORTICAL REORGANIZATION FOLLOWING DAMAGE IN HUMANS.

Demonstrations of cortical reorganization in controlled experiments on nonhumans provided an incentive to search for similar effects in human clinical populations. One such line of research has used brain-imaging technology to study the cortices of blind individuals. The findings are consistent with the hypothesis that there is continuous competition for cortical space by functional circuits. Without visual input to the cortex, there is an expansion of auditory and somatosensory cortex (see Elbert et al., 2002), and auditory and somatosensory input is processed in formerly visual areas (see Amedi et al., 2005). There seems to be a functional consequence to this reorganization: Blind volunteers have skills superior to those of sighted control volunteers on a variety of auditory and somatosensory tasks (see Merabet & Pascual-Leone, 2010).

MECHANISMS OF NEURAL REORGANIZATION.

Two kinds of mechanisms have been proposed to account for the reorganization of neural circuits: a strengthening of existing connections, possibly through release from inhibition, and the establishment of new connections by collateral sprouting (see Cafferty, McGee, & Strittmatter, 2008). Indirect support for the first mechanism comes from two observations: Reorganization often occurs too quickly to be explained by neural growth, and rapid reorganization never involves changes of more than 2 millimeters of cortical surface. Indirect support for the second mechanism comes from the observation that the magnitude of long-term reorganization can be too great to be explained by changes in existing connections. Figure 10.19 illustrates how these two mechanisms might account for the reorganization that occurs after damage to a peripheral somatosensory nerve.

Although sprouting and release from inhibition are considered to be the likely mechanisms of reorganization following brain damage, these are not the only possibilities. For example, neural degeneration, adjustment of dendritic trees, and adult neurogenesis may all be involved. It is also important to appreciate that reorganization following damage is not necessarily mediated by changes to the damaged area itself (see Grefkes & Fink, 2011; Rehme et al., 2011; Rossignol & Frigon, 2011).

Figure 10.19 Two proposed mechanisms for the reorganization of neural circuits: (1) strengthening of existing connections through release from inhibition and (2) establishment of new connections by collateral sprouting.

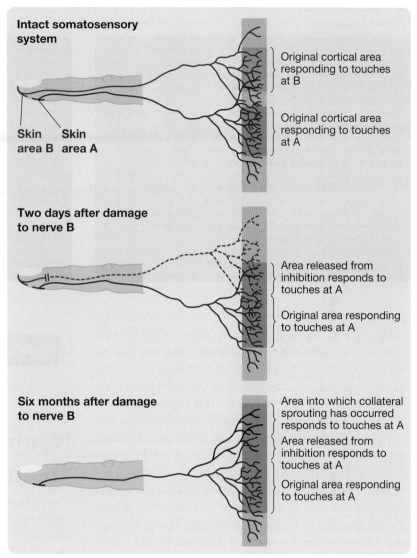

Recovery of Function after CNS Damage

LO 10.19 Describe the concept of "cognitive reserve," and discuss the potential role of adult neurogenesis in recovery following CNS damage.

Recovery of function after central nervous system damage in adult humans is poorly understood. In large part, this is so because improvements tend to be modest or nonexistent (see Teuber, 1975)—not the positive picture usually portrayed by the entertainment media, where all that is needed is lots of effort to guarantee a positive outcome. Another difficulty in studying recovery of function after CNS damage is that there are other compensatory changes that can easily be confused with it. For example, any improvement in the week or two after damage could reflect a decline in *cerebral edema* (brain swelling) rather than a recovery from the neural damage itself,

Figure 10.20 Increased neurogenesis in the dentate gyrus following damage. The left panel shows (1) an electrolytic lesion in the dentate gyrus (damaged neurons are stained turquoise) and (2) the resulting increase in the formation of new cells (stained red), many of which develop into mature neurons (stained dark blue). The right panel displays the control area in the unlesioned hemisphere, showing the normal number of new cells (stained red). (Images courtesy of Carl Ernst and Brian Christie, Department of Psychology, University of British Columbia.)

and any gradual improvement in the months after damage could reflect the learning of new cognitive and behavioral strategies (i.e., substitution of functions) rather than the return of lost functions. Despite these difficulties, it is clear that recovery is most likely when lesions are small and patients are young (see Marquez de la Plata et al., 2008; Yager et al., 2006).

Cognitive reserve (roughly equivalent to education and intelligence) is thought to play a role in the improvements observed after brain damage that do not result from true recovery of brain function. Let us explain. Kapur (1997) conducted a biographical study of doctors and neuroscientists with brain damage, and he observed a surprising degree of what appeared to be cognitive recovery. His results suggested, however, that the observed improvement did not occur because these patients had actually recovered lost brain function but because their cognitive reserve allowed them to accomplish tasks in alternative ways. Cognitive reserve has also been used to explain why highly educated people are less susceptible to the effects of brain deterioration associated with aging (see Barulli & Stern, 2013).

Does adult neurogenesis contribute to recovery from brain damage? In adult laboratory animals, there is an increased migration of stem cells into nearby [**Neuroplasticity**] damaged areas (see Figure 10.20), and some of these develop into neurons that can survive for a few months (see Machado et al., 2015; Sun, 2015). This finding has been replicated in one human patient who died 1 week after suffering a stroke (see Minger et al., 2007). However, although stem cells can migrate short distances, there is no evidence that they can migrate from their sites of genesis in the hippocampus and subventricular zone to distant areas of damage in the adult human brain. In any case, there is no direct evidence that stem cells contribute to recovery.

[**Neuroplasticity**] Given that brain damage seems to induce adult neurogenesis, what adaptive role, if any, might these new cells be playing?

Neuroplasticity and the Treatment of CNS Damage

This module reveals one reason for all the excitement about the phenomenon of neuroplasticity: the dream that recent discoveries about neuroplasticity can be applied to the treatment of CNS damage in human patients. The following sections describe [**Clinical Implications**] research on some major new treatment approaches that have been stimulated by the discovery of neuroplasticity.

Watch this video on MyPsychLab
BRAIN DAMAGE AND NEUROPLASTICITY

Neurotransplantation as a Treatment for CNS Damage: Early Research

LO 10.20 Discuss early work on neurotransplantation for the treatment of CNS damage.

In the late 1980s, researchers, stimulated by research on neurodevelopment, began to explore the possibility of repairing damaged CNS tissue by implanting embryonic tissue near the damaged area. Their hope was that the embryonic tissue would mature and replace the damaged cells. Could the *donor* tissue develop and become integrated into the *host* brain and, in so doing, alleviate the symptoms? This approach focused on Parkinson's disease. Parkinson's patients lack the dopamine-releasing cells of the nigrostriatal pathway: Could they be cured by transplanting the appropriate fetal tissue into the substantia nigra?

Neuroplasticity

Early signs were positive. Bilateral transplantation of fetal substantia nigra cells was successful in treating the MPTP monkey model of Parkinson's disease (see Bankiewicz et al., 1990; Sladek et al., 1987). Fetal substantia nigra transplants survived in the MPTP-treated monkeys; the transplanted cells innervated adjacent striatal tissue, released dopamine, and, most importantly, alleviated the severe poverty of movement, tremor, and rigidity produced by the MPTP.

Soon after the favorable effects of neurotransplants in the MPTP monkey model were reported, neurotransplantation was prematurely offered as a treatment for Parkinson's disease at major research hospitals. The results of the first case studies were promising. The fetal substantia nigra implants survived, and they released dopamine into the host striatum (see Sawle & Myers, 1993). More importantly, some of the patients improved.

These preliminary results triggered a large-scale double-blind evaluation study of neurotransplants in patients suffering from advanced Parkinson's disease. The initial results were encouraging: The implants survived, and there was a modest reduction of symptoms. Unfortunately, however, some of the patients started to display a variety of uncontrollable writhing and chewing movements about a year after the surgery (see Greene et al., 1999).

The negative results of this large-scale study had two positive effects. First, it all but curtailed the premature clinical use of neurotransplantation to treat human patients with Parkinson's disease. Many had warned that it was inappropriate to use such an invasive treatment without a solid foundation of research identifying its mechanisms, its hazards, and the best ways of maximizing its effectiveness (see Dunnett, Björkland, & Lindvall, 2001). Second, it stimulated researchers to take a more careful and systematic look at the effects of various kinds of neurotransplantation in animal models to answer fundamental questions.

In Chapter 4, you were introduced to Roberto Garcia d'Orta—the Lizard. D'Orta, who suffered from Parkinson's disease, initially responded to L-dopa therapy; but, after 3 years of therapy, his condition worsened. D'Orta was in a desperate state when he heard about *adrenal medulla autotransplantation* (transplanting a patient's own adrenal medulla cells into their striatum, usually for the treatment of Parkinson's disease). Adrenal medulla cells release small amounts of dopamine, and there were some early indications that adrenal medulla autotransplantation might alleviate the symptoms of Parkinson's disease.

Clinical Implications

D'Orta demanded adrenal medulla autotransplantation from his doctor. When his doctor refused, on the grounds that the effectiveness and safety of the treatment were unproven, d'Orta found another doctor—a neurosurgeon who was not so responsible (Klawans, 1990).

The Case of Roberto Garcia d'Orta: The Lizard Gets an Autotransplant

Roberto flew to Juarez for surgery. As long as Roberto would pay, the neurosurgeon would perform the autotransplantation.

Were there any risks? The neurosurgeon seemed insulted by the question. If Señor d'Orta didn't trust him, he could go elsewhere.

Roberto flew home 2 weeks after the surgery even though his condition had not improved. He was told to be patient and to wait for the cells to grow.

A few weeks later, Roberto died of a stroke. Was the stroke a complication of his surgery? It was more than a mere possibility.

Another approach to neurotransplantation research was developed in the late 1990s. Instead of implanting developing cells, researchers implanted nonneural cells to block neural degeneration or to stimulate and guide neural regeneration. For example, Xu and colleagues (1999) induced cerebral ischemia in rats by limiting blood flow to the brain. This had two major effects on rats in the control group: It produced damage to the hippocampus, a structure particularly susceptible to ischemic damage, and it produced deficits in the rats' performance in the Morris water maze (see Chapter 5). The hippocampuses of rats in the experimental group were treated with viruses genetically engineered to release *apoptosis inhibitor protein*. Amazingly, the apoptosis inhibitor protein reduced both the loss of hippocampal neurons and the deficits in Morris water maze performance. Many other neurotrophic factors have been shown to reduce degeneration—*brain-derived neurotrophic factor* (BDNF) and *glial-cell-line-derived factor* (GDNF) have been among the most widely studied (see Wang et al., 2011; Zhu et al., 2011).

A slightly different technique of this type involves implanting *Schwann cell sheaths*, which promote regeneration and guide axon growth. For example, Cheng, Cao, and Olson (1996) transected the spinal cords of rats, thus rendering them *paraplegic* (paralyzed in the posterior portion of their bodies). The researchers then transplanted sections of myelinated peripheral nerve across the transection. As a result, spinal cord neurons regenerated through the implanted Schwann cell myelin sheaths, and the regeneration allowed the rats to regain use of their hindquarters.

Modern Research on Neurotransplantation

LO 10.21 Discuss the methods and findings of modern research on neurotransplantation.

It was feared that the adverse consequences of prematurely rushing neurotransplantation to clinical practice for the treatment of Parkinson's disease might stifle further neurotransplantation research. It hasn't. In fact, since the failure of neurotransplantation to benefit human Parkinson's disease sufferers, neurotransplantation has become one of the most active areas of clinical neuroscientific research. The need for a method of repairing brain damage is simply too great for research on neurotransplantation to be deterred.

So, how active is the study of neurotransplantation? Hundreds of studies of neurotransplantation have been conducted since the turn of the century, involving animal models of virtually all common neurological disorders. And several of the protocols that have been developed in these studies have entered preliminary tests on human patients (see De Feo et al., 2012; Lemmens & Steinberg, 2013; Steinbeck & Studer, 2015). Given all this research activity, it is not surprising that there have been some major advances. Here are some of them.

At the turn of the century, stem cells were successfully isolated from the human embryo and maintained in tissue culture (see Hochedlinger, 2010). Because stem cells (see Chapter 9) divide indefinitely and are *pluripotent* (capable of developing into many, but not all, classes of adult cells), it seemed that stem-cell cultures would provide lasting sources of cells for transplantation, thus circumventing the ethical and technical difficulties in transplanting tissue obtained from human embryos. However, this did not prove to be the case: In practice, stem-cell cultures deteriorate as chromosomal abnormalities gradually accumulate during repeated cell division (see Hochedlinger, 2010). That is why the report in 2007 that human skin cells could be induced to return to stem cells (i.e., to return to a pluripotent state) generated great excitement (Takahashi et al., 2007). Induced stem cells have been the focus of a massive research effort; however, the genetic manipulation required to create them (i.e., the insertion of four genes) makes it difficult to predict how they might behave in a human patient (see Asuelime & Shi, 2012).

It is often assumed that the therapeutic effect of neurotransplantation results from the replacement of dead or dying neurons with healthy ones (see Gaillard & Jaber, 2011; Olson et al., 2012). However, in many cases this does not appear to be the mechanism (see Bonnamain, Neveu, & Naveilhan, 2012; Olson et al., 2012). In animal models, implants have been shown to stimulate remyelination of injured axons (Hwang et al., 2009; Yasuda et al., 2011), to release *neurotrophic* and *guidance molecules* (De Feo et al., 2012), and to develop into glial cells (Hwang et al., 2009). Any of these effects could have therapeutic effects. Indeed, the effects of implanting stem cells genetically programmed to release neurotrophins or to develop into glial cells are currently under investigation (see Aron & Klein, 2010; Trounson et al., 2011). Perhaps implants that include a variety of cells will prove to be most effective.

Promoting Recovery from CNS Damage by Rehabilitative Training

LO 10.22 Discuss methods of promoting recovery from CNS damage through rehabilitative treatment.

Several demonstrations of the important role of experience in the organization of the developing and adult brain kindled a renewed interest in the use of rehabilitative training to promote recovery from CNS damage. The following innovative rehabilitative training programs were derived from such findings. Perhaps neurotransplants would be more effective if accompanied by the appropriate training?

Neuroplasticity

Clinical Implications

TREATING STROKES. Small strokes produce a core of brain damage, which is often followed by a gradually expanding loss of neural function in the surrounding penumbra. Nudo and colleagues (1996) produced small *ischemic lesions* in the hand area of the motor cortex of monkeys. Then, 5 days later, a program of hand training and practice was initiated. During the ensuing 3 or 4 weeks, the monkeys plucked hundreds of tiny food pellets from food wells of different sizes. This practice substantially reduced the expansion of cortical damage into the surrounding penumbra. The monkeys that received the rehabilitative training also showed greater recovery in the use of their affected hand.

One of the principles that has emerged from the study of neurodevelopment is that neurons seem to be in a competitive situation: They compete with other neurons for synaptic sites and neurotrophins, and the losers die. Weiller and Rijntjes (1999) designed a rehabilitative program based on this principle. Their procedure, called *constraint-induced therapy* (see Kwakkel et al., 2015), was to tie down the functioning arm for 2 weeks while the affected arm received intensive training. Performance with the affected arm improved markedly over the 2 weeks, and there was an increase in the area of motor cortex controlling that arm.

TREATING SPINAL INJURY. In one approach to treating spinal injuries (see Wolpaw & Tennissen, 2001), patients who were incapable of walking were supported by a harness over a moving treadmill. With most of their weight supported and the treadmill providing feedback, the patients gradually learned to make walking movements. Then, as they improved, the amount of support was gradually reduced. In one study using this technique, more than 90 percent of the trained patients eventually became independent walkers compared with only 50 percent of those receiving conventional physiotherapy. The effectiveness of this treatment has been confirmed and extended in human patients (e.g., Herman et al., 2002) and in nonhuman subjects (Frigon & Rossignol, 2008).

BENEFITS OF COGNITIVE AND PHYSICAL EXERCISE. Individuals who are cognitively and physically active are less likely to contract neurological disorders; and if they do, their symptoms tend to be less severe and their recovery

Thinking Creatively

better (see Stranahan & Mattson, 2012; Voss et al., 2013). However, in such correlational studies, there are always problems of causal interpretation: Do more active individuals tend to have better neurological outcomes because they are more active, or do they tend to be more active because they are more healthy? Because of these problems of causal interpretation, research in this area has relied heavily on controlled experiments using animal models (see Fryer et al., 2011; Gitler, 2011).

Thinking Creatively — Someone tells you that physical activity protects one from the development of Alzheimer's disease. What would be your response to that person?

One experimental approach to studying the benefits of cognitive and physical activity has been to assess the neurological benefits of housing animals in enriched environments. **Enriched environments** are those designed to promote cog-

Evolutionary Perspective

nitive and physical activity—they typically involve group housing, toys, activity wheels, and changing stimulation (see Figure 10.21). The health-promoting effects of enriched environments have already been demonstrated in animal models of epilepsy, Huntington's disease, Alzheimer's disease, Parkinson's disease, Down syndrome, brain tumors, and various forms of stroke and traumatic brain injury (see Garofalo et al., 2015; Hannan, 2014; Mering & Jolkkonen, 2015). Although the mechanisms underlying the neurological benefits of enriched environments are unclear, there are many possibilities: Enriched environments have been shown to increase dendritic branching, the size and number of dendritic spines, the size of synapses, the rate of adult neurogenesis, and the levels of various neurotrophic factors.

Physical exercise in the form of daily wheel running has also been shown to have a variety of beneficial effects on the rodent brain (see Cotman, Berchtold, & Christie, 2007):

Figure 10.21 A rodent in an enriched laboratory environment.

increased adult neurogenesis in the hippocampus, reduced age-related declines in the number of neurons in the hippocampus, and improved performance on tests of memory and navigation (two abilities linked to the hippocampus). Also, Adlard and colleagues (2005) found that wheel running reduced the development of amyloid plaques in mice genetically predisposed to develop a model of Alzheimer's disease.

TREATING PHANTOM LIMBS. Most amputees continue to experience the limbs that have been amputated—a condition referred to as **phantom limb**. Even some individuals (20 percent) born with a missing limb report experiencing a phantom limb (see Melzack et al., 1997).

The most striking feature of phantom limbs is their reality. Their existence is so compelling that a patient may try to jump out of bed onto a nonexistent leg or to lift a cup with a nonexistent hand. In most cases, the amputated limb behaves like a normal limb; for example, as an amputee walks, a phantom arm seems to swing back and forth in perfect coordination with the intact arm. However, sometimes an amputee feels that the amputated limb is stuck in a peculiar position.

Watch this video on MyPsychLab
DRUMMING

About 50 percent of amputees experience severe chronic pain in their phantom limbs. A typical complaint is that an amputated hand is clenched so tightly that the fingernails are digging into the palm of the hand. Phantom limb pain can occasionally be treated by having the amputee concentrate on opening the amputated hand, but often surgical treatments are attempted. Based on the premise that phantom limb pain results from irritation at the stump, surgical efforts to control it have often involved cutting off the stump or various parts of the neural pathway between the stump and the cortex. Unfortunately, these treatments haven't worked (see Melzack, 1992).

Carlos and Philip experienced phantom limbs. Their neuropsychologist was the esteemed V. S. Ramachandran.

Cases of Carlos and Philip: Phantom Limbs and Ramachandran

Dr. Ramachandran read about the study of Pons and colleagues (1991), which you have already encountered in this chapter. In this study, severing the sensory neurons in the arms of monkeys led to a reorganization of somatosensory cortex: The area of the somatosensory cortex that originally received input from the damaged arm now received input from areas of the body normally

Clinical Implications

Thinking Creatively

Figure 10.22 The places on Carlos's body where touches elicited sensations in his phantom hand. (Based on Ramachandran & Blakeslee, 1998.)

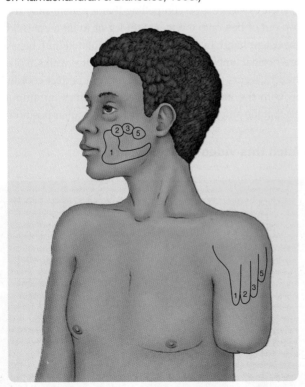

mapped onto adjacent areas of somatosensory cortex. Ramachandran was struck by a sudden insight: Perhaps phantom limbs were not in the stump at all, but in the brain; perhaps the perception of a phantom arm originated from parts of the body that now innervated the original arm area of the somatosensory cortex (see Ramachandran & Blakeslee, 1998).

Excited by his hypothesis, Dr. Ramachandran asked one of his patients, Carlos, if he would participate in a simple test. He touched various parts of Carlos's body and asked Carlos what he felt. Remarkably, when he touched the side of Carlos's face on the same side as his amputated arm, Carlos felt sensations from various parts of his phantom hand as well as his face. A second map of his hand was found on his shoulder (see Figure 10.22).

Neuroplasticity

Philip, another patient of Dr. Ramachandran, suffered from severe chronic pain in his phantom arm. For a decade, Philip's phantom arm had been frozen in an awkward position (Ramachandran & Rogers-Ramachandran, 2000), and Philip suffered great pain in his elbow.

Could Philip's pain be relieved by teaching him to move his phantom arm? Knowing how important feedback is in movement (see Chapter 8), Dr. Ramachandran constructed a special feedback apparatus for Philip. This was a box divided in two by a vertical mirror. Philip was instructed to put his good right hand into the box through a hole in the front and view it through a hole in the top. When he looked at his hand, he could see it and its mirror image. He was instructed to put his phantom limb in the box and try to position it, as best he could, so that it corresponded to the mirror image of his good hand. Then, he was instructed to make synchronous, bilaterally symmetrical movements of his arms—his actual right arm and his phantom left arm—while viewing his good arm and its mirror image. Ramachandran sent Philip home with the box and instructed him to use it frequently. Three weeks later, Philip's pain had subsided.

The Ironic Case of Professor P.: Recovery

If you remember the chapter-opening case study, I (JP) am sure you will appreciate why this chapter has special meaning for me. Writing it played a part in my recovery.

When I was released from the hospital, I had many problems related to my neurosurgery. I knew that I would have to live with hearing and balance problems because I no longer had a right auditory-vestibular nerve. My other problems concerned me more. The right side of my face sagged, and making facial expressions was difficult. My right eye was often painful—likely because of inadequate tearing. I had difficulty talking, and I experienced debilitating attacks of fatigue. Unfortunately, neither my neurosurgeon nor GP seemed to know how to deal with these problems, and I was pretty much left to fend for myself.

I used information that I had learned from writing this chapter. Little about recovery from brain damage had been

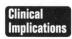

Thinking Creatively proven, but the results of experiments on animal models were suggestive. I like to think that the program I devised contributed to my current good health, but, of course, there is no way of knowing for sure.

I based my program of recovery on evidence that cognitive and physical exercise promotes recovery and other forms of neuroplasticity. My job constituted the cognitive part of my recovery program. Because I was influenced by recent evidence that the beneficial effects of exercise are greatest soon after the brain trauma, I returned to work 2 weeks after leaving the hospital.

Once back at work, I got more mental, oral, and facial exercise than I had anticipated. A few conversations were enough to make my throat and face ache and to totally exhaust me, at which point I would retreat to my office until I was fit to emerge once again for more "treatment."

Being a university professor is not physically demanding—perhaps you've noticed. I needed some physical exercise, but my balance problems limited my options. I turned to African hand drumming. I love the rhythms, and I found that learning and playing them could be a serious cognitive and physical challenge—particularly for somebody as enthusiastic and inept as I. So I began to practice, take lessons, and drum with my new friends at every opportunity. Gradually, I worked, talked, smiled, and drummed myself to recovery. Today, my face is reasonably symmetrical, my speech is good, I am fit, and my balance has improved.

Themes Revisited

This is the second chapter of the text to focus on neuroplasticity. It covered the neuroplastic changes associated

with neurological disease and brain damage and the efforts to maximize various neuroplastic changes to promote recovery.

Because this entire chapter dealt with clinical issues, the clinical implications tab made numerous appearances. In

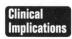

particular, it drew attention to the many cases in the chapter: the ironic case of Professor P.; Junior Seau, the all-star American football player; the cases of complex partial epilepsy; the cases of MPTP poisoning; and Carlos and Philip, the amputees with phantom limbs.

The chapter stressed creative thinking in several places. Attention was drawn to thinking about the need to identify the primary symptom of Alzheimer's disease,

about the applicability of animal models to humans, and about the correlation between

exercise and recovery of function after nervous system damage. Particularly interesting was the creative approach that Dr. Ramachandran took in treating Philip, who suffered from phantom limb pain.

The evolutionary perspective theme was also highlighted at several points. You were introduced to the concept of animal models, which is based on the comparative approach, and you learned that most of the research on neural regeneration and reorganization following brain damage has been done with animal models. Finally, you learned that research into the mechanisms of neural regeneration has been stimulated by the fact that this process occurs accurately in some species.

Key Terms

Causes of Brain Damage

Tumor (neoplasm), p. 268
Meningiomas, p. 268
Encapsulated tumors, p. 268
Benign tumors, p. 268
Infiltrating tumors, p. 269
Malignant tumors, p. 269
Gliomas, p. 269
Metastatic tumors, p. 269
Strokes, p. 269
Penumbra, p. 269
Cerebral hemorrhage, p. 270
Aneurysm, p. 270
Congenital, p. 270
Cerebral ischemia, p. 270
Thrombosis, p. 270

Embolism, p. 270
Arteriosclerosis, p. 270
Glutamate, p. 270
NMDA (N-methyl-D-aspartate) receptors, p. 270
Contusions, p. 271
Hematoma, p. 271
Contrecoup injuries, p. 271
Concussion, p. 271
Chronic traumatic encephalopathy, (CTE) p. 271
Dementia, p. 271
Encephalitis, p. 272
Meningitis, p. 272
General paresis, p. 272
Toxic psychosis, p. 273

Tardive dyskinesia (TD), p. 273
Down syndrome, p. 273
Apoptosis, p. 274

Neurological Diseases

Epilepsy, p. 274
Convulsions, p. 274
Epileptic auras, p. 274
Focal seizure, p. 275
Simple partial seizures, p. 275
Complex partial seizures, p. 275
Generalized seizures, p. 275
Tonic-clonic seizure, p. 276
Hypoxia, p. 276
Absence seizure, p. 276

Chapter 11
Learning, Memory, and Amnesia

How Your Brain Stores Information

 ## Chapter Overview and Learning Objectives (LOs)

Amnesic Effects of Bilateral Medial Temporal Lobectomy

LO 11.1 Describe the specific memory tests used to assess H.M.'s anterograde amnesia.

LO 11.2 Describe three major scientific contributions of H.M.'s case.

LO 11.3 Discuss what research on medial temporal lobe amnesias has taught us about learning and memory.

LO 11.4 Describe the difference between semantic and episodic memories.

LO 11.5 Describe the case of R.B. and the phenomenon known as transient global amnesia.

Learning and memory are two ways of thinking about the same thing: Both are neuroplastic processes; they deal with the ability of the brain to change its functioning in response to experience. **Learning** deals with how experience changes the brain, and **memory** deals with how these changes are stored and subsequently reactivated. Without the ability to learn and remember, we would experience every moment as if waking from a lifelong sleep—each person would be a stranger, each act a new challenge, and each word incomprehensible.

This chapter focuses on the roles played by various brain structures in the processes of learning and memory. Our knowledge of these roles has come to a great extent from the study of neuropsychological patients with brain-damage–produced **amnesia** (any pathological loss of memory) and from research on animal models of the same memory problems.

Amnesic Effects of Bilateral Medial Temporal Lobectomy

Ironically, the person who contributed more than any other to our understanding of the neuropsychology of memory was not a neuropsychologist. In fact, although he collaborated on dozens of studies of memory, he had no formal research training and not a single degree to his name. He was

Clinical Implications

H.M., a man who in 1953, at the age of 27, had the medial portions of his temporal lobes removed for the treatment of a severe case of epilepsy. Just as the Rosetta Stone provided archaeologists with important clues to the meaning of Egyptian hieroglyphics, H.M.'s memory deficits were instrumental in the achievement of our current understanding of the neural bases of memory (see Corkin, 2002).

Watch this video on MyPsychLab
WHEN MEMORY FAILS

The Case of H.M., the Man Who Changed the Study of Memory

During the 11 years preceding his surgery, H.M. suffered an average of one generalized seizure each week and many focal seizures each day, despite massive doses of anticonvulsant medication. Electroencephalography suggested that H.M.'s seizures arose from foci in the medial portions of

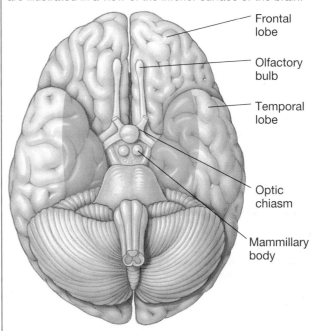

Figure 11.1 Medial temporal lobectomy. The portions of the medial temporal lobes removed from H.M.'s brain are illustrated in a view of the inferior surface of the brain.

- Frontal lobe
- Olfactory bulb
- Temporal lobe
- Optic chiasm
- Mammillary body

▓ Tissue typically excised in medial temporal lobectomy

both his left and right temporal lobes. Because the removal of one medial temporal lobe had proved to be an effective treatment for patients with a unilateral temporal lobe focus, the decision was made to perform a **bilateral medial temporal lobectomy**—the removal of the medial portions of both temporal lobes, including most of the **hippocampus**, **amygdala**, and adjacent cortex (see Figure 11.1). (A **lobectomy** is an operation in which a lobe, or a major part of one, is removed from the brain; a **lobotomy** is an operation in which a lobe, or a major part of one, is separated from the rest of the brain by a large cut but is not removed.)

In several respects, H.M.'s bilateral medial temporal lobectomy was an unqualified success. His generalized seizures were all but eliminated, and the incidence of partial seizures was reduced to one or two per day, even though the level of his anticonvulsant medication was substantially reduced. Furthermore, H.M. entered surgery a reasonably well-adjusted individual with normal perceptual and motor abilities and normal intelligence, and he left it in nearly the same condition. Indeed, H.M.'s IQ increased from 104 to 118 as a result of his surgery, presumably because of the decline in the incidence of his seizures. Be that as it may, H.M. was the last patient to receive a bilateral medial temporal lobectomy—because of its devastating amnesic effects.

In assessing the amnesic effects of brain surgery, it is usual to administer tests of the patient's ability to remember things learned before the surgery and tests of the patient's ability to remember things learned after the surgery. Deficits on the former tests lead to a diagnosis of **retrograde** (backward-acting) **amnesia**; those on the latter tests lead to a diagnosis of **anterograde** (forward-acting) **amnesia**. If a patient is found to have anterograde amnesia, the next step is usually to determine whether the difficulty in storing new memories influences **short-term memory** (storage of new information for brief periods of time while a person attends to it), **long-term memory** (storage of new information once the person stops attending to it), or both.

Like his intellectual abilities, H.M.'s memory for events predating his surgery remained largely intact. Although he had a mild retrograde amnesia for those events that occurred in the 2 years before his surgery, his memory for more remote events (e.g., for the events of his childhood) was reasonably normal.

H.M.'s short-term anterograde memory also remained normal: For example, his **digit span**, the classic test of short-term memory (see Chapter 5), was six digits (see Wickelgren, 1968)—this means that if a list of six digits was read to him, he could usually repeat the list correctly, but he would have difficulty repeating longer lists.

In contrast, H.M. had an almost total inability to form new long-term memories: Once he stopped thinking about a new experience, it was lost forever. In effect, H.M. became suspended in time on that day in 1953 when he regained his health but lost his future. His family moved shortly after his surgery, but he was never able to remember his new address or where commonly used items were kept in his new residence. He never learned to recognize people (e.g., doctors and nurses) who he did not meet until after his surgery, and he read the same magazines over and over without finding them familiar. If you met H.M. at a party he could chat quite normally until he was distracted (e.g., by the phone); then he would not remember you, the conversation, or where he was. It was as if he was continually regaining consciousness.

> In effect, H.M. became suspended in time on that day in 1953 when he regained his health but lost his future… It was as if he was continually regaining consciousness.

Formal Assessment of H.M.'s Anterograde Amnesia: Discovery of Unconscious Memories

LO 11.1 Describe the specific memory tests used to assess H.M.'s anterograde amnesia.

In order to characterize H.M.'s anterograde memory problems, researchers began by measuring his performance on objective tests of various kinds of memory. This subsection describes five tests that were used to assess H.M.'s long-term memory. The results of the first two tests documented H.M.'s severe deficits in long-term memory, whereas the results of the last three indicated that H.M.'s brain was capable of storing long-term memories but that H.M. had no conscious awareness of those memories. This finding changed the way biopsychologists think about the brain and memory.

DIGIT SPAN + 1 TEST. H.M.'s inability to form certain long-term memories was objectively illustrated by his performance on the *digit span + 1 test,* a classic test of verbal long-term memory. H.M. was asked to repeat 5 digits that were read to him at 1-second intervals. He repeated the sequence correctly. On the next trial, the same 5 digits were presented in the same sequence with 1 new digit added on the end. This same 6-digit sequence was presented a few times until he got it right, and then another digit was added to the end of it, and so on. After 25 trials, H.M. had not managed to repeat the 8-digit sequence. Most people can correctly repeat about 15 digits after 25 trials of the digit span + 1 test (see Drachman & Arbit, 1966).

BLOCK-TAPPING MEMORY-SPAN TEST. H.M. had **global amnesia**—amnesia for information presented in all sensory modalities. Milner (1971) demonstrated that H.M.'s amnesia was not restricted to verbal material by assessing his performance on the + 1 version of the *block-tapping memory-span test.* An array of 9 blocks was spread out on a board in front of H.M., and he was asked to watch the neuropsychologist touch a sequence of them and then to repeat the same sequence of touches. H.M. had a *block-tapping span* of 5 blocks, which is in the normal range; but he could not learn to correctly touch a sequence of 6 blocks, even when the same sequence was repeated 12 times.

MIRROR-DRAWING TEST. The first indication that H.M.'s anterograde amnesia did not involve all long-term memories came from the results of a *mirror-drawing test* (see Milner, 1965). H.M.'s task was to draw a line within the boundaries of a star-shaped target by watching his hand in a mirror. H.M. was asked to trace the star 10 times on each of 3 consecutive days, and the number of times he went outside the boundaries on each trial was recorded. As Figure 11.2 shows, H.M.'s performance improved over the 3 days, which indicates retention of the task. However, despite his improved performance, H.M. could not recall ever having completed the task before.

INCOMPLETE-PICTURES TEST. The discovery that H.M. was capable of forming long-term memories for mirror drawing suggested that sensorimotor tasks were the one exception to his inability to form long-term memories. However, this view was challenged by the demonstration that H.M. could also form new long-term memories for the **incomplete-pictures test** (see Gollin, 1960)—a nonsensorimotor

Figure 11.2 The learning and retention of the mirror-drawing task by H.M. Despite his good retention of the task, H.M. had no conscious recollection of having performed it before. (Based on Milner, 1965.)

test of memory that employs five sets of fragmented drawings. Each set contains drawings of the same 20 objects, but the sets differ in their degree of completeness: Set 1 contains the most fragmented drawings, and set 5 contains the complete drawings. The subject is asked to identify the 20 objects from the most fragmented set (set 1); then, those objects that go unrecognized are presented in their set 2 versions, and so on, until all 20 items have been identified. Figure 11.3 illustrates the performance of H.M. on this test and his improved performance 1 hour later (Milner et al., 1968). Despite his improved performance, H.M. could not recall previously performing the task.

PAVLOVIAN CONDITIONING. H.M. learned an eyeblink Pavlovian conditioning task, albeit at a retarded rate (Woodruff-Pak, 1993). A tone was sounded just before a puff of air was administered to his eye; these trials were repeated until the tone alone elicited an eye blink. Two years later,

H.M. retained this conditioned response almost perfectly, although he had no conscious recollection of the training.

Three Major Scientific Contributions of H.M.'s Case

LO 11.2 Describe three major scientific contributions of H.M.'s case.

H.M.'s case is a story of personal tragedy, but his contributions to the study of the neural basis of memory were immense. The following three contributions proved to be particularly influential.

First, by showing that the medial temporal lobes play an especially important role in memory, H.M.'s case challenged the then-prevalent view that memory functions are diffusely and equivalently distributed throughout the brain. In so doing, H.M.'s case renewed efforts to relate individual brain structures to specific *mnemonic* (memory-related) processes; in particular, H.M.'s case spawned a massive research effort aimed at clarifying the mnemonic functions of the hippocampus and other medial temporal lobe structures.

Second, the discovery that bilateral medial temporal lobectomy abolished H.M.'s ability to form certain kinds of long-term memories without disrupting his performance on tests of short-term memory or his **remote memory** (memory for experiences in the distant past) supported the theory that there are different modes of storage for short-term, long-term, and remote memory. H.M.'s specific problem appeared to be a difficulty in **memory consolidation** (the translation of short-term memories into long-term memories).

Third, H.M.'s case was the first to reveal that an amnesic patient might claim no recollection of a previous experience while demonstrating memory for it by improved performance (e.g., on the mirror-drawing and incomplete-pictures tests). This discovery led to the creation of two distinct categories of long-term memories: Conscious long-term memories became known as **explicit** memories (or *declarative memories*), and long-term memories demonstrated by improved test performance without conscious awareness became known as **implicit memories**. As you will soon learn, this distinction is of general relevance: Many people with amnesia lose their ability to form explicit memories while maintaining their ability to form implicit memories.

> **Clinical Implications** Using examples from your own experience, compare implicit and explicit memory.

H.M. died in 2008 of respiratory failure. His real name was Henry Molaison.

Figure 11.3 Two items from the incomplete-pictures test. H.M.'s memory for the 20 items on the test was indicated by his ability to recognize the more fragmented versions of them when he was retested. Nevertheless, he had no conscious awareness of having previously seen the items.

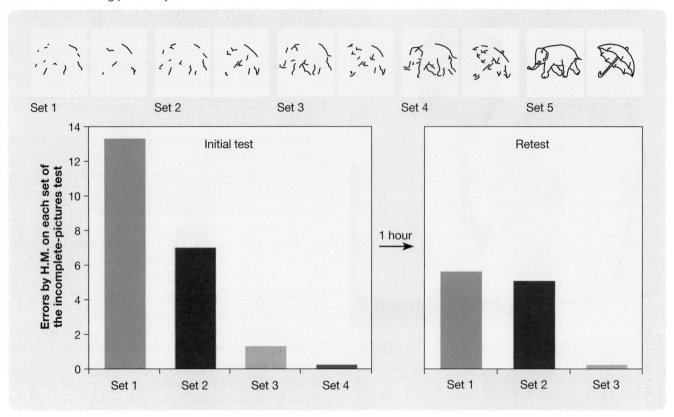

Medial Temporal Lobe Amnesia

LO 11.3 Discuss what research on medial temporal lobe amnesias has taught us about learning and memory.

Neuropsychological patients with a profile of mnemonic deficits similar to those of H.M., with preserved intellectual functioning, and with evidence of medial temporal lobe damage are said to suffer from **medial temporal lobe amnesia**.

Research on medial temporal lobe amnesia has shown that H.M.'s difficulty in forming explicit long-term memories while retaining the ability to form implicit long-term memories of the same experiences is not unique to him. This problem has proved to be a symptom of medial temporal lobe amnesia, as well as many other amnesic disorders. As a result, the assessment of implicit long-term memories now plays an important role in the study of human memory (see Reber, 2013).

Clinical Implications

Tests that assess implicit memory are called **repetition priming tests**. The incomplete-pictures test is an example, but repetition priming tests that involve memory for words are more common. First, the participants are asked to examine a list of words; they are not asked to learn or remember anything. Later, they are shown a series of fragments (e.g., _ O B _ _ E R) of words from the original list and are simply asked to complete them. Controls who have seen the original words perform well. Surprisingly, participants with amnesia often perform equally well, even though they have no explicit memory of seeing the original list. (By the way, the correct answer to the repetition priming example is "lobster.")

The discovery that there are two memory systems—explicit and implicit—raises an important question: Why do we have two parallel memory systems, one conscious (explicit) and one unconscious (implicit)? Presumably, the implicit system was the first to evolve because it is more simple (it does not involve consciousness), so the question is actually this: What is the advantage in having a second, conscious system?

Two experiments, one with amnesic patients (Reber, Knowlton, & Squire, 1996) and one with amnesic monkeys with medial temporal lobe lesions (Buckley & Gaffan, 1998), suggest that the answer is "flexibility." In both experiments, the amnesic subjects learned an implicit learning task as well as control subjects did; however, if they were asked to use their implicit knowledge in a different way or in a different context, they failed miserably. Presumably, the evolution of explicit memory systems provided for the flexible use of information.

Semantic and Episodic Memories

LO 11.4 Describe the difference between semantic and episodic memories.

H.M. was able to form very few new explicit memories. However, most people with medial temporal lobe amnesia display memory deficits that are less complete. The study of these amnesics has found that explicit memories fall into two categories and that many of these amnesics tend to have far greater difficulties with one category than the other.

Explicit long-term memories come in two varieties: semantic and episodic (see Squire et al., 2015). **Semantic memories** are explicit memories for general facts or information; **episodic memories** are explicit memories for the particular events (i.e., episodes) of one's life (see Rugg & Vilberg, 2013). People with medial temporal lobe amnesia have particular difficulty with episodic memories. In other words, they have difficulty remembering specific events from their lives, even though their memory for general information is often normal. Although they can't remember having lunch, going to a movie, chatting with a friend, or attending a lecture, they often remember what their friends are like, a movie they have seen, a language they learned, writing, world events, and the sorts of things learned at school.

Endel Tulving has been a major force in research on the semantic-episodic dichotomy (Tulving, 2002). Following is a description of Tulving's patient K.C. Episodic memory (also called *autobiographical memory*) has been likened to traveling back in time mentally and experiencing one's past.

The Case of K.C., the Man Who Can't Time Travel

K.C. had a motorcycle accident in 1981. He suffered diffuse brain damage, including damage to the medial temporal lobes. Despite severe amnesia, K.C.'s other cognitive abilities remain remarkably normal. His general intelligence and use of language are normal; he has no difficulty concentrating; he plays the organ, chess, and various card games; and his reasoning abilities are good. His knowledge of mathematics, history, science, geography, and other school subjects is good.

Similarly, K.C. has good retention of many of the facts of his early life. He knows his birth date, where he lived as a youth, where his parents' summer cottage was located, the names of schools he attended, the makes and colors of cars that he has owned.

Still, in the midst of these normal memories, K.C. has severe amnesia for personal experiences. He cannot recall a single personal event for more than a minute or two. This inability to recall any episodes (events) at which he was present covers his entire life. Despite these serious memory problems, K.C. has no difficulty having a conversation, and his memory problems are far less obvious to others than one would expect. Basically, he does quite well using his semantic memory.

K.C. understands time but cannot "time travel," into either the past or the future. He cannot imagine his future any better than he can recall his past: He can't imagine what he will be doing for the rest of the day, the week, or his life.

Vargha-Khadem and colleagues (1997) followed the maturation of three patients with medial temporal lobe amnesia who experienced bilateral medial temporal lobe damage early in life. Remarkably, although they could remember few of the experiences they had during their daily lives (episodic memory), they progressed through mainstream schools and acquired reasonable levels of language ability and factual knowledge (semantic memory). However, despite their academic success, their episodic memory did not improve (de Haan et al., 2006).

It is difficult to spot episodic memory deficits, even when the deficits are extreme. This occurs in part because neuropsychologists usually have no way of knowing the true events of a patient's life and in part because the patients become very effective at providing semantic answers to episodic questions. The following paraphrased exchange illustrates why neuropsychologists have difficulty spotting episodic memory problems.

The Case of the Clever Neuropsychologist: Spotting Episodic Memory Deficits

Neuropsychologist: I understand that you were a teacher.
Patient: That's right, I taught history.
Neuropsychologist: You must have given some good lectures in your time. Can you recall one of them that stands out?
Patient: Sure. I have given thousands of lectures. I especially liked Greek history.
Neuropsychologist: Was there any particular lecture that stood out—perhaps because it was very good or because something funny happened?
Patient: Oh, yes. Many stand out. My students liked my lectures—at least some of them—and sometimes I was quite funny.
Neuropsychologist: But is there one—just one—that you remember? And can you tell me something about it?
Patient: Oh yes, no problem. I didn't understand what you wanted. I can remember giving lectures and all my students were there watching and smiling.

Neuropsychologist: But can you describe a lecture where something happened that never happened in any other lecture? Perhaps something funny or disturbing.

Patient: That's hard.

Neuropsychologist: Before I go, I have some news for you that I think you will like. I understand that you are a hockey fan and follow the Toronto Maple Leafs.

Patient: Jeez, you guys know everything.

Neuropsychologist: Last night was a great night for Toronto. They beat New York 6–0. Do you think that you can remember that score for me? I will ask you about it a bit later.

Patient: That's great news. I will have no problem remembering that.

[Neuropsychologist leaves the room and returns an hour later.]

Neuropsychologist: I asked you to remember something the last time we chatted. Do you remember it?

Patient: I don't think so. I seem to have forgotten. It must have been a long time ago.

Neuropsychologist: That's strange. Do you remember anything specific about our last meeting, or even when it was?

Patient: Yes, we chatted for a time, I think about my memory.

Neuropsychologist: I understand that you are a Toronto Maple Leafs fan. Are they a good team?

Patient: Yes, they are very good. I used to go to every game with my father when I was a kid. They had great players; they were fast skaters and worked very hard. Did you know that they beat the New York Rangers 6–0? Now that's good.

Effects of Global Cerebral Ischemia on the Hippocampus and Memory

LO 11.5 Describe the case of R.B. and the phenomenon known as transient global amnesia.

Patients who have experienced **global cerebral ischemia**—that is, have experienced an interruption of blood supply to their entire brains—often suffer from medial temporal lobe amnesia. R.B. is one such individual (Zola-Morgan, Squire, & Amaral, 1986).

Clinical Implications

The Case of R.B., Product of a Bungled Operation

At the age of 52, R.B. underwent cardiac bypass surgery. The surgery was bungled, and, as a consequence, R.B. suffered brain damage. The pump that was circulating R.B.'s blood to his body while his heart was disconnected broke down, and it was several minutes before a replacement arrived from another

part of the hospital. R.B. lived, but the resulting ischemic brain damage left him amnesic.

Although R.B.'s amnesia was not as severe as H.M.'s, it was comparable in many aspects. R.B. died in 1983 of a heart attack, and a detailed postmortem examination of his brain was carried out with the permission of his family. Obvious brain damage was restricted largely to the **pyramidal cell layer** of just one part of the hippocampus—the **CA1 subfield** (see Figure 11.4).

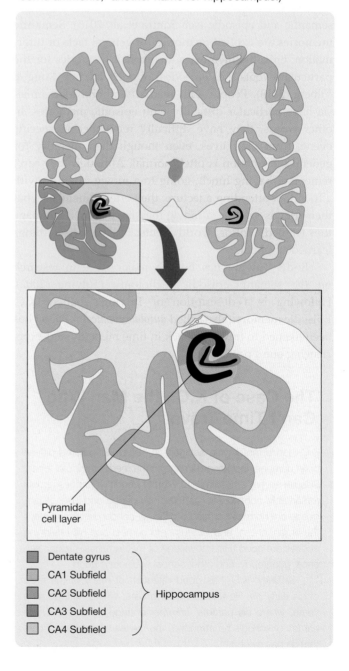

Figure 11.4 The major components of the hippocampus: CA1, CA2, CA3, and CA4 subfields and the dentate gyrus. R.B.'s brain damage appeared to be restricted largely to the pyramidal cell layer of the CA1 subfield. (*CA* stands for "cornu ammonis," another name for hippocampus.)

Pyramidal cell layer

Dentate gyrus
CA1 Subfield
CA2 Subfield } Hippocampus
CA3 Subfield
CA4 Subfield

R.B.'s case suggested that hippocampal damage by itself can produce medial temporal lobe amnesia. However, in such cases of cerebral ischemia, it is difficult to rule out the possibility of subtle damage to other areas of the brain.

Arguably, the strongest evidence that selective hippocampal damage can cause medial temporal lobe amnesia comes from cases of transient global amnesia. **Transient global amnesia** is defined by its sudden onset in the absence of any obvious cause in otherwise normal adults. As in other cases of medial temporal lobe amnesia, there is severe anterograde amnesia and moderate retrograde amnesia for explicit episodic memories (see Arena & Rabinstein, 2015; Bartsch & Butler, 2013). However, in the case of transient global amnesia, the amnesia is transient, typically lasting only 4 to 6 hours. Imagine the distress of the otherwise-healthy people who suddenly develop the symptoms of medial temporal lobe amnesia.

The sudden onset of transient global amnesia suggested it was caused by stroke; however, until recently no brain pathology could be linked to the disorder. But, in recent years, investigators have identified abnormalities to the CA1 subfield of the hippocampus (see Arena & Rabinstein, 2015; Bartsch & Butler, 2013). The time course of these abnormalities—they are not usually apparent for several hours after the beginning of the attack and have usually cleared up 10 days later—are suggestive of stroke-induced damage (see Hunter, 2011).

Amnesias of Korsakoff's Syndrome and Alzheimer's Disease

Amnesia of Korsakoff's Syndrome

LO 11.6 Describe the symptoms and etiology of the amnesia of Korsakoff's syndrome.

As you learned in Chapter 1, **Korsakoff's syndrome** is a disorder of memory common in people who have consumed large amounts of alcohol; the disorder is largely attributable to the brain damage associated with the thiamine deficiency that often accompanies heavy alcohol consumption. In its advanced stages, it is characterized by a variety of sensory and motor problems, extreme confusion, personality changes, and a risk of death from liver, gastrointestinal, or heart disorders. Postmortem examination typically reveals lesions to the *medial diencephalon* (the medial thalamus and the medial hypothalamus) and diffuse damage to several other brain structures, most notably the neocortex, hippocampus, and cerebellum (see Fama, Pitel, & Sullivan, 2012; Kril & Harper, 2012; Savage, Hall, & Resende, 2012).

The amnesia of Korsakoff's syndrome is similar to medial temporal lobe amnesia in some respects. For example, during the early stages of the disorder, anterograde amnesia for explicit episodic memories is the most prominent symptom. However, as the disorder progresses, retrograde amnesia, which can eventually extend back into childhood, also develops. Deficits in implicit memory depend on the particular test used, but in general they are less severe than those in explicit memory (see Oudman et al., 2011; Van Tilborg et al., 2011).

The gradual, insidious onset and progressive development of Korsakoff's syndrome complicate the study of the resulting retrograde amnesia. It is never entirely clear to what extent Korsakoff amnesia for recent events reflects the retrograde disruption of existing memories or the gradually increasing anterograde blockage of the formation of new ones.

Because the brain damage associated with Korsakoff's syndrome is diffuse, it has not been easy to identify which part of it is specifically responsible for the amnesia. The first hypothesis, which was based on several small postmortem studies, was that damage to the *mammillary bodies* of the hypothalamus was responsible for the memory deficits of Korsakoff patients; however, subsequent studies revealed cases of Korsakoff amnesia with no mammillary body damage. But in all of these exceptional cases, there was damage to another pair of medial diencephalic nuclei: the **mediodorsal nuclei** of the thalamus. However, it is unlikely that the memory deficits of Korsakoff patients are attributable to the damage of any single structure.

N.A. is a particularly well-known patient with **medial diencephalic amnesia** (amnesia, such as Korsakoff amnesia, associated with damage to the medial diencephalon). Although his memory deficits were conventional, their cause was not (Teuber, Milner, & Vaughan, 1968).

The Up-Your-Nose Case of N.A.

N.A. joined the U.S. Air Force after a year of college, serving as a radar technician until his accident. On the fateful day, N.A.'s roommate was playing with a fencing foil behind N.A.'s chair. N.A. turned unexpectedly and was stabbed up the right nostril. The foil punctured the *cribriform plate* (the thin bone around the base of the frontal lobes), taking an upward course into N.A.'s brain.

When tested a few weeks after his accident, N.A. was unable to recall any significant personal, national, or international events that had occurred in the 2 years preceding his accident. However, when retested 3 years later, his retrograde amnesia had decreased in duration, covering only those events that occurred in the 2 weeks before the accident.

The patient's recall of day-to-day events that occurred after the accident has been extremely poor. On initial testing, he could not remember what he ate for breakfast, people whom he had recently met, or visits from his family. However, unpredictably he would sometimes recall specific experiences of no particular significance. Although his ability to remember new experiences has improved somewhat since he was first tested, he has not been able to function well enough to gain employment.

An MRI of N.A.'s brain was taken in the late 1980s (Squire et al., 1989). It revealed extensive medial diencephalic damage, including damage to the mediodorsal nuclei and mammillary bodies.

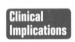
Clinical Implications How have case studies played an important role in the study of memory?

Amnesia of Alzheimer's Disease

LO 11.7 Describe the symptoms and etiology of the amnesia of Alzheimer's disease.

Alzheimer's disease is another major cause of amnesia. The first sign of Alzheimer's disease is often a mild deterioration of memory. However, the disorder is progressive: Eventually, *dementia* develops and becomes so severe that the patient is incapable of even simple activities (e.g., eating, speaking, recognizing a spouse, or bladder control). Alzheimer's disease is terminal.

Efforts to understand the neural basis of Alzheimer's amnesia have focused on *predementia Alzheimer's patients* (Alzheimer's patients who have yet to develop dementia). The memory deficits of these patients are more general than those associated with medial temporal lobe damage, medial diencephalic damage, or Korsakoff's syndrome. In addition to major anterograde and retrograde deficits in tests of explicit memory, predementia Alzheimer's patients often display deficits in short-term memory and in some types of implicit memory: Their implicit memory for verbal and perceptual material is often deficient, whereas their implicit memory for sensorimotor learning is not (see Postle, Corkin, & Growdon, 1996).

The level of acetylcholine is greatly reduced in the brains of Alzheimer's patients. This reduction results from the degeneration of the **basal forebrain** (a midline area located just above the hypothalamus; see Figure 11.17), which is the brain's main source of acetylcholine. This finding, coupled with the finding that strokes in the basal forebrain area can cause amnesia, led to the view that acetylcholine depletion is the cause of Alzheimer's amnesia.

Although acetylcholine depletion resulting from damage to the basal forebrain may contribute to Alzheimer's amnesia, it is clearly not the only factor. The brain damage associated with Alzheimer's disease is extremely diffuse (see Figure 10.14), involving many areas including the medial temporal lobes and the prefrontal cortex, which play major roles in memory (see Braskie & Thompson, 2013).

Amnesia after Concussion: Evidence for Consolidation

Blows to the head that do not penetrate the skull but are severe enough to produce *concussion* (a temporary disturbance of consciousness produced by a nonpenetrating head injury) are the most common causes of amnesia. Amnesia following a nonpenetrating blow to the head is called **posttraumatic amnesia (PTA)**. **Clinical Implications**

Posttraumatic Amnesia

LO 11.8 Summarize the effects of a closed-head injury on memory.

The *coma* (pathological state of unconsciousness) following a severe blow to the head usually lasts a few seconds or minutes, but in severe cases it can last weeks. Once the patient regains consciousness, he or she experiences a period of confusion. Victims of concussion are typically not tested by a neuropsychologist until after the period of confusion—if they are tested at all. Testing usually reveals that the patient has permanent retrograde amnesia for the events that led up to the blow and permanent anterograde amnesia for many of the events that occurred during the subsequent period of confusion.

The anterograde memory deficits that follow a nonpenetrating head injury are often quite puzzling to the friends and relatives who have talked to the patient during the period of confusion—for example, during a hospital visit. The patient may seem reasonably lucid at the time, because short-term memory is normal, but later may have no recollection whatsoever of the conversation.

Figure 11.5 summarizes the effects of a closed-head injury on memory. Note that the duration of the period of confusion and anterograde amnesia is typically longer than that of the coma, which is typically longer than the period of retrograde amnesia. More severe blows to the head tend to produce longer comas, longer periods of confusion, and longer periods of amnesia. Not illustrated in Figure 11.5 are *islands of memory*—surviving memories for isolated events that occurred during periods for which other memories have been wiped out.

Figure 11.5 The retrograde amnesia and anterograde amnesia associated with a concussion-producing blow to the head.

1 A blow to the head produces coma.

2 When the victim regains consciousness, there is a period of confusion.

3 When the period of confusion ends, the victim has retrograde amnesia for events that occurred during the period just before the blow and anterograde amnesia for events that occurred during the period of confusion.

BLOW TO HEAD

| Normal Cognitive Function | Retro-grade Amnesia | Coma | Confusion and Anterograde Amnesia | Normal Cognitive Function |

TIME   TIME   TIME

Many studies have employed ECS to study the duration of consolidation. Some studies have been conducted on human patients receiving ECS for the treatment of depression; others have been conducted with laboratory animals. Since the 1950s, hundreds of studies have examined ECS-produced gradients of retrograde amnesia in order to estimate the duration of memory consolidation. Hebb's theory implies that memory consolidation is relatively brief, a few seconds or minutes, about as long as specific patterns of reverberatory neural activity could conceivably maintain a memory. However, many studies found evidence for much longer gradients.

Gradients of Retrograde Amnesia and Memory Consolidation

LO 11.9 Describe the classic view of memory consolidation and some of the evidence it rests upon. Contrast that view with the current view of memory consolidation.

Gradients of retrograde amnesia after concussion seem to provide evidence for *memory consolidation*. The fact that concussions preferentially disrupt recent memories suggests that the storage of older memories has been strengthened (i.e., consolidated).

The classic theory of memory consolidation is Hebb's theory. He argued that memories of experiences are stored in the short term by neural activity *reverberating* (circulating) in closed circuits. These reverberating patterns of neural activity are susceptible to disruption—for example, by a blow to the head—but eventually they induce structural changes in the involved synapses, which provide stable long-term storage.

Electroconvulsive shock seemed to provide a controlled method of studying memory consolidation. **Electroconvulsive shock (ECS)** is an intense, brief, diffuse, seizure-inducing current that is administered to the brain through large electrodes attached to the scalp. The rationale for using ECS to study memory consolidation was that by disrupting neural activity, ECS would erase from storage only those memories that had not yet been converted to structural synaptic changes; the length of the period of retrograde amnesia produced by an ECS would thus provide an estimate of the amount of time needed for memory consolidation.

Evolutionary Perspective From an evolutionary perspective, why do you think consolidation should take so much longer than Hebb had originally envisioned?

The classic study of Squire, Slater, and Chace (1975) is an example of a study that found a long gradient of ECS-produced retrograde amnesia. They measured the memory of a group of ECS-treated patients for television shows that had played for only one season in different years prior to their electroconvulsive therapy. They tested each patient twice on different forms of the test: once before they received a series of five electroconvulsive shocks and once after. The difference between the before- and after-scores served as an estimate of memory loss for the events of each year. Figure 11.6 illustrates that five electroconvulsive shocks disrupted the retention of television shows that had played in the 3 years prior to treatment but not those that had played earlier.

The current view of memory consolidation is that it continues for a very long time if not indefinitely (see Dudai, Karni, & Born, 2015; Dudai & Morris, 2013). In other words, the evidence indicates that lasting memories become more and more resistant to disruption throughout a person's life. Each time a memory is activated, it is updated and linked to additional memories (see Sandrini, Cohen, & Censor, 2015). These additional links increase the memory's resistance to disruption by cerebral trauma such as concussion or ECS.

HIPPOCAMPUS AND CONSOLIDATION. The case of H.M. provided evidence of memory consolidation, and it seemed to suggest that the hippocampus played a special role in it. To account for the fact that the bilateral

Figure 11.6 Demonstration of a long gradient of ECS-produced retrograde amnesia. A series of five electroconvulsive shocks produced retrograde amnesia for television shows that played for only one season in the 3 years before the shocks; however, the shocks did not produce amnesia for one-season shows that had played prior to that. (Based on Squire, Slater, & Chace, 1975.)

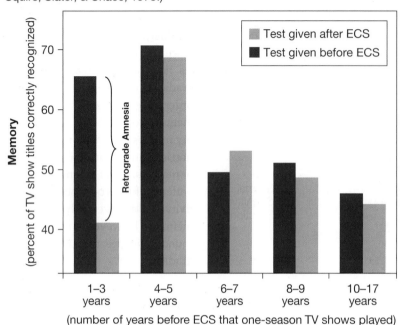

medial temporal lobectomy disrupted only those retrograde memories acquired in the few years before H.M.'s surgery, Scoville and Milner (1957) suggested that memories are temporarily stored in the hippocampus until they can be transferred to a more stable cortical storage system. This theory has become known as the **standard consolidation theory** or **dual-trace theory** (see Dudai, Karni, & Born 2015; Dudai & Morris, 2013).

Today, there are few adherents to standard consolidation theory. As you have just read, temporally graded retrograde amnesia is a feature of many forms of human amnesia (e.g., Alzheimer's amnesia, Korsakoff's amnesia); consequently, it seems unlikely that the hippocampus plays a special role in consolidation. It appears that when a conscious experience occurs, it is rapidly and sparsely encoded in a distributed fashion throughout the hippocampus and other involved structures. According to Nadel and Moscovitch, retained memories become progressively more resistant to disruption by hippocampal damage because each time a similar experience occurs or the original memory is recalled, a new **engram** (a change in the brain that stores a memory) is established and linked to the original engram, making the memory easier to recall and the original engram more difficult to disrupt.

RECONSOLIDATION. One theoretical construct that has recently attracted researchers' attention is **reconsolidation** (see Bonin & De Koninck, 2015). The hypothesis is that each time a memory is retrieved from long-term storage, it is temporarily held in *labile* (changeable or unstable) short-term memory, where it is once again susceptible to posttraumatic amnesia until it is reconsolidated.

Interest in the process of reconsolidation originated with several studies in the 1960s, but then faded until a key study by Nader, Schafe, and LeDoux (2000) rekindled it. These researchers infused the protein-synthesis inhibitor *anisomycin* into the amygdalae of rats shortly after the rats had been required to recall a fear-conditioning trial. The infusion produced retrograde amnesia for the fear conditioning, even though the original conditioning trial had occurred many days before. Most research on reconsolidation has involved fear conditioning, but some evidence suggests that it may be a general phenomenon in the nervous system (see Bonin & De Koninck, 2015).

Scan Your Brain

This chapter is about to move from discussion of human memory disorders to consideration of animal models of human memory disorders. Are you ready? Scan your brain to assess your knowledge of human memory disorders by filling in the blanks in the following sentences. The correct answers are provided at the end of the exercise. Before proceeding, review the material related to your errors and omissions.

1. _____ deals with how experiences changes the brain.
2. Any pathological loss to memory is called _____.
3. _____ deals with how changes are stored and subsequently reactivated.
4. H.M. learned an eye-blink _____ conditioning task.
5. _____ refers to translation of short-term memories into long-term memories.

6. Conscious long-term memories are called _____ memories.

7. Tests that assess implicit memory are called _____.

8. _____ memories are explicit memories for general facts or information.

9. _____ is defined by its sudden onset in the absence of any obvious cause in otherwise normal adults.

10. _____ is a disorder of memory common in people who have consume large amounts of alcohol.

11. Amnesia following a nonpenetrating blow to the head is called _____.

12. A _____ is a pathological state of unconsciousness.

13. _____ refer to surviving memories for isolated events that occurred during periods where other memories have been wiped out.

Scan Your Brain answers: (1) Learning, (2) amnesia, (3) Memory, (4) Pavlovian, (5) Memory consolidation, (6) explicit, (7) repetition priming tests, (8) Semantic, (9) Transient global amnesia, (10) Korsakoff's syndrome, (11) posttraumatic amnesia, (12) coma, (13) Islands of memory.

Evolving Perspective of the Role of the Hippocampus in Memory

As interesting and informative as the study of patients with amnesia can be, it has major limitations. Many important questions about the neural bases of amnesia can be answered only by controlled experiments. For example, in order to identify the particular structures of the brain that participate in various kinds of memory, it is necessary to make precise lesions in various structures and to control what and when the subjects learn and how and when their retention is tested. Because such experiments are not feasible with humans, a major effort has been made to develop animal models of human brain-damage–produced amnesia.

The first reports of H.M.'s case in the 1950s triggered a massive effort to develop an animal model of his disorder so that it could be subjected to experimental analysis. In its early years, this effort was a dismal failure; lesions of medial temporal lobe structures did not produce severe anterograde amnesia in rats, monkeys, or other nonhuman species.

In retrospect, there were two reasons for the initial difficulty in developing an animal model of medial temporal lobe amnesia. First, it was not initially apparent that H.M.'s anterograde amnesia did not extend to all kinds of long-term memory—that is, it was specific to explicit long-term memories—and most animal memory tests widely used in the 1950s and 1960s were tests of implicit memory (e.g., Pavlovian and operant conditioning). Second, it was incorrectly assumed that the amnesic effects of medial temporal lobe lesions were largely, if not entirely, attributable to hippocampal damage; and most efforts to develop animal models of medial temporal lobe amnesia thus focused on hippocampal lesions.

Evolutionary Perspective

Animal Models of Object-Recognition Amnesia: The Delayed Nonmatching-to-Sample Test

LO 11.10 Describe the delayed nonmatching-to-sample tests for monkeys and rats.

Finally, in the mid-1970s, more than two decades after the first reports of H.M.'s remarkable case, an animal model of his disorder was developed. It was hailed as a major breakthrough because it opened up the neuroanatomy of medial temporal lobe amnesia to experimental investigation.

Evolutionary Perspective

MONKEY VERSION OF THE DELAYED NON-MATCHING-TO-SAMPLE TEST. In separate laboratories, Gaffan (1974) and Mishkin and Delacour (1975) showed that monkeys with bilateral medial temporal lobectomies have major problems forming long-term memories for objects encountered in the **delayed nonmatching-to-sample test**. In this test, a monkey is presented with a distinctive object (the *sample object*), under which it finds food (e.g., a banana pellet). Then, after a delay, the monkey is presented with two test objects: the sample object and an unfamiliar object. The monkey must remember the sample object so that it can select the unfamiliar object to obtain food concealed beneath it. The correct performance of a trial is illustrated in Figure 11.7.

Intact, well-trained monkeys performed correctly on about 90 percent of delayed nonmatching-to-sample trials when the retention intervals were a few minutes or less. In contrast, monkeys with bilateral medial temporal lobe lesions had major object-recognition deficits (see Figure 11.8). These deficits modeled those of H.M. in key respects. For example, the monkeys' performance was normal at delays of a few seconds but fell off to near chance levels at delays of several minutes, and their performance was extremely susceptible to the disruptive effects of distraction (see Squire & Zola-Morgan, 1985). In fact, humans

Figure 11.7 Performance of a delayed nonmatching-to-sample trial.

1 The monkey moves the sample object to obtain food from the well beneath it.

2 A screen is lowered in front of the monkey during the delay period.

3 The monkey is confronted with the sample object and an unfamiliar object.

4 The monkey must remember the sample object and then select the unfamiliar object to obtain the food beneath it.

Figure 11.8 The performance deficits of monkeys with large bilateral medial temporal lobe lesions on the delayed nonmatching-to-sample test. There were significant deficits at all but the shortest retention interval. These deficits parallel the memory deficits of humans with medial temporal lobe amnesia on the same task. (Based on Squire & Zola-Morgan, 1991.)

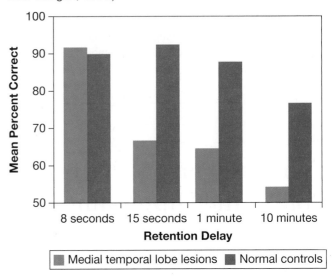

Watch this video on MyPsychLab

CHALK IT UP! THE DELAYED NONMATCHING-TO-SAMPLE TEST

The development of the delayed nonmatching-to-sample test for monkeys provided a means of testing the assumption that the amnesia resulting from medial temporal lobe damage is entirely the consequence of hippocampal damage—Figure 11.9 illustrates the locations in the monkey brain of three major temporal lobe structures: hippocampus, amygdala, and adjacent **medial temporal cortex**. But before we consider this important line of research, we need to look at another important methodological development: the rat version of the delayed nonmatching-to-sample test.

RAT VERSION OF THE DELAYED NON-MATCHING-TO-SAMPLE TEST. In order to understand why the development of the rat version of the delayed

with medial temporal lobe amnesia have been tested on the delayed nonmatching-to-sample test—their rewards were coins rather than banana slices—and their performance mirrored that of monkeys with similar brain damage.

Figure 11.9 The three major structures of the medial temporal lobe, illustrated in the monkey brain: the hippocampus, the amygdala, and the medial temporal cortex.

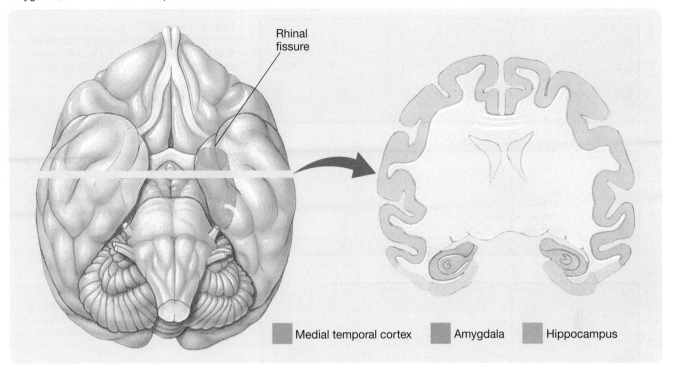

Rhinal fissure

Medial temporal cortex   Amygdala   Hippocampus

nonmatching-to-sample test played an important role in assessing the specific role of hippocampal damage in medial temporal lobe amnesia, examine Figure 11.10, which illustrates the usual methods of making hippocampal lesions in monkeys and rats. Because of the size and location of the hippocampus, almost all studies of hippocampal lesions in monkeys have involved *aspiration* (suction) of large portions of the medial temporal cortex in addition to the hippocampus. However, in rats, the extraneous damage associated with aspiration lesions of the hippocampus is typically limited to a small area of parietal neocortex. Furthermore, the rat hippocampus is small enough that it can be lesioned electrolytically or with intracerebral neurotoxin injections—methods that produce less extraneous damage.

Evolutionary Perspective

The version of the delayed nonmatching-to-sample test for rats that most closely resembles that for monkeys was developed by David Mumby using an apparatus that has become known as the **Mumby box**. This rat version of the test is illustrated in Figure 11.11.

It was once assumed that rats could not perform a task as complex as that required

Figure 11.10 Aspiration lesions of the hippocampus in monkeys and rats. Because of differences in the size and location of the hippocampus (pink) in monkeys and in rats, hippocampectomy typically involves the removal of large amounts of medial temporal cortex (red) in monkeys, but not in rats.

In monkeys, the hippocampus is usually removed by aspiration via the inferior surface of the brain, thus destroying substantial amounts of adjacent medial temporal cortex.

In rats, aspiration of the hippocampus is usually performed via the dorsal surface of the brain, thus destroying small amounts of parietal neocortex.

Figure 11.11 The Mumby box and the rat version of the delayed nonmatching-to-sample test.

The sample object is placed over one food cup at one end. An object identical to the sample object and a novel object are placed over the two food cups at the other end.

Food cup

Sample

When the sliding door is raised, exposing the sample object, a trained food-deprived rat runs down to the sample object and pushes it aside. Then, a piece of food is deposited by a food-delivery mechanism into the exposed food cup.

Food

The sample object is immediately removed by the experimenter, and the rat remains at the same end of the Mumby box until the prescribed delay period is over (e.g., 1 minute).

Then, the other sliding door is raised to expose the two objects at the other end. Trained rats, remembering their previous encounter with the sample object run to the novel object and push it aside; and food is delivered to the exposed food cup. The sliding door at the other end is lowered behind the rat.

The rat then runs to the center of the Mumby box, and the sliding door is closed behind it. Then, new objects are arranged for the next trial. One advantage of the Mumby box is that the rats do not have to be handled either during or between trials.

for the delayed nonmatching-to-sample test; Figure 11.12 indicates otherwise. Rats perform almost as well as monkeys with delays of up to 1 minute (Mumby, Pinel, & Wood, 1989).

The validity of the rat version of the delayed nonmatching-to-sample test has been established by studies of the effects of medial temporal lobe lesions. As in humans and monkeys, bilateral lesions of the rats' hippocampus, amygdala, and medial temporal cortex combined produce major deficits at all but the shortest retention intervals (Mumby, Wood, & Pinel, 1992).

Neuroanatomical Basis of the Object-Recognition Deficits Resulting from Bilateral Medial Temporal Lobectomy

LO 11.11 Describe the neuroanatomical basis for the object-recognition deficits that result from bilateral medial temporal lobectomy.

To what extent are the object-recognition deficits following bilateral medial temporal lobectomy a consequence of hippocampal damage? In **Evolutionary Perspective**

Figure 11.12 A comparison of the performance of intact monkeys (Zola-Morgan, Squire, & Mishkin, 1982) and intact rats (Mumby, Pinel, & Wood, 1989) on the delayed nonmatching-to-sample test.

the early 1990s, researchers began assessing the relative effects of lesions to various medial temporal lobe structures on performance in the delayed nonmatching-to-sample test, in both monkeys and rats. Challenges to the view that hippocampal damage is the critical factor in medial temporal amnesia quickly accumulated. Most reviewers of this research (see Bussey & Saksida, 2005;

Duva, Kornecook, & Pinel, 2000; Mumby, 2001) reached similar conclusions: Bilateral surgical removal of the medial temporal cortex consistently produces severe and permanent deficits in performance on the delayed nonmatching-to-sample test and other tests of object recognition. In contrast, bilateral surgical removal of the hippocampus produces only modest deficits, and bilateral destruction of the amygdala produces none. Figure 11.13 compares the effects of medial temporal cortex lesions and hippocampus-plus-amygdala lesions on object recognition memory in rats.

The reports that object-recognition memory is severely disrupted by medial temporal cortex lesions but only moderately by hippocampal lesions led to a resurgence of interest in the case of R.B. and others like it. Earlier in this chapter, you learned that R.B. was left amnesic following an ischemic accident that occurred during heart surgery and that subsequent analysis of his brain revealed that obvious cell loss was restricted largely to the pyramidal cell layer of his CA1 hippocampal subfield (see Figure 11.4). This result

Figure 11.13 Effects of medial temporal cortex lesions and hippocampus-plus-amygdala lesions in rats. Lesions of the medial temporal cortex, but not of the hippocampus and amygdala combined, produced severe deficits in performance of the delayed nonmatching-to-sample test in rats. (Based on Mumby & Pinel, 1994; Mumby, Wood, & Pinel, 1992.)

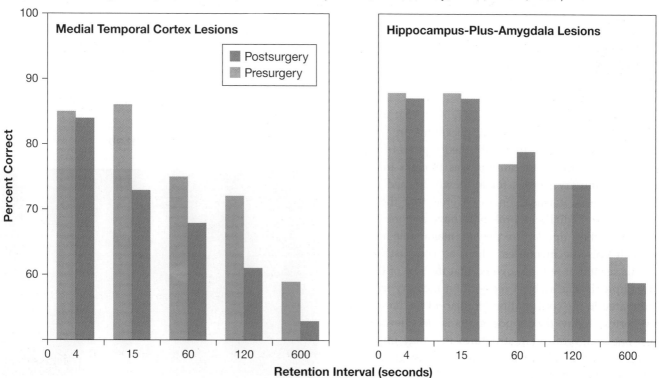

has been replicated in both monkeys (Zola-Morgan et al., 1992) and rats (Wood et al., 1993). In both monkeys and rats, global cerebral ischemia leads to a loss of CA1 hippocampal pyramidal cells and severe deficits in performance on the delayed nonmatching-to-sample test.

The relation between ischemia-produced hippocampal damage and object-recognition deficits in humans, monkeys, and rats seems to provide strong support for the theory that the hippocampus plays a key role in object-recognition memory. However, there is a gnawing problem with this conclusion: How can ischemia-produced lesions to one small part of the hippocampus be associated with severe deficits in performance on the delayed nonmatch-

Thinking Creatively ing-to-sample test when the deficits associated with total removal of the hippocampus are only modest? This line of evidence suggests that damage to brain structures other than the hippocampus contributes to the amnesia observed in patients following global cerebral ischemia (see Mumby et al., 1996). Indeed, although the most obvious damage following cerebral ischemia is in the CA1 subfield of the hippocampus, there is substantial damage to other areas that is more diffuse and thus more difficult to quantify (see Katsumata et al., 2006; van Groen et al., 2005). Allen and colleagues (2006) found that ischemic patients with a greatly reduced hippocampal volume were much more likely to suffer from anterograde amnesia; however, these same patients also tended to have extensive neocortical damage.

Thinking Creatively Before proceeding further, explain why ischemia-produced lesions to one small part of the hippocampus are associated with severe deficits in performance on the delayed nonmatching-to-sample test when the deficits associated with total removal of the hippocampus are only modest.

So far in this chapter, you have seen that our perspective of the role of the hippocampus in memory has changed since the first published reports of H.M.'s case. Initially, the hippocampus was thought to be the site of temporary storage for all newly formed memories. However, it was soon discovered that the structures of the medial temporal lobes have a more specific function—they appear to play a major role only in explicit episodic memories. Then, as you just learned in this section, it was discovered that the role of the hippocampus in one's object-recognition memory is minor compared to the contribution of adjacent medial temporal cortex. Today, the hippocampus is considered to be just one of several brain structures that play important roles in memory. The next module considers its particular mnemonic function.

Neurons of the Medial Temporal Lobes and Memory

Although the first suggestion that the medial temporal lobes play a major role in memory came from the study of the effects of damage to that area, the study of the responses of medial temporal lobe neurons have also been enlightening. The first major studies of the responses of medial temporal lobe neurons focused on the study of hippocampal neurons in rats. This research was stimulated by the finding that bilateral lesions of the hippocampus invariably disrupt the performance of tasks that involve memory for spatial location. For example, hippocampal lesions disrupt performance on the Morris water maze test and the radial arm maze test.

MORRIS WATER MAZE TEST.   In the **Morris water maze test**, intact rats placed at various locations in a circular pool of murky water rapidly learn to swim to a stationary platform hidden just below the surface. Rats with hippocampal lesions learn this simple task with great difficulty.

RADIAL ARM MAZE TEST.   In the **radial arm maze test**, several (e.g., eight) arms radiate out from a central starting chamber, and the same few arms are baited with food each day. Intact rats readily learn to visit only those arms that contain food and do not visit the same arm more than once each day. The ability to visit only the baited arms of the radial arm maze is a measure of **reference memory** (memory for the general principles and skills that are required to perform a task), and the ability to refrain from visiting an arm more than once in a given day is a measure of **working memory** (temporary memory that is necessary for the successful performance of a task on which one is currently working). Rats with hippocampal lesions display major deficits on both the reference memory and the working memory measures of radial arm maze performance.

Watch this video on MyPsychLab
WHAT IS WORKING MEMORY?

Hippocampal Place Cells and Entorhinal Grid Cells

LO 11.12 Describe hippocampal place cells and entorhinal grid cells and the relationship between these two cell types.

Consistent with the view that the hippocampus plays a role in spatial processing is the fact that many hippocampal neurons are **place cells** (see Moser & Moser, 2016; Rich, Liaw, & Lee, 2014; Wills & Cacucci, 2014)—neurons that respond only when a subject is in specific locations (i.e., in the *place fields* of the neurons). For example, when a rat is first placed in an unfamiliar test environment, none of its hippocampal neurons have a place field in that environment; then, as the rat familiarizes itself with the environment, many hippocampal neurons acquire a place field in it (see Silva, Feng, & Foster, 2015)—that is, each fires only when the rat is in a particular part of the test environment. Each place cell has a place field in a different part of the environment. Place cells have been identified in a variety of species (see Moser et al., 2014)—including human patients (Miller et al., 2013).

By placing a rat in an ambiguous situation in a familiar test environment, it is possible to determine where the rat thinks it is from the route that it takes to get to the location in the environment where it has previously been rewarded. Using this strategy, researchers (see Kubie et al., 2007) have shown that the firing of a rat's place cells indicates where the rat "thinks" it is in the test environment, not necessarily where it actually is.

One line of research on hippocampal place cells has focused on the **entorhinal cortex** (an area of the medial temporal cortex that is a major source of neural signals to the hippocampus)—see Figure 11.15. A possible answer to the question of how hippocampal place cells obtain their spatial information came from the discovery of so-called grid cells in the entorhinal cortex. **Grid cells** are entorhinal neurons that each have an extensive array of evenly spaced place fields, producing a pattern reminiscent of graph paper (see Moser & Moser, 2013; Rowland & Moser, 2014; Underwood, 2014). The distance between the evenly spaced place fields is flexible; in experimental animals kept in smaller or oddly shaped environments, the fields are closer together or sheared, respectively (see Krupic et al., 2015; Stensola et al., 2015). The even spacing of the place fields in the grid cells could enable spatial computations in hippocampal place cells. Grid cells have also been identified in other species including human patients (see Jacobs et al., 2013; Whalley, 2013). Other types of neurons in the entorhinal cortex are associated with spatial location: For example, *head-direction cells* are tuned to the direction of head orientation, and *border cells* fire when the subject is near the borders of its immediate environment (see Rowland & Moser, 2015; Sanders et al., 2015; Winter, Clark, & Taube, 2015).

The nature of the relationship between entorhinal grid cells and hippocampal place cells is still a matter of ongoing debate (see Sanders et al., 2015). Two lines of evidence suggested that the responses of hippocampal place cells depend on input from entorhinal grid cells (but see Bush, Barry, & Burgess, 2014). First, there is a major pathway from the entorhinal cortex to the hippocampus. Second, entorhinal grid cells respond relatively reflexively to location, whereas hippocampal place cells respond to place in combination with other features of the test environment (see Poucet & Save, 2005; Wills et al., 2005). However, the discovery that the properties of hippocampal place cells emerge in developing rat pups prior to the emergence of stable entorhinal grid cell firing challenges the idea that input from entorhinal grid cells is essential for hippocampal place cell function (see Derdikman & Moser, 2010; Langston et al., 2010; Wills & Cacucci, 2014). Moreover, there is evidence that place cells can still function after entorhinal grid cells have been eliminated (see Sanders et al., 2015).

Watch this video on MyPsychLab

TYPES AND PROCESSES OF MEMORY

Comparative Studies of the Hippocampus and Spatial Memory

LO 11.13 Describe the role of the hippocampus in spatial memory and the other types of memory it supports.

Although much of the evidence that the hippocampus plays a role in spatial memory comes from research on rats, the hippocampus seems to perform a similar function in other species (see Barry & Doeller, 2013; Heys et al., 2013; Yartsev & Ulanovsky, 2013). Particularly noteworthy has been the research on food-caching birds (see Figure 11.14). Food-caching birds **Evolutionary Perspective** must have remarkable spatial memories because, in order to survive, they must remember the locations of hundreds of food caches scattered around their territories. In one study, Sherry and Vaccarino (1989) found that food-caching

Figure 11.14 A nuthatch caching food in a tree stump.

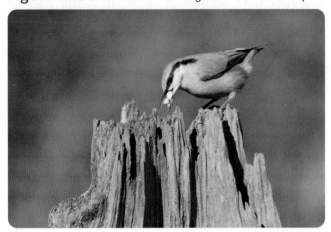

Figure 11.15 Areas of human medial temporal cortex. These areas are largely hidden from view in the lateral fissure.

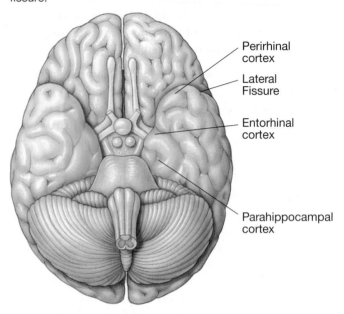

Perirhinal cortex

Lateral Fissure

Entorhinal cortex

Parahippocampal cortex

species tended to have larger hippocampuses than related nonfood-caching species.

Although research on a variety of species indicates that the hippocampus does play a role in spatial memory, the effects of hippocampal damage on the performance of spatial memory tasks in humans and other primates have been less consistent (e.g., Henke et al., 1999; Kessels et al., 2001; Maguire et al., 1998). One problem may be that spatial memory in humans and monkeys is often tested while they remain stationary and make judgments of locations on computer screens, whereas spatial memory in rats, mice, and birds is typically studied as they navigate through test environments (see Aghajan et al., 2015; Eichenbaum & Cohen, 2014; Nitz, 2015).

Recently, the hippocampus has been implicated in several forms of memory other than spatial memory. For example, certain cells in the hippocampus have recently been shown to code for the temporal aspects of an experience—so-called "time cells" (see Eichenbaum, 2014; Giacomo, 2015; Navratilova & Battaglia, 2015). Moreover, the hippocampus has been shown to play a role in learning about social organization ("social space") in humans (see Eichenbaum, 2015; Tavares et al., 2015) and in mice (see Hitti & Siegelbaum, 2014). And, as you will learn in the next section, cells in the hippocampus and its surrounding structures have been shown to play a role in the coding of concepts.

Jennifer Aniston Neurons: Concept Cells

LO 11.14 **Define a concept cell, and describe the key properties of concept cells with reference to the experimental evidence.**

Recording electrodes are sometimes implanted in the brains of patients with severe epilepsy, usually as a precursor to surgery. This provides an opportunity to record the activity of particular neurons in patients as they perform various tasks. Many of these electrodes are implanted in the structures of the medial temporal lobes because they are particularly susceptible to epileptic discharges.

As you have previously learned, the major structures of the medial temporal lobes are the hippocampus, amygdala, and medial temporal cortex. The medial temporal cortex (illustrated in Figure 11.15) is composed of entorhinal, perirhinal, and parahippocampal cortices.

In one of the first neurons to be studied in this way, the neuron fired in response to images of the actress Jennifer Aniston, but not to 80 other images (see Quiroga, 2012). Other medial temporal lobe neurons were discovered that responded to other individuals known to the patients (e.g., relatives, friends, or celebrities) or to known objects, but because the first neuron responded to Jennifer Aniston, they have all been termed **Jennifer Aniston neurons**.

Jennifer Aniston neurons are highly selective. Each neuron responded to only a small number of test objects or individuals—often only one could be found. Also, their responses are highly invariant: If a neuron responded to a particular object on test 1, it tended to respond to that object on all subsequent tests. The Jennifer Aniston cells of the hippocampus were more selective and more invariant than those of the other medial temporal lobe structures (i.e., parahippocampal cortex, perirhinal cortex, entorhinal cortex, and amygdala).

Without question, the most remarkable feature of Jennifer Aniston neurons is that they respond to ideas or concepts rather than to particulars, which is why they are also known as **concept cells** (see Quiroga, Fried, & Koch, 2013). For example, a Halle Berry neuron responded to all photos of the actress (even when she was dressed in her Cat Woman costume), to her printed name, and to the sound of her name. In one case, a neuron that invariably responded to the Sidney Opera House responded to photos of the Bahai temple in India. When questioned about it later, the patient said she thought the Bahai temple photos were photos of the Sidney Opera House. Similarly, when participants are given ambiguous human faces (faces that are the average of two well-known faces, such as Whoopi Goldberg and Bob Marley), these concept cells respond only when the viewer perceives the concept to which the cells are attuned to—for example, only when the viewer perceives Whoopi Goldberg, as opposed to Bob Marley (see Quiroga et al., 2014; Reddy & Thorpe, 2014).

Interestingly, when Jennifer Aniston neurons (concept cells) have been found to respond to more than one concept, there is usually an obvious relation between them. For example, on a second day of testing, it was discovered that the first Jennifer Aniston cell also responded to Lisa Kudrow, Jennifer Aniston's costar in the television series *Friends*. Another neuron responded to both Luke Skywalker and Yoda, both characters from the movie series *Star Wars*. Accordingly, it has been suggested that images trigger activity in circuits of concept cells in the medial temporal lobes (see Quiroga, 2012).

Figure 11.16 If researchers identified a "Harry Potter neuron" in a patient's brain, what other stimuli might it fire in response to?

Although it is not yet clear how Jennifer Aniston neurons contribute to the storage of memories, it is clear that they play a role, and their discovery is a major step forward.

Engram Cells

LO 11.15 Explain what an engram cell is, and describe how these cells were identified using optogenetics.

As you learned in Chapter 5, one new approach in the toolkit available to biopsychologists is *optogenetics*. If you recall, in optogenetics, neuroscientists insert an opsin gene into particular neurons, after which they can then use light to either hyperpolarize or depolarize those neurons. In recent years, this tool has been used extensively in studies of learning and memory in mice (see Goshen, 2014). One line of research has been particularly interesting because it can shed light on the location of the neurons that maintain an engram (**engram cells**)—see Josselyn, Köhler, and Frankland (2015).

The identification of an engram cell via optogenetics is typically a two-stage process. In the first stage, the *tagging stage*, the neurons that are active during the learning task are induced to express opsins while an animal engages in a particular learning task. In the second stage, the *manipulate stage*, the previously active neurons are now either inhibited or excited by using light to influence the activity of the opsin-tagged neurons (see Josselyn, Köhler, & Frankland, 2015; Redondo et al., 2014; Ryan et al., 2015; Takeuchi & Morris, 2014).

In essence, researchers are now able to observe, suppress, or activate engram cells in different parts of the nervous system. For example, researchers have been able to reverse depressive-like behavior in mice by optogenetically reactivating hippocampal dentate granule cells that had previously been active during the encoding of a positive experience (Ramirez et al., 2015). Moreover, researchers have shown that in transgenic mouse 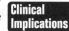 models of Alzheimer's disease, activating engram cells leads to the retrieval of memories that are otherwise inaccessible—suggesting that the memory deficits of Alzheimer's disease are retrieval deficits rather than encoding deficits (see Roy et al., 2016; Shrestha & Klann, 2016).

> **Clinical Implications** Do you think that optogenetics might have clinical implications for humans sometime in the future? If so, what do you think such interventions might look like?

Where Are Memories Stored?

As you learned in Chapter 1, modern biopsychology began in the mid-20th century. At that time, there was a major push to identify the areas in the brain where memories are stored. The search was largely championed by Karl Lashley, who wrote a famous review paper, *In Search of the Engram*, in which he described his fruitless efforts. Lashley and many who subsequently took up the search used the lesion method. If a particular structure were the storage site for all memories of a particular type, then destruction of that structure should eliminate all memories of that type that were acquired prior to the lesion. No brain structure has shown this result: Lesions of particular structures tend to produce either no retrograde amnesia at all or retrograde amnesia for only the experiences that occurred in the days or weeks just before the surgery. These findings have led to two major conclusions: (1) Memories are stored diffusely in the brain and thus can survive destruction of any single structure; and (2) memories become more resistant to disruption over time.

So far, this chapter has focused on four neural structures that appear to play some role in the storage of memories: (1) The hippocampus and (2) the medial temporal cortex have roles in episodic memory; and (3) the mediodorsal nucleus of the thalamus and (4) the basal forebrain have been implicated in the memory deficits of Korsakoff's and Alzheimer's diseases, respectively. In this module, we take a brief look at five other areas of the brain that have been implicated in memory: inferotemporal cortex, amygdala, prefrontal cortex, cerebellum, and striatum. See Figure 11.17.

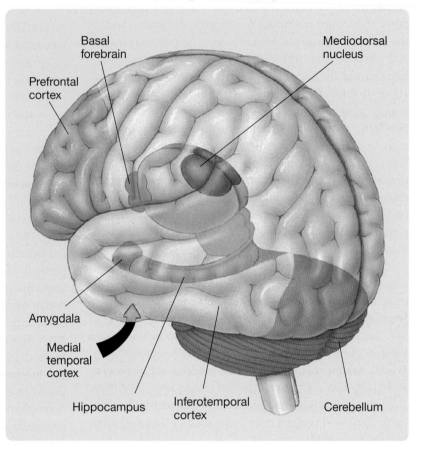

Figure 11.17 The structures of the brain that have been shown to play a role in memory. Because it would have blocked the view of other structures, the striatum is not included. (See Figure 3.27 on page 97.)

Watch this video on MyPsychLab

MEMORY: BRAIN REGIONS

Five Brain Areas Implicated in Memory

LO 11.16 List the types of memories that are stored in each of the following structures: inferotemporal cortex, amygdala, prefrontal cortex, cerebellum, and striatum.

INFEROTEMPORAL CORTEX. Numerous electrophysiological recording and functional brain-imaging studies of memory have led to the same important conclusion: Areas of the brain that are active during the retention of an experience tend to be the same ones active during the original experience. This has focused attention on the mnemonic functions of the sensory and motor areas of the brain. In particular, attention has focused on **inferotemporal cortex** (cortex of the inferior temporal cortex), which has complex visual functions—see Lehky and Tanaka (2016); Naya and Suzuki (2011); Suzuki (2010).

Bussey and Saksida (2005) have argued that the inferior temporal cortex, in concert with adjacent perirhinal cortex (see Suzuki & Naya, 2014), plays an important role in storing memories of visual input. In support of this view, Naya, Yoshida, and Miyashita (2001) recorded the responses of neurons in inferotemporal cortex and perirhinal cortex while monkeys learned the relation between the two items in pairs of visual images. When a pair was presented, responses were first recorded in inferotemporal neurons and then in perirhinal neurons; however, when the monkeys were required to recall that pair, activity was recorded in perirhinal neurons before inferotemporal neurons. Naya and colleagues concluded that this reversed pattern of activity reflected the retrieval of visual memories from inferotemporal cortex.

AMYGDALA. The amygdala is thought to play a special role in memory for the emotional significance of experiences (see Herry & Johansen, 2014; Paz & Pare, 2013). Rats with amygdalar lesions, unlike intact rats, do not respond with fear to a neutral stimulus that has previously been followed by electric foot shock (see Maren, 2015; Nader, 2015). Also, Bechara and colleagues (1995) reported the case of a neuro-psychological patient with bilateral damage to the amyg-

dala who could not acquire conditioned autonomic startle responses to various visual or auditory stimuli but had good explicit memory for the training. However, there is little evidence that the amygdala stores memories; it appears to be involved in strengthening emotionally significant memories stored in other structures (Do-Monte, Quiñones-Laracuente, & Quirk, 2015; Likhtik & Paz, 2015). The amygdala might be the reason why emotion-provoking events are remembered better than neutral events (see Dunsmoor et al., 2015; McGaugh, 2015; Yonelinas & Ritchey, 2015).

PREFRONTAL CORTEX. Patients with damage to the **prefrontal cortex** (the area of frontal cortex anterior to motor cortex) are not grossly amnesic; they often display no deficits at all on conventional tests of memory. This lack of reliable memory deficits in patients with prefrontal damage may in part result from the fact that different parts of the prefrontal cortex play different roles in memory, and that patients with damage to different areas of prefrontal cortex are often combined for analysis.

Be that as it may, two episodic memory abilities are often lost by patients with large prefrontal lesions. Patients with large prefrontal lesions often display both anterograde and retrograde deficits in memory for the temporal order of events, even when they can remember the events themselves. They also display deficits in *working memory* (the ability to

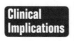

maintain relevant memories while a task is being completed)—see D'Esposito and Postle (2015); Ma, Husain, and Bays (2014). As a result of these two deficits, patients with prefrontal cortex damage often have difficulty performing tasks that involve a series of responses (see Colvin, Dunbar, & Grafman, 2001).

 The study of the anatomy of memory has come a long way since H.M.'s misfortune. What kind of advances do you think will be made in the next decade?

The prefrontal cortex is a large structure that is composed of many anatomically distinct areas that have different connections and, presumably, different functions. Functional brain-imaging studies are finding that specific complex patterns of prefrontal activity are associated with various memory functions. Some regions of prefrontal

The Case of the Cook Who Couldn't

The story of one patient with prefrontal cortex damage is very well known because she was the sister of Wilder Penfield, the famous Montreal neurosurgeon (Penfield & Evans, 1935). Before her brain damage, she had been an excellent cook; and afterward, she still remembered her favorite recipes and how to perform each individual cooking technique. However, she was incapable of preparing even simple meals because she could not carry out the various steps in proper sequence.

cortex seem to perform fundamental cognitive processes (e.g., attention and task management) during working memory tasks, and other regions of prefrontal cortex participate in other memory processes (e.g., Lehky & Tanaka, 2016; Morici, Bekinschtein, & Weisstaub, 2015).

CEREBELLUM AND STRIATUM. Just as explicit memories of experiences are presumed to be stored in the circuits of the brain that mediated their original perception, implicit memories of sensorimotor learning are presumed to be stored in sensorimotor circuits (see Graybiel & Grafton, 2015). Most research on the neural mechanisms of memory for sensorimotor tasks has focused on two structures: the cerebellum and the striatum.

The **cerebellum** is thought to participate in the storage of memories of learned sensorimotor skills through its various neuroplastic mechanisms (see Gao, van Beugen, & De Zeeuw, 2012). Its role in the Pavlovian conditioning of the eye-blink response of rabbits has been most intensively investigated (see Freeman, 2015). In this paradigm, a tone (conditional stimulus) is sounded just before a puff of air (unconditional stimulus) is delivered to the eye. After several trials, the tone comes to elicit an eye blink. The convergence of evidence from stimulation, recording, and lesion studies suggests that the effects of this conditioning are stored in the form of changes in the way that cerebellar neurons respond to the tone (see De Zeeuw & Ten Brinke, 2015; Freeman, 2015).

The **striatum** is thought to store memories for consistent relationships between stimuli and responses—the type of memories that develop incrementally over many trials (see Graybiel & Grafton, 2015). Sometimes this striatum-based form of learning is referred to as *habit formation* (see O'Tousa & Grahame, 2014).

Although few would disagree that the cerebellum and the striatum play a role in sensorimotor memory, there is growing evidence that these structures also play a role in certain types of memory with no obvious motor component (e.g., Maddox et al., 2005). For example, Knowlton, Mangels, and Squire (1996) found that the Parkinson's patients, who had striatal damage, could not solve a probabilistic discrimination problem. The problem was a computer "weather forecasting" game, and the task was to correctly predict the weather by pressing one of two keys, rain or shine. The patients based their predictions on stimulus cards presented on the screen—each card had a different probability of leading to sunshine, which the patients had to learn and remember. The Parkinson's patients

did not improve over 50 trials, although they displayed normal explicit (conscious) memory for the training episodes. In contrast, amnesic patients with medial temporal lobe or medial diencephalic damage displayed marked improvement in performance but had no explicit memory of their training.

Scan Your Brain

The preceding modules of this chapter have dealt with the gross neuroanatomy of memory—with the structures of the brain that are involved in various aspects. Before you proceed to the next module, which deals with the synaptic mechanisms of learning and memory, test your knowledge by writing the name of the relevant brain structure in each of the following blanks. The correct answers are provided at the end of the exercise. Before proceeding, review the material related to your errors and omissions.

1. The _____ is as an apparatus that is used in the rat version of the delayed non-matching-to-sample test.

2. A _____ is a maze in which several arms radiate out from a central starting chamber.

3. _____ refer to neurons that respond only when a subject is at specific locations.

4. _____ refers to the memory for the general principles and skills that are required to perform a task.

5. _____ are entorhinal cells that each have an extensive array of evenly spaced place fields.

6. The medial temporal cortex comprises the entorhinal, perirhinal, and _____ cortices.

7. _____ is a method that uses genetic engineering techniques to insert the opsin gene, or variants of the opsin gene, into particular types of neurons.

8. Identification of an engram cell is a two-stage process involving the _____ and manipulate stages.

9. Patients with large prefrontal lesions often display anterograde and _____ deficits in memory.

10. Regions of the prefrontal cortex perform fundamental _____ processes during working memory tasks.

Scan Your Brain answers: (1) Mumby box, (2) radial arm, (3) Place cells, (4) Reference memory, (5) Grid cells, (6) parahippocampal, (7) Optogenetics, (8) tagging, (9) retrograde, (10) cognitive.

Synaptic Mechanisms of Learning and Memory

So far, this chapter has focused on the particular structures of the human brain that are involved in learning and memory and on what happens when these structures are damaged. In this module, the level of analysis changes: The focus shifts to the neuroplastic mechanisms within these structures that are thought to be the fundamental bases of learning and memory.

Most modern thinking about the neural mechanisms of memory began with Hebb (1949). Hebb argued so convincingly that enduring changes in the efficiency of synaptic transmission were the basis of long-term memory that the search for the neural bases of learning and memory has focused almost exclusively on the synapse.

Long-Term Potentiation

LO 11.17 Describe the phenomenon known as long-term potentiation (LTP), and provide evidence for its role in learning and memory.

Because Hebb's hypothesis that enduring facilitations of synaptic transmission are the neural bases of learning

and memory was so influential, there was great excitement when such an effect was discovered. In 1973, Bliss and Lømo showed that there is a facilitation of synaptic transmission following high-frequency electrical stimulation applied to presynaptic neurons. This phenomenon has been termed **long-term potentiation (LTP)**.

LTP has been demonstrated in many species and in many parts of their brains, but it has been most frequently studied in the rodent hippocampus. Figure 11.18 illustrates three hippocampal synapses at which LTP has been commonly studied.

Evolutionary Perspective

Figure 11.19 illustrates LTP in the granule cell layer of the rat hippocampal dentate gyrus. First, a single low-intensity pulse of current was delivered to the perforant path (the major input to the dentate gyrus), and the response was recorded through an extracellular multiple-unit electrode in the granule cell layer of the hippocampal dentate gyrus; the purpose of this initial stimulation was to determine the initial response baseline. Second, high-intensity, high-frequency stimulation lasting 10 seconds was delivered to the perforant path to induce the LTP. Third, the granule cells' responses to single pulses of low-intensity current were measured again after various delays. Figure 11.19 shows that transmission at the

Figure 11.18 A slice of rat hippocampal tissue that illustrates the three synapses at which LTP is most commonly studied: (1) the dentate granule cell synapse, (2) the CA3 pyramidal cell synapse, and (3) the CA1 pyramidal cell synapse.

Cell bodies of pyramidal cells
Cell bodies of granule cells

CA1 subfield

CA3 subfield

Perforant path axon

Hippocampal dentate gyrus

granule cells' synapses was still potentiated 1 week after the high-frequency stimulation.

LTP is among the most widely studied neuroscientific phenomena. Why? The reason goes back to 1949 and Hebb's influential theory of memory. The synaptic changes that Hebb hypothesized as underlying long-term memory seemed to be the same kind of changes that underlie LTP (see Lisman, Grace, & Duzel, 2011).

LTP has two key properties that Hebb proposed as characteristics of the physiological mechanisms of learning and memory. First, LTP can last for a long time—for several months after multiple high-frequency stimulations (see Abraham, 2006). Second, LTP develops

only if the firing of the presynaptic neuron is followed by the firing of the postsynaptic neuron; it does not develop when the presynaptic neuron fires and the postsynaptic neuron does not, and it does not develop when the presynaptic neuron does not fire and the postsynaptic neuron does (see Bi & Poo, 2001; but see Gambino et al., 2014). The *co-occurrence* of firing in presynaptic and postsynaptic cells is now recognized as the critical factor in LTP, and the assumption that co-occurrence is a physiological necessity for learning and memory is often referred to as *Hebb's postulate for learning*.

Additional support for the idea that LTP is related to the neural mechanisms of learning and memory has come from several observations: (1) LTP can be elicited by low levels of stimulation that mimic normal neural activity; (2) LTP effects are most prominent in structures that have been implicated in learning and memory, such as the hippocampus; (3) learning can produce LTP-like changes in the hippocampus; (4) many drugs that influence learning and memory have parallel effects on LTP; (5) the induction of maximal LTP blocks the learning of a Morris water maze until the LTP has subsided; (6) mutant mice that display little hippocampal LTP have difficulty learning the Morris water maze; (7) behavioral changes that appear to be memories can be induced in mice via LTP (Nabavi et al., 2014); and (8) LTP occurs at specific synapses that have been shown to participate in learning and memory in simple invertebrate nervous systems. Still, it is important to keep in mind that all of this evidence is indirect and that LTP as induced in the laboratory by electrical stimulation is at best a caricature of the subtle cellular events that underlie learning and memory.

Conceiving of LTP as a three-part process, many researchers are investigating the mechanisms of *induction, maintenance,* and *expression*—that is, the processes by which high-frequency stimulations induce LTP (learning), the changes responsible for the maintenance of LTP

Figure 11.19 Long-term potentiation in the granule cell layer of the rat hippocampal dentate gyrus. (Traces courtesy of Michael Corcoran, Department of Psychology, University of Saskatchewan.)

A single pulse of stimulation was administered to the perforant path, and the baseline response was recorded by an extracellular electrode in the granule cell layer. Then, several trains of intense high-frequency stimulation were applied to the perforant path to induce the LTP.

A single pulse of stimulation was administered 1 day later and again 1 week later to assess the magnitude of and duration of the potentiation. One measure of LTP is the increased amplitude of the *population spike*, in this case, the spike created by the firing of a greater number of granule cells.

Watch this video on MyPsychLab

LTD AND LTP

(memory), and the changes that allow it to be expressed during the test (recall).

Induction of LTP: Learning

LO 11.18 Describe the mechanisms underlying the induction of LTP.

The NMDA (or N-methyl-D-aspartate) receptor is prominent at the synapses at which LTP is commonly studied. The **NMDA receptor** is a receptor for **glutamate**—the main excitatory neurotransmitter of the brain, as you learned in Chapter 4. An NMDA receptor does not respond maximally unless two events occur simultaneously: Glutamate must bind to it, and the postsynaptic neuron must already be partially depolarized. This dual requirement stems from the fact that the calcium channels associated with NMDA receptors allow only small numbers of calcium ions to enter the neuron unless the neuron is already depolarized when glutamate binds to the receptors; it is the influx of calcium ions that triggers the cascade of events in the postsynaptic neuron that induces LTP.

An important characteristic of the induction of LTP at glutaminergic synapses stems from the nature of the NMDA receptor and the requirement for co-occurrence of firing for LTP to occur. This characteristic is not obvious under the usual, but unnatural, experimental condition in which LTP is induced by high-intensity, high-frequency stimulation, which always activates the postsynaptic neurons through massive temporal and spatial summation. However, when a more natural, low-intensity stimulation is applied, the postsynaptic neurons do not fire, and thus LTP is not induced—unless the postsynaptic neurons are already partially depolarized so that their calcium channels open wide when glutamate binds to their NMDA receptors.

The requirement for the postsynaptic neurons to be partially depolarized when the glutamate binds to the NMDA receptors is an extremely important characteristic of conventional LTP because it permits neural networks to learn associations. Let us explain. If one glutaminergic neuron were to fire by itself and release its glutamate neurotransmitter across a synapse onto the NMDA receptors of a postsynaptic neuron, there would be no potentiation of transmission at that synapse because the postsynaptic cell would not fire. However, if the postsynaptic neuron were partially depolarized by input from other neurons when the presynaptic neuron fired, the binding of the glutamate to the NMDA receptors would open wide the calcium channels, calcium ions would flow into the postsynaptic neuron, and transmission across the synapses between the presynaptic and postsynaptic neuron would be potentiated. Accordingly, the requirement for co-occurrence and the dependence of NMDA receptors on simultaneous binding and partial depolarization mean that, under natural conditions, synaptic facilitation records the fact that there has been simultaneous activity in at least two converging inputs to the postsynaptic neuron—as would be produced, for example, by the "simultaneous" presentation of a conditional stimulus and an unconditional stimulus. Figure 11.20 summarizes the induction of NMDA-receptor–mediated LTP.

Figure 11.20 The induction of NMDA-receptor–mediated LTP.

1 If the postsynaptic neuron is not depolarized when glutamate binds to its receptors, the NMDA receptors permit the influx of only a few calcium ions, and no LTP is produced.

Calcium ion

Glutamate

NMDA receptor

Dendritic spine

Calcium channel

2 If the postsynaptic neuron is depolarized when glutamate binds to its receptors, the NMDA receptors permit the entry of many calcium ions, which induce LTP.

Watch this video on MyPsychLab

CHANGES TO NEURONS

Maintenance and Expression of LTP: Storage and Recall

LO 11.19 Describe four findings that have emerged from the study of the maintenance and expression phases of LTP.

The search for the mechanisms underlying the maintenance and expression of LTP began with attempts to determine whether these mechanisms occur in presynaptic or postsynaptic neurons. This question has been answered: The maintenance and expression of LTP involve changes in both presynaptic and postsynaptic neurons. This discovery indicated that the mechanisms underlying the maintenance and expression of LTP are complex. Indeed, after more than four decades of research, we still do not have satisfactory answers. However, the quest for the neural mechanisms of LTP maintenance and expression has contributed to several important discoveries. Here are three of them:

- Once it became apparent that LTP occurs only at specific synapses on a postsynaptic neuron, it was clear that there must be a mechanism for keeping the events at one set of synapses on a postsynaptic neuron from affecting other synapses on the same neuron. This specificity is due to the **dendritic spines**; the calcium ions that enter a dendritic spine do not readily pass out of it, and thus they exert their effects locally (see Attardo, Fitzgerald, & Schnitzer, 2015; Colgan & Yasuda, 2014; Lisman, Yasuda, & Raghavachari, 2012).

- It became apparent that maintenance of LTP involves structural changes, which depend on protein synthesis. The discovery that LTP causes structural changes was exciting because the structure of neurons and neural circuits had been assumed to be static. Many kinds of structural changes have been described (e.g., increases in number and size of synapses, increases in number and size of postsynaptic dendritic spines, changes in presynaptic and postsynaptic membranes, and changes in dendritic branching), and the changes have turned out to occur far more rapidly and more frequently than was once assumed (see Bliss & Collingridge, 2013; Wiegert & Oertner, 2015; Zhang et al., 2015).

- The discovery of structural changes in neurons following the induction of LTP stimulated a search for a mechanism by which a neuron's activity could change its structure. This led to the discovery of numerous **transcription factors** (intracellular proteins that bind to DNA and influence the operation of particular genes) that were activated by neural activity (see Ryan et al., 2015).

Variability of LTP

LO 11.20 Define long-term depression (LTD) and metaplasticity.

When we first learned about LTP, we were excited. LTP seemed like a good model of learning and memory, and its simplicity suggested that its mechanisms could be identified. A generation of neuroscientists has shared our view, and LTP has become the focus of a massive research effort. However, it seems that researchers are further from ultimate answers than we naively thought they were about a quarter century ago. What has happened? Many important discoveries have been made, but rather than leading to solutions, they have revealed that LTP is far more complex than first thought.

Most of the research on LTP has focused on NMDA-receptor–mediated LTP in the hippocampus. It is now clear that NMDA-receptor–mediated LTP involves a complex array of changes that are difficult to sort out. In addition, LTP has been documented in many other parts of the CNS, where it tends to be mediated by different mechanisms (see Grau, 2014; Gruart et al., 2015). There is also LTD (**long-term depression**), which is the flip side of LTP and occurs in response to prolonged low-frequency stimulation of presynaptic neurons (see Atwood, Lovinger, & Mathur, 2014; Connor & Wang, 2015). And then there is **metaplasticity**, which refers to the fact that LTP and/or LTD induction can be modulated by prior synaptic activity (see Hulme, Jones, & Abraham, 2013; Müller-Dahlhaus & Ziemann, 2015). Presumably, a full understanding of LTP and its role in memory will require an understanding of LTD and metaplasticity. And we still don't know what role glial cells play in LTP (see Jones, 2015; Jones & Lynch, 2014; Paixão & Klein, 2010).

 Neuroplasticity LTP is one of the most intensely studied of all neuroscientific phenomena. Why do you think that is?

The dream of discovering the neural basis of learning and memory has attracted many neuroscientists to the study of LTP. Although this dream has not yet been fulfilled, the study of LTP has led to several important discoveries about the function and plasticity of neural systems. By this criterion, its study has been a great success.

Conclusion: Biopsychology of Memory and You

Because this chapter has emphasized the amnesic effects of brain damage, you may have been left with the impression that the biopsychological study of memory has little direct relevance to individuals, like you, with intact healthy brains. This final module shows that such is not the case. It makes this point by describing two interesting lines of research and one provocative case study.

Infantile Amnesia

LO 11.21 Define infantile amnesia, and describe two experiments that investigated whether infantile amnesia extends to implicit memories.

We all experience **infantile amnesia**; that is, we remember virtually nothing of the events of our infancy (see Callaghan,

Li, & Richardson, 2014; Sneed, 2014). Newcombe and her colleagues (2000) addressed the following question: Do normal children who fail to explicitly recall or recognize things from their early childhood display preserved implicit memories for these things? The results of two experiments indicate that the answer is "yes."

In one study of infantile amnesia (Newcombe & Fox, 1994), children were shown a series of photographs of preschool-aged children, some of whom had been their preschool classmates. The children recognized a few of their former preschool classmates. However, whether they explicitly remembered a former classmate or not, they consistently displayed a large skin conductance response to the photographs of their former classmates but not to the control photographs.

In a second study of infantile amnesia, Drummey and Newcombe (1995) used a version of the incomplete-pictures test. First, they showed a series of drawings to 3-year-olds, 5-year-olds, and adults. Three months later, the researchers assessed the implicit memories for these drawings by asking each participant to identify them ("It's a car," "It's a chair," etc.) and some control drawings as quickly as they could. During the test, the drawings were first presented badly out of focus, but became progressively sharper over time. Following this test of implicit memory, explicit memory was assessed by asking the participants which of the drawings they remembered seeing before. The 5-year-olds and adults showed better explicit memory than the 3-year-olds did; that is, they were more likely to recall seeing drawings from the original series. However, all three groups displayed substantial implicit memory: All participants were able to identify the drawings they had previously seen sooner, even when they had no conscious recollection of them.

Smart Drugs: Do They Work?

LO 11.22 Discuss the findings on the efficacy of smart drugs.

Nootropics, or **smart drugs**, are substances (drugs, supplements, herbal extracts, etc.) that are thought to improve memory. The shelves of health food stores are full of them, and even more are available on the Internet. Perhaps you have heard of, or even tried, some of them: *ginkgo biloba* extracts, ginseng extracts, multivitamins, glucose, cholinergic agonists, Piracetam, antioxidants, phospholipids, stimulants (e.g., amphetamine, methylphenidate), and many more. Those offering nootropics for sale claim that scientific evidence has proven that these substances improve the memories of healthy children and adults and block the adverse effects of aging on memory. Are these claims really supported by valid scientific evidence?

The evidence that nootropics enhance memory has been reviewed several times by independent scientists (see Husain

& Mehta, 2011; Partridge et al., 2012; Stix, 2009). The following pattern of conclusions has emerged from these reviews:

- Although nootropics are often marketed to healthy adults, most research has been done on either nonhumans or humans with memory difficulties (i.e., the elderly).
- The relevant research with humans tends to be of low quality, with few participants and poor controls.
- For each purported nootropic, there are typically a few positive findings on which the vendors focus; however, these findings are often difficult to replicate or represent very small effect sizes (see Farah, 2015).

In short, no purported nootropic has been convincingly shown to have memory-enhancing effects. There may be enough positive evidence to warrant continued investigation of some potential nootropics (e.g., Hinnebusch, 2015), but there is not nearly enough to justify the various claims that are made in advertisements for these substances. Why do you think there is such a huge gulf between the evidence and the claims?

Thinking Creatively	Address the question posed to you in this paragraph: With respect to nootropics, why do you think there is such a huge gulf between the evidence and the claims?

POSTTRAUMATIC AMNESIA AND EPISODIC MEMORY
This chapter began with the case of H.M.; it ends with the case of R.M. The case of R.M. is one of the most ironic that we have encountered. R.M. is a biopsychologist, and, as you will learn, his vocation played an important role in one of his symptoms.

The Case of R.M., the Biopsychologist Who Remembered H.M.

R.M. fell on his head while skiing; when he regained consciousness, he was suffering from both retrograde and anterograde amnesia. For several hours, he could recall few of the events of his previous life. He could not remember if he was married, where he lived, or where he worked. He had lost most of his episodic memory.

Also, many of the things that happened to him in the hours after his accident were forgotten as soon as his attention was diverted from them. For example, in the car on his way to the hospital, R.M. chatted with the person sitting next to him—a friend of a friend with whom he had skied all day. But each time his attention was drawn elsewhere—for example, by the mountain scenery—he completely forgot this person and reintroduced himself.

This was a classic case of posttraumatic amnesia. Like H.M., R.M. was trapped in the present, with only a cloudy past and seemingly no future. The irony of the situation was that during those few hours, when R.M. could recall few of the events of his own life, his thoughts repeatedly drifted to one semantic memory—his memory of a person he remembered learning about somewhere in his muddled past. Through the haze, he remembered H.M., his fellow prisoner of the present and wondered if the same fate lay in store for him.

R.M. recovered fully and looks back on what he can recall of his experience with relief and a feeling of empathy for H.M. Unlike H.M., R.M. received a reprieve, but his experience left him with a better appreciation for the situation of those like H.M., who served a life sentence.

Themes Revisited

All four of the book's themes played major roles in this chapter. The biopsychology of memory is a neuroplastic phenomenon—it focuses on the changes in neural function that store experiences. Thus, the neuroplasticity theme was implicit throughout the chapter.

Because the study of the neural mechanisms of memory is based largely on the study of humans with amnesia, the clinical implications theme played a significant role. The study of memory disorders 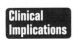 has so far been a one-way street: We have learned much about memory and its neural mechanisms from studying amnesic patients, but we have not yet learned enough to treat their memory problems.

Animal models have also played a major role in the study of memory disorders. Only so much progress can be made studying human clinical cases; questions of causation must be addressed with animal models. The study of medial temporal lobe amnesia illustrates the comparative approach at its best.

Finally, the thinking creatively tab marked three points in the chapter where you were encouraged to think in unconventional ways. You were encouraged to consider (1) why it proved so difficult to develop an animal model of medial temporal lobe amnesia; (2) why cases of cerebral ischemia do not provide strong evidence for involvement of the hippocampus in object recognition memory; and (3) the gulf between the actual evidence for smart drugs and the advertised claims.

Key Terms

Learning, p. 296
Memory, p. 296
Amnesia, p. 297

Amnesic Effects of Bilateral Medial Temporal Lobectomy

Bilateral medial temporal lobectomy, p. 297
Hippocampus, p. 297
Amygdala, p. 297
Lobectomy, p. 297
Lobotomy, p. 297
Retrograde amnesia, p. 297
Anterograde amnesia, p. 297
Short-term memory, p. 298
Long-term memory, p. 298
Digit span, p. 298
Global amnesia, p. 298
Incomplete-pictures test, p. 299
Remote memory, p. 299
Memory consolidation, p. 299
Explicit memories, p. 299

Implicit memories, p. 299
Medial temporal lobe amnesia, p. 300
Repetition priming tests, p. 300
Semantic memories, p. 301
Episodic memories, p. 301
Global cerebral ischemia, p. 302
Pyramidal cell layer, p. 302
CA1 subfield, p. 302
Transient global amnesia, p. 303

Amnesias of Korsakoff's Syndrome and Alzheimer's Disease

Korsakoff's syndrome, p. 303
Mediodorsal nuclei, p. 303
Medial diencephalic amnesia, p. 303
Alzheimer's disease, p. 304
Basal forebrain, p. 304

Amnesia after Concussion: Evidence for Consolidation

Posttraumatic amnesia (PTA), p. 304

Electroconvulsive shock (ECS), p. 305
Standard consolidation theory, p. 306
Dual-trace theory, p. 306
Engram, p. 306
Reconsolidation, p. 306

Evolving Perspective of the Role of the Hippocampus in Memory

Delayed nonmatching-to-sample test, p. 307
Medial temporal cortex, p. 308
Mumby box, p. 309

Neurons of the Medial Temporal Lobes and Memory

Morris water maze test, p. 312
Radial arm maze test, p. 312
Reference memory, p. 312
Working memory, p. 312
Place cells, p. 313
Entorhinal cortex, p. 313
Grid cells, p. 313

Chapter 12
Hunger, Eating, and Health

Why Do Many People Eat Too Much?

 ## Chapter Overview and Learning Objectives (LOs)

Digestion, Energy Storage, and Energy Utilization	**LO 12.1** Summarize the process of digestion, and explain how energy is stored in the body.
	LO 12.2 Explain the three phases of energy metabolism.
Theories of Hunger and Eating: Set Points versus Positive Incentives	**LO 12.3** Describe the set-point assumption, and describe the glucostatic and lipostatic set-point theories of hunger and eating. Also, outline three problems with set-point theories of hunger and eating.
	LO 12.4 Describe the positive-incentive perspective on hunger and eating.
Factors That Determine What, When, and How Much We Eat	**LO 12.5** Describe at least two factors that determine what we eat.
	LO 12.6 Describe at least two factors that influence when we eat.
	LO 12.7 Describe the various factors that influence how much we eat.

Physiological Research on Hunger and Satiety	**LO 12.8**	Explain the nature of the relationship between blood glucose levels and hunger and satiety.
	LO 12.9	Critically evaluate the concept of hypothalamic hunger and satiety centers.
	LO 12.10	Describe the role of the gastrointestinal tract in satiety.
	LO 12.11	Describe the discovery of the hunger and satiety peptides, and name several.
	LO 12.12	Describe the role of serotonin in satiety.
	LO 12.13	Describe the symptoms and etiology of Prader-Willi syndrome.
Body-Weight Regulation: Set Points versus Settling Points	**LO 12.14**	Evaluate the evidence for set-point assumptions about body weight and eating.
	LO 12.15	Compare and evaluate set-point and settling-point models of body-weight regulation.
Human Obesity: Causes, Mechanisms, and Treatments	**LO 12.16**	Explain why there is cause for concern surrounding the obesity epidemic.
	LO 12.17	Describe, from an evolutionary perspective, why there is a current epidemic of obesity.
	LO 12.18	Give some reasons as to why some people become obese whereas others do not.
	LO 12.19	Explain why weight-loss programs are typically ineffective.
	LO 12.20	Explain how leptin and insulin are feedback signals for the regulation of body fat.
	LO 12.21	Describe two sorts of treatments for obesity.
Anorexia and Bulimia Nervosa	**LO 12.22**	Describe the symptoms of anorexia nervosa and bulimia nervosa.
	LO 12.23	Explain how anorexia and bulimia are, and are not, related.
	LO 12.24	Explain why those starving due to anorexia do not appear to be as hungry as they should.
	LO 12.25	Explain how anorexia might result from conditioned taste aversions.

Eating is a behavior that is of interest to virtually everyone. We all do it, and most of us derive great pleasure from it. But for many of us, it becomes a source of serious personal and health problems.

Most eating-related health problems in industrialized nations are associated with eating too much—the average American consumes 3,800 calories per day, about twice the average daily requirement. For example, it is estimated that 68 percent of the adult U.S. population is either overweight or clinically obese, qualifying this problem for epidemic status (see Ogden et al., 2014). The resulting financial and personal costs are huge. Each year in the United States, about $150 billion is spent treating obesity-related disorders (see Finkelstein et al., 2009). Moreover, each year, an estimated 400,000 U.S. citizens die unnecessarily from disorders caused by excessive eating (see Masters et al., 2013). Although the United States is a trendsetter when it comes to overeating and obesity, many other countries are not far behind (see Scully, 2014). Ironically, as overeating and obesity have reached epidemic proportions, there has been a related increase in disorders associated with eating too little. For example, about 1.2 percent of Americans will suffer from *anorexia* or *bulimia* at some point in their lives; and these conditions can be life-threatening in extreme cases (see Swanson et al., 2011).

The massive increases in obesity and other eating-related disorders that have occurred over the past few decades in many countries stand in direct opposition to most people's thinking about hunger and eating. Many people—and we assume this includes you—believe that hunger and eating are normally triggered when the body's energy resources fall below a prescribed optimal level, or **set point**. They appreciate that many factors influence hunger and eating, but they assume that in general the hunger and eating system has evolved to supply the body with just the right amount of energy.

This chapter explores the incompatibility of the set-point assumption with the current epidemic of eating disorders. If we all have hunger and eating systems whose primary function is to maintain energy resources at optimal levels, then eating disorders should be rare. The fact that they are so prevalent suggests that hunger and eating are regulated in some other way. This chapter will repeatedly challenge you to think in new ways about issues that impact your health and longevity and will provide new insights of great personal relevance—we guarantee it.

Before you move on to the body of the chapter, we would like you to pause to consider a case study that links this chapter with the preceding one (Rozin et al., 1998). What would a severely amnesic patient do if offered a meal shortly after finishing one? If his hunger and eating were controlled by energy set points, he would refuse the second meal. Did he?

The Case of the Man Who Forgot Not to Eat

R.H. was a 48-year-old male whose progress in graduate school was interrupted by the development of severe amnesia for long-term explicit memory. His amnesia was similar in pattern and severity to that of H.M., whom you met in Chapter 11, and an MRI examination revealed bilateral damage to the medial temporal lobes.

The meals offered to R.H. were selected on the basis of interviews with him about the foods he liked: veal parmigiana (about 750 calories) plus all the apple juice he wanted. On one occasion, he was offered a second meal about 15 minutes after he had eaten the first, and he ate it. When offered a third meal 15 minutes later, he ate that, too. When offered a fourth meal he rejected it, claiming that his "stomach was a little tight."

Then, a few minutes later, R.H. announced that he was going out for a good walk and a meal. When asked what he was going to eat, his answer was "veal parmigiana."

Clearly, R.H.'s hunger (i.e., motivation to eat) did not result from an energy deficit. Other cases like that of R.H. have been reported by Higgs and colleagues (2008).

Digestion, Energy Storage, and Energy Utilization

The primary purpose of hunger is to increase the probability of eating, and the primary purpose of eating is to supply the body with the molecular building blocks and energy it needs to survive and function. This module provides the foundation for our consideration of hunger and eating by providing a brief overview of the processes by which food is digested, stored, and converted to energy.

Digestion and Energy Storage in the Body

LO 12.1 Summarize the process of digestion, and explain how energy is stored in the body.

DIGESTION. The *gastrointestinal tract* and the process of digestion are illustrated in Figure 12.1. **Digestion** is the gastrointestinal process of breaking down food and absorbing its constituents into the body. In order to appreciate the basics of digestion, it is useful to consider the body without its protuberances, as a simple living tube with a hole at each end. To supply itself with energy and other nutrients, the tube puts food into one of its two holes—the one with teeth—and passes the food along its internal canal so that the food can be broken down and partially absorbed from the canal into the body. Much of the work of breaking down the food we ingest is done by the constituents of our **gut microbiome** (the bacteria and other organisms that live inside our gastrointestinal tract). The leftovers of what we ingest are jettisoned from the other end. Although this is not a particularly appetizing description of eating, it does serve to illustrate that, strictly speaking, food has not been consumed until it has been digested.

ENERGY STORAGE IN THE BODY. As a consequence of digestion, energy is delivered to the body in three forms: (1) **lipids** (fats), (2) **amino acids** (the breakdown products of proteins), and (3) **glucose** (a simple sugar that is the breakdown product of complex *carbohydrates,* that is, starches and sugars).

The body uses energy continuously, but its consumption is intermittent; therefore, it must store energy for use in the intervals between meals. Energy is stored in three forms: *fats, glycogen,* and *proteins*. Most of the body's energy reserves are stored as fats, relatively little as glycogen

Figure 12.1 The gastrointestinal tract and the process of digestion. Not shown in the figure is the gut microbiome, which includes the bacteria and other organisms that live inside our gastrointestinal tract and help break down the food we ingest.

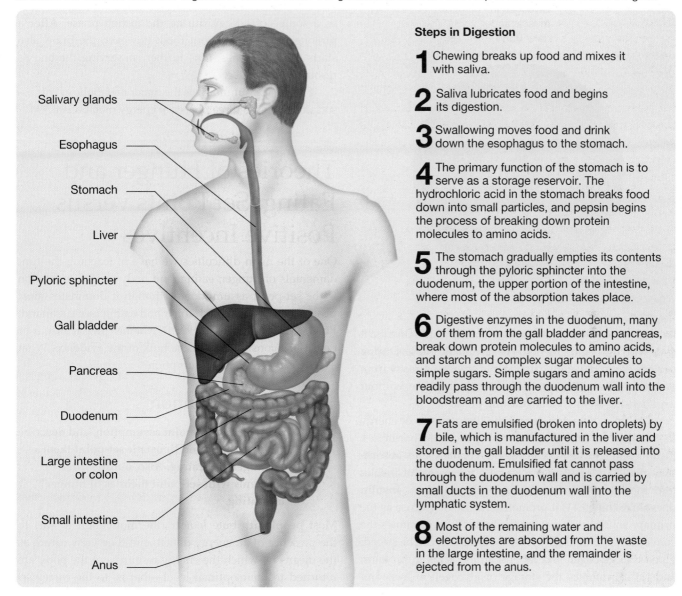

Steps in Digestion

1 Chewing breaks up food and mixes it with saliva.

2 Saliva lubricates food and begins its digestion.

3 Swallowing moves food and drink down the esophagus to the stomach.

4 The primary function of the stomach is to serve as a storage reservoir. The hydrochloric acid in the stomach breaks food down into small particles, and pepsin begins the process of breaking down protein molecules to amino acids.

5 The stomach gradually empties its contents through the pyloric sphincter into the duodenum, the upper portion of the intestine, where most of the absorption takes place.

6 Digestive enzymes in the duodenum, many of them from the gall bladder and pancreas, break down protein molecules to amino acids, and starch and complex sugar molecules to simple sugars. Simple sugars and amino acids readily pass through the duodenum wall into the bloodstream and are carried to the liver.

7 Fats are emulsified (broken into droplets) by bile, which is manufactured in the liver and stored in the gall bladder until it is released into the duodenum. Emulsified fat cannot pass through the duodenum wall and is carried by small ducts in the duodenum wall into the lymphatic system.

8 Most of the remaining water and electrolytes are absorbed from the waste in the large intestine, and the remainder is ejected from the anus.

Labels (top to bottom):
Salivary glands
Esophagus
Stomach
Liver
Pyloric sphincter
Gall bladder
Pancreas
Duodenum
Large intestine or colon
Small intestine
Anus

and proteins (see Figure 12.2). Thus, changes in the body weights of adult humans are largely a consequence of changes in the amount of their stored body fat.

Why is fat the body's preferred way of storing energy? Glycogen, which is largely stored in the liver and muscles, might be expected to be the body's preferred mode of energy storage because it is so readily converted to glucose—the body's main directly utilizable source of energy. But there are two reasons why fat, rather than glycogen, is the primary mode of energy storage: (1) a gram of fat can store almost twice as much energy as a gram of glycogen, and (2) glycogen, unlike fat, attracts and holds substantial quantities of water. Consequently, if all your fat calories were stored as glycogen, you would likely weigh well over 275 kilograms (600 pounds).

Three Phases of Energy Metabolism

LO 12.2 Explain the three phases of energy metabolism.

There are three phases of *energy metabolism* (the chemical changes by which energy is made available for an organism's use): the cephalic phase, the absorptive phase, and the fasting phase. The **cephalic phase** is the preparatory phase; it often begins with the sight, smell, or even just the thought of food, and it ends when the food starts to be absorbed into the bloodstream. The **absorptive phase** is the period during which the energy absorbed into the bloodstream from the meal is meeting the body's immediate energy needs. The **fasting phase** is the period during which all of the unstored energy from the previous meal has been used and the body is withdrawing energy from

Figure 12.2 Distribution of stored energy in an average person.

Glycogen in muscle and liver 0.5%

Protein in muscle 14.5%

Fat in adipose 85%

its reserves to meet its immediate energy requirements; it ends with the beginning of the next cephalic phase. During periods of rapid weight gain, people often go directly from one absorptive phase into the next cephalic phase, without experiencing an intervening fasting phase.

The flow of energy during the three phases of energy metabolism is controlled by two pancreatic hormones: insulin and glucagon. During the cephalic and absorptive phases, the pancreas releases a great deal of insulin into the bloodstream and very little glucagon. **Insulin** does three things: (1) it promotes the use of glucose as the primary source of energy by the body; (2) it promotes the conversion of bloodborne fuels to forms that can be stored: glucose to glycogen and fat and amino acids to proteins; and (3) it promotes the storage of glycogen in liver and muscle, fat in adipose tissue, and proteins in muscle. In short, the function of insulin during the cephalic phase is to lower the levels of bloodborne fuels, primarily glucose, in anticipation of the impending influx; and its function during the absorptive phase is to minimize the increasing levels of bloodborne fuels by utilizing and storing them.

In contrast to the cephalic and absorptive phases, the fasting phase is characterized by high blood levels of **glucagon** and low levels of insulin. Without high levels of insulin, glucose has difficulty entering most body cells; thus, glucose stops being the body's primary fuel. In effect, this saves the body's glucose for the brain, because insulin is not required for glucose to enter most brain cells. The low levels of insulin also promote the conversion of glycogen and protein to glucose. (The conversion of protein to glucose is called **gluconeogenesis**.)

On the other hand, the high levels of fasting-phase glucagon promote the release of **free fatty acids** from adipose tissue and their use as the body's primary fuel. The high glucagon levels also stimulate the conversion of free fatty acids to **ketones**, which are used by muscles as a source of energy during the fasting phase. After a prolonged period without food, however, the brain also starts to use ketones, thus further conserving the body's resources of glucose.

Figure 12.3 summarizes the major metabolic events associated with the three phases of energy metabolism.

Theories of Hunger and Eating: Set Points versus Positive Incentives

One of the main difficulties we have in teaching the fundamentals of hunger, eating, and body-weight regulation is the set-point assumption. Although it dominates most people's thinking about hunger and eating (see Assanand, Pinel, & Lehman, 1998a, 1998b), whether they realize it or not, it is inconsistent with the bulk of the evidence. What exactly is the set-point assumption?

Set-Point Assumption

LO 12.3 Describe the set-point assumption, and describe the glucostatic and lipostatic set-point theories of hunger and eating. Also, outline three problems with set-point theories of hunger and eating.

Most people attribute *hunger* (the motivation to eat) to the presence of an energy deficit, and they view eating as the means by which the energy resources of the body are returned to their optimal level—that is, to the *energy set point*. Figure 12.4 summarizes this **set-point assumption**. After a *meal* (a bout of eating), a person's energy resources are assumed to be near their set point and to decline thereafter as the body uses energy to fuel its physiological processes. When the level of the body's energy resources falls far enough below the set point, a person becomes motivated by hunger to initiate another meal. The meal continues, according to the set-point assumption, until the energy level returns to its set point and the person feels *satiated* (not hungry).

Set-point models assume that hunger and eating work in much the same way as a thermostat-regulated heating system in a cool climate. The heater increases the house temperature until it reaches its set point (the thermostat setting). The heater then shuts off, and the temperature of the house gradually declines until it becomes low enough to turn the heater back on. All set-point systems have three components: a set-point mechanism, a detector

Figure 12.3 The major events associated with the three phases of energy metabolism: the cephalic, absorptive, and fasting phases.

Figure 12.4 The energy set-point view that is the basis of many people's thinking about hunger and eating.

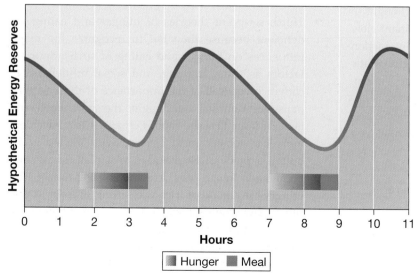

mechanism, and an effector mechanism. The *set-point mechanism* defines the set point, the *detector mechanism* detects deviations from the set point, and the *effector mechanism* acts to eliminate the deviations. For example, the set-point, detector, and effector mechanisms of a heating system are the thermostat, the thermometer, and the heater, respectively.

All set-point systems are **negative feedback systems**—systems in which feedback from changes in one direction elicit compensatory effects in the opposite direction. Negative feedback systems are common in mammals because they act to maintain **homeostasis**—a stable internal environment—which is critical for mammals' survival (see Kotas & Medzhitov, 2015;

Ramsay & Woods, 2014). Set-point systems combine negative feedback with a set point to keep an internal environment fixed at the prescribed point. Set-point systems seemed necessary when the adult human brain was assumed to be immutable: Because the brain couldn't change, energy resources had to be highly regulated. However, we now know that the adult human brain is plastic and capable of considerable adaptation. Thus, there is no longer a logical imperative for the set-point regulation of eating. Throughout this chapter, you will need to put aside your preconceptions and base your thinking about hunger and eating entirely on the empirical evidence.

GLUCOSTATIC THEORY. In the 1940s and 1950s, researchers working under the assumption that eating is regulated by some type of set-point system speculated about the nature of the regulation. Several researchers suggested that eating is regulated by a system designed to maintain a blood glucose set point—the idea being that we become hungry when our blood glucose levels drop significantly below their set point and that we become satiated when eating returns our blood glucose levels to their set point. The various versions of this theory are collectively referred to as the **glucostatic theory**. It seemed to make good sense that the main purpose of eating is to defend a blood glucose set point because glucose is the brain's primary fuel.

LIPOSTATIC THEORY. The **lipostatic theory** is another set-point theory proposed in various forms in the 1940s and 1950s. According to this theory, every person has a set point for body fat, and deviations from this set point produce compensatory adjustments in the level of eating that return levels of body fat to their set point. The most frequently cited support for the theory is the fact that the body weights of adults stay relatively constant.

The glucostatic and lipostatic theories were viewed as complementary, not mutually exclusive. The glucostatic theory was thought to account for meal initiation and termination, whereas the lipostatic theory was thought to account for long-term regulation. Thus, the dominant view in the 1950s was that eating is regulated by the interaction between two set-point systems: a short-term glucostatic system and a long-term lipostatic system. The simplicity of these 1950s theories is appealing. Remarkably, they are still being presented as the latest word in some textbooks; perhaps you have encountered them.

> **Thinking Creatively** Why do you think set-point theories of hunger and eating are so popular?

PROBLEMS WITH SET-POINT THEORIES OF HUNGER AND EATING. Set-point theories of hunger and eating have several serious weaknesses. You have already learned one fact that undermines these theories: There is an epidemic of obesity and overweight, which should not occur if eating is regulated by a set point. Let's look at three more major weaknesses of set-point theories of hunger and eating.

- First, set-point theories of hunger and eating are inconsistent with basic eating-related evolutionary pressures as we understand them. The major eating-related problem faced by our ancestors was the inconsistency and unpredictability of the food supply. Thus, in order to survive, it was important for them to eat large quantities of good food when it was available so that calories could be banked in the form of body fat. For any warm-blooded species to survive under natural conditions, it needs a hunger and eating system that prevents energy deficits, rather than one that merely responds to them once they have developed. From this perspective, it is difficult to imagine how a hunger and feeding system based entirely on set points could have evolved in mammals (see Johnson, 2013).

- Second, major predictions of the set-point theories of hunger and eating have not been confirmed. Early studies seemed to support the set-point theories by showing that large reductions in body fat, produced by starvation, or large reductions in blood glucose, produced by insulin injections, induce increases in eating in laboratory animals. The problem is that reductions in blood glucose of the magnitude needed to reliably induce eating rarely occur naturally. Indeed, as you have already learned in this chapter, about 68 percent of U.S. adults have a significant excess of fat deposits when they begin a meal. Conversely, efforts to reduce meal size by having volunteers unknowingly consume a high-calorie drink before eating have been unsuccessful.

- Third, set-point theories of hunger and eating are deficient because they fail to recognize the major influences on hunger and eating of such important factors as taste, learning, and social influences. To convince yourself of the importance of these factors, pause for a minute and imagine the sight, smell, and taste of your favorite food. Perhaps it is a succulent morsel of lobster meat covered with melted garlic butter, a piece of cheesecake, or a plate of sizzling homemade french fries. Are you starting to feel a bit hungry? If a plate of fries was sitting in front of you right now, wouldn't you eat one, or maybe eat the whole plateful? Have you not on occasion felt discomfort after a large main course, only to polish off a substantial dessert? The usual positive answers to these questions lead unavoidably to the conclusion that hunger and eating are not rigidly controlled by deviations from energy set points.

Positive-Incentive Perspective

LO 12.4 Describe the positive-incentive perspective on hunger and eating.

The inability of set-point theories to account for the basic phenomena of eating and hunger led to the development of an alternative theoretical perspective (see Berridge, 2004). The central assertion of this perspective, commonly referred to as **positive-incentive theory**, is that humans and other animals are not normally driven to eat by internal energy deficits but are drawn to eat by the anticipated pleasure of eating—the anticipated pleasure of a behavior is called its **positive-incentive value** (see Bolles, 1980; Booth, 1981; Collier, 1980; Rolls, 1981; Toates, 1981). There are several different positive-incentive theories, and we refer generally to all of them as the *positive-incentive perspective*.

The major tenet of the positive-incentive perspective on eating is that eating is controlled in much the same way as sexual behavior: We engage in sexual behavior not because we have an internal deficit but because we have evolved to crave it. The evolutionary pressures of unexpected food shortages have shaped us and all other

Evolutionary Perspective

warm-blooded animals, who need a continuous supply of energy to maintain their body temperatures, to take advantage of good food when it is present and eat it. According to the positive-incentive perspective, it is the presence of good food, or the anticipation of it, that normally makes us hungry, not an energy deficit.

According to the positive-incentive perspective, the degree of hunger you feel at any particular time depends on the interaction of all the factors that influence the positive-incentive value of eating (see Palmiter, 2007). These include the following: the flavor of the food you are likely to consume, what you have learned about the effects of this food either from eating it previously or from other people, the amount of time since you last ate, the type and quantity of food in your gut, whether or not other people are present and eating, whether or not your blood glucose levels are within the normal range. This partial list illustrates one strength of the positive-incentive perspective. Unlike set-point theories, positive-incentive theories do not single out one factor as the major determinant of hunger and ignore the others.

In this module, you learned that most people think about hunger and eating in terms of energy set points and were introduced to an alternative way of thinking—the positive-incentive perspective. Which way is correct? If you are like most people, you have an attachment to

familiar ways of thinking and a resistance to new ones. Try to put this tendency aside and base your views about this important issue entirely on the evidence.

The next module describes some of the things that biopsychological research has taught us about hunger and eating. As you progress through the module, notice the superiority of the positive-incentive theories over set-point theories in accounting for the basic facts.

Factors That Determine What, When, and How Much We Eat

This module describes major factors that commonly determine what we eat, when we eat, and how much we eat. Notice that energy deficits are not included among these factors. Although major energy deficits clearly increase hunger and eating, they are not a common factor in the eating behavior of people like us, who live in food-replete societies. Although you may believe your body is usually short of energy just before a meal, it is not.

Factors That Influence What We Eat

LO 12.5 Describe at least two factors that determine what we eat.

Certain tastes have a high positive-incentive value for virtually all members of a species. For example, most humans have a special fondness for sweet, fatty, and salty tastes. This species-typical pattern of human taste preferences is adaptive because in nature sweet and fatty tastes are typically characteristic of high-energy foods rich in vitamins and minerals, and salty tastes are characteristic of sodium-rich foods. In contrast, bitter tastes, for which most humans have an aversion, are often associated with toxins. Superimposed on our species-typical taste preferences and aversions, each of us has the ability to learn specific taste preferences and aversions (see Clouard, Meunier-Salaün, & Val-Laillet, 2012).

LEARNED TASTE PREFERENCES AND AVERSIONS. Animals learn to prefer tastes that are followed by an infusion of calories, and they learn to avoid tastes that are followed by illness. In addition, humans and other animals learn what to eat from their conspecifics. For example, rats learn to prefer flavors they experience in mother's milk and those that they smell on the breath of other rats (see Galef, Whishkin, & Bielavska, 1997). Similarly, in humans, many food preferences are culturally specific—for example, in some cultures, various nontoxic insects are considered to be a delicacy.

LEARNING TO EAT VITAMINS AND MINERALS. How do animals select a diet that provides all of the vitamins and minerals they need? To answer this question, researchers have studied how dietary deficiencies influence diet selection. Two patterns of results have emerged: one for sodium and one for the other essential vitamins and minerals. When an animal is deficient in sodium, it develops an immediate and compelling preference for the taste of sodium salt (see Geerling & Loewy, 2008). In contrast, an animal deficient in some vitamin or mineral other than sodium must learn to consume foods that are rich in the missing nutrient by experiencing their positive effects; this is because vitamins and minerals other than sodium normally have no detectable taste in food. For example, rats maintained on a diet deficient in *thiamine* (vitamin B$_1$) develop an aversion to the taste of that diet, and if they are offered two new diets, one deficient in thiamine and one rich in thiamine, they often develop a preference for the taste of the thiamine-rich diet over the ensuing days, as it becomes associated with improved health.

If we, like rats, are capable of learning to select diets rich in the vitamins and minerals we need, why are dietary deficiencies so prevalent in our society? One reason is that, in order to maximize profits, manufacturers produce foods that have the tastes we prefer but lack many of the nutrients we need to maintain our health. (Even rats prefer chocolate chip cookies to nutritionally complete rat chow.) The second reason is illustrated by the classic study of Harris and associates (1933). When thiamine-deficient rats were offered two new diets, one with thiamine and one without, almost all of them learned to eat the complete diet and avoid the deficient one. However, when they were offered 10 new diets, only one of which contained the badly needed thiamine, few developed a preference for the complete diet. The number of different substances, both nutritious and not, consumed each day by most people in industrialized societies is immense, and this makes it difficult, if not impossible, for their bodies to learn which foods are beneficial and which are not.

Factors That Influence When We Eat

LO 12.6 Describe at least two factors that influence when we eat.

Collier and his colleagues (see Collier, 1986) found that most mammals choose to eat many small meals (snacks) each day if they have ready access to a continuous supply of food. In contrast to the usual mammalian preference, most people, particularly those living in family groups, tend to eat a few large meals each day at regular times. Interestingly, each person's regular mealtimes are the very same times at which that person is likely to feel most hungry; in fact, many people experience attacks of malaise (headache, nausea, and an inability to concentrate) when they miss a regularly scheduled meal.

PREMEAL HUNGER. We are sure you have experienced attacks of premeal hunger. Subjectively, they seem to provide compelling support for set-point theories. Your body seems to be crying out: "I need more energy. I cannot function without it. Please feed me." But things are not always the way they seem. Woods has straightened out the confusion (see Begg & Woods, 2013; Woods & Begg, 2015).

According to Woods, the key to understanding hunger is to appreciate that eating meals stresses the body. Before a meal, the body's energy reserves are in reasonable homeostatic balance; then, as a meal is consumed, there is a major homeostasis-disturbing influx of fuels into the bloodstream. The body does what it can to defend its homeostasis. At the first indication that a person will soon be eating—for example, when the usual mealtime approaches—the body enters the cephalic phase and takes steps to soften the impact of the impending homeostasis-disturbing influx by releasing insulin into the blood and thus reducing blood glucose. Woods's message is that the strong, unpleasant feelings of hunger you may experience at mealtimes are not cries from your body for food; they are the sensations of your body's preparations for the expected homeostasis-disturbing meal. Mealtime hunger is caused by the expectation of food, not by an energy deficit.

As a high school student, I (JP) ate lunch at exactly 12:05 every day and was overwhelmed by hunger as the time approached. Now, my eating schedule is different, and I never experience noontime hunger pangs; I now get hungry just before the time at which I usually eat. Have you had a similar experience?

Thinking Creatively

PAVLOVIAN CONDITIONING OF HUNGER. In a classic series of Pavlovian conditioning experiments on laboratory rats, Weingarten (1983, 1984, 1985) provided strong support for the view that hunger is often caused by the expectation of food, not by an energy deficit. During the conditioning phase of one of his experiments, Weingarten presented rats with six meals per day at irregular intervals, and he signaled the impending delivery of each meal with a buzzer-and-light conditional stimulus. This conditioning procedure was continued for 11 days. Throughout the ensuing test phase of the experiment, the food was continuously available. Despite the fact that the subjects were never deprived during the test phase, the rats started to eat each time the buzzer and light were presented—even if they had recently completed a meal (see Johnson, 2013).

Factors That Influence How Much We Eat

LO 12.7 Describe the various factors that influence how much we eat.

The motivational state that causes us to stop eating a meal when there is food remaining is **satiety**. Satiety mechanisms play a major role in determining how much we eat.

SATIETY SIGNALS. As you will learn in the next module of the chapter, food in the gut and glucose entering the blood can induce satiety signals, which inhibit subsequent consumption. These signals depend on both the volume and the **nutritive density** (calories per unit volume) of the food.

The effects of nutritive density have been demonstrated in studies in which laboratory rats have been maintained on a single diet. Once a stable baseline of consumption has been established, the nutritive density of the diet is changed. Some rats eventually learn to adjust the volume of food they consume to keep their caloric intake and body weights relatively stable. However, there are major limits to this adjustment: Rats rarely increase their intake sufficiently to maintain their body weights if the nutritive density of their conventional laboratory feed is reduced by more than 50 percent or if there are major changes in the diet's palatability.

Evolutionary Perspective

SHAM EATING. The study of **sham eating** indicates that satiety signals from the gut or blood are not necessary to terminate a meal. In sham-eating experiments, food is chewed and swallowed by the subject; but rather than passing down the subject's esophagus into the stomach, it passes out of the body through an implanted tube (see Figure 12.5).

Because sham eating adds no energy to the body, set-point theories predict that all sham-eaten meals should be huge. But this is not the case. The first sham meal of rats sham eating their usual diet is typically the same size as previous normal meals, thus indicating that satiety is a function of previous experience, not the current increases in the body's energy resources. However, after the first few sham meals, rats begin to sham eat larger meals.

APPETIZER EFFECT AND SATIETY. The next time you attend a dinner party, you may experience a major weakness of the set-point theory of satiety. If appetizers are served, you will notice that small amounts of food consumed before a meal actually increase hunger rather than reduce it. This is the **appetizer effect**. Presumably, it occurs because the consumption of small amounts of food is particularly effective in eliciting cephalic-phase responses.

Thinking Creatively

Figure 12.5 The sham-eating preparation.

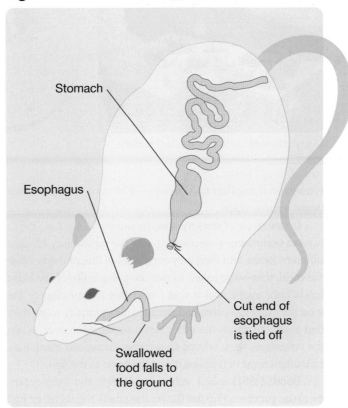

SERVING SIZE AND SATIETY. Many experiments have shown that the amount of consumption is influenced by serving size (see Hollands et al., 2015). The larger the servings, the more we tend to eat.

SOCIAL INFLUENCES AND SATIETY. Feelings of satiety also depend on whether we are eating alone or with others. People consume more when eating with others. Laboratory rats do the same.

SENSORY-SPECIFIC SATIETY. The number of different tastes available at each meal has a major effect on meal size. For example, the effect of offering a laboratory rat a varied diet of highly palatable foods—a **cafeteria diet**—is dramatic. Adult rats that were offered bread and chocolate in addition to their usual laboratory diet increased their average intake of calories by 84 percent, and after 120 days they had increased their average body weights by 49 percent (Rogers & Blundell, 1980). The spectacular effects of cafeteria diets on consumption and body weight clearly run counter to the idea that eating is rigidly controlled by internal energy set points.

The effect on meal size of cafeteria diets results from the fact that satiety is to a large degree sensory-specific. As you eat one food, the positive-incentive value of all foods declines slightly, but the positive-incentive value of that particular food plummets. As a result, you soon become satiated on that food and stop eating it.

Many different factors can affect satiety.

However, if another food is offered to you, you will often begin eating again.

In one study of **sensory-specific satiety** (Rolls et al., 1981), human volunteers were asked to rate the palatability of eight different foods, and then they ate a meal of one of them. After the meal, they were asked to rate the palatability of the eight foods once again, and it was found that their rating of the food they had just eaten had declined substantially more than had their ratings of the other seven foods. Moreover, when the volunteers were offered an unexpected second meal, they consumed most of it unless it was the same as the first.

Booth (1981) asked volunteers to rate the momentary pleasure produced by the flavor, the smell, the sight, or just the thought of various foods at different times after consuming a large, high-calorie, high-carbohydrate liquid meal. There was an immediate sensory-specific decrease in the palatability of foods of the same or similar flavor as soon as the liquid meal was consumed. This was followed by a general decrease in the palatability of all substances about 30 minutes later. Thus, it appears that signals from taste receptors produce an immediate decline in the positive-incentive value of similar tastes and that signals associated with the postingestive consequences of eating produce a general decrease in the positive-incentive value of all foods.

Rolls (1990) suggested that sensory-specific satiety has two kinds of effects: (1) relatively brief effects that influence the selection of foods within a single meal and (2) relatively enduring effects that influence the selection of foods from meal to meal. Some foods seem to be relatively immune to long-lasting sensory-specific satiety; foods such as rice, bread, potatoes, sweets, and green salads can be eaten almost every day with only a slight decline in their palatability (see Rolls, 1986).

The phenomenon of sensory-specific satiety has two adaptive consequences. First, it encourages the consumption of a varied diet. If there were no sensory-specific satiety, a person would tend to eat their preferred food and nothing else, and the result would be malnutrition. Second, sensory-specific satiety encourages animals that have access to a variety of foods to eat a lot; an animal that has eaten its fill of one food will often begin eating again if it encounters a different one (see Raynor & Epstein, 2001). This encourages animals to take full advantage of times of abundance, which are all too rare in nature.

Evolutionary Perspective

This module has introduced you to several important properties of hunger and eating. How many support the set-point assumption, and how many are inconsistent with it?

Thinking Creatively

Thinking Creatively Briefly summarize the evidence for and against the set-point theory of hunger and eating.

Scan Your Brain

Are you ready to move on to the discussion of the physiology of hunger and satiety in the following module? Find out by completing the following sentences with the most appropriate terms. The correct answers are provided at the end of the exercise. Before proceeding, review material related to your incorrect answers and omissions.

1. _____ is the gastrointestinal process of breaking down food and absorbing its constituents into the body.
2. Energy is delivered in the body in three forms: lipids, amino acids, and _____.
3. The phase during which the meal meets the body's immediate energy needs is called the _____ phase.
4. Conversion of protein to glucose is called _____.
5. _____ is the assumption that hunger is typically triggered by a decline in the body's energy reserves below their set point.
6. In _____ systems, feedback changes in one direction elicit compensatory effects in the opposite direction.
7. Pre-meal hunger and _____ conditioning of hunger are the factors that influence what we eat.

8. _____ refers to calories per unit volume of a food.

9. Snacks served before a meal increase hunger rather than reduce it. This is called the _____ effect.

10. The _____ the servings, the more we tend to eat.

11. Aside from satiety, _____ influences affect the amount we eat.

12. _____ produce an immediate decline in the positive-incentive value of similar tastes.

Physiological Research on Hunger and Satiety

Now that you have been introduced to set-point theories, the positive-incentive perspective, and some basic factors that affect why, when, and how much we eat, this module will introduce you to six prominent lines of research on the physiology of hunger and satiety.

Watch this video on MyPsychLab
HUNGER

Role of Blood Glucose Levels in Hunger and Satiety

LO 12.8 Explain the nature of the relationship between blood glucose levels and hunger and satiety.

As we have already explained, efforts to link blood glucose levels to eating have been largely unsuccessful. However, there was a renewed interest in the role of glucose in the regulation of eating in the 1990s, following the development of methods of continually monitoring blood glucose levels (see Grayson, Seeley, & Sandoval, 2013). In the classic experiment of Campfield and Smith (1990), rats were housed with free access to food and water, and their blood glucose levels were continually monitored. In this situation, baseline blood glucose levels rarely fluctuated more than 2 percent. However, about 10 minutes before a meal was initiated, the levels quickly dropped about 8 percent.

Evidence does not support the glucostatic interpretation of this observation: that the premeal decline in blood glucose produces hunger and eating. Indeed, evidence suggests that the causation goes in the opposite direction: that the intention to start eating triggers the decline in blood glucose. The following are four relevant observations:

- The time course of the glucose decline is not consistent with the idea that it reflects a gradual decline in the body's energy—it occurs suddenly just before eating begins.

- Eliminating the premeal drop in blood glucose does not eliminate the meal (see Geiselman, 1987; Strubbe & Stevens, 1977).

- If an expected meal is not served, blood glucose soon returns to its previous level.

- The glucose levels in the extracellular fluids that surround CNS neurons stay relatively constant, even when blood glucose levels drop (see Seeley & Woods, 2003).

Myth of Hypothalamic Hunger and Satiety Centers

LO 12.9 Critically evaluate the concept of hypothalamic hunger and satiety centers.

In the 1950s, experiments on rats seemed to suggest that eating behavior is controlled by two different regions of the hypothalamus: satiety by the **ventromedial hypothalamus (VMH)** and feeding by the **lateral hypothalamus (LH)**—see Figure 12.6. This theory turned out to be wrong, but it stimulated several important discoveries.

VMH SATIETY CENTER. In 1940, it was discovered that large bilateral electrolytic lesions to the ventromedial hypothalamus produce **hyperphagia** (excessive eating) and extreme obesity in rats (Hetherington & Ranson, 1940). This *VMH syndrome* has two different phases: dynamic and static. The **dynamic phase**, which begins as soon as the subject regains consciousness after the operation, is characterized by several weeks of grossly excessive eating and rapid weight gain. However, after that, consumption gradually declines to a level just sufficient to maintain a stable level of obesity; this marks the beginning of the

Figure 12.6 The locations in the rat brain of the ventromedial hypothalamus and the lateral hypothalamus.

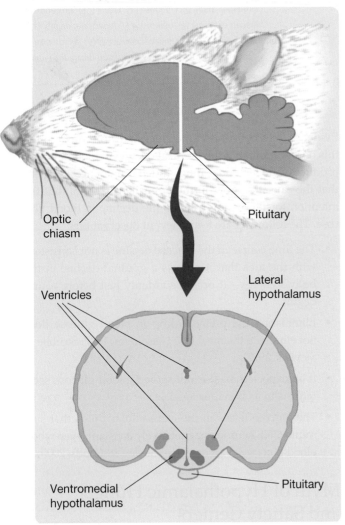

Second, they found that LH-lesioned rats partially recover if they are kept alive by tube feeding. First, they begin to eat wet, palatable foods, such as chocolate chip cookies soaked in milk, and eventually they will eat dry food pellets if water is concurrently available.

REINTERPRETATION OF THE EFFECTS OF VMH AND LH LESIONS. The theory that the VMH is a satiety center crumbled in the face of two lines of evidence. One of these lines showed that the primary role of the hypothalamus is the regulation of energy metabolism, not the regulation of eating. The initial interpretation was that VMH-lesioned animals become obese because they overeat; however, the evidence suggests the converse—that they overeat because they become obese. Bilateral VMH lesions increase blood insulin levels, which increases **lipogenesis** (the production of body fat) and decreases **lipolysis** (the breakdown of body fat to utilizable forms of energy)—see Powley et al. (1980). Both are likely to be the result of the increases in insulin levels that occur following the lesion. Because the calories ingested by VMH-lesioned rats are converted to fat at a high rate, the rats must keep eating to ensure they have enough calories in their blood to meet their immediate energy requirements (e.g., Hustvedt & Løvø, 1972); they are like misers who run to the bank each time they make a bit of money and deposit it in a savings account from which withdrawals cannot be made.

static phase. Figure 12.7 illustrates the weight gain and food intake of an adult rat with bilateral VMH lesions.

The most important feature of the static phase of the VMH syndrome is that the animal maintains its new body weight. If a rat in the static phase is deprived of food until it has lost a substantial amount of weight, it will regain the lost weight once the deprivation ends; conversely, if it is made to gain weight by forced feeding, it will lose the excess weight once the forced feeding is curtailed.

LH FEEDING CENTER. In 1951, Anand and Brobeck reported that bilateral electrolytic lesions to the *lateral hypothalamus* produce **aphagia**—a complete cessation of eating. Even rats that were first made hyperphagic by VMH lesions were rendered aphagic by the addition of LH lesions. Anand and Brobeck concluded that the lateral region of the hypothalamus is a feeding center. Teitelbaum and Epstein (1962) subsequently discovered two important features of the *LH syndrome*. First, they found that the aphagia was accompanied by **adipsia**—a complete cessation of drinking.

Figure 12.7 Postoperative hyperphagia and obesity in a rat with bilateral VMH lesions. (Based on Teitelbaum, P. (1961). Disturbances in feeding and drinking behavior after hypothalamic lesions. In M. R. Jones (Ed.), *Nebraska symposium on motivation* (pp. 63–93). Lincoln: University of Nebraska Press.)

Thinking Creatively Try to briefly summarize the evidence that undermined the theory of a VMH satiety center.

The second line of evidence that undermined the theory of a VMH satiety center has shown that many of the effects of VMH lesions are not attributable to VMH damage. A large fiber bundle, the *ventral noradrenergic bundle,* courses past the VMH and is thus inevitably damaged by large electrolytic VMH lesions; in particular, fibers that project from the nearby **paraventricular nuclei** of the hypothalamus are damaged (see Figure 12.8). Bilateral lesions of the noradrenergic bundle (e.g., Gold et al., 1977) or the paraventricular nuclei (Leibowitz, Hammer, & Chang, 1981) produce hyperphagia and obesity, just as VMH lesions do.

Most of the evidence against the notion that the LH is a feeding center has come from a thorough analysis of the effects of bilateral LH lesions. Early research focused exclusively on the aphagia and adipsia that are produced by LH lesions, but subsequent research has shown that LH lesions

Figure 12.8 Location of the paraventricular nucleus in the rat hypothalamus. Note that the section through the hypothalamus is slightly different than the one in Figure 12.6.

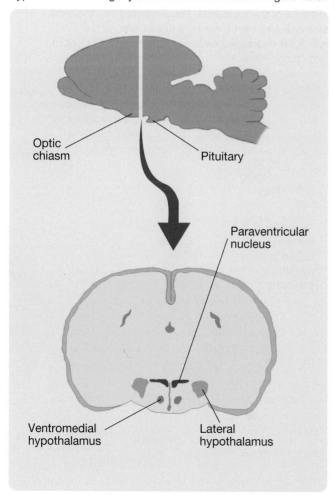

produce a wide range of severe motor disturbances and a general lack of responsiveness to sensory input (of which food and drink are but two examples). Consequently, the idea that the LH is a center specifically dedicated to feeding no longer warrants serious consideration.

MODERN RESEARCH ON THE ROLE OF HYPOTHALAMIC NUCLEI IN HUNGER AND SATIETY. Despite the failure of the concept of the LH and VMH as nuclei that control hunger and satiety, respectively, recent evidence suggests that certain distinct cell populations within the hypothalamus can influence hunger and satiety. For example, certain neurons within the paraventricular nucleus of the hypothalamus have been shown to act as nutrient sensors that can influence feeding and satiety (see Lagerlöf et al., 2016; Schwartz, 2016). Moreover, several distinct neuronal populations within the **arcuate nucleus** of the hypothalamus have been shown to either: (1) control the metabolism of adipose tissue (see Lagerlöf et al., 2016; Schwartz, 2016), (2) reduce feeding (see Carr, 2015), or (3) increase feeding (see Sternson, Betley, & Cao, 2013).

Role of the Gastrointestinal Tract in Satiety

LO 12.10 Describe the role of the gastrointestinal tract in satiety.

One of the most influential early studies of hunger was published by Cannon and Washburn in 1912. It was a perfect collaboration: Cannon had the ideas, and Washburn had the ability to swallow a balloon. First, Washburn swallowed an empty balloon tied to the end of a thin tube. Then, Cannon pumped some air into the balloon and connected the end of the tube to a water-filled glass U-tube so that Washburn's stomach contractions produced a momentary increase in the level of the water at the other end of the U-tube. Washburn reported a "pang" of hunger each time a large stomach contraction was recorded (see Figure 12.9).

Cannon and Washburn's finding led to the theory that hunger is the feeling of contractions caused by an empty stomach, whereas satiety is the feeling of stomach distention. However, support for this theory and interest in the role of the gastrointestinal tract in hunger and satiety quickly waned with the discovery that human patients whose stomach had been surgically removed and whose esophagus had been hooked up directly to their **duodenum** (the first segment of the small intestine, which normally carries food away from the stomach) continued to report feelings of hunger and satiety and continued to maintain their normal body weight by eating more meals of smaller size.

In the 1980s, there was a resurgence of interest in the role of the gastrointestinal tract in eating. It was

Figure 12.9 The system developed by Cannon and Washburn in 1912 for measuring stomach contractions. They found that large stomach contractions were related to pangs of hunger.

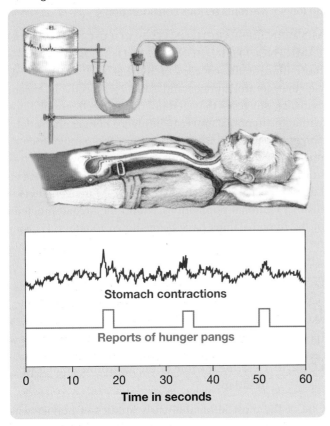

brain, evidence began to accumulate that these chemicals were *peptides*, short chains of amino acids that can function as hormones and neurotransmitters. Ingested food interacts with receptors in the gastrointestinal tract and in so doing causes the tract to release peptides into the bloodstream. In 1973, Gibbs, Young, and Smith injected one of these gut peptides, **cholecystokinin (CCK)**, into hungry rats and found that they ate smaller meals. This led to the hypothesis that circulating gut peptides provide the brain with information about the quantity and nature of food in the gastrointestinal tract and that this information plays a role in satiety (see Dockray, 2014; Woods, 2013).

Evolutionary Perspective

There has been considerable support for the hypothesis that peptides can function as satiety signals (see Gao & Horvath, 2007). Several gut peptides have been shown to bind to receptors in the brain, particularly in areas of the hypothalamus involved in energy metabolism, and a dozen or so (e.g., CCK, bombesin, glucagon,

Figure 12.10 Transplantation of an extra stomach and length of intestine in a rat. Koopmans (1981) implanted an extra stomach and length of intestine in each of his experimental subjects. He then connected the major blood vessels of the implanted stomachs to the circulatory systems of the recipients. Food injected into the extra stomach and kept there by a noose around the pyloric sphincter decreased eating in proportion to its volume and caloric value.

stimulated by a series of experiments that indicated the gastrointestinal tract is the source of satiety signals. For example, Koopmans (1981) transplanted an extra stomach and length of intestine into rats and then joined the major arteries and veins of the implants to the recipients' circulatory systems (see Figure 12.10). Koopmans found that food injected into the transplanted stomach and kept there by a noose around the *pyloric sphincter* decreased eating in proportion to both its caloric content and volume. Because the transplanted stomach had no functional nerves, the gastrointestinal satiety signal had to be reaching the brain through the blood. And because nutrients are not absorbed from the stomach, the bloodborne satiety signal could not have been a nutrient. It had to be some chemical or chemicals that were released from the stomach in response to the caloric value and volume of the food—which leads us nicely into the next section.

Hunger and Satiety Peptides

LO 12.11 Describe the discovery of the hunger and satiety peptides, and name several.

Soon after the discovery that the stomach and other parts of the gastrointestinal tract release chemical signals to the alpha-melanocyte-stimulating hormone, and somatostatin) have been reported to reduce food intake (see Crespo et al., 2014). These have become known as *satiety peptides* (peptides that decrease appetite).

In studying the appetite-reducing effects of peptides, researchers had to rule out the possibility that these effects are not merely the consequence of illness. Indeed, evidence suggests that one peptide in particular, CCK, induces illness: CCK administered to rats after they have eaten an unfamiliar substance induces a *conditioned taste aversion* for that substance, and CCK induces nausea in humans. However, CCK reduces appetite and eating at doses substantially below those required to induce taste aversion in rats, and thus it qualifies as a legitimate satiety peptide.

Several *hunger peptides* (peptides that increase appetite) have also been discovered. These peptides tend to be synthesized in the brain, particularly in the hypothalamus. The most widely studied of these are neuropeptide Y, galanin, orexin-A, and ghrelin (see Liu & Borgland, 2015; Wilson et al., 2014).

The discovery of the hunger and satiety peptides has had two major effects on the search for the neural mechanisms of hunger and satiety. First, the sheer number of these hunger and satiety peptides indicates that the neural system that controls eating likely reacts to many different signals, not just to one or two (e.g., not just to glucose and fat). Second, the discovery that many of the hunger and satiety peptides have receptors in the hypothalamus has renewed interest in the role of the hypothalamus in hunger and eating (see Betley et al., 2015; Dietrich & Horvath, 2013; Jennings et al., 2014; Krashes et al., 2014). This interest was further stimulated by the discovery that microinjection of gut peptides into some sites in the hypothalamus can have major effects on eating. Still it is clear that hypothalamic circuits are only one part of a two-way communication system between the brain and gut that influences hunger, eating, digestion, and the regulation of energy resources (see Grayson et al., 2013; Morton, Meek, & Schwartz, 2014; Sohn, Elmquist, & Williams, 2013; Trivedi, 2014).

Serotonin and Satiety

LO 12.12 Describe the role of serotonin in satiety.

The monoaminergic neurotransmitter serotonin is another chemical that plays a role in satiety. The initial evidence for this role came from a line of research in rats. In these studies, serotonin-produced satiety was found to have three major properties (see Blundell & Halford, 1998):

- It caused the rats to resist the powerful attraction of highly palatable cafeteria diets.

- It reduced the amount of food consumed during each meal rather than reducing the number of meals (see Clifton, 2000).

- It was associated with a shift in food preferences away from fatty foods.

This profile of effects suggested that serotonin might be useful in combating obesity in humans. Indeed, serotonin agonists (e.g., fenfluramine, dexfenfluramine, fluoxetine) have been shown to reduce hunger, eating, and body weight in obese humans under some conditions (see Voigt & Fink, 2015). Later in this chapter, you will learn about the use of serotonin to treat human obesity.

Prader-Willi Syndrome: Patients with Insatiable Hunger

LO 12.13 Describe the symptoms and etiology of Prader-Willi syndrome.

Prader-Willi syndrome could prove critical in the discovery of the neural mechanisms of hunger and satiety (see Tauber et al., 2014). Individuals with **Prader-Willi syndrome**, which results from an accident of chromosomal replication, experience insatiable hunger, little or no satiety, and an exceptionally slow metabolism (see Griggs, Sinnayah, & Mathai, 2015). In short, the Prader-Willi patient acts as though he or she is starving. Other common physical and neurological symptoms include weak muscles, small hands and feet, feeding difficulties in infancy, tantrums, compulsivity, and skin picking. If untreated, most patients become extremely obese, and they often die in early adulthood from diabetes, heart disease, or other obesity-related disorders. Some have even died from gorging until their stomachs split open. Miss A. was diagnosed in infancy and received excellent care, which kept her from becoming obese (Martin et al., 1998).

Prader-Willi Syndrome: The Case of Miss A.

Miss A. was born with little muscle tone. Because her sucking reflex was so weak, she was tube fed. By the time she was 2 years old, her *hypotonia* (below-normal muscle tone) had resolved itself, but a number of characteristic deformities and developmental delays began to appear.

At 3½ years of age, Miss A. suddenly began to display a voracious appetite and quickly gained weight. Fortunately, her family maintained her on a low-calorie diet and kept all food locked away.

Miss A. is moderately intellectually disabled, and she suffers from psychiatric problems. Her major problem is her tendency to have tantrums any time something changes in her environment (e.g., a substitute teacher at school). Thanks largely to her family and pediatrician, she has received excellent care, which has minimized the complications that arise with Prader-Willi syndrome—most notably those related to obesity and its pathological effects.

Although the study of Prader-Willi syndrome has yet to provide any direct evidence about the neural mechanisms of hunger and eating, there has been a marked surge in its investigation. This increase has been stimulated by the recent identification of the genetic cause of the condition: an accident of reproduction that deletes or disrupts a section of chromosome 15 coming from the father.

Body-Weight Regulation: Set Points versus Settling Points

One strength of set-point theories of eating is that they also explain body-weight regulation. You have already learned that set-point theories are largely inconsistent with the facts of eating, but how well do they account for the regulation of body weight? Certainly, many people in our culture believe that body weight is regulated by a body-fat set point (see Assanand, Pinel, & Lehman, 1998a, 1998b). They believe that when fat deposits are below a person's set point, a person becomes hungrier and eats more, which results in a return of body-fat levels to that person's set point. And, conversely, they believe that when fat deposits are above a person's set point, a person becomes less hungry and eats less, which results in a return of body-fat levels to their set point.

Set-Point Assumptions about Body Weight and Eating

LO 12.14 Evaluate the evidence for set-point assumptions about body weight and eating.

You have already learned that set-point theories do a poor job of explaining the characteristics of hunger and eating. Do they do a better job of accounting for the facts of body-weight regulation? Let's begin by looking at three lines of evidence that challenge fundamental aspects of many set-point theories of body-weight regulation.

VARIABILITY OF BODY WEIGHT. A set-point mechanism should make it virtually impossible for an adult to gain or lose large amounts of weight. Yet, many adults experience large and lasting changes in body weight. Set-point thinking crumbles in the face of the epidemic of obesity currently sweeping fast-food societies (see Morris et al., 2014).

Set-point theories of body-weight regulation suggest that the best method of maintaining a constant body weight is to eat each time there is a motivation to eat because, according to the theory, the main function of hunger is to defend the set point. However, many people avoid obesity only by resisting their urges to eat.

SET POINTS AND HEALTH. One implication of set-point theories of body-weight regulation is that each person's set point is optimal for that person's health—or at least not incompatible with good health. This is why popular psychologists commonly advise people to "listen to the wisdom of their bodies" and eat as much as they need to satisfy their hunger. Experimental results indicate that this common prescription for good health could not be further from the truth.

Two kinds of evidence suggest that typical *ad libitum* (free-feeding) levels of consumption are unhealthy. First are the results of nonexperimental studies of humans who consume fewer calories than others. For example, people living on the Japanese island of Okinawa eat so few calories that their eating habits became a concern of health officials. When the health officials took a closer look, here is what they found (see Kagawa, 1978). Adult Okinawans were found to consume, on average, 20 percent fewer calories than other adult Japanese, and Okinawan schoolchildren were found to consume 38 percent fewer calories than recommended by public health officials. It was somewhat surprising then that rates of mortality and of all aging-related diseases were found to be substantially lower in Okinawa than in other parts of Japan, a country in which overall levels of caloric intake and obesity are far below Western norms. For example, the death rates from stroke, cancer, and heart disease in Okinawa were only 59 percent, 69 percent, and 59 percent, respectively, of those in the rest of Japan. Indeed, the proportion of Okinawans living to be over 100 years of age was up to 4 times greater than inhabitants of the United States. In short, low-calorie diets seem to slow down the aging process (see Fontana & Partridge, 2015).

Because the Okinawan study and other nonexperimental studies of humans who eat less are not controlled, they must be interpreted with caution. For example, perhaps it is not simply the consumption of fewer calories that leads to health and longevity; perhaps people who eat less tend to eat healthier diets. **Thinking Creatively**

Controlled experiments of calorie restriction in more than a dozen different mammalian species, including monkeys and humans (see Colman et al., 2014; Ravussin et al., 2015), constitute the second kind of evidence that *ad libitum* levels of consumption are unhealthy. In typical *calorie-restriction experiments*, one group of subjects is allowed to eat as much as they choose, while other groups of subjects have their caloric intake of the same diets substantially reduced (by between 25 and 65 percent in various studies). Results of such experiments have been remarkably consistent (see Bucci, 1992; Masoro, 1988; Weindruch, 1996; Weindruch & Walford, 1988): In experiment after experiment, substantial reductions in the caloric intake of balanced diets have improved numerous indices of health and increased longevity. For example, in one experiment (Weindruch et al., 1986), groups of mice had their caloric intake of a well-balanced commercial diet reduced below free-feeding levels by either 25 percent, 55 percent, or 65 percent after weaning. All levels of dietary restriction substantially improved health and increased longevity, but the benefits were greatest in the mice whose intake was reduced the most. These mice had the lowest incidence of cancer, the best immune responses, and the greatest maximum life span—they lived 67 percent longer than mice that ate as much as they liked. Evidence suggests that dietary restriction can have beneficial effects even if it is not initiated until later in life (see Mair et al., 2003; Vaupel, Carey, & Christensen, 2003). The few experiments of calorie restriction in humans have been conducted over shorter periods of time (e.g., 2 years), but they support the findings in nonhumans (see Ravussin et al., 2015).

 Briefly explain why you think there is an *evolutionary perspective* icon at this particular location in the text.

Remarkably, there is evidence that dietary restriction can be used to treat some neurological conditions. Caloric restriction has been shown to reduce seizure susceptibility in human epileptics (see Maalouf, Rho, & Mattson, 2008) and to improve memory in the elderly (see Witte et al., 2009).

Please stop and think about the implications of all these findings about calorie restriction. How much do you eat?

REGULATION OF BODY WEIGHT BY CHANGES IN THE EFFICIENCY OF ENERGY UTILIZATION. Of course, how much someone eats plays a role in his or her body weight, but it is now clear that the body controls its fat levels, to a large degree, by changing the efficiency with which it uses energy. As a person's level of body fat declines, that person starts to use energy resources more efficiently, which limits further weight loss (see Tremblay et al., 2013); conversely, weight gain is limited by a progressive decrease in the efficiency of energy utilization. Rothwell and Stock (1982) created a group of obese rats by maintaining them on a cafeteria diet, and they found that the resting level of energy expenditure in these obese rats was 45 percent greater than in control rats.

This point is illustrated by the progressively declining effectiveness of weight-loss programs. Initially, low-calorie diets produce substantial weight loss. But the rate of weight loss diminishes with each successive week on the

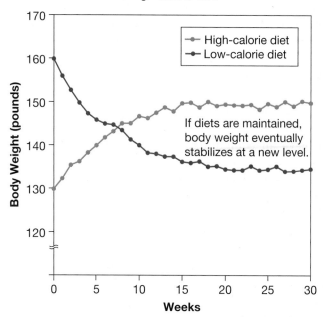

Figure 12.11 The diminishing effects on body weight of a low-calorie diet and a high-calorie diet.

diet, until an equilibrium is achieved and little or no further weight loss occurs. Most dieters are familiar with this disappointing trend. A similar effect occurs with weight-gain programs (see Figure 12.11).

The mechanism by which the body adjusts the efficiency of its energy utilization in response to its levels of body fat has been termed **diet-induced thermogenesis**. Increases in the levels of body fat produce increases in body temperature, which require additional energy to maintain them—and decreases in the level of body fat have the opposite effects (see Jun et al., 2014).

There are major differences among humans both in **basal metabolic rate** (the rate at which energy is utilized to maintain bodily processes when resting) and in the ability to adjust the metabolic rate in response to changes in the levels of body fat. We all know people who remain slim even though they eat gluttonously. However, the research on calorie-restricted diets suggests that these people may not eat with impunity: There seems to be a health cost to pay for overeating even in the absence of obesity.

Set Points and Settling Points in Weight Control

LO 12.15   Compare and evaluate set-point and settling-point models of body-weight regulation.

Several prominent reviews of research on hunger and weight regulation generally acknowledge that a strict set-point model cannot account for the facts of weight regulation, and they argue for a more flexible model (see Berthoud, 2002; Mercer & Speakman, 2001; Woods et al., 2000). Because the body-fat set-point model still dominates the thinking of many people, we want to review the main advantages of an alternative and more flexible regulatory model: the settling-point model. Can you change your thinking?

Thinking Creatively

According to the settling-point model, body weight tends to drift around a natural **settling point**—the level at which the various factors that influence body weight achieve an equilibrium. The idea is that as body-fat levels increase, changes occur that tend to limit further increases until a balance is achieved between all factors that encourage weight gain and all those that discourage it.

The settling-point model provides a loose kind of homeostatic regulation, without a set-point mechanism or mechanisms to return body weight to a set point. According to the settling-point model, body weight remains stable as long as there are no long-term changes in the factors that influence it; and if there are such changes, their impact is limited by negative feedback. In the settling-point model, the negative feedback merely limits further changes in the same direction, whereas in the set-point model, negative feedback triggers a return to the set point. A neuron's resting potential is a well-known biological settling point—see Chapter 4.

The seductiveness of the set-point mechanism is attributable in no small part to the existence of the thermostat model, which provides a vivid means of thinking about it. Figure 12.12 presents an analogy we like to use to think about the settling-point mechanism. We call it the **leaky-barrel model**: (1) the amount of water entering the hose is analogous to the amount of food available to the subject; (2) the water pressure at the nozzle is analogous to the positive-incentive value of the available food; (3) the amount of water entering the barrel is analogous to the amount of energy consumed; (4) the water level

Figure 12.12 The leaky-barrel model: a settling-point model of eating and body-weight homeostasis.

in the barrel is analogous to the level of body fat; (5) the amount of water leaking from the barrel is analogous to the amount of energy being expended; and (6) the weight of the barrel on the hose is analogous to the strength of the satiety signal.

The main advantage of the settling-point model of body-weight regulation over the body-fat set-point model is that it is more consistent with the data. Another advantage is that in those cases in which both models make the same prediction, the settling-point model does so more parsimoniously—that is, with a simpler mechanism that requires fewer assumptions. Let's use the leaky-barrel analogy to see how the two models account for four key facts of weight regulation.

- Body weight remains relatively constant in many adults. On the basis of this fact, it has been argued that body fat must be regulated around a set point. However, constant body weight does not require, or even imply, a set point. Consider the leaky-barrel model. As water from the tap begins to fill the barrel, the weight of the water in the barrel increases. This increases the amount of water leaking out of the barrel and decreases the amount of water entering the barrel by increasing the pressure of the barrel on the hose. Eventually, this system settles into an equilibrium where the water level stays constant; but because this level is neither predetermined nor actively defended, it is a settling point, not a set point.

- Many adults experience enduring changes in body weight. Set-point systems are designed to maintain internal constancy in the face of fluctuations of the external environment. Thus, the fact that many adults experience long-term changes in body weight is a strong argument against the set-point model. In contrast, the settling-point model predicts that when there is an enduring change in one of the parameters that affect body weight—for example, a major increase in the positive-incentive value of available food—body weight will drift to a new settling point.

- If a person's intake of food is reduced, metabolic changes that limit the loss of weight occur; the opposite happens when the subject overeats. This fact is often cited as evidence for set-point regulation of body weight; however, because the metabolic changes merely limit further weight changes rather than eliminating those that have occurred, they are more consistent with a settling-point model. For example, when water intake in the leaky-barrel model is reduced, the water level in the barrel begins to drop; but the drop is limited by a decrease in leakage and an increase in inflow attributable to the falling water pressure in the barrel. Eventually, a new settling point is achieved, but the reduction in water level is not as great as one might expect because of the loss-limiting changes.

- After an individual has lost a substantial amount of weight (by dieting, exercise, or the surgical removal of fat), there is a tendency for the original weight to be regained once he or she returns to the previous eating- and energy-related lifestyle. Although this finding is often offered as irrefutable evidence of a body-weight set point, the settling-point model readily accounts for it. When the water level in the leaky-barrel model is reduced—by temporarily decreasing input (dieting), by temporarily increasing output (exercising), or by scooping out some of the water (surgical removal of fat)—only a temporary drop in the settling point is produced. When the original conditions are reinstated, the water level inexorably drifts back to the original settling point.

Does it really matter whether we think about body-weight regulation in terms of set points or settling points—or is making such a distinction just splitting hairs? It certainly matters to biopsychologists: Understanding that body weight is regulated by a settling-point system helps them better understand, and more accurately predict, the changes in body weight likely to occur in various situations; it also indicates the kinds of physiological mechanisms that are likely **Thinking Creatively** to mediate these changes. And it should matter to you. If the set-point model is correct, attempting to change your body weight would be a waste of time; you would inevitably be drawn back to your body-weight set point. On the other hand, the leaky-barrel model suggests that it is possible to permanently change your body weight by permanently changing any of the factors that influence energy intake or output.

Watch this video on MyPsychLab
CHALK IT UP! SET POINTS VS. SETTLING POINTS

Scan Your Brain

Are you ready to move on to the final two modules of the chapter, which deal with eating disorders? This is a good place to pause and scan your brain to see if you understand the physiological mechanisms of eating and weight regulation. Complete the following sentences by filling in the blanks. The correct answers are provided at the end of the exercise. Before proceeding, review material related to your incorrect answers and omissions.

1. _____ is the complete cessation of drinking.
2. _____ refers to the production of body fat.
3. _____ are short chains of amino acids that can function as hormones and neurotransmitters.
4. _____ is an avoidance response to the taste of food whose consumption has been followed by illness.
5. _____ results from an accident of chromosomal replication, and patients suffer from lack of satiety and slow metabolism.

6. _____ is limited by a progressive decrease in the efficiency of energy utilization.
7. Low-calorie diets slow down the _____ process.
8. The rate at which energy is utilized to maintain bodily processes when resting is referred to as the _____ rate.
9. The _____ is the first segment of the small intestine and normally carries food away from the stomach.
10. The _____ is an analogy for the setting-point model of body-fat regulation.
11. _____ is the term for excessive eating.
12. VMH syndrome has two different phases: dynamic and _____.

Scan Your Brain answers: (1) Adipsia, (2) Lipogenesis, (3) Peptides, (4) Conditioned taste aversion, (5) Prader-Willi syndrome, (6) Weight gain, (7) aging, (8) basal metabolic, (9) duodenum, (10) leaky-barrel model, (11) Hyperphagia, (12) static.

Human Obesity: Causes, Mechanisms, and Treatments

This is an important point in this chapter. The chapter opened by describing the current epidemic of obesity and its adverse effects on health and longevity. Then, as the chapter progressed, you learned that many common beliefs about eating and weight regulation are incompatible with the evidence. Most importantly, you were challenged to think about eating and weight regulation in new ways that are more consistent with current evidence. Now that you are armed with these new ways of thinking, the chapter concludes with a discussion of obesity, anorexia, and bulimia and their treatment.

Obesity: Who Needs to Be Concerned?

LO 12.16 Explain why there is cause for concern surrounding the obesity epidemic.

Almost everyone needs to be concerned about the problem of obesity. If you are currently overweight, the reason for concern is obvious: The relation between obesity and poor health has been repeatedly documented (see Flegal et al., 2013; Simonds & Cowley, 2013). Moreover, some studies

have shown that even obese individuals who are metabolically healthy run a greater risk of developing health problems (see Kramer, Zinman, & Retnakaran, 2013). And the risk is not only to one's own health: Obese women are at increased risk of having infants with health problems (see Avci et al., 2015; Crane et al., 2013). Even if you are currently slim, there is cause for concern; many people who are slim as youths develop serious weight problems as they age.

There is cause for special concern for the next generation. Because rates of obesity are increasing in most parts of the world (see Rosenheck, 2008; Sofsian, 2007), public health officials are concerned about how they are going to handle the growing obesity-related health problem. For example, it has been estimated that more than one third of the children born in the United States in 2000 will eventually develop diabetes, and 10 percent of these will develop related life-threatening conditions (see Haslam, Sattar, & Lean, 2006; Olshansky et al., 2005).

Obesity: Why Is There An Epidemic?

LO 12.17 Describe, from an evolutionary perspective, why there is a current epidemic of obesity.

Let's begin our analysis of obesity by considering the pressures that are likely to have led to the evolution of our eating and weight-regulation systems (see Genné-Bacon, 2014). During the course of evolution, inconsistent food supplies were one of the main threats to survival. As a result, the fittest individuals were those who preferred high-calorie

Evolutionary Perspective foods, ate to capacity when food was available, stored as many excess calories as possible in the form of body fat, and used their stores of calories as efficiently as possible. Individuals who did not have these characteristics were unlikely to survive a food shortage or a harsh winter, and so these characteristics were passed on to future generations (see also Genné-Bacon, 2014; Sellayah, Cagampang, & Cox, 2014; Speakman, 2013).

The development of numerous cultural practices and beliefs that promote consumption has augmented the effects of evolution. For example, in our culture, it is commonly believed that one should eat three meals per day at regular times, whether one is hungry or not; that food should be the focus of most social gatherings; that meals should be served in courses of progressively increasing palatability; and that salt, sweets (e.g., sugar), and fats (e.g., butter or cream) should be added to foods to improve their flavor and thus increase their consumption. Moreover, the tendency to make unhealthy food choices by parents tends to be passed on to their offspring (see Campbell et al., 2007).

Each of us possesses an eating and weight-regulation system that evolved to deal effectively with periodic food shortages, and many of us live in cultures whose eating-related practices evolved for the same purpose. However, our current environment differs from our "natural" environment in critical food-related ways. We live in an environment in which an endless variety of foods of the highest positive-incentive and caloric value are readily and continuously available. The consequence is an appallingly high level of consumption.

Why Do Some People Become Obese While Others Do Not?

LO 12.18 Give some reasons as to why some people become obese whereas others do not.

Why do some people become obese while others living under the same obesity-promoting conditions do not? At a superficial level, the answer is obvious: Those who are obese are those whose energy intake has exceeded their energy output; those who are slim are those whose energy intake has not exceeded their energy output (see Drenowatz, 2015). Although this answer provides little insight, it does serve to emphasize that two kinds of individual differences play a role in obesity: those that lead to differences in energy input and those that lead to differences in energy output. Other differences also play a role.

DIFFERENCES IN CONSUMPTION. Many factors lead some people to eat more than others who have comparable access to food. For example, some people consume more energy because they have strong preferences for the taste of high-calorie foods (see Blundell & Finlayson, 2004; Epstein et al., 2007); some consume more because they were raised in families and/or cultures that promote excessive eating; and some consume more because they have particularly large cephalic-phase responses to the sight or smell of food (see Rodin, 1985).

DIFFERENCES IN ENERGY EXPENDITURE. With respect to energy output, people differ markedly from one another in the degree to which they can dissipate excess consumed energy. The most obvious difference is that people differ substantially in the amount of exercise they get; however, there are others. You have already learned about two of them: differences in *basal metabolic rate* and in the ability to react to fat increases by *diet-induced thermogenesis*. The third factor is called **NEAT**, or *nonexercise activity thermogenesis*, which is generated by activities such as fidgeting and the maintenance of posture and muscle tone; NEAT plays a small role in dissipating excess energy (see Villiblanca et al., 2015).

DIFFERENCES IN GUT MICROBIOME COMPOSITION. Our gastrointestinal tract is replete with microbes, such as bacteria, that help us digest the food we eat—collectively known as our gut microbiome. Indeed, these microbes are so numerous that they outnumber our own bodily cells by 10 to 1 (see Ackerman, 2012; Wallis, 2014). In recent years, there has been a growing appreciation that these microbes that reside inside us can have major influences on brain and behavior (see Walker & Parkhill, 2013). For example, they can influence neurodevelopment, the blood–brain barrier, and even myelination of certain CNS axons (see Flight, 2014; Reardon, 2014; Smith, 2015).

Several recent findings have raised the question of whether our personal gut microbiome might protect us from, or predispose us to, obesity (see Deweerdt, 2014). For example, Ridaura and colleagues (2013) reported on the effects of taking mice raised in a germ-free environment and colonizing them with the fecal microbiota of twin pairs that were discordant for obesity (i.e., one twin was obese whereas the other was not). That is, half the mice were colonized by microbes from the lean twins, and the other half were colonized by microbes from their obese co-twins. Those mice that were colonized with microbes from the obese co-twins gained more weight and had greater amounts of body fat compared with those colonized with microbes from the lean co-twins.

GENETIC AND EPIGENETIC FACTORS. Given the number of factors that can influence food consumption and energy metabolism, it is not surprising that many genes can influence body weight. Indeed, about 100 human chromosome loci (regions) have already been linked to obesity (see Locke et al., 2015). Interestingly, some of these genes seem to influence the likelihood of obesity by affecting one's gut microbiome (see Pennisi, 2014; van Opstal & Bordenstein, 2015).

Although it is proving difficult to unravel the interactions among the various genetic factors that influence variations in body weight among healthy people, single gene mutations have been linked to pathological conditions that involve obesity. You will encounter an example of such a condition later in this module. In addition, there is evidence that transgenerational epigenetic effects (see Chapter 2) can predispose subsequent generations to obesity (see Drummond & Gibney, 2013; Willyard, 2014).

Why Are Weight-Loss Programs Often Ineffective?

LO 12.19 Explain why weight-loss programs are typically ineffective.

Figure 12.13 describes the course of the typical weight-loss program. Most weight-loss programs are unsuccessful in the sense that, as predicted by the settling-point model, most of the lost weight is regained once the dieter stops following the program and the original conditions are reestablished. The key to permanent weight loss is a permanent lifestyle change.

Exercise has many health-promoting effects; however, despite the general belief that exercise is the most effective method of losing weight, several studies have shown that it often contributes little to weight loss (see Dhurandhar et

al., 2015; Riou et al., 2015). One reason is that physical exercise normally accounts for only a small proportion of total energy expenditure: Most of the energy you expend is used to maintain the resting physiological processes of your body (e.g., body temperature) and to digest your food (see Hills, Mokhtar, & Byrne, 2014). Another reason is that our bodies are efficient machines, burning only a small number of calories during a typical workout. Moreover, after exercise, many people feel free to consume extra drinks and foods that contain more calories than the relatively small number that were expended during the exercise (see Freedman, 2011).

Leptin and the Regulation of Body Fat

LO 12.20 Explain how leptin and insulin are feedback signals for the regulation of body fat.

Fat is more than a passive storehouse of energy; it actively releases a peptide hormone called **leptin**. The following three subsections describe (1) the discovery of leptin, (2) how its discovery has fueled the development of a new approach to the treatment of human obesity, and (3) how the understanding that leptin and insulin are feedback signals led to the discovery of a hypothalamic nucleus that plays an important role in the regulation of body fat.

Figure 12.13 The five stages of a typical weight-loss program.

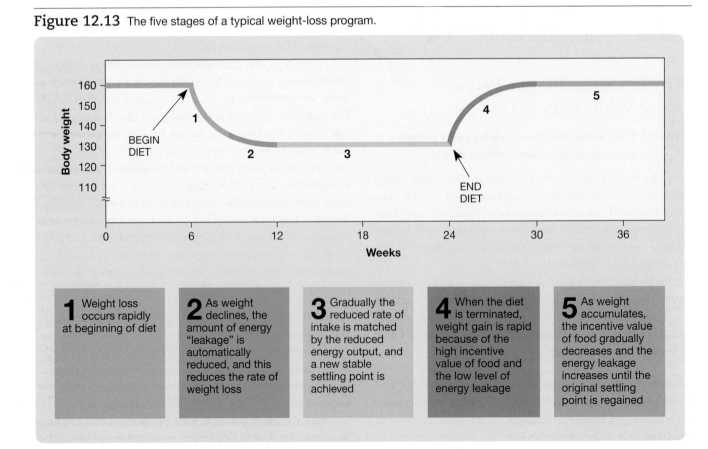

Figure 12.14 An ob/ob mouse and a control mouse.

OBESE MICE AND THE DISCOVERY OF LEPTIN. In 1950, a spontaneous genetic mutation occurred in the mouse colony being maintained in the Jackson Laboratory at Bar Harbor, Maine. The mutant mice were *homozygous* for the gene (ob), and they were grossly obese, weighing up to three times as much as typical mice. These mutant mice are commonly referred to as **ob/ob mice**. See Figure 12.14.

Ob/ob mice eat more than control mice; they convert calories to fat more efficiently; and they use their calories more efficiently. Coleman (1979) hypothesized that ob/ob mice lack a critical hormone that normally inhibits fat production and maintenance.

Evolutionary Perspective

In 1994, Friedman and his colleagues characterized and cloned the gene that is mutated in ob/ob mice. They found that this gene is expressed only in fat cells, and they characterized the protein it normally encodes, a peptide hormone they named leptin. Because of their mutation, ob/ob mice lack leptin. This finding led to an exciting hypothesis: Perhaps leptin is a negative feedback signal normally released from fat stores to decrease appetite and increase fat metabolism. Could leptin be administered to obese humans to reverse the current epidemic of obesity?

LEPTIN, INSULIN, AND THE ARCUATE MELANO-CORTIN SYSTEM. There was great fanfare when leptin was discovered. However, it was not the first peptide hormone to be discovered that seems to function as a negative feedback signal in the regulation of body fat (see Schwartz, 2000; Woods, 2004). More than 30 years ago, Woods and colleagues (1979) suggested that the pancreatic peptide hormone insulin serves such a function.

At first, the suggestion that insulin serves as a negative feedback signal for body fat regulation was viewed with skepticism. After all, how could the level of insulin in the body, which goes up and then comes back down to normal following each meal, provide the brain with information about gradually changing levels of body fat? It turns out that insulin does not readily penetrate the blood–brain barrier, and its levels in the brain were found

to stay relatively stable (see Tomlinson & Gardiner, 2008). The following findings supported the hypothesis that insulin serves as a negative feedback signal in the regulation of body fat:

- Brain levels of insulin were found to be positively correlated with levels of body fat (see Seeley et al., 1996).
- Receptors for insulin were found in the brain (see Baura et al., 1993).
- Infusions of insulin into the brains of laboratory animals were found to reduce eating and body weight (see Campfield et al., 1995; Chavez, Seeley, & Woods, 1995; but see Mc Allister et al., 2015; Woods & Begg, 2015).

Why are there two fat feedback signals? One reason may be that leptin levels are more closely correlated with **subcutaneous fat** (fat stored under the skin), whereas insulin levels are more closely correlated with **visceral fat** (fat stored around the internal organs of the body cavity)—see Heni et al. (2015). Thus, each fat signal could provide different information. Visceral fat is more common in males than females and poses the greater threat to health (see Palmer & Clegg, 2015).

The discovery that leptin and insulin are signals that provide information to the brain about fat levels in the body provided a means for discovering the neural circuits that participate in fat regulation. Receptors for both peptide hormones are located in many parts of the nervous system, but most are in the hypothalamus, particularly in the **arcuate nucleus**.

A closer look at the distribution of leptin and insulin receptors in the arcuate nucleus indicated that these receptors are not randomly distributed throughout the nucleus. They are located in two classes of neurons: neurons that release **neuropeptide Y** (the gut hunger peptide that you read about earlier in the chapter) and neurons that release **melanocortins**, a class of peptides that includes the gut satiety peptide α-*melanocyte-stimulating hormone* (alpha-melanocyte-stimulating hormone). Attention has been mostly focused on the melanocortin-releasing neurons in the arcuate nucleus (often referred to as the **melanocortin system**) because injections of α-melanocyte-stimulating hormone have been shown to suppress eating and promote weight loss (see Kim, Leyva, & Diano, 2014). It seems, however, that the melanocortin system is only a minor component of a much larger system: Elimination of leptin receptors in the melanocortin system produces only a slight weight gain (see Münzberg & Myers, 2005).

LEPTIN AS A TREATMENT FOR HUMAN OBESITY. The early studies of leptin seemed to confirm the hypothesis that it could function as an effective treatment for obesity. Receptors for leptin were found in the brain, and injecting it into ob/ob mice reduced both their eating and their body fat (see Seeley & Woods, 2003). All that remained was to prove leptin's effectiveness in human patients.

However, when research on leptin turned from ob/ob mice to obese humans, the program ran into two major snags. First, obese humans—unlike ob/ob mice—were found to have high, rather than low, levels of leptin (see Münzberg & Myers, 2005). Second, injections of leptin did not reduce either the eating or the body fat of obese humans (see Heymsfield et al., 1999).

Why the actions of leptin are different in humans and ob/ob mice has yet to be explained. Nevertheless, efforts 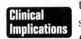 to use leptin in the treatment of human obesity have not been a total failure. Although few obese humans have low leptin levels (see Blüher & Mantzoros, 2015), leptin may be a panacea for those who do. Consider the following case.

The Case of the Child with No Leptin

The patient was of normal weight at birth, but her weight soon began to increase at an excessive rate. She demanded food continually and was disruptive when denied food. As a result of her extreme obesity, deformities of her legs developed, and surgery was required.

She was 9 when she was referred for treatment. At this point, she weighed 94.4 kilograms (about 210 pounds), and her weight was still increasing at an alarming rate. She was found to be homozygous for the ob gene and had no detectable leptin. Thus, leptin therapy was commenced.

The leptin therapy immediately curtailed the weight gain. She began to eat less, and she lost weight steadily over the 12-month period of the study, a total of 16.5 kilograms (about 36 pounds), almost all in the form of fat. There were no obvious side effects (Farooqi et al., 1999).

Treatment of Obesity

LO 12.21 Describe two sorts of treatments for obesity.

Because obesity is such a severe health problem, there have been many efforts to develop an effective treatment. Some of these—such as the leptin treatment you just read about—have worked for a few, but the problem of obesity continues to grow. The following two subsections discuss two treatments that are at different stages of development: serotonergic agonists and gastric surgery.

SEROTONERGIC AGONISTS. Because—as you have already learned—serotonin agonists have been shown to reduce food consumption in both human and nonhuman subjects, they have considerable potential in the treatment of obesity (Voigt & Fink, 2015). Serotonin agonists seem to act by a mechanism different from that for leptin and

insulin, which produce long-term satiety signals based on fat stores. Serotonin agonists seem to increase short-term satiety signals associated with the consumption of a meal (Halford & Blundell, 2000).

Serotonin agonists have been found in various studies of obese patients to reduce the following: the urge to eat high-calorie foods, the consumption of fat, the subjective intensity of hunger, the size of meals, the number of between-meal snacks, and bingeing. Because of this extremely positive profile of effects and the severity of the obesity problem, serotonin agonists (fenfluramine and dexfenfluramine) were rushed into clinical use. However, they were subsequently withdrawn from the market because chronic use was found to be associated with heart disease in a small but significant number of users.

Currently, there is only one approved serotonin agonist for the treatment of obesity that has a more favorable side-effect profile: lorcaserin (see Halpern & Halpern, 2015; Nigro, Luon, & Baker, 2013). However, the efficacy of lorcaserin for the treatment of obesity is only modest (see Adan, 2013).

GASTRIC SURGERY. Cases of extreme obesity sometimes warrant extreme treatment. **Gastric bypass** is a surgical treatment for extreme obesity that involves short-circuiting the normal path of food through the digestive tract so that its absorption is reduced. The first gastric bypass was done in 1967, and it is currently the most commonly prescribed surgical treatment for extreme obesity (see Berthoud, 2013). An alternative is the **adjustable gastric band procedure**, which involves surgically positioning a hollow silicone band around the stomach to reduce the flow of food through it; the circumference of the band can be adjusted by injecting saline into the band through a port that is implanted in the skin. One advantage of the gastric band over the gastric bypass is that the band can readily be removed.

The gastric bypass and adjustable gastric band are illustrated in Figure 12.15. A meta-analysis of studies comparing the two procedures found both to be highly effective (see Chang et al., 2014). In general, gastric bypass was found to be more effective than the adjustable gastric band procedure (see also Hughes, 2014) but was associated with more surgery-related complications. However, neither procedure is effective unless patients change their eating habits.

Anorexia and Bulimia Nervosa

This chapter concludes with a discussion of two eating disorders of underconsumption: anorexia nervosa and bulimia nervosa.

Figure 12.15 Two surgical methods for treating extreme obesity: gastric bypass and adjustable gastric band. The gastric band can be tightened by injecting saline into the access port implanted just beneath the skin.

Gastric Bypass

Adjustable Gastric Band

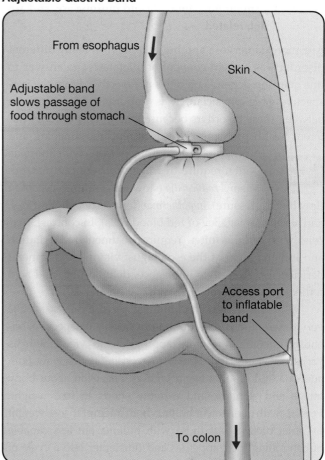

Anorexia and Bulimia Nervosa

LO 12.22 Describe the symptoms of anorexia nervosa and bulimia nervosa.

ANOREXIA NERVOSA. **Anorexia nervosa** is a disorder of underconsumption (see Kaye et al., 2013). Individuals with anorexia eat so little that they experience health-threatening weight loss, and despite their emaciated appearance, they often perceive themselves as fat (see Gardner & Brown, 2014). Anorexia nervosa is a serious condition: In approximately 4 percent of diagnosed cases, complications from starvation result in death, and there is a high rate of suicide among persons with anorexia.

BULIMIA NERVOSA. **Bulimia nervosa** is a disorder characterized by periods of not eating interrupted by *bingeing* (eating huge amounts of food in short periods of time) followed by efforts to immediately eliminate the consumed calories from the body by voluntary *purging* (via vomiting or excessive use of laxatives, enemas, or diuretics) or by extreme exercise.

Watch this video on MyPsychLab

NATASHA: ANOREXIA NERVOSA

Persons with bulimia may be obese or of normal weight. If they are underweight, they are diagnosed with *binge-eating/purging anorexia*. Bulimia nervosa is a serious condition: The mortality rate for individuals with bulimia is about 4 percent.

Relation between Anorexia and Bulimia

LO 12.23 Explain how anorexia and bulimia are, and are not, related.

Are anorexia nervosa and bulimia nervosa really different disorders, as current convention dictates? The answer to this question depends on one's perspective. From the perspective of a physician, it is important to distinguish between these disorders because starvation produces different health problems than does repeated bingeing and purging. For example, persons with anorexia often require treatment for reduced metabolism, *bradycardia* (slow heart rate), *hypotension* (low blood pressure), *hypothermia* (low body temperature), and *anemia* (deficiency of red blood cells). In contrast, persons with bulimia often require treatment for irritation and inflammation of the esophagus, vitamin and mineral deficiencies, electrolyte imbalance, dehydration, and acid reflux (see Westmoreland, Krantz, & Mehler, 2015).

Thinking Creatively

Although anorexia and bulimia nervosa may seem like very different disorders from a physician's perspective, scientists often find it more appropriate to view them as variations of the same disorder. According to this view, both anorexia and bulimia begin with an obsession about body image and slimness and extreme efforts to lose weight. Persons with anorexia or bulimia both attempt to lose weight by strict dieting, but those with bulimia are less capable of controlling their appetites and thus enter into a cycle of starvation, bingeing, and purging. The following are other similarities that support the view that anorexia and bulimia are variants of the same disorder (see Kaye et al., 2005):

- Individuals with anorexia or bulimia both tend to have distorted body images, seeing themselves as much fatter and less attractive than they are in reality (see Tabri et al., 2015).

- In practice, many patients seem to straddle the two diagnoses and cannot readily be assigned to one or the other categories, and many patients flip-flop between the two diagnoses as their circumstances change (see Kaye et al., 2013).

- Both anorexia and bulimia are highly correlated with obsessive-compulsive disorder and depression (see Kaye et al., 2004).

Anorexia and Positive Incentives

LO 12.24 Explain why those starving due to anorexia do not appear to be as hungry as they should.

The positive-incentive perspective on eating suggests that the decline in eating that defines both anorexia and

Video

bulimia is likely a consequence of a corresponding decline in the positive-incentive value of food. However, the positive-incentive value of food for anorexia patients has received little attention—in part, because anorexia patients often display substantial interest in food. The fact that many anorexia patients are obsessed with food—continually talking about it, thinking about it, and preparing it for others (see Crisp, 1983)—seems to suggest that food still holds a high positive-incentive value for them. However, to avoid confusion, it is necessary to keep in mind that the positive-incentive value of *interacting* with food is not necessarily the same as the positive-incentive value of *eating* food—and it is the positive-incentive value of eating food that is critical when considering anorexia nervosa.

Thinking Creatively

A few studies have examined the positive-incentive value of various tastes in anorexia patients (see Drewnowski et al., 1987; Roefs et al., 2006; Sunday & Halmi, 1990). In general, these studies have found that the positive-incentive value of various tastes is lower in anorexia patients than in controls. However, these studies grossly underestimate the importance of reductions in the positive-incentive value of food in the etiology of anorexia nervosa, because the participants with anorexia have been compared to normal-weight control participants.

We can get some insight into the effects of anorexia nervosa on the positive-incentive value of food only by comparing individuals with anorexia to starving people of the same weight. Consider the behavior of volunteers undergoing semistarvation and compare it to people with anorexia. When asked how it felt to starve, one starving volunteer replied:

> I wait for mealtime. When it comes I eat slowly and make the food last as long as possible. The menu never gets monotonous even if it is the same each day or is of poor quality. It is food and all food tastes good. Even dirty crusts of bread in the street look appetizing. (Keys et al., 1950, p. 876)

Anorexia Nervosa: A Hypothesis

LO 12.25   Explain how anorexia might result from conditioned taste aversions.

The dominance of set-point theories in research into the regulation of hunger and eating has resulted in widespread inattention to one of the major puzzles of anorexia: Why does the adaptive massive increase in the positive-incentive value of eating that occurs in victims of starvation not occur in persons starving due to anorexia? Under conditions of starvation, the positive-incentive value of eating normally increases to such high levels that it is difficult to imagine how anybody who was starving—no matter how controlled, rigid, obsessive, and motivated that person was—could refrain from eating in the presence of palatable food. Why this protective mechanism is not activated in severe anorexia is a pressing question about the etiology of anorexia nervosa.

We believe part of the answer lies in the research of Woods and his colleagues on the aversive physiological effects of meals. At the beginning of meals, people are normally in reasonably homeostatic balance, and this homeostasis is disrupted by the sudden infusion of calories. The other part of the answer lies in the finding that the aversive effects of meals are much greater in people who have been eating little (see Brooks & Melnik, 1995). Meals, which produce adverse, but tolerable, effects in healthy individuals, may be extremely aversive for individuals who have undergone food deprivation. Evidence for the extremely noxious effects that eating meals has on starving humans is found in the reactions of World War II concentration camp victims to refeeding—many were rendered ill and some were even killed by the food given to them by their liberators (see Keys et al., 1950; Soloman & Kirby, 1990).

So why do individuals with severe anorexia not experience a massive increase in the positive-incentive value of eating, similar to the increase experienced by other starving individuals? The answer may be *meals*. Meals consumed by a person with anorexia may produce a variety of conditioned taste aversions that reduce the motivation to eat. This hypothesis needs to be addressed because of its implication for treatment: Patients with anorexia—or anybody else who is severely undernourished—should not be encouraged, or even permitted, to eat meals. They should be fed—or infused with—small amounts of food intermittently throughout the day.

We have described the preceding hypothesis to show you the value of the new ideas you have encountered in this chapter: The major test of a new theory is whether it leads to innovative hypotheses.

A few years ago, as I (JP) was perusing an article on global famine and malnutrition, I noticed an intriguing comment: One of the clinical complications that results from feeding meals to famine victims is anorexia (Blackburn, 2001). What do you make of this?

 Thinking Creatively   What do you think causes anorexia nervosa? Summarize the evidence that supports your view.

The Case of the Student with Anorexia

In a society in which obesity is the main disorder of consumption, individuals with anorexia are out of step. People who are struggling to eat less have difficulty understanding those who have to struggle to eat. Still, when you stare anorexia in the face, it is difficult not to be touched by it.

She began by telling me (JP) how much she had been enjoying the course and how sorry she was to be dropping out of the university. She was articulate and personable, and her grades were high—very high. Her problem was anorexia; she weighed only 82 pounds, and she was about to be hospitalized.

"But don't you want to eat?" I asked naively. "Don't you see that your plan to go to medical school will go up in smoke if you don't eat?"

"Of course I want to eat. I know I am terribly thin—my friends tell me I am. Believe me, I know this is wrecking my life. I try to eat, but I just can't force myself. In a strange way, I am pleased with my thinness."

She was upset, and I was embarrassed by my insensitivity. "It's too bad you're dropping out of the course before we cover the chapter on eating," I said, groping for safer ground.

"Oh, I've read it already," she responded. "The bit about positive incentives and learning was really good. I think my problem began when eating started to lose its positive-incentive value for me—in my mind, I kind of associated eating with being fat and all the boyfriend problems I was having. This made it easy to diet, but every once in a while I would get hungry and binge, or my parents would force me to eat a big meal. I would eat so much that I would feel ill. So I would put my finger down my throat and make myself throw up. This kept me from gaining weight, but I think it also taught my body to associate my favorite foods with illness—kind of a conditioned taste aversion. What do you think of my theory?"

After a lengthy chat, she got up to leave, and I walked her to the door of my office. I wished her luck and made her promise to come back for a visit. I never saw her again, but the image of her emaciated body walking down the hallway from my office has stayed with me.

Themes Revisited

Three of the text's four themes played prominent roles in this chapter. The thinking creatively theme was prevalent as you were challenged to critically evaluate your own beliefs and ambiguous research findings, to con-

Thinking Creatively sider the scientific implications of your own experiences, and to think in new ways about phenomena with major personal and clinical implications. The chapter ended by using these new ideas to develop a potentially important hypothesis about the etiology of anorexia nervosa. Because of its emphasis on thinking, this chapter is our personal favorite.

Both aspects of the evolutionary perspective theme were emphasized repeatedly. First, you saw how thinking about hunger

 Evolutionary Perspective

and eating from an evolutionary perspective leads to important insights. Second, you saw how controlled research on nonhuman species has contributed to our current understanding of human hunger and eating.

Finally, the clinical implications theme pervaded the chapter, but it was featured in the cases of the man who forgot not to eat, the child with Prader-Willi syndrome, the child with no leptin, and the **Clinical Implications** student with anorexia.

Key Terms

Chapter 13
Hormones and Sex

What's Wrong with the Mamawawa?

Chapter Overview and Learning Objectives (LOs)

Neuroendocrine System

LO 13.1 Explain the distinction between exocrine glands and endocrine glands, describe the functions of the gonads, and distinguish between the X chromosome and the Y chromosome.

LO 13.2 Describe the three classes of hormones, and then describe three classes of gonadal hormones.

LO 13.3 Explain why the pituitary is sometimes called the *master gland*, and describe its anatomy. Discuss the female vs. male patterns of gonadal and gonadotropic hormone release, and explain the evidence that discounted a role for the anterior pituitary in those patterns of release.

LO 13.4 Explain how the anterior and posterior pituitary are controlled.

LO 13.5 Describe the research that led to the discovery of the hypothalamic releasing hormones.

355

This chapter is about hormones and sex, a topic that some regard as unfit for conversation but that fascinates many others. Perhaps the topic of hormones and sex is so fascinating because we are intrigued by the fact that our sex is so greatly influenced by the secretions of a small pair of glands. Because we each think of our gender as fundamental and immutable, it is a bit disturbing to think that it could be altered with a few surgical snips and some hormone injections. And there is something intriguing about the idea that our sex lives might be enhanced by the application of a few hormones. For whatever reason, the topic of hormones and sex is always a hit with our students. Some remarkable things await you in this chapter.

MEN-ARE-MEN-AND-WOMEN-ARE-WOMEN ASSUMPTION. Let's start with the fact that many students bring a piece of excess baggage to the topic of hormones and sex: the men-are-men-and-women-are-women assumption—or "mamawawa." This assumption is seductive; it seems so right that we are continually drawn to it without considering alternative views. Unfortunately, it is fundamentally flawed.

The men-are-men-and-women-are-women assumption is the tendency to think about femaleness and maleness as discrete, mutually exclusive, opposite categories. In thinking about hormones and sex, this general attitude leads one to assume that females have female sex hormones that give them female bodies and make them do "female" things, and that males have male sex hormones that give them male bodies and make them do opposite "male" things. Despite the fact that this approach to hormones and sex is inconsistent with the evidence, its simplicity, symmetry, and comfortable social implications draw us to it (see Carothers & Reis, 2013; Jordan-Young & Rumiati, 2012). That's why this chapter grapples with it throughout. In so doing, this chapter encourages you to think about hormones and sex in new ways that are more consistent with the evidence.

DEVELOPMENTAL AND ACTIVATIONAL EFFECTS OF SEX HORMONES. Before we begin discussing hormones and sex, you need to know that hormones influence sex in two fundamentally different ways (see Bale & Epperson, 2015): (1) by influencing the development from conception to sexual maturity of the anatomical, physiological, and behavioral characteristics that distinguish one as female or male; and (2) by activating the reproduction-related behavior of sexually mature adults (see Wu & Shah, 2011). The *developmental* (also called *organizational*) and *activational* effects of sex hormones are discussed in different parts of this chapter. However, in real life the two effects can occur simultaneously—for example, because the brain continues to develop into the late teens, adolescent hormone surges can have both effects.

Neuroendocrine System

This module starts off by introducing the general principles of neuroendocrine function. It introduces these principles by focusing on the glands and hormones directly involved in sexual development and behavior.

The endocrine glands are illustrated in Figure 13.1. By convention, only the organs whose primary function appears to be the release of hormones are referred to as *endocrine glands*. However, other organs (e.g., the stomach, liver, and intestine) and body fat also release hormones into general circulation (see Chapter 12), and they are thus, strictly speaking, also part of the endocrine system.

Glands

LO 13.1 Explain the distinction between exocrine glands and endocrine glands, describe the functions of the gonads, and distinguish between the X chromosome and the Y chromosome.

There are two types of glands: exocrine glands and endocrine glands. **Exocrine glands** (e.g., sweat glands) release their chemicals into ducts, which carry them to their targets, mostly on the surface of the body. **Endocrine glands** (ductless glands) release their chemicals, which are called **hormones**, directly into the circulatory system. Once released by an endocrine gland, a hormone travels via the circulatory system until it reaches the targets on which it

Figure 13.1 The endocrine glands.

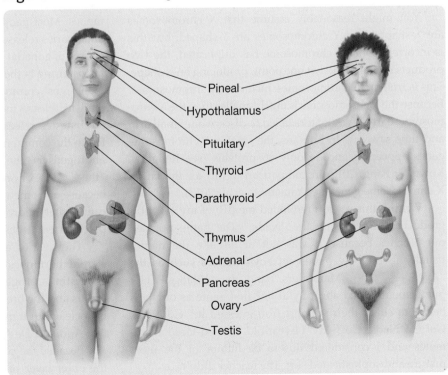

normally exerts its effect (e.g., other endocrine glands, sites in the nervous system).

GONADS. Central to any discussion of hormones, sex, and glands are the **gonads**—the male **testes** (pronounced TEST-eez) and the female **ovaries** (see Figure 13.1). As you learned in Chapter 2, the primary function of the testes and ovaries is the production of *sperm cells* and *ova*, respectively. After **copulation** (sexual intercourse), a single sperm cell may *fertilize* an *ovum* to form one cell called a **zygote**, which contains all of the information necessary for the typical growth of a complete adult organism in its natural environment. With the exception of ova and sperm cells, each cell of the human body has 23 pairs of chromosomes. In contrast, the ova and sperm cells contain only half that number, one member of each of the 23 pairs. Thus, when a sperm cell fertilizes an ovum, the resulting zygote ends up with the full complement of 23 pairs of chromosomes—one of each pair from the father and one of each pair from the mother.

Of particular interest in the context of this chapter is the pair of chromosomes called the **sex chromosomes**, so named because they contain the genetic programs that direct sexual development. The cells of females have two large sex chromosomes, called *X chromosomes*. In males, one sex chromosome is an X chromosome, and the other is called a *Y chromosome*. Consequently, the sex chromosome of every ovum is an X chromosome, whereas half the sperm cells have X chromosomes and half have Y chromosomes. Your sex with all its social, economic, and personal ramifications was determined by which of your father's sperm cells won the dash to your mother's ovum. If a sperm cell with an X sex chromosome won, you are a female; if one with a Y sex chromosome won, you are a male.

You might reasonably assume that X chromosomes are X-shaped and Y chromosomes are Y-shaped, but this is incorrect. Once a chromosome has duplicated, the two products remain joined at one point, producing an X shape. This is true of all chromosomes, including Y chromosomes. Because the Y chromosome is much smaller than the X chromosome, early investigators failed to discern one small arm and thus saw a Y. In humans, the smaller Y-chromosome genes appear to encode only 66 proteins (see Rengaraj, Kown, & Pang, 2015) in comparison to 615 for the larger X-chromosome genes (see Yamamoto et al., 2013).

Writing this section reminded me (JP) of my seventh-grade basketball team, the "Nads." The name puzzled our teacher because it was not at all like the names usually favored by pubescent boys—names such as the "Avengers," the "Marauders," and the "Vikings." Her puzzlement ended abruptly at our first game as our fans began to chant their support. You guessed it: "Go Nads, Go! Go Nads, Go!" My 14-year-old spotted-faced teammates and I considered this to be humor of the most mature and sophisticated sort. The teacher didn't.

Hormones

LO 13.2 **Describe the three classes of hormones, and then describe three classes of gonadal hormones.**

Vertebrate hormones fall into one of three classes: (1) amino acid derivatives, (2) peptides and proteins, and (3) steroids. **Amino acid derivative hormones** are hormones that are synthesized in a few simple steps from an amino acid molecule; an example is *epinephrine*, which is released from the *adrenal medulla* and synthesized from *tyrosine*. **Peptide hormones** and **protein hormones** are chains of amino acids—peptide hormones are short chains, and protein hormones are long chains. **Steroid hormones** are hormones that are synthesized from *cholesterol*, a type of fat molecule.

The hormones that influence sexual development and the activation of adult sexual behavior (i.e., the sex hormones) are all steroid hormones. Most other hormones produce their effects by binding to receptors in cell membranes. Steroid hormones can influence cells in this fashion; however, because they are small and fat-soluble, they can readily penetrate cell membranes and often affect cells in a second way. Once inside a cell, the steroid molecules can bind to receptors in the cytoplasm or nucleus and, by so doing, directly influence gene expression (amino acid derivative hormones and peptide hormones affect gene expression less commonly and by less direct mechanisms). Consequently, of all the hormones, steroid hormones tend to have the most diverse and long-lasting effects on cellular function.

SEX STEROIDS. The gonads do more than create sperm and egg cells; they also produce and release steroid hormones. Most people are surprised to learn that the testes and ovaries release the very same hormones. The two main classes of gonadal hormones are **androgens** and **estrogens**; **testosterone** is the most common androgen, and **estradiol** is the most common estrogen. The fact that adult ovaries tend to release more estrogens than androgens and that adult testes release more androgens than estrogens has led to the common, but misleading, practice of referring to androgens as "the *male* sex hormones" and to estrogens as "the *female* sex hormones." This practice should be avoided because of its men-are-men-and-women-are-women implication that androgens produce maleness and estrogens produce femaleness. They don't.

The ovaries and testes also release a third class of steroid hormones called **progestins**. The most common progestin is **progesterone**, which in females prepares the uterus and the breasts for pregnancy. Its function in males is unclear, but it may play a role in sperm cell metabolism (see Aquila & De Amicis, 2014).

Because the primary function of the **adrenal cortex**—the outer layer of the *adrenal glands* (see Figure 13.1)—is the regulation of glucose and salt levels in the blood, it is not generally thought of as a sex gland. However, in addition to its principal steroid hormones, it does release small amounts of all of the sex steroids released by the gonads.

The Pituitary

LO 13.3   Explain why the pituitary is sometimes called the *master gland*, and describe its anatomy. Discuss the female vs. male patterns of gonadal and gonadotropic hormone release, and explain the evidence that discounted a role for the anterior pituitary in those patterns of release.

The pituitary gland is frequently referred to as the *master gland* because most of its hormones are tropic hormones. *Tropic hormones'* primary function is to influence the release of hormones from other glands (*tropic* means "able to stimulate or change something"). For example, **gonadotropin** is a pituitary tropic hormone that travels through the circulatory system to the gonads, where it stimulates the release of gonadal hormones.

The pituitary gland is really two glands, the posterior pituitary and the anterior pituitary, which fuse during the course of embryological development. The **posterior pituitary** develops from a small outgrowth of hypothalamic tissue that eventually comes to dangle from the *hypothalamus* on the end of the **pituitary stalk** (see Figure 13.2). In contrast, the **anterior pituitary** begins as part of the same

embryonic tissue that eventually develops into the roof of the mouth; during the course of development, it pinches off and migrates upward to assume its position next to the posterior pituitary. It is the anterior pituitary that releases tropic hormones; thus, it is the anterior pituitary in particular, rather than the pituitary in general, that qualifies as the master gland.

FEMALE GONADAL HORMONE LEVELS ARE CYCLIC; MALE GONADAL HORMONE LEVELS ARE STEADY. Although males and females possess the same hormones, these hormones are not present at the same levels, and they do not necessarily perform the same functions. The major difference between the endocrine function of females and males is that in human females, the levels of gonadal and gonadotropic hormones go through a cycle that repeats itself every 28 days or so. It is these more-or-less regular hormone fluctuations that control the female **menstrual cycle**. In contrast, human males are, from a neuroendocrine perspective, rather dull creatures; males' levels of gonadal and gonadotropic hormones change little from day to day.

Because the anterior pituitary is the master gland, many early scientists assumed that an inherent difference between the male and female anterior pituitary was the basis for the difference in male and female patterns of gonadotropic and gonadal hormone release. However, this hypothesis was discounted by a series of clever transplant studies conducted by Geoffrey Harris in the 1950s (see Raisman, 2015). In these studies, a cycling **Evolutionary Perspective** pituitary removed from a mature female rat became a steady-state pituitary when transplanted at the appropriate site in a male, and a steady-state pituitary removed from a mature male rat began to cycle once transplanted into a female. What these studies established was that anterior pituitaries are not inherently female (cyclical) or male (steady-state); their patterns of hormone release are controlled by some other part of the body. The master gland seemed to have its own master. Where was it?

Control of the Pituitary

LO 13.4   Explain how the anterior and posterior pituitary are controlled.

The nervous system was implicated in the control of the anterior pituitary by behavioral research on birds and other animals that breed only during a specific time of the year. It was **Evolutionary Perspective** found that the seasonal variations in the light–dark cycle triggered many of the breeding-related changes in hormone

Figure 13.2 A midline view of the posterior and anterior pituitary and surrounding structures.

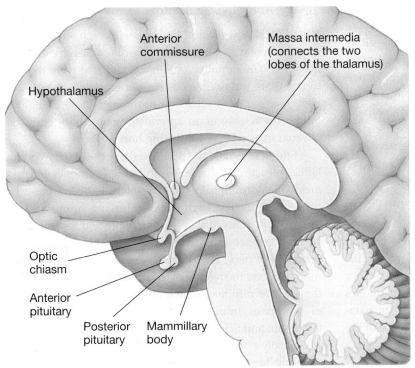

Figure 13.3 The neural connections between the hypothalamus and the pituitary. All neural input to the pituitary goes to the posterior pituitary; the anterior pituitary has no neural connections.

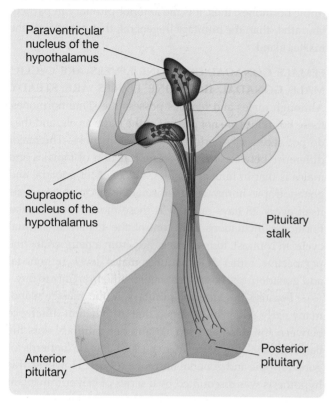

Paraventricular nucleus of the hypothalamus

Supraoptic nucleus of the hypothalamus

Pituitary stalk

Anterior pituitary

Posterior pituitary

release. If the lighting conditions under which the animals lived were reversed, for example, by having the animals transported across the equator, the breeding seasons were also reversed. Somehow, visual input to the nervous system was controlling the release of tropic hormones from the anterior pituitary.

The search for the particular neural structure that controlled the anterior pituitary turned, naturally enough, to the hypothalamus, the structure from which the pituitary is suspended. Hypothalamic stimulation and lesion experiments quickly established that the hypothalamus is the regulator of the anterior pituitary, but how the hypothalamus carries out this role remained a mystery. You see, the anterior pituitary, unlike the posterior pituitary, receives no neural input whatsoever from the hypothalamus, or from any other neural structure (see Figure 13.3).

CONTROL OF THE ANTERIOR AND POSTERIOR PITUITARY BY THE HYPOTHALAMUS. There are two different mechanisms by which the hypothalamus controls the pituitary: one for the posterior pituitary and one for the anterior pituitary. The two major hormones of the posterior pituitary, **vasopressin** and **oxytocin**, are peptide hormones that are synthesized in the cell bodies of neurons in the **paraventricular nuclei** and **supraoptic nuclei** on each side of the hypothalamus (see Figure 13.3 and Appendix VI). They are then transported along the axons of these neurons to their terminals in the posterior pituitary and are stored there until the arrival of action potentials causes them to be released into the bloodstream. (Neurons that release hormones into general circulation are called *neurosecretory cells*.) Oxytocin stimulates contractions of the uterus during labor and the ejection of milk during suckling; vasopressin (also called *antidiuretic hormone*) facilitates the reabsorption of water by the kidneys; and both seem to influence stress-coping and social responses (see Benarroch, 2013; Hammock, 2015; Shen, 2015).

The means by which the hypothalamus controls the release of hormones from the neuron-free anterior pituitary was more difficult to explain. Harris (1955) suggested that the release of hormones from the anterior pituitary was itself regulated by hormones released from the hypothalamus. Two findings provided early support for this hypothesis. The first was the discovery of a vascular network, the **hypothalamopituitary portal system**, that seemed well suited to the task of carrying hormones from the hypothalamus to the anterior pituitary. As Figure 13.4 illustrates, a network of hypothalamic capillaries feeds a bundle of portal veins that carries blood down the pituitary stalk into another network of capillaries in the anterior pituitary. (A *portal vein* is a vein that connects one capillary network with another.) The second finding was the discovery that cutting the portal veins of the pituitary stalk disrupts the release of anterior pituitary hormones until the damaged veins regenerate (Harris, 1955).

Discovery of Hypothalamic Releasing Hormones

LO 13.5 Describe the research that led to the discovery of the hypothalamic releasing hormones.

It was hypothesized that the release of each anterior pituitary hormone is controlled by a different hypothalamic hormone. The hypothalamic hormones that were thought to stimulate the release of an anterior pituitary hormone were referred to as **releasing hormones**; those thought to inhibit the release of an anterior pituitary hormone were referred to as **release-inhibiting hormones**.

Efforts to isolate the putative (hypothesized) hypothalamic releasing and release-inhibiting hormones led to a major breakthrough in the late 1960s. Guillemin and his colleagues isolated **thyrotropin-releasing hormone** from the hypothalamus of sheep, and Schally and his colleagues isolated the same hormone from the hypothalamus of pigs. Thyrotropin-releasing hormone triggers the release of **thyrotropin** from the anterior pituitary, which in turn stimulates the release of hormones from the *thyroid gland*. For their efforts, Guillemin and Schally were awarded Nobel Prizes in 1977.

Schally's and Guillemin's isolation of thyrotropin-releasing hormone confirmed that hypothalamic releasing

Figure 13.4 Control of the anterior and posterior pituitary by the hypothalamus.

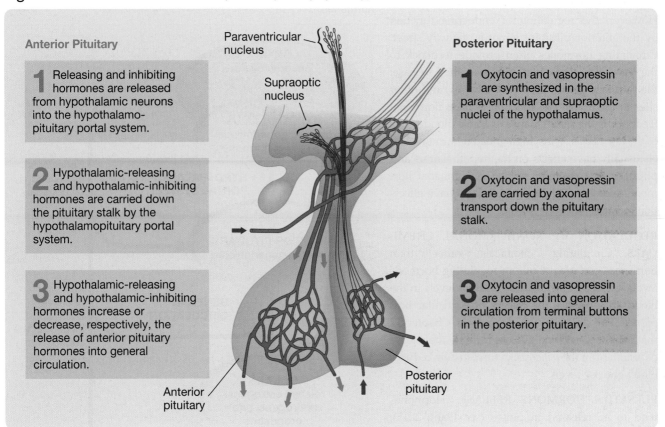

Anterior Pituitary

1 Releasing and inhibiting hormones are released from hypothalamic neurons into the hypothalamo-pituitary portal system.

2 Hypothalamic-releasing and hypothalamic-inhibiting hormones are carried down the pituitary stalk by the hypothalamopituitary portal system.

3 Hypothalamic-releasing and hypothalamic-inhibiting hormones increase or decrease, respectively, the release of anterior pituitary hormones into general circulation.

Paraventricular nucleus

Supraoptic nucleus

Posterior Pituitary

1 Oxytocin and vasopressin are synthesized in the paraventricular and supraoptic nuclei of the hypothalamus.

2 Oxytocin and vasopressin are carried by axonal transport down the pituitary stalk.

3 Oxytocin and vasopressin are released into general circulation from terminal buttons in the posterior pituitary.

Anterior pituitary

Posterior pituitary

hormones control the release of hormones from the anterior pituitary and thus provided the major impetus for the isolation and synthesis of other releasing and release-inhibiting hormones. Of direct relevance to the study of sex hormones was the subsequent isolation of **gonadotropin-releasing hormone** by Schally and his group (Schally, Kastin, & Arimura, 1971). This releasing hormone stimulates the release of both of the anterior pituitary's gonadotropins: **follicle-stimulating hormone (FSH)** and **luteinizing hormone (LH)**. All hypothalamic releasing hormones, like all tropic hormones, have proven to be peptides.

Regulation of Hormone Levels

LO 13.6 Describe three different types of signals that regulate hormone release. Also, describe how hormones are released over time and the effect this pattern of release has on levels of circulating hormones.

Hormone release is regulated by three different kinds of signals: signals from the nervous system, signals from circulating hormones, and signals from circulating nonhormonal chemicals.

REGULATION BY NEURAL SIGNALS. All endocrine glands, with the exception of the anterior pituitary, are directly regulated by signals from the nervous system.

Endocrine glands located in the brain (i.e., the pituitary and pineal glands) are regulated by cerebral neurons; those located outside the CNS are innervated by the *autonomic nervous system*—usually by both the *sympathetic* and *parasympathetic* branches, which often have opposite effects on hormone release.

The effects of experience on hormone release are usually mediated by signals from the nervous system. It is extremely important to remember that hormone release can be regulated by experience—for example, many species that breed only in the spring are often prepared for reproduction by the release of sex hormones triggered by the increasing daily duration of daylight. This means that an explanation of any behavioral phenomenon in terms of a hormonal mechanism does not necessarily rule out an explanation in terms of an experiential mechanism.

> **Thinking Creatively** Given what you have just learned, how would you respond if someone told you the following: "Ray gets angry easily because he has high testosterone levels"?

REGULATION BY HORMONAL SIGNALS. The hormones themselves also influence hormone release. You have already learned, for example, that the tropic hormones of the anterior pituitary influence the release of hormones from their respective target glands. However, the regulation of endocrine function by the anterior pituitary is not a one-way street. Circulating hormones often provide feedback to the very structures that influence their release: the pituitary gland, the hypothalamus, and other sites in the brain. The function of most hormonal feedback is the maintenance of stable blood levels of the hormones. Thus, high gonadal hormone levels usually have effects on the hypothalamus and pituitary that decrease subsequent gonadal hormone release, and low levels usually have effects that increase hormone release.

REGULATION BY NONHORMONAL CHEMICALS. Circulating chemicals other than hormones can play a role in regulating hormone levels. Glucose, calcium, and sodium levels in the blood all influence the release of particular hormones. For example, you learned in Chapter 12 that increases in blood glucose increase the release of *insulin* from the *pancreas*; in turn, insulin reduces blood glucose levels.

PULSATILE HORMONE RELEASE. Hormones tend to be released in pulses (see Plant, 2015); they are discharged several times per day in large surges, which typically last no more than a few minutes. Hormone levels in the blood are regulated by changes in the frequency and duration of the hormone pulses. One consequence of **pulsatile hormone release** is that there are often large minute-to-minute fluctuations in the levels of circulating hormones (see Lightman & Conway-Campbell, 2010). Accordingly, when the pattern of human male gonadal hormone release is referred to as "steady," it means that there are no major systematic changes in circulating gonadal hormone levels from day to day, not that the levels never vary.

Summary Model of Gonadal Endocrine Regulation

LO 13.7 Summarize the model of gonadal endocrine regulation.

Figure 13.5 is a summary model of the regulation of gonadal hormones. According to this model, the brain controls the release of gonadotropin-releasing hormone from the hypothalamus into the hypothalamopituitary portal system, which carries it to the anterior pituitary. In the anterior pituitary, the gonadotropin-releasing hormone stimulates the release of gonadotropins, which are carried by the circulatory system to the gonads. In response to the

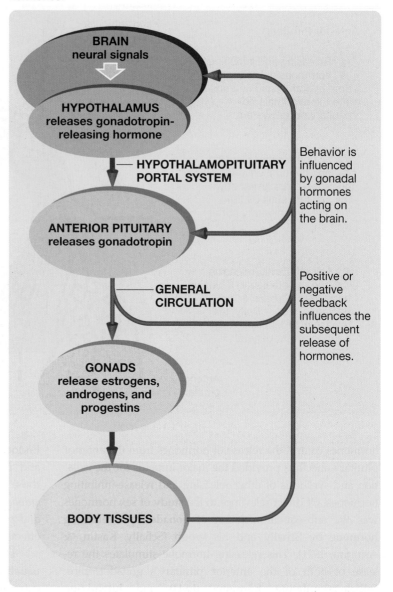

Figure 13.5 A summary model of the regulation of gonadal hormones.

gonadotropins, the gonads release androgens, estrogens, and progestins, which feed back into the pituitary and hypothalamus to regulate subsequent gonadal hormone release. Armed with this general perspective of neuroendocrine function, you are ready to consider how gonadal hormones direct sexual development and activate adult sexual behavior.

Hormones and Sexual Development of the Body

You have undoubtedly noticed that humans are *dimorphic*—that is, most come in one of two models: female and male. This module describes how the development of female and male bodily characteristics is directed by hormones.

Sexual Differentiation

LO 13.8 Describe the development of the internal and external reproductive organs.

Sexual differentiation in mammals begins at fertilization with the production of one of two different kinds of zygotes: either one with an XX (female) pair of sex chromosomes or one with an XY (male) pair. It is the genetic information on the sex chromosomes that usually determines whether development will occur along female or male lines. But be cautious here: Do not fall into the seductive embrace of the men-are-men-and-women-are-women assumption. Do not begin by assuming that there are two parallel but opposite genetic programs for sexual development, one for female development and one for male development. As you are about to learn, sexual development seems to unfold according to an entirely different principle. This principle is that, in general, we are all genetically programmed to develop female bodies; genetic males develop male bodies only when their female program of development has been overruled.

Thinking Creatively

FETAL HORMONES AND DEVELOPMENT OF REPRODUCTIVE ORGANS. Figure 13.6 illustrates the structure of the gonads as they appear 6 weeks after fertilization. Notice that at this stage of development, each fetus, regardless of its genetic sex, has the same pair of gonadal structures, called *primordial gonads* (*primordial* means "existing at the beginning"). Each primordial gonad has an outer covering, or *cortex*, which has the potential to develop into an ovary; and each has an internal core, or *medulla*, which has the potential to develop into a testis.

In the seventh week after conception, the **Sry gene** on the Y chromosome of the male triggers the synthesis of **Sry protein** (see Sekido & Lovell-Badge, 2013; Wu et al., 2012; but see M'charek, 2014), and this protein causes the medulla of each primordial gonad to grow and to develop into a testis. In the absence of Sry protein, the cortical cells of the primordial gonads develop into ovaries. Accordingly, if Sry protein is injected into a genetic female fetus 6 weeks after conception, the result is a genetic female with testes; or if drugs that block the effects of Sry protein are injected into a male fetus, the result is a genetic male with ovaries. Such **intersexed persons** expose in a dramatic fashion the weakness of mamawawa thinking (thinking of "male" and "female" as mutually exclusive, opposite categories).

INTERNAL REPRODUCTIVE DUCTS. Six weeks after fertilization, both males and females have two complete sets of reproductive ducts. They have a male **Wolffian system**, which has the capacity to develop into the male reproductive ducts (e.g., the *seminal vesicles*, which hold

Figure 13.6 The development of an ovary and a testis from the cortex and the medulla, respectively, of the primordial gonadal structure that is present 6 weeks after conception.

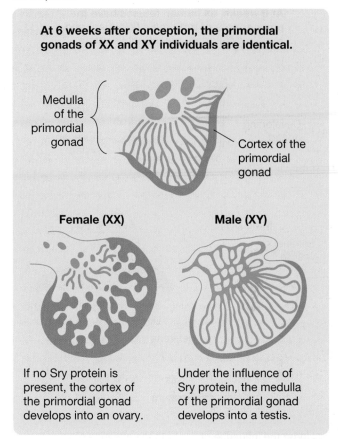

At 6 weeks after conception, the primordial gonads of XX and XY individuals are identical.

Medulla of the primordial gonad

Cortex of the primordial gonad

Female (XX)

Male (XY)

If no Sry protein is present, the cortex of the primordial gonad develops into an ovary.

Under the influence of Sry protein, the medulla of the primordial gonad develops into a testis.

the fluid in which sperm cells are ejaculated; and the *vas deferens*, through which the sperm cells travel to the seminal vesicles). And they have a female **Müllerian system**, which has the capacity to develop into the female ducts (e.g., the *uterus*; the upper part of the *vagina*; and the *fallopian tubes*, through which ova travel from the ovaries to the uterus).

In the third month of male fetal development, the testes secrete testosterone and **Müllerian-inhibiting substance**. As Figure 13.7 illustrates, the testosterone stimulates the development of the Wolffian system, and the Müllerian-inhibiting substance causes the Müllerian system to degenerate and the testes to descend into the **scrotum**—the sac that holds the testes outside the body cavity. Because it is testosterone—not the sex chromosomes—that triggers Wolffian development, genetic females who are injected with testosterone during the appropriate fetal period develop male reproductive ducts along with their female ones.

The differentiation of the internal ducts of the female reproductive system (see Figure 13.7) is not under the control of ovarian hormones; the ovaries are almost completely inactive during fetal development. The development of the Müllerian system occurs in any fetus that is not exposed

Figure 13.7 The development of the internal ducts of the male and female reproductive systems from the Wolffian and Müllerian systems, respectively.

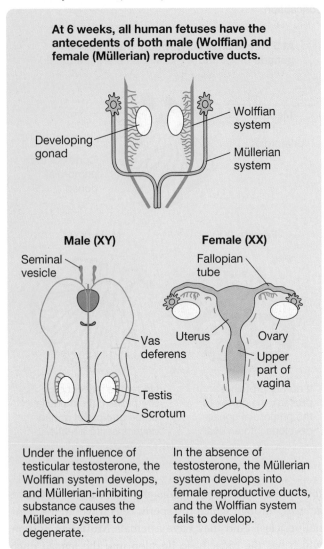

At 6 weeks, all human fetuses have the antecedents of both male (Wolffian) and female (Müllerian) reproductive ducts.

Developing gonad

Wolffian system

Müllerian system

Male (XY)

Seminal vesicle

Vas deferens

Testis

Scrotum

Female (XX)

Fallopian tube

Uterus

Ovary

Upper part of vagina

Under the influence of testicular testosterone, the Wolffian system develops, and Müllerian-inhibiting substance causes the Müllerian system to degenerate.

In the absence of testosterone, the Müllerian system develops into female reproductive ducts, and the Wolffian system fails to develop.

male or female, develops. In contrast, both male and female **genitals**—external reproductive organs—develop from the same precursor. This *bipotential precursor* and its subsequent differentiation are illustrated in Figure 13.8.

At the end of the second month of pregnancy, the bipotential precursor of the external reproductive organs consists of four parts: the glans, the urethral folds, the lateral bodies, and the labioscrotal swellings. Then it begins to differentiate. The *glans* grows into the head of the *penis* in the male or the *clitoris* in the female; the *urethral folds* fuse in the male or enlarge to become the *labia minora* in the female; the *lateral bodies* form the shaft of the penis in the male or the hood of the clitoris in the female; and the *labioscrotal swellings* form the *scrotum* in the male or the *labia majora* in the female.

Like the development of the internal reproductive ducts, the development of the external genitals is controlled by the presence or absence of testosterone. If testosterone is present at the appropriate stage of fetal development, male external genitals develop from the bipotential precursor; if testosterone is not present, development of the external genitals proceeds along female lines.

Watch this video on MyPsychLab

SEX AND GENDER

Video

to testicular hormones during the critical fetal period. Accordingly, typical female fetuses, ovariectomized female fetuses, and orchidectomized male fetuses all develop female reproductive ducts (Jost, 1972). **Ovariectomy** is the removal of the ovaries, and **orchidectomy** is the removal of the testes (the Greek word *orchis* means "testicle"). **Gonadectomy**, or *castration*, is the surgical removal of gonads—either ovaries or testes.

EXTERNAL REPRODUCTIVE ORGANS. There is a basic difference between the differentiation of the external reproductive organs and the differentiation of the internal reproductive organs (i.e., the gonads and reproductive ducts).

As you have just read, every typical fetus develops separate precursors for the male (medulla) and female (cortex) gonads and for the male (Wolffian system) and female (Müllerian system) reproductive ducts; then, only one set,

Puberty: Hormones and Development of Secondary Sex Characteristics

LO 13.9 Describe the male and female secondary sex characteristics and the role of hormones in their development.

During childhood, levels of circulating gonadal hormones are low, reproductive organs are immature, and males and females differ little in general appearance. This period of developmental quiescence ends abruptly with the onset of *puberty*—the transitional period between childhood and adulthood during which fertility is achieved, the adolescent growth spurt occurs, and the secondary sex characteristics develop. **Secondary sex characteristics** are those features other than the reproductive organs that distinguish sexually mature males and females. Some of the body changes that occur during puberty are illustrated in Figure 13.9.

Puberty is associated with an increase in the release of hormones by the anterior pituitary. The increase in the release of **growth hormone**—the only anterior pituitary hormone that does not have a gland as its primary target—acts directly on bone and muscle tissue to produce the pubertal growth spurt (see Russell et al., 2011). Increases in the release of gonadotropic hormone and **adrenocorticotropic hormone** cause the gonads and adrenal cortex to increase their release of gonadal and adrenal hormones, which in turn initiate the maturation of the genitals and the development of secondary sex characteristics.

The general principle guiding typical pubertal sexual maturation is a simple one: In pubertal males, androgen levels are higher than estrogen levels, and masculinization is the result; in pubertal females, the estrogens predominate, and the result is feminization. Individuals castrated prior to puberty do not become sexually mature unless they receive replacement injections of androgens or estrogens.

But even during puberty, the men-are-men-and-women-are-women assumption stumbles badly. You see, **androstenedione**, an androgen that is released primarily by the adrenal cortex, is typically responsible for the growth of pubic hair and *axillary hair* (underarm hair) in females. It is hard to take seriously the practice of referring to androgens as "male hormones" when one of them is responsible for the development of the female pattern of pubic hair growth. The male pattern is a pyramid, and the female pattern is an inverted pyramid (see Figure 13.9).

Hormones and Sexual Development of Brain and Behavior

Biopsychologists have been particularly interested in the effects of hormones on the sexual differentiation of the brain and the resulting effects on behavior. This module reveals how seminal studies conducted in the 1930s

Figure 13.8 The development of male and female external reproductive organs from the same bipotential precursor.

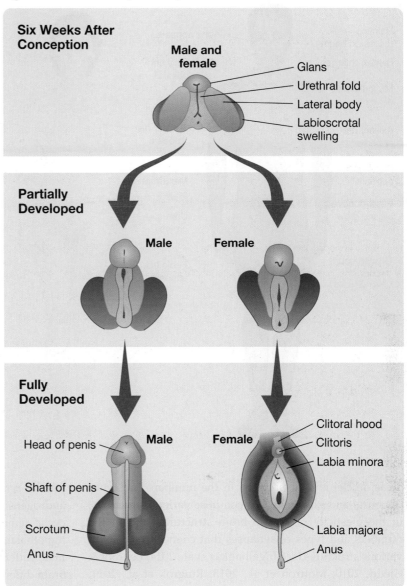

generated theories that have morphed, under the influence of subsequent research, into our current views.

Sex Differences in the Brain

LO 13.10 Describe the evolution of research and thinking about sex differences in the brain.

The brains of males and females may look the same on casual inspection, and it may be politically correct to believe that they are—but they are not. The brains of males tend to be about 15 percent larger than those of females, and many other anatomical differences between male and female brains have been documented. There are differences in the average volumes of various cortical

Figure 13.9 The changes that typically occur in males and females during puberty.

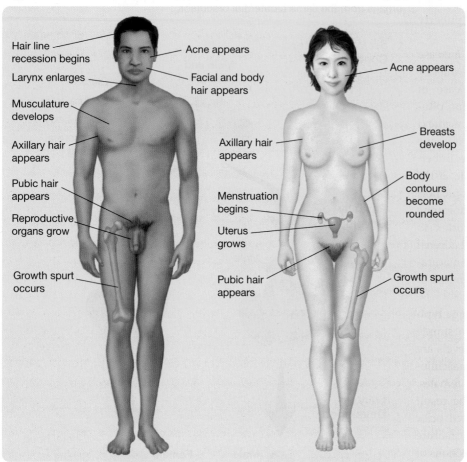

(Male labels, from top: Hair line recession begins; Larynx enlarges; Musculature develops; Axillary hair appears; Pubic hair appears; Reproductive organs grow; Growth spurt occurs; Acne appears; Facial and body hair appears.)

(Female labels: Acne appears; Breasts develop; Body contours become rounded; Growth spurt occurs; Pubic hair appears; Uterus grows; Menstruation begins; Axillary hair appears.)

areas, nuclei and fiber tracts, in the numbers and types of neural and glial cells that compose various structures, in the plasticity of certain brain structures, and in the numbers and types of synapses that connect the cells in various structures (see Ingalhalikar et al., 2014; Lenroot & Giedd, 2010; Mottron et al., 2015; Ruigrok et al., 2014; Zaidi, 2010).

Let's begin with the first functional sex difference to be identified in mammalian brains.

FIRST DISCOVERY OF A SEX DIFFERENCE IN MAMMALIAN BRAIN FUNCTION. The first attempts to discover sex differences in the mammalian brain focused on the factors that control the development of the steady and

cyclic patterns of gonadotropin release in males and females, respectively. The seminal experiments were conducted by Pfeiffer in 1936. In his experiments, some neonatal rats (males and females) were gonadectomized and some were not, and some received gonad transplants (ovaries or testes) and some did not.

Remarkably, Pfeiffer found that gonadectomizing neonatal rats of either genetic sex caused them to develop into adults with the female cyclic pattern of

gonadotropin release. In contrast, transplantation of testes into gonadectomized or intact female neonatal rats caused them to develop into adults with the steady male pattern of gonadotropin release. Transplantation of ovaries had no effect on the pattern of hormone release. Pfeiffer concluded that the female cyclic pattern of gonadotropin release develops unless the preprogrammed female cyclicity is overridden by testosterone during perinatal development.

Pfeiffer incorrectly concluded that the presence or absence of testicular hormones in neonatal rats influenced the development of the pituitary because he was not aware of something we know today: The release of gonadotropins from the anterior pituitary is controlled by the hypothalamus. Once this was discovered, it became apparent that Pfeiffer's experiments had provided the first evidence of the role of *perinatal* (around the time of birth) androgens in overriding the preprogrammed cyclic female pattern of gonadotropin release from the hypothalamus and initiating the development of the steady male pattern. This 1960s modification of Pfeiffer's theory of brain differentiation to include the hypothalamus was consistent with the facts of brain differentiation as understood at that time, but subsequent research necessitated major revisions. The first of these major revisions became known as the aromatization hypothesis.

> **Neuroplasticity** Explain why the neuroplasticity icon is present in this particular location in the text.

AROMATIZATION HYPOTHESIS. What is aromatization? All gonadal and adrenal sex hormones are steroid hormones, and because all steroid hormones are derived from cholesterol, they have similar structures and are readily converted from one to the other. For example, a slight change to the testosterone molecule that occurs under the influence of the *enzyme* (a protein that influences a biochemical reaction without participating in it)

aromatase converts testosterone to estradiol. This process is called **aromatization**.

According to the **aromatization hypothesis**, perinatal testosterone does not directly masculinize the brain; the brain is masculinized by estradiol that has been aromatized from perinatal testosterone. Although the idea that estradiol—the alleged female hormone—masculinizes the brain may seem counterintuitive, there is strong evidence for it. Most of the evidence is of two types, both coming from experiments on rats and mice: (1) findings demonstrating masculinizing effects on the brain of early estradiol injections, and (2) findings showing masculinization of the brain does not occur in response to testosterone administered with agents that block aromatization or in response to androgens that cannot be aromatized (e.g., dihydrotestosterone).

How do genetic females of species whose brains are masculinized by estradiol keep from being masculinized by their mothers' estradiol, which circulates through the fetal blood supply? Alpha fetoprotein is the answer. **Alpha fetoprotein** is present in the blood of rodents during the perinatal period, and it deactivates circulating estradiol by binding to it (see Yang & Shah, 2014). Although the role of alpha fetoprotein in deactivating estradiol is firmly established in rodents, its function in humans remains controversial (see Koebele & Bimonte-Nelson, 2015).

How, then, does estradiol masculinize the brain of the male rodent fetus in the presence of the deactivating effects of alpha fetoprotein? Because testosterone is immune to alpha fetoprotein, it can travel unaffected from the testes to the brain cells where it is converted to estradiol. Estradiol is not broken down in the rodent brain because alpha fetoprotein does not readily penetrate the blood–brain barrier.

SEX DIFFERENCES IN THE BRAIN: THE MODERN PERSPECTIVE. So far, our discussion of the development of sex differences has focused on the reproductive organs, secondary sex characteristics, and the hypothalamus. You have learned from this discussion that one theory accounts for the development of many sex differences: The default program of development is the female program, which is overridden in genetic males by perinatal exposure to testosterone. The initial assumption was that this same mechanism would prove to be the sole mechanism responsible for the development of other differences between male and female brains. However, this has not proven to be the case (see Lenz, Nugent, & McCarthy, 2012).

Before considering the mechanisms by which sex differences in the brain develop, it is important to understand the nature of the differences. The vast majority of sex differences in the brain are not all-or-none, men-are-men-and-women-are-women differences. Most of the sex differences in the brain that have been documented are slight, variable, and statistical. In short, many differences exist between average male and female brains, but there is usually plenty of overlap (see Lenroot & Giedd, 2010).

In thinking about the meaning of these statistical sex differences in the brain, it is important to understand that in no case has the behavioral significance of such a difference been identified (see Hines, 2010; McCarthy et al., 2012). It is unlikely that such sex differences in the brain would not be reflected in behavioral differences (see Cahill, 2014), but so far no such brain–behavior links have been clearly identified.

Although research on the development of sex differences in the brain is still in its infancy, one important principle has emerged. Brains are not masculinized or feminized as a whole: Sex differences develop independently in different parts of the brain at different points in time and by different mechanisms. For example, aromatase is found in only a few areas of the rat brain (e.g., the hypothalamus), and it is only in these areas that aromatization is critical for testosterone's masculinizing effects (see Lentini et al., 2012; McCarthy & Arnold, 2011). Also, some sex differences in the brain are not manifested until puberty, and these differences are unlikely to be the product of perinatal hormones (see Ingalhalikar et al., 2014), which, as you have just learned, play a role in the development of some sex differences in the brain.

Further complicating the study of the development of sex differences in the brain is the fact that two factors that have proven to play little or no role in the sexual differentiation of the reproductive organs do play a role in the sexual differentiation of the brain. First, sex chromosomes have been found to influence brain development independent of their effect on hormones (see Hines, 2011; Maekawa et al., 2014; Ngun et al., 2011); for example, different patterns of gene expression exist in the brains of male and female mice even before the gonads become functional (e.g., Wolstenholme, Rissman, & Bekiranov, 2013). Second, although the female program of reproductive organ development proceeds typically in the absence of gonadal steroids, recent evidence suggests that estradiol plays an active role; knockout mice without the gene that forms estradiol receptors do not display a typical female pattern of brain development (see Maekawa et al., 2014).

Thus, although the conventional view that a female program of development is the default program does a good job of explaining differentiation of the reproductive organs and hypothalamus, it falters badly when it comes to differentiation of other parts of the brain.

The mechanisms of brain differentiation appear to be much more complex and selective. Complicating their study is the fact that these complex mechanisms are different in different mammalian species (see Sekido, 2014); for example, **Evolutionary Perspective** aromatization seems to play a less prominent role in primates than in rats and mice (see Gillies & McArthur, 2010; Zuloaga et al., 2008).

Development of Sex Differences in Behavior

LO 13.11 Describe the results of studies of sex differences in behavior in humans and nonhumans.

Because it is not ethical to conduct experiments on the development of sex differences in humans, most of the research on this topic has focused on the development of reproductive behavior in laboratory animals. Until recently, this research has focused on the effects of perinatal hormones.

DEVELOPMENT OF REPRODUCTIVE BEHAVIORS IN LABORATORY ANIMALS. Phoenix and colleagues (1959) were among the first to demonstrate that the perinatal injection of testosterone **masculinizes** and **defeminizes** a genetic female's adult reproductive behavior. First, they injected pregnant guinea pigs with testosterone. Then, when the litters were born, the researchers ovariectomized the female offspring. Finally, when these ovariectomized female guinea pigs reached maturity, the researchers injected them with testosterone and assessed their copulatory behavior. Phoenix and his colleagues found that the females exposed to perinatal testosterone displayed more male-like mounting behavior in response to testosterone injections in adulthood than adult females who had not been exposed to perinatal testosterone. And when as adults the female guinea pigs were injected with progesterone and estradiol and mounted by males, they displayed less **lordosis** (the intromission-facilitating arched-back posture that signals female rodent receptivity).

Evolutionary Perspective

In a study complementary to that of Phoenix and colleagues, Grady, Phoenix, and Young (1965) found that the lack of early exposure of male rats to testosterone both **feminizes** and **demasculinizes** their reproductive behavior as adults. Male rats castrated shortly after birth failed to display the typical male copulatory pattern of mounting, **intromission** (penis insertion), and **ejaculation** (ejection of sperm) when as adults they were treated with testosterone and given access to a sexually receptive female, and when they were injected with estrogen and progesterone as adults, they exhibited more lordosis than uncastrated controls.

The aromatization of perinatal testosterone to estradiol seems to be important for both the defeminization and the masculinization of rodent copulatory behavior (see Goy & McEwen, 1980; Shapiro, Levine, & Adler, 1980). In contrast, aromatization does not seem to be critical for these effects in monkeys (Wallen, 2005).

When it comes to the effects of perinatal testosterone on behavioral development, timing is critical. The ability of single injections of testosterone to masculinize and defeminize rat reproductive behavior seems to be restricted to the first 11 days after birth.

Because much of the research on hormones and the development of reproductive behavior has focused on the copulatory act, we know less about the role of hormones in the development of **proceptive behaviors** (solicitation behaviors) and in the development of sex-related behaviors that are not directly related to reproduction. However, perinatal testosterone has been found to disrupt the proceptive hopping, darting, and ear wiggling of receptive female rats.

Before you finish this section, we want to clarify an important point. If you are like many of our students, you may be wondering why biopsychologists who study the development of male–female behavioral differences always measure *masculinization* separately from *defeminization* and *feminization* separately from *demasculinization*. If you think that masculinization and defeminization are the same thing and that feminization and demasculinization are the same thing, you have likely fallen into the trap of the men-are-men-and-women-are-women assumption—that is, into the trap of thinking of maleness and femaleness as discrete, mutually exclusive, opposite categories. In fact, male behaviors and female behaviors can coexist in the same individual, and they do not

Thinking Creatively

necessarily change in opposite directions if the individual receives physiological treatment such as hormones or brain lesions. For example, "male" behaviors (e.g., mounting receptive females) have been observed in the females of many different mammalian species, and "female" behaviors (e.g., lordosis) have been observed in males (see Dulac & Kimchi, 2007). Furthermore, lesions in medial preoptic areas have been shown to abolish male reproductive behaviors in both male and female rats without affecting female behaviors (see Singer, 1968; Will, Hull, & Dominguez, 2014). Think about this idea carefully; it plays an important role in later parts of the chapter.

DEVELOPMENT OF SEX DIFFERENCES IN THE BEHAVIOR OF HUMANS. There is much research on the development of behavioral differences in human females and males. However, because experimental investigations of this process are not ethical, virtually all of the research is based on case studies and correlational studies, which are difficult to interpret (see Chapter 1). Still, three general conclusions have emerged.

First, some sex differences in human behavior appear to be **sexual dimorphisms** (see McCarthy et al., 2012; Rigby & Kulathinal, 2015; Yang & Shaw, 2014). Sexual dimorphisms are instances where a behavior (or a structure) typically comes in two distinctive classes (male or female) into which most individuals can be unambiguously assigned.

In the case of humans, it appears to be only reproduction-related behaviors that clearly fall into this category. The presence or absence of prenatal testosterone appears to be a major factor in the development of these behaviors (see Balthazart, 2011; Kreukels & Cohen-Kettenis, 2012).

Second, most differences between the behavior of average human males and average human females are small and characterized by substantial overlap between individuals of the two groups (see Hines, 2011; McCarthy et al., 2012; Miller & Halpern, 2014). For example, there are human behavioral sex differences of this type in play behavior, social interaction, reaction to pain, language, cognition, emotionality, drug sensitivity, and responses to stress (see Bale & Epperson, 2015; Eisenegger, Haushofer, & Fehr, 2011; Loyd & Murphy, 2014; Miller & Halpern, 2014; Mogil, 2012). The presence or absence of prenatal testosterone exposure has been shown to contribute to the development of these kinds of sex differences, but in general they account for only a portion of each difference.

The third conclusion that has emerged from the study of human behavioral sex differences is that there are often differences in the susceptibility of human males and females to behavioral disorders (see McCarthy et al., 2012; ter Horst et al., 2012; Zhao, Woosy, & Chhibber, 2015). For example, *dyslexia* (reading difficulties), early-onset schizophrenia, stuttering, and autism spectrum disorders are each about three times more prevalent in males; and attention deficit hyperactivity disorder is 10 times more likely in males. In contrast, females are twice as likely to be diagnosed with depression, anxiety disorders, and Alzheimer's disease; and about 10 times as many females are diagnosed with certain eating disorders. The mechanisms leading to the development of any of these sex differences in susceptibility to behavioral disorders is unclear (see Cahill, 2014; ter Horst et al., 2012).

Before leaving the topic of sex differences in brain and behavior, we want to emphasize that the frequent finding that prenatal testosterone exposure influences the development of sex differences does not preclude other factors (see Hines, 2011). For example, cultural factors have been shown to play a major role in the development of many sex differences, perhaps by acting on the same brain mechanisms influenced by prenatal hormones.

Scan Your Brain

Before you proceed to a consideration of three cases of exceptional human sexual development, scan your brain to see whether you understand the basics of typical sexual development. Fill in the blanks in the following sentences. The correct answers are provided at the end of the exercise. Review material related to your errors and omissions before proceeding.

1. Glands that release chemicals into ducts that carry them to targets mostly on the surface of the body are called _____.

2. The ovaries and testes release steroid hormones called _____.

3. The pituitary gland is made up of two glands: _____.

4. Neurons that release hormones into general circulation are called _____ cells.

5. _____ is the anterior pituitary hormone that stimulates the release of hormones from the thyroid gland.

6. _____, calcium, and sodium levels in the blood influence the release of hormones.

7. A typical pattern of hormone release, where hormones are discharged several times per day in large surges, is _____.

8. Cells formed from the amalgamation of a sperm cell and an ovum are reformed as a _____.

9. The hormone that triggers the release of adrenal hormones from the adrenal cortices is called the _____.

Scan Your Brain answers: (1) exocrine glands, (2) progestin, (3) posterior and anterior, (4) neurosecretory, (5) Thyrotropin, (6) Glucose, (7) pulsatile hormone release, (8) zygote, (9) adrenocorticotropic hormone.

Three Cases of Exceptional Human Sexual Development

This module discusses three cases of exceptional sexual development. We are sure you will be intrigued by these three cases, but that is not the only reason we have chosen to present them. Our main reason is expressed by a proverb: The exception proves the rule. Most people think this proverb means that the exception "proves" the rule in the sense that it establishes its truth, but this is clearly wrong: The truth of a rule is challenged by, not confirmed by, exceptions to it. The word *proof* comes from the Latin *probare*, which means "to test"—as in *proving ground* or printer's *proof*—and this is the sense in which it is used in the proverb. Hence, the proverb means that the explanation of exceptional cases is a major challenge for any theory.

Exceptional Cases of Human Sexual Development

LO 13.12 Explain what androgen insensitivity syndrome, adrenogenital syndrome, and ablatio penis have taught us about human sexual development.

So far in this chapter, you have learned the "rules" according to which hormones seem to influence typical sexual development. Now, three exceptional cases are offered to prove (to test) these rules.

The Case of Anne S., the Woman Who Wasn't

Anne S., an attractive 26-year-old female, sought treatment for two sex-related disorders: lack of menstruation and pain during sexual intercourse (Jones & Park, 1971). She sought help because she and her husband of 4 years had been trying without success to have children, and she correctly surmised that her lack of a menstrual cycle was part of the problem. A physical examination revealed that Anne was a healthy young female. Her only readily apparent peculiarity was the sparseness and fineness of her pubic and axillary hair. Examination of her external genitals revealed nothing atypical; however, there were some differences with her internal genitals. Her vagina was only 4 centimeters long, and her uterus was underdeveloped.

At the start of this chapter, we said that you would encounter some remarkable things, and the diagnosis of Anne's case certainly qualifies as one of them. Anne's doctors concluded that her sex chromosomes were XY; they concluded that Anne, the attractive young female, had the genes of a genetic male. Three lines of evidence supported their diagnosis. First, analysis of cells scraped from the inside of Anne's mouth revealed that they were of the XY type. Second, a tiny incision in Anne's abdomen, which enabled Anne's physicians to look inside, revealed a pair of internalized testes but no ovaries. Finally, hormone tests revealed that Anne's hormone levels were those typical of a male.

Anne suffers from complete **androgen insensitivity syndrome**; all her symptoms stem from a mutation to the androgen receptor gene that rendered her androgen receptors totally unresponsive (see Chen et al., 2015; Mongan et al., 2015). Complete androgen insensitivity syndrome is rare, occurring in about 1 of 100,000 genetic male births (see Wang et al., 2014).

During development, Anne's testes released male-typical levels of androgens, but her body could not respond to them because of the mutation to her androgen receptor gene; thus, her development proceeded as if no androgens had been released. Her external genitals, her brain, and her behavior developed along female lines, without the effects of androgens to override the female program, and her testes could not descend from her body cavity with no scrotum for them to descend into. Furthermore, Anne did not develop typical internal female reproductive ducts because, like other genetic males, her testes released Müllerian-inhibiting substance; that is why her vagina was short and her uterus underdeveloped. At puberty, Anne's testes released enough estrogens to feminize her body in the absence of the counteracting effects of androgens; however, adrenal androstenedione was not able to stimulate the growth of pubic and axillary hair.

Although the samples are small, patients with complete androgen insensitivity syndrome have been found to be comparable to genetic females. All aspects of their behavior that have been studied—including gender identity, sexual orientation, interests, and cognitive abilities—have been found to be typical of many females (see Cohen-Bendahan, van de Beek, & Berenbaum, 2005).

An interesting issue of medical ethics is raised by the androgen insensitivity syndrome. Many people believe that physicians should always disclose all relevant findings to their patients. If you were Anne's physician, would you tell her that she is a genetic male? Would you tell her husband? Her doctor did not. Anne's vagina was surgically enlarged, she was counseled to consider adoption, and, as far as we know, she is still happily married and unaware of her genetic sex. On the other hand, we have heard from several genetic females who have partial androgen insensitivity, and they recommended full disclosure. They had faced a variety of sexual ambiguities throughout their lives, and learning the cause helped them.

The Case of the Little Girl Who Grew into a Boy

The patient—let's call her Elaine—sought treatment in 1972. Elaine was born with somewhat ambiguous external genitals, but she was raised by her parents as a girl without incident until the onset of puberty, when she suddenly began to develop male secondary sex characteristics. This was extremely distressing. Her treatment had two aspects: surgical and hormonal. Surgical treatment was used to increase 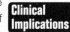 the size of her vagina and decrease the size of her clitoris; hormonal treatment was used to suppress androgen release so that her own estrogen could feminize her body. Following treatment, Elaine developed into an attractive young female—narrow hips and a husky voice being the only signs of her brush with masculinity (see Money & Ehrhardt, 1972).

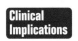 What treatment(s) do you think should be given to infants born with ambiguous external genitals? Why?

Elaine suffered from adrenogenital syndrome, which is the most common atypical form of sexual development, affecting about 1 in 10,000. **Adrenogenital syndrome** is caused by **congenital adrenal hyperplasia**—a congenital deficiency in the release of the hormone *cortisol* from the adrenal cortex, which results in compensatory adrenal hyperactivity and the excessive release of adrenal androgens. This produces an array of serious health problems (see Turcu & Auchus, 2015), but its most widely studied effect is on sexual development. There is little effect on the sexual development of males, other than accelerating the onset of puberty, but it has major effects on the development of genetic females. Females who suffer from the adrenogenital syndrome are usually born with an enlarged clitoris and partially fused labia. Their gonads and internal ducts are usually typical because the adrenal androgens are released too late to stimulate the development of the Wolffian system.

The mere existence of…transsexualism is a challenge to the mamawawa.

Most female cases of adrenogenital syndrome are diagnosed at birth. In such cases, the external genitals are altered to be more typically female, and cortisol is administered to reduce the levels of circulating adrenal androgens. Following early treatment, adrenogenital females grow up to be physically typical females except that the onset of menstruation is likely to be later than for most females. This makes them good participants for studies of the effects of fetal androgen exposure on psychosexual development.

Adrenogenital teenage girls who have received early treatment tend to display more tomboyishness, greater strength, and more aggression than most teenage girls, and they tend to prefer boys' clothes and toys, and play mainly with boys (e.g., Matthews et al., 2009; Pasterski et al., 2011). However, it is important not to lose sight of the fact that many teenage girls display similar characteristics—and why not? Accordingly, the behavior of treated adrenogenital females, although tending toward the masculine, is usually within the range considered to be typical female behavior by the current standards of our culture.

The most interesting questions about the development of females with adrenogenital syndrome concern their romantic and sexual preferences as adults. They seem to lag behind typical females in dating and marriage—perhaps because of the delayed onset of their menstrual cycle. Most are heterosexual, although a few studies have found an increased tendency for these females to express an interest in other females and a tendency to be less **Thinking Creatively** involved in heterosexual relationships (see Piaggio, 2014). Complicating the situation further is the fact that these slight differences may not be direct consequences of early androgen exposure but may arise from the fact that some adrenogenital girls have ambiguous genitalia and certain male characteristics (e.g., body hair), which may result in different experiential influences (see Jordan-Young, 2012).

Prior to the development of cortisol therapy in 1950, genetic females with adrenogenital syndrome were left untreated. Some were raised as boys and some as girls, but the direction of their pubertal development was unpredictable. In some cases, adrenal androgens predominated and masculinized their bodies; in others, ovarian estrogens predominated and feminized their bodies. Thus, some who were raised as boys were transformed at puberty into females and some who were raised as girls were transformed into males—sometimes with devastating emotional consequences.

The Case of the Twin Who Lost His Penis

One of the most famous cases in the literature on sexual development is David Reimer, an identical twin whose penis was accidentally destroyed during circumcision at the age of 7 months. Because there was no satisfactory way of surgically replacing the lost penis, an expert in such matters, John Money, recommended that he be castrated and raised as a girl, that an artificial vagina be created, and that estrogen be administered at puberty to feminize the body. After a great deal of anguish, the parents followed Money's advice.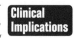

Money's (1975) report of this case of **ablatio penis** was influential. It was seen by some as the ultimate test of the *nature–nurture controversy* (see Chapter 2) with respect to the development of gender identity and behavior. It seemed to pit the masculinizing effects of male genes and male prenatal hormones against the effects of being reared as a girl. And the availability of a genetically identical control, the twin brother, made the case all the more interesting. According to Money, the outcome strongly supported the *social-learning theory* of gender identity. Money reported in 1975, when the patient was 12, that "she" had developed as a typical female, thus confirming his prediction that being gonadectomized, having the genitals surgically altered, and being raised as a girl would override the masculinizing effects of male genes and early androgens.

A long-term follow-up study published by impartial experts tells an entirely different story (see Diamond & Sigmundson, 1997). Despite having female genitalia and being treated as a female, he/she developed along male lines. Apparently, the organ that determines the course of psychosocial development is the brain, not the genitals (see Reiner, 1997). The following description gives you a glimpse of her/his life:

> From an early age, she tended to act in a masculine way, preferring boys' activities and games and displaying little interest in dolls, sewing, or other conventional female activities. At the age of four, she refused to put on mother's make-up, demanding instead to shave like dad. And by seven, she felt like a boy. Despite the absence of a penis, she often tried to urinate while standing and would sometimes go to the boys' lavatory.
>
> She was attractive as a girl, but when she moved or talked her masculinity became apparent. She was teased by the other girls, and she often retaliated violently, which resulted in her expulsion from school. Put on an estrogen regimen at the age of 12, she rebelled. She did not want to be feminized; she hated her developing breasts and refused to wear a bra.
>
> At 14, she changed her name to David and decided to live as a male. At that time, David's father revealed David's entire early history to him. All of a sudden everything clicked; for the first time, he understood who and what he was.
>
> David requested androgen treatment, a *mastectomy* (surgical removal of breasts), and *phalloplasty* (surgical creation of a penis). He became a handsome and popular young man (see Figure 13.10). He married at the age of 25 and adopted his wife's children. He was strictly heterosexual, and his ability to ejaculate and experience orgasm returned following his androgen treatments. However, his early castration permanently eliminated his reproductive capacity.

Figure 13.10 David Reimer, the twin whose penis was accidentally destroyed.

David remained bitter about his early treatment and his inability to produce offspring. To save others from his experience, he cooperated in writing his biography, *As Nature Made Him* (Colapinto, 2000). However, David never recovered from his emotional scars, and he committed suicide. His case suggests that the clinical practice of surgically modifying a person's sex at birth should be curtailed—irrevocable treatments should await early puberty and the emergence of the patient's gender identity. At that stage, a compatible course of treatment can be selected.

DO THE EXCEPTIONAL CASES PROVE THE RULE? Do current theories of hormones and sexual development pass the test of the three preceding cases of exceptional sexual development? In our view, the answer is "yes." Although current theories do not supply all of the answers, especially when it comes to brain and behavior, they have contributed greatly to the understanding of exceptional patterns of sexual differentiation of the body.

Notice one more thing about the three cases: Each of the three was male in some respects and female in others. Accordingly, each case is a serious challenge to the men-are-men-and-women-are-women assumption: Male and female are not opposite, mutually exclusive categories (see Ainsworth, 2015; Carothers & Reis, 2013).

Thinking Creatively

Effects of Gonadal Hormones on Adults

Once an individual reaches sexual maturity, gonadal hormones begin to play a role in activating reproductive behavior. These activational effects are the focus of the first two sections of this module. They deal with the role of hormones in activating the sexual behavior of males and females, respectively. The third section of this module deals with anabolic steroids.

Male Sexual Behavior and Testosterone

LO 13.13 Describe the role of testosterone in male sexual behavior.

The important role played by gonadal hormones in the activation of male sexual behavior is clearly demonstrated by the asexualizing effects of orchidectomy. Bremer (1959) reviewed the cases of 215 orchidectomized Norwegians. Many had committed sex-related offenses and had agreed to castration to reduce the length of their prison terms.

Two important generalizations can be drawn from Bremer's study. The first is that orchidectomy leads to a reduction in sexual interest and behavior; the second is that the rate and the degree of the loss are variable. About half the males became completely asexual within a few weeks of the operation; others quickly lost their ability to achieve an erection but continued to experience some sexual interest and pleasure; and a few continued to copulate successfully, although somewhat less enthusiastically, for the duration of the study. There were also body changes: a reduction of hair on the torso, limbs, and face; the deposition of fat on the hips and chest; a softening of the skin; and a reduction in muscle mass.

Of the 102 sex offenders in Bremer's study, only 3 were reconvicted of sex offenses. Accordingly, he recommended castration as an effective treatment of last resort for male sex offenders.

Why do some males remain sexually active for months after orchidectomy, despite the fact that testicular hormones are cleared from their bodies within days? It has been suggested that adrenal androgens may play some role in the maintenance of sexual activity in some castrated males, but there is no direct evidence for this hypothesis.

Orchidectomy removes, in one fell swoop—or, to put it more precisely, in two fell swoops—a pair of glands that release many hormones. Because testosterone is the major testicular hormone, the major symptoms of orchidectomy have been generally attributed to the loss of testosterone rather than to the loss of some other testicular hormone or to some nonhormonal consequence of the surgery. The therapeutic effects of **replacement injections** of testosterone have confirmed this assumption.

The Case of the Man Who Lost and Regained His 'Manhood'

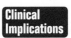 The very first case report of the effects of testosterone replacement therapy concerned an unfortunate 38-year-old World War I veteran, who was castrated in 1918 at the age of 19 by a shell fragment that removed his testes but left his penis undamaged (de Kruif, 1945).

His body was soft, as if he had little muscle, and his hips had grown wider and his shoulders narrower.

He got married—though the doctors had told him he would surely be **impotent** (unable to achieve an erection). He made some attempts at sexual intercourse for his wife's sake, but he had been unable to satisfy her.

Dr. Foss began injections of testosterone into the muscles of his patient, and after the fifth injection, erections became rapid and prolonged. Moreover, after 12 weeks of treatment he had gained 18 pounds, mainly of muscle, and all his clothes had become too small. Testosterone had resurrected a broken man to the 'manhood' that had been taken

from him by the shell fragment. Since this first clinical trial, testosterone has breathed sexuality into the lives of many males. Testosterone does not, however, eliminate the *sterility* (inability to reproduce) of males who lack functional testes.

The fact that testosterone is necessary for male sexual behavior has led to two widespread assumptions: (1) that the level of a man's sexuality is a function of the amount of testosterone he has in his blood, and (2) that a man's sex drive can be increased by increasing his testosterone levels. Both assumptions are incorrect. Sex drive and testosterone levels are uncorrelated in healthy males, and testosterone injections do not increase sex drive.

It seems that each healthy male has far more testosterone than required to activate the neural circuits that produce his sexual behavior, and having more than the minimum is of no advantage in this respect. A classic experiment by Grunt and Young (1952) clearly illustrates this point.

First, Grunt and Young rated the sexual behavior of each of the male guinea pigs in their experiment. Then, on the basis of the ratings, the researchers divided the male guinea pigs into three experimental groups: low, medium, and high sex drive. Following castration, the sexual behavior of all of the guinea pigs fell to negligible levels within a few weeks (see Figure 13.11), but it recovered after the initiation of a series of testosterone replacement injections. The important point is that although each subject received the same, very large replacement injections of testosterone, the injections simply returned each to its previous level of copulatory activity. The conclusion is clear: With respect to the effects of testosterone on sexual behavior, more is not necessarily better.

Dihydrotestosterone, a nonaromatizable androgen, restores the copulatory behavior of castrated male primates; however, it fails to restore the copulatory behavior of castrated male rodents (see Hull & Dominguez, 2007). These findings indicate that the restoration of copulatory behavior by testosterone occurs by different mechanisms in rodents and primates: It appears to be a direct effect of testosterone in primates, but it appears to be produced by estradiol aromatized from testosterone in rodents.

Female Sexual Behavior and Gonadal Hormones

LO 13.14 Describe the role of testosterone in female sexual behavior.

Sexually mature female rats and guinea pigs display 4-day cycles of gonadal hormone release. There is a gradual

Figure 13.11 The sexual behavior of male guinea pigs with low, medium, and high sex drive. Sexual behavior was disrupted by castration and returned to its original level by very large replacement injections of testosterone.

(Based on Grunt, J. A., & Young, W. C. (1952). Differential reactivity of individuals and the response of the male guinea pig to testosterone propionate. *Endocrinology, 51,* 237–248.)

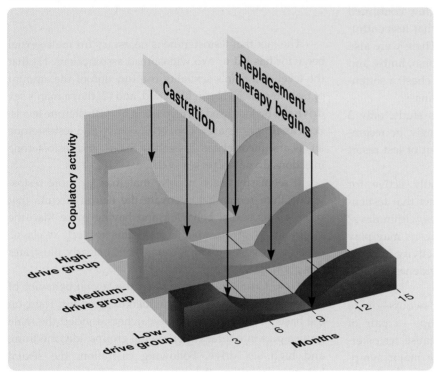

(Ziegler, 2007). However, in one study, human females were more likely to engage in masturbation and other sexual activity during periods of fertility, and they preferred masculine faces more on their fertile days than on their nonfertile days (see Gangestad, Thornhill, & Garver-Apgar, 2005). Moreover, ovariectomy has been shown to reduce sexual desire and frequency of sexual fantasies (see Cappalletti & Wallen, 2015).

So which particular ovarian hormone is responsible for sexual desire in females? Is it estradiol, progesterone, or testosterone?

- Roney and Simons (2013) found that only high estradiol levels were related to human females' sexual desire.

- In experiments on nonhuman female primates, replacement injections of testosterone, but not estradiol, increased the proceptivity of ovariectomized and adrenalectomized rhesus monkeys (see Everitt & Herbert, 1972).

- Some studies of postmenopausal human females found that estrogen therapy renewed sexual interest, whereas other studies did not. Likewise, some studies found that testosterone renewed sexual interest, whereas other studies did not (see Cappalletti & Wallen, 2015; Wylie et al., 2010).

- Still other studies found that testosterone increased sexual desire in postmenopausal human females but only at *supraphysiological levels* (i.e., levels above natural levels)—see Cappalletti and Wallen (2015); Davis and Braunstein (2012).

So, the jury is still out as to whether estradiol or testosterone is responsible for a female's sexual drive.

Anabolic Steroid Abuse

LO 13.15 Describe the dangers associated with anabolic steroid use.

Anabolic steroids are steroids, such as testosterone, that have *anabolic* (growth-promoting) effects. Testosterone itself is not very useful as an anabolic drug because it is broken down soon after injection and because it has undesirable side effects. Chemists have managed to synthesize a number of potent anabolic steroids that are long-acting, but they have not managed to synthesize one that does not have side effects.

increase in the secretion of estrogens by the developing *follicle* (ovarian structure in which eggs mature) in the 2 days prior to ovulation, followed by a sudden surge in progesterone as the egg is released. These surges of estrogens and progesterone initiate **estrus**—a period of 12 to 18 hours during which the female is *fertile, receptive* (likely to assume the lordosis posture when mounted), *proceptive* (likely to engage in behaviors that serve to attract the male), and *sexually attractive* (smelling of chemicals that attract males).

The close relation between the cycle of hormone release and the **estrous cycle**—the cycle of sexual receptivity—in female rats and guinea pigs and in many other mammalian species suggests that female sexual behavior in these species is under hormonal control. The effects of ovariectomy confirm this conclusion: Ovariectomy of female rats and guinea pigs produces a rapid decline of both proceptive and receptive behaviors. Furthermore, estrus can be induced in ovariectomized rats and guinea pigs by an injection of estradiol followed a day and a half later by an injection of progesterone.

Female primates are different from female rats, guinea pigs, and other mammals when it comes to the hormonal control of their sexual behavior: Female primates are the only female mammals motivated to copulate during periods of nonfertility

We are currently in the midst of an epidemic of anabolic steroid abuse. Many competitive athletes and bodybuilders are self-administering appallingly large doses, and many others use them for cosmetic purposes. Because steroids are illegal, estimates of the numbers who use them are likely underestimates. Still, the results of numerous surveys have been disturbing. Elite athletes began to use anabolic steroids in the 1950s to improve their athletic performance, but by the 1980s they were in widespread use by the general population, often for cosmetic reasons (see Figueiredo & Silva, 2014). Particularly troubling is the scale of anabolic steroid use: Global estimates of lifetime prevalence rates for anabolic steroid are 6.4 percent for males and 1.6 percent for females (see Sagoe et al., 2014).

Although it is about 40 years since anabolic steroids began to be used by the general public, we still do not fully understand all the risks. This is because anabolic steroid use is illegal, because there are more than 100 different testosterone derivatives (see Yavari, 2009), and because users vary greatly in their patterns and doses of administration. Hazardous effects, although well documented, typically occur in only a small proportion of users (see van Amsterdam, Opperhuizen, & Hartgens, 2010).

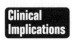

> **Clinical Implications** What should be done about the current epidemic of anabolic steroid abuse? Would you make the same recommendation if a safe anabolic steroid were developed?

Anabolic steroids have been shown to have a variety of cardiovascular effects, which have been linked to premature death (see Angell et al., 2012; Kanayama et al., 2010). Also, oral anabolic steroids have been shown to have adverse effects on the liver, including liver tumors. Less dangerous, but still disturbing, are the muscle spasms, muscle pains, blood in the urine, acne, general swelling from the retention of water, bleeding of the tongue, nausea, vomiting, and fits of depression and anger (see Kanayama et al., 2008; Kraus et al., 2012).

The main question of relevance in the context of this chapter is the following: Do the outrageously large doses of anabolic steroids routinely administered by many users enhance their sexual function? The answer is an emphatic "no." In fact, the effects appear to be uniformly disruptive.

In males, the negative feedback from high levels of anabolic steroids reduces gonadotropin release; this leads to a reduction in testicular activity, which can result in *testicular atrophy* (wasting away of the testes) and sterility. *Gynecomastia* (breast growth in males) can also occur, presumably as the result of the aromatization of anabolic steroids to estrogens. In females, anabolic steroids can produce *amenorrhea* (cessation of menstruation), sterility, *hirsutism* (excessive growth of body hair), growth of the clitoris, development of a masculine body shape, baldness, shrinking of the breasts, and deepening and coarsening of the voice. Unfortunately, some of the masculinizing effects of anabolic steroids on females appear to be irreversible.

There are two major points of concern about the adverse health consequences of anabolic steroids. First, the use of anabolic steroids in puberty, before developmental programs of sexual differentiation are complete, is particularly risky. Second, many of the adverse effects of anabolic steroids may take years to be manifested—steroid users who experience few immediate adverse effects may pay the price later.

Scan Your Brain

You encountered many forms of atypical sexual development and also many clinical problems in the preceding two modules of the chapter. Do you remember them? Write the name of the appropriate condition or syndrome in each blank based on the clues provided. The answers appear at the end of the exercise. Before proceeding, review material related to your errors and omissions.

Name of condition	Clues or syndrome
1. _____	Genetic male, sparse pubic hair, short vagina
2. _____	Congenital adrenal hyperplasia, elevated androgen levels
3. _____	David Reimer, destruction of penis
4. _____	Castrated males, gonadectomized males
5. _____	Castrated females, gonadectomized females
6. _____	Unable to achieve erection
7. _____	Enlargement of a male's breasts
8. _____	Cessation of menstruation
9. _____	Excessive body hair in females

Scan Your Brain answers: (1) androgen insensitivity syndrome, (2) adrenogenital syndrome, (3) ablatio penis, (4) orchidectomized, (5) ovariectomized, (6) impotent, (7) gynecomastia, (8) amenorrhea, (9) hirsutism

Brain Mechanisms of Sexual Behavior

Human sexual behavior is complex and varied. Sexual practices vary from culture to culture, and from person to person within each culture. Furthermore, behavioral preferences of individuals are often changed by experience (see Hoffman, Peterson, & Garner, 2012). However, there are four brain structures whose role in sexual behavior has been well established: cortex, hypothalamus, amygdala, and ventral striatum. This module focuses on these four structures.

Four Brain Structures Associated with Sexual Activity

LO 13.16 Describe the roles of the cortex, hypothalamus, amygdala, and ventral striatum in sexual activity.

Our current knowledge of the brain mechanisms of sexual behavior is based on the study of both human volunteers and nonhuman subjects (see Georgiadis, Kringelbach, & Pfaus, 2012). Because functional brain imaging is the main technology used to study the relation between brain activity and sexual behavior in human volunteers, there are some major limitations. Specifically, it is virtually impossible using current imaging technology to investigate the neural activity associated with *coitus* (copulation) between a female and a male—given cultural constraints, the requirement to remain motionless during brain scans, and the difficulty of squeezing two active adults into a conventional brain scanner. Consequently, research on humans has focused on sexual arousal, occasionally to orgasm, triggered by sexually provocative visual images or masturbation.

The study of the brain mechanisms of sexual behavior in laboratory animals—most commonly rats—circumvents the problems associated with studies of human volunteers. First, it is possible to study brain mechanisms in more detail by using invasive techniques. Second, it is possible to study natural patterns of copulatory activity. Conversely, several important aspects of sexual activity are difficult or impossible to study in laboratory animals: for example, sexual imagery, delayed orgasm, female orgasm, and feelings of love. The important point here is that both humans and nonhumans have major weaknesses as subjects in the investigation of the brain mechanisms of sexual behavior, but the weaknesses tend to be complementary. Thus, knowledge in this area often depends on an amalgamation of both lines of research (see Georgiadis et al., 2012).

CORTEX AND SEXUAL ACTIVITY. Because of its fundamental role in reproduction, and thus the very survival of our species, sexual behavior was once assumed to be regulated by archaic circuits in the brain stem of early evolutionary origin. This assumption is no longer tenable. Widespread cortical activation has been routinely recorded during functional brain imaging studies of volunteers exposed to sexually arousing stimuli (see Georgiadis, 2012; Stoléru et al., 2012). In both males and females, the following areas are often activated: occipitotemporal, inferotemporal, parietal, orbitofrontal, medial prefrontal, insular, cingulate, and premotor cortices. Interestingly, the activity in secondary visual cortex (occipitotemporal and inferotemporal cortices) occurs during sexual arousal even when eyes are closed (see Georgiadis, 2012), and the activity in prefrontal cortex is suppressed during orgasm (see Stoléru et al., 2012).

Presumably cortical activation mediates the most complex aspects of sexual experience. These may include feelings of release and loss of control, changes in self-awareness, disturbances of perceptions of space and time, and feelings of love.

HYPOTHALAMUS AND SEXUAL ACTIVITY. Interest in the role of the hypothalamus in sexual behavior was driven by the discovery of a specific structural difference in the male and female hypothalamus. In 1978, Gorski and his colleagues discovered a nucleus in the **medial preoptic area** of the rat hypothalamus that was several times larger in males. They called this nucleus the **sexually dimorphic nucleus**.

At birth, the sexually dimorphic nuclei of male and female rats are the same size. In the first few days after birth, the male sexually dimorphic nuclei grow at a high rate and the female sexually dimorphic nuclei do not. The growth of the male sexually dimorphic nuclei is normally triggered by estradiol, which has been aromatized from testosterone (Gorski, 1980)—see Figure 13.12. Since the discovery of the sexually dimorphic nuclei in rats, many other sex differences in hypothalamic anatomy have been identified in rats and in other species. These sex differences in the hypothalamus include differences in volume of various nuclei, cell number, connectivity, cell morphology, neural activity, and neurotransmitter type—all of which are influenced by perinatal exposure to estradiol (see Lenz & McCarthy, 2010).

The medial preoptic area (which includes the sexually dimorphic nucleus) is one area of the hypothalamus that plays a key role in male sexual behavior (see Will, Hull, & Dominguez, 2014). Destruction of the entire area abolishes sexual behavior in **Evolutionary Perspective** the males of all mammalian species that have been studied (see Hull et al., 1999). In contrast, medial preoptic area lesions do not eliminate the female sexual behaviors of females, but they do eliminate the male sexual behaviors (e.g., mounting) that are sometimes observed in females (see Singer, 1968). Conversely, electrical stimulation of the

Figure 13.12 The effects of neonatal testosterone exposure on the size of the sexually dimorphic nuclei in male and female adult rats, as reported by Gorski (1980).

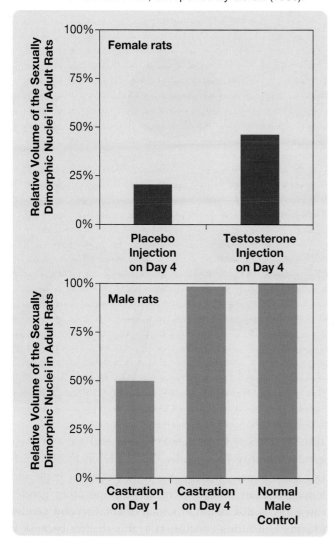

VMN do not display lordosis, and they are likely to attack suitors who become too ardent.

The influence of the VMN on the sexual behavior of female rats appears to be mediated by a tract that descends to the *periaqueductal gray (PAG)* of the tegmentum. Destruction of this tract eliminates female sexual behavior (see Hennessey et al., 1990), as do lesions of the PAG itself (see Sakuma & Pfaff, 1979)—see Figure 13.13.

AMYGDALA AND SEXUAL ACTIVITY. The amygdalas, located in the left and right medial temporal lobes, play a general role in the experience of emotions and social cognition (see Olson et al., 2013; Rolls, 2015). With respect to sexual behavior, they seem to play a role in the identification of potential mating partners based on sensory social signals, which are primarily visual in humans and olfactory in rats. Support for this view comes from three lines of research.

Evolutionary Perspective

The first line of evidence involves the study of bilateral amygdala lesions in male and female primates, including humans. Such lesions have a variety of effects on primate behavior, which together have been termed the *Kluver-Bucy syndrome* (see Chapter 17). The effects on sexual behavior are particularly striking (see Baird et al., 2004). For example, humans display flat affect, hypersexuality, and a complete inability to limit their sexual advances to appropriate partners or locations (see Anson & Kuhlman, 1993).

The second line of research stems from Everitt's (1990) classic study of bilateral amygdalar lesions in male rats. The lesions disrupted copulatory behavior, but

Figure 13.13 The hypothalamus-tegmentum circuits that play a role in female and male sexual behavior in rats.

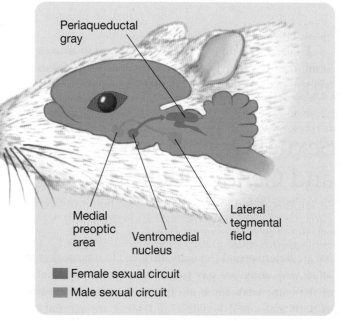

Periaqueductal gray

Medial preoptic area

Ventromedial nucleus

Lateral tegmental field

■ Female sexual circuit
■ Male sexual circuit

medial preoptic area elicits copulatory behavior in male rats (see Rodriguez-Manzo et al., 2000), and copulatory behavior can be reinstated in castrated male rats by medial preoptic implants of testosterone (see Davidson, 1980).

The medial preoptic area appears to control male sexual behavior via a tract that projects to an area of the midbrain called the *lateral tegmental field.* Destruction of this tract disrupts the sexual behavior of male rats (see Brackett & Edwards, 1984). Moreover, the activity of individual neurons in the lateral tegmental field of male rats is often correlated with aspects of the copulatory act (see Shimura & Shimokochi, 1990); for example, some neurons in the lateral tegmental field fire at a high rate only during intromission.

The **ventromedial nucleus (VMN)** of the rat hypothalamus contains circuits that appear to be critical for female sexual behavior. Female rats with bilateral lesions of the this did not occur because the males had difficulty copulating. The deficit occurred because the males were incapable of responding to the olfactory and visual cues from receptive females.

And the third line of evidence comes from the study of the reactions of human males and females to erotic images. Males are more likely than females to be sexually aroused by erotic images (see Rupp & Wallen, 2008), and this difference is reflected in differences in amygdalar activation. In several studies, erotic images presented to male and female volunteers undergoing functional brain scans produced greater amygdalar activation in males (see Hamann, 2005; Stoléru, 2012).

VENTRAL STRIATUM AND SEXUAL ACTIVITY. Sexual activity is clearly among the most pleasurable human activities (see Georgiadis & Kringelbach, 2012). Accordingly, it is not surprising that sexual activity can serve as a powerful reinforcer. Indeed, Pfaus and colleagues (2012) have shown that both male and female rats learn to prefer partners, locations, and odors associated with copulation.

Because orgasm is associated with pleasure, it comes as no surprise that the ventral striatum is activated in human volunteers by sexually provocative visual images (see Stoléru et al., 2012). Research on rats has shown that the activity in this area is associated with the anticipation and experience of sex and other forms of pleasure (see Matsumoto et al., 2012; Pitchers et al., 2010).

Figure 13.14 summarizes this module. It illustrates the location of the four brain structures that were discussed and summarizes their putative roles in sexual activity.

Figure 13.14 The cortex, hypothalamus, amygdala, and ventral striatum: their putative roles in sexual activity. The amygdala and ventral striatum are hidden in this view.

Cortex
Mediates the most complex aspects of sexual experience.

Ventral Striatum
Associated with the anticipation and experience of sexual activity and other pleasurable activities.

Hypothalamus
The ventromedial nucleus plays a role in female sexual behavior; the medial preoptic area plays a role in male sexual behavior.

Amygdala
Plays a role in the identification of potential mating partners.

Sexual Orientation and Gender Identity

So far, this chapter has not systematically addressed the topics of sexual orientation and gender identity. As you know, people differ in their sexual orientation: Some people are **heterosexual** (sexually attracted to members of the other sex), some are **gay** (sexually attracted to members of the same sex), some are **bisexual** (sexually attracted to both males and females), and some are **asexual** (not sexually attracted to others). People also vary in their **gender identity** (the gender that a person most identifies with: female, male, some combination of male and female, neither female or male, or some other gender category). A discussion of sexual orientation and gender identity is a fitting conclusion to this chapter because it further underscores its anti-mamawawa theme.

Sexual Orientation

LO 13.17 Describe the results of the two studies on the genetics of sexual orientation by Bailey and Pillard (1991, 1993), and describe the fraternal birth order effect and why it is thought to occur.

SEXUAL ORIENTATION AND GENES. Research has shown that differences in sexual orientation are influenced by genes. For example, Bailey and Pillard (1991) studied a group of gay males who had twin brothers, and they found that 52 percent of the monozygotic twin brothers and 22 percent of the dizygotic twin brothers were gay. In a comparable study of female twins by the same research group (Bailey et al., 1993), it was found that 48 percent of the monozygotic twin sisters and 16 percent of the dizygotic twin sisters were gay.

SEXUAL ORIENTATION AND EARLY HORMONES.
Many people mistakenly assume that gay persons have lower levels of sex hormones. They don't: Heterosexuals and gay persons do not differ in their levels of circulating hormones. Moreover, orchidectomy reduces the sexual behavior of both heterosexual and gay males, but it does not redirect it; and replacement injections simply reactivate the preferences that existed prior to surgery.

Many people also assume that sexual orientation is a matter of choice. It isn't. People discover their sexual orientation; they don't choose it. Sexual orientation seems to develop very early, and a child's first indication of their sexual orientation usually does not change as they mature. Could perinatal hormone exposure be the early event that shapes sexual orientation?

Because experiments involving levels of perinatal hormone exposure are not feasible with humans, efforts to determine whether perinatal hormone levels influence the development of sexual orientation have focused on nonhuman species. A consistent pattern of findings has

Evolutionary Perspective

emerged. In those species whose exposure to early sex hormones has been modified (e.g., rats, hamsters, ferrets, pigs, zebra finches, and dogs), it has not been uncommon to see males engaging in female-typical sexual behavior such as being mounted by other males. Nor has it been uncommon to see females engaging in male-typical sexual behavior such as mounting other females. However, because the defining feature of sexual orientation is sexual preference, the key studies have examined the effect of early hormone exposure on the sex of preferred sexual partners. In general, the perinatal castration of males has increased their preference as adults for male sex partners; similarly, prenatal testosterone exposure in females has increased their preference as adults for female sex partners (see Henley, Nunez, & Clemens, 2011).

On the one hand, we need to exercise prudence in drawing conclusions about the development of sexual orientation in humans based on the results of experiments on laboratory species; it would be a mistake to ignore the profound cognitive and emotional components of human sexuality, which have no counterpart in laboratory animals. On the other hand, it would also be a mistake to think that a pattern of results that runs so consistently through so many species has no relevance to humans.

There are some indications that perinatal hormones do influence sexual orientation in humans—although the evidence is sparse (see Balthazart, 2011; Diamond, 2009). Support comes from the quasiexperimental study of Ehrhardt and her colleagues (1985). They interviewed adult females whose mothers had been exposed to *diethylstilbestrol* (a synthetic estrogen) during pregnancy. The females' responses indicated that they were significantly

more sexually attracted to females than was a group of matched controls. Ehrhardt and her colleagues concluded that perinatal estrogen exposure does encourage lesbianism and bisexuality in females but that its effect is relatively weak: The sexual behavior of all but 1 of the 30 participants in this study was primarily heterosexual.

One promising line of research on sexual orientation focuses on the **fraternal birth order effect**, the finding that the probability of a male being gay increases as a function of the number of older brothers he has (see Alexander et al., 2011; Blanchard & Lippa, 2007). A recent study of blended families (families in which biologically related siblings were raised with adopted siblings or step-siblings) found that the effect is related to the number of males previously born to the mother, not the number of older males one is reared with (see Bogaert, 2007). The effect is relatively large: The probability of a male being gay increases by 33.3 percent for every older brother he has (see Puts, Jordan, & Breedlove, 2006).

The **maternal immune hypothesis** has been proposed to explain the fraternal birth order effect. This hypothesis is that some mothers become progressively more immune to masculinizing hormones in male fetuses (see Bogaert & Skorska, 2011), and a mother's immune system might deactivate masculinizing hormones in her younger sons.

What Triggers the Development of Sexual Attraction?

LO 13.18 Describe the hypothesized role of adrenal cortex steroids in the emergence of sexual attraction.

The evidence indicates that most females and males living in Western countries experience their first feelings of sexual attraction at about 10 years of age, whether they are heterosexual, bisexual, gay (see Quinsey, 2003). This finding is at odds with the usual assumption that sexual interest is triggered by puberty, which currently tends to occur at 10.5 years of age in females and at 11.5 years in males.

McClintock and Herdt (1996) have suggested that the emergence of sexual attraction may be stimulated by adrenal cortex steroids. Unlike gonadal maturation, adrenal maturation occurs at about the age of 10.

Is There a Difference in the Brains of Gay Persons and Heterosexuals?

LO 13.19 Describe the famous study of LeVay (1991) and the major problem with its finding.

The brains of gay persons and heterosexuals must differ in some way, but how? Many studies have attempted to identify neuroanatomical, neuropsychological, neurophysiological, and hormonal response differences between gay persons and heterosexuals.

In a highly publicized study, LeVay (1991) found that the structure of one hypothalamic nucleus in gay males was intermediate between that in female heterosexuals and that in male heterosexuals. This study has not been consistently replicated, however. Indeed, no reliable difference between the brains of heterosexuals and gay persons has yet been discovered.

Gender Identity

LO 13.20 Explain what transsexualism is, and describe the process of sexual reassignment.

Gender identity is the gender (male, female, some combination of female and male, neither male or female, or some other gender category) that a person most identifies with. Gender identity usually coincides with a person's anatomical sex, but not always.

Transsexualism is a condition where a person has a gender identity that is inconsistent with their anatomical sex (see Kreukels & Cohen-Kettenis, 2012). To put it mildly, the transsexual person faces a strong conflict: "I am a woman (or man) trapped in the body of a man (or woman). Help!" It is important to appreciate the desperation of these individuals; they do not merely think that life might be better if their gender were different. Today, many transsexual persons seek *surgical sexual reassignment* (surgery to change their sex), but their desperation is better indicated by how some of them dealt with their problem before surgical sexual reassignment was an option: Some biological males with female gender identities attempted self-castration, and others consumed copious quantities of estrogen-containing face creams in an attempt to feminize their bodies.

How does surgical sexual reassignment work? We will describe the male-to-female procedure; the female-to-male procedure is more complex (because a penis must be

Watch this video on MyPsychLab

BEING A TRANSSEXUAL PERSON: PROFILE 1

Watch this video on MyPsychLab

BEING A TRANSSEXUAL PERSON: PROFILE 2

created), and the male-to-female procedure is four times more prevalent (see Sutcliffe et al., 2009).

The first step in male-to-female reassignment is psychiatric assessment to establish that the candidate for surgery is a true transsexual individual. Once accepted for surgical reassignment, each transsexual person receives in-depth counseling to prepare for the difficulties that will ensue. If the candidate is still interested in reassignment after counseling, estrogen administration is initiated to feminize the body; the hormone regimen continues for life to maintain the changes. Then comes the surgery. 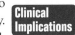 The penis and testes are surgically removed, and female external genitalia and a vagina are constructed—the vagina is lined with skin and nerves from the former penis so that it will have sensory nerve endings that will respond to sexual stimulation. Finally, some patients have cosmetic surgery to feminize the face (e.g., to reduce the size of the Adam's apple). Generally, the adjustment of transsexual persons after surgical sexual reassignment is good.

The causes of transsexualism are unknown. Transsexualism was once thought to be a product of social learning, that is, of atypical child-rearing practices (e.g., mothers dressing their little boys in dresses). The occasional case that is consistent with this view can be found, but in most cases, there is no obvious cause (see Smith et al., 2015). One of the major difficulties in identifying the causes and mechanisms of transsexualism is that there is no comparable condition in other species.

Independence of Sexual Orientation and Gender Identity

LO 13.21 Sexual attraction, gender identity, and body type are independent. Explain and give an example.

To complete this chapter, we would like to remind you of two of its main themes and show you how useful they are in thinking about one of the puzzles of human sexuality. One of the two themes is that the exception proves the rule: that a powerful test of any theory is its ability to explain exceptional cases. The second is that the mamawawa is seriously flawed: We have seen that males and females are similar in some ways and different in others, but they are certainly not opposites, and their programs of development are neither parallel nor opposite. Moreover, some people do not fall unambiguously into one or either of these two categories.

Here, we want to focus on the puzzling fact that sexual orientation, gender identity, and body type are sometimes unrelated (see Bao & Swaab, 2011; Garcia-Falgueras & Swaab, 2010). For example, consider transsexual persons: They, by definition, have a body type that is inconsistent with their gender identity, but their sexual orientation is an independent matter. Some transsexual persons **Thinking Creatively** with a male body type are sexually attracted to females, others are sexually attracted to males, and others are sexually attracted to neither—and this is not changed by sexual reassignment (see Van Goozen et al., 2002).

> **Thinking Creatively** Somebody tells you that all male-to-female transsexual persons prefer males as their sexual partners. What would your response be?

Obviously, the mere existence of non-heterosexual sexual orientations and transsexualism is a challenge to the mamawawa, the assumption that males and females belong to distinct and opposite categories. Many people tend to think of "femaleness" and "maleness" as being at opposite ends of a continuum, with a few atypical cases somewhere between the two. Perhaps this is what you think. However, the fact that body type, sexual orientation, and gender identity are often independent constitutes a serious attack on any assumption that femaleness and maleness lie at opposite ends of a single scale. Clearly, femaleness or maleness is a combination of many different attributes (e.g., body type, sexual orientation, and gender identity), each of which can develop quite independently. This is a real puzzle for many people, including scientists, but what you have already learned in this chapter suggests a solution.

Think back to the section on brain differentiation. Until recently, it was assumed that the differentiation of the human brain into its typical female and male forms occurred through a single testosterone-based mechanism. However, a different notion has developed from recent evidence. Now, it is clear that male and female brains differ in many ways and that the differences develop at different times and by different mechanisms. If you keep this developmental principle in mind, you will have no difficulty understanding how it is possible for some individuals to be female in some ways and male in others, and to lie somewhere between the two in still other ways.

This analysis exemplifies a point we make many times in this text. The study of biopsychology often has important personal and social implications: The search for the neural basis of a behavior frequently provides us with a greater understanding of that behavior. We hope that you now have a greater understanding of, and acceptance of, differences in human sexuality.

Themes Revisited

Three of the book's four major themes were repeatedly emphasized in this chapter: the evolutionary perspective, clinical implications, and thinking creatively themes.

The evolutionary perspective theme was pervasive. It received frequent attention because most experimental **Evolutionary Perspective** studies of hormones and sex have been conducted in nonhuman species. The other major source of information about hormones and sex has been the study of human clinical cases, which is why the clinical implications theme was prominent in the cases of the woman who wasn't, the little girl who grew into a boy, the twin who lost his penis, **Clinical Implications** and the man who lost and regained his 'manhood.'

The thinking creatively theme was emphasized throughout the chapter because conventional ways of thinking about hormones and sex have often been at odds with the results of biopsycho- **Thinking Creatively** logical research. If you are now better able to resist the seductive appeal of the men-are-men-and-women-are-women assumption, you are a more broadminded and understanding person than when you began this chapter. We hope you have gained an abiding appreciation of the fact that maleness and femaleness are multidimensional and, at times, ambiguous variations of each other.

The fourth major theme of the book, neuroplasticity, arose during the discussions of the effects of hormones on the development of sex differ- ences in the brain.

Key Terms

Neuroendocrine System
Exocrine glands, p. 357
Endocrine glands, p. 357
Hormones, p. 357
Gonads, p. 358
Testes, p. 358
Ovaries, p. 358
Copulation, p. 358
Zygote, p. 358
Sex chromosomes, p. 358
Amino acid derivative
    hormones, p. 358
Peptide hormones, p. 358
Protein hormones, p. 358
Steroid hormones, p. 358
Androgens, p. 358
Estrogens, p. 358
Testosterone, p. 358
Estradiol, p. 358
Progestins, p. 358
Progesterone, p. 358
Adrenal cortex, p. 358
Gonadotropin, p. 359
Posterior pituitary, p. 359
Pituitary stalk, p. 359
Anterior pituitary, p. 359
Menstrual cycle, p. 359
Vasopressin, p. 360
Oxytocin, p. 360
Paraventricular nuclei, p. 360
Supraoptic nuclei, p. 360
Hypothalamopituitary portal system,
    p. 360
Releasing hormones, p. 360
Release-inhibiting hormones, p. 360
Thyrotropin-releasing hormone, p. 360
Thyrotropin, p. 360

Gonadotropin-releasing hormone,
    p. 361
Follicle-stimulating hormone (FSH),
    p. 361
Luteinizing hormone (LH), p. 361
Pulsatile hormone release, p. 362

Hormones and Sexual Development of the Body
Sry gene, p. 363
Sry protein, p. 363
Intersexed person, p. 363
Wolffian system, p. 363
Müllerian system, p. 363
Müllerian-inhibiting substance, p. 363
Scrotum, p. 363
Ovariectomy, p. 364
Orchidectomy, p. 364
Gonadectomy, p. 364
Genitals, p. 364
Secondary sex characteristics, p. 364
Growth hormone, p. 365
Adrenocorticotropic hormone, p. 365
Androstenedione, p. 365

Hormones and Sexual Development of Brain and Behavior
Aromatase, p. 367
Aromatization, p. 367
Aromatization hypothesis, p. 367
Alpha fetoprotein, p. 367
Masculinizes, p. 368
Defeminizes, p. 368
Lordosis, p. 368
Feminizes, p. 368
Demasculinizes, p. 368
Intromission, p. 368

Ejaculation, p. 368
Proceptive behaviors, p. 368
Sexual dimorphisms, p. 368

Three Cases of Exceptional Human Sexual Development
Androgen insensitivity
    syndrome, p. 370
Adrenogenital syndrome, p. 371
Congenital adrenal hyperplasia, p. 371
Ablatio penis, p. 371

Effects of Gonadal Hormones on Adults
Replacement injections, p. 373
Impotent, p. 373
Estrus, p. 374
Estrous cycle, p. 374
Anabolic steroids, p. 374

Brain Mechanisms of Sexual Behavior
Medial preoptic area, p. 376
Sexually dimorphic nucleus, p. 376
Ventromedial nucleus
    (VMN), p. 377

Sexual Orientation and Gender Identity
Heterosexual, p. 378
Gay, p. 378
Bisexual, p. 378
Asexual, p. 378
Gender identity, p. 378
Fraternal birth order effect, p. 379
Maternal immune hypothesis, p. 379
Transsexualism, p. 380

Chapter 14
Sleep, Dreaming, and Circadian Rhythms

How Much Do You Need to Sleep?

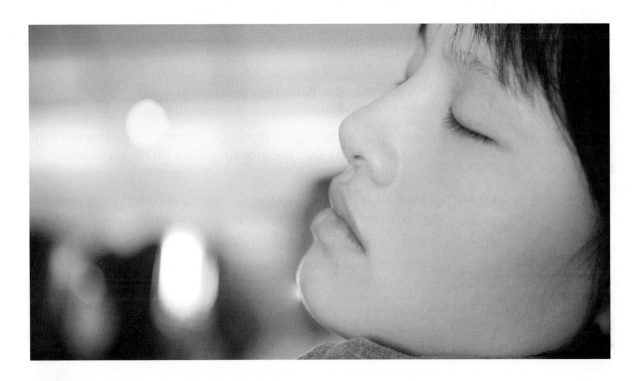

Chapter Overview and Learning Objectives (LOs)

Stages of Sleep	**LO 14.1**	Describe the three standard physiological measures of sleep.
	LO 14.2	Describe the three stages of the sleep EEG, and explain the difference between REM and non-REM sleep.
	LO 14.3	Describe the relationship between REM sleep and dreaming. Also, describe five common beliefs about dreaming and assess their validity. Finally, describe the activation-synthesis theory of dreams.
Why Do We Sleep, and Why Do We Sleep When We Do?	**LO 14.4**	Describe the two kinds of theories of sleep.
	LO 14.5	Explain four conclusions that have resulted from the comparative analysis of sleep.

Effects of Sleep Deprivation	**LO 14.6**	Explain how stress can often be a confounding variable when considering the effects of sleep deprivation.
	LO 14.7	List the three predictions that recuperation theories make about the effects of sleep deprivation.
	LO 14.8	Describe two classic sleep-deprivation case studies.
	LO 14.9	Describe the major effects of sleep deprivation in humans.
	LO 14.10	Describe the key studies of sleep deprivation in laboratory animals. Provide a critique of the carousel apparatus as a method of sleep deprivation.
	LO 14.11	Describe the effects of REM-sleep deprivation.
	LO 14.12	Describe six pieces of evidence that indicate that less sleep is associated with more efficient sleep.
Circadian Sleep Cycles	**LO 14.13**	Describe the circadian sleep–wake cycle and the role of zeitgebers in maintaining circadian rhythms.
	LO 14.14	Describe free-running rhythms and internal desynchronization, and explain why they are incompatible with recuperation theories of sleep.
	LO 14.15	Describe the disruptive effects of jet lag and shift work on circadian rhythmicitiy and how one can minimize such effects.
	LO 14.16	Describe the research that led to the discovery of a circadian clock in the suprachiasmatic nucleus (SCN) of the hypothalamus.
	LO 14.17	Explain the mechanism by which SCN neurons are entrained by the 24-hour light–dark cycles.
	LO 14.18	Understand the genetics of circadian rhythms and the important discoveries that have resulted from the discovery of circadian genes.
Four Areas of the Brain Involved in Sleep	**LO 14.19**	Describe the research that led to the identification of the anterior and posterior hypothalamus as brain regions involved in the regulation of sleep and wakefulness.
	LO 14.20	Describe the research that led to the identification of the reticular formation as a brain region involved in the regulation of sleep and wakefulness.
	LO 14.21	Discuss how REM sleep is controlled by the reticular formation and what implications this has for understanding the neural mechanisms of behavior.
Drugs That Affect Sleep	**LO 14.22**	Describe three classes of hypnotic drugs. Compare and contrast them in terms of their efficacy and side effects.
	LO 14.23	Describe three classes of antihypnotic drugs.

Most of us have a fondness for eating and sex—the two highly esteemed motivated behaviors discussed in Chapters 12 and 13. But the amount of time devoted to these behaviors by even the most amorous gourmands pales in comparison to the amount of time spent sleeping: Most of us will sleep for well over 175,000 hours in our lifetimes. This extraordinary commitment of time implies that sleep fulfills a critical biological function. But what is it? And what about dreaming: Why do we spend so much time dreaming? And why do we tend to get sleepy at about the same time every day? Answers to these questions await you in this chapter.

Almost every time we lecture about sleep, somebody asks, "How much sleep do we need?" Each time, we provide the same unsatisfying answer: We explain that there are two fundamentally different answers to this question, but neither has emerged a clear winner. One answer stresses the presumed health-promoting and recuperative powers of sleep and suggests that people need as much sleep as they can comfortably get—the usual prescription being at least 8 hours per night. The other answer is that many of us sleep more than we need to and are consequently sleeping part of our life away. Just think how your life could change if you slept 5 hours per night instead of 8. You would have an extra 21 waking hours each week, a mind-boggling 10,952 hours each decade.

As we prepared to write this chapter, I (JP) began to think of the personal implications of the idea that we get more sleep than we need. That is when I decided to do something a bit unconventional. I am going to be trying to get no more than 5 hours of sleep per night—11:00 p.m. to 4:00 a.m.—until this chapter is written. As I begin, I am excited by the

Thinking Creatively

prospect of having more time to write but a little worried that this extra time might cost me too dearly.

It is now the next day—4:50 Saturday morning to be exact—and I am just sitting down to write. There was a party last night, and I didn't make it to bed by 11:00; but considering that I slept for only 3 hours and 35 minutes, I feel quite good. I wonder what I will feel like later in the day. In any case, I will report my experiences to you at the end of the chapter.

The following case study challenges several common beliefs about sleep (Meddis, 1977). Ponder its implications before proceeding to the body of the chapter.

The Case of the Woman Who Wouldn't Sleep

Miss M usually sleeps only 1 hour per night. Although she is retired, she keeps busy painting, writing, and volunteering in the community. Although she becomes tired physically, she never reports feeling sleepy. During the night she sits on her bed reading, writing, crocheting, or painting. At about 2:00 a.m., she often falls asleep without any preceding drowsiness, and when she wakes about 1 hour later, she feels wide awake.

She came to the laboratory for some sleep tests, but on the first night we ran into a snag. She told us she did not sleep at all if she had interesting things to do, and she found her visit to a sleep laboratory very interesting. She had someone to talk to for the whole of the night.

In the morning, we broke into shifts so that some could sleep while at least one person stayed with her. The second night was the same as the first.

Finally, on the third night, she promised to try to sleep, and she did. The only abnormal thing about her sleep was that it was brief. After 99 minutes, she could sleep no more.

...es of Sleep

...anges occur in the body during sleep. This module introduces you to the major ones.

Three Standard Psychophysiological Measures of Sleep

LO 14.1 Describe the three standard physiological measures of sleep.

There are major changes in the human EEG during the course of a night's sleep. Although the EEG waves that accompany sleep are generally high-voltage and slow, there are periods throughout the night that are dominated by low-voltage, fast waves similar to those in nonsleeping individuals. In the 1950s, it was discovered that *rapid eye movements (REMs)* occur under the closed eyelids of sleepers during these periods of low-voltage, fast EEG activity. And in 1962, Berger and Oswald discovered that there is also a loss of electromyographic activity in the neck muscles during these same sleep periods. Subsequently, the **electroencephalogram (EEG)**, the **electrooculogram (EOG)**, and the neck **electromyogram (EMG)** became the three standard psychophysiological bases for defining the stages of sleep.

Figure 14.1 depicts a volunteer participating in a sleep experiment. A participant's first night of sleep in a laboratory is often fitful. That's why the usual practice is to have each participant sleep several nights in the laboratory before commencing a sleep study. The disturbance of sleep observed during the first night in a sleep laboratory is called the *first-night phenomenon*. It is well known to graders of introductory psychology examinations because of the creative definitions of it that are offered by students who forget that it is a sleep-related, rather than a sex-related, phenomenon.

Three Stages of Sleep EEG

LO 14.2 Describe the three stages of the sleep EEG, and explain the difference between REM and non-REM sleep.

According to the American Academy of Sleep Medicine, there are three

Figure 14.1 A participant in a sleep experiment.

stages of sleep EEG: stage 1, stage 2, and stage 3 (see Grigg-Damberger, 2012). Examples of these three stages are presented in Figure 14.2.

After the eyes are shut and a person prepares to go to sleep, **alpha waves**—waxing and waning bursts of 8- to 12-Hz EEG waves—begin to punctuate the low-voltage,

Figure 14.2 The EEG of alert wakefulness, the EEG that precedes sleep onset, and the three stages of sleep EEG. Each trace is about 10 seconds long.

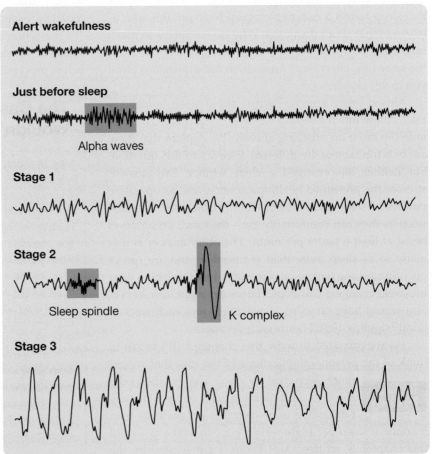

high-frequency waves of alert wakefulness. Then, as the person falls asleep, there is a sudden transition to a period of stage 1 sleep EEG. The stage 1 sleep EEG is a low-voltage, high-frequency signal that is similar to, but slower than, that of alert wakefulness.

There is a gradual increase in EEG voltage and a decrease in EEG frequency as the person progresses from stage 1 sleep through stages 2 and 3. Accordingly, the stage 2 sleep EEG has a slightly higher amplitude and a lower frequency than the stage 1 EEG; in addition, it is punctuated by two characteristic wave forms: K complexes and sleep spindles. Each *K complex* is a single large negative wave (upward deflection) followed immediately by a single large positive wave (downward deflection)—see Mak-McCully and colleagues (2014). Each *sleep spindle* is a 0.5- to 3-second waxing and waning burst of 9- to 15-Hz waves—see Astori, Wimmer, and Lüthi (2013). The stage 3 sleep EEG is defined by a predominance of **delta waves**—the largest and slowest EEG waves, with a frequency of 1 to 2 Hz.

Once sleepers reach stage 3 EEG sleep, they stay there for a time, and then they retreat back through the stages of sleep to stage 1. However, when they return to stage 1, things are not at all the same as they were the first time through. The first period of stage 1 EEG during a night's sleep (**initial stage 1 EEG**) is not marked by any striking electromyographic or electrooculographic changes, whereas subsequent periods of stage 1 sleep EEG (**emergent stage 1 EEG**) are accompanied by REMs and by a loss of tone in the muscles of the body core.

After the first cycle of sleep EEG—from initial stage 1 to stage 3 and back to emergent stage 1—the rest of the night is spent going back and forth through the stages. Figure 14.3 illustrates the EEG cycles of a typical night's sleep and the close relation between emergent stage 1 sleep, REMs, and the loss of tone in core muscles. Notice that each cycle tends to be about 90 minutes long and that, as the night progresses, more and more time is spent in emergent stage 1 sleep, and less and less time is spent in the other stages, particularly stage 3. Notice also that there are brief periods during the night when the person is awake, although he or she usually does not remember these periods of wakefulness in the morning.

Let's pause here to get some sleep-stage terms straight. The sleep associated with emergent stage 1 EEG is often called **REM sleep** (pronounced "rehm"), after the associated rapid eye movements; whereas all other stages of sleep together are called *NREM sleep* (non-REM sleep). Accordingly, initial stage 1, stage 2, and stage 3 sleep are sometimes referred to as NREM 1 (N1), NREM 2 (N2), and

Figure 14.3 The course of EEG stages during a typical night's sleep and the relation of emergent stage 1 EEG to REMs and lack of tone in core muscles.

NREM 3 (N3), respectively (see Grigg-Damberger, 2012). NREM 3 is often referred to as **slow-wave sleep (SWS)**, after the delta waves that characterize it. Table 14.1 summarizes the various sleep-stage terms.

REMs, loss of core-muscle tone, and a low-amplitude, high-frequency EEG are not the only physiological correlates of REM sleep. Cerebral activity (e.g., oxygen consumption, blood flow, and neural firing) increases to waking levels in many brain structures, and there is a general increase in the variability of autonomic nervous system activity (e.g., in blood pressure, pulse, and respiration). Also, the muscles of the extremities occasionally twitch, and there is almost always some degree of penile or clitoral erection.

Dreaming

LO 14.3 Describe the relationship between REM sleep and dreaming. Also, describe five common beliefs about dreaming and assess their validity. Finally, describe the activation-synthesis theory of dreams.

REM SLEEP AND DREAMING. Nathaniel Kleitman's laboratory was an exciting place in 1953. REM sleep had just been discovered, and Kleitman and his students were driven by the fascinating implication of the discovery. With the exception of the loss of tone in the core muscles, all of the other measures suggested that REM sleep episodes were emotion-charged. Could REM sleep be the physiological correlate of dreaming?

Table 14.1 Summary of Various Sleep-Stage Terms

REM sleep	Emergent stage 1 EEG
NREM sleep	Initial stage 1 EEG (NREM 1; N1)
	Stage 2 EEG (NREM 2; N2)
	Stage 3 EEG (NREM 3; N3)
Slow-wave sleep	Stage 3 EEG (NREM 3; N3)

Support for the theory that REM sleep is the physiological correlate of dreaming came from the observation that 80 percent of awakenings from REM sleep, but only 7 percent of awakenings from NREM sleep, led to dream recall. The dreams recalled from NREM sleep tended to be isolated experiences (e.g., "I was falling"), while those associated with REM sleep tended to take the form of stories, or narratives. While there are still many adherents to the theory that REM sleep and dreaming can be equated (e.g., Desseilles et al., 2011), the situation has been complicated by the discovery that dreaming is much more prevalent during NREM than first assumed (e.g., Siclari et al., 2013) and that many NREM dreams are comparable to REM dreams (see McNamara et al., 2010). More problematic is that REM sleep and dreaming can be dissociated (see Siegel, 2011). For example, antidepressants greatly reduce or abolish REM sleep without affecting aspects of dream recall (see Oudiette et al., 2012). Conversely, cortical lesions can abolish dreaming without affecting REM sleep (see Nir & Tononi, 2010).

TESTING COMMON BELIEFS ABOUT DREAMING. The correlation between REM sleep and dream recall that Kleitman and colleagues discovered provided them with an opportunity to test some common beliefs about dreaming. The following five beliefs were among the first to be addressed:

- Many people believe that external stimuli can become incorporated into their dreams. Dement and Wolpert (1958) sprayed water on sleeping volunteers after they had been in REM sleep for a few minutes and then awakened them a few seconds later. In 14 of 33 cases, the water was incorporated into the dream report. The following narrative was reported by one participant who had been dreaming that he was acting in a play:

  > I was walking behind the leading lady when she suddenly collapsed and water was dripping on her. I ran over to her and water was dripping on my back and head. The roof was leaking....I looked up and there was a hole in the roof. I dragged her over to the side of the stage and began pulling the curtains. Then I woke up. (p. 574)

- Some people believe dreams last only an instant, but research suggests that dreams run on "real time." In one study (Dement & Kleitman, 1957), volunteers were awakened 5 or 15 minutes after the beginning of a REM episode and asked to decide on the basis of the duration of the events in their dreams whether they had been dreaming for 5 or 15 minutes. They were correct in 92 of 111 cases.

- Some people claim that they do not dream. However, these people have just as much REM sleep as normal

dreamers. Moreover, most report dreams if they are awakened during REM episodes (see Goodenough et al., 1959), although they do so less frequently than do normal dreamers.

- Penile erections are commonly assumed to be indicative of dreams with sexual content. However, erections are no more complete during dreams with frank sexual content than during those without it (Karacan et al., 1966). Even babies have REM-related penile erections.

- Many people believe sleeptalking (*somniloquy*) and sleepwalking (*somnambulism*) occur during REM sleep. This is not so (see Dyken, Yamada, & Lin-Dyken, 2001). Sleeptalking has no special association with REM sleep—it can occur during any stage but often occurs during the transition to wakefulness. Sleepwalking usually occurs during slow-wave sleep, and it never occurs during REM sleep, when core muscles tend to be totally relaxed (see Januszko et al., 2015).

INTERPRETATION OF DREAMS. Sigmund Freud believed that dreams are triggered by unacceptable repressed wishes, often of a sexual nature. He argued that because dreams represent unacceptable wishes, the dreams we experience (our *manifest dreams*) are merely disguised versions of our real dreams (our *latent dreams*): He hypothesized an unconscious censor that disguises and subtracts information from our real dreams so that we can endure them. Freud thus concluded that one of the keys to understanding people and dealing with their psychological problems is to expose the meaning of their latent dreams through the interpretation of their manifest dreams.

There is no convincing evidence for the Freudian theory of dreams; indeed, the brain science of the 1890s, which served as its foundation, is now obsolete. Yet many people accept the notion that dreams bubble up from a troubled subconscious and that they represent repressed thoughts and wishes.

One widely held alternative to the Freudian theory of dreams is Hobson's (1989) activation-synthesis hypothesis (see Palagini & Rosenlicht, 2011). It is based on the observation that, during REM sleep, many brain-stem circuits become active and bombard the cerebral cortex with neural signals. The essence of the **activation-synthesis hypothesis** is that the information supplied to the cortex during REM sleep is largely random and that the resulting dream is the cortex's effort to make sense of these random signals. You might liken this process to what happens when you stare up at the clouds and happen to see faces or figures among them: The clouds are randomly patterned, but your brain is trying its best to make sense of that random pattern.

What do you see when you look at these clouds?

Why Do We Sleep, and Why Do We Sleep When We Do?

Now that you have been introduced to the properties of sleep and its various stages, the focus of this chapter shifts to a consideration of two fundamental questions about sleep: Why do we sleep? And why do we sleep when we do?

Two Kinds of Theories of Sleep

LO 14.4 Describe the two kinds of theories of sleep.

Two kinds of theories for sleep have been proposed: *recuperation theories* and *adaptation theories*. The differences between these two theoretical approaches are revealed by the answers they offer to the two fundamental questions about sleep.

The essence of **recuperation theories of sleep** is that being awake disrupts the *homeostasis* (internal physiological stability) of the body in some way and sleep is required to restore it. Various recuperation theories differ in terms of the particular physiological disruption they propose as the trigger for sleep. For example, the two most common recuperation theories of sleep are that the function of sleep is to: (1) restore energy levels that decline during wakefulness (see Porkka-Heiskanen, 2013), or (2) clear toxins (e.g., beta-amyloid—see Chapter 10) from the brain and other tissues that accumulate during wakefulness (see Herculano-Houzel, 2013; Lucey & Holtzman, 2015; Mander et al., 2015; Nedergard & Goldman, 2016; Xie et al., 2013). However, regardless of the particular function postulated by recuperation theories of sleep, they all imply that sleepiness is triggered by a deviation from homeostasis caused by wakefulness and that sleep is terminated by a return to homeostasis.

The essence of **adaptation theories of sleep** is that sleep is not a reaction to the disruptive effects of being awake but

the result of an internal 24-hour timing mechanism—that is, we humans are programmed to sleep at night regardless of what happens to us during the day. Adaptation theories of sleep focus more on when we sleep than on the function of sleep. Some of these theories even propose that sleep plays no role in the efficient physiological functioning of the body. According to these theories, early humans had enough time to get their eating, drinking, and reproducing out of the way during the daytime, and their strong motivation to sleep at night evolved to conserve their energy resources and to make them less susceptible to mishap (e.g., predation) in the dark (Rattenborg, Martinez-Gonzales, & Lesku, 2009; Siegel, 2009). **Evolutionary Perspective** Adaptation theories suggest that sleep is like reproductive behavior in the sense that we are highly motivated to engage in it, but we don't need it to stay healthy.

Comparative Analysis of Sleep

LO 14.5 Explain four conclusions that have resulted from the comparative analysis of sleep.

Sleep has been studied in only a small number of species, but the evidence so far suggests that most mammals and birds sleep. Furthermore, the sleep of mammals and birds, like ours, is characterized by high-amplitude, low-frequency EEG waves punctuated by periods of low-amplitude, high-frequency waves (see Siegel, 2008). The evidence for sleep in amphibians, reptiles, fish, and insects is less clear: Some display periods **Evolutionary Perspective** of inactivity and unresponsiveness, but the relation of these periods to mammalian sleep has not been established (see Siegel, 2008; Zimmerman et al., 2008). Table 14.2 gives the average number of hours per day that various mammalian species spend sleeping.

> **Evolutionary Perspective** If you were a sleep researcher studying sleep in various organisms, how would you define sleep?

The comparative investigation of sleep **Evolutionary Perspective** has led to several important conclusions. Let's consider four of these.

First, the fact that most mammals and birds sleep (see Siegel, 2012) suggests that sleep serves some important physiological function, rather than merely protecting animals from mishap and conserving energy. The evidence is strongest in species that are at increased risk of predation when they sleep (e.g., antelopes) and in species that have evolved complex mechanisms that enable them to sleep. For example, some marine mammals, such as dolphins, sleep with only half of their brain at a time so that the other half can control resurfacing for air (e.g., Dell et al., 2015a, 2015b). It is against the logic of natural selection for some animals to risk predation while sleeping and for others to have evolved complex mechanisms to permit them to safely sleep, unless sleep itself serves some critical function.

Second, the fact that most mammals and birds sleep suggests that the primary function of sleep is not some special, higher-order human function. For example, suggestions that sleep helps humans reprogram our complex brains or that it permits some kind of emotional release to maintain our mental health are improbable in view of the comparative evidence.

Third, the large between-species differences in sleep time suggest that although sleep may be essential for survival, it is not necessarily needed in large quantities (see Table 14.2). Horses and many other animals get by quite nicely on 2 or 3 hours of sleep per day. Moreover, it is important to realize that the sleep patterns of mammals and birds in their natural environments can vary substantially from their patterns in captivity, which is where they are typically studied (see Horne, 2009). For example, some animals that sleep a great deal in captivity sleep little in the wild when food is in short supply or during periods of migration or mating (see Lesku et al., 2012; Siegel, 2012).

Fourth, many studies have tried to identify the reasons why some species are long sleepers and others are short sleepers. Why do cats tend to sleep about 14 hours a day and horses only about 2? Under the influence of recuperation theories, researchers have focused on energy-related factors in their efforts. However, there is no strong relationship between a species' sleep time and its level of activity, its

Figure 14.4 After gorging themselves on a kill, African lions often sleep almost continuously for 2 or 3 days. And where do they sleep? Anywhere they want!

body size, or its body temperature (see Siegel, 2005). The fact that giant sloths sleep 20 hours per day is a strong argument against the theory that sleep is a compensatory reaction to energy expenditure—similarly, energy expenditure has been shown to have little effect on subsequent sleep in humans (see Driver & Taylor, 2000; Youngstedt & Kline, 2006). In contrast, adaptation theories correctly predict that the daily sleep time of each species is related to how vulnerable it is while it is asleep and how much time it must spend each day to feed itself and to take care of its other survival requirements. For example, zebras must graze almost continuously to get enough to eat and are extremely vulnerable to predatory attack when they are asleep—and they sleep only about 2 hours per day. In contrast, African lions often sleep more or less continuously for 2 or 3 days after they have gorged themselves on a kill. Figure 14.4 says it all.

Effects of Sleep Deprivation

One way to identify the functions of sleep is to determine what happens when a person is deprived of sleep. This module begins with a cautionary note about the interpretation of the effects of sleep deprivation, a description of the predictions that recuperation theories make about sleep deprivation, and two classic case studies of sleep deprivation. Then, it summarizes the results of sleep-deprivation research.

Interpretation of the Effects of Sleep Deprivation: The Stress Problem

LO 14.6 Explain how stress can often be a confounding variable when considering the effects of sleep deprivation.

When you sleep substantially less than you are used to, the next day you feel out of sorts and unable to function

Table 14.2 Average Number of Hours Slept per Day by Various Mammalian Species

Mammalian Species	Hours of Sleep per Day
Giant sloth	20
Opossum, brown bat	19
Giant armadillo	18
Owl monkey, nine-banded armadillo	17
Arctic ground squirrel	16
Tree shrew	15
Cat, golden hamster	14
Mouse, rat, gray wolf, ground squirrel	13
Arctic fox, chinchilla, gorilla, raccoon	12
Mountain beaver	11
Jaguar, vervet monkey, hedgehog	10
Rhesus monkey, chimpanzee, baboon, red fox	9
Human, rabbit, guinea pig, pig	8
Gray seal, gray hyrax, Brazilian tapir	6
Tree hyrax, rock hyrax	5
Cow, goat, elephant, donkey, sheep	3
Roe deer, horse, zebra	2

as well as you usually do. Although such experiences of sleep deprivation are compelling, you need to be cautious in interpreting them. In Western cultures, most people who sleep little or irregularly do so because they are under stress (e.g., from illness, excessive work, shift work, drugs, or examinations), which could have adverse effects independent of any sleep loss. Even when sleep-deprivation studies are conducted on healthy volunteers in controlled laboratory environments, stress can be a contributing factor because many of the volunteers will find the sleep-deprivation procedure itself stressful. Accordingly, because it is difficult to separate the effects of sleep loss from the effects of stressful conditions that may have induced the loss, results of sleep-deprivation studies must be interpreted with caution.

Be that as it may, almost every week we read a news article decrying the effects of sleep loss in the general population. Such articles will typically point out that many people who are pressured by the demands of their work schedule sleep little and experience a variety of health and accident problems. There is a place for this kind of research because it identifies a problem that requires public attention; however, because the low levels of sleep are hopelessly confounded with high levels of stress, most sleep-deprivation studies tell us little about the functions of sleep and how much we need.

Predictions of Recuperation Theories about Sleep Deprivation

LO 14.7 List the three predictions that recuperation theories make about the effects of sleep deprivation.

Because recuperation theories of sleep are based on the premise that sleep is a response to the accumulation of some debilitating effect of wakefulness, they make the following three predictions about sleep deprivation:

- Long periods of wakefulness will produce physiological and behavioral disturbances.
- These disturbances will grow worse as the sleep deprivation continues.
- After a period of deprivation has ended, much of the missed sleep will be regained.

Have these predictions been confirmed?

Two Classic Sleep-Deprivation Case Studies

LO 14.8 Describe two classic sleep-deprivation case studies.

Let's look at two widely cited sleep-deprivation case studies. First is the groundbreaking study of a group of

sleep-deprived students (Kleitman, 1963); second is the bizarre case of Randy Gardner (Dement,1978).

The Case of the Sleep-Deprived Students

Most of the volunteer students subjected to total sleep deprivation by Kleitman experienced the same effects. During the first night, they read or studied with little difficulty until after 3:00 a.m., when they experienced an attack of sleepiness. At this point, their watchers had to be particularly careful that they did not sleep. The next day the students felt alert as long as they were active. During the second night, reading or studying was next to impossible because sleepiness was so severe, and as on the first night, there came a time after 3:00 a.m. when sleepiness became overpowering. However, as before, later in the morning, there was a decrease in sleepiness, and the students could perform tasks around the lab during the day as long as they were standing and moving.

The cycle of sleepiness on the third and fourth nights resembled that on the second, but the sleepiness became even more severe. Surprisingly, things did not grow worse after the fourth night, and those students who persisted repeatedly went through the same daily cycle.

The Case of Randy Gardner

Randy Gardner and two classmates, who were entrusted with keeping him awake, planned to break the then world record of 260 hours of consecutive wakefulness. Dement learned about the project and, seeing an opportunity to collect some important data, joined the team, much to the comfort of Randy's parents. Randy did complain vigorously when his team would not permit him to close his eyes. However, in no sense could Randy's behavior be considered disturbed. Near the end of his vigil, Randy held a press conference, and he conducted himself impeccably. Randy went to sleep exactly 264 hours and 12 minutes after he had awakened 11 days before. And how long did he sleep? Only 14 hours the first night, and thereafter he returned to his usual 8-hour schedule. Although you may be surprised that Randy did not have to sleep longer to "catch up" on his lost sleep, the lack of substantial recovery sleep is typical of such cases.

Experimental Studies of Sleep Deprivation in Humans

LO 14.9 Describe the major effects of sleep deprivation in humans.

Since the first studies of sleep deprivation by Dement and Kleitman in the mid-20th century, there have been hundreds of studies assessing the effects on humans of sleep-deprivation schedules ranging from a slightly reduced amount of sleep during one night to total sleep deprivation for several nights (see Lim & Dinges, 2010). The studies have assessed the effects of these schedules on many different measures of sleepiness, mood, cognition, motor performance, physiological function, and even molecular function (see Cirelli, 2013).

Even moderate amounts of sleep deprivation—for example, sleeping 3 or 4 hours less than normal for one night—have been found to have three consistent effects. First, sleep-deprived individuals display an increase in sleepiness: They report being more sleepy, and they fall asleep more quickly if given the opportunity. Second, sleep-deprived individuals display negative affect on various written tests of mood. And third, they perform poorly on tests of sustained attention (e.g., watching for a moving light on a computer screen)—see Kirszenblat and van Swinderen (2015).

The effects of sleep deprivation on complex cognitive functions have been less consistent (see Basner et al., 2013). Consequently, researchers have preferred to assess performance on the simple, dull, monotonous tasks most sensitive to the effects of sleep deprivation. Nevertheless, a small but growing number of studies have been able to demonstrate disruption of the performance of some complex cognitive tasks by sleep deprivation (see Basner et al., 2013).

The inconsistent effects of sleep deprivation on cognitive function in various studies may have been clarified by the discovery that only some cognitive functions appear to be susceptible. Many early studies of the effects of sleep deprivation on cognitive function used tests of logical deduction or critical thinking, and these tests proved to be largely immune to disruption. In contrast, performance on tests of **executive function** (cognitive abilities that appear to depend on the *prefrontal cortex*) proved to be more susceptible to disruption by sleep loss—executive function includes innovative thinking, lateral thinking, insightful thinking, and assimilating new information to update plans and strategies (see Nilsson et al., 2005).

The hypothesis that only some cognitive processes are susceptible to disruption by sleep loss clearly requires more systematic investigation. For example, several researchers have pointed out the need to determine the degree to which the deficits in vigilance and motivation produced by sleep loss can be mistaken for cognitive deficits (see Basner et al., 2013; Engle-Friedman, 2014).

> **Thinking Creatively**
> Why would deficits in vigilance and motivation lead to cognitive deficits? Give an example as part of your answer.

The adverse effects of sleep deprivation on physical performance have been surprisingly inconsistent considering the general belief that a good night's sleep is essential for optimal motor performance. Only a few measures tend to be affected, even after lengthy periods of deprivation (see Fullager et al., 2015).

Sleep deprivation has been found to have a variety of physiological consequences such as reduced body temperature, increases in blood pressure, decreases in some aspects of immune function, hormonal changes, and metabolic changes (see Cedernaes, Schiöth, & Benedict, 2015; Irwin, Olmstead, & Carroll, 2015; Maggio et al., 2013). The problem is that there is little evidence that these changes have any consequences for health or performance. For example, the fact that a decline in immune function was discovered in sleep-deprived volunteers does not necessarily mean that they would be more susceptible to infection—the immune system is extremely complicated and a decline in one aspect is often compensated for by other changes. This is why we want to single out a study by Prather and colleagues (2015) for commendation: Rather than studying immune function, these researchers focused directly on susceptibility to infection and illness.

Prather and colleagues exposed 164 healthy volunteers to a cold virus. Those who slept less than 6 hours a night were not less likely to become infected, but they were more likely to develop a cold. This is only a *correlational study* (see Chapter 1), and thus it cannot directly implicate sleep duration as the causal factor in whether participants developed a cold. Still, the suggestion that there may be a causal relation between sleep and susceptibility to colds warrants further research.

After 2 or 3 days of continuous sleep deprivation, most volunteers experience microsleeps, unless they are in a laboratory environment where the microsleeps can be interrupted as soon as they begin. **Microsleeps** are brief periods of sleep, typically about 2 or 3 seconds long, during which the eyelids droop and the volunteers become less responsive to external stimuli, even though they remain sitting or standing (see Toppi et al., 2016). As one would expect, microsleeps severely disrupt the performance of tests of vigilance, but even sleep-deprived individuals not experiencing microsleeps experience some vigilance problems (see Ferrara, De Gennaro, & Bertini, 1999).

It can be useful to compare sleep deprivation with the deprivation of the motivated behaviors discussed in Chapters 12 and 13. If people were deprived of the opportunity to eat or engage in sexual activity, the effects would be severe and unavoidable: In the first case, starvation and death would ensue; in the second, there would be a total loss of reproductive capacity. Despite our powerful drive to sleep, the effects of sleep deprivation tend to be comparatively subtle, selective, and variable. This is puzzling. Another puzzling thing is that performance deficits observed after extended periods of sleep deprivation disappear so readily—for example, in one study, 4 hours of sleep eliminated the performance deficits produced by 64 hours of sleep deprivation (Rosa, Bonnett, & Warm, 2007).

Sleep-Deprivation Studies of Laboratory Animals

LO 14.10 Describe the key studies of sleep deprivation in laboratory animals. Provide a critique of the carousel apparatus as a method of sleep deprivation.

The **carousel apparatus** (see Figure 14.5) has been used to deprive rats of sleep. Two rats, an experimental rat and its *yoked control*, are placed in separate chambers of the apparatus. Each time the EEG activity of the experimental rat indicates that it is sleeping, the disk, which serves as the floor of half of both chambers, starts to slowly rotate. As a result, if the sleeping experimental rat does not awaken immediately, it gets shoved off the disk into a shallow pool of water. The yoked control is exposed to exactly the same pattern of disk rotations; but if it is not sleeping, it can easily avoid getting dunked by walking in the direction opposite to the direction of disk rotation. The experimental rats typically died after about 12 days, while the yoked controls stayed reasonably healthy (see Rechtschaffen & Bergmann, 1995).

The fact that humans and rats have been sleep-deprived by other means for similar periods of time without dire consequences argues for caution in **Evolutionary Perspective** interpreting the results of the carousel sleep-deprivation experiments (see Rial et al., 2007;

Figure 14.5 The carousel apparatus used to deprive an experimental rat of sleep while a yoked control rat is exposed to the same number and pattern of disk rotations. The disk on which both rats stand rotates every time the experimental rat displays sleep EEG. If the sleeping rat does not awaken immediately, it is deposited in the water.

(Based on Rechtschaffen, A., Gilliland, M. A., Bergmann, B. M., & Winter, J. B. (1983). Physiological correlates of prolonged sleep deprivation in rats. *Science, 221,* 182–184.)

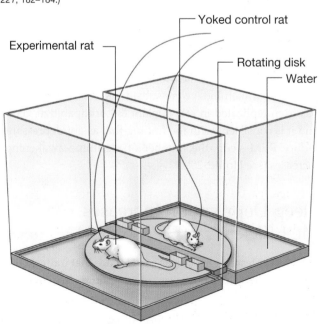

Siegel, 2009, 2012). It may be that repeatedly being awakened by this apparatus kills the experimental rats not because it keeps them from sleeping but because it is stressful. This interpretation is consistent with the pathological problems in the experimental rats that were revealed by postmortem examination: swollen adrenal glands, gastric ulcers, and internal bleeding.

You have already encountered many examples in this text of the value of the comparative approach. However, sleep deprivation may be one phenomenon that cannot be productively studied **Thinking Creatively** in nonhumans because of the unavoidable confounding effects of extreme stress (see Horne, 2000; McEwen & Karatsoreos, 2015; Minkel et al., 2014).

Watch this video on MyPsychLab
CHALK IT UP! SLEEP DEPRIVATION: CAROUSEL APPARATUS AND STRESS

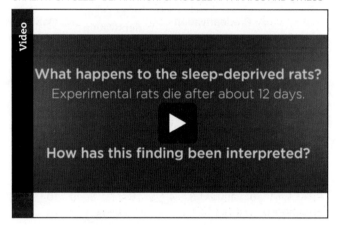

REM-Sleep Deprivation

LO 14.11 Describe the effects of REM-sleep deprivation.

Because of its association with dreaming, REM sleep has been the subject of intensive investigation. In an effort to reveal the particular functions of REM sleep, sleep researchers have specifically deprived sleeping volunteers of REM sleep by waking them up each time a bout of REM sleep begins.

REM-sleep deprivation has been shown to have two consistent effects (see Figure 14.6). First, following REM-sleep deprivation, participants display a *REM rebound*; that is, they have more than their usual amount of REM sleep for the first two or three nights (Endo et al., 1998). Second, with each successive night of deprivation, there is a greater tendency for participants to initiate REM sequences. Thus, as REM-sleep deprivation proceeds, participants have to be awakened more and more frequently to keep them from accumulating significant amounts of REM sleep. For example, during the first night of REM-sleep deprivation in one experiment (Webb & Agnew, 1967), the participants had to be awakened 17 times to keep them from having extended periods of REM sleep; but during the seventh night of deprivation, they had to be awakened 67 times.

Figure 14.6 The two effects of REM-sleep deprivation.

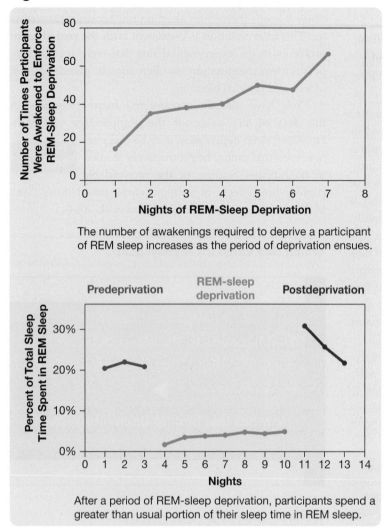

The number of awakenings required to deprive a participant of REM sleep increases as the period of deprivation ensues.

After a period of REM-sleep deprivation, participants spend a greater than usual portion of their sleep time in REM sleep.

The compensatory increase in REM sleep following a period of REM-sleep deprivation suggests that the amount of REM sleep is regulated separately from the amount of slow-wave sleep and that REM sleep serves a special function (see Hayashi et al., 2015; Vyazovskiy, 2015). This finding, coupled with the array of interesting physiological and psychological events that define REM sleep, has led to much speculation about its function.

Considerable attention has focused on the role of sleep in strengthening memory. For example, some researchers believe that REM sleep strengthens explicit memories (see Diekelmann & Born, 2010)—particularly those with emotional content (see Morgenthaler et al., 2014; Wiesner et al., 2015), other researchers believe that slow-wave sleep promotes memory consolidation (see Euston & Steenland, 2014; Inostroza & Born, 2013; Tononi & Cirelli, 2013), and still others believe that the memories of our daily experiences are processed (e.g., modified) prior to consolidation during sleep (see Chatburn, Lushington, & Kohler, 2014; Dudai, Karni, & Born, 2015; Stickgold & Walker, 2013). However, overall the results are still not convincing:

Some studies have not observed any relationship between memory and sleep (see Ackermann et al., 2015; Vertes & Siegel, 2005).

The sleep of depressed patients constitutes a serious challenge to the hypothesis that sleep influences memory. Depressed patients tend to get much less slow-wave sleep yet experience no disturbance of memory (see Genzel et al., 2014), and once they have been treated with antidepressant drugs, they may experience no REM sleep for years, again with no experience of memory deficits (see Tribl, Wetter, & Schredl, 2013).

The *default theory* of REM sleep is a different approach to understanding the functions of REM sleep (see Horne, 2000, 2013). According to this theory, it is difficult to stay continuously in NREM sleep, so the brain periodically switches to one of two other states. If there are any immediate bodily needs to be taken care of (e.g., the need for food or water), the brain switches to wakefulness; if there are no immediate needs, it switches to REM sleep. According to the default theory, REM sleep is more adaptive than wakefulness when there are no immediate bodily needs. In addition, according to the default theory, REM sleep functions to prepare organisms for wakefulness in natural environments where immediate effective activity may be required upon wakening (see Horne, 2013; Klemm, 2011).

Most support for the default theory of REM sleep is indirect, coming from the many similarities between REM sleep and wakefulness. However, the surprising results of Nykamp and colleagues (1998) provide more direct support. They awakened young adults every time they entered REM sleep, but instead of letting them go back to sleep immediately, they substituted a 15-minute period of wakefulness for each lost REM period. Under these conditions, the participants were not tired the next day, despite getting only 5 hours of sleep, and they displayed no REM rebound. In other words, there seemed to be no need for REM sleep if periods of wakefulness were substituted for it. This finding has been replicated in rats (Oniani & Lortkipanidze, 2003), and it is consistent with the finding that as antidepressants reduce REM sleep, the number of nighttime awakenings increases (see Horne, 2000).

Sleep Deprivation Increases the Efficiency of Sleep

LO 14.12 Describe six pieces of evidence that indicate that less sleep is associated with more efficient sleep.

One of the most important findings of human sleep-deprivation research is that individuals who are deprived of sleep become more efficient sleepers (see Elmenhorst et al., 2008). In particular, their sleep has a higher proportion of slow-wave sleep (NREM 3), which seems to serve the main restorative function. Because this is such an important finding, let's look at six major pieces of evidence that support it:

- Although people regain only a small proportion of their total lost sleep after a period of sleep deprivation, they regain most of their lost slow-wave sleep (see De Gennaro, Ferrara, & Bertini, 2000; Lucidi et al., 1997).

- After sleep deprivation, the slow-wave sleep EEG of humans is characterized by an even higher proportion of slow waves than usual (see Aeschbach et al., 1996).

- People who sleep 6 hours or less per night normally get as much slow-wave sleep as people who sleep 8 hours or more (see Jones & Oswald, 1966; Webb & Agnew, 1970).

- If individuals take a nap in the morning after a full night's sleep, their naptime EEG shows few slow waves, and the nap does not reduce the duration of the following night's sleep (see Åkerstedt & Gillberg, 1981; Hume & Mills, 1977).

- People who reduce their usual sleep time get less NREM 1 and NREM 2 sleep, but the duration of their slow-wave sleep remains about the same as before (see Mullaney et al., 1977; Webb & Agnew, 1975).

- Repeatedly waking individuals during REM sleep produces little increase in the sleepiness they experience the next day, whereas repeatedly waking individuals during slow-wave sleep has major effects (see Nykamp et al., 1998).

The fact that sleep becomes more efficient in people who sleep less means that conventional sleep-deprivation studies are virtually useless for discovering how much sleep people need. Certainly, our bodies respond negatively when we get less sleep than we are used to getting. However, the negative consequences of sleep loss in inefficient sleepers do not indicate whether the lost sleep was really needed. The true need for sleep can be assessed only by experiments in which sleep is regularly reduced for many weeks, to give the participants the opportunity to adapt to getting less sleep by maximizing their sleep efficiency. Only when people are sleeping at their maximum efficiency is it possible to determine how much sleep they really need. Such sleep-reduction studies are discussed later in the chapter, but please pause here to think about this point—it is extremely important. Still, many do not appreciate it (see Basner, 2011; Brown, 2012).

Thinking Creatively

Neuroplasticity

This is an appropriate time, here at the end of the module on sleep deprivation, for me (JP) to file a brief progress report. It has now been 2 weeks since I began my 5-hours-per-night sleep schedule. Generally, things are going well. My progress on this chapter has been faster than usual. I am not having any difficulty getting up on time or getting my work done, but I am finding that it takes a major effort to stay awake in the evening. If I try to read or watch a bit of television after 10:30, I experience microsleeps. My so-called friends delight in making sure that my transgressions are quickly punished.

Scan Your Brain

Before continuing with this chapter, scan your brain by completing the following exercise to make sure you understand the fundamentals of sleep. The correct answers appear at the end of the exercise. Before proceeding, review material related to your errors and omissions.

1. REM sleep is characterized by rapid eye movement, loss of core muscle tone, and _____.

2. _____ believed that dreams are triggered by unacceptable repressed wishes.

3. Freud referred to dreams that we experience as _____.

4. The _____ hypothesis states that the information supplied to the cortex during REM sleep is largely random, and the resulting dream is the cortex's effort to make sense of random signals.

5. _____ are brief periods of sleep that are typically about two or three seconds long.

6. The effects of sleep deprivation are often difficult to study because they are often confounded by _____.

7. Convincing evidence that REM-sleep deprivation does not produce severe memory problems comes from the study of patients taking certain _____ drugs.

8. After a lengthy period of sleep deprivation (e.g., several days), a person's first night of sleep is only slightly longer than usual, but it contains a much higher proportion of _____ waves.

9. _____ sleep in particular, rather than sleep in general, appears to play the major restorative role.

Scan Your Brain answers: (1) emergent Stage I EEG, (2) Sigmund Freud, (3) manifest dreams, (4) activation-synthesis, (5) Microsleeps, (6) stress, (7) antidepressant, (8) slow (or delta), (9) Slow-wave (or stage 3).

Circadian Sleep Cycles

This module explores the topic of circadian rhythms. We begin by describing what circadian rhythms are, then we move on to examples of what happens when circadian rhythms are disrupted. The module concludes with a discussion of the neural mechanisms and genetics of circadian rhythms.

Circadian Rhythms

LO 14.13 Describe the circadian sleep–wake cycle and the role of zeitgebers in maintaining circadian rhythms.

The world in which we live cycles from light to dark and back again once every 24 hours. Most surface-dwelling species have adapted to this regular change in their environment with a variety of **circadian rhythms** (*circadian* means "lasting about a day"). For example, most species display a regular circadian sleep–wake cycle. Humans take advantage of the light of day to take care of their biological needs, and then they sleep for much of the night; in contrast, *nocturnal animals*, such as rats, sleep for much of the day and stay awake at night.

Although the sleep–wake cycle is the most obvious circadian rhythm, it is difficult to find a physiological, biochemical, or behavioral process in animals that does not display some measure of circadian rhythmicity (see Bechtold & Loudon, 2012; Masri & Sassone-Corsi, 2013). Each day, our bodies adjust themselves in a variety of ways to meet the demands of the two environments in which we live: light and dark.

Our circadian cycles are kept right on their once-every-24-hours schedule by temporal cues in the environment. The most important of these cues for the regulation of mammalian circadian rhythms is the daily cycle of light and dark. Environmental cues, such as the light–dark cycle, that can *entrain* (control the timing of) circadian rhythms are called **zeitgebers** (pronounced "ZITE-gay-bers"), a German word that means "time givers." In controlled laboratory environments, it is possible to lengthen or shorten circadian cycles somewhat by adjusting the duration of the light–dark cycle; for example, when exposed to alternating 11.5-hour periods of light and 11.5-hour periods of dark, subjects' circadian cycles begin to conform to a 23-hour day. In a world without 24-hour cycles of light and dark, other *zeitgebers* can entrain circadian cycles. For example, the circadian sleep–wake cycles of hamsters living in continuous darkness or in continuous light can be entrained by regular daily bouts of social interaction, hoarding, eating, or exercise (see Mistlberger, 2011). Hamsters display particularly clear circadian cycles and thus are frequent subjects of research on circadian rhythms.

Free-Running Circadian Sleep–Wake Cycles

LO 14.14 Describe free-running rhythms and internal desynchronization, and explain why they are incompatible with recuperation theories of sleep.

What happens to sleep–wake cycles and other circadian rhythms in an environment that is devoid of *zeitgebers*? Remarkably, under conditions in which there are absolutely no temporal cues, humans and other animals maintain all of their circadian rhythms. Circadian rhythms in constant environments are said to be **free-running rhythms**, and their duration is called the **free-running period**. Free-running periods vary in length from individual to individual, are of relatively constant duration within a given individual, and are usually longer than 24 hours—about 24.2 hours is typical in humans living under constant moderate illumination (see Czeizler et al., 1999). It seems that we all have an internal *biological clock* that habitually runs a little slow unless it is entrained by time-related cues in the environment.

A typical free-running circadian sleep–wake cycle is illustrated in Figure 14.7. Notice its regularity. Without any external cues, this man fell asleep at intervals of approximately 25.3 hours for an entire month. The regularity of free-running sleep–wake cycles despite variations in physical and mental activity provides support for the dominance of circadian factors over recuperative factors in the regulation of sleep.

Free-running circadian cycles do not have to be learned. Even rats that are born and raised in an unchanging laboratory environment (in continuous light or in continuous darkness) display regular free-running sleep–wake cycles that are slightly longer than 24 hours (Richter, 1971).

Many animals display a circadian cycle of body temperature that is related to their circadian sleep–wake cycle: They tend to sleep during the falling phase of their circadian body temperature cycle and awaken during its rising phase. However, when subjects are housed in constant laboratory environments, their sleep–wake and body temperature cycles sometimes break away from one another. This phenomenon is called **internal desynchronization** (see Daan, Honma & Honma, 2013). For example, in one human volunteer, the free-running periods of *both* the sleep–wake and body temperature cycles were initially 25.7 hours; then, for some unknown reason, there was an increase in the free-running period of the sleep–wake cycle to 33.4 hours and a decrease in the free-running period of the body temperature cycle to 25.1 hours. The potential for the simultaneous existence of two different free-running periods was the first evidence that there is more than one circadian timing mechanism, and that sleep is not causally related to the decreases in body temperature normally associated with it.

Figure 14.7 A free-running circadian sleep–wake cycle 25.3 hours in duration. Despite living in an unchanging environment with no time cues, the man went to sleep each day approximately 1.3 hours later than he had the day before.

(Based on Wever, R. A. (1979). *The circadian system of man*. Seewiesen-Andechs, Germany: Max-Planck-Institut für Verhaltensphysiologie.)

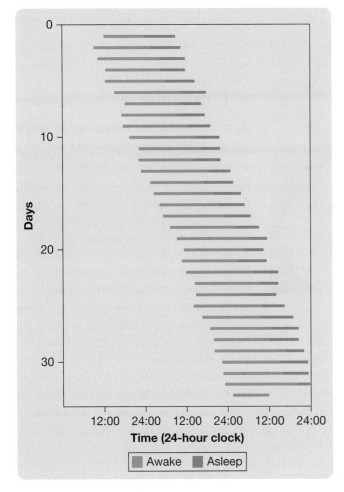

There is another point about free-running circadian sleep–wake cycles that is incompatible with recuperation theories of sleep. On occasions when volunteers stay awake longer than usual, the following sleep time is shorter rather than longer (Wever, 1979). Humans and other animals are programmed to have sleep–wake cycles of approximately 24 hours; hence, the more wakefulness there is during a cycle, the less time there is for sleep.

Jet Lag and Shift Work

LO 14.15   Describe the disruptive effects of jet lag and shift work on circadian rhythmicitiy and how one can minimize such effects.

People in modern industrialized societies are faced with two different disruptions of circadian rhythmicity: jet lag and shift work. **Jet lag** occurs when the *zeitgebers* that control the phases of various circadian rhythms are accelerated during east-bound flights (*phase advances*) or

decelerated during west-bound flights (*phase delays*). In *shift work*, the *zeitgebers* stay the same, but workers are forced to adjust their natural sleep–wake cycles in order to meet the demands of changing work schedules. Both of these disruptions produce sleep disturbances, fatigue, general malaise, and deficits on tests of physical and cognitive function (see Lewis, 2014). The disturbances can last for many days; for example, it typically takes about 10 days to completely adjust to the phase advance of 10.5 hours that one experiences on a Tokyo-to-Boston flight.

What can be done to reduce the disruptive effects of jet lag and shift work? Two behavioral approaches have been proposed for the reduction of jet lag. One is gradually shifting one's sleep–wake cycle in the days prior to the flight. The other is administering treatments after the flight that promote the required shift in the circadian rhythm. For example, melatonin can be taken before bedtime at the new location (see Reid & Abbott, 2015).

Companies that employ shift workers have had success in improving the productivity and job satisfaction of those workers by scheduling phase delays rather than phase advances; whenever possible, shift workers are transferred from their current schedule to one that begins later in the day (see Driscoll, Grunstein, & Rogers, 2007). It is much more difficult to go to sleep 4 hours earlier and get up 4 hours earlier (a phase advance) than it is to go to sleep 4 hours later and get up 4 hours later (a phase delay). This is also why east-bound flights tend to be more problematic for travelers than west-bound flights.

A Circadian Clock in the Suprachiasmatic Nuclei

LO 14.16   Describe the research that led to the discovery of a circadian clock in the suprachiasmatic nucleus (SCN) of the hypothalamus.

The fact that circadian sleep–wake cycles persist in the absence of temporal cues from the environment indicates that the physiological systems that regulate sleep are controlled by an internal timing mechanism—the **circadian clock**.

The first breakthrough in the search for the circadian clock was Richter's 1967 discovery that large medial hypothalamic lesions disrupt circadian cycles of eating, drinking, and activity in rats. Next, specific lesions of the **suprachiasmatic nuclei (SCN)** of the medial hypothalamus were shown to disrupt various circadian cycles, including sleep–wake cycles (see Figure 14.8). Although SCN lesions do not greatly affect the amount of time mammals spend sleeping, they do abolish the circadian periodicity of sleep cycles. Further support for the conclusion that the suprachiasmatic nuclei contain a circadian timing mechanism comes from the observation that the nuclei display circadian cycles of electrical, metabolic, and biochemical activity that can

Figure 14.8 Location of suprachiasmatic nuclei (SCN).

Suprachiasmatic nuclei (SCN)

be entrained by the light–dark cycle (see Sollars & Pickard, 2015; Zelinski, Deibel, & McDonald, 2014).

If there was any lingering doubt about the location of the circadian clock, it was eliminated by the brilliant experiment of Ralph and colleagues (1990). They removed the SCN from the fetuses of a strain of mutant hamsters that had an abnormally short (20-hour) free-running sleep–wake cycle. Then, they transplanted the SCN into normal adult hamsters whose free-running sleep–wake cycles of 25 hours had been abolished by SCN lesions. These transplants restored free-running sleep–wake cycles in the recipients; but, remarkably, the cycles were about 20 hours long rather than the original 25 hours. Transplants in the other direction—that is, from normal hamster fetuses to SCN-lesioned adult mutants—had the complementary effect: They restored free-running sleep–wake cycles to about 25 hours long rather than the original 20 hours.

Although the suprachiasmatic nuclei are unquestionably the major circadian clocks in mammals, they are not the only ones (see Rosenwasser & Turek, 2015). Three lines of experiments, largely conducted in the 1980s and 1990s, pointed to the existence of other circadian timing mechanisms:

- Under certain conditions, bilateral SCN lesions have been shown to leave some circadian rhythms unaffected while abolishing others.

- Bilateral SCN lesions do not eliminate the ability of all environmental stimuli to entrain circadian rhythms (see Saper, 2013); for example, SCN lesions can block entrainment by light but not by regular food or water availability (see Mistlberger, 2011).

- Just like suprachiasmatic neurons, cells from other parts of the body often display free-running circadian cycles of activity when maintained in tissue culture.

Neural Mechanisms of Entrainment

LO 14.17 Explain the mechanism by which SCN neurons are entrained by the 24-hour light–dark cycles.

How do the SCN control circadian rhythms? The timing mechanisms of the SCN depend on the firing patterns of SCN neurons. SCN neurons tend to be inactive at night, start to fire at dawn, and fire at a slow steady pace all day (see Belle & Piggins, 2012; Colwell, 2011; Mohawk & Takahashi, 2011).

How does the 24-hour light–dark cycle entrain the sleep–wake cycle and other circadian rhythms? To answer this question, researchers began at the obvious starting point: the eyes (see Morin & Allen, 2006). They tried to identify and track the specific neurons that left the eyes and carried the information about light and dark that entrained the biological clock. Cutting the *optic nerves* before they reached the *optic chiasm* eliminated the ability of the light–dark cycle to entrain circadian rhythms; however, when the *optic tracts* were cut at the point where they left the optic chiasm, the ability of the light–dark cycle to entrain circadian rhythms was unaffected. As Figure 14.9 illustrates, these two findings indicated that visual axons critical for the entrainment of circadian rhythms branch off from the optic nerve in the vicinity of the optic chiasm. This finding led to the discovery of the *retinohypothalamic tracts*, which leave the optic chiasm and project to the adjacent suprachiasmatic nuclei (see Canteras et al., 2010).

Surprisingly, although the retinohypothalamic tracts mediate the ability of light to entrain circadian rhythms, neither rods nor cones are necessary for the entrainment. The critical photoreceptors have proven to be neurons, *retinal ganglion cells* with distinctive functional properties (see Roecklein et al., 2013). During the course of evolution, these photoreceptors have sacrificed the ability to respond quickly and briefly to rapid changes of light in favor of the ability to respond consistently to slowly changing levels of background illumination. Their photopigment is **melanopsin** (see Renna et al., 2015).

Figure 14.9 The discovery of the retinohypothalamic tracts. Neurons from each retina project to both suprachiasmatic nuclei.

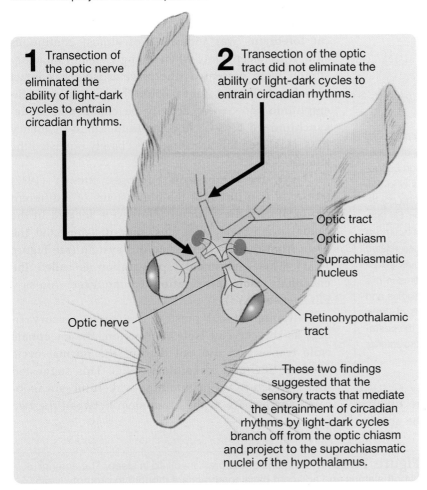

1 Transection of the optic nerve eliminated the ability of light-dark cycles to entrain circadian rhythms.

2 Transection of the optic tract did not eliminate the ability of light-dark cycles to entrain circadian rhythms.

Optic tract

Optic chiasm

Suprachiasmatic nucleus

Optic nerve

Retinohypothalamic tract

These two findings suggested that the sensory tracts that mediate the entrainment of circadian rhythms by light-dark cycles branch off from the optic chiasm and project to the suprachiasmatic nuclei of the hypothalamus.

The identification of circadian genes has led to three important discoveries:

- The same or similar circadian genes have been found in many species of different evolutionary ages (e.g., bacteria, flies, fish, frogs, mice, and humans), **Evolutionary Perspective** indicating that circadian genes evolved early in evolutionary history and have been conserved in various descendant species (see Cirelli, 2009).

- Once the circadian genes were discovered, the fundamental molecular mechanism of circadian rhythms was quickly clarified. The key mechanism seems to be gene expression; the transcription of proteins by the circadian genes displays a circadian cycle (see Brancaccio et al., 2014).

- The identification of circadian genes provided a more direct method of exploring the circadian timing capacities of parts of the body other than the SCN. Molecular circadian timing mechanisms similar to those in the SCN exist in most cells of the body (see Crane, 2012; Huang et al., 2012; Masri & Sassone-Corsi, 2013). Although most cells contain potential circadian timing mechanisms, these cellular clocks are normally regulated by neural and hormonal signals from the SCN.

Genetics of Circadian Rhythms

LO 14.18 Understand the genetics of circadian rhythms and the important discoveries that have resulted from the discovery of circadian genes.

An important breakthrough in the study of circadian rhythms came in 1988 when routine screening of a shipment of hamsters revealed that some of them had abnormally short 20-hour free-running circadian rhythms. Subsequent breeding experiments showed that the abnormality was the result of a genetic mutation, and the gene that was mutated was named **tau** (Ralph & Menaker, 1988).

Although tau was the first mammalian circadian gene to be identified, it was not the first to have its molecular structure characterized. This honor went to *clock*, a mammalian circadian gene discovered in mice. The structure of the clock gene was characterized in 1997, and that of the tau gene was characterized in 2000 (Lowrey et al., 2000). The molecular structures of several other mammalian circadian genes have since been specified (see Brancaccio et al., 2014; FitzGerald, 2014).

Four Areas of the Brain Involved in Sleep

You have just learned about the neural structures involved in controlling the circadian timing of sleep. This module describes four areas of the brain that are directly involved in producing or reducing sleep. You will learn more about their effects in the later module on sleep disorders.

Two Areas of the Hypothalamus Involved in Sleep

LO 14.19 Describe the research that led to the identification of the anterior and posterior hypothalamus as brain regions involved in the regulation of sleep and wakefulness.

It is remarkable that two areas of the brain involved in the regulation of sleep were discovered early in the

20th century—long before the advent of modern behavioral neuroscience. The discovery was made by Baron Constantin von Economo, a Viennese neurologist (see Saper, Scammell, & Lu, 2005).

The Case of Constantin von Economo, the Insightful Neurologist

During World War I, the world was swept by a serious viral infection of the brain: *encephalitis lethargica*. Many of its victims slept almost continuously. Baron Constantin von Economo discovered that the brains of deceased victims who had problems with excessive sleep all had damage in the *posterior hypothalamus* and adjacent parts of the midbrain. He then turned his attention to the brains of a small group of victims of encephalitis lethargica who had had the opposite sleep-related problem: In contrast to most victims, they had difficulty sleeping. He found that the brains of the deceased victims in this minority always had damage in the *anterior hypothalamus* and adjacent parts of the basal forebrain. On the basis of these clinical observations, von Economo concluded that the posterior hypothalamus promotes wakefulness, whereas the anterior hypothalamus promotes sleep.

Since von Economo's discovery of the involvement of the posterior hypothalamus and the anterior hypothalamus in human wakefulness and sleep, respectively, that involvement has been confirmed by lesion and recording studies in experimental animals (see Schwartz & Kilduff, 2015). The locations of the posterior and anterior hypothalamus are shown in Figure 14.10.

Reticular Formation and Sleep

LO 14.20 Describe the research that led to the identification of the reticular formation as a brain region involved in the regulation of sleep and wakefulness.

Another area involved in sleep was discovered through the comparison of the effects of two different brain-stem transections in cats. First, in 1936, Bremer severed the brain stems of cats between their *inferior colliculi* and *superior colliculi* in order to disconnect their forebrains from ascending sensory input (see Figure 14.11). This surgical preparation is called a **cerveau isolé preparation** (pronounced "ser-VOE ees-o-LAY"—literally, "isolated forebrain").

Bremer found that the cortical EEG of the isolated cat forebrains was indicative of almost continuous slow-wave sleep. Only when strong visual or olfactory stimuli were presented (the cerveau isolé has intact visual and olfactory input) could the continuous high-amplitude, slow-wave activity be changed to a **desynchronized EEG**—a low-amplitude, high-frequency EEG. However, this arousing effect barely outlasted the stimuli.

Next, for comparison purposes, Bremer (1937) *transected* (cut through) the brain stems of a different group of cats. These transections were located in the caudal brain stem, and thus, they disconnected the brain from the rest of the nervous system (see Figure 14.11). This experimental preparation is called the **encéphale isolé preparation** (pronounced "on-say-FELL ees-o-LAY").

Although it cut most of the same sensory fibers as the cerveau isolé transection, the encéphale isolé transection did not disrupt the normal cycle of sleep EEG and wakefulness EEG. This suggested that a structure for maintaining wakefulness was located somewhere in the brain stem between the two transections.

Figure 14.10 Two regions of the brain involved in sleep. The anterior hypothalamus and adjacent basal forebrain are thought to promote sleep; the posterior hypothalamus and adjacent midbrain are thought to promote wakefulness.

Anterior hypothalamus, basal-forebrain area (sleep)

Posterior hypothalamus, midbrain area (wakefulness)

Later, two important findings suggested that this wakefulness structure in the brain stem was the *reticular formation*. First, it was shown that partial transections at the cerveau isolé level disrupted normal sleep–wake cycles of cortical EEG only when they severed the reticular formation core of the brain stem; when the partial transections were restricted to more lateral areas, which contain the ascending sensory tracts, they had little effect on the cortical EEG (Lindsey, Bowden, & Magoun, 1949). Second, it was shown that electrical stimulation of the reticular formation of sleeping cats awakened them and produced a lengthy period of EEG desynchronization (Moruzzi & Magoun, 1949).

In 1949, Moruzzi and Magoun considered these four findings together: (1) the effects on cortical EEG of the cerveau isolé preparation, (2) the effects on cortical EEG of the encéphale isolé preparation, (3) the effects of reticular formation lesions, and (4) the effects on sleep of stimulation of the reticular formation. From these four key findings, Moruzzi and Magoun proposed that low levels of activity in the reticular formation produce sleep and that high levels produce wakefulness (see Larson-Prior, Ju, & Galvin, 2014). Indeed, this theory is so widely accepted that the reticular formation is commonly referred to as the **reticular activating system**, even though maintaining wakefulness is only one of the functions of the many nuclei it comprises.

Reticular REM-Sleep Nuclei

LO 14.21 Discuss how REM sleep is controlled by the reticular formation and what implications this has for understanding the neural mechanisms of behavior.

The fourth area of the brain involved in sleep controls REM sleep and is included in the brain area we have just described—it is part of the caudal reticular formation. It makes sense that an area of the brain involved in maintaining wakefulness would also be involved in the production of REM sleep because of the similarities between the two states. Indeed, REM sleep is controlled by a variety of nuclei scattered throughout the caudal reticular formation. Each site is responsible for controlling one of the major indices of REM sleep (see Peever, Luppi, & Montplaisir,

Figure 14.11 Four pieces of evidence that the reticular formation is involved in sleep.

2014; Weber et al., 2015)—a site for the reduction of core-muscle tone, a site for EEG desynchronization, a site for rapid eye movements, and so on. The approximate location in the caudal brain stem of each of these REM-sleep nuclei is illustrated in Figure 14.12.

Please think for a moment about the broad implications of these various REM-sleep nuclei. In thinking about the brain mechanisms of behavior, many people assume that if there is one name for a behavior, there must be a single structure for it in the brain; in other words, they assume that evolutionary pressures have acted to shape the human brain according to our current language and theories. Here we see the weakness of this assumption: The brain is organized along different principles, and REM sleep occurs only when a network of independent structures becomes active together. Relevant to this is the fact that the physiological changes that go together to define REM sleep sometimes break apart and go their separate ways—and the same is true of the changes that define slow-wave sleep. For example, during REM-sleep deprivation, penile erections, which normally occur during REM sleep, begin to occur during slow-wave sleep. And

Figure 14.12 A sagittal section of the brain stem of the cat illustrating the areas that control the various physiological indices of REM sleep.

(Vertes, R. P. (1983). Brainstem control of the events of REM sleep. *Progress in Neurobiology, 22,* 241–288.)

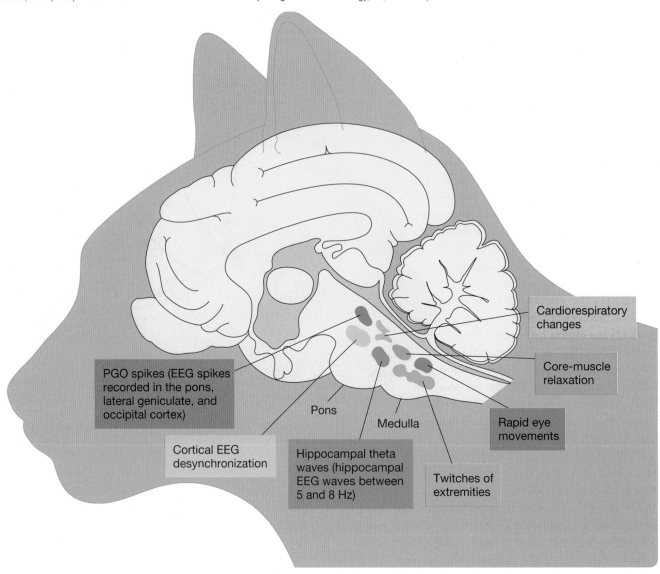

during total sleep deprivation, slow waves, which normally occur only during slow-wave sleep, begin to occur during wakefulness. This suggests that REM sleep, slow-wave sleep, and wakefulness are not each controlled by a single mechanism. Each state seems to result from the interaction of several mechanisms that are capable under certain conditions of operating independently of one another.

 Thinking Creatively Someone tells you that the prefrontal cortex is the brain structure responsible for higher cognition. What would your response be?

Scan Your Brain

Before continuing with this chapter, scan your brain by completing the following exercise to make sure you understand the fundamentals of sleep. The correct answers appear at the end of the exercise. Before proceeding, review material related to your errors and omissions.

1. _____ means lasting about one day.
2. Free-running rhythms are those that occur in environments devoid of _____.
3. The major circadian clock seems to be located in the _____ nuclei of the hypothalamus.

4. The _____ tracts conduct information about light–dark cycles to the SCN.

5. The first mammalian circadian gene to have its structure characterized was _____.

6. Patients with damage to the _____ hypothalamus and adjacent basal forebrain often have difficulty sleeping.

7. Damage to the _____ hypothalamus and adjacent areas of the midbrain often cause excessive sleepiness.

8. The low-amplitude high-frequency EEG of wakefulness is said to be _____.

9. In Bremer's classic study, cats with a _____ preparation displayed an EEG characteristic of continuous slow-wave sleep.

10. The indices of REM sleep are controlled by a variety of nuclei located in the caudal _____.

Drugs That Affect Sleep

Most drugs that influence sleep fall into two different classes: hypnotic and antihypnotic. **Hypnotic drugs** are drugs that increase sleep; **antihypnotic drugs** are drugs that reduce sleep. A third class of sleep-influencing drugs comprises those that influence its circadian rhythmicity; the main drug of this class is **melatonin**.

Hypnotic Drugs

LO 14.22 Describe three classes of hypnotic drugs. Compare and contrast them in terms of their efficacy and side effects.

The **benzodiazepines** (e.g., diazepam, clonazepam), which are GABA$_A$ agonists, were developed and tested for the treatment of anxiety, yet they are some of the most commonly prescribed hypnotic medications. In the short term, they increase drowsiness, decrease the time it takes to fall asleep, reduce the number of awakenings during a night's sleep, and increase total sleep time (Krystal, 2008). Thus, they can be effective in the treatment of occasional difficulties in sleeping.

Although benzodiazepines can be effective therapeutic hypnotic agents in the short term, their prescription for the treatment of chronic sleep difficulties, though common, is ill-advised (see Bourgeois et al., 2014; Mignot, 2013). Five complications are associated with the chronic use of benzodiazepines as hypnotic agents:

- Tolerance develops to the hypnotic effects of benzodiazepines; thus, patients must take larger and larger doses to maintain the drugs' efficacy.

- Cessation of benzodiazepine therapy after chronic use causes *insomnia* (sleeplessness), which can exacerbate the very problem that the benzodiazepines were intended to correct.

- Benzodiazepines distort the normal pattern of sleep; they increase the duration of NREM 2 sleep while actually decreasing the duration of both slow-wave and REM sleep.

- Benzodiazepines lead to next-day drowsiness (Ware, 2008) and increase the incidence of traffic accidents (Gustavsen et al., 2008).

- Most troubling is that chronic use of benzodiazepines has been shown to substantially reduce life expectancy (see Siegel, 2010).

Clinical Implications Given all the problems associated with the long-term use of benzodiazepines actually, why do you think they are they so commonly prescribed for the treatment of insomnia?

Problems with the benzodiazepines have led to a search for other pharmacological agents with the same hypnotic effects as the benzodiazepines but fewer side effects. In the early 1990s, a new class of GABA$_A$ agonists, the **imidazopyridines**, was marketed for the treatment of insomnia. It was claimed that they have fewer adverse side effects and less potential for addiction. One of the most widely prescribed imidazopyridines is Zolpidem (see Krystal, 2015; Neubauer, 2014), yet Zolpidem has been found to be no safer or more effective than benzodiazepines (see Arbon, Knurowska, & Dijk, 2015; Greenblatt & Roth, 2012).

Evidence that the raphé nuclei, which are serotonergic, play a role in sleep suggested that serotonergic drugs might be effective hypnotics. Efforts to demonstrate the hypnotic effects of such drugs have focused on **5-hydroxytryptophan (5-HTP)**—the precursor of serotonin—because 5-HTP, but not serotonin, readily passes through the blood–brain barrier. Injections of 5-HTP do reverse the insomnia produced in both cats and rats by the serotonin antagonist PCPA; however, they appear to be of no therapeutic benefit in the treatment of human insomnia.

Antihypnotic Drugs

LO 14.23 Describe three classes of antihypnotic drugs.

The mechanisms of the following three classes of antihypnotic drugs are well understood: *cocaine-derived stimulants, amphetamine-derived stimulants,* and *tricyclic antidepressants.* The drugs in these three classes seem to promote wakefulness by boosting the activity of catecholamines (norepinephrine, epinephrine, and dopamine)—by increasing their release into synapses, by blocking their reuptake from synapses, or both.

The regular use of antihypnotic drugs is risky. Antihypnotics tend to produce a variety of adverse side effects, such as loss of appetite, anxiety, tremor, addiction, and disturbance of normal sleep patterns. Moreover, they may mask the pathology that is causing the excessive sleepiness.

Melatonin

LO 14.24 Recognize the relationship between the pineal gland and melatonin, and how melatonin affects sleep.

Melatonin is a hormone synthesized from the neurotransmitter serotonin in the **pineal gland** (see Cecon et al., 2015). The pineal gland is an inconspicuous gland that René Descartes, whose dualistic philosophy was discussed in Chapter 2, once believed to be the seat of the soul. The pineal gland is located on the midline of the brain just ventral to the rear portion of the corpus callosum (see Figure 14.13).

The pineal gland has important functions in birds, reptiles, amphibians, and fish (see Sapède & Cau, 2013). The pineal gland of these species has inherent timing properties

and regulates circadian rhythms and seasonal changes in reproductive behavior through its release of melatonin. In humans and other mammals, however, the functions of the pineal gland and melatonin are not as apparent.

In humans and other mammals, circulating levels of melatonin display circadian rhythms under control of the suprachiasmatic nuclei (see Videnovic et al., 2014), with the highest levels being associated with darkness and sleep (see Morris, Aeschbach, & Scheer, 2012). On the basis of this correlation, it has long been assumed that melatonin plays a role in promoting sleep or in regulating its timing in mammals.

In order to put the facts about melatonin in perspective, it is important to keep one significant point firmly in mind. In adult mammals, pinealectomy and the consequent elimination of melatonin appear to have little effect. The pineal gland plays a role in the development of mammalian sexual maturity, but its functions after puberty are not at all obvious.

Does *exogenous* (externally produced) melatonin improve sleep, as widely believed? A *meta-analysis* (a combined analysis of results of more than one study) of 19 studies indicated that exogenous melatonin has a slight, but statistically significant, *soporific* (sleep-promoting) effect (Ferracioli-Oda, Qawasmi, & Bloch, 2013).

There is also good evidence that melatonin can shift the timing of mammalian circadian cycles. Indeed, several researchers have argued that melatonin is better classified as a **chronobiotic** (a substance that adjusts the timing of internal biological rhythms) than as a soporific (see Golombek et al., 2015). Arendt and Skene (2005) have argued that administration of melatonin in the evening increases sleep by accelerating the start of the nocturnal phase of the circadian rhythm and that administration at dawn increases sleep by delaying the end of the nocturnal phase.

Table 14.3 offers a summary of the drugs that affect sleep.

Figure 14.13 The location of the pineal gland, the source of melatonin.

Pineal gland

Table 14.3 Summary of Drugs That Affect Sleep

Effects on Sleep	Drug Class or Name
Hypnotic	Benzodiazepines
	Imidazopyridines
	5-hydroxytryptophan (5-HTP)
Antihypnotic	Cocaine-derived stimulants
	Amphetamine-derived stimulants
	Tricyclic antidepressants
Chronobiotic	Melatonin

Sleep Disorders

Many sleep disorders fall into one of two complementary categories: insomnia and hypersomnia. **Insomnia** includes

all disorders of initiating and maintaining sleep (see Ellis et al., 2011; Fortier-Brochu, 2012). **Hypersomnia** includes disorders of excessive sleep or sleepiness (see Billiard et al., 2011). A third major class of sleep disorders includes all those disorders that are specifically related to REM-sleep dysfunction (see Mahowald & Schenck, 2009). Both insomnia and hypersomnia are common symptoms of depression and bipolar disorders (see Rumble, White, & Benca, 2015).

Watch this video on MyPsychLab

SLEEP DISORDERS

In various surveys, approximately 30 percent of respondents report significant sleep-related problems. However, it is important to recognize that complaints of sleep problems often come from people whose sleep appears normal in laboratory sleep tests. For example, many people normally sleep 6 hours or less a night and seem to do well sleeping that amount, but they are pressured by their doctors, their friends, and their own expectations to sleep more (e.g., at least 8 hours). As a result, they spend more time in bed than they should and have difficulty getting to sleep. Often, the anxiety associated with their inability to sleep more makes it even more difficult for them to sleep (see Harvey & Tang, 2012; Khoury & Doghramji,

2015). Such patients can often be helped by counseling that persuades them to go to bed only when they are very sleepy. Others with disturbed sleep have more serious problems (see Khoury & Doghramji, 2015).

Insomnia

LO 14.25 Describe four causes of insomnia.

Many cases of insomnia are **iatrogenic** (physician-created)—in large part because sleeping pills (e.g., benzodiazepines), which are usually prescribed by physicians, are a major cause of insomnia. At first, hypnotic drugs may be effective in increasing sleep, but soon the patient may become trapped in a rising spiral of drug use, as *tolerance* to the drug develops and progressively more of it is required to produce its original hypnotic effect. Soon, the patient cannot stop taking the drug without running the risk of experiencing *withdrawal symptoms*, which include insomnia. The case of Mr. B. illustrates this problem (Dement, 1978).

Mr. B., the Case of Iatrogenic Insomnia

Mr. B. was studying for an exam, the outcome of which would affect his life. He was under stress and found it difficult to sleep. He consulted his physician who prescribed a moderate dose of barbiturate (i.e., sodium amytal) at bedtime. Mr. B. found the medication to be effective for a few nights, but after a week, he started having trouble sleeping again. So, he decided to take two sleeping pills each night. Twice more this cycle was repeated, so that on the night before his exam he was taking four times the original dose.

The next night, with the pressure off, Mr. B. took no pills, but he couldn't sleep. Accordingly, Mr. B. decided he had a serious case of insomnia and returned to the pills. By the time he consulted a sleep clinic several years later, he was taking approximately 1,000 mg sodium amytal every night, and his sleep was more disturbed than ever. Patients may go on for years with ever-increasing doses of one medication after another, never realizing that their troubles are caused by the pills.

Watch this video on MyPsychLab

ROBERTA: INSOMNIA

In one study, insomniacs claimed to take an average of 1 hour to fall asleep and to sleep an average of only 4.5 hours per night; but when they were tested in a sleep laboratory, they were found to have an average *sleep latency* (time to fall asleep) of only 15 minutes and an average nightly sleep duration of 6.5 hours. It used to be common medical practice to assume that people who claimed to suffer from insomnia but slept more than 6.5 hours per night were neurotic. However, this practice stopped when some of those diagnosed with *neurotic pseudoinsomnia* were subsequently found to be suffering from sleep apnea, nocturnal myoclonus, or other sleep-disturbing problems. Insomnia is not necessarily a problem of too little sleep; it is often a problem of too little undisturbed sleep.

The insomnia associated with **sleep apnea** is well documented. The patient with sleep apnea stops breathing many times each night. Each time, the patient awakens, begins to breathe again, and drifts back to sleep. Sleep apnea usually leads to a sense of having slept poorly and is thus often diagnosed as insomnia. However, some patients are totally unaware of their multiple awakenings and instead complain of excessive sleepiness during the day, which can lead to a diagnosis of *hypersomnia*. Sleep apnea disorders are of two types: (1) *obstructive sleep apnea* results from obstruction of the respiratory passages by muscle spasms or *atonia* (lack of muscle tone) and often occurs in individuals who are vigorous snorers; (2) *central sleep apnea* results from the failure of the central nervous system to stimulate respiration (see Aurora et al., 2012). Sleep apnea is more common in males, in people who are overweight, and in the elderly (see Badran et al., 2015).

Two other specific causes of insomnia are related to the legs: periodic limb movement disorder and restless legs syndrome. **Periodic limb movement disorder** is characterized by periodic, involuntary movements of the limbs, often involving twitches of the legs during sleep. Most patients suffering from this disorder complain of poor sleep and daytime sleepiness but are unaware of the nature of their problem. In contrast, people with **restless legs syndrome** are all too aware of their problem. They complain of a hard-to-describe tension or uneasiness in their legs that keeps them from falling asleep. Once established, both of these disorders are chronic (see Aurora et al., 2012; Stevens, 2015). There are no effective treatments for these disorders, although L-dopa (see Chapter 10) can help some patients (see Aurora et al., 2012).

One of the most effective treatments for insomnia is *sleep restriction therapy* (see Trauer et al., 2015). First, the amount of time that an insomniac is allowed to spend in bed is substantially reduced. Then, after a period of sleep restriction, the amount of time spent in bed is gradually increased in small increments, as long as sleep latency remains in the normal range. Even severe insomniacs often benefit from this treatment.

Someone suffering from insomnia

Hypersomnia

LO 14.26 Describe the symptoms of narcolepsy and the role of orexin (hypocretin) in this disorder.

Narcolepsy is the most widely studied disorder of hypersomnia. It occurs in about 1 out of 2,000 individuals (see Arango, Kivity, & Schoenfeld, 2015) and has two prominent symptoms. First, persons with narcolepsy experience severe daytime sleepiness and repeated, brief (10- to 15-minute) daytime sleep episodes. Individuals with narcolepsy typically sleep only about an hour per day more than average; it is the inappropriateness of their sleep episodes that most clearly defines their condition. Most of us occasionally fall asleep on the beach, in front of the television, or in that most soporific of all daytime sites—the large, stuffy, dimly lit lecture hall. But individuals with narcolepsy fall asleep in the middle of a conversation, while eating, while scuba diving, or even while making love.

Watch this video on MyPsychLab
MALI: NARCOLEPSY

The second prominent symptom of narcolepsy is cataplexy (see Dauvilliers et al., 2014). **Cataplexy** is characterized by recurring losses of muscle tone during wakefulness, often triggered by an emotional experience. In its mild form, it may simply force the patient to sit down for a few seconds until it passes. In its extreme form, the patient drops to the ground as if shot and remains there for a minute or two, fully conscious.

In addition to the two prominent symptoms of narcolepsy (daytime sleep attacks and cataplexy), people with narcolepsy often experience two other symptoms: sleep paralysis and hypnagogic hallucinations. **Sleep paralysis** is the inability to move just as one is falling asleep or waking up. **Hypnagogic hallucinations** are dreamlike experiences during wakefulness. Many healthy people occasionally experience sleep paralysis and hypnagogic hallucinations (see Sharpless & Barber, 2011). Have you experienced them?

Three lines of evidence suggested to early researchers that narcolepsy results from an abnormality in the mechanisms that trigger REM sleep. First, unlike people without narcolepsy, those with narcolepsy often go directly into REM sleep when they fall asleep. Second and third, as you have already learned, narcoleptics often experience two REM-sleep characteristics (dreamlike states and loss of muscle tone) during wakefulness.

Some of the most exciting research on the neural mechanisms of sleep in general and narcolepsy in particular began with the study of a strain of narcoleptic dogs. After 10 years of studying the genetics of these narcoleptic dogs, Lin and

colleagues (1999) finally isolated the gene that causes the disorder. The gene encodes a receptor protein that binds to a neuropeptide called **orexin** (sometimes called *hypocretin*; Richter, Woods, & Schier, 2014), which exists in two forms: orexin-A and orexin-B. Although discovery of the orexin gene has drawn attention to genetic factors in narcolepsy, the concordance rate for narcolepsy in monozygotic twins is only about 25 percent (see Liblau et al., 2015).

Several studies have documented reduced levels of orexin in the cerebrospinal fluid of individuals living with narcolepsy and in the brains of deceased individuals who had narcolepsy (see Nishino & Kanbayashi, 2005). Also, the number of orexin-releasing neurons has been found to be reduced in the brains of persons with narcolepsy (see Shan, Dauvilliers, & Siegel, 2015). One popular explanation for the loss of orexin-releasing neurons in narcolepsy is that it is the result of an autoimmune response (see Arango, Kivity, & Shoenfeld, 2015; Liblau et al., 2015).

Where is orexin synthesized in the brain? Orexin is synthesized by neurons in the region of the hypothalamus that has been linked to the promotion of wakefulness: the posterior hypothalamus (mainly its lateral regions). The orexin-producing neurons project diffusely throughout the brain, but they show many connections with neurons in the other wakefulness-promoting area of the brain: the reticular formation. Currently, there is considerable interest in understanding the role of the orexin circuits in normal sleep (see Luppi et al., 2010; Mignot, 2013).

Narcolepsy has traditionally been treated with stimulants (e.g., amphetamine, methylphenidate), but these have a potential for addiction and produce many undesirable side effects. The antihypnotic stimulant modafinil has been shown to be effective in the treatment of some cases of narcolepsy, and antidepressants can be effective against cataplexy (see Scammell, 2015).

REM-Sleep–Related Disorders

LO 14.27 Describe one REM-sleep–related disorder and its presumed neural mechanisms.

Several sleep disorders are specific to REM sleep; these are classified as *REM-sleep–related disorders*. Even narcolepsy, which is usually classified as a hypersomnic disorder, can be considered to be a REM-sleep–related disorder—for reasons you have just encountered.

Occasionally, patients who have little or no REM sleep are discovered. Although this disorder is rare, it is important because of its theoretical implications. Lavie and colleagues (1984) described a patient who had suffered a brain injury that presumably involved damage to the REM-sleep controllers in the caudal reticular formation. The most important finding of this case study was that the patient did not appear to be adversely affected by his lack of REM sleep. After receiving his injury, he completed high school, college, and law school and established a thriving law practice.

Some patients experience REM sleep without core-muscle atonia. This condition is known as **REM-sleep behavior disorder** (see Schenck et al., 2013) and is common in individuals with Parkinson's disease (see Neikrgu et al., 2014). It has been suggested that the function of REM-sleep atonia is to prevent the acting out of dreams. This theory receives support from case studies of people who suffer from this disorder—case studies such as the following one (Schenck et al., 1986).

The Case of the Sleeper Who Ran Over Tackle

(The patient was dreaming about football.) The quarterback lateraled the ball to me and I was supposed to cut back over tackle and—this is very vivid—as I cut back there is this 280-pound tackle waiting, so I gave him my shoulder and knocked him out of the way. When I awoke I was standing in front of our dresser. I had knocked lamps, mirrors, and everything off the dresser; hit my head against the wall; and banged my knee against the dresser.

Presumably, REM sleep without atonia is caused by damage to the nucleus magnocellularis or to an interruption of its output. The **nucleus magnocellularis** is a structure of the caudal reticular formation that evolved to control muscle relaxation during REM sleep. In normal dogs, it is active only during REM sleep; in narcoleptic dogs, it is also active during their attacks of cataplexy.

Effects of Long-Term Sleep Reduction

When people sleep less than they are used to sleeping, they do not feel or function well. We are sure you have experienced these effects. But what do they mean? Most people—nonexperts and experts alike—believe the adverse effects of sleep loss indicate that we need the sleep we typically get. However, there is an alternative interpretation—one that is more consistent with the plasticity of the adult human brain. Perhaps the brain needs a small amount of sleep each day but will sleep much more under ideal conditions because of sleep's high positive incentive value. The brain then slowly adapts to the amount of sleep it is getting— even though this amount may be far more than it needs— and is disturbed when there is a sudden reduction.

Fortunately, there are ways to determine which of these two interpretations of the effects of sleep loss is correct. The key is to study individuals who sleep little, either because they have always done so or because they have purposefully reduced their sleep times. If people need at least 8 hours of sleep each night, short sleepers should be suffering from a variety of health and performance problems. Before we summarize the results of this key area of research, we want to emphasize one point: Because they are so time-consuming, few studies of long-term sleep patterns have been conducted, and some of those that have been conducted are not sufficiently thorough. Nevertheless, there have been enough of them for a clear pattern of results to have emerged. We think they will surprise you.

This final module begins with a comparison of short and long sleepers. Then, it discusses two kinds of long-term sleep-reduction studies: studies in which volunteers reduced the amount they slept each night and studies in which volunteers reduced their sleep by restricting it to naps. Next comes a discussion of studies that have examined the relation between sleep duration and health. Finally, I (JP) relate my own experience of long-term sleep reduction.

Differences between Short and Long Sleepers

LO 14.28 List the main differences between short and long sleepers.

Numerous studies have compared short sleepers (those who sleep 6 hours or less per night) and long sleepers (those who sleep 8 hours or more per night). We focus here on the 2004 study of Fichten and colleagues because it is the most thorough. The study had three strong features:

- It included a relatively large sample (239) of adult short sleepers and long sleepers.

- It compared short and long sleepers in terms of 48 different measures, including daytime sleepiness, daytime naps, regularity of sleep times, busyness, regularity of meal times, stress, anxiety, depression, life satisfaction, and worrying.

- Before the study began, the researchers carefully screened out volunteers who were ill or under various kinds of stress or pressure; thus, the study was conducted with a group of healthy volunteers who slept the amount that they felt was right for them.

The findings of Fichten and colleagues are nicely captured by the title of their paper, "Long sleepers sleep more and short sleepers sleep less." In other words, other than the differences in sleep time, there were no differences between the two groups on any of the other measures—no indication that the short sleepers were suffering in any way from their shorter sleep time. Fichten and colleagues report that these results are consistent with most previous comparisons of short and long sleepers (e.g., Monk et al., 2001), except for a few studies that did not screen out participants who were sleeping little because they were under stress (e.g., from worry, illness, or a demanding work schedule). Those studies did report some negative characteristics in the short-sleep group, which likely reflected the stress experienced by some in that group.

Long-Term Reduction of Nightly Sleep

LO 14.29 Describe the results of studies of long-term reduction of nightly sleep.

Are short sleepers able to live happy, productive lives because they are genetically predisposed to be short sleepers, or is it possible for average people to adapt to a short sleep schedule? There have been only two published studies in which healthy volunteers have reduced their nightly sleep for several weeks or longer. In one (Webb & Agnew, 1974), a group of 16 volunteers slept for only 5.5 hours per night for 60 days, with only one detectable deficit on an extensive battery of mood, medical, and performance tests: a slight deficit on a test of vigilance.

In the other systematic study of long-term nightly sleep reduction (Friedman et al., 1977; Mullaney et al., 1977), eight volunteers reduced their nightly sleep by 30 minutes every 2 weeks until they reached 6.5 hours per night, then by 30 minutes every 3 weeks until they reached 5 hours, and then by 30 minutes every 4 weeks thereafter.

After a participant indicated a lack of desire to reduce sleep further, the person spent 1 month sleeping the shortest duration of nightly sleep that had been achieved. Finally, each participant slept at the shortest duration plus 30 minutes for 1 year.

The minimum duration of nightly sleep achieved during this experiment was 5.5 hours for 2 participants, 5.0 hours for 4 participants, and an impressive 4.5 hours for 2 participants. In each participant, a reduction in sleep time was associated with an increase in sleep efficiency: a decrease in the amount of time it took to fall asleep after going to bed, a decrease in the number of nighttime awakenings, and an increase in the proportion of slow-wave sleep. After the participants had reduced their sleep to 6 hours per night, they began to experience daytime sleepiness, and this became a problem as sleep time was further reduced. Nevertheless, there were no deficits on any of the mood, medical, or performance tests administered throughout the experiment. The most encouraging result was that an unexpected follow-up 1 year after the end of the study found that all participants were sleeping less than they had before the study—between 7 and 18 hours less each week—with no excessive sleepiness.

Long-Term Sleep Reduction by Napping

LO 14.30 Describe the results of studies of long-term reduction of sleep by napping.

Most mammals and human infants display **polyphasic sleep cycles**; that is, they regularly sleep more than once per day. In contrast, most adult humans display **monophasic sleep cycles**; that is, they sleep once per day. Nevertheless, most adult humans do display polyphasic cycles of sleepiness, with periods of sleepiness occurring in late afternoon and late morning. Have you ever experienced them?

Do adult humans need to sleep in one continuous period per day, or can they sleep effectively in several naps as human infants and other mammals do? Which of the two sleep patterns is more efficient? Research has shown that naps have recuperative powers out of proportion with their brevity (see Ficca et al., 2010; Milner & Cote, 2008), suggesting that polyphasic sleep might be particularly efficient.

Interest in the value of polyphasic sleep was stimulated by the legend that Leonardo da Vinci managed to generate a steady stream of artistic and engineering accomplishments during his life by napping for 15 minutes every 4 hours, thereby limiting his sleep to 1.5 hours per day. As unbelievable as this sleep schedule may seem, it has been replicated in several experiments (see Stampi, 1992). Here are the main findings of these truly mind-boggling experiments: First, participants required several weeks to adapt

to a polyphasic sleep schedule. Second, once adapted to polyphasic sleep, participants were content and displayed no deficits on the performance tests they were given. Third, Leonardo's 4-hour schedule worked quite well, but in unstructured working situations (e.g., around-the-world solo sailboat races), individuals often varied the duration of the cycle without feeling negative consequences. Fourth, most people displayed a strong preference for particular sleep durations (e.g., 25 minutes) and refrained from sleeping too little, which left them unrefreshed, or too much, which left them groggy for several minutes when they awoke—an effect called **sleep inertia** (see Fushimi & Hayashi, 2008; Ikeda & Hayashi, 2008). Fifth, when individuals first adopted a polyphasic sleep cycle, most of their sleep was slow-wave sleep, but eventually they returned to a mix of REM and slow-wave sleep.

The following are the paraphrased words of artist Giancarlo Sbragia (1992), who adopted Leonardo's purported sleep schedule:

> At first, the schedule was difficult to follow. It took about 3 weeks to get used to. But I soon reached a point of comfort, and it turned out to be a thrilling experience. How beautiful my life became: I discovered dawns, silence, and concentration. I had far more time for myself, for painting, and for developing my career.

Effects of Shorter Sleep Times on Health

LO 14.31 Recognize how shorter sleep times relate to longevity.

For decades, it was believed that sleeping 8 hours or more per night is ideal for promoting optimal health and longevity. Then, a series of large-scale epidemiological studies conducted in both the United States and Japan challenged this belief (see Ayas et al., 2003; Kripke et al., 2002; Patel et al., 2003; Tamakoshi & Ohno, 2004). These studies did not include participants who were a potential source of bias, for example, people who slept little because they were ill, depressed, or under stress. The studies started with a sample of healthy volunteers and followed their health for several years.

A meta-analysis found that the results of these studies were remarkably uniform (see Cappuccio et al., 2010). Figure 14.14 presents data from Tamakoshi and Ohno (2004), who followed 104,010 volunteers for 10 years. You will immediately see that sleeping 8 hours per night is not the healthy ideal it has been assumed to be: The fewest deaths occurred among people sleeping between 5 and 7 hours per night, far fewer than among those who slept 8 hours. You should be aware that other studies that are not as careful in excluding volunteers who sleep little because of stress or ill health do find more problems associated

Figure 14.14 The mortality rates associated with different amounts of sleep, based on 104,010 volunteers followed over 10 years. The mortality rate at 7 hours of sleep per night has been arbitrarily set at 100 percent, and the other mortality rates are presented in relation to it.

(Tamakoshi, A., & Ohno, Y. (2004). Self-reported sleep duration as a predictor of all-cause mortality: Results from the JACC study, Japan. Sleep, 27, 51–54.)

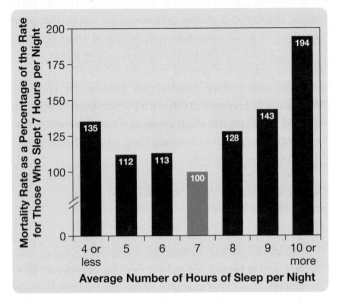

with short sleep (see Cappuccio et al., 2008), but any such finding is likely an artifact of preexisting ill health or stress, which is more prevalent among short sleepers.

Because these epidemiological data are correlational, it is important not to interpret them causally (see Grandner & Drummond, 2007; Stamatakis & Punjabi, 2007). They do not prove that sleeping 8 or more hours a night causes health problems: Perhaps there is something about people who sleep 8 hours or more per night that leads them to die sooner than people who sleep less. Thus, these studies do not prove that reducing your sleep will cause you to live longer—although some experts are advocating sleep reduction as a means of improving health (see Youngstedt & Kripke, 2004). These studies do, however, provide strong evidence that sleeping less than 8 hours is not the risk to life and health that it is often made out to be. Consistent with this idea is the recent finding that adults who live in pre-industrial hunter-gatherer societies tend to sleep less than 8 hours per day—the sleep times in these societies range from 5.7 to 7.1 hours per day—yet they have a lower incidence of many illnesses and higher levels of physical fitness than people living in industrial societies (Yetish et al., 2015).

Long-Term Sleep Reduction: A Personal Case Study

We began this chapter 4 weeks ago with both zeal and trepidation. One of us (JP) was fascinated by the idea that

one could wring 2 or 3 extra hours of living out of each day by sleeping less, and I hoped that adhering to a sleep-reduction program while writing about sleep would create an enthusiasm for the subject that would color our writing and be passed on to you. I began with a positive attitude because I was aware of the relevant evidence; still, I was more than a little concerned about the negative effect that reducing my sleep by 3 hours per night might have on my writing.

The Case of the Author Who Reduced His Sleep

Rather than using the gradual stepwise reduction method of Friedman and his colleagues, I jumped directly into my 5-hours-per-night sleep schedule. This proved to be less difficult than you might think. I took advantage of a trip to the East Coast from my home on the West Coast to reset my circadian clock. While I was in the East, I got up at 7:00 a.m., which is 4:00 a.m. on the West Coast, and I just kept on the same schedule when I got home. I decided to add my extra waking hours to the beginning of my day rather than to the end so there would be no temptation for me to waste them—there are not too many distractions around my university at 5:00 a.m.

Figure 14.15 is a record of my sleep times for the 4-week period that it took us to write a first draft of this chapter. I didn't quite meet my goal of sleeping less than 5 hours every night, but I didn't miss by much: My overall mean was 5.05 hours per night. Notice that in the last week, there was a tendency for my circadian clock to run a bit slow; I began sleeping in until 4:30 a.m. and staying up until 11:30 p.m.

Figure 14.15 Sleep record of Pinel during a 4-week sleep-reduction program.

What were the positives and negatives of my experience? The main positive was the added time to do things: Having an extra 21 hours per week was wonderful. Furthermore, because my daily routine was out of synchrony with everybody else's, I spent little time sitting in traffic or waiting in lines. The only negative of the experience was sleepiness. It was no problem during the day, when I was active. However, staying awake during the last hour before I went to bed—an hour during which I usually engaged in sedentary activities, such as reading—was at times a problem. This is when I became personally familiar with the phenomenon of microsleeps, and it was then that I required some assistance in order to stay awake. Each night of sleep became a highly satisfying but all too brief experience.

We began this chapter with this question: How much sleep do we need? Then, we gave you our best professorial it-could-be-this, it-could-be-that answer. However, that was a month ago. Now, after one of us experienced sleep reduction firsthand and we have reviewed the evidence yet again, we are less inclined toward wishy-washiness on the topic of sleep. The fact that most committed volunteers who are active during the day can reduce their sleep to about 5.5 hours per night without great difficulty or major adverse consequences suggested to us that the answer is 5.5 hours of sleep—not substantially different from the 6-hour daily sleep requirement advocated by one esteemed sleep expert (see Horne, 2010, 2011). However, we reached this conclusion before we learned about polyphasic sleep schedules. Now, we must revise our estimate downward.

Themes Revisited

The thinking creatively theme pervaded this chapter. In this chapter, you learned that many people sleep little with no apparent ill effects and that people who are average sleepers can reduce their sleep time substantially, again with few apparent ill effects. You also learned that epidemiological studies indicate that people who sleep between 5 and 7 hours a night live the longest. Together, this evidence challenges the widely held belief that humans have a fundamental need for at least 8 hours of sleep per night. Has this chapter changed your thinking about sleep? Writing it changed ours.

The evolutionary perspective theme also played a prominent role in this chapter. You learned how thinking about the adaptive function of sleep and comparing sleep in different species have led to interesting insights. Also, you saw how research into the physiology and genetics of sleep has been conducted on nonhuman species.

The clinical implications theme received emphasis in the module on sleep disorders. Perhaps most exciting and interesting were the recent breakthroughs in understanding the genetics and physiology of narcolepsy.

Finally, the neuroplasticity theme arose in a fundamental way. The fact that the adult human brain has the capacity to change and adapt raises the possibility that it might successfully adapt to a consistent long-term schedule of sleep that is of shorter duration than most people currently choose.

Key Terms

Stages of Sleep

Electroencephalogram (EEG), p. 386
Electrooculogram (EOG), p. 386
Electromyogram (EMG), p. 386
Alpha waves, p. 386
Delta waves, p. 387
Initial stage 1 EEG, p. 387
Emergent stage 1 EEG, p. 387
REM sleep, p. 387
Slow-wave sleep (SWS), p. 387
Activation-synthesis hypothesis, p. 388

Why Do We Sleep, and Why Do We Sleep When We Do?

Recuperation theories of sleep, p. 389
Adaptation theories of sleep, p. 389

Effects of Sleep Deprivation

Executive function, p. 392
Microsleeps, p. 392
Carousel apparatus, p. 393

Circadian Sleep Cycles

Circadian rhythms, p. 396
Zeitgebers, p. 396
Free-running rhythms, p. 396
Free-running period, p. 396
Internal desynchronization, p. 396
Jet lag, p. 397
Circadian clock, p. 397
Suprachiasmatic nuclei (SCN), p. 397
Melanopsin, p. 398
Tau, p. 399

Four Areas of the Brain Involved in Sleep

Cerveau isolé preparation, p. 400
Desynchronized EEG, p. 400
Encéphale isolé preparation, p. 400
Reticular activating system, p. 401

Drugs That Affect Sleep

Hypnotic drugs, p. 403
Antihypnotic drugs, p. 403
Melatonin, p. 403
Benzodiazepines, p. 403
Imidazopyridines, p. 403
5-hydroxytryptophan (5-HTP), p. 403
Pineal gland, p. 404
Chronobiotic, p. 404

Chapter 15
Drug Use, Drug Addiction, and the Brain's Reward Circuits

Chemicals That Harm with Pleasure

Chapter Overview and Learning Objectives (LOs)

Basic Principles of Drug Action	**LO 15.1**	Compare the various routes of drug administration.
	LO 15.2	Explain the ways in which drugs can influence the nervous system and how they are eliminated from the body.
	LO 15.3	Describe how the body becomes tolerant to drugs and the process of drug withdrawal. Explain what it means to be physically dependent on a drug.
	LO 15.4	Define drug addiction.
Role of Learning in Drug Tolerance	**LO 15.5**	Explain contingent drug tolerance.
	LO 15.6	Describe conditioned drug tolerance and conditioned compensatory responses.

Drug addiction is a serious problem in most parts of the world. Globally, more than 1 billion people are addicted to nicotine; more than 76 million are addicted to alcohol; more than 40 million are addicted to illegal drugs; and many millions are addicted to prescription drugs (Degenhardt & Hall, 2012). Pause for a moment and think about the sheer magnitude of the problem represented by such figures—more than a billion addicted people worldwide. The incidence of drug addiction is so high that it is almost certain that you or somebody dear to you will be adversely affected by drugs.

This chapter introduces you to some basic **pharmacological** (pertaining to the scientific study of drugs) principles and concepts, compares the effects of five commonly used drugs, and reviews the research on the neural mechanisms of addiction. You likely already have strong views about drug addiction; thus, as you progress through this chapter, it is particularly important that you do not let your thinking be clouded by preconceptions. In particular, it is important that you do not fall into the trap of assuming that a drug's legal status has much to say about its safety (see Nutt, King, & Nichols, 2013). You will be less likely to assume that legal drugs are safe and illegal drugs are dangerous if you remember that most laws governing drug use in various parts of the world were enacted in the early part of the 20th century, long before there was any scientific research on the topic.

Case of the Drugged High School Teachers

People's tendency to equate drug legality with drug safety was once conveyed to me (JP) in a particularly ironic fashion: I was invited to address a convention of high school teachers on the topic of drug misuse. When I arrived at the convention center to give my talk, I was escorted to a special suite, where I was encouraged to join the executive committee in a round of drug taking—the drug being a special single-malt whiskey. Later, the irony of the situation had its full impact. As I stepped to the podium under the influence of a psychoactive drug (the whiskey), I looked out through the haze of cigarette smoke at an audience of educators who had invited me to speak to them because they were concerned about the unhealthy impact of drugs on their students. The welcoming applause gradually gave way to the melodic tinkling of ice cubes in liquor glasses, and I began. They did not like what I had to say.

Basic Principles of Drug Action

This module focuses on the basic principles of drug action, with an emphasis on **psychoactive drugs**—drugs that influence subjective experience and behavior by acting on the nervous system.

Drug Administration, Absorption, and Penetration of the Central Nervous System

LO 15.1 **Compare the various routes of drug administration.**

Drugs are usually administered in one of four ways: oral ingestion, injection, inhalation, or absorption through the mucous membranes of the nose, mouth, or rectum. The route of administration influences the rate at which and the degree to which the drug reaches its sites of action in the body.

ORAL INGESTION. The oral route is the preferred route of administration for many drugs. Once they are swallowed, drugs dissolve in the fluids of the stomach and are carried to the intestine, where they are absorbed into the bloodstream. However, some drugs readily pass through the stomach wall (e.g., alcohol), and these take effect sooner because they do not have to reach the intestine to be absorbed. Drugs that are not readily absorbed from the digestive tract or that are broken down into inactive *metabolites* (breakdown products of the body's chemical reactions) before they can be absorbed must be taken by some other route.

The two main advantages of the oral route of administration over other routes are its ease and relative safety. Its main disadvantage is its unpredictability: Absorption from the digestive tract into the bloodstream can be greatly influenced by such difficult-to-gauge factors as the amount and type of food in the stomach.

INJECTION. Drug injection is common in medical practice because the effects of injected drugs are strong, fast, and predictable. Drug injections are typically made *subcutaneously* (*SC*), into the fatty tissue just beneath the skin; *intramuscularly* (*IM*), into the large muscles; or *intravenously* (*IV*), directly into veins at points where they run just beneath the skin. Many drug-addicted persons prefer the intravenous route because the bloodstream delivers the drug directly to the brain. However, the speed and directness of the intravenous route are mixed blessings; after an intravenous injection, there is little or no opportunity to counteract the effects of an overdose, an impurity, or an allergic reaction. Furthermore, many drug users develop scar tissue, infections, and collapsed veins at the few sites on their bodies where there are large accessible veins.

INHALATION. Some drugs can be absorbed into the bloodstream through the rich network of capillaries in the lungs. Many anesthetics are typically administered by *inhalation*, as are tobacco and marijuana. The two main shortcomings of this route are that it is difficult to precisely regulate the dose of inhaled drugs, and many substances damage the lungs if they are inhaled chronically.

ABSORPTION THROUGH MUCOUS MEMBRANES. Some drugs can be administered through the mucous membranes of the nose, mouth, and rectum. Cocaine, for example, is commonly self-administered through the nasal membranes (snorted)—but not without damaging them.

Drug Action, Metabolism, and Elimination

LO 15.2 **Explain the ways in which drugs can influence the nervous system and how they are eliminated from the body.**

DRUG PENETRATION OF THE CENTRAL NERVOUS SYSTEM. Once a drug enters the bloodstream, it is carried to the blood vessels of the central nervous system. Fortunately, a protective filter, the *blood–brain barrier* (see Chapter 3), makes it difficult for many potentially dangerous bloodborne chemicals to pass from the blood vessels of the CNS into the extracellular space around CNS neurons and glia.

MECHANISMS OF DRUG ACTION. Psychoactive drugs influence the nervous system in many ways. Some drugs (e.g., alcohol and many of the general anesthetics) act diffusely on neural membranes throughout the CNS. Others act in a more specific way: by binding to particular synaptic receptors; by influencing the synthesis, transport, release, or deactivation of particular neurotransmitters; or by influencing the chain of chemical reactions elicited in postsynaptic neurons by the activation of their receptors (see Chapter 4).

DRUG METABOLISM AND ELIMINATION.   The actions of most drugs are terminated by enzymes synthesized by the *liver*. These liver enzymes stimulate the conversion of active drugs to nonactive forms—a process referred to as **drug metabolism**. In many cases, drug metabolism eliminates a drug's ability to pass through lipid membranes of cells so that it can no longer penetrate the blood–brain barrier. In addition, small amounts of some psychoactive drugs are passed from the body in urine, sweat, feces, breath, and mother's milk.

Drug Tolerance, Drug Withdrawal Effects, and Physical Dependence

LO 15.3 Describe how the body becomes tolerant to drugs and the process of drug withdrawal. Explain what it means to be physically dependent on a drug.

DRUG TOLERANCE. **Drug tolerance** is a state of decreased sensitivity to a drug that develops as a result of exposure to it. Drug tolerance can be demonstrated in two ways: by showing that a given dose of the drug has less effect than it had before drug exposure or by showing that it takes more of the drug to produce the same effect. In essence, what this means is that drug tolerance is a shift in the *dose-response curve* (a graph of the magnitude of the effect of different doses of the drug) to the right (see Figure 15.1).

There are three important points to remember about the specificity of drug tolerance.

- One drug can produce tolerance to other drugs that act by the same mechanism; this is known as **cross tolerance**.

- Drug tolerance often develops to some effects of a drug but not to others (e.g., Castello et al., 2014). Failure to understand this second point can have tragic consequences for people who think that because they have become tolerant to some effects of a drug (e.g., to the nauseating effects of alcohol), they are tolerant to all of them. In fact, tolerance may develop to some effects of a drug while sensitivity to other effects of the same drug increases. Increasing sensitivity to a drug is called **drug sensitization**.

- Drug tolerance is not a unitary phenomenon; that is, there is no single mechanism that underlies all examples of it (Littleton, 2001). When a drug is administered at doses that affect nervous system function, many kinds of adaptive changes can occur to reduce its effects.

Two categories of changes underlie drug tolerance: metabolic and functional. Drug tolerance that results from changes that reduce the amount of the drug getting to its sites of action is called **metabolic tolerance**. Drug tolerance that results from changes that reduce the reactivity of the sites of action to the drug is called **functional tolerance**.

Tolerance to psychoactive drugs is largely functional. Functional tolerance to psychoactive drugs can result from several different types of adaptive neural changes (see Treistman & Martin, 2009). For example, exposure to a psychoactive drug can reduce the number of receptors for it, decrease the efficiency with which it binds to existing receptors, or diminish the impact of receptor binding on the activity of the cell. At least some of these adaptive neural changes are the result of epigenetic mechanisms (e.g., Ghezzi et al., 2013; Liang et al., 2013).

DRUG WITHDRAWAL EFFECTS AND PHYSICAL DEPENDENCE After significant amounts of a drug have been in the body for a period of time (e.g., several days), its sudden elimination can trigger an adverse physiological reaction called a **withdrawal syndrome**. The effects of drug withdrawal are virtually always opposite to the initial effects of the drug. For example, the withdrawal of anticonvulsant drugs often triggers convulsions, and the withdrawal of sleeping pills often produces insomnia. Individuals who suffer withdrawal reactions when they stop taking a drug are said to be **physically dependent** on that drug.

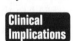

Figure 15.1 Drug tolerance is a shift in the dose-response curve to the right as a result of exposure to the drug.

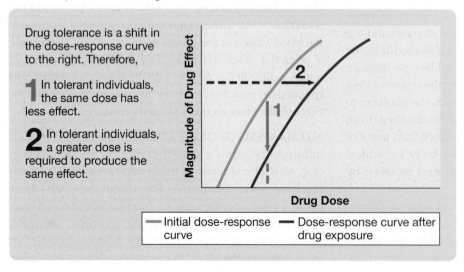

Drug tolerance is a shift in the dose-response curve to the right. Therefore,

1 In tolerant individuals, the same dose has less effect.

2 In tolerant individuals, a greater dose is required to produce the same effect.

Magnitude of Drug Effect

Drug Dose

— Initial dose-response curve   — Dose-response curve after drug exposure

Clinical Implications

What do you think the withdrawal reaction might be when one suddenly stops taking an antidepressant medication after having taken it for many years?

The fact that withdrawal effects are frequently opposite to the initial effects of the drug suggests that withdrawal effects may be produced by the same neural changes that produce drug tolerance (see Figure 15.2). According to this theory, exposure to a drug produces compensatory changes in the nervous system that offset the drug's effects and produce tolerance. Then, when the drug is eliminated from the body, these compensatory neural changes—without the drug to offset them—manifest themselves as withdrawal symptoms that are opposite to the initial effects of the drug.

The severity of withdrawal symptoms depends on the particular drug in question, on the duration and degree of the preceding drug exposure, and on the speed with which the drug is eliminated from the body. In general, longer exposure to greater doses followed by more rapid elimination produces greater withdrawal effects.

Watch this video on MyPsychLab

CHALK IT UP! DRUG TOLERANCE, WITHDRAWAL EFFECTS, AND PHYSICAL DEPENDENCE

Figure 15.2 The relation between drug tolerance and withdrawal effects. The same adaptive neurophysiological changes that develop in response to drug exposure and produce drug tolerance manifest themselves as withdrawal effects once the drug is removed. As the neurophysiological changes develop, tolerance increases; as they subside, the severity of the withdrawal effects decreases.

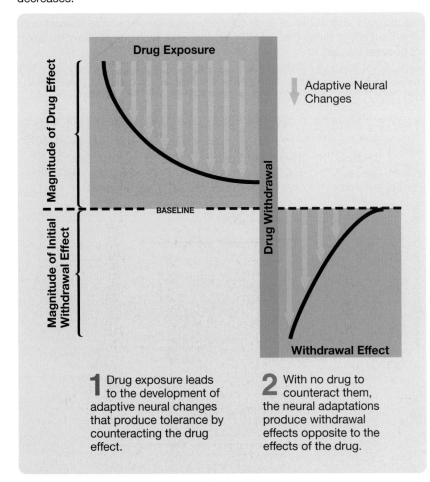

1 Drug exposure leads to the development of adaptive neural changes that produce tolerance by counteracting the drug effect.

2 With no drug to counteract them, the neural adaptations produce withdrawal effects opposite to the effects of the drug.

Drug Addiction: What Is It?

LO 15.4 Define drug addiction.

Drug-addicted individuals are habitual drug users, but not all habitual drug users are drug-addicted individuals. **Drug-addicted individuals** are those habitual drug users who continue to use a drug despite its adverse effects on their health and social life, and despite their repeated efforts to stop using it.

The greatest confusion about the nature of drug addiction concerns its relation to physical dependence. Many people equate the two: They see addicted persons as people who are trapped on a merry-go-round of drug taking, withdrawal symptoms, and further drug taking to combat the withdrawal symptoms. Although appealing in its simplicity, this conception of drug addiction is inconsistent with the evidence. Addicted individuals sometimes take drugs to prevent or alleviate their withdrawal symptoms, but this is often not the major motivating factor in their addiction. If it were, drug-addicted individuals could be easily cured by hospitalizing them for a few days, until their withdrawal symptoms subsided. However, most addicted individuals renew their

Thinking Creatively

drug taking even after months of enforced abstinence. This is an important issue, and it will be revisited later in this chapter.

Drugs are not the only substances to which humans become addicted. Indeed, people who risk their health by continually bingeing on high-calorie foods or risk their economic stability through compulsive gambling clearly have an addiction (see Clark, 2014; Ko et al., 2013; Robbins & Clark, 2015). Although this chapter focuses on drug addiction, other addictions—such as food, gambling, and Internet addictions—may be based on similar neural mechanisms.

Role of Learning in Drug Tolerance

An important line of psychopharmacologic research has shown that learning plays a major role in drug tolerance. In addition to contributing to our understanding of drug tolerance, this research has established that efforts to understand the effects of psychoactive drugs without considering the experience and behavior of the subjects can provide only partial answers.

Research on the role of learning in drug tolerance has focused on two phenomena: contingent drug tolerance and conditioned drug tolerance. These two phenomena are discussed in the following sections.

Contingent Drug Tolerance

LO 15.5 Explain contingent drug tolerance.

Contingent drug tolerance refers to demonstrations that tolerance develops only to drug effects that are actually experienced. Most studies of contingent drug tolerance employ the **before-and-after design**. In before-and-after experiments, two groups of subjects receive the same series of drug injections and the same series of repeated tests, but the subjects in one group receive the drug before each test of the series and those in the other group receive the drug after each test of the series. At the end of the experiment, all subjects receive the same dose of the drug followed by a final test so that the degree

to which the drug disrupts test performance in the two groups can be compared.

My colleagues and I (Pinel, Mana, & Kim, 1989) used the before-and-after design to study contingent tolerance to the anticonvulsant effect of alcohol. In one study, two groups of rats received exactly the same regimen of alcohol injections: one injection every 2 days for the duration of the experiment. During the tolerance development phase, the rats in one group received each alcohol injection 1 hour before a mild convulsive amygdala stimulation so that the anticonvulsant effect of the alcohol could be experienced on each trial. The rats in the other group received their injections 1 hour after each convulsive stimulation so that the anticonvulsant effect of the alcohol could not be experienced. At the end of the experiment, all of the subjects received a test injection of alcohol, followed 1 hour later by a convulsive stimulation so that the amount of tolerance to the anticonvulsant effect of alcohol could be compared in the two groups. As Figure 15.3 illustrates, the rats that received alcohol on each trial before a convulsive stimulation became almost completely tolerant to alcohol's anticonvulsant effect, whereas those that received the same injections and stimulations in the reverse order developed no tolerance whatsoever to alcohol's anticonvulsant effect. Contingent

Figure 15.3 Contingent tolerance to the anticonvulsant effect of alcohol. The rats that received alcohol before each convulsive stimulation became tolerant to its anticonvulsant effect; those that received alcohol after each convulsive stimulation did not become tolerant.

(Based on Pinel, J. P. J., Mana, M. J., & Kim, C. K. (1989). Effect-dependent tolerance to ethanol's anticonvulsant effect on kindled seizures. In R. J. Porter, R. H. Mattson, J. A. Cramer, & I. Diamond (Eds.), *Alcohol and seizures: Basic mechanisms and clinical implications* (pp. 139–149). Philadelphia, PA: F. A. Davis.)

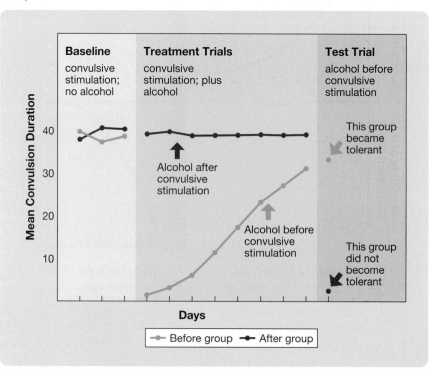

drug tolerance has been demonstrated to many other drug effects in many species, including humans (see Wolgin & Jakubow, 2003).

Conditioned Drug Tolerance

LO 15.6 Describe conditioned drug tolerance and conditioned compensatory responses.

Whereas studies of contingent drug tolerance focus on what subjects do while they are under the influence of drugs, studies of conditioned drug tolerance focus on the situations in which drugs are taken. **Conditioned drug tolerance** refers to demonstrations that tolerance effects are maximally expressed only when a drug is administered in the same situation in which it has previously been administered (see Siegel, 2011).

In one demonstration of conditioned drug tolerance (Crowell, Hinson, & Siegel, 1981), two groups of rats received 20 alcohol and 20 saline injections in an alternating sequence, one injection every other day. The only difference between the two groups was that the rats in one group received all 20 alcohol injections in a distinctive test room and the 20 saline injections in their colony room, while the rats in the other group received the alcohol in the colony room and the saline in the distinctive test room. At the end of the injection period, the

Evolutionary Perspective

tolerance of all rats to the *hypothermic* (temperature-reducing) effects of alcohol was assessed in both environments. As Figure 15.4 illustrates, tolerance was observed only when the rats were injected in the environment that had previously been paired with alcohol administration. There have been dozens of other demonstrations of the *situational specificity of drug tolerance*: The effects are large, reliable, and general.

The situational specificity of drug tolerance led Siegel and his colleagues to propose that drug users may be particularly susceptible to the lethal effects of a drug overdose when the drug is administered in a new context. Their hypothesis is that drug users become tolerant when they repeatedly self-administer their drug in the same environment and, as a result, begin taking larger and larger doses to counteract the diminution of drug effects. Then, if the drug user administers the usual massive dose in an unusual situation, tolerance effects are not present to counteract the effects of the drug, and there is a greater risk of death from overdose. In support of this hypothesis, Siegel and colleagues (1982) found that many more heroin-tolerant rats died following a high dose of heroin administered in a novel environment than died in the usual injection environment. (Heroin, as you will learn later in this chapter, kills by suppressing respiration.)

Siegel views each incidence of drug administration as a Pavlovian conditioning (see Chapter 5) trial in which various environmental stimuli (e.g., particular rooms, drug paraphernalia, or other drug users) that regularly predict the administration of the drug are conditional stimuli and the drug effects are unconditional stimuli. The central assumption of the theory is that conditional stimuli that predict drug administration come to elicit conditional responses opposite to the unconditional effects of the drug. Siegel has termed these hypothetical opposing conditional responses **conditioned compensatory responses**. The theory is that conditional stimuli that repeatedly predict the effects of a drug come to elicit greater and greater conditioned compensatory responses; and those conditioned compensatory responses increasingly counteract the unconditional effects of the drug and produce situationally specific tolerance.

Alert readers will have recognized the relation between Siegel's theory of drug tolerance and Woods's theory of mealtime hunger, which you learned about in Chapter 12. Stimuli that predict the homeostasis-disrupting effects of

Thinking Creatively

Figure 15.4 The situational specificity of tolerance to the hypothermic effects of alcohol in rats.

(Based on Crowell, C. R., Hinson, R. E., & Siegel, S. (1981). The role of conditional drug responses in tolerance to the hypothermic effects of ethanol. *Psychopharmacology, 73,* 51–54.)

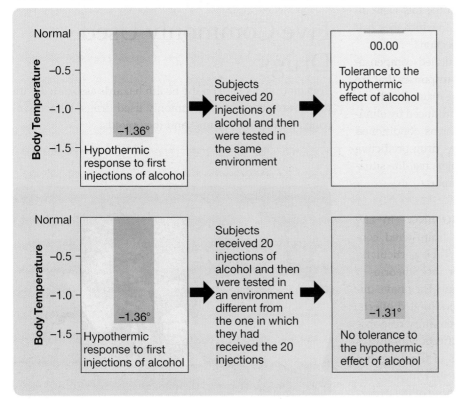

meals trigger conditioned compensatory responses to minimize a meal's disruptive effects in the same way that stimuli that predict the homeostasis-disrupting effects of a drug trigger conditioned compensatory responses to minimize the drug's disruptive effects.

> **Thinking Creatively** What other external stimuli, besides the drug-administration environment, do you think might serve as effective conditional stimuli for the development of conditioned drug tolerance?

Most demonstrations of conditioned drug tolerance have employed **exteroceptive stimuli** (external, public stimuli, such as the drug-administration environment) as the conditional stimuli. However, **interoceptive stimuli** (internal, private stimuli) are just as effective in this role. For example, both the thoughts and feelings produced by the drug-taking ritual and the drug effects experienced soon after administration can, through conditioning, come to reduce the full impact of a drug (Siegel, 2008). This point about interoceptive stimuli is important because it indicates that just thinking about a drug can evoke conditioned compensatory responses.

Although tolerance develops to many drug effects, sometimes the opposite occurs, that is, drug sensitization. *Drug sensitization*, like drug tolerance, can be situationally specific (e.g., Singer et al., 2014). For example, Anagnostaras and Robinson (1996) demonstrated the situational specificity of sensitization to the motor stimulant effects of amphetamine. They found that 10 amphetamine injections, one every 3 or 4 days, greatly increased the ability of amphetamine to activate the motor activity of rats—but only when the rats were injected and tested in the same environment in which they had experienced the previous amphetamine injections.

Drug withdrawal effects and conditioned compensatory responses are similar: They are both responses that are opposite to the unconditioned effect of the drug. The difference is that drug withdrawal effects are produced by elimination of the drug from the body, whereas conditioned compensatory responses are elicited by drug-predictive cues in the absence of the drug. In complex, real-life situations, it is nearly impossible to tell them apart.

THINKING ABOUT DRUG CONDITIONING. In any situation in which drugs are repeatedly administered, conditioned effects are inevitable. That is why it is particularly important to understand them. However, most theories of drug conditioning have a serious problem: They have difficulty predicting the direction of the conditioned effects. For example, Siegel's conditioned compensatory response theory predicts that conditioned drug effects will always be opposite to the unconditioned effects of the drug, but there are many documented instances in which conditional stimuli elicit responses similar to those of the drug.

Ramsay and Woods (1997) contend that much of the confusion about conditioned drug effects stems from a misunderstanding of Pavlovian conditioning. In particular, they criticize the common assumption that the unconditional stimulus (i.e., the stimulus to which the subject reflexively reacts) in a drug-tolerance experiment is the drug and that the unconditional responses are whatever changes in physiology or behavior the experimenter happens to be recording. They argue instead that the unconditional stimulus is the disruption of neural functioning that has been directly produced by the drug, and that the unconditional responses are the various neurally mediated compensatory reactions to the unconditional stimulus, which the experimenter may or may not be recording.

This change in perspective makes a big difference. For example, in the previously described alcohol tolerance experiment by Crowell and colleagues (1981), alcohol was designated as the unconditional stimulus and the resulting hypothermia as the unconditional response. Instead, Ramsay and Woods would argue that the unconditional stimulus was the hypothermia directly produced by the exposure to alcohol, and the compensatory changes that tended to counteract the reductions in body temperature were the unconditional responses. The important point about all of this is that once one determines the unconditional stimulus and unconditional response, it **Thinking Creatively** is easy to predict the direction of the conditional response in any drug-conditioning experiment: The conditional response is always similar to the unconditional response.

Five Commonly Used Drugs

This module focuses on the health hazards associated with the chronic use of five commonly used drugs: tobacco, alcohol, marijuana, cocaine, and the opioids.

Tobacco

LO 15.7 Describe the health hazards associated with smoking tobacco.

When a cigarette is smoked, **nicotine**—the major psychoactive ingredient of tobacco—and some 4,000 other chemicals, collectively referred to as *tar*, are absorbed through the lungs. Nicotine acts on nicotinic cholinergic receptors in the brain (see Nees, 2014; Pistillo et al., 2014). Tobacco is a leading cause of preventable death around the world. It contributes to more than 5 million premature deaths a year—about 1 in every 10 deaths (Degenhardt & Hall, 2012).

Because considerable tolerance develops to some of the immediate effects of tobacco, the effects of smoking a cigarette on nonsmokers and smokers can be quite different. Nonsmokers often respond to a few puffs of a cigarette with various combinations of nausea, vomiting, coughing, sweating, abdominal cramps, dizziness, flushing, and diarrhea. In contrast, smokers report that they are more relaxed, more alert, and less hungry after a cigarette.

There is no question that heavy smokers are addicted in every sense of the word. Can you think of any other psychoactive drug that is self-administered almost continually—even while the addicted person is walking along the street? The compulsive **drug craving** (an affective state in which there is a strong desire for the drug), which is a major defining feature of addiction, is readily apparent in any habitual smoker who has run out of cigarettes or who is forced by circumstance to refrain from smoking for several hours. Furthermore, habitual smokers who stop smoking experience a variety of withdrawal effects, such as depression, anxiety, restlessness, irritability, constipation, and difficulties in sleeping and concentrating.

About 70 percent of all people who experiment with smoking become addicted—this figure compares unfavorably with 10 percent for alcohol and 30 percent for heroin. Moreover, nicotine addiction typically develops quickly, within a few weeks (Di Franza, 2008), and only about 20 percent of all attempts to stop smoking are successful for 2 years or more. Twin studies confirm that nicotine addiction, like other addictions, has a major genetic component. The heritability estimate is about 55 percent (see Ducci & Goldman, 2012).

The consequences of long-term tobacco use are alarming. **Smoker's syndrome** is characterized by chest pain, labored breathing, wheezing, coughing, and a heightened susceptibility to infections of the respiratory tract. Chronic smokers are highly susceptible to a variety of potentially lethal lung disorders, including pneumonia, *bronchitis* (chronic inflammation of the bronchioles of the lungs), *emphysema* (loss of elasticity of the lung from chronic irritation), and lung cancer. Although the increased risk of lung cancer receives the greatest publicity, smoking also increases the risk of

cancer of the larynx (voice box), mouth, esophagus, kidneys, pancreas, bladder, and stomach. Smokers also run a greater risk of developing a variety of cardiovascular diseases, which may culminate in heart attack or stroke.

Sufferers from Buerger's disease provide a shocking illustration of the addictive power of nicotine. In **Buerger's disease**—which occurs in about 15 of 100,000 individuals, mostly in male smokers—the blood vessels, especially those supplying the legs, become constricted.

> If a patient with this condition continues to smoke, gangrene may eventually set in. First a few toes may have to be amputated, then the foot at the ankle, then the leg at the knee, and ultimately at the hip. Somewhere along this gruesome progression gangrene may also attack the other leg. Patients are strongly advised that if they will only stop smoking, it is virtually certain that the otherwise inexorable march of gangrene up the legs will be curbed. Yet surgeons report that it is not at all uncommon to find a patient with Buerger's disease vigorously puffing away in his hospital bed following a second or third amputation operation. (Brecher, 1972, pp. 239–240)

The adverse effects of tobacco smoke are unfortunately not restricted to those who smoke. Individuals who live or work with smokers are more likely to develop heart disease and cancer than those who don't. Even the unborn are vulnerable (see Abbott & Winzer-Serhan, 2012). Nicotine is a **teratogen** (an agent that can disturb the normal development of the fetus): Smoking during pregnancy increases the likelihood of miscarriage, stillbirth, and early death of the child.

If you or a loved one is a cigarette smoker, we have some good news and some bad news. First the bad news: Treatments for nicotine addiction are only marginally effective (see Zwar, Mendelsohn, & Richmond, 2014). The good news: Many people do stop smoking, and they experience major health benefits (see Godtfredsen & Prescott, 2011). Indeed, even the replacement of tobacco with another form of nicotine administration (e.g., nicotine gum, nicotine skin patch, nicotine mouth spray) is likely to lead to major health benefits (see Fagerström & Bridgman, 2014; Kupferschmidt, 2014).

Alcohol

LO 15.8 Describe the health hazards associated with alcohol consumption and the various stages of the full-blown alcohol withdrawal syndrome.

This section discusses another commonly misused drug: alcohol. Alcohol is involved in more than 2 million deaths each year across the globe, including deaths from birth defects, ill health, accidents, and violence (see Degenhardt & Hall, 2012; Mokdad et al., 2004). Worldwide, approximately 76 million people are heavy users of alcohol. Because alcohol molecules are small and soluble in both fat and water, they invade all parts of the body. Alcohol is classified as a depressant because at moderate-to-high doses it depresses neural firing; however, at low doses, it can stimulate neural firing and facilitate social interaction. Alcohol addiction has a major genetic component: Heritability estimates are about 50 percent (Enoch, 2012).

With moderate doses, the alcohol drinker experiences various degrees of cognitive, perceptual, verbal, and motor impairment, as well as a loss of control that can lead to a variety of socially unacceptable actions. High doses result in unconsciousness; and if blood levels reach 0.5 percent, there is a risk of death from respiratory depression. The telltale red facial flush of alcohol intoxication is produced by the dilation of blood vessels in the skin; this dilation increases the amount of heat lost from the blood to the air and leads to a decrease in body temperature (*hypothermia*). Alcohol is also a *diuretic*; that is, it increases the production of urine by the kidneys.

Alcohol, like many addictive drugs, produces both tolerance and physical dependence. The livers of heavy drinkers metabolize alcohol more quickly than the livers of nondrinkers, but this increase in metabolic efficiency contributes only slightly to overall alcohol tolerance; most alcohol tolerance is functional. Withdrawal from alcohol, even after a single bout of drinking, can produce a withdrawal syndrome of headache, nausea, vomiting, and tremulousness, which is euphemistically referred to as a *hangover*.

Withdrawal from alcohol after a long bout of heavy drinking produces a full-blown alcohol withdrawal syndrome comprising four phases (see Perry, 2014). The first phase begins 6 to 8 hours after the cessation of alcohol consumption and is characterized by anxiety, tremor, nausea, and *tachycardia* (rapid heartbeat). The second phase begins 10 to 30 hours after cessation of drinking, and is characterized by hyperactivity, insomnia, and hallucinations. The defining feature of the third phase, which typically occurs between 12 and 48 hours after cessation of drinking, is convulsive activity. The fourth phase, which usually begins 3 to 5 days after the cessation of drinking and lasts

Clinical Implications

up to a week, is called **delirium tremens (DTs)**. The DTs are characterized by disturbing hallucinations, bizarre delusions, disorientation, agitation, confusion, *hyperthermia* (high body temperature), and tachycardia. The convulsions and the DTs produced by alcohol withdrawal can be lethal.

Alcohol attacks almost every tissue in the body (see González-Reimers et al., 2014). Chronic alcohol consumption produces extensive brain damage. This damage is produced both directly (see Zahr, Kaufman, & Harper, 2011) and indirectly. For example, you learned in Chapter 1 that alcohol indirectly causes **Korsakoff's syndrome** (a neuropsychological disorder characterized by memory loss, sensory and motor dysfunction, and, in its advanced stages, severe dementia) by inducing thiamine deficiency. Alcohol affects the brain function of drinkers in other ways as well. For example, it interferes with the function of second messengers inside neurons; it disrupts GABAergic and glutaminergic transmission; it leads to DNA methylation; and it triggers apoptosis (see ali Shah et al., 2013).

Chronic alcohol consumption also causes extensive scarring, or **cirrhosis**, of the liver, which is the major cause of death among heavy alcohol users. Alcohol erodes the muscles of the heart and thus increases the risk of heart attack. It irritates the lining of the digestive tract and, in so doing, increases the risk of oral and liver cancer, stomach ulcers, *pancreatitis* (inflammation of the pancreas), and *gastritis* (inflammation of the stomach). And not to be forgotten is the carnage that alcohol produces from accidents on our roads, in our homes, in our workplaces, and at recreational sites—in the United States, more than 10,000 people die each year in alcohol-related traffic accidents alone.

Many people assume the adverse effects of alcohol occur only in people who drink a lot—they tend to define "a lot" as "much more than they themselves consume." But they are wrong. Several large-scale studies have shown that even low-to-moderate regular drinking (a drink or two per day) is associated with elevated levels of many cancers, including breast, oral cavity, and colorectal cancer (Bagnardi et al., 2013; Castro & Castro, 2014; Huber & Tantiwongkosi, 2014; Stone et al., 2014).

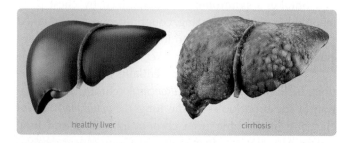

Comparison of healthy liver with cirrhosis liver.

The offspring of mothers who consume substantial quantities of alcohol during pregnancy can develop **fetal alcohol syndrome (FAS)**—see Valenzuela et al. (2012). A child with FAS suffers from some or all of the following symptoms: brain damage, intellectual disability poor co-ordination, poor muscle tone, low birth weight, retarded growth, and/or physical deformity (see Landgraf et al., 2014). Because alcohol can disrupt brain development in so many ways (e.g., by disrupting the production of cell-adhesion molecules or by disrupting normal patterns of apoptosis), there is no time during pregnancy when alcohol consumption is safe (see Paintner, Williams, & Burd, 2012). Moreover, there seems to be no safe amount (see Charness, Riley, & Sowell, 2016). Although full-blown FAS is rarely seen in the babies of mothers who never had more than one drink a day during pregnancy, children of mothers who drank only moderately while pregnant are sometimes found to have a variety of cognitive problems, even though they are not diagnosed with FAS (see Koren et al., 2014).

There is evidence that alcohol consumption might have effects on subsequent generations, even when consumed by the male parent; that is, alcohol consumption has been shown to produce *transgenerational epigenetic effects* (see Chapter 2)—see Kippin (2014); Vassoler, Byrnes, and Pierce (2014). For example, the offspring of alcohol-consuming male rats display impairments in spatial learning (see Chapter 11)—see Vassoler, Byrnes, and Pierce (2014). Moreover, there have been reports of human children born with characteristics of FAS whose mothers did not drink but whose fathers were alcoholics (see Vassoler, Byrnes, & Pierce, 2014).

One of the most widely publicized findings about alcohol is that moderate drinking reduces the risk of coronary heart disease. This conclusion is based on the finding that the incidence of coronary heart disease is less among moderate drinkers than among abstainers. You learned in Chapter 1 about the difficulty in basing causal interpretations on correlational data, and researchers worked diligently to identify and rule out factors other than the alcohol that might protect moderate drinkers from coronary heart disease. They seemed to rule out every other possibility. However, a thoughtful analysis led to a different conclusion. Let us explain. In a culture in

which alcohol consumption is the norm, any large group of abstainers will always include some people who have stopped drinking because they are ill—perhaps this is why abstainers have more heart attacks than moderate drinkers (see Naimi et al., 2005; Roerecke & Rehm, 2011). This hypothesis was tested by including in a meta-analysis only those studies that used an abstainers control group consisting of individuals who had never consumed alcohol. This meta-analysis indicated that alcohol in moderate amounts does not prevent coronary heart disease; that is, moderate drinkers did not suffer less coronary heart disease than lifelong abstainers

(Fillmore et al., 2006; Stockwell, 2012). Furthermore, a recent meta-analysis found that moderate alcohol consumption had no benefit in terms of reducing mortality risk (see Stockwell et al., 2016).

> **Thinking Creatively**
> Before reading this section, what were your views on the effects of moderate drinking? Have your views changed at all now? Why or why not?

Marijuana

LO 15.9 Explain the health effects of marijuana and the mechanism of action of THC.

Marijuana is the name commonly given to the dried flower buds of *Cannabis*—the common hemp plant of which there are three species: *Cannabis sativa*, *Cannabis indica*, and *Cannabis ruderalis*. More than 124 million people used marijuana in the past year across the globe (Degenhardt & Hall, 2012). The usual mode of consumption is to smoke these flowers in a *joint* (a cigarette of marijuana) or a pipe, but marijuana is also effective when ingested orally if first baked into an oil-rich substrate, such as a chocolate brownie, to promote absorption from the gastrointestinal tract.

The psychoactive effects of marijuana are largely attributable to a constituent called **THC** (delta-9-tetrahydrocannabinol). However, marijuana contains more than 80 *cannabinoids* (chemicals of the same chemical class as THC), which may also be psychoactive. For example, one cannabinoid, THCV (delta-9-tetrahydrocannabivarin), has been shown to have antipsychotic effects (see Chapter 18)—see Cascio et al. (2014). Most of the cannabinoids are found in a sticky resin covering the leaves and flowers of the plant; this resin can be extracted and dried to form a dark corklike material called **hashish**.

Written records of *Cannabis* use go back 6,000 years in China, where its stems were used to make rope, its seeds were used as a grain, and its leaves and flowers were used for their psychoactive and medicinal effects. In the Middle Ages, cannabis cultivation spread into Europe, where it was grown primarily for the manufacture of rope. During the period of European imperialism, rope was in high demand for sailing vessels, and the American colonies responded to this demand by growing cannabis as a cash crop. George Washington was one of the more notable cannabis growers.

The practice of smoking the flower buds of the *Cannabis* plant and the word *marijuana* itself seem to have been introduced to the southern United States in the early part of the 20th century. In 1926, an article appeared in a New Orleans newspaper exposing the "menace of marijuana," and soon similar stories were appearing in newspapers all over the United States claiming that marijuana turns people into violent, drug-crazed criminals. The misrepresentation of the effects of marijuana by the news media led to the rapid enactment of laws against the drug. In many states, marijuana was legally classified a **narcotic** (a legal term generally used to refer to opioids), and punishment for its use was dealt out accordingly. Marijuana bears no resemblance to opioid narcotics.

Popularization of marijuana smoking among the middle and upper classes in the 1960s stimulated a massive program of research. One of the difficulties in studying the effects of marijuana is that they are subtle, difficult to measure, and greatly influenced by the social situation:

> At low, usual "social" doses, the intoxicated individual may experience an increased sense of well-being: initial restlessness and hilarity followed by a dreamy, carefree state of relaxation; alteration of sensory perceptions including expansion of space and time; and a more vivid sense of touch, sight, smell, taste, and sound; a feeling of hunger, especially a craving for sweets; and subtle changes in thought formation and expression. To an unknowing observer, an individual in this state of consciousness would not appear noticeably different. (National Commission on Marijuana and Drug Abuse, 1972, p. 92)

Although the effects of typical social doses of marijuana are subtle, high doses do impair psychological functioning. At high doses, short-term memory is impaired, and the ability to carry out tasks involving multiple steps to reach a specific goal declines. Speech becomes slurred, and meaningful conversation becomes difficult. A sense of unreality, emotional intensification, sensory distortion, feelings of paranoia, and motor impairment are also common. Driving under the influence of marijuana is obviously dangerous (see Neavyn et al., 2014).

Some people do become addicted to marijuana, but its addiction potential is low. Most people who use marijuana do so only occasionally, with only about 10 percent of them using daily; moreover, most people who try marijuana do so in their teens and curtail their use by their 30s or 40s (see Room et al., 2010). Tolerance to marijuana develops during periods of sustained use; however, obvious withdrawal

symptoms (e.g., nausea, diarrhea, sweating, chills, tremor, sleep disturbance) are rare, except in contrived laboratory situations in which massive oral doses are administered.

What are the health hazards of marijuana use? Only one has been consistently documented: Because marijuana produces *tachycardia* (elevated heart rate), single large doses can trigger heart attacks in susceptible individuals who have previously suffered a heart attack.

Clinical Implications

You have likely heard that marijuana causes brain damage. This claim has been spread by governmental and social agencies attempting to discourage marijuana use. But what is the actual evidence?

Surprisingly, no damage that can reasonably be attributed to marijuana use has been found in the brains of living or deceased marijuana users (see Hall & Degenhardt, 2014). However, three lines of indirect correlational (see Chapter 1) evidence have a bearing on the question:

- Brain-imaging studies have found that hippocampal volumes tend to be slightly reduced in some heavy marijuana users (see Batalla et al., 2013; Rochetti et al., 2013). However, such findings might be the result of preexisting differences between users and nonusers (e.g., Goldman, 2015; Pagliaccio et al., 2015).

- Heavy marijuana users tend to have memory problems (see Crane et al., 2013; Hall & Degenhardt, 2014). However, because it is not clear whether the memory deficits persist after the cessation of marijuana use, it is not clear if they are indicative of persistent brain damage (see Mechoulam & Parker, 2013).

- Heavy marijuana users are slightly more likely to be diagnosed with schizophrenia (see Chapter 18)—especially if they began using marijuana during adolescence (see Radhakrishnan et al., 2014). Until the reasons for this correlation are sorted out (see Hill, 2015; Renard et al., 2014), youths with a history of schizophrenia in their families should refrain from marijuana use (see Burns, 2013).

In short, regardless of what you have heard to the contrary, there is no convincing evidence that marijuana causes brain damage. Complicating the situation further is that marijuana may actually have neuroprotective effects. For example, Nguyen and colleagues (2014) reviewed the data of adults that were treated for traumatic brain injury and found that those individuals who tested positive for marijuana use were 80 percent less likely to die from the brain injury than nonusers of marijuana.

Research on THC changed irrevocably in the early 1990s with the discovery of two receptors for it: CB_1 and CB_2. CB_1 turned out to be one of the most prevalent G-protein–linked receptors in the brain (see Chapter 4)—see Parsons and Hurd (2015), and it is present in other parts of the body as well (e.g., Hedlund, 2014); CB$_2$ is found throughout the CNS and in the cells of the immune system (see Mechoulam & Parker, 2013; Parsons & Hurd, 2015). But why are there receptors for THC in the brain? They could hardly have evolved to mediate the effects of marijuana smoking. This puzzle was quickly solved with the discovery of a class of endogenous cannabinoid neurotransmitters: the endocannabinoids (see McPartland et al., 2014). The first endocannabinoid neurotransmitter to be isolated and characterized was named **anandamide** (see Piomelli, 2014), from a word that means "internal bliss" (see Nicoll & Alger, 2004).

THC has been shown to have several therapeutic effects (see Noonan, 2015). Since the early 1990s, it has been used to suppress nausea and vomiting in cancer patients and to stimulate the appetite of patients with AIDS (see Robson, 2014). THC has also been shown to block seizures; to dilate the bronchioles of asthmatics; to decrease the severity of *glaucoma* (a disorder characterized by an increase in the pressure of the fluid inside the eye); and to reduce anxiety, some kinds of pain, and the symptoms of multiple sclerosis (see Koppel et al., 2014). In 2010, *Sativex*, a mouth spray that contains THC and other cannabinoids, was introduced into several countries for the treatment of multiple sclerosis symptoms (see Pertwee, 2012; Cressey, 2015). Medical use of THC does not appear to be associated with any serious adverse side effects (see Hosking & Zajicek, 2014).

We cannot end this discussion of marijuana (e.g., *Cannabis sativa*) without telling you the following story:

> You can imagine how surprised I (JP) was when my colleague went to his back door, opened it, and yelled, "Sativa, here Sativa, dinner time."
>
> "What was that you called your dog?" I asked as he returned to his beer.
>
> "Sativa," he said. "The kids picked the name. I think they learned about it at school; a Greek goddess or something. Pretty, isn't it? And catchy too: Every kid on the street seems to remember her name."
>
> "Yes," I said. "Very pretty."

Cocaine and Other Stimulants

LO 15.10 Describe the health hazards associated with the consumption of cocaine and other stimulants.

Stimulants are drugs whose primary effect is to produce general increases in neural and behavioral activity. Although stimulants all have a similar profile of effects, they differ greatly in their potency. Coca-Cola is a mild commercial stimulant preparation consumed by many people around the world. Today, its stimulant action is attributable to *caffeine*, but when it was first introduced, it packed a real wallop in the form of small amounts of cocaine. **Cocaine** and its derivatives are the focus of this section; but we will also be discussing other stimulants.

Cocaine is prepared from the leaves of the coca shrub, which grows primarily in western South America. For centuries, a crude extract called *coca paste* has been made directly from the leaves and eaten. Today, it is more common to treat the coca paste and extract *cocaine hydrochloride*, the nefarious white powder that is referred to simply as *cocaine* and typically consumed by snorting or by injection. Cocaine hydrochloride may be converted to its base form by boiling it in a solution of baking soda until the water has evaporated. The impure residue of this process is **crack**, a potent, cheap, smokeable form of cocaine. However, because crack is impure and consumed by smoking, it is difficult to study, and most research on cocaine derivatives has thus focused on pure cocaine hydrochloride. More than 14 million people used cocaine in the past year across the globe (Degenhardt & Hall, 2012).

Cocaine hydrochloride is an effective local anesthetic and was once widely prescribed as such until it was supplanted by synthetic analogues such as *procaine* and *lidocaine*. It is not, however, cocaine's anesthetic actions that are of interest to users. People eat, smoke, snort, or inject cocaine or its derivatives in order to experience its psychological effects. Users report being swept by a wave of well-being; they feel self-confident, alert, energetic, friendly, outgoing, fidgety, and talkative; and they have less than their usual desire for food and sleep.

Individuals who are addicted to cocaine tend to go on so-called **cocaine sprees**, binges in which extremely high levels of intake are maintained for periods of a day or two. During a cocaine spree, users become increasingly tolerant to the euphoria-producing effects of cocaine. Accordingly, larger and larger doses are often administered. The spree usually ends when the cocaine is gone or when it begins to have serious toxic effects. The effects of cocaine sprees include sleeplessness, tremors, nausea, hyperthermia, and, in rare cases, psychotic symptoms, which is called **cocaine psychosis** and has sometimes been mistakenly diagnosed as *schizophrenia* (see Chapter 18). During cocaine sprees, there is a risk of loss of consciousness, seizures, respiratory arrest, heart attack, or

Clinical Implications

stroke (see Zimmerman, 2012; Stankowski, Kloner, & Rezkalla, 2014). Although tolerance develops to most effects of cocaine (e.g., to the euphoria), repeated cocaine exposure sensitizes subjects (i.e., makes them even more responsive) to its motor effects (see Li & Wolf, 2012). The withdrawal effects triggered by abrupt termination of a cocaine spree are relatively mild. Common cocaine withdrawal symptoms include a negative mood swing and insomnia.

Although cocaine and its derivatives are widely misused, **amphetamine** and its relatives are currently the most widely misused stimulants (UN Global ATS Assessment, 2011). Amphetamine has been in wide use since the 1960s. It is usually consumed orally in the potent form called *d-amphetamine* (dextroamphetamine). Some of the effects of *d*-amphetamine are comparable to those of cocaine; for example, it can also produce a syndrome of psychosis called *amphetamine psychosis*.

In the 1990s, *d*-amphetamine was supplanted as the favored amphetamine-like drug by several more potent relatives. One is *methamphetamine*, or "meth" (see Hsieh et al., 2014), which is commonly used in its even more potent, smokeable, crystalline form (crystal meth). Another potent relative of amphetamine is *3,4-methylenedioxymethamphetamine* (MDMA, or ecstasy), which is taken orally (see Cole, 2014). Besides being a stimulant, MDMA is also considered an empathogen. **Empathogens** are psychoactive drugs that produce feelings of empathy (see Bedi, Hyman, & de Wit, 2010).

The primary mechanism by which cocaine and its derivatives exert their effects is by altering the activity of **dopamine transporters**, molecules in the presynaptic membrane that normally remove dopamine from synapses and transfer it back into presynaptic neurons. Other stimulants increase the release of monoamines into synapses (see Sitte & Freissmuth, 2015).

Do stimulants have long-term adverse effects on the health of habitual users? There is some evidence that they do. For example, many studies have reported cognitive impairments in both methamphetamine and MDMA users (see Marshall & O'Dell, 2012; Parrott, 2013), though the effects have often been small or difficult to reproduce (see Hart et al., 2012). In addition, methamphetamine and amphetamine users, but not cocaine users, have a greater risk of developing Parkinson's disease (see Callaghan et al., 2012; Curtin et al., 2015). There is also evidence of heart pathology: Many cocaine-dependent, amphetamine-dependent, and methamphetamine-dependent patients have been found to have electrocardiographic abnormalities (see Carvalho et al., 2012; Maceira et al., 2014). Finally, there is evidence that stimulant-dependent individuals have less gray matter in their prefrontal cortex (see Ersche et al., 2013). However, because these results are correlational, one cannot rule out other explanations (see Hart et al., 2012; Krebs & Johansen, 2012).

Clinical Implications

The Opioids: Heroin and Morphine

LO 15.11 Describe the health hazards associated with the consumption of opioids and the opioid withdrawal syndrome.

Opium—the dried form of sap exuded by the seedpods of the opium poppy—has several psychoactive ingredients. Most notable are **morphine** and **codeine**, its weaker relative. Morphine, codeine, and other drugs that have similar structures or effects are commonly referred to as **opioids**. The opioids exert their effects by binding to receptors whose normal function is to bind to endogenous opioids. The endogenous opioid neurotransmitters that bind to such receptors are of two classes: *endorphins* and *enkephalins* (see Chapter 4).

The opioids have a Jekyll-and-Hyde character. On their Dr. Jekyll side, the opioids are effective as **analgesics** (painkillers; see Weibel et al., 2013); they are also extremely effective in the treatment of cough and diarrhea. But, unfortunately, the kindly Dr. Jekyll brings with him the evil Mr. Hyde—the risk of addiction.

The practice of eating opium spread from the Middle East sometime before 4000 B.C. Three historic events fanned the flame of opioid addiction. First, in 1644, the Emperor of China banned tobacco smoking, and this contributed to a gradual increase in opium smoking in China, spurred on by the smuggling of opium into China by the

British East India Company. Because smoking opium has a greater effect on the brain than does eating it, many more people became addicted. Second, morphine, the most potent constituent of opium, was isolated in 1803, and it became available commercially in the 1830s. Third, the hypodermic needle was invented in 1856, and soon the injured were introduced to morphine through a needle.

Until the early part of the 20th century, opium was available legally in many parts of the world, including Europe and North America. Indeed, opium was an ingredient in cakes, candies, and wines, as well as in a variety of over-the-counter medicinal offerings. Opium potions such as *laudanum* (a very popular mixture of opium and alcohol), *Godfrey's Cordial*, and *Dalby's Carminative* were very popular. (The word *carminative* should win first prize for making a sow's ear at least sound like a silk purse: A carminative is a drug that expels gas from the digestive tract, thereby reducing stomach cramps and flatulence. *Flatulence* is the obvious pick for second prize.) There were even over-the-counter opium potions just for baby—such as *Mrs. Winslow's Soothing Syrup* and the aptly labeled *Street's Infant Quietness*. Although pure morphine required a prescription at the time, physicians prescribed it for so many different maladies that morphine addiction was common among those who could afford a doctor.

The **Harrison Narcotics Act**, passed in 1914, made it illegal to sell or use opium, morphine, or cocaine in the United States—although morphine and its analogues are still legally prescribed for their medicinal properties. However, the act did not include the semisynthetic opioid **heroin**. Heroin was synthesized in 1870 by the addition of two acetyl groups to the morphine molecule, which greatly increased its ability to penetrate the blood–brain barrier. In 1898, heroin was marketed by the Bayer Drug Company; it was freely available without prescription and was widely advertised as a superior kind of aspirin. Tests showed that it was a more potent analgesic than morphine and that it was less likely to induce nausea and vomiting. Moreover, the Bayer Drug Company, on the basis of flimsy evidence, claimed that heroin was not addictive; this is why it was not covered by the Harrison Narcotics Act. The consequence of omitting heroin from the Harrison Narcotics Act was that opioid-dependent individuals in the United States, forbidden by law to use opium or morphine, turned to the readily available and much more potent heroin—and the flames of addiction were further fanned. In 1924, the U.S. Congress made it illegal for anybody to possess, sell, or use heroin. Unfortunately, the laws enacted to stamp out opioid use in the United States have been far from successful: An estimated 507,000 Americans currently use heroin (U.S. Department of Health and Human Services, 2010), and organized crime flourishes on the proceeds.

The effect of opioids most valued by users is the *rush* that follows intravenous injection. The *heroin rush* is a wave of intense abdominal, orgasmic pleasure that evolves into a state of serene, drowsy euphoria. Many opioid users, drawn by these pleasurable effects, begin to use the drug more and more frequently. Then, once they reach a point where they keep themselves drugged much of the time, tolerance and physical dependence develop and contribute to the problem. Opioid tolerance encourages users to progress to higher doses, to more potent drugs (e.g., heroin, fentanyl), and to more direct routes of administration (e.g., IV injection); and physical dependence adds to the already high motivation to take the drug.

The classic opioid withdrawal syndrome usually begins 6 to 12 hours after the last dose. The first withdrawal sign is typically an increase in restlessness; the opioid user begins to pace and fidget. Watering eyes, running nose, yawning, and sweating are also common during the early stages of opioid withdrawal. Then, the person often falls into a fitful sleep, which typically lasts for several hours. Once they wake up, the original symptoms may be joined in extreme cases by chills, shivering, profuse sweating, gooseflesh, nausea, vomiting, diarrhea, cramps, dilated pupils, tremor, and muscle pains and spasms. The gooseflesh skin and leg spasms of the opioid withdrawal syndrome are the basis for the expressions "going cold turkey" and "kicking the habit." The symptoms of opioid withdrawal are typically most severe in the second or third day after the last injection, and by the seventh day they have all but disappeared. In short, opioid withdrawal is about as serious as a bad case of the flu:

> [Opioid] withdrawal is probably one of the most misunderstood aspects of drug use. This is largely because of the image of withdrawal that has been portrayed in the movies and popular literature for many years….Few…take enough drug to cause the…severe withdrawal symptoms that are shown in the movies. Even in its most severe form, however, [opioid] withdrawal is not as dangerous or terrifying as withdrawal from barbiturates or alcohol. (McKim, 1986, p. 223)

Although many opioids are highly addictive, the direct health hazards of chronic exposure are surprisingly minor. The main direct risks are constipation, pupil constriction, menstrual irregularity, and reduced sex drive. Many opioid users **Clinical Implications** have taken pure heroin or morphine for years with no serious ill effects. In fact, opioid addiction is more prevalent among doctors, nurses, and dentists than among other professionals (e.g., Brewster, 1986):

> An individual tolerant to and dependent upon an [opioid] who is socially or financially capable of obtaining an adequate supply of good quality drug, sterile syringes and needles, and other paraphernalia may maintain his or her proper social and occupational functions, remain in fairly good health, and suffer little serious incapacitation as a result of the dependence. (Julien, 1981, p. 141)

One such individual was Dr. William Steward Halsted, one of the founders of Johns Hopkins Medical School and one of the most brilliant surgeons of his day…known as "the father of modern surgery." And yet, during his career he was addicted to morphine, a fact that he was able to keep secret from all but his closest friends. In fact, the only time his habit caused him any trouble was when he was attempting to reduce his dosage. (McKim, 1986, p. 221)

Most medical risks of opioid addiction are indirect—that is, not entirely attributable to the drug itself. Many of the medical risks arise out of the battle between the relentless addictive power of opioids and the attempts of governments to eradicate addiction by making opioids illegal. The opioid user who cannot give up their habit—treatment programs report success rates of only about 10 percent—are caught in the middle. Because most opioid users must purchase their morphine and heroin from illicit dealers at greatly inflated prices, those who are not wealthy become trapped in a life of poverty and petty crime. They are poor, they are undernourished, they receive poor medical care, and they run great risk of contracting HIV and other infections from unsterile needles. Moreover, they never know for sure what they are injecting: Some street drugs are poorly processed, and virtually all have been *cut* (stretched by the addition of some similar-appearing substance) to an unknown degree.

Death associated with heroin overdose is a serious problem—high doses of heroin kill by suppressing breathing (see Darke, Duflou, & Torok. 2010). However, death from heroin overdose is not well understood: Medical examiners often attribute death to heroin overdose without assessing blood levels of heroin. Yet, careful toxicological analysis at autopsy often reveals that this diagnosis is questionable. In some cases, the deceased have low levels of heroin in the blood and high levels of other CNS depressants such as alcohol and benzodiazepines. In short, some so-called heroin overdose deaths appear to be a product of drug interaction (Darke, Duflou, & Torok, 2010).

The primary treatments for heroin addiction in most countries are *methadone* and *buprenorphine*. Both methadone and buprenorphine have a high and long-lasting affinity for opioid receptors. Ironically, they are both opioids with many of the same adverse effects as heroin. However, because they produce less pleasure than heroin, the strategy has been to block heroin withdrawal effects with either methadone or buprenorphine and then maintain the individual on one of those drugs until they can be weaned from it. Methadone replacement has been shown to improve the success rate of some treatment programs, but its adverse effects are problematic (see Nutt, 2015). Buprenorphine has fewer adverse side effects than

methadone (see Nutt, 2015) but is considered less effective than methadone (see Mattick et al., 2014).

In 1994, the Swiss government took an alternative approach to the problem of heroin addiction. It established a series of clinics in which, as part of a total treatment package, Swiss heroin users could receive heroin injections from a physician for a small fee. The Swiss government wisely funded a major research program to evaluate the clinics (see Khan et al., 2014). The results have been uniformly positive. 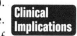 Once they had a cheap reliable source of heroin, most heroin users gave up their criminal lifestyles, and their health improved once they were exposed to the specialized medical and counseling staff at the clinics. Many heroin users returned to their family and jobs, and many opted to reduce or curtail their heroin use. As a result, heroin use is no longer present in Swiss streets and parks; drug-related crime has substantially declined; and the physical and social well-being of the heroin users has greatly improved. Furthermore, the number of new cases of heroin addiction has declined (see Uchtenhagen, 2010).

These positive results have led to the establishment of similar experimental programs in other countries (e.g., Canada, Germany, Netherlands, Spain, Switzerland, and United Kingdom) with similar success. Indeed, in a large randomized trial, supervised treatment with heroin was shown to be more effective and less costly than methadone (Nosyk et al., 2012). Furthermore, safe injection facilities have managed to reduce the spread of infection and death from heroin overdose in many cities (e.g., Marshall et al., 2011). Given the unqualified success of such programs in dealing with the drug problem, it is interesting to consider why some governments have not adopted them (e.g., Kupferschmidt, 2014). What do you think?

Comparing the Health Hazards of Commonly Used Drugs

Interpreting Studies of the Health Hazards of Drugs

LO 15.12 Explain why it is difficult to determine causality in studies of the health hazards of drugs.

The previous module described the health hazards of five commonly used drugs, some legal, some illegal. You probably noticed a repeated disclaimer: Interpretation of the adverse effects observed in drug users is almost always complicated by the fact that the relevant research is corre-

lational. Because most studies compare the health of known drug users with that of non-users, one can never be certain that any observed differences in health are due to the drug or to some other difference between the two groups. An additional complication arises from the fact that most studies recruit drug users from addiction treatment clinics. Such users are typically the most severe. Indeed, when studies use samples of drug users from the general population, the outcomes can be quite different (see Krebs & Johansen, 2012; Krebs et al., 2009). For example, studies that recruit samples of drug users from addiction treatment clinics typically find that drug addiction is difficult to treat. In contrast, studies that recruit samples of drug users from the general population have found that many drug users can successfully treat their own addictions without professional help and live productive lives thereafter (see Blanco et al., 2013; Chapman & MacKenzie, 2010; Klingemann, Sobell, & Sobell, 2009). The following quote from a former student, who was a heavy user of methamphetamine, illustrates this point:

* "I dropped out of high school 17 years ago…Somewhere along the line, knowing full well I was playing with fire, I developed a methamphetamine habit. For 3 years I used almost daily, most often injecting. I never lost my job or my house, never experienced psychiatric symptoms, and never received any treatment for medical conditions related to my drug use—but it did permeate my life and interfere with my goals. Eventually I fell in love with the woman who would later become my wife, and that relationship provided all the motivation I needed to stop using regularly. Until we decided to get pregnant (5 years later) I continued to use meth at parties, but never more than twice a year…More than a decade after dropping out of high school I enrolled in university and found I was able to do my homework and get good grades."

*Student Excerpt. Anonymous.

Comparison of the Hazards of Tobacco, Alcohol, Marijuana, Cocaine, and Heroin

LO 15.13 Compare the direct health hazards of alcohol, tobacco, marijuana, heroin, and cocaine.

One way of comparing the adverse effects of tobacco, alcohol, marijuana, cocaine, and heroin is to compare the prevalence of their use in society as a whole. In terms of this criterion, it is clear that tobacco and alcohol have a greater negative impact than marijuana, cocaine, and heroin (see Figure 15.5). Another method of comparison is based on global death rates: Tobacco has been implicated in approximately 5 million deaths per year; alcohol in approximately 2 million deaths per year; and all other drugs combined in about 250,000 deaths per year (see Degenhardt & Hall, 2012).

> Thinking Creatively — Do you or somebody you love use a hard drug such as nicotine or alcohol? How would you summarize the relevant data to someone who you wanted to stop using the drug?

But what about the individual drug user? Who is taking greater health risks: the cigarette smoker, the alcohol

Figure 15.5 Prevalence of drug use in the United States. Figures are based on a survey of people 12 years of age and over who live in households and used the drug in question at least once in the past month.

(Based on the National Survey on Drug Use and Health, 2011.)

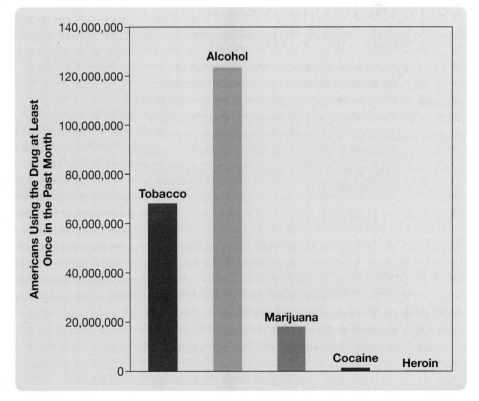

drinker, the marijuana smoker, the cocaine user, or the **Thinking Creatively** heroin user? You now have the information to answer this question. Would you have ranked the health risks of these drugs in the same way before you began this chapter? How have the laws, or lack thereof, influenced the hazards associated with the five drugs?

Scan Your Brain

So far in this chapter, you have been introduced to the principles of drug action, the role of learning in drug tolerance, and five commonly used drugs. This is a good place to pause and reinforce what you have learned. In each blank, write the appropriate term. The correct answers are provided at the end of the exercise. Review material related to your errors and omissions before proceeding.

1. Broken down products of the body's chemical reactions are called _____.
2. _____ is a state of decreased sensitivity to a drug that develops as a result of exposure to it.
3. A graph of the magnitude of the effect of different doses of a drug is referred to as a _____.
4. _____ are hypothetical conditional physiological responses that are opposite to the effects of a drug.
5. Psychoactive drugs that produce feelings of affection and compassion are called _____.
6. _____ stimuli arise from outside the body.
7. _____ is described as the phase of alcohol withdrawal syndrome characterized by hallucinations, delusions, disorientation, agitation, confusion, and hyperthermia.
8. Chronic alcohol consumption causes extensive scarring of the liver, also called _____.
9. The offspring of mothers who consume substantial quantities of alcohol during pregnancy may develop _____.
10. _____ are drugs whose primary effect produces a general increase in neural and behavioral activity.
11. Morphine and codeine are constituents of _____.
12. _____ is a semisynthetic opioid that penetrates the blood–brain barrier more effectively than morphine.
13. _____ heroin users were among the first to legally receive heroin injections from a physician for a small fee.

Scan Your Brain answers: (1) metabolites, (2) Drug tolerance, (3) dose-response curve, (4) Conditioned compensatory responses, (5) empathogens, (6) Exteroceptive, (7) Delirium tremens, (8) cirrhosis, (9) fetal alcohol syndrome, (10) Stimulants, (11) opium, (12) Heroin, (13) Swiss.

Early Biopsychological Research on Addiction

This module begins by introducing two diametrically different ways of thinking about drug addiction: Are drug-addicted individuals driven to take drugs by an internal need, or are they drawn to take drugs by the anticipated positive effects? After having read the preceding chapters, you will recognize this is the same fundamental question that has been the focus of biopsychological research on the motivation to eat and sleep.

Physical-Dependence and Positive-Incentive Perspectives of Addiction

LO 15.14 Explain the physical-dependence and positive-incentive perspectives of addiction.

Early attempts to explain the phenomenon of drug addiction attributed it to physical dependence. According to various **physical-dependence theories of addiction**, physical dependence traps addicted individuals in a vicious circle of drug taking and withdrawal symptoms.

The idea was that drug users whose intake has reached a level sufficient to induce physical dependence are driven by their withdrawal symptoms to self-administer the drug each time they attempt to curtail their intake.

Early drug addiction treatment programs were based on the physical-dependence perspective. They attempted to break the vicious cycle of drug taking by gradually withdrawing drugs from addicted individuals in a hospital environment. Unfortunately, once discharged, almost all detoxified drug misusers return to their former drug-taking habits.

The failure of detoxification as a treatment for addiction is not surprising, for two reasons. First, some highly addictive drugs, such as cocaine and amphetamines, do not produce severe withdrawal distress (see Gawin, 1991). Second, the pattern of drug taking routinely displayed by many habitual drug users involves an alternating cycle of binges and detoxification (Mello & Mendelson, 1972). There are a variety of reasons for this pattern of drug use. For example, some addicted individuals adopt it because weekend binges are compatible with their work schedules, others adopt it because they do not have enough money to use drugs continuously, and others have it forced on them by their repeated unsuccessful efforts to shake their habit.

However, whether detoxification is by choice or necessity, it does not stop addicted individuals from renewing their drug-taking habits (see Leshner, 1997).

As a result of these problems with physical-dependence theories of addiction, a different approach began to predominate in the 1970s and 1980s (see Higgins, Heil, & Lussier, 2004). This approach was based on the assumption that most addicted individuals take drugs not to escape or to avoid the unpleasant consequences of withdrawal, but rather to obtain the drugs' positive effects. Theories of addiction based on this premise are called **positive-incentive theories of addiction**. They hold that the primary factor in most cases of addiction is the craving for the positive-incentive (expected pleasure-producing) properties of the drug.

There is no question that physical dependence does play a role in addiction: Addicted individuals do sometimes consume the drug to alleviate their withdrawal symptoms. However, most researchers now assume that the more important factor in addiction is the drugs' *hedonic* (pleasurable) effects (see Cardinal & Everitt, 2004; Everitt, Dickinson, & Robbins, 2001).

The remainder of this module summarizes the early biopsychological research into the brain mechanisms of addiction. As you will learn, this research was largely based on the positive-incentive theory of addiction.

Intracranial Self-Stimulation and the Mesotelencephalic Dopamine System

LO 15.15 Describe the intracranial self-stimulation (ICSS) paradigm.

Rats, humans, and many other species will administer brief bursts of weak electrical stimulation to specific sites in their own brains (see Figure 15.6). This phenomenon is known as **intracranial self-stimulation (ICSS)**, and the brain sites capable of mediating the phenomenon are often called *pleasure centers*. When research on addiction turned to positive incentives in the 1970s and 1980s, what had been learned about the neural mechanisms of pleasure from studying intracranial self-stimulation served as a starting point for the study of the neural mechanisms of addiction.

Olds and Milner (1954), the discoverers of intracranial self-stimulation, argued that the specific brain sites that mediate self-stimulation are those that normally mediate the pleasurable effects of natural rewards (i.e., food, water, and sex). Accordingly, researchers studied the self-stimulation of various brain sites in order to map the neural circuits that mediate the experience of pleasure.

It was initially assumed that intracranial self-stimulation was a unitary phenomenon—that is, that its fundamental properties were the same regardless of the site of stimulation. Most early studies of intracranial self-stimulation involved septal or lateral hypothalamic stimulation because the rates of self-stimulation from these sites are spectacularly high: Rats typically press a lever thousands of times per hour for stimulation of these sites, stopping only when they become exhausted. However, self-stimulation of many other brain structures has been documented.

The mesotelencephalic dopamine system plays an important role in intracranial self-stimulation. The **mesotelencephalic dopamine system** is a system of dopaminergic neurons that projects from the mesencephalon (the midbrain) into various regions of the telencephalon. As Figure 15.7 indicates, the neurons that compose the mesotelencephalic dopamine system have their cell bodies in two midbrain nuclei—the **substantia nigra** and the **ventral tegmental area**. Their axons project to a variety of telencephalic sites, including specific regions of the prefrontal cortex, the limbic cortex, the olfactory tubercle, the amygdala, the septum, the dorsal striatum, and, in particular, the **nucleus accumbens** (a nucleus of the ventral striatum)—see Kringelbach and Berridge (2012).

Most of the axons of dopaminergic neurons that have their cell bodies in the substantia nigra project to the dorsal striatum; this component of the mesotelencephalic dopamine system is called the *nigrostriatal pathway*. It is degeneration in this pathway that is associated with Parkinson's disease (see Chapter 10).

Most of the axons of dopaminergic neurons that have their cell bodies in the ventral tegmental area project to various cortical and limbic sites. This component of the mesotelencephalic dopamine system is called the **mesocorticolimbic pathway**. Although there is some intermingling of the neurons between these two dopaminergic pathways, several pieces of evidence have supported the view that the mesocorticolimbic pathway plays an important

Figure 15.6 A rat pressing a lever to obtain rewarding brain stimulation.

Suspending elastic band

Stimulator delivers electrical stimulation

Lever

Lever press activates stimulator

Stimulator

Figure 15.7 The mesotelencephalic dopamine system in the human brain, consisting of the nigrostriatal pathway (green) and the mesocorticolimbic pathway (red).

(Based on Klivington, 1992.)

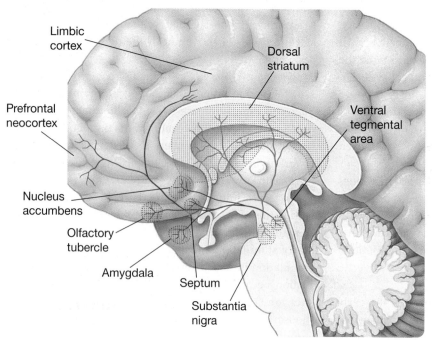

Limbic cortex
Dorsal striatum
Prefrontal neocortex
Ventral tegmental area
Nucleus accumbens
Olfactory tubercle
Amygdala
Septum
Substantia nigra

(see Badiani et al., 2011). These two methods, still in use today, are illustrated in Figure 15.8.

 Evolutionary Perspective What do you think are some of the limitations of using nonhuman animals to study the neural basis of drug addiction?

In the **drug self-administration paradigm**, nonhuman animals press a lever to inject drugs into themselves through implanted *cannulas* (thin tubes). They readily learn to self-administer intravenous injections of drugs to which humans become addicted (see O'Connor et al., 2011). Studies in which microinjections have been self-administered directly into particular brain structures have proved particularly enlightening.

In the **conditioned place-preference paradigm**, nonhuman animals repeatedly receive a drug in one compartment (the *drug compartment*) of a two-compartment box. Then, during the test phase, the drug-free rat is placed in the box, and the proportion of time it spends in the drug compartment, as opposed to the equal-sized but distinctive *control compartment*, is measured. Subjects usually prefer the drug compartment over the control compartment when the drug compartment has been associated with the effects of drugs to which humans become addicted. The main advantage of the conditioned place-preference paradigm is that the subjects are tested while they are drug-free, which means that the measure of the incentive value of a drug is not confounded by other effects the drug might have on behavior.

Experiments that used these methods showed that dopamine played an important role in the rewarding effects of addictive drugs and natural reinforcers. For example, in rats, dopamine antagonists blocked the self-administration of, or the conditioned **Evolutionary Perspective** preference for, several different addictive drugs, and they reduced the reinforcing effects of food. These findings suggested that dopamine signaled something akin to reward value or pleasure.

role in mediating intracranial self-stimulation. The following are four of them:

- Many of the brain sites at which self-stimulation occurs are part of the mesocorticolimbic pathway.
- Intracranial self-stimulation is often associated with an increase in dopamine release in the mesocorticolimbic pathway.
- Dopamine agonists tend to increase intracranial self-stimulation, and dopamine antagonists tend to decrease it.
- Lesions of the mesocorticolimbic pathway tend to disrupt intracranial self-stimulation.

Early Evidence of the Involvement of Dopamine in Drug Addiction

LO 15.16 Describe two methods for measuring the rewarding effects of drugs.

In the 1970s, following much research on the role of dopamine in intracranial self-stimulation, experiments began to implicate dopamine in the rewarding effects of natural reinforcers and addictive drugs (mainly stimu- **Evolutionary Perspective** lants). These experiments, which were largely conducted in nonhumans, used one of two methods for measuring the rewarding effects of drugs: the drug self-administration paradigm and the conditioned place-preference paradigm

Nucleus Accumbens and Drug Addiction

LO 15.17 Explain the role of the nucleus accumbens in drug addiction.

Once evidence had accumulated linking dopamine to natural reinforcers and drug-induced reward, investigators

Figure 15.8 Two behavioral paradigms that are used extensively in the study of the neural mechanisms of addiction: the drug self-administration paradigm and the conditioned place-preference paradigm.

Drug Self-Administration

From infusion pump

The rat presses the lever to self-inject a drug, either into an area of its brain or into general circulation.

Conditioned Place Preference

A rat repeatedly receives a drug in one of two distinctive compartments. Then, on the test, the tendency of the rat, now drug-free, to prefer the drug compartment is assessed.

began to explore particular sites in the mesocorticolimbic dopamine pathway by conducting experiments on laboratory animals. Their findings soon focused attention on the nucleus accumbens. Events occurring in the nucleus accumbens and dopaminergic input to it from the ventral tegmental area appeared to be most clearly related to the experience of reward and pleasure.

The following are four kinds of findings from research on laboratory animals that focused attention on the nucleus accumbens (see Deadwyler et al., 2004; Nestler, 2005; **Evolutionary Perspective** Pierce & Kumaresan, 2006). Most of the early studies focused on stimulants.

- Laboratory animals self-administered microinjections of addictive drugs directly into the nucleus accumbens.

- Microinjections of addictive drugs into the nucleus accumbens produced a conditioned place preference for the compartment in which they were administered.

- Lesions to either the nucleus accumbens or the ventral tegmental area blocked the self-administration of addictive drugs into general circulation or the development of drug-associated conditioned place preferences.

- Both the self-administration of addictive drugs and the experience of natural reinforcers were found to be associated with elevated levels of extracellular dopamine in the nucleus accumbens.

Current Approaches to the Mechanisms of Addiction

The previous module brought us from the beginnings of research on the brain mechanisms of addiction to current research, which will be discussed in this module. Figure 15.9 summarizes the major shifts in thinking about the brain mechanisms of addiction that have occurred over time.

Figure 15.9 shows that two lines of thinking about the brain mechanisms of addiction both had their origins in classic research on drug tolerance and physical dependence. One line developed into physical-dependence theories of addiction, which, though appealing in their simplicity, proved to be inconsistent with the evidence, and these inconsistencies led to the emergence of positive-incentive theories. The positive-incentive approach to addiction, in combination with research on dopamine and intracranial self-stimulation, led to a focus on the mesocorticolimbic pathway and the mechanisms of reward. The second line of thinking about the brain mechanisms of addiction also began with early research on drug tolerance and physical dependence. This line moved ahead with the discovery that drug-associated cues come to elicit conditioned compensatory responses through a Pavlovian conditioning mechanism and that these conditioned responses are largely responsible for functional drug

Figure 15.9 Historic influences that shaped current thinking about the brain mechanisms of addiction.

Why does someone choose to take a drug those first few times? Price and availability of the drug, peer pressure, and prior life experiences are all well-known factors in initial drug taking; however, research has suggested a role for several others.

Experimental studies of drug self-administration in rats have pointed to a variety of factors that facilitate, or protect from, initial drug taking. Food restriction (Carroll & Meisch, 1984), social stress (see Ahmed, 2005), and environmental stress (Ambroggi et al., 2009; Lu et al., 2003) facilitate the acquisition of drug self-administration by rats. In contrast, environmental enrichment (Puhl et al., 2012), social interaction (Raz & Berger, 2010), and access to nondrug reinforcers (Ahmed, Lenoir, & Guillem, 2013) all protect against the acquisition of drug self-administration.

The acquisition of drug self-administration can also be predicted from certain behavioral traits. For example, rats that prefer to drink sweetened water and rats that are more active in a novel environment are both more likely to self-administer cocaine. These two behavioral traits have been likened to *novelty seeking*, a behavioral trait commonly associated with initial drug taking in humans (Wills, Vaccaro, & McNamara, 1994).

When drugs are viewed as tools, or *instruments* (see Müller & Schumann, 2011), the answer to the question of why people start taking them is simple: People first take a drug to determine if it will be useful to them in some way (or to confirm rumors of its usefulness); and their choice to continue taking that drug will depend on whether they find some use in it (Boys & Marsden, 2003). As an example, I (SB) often have a coffee in the morning before driving to campus to ensure that I am alert behind the wheel. In other words, I use caffeine as an instrument to increase my alertness. Other stimulants, and nicotine, are often used for this same reason. Alcohol, in low doses, can be used as an instrument to facilitate social interaction and sexual intercourse (see Patrick & Maggs, 2009). Alcohol is also commonly used as an instrument to relieve stress and anxiety,

tolerance. This finding gained further prominence when researchers discovered that conditioned responses elicited by drug-associated cues were major factors in drug craving and **relapse** (the return to one's drug-taking habit after a period of voluntary abstinence).

These two lines of research together have shaped modern thinking about the brain mechanisms of addiction, but as you can see from Figure 15.9, this was not the end of the story. In this module you will learn about modern approaches to the study of drug addiction.

Three Stages in the Development of an Addiction

LO 15.18 Describe the three stages in the development of a drug addiction.

Modern approaches to drug addiction are increasingly concerned with modeling each of the three stages involved in the development of an addiction: (1) initial drug taking, (2) habitual drug taking, and (3) drug craving and repeated relapse.

INITIAL DRUG TAKING. Not everyone given access to a drug will consume it, and of those that do, many will never take the drug more than once.

Figure 15.10 Three Stages in the Development of an Addiction

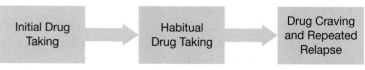

and the same is true for cannabis (Müller & Schumann, 2011). Furthermore, people with medical conditions often take specific drugs to self-medicate. For example, many individuals with schizophrenia use nicotine to alleviate any cognitive impairments and **anhedonia** (a general inability to experience pleasure)—see Rezvani and Levin (2001). Of course, many people use drugs simply for their pleasurable effects (see Hart, 2013).

HABITUAL DRUG TAKING. Habitual drug use, a necessary component of an addiction, is not the inevitable outcome of taking a drug. Many people periodically use addictive drugs and experience their hedonic effects without becoming habitual users (see Badiani et al., 2011). What is responsible for the transition from initial drug taking to habitual drug taking?

Positive-incentive theories of drug addiction have trouble explaining why some users become habitual users and others do not. Another challenge faced by positive-incentive theories is that they are unable to explain why addicted individuals often experience a big discrepancy between the hedonic value (*liking*) and the positive-incentive value (*wanting*) of their preferred drug. **Positive-incentive value** refers specifically to the anticipated pleasure associated with an action (e.g., taking a drug), whereas **hedonic value** refers to the amount of pleasure that is actually experienced. Addicted individuals often report that they are compulsively driven to take their drug by its positive-incentive value (they *want* the drug), although taking the drug is often not as pleasurable as it once was (they no longer *like* the drug)—see Ahmed (2004).

One recent theory of drug addiction, the **incentive-sensitization theory**, is able to explain why some drug users become habitual users and others do not. It is also able to explain the discrepancy between the hedonic value and the positive-incentive value of drug taking in addicted persons (see Berridge, Robinson, & Aldridge, 2009). The central tenet of the incentive-sensitization theory is that the positive-incentive value of addictive drugs increases (i.e., becomes sensitized) with repeated drug use in addiction-prone individuals (see Miles et al., 2004; Robinson & Berridge, 2003). This renders addiction-prone individuals highly motivated to seek and consume the drug. A key point of the incentive-sensitization theory is that it isn't the pleasure (*liking*) of taking the drug that is the basis of habitual drug use and addiction; it is the anticipated pleasure of drug taking (i.e., the drug's positive-incentive value)—the *wanting* or *craving* for the drug. Initially, a drug's positive-incentive value is closely tied to its pleasurable effects; but tolerance often develops to the pleasurable effects, whereas the drug-addicted individuals craving for the drug is sensitized. Thus, in drug-addicted individuals, the positive-incentive value of the drug is often out of proportion with the pleasure actually derived from it: Many

addicted individuals are miserable, their lives are in ruin, and the drug effects are not that great anymore; but they crave the drug more than ever.

Inspired by this important distinction between the wanting (positive-incentive value) vs. liking (hedonic value) of a drug, researchers have been trying to identify the brain circuitry responsible for each. There is now general agreement that there are differences in the circuitry for wanting vs. liking, and that dopamine release in the nucleus accumbens (via the mesocorticolimbic pathway) is more closely associated with the wanting of a drug, rather than the liking of it (see Berridge & Kringelbach, 2015; Kringelbach & Berridge, 2012). For example, studies have shown that neutral stimuli that signal the impending delivery of a reward (e.g., food or an addictive drug) are sufficient to trigger dopamine release in the nucleus accumbens (see Floresco, 2015). Researchers are still determining the brain circuitry responsible for the liking of a drug, but we do know that dopamine is less important for this aspect of drug taking than was once believed and that the structures involved only partially overlap with those that mediate the wanting of a drug (see Kringelbach & Berridge, 2012; Liu et al., 2011).

Several changes in brain function have been associated with the transition from initial drug taking to habitual drug taking. First, there is a difference in how the striatum of drug-addicted individuals reacts to drugs and drug-associated cues. In addicted individuals, striatal control of drug taking is shifted from the nucleus accumbens (i.e., the ventral striatum) to the dorsal striatum (Pierce & Vanderschuren, 2010), an area that is known to play a role in habit formation and retention (see Chapter 11). Also, at the same time, there are impairments in the function of the prefrontal cortex, which likely relates to the loss of self-control that accompanies addiction (George & Koob, 2010; Goldstein & Volkow, 2011; Volkow & Warren, 2011). It was originally believed that these brain differences merely accompanied the transition to habitual drug taking, but Ersche and colleagues (2012) showed that these differences predispose an individual to that transition (Volkow & Baler, 2012).

There has been a growing appreciation that drug addiction is a specific expression of a more general behavioral problem: the inability to refrain from a behavior despite its adverse effects. Addicted individuals have been found to make poor decisions, to engage in excessive risk taking, and to have deficits in self-control (see Volkow et al., 2013). These behavioral problems are not limited to drug-addicted individuals. A lot of attention has recently been paid to overeating, compulsive gambling, kleptomania (compulsive shoplifting), and compulsive shopping as addictive behaviors (see Jabr, 2013; Potenza, 2015; Robbins & Clark, 2015).

Another change that habitual drug users often experience is *anhedonia* (a general inability to experience pleasure in response to natural reinforcers)—see Ahmed (2005); Robbins

(2016). Those things that most of us find pleasurable (e.g., sex, eating, sleeping) are often less pleasurable to the habitual drug user. This devaluation of natural reinforcers poses a major problem for the treatment of addiction because it persists even after stopping the drug. Without the experience of pleasure from natural reinforcers, many abstinent drug users experience craving for their drug and then relapse.

DRUG CRAVING AND ADDICTION RELAPSE. Addiction is not necessarily a life sentence; many addicted individuals successfully treat their addiction by either stopping or reducing their drug intake (see Klingemann, Sobell, & Sobell, 2009). Others manage to stop or reduce their drug intake with the help of a treatment program. However, weeks, months, or even years later, some abstainers may experience

Clinical Implications drug craving. Such craving can lead to a relapse. This propensity to relapse, even after a long period of voluntary abstinence, is a hallmark of addiction. Thus, understanding the causes of relapse is one key to understanding addiction and its treatment.

Three different causes of relapse in addicted individuals have been identified (see Badiani et al., 2011; Pickens et al., 2011):

- Many therapists and patients point to stress as a major factor in relapse. The impact of stress on drug taking was illustrated in a dramatic fashion by the marked increases in cigarette, alcohol, and marijuana consumption by New Yorkers following the terrorist attacks of September 11, 2001 (see Vlahov et al., 2004).

- **Drug priming** (a single exposure to the formerly misused drug) is another cause of relapse. Many addicted individuals who have managed to abstain feel they have their addiction under control. Reassured by this feeling, they sample their addictive drug just once and are immediately plunged back into full-blown addiction.

- Exposure to cues (e.g., people, times, places, or objects) that have previously been associated with drug taking has been shown to precipitate relapse (see Milton & Everitt, 2012; Steketee & Kalivas, 2011). The fact that the many U.S. soldiers who became addicted to heroin while fighting in the Vietnam War easily shed their addiction when they returned home has been attributed to removal from their drug-associated environment.

Explanation of the effects of drug-associated cues on relapse is related to our discussion of conditioned drug tolerance earlier in the chapter. You may recall from earlier in this chapter that cues that predict drug exposure come to elicit conditioned compensatory responses through a Pavlovian conditioning mechanism, and because conditioned compensatory responses are usually opposite to the original drug effects, they produce tolerance. The point here is that conditioned compensatory responses seem to increase craving in abstinent drug-addicted individuals

and, in so doing, trigger relapse. Indeed, just thinking about a drug is enough to induce craving and relapse.

It turns out that exactly when a drug-associated cue is presented is an important determinant of its effects: Cues presented soon after drug withdrawal are less likely to elicit craving and relapse than cues presented later. This time-dependent increase in cue-induced drug craving and relapse is known as the **incubation of drug craving** (Pickens et al., 2011). This phenomenon is illustrated in Figure 15.11. Notice in Figure 15.11 that shortly after cocaine withdrawal a drug-associated cue elicited few presses to a lever that had always delivered drug before withdrawal. However, as time passed, there was a gradual increase in lever pressing in response to presentations of a drug-associated cue. In addition to cocaine, the incubation of drug craving has also been demonstrated with heroin, methamphetamine, alcohol, and nicotine (see Pickens et al., 2011). This important phenomenon may help explain why some individuals who have seemingly recovered from an addiction, experience craving and relapse even after years of abstinence (Bedi et al., 2011).

The animal literature on drug self-administration has suggested two additional factors that may play a role in drug craving and relapse. First, environmental enrichment after drug withdrawal has reduced cue- and stress-induced, but not drug-priming-induced, relapse of drug self-administration (Chauvet et al., 2009, 2012). Second, even a few brief exposures to nondrug reinforcers can reliably reduce relapse of cocaine self-administration (e.g., Liu & Grigson, 2005; Quick et al., 2011). Perhaps the best way of preventing

Figure 15.11 Incubation of cocaine craving in rats that were previously self-administering cocaine. After cocaine withdrawal, there was a time-dependent increase in the number of lever presses the rats made in response to a drug-associated cue.

Data redrawn from Pickens et al. (2011).

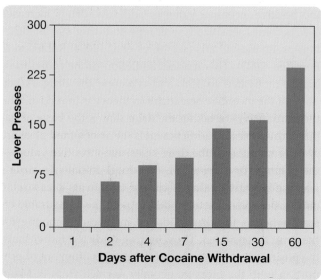

relapse in recovered drug-addicted individuals is to improve their opportunities and surroundings. Indeed, such interventions have proven successful (e.g., Cao et al., 2011; Dutra et al., 2008; Friedmann et al., 2004).

Current Concerns about the Drug Self-Administration Paradigm

LO 15.19 Describe two sets of findings that have challenged the relevance of drug self-administration studies.

Much of what we now know about the neurobiology of drug addiction has been derived from animal studies of drug self-administration. Two sets of recent findings have challenged the relevance of drug self-administration studies and have opened new avenues of research.

UNNATURAL HOUSING AND TESTING CONDITIONS. In conventional drug self-administration studies, rats are housed individually and tested in a barren test chamber where the only rewarding thing they can do is press a lever for a drug injection (see Figure 15.8). What would happen

if the rats had more natural housing and testing conditions? When rats were either group housed (Raz & Berger, 2010), given access to enriched environments (Nader et al., 2008; Solinas et al., 2010), provided with the opportunity to obtain nondrug reinforcers (Ahmed, 2010, 2012), or housed in a large naturalistic environment (Alexander et al., 1981), they were much less likely to self-administer drugs. For example, only 10 percent of rats given a choice between consuming sucrose and self-administering cocaine displayed a preference for the cocaine (Lenoir et al., 2007).

The finding that more naturalistic housing and testing conditions reduce drug self-administration has led some researchers to question the relevance of conventional drug self-administration research to human addiction (Ahmed,

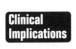

Lenoir, & Guillem, 2013). However, when viewed another way, these findings suggest that human drug addiction might be prevented by improving the environment and life choices of those most vulnerable to addiction.

> **Clinical Implications**
> If you could change those policies related to how we treat drug-addicted individuals, what would be the first thing you would change?

EXCESSIVE FOCUS ON STIMULANTS. It has long been assumed that the mechanisms of addiction are independent of the specific addictive drug. Thus, there has been little concern over the specific drug used in studies of addiction (see Badiani et al., 2011). Indeed, most drug self-administration studies have been done with stimulants,

and most biopsychological theories of drug addiction have been built on the results of such studies.

Research on the self-administration of stimulants has led to two major conclusions about the mechanisms of drug addiction: (1) that all addictive drugs activate the mesocorticolimbic pathway and (2) that dopamine is important for the reinforcing properties of all addictive drugs. However, studies of opioid **Thinking Creatively** self-administration have led to different conclusions (see Nutt et al., 2015). For example, although mesocorticolimbic pathway lesions or dopamine antagonists disrupt habitual cocaine self-administration, they did not disrupt habitual heroin self-administration (see Badiani et al., 2011).

A Noteworthy Case of Addiction

LO 15.20 Explain the significance of the case of Sigmund Freud.

To illustrate in a more personal way some of the things you have learned about addiction, this chapter concludes with a case study of one drug-addicted individual: Sigmund Freud, a man of great significance to psychology.

Freud's case is particularly important for two reasons. First, it shows that nobody, no matter how powerful their intellect, is immune to the addictive effects of drugs.

Second, it allows comparisons between the two addictive drugs with which Freud had problems.

The Case of Sigmund Freud

In 1883, a German army physician prescribed cocaine, which had recently been isolated, to Bavarian soldiers to help them deal with the demands of military maneuvers. **Clinical Implications** When Freud read about this, he decided to procure some of the drug.

In addition to taking cocaine himself, Freud pressed it on his friends and associates, both for themselves and for their patients. He even sent some to his fiancée. In short, by today's standards, Freud was a public menace.

Freud's famous essay "Song of Praise" was about cocaine and was published in July 1884. Freud wrote in such glowing terms about his own personal experiences with cocaine that he created a wave of interest in the drug. But within a year, there was a critical reaction to Freud's premature advocacy of the drug. As evidence accumulated that cocaine was highly addictive and produced a psychosis-like state at high doses, so too did published criticisms of Freud.

Freud continued to praise cocaine until the summer of 1887, but soon thereafter he suddenly stopped all use of cocaine—both personally and professionally. Despite the fact that he had used cocaine for 3 years, he seems to have had no difficulty stopping.

Some 7 years later, in 1894, when Freud was 38, his physician and close friend ordered him to stop smoking because it was causing a heart arrhythmia. Freud was a heavy smoker; he smoked approximately 20 cigars per day.

Freud did stop smoking, but 7 weeks later he started again. On another occasion, Freud stopped for 14 months, but at the age of 58, he was still smoking 20 cigars a day—and still struggling against his addiction. He wrote to friends that smoking was adversely affecting his heart and making it difficult for him to work...yet he kept smoking.

In 1923, at the age of 67, Freud developed sores in his mouth. They were cancerous. When he was recovering from oral surgery, he wrote to a friend that smoking was the cause of his cancer...yet he kept smoking.

In addition to the cancer, Freud began to experience severe heart pains (tobacco angina) whenever he smoked...still he kept smoking.

At 73, Freud was hospitalized for his heart condition and stopped smoking. He made an immediate recovery. But 23 days later, he started to smoke again.

In 1936, at the age of 79, Freud was experiencing more heart trouble, and he had had 33 operations to deal with his recurring oral cancer. His jaw had been entirely removed and replaced by an artificial one. He was in constant pain, and he could swallow, chew, and talk only with difficulty...yet he kept smoking.

Freud died of cancer in 1939 (see Sheth, Bhagwate, & Sharma, 2005).

Themes Revisited

Two of this text's themes—thinking creatively and clinical implications—received strong emphasis in this chapter because they are integral to its major objective: to sharpen your thinking about the effects of addiction on people's health. You were repeatedly challenged to think about drug addiction in ways that may have been new to you but are more consistent with the evidence.

The evolutionary perspective theme was also highlighted frequently in this chapter, largely because of the nature of biopsychological research into drug addiction.

Because of the risks associated with the administration of addictive drugs and the direct manipulation of brain structures, the majority of biopsychological studies of drug addiction involve nonhumans—mostly rats and monkeys. Also, in studying the neu- ral mechanisms of addiction, there is a need to maintain an evolutionary perspective. It is important not to lose sight of the fact that brain mechanisms did not evolve to support addiction; they evolved to serve natural adaptive functions and have somehow been co-opted by addictive drugs.

Key Terms

Chapter 16
Lateralization, Language, and the Split Brain

The Left Brain and Right Brain

⌄ Chapter Overview and Learning Objectives (LOs)

Cerebral Lateralization of Function: Introduction	**LO 16.1**	Summarize early studies of the cerebral lateralization of function.
	LO 16.2	Describe three techniques for assessing cerebral lateralization of function.
	LO 16.3	Outline the discovery of the relationship between speech laterality and handedness.
	LO 16.4	Describe and evaluate the hypothesis that male brains are more lateralized than female brains.
The Split Brain	**LO 16.5**	Outline the groundbreaking experiment of Myers and Sperry on split-brain cats.
	LO 16.6	Describe the method used to demonstrate the hemispheric independence of visual experience in human split-brain patients.

LO 16.7 Describe the evidence that indicates that the hemispheres of split-brain patients can function independently.

LO 16.8 Outline the process of cross-cuing in split-brain patients.

LO 16.9 Describe the helping-hand phenomenon and the use of the chimeric figures test in experiments on split-brain patients.

LO 16.10 Explain the Z lens and how it was used to study split-brain patients.

LO 16.11 Describe a case where the right hemisphere tried to take control of a split-brain patient's everyday behavior.

LO 16.12 Explain how complete hemispheric independence is not an inevitable consequence of split-brain surgery.

Differences between Left and Right Hemispheres

LO 16.13 Describe five examples of abilities that have been found to be lateralized, and explain what is meant by the "left hemisphere interpreter."

LO 16.14 Discuss how we've come to understand that the lateralization of function is better understood in terms of individual cognitive processes rather than clusters of abilities.

LO 16.15 Describe three anatomical asymmetries in the human brain.

Evolutionary Perspective of Cerebral Lateralization and Language

LO 16.16 Describe and evaluate three theoretical explanations for why cerebral lateralization of function evolved.

LO 16.17 Outline how cerebral lateralization evolved.

LO 16.18 List two survival advantages of cerebral lateralization.

LO 16.19 Describe what the study of nonhuman primates has suggested about the evolution of human language.

Cortical Localization of Language: Wernicke-Geschwind Model

LO 16.20 Describe the historical antecedents of the Wernicke-Geschwind model. Include descriptions of the following disorders: Broca's and Wernicke's aphasia, conduction aphasia, agraphia, and alexia.

LO 16.21 Describe the Wernicke-Geschwind model.

Wernicke-Geschwind Model: The Evidence

LO 16.22 Identify the effects of cortical damage and brain stimulation on language abilities, and evaluate the Wernicke-Geschwind model in light of these findings.

LO 16.23 Summarize the current status of the Wernicke-Geschwind model.

Cognitive Neuroscience of Language

LO 16.24 Describe the three premises that define the cognitive neuroscience approach to language, and compare them with the premises on which the Wernicke-Geschwind model is based.

LO 16.25 Describe two influential functional imaging studies of the localization of language, and explain what their findings indicate.

Cognitive Neuroscience of Dyslexia

LO 16.26 Describe the causes and neural mechanisms of developmental dyslexia.

LO 16.27 Describe research that helped discredit the notion that dyslexia could not be a brain disorder because it is influenced by culture.

LO 16.28 Describe the difference between the lexical procedure and the phonetic procedure for reading aloud. Then describe the difference between surface dyslexia and deep dyslexia.

With the exception of a few midline orifices, we humans have two of almost everything—one on the left and one on the right. Even the brain, which most people view as the unitary and indivisible basis of self, reflects this general principle of bilateral duplication. In its upper reaches, the brain comprises two structures—the left and right cerebral hemispheres—which are entirely separate except for the **cerebral commissures** connecting them. The fundamental duality of the human forebrain and the locations of the cerebral commissures are illustrated in Figure 16.1.

Although the left and right hemispheres are similar in appearance, there are major differences between them in function. This chapter is about these differences, a topic commonly referred to as **lateralization of function**. The study of **split-brain patients**—patients whose left and right hemispheres have been separated by **commissurotomy**—is a major focus of discussion. Another focus is the cortical localization of language abilities in the left hemisphere; language abilities are the most highly lateralized of all cognitive abilities.

You will learn in this chapter that your left and right hemispheres have different abilities and that they have the capacity to function independently—to have different thoughts, memories, and emotions. Thus, this chapter will challenge the concept you have of yourself as a unitary being. We hope you both enjoy it.

Figure 16.1 The cerebral hemispheres and cerebral commissures.

Frontal section of the human brain, which illustrates the fundamental duality of the human forebrain.

Midsagittal section of the human brain, which illustrates the corpus callosum and other commissures.

Cerebral Lateralization of Function: Introduction

In 1836, Marc Dax, an unknown country doctor, presented a short report at a medical society meeting in France. It was his first and only scientific presentation. Dax was struck by the fact that of the 40 or so brain-damaged patients with speech problems whom he had seen during his career, not a single one had damage restricted to the right hemisphere. His report aroused little interest, and Dax died the following year unaware that he had anticipated one of the most important areas of modern neuropsychological research.

Discovery of the Specific Contributions of Left-Hemisphere Damage to Aphasia and Apraxia

LO 16.1 Summarize early studies of the cerebral lateralization of function.

One reason Dax's important paper had so little impact was that most of his contemporaries believed that the brain acted as a whole and that specific functions could not be attributed to particular parts of it. This view began to change 25 years later in 1861, when Paul Broca reported his post-mortem examination of two aphasic patients. **Aphasia** is a brain damage–produced deficit in the ability to produce or comprehend language.

Both of Broca's patients had a left-hemisphere lesion that involved an area in the frontal cortex just in front of the

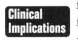 **Clinical Implications**

face area of the primary motor cortex. Broca at first did not recognize the relation between aphasia and the side of the brain damage; he did not know about Dax's report. However, by 1864, Broca had performed postmortem examinations on seven more aphasic patients, and he was struck by the fact that, like the first two, they all had damage to the *inferior prefrontal cortex* of the left hemisphere—which by then had become known as **Broca's area** (see Figure 16.2).

In the early 1900s, another example of *cerebral lateralization of function* was discovered. Hugo-Karl Liepmann found that **apraxia**, like aphasia, is almost always associated with left-hemisphere damage, despite the fact that its

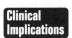 **Clinical Implications**

symptoms are *bilateral* (involving both sides of the body). Apraxic patients have difficulty performing movements when asked to perform them out of context, even though they often have no difficulty performing the same movements when they are not thinking about doing so (see Chapter 8).

The combined impact of the evidence that the left hemisphere plays a special role in both language and voluntary movement led to the theory of *cerebral dominance*. According

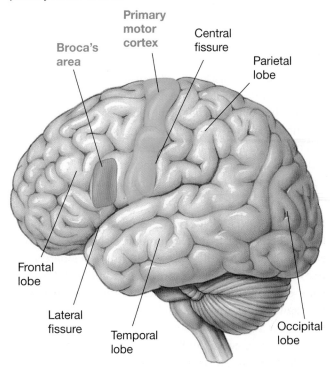

Figure 16.2 The location of Broca's area: in the inferior left prefrontal cortex, just anterior to the face area of the left primary motor cortex.

to this theory, one hemisphere—usually the left—assumes the dominant role in the control of all complex behavioral and cognitive processes, and the other plays only a minor role. This thinking led to the practice of referring to the left hemisphere as the **dominant hemisphere** and the right hemisphere as the **minor hemisphere**.

In addition, the discovery that language and motor abilities are lateralized to the left hemisphere triggered a search for other lateralized functions. In effect, the discovery of language and motor lateralization established *lateralization of function* as a major area of neuroscientific research.

Tests of Cerebral Lateralization

LO 16.2 Describe three techniques for assessing cerebral lateralization of function.

Early research on the cerebral lateralization of function compared the effects of left-hemisphere and right-hemisphere lesions. Now, however, other techniques are also used for this purpose. The sodium amytal test, the dichotic listening test, and functional brain imaging are three of them.

SODIUM AMYTAL TEST. The **sodium amytal test** of language lateralization (Wada, 1949) is often given to patients prior to neurosurgery (see Bauer et al., 2014). The neurosurgeon uses the results of the test to plan the surgery; every effort is made to avoid damaging areas of the cortex that are likely to be involved in language. The sodium amytal test involves the injection of a small amount of sodium amytal into the carotid artery on one side of the neck. The injection anesthetizes the hemisphere on that side for a few minutes, thus allowing the capacities of the other hemisphere to be assessed. During the test, the patient is asked to recite well-known series (e.g., letters of the alphabet, days of the week, months of the year) and to name pictures of common objects. Then, an injection is administered to the other side, and the test is repeated. When the hemisphere specialized for speech, usually the left hemisphere, is anesthetized, the patient is rendered completely mute for a minute or two; and once the ability to talk returns, there are errors of serial order and naming. In contrast, when the other hemisphere, usually the right, is anesthetized, mutism often does not occur at all, and errors are few.

DICHOTIC LISTENING TEST. Unlike the sodium amytal test, the **dichotic listening test** is noninvasive; thus, it can be administered to healthy individuals. In the standard dichotic listening test (see Blass et al., 2015; Kimura, 2011), three pairs of spoken digits are presented through earphones; the digits of each pair are presented simultaneously, one to each ear. For example, a person might hear the sequence *3, 9, 2* through one ear and at the same time *1, 6, 4* through the other. The person is then asked to report all of the digits. Kimura found that most people report slightly more of the digits presented to the right ear than the left, which is indicative of left-hemisphere specialization for language. In contrast, Kimura found that all the patients who had been identified by the sodium amytal test as having right-hemisphere specialization for language performed better with the left ear than the right. Kimura argued that although the sounds from each ear are projected to both hemispheres, the contralateral connections are stronger and take precedence when two different sounds are simultaneously competing for access to the same cortical auditory centers.

FUNCTIONAL BRAIN IMAGING. Lateralization of function has also been studied using functional brain-imaging techniques. While a volunteer engages in some activity, such as reading, the activity of the brain is monitored by positron emission tomography (PET) or functional magnetic resonance imaging (fMRI). On language tests, functional brain-imaging techniques typically reveal far greater activity in the left hemisphere than in the right hemisphere (see Bauer et al., 2014; Vigneau et al., 2011).

Discovery of the Relation between Speech Laterality and Handedness

LO 16.3 Outline the discovery of the relationship between speech laterality and handedness.

Lesion studies have clarified the relation between the cerebral lateralization of speech and handedness. For example, one study involved military personnel who suffered brain damage in World War II (Russell & Espir, 1961), and another focused on neurological patients who underwent unilateral excisions for the treatment of neurological disorders (Penfield & Roberts, 1959). In both studies, approximately 60 percent of **dextrals** (right-handers) with left-hemisphere lesions and 2 percent of those with right-hemisphere lesions were diagnosed as aphasic; the comparable figures for **sinestrals** (left-handers) were about 30 and 24 percent, respectively. These results indicate that the left hemisphere is dominant for language-related abilities in almost all dextrals and in the majority of sinestrals. In effect, sinestrals are more variable (less predictable) than dextrals with respect to their hemisphere of language lateralization. This increased variability also holds for other aspects of brain function; for example, sinestrals show greater variability in their lateralization of certain aspects of visual system function (see Willems, Peelen, & Hagoort, 2010).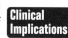

Results of the sodium amytal test have confirmed the relation between handedness and language lateralization that was first observed in early lesion studies. For example, Milner (1974) found that almost all right-handed patients without early left-hemisphere damage had left-hemisphere specialization for speech (92 percent), most left-handed and ambidextrous patients without early left-hemisphere damage had left-hemisphere specialization for speech (69 percent), and early left-hemisphere damage decreased left-hemisphere specialization for speech in left-handed and ambidextrous patients (30 percent).

Sex Differences in Brain Lateralization

LO 16.4 Describe and evaluate the hypothesis that male brains are more lateralized than female brains.

Interest in the possibility that the brains of females and males differ in their degree of lateralization was stimulated by McGlone's (1977, 1980) observation that male victims of unilateral strokes were three times more likely to suffer from aphasia than female victims. McGlone concluded that male brains are more lateralized than female brains.

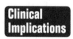 What other clinical implications might this observed sex difference in brain lateralization have?

McGlone's hypothesis of a sex difference in brain lateralization has been widely embraced, and it has been used to explain almost every imaginable behavioral difference between the sexes. But support for McGlone's hypothesis has been mixed. Some researchers have failed to confirm her report of a sex difference in the effects of unilateral brain lesions (see Inglis & Lawson, 1982). Even more problematic, a meta-analysis of 14 functional brain-imaging studies did not find a significant effect of sex on language lateralization (Sommer et al., 2004).

In this module, you have been introduced to early research on the lateralization of function, and you learned about four methods of studying cerebral lateralization of function: comparing the effects of unilateral left- and right-hemisphere brain lesions, the sodium amytal test, the dichotic listening test, and functional brain imaging. The next module focuses on a fifth method.

The Split Brain

In the early 1950s, the **corpus callosum**—the largest cerebral commissure—constituted a paradox of major proportions. Its size, an estimated 200 million axons, and its central position, right between the two cerebral hemispheres, implied that it performed an extremely important function; yet research in the 1930s and 1940s seemed to suggest that it did nothing at all. The corpus callosum had been cut in monkeys and in several other laboratory species, but the animals seemed no different after the surgery than they had been before. Similarly, human patients who were born without a corpus callosum or had it damaged seemed quite normal. In the early 1950s, Roger Sperry, whom you may remember for the eye-rotation experiments described in Chapter 9, and his colleagues were intrigued by this paradox.

Groundbreaking Experiment of Myers and Sperry

LO 16.5 Outline the groundbreaking experiment of Myers and Sperry on split-brain cats.

The solution to the puzzle of the corpus callosum was provided in 1953 by an experiment on cats by Myers and Sperry. The experiment made **Evolutionary Perspective** two astounding theoretical points. First, it showed that one function of the corpus callosum is to transfer learned information from one hemisphere to the other. Second, it showed that when the corpus

callosum is cut, each hemisphere can function independently; each split-brain cat appeared to have two brains. If you find the thought of a cat with two brains provocative, you will almost certainly be bowled over by similar observations about split-brain humans. But we are getting ahead of ourselves. Let's first consider the research on cats.

In their experiment, Myers and Sperry trained cats to perform a simple visual discrimination task. On each trial, each cat was confronted by two panels, one with a circle on it and one with a square on it. The relative positions of the circle and square (right or left) were varied randomly from trial to trial, and the cats had to learn which symbol to press in order to get a food reward. Myers and Sperry correctly surmised that the key to split-brain research was to develop procedures for teaching and testing one hemisphere at a time. Figure 16.3 illustrates the method they used to isolate visual-discrimination learning in one hemisphere of the cats. There are two routes by which visual information can cross from one eye to the contralateral hemisphere: via the corpus callosum or via the optic chiasm. Accordingly, in their key experimental group, Myers and Sperry *transected* (cut completely through) both the optic chiasm and the corpus callosum of each cat and put a patch on one eye. This restricted all incoming visual information to the hemisphere ipsilateral to the uncovered eye.

The results of Myers and Sperry's experiment are illustrated in Figure 16.4. In the first phase of the study, all cats learned the task with a patch on one eye. The cats

Figure 16.3 Restricting visual information to one hemisphere in cats. To restrict visual information to one hemisphere, Myers and Sperry (1) cut the corpus callosum, (2) cut the optic chiasm, and (3) blindfolded one eye. This restricted the visual information to the hemisphere ipsilateral to the uncovered eye.

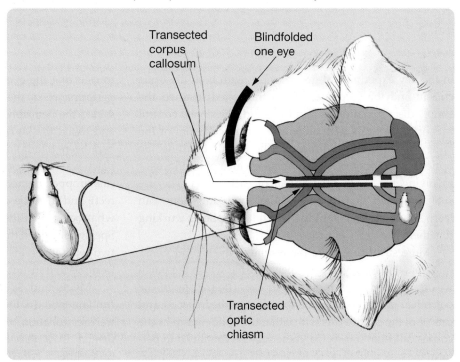

Figure 16.4 Schematic illustration of Myers and Sperry's (1953) groundbreaking split-brain experiment. There were four groups: (1) the key experimental group with both the optic chiasm and corpus callosum transected, (2) a control group with only the optic chiasm transected, (3) a control group with only the corpus callosum transected, and (4) an unlesioned control group. The performance of the three control groups did not differ, so they are illustrated together here.

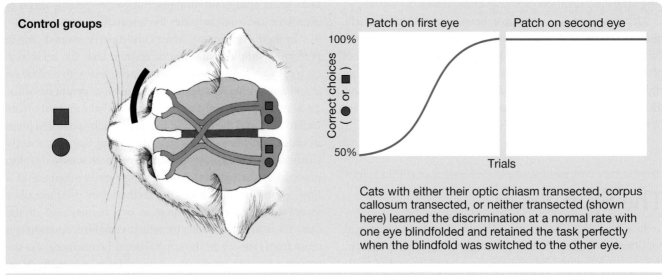

Control groups

Patch on first eye | Patch on second eye

Cats with either their optic chiasm transected, corpus callosum transected, or neither transected (shown here) learned the discrimination at a normal rate with one eye blindfolded and retained the task perfectly when the blindfold was switched to the other eye.

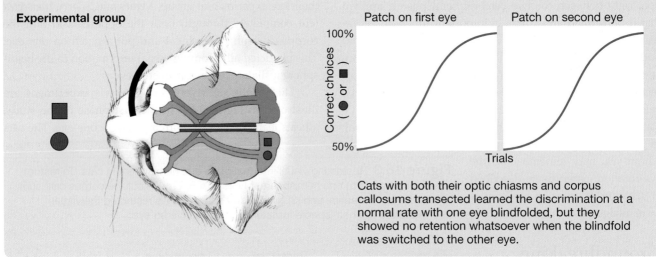

Experimental group

Patch on first eye | Patch on second eye

Cats with both their optic chiasms and corpus callosums transected learned the discrimination at a normal rate with one eye blindfolded, but they showed no retention whatsoever when the blindfold was switched to the other eye.

in the key experimental group (those with both the optic chiasm and the corpus callosum transected) learned the simple discrimination as rapidly as did unlesioned control cats or control cats with either the corpus callosum or the optic chiasm transected, despite the fact that cutting the optic chiasm produced a **scotoma**—an area of blindness—involving the entire medial half of each retina. This result suggested that one hemisphere working alone can learn simple tasks as rapidly as two hemispheres working together.

More surprising were the results of the second phase of Myers and Sperry's experiment, during which the patch was transferred to each cat's other eye. The transfer of the patch had no effect on the performance of the intact control cats or of the control cats with either the optic chiasm or the corpus callosum transected; these subjects continued to perform the task with close to 100 percent accuracy. In contrast,

transferring the eye patch had a devastating effect on the performance of the experimental cats. In effect, it blindfolded the hemisphere that had originally learned the task and tested the knowledge of the other hemisphere, which had been blindfolded during initial training. When the patch was transferred, the performance of the experimental cats dropped immediately to baseline (i.e., to 50 percent correct); and then the cats relearned the task with no savings whatsoever, as if they had never seen it before. Myers and Sperry concluded that the cat brain has the capacity to act as two separate brains and that the function of the corpus callosum is to transmit information between them.

Myers and Sperry's startling conclusions about the fundamental duality of the cat brain and the information-transfer function of the corpus callosum have been confirmed in a variety of species with a variety of test procedures. For example, split-brain monkeys cannot perform tasks requiring fine tactual discriminations (e.g., rough versus smooth) or fine motor responses (e.g., unlocking a puzzle) with one hand if they have learned them with the other—provided they are not allowed to watch their hands, which would allow the information to enter both hemispheres. This failure of intermanual transfer of fine tactual and motor information in split-brain monkeys occurs because the somatosensory and motor fibers involved in fine sensory and motor discriminations are all contralateral and because the hemispheres have lost their ability to communicate directly.

Commissurotomy in Human's with Epilepsy

LO 16.6 **Describe the method used to demonstrate the hemispheric independence of visual experience in human split-brain patients.**

In the first half of the 20th century, when the normal function of the corpus callosum was still a mystery, it was known that epileptic discharges often spread from one hemisphere to the other through the corpus callosum. This, along with the fact that cutting the corpus callosum had proven in numerous studies to have no obvious effect on performance outside the contrived conditions of Sperry's laboratory, led two neurosurgeons, Vogel and Bogen, to initiate a program of commissurotomy for the treatment of severe intractable cases of epilepsy—despite the fact that a previous similar attempt had failed, presumably because of incomplete transections 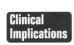 (Van Wagenen & Herren, 1940). The rationale underlying therapeutic commissurotomy— which typically involves transecting the corpus callosum and leaving the smaller commissures intact—was that the severity of the patient's convulsions might be reduced if the discharges could be limited to the hemisphere of their origin. The therapeutic benefits of commissurotomy turned out to be even greater than anticipated: Despite the fact that commissurotomy is performed in only the most severe cases, many commissurotomized patients do not experience another major convulsion.

 The decision to perform commissurotomies on patients with epilepsy turned out to be a good one. In Chapter 1, you learned that the decision to perform prefrontal lobotomies on patients with mental illness turned out to be a bad one. Was this just the luck of the draw? (Hint: Make one list for commissurotomy, and one list for prefrontal lobotomy, of the evidence for and against each that existed when they were first adopted.)

Evaluation of the neuropsychological status of Vogel and Bogen's split-brain patients was conducted by Sperry and his associate Gazzaniga, and this work was a major factor in Sperry receiving a Nobel Prize in 1981 (see Table 1.1). Sperry and Gazzaniga began by developing a battery of tests based on the same methodological strategy that had proved so informative in Sperry's studies of laboratory animals: delivering information to one hemisphere while keeping it out of the other (see Gazzaniga, 2005; Uddin, 2011).

They could not use the same visual-discrimination procedure that had been used in studies of split-brain laboratory animals (i.e., cutting the optic chiasm and blindfolding one eye) because cutting the optic chiasm produces a scotoma. Instead, they employed the procedure illustrated in Figure 16.5. Each split-brain patient was asked to fixate on the center of a display screen; then, visual stimuli were flashed onto the left or right side of the screen for 0.1 second. The 0.1-second exposure time was long enough for the subjects to perceive the stimuli but short enough to preclude the confounding effects of eye movement. All stimuli thus presented in the left visual field were transmitted to the right visual cortex, and all stimuli thus presented in the right visual field were transmitted to the left visual cortex.

Fine tactual and motor tasks were performed by each hand under a ledge. This procedure was used so that the nonperforming hemisphere—that is, the ipsilateral hemisphere—could not monitor the performance via the visual system.

The results of the tests on split-brain patients have confirmed the findings in split-brain laboratory animals in one major respect but not in another. Like split-brain laboratory animals, human split-brain patients seem to have in some respects two independent brains, each with its own stream of consciousness, abilities, memories, and emotions (e.g., Gazzaniga, 1967; Gazzaniga & Sperry, 1967; Sperry, 1964). But unlike the hemispheres of split-brain laboratory animals, the hemispheres of split-brain patients are far from equal in their ability to perform certain tasks. Most notably, the left hemisphere of most split-brain patients is capable of speech, whereas the right hemisphere is not.

Before we recount some of the key results of the tests on split-brain humans, let us give you some advice. Some students become confused by the results of these tests because their tendency to think of the human brain as a single unitary organ is deeply engrained. If you become confused, think of each split-brain patient as two separate individuals: Ms. or Mr. Right Hemisphere, who understands a few simple instructions but cannot speak, who receives sensory information from the left visual field and left hand, and who controls the fine motor responses of the left hand; and Ms. or Mr. Left Hemisphere, who is verbally adept, who receives sensory information from the right visual field and right hand, and who controls the fine motor responses

Figure 16.5 The testing procedure used to evaluate the neuropsychological status of split-brain patients. Visual input goes from each visual field to the contralateral hemisphere; fine tactile input goes from each hand to the contralateral hemisphere; and each hemisphere controls the fine motor movements of the contralateral hand.

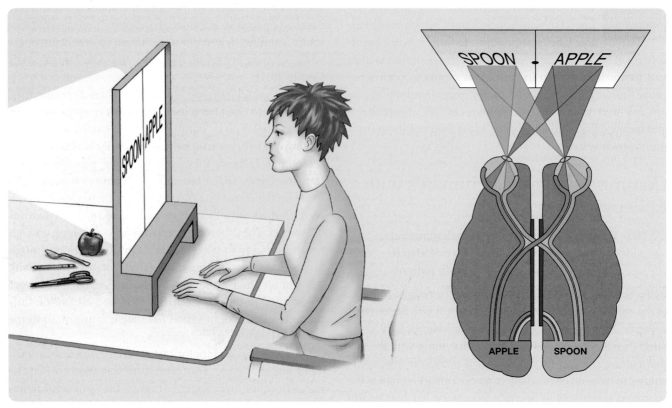

of the right hand. In everyday life, the behavior of split-brain patients is reasonably normal because their two brains go through life together and acquire much of the same information; however, in the neuropsychological laboratory, major discrepancies in what the two hemispheres learn can be created. As you are about to find out, this situation has interesting consequences.

Evidence That the Hemispheres of Split-Brain Patients Can Function Independently

LO 16.7 Describe the evidence that indicates that the hemispheres of split-brain patients can function independently.

If a picture of an apple were flashed in the right visual field of a split-brain patient, the left hemisphere could do one of two things to indicate that it had received and stored the information. Because it is the hemisphere that speaks, the left hemisphere could simply tell the experimenter that it saw a picture of an apple. Or the patient could reach under a ledge with the right hand, feel the test objects, and pick out the apple. Similarly, if the apple were presented to the left hemisphere by being placed in the patient's right hand, the left hemisphere could indicate to the experimenter

that it was an apple either by saying so or by putting the apple down and picking out another apple with the right hand from the test objects under the ledge. If, however, the nonspeaking right hemisphere were asked to indicate the identity of an object that had previously been presented to the left hemisphere, it could not do so. Although objects that have been presented to the left hemisphere can be accurately identified with the right hand, performance is no better than chance with the left hand.

When test objects are presented to the right hemisphere either visually (in the left visual field) or tactually (in the left hand), the pattern of responses is entirely different. A split-brain patient asked to name an object flashed in the left visual field is likely to claim that nothing appeared on the screen. (Remember that it is the left hemisphere who is talking and the right hemisphere who has seen the stimulus.) A patient asked to name an object placed in the left hand is usually aware that something is there, presumably because of the crude tactual information carried by ipsilateral somatosensory fibers, but is unable to say what it is (see Fabri et al., 2001). Amazingly, all the while the patient is claiming (i.e., all the while the left hemisphere is claiming) the inability to identify a test object presented in the left visual field or left hand, the left hand (i.e., the right hemisphere) can identify the correct object. Imagine how confused the patient must become when, in trial after trial, the left hand can feel an object and then fetch another just like it from a collection of test items under the ledge, while the left hemisphere is vehemently claiming that it does not know the identity of the test object.

Cross-Cuing

LO 16.8 Outline the process of cross-cuing in split-brain patients.

Although the two hemispheres of a split-brain patient have no means of direct neural communication, they can communicate neurally via indirect pathways through the brain stem. They can also communicate with each other by an external route, by a process called **cross-cuing**. An example of cross-cuing occurred during a series of tests designed to determine whether the left hemisphere could respond to colors presented in the left visual field. To test this possibility, a red or a green stimulus was presented in the left visual field, and the split-brain patient was asked to verbally report the color: red or green. At first, the patient performed at a chance level on this task (50 percent correct); but after a time, performance improved appreciably, thus suggesting that the color information was somehow transferred over neural pathways from the right hemisphere to the left.

However, this proved not to be the case:

> If a green light was presented and the patient happened to correctly guess green, she would be correct and the trial would end. However, if the green light was presented and the patient guessed red, after a pause, she would frown, shake her head, and then change her answer: "Oh no, I meant green." The right hemisphere saw the green light and heard the left hemisphere guess "red." Knowing that red was wrong, the right hemisphere initiated a frown and shook her head, no. This signaled to the left hemisphere that the answer was wrong and that it needed to be corrected.

This example demonstrates how neurological patients can use different cognitive strategies to perform the same task. The fact that neurological patients can perform the same task in different ways often clouds their deficits and greatly complicates the assessment of their neurological status.

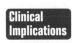

Doing Two Things at Once

LO 16.9 Describe the helping-hand phenomenon and the use of the chimeric figures test in experiments on split-brain patients.

In many of the classes we teach, a student fits the following stereotype: He sits—or rather sprawls—near the back of the class; and despite good grades, he tries to create the impression he is above it all by making sarcastic comments. Such a student inadvertently triggered an interesting discussion

in one of our classes. His comment went something like this: "If getting my brain cut in two can create two separate brains, perhaps I should get it done so that I can study for two different exams at the same time."

The question raised by this comment is a good one. If the two hemispheres of a split-brain patient are capable of independent functioning, then they should be able to do two different things at the same time—in this case, learn two different things at the same time. Can they? Indeed they can. For example, in one test, two different visual stimuli appeared simultaneously on the test screen—let's say a pencil in the left visual field and an orange in the right visual field. The split-brain patient was asked to simultaneously reach into two bags—one with each hand—and grasp in each hand the object that was on the screen. After grasping the objects, but before withdrawing them, the patient was asked to tell the experimenter what was in the two hands; the patient (i.e., the left hemisphere) replied, "Two oranges." Much to the bewilderment of the verbal left hemisphere, when the hands were withdrawn, there was an orange in the right hand and a pencil in the left. The two hemispheres of the split-brain patient had learned two different things at exactly the same time.

In another test in which two visual stimuli were presented simultaneously—again, let's say a pencil to the left visual field and an orange to the right—the split-brain patient was asked to pick up the presented object from an assortment of objects on a table, this time in full view. As the right hand reached out to pick up the orange under the direction of the left hemisphere, the right hemisphere saw what was happening and thought an error was being made (remember that the right hemisphere saw a pencil). On some trials, the right hemisphere dealt with this problem in the only way that it could: The left hand shot out, grabbed the right hand away from the orange, and redirected it to the pencil. This response is called the **helping-hand phenomenon**.

The special ability of split brains to do two things at once has also been demonstrated on tests of attention. Each hemisphere of split-brain patients appears to be able to maintain an independent focus of attention (see Gazzaniga, 2005). This leads to an ironic pattern of results: Split-brain patients can search for, and identify, a visual target item in an array of similar items more quickly than healthy controls can (Luck et al., 1989)—presumably because the two split hemispheres are conducting two independent searches.

Yet another example of the split brain's special ability to do two things at once involves the phenomenon of **visual completion**. As you may recall from Chapter 6, individuals with scotomas are often unaware of them because their brains have the capacity to fill them in (to complete them) by using information from the surrounding areas of the visual field. In a sense, each hemisphere of a split-brain patient is a participant with a scotoma covering the entire ipsilateral visual field. The ability of the hemispheres of a split-brain patient to simultaneously and independently engage in completion has been demonstrated in studies using the **chimeric figures test**—named after *Chimera*, a mythical monster composed of parts of different animals. Levy, Trevarthen, and Sperry (1972) flashed photographs composed of fused-together half-faces of two different people onto the center of a screen in front of split-brain patients—see Figure 16.6. The patients were then asked to describe what they saw or to indicate what they saw by pointing to it in a series of photographs of intact faces. Amazingly, each patient (i.e., each left hemisphere) reported seeing a complete, bilaterally symmetrical face, even when asked such leading questions as "Did you notice anything peculiar about what you just saw?" When the patients were asked to describe what they saw, they usually described a completed version of the half that had been presented to the right visual field (i.e., the left hemisphere).

The Z Lens

LO 16.10 Explain the Z lens and how it was used to study split-brain patients.

Once it was firmly established that the two hemispheres of each split-brain patient can function independently, it became clear that the study of split-brain patients provided a unique opportunity to compare the abilities of left and right hemispheres. However, early studies of the lateralization of function in split-brain patients were limited by the fact that visual stimuli requiring more than 0.1 second to perceive could not be studied using the conventional method for restricting visual input to one hemisphere. This methodological barrier was eliminated by Zaidel in 1975. Zaidel developed a lens, called the **Z lens**, that limits visual input to one hemisphere of split-brain patients while they scan complex visual material such as the pages of a book. As Figure 16.7 illustrates, the Z lens is a contact lens that is opaque on one side (left or right). Because it moves with the eye, it permits visual input to enter only one hemisphere, irrespective of eye movement. Zaidel used the Z lens to compare the ability of the left and right hemispheres of split-brain patients to perform on various tests.

The usefulness of the Z lens is not restricted to purely visual tests. For example, it has been used to compare the ability of the left and right hemispheres to comprehend speech. Because each ear projects to both hemispheres, it is not possible to present spoken words to only one hemisphere. Thus, to assess the ability of a hemisphere to comprehend spoken words or sentences, Zaidel presented them

Figure 16.6 The chimeric figures test. When a split-brain patient focuses on a chimeric face, the left hemisphere sees a single normal face that is a completed version of the half face on the right. At the same time, the right hemisphere sees a single normal face that is a completed version of the half face on the left.

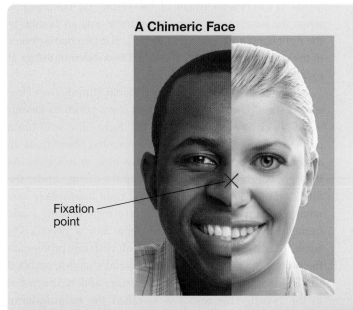

A Chimeric Face

Fixation point

Left hemisphere of a split-brain patient sees this.

Right hemisphere of a split-brain patient sees this.

Figure 16.7 The Z lens, which was developed by Zaidel to study functional asymmetry in split-brain patients. It is a contact lens that is opaque on one side (left or right), so that visual input reaches only one hemisphere.

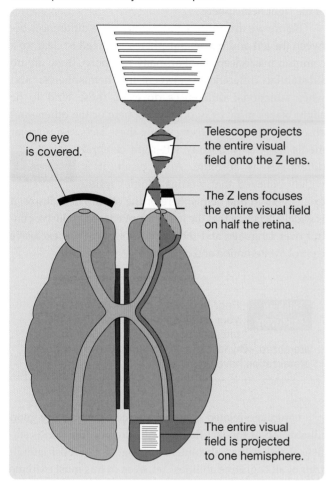

One eye is covered.

Telescope projects the entire visual field onto the Z lens.

The Z lens focuses the entire visual field on half the retina.

The entire visual field is projected to one hemisphere.

active role in controlling behavior, and in these cases, there can be serious conflicts between the left and right hemispheres (see Verleger et al., 2011). One patient (let's call him Peter) was such a case.

The Case of Peter, the Split-Brain Patient Tormented by Conflict

At the age of 8, Peter began to suffer from complex partial seizures. Antiepileptic medication was ineffective, and at 20, he received a commissurotomy, which greatly improved his condition but did not completely block his seizures. A sodium amytal test administered prior to surgery showed that he was left-hemisphere dominant for language.

Clinical Implications

Following surgery, the independent mischievous behavior of Peter's right hemisphere often caused him (his left hemisphere) considerable frustration. He (his left hemisphere) complained that his left hand would turn off television shows that he was enjoying, that his left leg would not always walk in the intended direction, and that his left arm would sometimes perform embarrassing, socially unacceptable acts (e.g., striking a relative).

In the laboratory, Peter (his left hemisphere) sometimes became angry with his left hand, swearing at it, striking it, and trying to force it with his right hand to do what he (his left hemisphere) wanted (Joseph, 1988).

to both ears, and then he asked the split-brain patients to pick the correct answer or to perform the correct response under the direction of only that hemisphere. For example, to test the ability of the right hemisphere to understand oral commands, the patients were given an oral instruction (such as "Put the green square under the red circle"), and then the right hemisphere's ability to comprehend the direction was tested by allowing only the right hemisphere to see the colored tokens while the task was completed.

Dual Mental Functioning and Conflict in Split-Brain Patients

LO 16.11 Describe a case where the right hemisphere tried to take control of a split-brain patient's everyday behavior.

In most split-brain patients, the right hemisphere does not seem to have a strong will of its own; the left hemisphere seems to control most everyday activities. However, in a few split-brain patients, the right hemisphere takes a more

Independence of Split Hemispheres: Current Perspective

LO 16.12 Explain how complete hemispheric independence is not an inevitable consequence of split-brain surgery.

Discussions of split-brain patients tend to focus on cases in which there seems to be a complete separation of left-hemisphere and right-hemisphere function, and this is what we have done here. But complete hemispheric independence is not an inevitable consequence of split-brain surgery. In most split-brain patients, it is possible to demonstrate some communication of information between hemispheres, depending on the particular surgery, the time since surgery, the particular information, and the method of testing. For example, feelings of emotion appear to be readily passed between the hemispheres of most split-brain patients. This is easily demonstrated by presenting emotionally loaded images to the right hemisphere and asking patients to respond verbally to the images. Their verbal left hemisphere often responds with the appropriate emotion, even when the left hemisphere is unaware of the image (Sperry, Zaidel, & Zaidel, 1979).

Consider the following remarkable exchange (paraphrased from Sperry, Zaidel, & Zaidel, 1979, pp. 161–162).

The patient's right hemisphere was presented with an array of photos, and the patient was asked if one was familiar. He pointed to the photo of his aunt.

> *Experimenter:* "Is this a neutral, a thumbs-up, or a thumbs-down person?"
> *Patient:* With a smile, he made a thumbs-up sign and said, "This is a happy person."
> *Experimenter:* "Do you know him personally?"
> *Patient:* "Oh, it's not a him, it's a her."
> *Experimenter:* "Is she an entertainment personality or an historical figure?"
> *Patient:* "No, just..."
> *Experimenter:* "Someone you know personally?"
> *Patient:* He traced something with his left index finger on the back of his right hand, and then he exclaimed, "My aunt, my Aunt Edie."
> *Experimenter:* "How do you know?"
> *Patient:* "By the E on the back of my hand."

Another factor that has been shown to contribute substantially to the hemispheric independence of split-brain patients is task difficulty (Weissman & Banich, 2000). As tasks become more difficult, they are more likely to involve both hemispheres of split-brain patients. It appears that simple tasks are best processed in one hemisphere, the hemisphere specialized for the specific activity, but complex tasks require the cognitive power of both hemispheres.

Watch this video on MyPsychLab

CHALK IT UP! HOW TO TEST A SPLIT BRAIN

Differences Between Left and Right Hemispheres

So far in this chapter, you have learned about five methods of studying cerebral lateralization of function: unilateral lesions, the sodium amytal test, the dichotic listening test, functional brain imaging, and studies of split-brain patients. This module takes a look at some of the major functional differences between the left and right cerebral hemispheres

that have been discovered using these methods. Because the verbal and motor abilities of the left hemisphere are readily apparent, most research on the lateralization of function has focused on uncovering the not-so-obvious special abilities of the right hemisphere.

Before we introduce you to some of the differences between the left and right hemispheres, we need to clear up a common misconception: For many functions, there are no substantial differences between the hemispheres; and when functional differences do exist, these tend to be slight biases in favor of one hemisphere or the other—not absolute differences. Disregarding these facts, the popular media inevitably portray left–right cerebral differences as absolute. As a result, it is widely believed that various abilities reside exclusively in one hemisphere or the other. For example, it is widely believed that the left hemisphere has exclusive control over language and the right hemisphere has exclusive control over emotion and creativity.

Thinking Creatively

Thinking Creatively Prior to delving into this module, list your preconceptions about cerebral lateralization of function. (Hint: What is lateralized, why is it lateralized, and what effect does lateralization have on behavior?)

Language-related abilities provide a particularly good illustration of the fact that lateralization of function is statistical rather than absolute. Language is the most lateralized of all cognitive abilities. Yet, even in this most extreme case, lateralization is far from total; there is substantial language-related activity in the right hemisphere. For example, on the dichotic listening test, people who are left-hemisphere dominant for language tend to identify more digits with the right ear than the left ear, but this right-ear advantage is only 55 to 45 percent. Furthermore, the right hemispheres of most left-hemisphere dominant split-brain patients can understand many spoken or written words and simple sentences (see Gazzaniga, 2013).

Examples of Cerebral Lateralization of Function

LO 16.13 Describe five examples of abilities that have been found to be lateralized, and explain what is meant by the "left hemisphere interpreter."

Table 16.1 lists some of the abilities that are often found to be lateralized. They are arranged in two columns: those that seem to be controlled more by the left hemisphere and those that seem to be controlled more by the right hemisphere. Let's consider several examples of cerebral lateralization of function.

Table 16.1 Abilities that display some degree of cerebral lateralization.

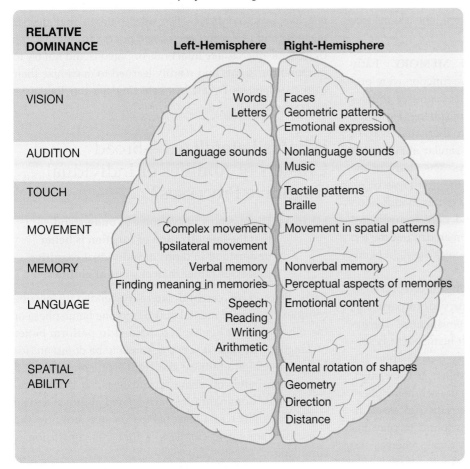

RELATIVE DOMINANCE	Left-Hemisphere	Right-Hemisphere
VISION	Words Letters	Faces Geometric patterns Emotional expression
AUDITION	Language sounds	Nonlanguage sounds Music
TOUCH		Tactile patterns Braille
MOVEMENT	Complex movement Ipsilateral movement	Movement in spatial patterns
MEMORY	Verbal memory Finding meaning in memories	Nonverbal memory Perceptual aspects of memories
LANGUAGE	Speech Reading Writing Arithmetic	Emotional content
SPATIAL ABILITY		Mental rotation of shapes Geometry Direction Distance

SUPERIORITY OF THE LEFT HEMISPHERE IN CONTROLLING IPSILATERAL MOVEMENT. One unexpected left-hemisphere specialization was revealed by functional brain-imaging studies (see Hervé et al., 2013). When complex, cognitively driven movements are made by one hand, most of the activation is observed in the *contralateral* hemisphere, as expected. However, some activation is also observed in the *ipsilateral* hemisphere, and these ipsilateral effects are substantially greater in the left hemisphere than in the right (see Hervé et al., 2013). Consistent with this observation is the finding that left-hemisphere lesions are more likely than right-hemisphere lesions to produce ipsilateral motor problems—for example, left-hemisphere lesions are more likely to reduce the accuracy of left-hand movements than right-hemisphere lesions are to reduce the accuracy of right-hand movements.

SUPERIORITY OF THE RIGHT HEMISPHERE IN SPATIAL ABILITY. In a classic early study, Levy (1969) placed a three-dimensional block of a particular shape in either the right hand or the left hand of split-brain patients. Then, after they had thoroughly *palpated* (tactually investigated) it, she asked them to point to the two-dimensional test stimulus that best represented what the three-dimensional block would look like if it were made of cardboard and unfolded. She found a right-hemisphere superiority on this task, and she found that the two hemispheres seemed to go about the task in different ways. The performance of the left hand and right hemisphere was rapid and silent, whereas the performance of the right hand and left hemisphere was hesitant and often accompanied by a running verbal commentary that was difficult for the patients to inhibit. Levy concluded that the right hemisphere is superior to the left at spatial tasks. This conclusion has been frequently confirmed (see Dietz et al., 2014; Zaidel, 2013), and it is consistent with the finding that disorders of spatial perception (e.g., contralateral neglect—see Chapters 7 and 8) tend to be associated with right-hemisphere damage.

SPECIALIZATION OF THE RIGHT HEMISPHERE FOR EMOTION. According to the old concept of left-hemisphere dominance, the minor right hemisphere is not involved in emotion. This presumption has been proven false. Indeed, analysis of the effects of unilateral brain lesions indicates that the right hemisphere may be superior to the left at performing some tests of emotion—for example, in accurately identifying facial expressions of emotion (see Mitchell & Phillips, 2015; Prete et al., 2015). Although the study of unilateral brain lesions suggests a general right-hemisphere dominance for some aspects of emotional processing, functional brain-imaging studies have not provided unambiguous support for this view (see Bourne, 2010; Costanzo et al., 2015; Herrington et al., 2010).

SUPERIOR MUSICAL ABILITY OF THE RIGHT HEMISPHERE. Kimura (1964) compared the performance of 20 right-handers on the standard digit version of the dichotic listening test with their performance on a version of the test involving the dichotic presentation of melodies. In the melody version of the test, Kimura simultaneously played two different melodies—one to each ear—and then asked the participants to identify the two they had just heard from four that were subsequently played to them through both ears. The right ear (i.e., the left hemisphere) was superior in the perception of digits, whereas the left ear (i.e., the right hemisphere) was superior in the perception of melodies. This is consistent with the observation that right temporal lobe lesions are more likely to disrupt music discriminations than are left temporal lobe lesions (see Casey, 2013).

HEMISPHERIC DIFFERENCES IN MEMORY. Early studies of the lateralization of cognitive function were premised on the assumption that particular cognitive abilities reside in one or the other of the two hemispheres. However, the results of research have led to an alternative way of thinking: The two hemispheres have similar abilities that tend to be expressed in different ways. The study of the lateralization of memory was one of the first areas of research on cerebral lateralization to lead to this modification in thinking. You see, both the left and right hemispheres have the ability to perform on tests of memory, but the left hemisphere is better on some tests, whereas the right hemisphere is better on others.

There are two approaches to studying the cerebral lateralization of memory. One approach is to try to link particular memory processes with particular hemispheres—for example, it has been argued that the left hemisphere is specialized for encoding episodic memory (see Chapter 11). The other approach (e.g., Wolford, Miller, & Gazzaniga, 2004) is to link the memory processes of each hemisphere to specific materials rather than to specific processes. In general, the left hemisphere has been found to play the greater role in memory for verbal material, whereas the right hemisphere has been found to play the greater role in memory for nonverbal material (e.g., Willment & Golby, 2013). Whichever of these two approaches ultimately proves more fruitful, they represent an advance over the tendency to think that memory is totally lateralized to one hemisphere.

THE LEFT-HEMISPHERE INTERPRETER. Several lines of evidence suggest that the left and right hemispheres approach cognitive tasks in different ways. The cognitive approach that is typical of the left hemisphere is attributed to a mechanism that is metaphorically referred to as the **interpreter**—a hypothetical neuronal mechanism that continuously assesses patterns of events and tries to make sense of them.

The following experiment illustrates the kind of evidence that supports the existence of a left-hemisphere interpreter. The left and right hemispheres of split-brain patients were tested separately. The task was to guess which of two lights—top or bottom—would come on next. The top light came on 80 percent of the time in a random sequence, but the subjects were not given this information. Intact control participants quickly discovered that the top light came on more often than the bottom one; however, because they tried to figure out the nonexistent rule that predicted the exact sequence, they were correct only 68 percent of the time—even though they could have scored

80 percent if they always selected the top light. The left hemispheres of the split-brain patients performed on this test like intact controls: They attempted to find deeper meaning and as a result performed poorly. In contrast, the right hemispheres, like intact rats or pigeons, did not try to interpret the events and readily learned to maximize their correct responses by always selecting the top light (see Gazzaniga, 2013).

What Is Lateralized—Broad Clusters of Abilities or Individual Cognitive Processes?

LO 16.14 Discuss how we've come to understand that the lateralization of function is better understood in terms of individual cognitive processes rather than clusters of abilities.

Early theories of cerebral laterality tended to ascribe complex clusters of mental abilities to one hemisphere or the other. The left hemisphere tended to perform better on language tests, so it was presumed to be dominant for language-related abilities; the right hemisphere tended to perform better on some spatial tests, so it was presumed to be dominant for space-related abilities; and so on. Perhaps this was a reasonable first step, but now the consensus among researchers is that this conclusion is simplistic.

The problem is that categories such as language, emotion, musical ability, and spatial ability are each composed of dozens of different individual cognitive activities, and there is no reason to assume that all those activities associated with a general label (e.g., spatial ability) will necessarily be lateralized in the same hemisphere. Indeed, major exceptions to all broad categories of cerebral lateralization have emerged (see Cai & Van der Haegen, 2015; Crepaldi et al., 2013; Turner et al., 2015). How is it possible to argue that all language-related abilities are lateralized in the left hemisphere when the right hemisphere has been shown to be involved in speech perception and the understanding of word meaning (see Kreitewolf, Friederici, & von Kriegstein, 2014; Poeppel, 2014)?

Many researchers are taking a different approach to the study of cerebral lateralization. They are basing their studies on the work of cognitive psychologists, who have broken down complex cognitive tasks—such as reading, judging space, and remembering—into their *constituent cognitive processes*. Once the laterality of the individual cognitive elements has been determined, it should be possible to predict the laterality of cognitive tasks based on the specific cognitive elements that compose them.

Anatomical Asymmetries of the Brain

LO 16.15 Describe three anatomical asymmetries in the human brain.

The discovery of cerebral lateralization of function led to a search for anatomical asymmetries in the brain. In particular, it led to a search for those anatomical differences between the hemispheres that are the basis for their functional differences. For example, do anatomical differences between the left and right hemispheres make the left hemisphere more suited for the control of language?

Most efforts to identify interhemispheric differences in brain anatomy have focused on the size of three areas of cortex that are important for language, the most lateralized

of our cognitive abilities: the frontal operculum, the planum temporale, and Heschl's gyrus (see Figure 16.8). The **frontal operculum** is the area of frontal lobe cortex that lies just in front of the face area of the primary motor cortex; in the left hemisphere, it is the location of Broca's area. The planum temporale and Heschl's gyrus are areas of temporal lobe cortex. The **planum temporale** lies in the posterior region of the lateral fissure; it is thought to play a role in the comprehension of language and is often referred to as *Wernicke's area*. **Heschl's gyrus** is located in the lateral fissure just anterior to the planum temporale in the temporal lobe; it is the location of primary auditory cortex.

Many anatomical differences between the average left and right hemispheres of the human brain have been reported. There is no question that the average human cerebral hemispheres tend to be anatomically different, but the functional consequences of the differences have not been apparent. Let's consider research on the three cortical language areas.

There are two serious difficulties in studying anatomical asymmetry of the language areas. First, their boundaries are unclear, with no consensus on how best to define them (see Hagoort, 2014; Poeppel, 2014). Second, there are large differences among healthy people in the structure of these cortical language areas (see Amunts & Zilles, 2012; Warrier et al., 2009). Given these two difficulties, it is not surprising that reports of their anatomical asymmetry have been variable (see Amunts & Zilles, 2012). In many cases, the predicted size advantage of the left-hemisphere language areas is reported, but in other cases there is no asymmetry, or even a right-hemisphere size advantage.

Any report that one of the three cortical language areas tends to be larger in the left hemisphere typically leads to the suggestion that the anatomical asymmetry might have caused, or have been caused by, the lateralization of language to the left hemisphere. However, there is little support for such conjectures (see Bishop, 2013).

The fact that a particular cortical area is on the average larger in the left hemisphere does not suggest that it is causally linked to language lateralization, even if the cortical area has been linked to language (see Boles & Barth, 2011). At a bare minimum, it must be shown that the anatomical and functional asymmetries are correlated—that the degree of anatomical lateralization in a person reflects the degree of language lateralization in the same person. The fact that close to

Figure 16.8 Three language areas of the cerebral cortex that have been the focus of studies on neuroanatomical asymmetry: the frontal operculum, the planum temporale (Wernicke's area), and Heschl's gyrus (primary auditory cortex).

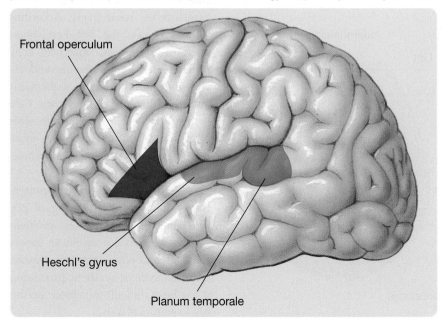

Frontal operculum

Heschl's gyrus

Planum temporale

90 percent of healthy people are left-hemisphere dominant for language, while reports of left-hemisphere anatomical biases in the three language areas do not typically exceed 65 percent is reason for skepticism.

In short, the search for anatomical differences between the two hemispheres has been only partially successful. Many anatomical asymmetries have been discovered, but few have been clearly related to functional asymmetries. Several researchers have suggested that studies of differences in the microstructure (e.g., differences in cell type, synapses, and neural circuitry) between the two hemispheres may prove more informative than comparisons of differences in the size of vaguely defined areas (see Chance, 2014).

One interesting study of planum temporale asymmetry was conducted by Schlaug and colleagues (1995). They used magnetic resonance imaging (MRI) to measure the asymmetry of the planum temporale and relate it to the presence of *perfect pitch* (the ability to identify the pitch of individual musical notes). The planum temporale tended to be larger in the left hemisphere in musicians with perfect pitch than in nonmusicians or in musicians without perfect pitch (see Figure 16.9).

The finding that many musicians have a larger left planum temporale has functional consequences beyond just being correlated with perfect pitch. For example, the size of the left planum temporale in musicians was found to be positively correlated with their ability to hear poorly pronounced syllables.

Evolutionary Perspective of Cerebral Lateralization and Language

You have already seen in this chapter how the discussion of cerebral lateralization inevitably leads to a discussion of language: Language is the most lateralized cognitive function. This module considers the evolution of cerebral lateralization and then the evolution of language.

Evolutionary Perspective

Theories of the Evolution of Cerebral Lateralization

LO 16.16 Describe and evaluate three theoretical explanations for why cerebral lateralization of function evolved.

Many theories have been proposed to explain why cerebral lateralization of function evolved. Most are based on the same general premise: that it is advantageous for areas of the brain that perform similar functions to be located in the same hemisphere. However, each theory of cerebral asymmetry postulates a different fundamental distinction between left and right hemisphere function. Consider the following three theories.

ANALYTIC–SYNTHETIC THEORY. The *analytic–synthetic theory of cerebral asymmetry* holds that there are two basic modes of thinking—an analytic mode and a synthetic mode—which have become segregated during the course of evolution in the left and right hemispheres, respectively. According to to this theory, the left hemisphere operates in a logical, analytical, computerlike fashion, analyzing and abstracting stimulus input sequentially and attaching verbal labels; the right hemisphere is primarily a synthesizer, which organizes and processes information in terms of gestalts, or wholes (Harris, 1978).

Although the analytic–synthetic theory has been the darling of pop psychology, its vagueness is a problem. Because it is not possible to specify the degree to which any task requires either analytic or synthetic processing, it has been difficult to subject the theory to empirical tests.

Figure 16.9 The anatomical asymmetry detected in the planum temporale of musicians by magnetic resonance imaging. In most people, the planum temporale is larger in the left hemisphere than in the right; this difference was found to be greater in musicians with perfect pitch than in either musicians without perfect pitch or controls.

(Based on Schlaug, G., Jäncke, L., Huang, Y., & Steinmetz, H. (1995). In vivo evidence of structural brain asymmetry in musicians. *Science, 267,* 699–701.)

Planum temporale

MOTOR THEORY. The *motor theory of cerebral asymmetry* (Kimura, 1979) holds that the left hemisphere is specialized not for the control of speech specifically but for the control of fine movements, of which speech is only one category. Support for this theory comes from reports that lesions that produce aphasia often produce other motor deficits (see Kimura, 2011). One shortcoming of the motor theory of cerebral asymmetry is that it does not suggest why motor function became lateralized in the first place (see Beaton, 2003).

LINGUISTIC THEORY. A third theory of cerebral asymmetry, the *linguistic theory of cerebral asymmetry,* posits that the primary role of the left hemisphere is language; this is in contrast to the analytic–synthetic and motor theories, which view language as a secondary specialization residing in the left hemisphere because of that hemisphere's primary specialization for analytic thought and skilled motor activity, respectively.

The linguistic theory of cerebral asymmetry is based to a large degree on the study of deaf people who use *American Sign Language* (a sign language with a structure similar to spoken language) and who suffer unilateral brain damage (see Campbell, MacSweeney, & Waters, 2008; Rogalsky et al., 2013). The fact that left-hemisphere damage can disrupt the use of sign language but not *pantomime gestures* (gestures that express meaning), as occurred in the case of W.L., suggests that the fundamental specialization of the left hemisphere may be language.

The Case of W.L., the Man Who Experienced Aphasia for Sign Language

W.L. is a congenitally deaf, right-handed male who grew up using American Sign Language. Seven months prior to testing, W.L. was admitted to hospital complaining of right-side weakness and motor problems. A CT scan revealed a large left frontotemporoparietal stroke. At that time, W.L.'s wife noticed he was making many uncharacteristic errors in signing and was having difficulty understanding the signs of others.

W.L.'s neuropsychologists managed to obtain a 2-hour videotape of an interview with him recorded 10 months before his stroke, which served as a valuable source of prestroke performance measures. Formal poststroke neuropsychological testing confirmed that W.L. had suffered a specific loss in his ability to use and understand sign language. The fact that he could produce and understand complex pantomime gestures suggested that his sign-language aphasia was specific to language (Corina et al., 1992).

When Did Cerebral Lateralization Evolve?

LO 16.17 Outline how cerebral lateralization evolved.

Until recently, cerebral lateralization had been assumed to be an exclusive feature of the hominin brain. For example, one version of the motor theory of cerebral asymmetry is that left-hemisphere specialization for motor control evolved in early hominins in response to their use of tools, and then the capacity for vocal language subsequently evolved in the left hemisphere because of its greater motor dexterity. However, there is evidence of lateralization of function in many vertebrates that evolved long before we humans did (see Hopkins & Cantalupo, 2008; Hopkins, Russell, & Cantalupo, 2007). Indeed, it has been suggested that lateralization of function may have been present in its basic form when vertebrates emerged about 425 million years ago (see Frasnelli, Vallortigara, & Rogers, 2012; MacNeilage, Rogers, & Vallortigara, 2009; Rilling, 2014). There is even some evidence of lateralization of function in certain invertebrate species (see Frasnelli, 2013).

> **Evolutionary Perspective** What do you think was the initial pressure for the lateralization of function in vertebrates? Explain why you favor your position.

Right-handedness may have evolved from a preference for the use of the right side of the body for feeding—such a right-sided preference has been demonstrated in species of all five classes of vertebrates (fishes, reptiles, birds, amphibians, and mammals). Then, once hands evolved, those species with hands (i.e., species of monkeys and apes) displayed a right- or left-hand preference for feeding and other complex responses such as tool use (see Cochet & Byrne, 2013; Frayer et al., 2012; Zhao, Hopkins, & Li, 2012).

A left-hemisphere specialization for communication is also present in species that existed prior to human evolution. For example, you learned in Chapter 2 that the left hemisphere plays the dominant role in birdsong, and the left hemispheres of dogs and monkeys have been found to be dominant in the perception of conspecific calls.

What Are the Survival Advantages of Cerebral Lateralization?

LO 16.18 List two survival advantages of cerebral lateralization.

The discovery of examples of cerebral lateralization in species from all five vertebrate classes suggests that cerebral lateralization must have survival advantages: But what are they? There seem to be two fundamental advantages. First, in some cases, it may be more efficient for the neurons performing a particular function to be concentrated in one hemisphere. For example, in most cases, it is advantageous to have one highly skilled hand rather than having two moderately skilled hands. Second, in some cases, two different kinds of cognitive processes may be more readily performed simultaneously if they are lateralized to different hemispheres (see Corballis, 2015).

Once the control of some abilities becomes lateralized, this may make the lateralization of other abilities advantageous. There may be situations in which there is an advantage to having the control of one ability lateralized in the hemisphere of another ability. For example, the motor theory of lateralization suggests that language became lateralized in the left hemisphere because fine motor control was already lateralized there.

Evolution of Human Language

LO 16.19 Describe what the study of nonhuman primates has suggested about the evolution of human language.

Human communication is different from the communication of other species. Human language is a system allowing a virtually limitless number of ideas to be expressed by combining a finite set of elements (see Hauser et al., 2014). Other species do have language of sorts, but it can't compare with human language. For example, monkeys have distinct warning calls for different threats, but they do not combine the calls to express new ideas. Also, birds and whales sing complex songs, but there is no creative recombination of the songs to express new ideas.

Language has been called a human instinct because it is so readily and universally learned by infants. At 10 months of age, infants say little, but 30-month-old infants speak in complete sentences and use more than 500 words (Golinkoff & Hirsh-Pasek, 2006). Also, over this same 20-month period, the plastic infant brain reorganizes itself to learn its parents' languages. At 10 months, human infants can distinguish the sounds of all human languages, but by 30 months, they can readily discriminate only those sounds that compose the languages to which they have been exposed (Kraus & Banai, 2007). Once the ability to discriminate particular speech sounds is lost, it is difficult to regain, which is one reason why adults usually have difficulty learning to speak new languages without an accent.

Words do not leave fossils, and thus, insights into the evolution of human language can be obtained only through the comparative study of existing species. Naturally enough, researchers interested in the evolution of human language turned first to the vocal communications of our primate relatives.

VOCAL COMMUNICATION IN NONHUMAN PRIMATES. As you have just learned, no other species has a language that can compare with human language. However, each nonhuman primate species has a variety of calls, each with a specific meaning that is understood by conspecifics. Moreover, the calls are not simply reflexive reactions to particular situations: They are dependent on the social context (see Seyfarth & Cheney, 2014). For example, vervet monkeys do not make alarm calls unless other vervet monkeys are nearby, and the calls are most likely to be made if the nearby vervets are relatives (see Oller & Griebel, 2014). And chimpanzees vary the screams they produce during aggressive encounters depending on the severity of the encounter, their role in it, and which other chimpanzees can hear them (see Slocombe et al., 2010).

A consistent pattern has emerged from studies of nonhuman vocal language: There is typically a substantial difference between the capacity for vocal production and the capacity for auditory comprehension. Even the most vocal nonhumans can produce relatively few calls, yet they are capable of interpreting a wide range of other sounds in their environments (see Hauser et al., 2014). This suggests that the ability of nonhumans to produce vocal language may be limited, not by their inability to interpret sounds, but by their inability to exert fine motor control over their voices—only humans have this ability (see Ghazanfar & Takahashi, 2014). It also suggests that human language may have evolved from a competence in comprehension of sounds already existing in our primate ancestors.

MOTOR THEORY OF SPEECH PERCEPTION. It was reasonable for Broca to believe that Broca's area played a specific role in language expression (speech): After all, Broca's area is part of the left premotor cortex. However, the **motor theory of speech perception** goes one step

Each nonhuman primate species has a variety of calls, each with a specific meaning that is understood by conspecifics.

further: It proposes that the perception and comprehension of speech depends on the words activating the same neural circuits in the motor system that would have been activated if the listener had said the words (see Cogan et al., 2014; Hicock, Houde, & Rong, 2011; but see Arsenault & Buchsbaum, 2015). General support for this theory has come from the discovery that just thinking about performing a particular action often activates the same areas of the brain as performing the action and from the discovery of *mirror neurons* (see Chapter 8), motor cortex neurons that fire when particular responses are either performed or observed (see Cook et al., 2014).

Further support for the motor theory of speech perception has come from many functional brain-imaging studies that have revealed activity in primary or secondary motor cortex during language comprehension tests that do not involve language expression (i.e., speaking or writing). Scott, McGettigan, and Eisner (2009) compiled and evaluated the results of studies that recorded activity in motor cortex during speech perception and concluded that the motor cortex is particularly active during the perception of conversational exchanges.

More direct support for the motor theory of speech perception has come from several studies that have applied transcranial magnetic stimulation (TMS) to areas of the motor cortex involved in speech articulation while volunteers listened to syllables and words. As hypothesized, the motor-cortex stimulation disrupted the perception of the syllables and words (see D'Ausilio et al., 2014; Schomers et al., 2015; Smalle, Rogers, & Möttönen, 2015).

However, there is some clinical evidence that contradicts the predictions of the motor theory of speech perception. Specifically, case studies of patients with damage to their motor cortex have failed to reveal the predicted deficits in speech perception (see Stasenko, Garcea, & Mahon, 2013; Stasenko et al., 2015).

GESTURAL LANGUAGE. Because only humans are capable of a high degree of motor control over their vocal apparatus, language in nonhuman primates might be mainly gestural, rather than vocal. To test this hypothesis, Pollick and de Waal (2007) compared the gestures and the vocalizations of chimpanzees. They found a highly nuanced vocabulary of hand gestures that were used in many situations and in various combinations. In short, the chimpanzees' gestures were much more like human language than their vocalizations. Could primate gestures have been a critical stage in the evolution of human language (see Gillespie-Lynch et al., 2014; Meunier, Vauclair, & Fagard, 2012)?

Scan Your Brain

The chapter now switches its focus to the cerebral mechanisms of language and language disorders. This is a good point for you to review what you have learned about cerebral lateralization by filling in the blanks in the following sentences. The correct answers are provided at the end of the exercise. Be sure to review material related to your errors and omissions before proceeding.

1. The cerebral _____ connect the two hemispheres.
2. Left-hemisphere damage plays a special role in both aphasia and _____.
3. Cortex of the left inferior prefrontal lobe became known as _____.
4. One common test of language lateralization is invasive; it involves injecting _____ into the carotid artery.
5. Some evidence suggests that the brains of males are _____ lateralized than the brains of females.
6. The _____ is the largest cerebral commissure.
7. _____ received a Nobel Prize for his research on split-brain patients.
8. Commissurotomy can be an effective treatment for severe cases of _____.
9. The two hemispheres of a split-brain patient can communicate via an external route; such external communication has been termed _____.
10. Damage to the _____ hemisphere is more likely to produce ipsilateral motor problems.
11. A neural mechanism metaphorically referred to as the *interpreter* is assumed to reside in the _____ hemisphere.
12. Because broad categories of abilities do not appear to be the units of cerebral lateralization, researchers have turned to studying the laterality of _____ cognitive processes.
13. Three common theories of cerebral asymmetry are the analytic–synthetic theory, the motor theory, and the _____ theory.
14. Broca's area plays a role in speech production, but there is now strong evidence that Broca's area and other areas of motor cortex also play a role in language _____.

Scan Your Brain answers: (1) commissures, (2) apraxia, (3) Broca's area, (4) sodium amytal, (5) more, (6) corpus callosum, (7) Sperry, (8) epilepsy, (9) cross-cuing, (10) left, (11) left, (12) constituent, (13) linguistic, (14) comprehension.

Cortical Localization of Language: Wernicke-Geschwind Model

This module focuses on the cerebral localization of language. In contrast to language lateralization, which refers to the relative control of language-related functions by the left and right hemispheres, *language localization* refers to the location within the hemispheres of the circuits that participate in language-related activities.

Like most introductions to language localization, the following discussion begins with the *Wernicke-Geschwind model*, the predominant theory of language localization. Because most of the research on the localization of language has been conducted and interpreted within the context of this model, reading about the localization of language without a basic understanding of the Wernicke-Geschwind model would be like watching a game of chess without knowing the rules.

Historical Antecedents of the Wernicke-Geschwind Model

LO 16.20 Describe the historical antecedents of the Wernicke-Geschwind model. Include descriptions of the following disorders: Broca's and Wernicke's aphasia, conduction aphasia, agraphia, and alexia.

The history of the localization of language and the history of the lateralization of function began at the same point, with Broca's assertion that a small area (Broca's area) in the inferior portion of the left prefrontal cortex is the center for speech production. Broca hypothesized that programs of

Clinical Implications articulation are stored within this area and that speech is produced when these programs activate the adjacent area of the precentral gyrus, which controls the muscles of the face and oral cavity. According to Broca, damage restricted to Broca's area should disrupt speech production without producing deficits in language comprehension.

> **Clinical Implications** As you have just learned, Broca's claim that a small area of human left prefrontal cortex (Broca's area) controls speech is considered to be the first evidence for localization of function in the human cortex. Before you encounter more discussion of this claim, please jot down the claim made by Broca and make several predictions about what subsequent research will reveal about it. Can you spot weaknesses in Broca's claim that will later emerge under the scrutiny of a more concerted research effort? (Hint: Consider when Broca made the claim (1861) and the nature of the damage typically found in diseased or otherwise damaged brains.)

The next major event in the study of the cerebral localization of language occurred in 1874, when Carl Wernicke (pronounced "VER-ni-key") concluded on the basis of 10 clinical cases that there is a language area in the left temporal lobe just posterior to the primary auditory cortex (i.e., in the left planum temporale). This second language area, which Wernicke argued was the cortical area of language comprehension, subsequently became known as **Wernicke's area**.

Wernicke suggested that selective lesions of Broca's area produce a syndrome of aphasia whose symptoms are primarily **expressive**—characterized by normal comprehension of both written and spoken language and by speech that retains its meaningfulness despite being slow, labored, disjointed, and poorly articulated. This hypothetical form of aphasia became known as **Broca's aphasia**. In contrast, Wernicke suggested that selective lesions of Wernicke's area produce a syndrome of aphasia whose deficits are primarily **receptive**—characterized by poor comprehension of both written and spoken language and speech that is meaningless but still retains the superficial structure, rhythm, and intonation of normal speech. This hypothetical form of aphasia became known as **Wernicke's aphasia**, and the normal-sounding but nonsensical speech of Wernicke's aphasia became known as *word salad*.

The following are examples of the kinds of speech presumed to be associated with selective damage to Broca's and Wernicke's areas (Geschwind, 1979, p. 183):

> *Broca's aphasia*: A patient who was asked about a dental appointment replied haltingly and indistinctly: "Yes...Monday...Dad and Dick...Wednesday nine o'clock...10 o'clock...doctors...and...teeth."

> *Wernicke's aphasia*: A patient who was asked to describe a picture that showed two boys stealing cookies reported smoothly: "Mother is away here working her work to get her better, but when she's looking the two boys looking in the other part. She's working another time."

Wernicke reasoned that damage to the pathway connecting Broca's and Wernicke's areas—the **arcuate fasciculus**—would produce a third type of aphasia, one

Watch this video on MyPsychLab
LEFT/RIGHT SPECIALIZATION

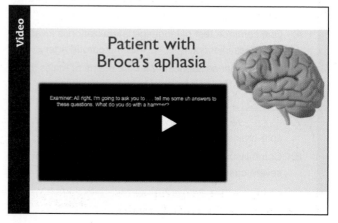

he called **conduction aphasia**. He contended that comprehension and spontaneous speech would be largely intact in patients with damage to the arcuate fasciculus but that they would have difficulty repeating words they had just heard.

The left **angular gyrus**—the area of left temporal and parietal cortex just posterior to Wernicke's area—is another cortical area that has been implicated in language. Its role in language was recognized in 1892 by neurologist Joseph Jules Dejerine on the basis of the postmortem examination of one special patient. The patient suffered from **alexia** (the inability to read) and **agraphia** (the inability to write). What made this case special was that the alexia and agraphia were exceptionally pure: Although the patient could not read or write, he had no difficulty speaking or understanding speech. Dejerine's postmortem examination revealed damage in the pathways connecting the visual cortex with the left angular gyrus. He concluded that the left angular gyrus is responsible for comprehending language-related visual input, which is received directly from the adjacent left visual cortex and indirectly from the right visual cortex via the corpus callosum.

During the era of Broca, Wernicke, and Dejerine, many influential scholars (e.g., Freud, Head, and Marie) opposed their attempts to localize various language-related abilities to specific neocortical areas. In fact, advocates of the holistic approach to brain function gradually gained the upper hand, and interest in the cerebral localization of language waned. However, in the mid-1960s, Norman Geschwind (1970) revived the old localizationist ideas of Broca, Wernicke, and Dejerine, added some new data and insightful interpretation, and melded the mix into a powerful theory: the Wernicke-Geschwind model.

The Wernicke-Geschwind Model

LO 16.21 Describe the Wernicke-Geschwind model.

The following are the seven components of the **Wernicke-Geschwind model**:

Figure 16.10 The seven components of the Wernicke-Geschwind model. All of the components are in the left hemisphere.

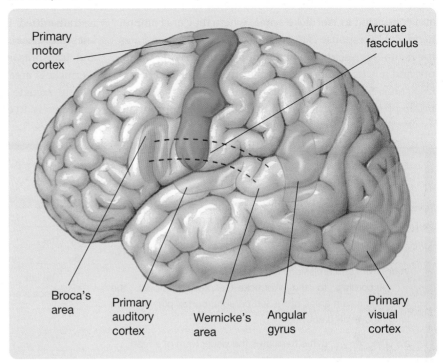

primary visual cortex, angular gyrus, primary auditory cortex, Wernicke's area, arcuate fasciculus, Broca's area, and primary motor cortex—all of which are in the left hemisphere. They are shown in Figure 16.10.

The following two examples illustrate how the Wernicke-Geschwind model is presumed to work

Figure 16.11 How the Wernicke-Geschwind model works in a person who is responding to a heard question and reading aloud. The hypothetical circuit that allows the person to respond to heard questions is in pink; the hypothetical circuit that allows the person to read aloud is in black.

(see Figure 16.11). First, when you are having a conversation, the auditory signals triggered by the speech of the other person are received by your primary auditory cortex and conducted to Wernicke's area, where they are comprehended. If a response is in order, Wernicke's area generates the neural representation of the thought underlying the reply, and it is transmitted to Broca's area via the left arcuate fasciculus. In Broca's area, this signal activates the appropriate program of articulation that drives the appropriate neurons of your primary motor cortex and ultimately your muscles of articulation. Second, when you are reading aloud, the signal received by your primary visual cortex is transmitted to your left angular gyrus, which translates the visual form of the word into its auditory code and transmits it to Wernicke's area for comprehension. Wernicke's area then triggers the appropriate responses in your arcuate fasciculus, Broca's area, and motor cortex, respectively, to elicit the appropriate speech sounds.

Scan Your Brain

Before proceeding to the following evaluation of the Wernicke-Geschwind model, scan your brain to confirm that you understand its fundamentals. The correct answers are provided at the end of the exercise. Review material related to your errors and omissions before proceeding.

According to the Wernicke-Geschwind model, the following seven areas of the left cerebral cortex play a role in language-related activities:

1. The _____ gyrus translates the visual form of a read word into an auditory code.

2. The _____ cortex controls the muscles of articulation.

3. The _____ cortex perceives the written word.

4. _____ area is the center for language comprehension.

5. The _____ cortex perceives the spoken word.

6. _____ area contains the programs of articulation.

7. The left _____ carries signals from Wernicke's area to Broca's area.

Scan Your Brain answers: (1) angular, (2) primary motor, (3) primary visual, (4) Wernicke's, (5) primary auditory, (6) Broca's, (7) arcuate fasciculus.

Wernicke-Geschwind Model: the Evidence

Unless you are reading this text from back to front, you should have read the preceding description of the Wernicke-Geschwind model with some degree of skepticism. By this point in the text, you will almost certainly recognize that any model of a complex cognitive process that involves a few localized neocortical centers joined in a serial fashion by a few arrows is sure to have major shortcomings, and you will appreciate that the neocortex is not divided into neat compartments whose cognitive functions conform to vague concepts such as language comprehension, speech motor programs, and conversion of written language to auditory language (see Cahana-Amitay & Albert, 2014). Initial skepticism aside, the ultimate test of a theory's validity is the degree to which its predictions are consistent with the empirical evidence.

Before we examine this evidence, we want to emphasize one point. The Wernicke-Geschwind model was initially based on case studies of aphasic patients with strokes, tumors, and penetrating brain injuries. Damage in such cases is often diffuse, and it inevitably encroaches on subcortical nerve fibers that connect the lesion site to other areas of the brain (see Bogen & Bogen, 1976). For example,

Thinking Creatively

Figure 16.12 shows the extent of the cortical damage in one of Broca's two original cases (see Mohr, 1976)—the damage is so diffuse that the case provides little evidence that Broca's area plays a role in speech.

Effects of Cortical Damage and Brain Stimulation on Language Abilities

LO 16.22 Identify the effects of cortical damage and brain stimulation on language abilities, and evaluate the Wernicke-Geschwind model in light of these findings.

In view of the fact that the Wernicke-Geschwind model grew out of the study of patients with cortical damage, it is appropriate to begin evaluating it by assessing its ability to predict the language-related deficits produced by damage to various parts of the cortex.

Clinical Implications

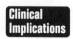
Before you read the rest of this module, write down your predictions derived from the Wernicke-Geschwind model. For each structure in the model, write down the predicted effect of damage. Later, compare your predictions with the evidence you will encounter in this module.

Figure 16.12 The extent of brain damage in one of Broca's two original patients. Like this patient, most aphasic patients have diffuse brain damage. It is thus difficult to determine from studying them the precise location of particular cortical language areas.

(Based on Mohr, J. P. (1976). Broca's area and Broca's aphasia. In H. Whitaker & H. A. Whitaker (Eds.), *Studies in neurolinguistics* (Vol. 1, pp. 201–235). New York, NY: Academic Press.)

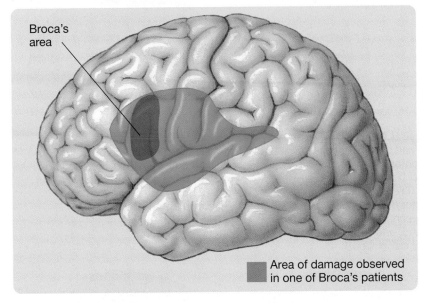

Broca's area

Area of damage observed in one of Broca's patients

EVIDENCE FROM STUDIES OF THE EFFECTS OF CORTICAL DAMAGE. The study of patients in whom discrete areas of cortex have been surgically removed has been particularly informative about the cortical localization of language, because the location and extent of these patients' lesions can be derived with reasonable accuracy from the surgeons' reports. The study of neurosurgical patients has not confirmed the predictions of the Wernicke-Geschwind model by any stretch of the imagination. See the six cases summarized in Figure 16.13.

Surgery that destroys all of Broca's area but little surrounding tissue typically has no lasting effects on speech (Penfield & Roberts, 1959; Rasmussen & Milner, 1975; Zangwill, 1975). Some speech problems were observed after the removal of Broca's area, but their temporal course suggested that they were products of postsurgical *edema* (swelling) in the surrounding neural tissue rather than of the *excision* (cutting out) of Broca's area itself. Prior to the use of effective anti-inflammatory drugs, patients with excisions of Broca's area often regained consciousness with their language abilities fully intact only to have serious language-related problems develop over the next few hours and then subside in the following weeks. Similarly, permanent speech difficulties were not produced by discrete surgical lesions to the arcuate fasciculus, and permanent alexia and agraphia were not produced by surgical lesions restricted to the cortex of the angular gyrus (Rasmussen & Milner, 1975).

The consequences of surgical removal of Wernicke's area are less well documented; surgeons have been hesitant to remove it in light of Wernicke's dire predictions. Nevertheless, in some cases, a good portion of Wernicke's area has been removed without lasting language-related deficits (e.g., Ojemann, 1979; Penfield & Roberts, 1959).

Hécaen and Angelergues (1964) published the first large-scale study of accidental or disease-related brain damage and aphasia. They rated the articulation, fluency, comprehension, naming ability, ability to repeat spoken sentences, reading, and writing of 214 right-handed patients with left-hemisphere damage. The extent and location of the damage in each case were estimated by either postmortem examination or visual inspection during subsequent surgery.

Hécaen and Angelergues found that small lesions to Broca's area seldom produced lasting language deficits and that small lesions restricted to Wernicke's area did not always produce lasting language deficits. Larger lesions did produce more lasting language deficits; but, in contrast to the predictions of the Wernicke-Geschwind model, problems of articulation were just as likely to occur following parietal or temporal lesions as they were following comparable lesions in the vicinity of Broca's area. It is noteworthy that none of the 214 patients studied by Hécaen and Angelergues displayed syndromes of aphasia that were either totally expressive (Broca's aphasia) or totally receptive (Wernicke's aphasia).

EVIDENCE FROM FUNCTIONAL NEUROIMAGING STUDIES. Since their development in the 1970s, CT and MRI techniques have been used extensively to analyze the brain damage associated with aphasia. Several large studies have assessed the CT and structural MRI scans of aphasic patients with accidental or disease-related brain damage (e.g., Alexander, 1989; Damasio, 1989; Naeser et al., 1981; Yourganov et al., 2015). In confirming and extending the results of earlier studies, they have not been kind to the Wernicke-Geschwind model. The following have been their major findings:

- No aphasic patients have damage restricted to Broca's area or Wernicke's area.

- Aphasic patients almost always have significant damage to subcortical white matter.

- Large anterior lesions are more likely to produce expressive symptoms, whereas large posterior lesions are more likely to produce receptive symptoms.

Figure 16.13 The lack of permanent disruption of language-related abilities after surgical excision (indicated in orange) of the classic Wernicke-Geschwind language areas (outlined with dotted lines).

(Based on Penfield, W., & Roberts, L. (1959). *Speech and brain mechanisms.* Princeton, NJ: Princeton University Press.)

Case J.M. No speech difficulties for 2 days after his surgery, but by Day 3 he was almost totally aphasic; 18 days after his operation he had no difficulty in spontaneous speech, naming, or reading, but his spelling and writing were poor.

Case H.N. After his operation, he had a slight difficulty in spontaneous speech, but 4 days later he was unable to speak; 23 days after surgery, there were minor deficits in spontaneous speech, naming, and reading aloud, and a marked difficulty in oral calculation.

Case J.C. There were no immediate speech problems; 18 hours after his operation he became completely aphasic, but 21 days after surgery, only mild aphasia remained.

Case P.R. He had no immediate speech difficulties; 2 days after his operation, he had some language-related problems, but they cleared up.

Case D.H. This operation was done in two stages; following completion of the second stage, no speech-related problems were reported.

Case A.D. He had no language-related problems after his operation, except for a slight deficit in silent reading and writing.

■ Area of Surgical Excision

- **Global aphasia** (a severe disruption of all language-related abilities) is usually related to massive lesions of anterior cortex, posterior cortex, and underlying white matter.

- Aphasic patients sometimes have brain damage that does not encroach on the Wernicke-Geschwind areas—aphasia has been observed in patients with visible damage to only the medial frontal lobe, subcortical white matter, basal ganglia, or thalamus.

In summary, large-scale, objective studies of the relationship between language deficits and brain damage—whether utilizing autopsy, direct observation during surgery, or brain scans—have not confirmed the major predictions of the Wernicke-Geschwind model. Has the model been treated more favorably by studies of electrical brain stimulation?

EVIDENCE FROM STUDIES OF ELECTRICAL STIMULATION OF THE CORTEX. The first large-scale electrical brain-stimulation studies of humans were conducted by Wilder Penfield and his colleagues in the 1940s at the Montreal Neurological Institute (see Feindel, 1986). One purpose of the studies was to map the language areas of each patient's brain so that tissue involved in language could be avoided during the surgery. The mapping was done by assessing the responses of conscious patients, who were under local anesthetic, to stimulation applied to various points on the cortical surface. The description of the effects of each stimulation was dictated to a stenographer—this was before the days of tape recorders—and then a tiny numbered card was dropped on the stimulation site for subsequent photography.

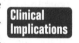

Figure 16.14 The responses of the left hemisphere of a 37-year-old right-handed person with epilepsy to electrical stimulation. Numbered cards were placed on the brain during surgery to mark the sites where brain stimulation had been applied.

(Based on Penfield & Roberts, 1959.)

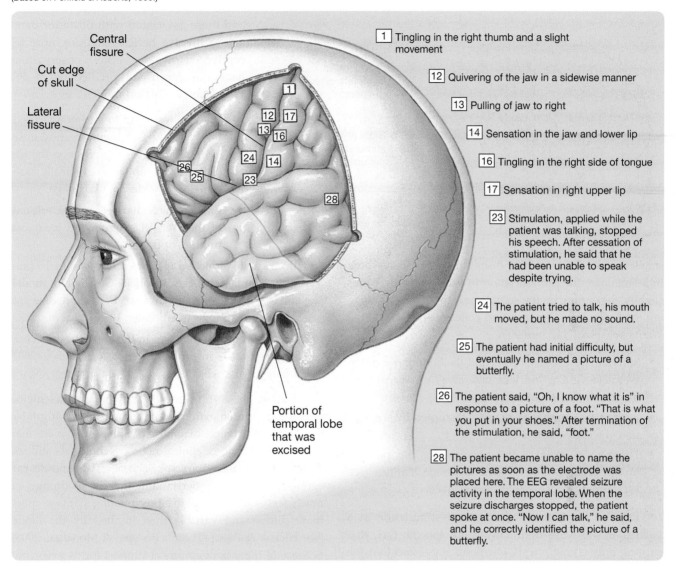

1 Tingling in the right thumb and a slight movement

12 Quivering of the jaw in a sidewise manner

13 Pulling of jaw to right

14 Sensation in the jaw and lower lip

16 Tingling in the right side of tongue

17 Sensation in right upper lip

23 Stimulation, applied while the patient was talking, stopped his speech. After cessation of stimulation, he said that he had been unable to speak despite trying.

24 The patient tried to talk, his mouth moved, but he made no sound.

25 The patient had initial difficulty, but eventually he named a picture of a butterfly.

26 The patient said, "Oh, I know what it is" in response to a picture of a foot. "That is what you put in your shoes." After termination of the stimulation, he said, "foot."

28 The patient became unable to name the pictures as soon as the electrode was placed here. The EEG revealed seizure activity in the temporal lobe. When the seizure discharges stopped, the patient spoke at once. "Now I can talk," he said, and he correctly identified the picture of a butterfly.

Figure 16.14 illustrates the responses to stimulation of a 37-year-old right-handed patient with epilepsy. He had started to have seizures about 3 months after receiving a blow to the head; at the time of his operation, in 1948, he had been suffering from seizures for 6 years, despite efforts to control them with medication. In considering his responses, remember that the cortex just posterior to the central fissure is primary somatosensory cortex and that the cortex just anterior to the central fissure is primary motor cortex.

Because electrical stimulation of the cortex is much more localized than a brain lesion, it has been a useful method for testing predictions of the Wernicke-Geschwind model. Penfield and Roberts (1959) published the first large-scale study of the effects of cortical stimulation on speech. They found that sites at which stimulation

blocked or disrupted speech in conscious neurosurgical patients were scattered throughout a large expanse of frontal, temporal, and parietal cortex, rather than being restricted to the Wernicke-Geschwind language areas (see Figure 16.15). They also found no tendency for particular kinds of speech disturbances to be elicited from particular areas of the cortex: Sites at which stimulation produced disturbances of pronunciation, confusion of counting, inability to name objects, or misnaming of objects were pretty much intermingled. Right-hemisphere stimulation almost never disrupted speech.

Ojemann and his colleagues (see Corina et al., 2010; Ojemann, 1983) assessed naming, reading of simple sentences, short-term verbal memory, ability to mimic movements of the face and mouth, and ability to recognize phonemes during cortical stimulation. A **phoneme** is the

Figure 16.15 The wide distribution of left hemisphere sites where cortical stimulation either blocked speech or disrupted it.

(Based on Penfield & Roberts, 1959.)

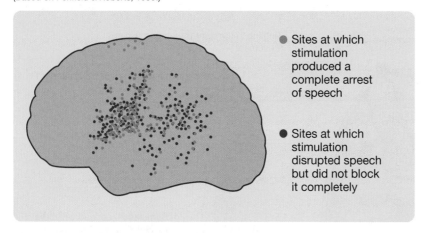

● Sites at which stimulation produced a complete arrest of speech

● Sites at which stimulation disrupted speech but did not block it completely

smallest unit of sound that distinguishes various words in a language; the pronunciation of each phoneme varies slightly, depending on the sounds next to it. The following are the findings of Ojemann and colleagues related to the Wernicke-Geschwind model:

- Stimulation to areas far beyond the boundaries of the Wernicke-Geschwind language areas was capable of disrupting the use of language.
- Each of the language tests was disrupted by stimulation at widely scattered sites.
- There were major differences among the patients in the organization of their language abilities (see McDermott, Watson, & Ojemann, 2005).

Because the disruptive effects of stimulation at a particular site were frequently quite specific (i.e., disrupting only a single test), Ojemann suggested that the language cortex is organized like a *mosaic*, with the discrete columns of tissue that perform a particular function widely distributed throughout the language areas of cortex.

Current Status of the Wernicke-Geschwind Model

LO 16.23 Summarize the current status of the Wernicke-Geschwind model.

Evidence from studies of brain damage and from observations of electrical stimulation of the brain has supported the Wernicke-Geschwind model in two general respects. First, the evidence has confirmed that Broca's and Wernicke's areas play important roles in language; many aphasics have diffuse cortical damage

that involves one or both of these areas. Second, there is a tendency for aphasias associated with anterior damage to involve deficits that are more expressive and those associated with posterior damage to involve deficits that are more receptive. However, other observations have not confirmed predictions of the Wernicke-Geschwind model:

- Damage restricted to the boundaries of the Wernicke-Geschwind cortical areas often has little lasting effect on the use of language—aphasia is typically associated with widespread damage.
- Brain damage that does not include any of the Wernicke-Geschwind areas can produce aphasia.
- Broca's and Wernicke's aphasias rarely exist in the pure forms implied by the Wernicke-Geschwind model; aphasia virtually always involves both expressive and receptive symptoms (see Benson, 1985).
- There are major differences in the locations of cortical language areas in different people (see Casey, 2002; Schlaggar et al., 2002).

Despite these problems, the Wernicke-Geschwind model has been an extremely important theory. It guided the study and clinical diagnosis of aphasia for more than four decades. Indeed, clinical neuropsychologists still use *Broca's aphasia* and *Wernicke's aphasia* as diagnostic categories, but with an understanding that the syndromes are much less selective and the precipitating damage much more diffuse and variable than implied by the model (see Hickok & Poeppel, 2007; Poeppel & Monahan, 2008). Because of the lack of empirical support for its major predictions, the Wernicke-Geschwind model has been largely abandoned by researchers, but it is still prominent in the classroom and clinic (see Dick, Bernal, & Tremblay, 2014; Poeppel et al., 2012).

Cognitive Neuroscience of Language

The *cognitive neuroscience approach*, which currently dominates research on language, is the focus of the final two modules of this chapter. Three premises define the cognitive neuroscience approach to language and differentiate it from the premises on which the Wernicke-Geschwind model is based.

Three Premises That Define the Cognitive Neuroscience Approach to Language

LO 16.24 Describe the three premises that define the cognitive neuroscience approach to language, and compare them with the premises on which the Wernicke-Geschwind model is based.

- *Premise 1:* The use of language is mediated by widespread activity in all the areas of the brain that participate in the cognitive processes involved in the particular language-related behavior. As you have just learned, the Wernicke-Geschwind model is based on the assumption that particular areas of the brain involved in language are each dedicated to a complex process such as speech production, language comprehension, or reading. In contrast, cognitive neuroscience research is based on the premise that each of these complex processes results from a combination of several *constituent cognitive processes*, which may be organized separately in different parts of the brain (see Bouchard, 2015). Accordingly, the specific constituent cognitive processes, not the general Wernicke-Geschwind processes, are assumed to be the appropriate level at which to conduct cognitive neuroscientific analysis. Cognitive neuroscientists typically divide analysis of the constituent cognitive processes involved in language into three categories: **phonological analysis** (analysis of the sound of language), **grammatical analysis** (analysis of the structure of language), and **semantic analysis** (analysis of the meaning of language).

- *Premise 2:* The areas of the brain involved in language are not dedicated solely to that purpose (see Friederici & Singer, 2015). In the Wernicke-Geschwind model, large areas of left cerebral cortex were thought to be dedicated solely to language, whereas the cognitive neuroscience approach assumes that many of the constituent cognitive processes involved in language also play roles in other kinds of behavior.

- *Premise 3:* Because many of the areas of the brain that perform specific language functions are also parts of other functional systems, these areas are likely to be small, widely distributed, and specialized (see Friederici & Singer, 2015). In contrast, the language areas of the Wernicke-Geschwind model are assumed to be large, circumscribed, and homogeneous (see Friederici & Gierhan, 2013).

In addition to these three premises, the methodology of the cognitive neuroscience approach to language distinguishes it from previous approaches. The Wernicke-Geschwind model rests heavily on the analysis of brain-damaged patients, whereas researchers using the cognitive neuroscience approach also employ an array of other techniques—most notably, functional brain imaging—in studying the localization of language in healthy volunteers.

It is important to remember that functional brain-imaging studies cannot prove causation (see Cloutman et al., 2010). There is a tendency to assume that brain activity recorded during a particular cognitive process plays a causal role in that process, but, as you learned in Chapter 1, correlation cannot prove causation. For example, substantial right-hemisphere activity is virtually always recorded during various language-related cognitive tasks, and it is tempting to assume that this activity is thus crucial to language-related cognitions. However, lesions of the right hemisphere are only rarely associated with lasting language-related deficits (see Hickok et al., 2008).

> **Thinking Creatively** Substantial right-hemisphere activity is virtually always recorded during various language-related cognitive tasks even though language tends to be lateralized to the left hemisphere. Why do you think this happens? (Hint: Think about the connectivity between the two hemispheres via the various cerebral commissures.)

Functional Brain Imaging and the Localization of Language

LO 16.25 Describe two influential functional imaging studies of the localization of language, and explain what their findings indicate.

Numerous PET and fMRI studies of volunteers engaging in various language-related tasks have been published (see Price, 2012). The following two have been particularly influential.

BAVELIER'S fMRI STUDY OF READING. Bavelier and colleagues (1997) used fMRI to measure the brain activity of healthy volunteers while they read silently. The methodology of these researchers was noteworthy in two respects. First, they used a particularly sensitive fMRI machine that allowed them to identify areas of activity with more accuracy than in most previous studies and without having to average the scores of several participants (see Chapter 5). Second, they recorded brain activity during the reading of sentences—rather than during simpler, controllable, unnatural tasks (e.g., listening to individual words) as in most functional brain-imaging studies of language.

The volunteers in Bavelier and colleagues' study viewed sentences displayed on a screen. Interposed between periods of silent reading were control periods, during which the participants were presented with strings of consonants. The differences in cortical activity during the reading and control periods served as the basis for determining those areas of cortical activity associated with reading.

Let's begin by considering the findings obtained for individual participants on individual trials before any averaging took place. Three important points emerged from this analysis:

- The areas of activity were patchy; that is, they were tiny areas of activity separated by areas of inactivity (see Leech & Saygin, 2011).

- The patches of activity were variable; that is, the areas of activity differed from participant to participant and even from trial to trial in the same participant.

- Although activity was often observed in parts of the classic Wernicke-Geschwind areas, it was widespread over the lateral surfaces of the brain.

Even though Bavelier and colleagues' fMRI machine was sensitive enough to render averaging unnecessary, they did average their data in the usual way to illustrate its misleading effects. Figure 16.16 illustrates the reading-related increases of activity averaged over all the trials and participants in the study by Bavelier and colleagues—as they are typically reported. The averaging creates the false impression that large, homogeneous expanses of tissue were active during reading, whereas the patches of activity induced on any given trial comprised only between

5 and 10 percent of the illustrated areas. Still, two points are clear from the averaged data: First, although there was significant activity in the right hemisphere, there was far more activity in the left hemisphere; second, the activity extended far beyond those areas predicted by the Wernicke-Geschwind model to be involved in silent reading (e.g., activity in Broca's area and the primary motor cortex would not have been predicted).

DAMASIO'S PET STUDY OF NAMING. The objective of the study of Damasio and colleagues (1996) was to look selectively at the temporal-lobe activity involved in naming objects within particular categories. PET activity was recorded from the left temporal lobes of healthy volunteers while they named images presented on a screen. The images were of three different types: famous faces, animals, and tools. To get a specific measure of the temporal-lobe activity involved in naming, the researchers subtracted from the activity recorded during this task the activity recorded while the volunteers judged the orientation of the images. The researchers limited the PET images to the left temporal lobe to permit a more fine-grained PET analysis.

Naming objects activated areas of the left temporal lobe outside the classic Wernicke's language area. Remarkably, the precise area activated by the naming depended on the category: Famous faces, animals, and tools each activated a slightly different area.

Other functional brain-imaging studies have confirmed category-specific encoding of words in the left temporal lobe (see Brambati et al., 2006). Moreover, aphasic patients who have naming difficulties that are specific to famous faces, animals, or tools have been

Figure 16.16 The areas in which reading-associated increases in activity were observed in the fMRI study of Bavelier and colleagues (1997). These maps were derived by averaging the scores of all participants, each of whom displayed patchy increases of activity in 5 to 10 percent of the indicated areas on any particular trial.

shown to have damage in one of the three areas of the left temporal lobe identified by Damasio and colleagues.

Cognitive Neuroscience of Dyslexia

This final module of the chapter looks at how the cognitive neuroscience approach to language views dyslexia, one of the major subjects of cognitive neuroscience research.

Dyslexia is a reading disorder, one that does not result from general visual, motor, or intellectual deficits. There are two fundamentally different types of dyslexias: **developmental dyslexias**, which become apparent 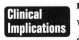 when a child is learning to read; and **acquired dyslexias**, which are caused by brain damage in individuals who were already capable of reading. Developmental dyslexia is a widespread problem. Estimates of the overall incidence of developmental dyslexia among English-speaking children range from 5 to 12 percent (see Norton, Beach, & Gabrieli, 2015), depending on the criteria that are employed to define dyslexia, and the incidence is two to three times higher among boys than girls. In contrast, acquired dyslexias are relatively rare.

 Do you or someone you know have dyslexia? What were some of the difficulties that you or the other person experienced?

Developmental Dyslexia: Causes and Neural Mechanisms

LO 16.26 Describe the causes and neural mechanisms of developmental dyslexia.

Because developmental dyslexia is far more common and its causes are less obvious, most research on dyslexia has focused on this form. There is a major genetic component to developmental dyslexia. The disorder has a heritability estimate of about 50 percent, and several genes have been linked to it (see Field et al., 2013; Giraud & Ramus, 2013).

The task of identifying the neural correlates of developmental dyslexia is complicated by the fact that the disorder occurs in various forms, which likely have different neural correlates (see O'Brien, Wolf, & Lovett, 2012; Peyrin et al., 2012). Another problem is that the ma- 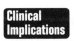 jor reduction of reading may induce changes in the brain itself, making it difficult to determine whether a difference in the brain of a person with developmental dyslexia is the cause or the result of the disorder (see Bishop, 2013).

One approach to dealing with the issue of whether any observed brain changes are a cause or a consequence of having dyslexia has been to compare dyslexic children to "ability-matched" children who are typically many years younger than them (see Norton, Beach, & Gabrieli, 2015). The rationale for such a comparison is that the two groups would be matched in terms of the amount of reading they have engaged in. In one such study by Hoeft et al. (2007), dyslexic children exhibited reduced fMRI activity in their left parietal and left occipito-temporal cortices relative to their ability-matched controls.

Many researchers who study the neural mechanisms of dyslexia have focused on one kind of brain pathology and have tried to attribute developmental dyslexia to it. For example, developmental dyslexia has been attributed to attentional, auditory, visual, and sensorimotor deficits (see Goswami, 2014; Harrar et al., 2014; Stoodley & Stein, 2013; Tse, 2012). However, although many dyslexic persons do experience a variety of subtle attentional, auditory, visual, and sensorimotor deficits, many do not. Moreover, even when these deficits are present in dyslexic persons, they do not account for all aspects of the disorder. As a result, there is now widespread agreement that dyslexia results most commonly from a specific disturbance of *phonological processing* (the representation and comprehension of speech sounds)—see Ramus and colleagues (2013); Hahn, Foxe, and Molholm (2014); but see Boets et al. (2013).

Developmental Dyslexia and Culture

LO 16.27 Describe research that helped discredit the notion that dyslexia could not be a brain disorder because it is influenced by culture.

Although it is established that developmental dyslexia is associated with abnormalities of brain function and specific genes (see Graham & Fisher, 2013), it was once considered to be a psychological rather than a neural disorder. Why? Because for many years, those whose thinking was affected by the physiology-or-psychology dichotomy (see Chapter 2) assumed that developmental dyslexia could not possibly be a brain disorder because it is influenced by culture. Paulesu and colleagues (2001) used the cognitive neuroscience approach to discredit this misguided way of thinking about dyslexia.

Paulesu and colleagues were intrigued by the finding that about twice as many English speakers as Italian speakers are diagnosed as dyslexic. They reasoned that this difference probably resulted from differences in the complexity of the two languages. English consists of 40 phonemes, which can be spelled, by one count, in 1,120 different ways. In contrast, Italian is composed of 25 phonemes, which can be spelled in 33 different ways.

Paulesu and colleagues (2000) began by comparing PET activity in the brains of typical English-speaking and Italian-speaking adults as they read. These researchers hypothesized that since the cognitive demands of reading aloud are different for Italian and English speakers, their volunteers might use different parts of their brains while reading. That is exactly what the researchers found. Although the same general areas were active during reading in both groups, Italian readers displayed more activity in the left superior temporal lobe, whereas English readers displayed more activity in the left inferior temporal and frontal lobes.

Next, Paulesu and colleagues (2001) turned their attention to Italian and English readers with developmental dyslexia. Despite the fact that the dyslexic Italians had less severe reading problems, both groups of dyslexic individuals displayed the same pattern of atypical PET activity when reading: less than typical reading-related activity in the posterior region of the temporal lobe. Thus, although dyslexia can manifest itself differently in people who speak different languages, the underlying neural pathology appears to be the same. Clearly, the fact that developmental dyslexia is influenced by cultural factors does not preclude the involvement of neural mechanisms.

Cognitive Neuroscience of Deep and Surface Dyslexia

LO 16.28 Describe the difference between the lexical procedure and the phonetic procedure for reading aloud. Then describe the difference between surface dyslexia and deep dyslexia.

Cognitive psychologists have long recognized that reading aloud can be accomplished in two entirely different ways. One is by a **lexical procedure**, which is based on specific stored information that has been acquired about written words: The reader simply looks at the word, recognizes it, and says it. The other way reading can be accomplished is by a **phonetic procedure**: The reader looks at the word, recognizes the letters, sounds them out, and says the word. The lexical procedure dominates in the reading of familiar words; the phonetic procedure dominates in the reading of unfamiliar words.

This simple cognitive analysis of reading aloud has proven useful in understanding the symptoms of two kinds of dyslexia resulting from brain damage (see Crisp & Ralph, 2006): *surface dyslexia* and *deep dyslexia*. (Two similar types of developmental dyslexia are also observed, but they tend to be less severe.)

In cases of **surface dyslexia**, patients have lost their ability to pronounce words based on their specific memories of the words (i.e., they have lost the *lexical procedure*), but they can still apply rules of pronunciation in their reading (i.e., they can still use the *phonetic procedure*). Accordingly,

they retain their ability to pronounce words whose pronunciation is consistent with common rules (e.g., *fish, river,* and *glass*) and their ability to pronounce nonwords according to common rules of pronunciation (e.g., *spleemer* and *twipple*); but they have great difficulty pronouncing words that do not follow common rules of pronunciation (e.g., *have, lose,* and *steak*). The errors they make often involve the misapplication of common rules of pronunciation; for example, *have, lose,* and *steak* are typically pronounced as if they rhymed with *cave, hose,* and *beak.*

In cases of **deep dyslexia** (also called *phonological dyslexia*), patients have lost their ability to apply rules of pronunciation in their reading (i.e., they have lost the *phonetic procedure*), but they can still pronounce familiar words based on their specific memories of them (i.e., they can still use the *lexical procedure*). Accordingly, they are completely incapable of pronouncing nonwords and have difficulty pronouncing uncommon words and words whose meaning is abstract. In attempting to pronounce words, patients with deep dyslexia try to react to them by using various lexical strategies, such as responding to the overall look of the word, the meaning of the word, or the derivation of the word. This leads to a characteristic pattern of errors. A patient with deep dyslexia might say "quill" for *quail* (responding to the overall look of the word), "hen" for *chicken* (responding to the meaning of the word), or "wise" for *wisdom* (responding to the derivation of the word).

If you have difficulty keeping these two types of acquired dyslexia straight, try this: Remember which is which by reminding yourself that persons with surface dyslexia have difficulty reacting to the overall shape of the word, which is metaphorically more superficial (less deep) than a problem in applying rules of pronunciation, which is experienced by persons with deep dyslexia.

Where are the lexical and phonetic procedures performed in the brain? Much of the research attempting to answer this question has focused on the study of deep dyslexia. Persons with deep dyslexia most often have extensive damage to the left-hemisphere language areas, suggesting that the disrupted phonetic procedure is widely distributed in the frontal and temporal areas of the left hemisphere. But which part of the brain maintains the lexical procedure in persons with deep dyslexia? There have been two theories, both of which have received some support. One theory is that the surviving lexical abilities of persons with deep dyslexia are mediated by activity in surviving parts of the left-hemisphere language areas. Evidence for this theory comes from the observation of neural activity in the surviving regions during reading (see Laine et al., 2000; Price et al., 1998). The other theory is that the surviving lexical abilities of persons with deep dyslexia are mediated by activity in the right hemisphere. The following remarkable case study provides support for this theory.

The Case of N.I., the Woman Who Read with Her Right Hemisphere

Prior to the onset of her illness, N.I. was a healthy girl. At the age of 13, she began to experience periods of aphasia, and several weeks later, she suffered a generalized convulsion. She subsequently had many convulsions, and her speech and motor abilities deteriorated badly. CT scans indicated ischemic brain damage to the left hemisphere.

Two years after the onset of her disorder, N.I. was experiencing continual seizures and blindness in her right visual field, and there was no meaningful movement or perception in her right limbs. In an attempt to relieve these symptoms, a total left **hemispherectomy** was performed; that is, her left hemisphere was totally removed. Her seizures were totally arrested by this surgery.

The reading performance of N.I. is poor, but she displays a pattern of retained abilities strikingly similar to those displayed by persons with deep dyslexia or split-brain patients reading with their right hemispheres. For example, she recognizes letters but is totally incapable of translating them into sounds; she can read concrete familiar words; she cannot pronounce even simple non-sense words (e.g., *neg*); and her reading errors indicate that she is reading on the basis of the meaning and appearance of words rather than by translating letters into sounds (e.g., when presented with the word *fruit*, she responded, "Juice…it's apples and pears and…fruit"). In other words, she suffers from a severe case of deep dyslexia (Patterson, Vargha-Khadem, & Polkey, 1989).

The case of N.I. completes the circle: The chapter began with a discussion of lateralization of function, and the case of N.I. concludes it on the same note.

Themes Revisited

In positioning the themes tabs throughout this chapter, we learned something. We learned why this is one of our favorite chapters: This chapter contributes most to developing the themes of the text. Indeed, several passages in this chapter are directly relevant to more than one of the themes, which made placing the tabs difficult for us. The clinical implications theme is the most prevalent because much of what we know about the lateralization of function and the localization of language in the brain comes from the study of neuropsychological patients.

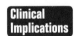

Because lateralization of function and language localization are often covered by the popular media, they have become integrated into pop culture, and many widely held ideas about these subjects are overly simplistic. In this chapter, thinking creatively tabs mark aspects of

laterality and language that require unconventional ways of thinking.

Evolutionary analysis has not played a major role in the study of the localization of language, largely because humans are the only species with well-developed language. However, it has played a key role in trying to understand why cerebral lateralization of function evolved in the first place, and the major breakthrough in understanding the split-brain phenomenon came from comparative research.

The neuroplasticity theme arose during the discussion of the sensitive period for the learning of new languages and during the discussion of the neurodevelopmental bases of developmental dyslexia. Damage to the brain always triggers a series of neuroplastic changes, which can complicate the study of the behavioral effects of the damage.

Key Terms

Chapter 17
Biopsychology of Emotion, Stress, and Health

Fear, the Dark Side of Emotion

Chapter Overview and Learning Objectives (LOs)

Biopsychology of Emotion: Introduction	**LO 17.1**	Summarize the major events in the history of research on the biopsychology of emotion.
	LO 17.2	Summarize the research on the relationship between the autonomic nervous system and emotions.
	LO 17.3	Describe research on the facial expression of emotions.
Fear, Defense, and Aggression	**LO 17.4**	Describe the work that led to the distinction between aggressive and defensive behaviors in mammals.
	LO 17.5	Describe the relation between testosterone levels and aggression in males.

This chapter is about the biopsychology of emotion, stress, and health. It begins with a historical introduction to the biopsychology of emotion and then focuses in the next two modules on the dark end of the emotional spectrum: fear. Biopsychological research on emotions has concentrated on fear not because biopsychologists are a scary bunch, but because fear has three important qualities: It is the easiest emotion to infer from behavior in various species; it plays an important adaptive function in motivating the avoidance of threatening situations; and chronic fear is one common source of stress. In the final two modules of the chapter, you will learn how some brain structures have been implicated in human emotion, and how stress increases susceptibility to illness.

Biopsychology of Emotion: Introduction

To introduce the biopsychology of emotion, this module reviews several classic early discoveries and then discusses the role of the autonomic nervous system in emotional experience and the facial expression of emotion.

Early Landmarks in the Biopsychological Investigation of Emotion

LO 17.1 Summarize the major events in the history of research on the biopsychology of emotion.

This section describes, in chronological sequence, six early landmarks in the biopsychological investigation of emotion. It begins with the 1848 case of Phineas Gage.

The Mind-Blowing Case of Phineas Gage

In 1848, Phineas Gage, a 25-year-old construction foreman for the Rutland and Burlington Railroad, was the victim of a tragic accident. In order to lay new tracks, the terrain had to be leveled, and Gage was in charge of the blasting. His task involved drilling holes in the rock, pouring some gunpowder into each hole, covering it with sand, and tamping the material down with a large tamping iron before detonating it with a fuse. On the fateful day, the gunpowder exploded while Gage was tamping it, launching the 3-cm-thick, 90-cm-long tamping iron through his face, skull, and brain and out the other side.

Amazingly, Gage survived his accident, but he survived it a changed man. Before the accident, Gage had been a responsible, intelligent, socially well-adapted person, who was well liked by his friends and fellow workers. Once recovered, he appeared to be as able-bodied and intellectually capable as before, but his personality and emotional life had totally changed. Formerly a religious, respectful, reliable man, Gage became irreverent and impulsive. In particular, his abundant profanity offended many. He became so unreliable and undependable that he soon lost his job, and was never again able to hold a responsible position.

Gage became itinerant, roaming the country for a dozen years until his death in San Francisco. His bizarre accident and apparently successful recovery made headlines around the world, but his death went largely unnoticed and unacknowledged.

Gage was buried next to the offending tamping iron. Five years later, neurologist John Harlow was granted permission from Gage's family to exhume the body and tamping iron to study them. Since then, Gage's skull and the tamping iron have been on display in the Warren Anatomical Medical Museum at Harvard University.

In 1994, Damasio and her colleagues brought the power of computerized reconstruction to bear on Gage's classic case. They began by taking an x-ray of the skull and measuring it precisely, paying particular attention to the position of the entry and exit holes. From these measurements, they reconstructed the accident and determined the likely region of Gage's brain damage (see Figure 17.1). It was apparent that the damage to Gage's brain affected both medial prefrontal lobes, which we now know are involved in planning, decision making, and emotion (see Jin & Maren, 2015; Lee & Seo, 2016; Simon, Wood & Moghaddam, 2015).

DARWIN'S THEORY OF THE EVOLUTION OF EMOTION. The first major event in the study of the biopsychology of emotion was the publication in 1872 of Darwin's book *The Expression of Emotions in Man and Animals*. In it, Darwin argued, largely on the basis of anecdotal evidence, that particular emotional responses, such as human facial expressions, tend to accompany the same emotional states in all members of a species.

Darwin believed that expressions of emotion, like other behaviors, are products of

evolution; he therefore tried to understand them by comparing them in different species (see Brecht & Freiwald, 2012; Panksepp, 2011). From such interspecies comparisons, Darwin developed a theory of the evolution of emotional expression that was composed of three main ideas:

- Expressions of emotion evolve from behaviors that indicate what an animal is likely to do next.

- If the signals provided by such behaviors benefit the animal that displays them, they will evolve in ways that enhance their communicative function, and their original function may be lost.

- Opposite messages are often signaled by opposite movements and postures, an idea called the *principle of antithesis*.

Consider how Darwin's theory accounts for the evolution of *threat displays*. Originally, facing one's enemies, rising up, and exposing one's weapons were the components of the early stages of combat. But once enemies began to recognize these behaviors as signals of impending aggression, a survival advantage accrued to attackers that could communicate their aggression most effectively and intimidate their victims without actually fighting. As a result, elaborate threat displays evolved, and actual combat declined.

To be most effective, signals of aggression and submission must be clearly distinguishable; thus, they tended to

Figure 17.1 A reconstruction of the brain injury of Phineas Gage. The damage focused on the medial prefrontal lobes.

(Based on Damasio, H., Grabowski, T., Frank, R., Galaburda, A. M., & Damasio, A. R. (1994). The return of Phineas Gage: Clues about the brain from the skull of a famous patient. *Science, 264*, 1102–1105.)

evolve in opposite directions. For example, gulls signal aggression by pointing their beaks at one another and submission by pointing their beaks away from one another; primates signal aggression by staring and submission by averting their gaze. Figure 17.2 reproduces the woodcuts Darwin used in his 1872 book to illustrate this principle of antithesis in dogs.

JAMES-LANGE AND CANNON-BARD THEORIES. The first physiological theory of emotion was proposed independently by James and Lange in 1884. According to the **James-Lange theory**, emotion-inducing sensory stimuli are received and interpreted by the cortex, which triggers changes in the visceral organs via the autonomic nervous system and in the skeletal

---

Figure 17.2 Two woodcuts from Darwin's 1872 book, *The Expression of Emotions in Man and Animals*, that he used to illustrate the principle of antithesis. The aggressive posture of dogs features ears forward, back up, hair up, and tail up; the submissive posture features ears back, back down, hair down, and tail down.

Aggression

Submission

muscles via the somatic nervous system. Then, the autonomic and somatic responses trigger the experience of emotion in the brain. In effect, what the James-Lange theory did was to reverse the usual commonsense way of thinking about the causal relation between the experience of emotion and its expression. James and Lange argued that the autonomic activity and behavior that are triggered by the emotional event (e.g., rapid heartbeat and running away) produce the feeling of emotion, not vice versa.

Around 1915, Cannon proposed an alternative to the James-Lange theory of emotion, and it was subsequently extended and promoted by Bard. According to the **Cannon-Bard theory**, emotional stimuli have two independent excitatory effects: They excite both the feeling of emotion in the brain and the expression of emotion in the autonomic and somatic nervous systems. That is, the Cannon-Bard theory, in contrast to the James-Lange theory, views emotional experience and emotional expression as parallel processes that have no direct causal relation.

The James-Lange and Cannon-Bard theories make different predictions about the role of feedback from autonomic and somatic nervous system activity in emotional experience. According to the James-Lange theory, emotional experience depends entirely on feedback from autonomic and somatic nervous system activity; according to the Cannon-Bard theory, emotional experience is totally independent of such feedback. Both extreme positions have proved to be incorrect. On the one hand, it seems that the autonomic and somatic feedback is not necessary for the experience of emotion: Human patients whose autonomic and somatic feedback has been largely eliminated by a broken neck are capable of a full range of emotional experiences. However, there does seem to be some dampening of certain emotional experiences (i.e., fear, anger) in these patients (see Pistoia et al., 2015). On the other hand, there have been numerous reports—some of which you will soon encounter—that autonomic and somatic responses to emotional stimuli can influence emotional experience.

Failure to find unqualified support for either the James-Lange or the Cannon-Bard theory led to the modern biopsychological view. According to this view, each of the three principal factors in an emotional response—the perception of the emotion-inducing stimulus, the autonomic and somatic responses to the stimulus, and the experience of the emotion—can influence the other two (see Figure 17.3).

SHAM RAGE. In the late 1920s, Bard (1929) discovered that **decorticate** cats—cats whose cortex has been removed—respond aggressively to the slightest

Figure 17.3 Four ways of thinking about the relations among the perception of emotion-inducing stimuli, the autonomic and somatic responses to the stimuli, and the emotional experience.

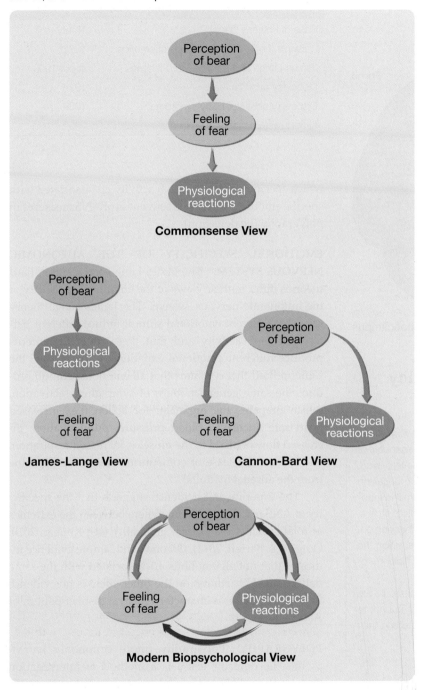

the hypothalamus; but it cannot be elicited if the hypothalamus is also removed. On the basis of this observation, Bard concluded that the hypothalamus is critical for the expression of aggressive responses and that the function of the cortex is to inhibit and direct these responses.

LIMBIC SYSTEM AND EMOTION. In 1937, Papez (pronounced "Payps") proposed that emotional expression is controlled by several interconnected nuclei and tracts that ring the thalamus. Figure 17.4 illustrates some of the key structures in this circuit, now known as the **limbic system** (*limbic* means "border"): the amygdala, mammillary body, hippocampus, fornix, cingulate cortex, septum, olfactory bulb, and hypothalamus. Papez proposed that emotional states are expressed through the action of the other structures of the circuit on the hypothalamus and that they are experienced through their action on the cortex. Papez's theory of emotion was revised and expanded by Paul MacLean in 1952 and became the influential *limbic system theory of emotion.*

KLÜVER-BUCY SYNDROME. In 1939, Klüver and Bucy observed a striking *syndrome* (pattern of behavior) in monkeys whose anterior temporal lobes had been removed. This syndrome, which is commonly referred to as the **Klüver-Bucy syndrome**, includes the following behaviors: the consumption of almost anything that is edible, increased sexual activity often directed at inappropriate objects, a tendency to repeatedly investigate familiar objects, a tendency to investigate objects with the mouth, and a lack of fear. Monkeys that could not be handled before surgery were transformed by bilateral anterior temporal lobectomy into tame subjects that showed no fear whatsoever—even in response to snakes, which terrify normal monkeys. In primates, most of the symptoms of the Klüver-Bucy syndrome appear to result from damage to the **amygdala** (see Phelps, 2006), a structure that has played a major role in research on emotion, as you will learn later in this chapter.

The Klüver-Bucy syndrome has been observed in several species. Following is a description of the syndrome in a human patient with a brain infection.

provocation: After a light touch, they arch their backs, erect their hair, hiss, and expose their teeth.

The aggressive responses of decorticate animals are abnormal in two respects: They are inappropriately severe, and they are not directed at particular targets. Bard referred to the exaggerated, poorly directed aggressive responses of decorticate animals as **sham rage**.

Sham rage can be elicited in cats whose cerebral hemispheres have been removed down to, but not including,

Figure 17.4 The location of the major limbic system structures. In general, they are arrayed near the midline in a ring around the thalamus. (See also Figure 3.26 on page 97)

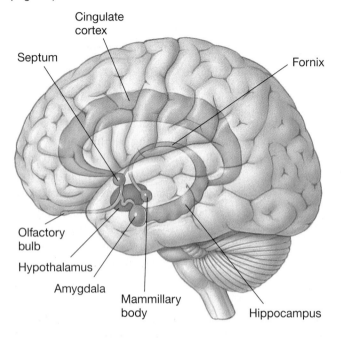

Cingulate cortex

Septum

Fornix

Olfactory bulb

Hypothalamus

Amygdala

Mammillary body

Hippocampus

A Human Case of Klüver-Bucy Syndrome

At first he was listless, but eventually he became very placid with flat affect. He reacted little to people or to other aspects of his environment. He spent much time staring at the television, even when it was not turned on. On occasion he would become extremely silly, smiling inappropriately and mimicking the actions of others, and once he began copying the movements of another person, he would persist for extended periods of time. In addition, he tended to engage in oral exploration, sucking, licking, or chewing all small objects that he could reach.

Although strictly heterosexual prior to his illness, in the hospital he made sexual advances to male patients, but not to female patients. This change prompted his fiancée to end their relationship.

The six early landmarks in the study of brain mechanisms of emotion just reviewed are listed in Table 17.1.

Emotions and the Autonomic Nervous System

LO 17.2 Summarize the research on the relationship between the autonomic nervous system and emotions.

Research on the role of the autonomic nervous system (ANS) in emotion has focused on two issues: the degree to

Table 17.1 Biopsychological Investigation of Emotion: Six Early Landmarks

Event	Date
Case of Phineas Gage	1848
Darwin's theory of the evolution of emotion	1872
James-Lange and Cannon-Bard theories	about 1900
Discovery of sham rage	1929
Discovery of Klüver-Bucy syndrome	1939
Limbic system theory of emotion	1952

which specific patterns of ANS activity are associated with specific emotions and the effectiveness of ANS measures in polygraphy (lie detection).

EMOTIONAL SPECIFICITY OF THE AUTONOMIC NERVOUS SYSTEM. The James-Lange and Cannon-Bard theories differ in their views of the emotional specificity of the autonomic nervous system. The James-Lange theory says that different emotional stimuli induce different patterns of ANS activity and that these different patterns produce different emotional experiences. In contrast, the Cannon-Bard theory claims that all emotional stimuli produce the same general pattern of sympathetic activation, which prepares the organism for action (i.e., increased heart rate, increased blood pressure, pupil dilation, increased flow of blood to the muscles, increased respiration, and increased release of epinephrine and norepinephrine from the adrenal medulla).

The experimental evidence suggests that the specificity of ANS reactions lies somewhere between the extremes of total specificity and total generality (see Kreibig, 2010; Quigley & Barrett, 2014). On one hand, ample evidence indicates that not all emotions are associated with the same pattern of ANS activity; on the other, there is no evidence that each emotion is characterized by a distinct pattern of ANS activity.

POLYGRAPHY. Polygraphy (more commonly known as the "lie detector test") is a method of interrogation that employs ANS indexes of emotion to infer the truthfulness of a person's responses. Polygraph tests administered by skilled examiners can be useful additions to normal interrogation procedures, but they are far from infallible.

The main problem in evaluating the effectiveness of polygraphy is that it is rarely possible in real-life situations to know for certain whether a suspect is guilty or innocent. Consequently, many studies of polygraphy have employed the *mock-crime procedure*: Volunteers participate in a mock crime and are then subjected to a polygraph test by an examiner who is unaware of their "guilt" or "innocence." The usual interrogation method is the **control-question technique**, in which the physiological response to the target question (e.g., "Did you steal that purse?") is compared with the physiological responses to control questions whose answers are known (e.g., "Have you ever been in jail before?"). The assumption is that lying will be associated with greater sympathetic activation. The average success rate in various mock-crime studies using the control-question technique is about 80 percent.

Despite being commonly referred to as *lie detection*, polygraphy detects ANS activity, not lies. Consequently, it is less likely to successfully identify lies in real life than in experiments. In real-life situations, questions such as "Did you steal that purse?" are likely to elicit an emotional reaction from all suspects, regardless of their guilt or innocence, making it difficult to detect deception. The **guilty-knowledge technique**, also known as the *concealed information test*, circumvents this problem. In order to use this technique, the polygrapher must have a piece of information concerning the crime that would be known only to the guilty person. Rather than attempting to catch the suspect in a lie, the polygrapher simply assesses the suspect's reaction to a list of actual and contrived details of the crime. Innocent suspects, because they have no knowledge of the crime, react to all such details in the same way; the guilty react differentially.

In the classic study of the guilty-knowledge technique (Lykken, 1959), volunteers waited until the occupant of an office went to the washroom. Then, they entered her office, stole her purse from her desk, removed the money, and left the purse in a locker. The critical part of the interrogation went something like this: "Where do you think we found the purse? In the washroom?... In a locker?...Hanging on a coat rack?..." Even though electrodermal activity was the only measure of ANS activity used in this study, 88 percent of the mock criminals were correctly identified; more importantly, none of the innocent control volunteers was judged guilty—see Ben-Shakhar (2012).

Emotions and Facial Expression

LO 17.3 Describe research on the facial expression of emotions.

Ekman and his colleagues have been preeminent in the study of facial expression (see Ekman, 2016). They began in the 1960s by analyzing hundreds of films and photographs of people experiencing various real emotions. From these, they compiled an atlas of the facial expressions that are normally associated with different emotions (Ekman & Friesen, 1975). For example, to produce the

facial expression for surprise, models were instructed to pull their brows upward so as to wrinkle their forehead, to open their eyes wide so as to reveal white above the iris, to slacken the muscles around their mouth, and to drop their jaw. Try it.

UNIVERSALITY OF FACIAL EXPRESSION. Several studies have found that people of different cultures make similar facial expressions in similar situations and that they can correctly identify the emotional significance of facial expressions displayed by people from cultures other than their own. The most convincing of these studies was a study of the members of an isolated New Guinea tribe who had had little or no contact with the outside world (see Ekman & Friesen, 1971).

PRIMARY FACIAL EXPRESSIONS. Ekman and Friesen concluded that the facial expressions of the following six emotions are primary: surprise, anger, sadness, disgust, fear, and happiness. They further concluded that all other facial expressions of genuine emotion are composed of mixtures of these six primaries. Figure 17.5 illustrates these six primary facial expressions and the combination of two of them to form a nonprimary expression.

FACIAL FEEDBACK HYPOTHESIS. Is there any truth to the old idea that putting on a happy face can make you feel better? Research suggests that there is. The hypothesis that our facial expressions influence our emotional experience is called the **facial feedback hypothesis**. In a test of the facial feedback hypothesis, Rutledge and Hupka (1985) instructed volunteers to assume one of two patterns of facial contractions while they viewed a series of slides; the patterns corresponded to happy or angry faces, although the volunteers were unaware of that. They reported that the slides made them feel more happy and less angry when they were making happy faces and less happy and more angry when they were making angry faces (see Figure 17.6).

Check It Out
Experiencing Facial Feedback

Why don't you try the facial feedback hypothesis? Pull your eyebrows down and together; raise your upper eyelids and tighten your lower eyelids, and narrow your lips and press them together. Now, hold this expression for a few seconds. If it makes you feel slightly angry and uncomfortable, you have just experienced the effect of facial feedback.

Figure 17.5 Ekman's six primary facial expressions of emotion and one combination facial expression.

(Generously supplied by Kyung Jae Lee and Stephen DiPaola of the iVizLab, Simon Fraser University. The expressions were created in video game character style using FaceFx 3D software, which allows DiPaola and Lee to create and control facial expressions of emotion in stills and animated sequences; see ivizlab.sfu.ca).

ANGER DISGUST FEAR SAD EYES / HAPPY MOUTH

HAPPINESS SADNESS SURPRISE

Figure 17.6 The effects of facial expression on the experience of emotion. Participants reported feeling more happy and less angry when they viewed slides while making a happy face and less happy and more angry when they viewed slides while making an angry face.

(Based on Rutledge, L. L., & Hupka, R. B. (1985). The facial feedback hypothesis: Methodological concerns and new supporting evidence. *Motivation and Emotion, 9,* 219–240.)

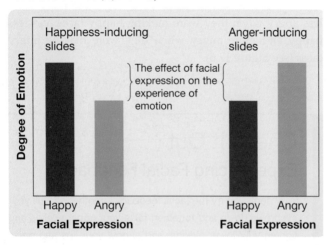

VOLUNTARY CONTROL OF FACIAL EXPRESSION. Because we can exert voluntary control over our facial muscles, it is possible to inhibit true facial expressions and to substitute false ones. There are many reasons for choosing to put on a false facial expression. Some of them are positive (e.g., putting on a false smile to reassure a worried friend), and some are negative (e.g., putting on a false smile to disguise a lie). In either case, it is difficult to fool an expert.

There are two ways of distinguishing true expressions from false ones (Ekman, 1985). First, *microexpressions* (brief facial expressions) of the real emotion often break through the false one (see Wang et al., 2015). Such microexpressions last only about 0.05 second, but with practice they can be detected without the aid of slow-motion photography. Second, there are often subtle differences between genuine facial expressions and false ones that can be detected by skilled observers.

The most widely studied difference between a genuine and a false facial expression was first described by the French anatomist Duchenne in 1862. Duchenne said that the smile of enjoyment could be distinguished from deliberately produced smiles by consideration of the two facial muscles that are contracted during genuine smiles: *orbicularis oculi*, which encircles the eye and pulls the skin from the cheeks and forehead toward the eyeball, and *zygomaticus major*, which pulls the lip corners up (see Figure 17.7). According to Duchenne, the zygomaticus major can be controlled voluntarily, whereas the orbicularis

Figure 17.7 A fake smile. The orbicularis oculi and the zygomaticus major are two muscles that contract during genuine (Duchenne) smiles. Because the lateral portion of the orbicularis oculi is difficult for most people to contract voluntarily, fake smiles usually lack this component. This young man is faking a smile for the camera. Look at his eyes.

Figure 17.8 An expression of pride.

(Reproduced with permission of Jessica Tracy, Department of Psychology, University of British Columbia.)

oculi is normally contracted only by genuine pleasure. Thus, inertia of the orbicularis oculi in smiling unmasks a false friend—a fact you would do well to remember. Ekman named the genuine smile the **Duchenne smile**.

FACIAL EXPRESSIONS: CURRENT PERSPECTIVES. Ekman's work on facial expression began before video recording became commonplace. Now, video recordings provide almost unlimited access to natural facial expressions made in response to real-life situations. This technology has contributed to four important qualifications to Ekman's original theory. First, it is now clear that Ekman's six primary facial expressions of emotion rarely occur in pure form—they are ideals with many subtle variations. Second, the existence of other primary emotions has been recognized (see Whalen et al., 2013). Third, it is now clear that body cues, not just facial expressions, play a major role in expressions of emotion (see Aviezer, Trope, & Todorov, 2012). For example, pride is expressed through a small smile, with the head tilted back slightly and the hands on the hips, raised above the head, or clenched in fists with the arms crossed on the chest—see Figure 17.8 (see Tracy & Robins, 2007). Fourth, there is evidence that Ekman's six primary facial expressions may not be as universal as originally believed. For example, there seem to be distinct differences, in terms of both the expression and recognition of facial expressions, between Western Caucasian and East Asian individuals (see Calvo & Nummenmaa, 2015; Jack et al., 2012; Wood et al., 2016).

Fear, Defense, and Aggression

Most biopsychological research on emotion has focused on fear and defensive behaviors. **Fear** is the emotional reaction to threat; it is the motivating force for defensive behaviors. **Defensive behaviors** are behaviors whose primary function is to protect the organism from threat or harm. In contrast, **aggressive behaviors** are behaviors whose primary function is to threaten or harm.

Although one purpose of this module is to discuss fear, defense, and aggression, it has another important purpose: to explain a common problem faced by biopsychologists and the way in which those who conduct research in this particular area have managed to circumvent it. Barrett (2006) pointed out that progress in the study of the neural basis of emotion has been limited because neuroscientists have often been guided by unsubstantiated cultural assumptions about emotion: Because we have words such as *fear*, *happiness*, and *anger* in our language, scientists have often assumed that these emotions exist as entities in the brain, and they have searched for them—often with little success. The following lines of research on fear, defense, and aggression illustrate how biopsychologists can overcome the problem of vague, subjective, everyday concepts by basing their search for neural mechanisms on

Thinking Creatively

the thorough descriptions of relevant behaviors, the environments in which they occur, and the putative adaptive

Evolutionary Perspective functions of such behaviors (see Kasai et al., 2015; Sachser, Kaiser, & Hennessy, 2013).

Thinking Creatively Many people treat "intelligence" as if it were a real entity, yet it is a complex construct that was developed by psychologists. Treating a psychological construct (e.g., intelligence) as if it actually exists is a logical error, known as an *error of reification*. Have you ever encountered such errors in the popular media? Give an example.

Types of Aggressive and Defensive Behaviors

LO 17.4 Describe the work that led to the distinction between aggressive and defensive behaviors in mammals.

Considerable progress in the understanding of aggressive and defensive behaviors has come from the research of Blanchard and Blanchard (see Blanchard, Summers, & Blanchard, 2013; Koolhaus et al., 2013) on the *colony-intruder model of aggression and defense* in rats.

Evolutionary Perspective Blanchard and Blanchard have derived rich descriptions of rat intraspecific aggressive and defensive behaviors by studying the interactions between the **alpha male**—the dominant male—of an established mixed-sex colony and a small male intruder: Upon encountering the intruder, the alpha male typically chases it away, repeatedly biting its back during the pursuit. The intruder eventually stops running and turns to face the alpha male. The intruder then rears up on its hind legs, still facing its attacker and using its forelimbs to ward off the attack. In response, the alpha male changes to a lateral orientation, with the side of its body perpendicular to the front of the defending intruder. Then, the alpha moves sideways toward the intruder, crowding and trying to push it off balance. If the defending intruder stands firm against this "lateral attack," the alpha often reacts by making a quick lunge around the defender's body in an attempt to bite its back. In response to such attacks, the defender pivots on its hind feet, in the same direction as the attacker is moving, continuing its frontal orientation to the attacker in an attempt to prevent the back bite.

Another excellent illustration of how careful observation of behavior has led to improved understanding of aggressive and defensive behaviors is provided by Pellis and colleagues' (1988) study of cats. They began by videotaping interactions between cats and mice. They found that different cats reacted to mice in different ways: Some were efficient mouse killers, some reacted defensively, and some seemed to play with the mice. Careful analysis of the

"play" sequences led to two important conclusions. The first conclusion was that, in contrast to the common belief, cats do not play with their prey; the cats that appeared to be playing with the mice were simply vacillating between attack and defense. The second conclusion was that one can best understand each cat's interactions with mice by locating the interactions on a linear scale, with total aggressiveness at one end, total defensiveness at the other, and various proportions of the two in between.

Pellis and colleagues tested their conclusions by reducing the defensiveness of the cats with an antianxiety drug. As predicted, the drug moved each cat along the scale toward more efficient killing. Cats that avoided mice before the injection "played with" them after the injection, those that "played with" them before the injection killed them after the injection, and those that killed them before the injection killed them more quickly after the injection.

Thinking Creatively

Based on the numerous detailed descriptions of aggressive and defensive behaviors provided by the Blanchards, Pellis and colleagues, and other biopsychologists who have followed their example, most researchers now distinguish among different categories of such behaviors. These categories of aggressive and defensive behaviors are based on three criteria: (1) their *topography* (form), (2) the situations that elicit them, and (3) their apparent function. Several of these categories for rats are described in Table 17.2 (see Blanchard et al., 2011; Eilam, Izhar, & Mort, 2011).

The analysis of aggressive and defensive behaviors has led to the development of the **target-site concept**—the idea that the aggressive and defensive behaviors of an animal are often designed to attack specific sites on the body of another animal while protecting specific sites on its own. For example, the behavior of a socially aggressive rat (e.g., lateral attack) appears to be designed to deliver bites to the defending rat's back and to protect its own face, the likely target of a defensive attack. Conversely, most of the maneuvers of the defending rat (e.g., boxing and pivoting) appear to be designed to protect the target site on its back.

The discovery that aggressive and defensive behaviors occur in a variety of stereotypical species-common forms was the necessary first step in the identification of their neural bases. Because the different categories of aggressive and defensive behaviors are mediated by different neural circuits, little progress was made in identifying these circuits before the categories were first delineated. For example, the lateral septum was once believed to inhibit all aggression, because lateral septal lesions rendered laboratory rats notoriously difficult to handle—the behavior of the lesioned rats was commonly referred to as *septal aggression* or *septal rage*. However, we now know that lateral septal lesions do not increase aggression: Rats with lateral septal lesions do not initiate more attacks, but they are hyperdefensive when threatened.

Table 17.2 Categories of Aggressive and Defensive Behaviors in Rats

Aggressive Behaviors	Predatory Aggression	The stalking and killing of members of other species for the purpose of eating them. Rats kill prey, such as mice and frogs, by delivering bites to the back of the neck.
	Social Aggression	Unprovoked aggressive behavior that is directed at a *conspecific* (member of the same species) for the purpose of establishing, altering, or maintaining a social hierarchy. In mammals, social aggression occurs primarily among males. In rats, it is characterized by piloerection, lateral attack, and bites directed at the defender's back.
Defensive Behaviors	Intraspecific Defense	Defense against social aggression. In rats, it is characterized by freezing and flight and by various behaviors, such as boxing, that are specifically designed to protect the back from bites.
	Defensive Attacks	Attacks that are launched by animals when they are cornered by threatening members of their own or other species. In rats, they include lunging, shrieking, and biting attacks that are usually directed at the face of the attacker.
	Freezing and Flight	Responses that many animals use to avoid attack. For example, if a human approaches a wild rat, it will often freeze until the human penetrates its safety zone, whereupon it will explode into flight.
	Maternal Defensive Behaviors	The behaviors by which mothers protect their young. Despite their defensive function, they are similar to male social aggression in appearance.
	Risk Assessment	Behaviors that are performed by animals in order to obtain specific information that helps them defend themselves more effectively. For example, rats that have been chased by a cat into their burrow do not emerge until they have spent considerable time at the entrance scanning the surrounding environment.
	Defensive Burying	Rats and other rodents spray sand and dirt ahead with their forepaws to bury dangerous objects in their environment, to drive off predators, and to construct barriers in burrows.

Aggression and Testosterone

LO 17.5 Describe the relation between testosterone levels and aggression in males.

The fact that social aggression in many species occurs more commonly among males than among females is usually explained with reference to the organizational and activational effects of testosterone. The brief period of testosterone release that occurs around birth in genetic males is thought to organize their nervous systems along masculine lines and hence to create the potential for male patterns of social aggression to be activated by the high testosterone levels that are present after puberty. These organizational and activational effects have been demonstrated in some mammalian species. For example, neonatal castration of male mice eliminates the ability of testosterone injections to induce social aggression in adulthood, and adult castration eliminates social aggression in male mice that do not receive testosterone replacement injections. Unfortunately, research on testosterone and aggression in other species has not been so straightforward (see Carré & Olmstead, 2015).

Soma and his colleagues have reviewed the extensive comparative research literature on testosterone and aggression (Demas et al., 2005; Soma, 2006). Here are their major conclusions:

- Testosterone increases social aggression in the males of many species; aggression is largely abolished by castration in these same species.

- In some species, castration has no effect on social aggression; in still others, castration reduces social aggression during the breeding season but not at other times.

- The relation between aggression and testosterone levels is difficult to interpret because engaging in aggressive activity can itself increase testosterone levels—for example, just playing with a gun increased the testosterone levels of male college students (Klinesmith, Kasser, & McAndrew, 2006).

- The blood level of testosterone, which is the only measure used in many studies, is not the best measure. What matters more are the testosterone levels in the relevant areas of the brain. Although studies focusing on brain levels of testosterone are rare, it has been shown that testosterone can be synthesized in particular brain sites and not in others.

It is unlikely that humans are an exception to the usual involvement of testosterone in mammalian social aggression. However, the evidence is far from clear. In human males, aggressive behavior does not increase at puberty as testosterone levels in the blood increase; aggressive behavior is not eliminated by castration; and it is not increased by testosterone injections that elevate blood levels of testosterone. A few studies have found that violent male criminals and aggressive male athletes tend to have higher testosterone levels than normal (see Batrinos, 2012); however, this correlation may indicate that aggressive behaviors increase testosterone, rather than vice versa.

The lack of strong evidence of the involvement of testosterone in human aggression could mean that hormonal and neural regulation of aggression in humans differs from that in many other mammalian species. Or, it could

mean that the research on human aggression and testosterone is flawed. For example, human studies are typically based on blood levels of testosterone (often inferred from saliva levels because collecting saliva is safer and easier than collecting blood) rather than on brain levels. However, the blood levels of a hormone aren't necessarily indicative of how much hormone is reaching the brain. Also, the researchers who study human aggression have often failed to appreciate the difference between social aggression, which is related to testosterone in many species, and defensive attack, which is not (see Montoya et al., 2012; Sobolewski, Brown, & Mitani, 2013). Most seemingly aggressive outbursts in humans are overreactions to real or perceived threat, and thus they are more appropriately viewed as defensive attack, not social aggression.

Neural Mechanisms of Fear Conditioning

Much of what we know about the neural mechanisms of fear has come from the study of fear conditioning. **Fear conditioning** is the establishment of fear in response to a previously neutral stimulus (the *conditional stimulus*) by presenting it, usually several times, before the delivery of an aversive stimulus (the *unconditional stimulus*).

In a standard fear-conditioning experiment, the subject, often a rat, hears a tone (conditional stimulus) and then receives a mild electric shock to its feet (unconditional stimulus). After several pairings of the tone and the shock, the rat responds to the tone with a variety of defensive behaviors (e.g., freezing and increased susceptibility to startle) and sympathetic nervous system responses (e.g., increased heart rate and blood pressure). LeDoux and his colleagues have mapped the neural mechanism that mediates this form of auditory fear conditioning (see Johansen et al., 2011; Ledoux, 2014).

Amygdala and Fear Conditioning

LO 17.6 Describe the role of the amygdala in fear conditioning.

LeDoux and his colleagues began their search for the neural mechanisms of *auditory fear conditioning* (fear conditioning that uses a sound as a conditional stimulus) by making lesions in the auditory pathways of rats. They found that bilateral lesions to the *medial geniculate nucleus* (the auditory relay nucleus of the thalamus) blocked fear conditioning to a

tone, but bilateral lesions to the auditory cortex did not. This indicated that for auditory fear conditioning to occur, it is necessary for signals elicited by the tone to reach the medial geniculate nucleus but not the auditory cortex. It also indicated that a pathway from the medial geniculate nucleus to a structure other than the auditory cortex plays a key role in fear conditioning. This pathway proved to be the pathway from the medial geniculate nucleus to the amygdala. Lesions of the amygdala, like lesions of the medial geniculate nucleus, blocked auditory fear conditioning. The amygdala receives input from all sensory systems, and it is believed to be the structure in which the emotional significance of sensory signals is learned and retained.

Several pathways (see Dampney, 2015) carry signals from the amygdala to brain-stem structures that control the various emotional responses. For example, a pathway to the periaqueductal gray of the midbrain elicits appropriate defensive responses (see Kim et al., 2013), whereas another pathway to the lateral hypothalamus elicits appropriate sympathetic responses.

The fact that auditory cortex lesions do not disrupt fear conditioning to simple tones does not mean that the auditory cortex is not involved in auditory fear conditioning. There are two pathways from the medial geniculate nucleus to the amygdala: the direct one, which you have already learned about, and an indirect one that projects via the auditory cortex. Both routes are capable of mediating fear conditioning to simple sounds; if only one is destroyed, conditioning progresses normally. However, only the cortical route is capable of mediating fear conditioning to complex sounds (see Change & Grace, 2015).

Figure 17.9 illustrates the circuit of the brain that is thought to mediate fear conditioning to auditory conditional stimuli (see Calhoun & Tye, 2015; Herry & Johansen, 2014). Sound signals from the medial geniculate nucleus of the thalamus reach the amygdala directly, or indirectly via the auditory cortex. The amygdala assesses the emotional significance of the sound on the basis of previous encounters with it, and then the amygdala activates the appropriate response circuits—for example, behavioral circuits in the periaqueductal gray and sympathetic circuits in the hypothalamus.

Contextual Fear Conditioning and the Hippocampus

LO 17.7 Describe the role of the hippocampus in contextual fear conditioning.

Environments, or *contexts*, in which fear-inducing stimuli are encountered can come to elicit fear. For example, if you repeatedly encountered a bear on a particular trail in the forest, the trail itself would begin to elicit fear. The process by which benign contexts come to elicit fear through their association with fear-inducing stimuli is called **contextual fear conditioning**.

Can you think of an instance where you have been subjected to contextual fear conditioning? Describe that instance.

Contextual fear conditioning has been produced in the laboratory in two ways. First, it has been produced by the conventional fear-conditioning procedure, which we just discussed. For example, if a rat repeatedly receives an electric shock following a conditional stimulus, such as a tone, the rat will become fearful of the conditional context (the test chamber) as well as the tone. Second, contextual fear conditioning has been produced by delivering aversive stimuli in a particular context in the absence of any other conditional stimulus. For example, if a rat receives shocks in a distinctive test chamber, the rat will become fearful of that chamber.

In view of the fact that the **hippocampus** plays a key role in memory for spatial location, it is reasonable to expect that it would be involved in contextual fear conditioning. This seems to be the case (see Maren, Phan, & Liberzon, 2013). Bilateral hippocampal lesions block the subsequent development of a fear response to the context without blocking the development of a fear response to the explicit conditional stimulus (e.g., a tone).

Amygdala Complex and Fear Conditioning

LO 17.8 Describe the role of two amygdalar nuclei in fear conditioning.

The preceding discussion has probably left you with the impression that the amygdala is a single brain structure; it isn't. It is actually a cluster of many nuclei, often referred to as the *amygdala complex*. The amygdala is composed of a dozen or so major nuclei, which are themselves divided into subnuclei. Each of these subnuclei is structurally distinct, has different connections, and is thus likely to have different functions (see Duvarci & Pare, 2014; Janak & Tye, 2015).

Figure 17.9 The structures thought to mediate the sympathetic and behavioral responses conditioned to an auditory conditional stimulus.

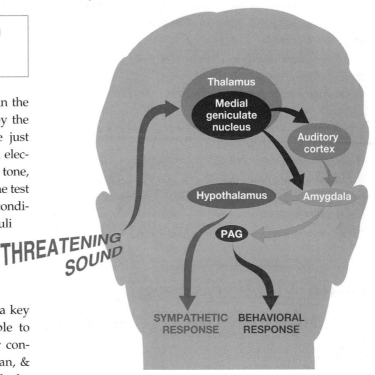

The study of fear conditioning provides a compelling demonstration of the inadvisability of assuming that the amygdala is a single structure. Evidence has been accumulating that the **lateral nucleus of the amygdala**—not the entire amygdala—is critically involved in the acquisition, storage, and expression of conditioned fear (see Duvarci & Pare, 2014; Janak & Tye, 2015; Tovote, Fadok, & Lüthi, 2015). Both the prefrontal cortex and the hippocampus project to the lateral nucleus of the amygdala: The **prefrontal cortex** is thought to act on the lateral nucleus of the amygdala to suppress conditioned fear (see Gilmartin, Balderston, & Helmstetter, 2014), and the hippocampus is thought to interact with that part of the amygdala to mediate learning about the context of fear-related events. The amygdala is thought to control defensive behavior via outputs from the **central nucleus of the amygdala** (see Janak & Tye, 2015).

Scan Your Brain

This chapter is about to change direction: The remaining two modules focus on the neural mechanisms of human emotion and on the effects of stress on health. This is a good point for you to scan your brain to see whether it has retained the introductory material on emotion and fear. Fill in each of the following blanks with the most appropriate term. The correct answers are provided at the end of the exercise. Before continuing, review material related to your errors and omissions.

1. The theory that the subjective experience of emotion is triggered by ANS responses is called the _____ theory.

2. The pattern of aggressive responses observed in decorticate animals is called _____.

3. Between the amygdala and the fornix in the limbic system is the _____.

4. A Duchenne smile, but not a false smile, involves appropriate contraction of the _____.

5. Aggression directed by the alpha male of a colony at a male intruder is called _____ aggression.

6. The usual target site of rat defensive attacks is the _____ of the attacking rat.

7. Testosterone increases _____ aggression in rats.

8. In humans, most violent outbursts that are labeled as aggression are more appropriately viewed as _____ attacks.

9. The establishing of a fear response to a previously neutral stimulus, such as a tone, is accomplished by fear _____.

10. In the typical auditory fear-conditioning experiment, the _____ is a tone.

11. Auditory fear conditioning to simple tones depends on a pathway from the _____ to the amygdala.

12. Unlike auditory fear conditioning to simple tones, fear conditioning to complex sounds involves the _____.

13. The prefrontal cortex is thought to act on the _____ of the amygdala to inhibit conditioned fear.

Scan Your Brain answers: (1) James-Lange, (2) sham rage, (3) hippocampus, (4) orbicularis oculi, (5) social, (6) face, (7) social, (8) defensive, (9) conditioning, (10) conditional stimulus, (11) medial geniculate nucleus, (12) auditory cortex, (13) lateral nucleus.

Brain Mechanisms of Human Emotion

This module deals with the brain mechanisms of human emotion. We still do not know how the brain controls the experience or expression of emotion, or how the brain interprets emotion in others, but progress has been made. Each of the following sections illustrates an area of progress.

Cognitive Neuroscience of Emotion

LO 17.9 Describe the current status of cognitive neuroscience research on emotion.

Cognitive neuroscience is currently the dominant approach being used to study the brain mechanisms of human emotion. There have been many functional brain-imaging studies of people experiencing or imagining emotions or watching others experiencing them. These studies have established three points that have advanced our understanding of the brain mechanisms of emotion in fundamental ways (see Neumann et al., 2014; Wood et al., 2016):

• Brain activity associated with each human emotion is diffuse—there is not a center

for each emotion (see Feinstein, 2013). Think "mosaic," not "center," for locations of brain mechanisms of emotion.

• There is virtually always activity in motor and sensory cortices when a person experiences an emotion or empathizes with a person experiencing an emotion (see Figure 17.10).

• Similar patterns of brain activity tend to be recorded when a person experiences an emotion, imagines that emotion, or sees somebody else experience that emotion.

Figure 17.10 Horizontal, sagittal, and coronal functional MRIs show areas of increased activity in the primary motor cortex (M1) and the premotor cortex (PMC) when volunteers watched facial expressions of emotion. The same areas were active when the volunteers made the expressions themselves.

(From Carr et al., 2003.)

These three fundamental findings are influencing how researchers are thinking about the neural mechanisms of emotion. For example, the activity observed in sensory and motor cortex during the experience of human emotions is now believed to be an important part of the mechanism by which the emotions are experienced. The re-experiencing of related patterns of motor, autonomic, and sensory neural activity during emotional experiences is generally referred to as the *embodiment of emotions* (see Wang et al., 2016). These findings may also help explain the remarkable ability of humans to empathize with others.

Amygdala and Human Emotion

LO 17.10 Describe the role of the amygdala in human emotion.

You have already learned that the amygdalae play an important role in fear conditioning in rats. Numerous functional brain-imaging studies have suggested that the function of the human amygdalae is more general. Although the human amygdalae appear to respond most robustly to fear, they also respond to other emotions (see Hsu et al., 2015; Koelsch & Skouras, 2014; Patin & Pause, 2015). Indeed, the amygdalae appear to play a role in the performance of any task with an emotional component, whether positive or negative (see Fastenrath et al., 2014; Stillman, Van Bavel, & Cunningham, 2015). This has led to the view that the amygdalae play a role in evaluating the emotional significance of situations.

Although the results of brain-imaging studies suggest that the amygdalae play a general role in emotions, the study of some patients with amygdalar damage suggests a specific role in fear. The following case illustrates this point.

The Case of S.P., the Woman Who Couldn't Perceive Fear

At the age of 48, S.P. had her right amygdala and adjacent tissues removed for the treatment of epilepsy. Because her left **Clinical Implications** amygdala had been damaged, she in effect had a bilateral amygdalar lesion.

Clinical Implications Before reading any further, based on the animal research on the amygdala that you read about in the previous module, try to predict the sorts of deficits you would expect to see in patient S.P.

Following her surgery, S.P. had an above-average I.Q., and her perceptual abilities were generally normal. Of particular relevance was the fact that she had no difficulty in identifying faces or extracting information from them (e.g., information about age or gender). However, S.P. did have a severe postsurgical deficit in recognizing facial expressions of fear and less striking deficits in recognizing facial expressions of disgust, sadness, and happiness.

In contrast, S.P. had no difficulty specifying which emotion would go with particular sentences. Also, she had no difficulty using facial expressions upon request to express various emotions (see Anderson & Phelps, 2000).

The case of S.P. is similar to reported cases of Urbach-Wiethe disease (see Meletti et al., 2014). **Urbach-Wiethe disease** is a genetic disorder that often results in *calcification* (hardening by conversion to calcium carbonate, the main component of bone) of the amygdala and surrounding anterior medial temporal-lobe structures in both hemispheres (see Figure 17.11). One Urbach-Wiethe patient with bilateral amygdalar damage was found to have lost the ability to recognize facial expressions of fear (see Adolphs, 2006). Indeed, she could not describe fear-inducing situations or produce fearful expressions, although she had no difficulty on tests involving other emotions. Although recent research has focused on the role of the amygdala in the recognition of fearful facial expressions, patients with Urbach-Wiethe disease sometimes have difficulty recognizing other complex visual stimuli (see Adolphs, 2010).

Medial Prefrontal Lobes and Human Emotion

LO 17.11 Describe the role of the medial prefrontal lobes in human emotion.

Emotion and cognition are often studied independently, but it is now believed that they are better studied as different

Figure 17.11 Bilateral calcification of the amygdalae in a patient with Urbach-Wiethe disease (right). The amygdalae of a healthy volunteer are also shown (left). The red circles indicate the location of the amygdalae.

(From Feinstein et al., 2013.)

components of the same system (see Barrett & Satpute, 2013). The medial portions of the prefrontal lobes (including the medial portions of the orbitofrontal cortex and anterior cingulate cortex) are the sites of emotion–cognition interaction that have received the most attention (e.g., Etkin, Büchel, & Gross, 2015). Functional brain-imaging studies have found evidence of activity in the medial prefrontal lobes when emotional reactions are being cognitively suppressed or re-evaluated (see Okon-Singer et al., 2015).

Many studies of medial prefrontal lobe activity employ suppression paradigms or reappraisal paradigms. In studies that use **suppression paradigms**, participants are directed to inhibit their emotional reactions to unpleasant films or pictures; in studies that use **reappraisal paradigms**, participants are instructed to reinterpret a picture to change their emotional reaction to it. The medial prefrontal lobes are active when both of these paradigms are used, and they seem to exert their cognitive control of emotion by interacting with the amygdala (see Sotres-Bayon & Quirk, 2010; Whalen et al., 2013).

Many theories of the specific functions of the medial prefrontal lobes have been proposed. The medial prefrontal lobes have been hypothesized to monitor the difference between outcome and expectancy (see Diekhof et al., 2012), to encode stimulus value over time (Tsetsos et al., 2014), to predict the likelihood of error (see Hoffman & Beste, 2015), to mediate the conscious awareness of emotional stimuli (see Mitchell & Greening, 2011), and to mediate social decision making (see Lee & Seo, 2016; Phelps, Lempert, & Sokol-Hessner, 2014). Which hypothesis is correct? Perhaps all are; the medial prefrontal cortex is large and complex, and it likely performs many functions. This point was made by the study of Kawasaki and colleagues (2005).

Kawasaki and colleagues used microelectrodes to record from 267 neurons in the anterior cingulate cortices (part of the medial prefrontal cortex) of four patients prior to surgery. They assessed the activity of the neurons when the patients viewed photographs with emotional content. Of these 267 neurons, 56 responded most strongly and consistently to negative emotional content. This confirms previous research linking the medial prefrontal lobes with negative emotional reactions, but it also shows that not all neurons in the area perform the same function—neurons directly involved in emotional processing appear to be sparse and widely distributed in the human medial prefrontal lobes.

Lateralization of Emotion

LO 17.12 Describe the research on the lateralization of emotion.

There is evidence suggesting that emotional functions are lateralized, that is, the left and right cerebral hemispheres are specialized to perform different emotional functions

(see Shaw et al., 2005)—as you learned in Chapter 16. This evidence has led to several theories of the cerebral lateralization of emotion; the following are the two most prominent:

- The *right-hemisphere model* of the cerebral lateralization of emotion holds that the right hemisphere is specialized for all aspects of emotional processing: perception, expression, and experience of emotion.
- The *valence model* proposes that the right hemisphere is specialized for processing negative emotion and the left hemisphere is specialized for processing positive emotion.

Which of the two theories does the evidence support? Most studies of the cerebral lateralization of emotion have employed functional brain-imaging methods, and the results have been complex and variable. Wager and colleagues (2003) performed a meta-analysis of the data from 65 such studies.

The main conclusion of Wager and colleagues was that the current theories of lateralization of emotion are too general from a neuroanatomical perspective. Overall comparisons between left and right hemispheres revealed no interhemispheric differences in either the amount of emotional processing or the valence of the emotions being processed. However, when the comparisons were conducted on a structure-by-structure basis, they revealed substantial evidence of lateralization of emotional processing. Some kinds of emotional processing were lateralized to the left hemisphere in certain structures and to the right in others. Functional brain-imaging studies of emotion have commonly observed lateralization in the amygdalae—more activity is often observed in the left amygdala. Clearly, neither the right-hemisphere model nor the valence model of the lateralization of emotion is supported by the evidence. The models are too general (see Lindquist et al., 2012).

Another approach to studying the lateralization of emotions is based on observing the asymmetry of facial expressions. In most people, each facial expression begins on the left side of the face and, when fully expressed, is more pronounced there—which implies right-hemisphere dominance for facial expressions (see Figure 17.12). Remarkably, the same asymmetry of facial expressions has been documented in monkeys (see Lindell, 2013).

Neural Mechanisms of Human Emotion: Current Perspectives

LO 17.13 Describe the current perspective on the neural mechanisms of human emotion that has emerged from brain-imaging studies.

Although there is a general consensus that the amygdalae and medial prefrontal cortex play major roles in the

Figure 17.12 The asymmetry of facial expressions. Notice that the expressions are more obvious on the left side of two well-known faces: those of Mona Lisa and Albert Einstein.

(Right-hand image from Science Source/Getty Images.)

perception and experience of human emotion, the results of brain-imaging studies have put this consensus into perspective (see Braver, Cole, & Barrett, 2012; Lindquist et al., 2012). Here are four important points.

- Emotional situations produce widespread increases in cerebral activity, not just in the amygdalae and prefrontal cortex.

- All brain areas activated by emotional stimuli are also activated during other psychological processes.

- No brain structure has been invariably linked to a particular emotion.

- The same emotional stimuli often activate different areas in different people.

Stress and Health

When the body is exposed to harm or threat, the result is a cluster of physiological changes generally referred to as the *stress response*—or just **stress**. All **stressors** (experiences that induce the stress response) produce the same core pattern of physiological changes, whether psychological (e.g., dismay at the loss of one's job) or physical (e.g., long-term exposure to cold). However, it is *chronic psychological stress* that has been most frequently implicated in ill health, which is the focus of this module.

The Stress Response

LO 17.14 Describe the components of the stress response.

Hans Selye (pronounced "SELL-yay") first described the stress response in the 1950s, and he emphasized its dual nature. In the short term, it produces adaptive changes that help the animal respond to the stressor (e.g., mobilization of energy resources); in the long term, however, it produces changes that are maladaptive (e.g., enlarged adrenal glands).

Clinical Implications

Selye attributed the stress response to the activation of the *anterior-pituitary adrenal-cortex system*. He concluded that stressors acting on neural circuits stimulate the release of **adrenocorticotropic hormone (ACTH)** from the anterior pituitary, that ACTH in turn triggers the release of **glucocorticoids** from the **adrenal cortex**, and that the glucocorticoids produce many of the components of the stress response (see Nicolaides et al., 2014; Shirazi et al., 2015; Spiga et al., 2014). The level of circulating glucocorticoids is the most commonly employed physiological measure of stress.

Selye largely ignored the contributions of the sympathetic nervous system to the stress response. However, stressors activate the sympathetic nervous system, thereby increasing the amounts of epinephrine and norepinephrine released from the **adrenal medulla**. Most modern theories of stress acknowledge the roles of both the anterior-pituitary adrenal-cortex system and the sympathetic-nervous-system adrenal-medulla system (see Carter & Goldstein, 2015; Herman et al., 2012). Figure 17.13 illustrates the two-system view.

Watch this video on MyPsychLab
FIGHT OR FLIGHT

Figure 17.13 The two-system view of the stress response.

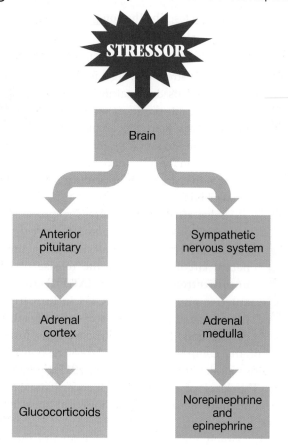

The major feature of Selye's landmark theory is its assertion that both physical and psychological stressors induce the same general stress response. This assertion has proven to be partly correct. There is good evidence that all kinds of common psychological stressors—such as losing a job, taking a final exam, or ending a relationship—act like physical stressors. However, Selye's contention that there is only one stress response has proven to be a simplification. Stress responses are complex and varied, with the exact response depending on the stressor, its timing, the nature of the stressed person, and how the stressed person reacts to the stressor (see Hostinar, Sullivan, & Gunnar, 2014; Oitzl et al., 2010; Oken, Chamine, & Wakeland, 2015). For example, in a study of women awaiting surgery for possible breast cancer, the levels of stress were lower in those who had convinced themselves that they could not possibly have cancer, that their prayers were certain to be answered, or that it was counterproductive to worry (see Katz et al., 1970).

In the 1990s, there was an important advance in the understanding of the stress response (see Grippo & Scotti, 2013). It was discovered that stressors produce physiological reactions that participate in the body's inflammatory responses. Most notably, it was found that stressors produce an increase in blood levels of **cytokines**, a group of peptide hormones that are released by many cells and participate in a variety of physiological and immunological

responses, causing inflammation and fever (see Padro & Sanders, 2014). The cytokines are now classified with the adrenal hormones as major stress hormones.

Animal Models of Stress

LO 17.15 Describe research on animal models of stress, including that on subordination stress.

Most of the early research on stress was conducted with nonhumans, and even today most lines of stress research begin with controlled experiments involving nonhumans before moving to correlational studies of humans. Early stress research on nonhumans tended to involve extreme forms of stress such as repeated exposure to electric shock or long periods of physical restraint. There are two problems with this kind of research. First is the problem of ethics. Any research that involves creating stressful situations is going to be controversial, but many of the early stress studies were "over the top" and would not be permitted today in many countries. The second problem is that studies that use extreme, unnatural forms of stress are often of questionable scientific value. Responses to extreme stress tend to mask normal variations in the stress response, and it is difficult to relate the results of such studies to common human stressors.

Better animal models of stress involve the study of social threat from *conspecifics* (members of the same species). Virtually all mammals—particularly males—experience threats from conspecifics at certain points in their lives. When conspecific threat becomes an enduring feature of daily life, the result is **subordination stress** (e.g., Rodriguez-Arias et al., 2016).

Subordination stress is most readily studied in social species that form *dominance hierarchies* (pecking orders; see Chapter 2). What do you think happens to subordinate male rodents who are continually attacked by more dominant males? They are more likely to attack juveniles, and they have smaller testes, shorter life spans, lower blood levels of testosterone, and higher blood levels of glucocorticoids (see Barik et al., 2013). If it has not already occurred to you, the chronic social threat that induces subordination stress in the members of many species is termed **bullying** in our own.

Psychosomatic Disorders: The Case of Gastric Ulcers

LO 17.16 Describe how our view of psychosomatic disorders has been refined by the results of research on gastric ulcers.

Interest in pathological effects of stress has increased as researchers have identified more and more **psychosomatic disorders** (medical disorders in which psychological factors play a causal role). So many adverse effects of stress on health (e.g., in heart disease, asthma, and skin disorders) have been documented that it is now more reasonable to think of most, if not all, medical disorders as psychosomatic.

Gastric ulcers were one of the first medical disorders to be classified as psychosomatic. **Gastric ulcers** are painful lesions to the lining of the stomach and duodenum, which in extreme cases can be life-threatening. About 500,000 new cases are reported each year in the United States.

The view of gastric ulcers as the prototypical psychosomatic disorder changed with the discovery that they seemed to be caused by bacteria. It was claimed that the bacteria *Helicobacter pylori* (i.e., *H. pylori*) are responsible for all cases of gastric ulcers except those caused by nonsteroidal anti-inflammatory agents such as aspirin. This seemed to rule out stress as a causal factor, but a consideration of the evidence suggests otherwise.

There is no denying that *H. pylori* damage the stomach wall or that antibiotic treatment of gastric ulcers helps many sufferers. The facts do, however, suggest that *H. pylori* infection alone is insufficient to produce the disorder in most people. Although most patients with gastric ulcers display signs of *H. pylori* infection, so too do many healthy individuals (see Maixner et al., 2016; Testerman & Morris, 2014). Also, antibiotics improve the condition of many patients with gastric ulcers, but so do psychological treatments—and they do it without reducing signs of *H. pylori* infection. Apparently, another factor increases the susceptibility of the stomach wall to damage from *H. pylori*, and this factor appears to be stress. Gastric ulcers occur more commonly in people living in stressful situations, and stressors can produce gastric ulcers in laboratory animals.

Psychoneuroimmunology: Stress, the Immune System, and the Brain

LO 17.17 Define psychoneuroimmunology, and describe the four components that make up our bodies' defenses against foreign pathogens.

A major change in the study of psychosomatic disorders came in the 1970s with the discovery that stress can increase susceptibility to infectious diseases. Up to that point, infectious diseases had been regarded as "strictly physical." The discovery that stress can increase susceptibility to infection led to the emergence of a new field of research in the early 1980s: **psychoneuroimmunology**— the study of interactions among psychological factors, the nervous system, and the immune system. Psychoneuroimmunological research is the focus of this section. Let's begin with an introduction to the immune system.

Microorganisms of every description revel in the warm, damp, nutritive climate of your body. However,

the body has four lines of defense to keep it from being overwhelmed. First is what has been termed the *behavioral immune systems:* Humans are motivated to avoid contact with individuals who are displaying symptoms of illness (see Murray & Schaller, 2016), and their bodies are primed to respond more aggressively to infection when they perceive signs of infection in others (see Schaller et al., 2010). Second are a variety of surface barriers that keep the body from being overwhelmed. The major surface barrier is skin, but there are other mechanisms that protect from invasions through bodily openings (e.g., respiratory tract, eyes, and gastrointestinal tract). These mechanisms include coughing, sneezing, tears, mucous, and numerous chemical barriers.

If microorganisms do manage to breach the surface barriers and enter the body, they are met by two additional lines of defense: the innate immune system and the adaptive immune system. Together, these two lines of defense constitute the **immune system** (see Pringle, 2013).

INNATE IMMUNE SYSTEM. The **innate immune system** is the first component of the immune system to react. It reacts quickly and generally near points of entry of **pathogens** (disease-causing agents) to the body. It is triggered when receptors called **toll-like receptors** (because they are similar to *toll*, a receptor previously discovered in fruit flies) bind to molecules on the surface of the pathogens or when injured cells send out alarm signals (see DeNardo, 2015). The reaction of the innate immune system includes a complex, but general, array of chemical and cellular reactions—they are general in the sense that the reactions to all pathogens are the same.

One of the first reactions of the innate immune system to the invasion of pathogens is *inflammation* (swelling). Inflammation is triggered by the release of chemicals from damaged cells. Particularly influential are the cytokines, which attract **leukocytes** (white blood cells) and other **phagocytes** (cells that engulf and destroy pathogens) into the infected area. Microglia are phagocytes that are specific to the central nervous system (see Aguzzi, Barres, & Bennett, 2013; Su et al., 2016). Cytokines also promote healing of the damaged tissue once the pathogens are destroyed (see Kyritsis et al., 2012; Stella, 2012).

Phagocytosis (destruction of pathogens by phagocytes) is thought to be one of the first immune reactions to have evolved. Phagocytes have been identified in all vertebrates and invertebrates that have been examined. A phagocyte is shown attacking bacteria in Figure 17.14.

ADAPTIVE IMMUNE SYSTEM. The **adaptive immune system** differs from the innate immune system in the following four respects: The adaptive immune system

- evolved more recently, first appearing in early vertebrates.

Figure 17.14 Phagocytosis: A phagocyte about to ingest and destroy bacteria (red blobs).

- is slower; its immune reaction to pathogens takes longer to be fully manifested.
- is specific in the sense that it reacts against specific antigens.
- has a memory; once it has reacted against a particular pathogen, it reacts more effectively against that same pathogen in the future.

The main cells of the adaptive immune system are specialized leukocytes called **lymphocytes**. Lymphocytes are produced in bone marrow and the thymus gland and are stored in the *lymphatic system* until they are activated. There are two major classes of lymphocytes: B cells and T cells (see Plesnila, 2016). **Cell-mediated immunity** is directed by **T cells** (T lymphocytes); **antibody-mediated immunity** is directed by **B cells** (B lymphocytes).

The cell-mediated immune reaction begins when a phagocyte ingests a foreign microorganism. The phagocyte then displays the microorganism's **antigens** (molecules, usually proteins, that can trigger an immune response) on the surface of its cell membrane, and this display attracts T cells. Each T cell has two kinds of receptors on its surface, one for molecules that are normally found on the surface of phagocytes and other body cells, and one for a specific foreign antigen. There are millions of different receptors for foreign antigens on T cells, but there is only one kind on each T cell, and there are only a few T cells with each kind of receptor. Once a T cell with a receptor for the foreign antigen binds to the surface of an infected macrophage, a series of reactions is initiated. Among these reactions is the

multiplication of the bound T cell, creating more T cells with the specific receptor necessary to destroy all invaders that contain the target antigens and all body cells that have been infected by the invaders.

The antibody-mediated immune reaction begins when a B cell binds to a foreign antigen for which it contains an appropriate receptor. This causes the B cell to multiply and to synthesize a lethal form of its receptor molecules. These lethal receptor molecules, called **antibodies**, are released into the intracellular fluid, where they bind to the foreign antigens and destroy or deactivate the microorganisms that possess them. Memory B cells for the specific antigen are also produced during the process; these cells have a long life and accelerate antibody-mediated immunity if there is a subsequent infection by the same microorganism.

The memory of the adaptive immune system is the mechanism that gives vaccinations their *prophylactic* (preventive) effect—**vaccination** involves administering a weakened form of a virus so that if the virus later invades, the adaptive immune system is prepared to act against it. For example, smallpox has been largely eradicated by programs of vaccination with the weakened form of its largely benign relative, cowpox. The process of creating immunity through vaccination is termed **immunization**.

Until recently, most immunological research has focused on the adaptive immune system; however, the discovery of the role of cytokines in the innate immune system stimulated interest in that system.

Watch this video on MyPsychLab
CHALK IT UP! ORGANIZATION OF THE IMMUNE SYSTEM

WHAT EFFECT DOES STRESS HAVE ON IMMUNE FUNCTION: DISRUPTIVE OR BENEFICIAL? It is widely believed that the main effect of stress on immune function is disruptive. We are sure you have heard this from family members, friends, and even physicians. But is this true?

One of the logical problems with the view that stress always disrupts immune function is that it is inconsistent with the principles of evolution. Virtually every individual organism encounters many stressors during the course of its life, and it is difficult to see how a maladaptive response to stress, such as a disruption of immune function, could have evolved—or could have survived if it had been created by a genetic accident or as a *spandrel* (a nonadaptive by-product of an adaptive evolutionary change; see Chapter 2).

Two events have helped clarify the relation between stress and immune function. The first was the *meta-analysis* of Segerstrom and Miller (2004), which reviewed about 300 previous studies of stress and immune function. Segerstrom and Miller found that the effects of stress on immune function depended on the kind of stress. They found that acute (brief) stressors (i.e., those lasting less than 100 minutes, such as public speaking, an athletic competition, or a musical performance) actually led to improvements in immune function. Not surprisingly, the improvements in immune function following acute stress occurred mainly in the innate immune system, whose components can be marshaled quickly. In contrast, chronic (long-lasting) stressors, such as caring for an ill relative or experiencing a period of unemployment, adversely affected the adaptive immune system. Stress that disrupts health or other aspects of functioning is called *distress*, and stress that improves health or other aspects of functioning is called *eustress*.

The second event that has helped clarify the relation between stress and immune function was the discovery of the bidirectional role played by the cytokines in the innate immune system. Short-term cytokine-induced inflammatory responses help the body combat infection, whereas long-term cytokine release is associated with a variety of adverse health consequences (see Dhabhar, 2014). This finding provided an explanation of the pattern of results discovered by Segerstrom and Miller's meta-analysis.

HOW DOES STRESS INFLUENCE IMMUNE FUNCTION?
The mechanisms by which stress influences immune function have been difficult to specify because there are so many possibilities. Stress produces widespread changes in the body through its effects on the anterior-pituitary adrenal-cortex system and the sympathetic-nervous-system adrenal-medulla system, and there are innumerable mechanisms by which those systems can influence immune function. For example, both T cells and B cells have receptors for glucocorticoids; and lymphocytes have receptors for epinephrine, norepinephrine, and glucocorticoids. In addition, many of the neuropeptides that are released by neurons are also released by cells of the immune system. Conversely, cytokines, originally thought to be produced only by cells of the immune system, have been found to be produced by cells of the nervous system (see Jin & Yamashita, 2016).

It is important to appreciate that there are behavioral routes by which stress can affect immune function. For example, people under severe stress often change their diet, exercise, sleep, and drug use, any of which could influence immune function. Also, the behavior of a stressed or ill person can produce stress and illness in others. For example, Wolf and colleagues (2007) found that stress in mothers aggravates asthmatic symptoms in their children; conversely, asthma in the children increases measures of stress in their mothers.

Watch this video on MyPsychLab
REDUCING STRESS, IMPROVING HEALTH

DOES STRESS AFFECT SUSCEPTIBILITY TO INFECTIOUS DISEASE?   You have just learned that stress influences immune function. Most people assume that this means that stress increases susceptibility to infectious diseases. But it doesn't mean this at all, and it is important that you understand why.

> Before reading further, try jotting down some reasons as to why it would be a mistake to think that stress increases susceptibility to infectious diseases.

There are at least three reasons why stress-produced decreases in immune function may not be reflected in an increased susceptibility to infectious disease:

- The immune system seems to have many redundant components; thus, disruption of one of them may have little or no effect on vulnerability to infection.

- Stress-produced changes in immune function may be too short-lived to have substantial effects on the probability of infection.

- Declines in some aspects of immune function may induce compensatory increases in others.

It has been difficult to prove that stress causes increases in susceptibility to infectious diseases in humans. One reason for this difficulty is that only correlational studies are possible. Numerous studies have reported *positive* correlations between stress and ill health in humans; for example, students in one study reported more respiratory infections during final exams (Glaser et al., 1987). However, interpretation of such correlations is never straightforward: People may report more illness during times of stress because they expect to be more ill, because their experience of illness during times of stress is more unpleasant, or because the stress changed their behavior in ways that increased their susceptibility to infection.

Despite the difficulties of proving a direct causal link between stress and susceptibility to infectious disease in humans, the evidence for such a link is strong. Three basic types of evidence, when considered together, are persuasive:

- Correlational studies in humans—as you have just learned—have found correlations between stress levels and numerous measures of health.

- Controlled experiments conducted with laboratory animals show that stress can increase susceptibility to infectious disease in these species.

- A few partially controlled studies of humans have added greatly to the weight of evidence.

One of the first partially controlled studies demonstrating stress-induced increases in the susceptibility of humans to infectious disease was conducted by Cohen and colleagues (1991). Using questionnaires, they assessed psychological stress levels in 394 healthy participants. Then, each participant randomly received saline nasal drops that contained a respiratory virus or only saline. Then, all of the participants were quarantined until the end of the study. A higher proportion of those participants who scored highly on the stress scales developed colds.

Early Experience of Stress

LO 17.18 Describe the effects of early exposure to severe stress.

Early exposure to severe stress can have a variety of adverse effects on subsequent development. Children subjected to maltreatment or other forms of severe stress display a variety of brain and endocrine system abnormalities (see Klengel & Binder, 2015). As you will learn in Chapter 18, some psychiatric disorders are thought to result from an interaction between an inherited susceptibility to a disorder and early exposure to severe stress. Also, early exposure to stress often increases the intensity of subsequent stress responses (e.g., increases the release of glucocorticoids in response to stressors).

It is important to understand that the developmental period during which early stress can adversely affect neural and endocrine development begins before birth. Many experiments have demonstrated the adverse effects of prenatal stress in laboratory animals; pregnant females have been exposed to stressors, and the adverse effects of that exposure on their offspring have subsequently been documented (e.g., Sowa et al., 2015).

Evolutionary Perspective

One particularly interesting line of research on the role of early experience in the development of the stress response began with the observation that handling of rat pups by researchers for a few minutes per day during the first few weeks of the rats' lives has a variety of salutary (health-promoting) effects (see Raineki, Lucion, & Weinberg, 2014). The majority of these effects seemed to result from a decrease in the magnitude of the handled pups' responses to stressful events. As adults, rats that had been handled as pups displayed smaller increases in circulating glucocorticoids in response to stressors (see Francis & Meaney, 1999). It seemed remarkable that a few hours of handling early in life could have such a significant and lasting effect. However, evidence supports an alternative interpretation.

Liu and colleagues (1997) found that handled rat pups are groomed (licked) more by their mothers, and they hypothesized that the salutary effects of the early handling resulted from the extra grooming, rather than from the handling itself. They confirmed this hypothesis by showing that unhandled rat pups that received a lot of grooming from their mothers developed the same profile of less glucocorticoid release that was observed in handled pups (see Champagne et al., 2008).

Early separation of rat pups from their mothers seems to have effects opposite to those that result from high levels of early grooming (see Zhang et al., 2013). For example, rats that are separated from their mothers in infancy display elevated behavioral and hormonal responses to stress as adults.

Stress and the Hippocampus

LO 17.19 Describe the effects of stress on the hippocampus.

Exposure to stress affects the structure and function of the brain in a variety of ways (see McEwen, Gray, & Nasca, 2015; Sandi & Haller, 2015). However, the hippocampus appears to be particularly susceptible to stress-induced effects (see Kim, Pellman, & Kim, 2015; McEwen, Nasca, & Gray, 2016). The reason for this susceptibility may be the particularly dense population of glucocorticoid receptors in the hippocampus.

Neuroplasticity

Stress has been shown to reduce dendritic branching in the hippocampus, to reduce adult neurogenesis in the hippocampus (see Egeland, Zunszain, & Pariante, 2015), to modify the structure of some hippocampal synapses, and to disrupt the performance of hippocampus-dependent tasks (see Kim, Pellman, & Kim, 2015). These effects of stress on the hippocampus appear to be mediated by elevated glucocorticoid levels: They can be induced by **corticosterone** (a major glucocorticoid) and can be blocked by **adrenalectomy** (surgical removal of the adrenal glands)—see Shirazi et al. (2015).

CONCLUSION. In this chapter, you have learned that the amygdala plays a role in emotion. The chapter ends with a troubling case that reinforces this point. Fortunately, not everybody reacts in the same way to amygdalar damage.

The Case of Charles Whitman, the Texas Tower Sniper

After having lunch with his wife and his mother, Charles Whitman went home and typed a letter of farewell—perhaps as an explanation for what would soon happen.

He stated in his letter that he was having many compelling and bizarre ideas. Psychiatric care had been no help. He asked that his brain be autopsied after he was through; he was sure they would find the problem.

 Clinical Implications

By all reports, Whitman had been a nice person. An Eagle Scout at 12 and a high school graduate at 17, he then enlisted in the Marine Corps, where he established himself as an expert marksman. After his discharge, he entered the University of Texas to study architectural engineering.

Nevertheless, in the evening of August 1, 1966, Whitman killed his wife and mother. He professed love for both of them, but he did not want them to face the aftermath of what was to follow.

The next morning, at about 11:30, Whitman went to the Tower of the University of Texas, carrying six guns, ammunition, several knives, food, and water. He clubbed the receptionist to death and shot four more people on his way to the observation deck. Once on the deck, he opened fire on people crossing the campus and on nearby streets. His accuracy was deadly: He killed people as far as 300 meters away—people who assumed they were out of range.

At 1:24 that afternoon, the police fought their way to the platform and shot Whitman to death. All told, 17 people, including Whitman, had been killed, and another 31 had been wounded (Helmer, 1986).

An autopsy was conducted. Whitman had been correct: They found a walnut-sized tumor in his right amygdala.

Scan Your Brain

Review the preceding module on stress and health. Fill in each of the following blanks. The correct answers are provided at the end of the exercise. Review material related to your errors or omissions before proceeding.

1. Glucocorticoids are released from the _____ as part of the stress response.
2. Stressors increase the release of epinephrine and norepinephrine from the _____.
3. Stressors trigger the release of _____, which participate in the body's inflammatory responses.
4. When threats from conspecifics become an enduring feature of daily life, the result is _____.
5. Gastric ulcers have been associated with *H. pylori* infection, but it seems likely that _____ is another causal factor in their development.
6. The field of science that focuses on the interactions among psychological factors, the nervous system, and the immune system is called _____.
7. There are two components of the immune system: the _____ immune system and the adaptive immune system.
8. Disease-causing agents are known as _____.
9. T cells and B cells are involved in cell-mediated and _____ immune reactions, respectively.
10. Adult rats groomed intensely as pups by their mothers display smaller increases in circulating _____ in response to stressors.
11. Corticosterone is a _____.
12. Stress has been shown to reduce adult neurogenesis in the _____ of laboratory animals.

Scan Your Brain answers: (1) adrenal cortex, (2) adrenal medulla, (3) cytokines, (4) subordination stress, (5) stress, (6) psychoneuroimmunology, (7) innate, (8) pathogens, (9) antibody-mediated, (10) glucocorticoids, (11) glucocorticoid, (12) hippocampus.

Themes Revisited

All four of the book's themes were prevalent in this chapter. The clinical implications theme appeared frequently, both be-

cause brain-damaged patients have taught us much about the neural mechanisms of emotion and because emotions have a major impact on health. The evolutionary perspective theme also occurred frequently because comparative research and the consideration of evolutionary pressures have also had a major impact on current thinking about the biopsychology of emotion.

The thinking creatively theme appeared where the text encouraged you to think in unconventional ways about the relation between testosterone

and human aggression and the interpretation of reports of correlations between stress and ill health.

Neuroplasticity was the major theme of the discussion of the effects of stress on the hippocampus.

Key Terms

Chapter 18
Biopsychology of Psychiatric Disorders

The Brain Unhinged

This chapter is about the biopsychology of **psychiatric disorders** (disorders of psychological function sufficiently severe to require treatment). One of the main difficulties in studying or treating psychiatric disorders is that they are difficult to diagnose. The psychiatrist or clinical psychologist must first decide whether a patient's psychological function is pathological or merely an extreme of normal human variation: For example, does a patient with a poor memory suffer from a pathological condition, or is he merely a healthy person with a poor memory?

Watch this video on MyPsychLab
WHAT DOES IT MEAN TO HAVE A MENTAL DISORDER?

If a patient is judged to be suffering from a psychiatric disorder, then the particular disorder must be diagnosed. Because we cannot yet identify the specific brain pathology associated with various disorders, their diagnosis usually rests entirely on the patient's symptom profile. Currently, the diagnosis is guided by the **DSM-5** (the current edition of the *Diagnostic and Statistical Manual* of the American Psychiatric Association). There are two main difficulties in diagnosing particular psychiatric disorders: (1) patients suffering from the same disorder often display different symptoms, and (2) patients suffering from different disorders often display many of the same symptoms. Consequently, experts often disagree on the diagnosis of particular cases, and the guidelines provided by the DSM change with each new edition (see Blashfield et al., 2014). One major purpose of this chapter is to help you understand why it is important to periodically revise the diagnosis of psychiatric disorders.

This chapter begins with discussions of five sorts of psychiatric disorders: schizophrenia, depressive disorders, bipolar disorders, anxiety disorders, and Tourette's disorder. It ends with a description of how new *psychotherapeutic* drugs are developed and tested.

Schizophrenia

Schizophrenia means "the splitting of psychic functions." The term was coined in the early years of the 20th century to describe what was assumed at the time to be the primary symptom of the disorder: the breakdown of integration among emotion, thought, and action.

Watch this video on MyPsychLab
LARRY: SCHIZOPHRENIA

Schizophrenia is considered to be a severe psychiatric disorder (see Uher, 2014). It attacks about 1 percent of individuals of all races and cultural groups, typically beginning in adolescence or early adulthood. Schizophrenia occurs in many forms, but the case of Lena introduces you to some of its common features (Meyer & Salmon, 1988).

Schizophrenia: The Case of Lena

Lena's mother was hospitalized with schizophrenia when Lena was 2. As a child, Lena displayed periods of hyperactivity; as an adolescent, she was viewed as odd. She enjoyed her classes and got good grades, but she had few friends. **Clinical Implications**

Shortly after their marriage, Lena's husband noticed that Lena was becoming more withdrawn. She would sit for hours barely moving a muscle, often having lengthy discussions with nonexistent people.

One day, Lena's husband found her sitting on the floor in an odd posture staring into space. She was totally unresponsive. When he tried to move her, Lena displayed *waxy flexibility*—that is, she reacted like a mannequin, not resisting movement and holding her new position until she was moved again. She was diagnosed with *schizophrenia with catatonia* (schizophrenia characterized by long periods of immobility and waxy flexibility).

In the hospital, Lena displayed a speech pattern exhibited by some individuals with schizophrenia: echolalia (vocalized repetition of some or all of what has just been heard).

Doctor: How are you feeling today?

Lena: I am feeling today, feeling the feelings today.

Doctor: Are you still hearing the voices?

Lena: Am I still hearing the voices, voices?

What Is Schizophrenia?

LO 18.1 Describe the positive and negative symptoms of schizophrenia, and provide specific examples of each.

The major difficulty in studying and treating schizophrenia is accurately defining it (see Bhati, 2013; Silveira, Marques-Teixeira, & Bastos-Leite, 2012). Its symptoms are complex and diverse; they overlap greatly with those of other psychiatric disorders and frequently change during the progression of the disorder. Also, various neurological disorders (e.g., complex partial epilepsy; see Chapter 10) have symptoms that might suggest a diagnosis of schizophrenia. Because the current definition of schizophrenia overlaps with that of several different disorders, the DSM-5 prefers to use the label *schizophrenia spectrum disorders* to refer to schizophrenia and related disorders (see Bhati, 2013).

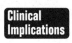 The DSM-5 made significant changes to many diagnostic categories. What problems do you foresee arising from such radical changes?

The following are some symptoms of schizophrenia, although none of them appears in all cases. In an effort to categorize cases of schizophrenia so that they can be studied and treated more effectively, it is common practice to consider **positive symptoms** (symptoms that seem to represent an excess of typical function) separately from **negative symptoms** (symptoms that seem to represent a reduction or loss of typical function).

Examples of positive symptoms:

- *Delusions.* Delusions of being controlled (e.g., "Martians are making me steal"), delusions of persecution (e.g., "My mother is poisoning me"), or delusions of grandeur (e.g., "Steph Curry admires my jump shot").

- *Hallucinations.* Imaginary voices making critical comments or telling patients what to do.

- *Inappropriate affect.* Failure to react with the appropriate emotion to positive or negative events.

- *Disorganized speech or thought.* Illogical thinking, peculiar associations among ideas, belief in supernatural forces.

- *Odd behavior.* Difficulty performing everyday tasks, lack of personal hygiene, talking in rhymes.

Examples of negative symptoms:

- *Affective flattening.* Diminished emotional expression.

- *Avolition.* Reduction or absence of motivation.

- *Catatonia.* Remaining motionless, often in awkward positions for long periods.

The frequent recurrence of any two of these symptoms for 1 month is currently sufficient for the diagnosis of schizophrenia—provided that one of the symptoms is delusions, hallucinations, or disorganized speech.

Causal Factors in Schizophrenia

LO 18.2 Describe the causal factors that have been implicated in the development of schizophrenia.

In the first half of the 20th century, the cloak of mystery began to be removed from mental illness by a series of studies that established schizophrenia's genetic basis (see Kotlar et al., 2015). First, it was discovered that although only 1 percent of the population develops schizophrenia, the probability of schizophrenia occurring in a close biological relative (i.e., a parent, child, or sibling) of a patient with schizophrenia is about 10 percent, even if the patient with schizophrenia was adopted shortly after birth by a healthy family (see Gejman, Sanders, & Kendler, 2011). Then, it was discovered that the concordance rates for schizophrenia are higher in monozygotic twins (45–50 percent) than in dizygotic twins (10–17 percent)—see Holzman and Matthyse (1990), Kallman (1946), and Singh et al. (2014). Finally, adoption studies found that the risk of schizophrenia is increased by the presence of the disorder in biological parents but not by its presence in adoptive parents (see Gejman, Sanders, & Kendler, 2011).

The concordance rate for schizophrenia in monozygotic twins is substantially less than 100 percent, suggesting that differences in experience have a significant effect on the development of schizophrenia. The current view is that some people inherit a potential for schizophrenia, which may or may not be activated by experience (see Uher, 2014). Supporting this view is a comparison of the offspring of a large sample of monozygotic twins who were themselves discordant for schizophrenia (i.e., one had the disorder and one did not); the incidence of schizophrenia was as great in the offspring of the twin without schizophrenia as in the offspring of the twin with schizophrenia (see Gejman, Sanders, & Kendler, 2011).

It is clear that schizophrenia has multiple causes. Many genes have been linked to the disorder (see Flint & Manufò, 2014; Reardon, 2014; Ripke et al., 2014), but no single gene seems capable of causing schizophrenia by itself, although certain genes have been more strongly implicated than others (see Dhindsa & Goldstein, 2016; Fromer et al., 2014; Sekar et al., 2016). Instead, the genes act in combination with one another and with experience to produce the disorder (see Bray et al., 2010). However, the mechanisms by which genes contribute to schizophrenia have yet to be determined (see Akil et al., 2010; Arguello & Gogos, 2011).

Also, a variety of early experiential factors have been implicated in the development of schizophrenia—for example, birth complications, maternal stress, prenatal infections, socioeconomic factors, urban birth or residing in an urban setting, and childhood adversity (see Owen, Sawa, & Mortensen, 2016). Such early experiences are thought to alter the typical course of neurodevelopment leading to schizophrenia in individuals who have a genetic susceptibility (see Negrón-Oyarzo et al., 2016; Owen, Sawa, & Mortensen, 2016), presumably through epigenetic mechanisms (see Chapter 2)—see Hannon et al. (2016), Jaffe et al. (2016), and Sharp and Akbarian (2016). Supporting this neurodevelopmental theory of schizophrenia are: (1) the fact that schizophrenia and autism spectrum disorders share many of the same causal factors (e.g., genetic risk factors, environmental triggers)—see Millan et al. (2016), and (2) the study of two 20th-century famines: the Nazi-induced Dutch famine of 1944–1945 and the Chinese famine of 1959–1961. Fetuses whose pregnant mothers suffered in those famines were more likely to develop schizophrenia as adults (see Li et al., 2015; Schmitt et al., 2014).

Discovery of the First Antipsychotic Drugs

LO 18.3 Describe the discovery of the first two widely prescribed antipsychotic drugs.

The first major breakthrough in the study of the biochemistry of schizophrenia was the accidental discovery in the early 1950s of the first **antipsychotic** drug (a drug that is 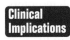 meant to treat certain symptoms of schizophrenia and bipolar disorders), **chlorpromazine**. Chlorpromazine was developed by a French drug company as an antihistamine. Then, in 1950, a French surgeon noticed that chlorpromazine given prior to surgery to counteract swelling had a calming effect on some of his patients, and he suggested that it might have a calming effect on difficult-to-handle patients with **psychosis** (a loss of touch with reality). His suggestion triggered research that led to the discovery that chlorpromazine alleviates the symptoms of schizophrenia: Agitated patients with schizophrenia were calmed by chlorpromazine, and emotionally blunted patients with schizophrenia were activated by it. Don't get the idea that chlorpromazine cures schizophrenia. It doesn't. But it often reduces the severity of symptoms enough to allow institutionalized patients to be discharged.

Shortly after the antipsychotic action of chlorpromazine was first documented, an American psychiatrist became interested in reports that the snakeroot plant had long been used in India for the treatment of mental illness. He gave **reserpine**—the active ingredient of the snakeroot plant—to his patients with schizophrenia and confirmed its antipsychotic action. Reserpine is no longer used in the treatment of schizophrenia because it produces a dangerous decline in blood pressure at the doses needed for successful treatment.

Although the chemical structures of chlorpromazine and reserpine are dissimilar, their antipsychotic effects are similar in two major respects. First, the antipsychotic effect of both drugs is manifested only after a patient has been medicated for 2 or 3 weeks. Second, the onset of this antipsychotic effect is usually associated with motor effects similar to the symptoms of Parkinson's disease (e.g., muscular rigidity, a general decrease in voluntary movement). These similarities suggested to researchers that chlorpromazine and reserpine were acting through the same mechanism—one that was related to Parkinson's disease.

Dopamine Theory of Schizophrenia

LO 18.4 Describe the evolution of the dopamine theory of schizophrenia.

Paradoxically, the next major breakthrough in the study of schizophrenia came from research on Parkinson's disease. In 1960, it was reported that the *striatums* (caudates plus putamens) of persons dying of Parkinson's disease had been depleted of dopamine (see Goetz, 2011). This finding suggested that a disruption of dopaminergic transmission might produce both Parkinson's disease and the antipsychotic effects of chlorpromazine and reserpine. Thus was born the *dopamine theory of schizophrenia*—the theory that schizophrenia is caused by too much dopamine and, conversely, that antipsychotic drugs exert their effects by decreasing dopamine levels.

Lending instant support to the dopamine theory of schizophrenia were two already well-established facts. First, the antipsychotic drug reserpine was known to deplete the brain of dopamine and other monoamines by breaking down the synaptic vesicles in which these neurotransmitters are stored. Second, drugs such as amphetamine and cocaine, which can trigger episodes that resemble schizophrenia in healthy users, were known to increase the extracellular levels of dopamine and other monoamines in the brain.

An important step in the evolution of the dopamine theory of schizophrenia came in 1963, when Carlsson and Lindqvist assessed the effects of chlorpromazine on extracellular levels of dopamine and its *metabolites* (substances that are created by the breakdown of another substance in cells). Although they expected to find that chlorpromazine, like reserpine, depletes the brain of dopamine, they didn't. The extracellular levels of dopamine were unchanged by chlorpromazine, and the extracellular levels of its metabolites were increased. The researchers concluded that both chlorpromazine and reserpine antagonize transmission at dopamine synapses but that they do it in different ways: reserpine by depleting the brain of dopamine and chlorpromazine by binding to dopamine receptors.

Carlsson and Lindqvist argued that chlorpromazine is a *receptor blocker* at dopamine synapses—that is, it binds to dopamine receptors without activating them and, in so

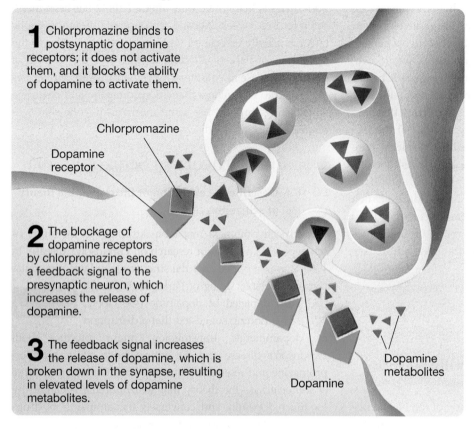

Figure 18.1 Chlorpromazine is a receptor blocker at dopamine synapses. Chlorpromazine was the first receptor blocker to be identified, and its discovery changed psychopharmacology.

1 Chlorpromazine binds to postsynaptic dopamine receptors; it does not activate them, and it blocks the ability of dopamine to activate them.

Chlorpromazine

Dopamine receptor

2 The blockage of dopamine receptors by chlorpromazine sends a feedback signal to the presynaptic neuron, which increases the release of dopamine.

3 The feedback signal increases the release of dopamine, which is broken down in the synapse, resulting in elevated levels of dopamine metabolites.

Dopamine

Dopamine metabolites

doing, keeps dopamine from activating them (see Figure 18.1). We now know that many psychoactive drugs are receptor blockers, but chlorpromazine was the first to be identified as such.

Carlsson and Lindqvist further postulated that the lack of activity at postsynaptic dopamine receptors sent a feedback signal to the presynaptic cells that increased their release of dopamine, which was broken down in the synapses. This explained why dopaminergic activity was reduced while extracellular levels of dopamine stayed about the same and extracellular levels of its metabolites were increased. Carlsson and Lindqvist's findings led to an important revision of the dopamine theory of schizophrenia: Rather than high dopamine levels, the main factor in schizophrenia was presumed to be high levels of activity at dopamine receptors.

In the mid-1970s, Snyder and his colleagues (see Creese, Burt, & Snyder, 1976; Madras, 2013) assessed the degree to which the various antipsychotic drugs that had been developed by that time bind to dopamine receptors. First, they added radioactively labeled dopamine to samples of dopamine-receptor–rich neural membrane obtained from calf striatums. Then, they rinsed away the unbound dopamine molecules from the samples and measured the amount of radioactivity left in them to obtain a measure of the number

of dopamine receptors. Next, in other samples, they measured each drug's ability to block the binding of radioactive dopamine to the sample; the assumption was that the drugs with a high affinity for dopamine receptors would leave fewer sites available for the dopamine. In general, they found that chlorpromazine and the other effective antipsychotic drugs had a high affinity for dopamine receptors, whereas ineffective antipsychotic drugs had a low affinity. There were, however, several major exceptions, including haloperidol. Although **haloperidol** was one of the most potent antipsychotic drugs of its day, it had a relatively low affinity for dopamine receptors.

A solution to the haloperidol puzzle came with the discovery that dopamine binds to more than one dopamine receptor subtype— five have been identified (see Beaulieu, Espinoza, & Gainetdinov, 2015). It turns out that chlorpromazine and other antipsychotic drugs in the same chemical class (the **phenothiazines**) all bind effectively to both D_1 and D_2 receptors, whereas haloperidol and the other antipsychotic drugs in its chemical class (the **butyrophenones**) all bind effectively to D_2 receptors but not to D_1 receptors.

This discovery of the selective binding of butyrophenones to D_2 receptors led to an important revision in the dopamine theory of schizophrenia. It suggested that schizophrenia is caused by hyperactivity specifically at D_2 receptors, rather than at dopamine receptors in general. Snyder and his colleagues (see Madras, 2013; Snyder, 1978) subsequently confirmed that the degree to which **typical antipsychotics** (the first generation of antipsychotic drugs) bind to D_2 receptors is highly correlated with their effectiveness in suppressing the symptoms of schizophrenia (see Figure 18.2). For example, the butyrophenone *spiroperidol* had the greatest affinity for D_2 receptors and the most potent antipsychotic effect.

Although the evidence implicating D_2 receptors in schizophrenia is strong, it has become apparent that the D_2 version of the dopamine theory of schizophrenia could not explain two general findings:

- Although typical antipsychotics block activity at D_2 receptors within hours, their therapeutic effects are usually not apparent for several weeks.

Figure 18.2 The positive correlation between the ability of various antipsychotics to bind to D_2 receptors and their clinical potency.

(Based on Snyder, 1978.)

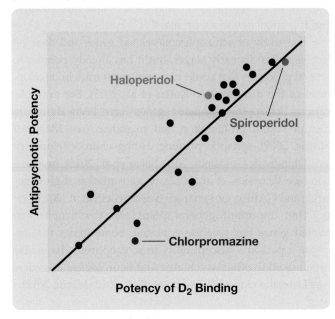

- Most antipsychotics are only effective in the treatment of schizophrenia's positive symptoms, but not its negative symptoms (see Arango et al., 2013; Carbon & Correll, 2014).

Appreciation of these limitations has led to the current version of the dopamine theory. This version holds that excessive activity at D_2 receptors is one factor in the disorder but that there are many other factors as well (see Laruelle, 2013; Poels et al., 2014). The major events in the development of the dopamine theory are summarized in Table 18.1.

Schizophrenia: Current Research and Treatment

LO 18.5 Describe four current lines of research on schizophrenia.

Although the dopamine theory of schizophrenia is still influential (see Laruelle, 2013), current lines of research into

(1) atypical antipsychotics, (2) psychedelic drug effects, (3) schizophrenia-related genes, and (4) brain changes associated with schizophrenia are leading to interesting new perspectives. These four areas of research will be described in the following four subsections.

ATYPICAL ANTIPSYCHOTICS. Currently, atypical antipsychotics (also known as second-generation antipsychotics) are often the drugs of choice for the treatment of schizophrenia. **Atypical antipsychotics** are drugs that are effective against schizophrenia but yet do not bind strongly to D_2 receptors. For example, **clozapine**, the first atypical antipsychotic to be approved for clinical use, has an affinity for D_1 receptors, D_4 receptors, and several serotonin and histamine receptors, but only a slight affinity for D_2 receptors (see Humbert-Claude et al., 2012).

It was initially claimed that atypical antipsychotics were more effective in the treatment of schizophrenia than the typical (D_2-blocking) antipsychotics and that they did this without producing Parkinsonian side effects (see Gründer, Hippius, & Carlsson, 2009). This is why these drugs were so quickly and widely adopted. Unfortunately, neither of these two claims has been unambiguously supported by recent research. Although atypical antipsychotics differ among themselves in their therapeutic efficacy, mechanisms of action, and production of side effects, as a group their effects do not seem to differ substantially from typical antipsychotics (see Crossley et al., 2010).

At first, the discovery of atypical antipsychotics appeared to discredit the dopamine theory of schizophrenia because none of them acted primarily as a D_2 receptor antagonist. However, all atypicals were subsequently shown to antagonize D_2 receptors, if only weakly. Thus, this line of evidence is somewhat inconclusive. Be that as it may, it is important to be aware that: (1) some D_2 receptor antagonists have no antipsychotic actions (see González-Maeso & Sealfon, 2009); (2) drugs that enhance the effects of glycine or block the effects of glutamate are proving to be effective treatments for schizophrenia in preliminary tests (see Laruelle, 2014); and (3) there is growing appreciation of the role of glutamatergic dysregulation in the development of schizophrenia (see Cannon, 2015; Elert, 2014).

Table 18.1 Key Events That Led to the Development and Refinement of the Dopamine Theory of Schizophrenia

Early 1950s	The antipsychotic effects of both chlorpromazine and reserpine were documented and related to their Parkinsonian side effects.
Late 1950s	The brains of recently deceased Parkinson's patients were found to be depleted of dopamine.
Early 1960s	It was hypothesized that schizophrenia was associated with excessive activity at dopaminergic synapses.
1960s and early 1970s	Chlorpromazine and other clinically effective first-generation antipsychotics were found to act as receptor blockers at dopamine synapses.
Mid-1970s	The affinity of antipsychotics for dopamine receptors was found to be only roughly correlated with their antipsychotic potency.
Late 1970s	The binding of existing antipsychotic drugs to D_2 receptors was found to be highly correlated with their antipsychotic potency.
1980s and 1990s	It became clear that the D_2 version of the dopamine theory of schizophrenia cannot account for all of the research findings.

RENEWED INTEREST IN HALLUCINOGENIC DRUGS.
The study of **psychedelic drugs** (drugs whose primary action is to alter perception, emotion, and cognition) began in the 1950s with the discovery of *LSD* (lysergic acid diethylamide). In addition to *classical hallucinogens* (such as LSD, psilocybin, and mescaline), psychedelic drugs include a variety of other drugs including *dissociative hallucinogens* (such as ketamine and phencyclidine) and cannabinoids.

Researchers have pursued two lines of research on psychedelics (see Vollenweider & Kometer, 2010). One line focused on those psychedelic drugs that produce effects similar to the symptoms of psychiatric disorders (e.g., illusions, hallucinations, paranoia, panic), and they used the drugs to model the disorders. The other line focused on the feelings of boundlessness, unity, and bliss reported by some users and attempted to use psychedelics in the treatment of psychiatric disorders. Unfortunately, these promising lines of research ground to a halt in the 1970s when many governments, troubled by the association of LSD and related drugs with cultural rebellion, made it extremely difficult for researchers to study their effects, particularly in humans.

In the 1990s, there was a gradual renewal of interest in utilizing psychedelic drugs to study the mechanisms of schizophrenia and other psychiatric disorders (see Kupferschmidt, 2014). This renewal was stimulated by the development of techniques for imaging the effects of drugs in the human brain and by an increased understanding of the mechanisms of psychedelic drug action (e.g., Tylš, Páleníček, & Horáček, 2014). This new research has led to two important conclusions: (1) the effects of classical hallucinogens, such as LSD, mimic the positive symptoms of schizophrenia (e.g., hallucinations and disorganized thought) by acting as agonists of particular serotonin receptors; and (2) dissociative hallucinogens (e.g., ketamine) mimic the negative symptoms of schizophrenia by acting as antagonists of glutamate receptors (see Laruelle, 2014; Paparelli et al., 2011; Vollenweider & Kometer, 2010).

MECHANISMS OF SCHIZO-PHRENIA-RELATED GENES.
Recent research has identified many genes associated with schizophrenia (see Flint & Manufò, 2014; Reardon, 2014;

Ripke et al., 2014), with each gene contributing only slightly to the development of schizophrenia (see Singh et al., 2014). This does not mean that investigating the genes involved in schizophrenia has been a waste: Identifying such genes can provide new insights into the causes, neural mechanisms, and treatment of schizophrenia.

The study of schizophrenia-related genes and their effects is still in its early stages, but it has already pointed to several processes that could play important roles in development of the disorder (see Kotlar et al., 2015). For example, various schizophrenia-related genes have been shown to disrupt neural proliferation and migration (see Meyer & Morris, 2009), synaptic pruning during neurodevelopment (see Dhindsa & Goldstein, 2016; Sekar et al., 2016), myelination (see Voineskos et al., 2012), or transmission at glutamatergic and GABAergic synapses (see Sacchetti et al., 2013).

One important general point about schizophrenia-related genes has recently emerged. Some genes that increase a person's susceptibility to schizophrenia have also been linked to other psychiatric and neurological disorders (see Demjaha et al., 2012; Gilman et al., 2012; Marin, 2012).

SCHIZOPHRENIA AND BRAIN STRUCTURE CHANGES.
With the development of neuroimaging techniques in the 1960s, reports of brain changes in patients with schizophrenia accumulated rapidly. The first generation of studies reported enlarged ventricles and fissures (see Figure 18.3), which indicated reduced brain volume. Subsequent studies focused on specific cortical areas and subcortical structures. For example, in a recent large-scale

Figure 18.3 Brain scans of a patient with schizophrenia and his healthy monozygotic twin.

Patient with Schizophrenia | Healthy Monozygotic Twin

Figure 18.4 Structural MRIs reveal cortical loss in adolescent patients with schizophrenia. Here red indicates areas of greatest tissue loss.

(From Thompson et al., 2001.)

study of several thousand persons with schizophrenia and healthy controls, the hippocampus, amygdala, thalamus, and nucleus accumbens were found to be significantly smaller in those with schizophrenia (van Erp et al., 2016). In general, schizophrenia-related volume reductions develop in both gray and white matter, and they are most consistently observed in the temporal lobes (see Bakhshi & Chance, 2015).

Figure 18.4 illustrates the amount of gray matter loss documented by structural MRIs in various cortical areas of a group of teenagers with schizophrenia (Thompson et al., 2001). Brain volume reductions in schizophrenia might be the result of reduced neuron size and reduced dendritic and axonal arborization, which have both been reported in persons with schizophrenia (see Bakhshi & Chance, 2015).

Many studies have assessed brain development in patients with, or at risk for, schizophrenia. Four important findings have emerged from various meta-analyses of those studies (see Fusar-Poli et al., 2010; Steen et al., 2006; Vita et al., 2006):

- Individuals who have not been diagnosed with schizophrenia but are at risk for the disorder (e.g., because they have close relatives with schizophrenia) display volume reductions in some parts of the brain.

- Extensive brain changes already exist when patients first seek medical treatment and receive their first brain scans.

- Subsequent brain scans reveal that the brain changes continue to develop after the initial diagnosis.

- Alterations to different areas of the brain develop at different rates (see Gogtay & Thompson, 2009).

CONCLUSION. Although there has been significant progress in our understanding of the mechanisms and treatment of schizophrenia, a careful reading of the research results suggests that ultimate answers will not be forthcoming until its diagnosis is "sharpened up." There is a general consensus that those patients diagnosed with schizophrenia under the current DSM-5 criteria do not suffer from a single unitary disorder resulting from the same neural pathology: The current diagnosis seems to lump together a group of related disorders under one label. This is suggested by the variability of psychological symptoms, related genes, and neural pathology, and by the fact that treatments have lasting major benefits for only a small proportion of patients.

Depressive Disorders

All of us have experienced depression. Depression is a normal reaction to grievous loss such as the loss of a loved one, the loss of self-esteem, or the loss of health. However, there are people whose tendency toward depression is out of proportion to actual events in their life. Such cases will be the focus of this module.

Defining Depressive Disorders

LO 18.6 Explain what a clinical depression is.

Some people experience deep depression and/or **anhedonia** (loss of the capacity to experience pleasure), often for no apparent reason (see Treadway & Zald, 2011). Their depression can be so extreme that it is almost impossible for them to meet the essential requirements of their daily lives—to keep a job, to maintain social contacts, to eat, or even to maintain an acceptable level of personal hygiene. Sleep disturbances and thoughts of suicide are common. When this condition lasts for 2 weeks or longer, these people are said to be suffering from a **clinical depression**, also known as **major depressive disorder**. The case of S.B. introduces you to some of the main features of clinical depression.

The Case of S.B., the Depressed Biopsychology Student

S.B. excelled during his first year at university—earning top marks in his program of study: biosychology. However, beginning in the second year of his studies, S.B. began to suffer from depression: He began to sleep excessively, he had trouble concentrating on his studies, and he thought about death and suicide frequently. He also suffered from delusions: He thought he was stupid and disliked, and he felt persecuted by his instructors and peers. Having seen these symptoms previously in certain members of his family, S.B. made the astute decision of seeking out help from a psychiatrist.

His psychiatrist offered him medications, but S.B. refused, as he was reminded of the many drug-related side effects he had seen in his family members. Rather, he attended psychotherapy for the remaining years of his degree. Although it helped to talk about his problems, S.B. saw little improvement in his condition during this period. Still, he was able to complete his degree with relatively high grades and subsequently applied and was admitted to graduate studies in biopsychology.

A few months after beginning graduate school, S.B.'s depression became so severe that he could no longer function. For example, S.B. had impairments in his memory and attention that affected his ability to read; delusional ideas and suicidal thoughts constantly plagued his mind. After seeing S.B. in this state, his psychiatrist immediately hospitalized him for a period of 2 weeks. While he was hospitalized, he was started on an antidepressant medication to calm his depression and an antipsychotic medication to help him deal with his delusional thoughts. Upon being released from the hospital, his psychiatrist advised him to take a leave of absence from his studies, which he did. S.B. returned to graduate school several months later. However, since his symptoms still persisted despite all the medications, albeit to a lesser degree, he was barely capable of keeping things together.

Don't forget S.B.; you will learn more about him later in this chapter.

Depression is often divided into two categories. Depression triggered by an obvious negative experience (e.g., the death of a friend, the loss of a job) is called **reactive depression**; depression with no apparent cause (as in the case of S.B.) is called **endogenous depression** (see Malki et al., 2014).

In most countries, the probability of suffering from a clinical depression during one's lifetime is about 10 percent (see Flint & Kendler, 2014). Women tend to be diagnosed with clinical depression about twice as frequently as men (see Schuch et al., 2014)—although the reasons for this are still unclear, gonadal-hormone-related explanations are currently popular (see Altemus, Sarvaiya, & Epperson, 2014; Bangasser & Valentino, 2014; Kokras & Dalla, 2014). The lifetime risk of completed suicide in an individual diagnosed with clinical depression has been found to range between 4 and 15 percent (see Wang et al., 2015).

Clinical depressions attack children, adolescents, and adults. In adults, clinical depression is often **comorbid** (the tendency for two health conditions to occur together in the same individual) with one or more other health conditions—for example, anxiety disorders, coronary heart disease, and diabetes (see Scott, 2014).

Watch this video on MyPsychLab
A CLOSER LOOK AT DEPRESSION

Causal Factors in Major Depressive Disorder

LO 18.7 Describe the causal factors that have been implicated in the development of major depressive disorder.

Genetic factors contribute to differences among people in the development of major depressive disorder. For example, twin studies of major depressive disorder yield heritability estimates of 30–40 percent (see Flint & Kendler, 2014; Klengel & Binder, 2013; Lolak, Suwannarat, & Lipsky, 2014). Genome sequencing studies of individuals with recurrent major depressive disorder have recently identified two loci on chromosome 10 as contributors to the risk for depression (see Cai et al., 2015; Sullivan, 2015).

Most of the research on the causal role of experience in major depressive disorder has focused on the role of stress and trauma in the etiology of depression. Some of that research has pointed toward epigenetic mechanisms (see Chapter 2) as being key mediators of depression onset in susceptible individuals (see Heller et al., 2014; Nestler, 2014; Whalley, 2014).

There are two subtypes of major depressive disorder whose cause is more apparent because of the timing of the episodes. One is **seasonal affective disorder (SAD)**, in which episodes of depression and lethargy typically recur during particular seasons—usually during the winter months. Two lines of evidence suggest that the episodes are triggered by the reduction in sunlight. One is that the incidence of the disorder is higher in Alaska (9 percent) than in Florida (1 percent) where the winter days are longer and brighter (see Melrose, 2015). The other is that *light therapy* (e.g., exposure to 15-30 minutes of very bright light each morning) is often effective in reducing the symptoms of SAD (see Oren, Koziorowski, & Desan, 2013; Song et al., 2015). The second subtype of major depressive disorder with an obvious cause is **peripartum depression**, the intense, sustained depression experienced by some women during pregnancy, after they give birth, or both (see Serati et al., 2016). Although estimates vary, the disorder seems to be associated with about 19 percent of pregnancies (see Figueiredo et al., 2015).

Antidepressant Drugs

LO 18.8 Describe the early research that led to the discovery of antidepressant medications. Also, list each of the five major classes of antidepressant drugs, and provide one specific example of each.

Five major classes of drugs have been used for the treatment of depressive disorders (see Willner, Scheel-Krüger, & Belzung, 2013): monoamine oxidase inhibitors, tricyclic antidepressants, selective monoamine-reuptake inhibitors, atypical antidepressants, and NMDA-receptor antagonists.

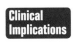

MONOAMINE OXIDASE INHIBITORS. **Iproniazid**, the first antidepressant drug, was originally developed for the treatment of tuberculosis, for which it proved to be a dismal flop. However, interest in the antidepressant potential of the drug was kindled by the observation that it left patients with tuberculosis less concerned about their disorder. As a result, iproniazid was tested on a mixed group of psychiatric patients and seemed to act against clinical depression. It was first marketed as an antidepressant drug in 1957.

Iproniazid is a monoamine agonist; it increases the levels of monoamines (e.g., norepinephrine and serotonin) by inhibiting the activity of *monoamine oxidase* (*MAO*), the enzyme that breaks down monoamine neurotransmitters in the *cytoplasm* (cellular fluid) of the neuron. **MAO inhibitors** have several side effects; the most dangerous is known as the **cheese effect** (see Finberg & Gillman, 2011). Foods such as cheese, wine, and pickles contain an amine called *tyramine*, which is a potent elevator of blood pressure. Normally, these foods have little effect on blood pressure because tyramine is rapidly metabolized in the liver by MAO. However, people who take MAO inhibitors and consume tyramine-rich foods run the risk of stroke caused by surges in blood pressure.

TRICYCLIC ANTIDEPRESSANTS. The **tricyclic antidepressants** are so named because of their antidepressant action and because their chemical structures include three rings of atoms. **Imipramine**, the first tricyclic antidepressant, was initially thought to be an antipsychotic drug. However, when its effects on a mixed sample of psychiatric patients were assessed, it had no effect against schizophrenia but seemed to help some depressed patients. Tricyclic antidepressants block the reuptake of both serotonin and norepinephrine, thus increasing their levels in the brain. They are a safer alternative to MAO inhibitors.

SELECTIVE MONOAMINE-REUPTAKE INHIBITORS. In the late 1980s, a new class of drugs—the selective serotonin-reuptake inhibitors—was introduced for treating clinical depression. **Selective serotonin-reuptake inhibitors (SSRIs)** are serotonin agonists that exert their agonistic effects by blocking the reuptake of serotonin from synapses—see Figure 18.5.

Fluoxetine (marketed as Prozac) was the first SSRI to be developed. Now there are many more (e.g., paroxetine, sertraline, fluvoxamine). Fluoxetine's structure is a slight variation of that of imipramine and other tricyclic antidepressants; in fact, fluoxetine is no more effective than imipramine in treating depression. Nevertheless, it was immediately embraced by the psychiatric community and has been prescribed in many millions of cases. The remarkable popularity of fluoxetine and other SSRIs is attributable to two things: First, they have fewer side effects than tricyclics and MAO inhibitors; second, they act against a wide range of psychological disorders in addition to depression.

The success of the SSRIs spawned the introduction of a similar class of drugs, the **selective norepinephrine-reuptake inhibitors (SNRIs)**. These (e.g., reboxetine) have proven to be just as effective as the SSRIs in the treatment of depression. Also effective against depression are drugs that block the reuptake of more than one monoamine neurotransmitter (e.g., venlafaxine).

ATYPICAL ANTIDEPRESSANTS. Beginning in the 1980s, several new antidepressants began to appear on the market that did not neatly fit into the three aforementioned classes (i.e., MAO inhibitors, tricyclic antidepressants, and selective monoamine-reuptake inhibitors). Accordingly, a new class of antidepressant medications emerged that is really just a catch-all class comprising drugs that have many different modes of action: the **atypical antidepressants** (see Willner, Scheel-Krüger, & Belzung, 2013). For example, one of the drugs in this class, *bupropion*, has several effects on neurotransmission: It is a blocker of dopamine and norepinephrine reuptake, and it is also a blocker of nicotinic acetylcholine receptors (see Carroll et al., 2014). Another example of a drug in this class is *agomelatine*—a melatonin receptor agonist (see Taylor et al., 2014). There are many other drugs in this class, each with its own unique mechanism of action (see Willner, Scheel-Krüger, & Belzung, 2013).

Figure 18.5 Blocking of serotonin reuptake by fluoxetine (Prozac).

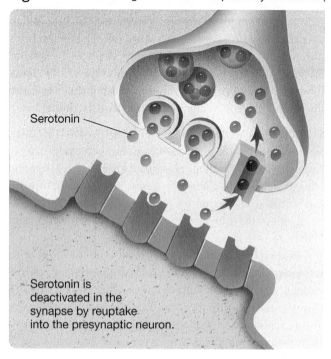

Serotonin

Serotonin is deactivated in the synapse by reuptake into the presynaptic neuron.

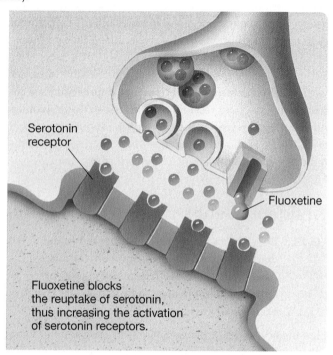

Serotonin receptor

Fluoxetine

Fluoxetine blocks the reuptake of serotonin, thus increasing the activation of serotonin receptors.

NMDA-RECEPTOR ANTAGONISTS. Beginning in the early 1990s, several studies reported a positive effect of antagonizing the glutamate *NMDA receptor* on depressive disorders. In the early 2000s, one agent in particular was shown to be remarkably effective: the dissociative hallucinogen **ketamine**. Remarkably, even a single low dose of ketamine rapidly reduces depression, even in patients who had been experiencing a severe episode (see Amit et al., 2015; McGirr et al., 2015; Monteggia, Malenka, & Deisseroth, 2014; Niciu et al., 2014). However, because ketamine has undesirable side effects, researchers are now in the process of trying to identify more selective NMDA-receptor antagonists with fewer side effects (see Duman & Aghajanian, 2012; Niciu et al., 2014).

EFFECTIVENESS OF DRUGS IN THE TREATMENT OF DEPRESSIVE DISORDERS. About $10 billion is spent in the United States each year on antidepressants (see Pratt, Brody, & Gi, 2012). But how effective are antidepressants? Numerous studies have evaluated the effectiveness of antidepressant drugs against major depressive disorder. Hollon, Thase, and Markowitz (2002) compared the efficacy of the various pharmacological treatments for depression. The results were about the same for MAO inhibitors, tricyclic antidepressants, and selective monoamine-reuptake inhibitors: About 50 percent of clinically depressed patients improved. This rate seems quite good; however, control groups showed a 25 percent rate of improvement, so only 25 percent of depressed individuals

were actually helped by the antidepressants (see Parikh, LeBlanc, & Ovanessian, 2010).

An important discovery was made by meta-analyses that focused on the effectiveness of antidepressant drugs as a function of the severity of the disorder (see Fournier et al., 2010; Kirsch et al., 2008). They found that antidepressants were not significantly better than placebo in treating patients with mild or moderate depression. Only the severely depressed seemed to benefit.

Brain Differences in Depression

LO 18.9 Describe the various brain differences associated with major depressive disorder.

Numerous structural MRI studies of the brains of depressed patients have been published. Consistent reductions in gray matter volumes in the prefrontal cortex, hippocampus, amygdala, and cingulate cortex have been observed (see Lener &

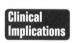

Iosifescu, 2015). For example, Figure 18.6 illustrates the loss of gray matter in the medial prefrontal cortex and the amygdala in a group of healthy volunteers who are genetically predisposed to developing depression. White matter reductions have also been noted in several brain regions—most reliably in the frontal cortex (see Russo & Nestler, 2013; Wang et al., 2014).

Similarly, fMRI studies have found atypical activity in frontal, cingulate, and insular cortices as well as in the amygdala, thalamus, and striatum. In addition,

Figure 18.6 Structural MRIs of healthy volunteers with a genetic predisposition to developing depression reveal cell loss in the medial prefrontal cortex and the amygdala.

Left hemisphere

Medial prefrontal cortex

Amygdala

Right hemisphere

Greatest cell loss

Significant cell loss

Medial prefrontal cortex

Amygdala

communication amongst these structures has been found to be atypical during a variety of cognitive states (see Lener & Iosifescu, 2015).

Theories of Depression

LO 18.10 Describe two theories of the etiology of major depressive disorder.

There are several theories of the etiology of major depressive disorder. As you will soon find out, most theories are based almost entirely on those therapies that have been found to be effective against depression.

MONOAMINE THEORY OF DEPRESSION. One prominent theory of clinical depression is the *monoamine theory*. The monoamine theory of depression holds that depression is associated with underactivity at serotonergic and noradrenergic synapses. The theory is largely based on the fact that monoamine oxidase inhibitors, tricyclic antidepressants, selective serotonin-reuptake inhibitors, and

selective norepinephrine-reuptake inhibitors are all agonists of serotonin, norepinephrine, or both.

Other support for the monoamine theory of depression has been provided by autopsy studies. Norepinephrine and serotonin receptors have been found to be more numerous in the brains of deceased depressed individuals who had not received pharmacological treatment. This implicates a deficit in monoamine release: When an insufficient amount of a neurotransmitter is released at a synapse, there is usually a compensatory increase in the number of receptors for that neurotransmitter—a process called **up-regulation**.

Two recent lines of evidence have challenged the monoamine theory of depression. First was the discovery that monoamine agonists, although widely prescribed, are not effective in the treatment of most depressed patients (see Fournier et al., 2010; Malhi, Langford-Hughes, & Young, 2016), and even when they are effective, they are only slightly better than placebo (see Khan et al., 2012; Linde et al., 2015). Second was the discovery that other neurotransmitters (e.g., GABA, glutamate, acetylcholine) play a role in the development of depression (see Baudry et al., 2011; Northoff, 2013; Pytka et al., 2016).

NEUROPLASTICITY THEORY OF DEPRESSION. Nearly all antidepressant drugs rapidly increase transmission at monoaminergic synapses, yet any therapeutic effects of those increases typically are not manifested until weeks after the beginning of drug therapy. Therefore, it is clear that the agonistic effects at monoaminergic synapses cannot be the critical therapeutic mechanism: There must be some change that occurs downstream from the synaptic changes (see Andrade & Rao, 2010; Berk et al., 2011). One theory is that the critical downstream change is an increase in neuroplasticity.

In a nutshell, the neuroplasticity theory of depression is that depression results from a decrease of neuroplastic processes in various brain structures (e.g., the hippocampus), which leads to neuron loss and other neural pathology (see Castrén & Hen, 2013; Miller & Hen, 2015). General support for the neuroplasticity theory of depression comes from two kinds of research: (1) research showing that stress and depression are associated with the disruption of various neuroplastic processes (e.g., a reduction in the synthesis of neurotrophins, a decrease in adult hippocampal neurogenesis; see Chapter 9) and (2) research showing that antidepressant treatments are associated with an enhancement of neuroplastic processes (e.g., an increase in the synthesis of neurotrophins, an increase in synaptogenesis, and an increase in adult hippocampal neurogenesis)—see Brandon and McKay (2015), Christian et al. (2014), Mahar et al. (2014), and Samuels et al. (2015).

Brain-derived neurotropic factor (BDNF) has been of particular interest to researchers because treatments that improve depression (both pharmacological and nonpharmacological) have been found to increase BDNF levels in those patients who show improvement (see Homberg et al., 2014). Indeed, it has been proposed that decreased blood levels of BDNF might be a *biomarker* (a biological state that is predictive of a particular disorder) for depression, and that increased blood levels of BDNF might be a biomarker for the successful treatment of depression (see Polyakova et al., 2015). Moreover, it has been hypothesized that antidepressants increase BDNF levels, which in turn increase certain neuroplastic processes (e.g., increase adult hippocampal neurogenesis) that lead to the alleviation of depression (see Björkholm & Monteggia, 2016).

Treatment of Depression with Brain Stimulation

LO 18.11 Describe two forms of treatment for depression that utilize brain stimulation.

Recently, two treatments involving brain stimulation have been developed for depression: repetitive transcranial magnetic stimulation and deep brain stimulation.

REPETITIVE TRANSCRANIAL MAGNETIC STIMULATION. **Repetitive transcranial magnetic stimulation (rTMS)** is a form of transcranial magnetic stimulation (TMS; see Chapter 5) that involves the noninvasive delivery of repetitive magnetic pulses 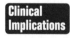 at either high frequencies (e.g., five pulses per second; high-frequency rTMS) or low frequencies (e.g., less than one pulse per second; low-frequency rTMS) to specific cortical areas—usually the prefrontal cortex (see Gaynes et al., 2014). High-frequency rTMS and low-frequency rTMS are believed to stimulate and inhibit, respectively, activity within those brain regions to which they are applied (see Berlim et al., 2013, 2014). Meta-analyses have shown reliable improvement of depressive symptoms after either low-frequency (see Berlim et al., 2013) or high-frequency (see Berlim et al., 2014) rTMS when compared with sham rTMS.

Clinical Implications There are many other treatments for depression that aren't discussed in this module. Name a few that you know of. What is the evidence for their efficacy?

Figure 18.7 Implantation of bilateral anterior cingulate electrodes and a stimulator for chronic deep brain stimulation for the treatment of depression.

Bilateral electrodes

Stimulator leads

Stimulator

DEEP BRAIN STIMULATION. Chronic brain stimulation through an implanted electrode (see Figure 18.7) has been shown to have a therapeutic effect in some depressed patients who have failed to respond to other treatments. Lozano and colleagues (2008) implanted the tip of a stimulation electrode into an area of the white matter of the anterior cingulate gyrus in the medial prefrontal cortex (see Figure 18.8). The stimulator, which was implanted under the skin, delivered continual pulses of electrical stimulation that could not be detected by the patients. The 20 patients in this study were selected because they had repeatedly failed to respond to conventional treatments.

Considering that patients had failed to respond to other treatments, the results were strikingly positive: 60 percent showed substantial improvements, 35 percent were largely symptom free, and most of the patients were improved for at least 1 year (the duration of the study). These positive results have since been replicated at other treatment centers (see Holtzheimer et al., 2011; Lozano et al., 2012; Lozano & Mayberg, 2015).

CONCLUSION. Although a number of promising lines of research currently focus on the mechanisms and treatment of clinical depression, treatments are not much better than they were 50 years ago. Many researchers contend that current diagnostic tools, such as those that

Figure 18.8 The site in the anterior cingulate gyrus at which chronic brain stimulation to subcortical white matter alleviated symptoms in treatment-resistant depressed patients.

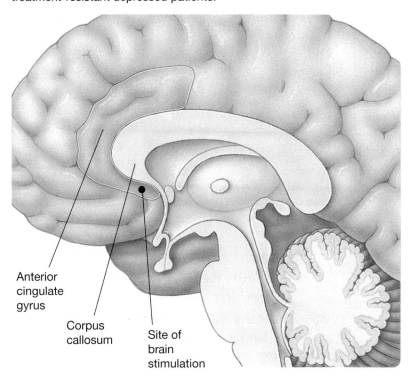

Anterior
cingulate
gyrus

Corpus
callosum

Site of
brain
stimulation

an extreme; it also has additional symptoms, such as delusions of grandeur, overconfidence, impulsivity, and distractibility. Mania usually involves psychosis (a loss of touch with reality). When mania is full-blown, the person often exhibits unbridled enthusiasm with an outflow of incessant chatter that hurtles from topic to topic. No task is too difficult. No goal is unattainable. This confidence and grandiosity, coupled with high energy, distractibility, and a leap-before-you-look impulsiveness, can result in a series of disasters. Mania often leaves behind a trail of unfinished projects, unpaid bills, and broken relationships.

Those persons who only experience bouts of depression and hypomania are said to have **bipolar disorder type II**; those who also experience bouts of mania are said to have **bipolar disorder type I**. The case of S.B., previously introduced to you in the module on depressive disorders, will introduce you to the main features of both forms of bipolar disorder.

generate large heterogeneous groups of patients—like the DSM-5—are misguiding research and that more precise approaches to diagnosis are necessary (see Casey et al., 2013; Insel & Cuthbert, 2015; Stein, Lund, & Nesse, 2013).

Bipolar Disorders

Some depressed persons experience periods of hypomania or mania. Those who do are said to suffer from a **bipolar disorder**. There is no sex difference in the incidence of bipolar disorders.

Defining Bipolar Disorders

LO 18.12 Describe the symptoms associated with each of the two categories of bipolar disorder.

Hypomania and mania are in some respects the opposite of depression. **Hypomania** is characterized by a reduced 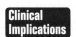 need for sleep, high energy, and positive affect. During periods of hypomania, people are talkative, energetic, impulsive, positive, and very confident. In this state, they can be very effective at certain jobs and can be great fun to be with. **Mania** has the same features as hypomania but taken to

The Case of S.B. Revisited: The Biopsychology Student with Bipolar Disorder

S.B. continued his graduate studies in biopsychology while still suffering from a residual depression. Although he struggled through the remaining years of his program, he was successful in attaining a master's degree in biopsychology.

S.B. subsequently began a Ph.D. program in biopsychology. During the first summer after beginning this new program, S.B. started to feel exceptionally good: His mood was elevated; he was sleeping less than 3 hours per night; he became highly sociable and very charismatic; and he found he could read faster and understand materials that he had previously found difficult. Moreover, he became very productive. Indeed, many of the ideas that would later form the basis of his Ph.D. thesis came to him during this period of elation. S.B. was experiencing all the symptoms of a hypomania. Because S.B. had experienced both depression and hypomania, he now met criteria for a diagnosis of bipolar disorder type II. His hypomania persisted for several months, but things were about to take a turn for the worse.

S.B. began to sleep less than 2 hours per night, and sometimes he would simply not sleep at all for several days. He read incessantly—his living room was transformed into a labyrinthian pile of books and academic papers. S.B. also began to believe that he had some unique talents and insights. For example, he believed that he had developed a comprehensive theory that explained every aspect of how society functioned and he began to see linkages between everything that he thought about and experienced. He filled many notebooks with diagrams and writings that he thought summarized his theory quite well; however, nobody seemed to understand his theory except for him. But this didn't deter him. In short, he was displaying delusions of grandeur: He believed he had intellectual capacities that surpassed all those around him. Moreover, whenever he spoke with anyone, they always told him to slow down, or they simply gave him funny looks. At this point, S.B. was in a state of mania and now met criteria for a diagnosis of bipolar disorder type I.

However, his enthusiasm and positive affect began to slowly dwindle. Because nobody seemed to understand him and his theories, he felt increasingly alone and rejected. Soon, suicidal thoughts began to dominate his mind. After several weeks of experiencing intense suicidal ideation, barely sleeping, and often forgetting to eat, S.B. contacted his psychiatrist. He told his psychiatrist over the phone about his "brilliant" theory. Feeling suspicious, she asked S.B. to come see her at the hospital to talk about his theory further. When she saw S.B. and talked with him, she immediately realized he was in a **mixed state**: He was displaying symptoms of both severe depression (e.g., suicidal ideation) and mania (e.g., delusions of grandeur). She promptly committed S.B., and he was subsequently placed on a psychiatric ward where he stayed for 6 weeks.

So far, the case of S.B. has introduced you to the features of both depression and bipolar disorders. Here, his case makes an important point about bipolar disorders: Contrary to a popular misconception, bipolar disorders do not involve rapid alternations in mood (i.e., alternations within hours to days); rather, the mood episodes often last weeks to months. To put things in context, there is a subtype of bipolar disorders known as *rapid cycling* bipolar disorders—these are defined as involving 4 or more mood episodes per year (see Carvalho et al., 2014). S.B.'s case also makes an 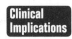 important point about psychiatric diagnoses in general: Psychiatric patients often careen from one diagnosis to another (see Phillips & Kupfer, 2013) For example, S.B.'s diagnosis changed from clinical depression to bipolar type II and then to bipolar type I. But stay tuned: There is more to the case of S.B.

Clinical Implications
Do you think that such careening between diagnoses represents an actual change in one's illness or a problem with psychiatric diagnoses in general? Discuss.

Watch this video on MyPsychLab
ANN: BIPOLAR DISORDER

Causal Factors in Bipolar Disorders

LO 18.13 Describe the various causal factors that have been identified for bipolar disorders.

Bipolar disorders are highly heritable. For example, twin studies of bipolar disorders yield heritability estimates ranging from 80–90 percent (see Harrison, 2016; Maletic & Raison, 2014). Genome sequencing studies of individuals with bipolar disorders have implicated many different genes in bipolar disorders—for example, genes that code for particular calcium channels and for particular proteins found at the nodes of Ranvier (see Harrison, 2016).

Mood Stabilizers

LO 18.14 Describe the discovery of the first mood stabilizer.

Ideally, **mood stabilizers** are drugs that effectively treat depression or mania without increasing the risk of mania or depression, respectively (see Karanti et al., 2016). Protection against the recurrence of mood episodes is important because mood episodes in bipolar disorder typically become both more severe and more frequent if left untreated (see Post, 2016; Post, Fleming, & Kapczinski, 2012). The mechanism by which mood stabilizers work is still a matter of debate (see Oruch et al., 2014; Rapoport, 2014), but for some reason many mood stabilizers are also effective in the treatment of both epilepsy (see Prabhavalkar, Poovanpallil, & Bhatt, 2015; Yildiz et al., 2011) and schizophrenia (see Post, 2016).

Lithium, a simple metallic ion, was the first drug found to act as a mood stabilizer. The discovery of lithium's antimania action is yet another important pharmacological breakthrough that occurred largely by accident. John Cade, an Australian psychiatrist, injected guinea pigs with the urine of various psychiatric inpatients and found that the urine of manic patients was the most toxic (i.e., it killed the most guinea pigs). Next, he set about investigating which chemical constituent of the manic patients' urine caused the increased toxicity: He began by injecting guinea pigs with urea (one constituent of urine) and found that it was toxic, but not nearly as toxic as the urine of the manic patients. Something else was contributing to the toxicity of the manic patients' urine. What was it? Cade thought it might be uric acid (another constituent of urine), so he injected both urea and lithium urate (a soluble form of uric acid that takes the form of a lithium salt) into a group of guinea pigs. Contrary to his hypothesis, he found that lithium urate protected the guinea pigs from the toxicity of the urea. Next, Cade injected some guinea pigs with both urea and lithium carbonate (another lithium salt) to check whether it was the lithium or the uric acid that was protective. He found that lithium carbonate also protected the guinea pigs from the toxicity of urea. Accordingly, Cade hypothesized that manic patients have lower levels of lithium than non-manic patients.

Cade wanted to test lithium carbonate on a group of manic patients, but he decided to first test it on a group of guinea pigs. The lithium carbonate seemed to calm the guinea pigs. However, we now know that at the doses he used, lithium carbonate produces extreme nausea; so, his subjects weren't calm—they were just sick. In any case, excited by what he thought was the success of his guinea pig experiments, in 1954 Cade gave lithium to a group of 10 manic patients, 6 patients with schizophrenia, and 3 depressed patients. The lithium had a dramatic effect, but only in the manic patients. The effect was so dramatic that some of the manic patients were even discharged from hospital (see Mitchell & Hadzi-Pavlovic, 2000), something unheard of in the predrug era of psychiatry.

Unfortunately, there was little immediate reaction to Cade's report—few scientists were impressed by his conference presentations, and few drug companies were interested in spending money to evaluate the therapeutic potential of a metallic ion that could not be protected by a patent. Consequently, it was not until the late 1960s that lithium was conclusively shown to be an effective mood stabilizer. Over the 50 years since its introduction, lithium is still considered by many to be the best mood stabilizer (see Oruch et al., 2014).

All mood stabilizers (i.e., lithium, certain anticonvulsants, and certain atypical antipsychotics) act against bouts of mania, some act against depression, and some act against both (see Prabhavalkar, Poovanpallil, & Bhatt, 2015; Yildiz et al., 2011), but they do not eliminate all symptoms. Moreover, many of them produce an array of adverse side effects (e.g., weight gain, tremor, blurred vision, dizziness; see Murru et al., 2015), which encourage nonadherence to these medications (see Jann, 2014; Schloesser, Martinowich, & Manji, 2012).

Brain Differences Associated with Bipolar Disorders

LO 18.15 Describe the brain differences associated with bipolar disorders.

Numerous MRI studies of the brains of patients with bipolar disorders have been published. Consistent overall reductions in gray matter volume have been reported (see Maletic & Raison, 2014). In addition, there have been reports of several specific brain structures being smaller in patients with bipolar disorders, including the medial prefrontal cortex, the left anterior cingulate, the left superior temporal gyrus, certain prefrontal regions, and the hippocampus (see Hanford et al., 2016; Knöchel et al., 2014; Otten & Meeter, 2015; Savitz, Price, & Drevets, 2014).

Meta-analyses of fMRI studies of patients with bipolar disorders have found atypical activation in the frontal cortex, medial temporal lobe structures, and basal ganglia, as well as atypical functional connectivity between some of these structures, in a variety of cognitive states (see Chen et al., 2011; Favre et al., 2014; Maletic & Raison, 2014; Vargas, López-Jaramillo, & Vieta, 2013).

Theories of Bipolar Disorders

LO 18.16 Describe some of the theories of the etiology of bipolar disorders.

An understanding of the mechanisms underlying the development and maintenance of bipolar disorders has been hampered by the lack of a clear understanding of the mechanisms underlying the efficacy of various mood stabilizers (e.g., Can, Schulze, & Gould, 2014) and by the lack of an adequate animal model of bipolar disorder (see Logan & McClung, 2016). However, several physiological disturbances have been identified that might be contributing to the onset and maintenance of bipolar disorders. For example, there is evidence of hypothalamic–pituitary–adrenal (HPA) axis dysregulation in bipolar disorders; there are marked disruptions in the circadian rhythms in both patients with bipolar disorders and their nonbipolar relatives; and there are also alterations to GABA, glutamate, and monoamine neurotransmission in patients with bipolar disorders (see Maletic & Raison, 2014). Finally, there is evidence that BDNF levels are lower in patients with bipolar disorders when they are either depressed or manic (see Maletic & Raison, 2014).

Anxiety Disorders

Anxiety—chronic fear that persists in the absence of any direct threat—is a common psychological correlate of stress (see Mahan & Ressler, 2012). Anxiety is adaptive if it motivates effective coping behaviors; however, when it becomes so severe that it disrupts functioning, it is referred to as an **anxiety disorder**. All anxiety disorders are associated with feelings of anxiety (e.g., fear, worry) and with a variety of physiological stress reactions—for example, *tachycardia* (rapid heartbeat), *hypertension* (high blood pressure), nausea, breathing difficulties, sleep disturbances, and high glucocorticoid levels.

Anxiety disorders are the most prevalent of all psychiatric disorders. Different estimates suggest that between 14 and 34 percent of people suffer from an anxiety disorder at some point in their lives, and the incidence seems to be almost twice as great in females as in males (Bandelow & Michaelis, 2015). M.R., a woman who was afraid to leave her home, suffered from one type of anxiety disorder.

The Case of M.R., the Woman Who Was Afraid to Go Out

 M.R. was a 35-year-old woman who developed a pathological fear of leaving her house. The onset of her problem was sudden. Following an argument with her husband, she went out to mail a letter and cool off, but before she could accomplish her task, she was overwhelmed by dizziness and fear. She immediately struggled back to her house and rarely left it again, for about 2 years. Then, she gradually started to improve.

Her recovery was abruptly curtailed, however, by the death of her sister and another argument with her husband. Following the argument, she tried to go shopping, panicked, and had to be escorted home by a stranger. Following that episode, she was not able to leave her house by herself without experiencing an anxiety attack. Shortly after leaving home by herself, she would feel dizzy and sweaty, and her heart would start to pound; at that point, she would flee home to avoid a full-blown panic attack.

Although M.R. could manage to go out if she was escorted by her husband or one of her children, she felt anxious the entire time.

Four Anxiety Disorders

LO 18.17 Describe four anxiety disorders.

The following are four anxiety disorders:

- **Generalized anxiety disorder** is characterized by stress responses and extreme feelings of anxiety and worry about a large number of different activities or events.
- **Specific phobias** involve a strong fear or anxiety about particular objects (e.g., birds, spiders) or situations (e.g., enclosed spaces, darkness). A person with a phobia will usually try to avoid those specific objects or situations that are anxiety producing.

- **Agoraphobia** is the pathological fear of public places and open spaces. Although it might be considered as a specific phobia (see above), it is generally considered to be more incapacitating than most specific phobias and is thus treated as a separate diagnostic category in the DSM-5. M.R., the woman who was afraid to go out, suffered from agoraphobia.
- **Panic disorder** is characterized by recurrent rapid-onset attacks of extreme fear and severe symptoms of stress (e.g., choking, heart palpitations, shortness of breath). Such **panic attacks** also occur in certain cases of generalized anxiety disorder, specific phobia, and agoraphobia (see Johnson, Federici, & Shekhar, 2014).

Etiology of Anxiety Disorders

LO 18.18 Describe the etiological factors that have been implicated in anxiety disorders.

Because anxiety disorders are often triggered by identifiable stressful events and because the anxiety is often focused on particular objects or situations, the role of experience in shaping the disorder is often apparent (see Chu et al., 2012; Moitra et al., 2011). For example, in addition to having agoraphobia, M.R. was obsessed by her health—particularly by high blood pressure, although hers was in the normal range. The fact that both her grandfather and her father suffered from high blood pressure and died of heart attacks clearly shaped this component of her disorder.

Like other psychiatric disorders, anxiety disorders have a significant genetic component—heritability estimates range from 30–50 percent (see Shimada-Sugimoto, Otowa, & Hettema, 2015). Moreover, the concordance rates for various anxiety disorders are substantially higher for monozygotic twins than for dizygotic twins. No specific genes have yet been linked to anxiety disorders (see Dias et al., 2013).

Pharmacological Treatment of Anxiety Disorders

LO 18.19 Describe three categories of drugs used in the treatment of anxiety disorders.

Three categories of drugs are commonly prescribed for the treatment of anxiety disorders: benzodiazepines, sero-

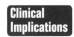

tonin agonists, and certain antidepressants (see Bandelow et al., 2012; Ravindran & Stein, 2010).

BENZODIAZEPINES. Benzodiazepines such as *chlordiazepoxide* (marketed as Librium) and *diazepam* (marketed as Valium) are widely prescribed for the treatment of anxiety disorders. They are also prescribed as *hypnotics* (sleep-inducing drugs), anticonvulsants, and muscle relaxants. Indeed, benzodiazepines are the most widely prescribed psychoactive drugs; approximately 10 percent of adult North Americans are currently taking them. The benzodiazepines have several adverse side effects: sedation, *ataxia* (disruption of motor activity), tremor, nausea, and a withdrawal reaction that includes rebound anxiety. Another serious problem with benzodiazepines is that they are addictive. Consequently, they should be prescribed for only short-term use. The behavioral effects of benzodiazepines are thought to be mediated by their agonistic action on GABA$_A$ receptors.

SEROTONIN AGONISTS. The serotonin agonist *buspirone* is also used for the treatment of anxiety disorders. Buspirone appears to have selective agonist effects at one subtype of serotonin receptor, the 5-HT$_{1A}$ receptor. Its mechanism of action is not entirely understood, but it does not function as an SSRI. The main advantage of buspirone over the benzodiazepines is its specificity: It produces *anxiolytic* (antianxiety) effects without producing ataxia, muscle relaxation, and sedation, the common side effects of the benzodiazepines. Buspirone does, however, have other side effects (e.g., dizziness, nausea, headache, and insomnia).

ANTIDEPRESSANT DRUGS. One of the complications in studying anxiety disorders is their high comorbidity with other psychiatric disorders. For example, about 47 percent of individuals with a bipolar disorder and about 53 percent of individuals with major depressive disorder have a comorbid anxiety disorder (see Moscati, Flint, & Kendler, 2015; Vázquez, Baldessarini, & Tondo, 2014).

Consistent with the comorbidity of anxiety disorders and clinical depression is the observation that antidepressants, such as SSRIs and SNRIs, are often effective against anxiety disorders, and **anxiolytic drugs** (antianxiety drugs) are often effective against clinical depression.

Furthermore, consistent with the comorbidity of anxiety disorders and bipolar disorders are the observations that atypical antipsychotics and anticonvulsants, some of which are effective mood stabilizers, are also effective treatments for certain anxiety disorders.

Although many drugs have been shown to produce slight, but statistically significant, improvements in groups of patients suffering from anxiety disorders, the treatment of anxiety disorders leaves a lot to be desired. Many patients are not helped at all by existing drug therapies, and many curtail therapy because of adverse side effects (see Batelaan, Van Balkom, & Stein, 2011; Ravindran & Stein, 2010).

Animal Models of Anxiety Disorders

LO 18.20 Describe three animal models of anxiety disorders.

Animal models have played an important role in the study of anxiety disorders and in the assessment of the anxiolytic potential of new drugs. A weakness of these models is that they typically involve animal defensive behaviors, the implicit assumption being that defensive behaviors are motivated by fear and that fear and anxiety are similar states (see Diaz et al., 2013; LeDoux, 2014). Three animal behaviors that model anxiety are elevated-plus-maze performance, defensive burying, and risk assessment.

 What do you think is wrong with assuming that the defensive behaviors of nonhuman animals are representative of anxiety? What clinical implications might this assumption have for the development of new therapies for anxiety disorders?

In the **elevated-plus-maze test**, rats are placed on a four-armed plus-sign-shaped maze that rests about 50 centimeters above the floor. Two arms have sides and two arms have no sides, and the measure of anxiety is the proportion of time the rats spend in the enclosed arms, rather than venturing onto the exposed arms.

In the **defensive-burying test** (see Figure 5.25), rats are shocked by a wire-wrapped wooden dowel mounted on the wall of a familiar test chamber. The measure of anxiety is the amount of time the rats spend spraying bedding material from the floor of the chamber at the source of the shock with forward thrusting movements of their head and forepaws.

In the **risk-assessment test**, after a single brief exposure to a cat on the surface of a laboratory burrow system, rats flee to their burrows and freeze. Then, they engage in a variety of risk-assessment behaviors (e.g., scanning the surface from the mouth of the burrow or exploring the surface in a cautious stretched posture) before their behavior eventually returns to normal. The measures of anxiety in this test are the amounts of time that the rats spend in freezing and in risk assessment.

The elevated-plus-maze, defensive-burying, and risk-assessment tests of anxiety have all been validated by demonstrations that benzodiazepines reduce the various indices of anxiety used in the tests, whereas nonanxiolytic drugs usually do not. However, a potential problem with this line of evidence stems from the fact that many cases of anxiety do not respond well to benzodiazepine therapy. Therefore, existing animal models of anxiety may be models of benzodiazepine-sensitive anxiety rather than of anxiety in general, and thus the models may not be sensitive to anxiolytic drugs that act by a different (i.e., a nonGABAergic) mechanism. For example, the serotonin agonist buspirone does not have a reliable anxiolytic effect on the elevated-plus-maze test.

Neural Bases of Anxiety Disorders

LO 18.21 Describe research findings related to the neural bases of anxiety disorders.

Like current theories of the neural bases of schizophrenia, depressive disorders, and bipolar disorders, current theories of the neural bases of anxiety disorders rest heavily on the analysis of therapeutic drug effects. The fact that many anxiolytic drugs are agonists at either $GABA_A$ receptors (e.g., the benzodiazepines) or serotonin receptors (e.g., buspirone, fluoxetine, and paroxetine) has focused attention on the possible role in anxiety disorders of deficits in GABAergic and serotonergic transmission.

There is substantial overlap between the brain structures involved in major depressive disorder and anxiety disorders. Indeed, the prefrontal cortex, hippocampus, and amygdala, which you have just learned are implicated in major depressive disorder, have also been implicated in anxiety disorders (see Calhoon & Tye, 2015). This is hardly surprising given the comorbidity of depression and anxiety disorders and the effectiveness of many drugs against both.

Although the prefrontal cortex, hippocampus, and amygdala have been implicated in both depression and anxiety disorders, the patterns of evidence differ. With major depressive disorder, you have already seen that there seems to be *atrophy* (shrinkage) of these structures; however, with anxiety disorders, there appears to be no significant atrophy. Most of the evidence linking these structures to anxiety disorders has come from functional brain-imaging studies in which atypical activity in these areas has been recorded during the performance of various emotional tasks (see Kim & Whalen, 2009; Nitschke et al., 2009).

Watch this video on MyPsychLab

BRAIN REGIONS INVOLVED IN ANXIETY

Tourette's Disorder

Tourette's disorder (formerly known as Tourette syndrome) is the last of the psychiatric disorders discussed in this chapter. It differs from the others that have already been discussed (i.e., schizophrenia, depressive disorders, bipolar disorders, and anxiety disorders) in the specificity of its symptoms. And, as you are about to learn, they are as interesting as they are specific. The case of R.G. introduces you to Tourette's disorder.

The Case of R.G.—Barking Like a Dog

When R.G. was 15, he developed *tics* (involuntary, repetitive, stereotyped movements or vocalizations). For the first week, his tics took the form of involuntary blinking, but after that they started to involve other parts of the body, particularly his arms and legs (Spitzer et al., 1983).

R.G. and his family were religious, so it was particularly distressing when his tics became verbal. He began to curse repeatedly and involuntarily. Involuntary cursing is a common symptom of Tourette's disorder and of several other psychiatric and neurological disorders. R.G. also started to bark like a dog. Finally, he developed echolalia: When his mother said, "Dinner is ready," he responded, "Is ready, is ready."

Prior to the onset of R.G.'s symptoms, he was a top student, he was happy, and he had an outgoing, engaging personality. Once his symptoms developed, he was jeered at, imitated, and ridiculed by his schoolmates. He responded by becoming anxious, depressed, and withdrawn. His grades plummeted.

Once R.G. was taken to a psychiatrist by his parents, his condition was readily diagnosed—the symptoms of Tourette's disorder are unmistakable. Medication eliminated 99 percent of his symptoms, and then his anxiety and depression lifted and he returned to his former outgoing manner.

Imagine how difficult it would be to get on with your life if you suffered from an extreme form of Tourette's disorder—for example, if you frequently made obscene gestures and barked like a dog. No matter how polite, intelligent, and kind you were inside, not many people would be willing to socialize with you or employ you (see Smith, Fox, & Trayner, 2015). However, if their friends, family members, and colleagues are understanding and supportive, people with Tourette's disorder can live happy, productive lives—for example, Tim Howard (shown in the photo—wearing the blue shirt) has Tourette's disorder and is goalkeeper for both the American national team and the Colorado Rapids.

What Is Tourette's Disorder?

LO 18.22 Describe the symptoms of Tourette's disorder.

Tourette's disorder is a disorder of **tics** (involuntary, repetitive, stereotyped movements or

 vocalizations). It typically begins early in life—usually in childhood or early adolescence—with simple motor tics, such as eye blinking or head movements, but the symptoms tend to become more complex and severe as the patient grows older. Common complex motor tics include hitting, touching objects, squatting, hopping, twirling, and sometimes even making lewd gestures. Common verbal tics include inarticulate sounds (e.g., barking, coughing, grunting),

coprolalia (uttering obscenities), *echolalia* (repetition of another's words), and *palilalia* (repetition of one's own words). The symptoms usually reach a peak after a few years and gradually subside as the patient matures.

Tourette's disorder develops in 0.3–1 percent of the population (see Serajee & Huq, 2015). It is four times more frequent in male children than in female children (see Hallett, 2015), but this sex difference is not as profound in adult patients (see Jackson et al., 2015). There is a significant genetic component: Concordance rates are 50 percent for monozygotic twins and 10 percent for dizygotic twins (see Serajee & Huq, 2015).

Some patients with Tourette's disorder also display signs of *attention-deficit/hyperactivity disorder, obsessive-compulsive disorder*, or both (see Serajee & Huq, 2015). For example, R.G. was obsessed by odd numbers and refused to sit in even-numbered seats.

Although the tics of Tourette's disorder are involuntary, they can be temporarily suppressed with concentration and effort by the patient. The effect of suppression has been widely misunderstood. Many medical professionals believe that tic suppression is inevitably followed by a *rebound* (that the tics become even worse following a period of suppression). However, this is not the case—see Figure 18.9.

Figure 18.9 No rebound effect above baseline was observed following periods of tic suppression by children with Tourette's disorder.

(Based on Himle & Woods, 2005.)

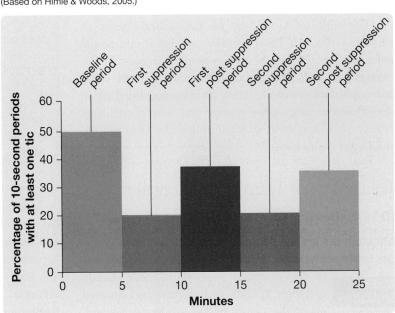

Neural Bases of Tourette's Disorder

LO 18.23 Describe the research findings related to the neural bases of Tourette's disorder.

Because Tourette's disorder is a well-defined disorder with clearly observable symptoms, its neural bases are more amenable to study than those of the other disorders that you have already encountered in this chapter. However, there are impediments to its study (e.g., the lack of a strong link to any particular gene is problematic). The greatest difficulty in studying Tourette's disorder is the fact that the symptoms usually subside as people age; because Tourette's patients are rarely under care for the disorder when they die, few postmortem studies of Tourette's disorder have been conducted. Consequently, the study of the disorder's neural bases is based almost exclusively on brain-imaging studies, which are difficult to conduct because of the requirement that the patients remain motionless.

Most research on the cerebral pathology associated with Tourette's disorder has focused on the striatum (caudate plus putamen). Patients with this disorder tend to have smaller striatal volumes (see Jackson et al., 2015), and when they suppress their tics, fMRI activity is recorded in both the prefrontal cortex and caudate nuclei (see Thomas & Cavanna, 2013). Presumably, the decision to suppress the tics comes from the prefrontal cortex, which initiates the suppression by acting on the caudate nuclei.

There is also evidence of dysfunctional dopaminergic and GABAergic signaling within the cortical-striatal-thalamic-cortical brain circuits in Tourette's disorder. This finding has been of particular interest because those brain circuits are implicated in motor learning—including habit formation (see Jackson et al., 2015).

Although most studies of the neural bases of Tourette's disorder have focused on the striatum, the brain differences appear to be more widespread. For example, an MRI study of children with Tourette's disorder (see Jackson et al., 2015) documented thinning in sensorimotor cortex gray matter that was particularly prominent in the areas that controlled the face, mouth, and *larynx* (voice box).

Treatment of Tourette's Disorder

LO 18.24 Describe how Tourette's disorder is treated.

Although tics are the defining feature of Tourette's disorder, treatment typically begins by focusing on other aspects 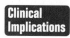 of the disorder. First, the patient, family members, friends, and teachers are educated about the nature of the syndrome. Second,

the treatment focuses on the ancillary emotional problems (e.g., anxiety and depression). Once these first two steps have been taken, attention turns to treating the tics.

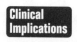 Tourette's disorder is a disorder of onlookers. Explain.

The tics of Tourette's disorder are usually treated with *antipsychotics*. Antipsychotics can reduce tics by about 70 percent, but patients or their caregivers often refuse them because of the adverse side effects (e.g., weight gain, fatigue, dry mouth). The success of antipsychotics in blocking Tourette's tics is consistent with the hypothesis that the disorder is related to changes in the cortical-striatal-thalamic-cortical circuit because that circuit relies heavily on dopaminergic signaling (see Greene & Schlaggar, 2012; Jackson et al., 2015).

P.H. is a scientist who counsels Tourette's patients and their families. He also has Tourette's disorder, which provides him with a useful perspective (Hollenbeck, 2001).

The Case of P.H., the Neuroscientist with Tourette's Disorder

Tourette's disorder has been P.H.'s problem for more than three decades. Taking advantage of his position as a medical school faculty member, he regularly offers a series of lectures on the topic. Along with students, many other Tourette's patients and their families are attracted to his lectures.

Encounters with Tourette's patients of his own generation taught P.H. a real lesson. He was astounded to learn that most of them did not have his thick skin. About half of them were still receiving treatment for psychological wounds inflicted during childhood.

For the most part, these patients' deep-rooted pain and anxiety did not result from the tics themselves. They derived from being ridiculed and tormented by others and from the self-righteous advice repeatedly offered by well-meaning "clods." The malfunction may be in a patient's striatum, but in reality this is more a disorder of the onlooker than of the patient.

We received an e-mail from a professor of biological sciences at Purdue University. He came across this text because it was used in his department's behavioral neurobiology course. He thanked us for our coverage of Tourette's disorder but said that he found the case study "a bit eerie." The message began with "From one case study to another," and it ended "All the best, P.H."

Clinical Trials: Development of New Psychotherapeutic Drugs

Almost daily, there are news reports of exciting discoveries that appear to be pointing to effective new therapeutic drugs or treatments for psychiatric disorders. But most often, the promise does not materialize. For example, almost 50 years after the revolution in molecular biology began, not a single form of gene therapy is yet in widespread use. The reason is that the journey of a drug or other medical treatment from promising basic research to useful reality is excruciatingly complex, time-consuming, and expensive. Research designed to translate basic scientific discoveries into effective clinical treatments is called **translational research**.

So far, the chapter has focused on early drug discoveries and their role in the development of theories of psychiatric disorders. In the early years, the development of psychotherapeutic drugs was largely a hit-or-miss process. New drugs were tested on patient populations with little justification and then quickly marketed to an unsuspecting public, often before it was discovered that they were dangerous or ineffective for their original purpose.

Things have changed. The testing of experimental drugs on human volunteers and their subsequent release for sale are now strictly regulated by government agencies.

The process of gaining permission from the government to market a new psychotherapeutic drug begins with the synthesis of the drug, the development of procedures for synthesizing it economically, and the collection of evidence from nonhuman subjects showing that the drug is likely safe for human consumption and has potential therapeutic benefits. These initial steps usually take a long time—at least 5 years—and only if the evidence is sufficiently promising is permission granted to proceed to clinical trials. **Clinical trials** are studies conducted on human volunteers to assess the therapeutic efficacy of an untested drug or other treatment. This process is summarized in Table 18.2. This final module of the chapter focuses on the process of conducting clinical trials.

Clinical Trials: The Three Phases

LO 18.25 Describe the three phases of clinical trials.

Once approval has been obtained from the appropriate government agencies, clinical trials of a new drug with therapeutic potential can commence. Clinical trials are conducted in three separate phases: (1) screening for safety, (2) establishing the testing protocol, and (3) final testing (see Zivin, 2000). The average duration and cost of each phase, based on estimates by Adams and Brantner (2010), are summarized in Figure 18.10.

PHASE 1: SCREENING FOR SAFETY. The purpose of the first phase of a clinical trial is to determine whether the drug is safe for human use and, if it is, to determine how much of the drug can be tolerated. Administering the drug to humans for the first time is always a risky process because there is no way of knowing for certain how they will respond. The subjects in phase 1 are typically healthy paid volunteers. Phase 1 clinical trials always begin with tiny injections, which are gradually increased as the tests proceed. The reactions of the volunteers are meticulously monitored, and if strong adverse reactions are observed, testing is curtailed.

Table 18.2 Phases of Drug Development

BASIC RESEARCH
Discovery of the drug, development of efficient methods of synthesis, and testing with animal models
Application to begin clinical trials and the review of basic research by government agency
HUMAN CLINICAL TRIALS
Phase 1 Screening for safety and finding the maximum safe dose
Phase 2 Establishing most effective doses and schedules of treatment
Phase 3 Clear demonstrations that the drug is therapeutic
Application to begin marketing and reviews of results of clinical trials by government agency
SELLING TO THE PUBLIC
Recovering development costs and continuing to monitor the safety of the drug

Source: Based on Zivin (2000).

Figure 18.10 The cost and duration of the three phases of drug testing on human volunteers.

protocol may be conducted. In most cases, two independent successful tests are required to convince government regulatory agencies. A successful test is one in which the beneficial effects outweigh any adverse side effects.

Controversial Aspects of Clinical Trials

LO 18.26 Identify five controversial aspects of clinical trials.

The clinical trial process is not without controversy. The following are five points that have been focuses of criticism and debate (see Goldacre, 2013; London, Kimmelman, & Carlisle, 2012).

REQUIREMENT FOR DOUBLE-BLIND DESIGN AND PLACEBO CONTROLS. In most clinical trials, patients are assigned to drug or placebo groups randomly and do not know for sure which treatment they are receiving. Thus, some patients whose only hope for recovery may be the latest experimental treatment will, without knowing it, receive the placebo. Drug companies and government agencies concede that this is true, but they argue that there can be no convincing evidence that the experimental treatment is effective until a double-blind, placebo-control trial has been completed. Because psychiatric disorders often improve after a placebo, a double-blind, placebo-control procedure is essential in the evaluation of any psychotherapeutic drug.

PHASE 2: ESTABLISHING THE TESTING PROTOCOL. The purpose of the second phase of a clinical trial is to establish the *protocol* (the conditions) under which the final tests are likely to provide a clear result. For example, in phase 2, researchers hope to discover which doses are likely to be therapeutically effective, how frequently they should be administered, how long they need to be administered to have a therapeutic effect, what benefits are likely to occur, and which patients are likely to be helped. Phase 2 tests are conducted on volunteer patients suffering from the target disorder; the tests usually include *placebo-control groups* (groups of patients who receive a control substance rather than the drug), and their designs are usually *double-blind*—that is, the tests are conducted so that neither the patients nor the physicians interacting with them know which treatment (drug or placebo) each patient has received.

PHASE 3: FINAL TESTING. Phase 3 of a clinical trial is typically a double-blind, placebo-control study on large numbers—often, many thousands—of patients suffering from the target disorder. The design of the phase 3 tests is based on the results of phase 2 so that the final tests are likely to demonstrate positive therapeutic effects if they exist. The first test of the final phase is often not conclusive, but if it is promising, a second test based on a redesigned

THE NEED FOR ACTIVE PLACEBOS. Conventional wisdom has been that the double-blind, placebo-control procedure is the perfect control procedure to establish the effectiveness of new drugs, but **Thinking Creatively** it isn't (see Benedetti, 2014). Here is a new way to think about the double-blind placebo-control procedure. At therapeutic doses, many drugs have side effects that are obvious to people taking them, and thus the participants in double-blind, placebo-control studies who receive the drug can be certain that they are not in the placebo group. This knowledge may greatly contribute to the positive effects of the drug, independent of any real therapeutic effect. Accordingly, it is now widely recognized that an active placebo is better than an inert placebo as the control drug. **Active placebos** are control drugs that have no therapeutic effect but produce side effects similar to those produced by the drug under evaluation.

LENGTH OF TIME REQUIRED. Patients desperately seeking new treatments are frustrated by the amount of time needed for clinical trials (see Figure 18.10). Therefore, researchers, drug companies, and government agencies are striving to speed up the evaluation process without sacrificing the quality of the procedures designed to protect patients from ineffective or dangerous treatments. It is imperative to strike the right compromise.

Figure 18.11 The probabilities that a drug that qualifies for testing in humans will reach each phase of testing and ultimately gain approval. Only 22 percent of the drugs that initially qualify for testing eventually gain approval.

FINANCIAL ISSUES. The drug companies pay the scientists, physicians, technicians, assistants, and patients involved in drug trials. Considering the millions these companies spend and the fact that only about 22 percent of the candidate drugs entering phase 1 testing ever gain final approval (see Figure 18.11), it should come as no surprise that the companies are anxious to recoup their costs. In view of this pressure, many have questioned the impartiality of those conducting and reporting the trials (see Normile, 2014; Roest et al., 2015). The scientists themselves have often complained that the sponsoring drug company makes them sign an agreement

Thinking Creatively

that prohibits them from publishing or discussing negative findings without the company's consent. This is a serious ongoing problem: Any new drug will look promising if all negative evidence is suppressed (see Goldacre, 2012).

Another financial issue is profitability—drug companies seldom develop drugs to treat rare disorders because such treatments will not be profitable. Drugs for which the market is too small for them to be profitable are called **orphan drugs**. Governments in Europe and North America have passed laws intended to promote the development of orphan drugs. Also, the massive costs of clinical trials have contributed to a **translational bottleneck**—only a small proportion of potentially valuable ideas or treatments receive funding for translational research.

TARGETS OF PSYCHOPHARMACOLOGY. Hyman and Fenton (2003) have argued that a major impediment to the development of effective psychotherapeutic drugs is that the

Thinking Creatively

effort is often aimed at curing disease entities as currently conceived—for example, as defined by the DSM-5. The current characterizations of various psychiatric disorders are the best they can be given the existing evidence; however, it is clear that most

psychiatric disorders, as currently conceived, are likely clusters of disorders, each with a different pattern of associated brain changes. Thus, effective new drugs are likely to benefit only a proportion of those patients who have been given a particular diagnosis, and thus their effectiveness might go unrecognized.

Effectiveness of Clinical Trials

LO 18.27 Discuss the relative effectiveness of clinical trials.

Despite the controversy that surrounds the clinical trial process, there is no question that it works.

A long, dismal history tells of charlatans who make unfounded promises and take advantage of people at the time when they are least able to care for themselves. The clinical trial process is the most objective method ever devised to assess the efficacy of a treatment. It is expensive and slow, and in need of constant refinements, and oversight, but the process is trustworthy. (Zivin, 2000, p. 75)

Certainly, the clinical trial process is far from perfect. For example, concerns about the ethics of randomized double-blind, placebo-control studies are warranted. Still, the vast majority of those in the medical and research professions accept that these studies are the essential critical test of any new therapy. This is particularly true of psychotherapeutic drugs because psychiatric disorders often respond to placebo **Thinking Creatively** treatments (see Rutherford & Roose, 2013; Wager & Atlas, 2015) and because assessment of their severity can be greatly influenced by the expectations of the therapist.

Everybody agrees that clinical trials are too expensive and take too long. But Zivin (2000) responds to this concern in the following way: Clinical trials can be trustworthy, fast, or cheap; but in any one trial, only two of the three are possible. Think about it.

It is important to realize that every clinical trial is carefully monitored as it is being conducted. Any time the results warrant it, changes to the research protocol are made to reduce costs, improve safety, and reduce the time to get the drug to patients. We think this system would be greatly improved if there was a legal requirement for all partial or completed clinical trials to be **Thinking Creatively** published so that patients, doctors, and scientists would have access to all of the evidence. What do you think?

Thinking Creatively What do you think Zivin means when he suggests that clinical trials can be trustworthy, fast, or cheap—but that in any one trial, only two of the three are possible?

CONCLUSION. Ideally, patients in the same diagnostic category should display the same symptoms associated with the same underlying pathology caused by the same genetic and environmental factors. But more importantly, they should all respond to the same treatments. When it comes to disorders of the brain, our most complex organ, this ideal is rarely met. However, when it comes to the diagnosis of psychiatric disorders, we have not even been close.

As you progressed through this chapter, we hope you recognized the signs that the diagnosis of psychiatric disorders needs to be improved (with the possible exception of Tourette's disorder). The symptoms of schizophrenia, depressive disorders, bipolar disorders, and anxiety disorders are so variable that two individuals with the same diagnosis may share few of the same symptoms. Moreover, a wide range of genetic and environmental factors have been implicated in each diagnosis, and patients with the same diagnosis display substantial variability in any associated neural changes. Most problematic is that, despite the fact that many drugs acting by several mechanisms are used in the treatment of each disorder, many patients do not substantially improve. It does seem that each diagnosis contains several different disorders and that research and treatment could benefit from distinguishing among them.

The chapter, and indeed the book, ends with the case of S.B., who, if you recall from the module on bipolar disorders, suffers from bipolar disorder type I. So far, the case of S.B. has introduced you to the features of both depressive disorders and bipolar disorders. The conclusion of his case study demonstrates the value of a biopsychological education that stresses independent thinking and the importance of taking responsibility for one's own health. You see, S.B. took a course similar to the one you are currently taking, and the things that he learned in the course enabled him to steer his own treatment to a positive outcome.

Conclusion of the Case of S.B.: The Biopsychology Student Who Took Control

Heavily sedated on benzodiazepines, S.B. slept for much of the first week after he was committed to a psychiatric ward by his psychiatrist. When he came out of his stupor, the ward's resident psychiatrist informed S.B. that he would be placed on a particular mood stabilizer and that he would

likely have to take it for the rest of his life. Two things made S.B. feel uncomfortable about this. First, many patients in the ward were taking this drug, and they seemed like bloated zombies; second, the resident psychiatrist seemed to know less about this drug and its mechanisms than S.B. did. So S.B. requested that he be given access to the hospital library so he could learn more about his disorder and the drugs used to treat it.

S.B. was amazed by what he found. The drug favored by the resident psychiatrist had been shown several months before to be no more effective in the long-term treatment of bipolar disorders than placebo. **Thinking Creatively** Moreover, a new drug that had recently cleared clinical trials was proving to be effective with fewer side effects. When S.B. confronted the resident psychiatrist with this evidence, he was surprised and agreed to prescribe the new drug.

Today, S.B. is feeling well and has finished graduate school. In fact, at the time of writing of this text, S.B. holds a faculty position at a leading university in Canada. In fact, S.B. is writing these very words. If it has not yet occurred to you, I (Steven Barnes) am S.B.

I still find it difficult to believe that I had enough nerve to question a psychiatrist and prescribe for myself. I never imagined that the lessons learned from Biopsychology would have such a positive impact on my life. Although I still experience mood episodes associated with my bipolar disorder, they aren't nearly as severe as they were before I started taking a mood stabilizer, and I have learned to manage the residual symptoms using both pharmacological and psychosocial methods (see Geddes & Miklowitz, 2013; Murray et al., 2011). I am glad that I could tell you my story and hope that you or someone you care for will benefit from it.

Watch this video on MyPsychLab

CHALK IT UP: THE CASE OF S.B.

Themes Revisited

This entire chapter focused on psychiatric disorders, so it should come as no surprise that the clinical implications theme was predominant. Nevertheless, the other three major themes of this text also received coverage.

The thinking creatively theme arose during the discussions of the following ideas: animal models of anxiety may

be models of benzodiazepine effects, active placebos are needed to establish the clinical efficacy of psychotherapeutic drugs, scientists should try to focus on treatments for specific measurable symptoms rather than general diseases as currently conceived, and there needs to be a way to force drug companies to publish negative findings.

The evolutionary perspective theme came up twice: in the discussions of animal models of anxiety and of the important role played by research on non-human subjects in gaining official clearance to commence human clinical trials.

The neuroplasticity theme was discussed only once, during the explanation of the neuroplasticity theory of depression.

Neuroplasticity

Key Terms

Psychiatric disorders, p. 498
DSM-5, p. 499

Schizophrenia

Positive symptoms, p. 500
Negative symptoms, p. 500
Antipsychotic drug, p. 501
Chlorpromazine, p. 501
Psychosis, p. 501
Reserpine, p. 501
Haloperidol, p. 502
Phenothiazines, p. 502
Butyrophenones, p. 502
Typical antipsychotics, p. 502
Atypical antipsychotics, p. 503
Clozapine, p. 503
Psychedelic drugs, p. 504

Depressive Disorders

Anhedonia, p. 505
Clinical depression (major depressive
    disorder), p. 505
Reactive depression, p. 506
Endogenous depression p. 506
Comorbid, p. 506
Seasonal affective disorder (SAD),
    p. 506

Peripartum depression, p. 507
Iproniazid, p. 507
MAO inhibitors, p. 507
Cheese effect, p. 507
Tricyclic antidepressants,
    p. 507
Imipramine, p. 507
Selective serotonin-reuptake
    inhibitors (SSRIs), p. 507
Fluoxetine, p. 507
Atypical antidepressants,
    p. 507
Ketamine, p. 508
Up-regulation, p. 509
Repetitive transcranial magnetic
    stimulation (rTMS), p. 510

Bipolar Disorders

Bipolar disorder, p. 511
Hypomania, p. 511
Mania, p. 511
Bipolar disorder type II, p. 511
Bipolar disorder type I, p. 511
Mixed state, p. 512
Mood stabilizers, p. 512
Lithium, p. 512

Anxiety Disorders

Anxiety, p. 513
Anxiety disorder, p. 514
Generalized anxiety disorder, p. 514
Specific phobia, p. 514
Agoraphobia, p. 514
Panic disorder, p. 514
Panic attacks, p. 514
Benzodiazepines, p. 515
Anxiolytic drugs, p. 515
Elevated-plus-maze test, p. 515
Defensive-burying test, p. 515
Risk-assessment test, p. 515

Tourette's Disorder

Tourette's disorder, p. 516
Tics, p. 517

Clinical Trials: Development of New Psychotherapeutic Drugs

Translational research, p. 519
Clinical trials, p. 519
Active placebos, p. 520
Orphan drugs, p. 521
Translational bottleneck, p. 521

Epilogue

We feel relieved to be finishing this edition of *Biopsychology*, which we began almost 2 years ago, and we are excited by the prospect of being able to speak to so many students like you through this new edition. We were especially excited by the process of converting this edition into an electronic format that allows for greater interactivity. We hope you enjoyed all the great features this new electronic format had to offer.

You must also feel relieved to be finishing this text; still, we hope that you feel a tiny bit of regret that our time together is over. Like good friends, we have shared good times and bad. We have shared the fun and wonder of Rhonelle, the dexterous cashier; the Nads basketball team; people who rarely sleep; the "mamawawa"; and split brains. But we have also been touched by many personal tragedies: for example, the victims of Alzheimer's disease and MPTP poisoning; Jimmie G.; H.M.; the man who mistook his wife for a hat; Professor P., the biopsychologist who experienced brain surgery from the other side of the knife; and S.B., the biopsychology student who guided the treatment of his own disease. Thank you for allowing us to share biopsychology with you. We hope you have found it to be an enriching experience.

Right now, John Pinel is sitting at his desk looking out over his garden and the Pacific Ocean, and Steven Barnes is sitting at his desk looking out at his art studio. Our writing of this edition is complete. John's garden is calling for his attention, and Steven's paintings are demanding completion. It is the evening of Saturday, April 30, 2016.

Appendix I

The Autonomic Nervous System (ANS)

Appendix II

Some Functions of Sympathetic and Parasympathetic Neurons

Organ	Sympathetic Effect	Parasympathetic Effect
Salivary gland	Decreases secretion	Increases secretion
Heart	Increases heart rate	Decreases heart rate
Blood vessels	Constricts blood vessels in most organs	Dilates blood vessels in a few organs
Penis	Ejaculation	Erection
Iris radial muscles	Dilates pupils	No effect
Iris sphincter muscles	No effect	Constricts pupils
Tear gland	No effect	Stimulates secretion
Sweat gland	Stimulates secretion	No effect
Stomach and intestine	No effect	Stimulates secretion
Lungs	Dilates bronchioles; inhibits mucous secretion	Constricts bronchioles; stimulates mucous secretion
Arrector pili muscles	Erects hair and creates gooseflesh	No effect

Appendix III

The Cranial Nerves

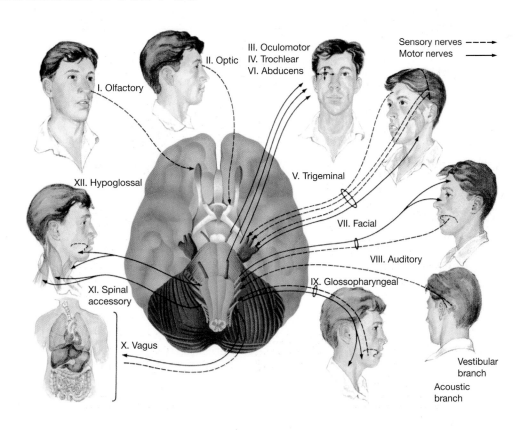

Appendix IV

Functions of the Cranial Nerves

Number	Name	General Function	Specific Functions
I	Olfactory	Sensory	Smell
II	Optic	Sensory	Vision
III	Oculomotor	Motor	Eye movement and pupillary constriction
		Sensory	Sensory signals from certain eye muscles
IV	Trochlear	Motor	Eye movement
		Sensory	Sensory signals from certain eye muscles
V	Trigeminal	Sensory	Facial sensations
		Motor	Chewing
VI	Abducens	Motor	Eye movement
		Sensory	Sensory signals from certain eye muscles
VII	Facial	Sensory	Taste from anterior two-thirds of tongue
		Motor	Facial expression, secretion of tears, salivation, cranial blood vessel dilation
VIII	Auditory-Vestibular	Sensory	Audition; sensory signals from the organs of balance in the inner ear
IX	Glossopharyngeal	Sensory	Taste from posterior third of tongue
		Motor	Salivation, swallowing
X	Vagus	Sensory	Sensations from abdominal and thoracic organs
		Motor	Control over abdominal and thoracic organs and muscles of the throat
XI	Spinal Accessory	Motor	Movement of neck, shoulders, and head
		Sensory	Sensory signals from muscles of the neck
XII	Hypoglossal	Motor	Tongue movements
		Sensory	Sensory signals from tongue muscles

NOTE: Some authors describe cranial nerves III, IV, VI, XI, and XII as purely motor. However, each of these cranial nerves contains a small proportion of sensory fibers that conduct information from receptors to the brain. This sensory information is necessary for directing the respective cranial nerve's motor responses. See the discussion of sensory feedback in Chapter 8.

Appendix V

Nuclei of the Thalamus

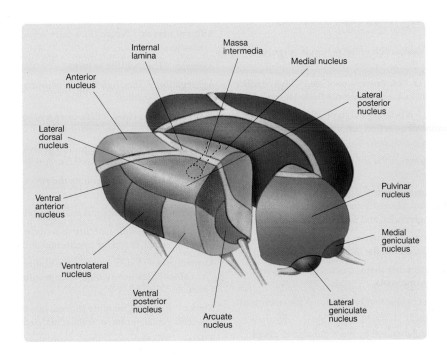

Appendix VI

Nuclei of the Hypothalamus

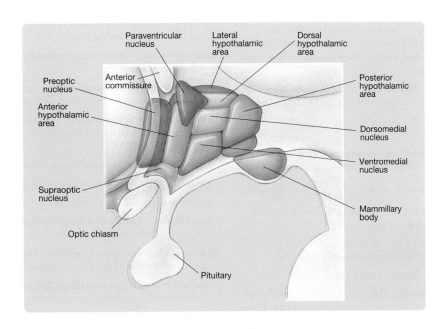

Glossary

3-per-second spike-and-wave discharge. The characteristic EEG pattern of the absence seizure.

5-hydroxytryptophan (5-HTP). The precursor of serotonin.

Ablatio penis. Accidental destruction of the penis via surgery.

Absence seizure. A type of generalized seizure whose primary behavioral symptom is a disruption of consciousness associated with a cessation of ongoing behavior, a vacant look, and sometimes fluttering eyelids.

Absolute refractory period. A brief period (typically 1 to 2 milliseconds) after the initiation of an action potential during which it is impossible to elicit another action potential in the same neuron.

Absorption spectrum. A graph of the ability of a substance to absorb light of different wavelengths.

Absorptive phase. The metabolic phase during which the body is operating on the energy from a recently consumed meal and is storing the excess as body fat, glycogen, and proteins.

Accommodation. The process of adjusting the configuration of the lenses to bring images into focus on the retina.

Acetylcholine. A neurotransmitter that is created by the addition of an acetyl group to a choline molecule.

Acetylcholinesterase. The enzyme that breaks down the neurotransmitter acetylcholine.

Acquired dyslexias. Dyslexias caused by brain damage in people previously capable of reading.

Action potential (AP). A massive momentary reversal of a neuron's membrane potential from about –70 mV to about +50 mV.

Activation-synthesis hypothesis. The theory that the information supplied to the cortex by the brain stem during REM sleep is largely random and that the resulting dream is the cortex's best effort to make sense of those random signals.

Active placebos. Control drugs that have no therapeutic effect but produce side effects similar to those produced by the drug under evaluation in a clinical trial.

Acuity. The ability to see the details of objects.

Adaptation theories of sleep. Theories of sleep based on the premise that sleep evolved to protect organisms from predation and accidents and to conserve their energy rather than to fulfill some particular physiological need.

Adaptive immune system. The division of the immune system that mounts targeted attacks on foreign pathogens by binding to antigens in their cell membranes.

Adipsia. Complete cessation of drinking.

Adjustable gastric band procedure. A surgical procedure for treating obesity in which an adjustable band is implanted around the stomach to reduce the flow of food.

Adrenal cortex. The outer layer of each adrenal gland, which releases glucocorticoids in response to stressors, as well as small amounts of steroid hormones.

Adrenal medulla. The core of each adrenal gland, which releases epinephrine and norepinephrine in response to stressors.

Adrenalectomy. Surgical removal of the adrenal glands.

Adrenocorticotropic hormone (ACTH). An anterior pituitary hormone that triggers the release of adrenal hormones from the adrenal cortices.

Adrenogenital syndrome. Caused by congenital adrenal hyperplasia, which results in the excessive release of adrenal androgens which have masculinizing effects in females.

Afferent nerves. Nerves that carry sensory signals to the central nervous system.

Ageusia. The inability to taste.

Aggregation. The alignment of neurons during the development of the nervous system.

Aggressive behaviors. Behaviors whose primary function is to threaten or harm other organisms.

Agnosia. A failure of recognition of sensory stimuli that is not attributable to a sensory or to verbal or intellectual impairment.

Agonists. Drugs that facilitate the effects of a particular neurotransmitter.

Agoraphobia. Pathological fear of public places and open spaces.

Agraphia. A specific inability to write; one that does not result from general visual, motor, or intellectual deficits.

Akinetopsia. A deficiency in the ability to see movement progress in a smooth fashion, which often results from damage to the MT area.

Alexia. A specific inability to read; one that does not result from general visual, motor, or intellectual deficits.

Alleles. The two genes that control the same trait.

All-or-none responses. Responses that are not graded; they either occur to their full extent or do not occur at all.

Alpha fetoprotein. A protein that is present in the blood of many mammals during the perinatal period and that deactivates circulating estradiol by binding to it.

Alpha male. The dominant male of a colony.

Alpha waves. Regular, 8- to 12-per-second, high-amplitude EEG waves that typically occur during relaxed wakefulness and just before falling asleep.

Alzheimer's disease. The most common form of dementia in the elderly. It's three defining characteristics are: neurofibrillary tangles, amyloid plaques, and neuron loss.

Amacrine cells. Retinal neurons that are specialized for lateral communication.

Amino acid derivative hormones. Hormones that are synthesized in a few simple steps from an amino acid molecule.

Amino acid neurotransmitters. A class of small-molecule neurotransmitters, which includes the amino acids glutamate, aspartate, glycine, and GABA.

Amino acids. The building blocks of proteins.

Amnesia. Any pathological loss of memory.

Amphetamine. A stimulant drug.

Amphibians. Species that must live in water during their larval phase; adult amphibians can survive on land.

Amygdala. A structure in the anterior temporal lobe, just anterior to the hippocampus; plays a role in emotion.

Anabolic steroids. Steroid drugs that are similar to testosterone and have powerful anabolic (growth-promoting) effects.

Analgesics. Drugs that reduce pain.

Analogous. Having a similar structure because of convergent evolution (e.g., a bird's wing and a bee's wing are analogous).

Anandamide. The first endogenous endocannabinoid to be discovered and characterized.

Androgen insensitivity syndrome. Results from a mutation to the androgen receptor gene that renders the androgen receptors unresponsive and leads to the development of a female body.

Androgens. The class of steroid hormones that includes testosterone.

Androstenedione. The adrenal androgen that is responsible for the growth of pubic hair and axillary hair in human females.

Aneurysm. A pathological balloonlike dilation that forms in the wall of an artery at a point where the elasticity of the artery wall is defective.

Angular gyrus. The gyrus of the posterior cortex at the boundary between the temporal and parietal lobes. According to the Wernicke-Geschwind model the left hemisphere angular gyrus plays a role in reading.

Anhedonia. A general inability to experience pleasure.

Anorexia nervosa. An eating disorder of underconsumption that results in health-threatening weight loss.

Anosmia. The inability to smell.

Anosognosia. The common failure of neuropsychological patients to recognize their own symptoms.

Antagonistic muscles. Pairs of muscles that act in opposition.

Antagonists. Drugs that inhibit the effects of a particular neurotransmitter.

Anterior. Toward the nose end of a vertebrate.

Anterior cingulate cortex. The cortex of the anterior cingulate gyrus.

Anterior pituitary. The part of the pituitary gland that releases tropic hormones.

Anterograde amnesia. Loss of memory for events occurring after the amnesia-inducing brain injury.

Anterograde degeneration. The degeneration of the distal segment of a cut axon.

Anterolateral system. A major somatosensory pathway that ascends in the anterolateral portion of the spinal cord and tends to carry information related to pain and temperature.

Antibodies. Proteins that bind to foreign antigens on the surface of microorganisms and in so doing promote the destruction of the microorganisms.

Antibody-mediated immunity. The immune reaction in which B cells destroy invading microorganisms via the production of antibodies.

Antidromic conduction. Axonal conduction opposite to the normal direction; conduction from axon terminals back toward the cell body.

Antihypnotic drugs. Sleep-reducing drugs.

Anxiety. Chronic fear that persists in the absence of any direct threat.

Anxiety disorder. A psychiatric disorder that involves anxiety that is so extreme and so pervasive that it disrupts normal functioning.

Anxiolytic drugs. Drugs that have antianxiety effects.

Anxiolytics. Antianxiety drugs.

Aphagia. Complete cessation of eating.

Aphasia. A brain damage–produced deficit in the ability to produce or comprehend language.

Apoptosis. Cell death that is actively induced by genetic programs; programmed cell death.

Appetizer effect. The increase in hunger that is produced by the consumption of small amounts of food.

Applied research. Research that is intended to bring about some direct benefit to humankind.

Apraxia. A disorder in which patients have great difficulty performing movements when asked to do so out of context but can readily perform them spontaneously in natural situations.

Arachnoid membrane. The meninx that is located between the dura mater and the pia mater and has the appearance of a gauzelike spiderweb.

Arcuate fasciculus. The major neural pathway between Broca's area and Wernicke's area.

Arcuate nucleus. A nucleus of the hypothalamus that contains high concentrations of both leptin receptors and insulin receptors.

Aromatase. An enzyme that promotes the conversion of testosterone to estradiol.

Aromatization. The chemical process by which testosterone is converted to estradiol.

Aromatization hypothesis. The hypothesis that the brain is masculinized by estradiol that is produced from perinatal testosterone through a process called *aromatization*.

Arteriosclerosis. A condition in which blood vessels are narrowed or blocked by the accumulation of fat deposits on their walls.

Asomatognosia. A deficiency in the awareness of parts of one's own body that is typically produced by damage to the right parietal lobe.

Aspartate. An amino acid neurotransmitter.

Aspiration. A lesion technique in which tissue is drawn off by suction through the fine tip of a glass pipette.

Association cortex. An area of cortex that receives input from more than one sensory system.

Astereognosia. An inability to recognize objects by touch that is not attributable to a simple sensory deficit or to an intellectual impairment.

Astrocytes. Large, star-shaped glial cells that play multiple roles in the CNS.

Ataxia. A loss of motor coordination.

Atropine. A receptor blocker that exerts its antagonistic effect by binding to muscarinic receptors.

Atypical antidepressants. A catch-all class for antidepressant drugs that do not fit into the other categories of antidepressants (e.g., monoamine oxidase inhibitors, tricyclic antidepressants). Each of the drugs in this class has its own unique mechanism of action.

Atypical antipsychotics. Drugs that are effective against schizophrenia but yet do not bind strongly to D_2 receptors. Also known as second-generation antipsychotics.

Auditory nerve. The branch of cranial nerve VIII that carries auditory signals from the hair cells in the basilar membrane.

Autism spectrum disorder (ASD). A complex neurodevelopmental disorder characterized by a reduced capacity for social interaction and communication and restricted and repetitive patterns of behavior, interests, or activities.

Autonomic nervous system (ANS). The part of the peripheral nervous system that participates in the regulation of the body's internal environment.

Autoradiography. The technique of photographically developing brain slices that have been exposed to a radioactively labeled substance (such as 2-deoxyglucose) so that regions of high uptake are made visible.

Autoreceptors. A type of metabotropic receptor located on the presynaptic membrane that bind to their neuron's own neurotransmitters.

Autosomal chromosomes. Chromosomes that come in matched pairs; in mammals, all of the chromosomes except the sex chromosomes are autosomal.

Axon hillock. The conical structure at the junction between the axon and cell body.

Axon initial segment. The segment of the axon where action potentials are generated—located immediately adjacent to the axon hillock.

B cells. B lymphocytes; lymphocytes that manufacture antibodies against antigens they encounter.

Basal forebrain. A midline area of the forebrain, which is located just in front of and above the hypothalamus and is the brain's main source of acetylcholine.

Basal ganglia. A collection of subcortical nuclei (e.g., striatum and globus pallidus).

Basal metabolic rate. The rate at which energy is utilized to maintain bodily processes when resting.

Basilar membrane. The membrane of the organ of Corti in which the hair cell receptors are embedded.

Before-and-after design. The experimental design used to demonstrate contingent drug tolerance; one group receives the drug before each of a series of behavioral tests and the other group receives the drug after each test.

Behavioral paradigm. A single set of procedures developed for the investigation of a particular behavioral phenomenon.

Benign tumors. Tumors that are surgically removable with little risk of further growth in the body.

Benzodiazepines. A class of GABA$_A$ agonists with anxiolytic, sedative, and anticonvulsant properties; drugs such as chlordiazepoxide (Librium) and diazepam (Valium).

Beta-amyloid. A protein that is present in normal brains in small amounts. Beta amyloid is a major constituent of the amyloid plaques of Alzheimer's disease.

Between-subjects design. An experimental design in which a different group of subjects is tested under each condition.

Betz cells. Large pyramidal neurons of the primary motor cortex whose axons form part of the dorsolateral corticospinal tract.

Bilateral medial temporal lobectomy. The removal of the medial portions of both temporal lobes, including the hippocampus, the amygdala, and the adjacent cortex.

Binocular. Cells in the visual system that are *binocular* respond to stimulation of either eye.

Binocular disparity. The difference in the position of the same image on the two retinas.

Biopsychology. The scientific study of the biology of behavior; a biological approach to the study of psychology.

Bipolar cells. Bipolar neurons that form the middle layer of the retina.

Bipolar disorders. A category of psychiatric disorders that involves alternate bouts of depression and mania or hypomania.

Bipolar disorder type I. A psychiatric disorder that involves alternate bouts of depression and mania.

Bipolar disorder type II. A psychiatric disorder that involves alternate bouts of depression and hypomania.

Bipolar neuron. A neuron with two processes extending from its cell body.

Bisexual. An individual who is sexually attracted to members of both sexes.

Blind spot. The area on the retina where the bundle of axons from the retinal ganglion cells leave the eye as the optic nerve.

Blindsight. The ability to respond to visual stimuli in a scotoma without conscious awareness of those stimuli.

Blobs. Peglike, cytochrome oxidase–rich, dual-opponent color columns.

Blood–brain barrier. The mechanism that impedes the passage of toxic substances from the blood into the brain.

BOLD signal. The blood-oxygen-level-dependent signal that is recorded by functional MRI (fMRI).

Botox. *Botulinium toxin*; a neurotoxin released by bacterium often found in spoiled food. It blocks the release of acetylcholine at neuromuscular junctions and has applications in medicine and cosmetics.

Bottom-up. A sort of neural mechanism that involves activation of higher cortical areas by lower cortical areas.

Brain stem. The part of the brain on which the cerebral hemispheres rest; in general, it regulates reflex activities that are critical for survival (e.g., heart rate and respiration).

Bregma. The point on the surface of the skull where two of the major sutures intersect; commonly used as a reference point in stereotaxic surgery on rodents.

Broca's aphasia. A hypothetical disorder of speech production with no associated deficits in language comprehension.

Broca's area. The area of the inferior prefrontal cortex of the left hemisphere hypothesized by Broca to be the center of speech production.

Buerger's disease. A condition in which the blood vessels, especially those supplying the legs, are constricted whenever tobacco is smoked. The disease can progress to gangrene and amputation.

Bulimia nervosa. An eating disorder characterized by periods of not eating interrupted by bingeing followed by purging.

Bullying. A chronic social threat that induces subordination stress in members of our species.

Butyrophenones. A class of antipsychotic drugs that bind primarily to D$_2$ receptors.

CA1 subfield. A region of the hippocampus that is commonly damaged by cerebral ischemia.

Cafeteria diet. A diet offered to experimental animals that is composed of a wide variety of palatable foods.

Cannabis. The common hemp plant, which is the source of marijuana.

Cannon-Bard theory. The theory that emotional experience and emotional expression are parallel processes that have no direct causal relation.

Cannula. A fine, hollow tube that is implanted in the body for the purpose of introducing or extracting substances.

Carbon monoxide. A soluble-gas neurotransmitter.

Carousel apparatus. An apparatus used to study the effects of sleep deprivation in laboratory rats.

Cartesian dualism. The philosophical position of René Descartes, who argued that the universe is composed of two elements: physical matter and the human mind.

Case studies. Studies that focus on a single case, or subject.

Cataplexy. A disorder that is characterized by recurring losses of muscle tone during wakefulness and is often seen in cases of narcolepsy.

Catecholamines. The three monoamine neurotransmitters that are synthesized from the amino acid tyrosine: dopamine, epinephrine, and norepinephrine.

Caudate. The tail-like structure that is part of the striatum.

Cell-adhesion molecules (CAMs). Molecules on the surface of cells that have the ability to recognize specific molecules on the surface of other cells and adhere to them.

Cell-mediated immunity. The immune reaction by which T cells destroy invading microorganisms.

Central canal. The small CSF-filled channel that runs the length of the spinal cord.

Central fissure. The large fissure that separates the frontal lobe from the parietal lobe.

Central nervous system (CNS). The portion of the nervous system within the skull and spine.

Central nucleus of the amygdala. A nucleus of the amygdala that is thought to control defensive behavior.

Central sensorimotor programs. Patterns of activity that are programmed into the sensorimotor system.

Cephalic phase. The metabolic phase during which the body prepares for food that is about to be absorbed.

Cerebellum. A metencephalic structure that is thought to participate in the storage of memories of learned sensorimotor skills.

Cerebral angiography. A contrast x-ray technique for visualizing the cerebral circulatory system by infusing a radio-opaque dye into a cerebral artery.

Cerebral aqueduct. A narrow channel that connects the third and fourth ventricles.

Cerebral commissures. Tracts that connect the left and right cerebral hemispheres.

Cerebral cortex. The layer of neural tissue covering the cerebral hemispheres of humans and other mammals.

Cerebral dialysis. A method for recording changes in brain chemistry in behaving animals in which a fine tube with a short semipermeable section is implanted in the brain and extracellular neurochemicals are continuously drawn off for analysis.

Cerebral hemorrhage. Bleeding in the brain.

Cerebral ischemia. An interruption of the blood supply to an area of the brain.

Cerebral ventricles. The four CSF-filled internal chambers of the brain: the two lateral ventricles, the third ventricle, and the fourth ventricle.

Cerebrospinal fluid (CSF). The fluid that fills the subarachnoid space, the central canal, and the cerebral ventricles.

Cerebrum. The portion of the brain that sits above the brain stem; in general, it plays a role in complex adaptive processes (e.g., learning, perception, and motivation).

Cerveau isolé preparation. An experimental preparation in which the forebrain is disconnected from the rest of the brain by a midcollicular transection.

Change blindness. The difficulty perceiving major changes to unattended-to parts of a visual image when the changes are introduced during brief interruptions in the presentation of the image.

Cheese effect. The surges in blood pressure that occur when individuals taking MAO inhibitors consume tyramine-rich foods, such as cheese.

Chemoaffinity hypothesis. The hypothesis that growing axons are attracted to the correct targets by different chemicals released by the target sites.

Chemotopic. Organized, like the olfactory bulb, according to a map of various odors.

Chimeric figures test. A test of visual completion in split-brain subjects that uses pictures composed of the left and right halves of two different faces.

Chlorpromazine. The first antipsychotic drug.

Cholecystokinin (CCK). A peptide that is released by the gastrointestinal tract and is thought to function as a satiety signal.

Chordates. Animals with dorsal nerve cords.

Choroid plexuses. The networks of capillaries that protrude into the ventricles from the pia mater and produce cerebrospinal fluid.

Chromosomes. Threadlike structures in the cell nucleus that contain the genes; each chromosome is a DNA molecule.

Chronic traumatic encephalopathy. The dementia and cerebral scarring observed in boxers, rugby players, American football players, and other individuals who have experienced repeated concussive, or even subconcussive, blows to the head.

Chronobiotic. A substance that influences the timing of internal biological rhythms.

Ciliary muscles. The eye muscles that control the shape of the lenses.

Cingulate cortex. The cortex of the cingulate gyri, which are located on the medial surfaces of the frontal lobes.

Cingulate gyri. Large gyri located on the medial surfaces of the frontal lobes, just superior to the corpus callosum.

Cingulate motor areas. Two small areas of secondary motor cortex located in the cortex of the cingulate gyrus of each hemisphere.

Circadian clock. An internal timing mechanism that is capable of maintaining daily cycles of physiological functions.

Circadian rhythms. Daily cycles of bodily functions.

Cirrhosis. Scarring of the liver, which is a major cause of death among heavy alcohol users.

Clinical. Pertaining to illness or treatment.

Clinical depression (major depressive disorder). Depression that is so severe that it is difficult for the patient to meet the essential requirements of daily life.

Clinical trials. Studies conducted on human subjects to assess the therapeutic efficacy of an untested drug or other treatment.

Clozapine. An atypical antipsychotic that is used to treat schizophrenia, does not produce Parkinsonian side effects, and has only a slight affinity for D_2 receptors.

Cocaine. A stimulant that exerts its effects by altering the activity of dopamine transporters.

Cocaine psychosis. Psychotic symptoms that are sometimes observed during cocaine sprees; similar in certain respects to schizophrenia.

Cocaine sprees. Binges of cocaine use.

Cochlea. The long, coiled tube in the inner ear that is filled with fluid and contains the organ of Corti and its auditory receptors.

Cocktail-party phenomenon. The ability to unconsciously monitor the contents of one conversation while consciously focusing on another.

Cocontraction. The simultaneous contraction of antagonistic muscles.

Codeine. A relatively weak psychoactive ingredient of opium.

Codon. A group of three consecutive nucleotide bases on a DNA or messenger RNA strand; each codon specifies the particular amino acid that is to be added to an amino acid chain during protein synthesis.

Coexistence. The presence of more than one neurotransmitter in the same neuron.

Cognition. Higher intellectual processes such as thought, memory, attention, and complex perceptual processes.

Cognitive neuroscience. A division of biopsychology that focuses on the use of functional brain imaging to study the neural mechanisms of human cognition.

Collateral sprouting. The growth of axon branches from mature neurons, usually to postsynaptic sites abandoned by adjacent axons that have degenerated.

Colony-intruder paradigm. A paradigm for the study of aggressive and defensive behaviors in male rats; a small male intruder rat is placed in an established colony in order to study the aggressive responses of the colony's alpha male and the defensive responses of the intruder.

Color constancy. The tendency of an object to appear the same color even when the wavelengths of light that it reflects change.

Columnar organization. The functional organization of the neocortex in vertical columns; the cells in each column form a mini-circuit that performs a single function.

Commissurotomy. Surgical severing of the cerebral commissures.

Comorbid. The tendency for two or more health conditions to occur together in the same individual.

Comparative approach. The study of biological processes by comparing different species—usually from the evolutionary perspective.

Comparative psychology. The division of biopsychology that studies the evolution, genetics, and adaptiveness of behavior, often by using the comparative approach.

Complementary colors. Pairs of colors that produce white or gray when combined in equal measure.

Completion. The visual system's automatic use of information obtained from receptors around the blind spot, or scotoma, to create a perception of the missing portion of the retinal image.

Complex cells. Neurons in the visual cortex that respond optimally to straight-edge stimuli in a certain orientation in any part of their receptive field.

Complex partial seizures. Seizures that are characterized by various complex psychological phenomena and are thought to originate in the temporal lobes.

Component theory. The theory that the relative amount of activity produced in three different classes of cones by light determines its perceived color (also called *trichromatic theory*).

Computed tomography (CT). A computer-assisted x-ray procedure that can be used to visualize the brain and other internal structures of the living body.

Concept cells. Cells, such as those found in the medial temporal lobe, that respond to ideas or concepts rather than to particulars. Also known as Jennifer Aniston neurons.

Concussion. Disturbance of consciousness following a blow to the head with no evidence of contusion or other structural damage.

Conditioned compensatory responses. Hypothetical conditional physiological responses that are opposite to the effects of a drug that are thought to be elicited by stimuli that are regularly associated with experiencing the drug effects.

Conditioned defensive burying. The burial of a source of aversive stimulation by rats.

Conditioned drug tolerance. Tolerance effects that are maximally expressed only when a drug is administered in the same situation in which it has previously been administered.

Conditioned place-preference paradigm. A test that assesses a laboratory animal's preference for an environment in which it has previously experienced drug effects relative to a control environment.

Conditioned taste aversion. An avoidance response that develops to the taste of food whose consumption has been followed by illness.

Conduction aphasia. A hypothetical aphasia that is thought to result from damage to the arcuate fasciculus—the pathway between Broca's and Wernicke's areas.

Cones. The visual receptors in the retina that mediate high acuity color vision in good lighting.

Confounded variable. An unintended difference between the conditions of an experiment that could have affected the dependent variable.

Congenital. Present at birth.

Congenital adrenal hyperplasia. A congenital deficiency in the release of cortisol from the adrenal cortex, which leads to the excessive release of adrenal androgens.

Conscious awareness. The awareness of one's perceptions; typically inferred from the ability to verbally describe them.

Conspecifics. Members of the same species.

Constituent cognitive processes. Simple cognitive processes that combine to produce complex cognitive processes.

Contextual fear conditioning. The process by which benign contexts (situations) come to elicit fear through their association with fear-inducing stimuli.

Contingent drug tolerance. Drug tolerance that develops as a reaction to the experience of the effects of drugs rather than to drug exposure alone.

Contralateral. Projecting from one side of the body to the other.

Contralateral neglect. A disturbance of the patient's ability to respond to stimuli on the side of the body opposite to a site of brain damage, usually the left side of the body following damage to the right parietal lobe.

Contrast enhancement. The intensification of the perception of edges.

Contrast x-ray techniques. X-ray techniques that involve the injection, into one compartment of the body, of a substance that absorbs x-rays either less than or more than surrounding tissues.

Contrecoup injuries. Contusions that occur on the side of the brain opposite to the side of a blow.

"Control of behavior" versus "conscious perception" theory. The theory that the dorsal stream mediates behavioral interactions with objects and the ventral stream mediates conscious perception of objects.

Control-question technique. A lie-detection interrogation method in which the polygrapher compares the physiological responses to target questions with the responses to control questions.

Contusions. Closed-head injuries that involve damage to the cerebral circulatory system, which produces internal hemorrhaging.

Convergent evolution. The evolution in unrelated species of similar solutions to the same environmental demands.

Converging operations. The use of several research approaches to solve a single problem.

Convolutions. Folds on the surface of the cerebral hemispheres.

Convulsions. Motor seizures.

Coolidge effect. The fact that a copulating male who becomes incapable of continuing to copulate with one sex partner can often recommence copulating with a new sex partner.

Copulation. Sexual intercourse.

Corpus callosum. The largest cerebral commissure.

Corticosterone. The predominant glucocorticoid in humans.

Crack. A potent, cheap, smokable form of cocaine.

Cranial nerves. The 12 pairs of nerves extending from the brain (e.g., optic nerves, olfactory nerves, and vagus nerves).

Critical period. A period during development in which a particular experience must occur for it to influence the course of subsequent development.

Critical thinking. The process of recognizing the weaknesses of existing ideas and the evidence on which they are based.

Cross-cuing. Communication between hemispheres that have been separated by commissurotomy via an external route.

Cross section. Section cut at a right angle to any long, narrow structure of the CNS.

Cross tolerance. Tolerance to the effects of one drug that develops as the result of exposure to another drug that acts by the same mechanism.

Cytochrome oxidase. An enzyme present in particularly high concentrations in the mitochondria of dual-opponent color cells of the visual cortex.

Cytokines. A group of peptide hormones that are released by many cells and participate in a variety of physiological and immunological responses, causing inflammation and fever.

Decorticate. Lacking a cortex.

Decussate. To cross over to the other side of the brain.

Deep brain stimulation. A treatment in which low intensity electrical stimulation is continually applied to an area of the brain through an implanted electrode.

Deep dyslexia. A reading disorder in which the phonetic procedure is disrupted while the lexical procedure is not.

Default mode. The pattern of brain activity that is present when humans sit quietly and let their minds wander.

Default mode network. The network of brain structures that tends to be active when the brain is in default mode.

Defeminizes. Suppresses or disrupts female characteristics.

Defensive behaviors. Behaviors whose primary function is protection from threat or harm.

Defensive-burying test. An animal model of anxiety; anxious rats will bury objects that generate anxiety.

Delayed nonmatching-to-sample test. A test in which the subject is presented with an unfamiliar sample object and then, after a delay, is presented with a choice between the sample object and an unfamiliar object, where the correct choice is the unfamiliar object.

Delirium tremens (DTs). The phase of alcohol withdrawal syndrome characterized by hallucinations, delusions, disorientation, agitation, confusion, hyperthermia, and tachycardia.

Delta waves. The largest and slowest EEG waves.

Demasculinizes. Suppresses or disrupts male characteristics.

Dementia. General intellectual deterioration.

Dendritic spines. Tiny protrusions of various shapes that are located on the surfaces of many dendrites.

Deoxyribonucleic acid (DNA). The double-stranded, coiled molecule of genetic material.

Dependent variable. The variable measured by the experimenter to assess the effect of the independent variable.

Depolarize. To decrease the resting membrane potential.

Depressant. A drug that depresses neural activity.

Dermatome. An area of the body that is innervated by the left and right dorsal roots of one segment of the spinal cord.

Desynchronized EEG. Low-amplitude, high-frequency EEG.

Developmental dyslexias. Dyslexias that become apparent when a child is learning to read.

Dextrals. Right-handers.

Dichotic listening test. A test of language lateralization in which two different sequences of three spoken digits are presented simultaneously, one to each ear, and the subject is asked to report all of the digits heard.

Dichotomous traits. Traits that occur in one form or the other, never in combination.

Diencephalon. One of the five major divisions of the brain; it is composed of the thalamus and hypothalamus.

Diet-induced thermogenesis. The homeostasis-defending increases in body temperature that are associated with increases in body fat.

Diffusion tensor imaging. A magnetic resonance imaging (MRI) technique that is used for identifying major tracts.

Digestion. The process by which food is broken down and absorbed through the lining of the gastrointestinal tract.

Digit span. The longest sequence of random digits that can be repeated correctly 50 percent of the time—most people have a digit span of 7.

Directed synapses. Synapses at which the site of neurotransmitter release and the site of neurotransmitter reception are in close proximity.

Distal. Far from something.

Distal segment. The segment of a cut axon between the cut and the axon terminals.

Dizygotic twins. Twins that develop from two zygotes and thus tend to be as genetically similar as any pair of siblings.

DNA methylation. An epigenetic mechanism wherein a methyl group attaches to a DNA molecule, usually at cytosine sites in mammals. DNA methylation can either decrease or increase gene expression.

Dominant hemisphere. A term used in the past to refer to the left hemisphere, based on the incorrect assumption that the left hemisphere is dominant in all complex behavioral and cognitive activities.

Dominant trait. The trait of a dichotomous pair that is expressed in the phenotypes of heterozygous individuals.

Dopamine. One of the three catecholamine neurotransmitters.

Dopamine transporters. Molecules in the presynaptic membrane of dopaminergic neurons that attract dopamine molecules in the synaptic cleft and deposit them back inside the neuron.

Dorsal. Toward the surface of the back of a vertebrate or toward the top of the head.

Dorsal-column medial-lemniscus system. The division of the somatosensory system that ascends in the dorsal portion of the spinal white matter and tends to carry signals related to touch and proprioception.

Dorsal columns. The somatosensory tracts that ascend in the dorsal portion of the spinal cord white matter.

Dorsal horns. The two dorsal arms of the spinal gray matter.

Dorsal root ganglia. Structures just outside the spinal cord that are composed of the cell bodies of dorsal root axons.

Dorsal stream. The group of visual pathways that flows from the primary visual cortex to the dorsal prestriate cortex to the posterior parietal cortex.

Dorsolateral corticorubrospinal tract. The descending motor tract that synapses in the red nucleus of the midbrain, decussates, and descends in the dorsolateral spinal white matter.

Dorsolateral corticospinal tract. The motor tract that leaves the primary motor cortex, descends to the medullary pyramids, decussates, and then descends in the contralateral dorsolateral spinal white matter.

Dorsolateral prefrontal association cortex. An area of the prefrontal cortex that plays a role in the evaluation of external stimuli and the initiation of complex voluntary motor responses.

Down syndrome. A disorder associated with the presence of an extra chromosome 21, resulting in disfigurement and intellectual impairment.

Drug-addicted individuals. Those habitual drug users who continue to use a drug despite its adverse effects on their health and social life and despite their repeated efforts to stop using it.

Drug craving. An affective state in which there is a strong desire for a particular drug.

Drug metabolism. The conversion of a drug from its active form to a nonactive form.

Drug priming. A single exposure to a formerly abused drug.

Drug self-administration paradigm. A test of the addictive potential of drugs in which laboratory animals can inject drugs into themselves by pressing a lever.

Drug sensitization. An increase in the sensitivity to a drug effect that develops as the result of exposure to the drug.

Drug tolerance. A state of decreased sensitivity to a drug that develops as a result of exposure to the drug.

DSM-5. The fifth and current edition of the *Diagnostic and Statistical Manual of Mental Disorders;* produced by the American Psychiatric Association.

Dual-opponent color cells. Neurons that respond to the differences in the wavelengths of light stimulating adjacent areas of their receptive field.

Dual-trace theory. The theory that memories are temporarily stored in the hippocampus until they can be transferred to a more stable cortical storage system. Also known as the *standard consolidation theory.*

Duchenne smile. A genuine smile, one that includes contraction of the facial muscles called the *orbicularis oculi.*

Duodenum. The upper portion of the intestine through which most of the glucose and amino acids are absorbed into the bloodstream.

Duplexity theory. The theory that cones and rods mediate photopic and scotopic vision, respectively.

Dura mater. The tough outer meninx.

Dynamic contraction. Contraction of a muscle that causes the muscle to shorten.

Dynamic phase. The first phase of the VMH syndrome, characterized by grossly excessive eating and rapid weight gain.

Dyslexia. A reading disorder that does not result from general visual, motor, or intellectual deficits.

Efferent nerves. Nerves that carry motor signals from the central nervous system to the skeletal muscles or internal organs.

Ejaculate. To eject sperm from the penis.

Ejaculation. Ejection of sperm.

Electrocardiogram (ECG or EKG). A recording of the electrical signals associated with heartbeats.

Electroconvulsive shock (ECS). An intense, brief, diffuse, seizure-inducing current administered to the brain via large electrodes attached to the scalp.

Electroencephalogram (EEG). A measure of the gross electrical activity of the brain, commonly recorded through scalp electrodes.

Electroencephalography. A technique for recording the gross electrical activity of the brain through electrodes, which in humans are usually attached to the surface of the scalp.

Electromyogram (EMG). A record of muscle tension.

Electromyography. A procedure for measuring muscle tension.

Electron microscopy. A microscopy technique used to study the fine details of cellular structure.

Electrooculogram (EOG). A measure of eye movement.

Electrooculography. A technique for recording eye movements through electrodes placed around the eye.

Elevated plus maze. An apparatus for recording defensiveness or anxiety in rats by assessing their tendency to avoid the two open arms of a plus sign–shaped maze mounted some distance above the floor.

Elevated-plus-maze test. An animal model of anxiety; anxious rats tend to stay in the enclosed arms of the maze rather than venturing onto the open arms.

Embolism. The blockage of blood flow in a smaller blood vessel by a plug that was formed in a larger blood vessel and carried by the bloodstream to the smaller one.

Emergent stage 1 EEG. All periods of stage 1 sleep EEG except initial stage 1; each is associated with REMs.

Empathogens. Psychoactive drugs that produce feelings of empathy.

Encapsulated tumors. Tumors that grow within their own membrane.

Encéphale isolé preparation. An experimental preparation in which the brain is separated from the rest of the nervous system by a transection of the caudal brain stem.

Encephalitis. The inflammation associated with brain infection.

Endocannabinoids. A class of unconventional neurotransmitters that are chemically similar to the active components of marijuana.

Endocrine glands. Ductless glands that release chemicals called hormones directly into the circulatory system.

Endogenous. Naturally occurring in the body (e.g., endogenous opioids).

Endogenous depression. Depression that occurs with no apparent cause.

Endorphins. A class of endogenous opioids.

Engram. A change in the brain that stores a memory.

Engram cells. Neurons that maintain an engram.

Enhancers. Stretches of DNA that control the rate of expression of target genes.

Enkephalins. The first class of endogenous opioids to be discovered.

Enriched environments. Laboratory environments designed to promote cognitive and physical activity by providing opportunities for a greater variety of sensory and motor experiences than available in conventional laboratory environments; commonly used to study the effects of experience on development in rats and mice.

Entorhinal cortex. An area of the medial temporal cortex that is a major source of neural signals to the hippocampus.

Enzymatic degradation. The breakdown of chemicals by enzymes—one of the two mechanisms for deactivating released neurotransmitters.

Enzymes. Proteins that stimulate or inhibit biochemical reactions without being affected by them.

Epidemiology. The study of the factors that influence the distribution of a disease in the general population.

Epigenetics. The study of all mechanisms of inheritance other than the genetic code and its expression.

Epigenetic. Not of the genes; refers to nongenetic means by which traits are passed from parents to offspring.

Epilepsy. A neurological disorder characterized by spontaneously recurring seizures.

Epileptic auras. Psychological changes that precede the onset of a seizure.

Epileptogenesis. Development of epilepsy.

Epinephrine. One of the three catecholamine neurotransmitters.

Episodic memories. Explicit memories for the particular events and experiences of one's life.

Estradiol. The most common estrogen.

Estrogens. The class of steroid hormones that are released in large amounts by the ovaries; an example is estradiol.

Estrous cycle. The cycle of sexual receptivity displayed by many female mammals.

Estrus. The portion of the estrous cycle characterized by proceptivity, sexual receptivity, and fertility (*estrus* is a noun and *estrous* an adjective).

Ethological research. The study of animal behavior in its natural environment.

Ethology. The study of the behavior of animals in their natural environments.

Event-related potentials (ERPs). The EEG waves that regularly accompany certain psychological events.

Evolutionary perspective. The approach that focuses on the environmental pressures that likely led to the evolution of the characteristics (e.g., of brain and behavior) of current species.

Evolve. To undergo gradual orderly change.

Exaptation. A characteristic that evolved because it performed one function but was later co-opted to perform another.

Excitatory postsynaptic potentials (EPSPs). Graded postsynaptic depolarizations, which increase the likelihood that an action potential will be generated.

Executive function. A collection of cognitive abilities (e.g., innovative thinking, lateral thinking, and insightful thinking) that appear to depend on the prefrontal cortex.

Exocrine glands. Glands that release chemicals into ducts that carry them to targets, mostly on the surface of the body.

Exocytosis. The process of releasing a neurotransmitter.

Explicit memories. Conscious memories.

Expressive. Pertaining to the generation of language; that is, pertaining to writing or talking.

Extensors. Muscles that act to straighten or extend a joint.

Exteroceptive stimuli. Stimuli that arise from outside the body.

Facial feedback hypothesis. The hypothesis that our facial expressions can influence the emotions we experience.

Far-field potentials. EEG signals recorded in attenuated form at the scalp because they originate far away—for example, in the brain stem.

Fasciculation. The tendency of developing axons to grow along the paths established by preceding axons.

Fasting phase. The metabolic phase that begins when energy from the preceding meal is no longer sufficient to meet the immediate needs of the body and during which energy is extracted from fat and glycogen stores.

Fear. The emotional reaction that is normally elicited by the presence or expectation of threatening stimuli.

Fear conditioning. Establishing fear of a previously neutral conditional stimulus by pairing it with an aversive unconditional stimulus.

Feminizes. Enhances or produces female characteristics.

Fetal alcohol syndrome (FAS). A syndrome produced by prenatal exposure to alcohol and characterized by brain damage, intellectual disability, poor coordination, poor muscle tone, low birth weight, retarded growth, and/or physical deformity.

Fissures. The large furrows in a convoluted cortex.

Fitness. According to Darwin, the ability of an organism to survive and contribute its genes to the next generation.

Fixational eye movements. Involuntary movements of the eyes (tremor, drifts, and saccades) that occur when a person tries to fix their gaze on (i.e., stare at) a point.

Flavor. The combined impression of taste and smell.

Flexors. Muscles that act to bend or flex a joint.

Fluorodeoxyglucose (FDG). A molecule that is similar to glucose, and is thus rapidly taken up by active cells. However, unlike glucose, fluorodeoxyglucose cannot be metabolized; it therefore accumulates in active cells until it is gradually broken down. A radioactive isotope of this molecule is commonly used in positron emission tomography (PET).

Fluoxetine. The first selective serotonin reuptake inhibitor (SSRI) to be developed. It was initially marketed under the tradename *Prozac*.

Focal seizure. A seizure that does not involve the entire brain.

Follicle-stimulating hormone (FSH). The gonadotropic hormone that stimulates development of ovarian follicles.

Fornix. The major tract of the limbic system; it connects the hippocampus with the septum and mammillary bodies.

Fourier analysis. A mathematical procedure for breaking down a complex wave form into component sine waves of various frequencies.

Fovea. The central indentation of the retina, which is specialized for high-acuity vision.

Fraternal birth order effect. The finding that the probability of a male being attracted to other males increases as a function of the number of older brothers he has.

Free fatty acids. The main source of the body's energy during the fasting phase; released from adipose tissue in response to high levels of glucagon.

Free nerve endings. Neuron endings that lack specialized structures on them and that detect cutaneous pain and changes in temperature.

Free-running period. The duration of one cycle of a free-running rhythm.

Free-running rhythms. Circadian rhythms that do not depend on environmental cues to keep them on a regular schedule.

Frontal eye field. A small area of prefrontal cortex that controls eye movements.

Frontal lobe. The most anterior of the four cerebral lobes.

Frontal operculum. The area of prefrontal cortex that in the left hemisphere is the location of Broca's area.

Frontal sections. Any slices of brain tissue cut in a plane that is parallel to the face; also termed *coronal sections*.

Functional MRI (fMRI). A magnetic resonance imaging technique for inferring brain activity by measuring increased oxygen flow into particular areas.

Functional segregation. Organization into different areas, each of which performs a different function; for example, in sensory systems, different areas of secondary and association cortex analyze different aspects of the same sensory stimulus.

Functional tolerance. Drug tolerance that results from changes that reduce the reactivity of the sites of action to the drug.

Fusiform face area. An area of human cortex, located at the boundary between the occipital and temporal lobes, that is selectively activated by human faces.

G proteins. Proteins that are located inside neurons (and some other cells) and are attached to metabotropic receptors in the cell membrane.

Gametes. Egg cells and sperm cells.

Gamma-aminobutyric acid (GABA). The amino acid neurotransmitter that is synthesized from glutamate; the most prevalent inhibitory neurotransmitter in the mammalian CNS.

Ganglia. Clusters of neuronal cell bodies in the peripheral nervous system (singular *ganglion*).

Gap junctions. Narrow spaces between adjacent neurons that are bridged by fine tubular channels containing cytoplasm, through which electrical signals and small molecules can pass readily.

Gastric bypass. A surgical procedure for treating obesity in which the intestine is cut and connected to the upper portion of the stomach, which is isolated from the rest of the stomach by a row of staples.

Gastric ulcers. Painful lesions to the lining of the stomach or duodenum.

Gay. Sexually attracted to members of the same sex.

Gender identity. The gender that a person most identifies with: female, male, some combination of male and female, neither female or male, or some other gender category.

Gene. A unit of inheritance; for example, the section of a chromosome that controls the synthesis of one protein.

Gene expression. The production of the protein specified by a particular gene.

Gene knockout techniques. Procedures for creating organisms that lack a particular gene.

Gene replacement techniques. Procedures for creating organisms in which a particular gene has been replaced with another.

General paresis. The mental illness and dementia resulting from a syphilitic infection.

Generalizability. The degree to which the results of a study can be applied to other individuals or situations.

Generalized anxiety disorder. An anxiety disorder characterized by stress responses and extreme feelings of anxiety and worry about a large number of different activities or events.

Generalized seizures. Seizures that involve the entire brain.

Genetic recombination. The meiotic process by which pairs of chromosomes cross over one another at random points, break apart, and exchange genes.

Genitals. The external reproductive organs.

Genotype. The traits that an organism can pass on to its offspring through its genetic material.

Glial cells. Several classes of nonneural cells of the nervous system.

Glia-mediated migration. One of two major modes of neural migration during development, by which immature neurons move away from the central canal along radial glial cells.

Gliomas. Brain tumors that develop from glial cells.

Global amnesia. Amnesia for information presented in all sensory modalities.

Global aphasia. Severe disruption of all language-related abilities.

Global cerebral ischemia. An interruption of blood supply to the entire brain.

Globus pallidus. A structure of the basal ganglia that is located between the putamen and thalamus.

Glucagon. A pancreatic hormone that promotes the release of free fatty acids from adipose tissue, their conversion to ketones, and the use of both as sources of energy.

Glucocorticoids. Steroid hormones that are released from the adrenal cortex in response to stressors.

Gluconeogenesis. The process by which protein is converted to glucose.

Glucose. A simple sugar that is the breakdown product of complex carbohydrates; it is the body's primary, directly utilizable source of energy.

Glucostatic theory. The theory that eating is controlled by deviations from a hypothetical blood glucose set point.

Glutamate. The most prevalent excitatory neurotransmitter in the CNS.

Glycine. An amino acid neurotransmitter.

Golgi complex. Structures in the cell bodies and terminal buttons of neurons that package neurotransmitters and other molecules in vesicles.

Golgi stain. A neural stain that completely darkens a few of the neurons in each slice of tissue, thereby revealing their silhouettes.

Golgi tendon organs. Receptors that are embedded in tendons and are sensitive to the amount of tension in the skeletal muscles to which their tendons are attached.

Gonadectomy. The surgical removal of the gonads (testes or ovaries); castration.

Gonadotropin. The pituitary tropic hormone that stimulates the release of hormones from the gonads.

Gonadotropin-releasing hormone. The hypothalamic releasing hormone that controls the release of the two gonadotropic hormones from the anterior pituitary.

Gonads. The testes and the ovaries.

Graded responses. Responses whose magnitude is proportional to the magnitude of the stimuli that elicit them.

Grammatical analysis. Analysis of the structure of language.

Gray matter. Portions of the nervous system that are gray because they are composed largely of cell bodies and unmyelinated interneurons.

Green fluorescent protein (GFP). A protein that is found in certain species of jellyfish and that fluoresces when exposed to blue light.

Grid cells. Entorhinal neurons that each have an extensive array of evenly spaced place fields, producing a pattern reminiscent of graph paper.

Growth cone. Amoebalike structure at the tip of each growing axon or dendrite that guides growth to the appropriate target.

Growth hormone. The anterior pituitary hormone that acts directly on bone and muscle tissue to produce the pubertal growth spurt.

Guilty-knowledge technique. A lie-detection method in which the polygrapher records autonomic nervous system responses to a list of control and crime-related information known only to the guilty person and the examiner; also known as the concealed information test.

Gut microbiome. The bacteria and other organisms that live inside our gastrointestinal tract.

Gyri. The cortical ridges that are located between fissures or sulci.

Hair cells. The receptors of the auditory system.

Haloperidol. A butyrophenone used as an antipsychotic drug.

Harrison Narcotics Act. The act passed in 1914 that made it illegal to sell or use opium, morphine, or cocaine in the United States.

Hashish. Dark corklike material extracted from the resin on the leaves and flowers of *Cannabis*.

Hedonic value. The amount of pleasure that is actually experienced as the result of some action.

Helping-hand phenomenon. The redirection of one hand of a split-brain patient by the other hand.

Hematoma. A localized collection of clotted blood in an organ or tissue; a bruise.

Hemianopsic. Having a scotoma that covers half of the visual field.

Hemispherectomy. The removal of one cerebral hemisphere.

Heritability estimate. A numerical estimate of the proportion of variability that occurred in a particular trait in a particular study and that resulted from the genetic variation among the subjects in that study.

Heroin. A semisynthetic opioid.

Heschl's gyrus. The temporal lobe gyrus that is the location of primary auditory cortex.

Heterosexual. Sexually attracted to members of the other sex.

Heterozygous. Possessing two different genes for a particular trait.

Hierarchical organization. Organization into a series of levels that can be ranked with respect to one another; for example, in sensory systems, primary cortex, secondary cortex, and association cortex perform progressively more detailed analyses.

Hippocampus. A structure of the medial temporal lobes that plays a role in various forms of memory.

Histone. A protein around which DNA is coiled.

Histone remodeling. An epigenetic mechanism wherein histones change their shape and in so doing influence the shape of the adjacent DNA. This can either increase or decrease gene expression.

Homeostasis. A stable internal environment.

Hominini. The tribe of primates that includes at least six genera: *Australopithecus, Paranthropus, Sahelanthropus, Orrorin, Pan,* and *Homo.*

Homologous. Having a similar structure because of a common evolutionary origin (e.g., a human's arm and a bird's wing are homologous).

Homozygous. Possessing two identical genes for a particular trait.

Horizontal cells. Retinal neurons whose specialized function is lateral communication.

Horizontal sections. Any slices of brain tissue cut in a plane that are parallel to the top of the brain.

Hormones. Chemicals released by the endocrine system directly into the circulatory system.

Human Genome Project. The international research effort to construct a detailed map of the human chromosomes.

Human proteome. A map of the entire set of proteins encoded for by human genes.

Huntingtin. Dominant gene that is mutated in cases of Huntington's disease.

Huntingtin protein. Protein whose synthesis is controlled by the huntingtin gene and is thus abnormal in individuals with Huntington's disease.

Huntington's disease. A progressive terminal disorder of motor and intellectual function that is produced in adulthood by a dominant gene.

Hyperphagia. Excessive eating.

Hyperpolarize. To increase the resting membrane potential.

Hypersomnia. Disorders characterized by excessive sleep or sleepiness.

Hypertension. Chronically high blood pressure.

Hypnagogic hallucinations. Dreamlike experiences that occur during wakefulness.

Hypnotic drugs. Sleep-promoting drugs.

Hypomania. A state that is characterized by a reduced need for sleep, high energy, and positive affect. During periods of hypomania, people are talkative, energetic, impulsive, positive, and very confident.

Hypothalamic peptides. One of the five classes of neuropeptide transmitters; it consists of those first identified as hormones released by the hypothalamus.

Hypothalamopituitary portal system. The vascular network that carries hormones from the hypothalamus to the anterior pituitary.

Hypothalamus. The diencephalic structure that sits just below the anterior portion of the thalamus.

Hypoxia. Shortage of oxygen supply to tissue—for example, to the brain.

Iatrogenic. Physician-created.

Imidazopyridines. A class of $GABA_A$ agonists that were marketed for the treatment of insomnia.

Imipramine. The first tricyclic antidepressant drug.

Immune system. The system that protects the body against infectious microorganisms.

Immunization. The process of creating immunity through vaccination.

Immunocytochemistry. A procedure for locating particular proteins in the brain by labeling their antibodies with a dye or radioactive element and then exposing slices of brain tissue to the labeled antibodies.

Implicit memories. Memories that are expressed by improved performance without conscious recall or recognition.

Impotent. Unable to achieve a penile erection.

In situ hybridization. A technique for locating particular proteins in the brain; molecules that bind to the mRNA that directs the synthesis of the target protein are synthesized and labeled, and brain slices are exposed to them.

Incentive-sensitization theory. Theory that addictions develop when drug use sensitizes the neural circuits mediating wanting of the drug—not necessarily liking of the drug.

Incomplete-pictures test. A test of memory measuring the improved ability to identify fragmented figures that have been previously observed.

Incubation of drug craving. The time-dependent increase in cue-induced drug craving and relapse.

Independent variable. The difference between experimental conditions that is arranged by the experimenter.

Indolamines. The class of monoamine neurotransmitters that are synthesized from tryptophan; serotonin is the only member of this class found in the mammalian nervous system.

Infantile amnesia. The normal inability to recall events from early childhood.

Inferior. Toward the bottom of the primate head or brain.

Inferior colliculi. The structures of the tectum that receive auditory input from the superior olives.

Inferotemporal cortex. The cortex of the inferior temporal lobe, in which is located an area of secondary visual cortex.

Infiltrating tumors. Tumors that grow diffusely through surrounding tissue.

Inhibitory postsynaptic potentials (IPSPs). Graded postsynaptic hyperpolarizations, which decrease the likelihood that an action potential will be generated.

Initial stage 1 EEG. The period of the stage 1 EEG that occurs at the onset of sleep; it is not associated with REMs.

Innate immune system. The first component of the immune system to react. It reacts quickly and generally near points of entry of pathogens.

Insomnia. Sleeplessness.

Instinctive behaviors. Behaviors that occur in all like members of a species, even when there seems to have been no opportunity for them to have been learned.

Instructive experiences. Particular experiences that contribute to the information in genetic programs and influence the course of development.

Insulin. A pancreatic hormone that facilitates the entry of glucose into cells and the conversion of bloodborne fuels to forms that can be stored.

Integration. Adding or combining a number of individual signals into one overall signal.

Internal desynchronization. The cycling on different schedules of the free-running circadian rhythms of two or more different processes.

Interneurons. Neurons with short axons or no axons at all, whose function is to integrate neural activity within a single brain structure.

Interoceptive stimuli. Stimuli that arise from inside the body.

Interpreter. A hypothetical mechanism that is assumed to reside in the left hemisphere and that continuously assesses patterns of events and tries to make sense of them.

Intersexed person. A term used to refer to a person who is born with sexual anatomy that does not clearly fit into typical definitions of male and female sexual anatomy.

Intracranial self-stimulation (ICSS). The repeated performance of a response that delivers electrical stimulation to certain sites in the animal's brain.

Intrafusal motor neuron. A motor neuron that innervates an intrafusal muscle.

Intrafusal muscle. A threadlike muscle that adjusts the tension on a muscle spindle.

Intromission. Insertion of the penis into the vagina.

Ion channels. Pores in neural membranes through which specific ions pass.

Ionotropic receptors. Receptors that are associated with ligand-activated ion channels.

Ions. Positively or negatively charged particles.

Iproniazid. The first antidepressant drug; a monoamine oxidase inhibitor.

Ipsilateral. On the same side of the body.

Isometric contraction. Contraction of a muscle that increases the force of its pull but does not shorten the muscle.

James-Lange theory. The theory that emotion-inducing sensory stimuli are received and interpreted by the cortex, which triggers changes in the visceral organs via the autonomic nervous system and in the skeletal muscles via the somatic nervous system. Then, the autonomic and somatic responses trigger the experience of emotion in the brain.

Jennifer Aniston neurons. Neurons, such as those found in the medial temporal lobe, that respond to ideas or concepts rather than to particulars. Also known as concept cells.

Jet lag. The adverse effects on body function of the acceleration of zeitgebers during eastbound flights or their deceleration during westbound flights.

Ketamine. A drug that is a type of dissociative hallucinogen.

Ketones. Breakdown products of free fatty acids that are used by muscles as a source of energy during the fasting phase.

Kindling phenomenon. The progressive development and intensification of convulsions elicited by a series of periodic low-intensity brain stimulations—most commonly by daily electrical stimulations to the amygdala.

Kluver-Bucy syndrome. The syndrome of behavioral changes (e.g., lack of fear and hypersexuality) that is induced in primates by bilateral damage to the anterior temporal lobes.

Korsakoff's syndrome. A neuropsychological disorder that is common in alcoholics and whose primary symptoms include memory loss, sensory and motor dysfunction, and, in its advanced stages, severe dementia.

L-Dopa. The chemical precursor of dopamine, which is used in the treatment of Parkinson's disease.

Lateral. Away from the midline of the body of a vertebrate, toward the body's lateral surfaces.

Lateral fissure. The large fissure that separates the temporal lobe from the frontal lobe.

Lateral geniculate nuclei. The six-layered thalamic structures that receive input from the retinas and transmit their output to the primary visual cortex.

Lateral hypothalamus (LH). The area of the hypothalamus once thought to be the feeding center.

Lateral inhibition. Inhibition of adjacent neurons or receptors in a topographic array.

Lateral nucleus of the amygdala. The nucleus of the amygdala that plays the major role in the acquisition, storage, and expression of conditioned fear.

Lateralization of function. The unequal representation of various psychological functions in the two hemispheres of the brain.

Leaky-barrel model. An analogy for the settling-point model of body-fat regulation.

Learning. The brain's ability to change in response to experience.

Leptin. A protein normally synthesized in fat cells; it is thought to act as a negative feedback signal normally released by fat stores to decrease appetite and increase fat metabolism.

Leucotome. A surgical device used in psychosurgery to cut out a core of brain tissue.

Leukocytes. White blood cells.

Lewy bodies. Clumps of proteins that can be found in the surviving dopaminergic neurons of the substantia nigra of Parkinson's patients.

Lexical procedure. A procedure for reading aloud that is based on specific stored information acquired about written words.

Ligand. A molecule that binds to another molecule; neurotransmitters are ligands of their receptors.

Limbic system. A collection of interconnected nuclei and tracts that ring the thalamus.

Lipids. Fats.

Lipogenesis. The production of body fat.

Lipolysis. The breakdown of body fat.

Lipostatic theory. The theory that eating is controlled by deviations from a hypothetical body-fat set point.

Lithium. A metallic ion that is a mood stabilizer; used in the treatment of bipolar disorders.

Lobectomy. An operation in which a lobe, or a major part of one, is removed from the brain.

Lobotomy. An operation in which a lobe, or a major part of one, is separated from the rest of the brain by a large cut but is not removed.

Longitudinal fissure. The large fissure that separates the two cerebral hemispheres.

Long-term depression (LTD). A long-lasting decrease in synaptic efficacy (the flip side of LTP) that occurs in response to prolonged low-frequency stimulation of presynaptic neurons.

Long-term memory. Memory for experiences that endures after the experiences are no longer the focus of attention.

Long-term potentiation (LTP). The enduring facilitation of synaptic transmission that occurs following activation of synapses by high-intensity, high-frequency stimulation of presynaptic neurons.

Lordosis.   The arched-back, rump-up, tail-to-the-side posture of female rodent sexual receptivity.

Lordosis quotient.   The proportion of mounts that elicit lordosis.

Luteinizing hormone (LH).   The gonadotropic hormone that causes the developing ovum to be released from its follicle.

Lymphocytes.   Specialized leukocytes that are produced in bone marrow and the thymus gland and play important roles in the body's immune reactions.

Magnetic resonance imaging (MRI).   A structural brain imaging procedure in which high-resolution images are constructed from the measurement of waves that hydrogen atoms emit when they are activated by radio-frequency waves in a magnetic field.

Magnetoencephalography (MEG).   A technique for measuring changes in magnetic fields on the surface of the scalp that are produced by changes in underlying patterns of neural activity.

Magnocellular layers.   The layers of the lateral geniculate nuclei that are composed of neurons with large cell bodies; the bottom two layers (also called *M layers*).

Malignant tumors.   Tumors that are difficult to remove or destroy, and continue to grow after attempts to remove or destroy them.

Mammals.   A class of animals whose young are fed from mammary glands.

Mammillary bodies.   The pair of spherical nuclei that are located on the inferior surface of the hypothalamus.

Mania.   A state that has the same features as hypomania but taken to an extreme; it also has additional symptoms, such as delusions of grandeur, overconfidence, and distractibility. Mania usually involves psychosis.

MAO inhibitors.   Antidepressant drugs that increase the level of monoamine neurotransmitters by inhibiting the action of the enzyme monoamine oxidase.

Masculinizes.   Enhances or produces male characteristics.

Massa intermedia.   The neural structure located in the third ventricle that connects the two lobes of the thalamus.

Maternal immune hypothesis.   The hypothesis that mothers become progressively more immune to some masculinizing hormone in their male fetuses; proposed to explain the fraternal birth order effect.

Mean difference image.   In the context of functional neuroimaging, the average of the difference images (obtained via paired-image subtraction) obtained from multiple participants.

Medial.   Toward the midline of the body.

Medial diencephalic amnesia.   Amnesia that is associated with damage to the medial diencephalon (e.g., Korsakoff's amnesia).

Medial dorsal nuclei.   The thalamic relay nuclei of the olfactory system.

Medial geniculate nuclei.   The auditory thalamic nuclei that receive input from the inferior colliculi and project to primary auditory cortex.

Medial lemniscus.   The somatosensory pathway between the dorsal column nuclei and the ventral posterior nucleus of the thalamus.

Medial preoptic area.   The area of the hypothalamus that includes the sexually dimorphic nuclei and that plays a key role in the control of male sexual behavior.

Medial temporal cortex.   Cortex in the medial temporal lobe that lies adjacent to the hippocampus and amygdala.

Medial temporal lobe amnesia.   Amnesia associated with bilateral damage to the medial temporal lobes; its major features are antero-grade and retrograde amnesia for explicit memories, with preserved intellectual functioning.

Mediodorsal nuclei.   A pair of thalamic nuclei, damage to which is thought to be responsible for many of the memory deficits associated with Korsakoff's syndrome.

Meiosis.   The process of cell division that produces cells (e.g., egg cells and sperm cells) with half the chromosomes of the parent cell.

Melanocortin system.   Neurons in the arcuate nucleus that release melanocortins.

Melanocortins.   A class of peptides that includes the gut satiety peptide α-melanocyte-stimulating hormone.

Melanopsin.   Photopigment found in certain retinal ganglion cells that responds to changes in background illumination and plays a role in the entrainment of circadian rhythms.

Melatonin.   A hormone that is synthesized from serotonin in the pineal gland, and is both a soporific and a chronobiotic.

Membrane potential.   The difference in electrical charge between the inside and the outside of a cell.

Memory.   The brain's ability to store and access the learned effects of experiences.

Memory consolidation.   The transfer of short-term memories to long-term storage.

Meninges.   The three protective membranes that cover the brain and spinal cord (singular *meninx*).

Meningiomas.   Tumors that grow between the meninges.

Meningitis.   Inflammation of the meninges, usually caused by bacterial infection.

Menstrual cycle.   The hormone-regulated cycle in females of follicle growth, egg release, buildup of the uterus lining, and menstruation.

Mesencephalon.   One of the five major divisions of the brain; it is composed of the tectum and tegmentum.

Mesocorticolimbic pathway.   The component of the mesotelencephalic dopamine system that has cell bodies in the ventral tegmental area that project to various cortical and limbic sites.

Mesoderm layer.   The middle of the three cell layers in the developing embryo.

Mesotelencephalic dopamine system.   The ascending projections of dopamine-releasing neurons from the substantia nigra and ventral tegmental area of the mesencephalon into various regions of the telencephalon.

Messenger RNA.   A strand of RNA that is transcribed from DNA and then moves out of the cell nucleus where it is translated into a protein.

Metabolic tolerance.   Tolerance that results from a reduction in the amount of a drug getting to its sites of action.

Metabotropic receptors.   Receptors that are associated with signal proteins and G proteins.

Metaplasticity.   The modulation of long term potentiation (LTP) and/or long-term depression (LTD) induction by prior synaptic activity.

Metastatic tumors.   Tumors that originate in one organ and spread to another.

Metencephalon.   One of the five major divisions of the brain; it includes the pons and cerebellum.

Microbleeds.   Small dot-like lesions found in the brains of some Alzheimer's patients that appear to be the result of microhemorrhages.

Microelectrodes.   Extremely fine recording electrodes, which are used for intracellular recording.

Microglia.   Glial cells that respond to injury or disease by engulfing cellular debris and triggering inflammatory responses.

Microsleeps.   Brief periods of sleep that occur in sleep-deprived subjects while they remain sitting or standing.

Migration.   The movement of cells from their site of creation in the ventricular zone of the neural tube to their appropriate target location.

Minor hemisphere. A term used in the past to refer to the right hemisphere, based on the incorrect assumption that the left hemisphere is dominant.

Mirror neurons. Neurons that fire when an individual performs a particular goal-directed hand movement or when they observe the same goal-directed movement performed by another.

Mirror-like system. Areas of the cortex that are active both when a person performs a particular response and when the person perceives somebody else performing the same response.

Miscellaneous peptides. One of the five categories of neuropeptide transmitters; it include those neuropeptide transmitters that don't fit into one of the other four categories.

Mitosis. The process of cell division that produces cells with the same number of chromosomes as the parent cell.

Mixed state. A state that can occur in bipolar disorder type I, where the patient simultaneously displays symptoms of both depression and mania.

Monoamine neurotransmitters. Small-molecule neurotransmitters that are synthesized from monoamines and comprise two classes: catecholamines and indolamines.

Monocular. Involving only one eye.

Monogamy. A pattern of mate bonding in which one male and one female form an enduring bond.

Monophasic sleep cycles. Sleep cycles that regularly involve only one period of sleep per day, typically at night.

Monozygotic twins. Twins that develop from the same zygote and are thus genetically identical.

Mood stabilizers. Drugs that effectively treat depression or mania without increasing the risk of mania or depression, respectively.

Morgan's Canon. The rule that the simplest possible interpretation for a behavioral observation should be given precedence.

Morphine. The major psychoactive ingredient in opium.

Morris water maze. A pool of milky water that has a goal platform invisible just beneath its surface and is used to study the ability of rats to learn spatial locations.

Morris water maze test. A widely used test of spatial memory in which rats must learn to swim directly to a platform hidden just beneath the surface of a circular pool of murky water.

Motor end-plate. The receptive area on a muscle fiber at a neuromuscular junction.

Motor equivalence. The ability of the sensorimotor system to carry out the same basic movement in different ways that involve different muscles.

Motor homunculus. The somatotopic map of the human primary motor cortex.

Motor pool. All of the motor neurons that innervate the fibers of a given muscle.

Motor theory of speech perception. The theory that the perception of speech involves activation of the same areas of the brain that are involved in the production of speech.

Motor units. A single motor neuron and all of the skeletal muscle fibers that are innervated by it.

MPTP. A neurotoxin that produces a disorder in primates that is similar to Parkinson's disease.

MT area. An area of cortex, located near the junction of the temporal, parietal, and occipital lobes, whose function appears to be the perception of motion.

Müllerian-inhibiting substance. The testicular hormone that causes the precursor of the female reproductive ducts (the Müllerian system) to degenerate and the testes to descend.

Müllerian system. The embryonic precursor of the female reproductive ducts.

Multiple sclerosis (MS). A progressive disease that attacks the myelin of axons in the CNS.

Multipolar neuron. A neuron with more than two processes extending from its cell body.

Multipotent. Capable of developing into different cells of only one class of cells (e.g., different kinds of blood cells).

Mumby box. An apparatus that is used in the rat version of the delayed nonmatching-to-sample test.

Muscle spindles. Receptors that are embedded in skeletal muscle tissue and are sensitive to changes in muscle length.

Mutations. Accidental alterations in individual genes.

Myelencephalon. The most posterior of the five major divisions of the brain; the medulla.

Myelin. A fatty insulating substance.

Myelin sheaths. Coverings on the axons of some neurons that are rich in myelin and increase the speed and efficiency of axonal conduction.

Narcolepsy. A disorder of hypersomnia that is characterized by repeated, brief daytime sleep attacks and cataplexy.

Narcotic. A legal term generally used to refer to opioids.

Nasal hemiretina. The half of each retina next to the nose.

Natural selection. The idea that those heritable traits that are associated with high rates of survival and reproduction are the most likely to be passed on to future generations.

Nature–nurture issue. The debate about the relative contributions of nature (genes) and nurture (experience) to the behavioral capacities of individuals.

NEAT. Nonexercise activity thermogenesis, which is generated by activities such as fidgeting and the maintenance of posture and muscle tone.

Necrosis. Passive cell death.

Negative feedback systems. Systems in which feedback from changes in one direction elicit compensatory effects in the opposite direction.

Negative symptoms. Symptoms of schizophrenia that seem to represent a reduction or loss of typical function.

Neocortex. Six-layered cerebral cortex of relatively recent evolution; it constitutes 90 percent of human cerebral cortex.

Neoplasm. Tumor; literally, "new growth."

Nerve growth factor (NGF). The first neurotrophin to be discovered.

Nerves. Bundles of axons in the peripheral nervous system.

Neural crest. A structure situated just dorsal to the neural tube. It is formed from cells that break off from the neural tube as it is being formed.

Neural plate. A small patch of ectodermal tissue on the dorsal surface of the vertebrate embryo, from which the neural groove, the neural tube, and, ultimately, the mature nervous system develop.

Neural proliferation. The rapid increase in the number of neurons that follows the formation of the neural tube.

Neural regeneration. The regrowth of damaged neurons.

Neural tube. The tube that is formed in the vertebrate embryo when the edges of the neural groove fuse and that develops into the central nervous system.

Neuroanatomy. The study of the structure of the nervous system.

Neurochemistry. The study of the chemical bases of neural activity.

Neuroendocrinology. The study of the interactions between the nervous system and the endocrine system.

Neurogenesis. The growth of new neurons.

Neuromuscular junctions. The synapses of a motor neuron on a muscle.

Neurons. Cells of the nervous system that are specialized for the reception, conduction, and transmission of electrochemical signals.

Neuropathic pain. Severe chronic pain in the absence of a recognizable pain stimulus.

Neuropathology. The study of nervous system disorders.

Neuropeptide. Short amino acid chains.

Neuropeptide transmitters. Peptides that function as neurotransmitters, of which about 100 have been identified; also called *neuropeptides*.

Neuropeptide Y. A gut hunger peptide.

Neuropharmacology. The study of the effects of drugs on neural activity.

Neurophysiology. The study of the functions and activities of the nervous system.

Neuropsychology. The division of biopsychology that studies the psychological effects of brain damage in human patients.

Neuroscience. The scientific study of the nervous system.

Neurotoxins. Neural poisons.

Neurotrophins. Chemicals that are supplied to developing neurons by their targets and that promote their survival.

Nicotine. The major psychoactive ingredient of tobacco.

Nigrostriatal pathway. The pathway along which axons from neurons in the substantia nigra project to the striatum.

Nissl stain. A neural stain that has an affinity for structures in neuron cell bodies.

Nitric oxide. A soluble-gas neurotransmitter.

NMDA (N-methyl-d-aspartate) receptors. Glutamate receptors that play key roles in the development of stroke-induced brain damage and long-term potentiation at glutaminergic synapses.

Nodes of Ranvier. The gaps between adjacent myelin sheaths on an axon.

Nondirected synapses. Synapses at which the site of neurotransmitter release and the site of neurotransmitter reception are not close together.

Nootropics (smart drugs). Drugs that purportedly improve memory.

Norepinephrine. One of the three catecholamine neurotransmitters.

Nuclei. The DNA-containing structures of cells; also, clusters of neuronal cell bodies in the central nervous system (singular *nucleus*).

Nucleotide bases. A class of chemical substances that includes adenine, thymine, guanine, and cytosine—constituents of DNA.

Nucleus accumbens. Nucleus of the ventral striatum and a major terminal of the mesocorticolimbic dopamine pathway.

Nucleus magnocellularis. The nucleus of the caudal reticular formation that promotes relaxation of the core muscles during REM sleep and during attacks of cataplexy.

Nutritive density. Calories per unit volume of a food.

Ob/ob mice. Mice that are homozygous for the mutant ob gene; their body fat produces no leptin, and they become very obese.

Occipital lobe. The most posterior of the four cerebral lobes; its function is primarily visual.

Off-center cells. Visual neurons that respond to lights shone in the center of their receptive fields with "off" firing and to lights shone in the periphery of their receptive fields with "on" firing.

Olfactory bulbs. Their output goes primarily to the amygdala and piriform cortex.

Olfactory glomeruli. Discrete clusters of neurons that lie near the surface of the olfactory bulbs.

Olfactory mucosa. The mucous membrane that lines the upper nasal passages and contains the olfactory receptor cells.

Oligodendrocytes. Glial cells that myelinate axons of the central nervous system; also known as *oligodendroglia*.

Oligodendroglia. Glial cells that myelinate CNS axons; also known as *oligodendrocytes*.

On-center cells. Visual neurons that respond to lights shone in the center of their receptive fields with "on" firing and to lights shone in the periphery of their receptive fields with "off" firing.

Ontogeny. The development of individuals over their life span.

Open-field test. In this test an animal is placed in a large, barren chamber and it's activity is recorded.

Operant conditioning paradigm. A paradigm in which the rate of a particular voluntary response is increased by reinforcement or decreased by punishment.

Opioids. Morphine, codeine, heroin, and other chemicals with similar structures or effects.

Opioid peptides. One of the five classes of neuropeptide transmitters; it consists of those with a structure similar to the active ingredients of opium.

Opium. The sap that exudes from the seed pods of the opium poppy.

Opponent-process theory. The theory that a visual receptor or a neuron signals one color when it responds in one way (e.g., by increasing its firing rate) and signals the complementary color when it responds in the opposite way (e.g., by decreasing its firing rate).

Opsins. Light-sensitive ion channels that are found in the cell membranes of certain bacteria and algae. When opsins are illuminated with light, they open and allow ions to enter the cell.

Optic chiasm. The X-shaped structure on the inferior surface of the diencephalon; the point where the optic nerves decussate.

Optic tectum. The main destination of retinal ganglion cells in non-mammalian vertebrates.

Optogenetics. A method that uses genetic engineering techniques to insert the opsin gene, or variants of the opsin gene, into particular types of neurons. By inserting an opsin gene into a particular type of neuron, a researcher can use light to hyperpolarize or depolarize those neurons.

Orbitofrontal cortex. The cortex of the inferior frontal lobes, adjacent to the orbits, which receives olfactory input from the thalamus.

Orchidectomy. The removal of the testes.

Orexin. A neuropeptide that has been implicated in narcolepsy; sometimes called hypocretin.

Organ of Corti. The auditory receptor organ, comprising the basilar membrane, the hair cells, and the tectorial membrane.

Orphan drugs. Drugs for which the market is too small for the necessary developmental research to be profitable.

Orthodromic conduction. Axonal conduction in the normal direction—from the cell body toward the terminal buttons.

Ossicles. The three small bones of the middle ear: the malleus, the incus, and the stapes.

Oval window. The membrane that transfers vibrations from the ossicles to the fluid of the cochlea.

Ovariectomy. The removal of the ovaries.

Ovaries. The female gonads.

Oxytocin. One of the two major peptide hormones of the posterior pituitary, which in females stimulates contractions of the uterus during labor and the ejection of milk during suckling.

Pacinian corpuscles. The largest and most deeply positioned cutaneous receptors, which are sensitive to sudden displacements of the skin.

Paired-image subtraction technique. The use of PET or fMRI to locate constituent cognitive processes in the brain by producing an image of the difference in brain activity associated with two cognitive tasks that differ in terms of a single constituent cognitive process.

Panic attacks. Rapid-onset attacks of extreme fear and severe symptoms of stress (e.g., choking, heart palpitations, shortness of breath).

Panic disorder. An anxiety disorder characterized by recurrent rapid-onset attacks of extreme fear and severe symptoms of stress (choking, heart palpitations, and shortness of breath).

Parallel processing. The simultaneous analysis of a signal in different ways by the multiple parallel pathways of a neural network.

Parasympathetic nerves. Those autonomic motor nerves that project from the brain to the sacral region of the spinal cord.

Paraventricular nuclei. Hypothalamic nuclei that play a role in eating and synthesize hormones released by the posterior pituitary.

Parietal lobe. One of the four cerebral lobes; it is located just posterior to the central fissure.

Parkinson's disease. A movement disorder that is associated with degeneration of dopaminergic neurons in the substantia nigra.

Parvocellular layers. The layers of the lateral geniculate nuclei that are composed of neurons with small cell bodies; the top four layers (also called *P layers*).

Patellar tendon reflex. The stretch reflex that is elicited when the patellar tendon is struck.

Pathogens. Disease-causing agents.

Pattern separation. The ability to separate distinct percepts into individual memories for storage.

Pavlovian conditioning paradigm. A paradigm in which the experimenter pairs an initially neutral stimulus (conditional stimulus) with a stimulus (unconditional stimulus) that elicits a reflexive response (unconditional response); after several pairings, the neutral stimulus elicits a conditional response.

Penumbra. The dysfunctional area of brain tissue around an infarct. The tissue in the penumbra may recover or die in the days following a stroke.

Peptide hormones. Hormones that are short chains of amino acids.

Perception. The higher-order process of integrating, recognizing, and interpreting complete patterns of sensations.

Periaqueductal gray (PAG). The gray matter around the cerebral aqueduct, which contains opiate receptors and activates a descending analgesia circuit.

Perimetry test. The procedure used to map scotomas.

Periodic limb movement disorder. Characterized by periodic, involuntary movements of the limbs often involving twitches of the legs during sleep; one cause of insomnia.

Peripartum depression. The intense, sustained depression experienced by some females during pregnancy, after they give birth, or both.

Peripheral nervous system (PNS). The portion of the nervous system outside the skull and spine.

Permissive experiences. Experiences that permit the information in genetic programs of brain development to be expressed and maintained.

Perseveration. The tendency to continue making a formerly correct response that is currently incorrect.

Phagocytes. Cells, such as macrophages and microglia, that destroy and ingest pathogens.

Phagocytosis. The destruction and ingestion of foreign matter by cells of the immune system.

Phantom limb. The vivid perception that an amputated limb still exists.

Pharmacological. Pertaining to the scientific study of drugs.

Phenothiazines. A class of antipsychotic drugs that bind effectively to both D_1 and D_2 receptors.

Phenotype. An organism's observable traits.

Phenylketonuria (PKU). A neurological disorder whose symptoms are vomiting, seizures, hyperactivity, hyperirritability, intellectual disability, brain damage, and high levels of phenylpyruvic acid in the urine.

Phenylpyruvic acid. A substance that is found in abnormally high concentrations in the urine of those suffering from phenylketonuria.

Pheromones. Chemicals that are released by an animal and elicit through their odor specific patterns of behavior in its conspecifics.

Phoneme. The smallest unit of sound that distinguishes among various words in a language.

Phonetic procedure. A procedure for reading aloud that involves the recognition of letters and the application of a language's rules of pronunciation.

Phonological analysis. Analysis of the sound of language.

Photopic spectral sensitivity curve. The graph of the sensitivity of cone-mediated vision to different wavelengths of light.

Photopic vision. Cone-mediated vision, which predominates when lighting is good.

Phylogeny. The evolutionary development of species.

Physical-dependence theories of addiction. Theories holding that the main factor that motivates drug-addicted individuals to keep taking drugs is the prevention or termination of withdrawal symptoms.

Physically dependent. Being in a state in which the discontinuation of drug taking will induce withdrawal reactions.

Physiological psychology. The division of biopsychology that studies the neural mechanisms of behavior through direct manipulation of the brains of nonhuman animal subjects in controlled experiments.

Pia mater. The delicate, innermost meninx.

Pineal gland. The endocrine gland that is the human body's sole source of melatonin.

Pioneer growth cones. The first growth cones to travel along a particular route in the developing nervous system.

Piriform cortex. An area of medial temporal cortex that is adjacent to the amygdala and that receives direct olfactory input.

Pituitary gland. The gland that dangles from, and is controlled by, the hypothalamus.

Pituitary peptides. One of the five categories of neuropeptide transmitters; it contains neuropeptides that were first identified as hormones released by the pituitary.

Pituitary stalk. The structure connecting the hypothalamus and the pituitary gland.

Place cells. Neurons that respond only when the subject is in specific locations (i.e., in the place fields of the neurons).

Planum temporale. An area of temporal lobe cortex that lies in the posterior region of the lateral fissure and, in the left hemisphere, roughly corresponds to Wernicke's area.

Plethysmography. Any technique for measuring changes in the volume of blood in a part of the body.

Pluripotent. Cells that can develop into many, but not all, classes of body cells.

Polyandry. A pattern of mate bonding in which one female bonds with more than one male.

Polygraphy. A method of interrogation that employs ANS indexes of emotion to infer the truthfulness of a person's responses.

Polygyny. A pattern of mate bonding in which one male bonds with more than one female; the most prevalent pattern of mate bonding in mammals.

Polyphasic sleep cycles. Sleep cycles that regularly involve more than one period of sleep per day.

Pons. The metencephalic structure that creates a bulge on the ventral surface of the brain stem.

Positive symptoms. Symptoms of schizophrenia that seem to represent an excess of typical function.

Positive-incentive theories of addiction. Theories holding that the primary factor in most cases of addiction is the craving for the positive-incentive (expected pleasure-producing) properties of the drug.

Positive-incentive theory. The idea that behaviors (e.g., eating and drinking) are motivated by their anticipated pleasurable effects.

Positive-incentive value. The anticipated pleasure associated with a particular action, such as taking a drug.

Positron emission tomography (PET). A technique for visualizing brain activity, usually by measuring the accumulation of radioactive fluorodeoxyglucose (FDG) in active areas of the brain.

Postcentral gyrus. The gyrus located just posterior to the central fissure; its function is primarily somatosensory.

Posterior. Toward the tail end of a vertebrate or toward the back of the head.

Posterior parietal association cortex. An area of association cortex that receives input from the visual, auditory, and somatosensory systems and is involved in the perception of spatial location and guidance of voluntary behavior.

Posterior pituitary. The part of the pituitary gland that contains the terminals of hypothalamic neurons.

Posttraumatic amnesia (PTA). Amnesia produced by a nonpenetrating head injury (a blow to the head that does not penetrate the skull).

Prader-Willi syndrome. A neurodevelopmental disorder that is characterized by insatiable appetite and exceptionally slow metabolism.

Precentral gyrus. The gyrus located just anterior to the central fissure; its function is primarily motor.

Prefrontal cortex. The areas of frontal cortex that are anterior to the frontal motor areas.

Prefrontal lobes. Areas of cortex, left and right, that are located at the very front of the brain—in the frontal lobes.

Prefrontal lobotomy. A surgical procedure in which the connections between the prefrontal lobes and the rest of the brain are cut, as a treatment for mental illness.

Premotor cortex. The area of secondary motor cortex that lies between the supplementary motor area and the lateral fissure.

Prestriate cortex. The band of tissue in the occipital lobe that surrounds the primary visual cortex and contains areas of secondary visual cortex.

Primary motor cortex. The cortex of the precentral gyrus, which is the major point of departure for motor signals descending from the cerebral cortex into lower levels of the sensorimotor system.

Primary sensory cortex. An area of sensory cortex that receives most of its input directly from the thalamic relay nuclei of one sensory system.

Primary visual cortex. The area of the cortex that receives direct input from the lateral geniculate nuclei (also called *striate cortex*).

Primates. One of 20 different orders of mammals; there are about a dozen families of primates.

Proceptive behaviors. Behaviors that solicit the sexual advances of members of the other sex.

Progesterone. A progestin that prepares the uterus and breasts for pregnancy.

Progestins. The class of steroid hormones that includes progesterone.

Prosopagnosia. Visual agnosia for faces.

Protein hormones. Hormones that are long chains of amino acids.

Proteins. Long chains of amino acids.

Proximal. Close to something.

Proximal segment. The segment of a cut axon between the cut and the cell body.

Psychedelic drugs. Drugs whose primary action is to alter perception, emotion, and cognition.

Psychiatric disorder. A disorder of psychological function sufficiently severe to require treatment by a psychiatrist or clinical psychologist.

Psychoactive drugs. Drugs that influence subjective experience and behavior by acting on the nervous system.

Psychoneuroimmunology. The study of interactions among psychological factors, the nervous system, and the immune system.

Psychopharmacology. The division of biopsychology that studies the effects of drugs on the brain and behavior.

Psychophysiology. The division of biopsychology that studies the relation between physiological activity and psychological processes in human subjects by noninvasive methods.

Psychosis. A loss of touch with reality.

Psychosomatic disorder. Any physical disorder that can be caused or exacerbated by stress.

Psychosurgery. Any brain surgery performed for the treatment of a psychological problem (e.g., prefrontal lobotomy).

P300 wave. The positive EEG wave that usually occurs about 300 milliseconds after a momentary stimulus that has meaning for the subject.

Pulsatile hormone release. The typical pattern of hormone release: Hormones are discharged several times per day in large surges.

Pure research. Research motivated primarily by the curiosity of the researcher and done solely for the purpose of acquiring knowledge.

Purkinje effect. In intense light, red and yellow wavelengths look brighter than blue or green wavelengths of equal intensity; in dim light, blue and green wavelengths look brighter than red and yellow wavelengths of equal intensity.

Putamen. A structure that is joined to the caudate by a series of fiber bridges; together the putamen and caudate compose the striatum.

Pyramidal cell layer. One of the major layers of cell bodies in the hippocampus.

Pyramidal cells. Large multipolar cortical neurons with a pyramid-shaped cell body, an apical dendrite, and a very long axon.

Quasiexperimental studies. Studies of groups of subjects who have been exposed to the conditions of interest in the real world; such studies have the appearance of experiments but are not true experiments because potential confounded variables have not been controlled for.

Radial arm maze. A maze in which several arms radiate out from a central starting chamber; commonly used to study spatial learning in rats.

Radial arm maze test. A widely used test of rats' spatial ability in which the same arms are baited on each trial, and the rats must learn to visit only the baited arms once per trial.

Radial glial cells. Glial cells that exist in the neural tube during the period of neural migration and that form a network along which radial migration occurs. Some radial glial cells are stem cells.

Radial migration. Movement of cells in the developing neural tube from the ventricular zone in a straight line outward toward the tube's outer wall.

Reactive depression. Depression that is triggered by a negative experience.

Reappraisal paradigm. An experimental method for studying emotion; subjects are asked to reinterpret a film or photo to change their emotional reaction to it while their brain activity is recorded.

Receptive. Pertaining to the comprehension of language and speech.

Receptive field. The area of the visual field within which it is possible for the appropriate stimulus to influence the firing of a visual neuron.

Receptor blockers. Antagonistic drugs that bind to postsynaptic receptors without activating them and block the access of the usual neurotransmitter.

Receptor subtypes. The different types of receptors to which a particular neurotransmitter can bind.

Receptors. Cells that are specialized to receive chemical, mechanical, or radiant signals from the environment; also proteins that contain binding sites for particular neurotransmitters.

Recessive trait. The trait of a dichotomous pair that is not expressed in the phenotype of heterozygous individuals.

Reciprocal innervation. The principle of spinal cord circuitry that causes a muscle to automatically relax when a muscle that is antagonistic to it contracts.

Recuperation theories of sleep. Theories based on the premise that being awake disturbs the body's homeostasis and the function of sleep is to restore it.

Recurrent collateral inhibition. The inhibition of a neuron that is produced by its own activity via a collateral branch of its axon and an inhibitory interneuron.

Red nucleus. A structure of the sensorimotor system that is located in the tegmentum of the mesencephalon.

Reference memory. Memory for the general principles and skills that are required to perform a task.

Relapse. The return to one's drug taking habit after a period of voluntary abstinence.

Relative refractory period. A period after the absolute refractory period during which a higher-than-normal amount of stimulation is necessary to make a neuron fire.

Release-inhibiting hormones. Hypothalamic hormones that inhibit the release of hormones from the anterior pituitary.

Releasing hormones. Hypothalamic hormones that stimulate the release of hormones from the anterior pituitary.

REM sleep. The stage of sleep characterized by rapid eye movements, loss of core muscle tone, and emergent stage 1 EEG.

REM-sleep behavior disorder. A disorder where the individual experiences REM sleep without core-muscle atonia.

Remote memory. Memory for experiences in the distant past.

Repetition priming tests. Tests of implicit memory; in one example, a list of words is presented, then fragments of the original words are presented and the subject is asked to complete them.

Repetitive transcranial magnetic stimulation (rTMS). A form of transcranial magnetic stimulation (TMS) that involves the delivery of repetitive magnetic pulses at either high frequencies (e.g., five pulses per second; high-frequency rTMS) or low frequencies (e.g., less than one pulse per second; low-frequency rTMS) to specific cortical areas.

Replacement injections. Injections of a hormone whose natural release has been curtailed by the removal of the gland that normally releases it.

Replication. The process by which the DNA molecule duplicates itself.

Reserpine. The first monoamine antagonist to be used in the treatment of schizophrenia; the active ingredient of the snakeroot plant.

Response-chunking hypothesis. The idea that practice combines the central sensorimotor programs that control individual responses into programs that control sequences (chunks) of behavior.

Resting potential. The steady membrane potential of a neuron at rest, usually about –70 mV.

Restless legs syndrome. Tension or uneasiness in the legs that keeps a person from falling asleep; one cause of insomnia.

Reticular activating system. The hypothetical arousal system in the reticular formation.

Reticular formation. A complex network of about 100 tiny nuclei that occupies the central core of the brain stem.

Retina-geniculate-striate pathway. The major visual pathway from each retina to the striate cortex (primary visual cortex) via the lateral geniculate nuclei of the thalamus.

Retinal ganglion cells. Retinal neurons whose axons leave the eyeball and form the optic nerve.

Retinex theory. Land's theory that the color of an object is determined by its reflectance, which the visual system calculates by comparing the ability of adjacent surfaces to reflect short, medium, and long wavelengths.

Retinotopic. Organized, like the primary visual cortex, according to a map of the retina.

Retrograde amnesia. Loss of memory for events or information learned before the amnesia-inducing brain injury.

Retrograde degeneration. Degeneration of the proximal segment of a cut axon.

Reuptake. The drawing back into the terminal button of neurotransmitter molecules after their release into the synapse; the most common mechanism for deactivating a released neurotransmitter.

Reversible lesions. Methods for temporarily eliminating the activity in a particular area of the brain while tests are being conducted.

Rhodopsin. The photopigment of rods.

Ribonucleic acid (RNA). A molecule that is similar to DNA except that it has the nucleotide base uracil and a phosphate and ribose backbone.

Ribosome. A structure in the cell's cytoplasm that translates strands of messenger RNA into proteins.

Risk-assessment test. An animal model of anxiety. After a single brief exposure to a cat on the surface of a laboratory burrow system, rats flee to their burrows and freeze. Then they engage in a variety of risk-assessment behaviors.

RNA editing. An epigenetic mechanism wherein messenger RNA is modified through the actions of small RNA molecules and other proteins.

Rods. The visual receptors in the retina that mediate achromatic, low-acuity vision under dim light.

Rubber-hand illusion. The feeling that an extraneous object, usually a rubber hand, is actually part of one's own body.

Saccades. The rapid movements of the eyes between fixations.

Sagittal sections. Any slices of brain tissue cut in a plane that is parallel to the side of the brain.

Saltatory conduction. Conduction of an action potential from one node of Ranvier to the next along a myelinated axon.

Satiety. The motivational state that terminates a meal when there is food remaining.

Savants. Individuals with developmental disabilities who nevertheless display amazing and specific cognitive or artistic abilities; savant abilities are sometimes associated with autism spectrum disorder.

Schwann cells. The glial cells that compose the myelin sheaths of PNS axons and promote the regeneration of PNS axons.

Scientific inference. The logical process by which observable events are used to infer the properties of unobservable events.

Scotoma. An area of blindness produced by damage to, or disruption of, an area of the visual system.

Scotopic spectral sensitivity curve. The graph of the sensitivity of rod-mediated vision to different wavelengths of light.

Scotopic vision. Rod-mediated vision, which predominates in dim light.

Scrotum. The sac that holds the male testes outside the body cavity.

Seasonal affective disorder (SAD). Type of major depressive disorder in which episodes of depression typically recur during particular seasons—usually during the winter months.

Second messenger. A chemical synthesized in a neuron in response to the binding of a neurotransmitter to a metabotropic receptor in its cell membrane.

Secondary motor cortex. An area of the cerebral cortex that receives much of its input from association cortex and sends much of its output to primary motor cortex.

Secondary sensory cortex. An area of sensory cortex that receives most of its input from the primary sensory cortex of one sensory system or from other areas of secondary cortex of the same system.

Secondary sex characteristics. Body features, other than the reproductive organs, that distinguish males from females.

Secondary visual cortex. Areas of cerebral cortex that receive most of their input from primary visual cortex.

Selective attention. The ability to focus on a small subset of the multitude of stimuli that are being received at any one time.

Selective serotonin-reuptake inhibitors (SSRIs). Class of drugs that exert agonistic effects by blocking the reuptake of serotonin from synapses; used to treat depression.

Self-stimulation paradigm. A paradigm in which animals press a lever to administer reinforcing electrical stimulation to particular sites in their own brains.

Semantic analysis. Analysis of the meaning of language.

Semantic memories. Explicit memories for general facts or knowledge.

Semicircular canals. The receptive organs of the vestibular system.

Sensation. The process of detecting the presence of stimuli.

Sensitive period. An interval of time during development when an experience can have a greater effect on development if it occurs during that interval, as opposed to outside that interval.

Sensitivity. In vision, the ability to detect the presence of dimly lit objects.

Sensorimotor phase. The second of the two phases of birdsong development, during which juvenile birds progress from subsongs to adult songs.

Sensory evoked potential. A change in the electrical activity of the brain (e.g., in the cortical EEG) that is elicited by the momentary presentation of a sensory stimulus.

Sensory feedback. Sensory signals that are produced by a response and are often used to guide the continuation of the response.

Sensory phase. The first of the two phases of birdsong development, during which young birds do not sing but form memories of the adult songs they hear.

Sensory relay nuclei. Those nuclei of the thalamus whose main function is to relay sensory signals to the appropriate areas of cortex.

Sensory-specific satiety. The fact that the consumption of a particular food produces greater satiety for foods of the same taste than for other foods.

Septum. A midline nucleus of the limbic system, located near the anterior tip of the cingulate cortex.

Serotonin. An indolamine neurotransmitter; the only member of this class of monoamine neurotransmitters found in the mammalian nervous system.

Set point. The value of a physiological parameter that is maintained constantly by physiological or behavioral mechanisms; for example, the body's energy resources are often assumed to be maintained at a constant optimal level by compensatory changes in hunger.

Set-point assumption. The assumption that hunger is typically triggered by a decline in the body's energy reserves below their set point.

Settling point. The point at which various factors that influence the level of some regulated function (such as body weight) achieve an equilibrium.

Sex chromosomes. The pair of chromosomes that determine an individual's genetic sex: XX for a female and XY for a male.

Sex-linked traits. Traits that are influenced by genes on the sex chromosomes.

Sexual dimorphisms. Instances where a behavior (or structure) comes in two distinct classes (male or female) into which most individuals can be unambiguously assigned.

Sexually dimorphic nucleus. The nucleus in the medial preoptic area of rats that is larger in males than in females.

Sham eating. The experimental protocol in which an animal chews and swallows food, after which the food immediately exits its body through a tube implanted in its esophagus.

Sham rage. The exaggerated, poorly directed aggressive responses of decorticate animals.

Short-term memory. Storage of information for brief periods of time while a person attends to it.

Signal averaging. A method of increasing the signal-to-noise ratio by reducing background noise.

Simple cells. Neurons in the visual cortex that respond maximally to straight-edge stimuli of a particular width and orientation.

Simple partial seizures. Focal seizures in which the symptoms are primarily sensory or motor or both.

Simultanagnosia. A difficulty attending to more than one stimulus at a time.

Sinestrals. Left-handers.

Skeletal muscle (extrafusal muscle). Striated muscle that is attached to the skeleton and is usually under voluntary control.

Skin conductance level (SCL). A measure of the background level of skin conductance associated with a particular situation.

Skin conductance response (SCR). The transient change in skin conductance associated with discrete experiences.

Sleep apnea. A condition in which sleep is repeatedly disturbed by momentary interruptions in breathing.

Sleep inertia. The unpleasant feeling of grogginess that is sometimes experienced for a few minutes after awakening.

Sleep paralysis. A sleep disorder characterized by the inability to move (paralysis) just as a person is falling asleep or waking up.

Slow-wave sleep (SWS). Stage 3 sleep, which is characterized by the largest and slowest EEG waves.

Smoker's syndrome. The chest pain, labored breathing, wheezing, coughing, and heightened susceptibility to infections of the respiratory tract commonly observed in tobacco smokers.

Sodium amytal test. A test involving the anesthetization of first one cerebral hemisphere and then the other to determine which hemisphere plays the dominant role in language.

Sodium–potassium pumps. An ion transporter that actively exchanges three Na^+ ions inside the neuron for two K^+ ions outside.

Solitary nucleus. The medullary relay nucleus of the gustatory system.

Soluble-gas neurotransmitters. A class of unconventional neurotransmitters that includes nitric oxide and carbon monoxide.

Somal translocation. One of two major modes of neural migration, in which an extension grows out from the undeveloped neuron and draws the cell body up into it.

Somatic nervous system (SNS). The part of the peripheral nervous system that interacts with the external environment.

Somatosensory homunculus. The somatotopic map in the primary somatosensory cortex.

Somatotopic. Organized, like the primary somatosensory cortex, according to a map of the surface of the body.

Spandrels. Incidental nonadaptive evolutionary by-products of some adaptive characteristic.

Spatial resolution. Ability of a recording technique to detect differences in spatial location (e.g., to pinpoint a location in the brain).

Spatial summation. The integration of signals that originate at different sites on the neuron's membrane.

Species. A group of organisms that is reproductively isolated from other organisms; the members of one species cannot produce fertile offspring by mating with members of other species.

Species-common behaviors. Behaviors that are displayed in the same manner by virtually all like members of a species.

Specific phobia. An anxiety disorder that involves strong fear or anxiety about particular objects (e.g., birds, spiders) or situations (e.g., enclosed spaces, darkness).

Spindle afferent neurons. Neurons that carry signals from muscle spindles into the spinal cord via the dorsal root.

Split-brain patients. Commissurotomized patients.

Sry gene. A gene on the Y chromosome that triggers the production of Sry protein.

Sry protein. A protein that causes the medulla of each primordial gonad to grow and develop into a testis.

Standard consolidation theory. The theory that memories are temporarily stored in the hippocampus until they can be transferred to a more stable cortical storage system. Also known as dual-trace theory.

Static phase. The second phase of the VMH syndrome, during which the obese animal maintains a stable level of obesity.

Stellate cells. Small star-shaped cortical interneurons.

Stem cells. Cells that have an almost unlimited capacity for self-renewal and the ability to develop into many different types of cells.

Stereognosis. The process of identifying objects by touch.

Stereotaxic atlas. A series of maps representing the three-dimensional structure of the brain that is used to determine coordinates for stereotaxic surgery.

Stereotaxic instrument. A device for performing stereotaxic surgery, composed of two parts: a head holder and an electrode holder.

Steroid hormones. Hormones that are synthesized from cholesterol.

Stimulants. Drugs that produce general increases in neural and behavioral activity.

Stress. The physiological changes that occur when the body is exposed to harm or threat.

Stressors. Experiences that induce a stress response.

Stretch reflex. A reflexive counteracting reaction to an unanticipated external stretching force on a muscle.

Striatum. A structure of the basal ganglia that is the terminal of the dopaminergic nigrostriatal pathway.

Strokes. Sudden-onset cerebrovascular disorders that cause brain damage.

Subarachnoid space. The space beneath the arachnoid membrane, which contains many large blood vessels and cerebrospinal fluid.

Subcutaneous fat. Fat stored under the skin.

Subordination stress. Stress experienced by animals, typically males, that are continually attacked by higher-ranking conspecifics.

Substantia nigra. The midbrain nucleus whose neurons project via the nigrostriatal pathway to the striatum of the basal ganglia; it is part of the mesotelencephalic dopamine system.

Subthalamic nucleus. A nucleus that lies just below the thalamus and is connected to the basal ganglia; deep brain stimulation applied to this site has been used to treat Parkinson's disease.

Sulci. Small furrows in a convoluted cortex.

Superior. Toward the top of the primate head.

Superior colliculi. Two of the four nuclei that compose the tectum; they receive major visual input.

Superior olives. Medullary nuclei that play a role in sound localization.

Superior temporal gyri. The plural of superior temporal gyrus.

Superior temporal gyrus. The large gyrus of the temporal lobe adjacent to the lateral fissure; the location of auditory cortex.

Supplementary motor area. The area of secondary motor cortex that is within and adjacent to the longitudinal fissure.

Suppression paradigm. An experimental method for studying emotion; subjects are asked to inhibit their emotional reactions to unpleasant films or photos while their brain activity is recorded.

Suprachiasmatic nuclei (SCN). Nuclei of the medial hypothalamus that control the circadian cycles of various body functions.

Supraoptic nuclei. Hypothalamic nuclei in which the hormones of the posterior pituitary are synthesized.

Surface dyslexia. A reading disorder in which the lexical procedure is disrupted while the phonetic procedure is not.

Surface interpolation. The process by which we perceive surfaces; the visual system extracts information about edges and from it infers the appearance of large surfaces.

Sympathetic nerves. Those motor nerves of the autonomic nervous system that project from the CNS in the lumbar and thoracic region areas of the spinal cord.

Synaptic vesicles. Small spherical membranes that store neurotransmitter molecules and release them into the synaptic cleft.

Synaptogenesis. The formation of new synapses.

Synergistic muscles. Pairs of muscles whose contraction produces a movement in the same direction.

T cells. T lymphocytes; lymphocytes that bind to foreign microorganisms and cells that contain them and, in so doing, destroy them.

Tangential migration. Movement of cells in the developing neural tube in a direction parallel to the tube's walls.

Tardive dyskinesia (TD). A motor disorder that results from chronic use of certain antipsychotic drugs.

Target-site concept. The idea that aggressive and defensive behaviors of an animal are often designed to attack specific sites on the body of another animal while protecting specific sites on its own.

Taste buds. Clusters of taste receptors found on the tongue and in parts of the oral cavity.

Tau. The first circadian gene to be identified in mammals.

Tectorial membrane. The cochlear membrane that rests on the hair cells.

Tectum. The "roof," or dorsal surface, of the mesencephalon; it includes the superior and inferior colliculi.

Tegmentum. The ventral division of the mesencephalon; it includes part of the reticular formation, substantia nigra, and red nucleus.

Telencephalon. The most superior of the brain's five major divisions.

Temporal hemiretina. The half of each retina next to the temple.

Temporal lobe. One of the four major cerebral lobes; it lies adjacent to the temples and contains the hippocampus and amygdala.

Temporal resolution. Ability of a recording technique to detect differences in time (i.e., to pinpoint when an event occurred).

Temporal summation. The integration of neural signals that occur at different times at the same synapse.

Teratogen. A drug or other chemical that causes birth defects.

Testes. The male gonads.

Testosterone. The most common androgen.

Thalamus. The large two-lobed diencephalic structure that constitutes the anterior end of the brain stem; many of its nuclei are sensory relay nuclei that project to the cortex.

THC. Delta-9-tetrahydrocannabinol, the main psychoactive constituent of marijuana.

Thigmotaxic. Tending to stay near the walls of an open space such as a test chamber.

Thinking creatively. Thinking in productive, unconventional ways.

Threshold of excitation. The level of depolarization necessary to generate an action potential; usually about –65 mV.

Thrombosis. The blockage of blood flow by a plug (a thrombus) at the site of its formation.

Thyrotropin. The anterior pituitary hormone that stimulates the release of hormones from the thyroid gland.

Thyrotropin-releasing hormone. The hypothalamic hormone that stimulates the release of thyrotropin from the anterior pituitary.

Tics. Involuntary, repetitive, stereotyped movements or vocalizations; the defining feature of Tourette's disorder.

Tinnitus. Ringing in the ears.

Token test. A preliminary test for language-related deficits that involves following verbal instructions to touch or move tokens of different shapes, sizes, and colors.

Toll-like receptors. Receptors found in the cell membranes of many cells of the innate immune system; they trigger phagocytosis and inflammatory responses.

Tonic-clonic seizure. A type of generalized seizure whose primary behavioral symptoms are loss of consciousness, loss of equilibrium, and a tonic-clonic convulsion—a convulsion involving both tonus and clonus.

Tonotopic. Organized, like the primary auditory cortex, according to the frequency of sound.

Top-down. A sort of neural mechanism that involves activation of lower cortical areas by higher cortical areas.

Topographic gradient hypothesis. The hypothesis that axonal growth is guided by the relative position of the cell bodies on intersecting gradients, rather than by point-to-point coding of neural connections.

Totipotent. Capable of developing into any type of body cell.

Tourette's disorder. A disorder of tics (involuntary, repetitive, stereotyped movements or vocalizations).

Toxic psychosis. A chronic psychiatric disorder produced by exposure to a neurotoxin.

Tracts. Bundles of axons in the central nervous system.

Transcranial direct current stimulation (tDCS). A technique that can be used to stimulate ("turn on") an area of the cortex by applying an electrical current through two electrodes placed directly on the scalp.

Transcranial magnetic stimulation (TMS). A technique that can be used to stimulate ("turn on") or turn off an area of the cortex by creating a magnetic field under a coil positioned next to the skull.

Transcription factors. Intracellular proteins that bind to DNA and influence the operation of particular genes.

Transduction. The conversion of one form of energy to another.

Transfer RNA. Molecules of RNA that carry amino acids to ribosomes during protein synthesis; each kind of amino acid is carried by a different kind of transfer RNA molecule.

Transgenerational epigenetics. A subfield of epigenetics that examines the transmission of experiences via epigenetic mechanisms across generations.

Transgenic. Containing the genes of another species, which have been implanted there for research purposes.

Transgenic mice. Mice into which the genetic material of another species has been introduced.

Transient global amnesia. A sudden onset severe anterograde amnesia and moderate retrograde amnesia for explicit episodic memory that is transient—typically lasting only between 4 to 6 hours.

Translational bottleneck. A barrier keeping promising ideas and treatments from becoming the focus of translational research; largely created by the massive cost of such research.

Translational research. Research designed to translate basic scientific discoveries into effective applications (e.g., into clinical treatments).

Transneuronal degeneration. Degeneration of a neuron caused by damage to another neuron to which it is linked by a synapse.

Transorbital lobotomy. A prefrontal lobotomy performed with an instrument inserted through the eye socket.

Transporters. Mechanisms in the membrane of a cell that actively transport ions or molecules across the membrane.

Transsexualism. When a person has a gender identity that is inconsistent with their anatomical sex.

Tricyclic antidepressants. Drugs with an antidepressant action and a three-ring molecular structure.

True-breeding lines. Breeding lines in which interbred members always produce offspring with the same trait, generation after generation.

Tumor (neoplasm). A mass of cells that grows independently of the rest of the body.

Tympanic membrane. The eardrum.

Typical antipsychotics. The first generation of antipsychotic drugs.

Unipolar neuron. A neuron with one process extending from its cell body.

Unipotent. Cells that can develop into only one type of cell.

Up-regulation. An increase in the number of receptors for a neurotransmitter in response to decreased release of that neurotransmitter.

Urbach-Wiethe disease. A genetic disorder that often results in the calcification of the amygdala and surrounding brain structures.

Vaccination. Administering a weakened form of a virus so that if the virus later invades, the adaptive immune system is prepared to deal with it.

Vasopressin. One of the two major peptide hormones of the posterior pituitary; it facilitates reabsorption of water by kidneys and is thus also called *antidiuretic hormone*.

Ventral. Toward the chest surface of a vertebrate or toward the bottom of the head.

Ventral horns. The two ventral arms of the spinal gray matter.

Ventral posterior nucleus. A thalamic relay nucleus in both the somatosensory and gustatory systems.

Ventral stream. The group of visual pathways that flows from the primary visual cortex to the ventral prestriate cortex to the inferotemporal cortex.

Ventral tegmental area. The midbrain nucleus of the mesotelencephalic dopamine system that is the major source of the mesoscorticolimbic pathway.

Ventricular zone. The region adjacent to the ventricle in the developing neural tube.

Ventromedial cortico-brainstem-spinal tract. The indirect ventromedial motor pathway, which descends bilaterally from the primary motor cortex to several interconnected brain stem motor structures and then descends in the ventromedial portions of the spinal cord.

Ventromedial corticospinal tract. The direct ventromedial motor pathway, which descends ipsilaterally from the primary motor cortex directly into the ventromedial areas of the spinal white matter.

Ventromedial hypothalamus (VMH). The area of the hypothalamus that was once thought to be a satiety center.

Ventromedial nucleus (VMN). A hypothalamic nucleus that is thought to be involved in female sexual behavior.

Vertebrates. Chordates that possess spinal bones.

Vestibular nucleus. The brain stem nucleus that receives information about balance from receptors in the semicircular canals.

Vestibular system. The sensory system that detects changes in the direction and intensity of head movements and that contributes to the maintenance of balance through its output to the motor system.

Visceral fat. Fat stored around the internal organs of the body cavity.

Visual agnosia. A failure to recognize visual stimuli that is not attributable to sensory, verbal, or intellectual impairment.

Visual association cortex. Areas of cerebral cortex that receive input from areas of secondary visual cortex as well as from secondary areas of other sensory systems.

Visual completion. The completion or filling in of a scotoma by the brain.

Voltage-activated ion channels. Ion channels that open and close in response to changes in the level of the membrane potential.

Wechsler Adult Intelligence Scale (WAIS). A widely used test of general intelligence that includes 11 subtests.

Wernicke-Geschwind model. An influential model of cortical language localization in the left hemisphere.

Wernicke's aphasia. A hypothetical disorder of language comprehension with no associated deficits in speech production.

Wernicke's area. The area of the left temporal cortex hypothesized by Wernicke to be the center of language comprehension.

"Where" versus "what" theory. The theory that the dorsal stream mediates the perception of where things are and the ventral stream mediates the perception of what things are.

White matter. Portions of the nervous system that are white because they are composed largely of myelinated axons.

Williams syndrome. A neurodevelopmental disorder characterized by intellectual disability, accompanied by preserved language and social skills.

Wisconsin Card Sorting Test. A neuropsychological test that evaluates a patient's ability to remember that previously learned rules of behavior are no longer effective and to learn to respond to new rules.

Withdrawal reflex. The reflexive withdrawal of a limb when it comes in contact with a painful stimulus.

Withdrawal syndrome. The illness brought on by the elimination from the body of a drug on which the person is physically dependent.

Within-subjects design. An experimental design in which the same subjects are tested under each condition.

Wolffian system. The embryonic precursor of the male reproductive ducts.

Working memory. Temporary memory that is necessary for the successful performance of a task on which one is currently working.

Z lens. A contact lens that is opaque on one side (left or right) and thus allows visual input to enter only one hemisphere of a split-brain subject, irrespective of eye movements.

Zeitgebers. Environmental cues, such as the light–dark cycle, that entrain circadian rhythms.

Zeitgeist. The general intellectual climate of a culture.

Zygote. The cell formed from the amalgamation of a sperm cell and an ovum.

References

Abbott, L. C., & Winzer-Serhan, U. H. (2012). Smoking during pregnancy: Lessons learned from epidemiological studies and experimental studies using animal models. *Clinical Reviews in Toxicology, 42*, 279–303.

Abraham, W. C. (2006). Memory maintenance: The changing nature of neural mechanisms. *Current Directions in Psychological Science, 15*, 5–8.

Ackerman, J. (2012). The ultimate social network. *Scientific American, 306*, 36–43.

Ackermann, S., Hartmann, F., Papassotiropoulos, A., de Quervain, D. J., & Rasch, B. (2015). No associations between interindividual differences in sleep parameters and episodic memory consolidation. *Sleep, 38*, 951–959.

Ackman, J. B., & Crair, M. C. (2014). Role of emergent neural activity in visual map development. *Current Opinion in Neurobiology, 24*, 166–175.

Adams, C. P., and Brantner, V. V. (2010). Spending on new drug development. *Health Economics, 19*, 130–141.

Adan, R. A. H. (2013). Mechanisms underlying current and future anti-obesity drugs. *Trends in Neurosciences, 36*, 133–140.

Adlard, P. A., Perreau, V. M., Pop, V., & Cotman, C. W. (2005). Voluntary exercise decreases amyloid load in a transgenic model of Alzheimer's diseases. *Journal of Neuroscience, 25*, 4217–4221.

Adler, D. S., Wilkinson, K. N., Blockley, S., Mark, D. F., Pinhasi, R., et al. (2014). Early Levallois technology and the lower to middle paleolithic transition in the Southern Caucasus. *Science, 345*, 1609–1613.

Adolphs, R. (2006). Perception and emotion: How we recognize facial expressions. *Current Directions in Psychological Science, 15*, 222–226.

Adolphs, R. (2010). What does the amygdala contribute to social cognition? *Annals of the New York Academy of Sciences, 1191*, 42–61.

Adrian, M., Kusters, R., Wierenga, C. J., Storm, C., Hoogenraad, C. C., & Kapitein, L. C. (2014). Barriers in the brain: Resolving dendritic spine morphology and compartmentalization. *Frontiers in Neuroanatomy, 8*, 142.

Aeschbach, D., Cajochen, C., Landolt, H., & Borbely, A. A. (1996). Homeostatic sleep regulation in habitual short sleepers and long sleepers. *American Journal of Regulatory, Integrative and Comparative Physiology, 270*, R41–R53.

Aflalo, T., Kellis, S., Klaes, C., Lee, B., Shi, Y., . . . & Andersen, R. A. (2015). Decoding motor imagery from the posterior parietal cortex of a tetraplegic human. *Science, 348*, 906–910.

Aghajan, Z. M., Acharya, L., Moore, J. J., Cushman, J. D., Vuong, C., & Mehta, M. R. (2015). Impaired spatial selectivity and intact phase precession in two-dimensional virtual reality. *Nature Neuroscience, 18*, 121–128.

Aguilera, O., Fernández, A. F., Muñoz, A., & Fraga, M. F. (2010). Epigenetics and environment: A complex relationship. *Journal of Applied Physiology, 109*, 243–251.

Aguzzi, A., Barres, B. A., & Bennett, M. L. (2013). Microglia: Scapegoat, saboteur, or something else? *Science, 339*, 156–161.

Ahmed, S. H. (2005). Imbalance between drug and non-drug reward availability: A major risk factor for addiction. *European Journal of Pharmacology, 526*, 9–20.

Ahmed, S. H. (2010). Validation crisis in animals models of drug addiction: Beyond non-disordered drug use toward drug addiction. *Neuroscience and Biobehavioral Reviews, 35*, 172–184.

Ahmed, S. H. (2012). The science of making drug addicted animals. *Neuroscience, 211*, 107–125.

Ahmed, S. H., Lenoir, M., & Guillem, K. (2013). Neurobiology of addiction versus drug use driven by lack of choice. *Current Opinion in Neurobiology, 23*, 1–7.

Aimone, J. B., Li, Y., Lee, S. W., Clemenson, G. D., Deng, W., & Gage, F. H. (2014). Regulation and function of adult neurogenesis: From genes to cognition. *Physiology Review, 94*, 991–1026.

Ainsworth, C. (2015). Sex redefined. *Nature, 518*, 288–291.

Akers, K. G., Martinez-Canabal, A., Restivo, L., Yiu, A. P., De Cristofaro, A., . . . & Frankland, P. W. (2014). Hippocampal neurogenesis regulates forgetting during adulthood and infancy. *Science, 344*, 598–602.

Åkerstedt, R., & Gillberg, M. (1981). The circadian variation of experimentally displaced sleep. *Sleep, 4*, 159–169.

Akil, H., Brenner, S., Kandel, E., Kendler, K. S., King, M-C., Scolnick, E., Watson, J., & Zoghbi, H. Y. (2010). The future of psychiatric research: Genomes and neural circuits. *Science, 327*, 1580–1581.

Aktas, O., Kieseier, B., & Hartung, H.P. (2009). Neuroprotection, regeneration and immunomodulation: Broadening the therapeutic repertoire in multiple sclerosis. *Trends in Neurosciences, 33*, 140–152.

Alabi, A. A., & Tsien, R. W. (2012). Synaptic vesicle pools and dynamics. *Cold Spring Harbor Perspectives in Biology, 4*, a013680.

Albright, T. D., Kandel, E. R., & Posner, M. I. (2000). Cognitive neuroscience. *Current Opinion in Neurobiology, 10*, 612–624.

Alexander, B. K., Beyerstein, B. L., Hadaway, P. F., & Coambs, R. B. (1981). Effects of early and later colony housing on oral ingestion of morphine in rats. *Psychopharmacology Biochemistry and Behavior, 58*, 176–179.

Alexander, B. M., Skinner, D. C., & Roselli, C. E. (2011). Wired on steroids: Sexual differentiation of the brain and its role in the expression of sexual partner preferences. *Frontiers in Endocrinology, 2*, 42.

Alexander, M. P. (1989). Clinical-anatomical correlations of aphasia following predominantly subcortical lesions. In H. Goodglass (Ed.), *Handbook of neuropsychology* (Vol. II, Pt. 2, pp. 47–66). New York, NY. Elsevier.

ali Shah, S., Ullah, I., Lee, H. Y., & Kim, M. O. (2013). Anthocyanin's protect against ethanol-induced neuronal apoptosis via GABA$_{B1}$ receptors intracellular signaling in prenatal rat hippocampal neurons. *Molecular Neurobiology, 48*, 257–269.

Allen, J. S., Tranel, D., Bruss, J., & Damasio, H. (2006). Correlations between regional brain volumes and memory in anoxia. *Journal of Clinical and Experimental Neuropsychology, 28*, 457–476.

Allen, N. J. (2013). Role of glia in developmental synapse formation. *Current Opinion in Neurobiology, 23*, 1027–1033.

Allen, N. J., & Barres, B. A. (2005). Signaling between glia and neurons: Focus on synaptic plasticity. *Current Opinion in Neurobiology, 15*, 542–548.

Altemus, M., Sarvaiya, N., & Epperson, C. N. (2014). Sex differences in anxiety and depression clinical perspectives. *Frontiers in Neuroendocrinology, 35*, 320–330.

Alvarez, J. I., Katayama, T., & Prat, A. (2013). Glial influence on the blood brain barrier. *Glia, 61*, 1939–1958.

Alvarez, V. A., & Sabatini, B. L. (2007). Anatomical and physiological plasticity of dendritic spines. *Annual Review of Neuroscience, 30*, 79–97.

Amanzio, M., Monteverdi, S., Giordano, A., Soliveri, P., Filippi, P., & Geminiani, G. (2010). Impaired awareness of movement disorders in Parkinson's disease. *Brain and Cognition, 72*, 337–346.

Amaral, D. G., Schumann, C. M., & Nordahl, C. W. (2008). Neuroanatomy of autism. *Trends in Neurosciences, 31*, 137–145.

Amato, D. (2015). Serotonin in antipsychotic drugs action. *Behavioural Brain Research, 277*, 125–135.

Ambroggi, F., Turiault, M., Milet, A., Deroche-Gamonet, V., Parnaudeau, S., Balado, E., Barik, J., van der Veen, R., Maroteaux, G., Lemberger, T., Schütz, G., Lazar, M., Marinelli, M., Piazza, P. V., & Tronche, F. (2009). Stress and addiction: Glucocorticoid receptor in dopaminoceptive neurons facilitates cocaine seeking. *Nature Neuroscience, 12*, 247–249.

Amedi, A., Merabet, L. B., Bermpohl, F., & Pascual-Leone, A. (2005). The occipital cortex in the blind. *Current Directions in Psychological Science, 14*, 306–311.

American Psychiatric Association. (2013). *Diagnostic and statistical manual of mental disorders* (5th ed.). Washington, DC: Author.

Amit, B. H., Caddy, C., McCloud, T. L., Rendell, J. M., Hawton, K., Diamond, P. R., . . . & Cipriani, A. (2015). Ketamine and other glutamate receptor modulators for depression in adults. *Cochrane Database of Systematic Reviews, 9*, CD011612.

Amso, D., & Scerif, G. (2015). The attentive brain: Insights from developmental cognitive neuroscience. *Nature Reviews Neuroscience, 16*, 606–619.

Amunts, K., & Zilles, K. (2012). Architecture and organizational principles of Broca's region. *Trends in Cognitive Sciences, 16*, 418–426.

Anagnostaras, S. G., & Robinson, T. E. (1996). Sensitization to the psychomotor stimulant effects of amphetamine: Modulation by associative learning. *Behavioral Neuroscience, 110*(6), 1397–1414.

Anand, B. K., & Brobeck, J. R. (1951). Localization of a "feeding center" in the hypothalamus of the rat. *Proceedings of the Society for Experimental Biology and Medicine, 77*, 323–324.

Andersen, R. A., Andersen, K. N., Hwang, E. J., & Hauschild, M. (2014). Optic ataxia: From Balint's syndrome to the parietal reach region. *Neuron, 81*, 967–983.

Anderson, A. K., & Phelps, E. A. (2000). Expression without recognition: Contributions of the human amygdala to emotional communication. *Psychological Science, 11*, 106–111.

Anderson, M. A., Burda, J. E., Ren, Y., Ao, Y., O'Shea, T. M., Kawaguchi, R., . . . & Sofroniew, M. V. (2016). Astrocyte scar formation aids central nervous system axon regeneration. *Nature, 532*, 195–200.

Anderson, S., & Vanderhaeghen, P. (2014). Cortical neurogenesis from pluripotent stem cells: Complexity emerging from simplicity. *Current Opinion in Neurobiology, 27*, 151–157.

Andrade-Moraes, C. H., Oliveira-Pinto, A. V., Castro-Fonseca, E., da Silva, C. G., Guimarães, D. M., . . . & Lent, R. (2013). Cell number changes in Alzheimer's disease relate to dementia, not to plaques and tangles. *Brain, 136*, 3738–3752.

Andrade, C., & Rao, N. S. K. (2010). How antidepressant drugs act: A primer on neuroplasticity as the eventual mediator of antidepressant efficacy. *Indian Journal of Psychiatry, 52,* 378–386.

Andreae, L. C., & Burrone, J. (2014). The role of neuronal activity and transmitter release on synapse formation. *Current Opinion in Neurobiology, 24,* 47–52.

Angell, P., Chester, N., Green, D., Somauroo, J., Whyte, G., & George, K. (2012). Anabolic steroids and cardiovascular risk. *Sports Medicine, 42,* 119–134.

Anson, J. A., & Kuhlman, D. T. (1993). Post-ictal Klüver-Bucy syndrome after temporal lobectomy. *Journal of Neurology, Neurosurgery, and Psychiatry, 56,* 311–313.

Anton-Erxleben, K., & Carrasco, M. (2013). Attentional enhancement of spatial resolution: Linking behavioral and neurophysiological evidence. *Nature Reviews Neuroscience, 14,* 188–200.

Antón, S. C., Potts, R., & Aiello, L. C. (2014). Evolution of early *Homo:* An integrated biological perspective. *Science, 345,* 45.

Antonini, A., & Stryker, M. P. (1993). Rapid remodeling of axonal arbors in the visual cortex. *Science, 260,* 1819–1821.

Apps, M. A. J., & Tsakiris, M. (2014). The free-energy self: A predictive coding account of self-recognition. *Neuroscience and Biobehavioral Reviews, 41,* 85–97.

Apps, R., & Hawkes, R. (2009). Cerebellar cortical organization: A one-map hypothesis. *Nature Reviews Neuroscience, 10,* 670–681.

Aquila, S., & De Amicis, F. (2014). Steroid receptors and their ligands: Effects on male gamete functions. *Experimental Cell Research, 328,* 303–313.

Arango, C., Garibaldi, G., & Marder, S. R. (2013). Pharmacological approaches to treating negative symptoms: A review of clinical trials. *Schizophrenia Research, 150,* 346–352.

Arango, M.-T., Kivity, S., & Shoenfeld, Y. (2015). Is narcolepsy a classical autoimmune disease? *Pharmacological Research, 92,* 6–12.

Araque, A., Carmignoto, G., Haydon, P. G., Oliet, S. H. R., Robitaille, R., & Volterra, A. (2014). Gliotransmitters travel in time and space. *Neuron, 81,* 728–739.

Araya, R., Tawk, M., Girdler, G. C., Costa, M., Carmone-Fontaine, C., & Clarke, J. D. (2014). Mesoderm is required for coordinated cell movements within zebrafish neural plate in vivo. *Neural Development, 9,* 9.

Araya, R. (2014). Input transformation by dendritic spines of pyramidal neurons. *Frontiers in Neuroanatomy, 8,* 141.

Arbon, E. L., Knurowska, M., & Dijk, D. J. (2015). Randomised clinical trial of the effects of prolonged-release melatonin, temazepam, and zolpidem on slow-wave activity during sleep in healthy people. *Journal of Psychopharmacology, 29,* 764–776.

Arena, J. E., & Rabinstein, A. A. (2015). Transient global amnesia. *Mayo Clinic Proceedings, 90,* 264–272.

Arendt, J., & Skene, D. J. (2005). Melatonin as a chronobiotic. *Sleep Medicine Reviews, 9,* 25–39.

Arguello, P. A., & Gogos, J. A. (2011). Genetic and cognitive windows into circuit mechanisms of psychiatric disease. *Trends in Neurosciences, 35,* 3–13.

Arnegard, M. E., McGee, M. D., Matthews, B., Marchinko, K. B., Conte, G. L., et al. (2014). Genetics of ecological divergence during speciation. *Nature, 511,* 307–311.

Arnott, S. R., & Alain, C. (2011). The auditory dorsal pathway: Orienting vision. *Neuroscience and Biobehavioral Reviews, 35,* 2162–2173.

Aron, L., & Klein, R. (2010). Repairing the parkinsonian brain with neurotrophic factors. *Trends in Neurosciences, 34,* 88–100.

Arsenault, J. S., & Buchsbaum, B. R. (2015). No evidence of somatotopic place of articulation feature mapping in motor cortex during passive speech perception. *Psychonomic Bulletin & Review.* Advance online publication. doi:10.3758/s13423-015-0988-z

Ashby, F. G., Turner, B. O., & Horvitz, J. C. (2010). Cortical and basal ganglia contributions to habit learning and automaticity. *Trends in Cognitive Sciences, 14,* 208–215.

Ashe, J., Lungu, O. V., Basford, A. T., & Lu, X. (2006). Cortical control of motor sequences. *Current Opinion in Neurobiology, 16,* 213–221.

Ascherio, A., & Munger, K. (2008). Epidemiology of multiple sclerosis: From risk factors to prevention. *Seminars in Neurology, 28,* 17–28.

Assali, A., Gaspar, P., & Rebsam, A. (2014). Activity dependent mechanisms of visual map formation—from retinal waves to molecular regulators. *Seminars in Cell and Developmental Biology, 35,* 136–146.

Assanand, S., Pinel, J. P. J., & Lehman, D. R. (1998a). Personal theories of hunger and eating. *Journal of Applied Social Psychology, 28,* 998–1015.

Assanand, S., Pinel, J. P. J., & Lehman, D. R. (1998b). Teaching theories of hunger and eating: Overcoming students' misconceptions. *Teaching Psychology, 25,* 44–46.

Ast, G. (April, 2005). The alternative genome. *Scientific American, 292,* 58–65.

Astori, S., Wimmer, R. D., & Lüthi, A. (2013). Manipulating sleep spindles–expanding views on sleep, memory, and disease. *Trends in Neurosciences, 36,* 738–748.

Asuelime, G. E., & Shi, Y. (2012). A case of cellular alchemy: Lineage reprogramming and its potential in regenerative medicine. *Journal of Molecular Cell Biology, 4,* 190–196.

Attardo, A., Fitzgerald, J. E., & Schnitzer, M. J. (2015). Impermanence of dendritic spines in live adult CA1 hippocampus. *Nature, 523,* 592–596.

Atwood, B. K., Lovinger, D. M., & Mathur, B. N. (2014). Presynaptic long-term depression mediated by Gi/o-coupled receptors. *Trends in Neurosciences, 37,* 663–673.

Aurora, R. N., Chowdhuri, S., Ramar, K., Bista, S. R., Casey, K. R.,…& Tracy, S. L. (2012). The treatment of central sleep apnea syndromes in adults: Practice parameters with an evidence-based literature review and meta-analyses. *Sleep, 35,* 17–40.

Aurora, R. N., Kristo, D. A., Bista, S. R., Rowley, J. A., Zak, R. S.,…& American Academy of Sleep Medicine. The treatment of restless legs syndrome and periodic limb movement disorder in adults—an update for 2012: Practice parameters with an evidence-based systematic review and meta-analyses: An American academy of sleep medicine clinical practice guideline. *Sleep, 35,* 1039–1062.

Autism Genome Project. (2007). Mapping autism risk loci using genetic linkage and chromosomal rearrangements. *Nature Genetics, 39,* 319–328.

Avci, M. E., Sanlikan, F., Çelik, M., Avci, A., Kocaer, M., & Göçmen, A. (2015). Effects of maternal obesity on antenatal, perinatal, and neonatal outcomes. *Journal of Maternal-Fetal and Neonatal Medicine, 28,* 2080–2083.

Aviezer, H., Trope, Y., & Todorov, A. (2012). Body cues, not facial expressions, discriminate between intense positive and negative emotions. *Science, 338,* 1225–1228.

Ayas, N. T., White, D. P., Manson, J. E., Stampfer, M. J., Speizer, F. E., Malhotra, A., & Hu, F. B. (2003). A prospective study of sleep duration and coronary heart disease in women. *Archives of Internal Medicine, 163,* 205–209.

Azad, T. D., Li, A., Pendharkar, A. V., Veeravagu, A., & Grant, G. A. (2016). Junior Seau: An illustrative case of chronic traumatic encephalopathy and update on chronic sports-related head injury. *World Neurosurgery, 86,* 515–e11.

Azevedo, F. A., Carvalho, L. R., Grinberg, L. T., Farfel, J. M., Ferretti, R. E., Leite, R. E.,…& Herculano-Houzel, S. (2009). Equal numbers of neuronal and nonneuronal cells make the human brain an isometrically scaled-up primate brain. *Journal of Comparative Neurology, 513,* 532–541.

Azim, E., Fink, A. J., & Jessell, T. M. (2014). Internal and external feedback circuits for skilled forelimb movement. *Cold Spring Harbor Symposia on Quantitative Biology, 79,* 81–92.

Bachevalier, J., & Loveland, K. A. (2006). The orbitofrontal-amygdala circuit and self-regulation of social-emotional behavior in autism. *Neuroscience and Biobehavioural Reviews, 30,* 97–117.

Baden, T., Berens, P., Franke, K., Rosón, M. R., Bethge, M., & Euler, T. (2016). The functional diversity of retinal ganglion cells in the mouse. *Nature, 529,* 345–350.

Badiani, A., Belin, D., Epstein, D., Calu, D., & Shaham, Y. (2011). Opiate versus psychostimulant addiction: The differences do matter. *Nature Reviews Neuroscience, 12,* 685–700.

Badran, M., Yassin, B. A., Fox, N., Laher, I., & Ayas, N. (2015). Epidemiology of sleep disturbances and cardiovascular consequences. *Canadian Journal of Cardiology, 31,* 873–879.

Bagnardi, V., Rota, M., Botteri, E., Tramacere, I., Islami, F., Fedirko, V., Scotti, L., Jenab, M., Turati, F., Pasquali, E., Pelucchi, C., Bellocco, R., Negri, E., Corrao, G., Rehm, J., Boffetta, P., & La Vecchia, C. (2013). Light alcohol drinking and cancer: A meta-analysis. *Annals of Oncology, 24,* 301–308.

Bailey, J. M., Pillard, R. C., Neale, M. C., & Agyei, Y. (1993). Heritable factors influence sexual orientation in women. *Archives of General Psychiatry, 50,* 217–223.

Bailey, M. J., & Pillard, R. C. (1991). A genetic study of male sexual orientation. *Archives of General Psychiatry, 48,* 1089–1096.

Baird, A. D., Wilson, S. J., Bladin, P. F., Saling, M. M., & Reutens, D. C. (2004). The amygdala and sexual drive: Insights from temporal lobe epilepsy surgery. *Annals of Neurology, 55,* 87–96.

Baker-Andresen, D., Ratnu, V. S., & Bredy, T. W. (2013). Dynamic DNA methylation: A prime candidate for genomic metaplasticity and behavioral adaptation. *Trends in Neurosciences, 36,* 3–13.

Bakhshi, K., & Chance, S. A. (2015). The neuropathology of schizophrenia: A selective review of past studies and emerging themes in brain structure and cytoarchitecture. *Neuroscience, 303,* 82–102.

Bale, T. L., & Epperson, C. N. (2015). Sex differences and stress across the lifespan. *Nature Neuroscience, 18,* 1413–1420.

Ball, G. F., & Balthazart, J. (2006). Androgen metabolism and the activation of male sexual behavior: It's more complicated than you think! *Hormones and Behavior, 49,* 1–3.

Balthazart, J. (2011). Minireview: Hormones and human sexual orientation. *Endocrinology, 152,* 2937–2947.

Baluch, F., & Itti, L. (2011). Mechanisms of top-down attention. *Trends in Neurosciences, 34,* 210–224.

Bandelow, B., & Michaelis, S. (2015). Epidemiology of anxiety disorders in the 21st century. *Dialogues in Clinical Neuroscience, 17,* 327.

Bandelow, B., Sher, L., Bunevicius, R., Hollander, E., Kasper, S., Zohar, J., Möller, H.-J., WFSBP Task Force on Mental Disorders in Primary Care, & WFSBP Task Force on Anxiety Disorders, OCD, and PTSD. (2012). Guidelines for the pharmacological treatment of anxiety disorders, obsessive-compulsive disorder and posttraumatic stress disorder in primary care. *International Journal of Psychiatry in Clinical Practice, 16,* 77–84.

Bangasser, D. A., & Valentino, R. J. (2014). Sex differences in stress-related psychiatric disorders: Neurobiological perspectives. *Frontiers in Neuroendocrinology, 35,* 303–319.

Bankiewicz, K. S., Plunkett, R. J., Jaconowitz, D. M., Porrino, L., di Porzio, U., London, W. T.,…&

Oldfield, E. H. (1990). The effect of fetal mesencephalon implants on primate MPTP-induced Parkinsonism: Histochemical and behavioral studies. *Journal of Neuroscience, 72,* 231–244.

Bao, A. M., & Swaab, D. F. (2011). Sexual differentiation of the human brain: Relation to gender identity, sexual orientation and neuropsychiatric disorders. *Frontiers in Neuroendocrinology, 32,* 214–226.

Bard P. (1929). The central representation of the sympathetic system. *Archives of Neurology and Psychiatry, 22,* 230–246.

Barik, J., Marti, F., Morel, C., Fernandez, S. P., Lanteri, C., Godeheu, G., Tassin, J.-P., Mombereau, C., Faure, P., & Tronche, F. (2013). Chronic stress triggers social aversion via glucocorticoid receptor in dopaminoceptive neurons. *Science, 339,* 332–335.

Barrett, L. F. (2006). Are emotions natural kinds? *Perspectives on Psychological Science, 1,* 28–58.

Barrett, L. F., & Satpute, A. B. (2013). Large-scale brain networks in affective and social neuroscience: Towards an integrative functional architecture of the brain. *Current Opinion in Neurobiology, 23,* 361–372.

Barretto, R. P. J., Gillis-Smith, S., Chandrashekar, J., Yarmolinsky, D. A.,...& Zuker, C. S. (2015). The neural representation of taste quality at the periphery. *Nature, 517,* 373–376.

Barrick, J. E., & Lenski, R. E. (2013). Genome dynamics during experimental evolution. *Nature Reviews Genetics, 14,* 827–839.

Barry, C., & Doeller, C. F. (2013). 3D mapping in the brain. *Science, 340,* 279–280.

Bartal, I. B.-A., Decety, J., & Mason, P. (2011). Empathy and pro-social behavior in rats. *Science, 334,* 1427–1430.

Bartsch, T., & Butler, C. (2013). Transient amnesic syndromes. *Nature Reviews Neurology, 9,* 86–97.

Barulli, D., & Stern, Y. (2013). Efficiency, capacity, compensation, maintenance, plasticity: Emerging concepts in cognitive reserve. *Trends in Cognitive Sciences, 17,* 502–509.

Basbaum, A. I., & Fields, H. L. (1978). Endogenous pain control mechanisms: Review and hypothesis. *Annals of Neurology, 4,* 451–462.

Basner, M. (2011). Sleep duration and chronic sleep debt: Are 6 hours enough? *Biological Psychology, 87,* 15–16.

Basner, M., Rao, H., Goel, N., & Dinges, D. F. (2013). Sleep deprivation and neurobehavioral dynamics. *Current Opinion in Neurobiology, 23,* 854–863.

Bassett, D. S., Yang, M., Wymbs, N. F., & Grafton, S. T. (2015). Learning-induced autonomy of sensorimotor systems. *Nature Neuroscience, 5,* 744–751.

Bastian, A. J. (2006). Learning to predict the future: The cerebellum adapts feedforward movement control. *Current Opinion in Neurobiology, 16,* 645–649.

Batalla, A., Bhattacharyya, S., Yücel, M., Fusar-Poli, P., Crippa, J. A., Nogué, S., Torrens, M., Pujol, J., Farré, M., & Martin-Santos, R. (2013). Structural and functional imaging studies in chronic cannabis users: A systematic review of adolescent and adult findings. *PLoS ONE, 8,* e55821.

Batelaan, N. M., Van Balkom, A. J. L. M., & Stein, D. J. (2012). Evidence-based pharmacotherapy of panic disorder: An update. *International Journal of Neuropsychopharmacology, 15,* 403–415.

Batrinos, M. L. (2012). Testosterone and aggressive behavior in man. *Endocrinology and Metabolism, 10,* 563–568.

Baudry, A., Mouillet-Richard, S., Launay, J. M., & Kellermann, O. (2011). New views on antidepressant action. *Current Opinion in Neurobiology, 21,* 858–865.

Bauer, P. R., Reitsma, J. B., Houweling, B. M., Ferrier, C. H., & Ramsey, N. F. (2014). Can fMRI safely replace the Wada test for preoperative assess-

ment of language lateralisation? A meta-analysis and systematic review. *Journal of Neurology, Neurosurgery & Psychiatry, 85,* 581–588.

Baura, G., Foster, D., Porte, D., Kahn, S. E., Bergman, R. N., Cobelli, C., & Schwartz, M. W. (1993). Saturable transport of insulin from plasma into the central nervous system of dogs in vivo: A mechanism for regulated insulin delivery to the brain. *Journal of Clinical Investigations, 92,* 1824–1830.

Bavelier, D., Corina, D., Jessard, P., Padmanabhan, S., Clark, V. P., Karni, A., et al. (1997). Sentence reading: A functional MRI study at 4 tesla. *Journal of Cognitive Neuroscience, 9,* 664–686.

Bean, B. P. (2007). The action potential in mammalian central neurons. *Nature Reviews Neuroscience, 8,* 451–465.

Beaton, A. A. (2003). The nature and determinants of handedness. In K. Hugdahl and R. J. Davidson (Eds.), *The asymmetrical brain* (pp. 105–158). Cambridge, MA: Bradford Books/MIT Press.

Beaulieu, J. M., Espinoza, S., & Gainetdinov, R. R. (2015). Dopamine receptors–IUPHAR review 13. *British Journal of Pharmacology, 172,* 1–23.

Bechara, A., Tranel, D., Damasio, H., Adolphs, R., Rockland, C., & Damasio, A. R. (1995). Double dissociation of conditioning and declarative knowledge relative to the amygdala and hippocampus in humans. *Science, 269,* 1115–1118.

Bechtold, D. A., & Loudon, A. S. I. (2012). Hypothalamic clocks and rhythms in feeding behaviour. *Trends in Neurosciences, 36,* 74–82.

Bedi, G., Hyman, D., & de Wit, H. (2010). Is ecstasy an "empathogen"? Effects of ±3,4—methylenedioxymethamphetamine on prosocial feelings and identification of emotional states in others. *Biological Psychiatry, 68,* 1134–1140.

Bedi, G., Preston, K. L., Epstein, D. H., Heishman, S. J., Marrone, G. F., Shaham, Y., & de Wit, H. (2011). Incubation of cue-induced cigarette craving during abstinence in human smokers. *Biological Psychiatry, 69,* 708–711.

Begg, D. P., & Woods, S. C. (2013). The endocrinology of food intake. *Nature Reviews Endocrinology, 9,* 584–597.

Beggs, S., & Salter, M. W. (2010). Microglia-neuronal signalling in neuropathic pain hypersensitivity 2.0. *Current Opinion in Neurobiology, 20,* 474–480.

Behrensmeyer, A. K. (2006). Climate change and human evolution. *Science, 311,* 476–478.

Behrmann, M., Avidan, G., Marotta, J. J., & Kimchi, R. (2005). Detailed exploration of face-related processing in congenital prosopagnosia: 1. Behavioral findings. *Journal of Cognitive Neuroscience, 17,* 1130–1149.

Bekkers, J. M., & Suzuki, N. (2013). Neurons and circuits for odor processing in the piriform cortex. *Trends in Neurosciences, 36,* 429–438.

Bell, C. C., Han, V., & Sawtell, N. B. (2008). Cerebellum-like structures and their implications for cerebellar function. *Annual Review of Neuroscience, 31,* 1–24.

Bell, J. T., & Saffery, R. (2012). The value of twins in epigenetic epidemiology. *International Journal of Epidemiology,* dyr179.

Bell, J. T., & Spector, T. D. (2011). A twin approach to unraveling epigenetics. *Trends in Genetics, 27,* 116–125.

Bell, K. F. S., & Hardingham, G. E. (2011). The influence of synaptic activity on neuronal health. *Current Opinion in Neurobiology, 21,* 299–305.

Belle, M. D. C., & Piggins, H. D. (2012). Circadian time redoxed. *Science, 337,* 805–806.

Belousov, A. B. (2011). The regulation and role of neuronal gap junctions during development. *Communicative & Integrative Biology, 4,* 579–581.

Belousov, A. B., & Fontes, J. D. (2013). Neuronal gap junctions: Making and breaking connections during development and injury. *Trends in Neurosciences, 36,* 227–236.

Ben-Shakhar, G. (2012). Current research and potential applications of the concealed

information test: An overview. *Frontiers in Psychology, 3,* 342.

Benarroch, E. E. (2013). Oxytocin and vasopressin: Social neuropeptides with complex neuromodulatory functions. *Neurology, 80,* 1521–1528.

Bendor, D., & Wang, X. (2005). The neuronal representation of pitch in primate auditory cortex. *Nature, 436,* 1161–1165.

Bendor, D., & Wang, S. (2006). Cortical representations of pitch in monkeys and humans. *Current Opinion in Neurobiology, 16,* 391–399.

Benedetti, F. (2014). Placebo effects: From the neurobiological paradigm to translational implications. *Neuron, 84,* 623–637.

Bennett, M. V. L., Contreras, J. E., Bukauskas, F. F., & Saez, J. C. (2003). New roles for astrocytes: Gap junction hemichannels have something to communicate. *Trends in Neurosciences, 26,* 610–617.

Bensmaia, S. J., & Miller, L. E. (2014). Restoring sensorimotor function through intracortical interfaces: Progress and looming challenges. *Nature Reviews Neuroscience, 15,* 313–325.

Benson, D. F. (1985). Aphasia. In K. M. Heilman & E. Valenstein (Eds.), *Clinical neuropsychology* (pp. 17–47). New York, NY: Oxford University Press.

Bentivoglio, M., & Kristensson, K. (2014). Tryps and trips: Cell trafficking across the 100-year-old blood-brain barrier. *Trends in Neurosciences, 37,* 325–333.

Bentivoglio, M., Mariotti, R., & Bertini, G. (2011). Neuroinflammation and brain infections: Historical context and current perspectives. *Brain Research Reviews, 66,* 152–173.

Benton, A. L. (1994). Neuropsychological assessment. *Annual Review of Psychology, 45,* 1–23.

Berardi, N., Sale, A., & Maffei, L. (2014). Brain structural and functional development: genetics and experience. *Developmental Medicine and Child Neurology, 57*(Suppl. 2), 4–9.

Berg, A. T., & Millichap, J. J. (2013). The 2010 revised classification of seizures and epilepsy. *Continuum, 19,* 571–597.

Berger, J. R., & Dean, D. (2014). Neurosyphilis. *Handbook of Clinical Neurology, 121,* 1461–1472.

Berger, R. J., & Oswald, I. (1962). Effects of sleep deprivation on behaviour, subsequent sleep, and dreaming. *Journal of Mental Science, 106,* 457–465.

Bergles, D. E., Jabs, R., & Steinhauser, C. (2010). Neuron-glia synapses in the brain. *Brain Research Reviews, 63,* 130–137.

Bergmann, O., & Frisén, J. (2013). Why adults need new brain cells. *Science, 340,* 695–696.

Berlim, M. T., Van den Eynde, F., & Daskalakis, Z. J. (2013). Clinically meaningful efficacy and acceptability of low-frequency repetitive transcranial magnetic stimulation (rTMS) for treating primary major depression: A meta-analysis of randomized, double-blind and sham-controlled trials. *Neuropsychopharmacology, 38,* 543–551.

Berlim, M. T., Van den Eynde, F., Tovar-Perdomo, S., & Daskalakis, Z. J. (2014). Response, remission and drop-out rates following high-frequency repetitive transcranial magnetic stimulation (rTMS) for treating major depression: A systematic review and meta-analysis of randomized, double-blind and sham-controlled trials. *Psychological Medicine, 44,* 225–239.

Berndt, A., & Deisseroth, K. (2015). Expanding the optogenetics toolkit. *Science, 349,* 590–591.

Bernhardt, B. C., & Singer, T. (2012). The neural basis of empathy. *Annual Review of Neuroscience, 35,* 1–23.

Bernstein, I. L., & Webster, M. M. (1980). Learned taste aversion in humans. *Physiology & Behavior, 25,* 363–366.

Berridge, K. C. (2004). Motivation concepts in behavioral neuroscience. *Physiology & Behavior, 81,* 179–209.

Berridge, K. C., & Kringelbach, M. L. (2015). Pleasure systems in the brain. *Neuron, 86,* 646–664.

Berridge, K. C., Robinson, T. E., & Aldridge, J. W. (2009). Dissecting components of reward: "Liking," "wanting," and learning. *Current Opinion in Pharmacology, 9*, 65–73.

Berthoud, H.-R. (2002). Multiple neural systems controlling food intake and body weight. *Neuroscience and Biobehavioural Reviews, 26*, 393–428.

Berthoud, H.-R. (2013). Why does gastric bypass surgery work? *Science, 341*, 351–352.

Bertram, E. H. (2014). Extratemporal lobe circuits in temporal lobe epilepsy. *Epilepsy & Behavior, 38*, 13–18.

Betley, J. N., Xu, S., Cao, Z. F. H., Gong, R., Magnus, C. J., Yu, Y., & Sternson, S. M. (2015). Neurons for hunger and thirst transmit a negative-valence teaching signal. *Nature, 521*, 180–185.

Bhati, M. T. (2013). Defining psychosis: the evolution of DSM-5 schizophrenia spectrum disorders. *Current Psychiatry Reports, 15*, 1–7.

Bi, G.-Q., & Poo, M.-M. (2001). Synaptic modification by correlated activity: Hebb's postulate revisited. *Annual Review of Neuroscience, 24*, 139–166.

Bichot, N. P., Heard, M. T., DeGennaro, E. M., & Desimone, R. (2015). A source for feature-based attention in the prefrontal cortex. *Neuron, 88*, 832–844.

Bidelman, G. M., & Grall, J. (2014). Functional organization for musical consonance and tonal pitch hierarchy in human auditory cortex. *NeuroImage, 101*, 204–214.

Billiard, M., Jaussent, I., Dauvilliers, Y., & Besset, A. (2011). Recurrent hypersomnia: A review of 339 cases. *Sleep Medicine Reviews, 15*, 247–257.

Billock, V. A., & Tsou, B. H. (2010, February). Seeing forbidden colors. *Scientific American, 302*, 72–77.

Bintu, L., Yong, J., Antebi, Y. E., McCue, K., Kazuki, Y., Uno, N.,…& Elowitz, M. B. (2016). Dynamics of epigenetic regulation at the single-cell level. *Science, 351*, 720–724.

Birney, E. (2012). Journey to the genetic interior. Interview by Stephen S. Hall. *Scientific American, 307*, 80–82.

Bishop, D. V. M. (2013). Cerebral asymmetry and language development: Cause, correlate, or consequence? *Science, 340*, 1302.

Biyani, S., Morgan, P. S., Hotchkiss, K., Cecchini, M., & Derkay, C. S. (2015). Autism spectrum disorder 101: A primer for pediatric otolaryngologists. *International Journal of Pediatric Otorhinolaryngology, 79*, 798–802.

Björkholm, C., & Monteggia, L. M. (2016). BDNF—a key transducer of antidepressant effects. *Neuropharmacology, 102*, 72–79.

Black, J. E., Isaacs, K. R., Anderson, B. J., Alcantara, A. A., & Greenough, W. T. (1990). Learning causes synaptogenesis, whereas motor activity causes angiogenesis, in cerebellar cortex of adult rats. *Proceedings of the National Academy of Science, USA, 87*, 5568–5572.

Blackburn, G. L. (2001). Pasteur's quadrant and malnutrition. *Nature, 409*, 397–401.

Blakemore, C., Clark, J. M., Nevalainen, T., Oberdorfer, M., & Sussman, A. (2012). Implementing the 3Rs in neuroscience research: A reasoned approach. *Neuron, 75*, 948–950.

Blakemore, S.-J. (2008). The social brain in adolescence. *Nature Reviews Neuroscience, 9*, 267–277.

Blanchard, D. C., & Blanchard, R. J. (1984). Affect and aggression: An animal model applied to human behavior. In D. C. Blanchard & R. J. Blanchard (Eds.), *Advances in the study of aggression* (pp. 1–62). Orlando, FL: Academic Press.

Blanchard, D. C., & Blanchard, R. J. (1988). Ethoexperimental approaches to the biology of emotion. *Annual Review of Psychology, 39*, 43–68.

Blanchard, D. C., Griebel, G., Pobbe, R., & Blanchard, R. J. (2011). Risk assessment as an evolved threat detection and analysis process. *Neuroscience and Biobehavioral Reviews, 35*, 991–998.

Blanchard, D. C., Summers, C. H., & Blanchard, R. J. (2013). The role of behavior in translational models for psychopathology: Functionality and dysfunctional behaviors. *Neuroscience & Biobehavioral Reviews, 37*, 1567–1577.

Blanchard, R., & Lippa, R. A. (2007). Birth order, sibling sex ratio, handedness, and sexual orientation of male and female participants in a BBC internet research project. *Archives of Sexual Behavior, 36*, 163–176.

Blanco, C., Secades-Villa, R., Garcia-Rodriguez, O., Labrador-Mendez, M., Wang, S., & Schwartz, R. P. (2013). Probability and predictors of remission from life-time prescription drug use disorders: Results from the national epidemiologic survey on alcohol and related conditions. *Journal of Psychiatric Research, 47*, 42–49.

Blanke, O., Landis, T., Safran, A. B., & Seeck, M. (2002). Direction-specific motion blindness induced by focal stimulation of human extrastriate cortex. *European Journal of Neuroscience, 15*, 2043–2048.

Blanke, O., Slater, M., & Serino, A. (2015). Behavioral, neural, and computational principles of bodily self-consciousness. *Neuron, 88*, 145–166.

Blankenship, A. G., & Feller, M. B. (2010). Mechanisms underlying spontaneous patterned activity in developing neural circuits. *Nature Reviews Neuroscience, 11*, 18–29.

Blashfield, R. K., Keeley, J. W., Flanagan, E. H., & Miles, S. R. (2014). The cycle of classification: DSM-I through DSM-5. *Annual Review of Clinical Psychology, 10*, 25–51.

Blesa, J., Phani, S., Jackson-Lewis, V., & Przedborski, S. (2012). Classic and new animal models of Parkinson's disease. *Journal of Biomedicine and Biotechnology, 2012*, article 845618.

Bless, J. J., Westerhausen, R., von Koss Torklidsen, J., Gudmundsen, M., Kompus, K., & Hughdahl, K. (2015). Laterality across languages: Results from a global dichotic listening study using a smartphone application. *Laterality, 20*, 434–452.

Bliss, T. V. P., & Collingridge, G. L. (2013). Expression of NMDA receptor-dependent LTP in the hippocampus: Bridging the divide. *Molecular Brain, 6*, 5.

Bliss, T. V. P., & Lømø, T. (1973). Long-lasting potentiation of synaptic transmission in the dentate area of the anaesthetized rabbit following stimulation of the perforant path. *Journal of Physiology, 232*, 331–356.

Bloch, G. J., & Mills, R. (1995). Prepubertal testosterone treatment of neonatally gonadectomized male rats: Defeminization and masculinization of behavioral and endocrine function in adulthood. *Neuroscience and Behavioral Reviews, 19*, 187–200.

Bloch, G. J., Mills, R., & Gale, S. (1995). Prepubertal testosterone treatment of female rats: Defeminization of behavioral and endocrine function in adulthood. *Neuroscience and Biobehavioural Reviews, 19*, 177–186.

Block, M. L., & Calderón-Garcidueñas, L. (2009). Air pollution: Mechanisms of neuroinflammation and CNS disease. *Trends in Neurosciences, 32*, 506–511.

Blüher, M., & Mantzoros, C. S. (2015). From leptin to other adipokines in health and disease: Facts and expectations at the beginning of the 21st century. *Metabolism, 61*, 131–145.

Blundell, J. E., & Finlayson, G. (2004). Is susceptibility to weight gain characterized by homeostatic or hedonic risk factors for overconsumption? *Physiology & Behavior, 82*, 21–25.

Blundell, J. E., & Halford, J. C. G. (1998). Serotonin and appetite regulation. *CNS Drugs, 9*, 473–495.

Boets, B., de Beeck, H. P. O., Vandermosten, M., Scott, S. K., Gillebert, C. R., Mantini, D.,…& Ghesquière, P. (2013). Intact but less accessible phonetic representations in adults with dyslexia. *Science, 342*, 1251–1254.

Bogaert, A. F. (2006). Biological versus nonbiological older brothers and men's sexual orientation. *Proceedings of the National Academy of Sciences, USA, 103*, 10771–10774.

Bogaert, A. F., & Skorska, M. (2011). Sexual orientation, fraternal birth order, and the maternal immune hypothesis: A review. *Frontiers in Neuroendocrinology, 32*, 247–254.

Bogen, J. G., & Bogen, G. M. (1976). Wernicke's region—where is it? *Annals of the New York Academy of Science, 280*, 834–843.

Boles, D. B., & Barth, J. M. (2011). "Does degree of asymmetry relate to performance?" A critical review. *Brain and Cognition, 76*, 1–4.

Bolhuis, J. J., & Moorman, S. (2015). Birdsong memory and the brain: In search of the template. *Neuroscience and Biobehavioral Reviews, 50*, 41–55.

Bolles, R. C. (1980). Some functionalistic thought about regulation. In F. M. Toates & T. R. Halliday (Eds.), *Analysis of motivational processes* (pp. 63–75). London, England: Academic Press.

Bolton, M. M., & Eroglu, C. (2009). Look who is weaving the neural web: Glial control of synapse formation. *Current Opinion in Neurobiology, 19*, 491–497.

Bonin, R. P., & De Koninck, Y. (2015). Reconsolidation and the regulation of plasticity: Moving beyond memory. *Trends in Neurosciences, 38*, 336–344.

Bonini, L., & Ferrari, P. F. (2011). Evolution of mirror systems: A simple mechanism for complex cognitive functions. *Annals of the New York Academy of Sciences, 1225*, 166–175.

Bonnamain, V., Neveu, I., & Naveilhan, P. (2012). Neural stem/progenitor cells as promising candidates for regenerative therapy of the central nervous system. *Frontiers in Cellular Neuroscience, 6*, 17.

Bonnel, A., Mottron, L., Peretz, I., Trudel, M., Gallun, E., & Bonnel, A. M. (2003). Enhanced pitch sensitivity in individuals with autism: A signal detection analysis. *Journal of Cognitive Neuroscience, 15*, 226–235.

Booth, D. A. (1981). The physiology of appetite. *British Medical Bulletin, 37*, 135–140.

Borbély, A. A. (1983). Pharmacological approaches to sleep regulation. In A. R. Mayes (Ed.), *Sleep mechanisms and functions in humans and animals* (pp. 232–261). Wokingham, England: Van Nostrand Reinhold.

Borodinsky, L. N., Belgacem, Y. H., & Swapna, I. (2012). Electrical activitiy as a developmental regulator in the formation of spinal cord circuits. *Current Opinion in Neurobiology, 22*, 624–630.

Boroviak, T., & Nichols, J. (2014). The birth of embryonic pluripotency. *Philosophical Transactions of the Royal Society B, 369*, 2.

Borrell, V., & Götz, M. (2014). Role of radial glial cells in cerebral cortex folding. *Current Opinion in Neurobiology, 27*, 39–46.

Bottjer, D. J. (2005, August). The early evolution of animals. *Scientific American, 293*, 43–47.

Bouchard, D. (2015). Brain readiness and the nature of language. *Frontiers in Psychology, 6*, 1376.

Bouchard, T. J., Jr. (1998). Genetic and environmental influences on adult intelligence and special mental abilities. *Human Biology, 70*, 257–279.

Bouchard, T. J., Jr., & Pederson, N. L. (1999). Twins reared apart: Natures double experiment. In M. C. LaBuda & E. L. Grigorenko (Eds.), *Current Methodological Issues in Behavioral Genetics* (pp. 71–93). Commack, N. Y.: Nova Scientific.

Bourgeois, J., Elseviers, M. M., Van Bortel, L., Petrovic, M., & Vander Stichele, R. H. (2014). One-year evolution of sleep quality in older users of benzodiazepines: A longitudinal cohort study in Belgian nursing home residents. *Drugs & Aging, 31*, 677–682.

Bourgeron, T. (2015). From the genetic architecture to synaptic plasticity in autism spectrum disorder. *Nature Reviews Neuroscience, 16*, 551–563.

Bourne, J. N., & Harris, K. M. (2012). Nanoscale analysis of structural synaptic plasticity. *Current Opinion in Neurobiology, 22*, 372–382.

Bourne, V. J. (2010). How are emotions lateralised in the brain? Contrasting exisiting hypotheses using the chimeric faces test. *Cognition and Emotion, 24*, 903–911.

Bouzier-Sore, A-K., & Pellerin, L. (2013). Unraveling the complex metabolic nature of astrocytes. *Frontiers in Cellular Neuroscience, 7*, 179.

Bowler, P. J. (2009). Darwin's originality. *Science, 323*, 223–226.

Boyden, E. S. (2014, November/December). Let there be light. *Scientific American Mind*, 62–69.

Boyden, E. S. (2015). Optogenetics and the future of neuroscience. *Nature Neuroscience, 18*, 1200–1201.

Boys, A., & Marsden, J. (2003). Perceived functions predict intensity of use and problems in young polysubstance users. *Addiction, 98*, 951–963.

Brackett, N. L., & Edwards, D. A. (1984). Medial preoptic connections with the midbrain tegmentum are essential for male sexual behavior. *Physiology & Behavior, 32*, 79–84.

Bradke, F., Fawcett, J. W., & Spira, M. E. (2012). Assembly of a new growth cone after axotomy: The precursor to axon regeneration. *Nature Reviews Neuroscience, 13*, 183–192.

Bragatti, J. A., Torres, C. M., Abrahim, C., Leistner-Segal, S., & Bianchin, M. M. (2014). Is interictal EEG activity a biomarker for mood disorders in temporal lobe epilepsy? *Clinical Neurophysiology, 125*, 1952–1958.

Braidy, N., Poljak, A., Jayasena, T., Mansour, H., Inestrosa, N. C., & Sachdev, P. S. (2015). Accelerating Alzheimer's reserach through "natural" animal models. *Current Opinion in Psychiatry, 28*, 155–164.

Brainard, M. S., & Doupe, A. J. (2013). Translating birdsong: Songbirds as a model for basic and applied medical research. *Annual Review of Neuroscience, 36*, 489–517.

Brambati, S. M., Myers, D., Wilson, A., Rankin, K. P., Allison, S. C., Rosen, H. J.,... & Gorno-Tempini, M. L. (2006). The anatomy of category-specific object naming in neurodegenerative diseases. *Journal of Cognitive Neuroscience, 18*, 1644–1653.

Brancaccio, M., Enoki, R., Mazuski, C. N., Jones, J., Evans, J. A., & Azzi, A. (2014). Network-mediated encoding of circadian time: The suprachiasmatic nucleus (SCN) from genes to neurons to circuits, and back. *Journal of Neuroscience, 34*, 15192–15199.

Brandon, N. J., & McKay, R. (2015). The cellular target of antidepressants. *Nature Neuroscience, 18*, 1537–1538.

Brang, D., Taich, Z. J., Hillyard, S. A., Grabowecky, M., & Ramachandran, V. S. (2013). Parietal connectivity mediates multisensory facilitation. *NeuroImage, 78*, 396–401.

Brann, J. H., & Firestein, S. J. (2014). A lifetime of neurogenesis in the olfactory system. *Frontiers in Neuroscience, 8*, 182.

Braskie, M. N., & Thompson, P. M. (2013). Understanding cognitive deficits in Alzheimer's disease based on neuroimaging findings. *Trends in Cognitive Sciences, 17*, 510–516.

Braver, T. S., Cole, M. W., & Yarkoni, T. (2010). Vive les differences! Individual variation in neural mechanisms of executive control. *Current Opinion in Neurobiology, 20*, 242–250.

Bray, N. J., Leweke, F. M., Kapur, S., & Meyer-Lindenberg, A. (2010). The neurobiology of schizophrenia: New leads and avenues for treatment. *Current Opinion in Neurobiology, 20*, 810–815.

Brecher, E. M. (1972). *Licit and illicit drugs.* Boston, MA: Little, Brown.

Brecht, M., & Freiwald, W. A. (2012). The many facets of facial interactions in mammals. *Current Opinion in Neurobiology, 22*, 259–266.

Bremen, P., & Middlebrooks, J. C. (2013). Weighting of spatial and spectro-temporal cues for auditory scene analysis by human listeners. *PLoS ONE, 8*, e59815.

Bremer, F. (1936). Nouvelles recherches sur le mécanisme du sommeil. *Comptes rendus de la Société de Biologie, 22*, 460–464.

Bremer, F. L. (1937). L'activité cérébrale au cours du sommeil et de la narcose. Contribution à l'étude du mécanisme du sommeil. *Bulletin de l'Académie Royale de Belgique, 4*, 68–86.

Bremer, J. (1959). *Asexualization.* New York, NY: Macmilan.

Brenner, S. (2012). The revolution in the life sciences. *Science, 338*, 1427–1428.

Bressler, S. L., & Richter, C. G. (2015). Interareal oscillatory synchronization in top-down neocortical processing. *Current Opinion in Neurobiology, 31*, 62–66.

Brettschneider, J., Del Tredici, K., Lee, V. M. Y., & Trojanowski, J. Q. (2015). Spreading of pathology in neurodegenerative diseases: A focus on human studies. *Nature Reviews Neuroscience, 16*, 109–120.

Brewster, J. M. (1986). Prevalence of alcohol and other drug problems among physicians. *Journal of the American Medical Association, 255*, 1913–1920.

Brichta, L., Greengard, P., & Flajolet, M. (2013). Advances in the pharmacological treatment of Parkinson's disease: Targeting neurotransmitter systems. *Trends in Neurosciences, 36*, 543–554.

Brinker, T., Stopa, E., Morrison, J., & Klinge, P. (2014). A new look at cerebrospinal fluid circulation. *Fluids and Barriers of the CNS, 11*, 10.

Brooks, M. J., & Melnik, G. (1995). The refeeding syndrome: An approach to understanding its complications and preventing its occurrence. *Pharmacotherapy, 15*, 713–726.

Brooks, S. P., & Dunnett, S. B. (2009). Tests to assess motor phenotype in mice: A user's guide. *Nature Reviews Neuroscience, 10*, 519–528.

Brooks, V. B. (1986). *The neural basis of motor control.* New York, NY: Oxford University Press.

Brown, G. C., & Neher, J. J. (2014). Microglial phagocytosis of live neurons. *Nature Reviews Neuroscience, 15*, 209–216.

Brown, J. W., & Braver, T. S. (2005). Learned predictions of error likelihood in the anterior cingulate cortex. *Science, 307*, 1118–1121.

Brown, L. K. (2012). Can sleep deprivation studies explain why human adults sleep? *Current Opinion in Pulmonary Medicine, 18*, 541–545.

Brown, R. D., & Broderick, J. P. (2014). Unruptured intracranial aneurysms: Epidemiology, natural history, management options, and familial screening. *The Lancet Neurology, 13*, 393–404.

Brown, R. E. (1994). *An introduction to neuroendocrinology.* Cambridge, England: Cambridge University Press.

Brown, R. E., & Milner, P. M. (2003). The legacy of Donald Hebb: More than the Hebb synapse. *Nature Reviews Neuroscience, 4*, 1013–1019.

Brunoni, A. R., Nitsche, M. A., Bolognini, N., Bikson, M., Wagner, T., Merabet, L.,... & Ferrucci, R. (2012). Clinical research with transcranial direct current stimulation (tDCS): Challenges and future directions. *Brain Stimulation, 5*, 175–195.

Bucci, T. J. (1992). Dietary restriction: Why all the interest? An overview. *Laboratory Animal, 21*, 29–34.

Buckingham-Howes, S., Berger, S. S., Scaletti, L. A., & Black, M. M. (2013). Systematic review of prenatal cocaine exposure and adolescent development. *Pediatrics, 131*, e1917.

Buckley, M. J., & Gaffan, D. (1998). Perirhinal cortex ablation impairs visual object identification. *Journal of Neuroscience, 18*(6), 2268–2275.

Buckner, R. L. (2013). The cerebellum and cognitive function: 25 years of insight from anatomy and neuroimaging. *Neuron, 80*, 807–815.

Budday, S., Steinmann, P., & Kuhl, E. (2015). Physical biology of human brain development. *Frontiers in Cellular Neuroscience, 9*, 257.

Buitrago-Delgado, E., Nordin, K., Rao, A., Geary, L., & LaBonne, C. (2015). Shared regulatory programs suggest retention of blastula-stage potential in neural crest cells. *Science, 348*, 1332–1335.

Burda, J. E., & Sofroniew, M. V. (2014). Reactive gliosis and the multicellular response to CNS damage and disease. *Neuron, 81*, 229–248.

Burke, D. (2014). Why isn't everyone an evolutionary psychologist? *Frontiers in Psychology, 5*, 910.

Burke, D. (2014). Why isn't everyone an evolutionary psychologist? *Frontiers in Psychology, 5*, 1–8.

Burns, J. K. (2013). Pathways from cannabis to psychosis: A review of the evidence. *Frontiers in Psychiatry, 4*, 128.

Busche, M. A., Grienberger, C., Keskin, A. D., Song, B., Neumann, U., Staufenbiel, M.,... & Konnerth, A. (2015). Decreased amyloid-beta and increased neuronal hyperactivity by immunotherapy in Alzheimer's models. *Nature Neuroscience, 18*, 1725–1728.

Buschman, T. J. (2015). Paying attention to the details of attention. *Neuron, 86*, 1111–1113.

Bush, D., Barry, C., & Burgess, N. (2014). What do grid cells contribute to place cell firing? *Trends in Neurosciences, 37*, 136–145.

Bushnell, M. C., Čeko, M., & Low, L. A. (2013). Cognitive and emotional control of pain and its disruption in chronic pain. *Nature Reviews Neuroscience, 14*, 502–511.

Buss, D. M. (1992). Mate preference mechanisms: Consequences for partner choice and intrasexual competition. In J. M. Barkow, L. Cosmides, & J. Tooby (Eds.), *The adapted mind* (pp. 249–265). New York, NY: Oxford University Press.

Bussey, T. J., & Saksida, L. M. (2005). Object memory and perception in the medial temporal lobe: An alternative approach. *Current Opinion in Neurobiology, 15*, 730–737.

Bussey, T. J., Warburton, E. C., Aggleton, J. P., & Muir, J. L. (1998). Fornix lesions can facilitate acquisition of the transverse patterning task: A challenge for "configural" theories of hippocampal function. *Journal of Neuroscience, 18*(4), 1622–1631.

Buzsáki, G. (2005). Similar is different in hippocampal networks. *Science, 309*, 568–569.

Cabezas, R., Avila, M., Gonzalez, J., El-Bachá, R. S., Báez, E., et al. (2014). Astrocytic modulation of blood brain barrier: Perspectives on Parkinson's disease. *Frontiers in Cellular Neuroscience, 8*, 211.

Cacioppo, J. T., & Decety, J. (2009). What are the brain mechanisms on which psychological processes are based? *Perspectives on Psychological Science, 4*, 10–18.

Cafferty, W. B. J., McGee, A. W., & Strittmatter, S. M. (2008). Axonal growth therapeutics: Regeneration or sprouting or plasticity? *Trends in Neurosciences, 31*, 215–220.

Caggiula, A. R. (1970). Analysis of the copulation-reward properties of posterior hypothalamic stimulation in male rats. *Journal of Comparative and Physiological Psychology, 70*, 399–412.

Cahana-Amitay, D., & Albert, M. L. (2014). Brain and language: Evidence for neural multifunctionality. *Behavioural Neurology, 2014*, 260–381.

Cahill, L. (2006). Why sex matters for neuroscience. *Nature Reviews Neuroscience, 7*, 477–484.

Cahill, L. (2014). Equal ≠ the same: Sex differences in the human brain. *Cerebrum, April 2014*, 1–19.

Cai, N., Bigdeli, T. B., Kretzschmar, W., Li, Y., Liang, J., Song, L.,... & Wang, G. (2015). Sparse whole-genome sequencing identifies two loci for major depressive disorder. *Nature, 523*, 588–591.

Cai, Q., & Van der Haegen, L. (2015). What can atypical language hemispheric specialization tell us about cognitive functions? *Neuroscience Bulletin, 31*, 220–226.

Cai, Y.-C., Lu, S., & Li, C.-Y. (2012). Interactions between surround suppression and interocular suppression in human vision. *PLoS ONE, 7*, e38093.

Calhoon, G. G., & Tye, K. M. (2015). Resolving the neural circuits of anxiety. *Nature Neuroscience, 18*, 1394–1404.

Calhoon, G. G., & Tye, K. M. (2015). Resolving the neural circuits of anxiety. *Nature Neuroscience, 18*, 1394–1404.

Calhoun, V. D., Miller, R., Pearlson, G., & Adal, T. (2014). The chronnectome: Time-varying connectivity networks as the next frontier in fMRI data discovery. *Neuron, 84*, 262–274.

Callaghan, B. L., Li, S., & Richardson, R. (2014). The elusive engram: What can infantile amnesia tell us about memory? *Trends in Neurosciences, 37*, 47–53.

Callaghan, R. C., Cunningham, J. K., Sykes, J., & Kish, S. J. (2012). Increased risk of Parkinson's disease in individuals hospitalized with conditions related to the use of methamphetamine or other amphetamine-type drugs. *Drug and Alcohol Dependence, 120*, 35–40.

Callaway, E., Sutikana, T., Roberts, R., Saptomo, W., Brown, P., et al. (2014). The discovery of *Homo floresiensis*: Tales of the hobbit. *Nature, 514*, 422–426.

Calmon, G., Roberts, N., Eldridge, P., & Thirion, J.-P. (1998). Automatic quantification of changes in the volume of brain structures. *Lecture Notes in Computer Science, 1496*, 761–769.

Calvo, M. G., & Nummenmaa, L. (2015). Perceptual and affective mechanisms in facial recognition: An integrative review. *Cognition and Emotion*, 1–26.

Camardese, G., Di Giuda, D., Di Nicola, M., Cocciolillo, F., Giordano, A., Janiri, L., & Guglielmo, R. (2014). Imaging studies on dopamine transporter and depression: A review of literature and suggestions for future research. *Journal of Psychiatric Research, 51*, 7–18.

Cameron, H. A., & Glover, L. R. (2015). Adult neurogenesis: Beyond learning and memory. *Annual Review of Psychology, 66*, 53–81.

Cameron, H. A., Woolley, C. S., McEwen, B. S., & Gould, E. (1993). Differentiation of newly born neurons and glia in the dentate gyrus of the adult rat. *Neuroscience, 56*, 337–344.

Caminiti, R., Innocenti, G. M., & Battaglia-Mayer, A. (2015). Organization and evolution of parieto-frontal processing streams in macaque monkeys and humans. *Neuroscience and Biobehavioral Reviews, 56*, 73–96.

Campbell, K. J., Crawford, D. A., Salmon, J., Carver, A., Garnett, S. P., & Baur, L. A. (2007). Associations between the home food environment and obesity-promoting eating behaviors in adolescence. *Obesity, 15*, 719–730.

Campbell, R., MacSweeney, M., & Waters, D. (2008). Sign language and the brain: A review. *Journal of Deaf Studies and Deaf Education, 13*, 3–20.

Campfield, L. A., Smith, F. J., Gulsez, Y., Devos, R., & Burn, J. (1995). Mouse Ob protein: Evidence for a peripheral signal linking adiposity and central neural networks. *Science, 269*, 546–550.

Campfield, L. A., & Smith, F. J. (1989). Transient declines in blood glucose signal meal initiation. *International Journal of Obesity, 14*, 15–31.

Can, A., Schulze, T. G., & Gould, T. D. (2014). Molecular actions and clinical pharmacogenetics of lithium therapy. *Pharmacology Biochemistry and Behavior, 123*, 3–16.

Candidi, M., Stienen, B. M., Aglioti, S. M., & de Gelder, B. (2015). Virtual lesion of right posterior superior temporal sulcus modulates conscious visual perception of fearful expressions in faces and bodies. *Cortex, 65*, 184–194.

Cang, J., & Feldheim, D. A. (2013). Developmental mechanisms of topographic map formation and alignment. *Annual Review of Neuroscience, 36*, 51–77.

Cannon, T. D. (2015). How schizophrenia develops: Cognitive and brain mechanisms underlying onset of psychosis. *Trends in Cognitive Sciences, 19*, 744–756.

Cannon, W. B., & Washburn, A. L. (1912). An explanation of hunger. *American Journal of Physiology, 29*, 441–454.

Canteras, N. S., Ribeiro-Barbosa, É. R., Goto, M., Cipolla-Nito, J., & Swanson, L. W. (2011). The retinohypothalamic tract: Comparison of axonal projection patterns from four major targets. *Brain Research Reviews, 65*, 150–183.

Cantor, J. M., Blanchard, R., Paterson, A. D., & Bogaert, A. F. (2004). How many gay men owe their sexual orientation to fraternal birth order? *Archives of Sexual Behavior, 31*, 63–71.

Cao, D., Marsh, J. C., Shun, H. C., & Andrews, C. M. (2011). Improving health and social outcomes with targeted services in comprehensive substance abuse treatment. *American Journal of Drug and Alcohol Abuse, 37*, 250–258.

Caporael, L. R. (2001). Evolutionary psychology: Toward a unifying theory and a hybrid science. *Annual Review of Psychology, 52*, 607–628.

Cappelletti, M., & Wallen, K. (2016). Increasing women's sexual desire: The comparative effectiveness of estrogens and androgens. *Hormones and Behavior, 78*, 178–193.

Cappuccio, F. P., D'Elia, L., Strazzullo, P., & Miller, M. A. (2008). Sleep duration and all-cause mortality: A systematic review and meta-analysis of prospective studies. *Sleep, 33*, 585–592.

Cappuccio, F. P., D'Elia, L., Strazzullo, P., & Miller, M. A. (2010). Sleep duration and all-cause mortality: A systematic review and meta-analysis of prospective studies. *Sleep, 33*, 585–592.

Caranci, F., Briganti, F., Cirillo, L., Leonardi, M., & Muto, M. (2013). Epidemiology and genetics of intracranial aneurysms. *European Journal of Radiology, 82*, 1598–1605.

Carbon, M., & Correll, C. U. (2014). Thinking and acting beyond the positive: The role of the cognitive and negative symptoms in schizophrenia. *CNS Spectrums, 19*, 35–53.

Cardinal, R. N., & Everitt, B. J. (2004). Neural and psychological mechanisms underlying appetitive learning: Links to drug addiction. *Current Opinion in Neurobiology, 14*, 156–162.

Carlsson, A., & Lindqvist, M. (1963). Effect of chlorpromazine or haloperidol on formation of 3-methoxytyramine and normetanephrine in mouse brains. *Acta Pharmacologica et Toxicologica, 20*, 140–144.

Carman, A. J., Ferguson, R., Cantu, R., Comstock, R. D., Dacks, P. A.,…& Fillit, H. M. (2015). Mind the gaps—advancing research into short-term and long-term neuropsychological outcomes of youth sports-related concussions. *Nature Neurology, 11*, 230–244.

Carothers, B. J., & Reis, H. T. (2013). Men and women are from Earth: Examining the latent structure of gender. *Journal of Personality and Social Psychology, 104*, 385.

Carr, F. (2015). Neuropharmacology: Driving the urge to eat. *Nature Reviews Neuroscience, 16*, 185–185.

Carr, L., Iacoboni, M., Dubeau, M.-C., Mazziotta, J. C., & Lenzi, G. L. (2003). Neural mechanisms of empathy in humans: A relay from neural systems for imitation to limbic areas. *Proceedings of the National Academy of Sciences, USA, 100*, 5497–5502.

Carré, J. M., & Olmstead, N. A. (2015). Social neuroendocrinology of human aggression: Examining the role of competition-induced testosterone dynamics. *Neuroscience, 286*, 171–186.

Carroll, F., Blough, B., Mascarella, S., Navarro, H. A., Lukas, R. J., & Damaj, M. I. (2014). Bupropion and bupropion analogs as treatments for CNS disorders. *Advances in Pharmacology, 69*, 177–216.

Carroll, M. E., & Meisch, R. A. (1984). Increased drug-reinforced behavior due to food deprivation. *Advances in Behavioral Pharmacology, 4*, 47–88.

Carson, R. A., & Rothstein, M. A. (1999). *Behavioral genetics: The clash of culture and biology*. New York, NY: Worth.

Carter, J. R., & Goldstein, D. S. (2015). Sympathoneural and adrenomedullary responses to mental stress. *Comprehensive Physiology, 5*, 119–146.

Carvalho, A. F., Dimellis, D., Gonda, X., Vieta, E., McIntyre, R. S., & Fountoulakis, K. N. (2014). Rapid cycling in bipolar disorder: A systematic review. *Journal of Clinical Psychiatry, 75*, 1–478.

Carvalho, M., Carmo, H., Costa, V. M., Capela, J. P., Pontes, H., Remião, F., Carvalho, F., & Bastos, M. D. (2012). Toxicity of amphetamines: An update. *Archives of Toxicology, 86*, 1167–1231.

Casadio, P., Fernandes, C., Murray, R. M., & Di Forti, M. (2011). Cannabis use in young people: The risk of schizophrenia. *Neuroscience and Biobehavioral Reviews, 35*, 1779–1787.

Cascio, M. G., Zamberletti, E., Marini, P., Parolaro, D., & Pertwee, R. G. (2014). The phytocannabinoid, delta-9-tetrahydrocannabivarin, can act through 5-HT1A receptors to produce antipsychotic effects. *British Journal of Pharmacology, 172*, 1305–1318.

Casey, B. J. (2002). Windows into the human brain. *Science, 296*, 1408–1409.

Casey, B. J., Craddock, N., Cuthbert, B. N., Hyman, S. E., Lee, F. S., & Ressler, K. J. (2013). DSM-5 and RDoC: progress in psychiatry research? *Nature Reviews Neuroscience, 14*, 810–814.

Casey, D. A. J. (2013). Aetiology of auditory dysfunction in amusia: A systematic review. *International Archives of Medicine, 6*, 16.

Casey, L. (2013). Caring for children with phenylketonuria. *Canadian Family Physician, 59*, 837–840.

Castelblanco, R. L., Lee, M., & Hasbun, R. (2014). Epidemiology of bacterial meningitis in the USA from 1997 to 2010: A population-based observational study. *The Lancet Infectious Diseases, 14*, 813–819.

Castello, S., Revile, D. A., Molina, J. C., & Arias, C. (2014). Ethanol-induced tolerance and sex-dependent sensitization in preweanling rats. *Physiology & Behavior, 139*, 50–58.

Castrén, E., & Hen, R. (2013). Neuronal plasticity and antidepressant actions. *Trends in Neurosciences, 36*, 259–267.

Castro, G. D., & Castro, J. A. (2014). Alcohol drinking and mammary cancer: Pathogenesis and potential dietary preventive alternatives. *World Journal of Clinical Oncology, 5*, 713–729.

Catterall, W. A., Raman, I. M., Robinson, H. P. C., Sejnowski, T. J., & Paulsen, O. (2012). The Hodgkin-Huxley heritage: From channels to circuits. *Journal of Neuroscience, 32*, 14064–14073.

Cavaliere, C., Aiello, M., Di Perri, C., Fernandez-Espajo, D., Owen, A. M., & Soddu, A. (2015). Diffusion tensor imaging and white matter abnormalities in patients with disorders of consciousness. *Frontiers in Human Neuroscience, 8*, 1028.

Cecon, E., Chen, M., Marçola, M., Fernandes, P. A., Jockers, R., & Markus, R. P. (2015). Amyloid β peptide directly impairs pineal gland melatonin synthesis and melatonin receptor signaling through the ERK pathway. *FASEB Journal, 29*, 2566–2582.

Cedernaes, J., Schiöth, H. B., & Benedict, C. (2015). Determinants of shortened, disrupted, and mistimed sleep and associated metabolic health consequences in healthy humans. *Diabetes, 64*, 1073–1080.

Cepko, C. (2015). Intrinsically different retinal progenitor cells produce specific types of progeny. *Nature Reviews Neuroscience, 15*, 615–627.

Cermakian, N., & Sassone-Corsi, P. (2002). Environmental stimulus perception and control of circadian clocks. *Current Opinion in Neurobiology, 12*, 359–365.

Chalfie, M., Tu, Y., Euskirchen, G., Ward, W., & Prasher, D. (1994). Green fluorescent protein as a marker for gene expression. *Science, 263*, 802–805.

Champagne, D. L., Bagot, R. C., van Hasselt, F., Ramakers, G., Meaney, M. J., de Kloet, E. R.,…& Krugers, H. (2008). Maternal care and hippocampal plasticity: Evidence for experience-dependent structural plasticity, altered synaptic functioning, and differential responsiveness to glucocorticoids and stress. *Journal of Neuroscience, 28*, 6037–6045.

Chance, S. A. (2014). The cortical microstructural basis of lateralized cognition: A review. *Frontiers in Psychology, 5*, 820.

Chang, C. H., & Grace, A. A. (2015). Dopaminergic modulation of lateral amygdala neuronal activity: Differential D1 and D2 receptor effects on thalamic and cortical afferent inputs. *International Journal of Neuropsychopharmacology, 18*, pyv015.

Chang, C. Y., Esber, G. R., Marrero-Garcia, Y., Yau, H. J., Bonci, A., & Schoenbaum, G. (2016). Brief optogenetic inhibition of dopamine neurons mimics endogenous negative reward prediction errors. *Nature Neuroscience, 19*, 111–116.

Chang, S. H., Stoll, C. R., Song, J., Varela, J. E., Eagon, C. J., & Colditz, G. A. (2014). The effectiveness and risks of bariatric surgery: An updated systematic review and meta-analysis, 2003–2012. *JAMA Surgery, 149*, 275–287.

Changeux, J.-P. (2013). The concept of allosteric interaction and its consequences for the chemistry of the brain. *Journal of Biological Chemistry, 288*, 26969–26986.

Chapman, S., & MacKenzie, R. (2010). The global research neglect of unassisted smoking cessation: Causes and consequences. *PLoS Medicine, 7*, e1000216.

Charles, A. C., & Baca, S. M. (2013). Cortical spreading depression and migraine. *Nature Reviews Neurology, 9*, 637–644.

Charness, M. E., Riley, E. P., & Sowell, E. R. (2016). Drinking during pregnancy and the developing brain: Is any amount safe? *Trends in Cognitive Sciences, 20*, 80–82.

Chatburn, A., Lushington, K., & Kohler, M. J. (2014). Complex associative memory processing and sleep: A systematic review and meta-analysis of behavioural evidence and underlying EEG mechanisms. *Neuroscience & Biobehavioral Reviews, 47*, 646–655.

Chattarji, S., Tomar, A., Suvrathan, A., Ghosh, S., & Rahman, M. M. (2015). Neighborhood matters: Divergent patterns of stress-induced plasticity across the brain. *Nature Neuroscience, 18*, 1364–1375.

Chatterjee, A., & Morison, A. M. (2011). Monozygotic twins: Genes are not the destiny? *Bioinformation, 7*, 369–370.

Chatterjee, S., & Callaway, E. M. (2003). Parallel colour-opponent pathways to primary visual cortex. *Nature, 426*, 668–671.

Chaudhuri, K. R., & Sauerbier, A. (2016). Parkinson disease: Unravelling the nonmotor mysteries of Parkinson disease. *Nature Reviews Neurology, 12*, 10–11.

Chaudhari, N., & Roper, S. D. (2010). The cell biology of taste. *The Journal of Cell Biology, 190*, 285–296.

Chauvet, C., Goldberg, S. R., Jaber, M., & Solinas, M. (2012). Effects of environmental enrichment on the incubation of drug craving. *Neuropharmacology, 63*, 635–641.

Chauvet, C., Lardeux, V., Goldberg, S. R., Jaber, M., & Solinas, M. (2009). Environmental enrichment reduces cocaine seeking and reinstatement induced by cues and stress but not by cocaine. *Neuropsychopharmacology, 34*, 2767–2778.

Chavez, M., Seeley, R. J., & Woods, S. C. (1995). A comparison between the effects of intraventricular insulin and intraperitoneal LiCl on three measures sensitive to emetic agents. *Behavioral Neuroscience, 109*, 547–550.

Cheetham, C. E., & Belluscio, L. (2014). An olfactory critical period. *Science, 344*, 157–158.

Chelazzi, L., Libera, C. D., Sani, I., & Santandrea, E. (2010). Neural basis of visual selective attention. *Wiley Interdisciplinary Reviews: Cognitive Science, 2*, 392–407.

Chen, C. H., Suckling, J., Lennox, B. R., Ooi, C., & Bullmore, E. T. (2011). A quantitative meta-analysis of fMRI studies in bipolar disorder. *Bipolar Disorders, 13*, 1–15.

Chen, C.-C., Syue, K.-S., Li, K.-C., & Yeh, S.-C. (2014). Neuronal correlates of a virtual-reality-based passive P300 network. *PLoS ONE, 9*, e112228.

Chen, E., Hanson, M. D., Paterson, L. Q., Griffin, M. J., Walker, H. A., & Miller, G. E. (2006). Socioeconomic status and inflammatory processes in childhood asthma: The role of psychological stress. *Journal of Allergy and Clinical Immunology, 117*, 1014–1020.

Chen, I. (2013a). Lead's buried legacy. *Scientific American, 309*, 28–30.

Chen, I. (2013b). Scanning for Alzheimer's. *Scientific American, 309*, 30–31.

Chen, J. L., Margolis, D. J., Stankov, A., Sumanovski, L. T., Schneider, B. L., & Helmchen, F. (2015). Pathway-specific reorganization of projection neurons in somatosensory cortex during learning. *Nature Neuroscience, 18*, 1101–1108.

Chen, M. J., Axelrad, M., Dietrich, J. E., Gargollo, P., Gunn, S.,… & Karaviti, L. P. (2015). Androgen insensitivity syndrome: Management considerations from infancy to adulthood. *Pediatric Endocrinology Reviews, 12*, 373–387.

Chen, M., & Zheng, B. (2014). Axon plasticity in the mammalian central nervous system after injury. *Trends in Neurosciences, 37*, 583–593.

Chen, W. R., Midtgaard, J., & Shepherd, G. M. (1997). Forward and backward propagation of dendritic impulses and their synaptic control in mitral cells. *Science, 278*, 463–466.

Chen, X., Gabitto, M., Peng, Y., Ryba, N. J. P., & Zuker, C. S. (2011). A gustatopic map of taste qualities in the mammalian brain. *Science, 333*, 1262–1266.

Chen, Y., Kelton, C. M., Jing, Y., Guo, J. J., Li, X., & Patel, N. C. (2008). Utilization, price, and spending trends for antidepressants in the US medicaid program. *Research in Social and Administrative Pharmacy, 4*, 244–257.

Cheng, J., Cao, Y., & Olson, L. (1996). Spinal cord repair in adult paraplegic rats: Partial restoration of hind limb function. *Science, 273*, 510–513.

Cheung, K. J., & Ewald, A. J. (2016). A collective route to metastasis: Seeding by tumor cell clusters. *Science, 352*, 167–169.

Chica, A. B., Bartolomeo, P., & Lupiáñez, J. (2013). Two cognitive and neural systems for endogenous and exogenous spatial attention. *Behavioural Brain Research, 237*, 107–123.

Chisholm, N. C., & Sohrabji, F. (2015). Astrocytic response to cerebral ischemia is influenced by sex differences and impaired by aging. *Neurobiology of Disease, 85*, 245–253.

Chotard, C., & Salecker, I. (2004). Neurons and glia: Team players in axon guidance. *Trends in Neurosciences, 27*, 655–661.

Chouraki, V., & Seshadri, S. (2014). Genetics of Alzheimer's disease. *Advances in Genetics, 87*, 245–294.

Chow, B. W., & Gu, C. (2015). The molecular constituents of the blood–brain barrier. *Trends in Neurosciences, 38*, 598–608.

Christensen, R., Shao, Z., & Colón-Ramos, D. A. (2013). The cell biology of synaptic specificity during development. *Current Opinion in Neurobiology, 23*, 1018–1026.

Christian, K. M., Song, H., & Ming, G. L. (2014). Functions and dysfunctions of adult hippocampal neurogenesis. *Annual Review of Neuroscience, 37*, 243–262.

Christison-Lagay, K. L., & Cohen, Y. E. (2014). Behavioral correlates of auditory streaming in rhesus macaques. *Hearing Research, 309*, 17–25.

Christison-Lagay, K. L., Gifford, A. M., & Cohen, Y. E. (2015). Neural correlates of auditory scene analysis and perception. *International Journal of Psychophysiology, 95*, 238–245.

Chu, D. A., Williams, L. M., Harris, A. W. F., Bryant, R. A., & Gatt, J. M. (2012). Early life trauma predicts self-reported levels of depressive and anxiety symptoms in nonclinical community adults: Relative contributions of early life stressor types and adult trauma exposure. *Journal of Psychiatric Research, 47*, 23–32.

Chuang, A. T., Margo, C. E., & Greenberg, P. B. (2014). Retinal implants: A systematic review. *British Journal of Ophthalmology, 98*, 852–856.

Churchland, P. C. (2002). Self-representation in nervous systems. *Science, 296*, 308–310.

Churchland, P. S. (2014). Looking-glass wars. *Nature, 511*, 532–533.

Cirelli, C. (2009). The genetic and molecular regulation of sleep: From fruit flies to humans. *Nature Reviews Neuroscience, 10*, 549–560.

Cirelli, C. (2013). Sleep and synaptic changes. *Current Opinion in Neurobiology, 23*, 841–846.

Cisek, P., & Kalaska, J. F. (2010). Neural mechanisms for interacting with a world full of action choices. *Annual Review of Neuroscience, 33*, 269–298.

Citron, M. (2004). Strategies for disease modification in Alzheimer's disease. *Nature Reviews Neuroscience, 5*, 677–685.

Clark, L. (2014). Disordered gambling: The evolving concept of behavioural addiction. *Annals of the New York Academy of Sciences, 1327*, 46–61.

Clarke, L. E., & Barres, B. A. (2013). Emerging roles of astrocytes in neural circuit development. *Nature Reviews Neuroscience, 14*, 311–321.

Clifton, P. G. (2000). Meal patterning in rodents: Psychopharmacological and neuroanatomical studies. *Neuroscience and Biobehavioural Reviews, 24*, 213–222.

Clouard, C., Meunier-Salaün, M. C., & Val-Laillet, D. (2012). Food preferences and aversions in human health and nutrition: How can pigs help the biomedical research. *Animal, 6*, 118–136.

Cloud, L. J., Zutshi, D., & Factor, S. A. (2014). Tardive dyskinesia: Therapeutic options for an increasingly common disorder. *Neurotherapeutics, 11*, 166–176.

Cloutman, L. L. (2013). Interaction between dorsal and ventral processing streams: Where, when and how? *Brain and Language, 127*, 251–263.

Cloutman, L. L., Newhart, M., Davis, C. L., Heidler-Gary, J., & Hillis, A. E. (2011). Neuroanatomical correlates of oral reading in acute left hemispheric stroke. *Brain and Language, 116*, 14–21.

Clutton-Brock, T. H., & Huchard, E. (2013). Social competition and selection in males and females. *Philosophical Transactions of the Royal Society B, 368*, 20130074.

Cochet, H., & Byrne, R. W. (2013). Evolutionary origins of human handedness: Evaluating contrasting hypotheses. *Animal Cognition, 16*, 531–542.

Coen-Cagli, R., Kohn, A., & Schwartz, O. (2015). Flexible gating of contextual influences in natural vision. *Nature Neuroscience, 18*, 1648–1655.

Cogan, G. B., Thesen, T., Carlson, C., Doyle, W., Devinsky, O., & Pesaran, B. (2014). Sensory-motor transformations for speech occur bilaterally. *Nature, 507*, 94–98.

Cohen-Bendahan, C. C., van de Beek, C., & Berenbaum, S. A. (2005). Prenatal sex hormone effects on child and adult sex-typed behavior: Methods and findings. *Neuroscience & Biobehavioral Reviews, 29*, 353–384.

Cohen, J. (2007). Relative differences: The myth of 1%. *Science, 316*, 1836.

Cohen, S., Tyrrell, D. A. J., & Smith, A. P. (1991). Psychological stress and susceptibility to the common cold. *New England Journal of Medicine, 325*, 606–612.

Cohen, Y. E. (2009). Multimodal activity in the parietal cortex. *Hearing Research, 258*, 100–105.

Colapinto, J. (2000). *As nature made him: The boy who was raised as a girl.* New York, NY: HarperCollins.

Cole, J. C. (2014). MDMA and the "Ecstasy Paradigm." *Journal of Psychoactive Drugs, 46*, 44–56.

Cole, M. W., Yeung, N., Freiwald, W. A., & Botvinick, M. (2009). Cingulate cortex: Diverging data from humans and monkeys. *Trends in Neurosciences, 32*, 566–574.

Coleman, D. L. (1979). Obesity genes: Beneficial effects in heterozygous mice. *Science, 203*, 663–665.

Colgan, L. A., & Yasuda, R. (2014). Plasticity of dendritic spines: Subcompartmentalization of signaling. *Annual Review of Physiology, 76*, 365–385.

Collaer, M. L., Brook, C. G. D., Conway, G. S., Hindmarsh, P. C., & Hines, M. (2008). Motor development in individuals with congenital adrenal hyperplasia: Strength, targeting, and fine motor skill. *Psychoneuroendocrinology, 34*, 249–258.

Collier, G. (1986). The dialogue between the house economist and the resident physiologist. *Nutrition and Behavior, 3*, 9–26.

Collier, G. H. (1980). An ecological analysis of motivation. In F. M. Toates & T. R. Halliday (Eds.), *Analysis of motivational processes* (pp. 125–151). London, England: Academic Press.

Collin, T., Marty, A., & Llano, I. (2005). Presynaptic calcium stores and synaptic transmission. *Current Opinion in Neurobiology, 15*, 275–281.

Collinger, J. L., Wodlinger, B., Downey, J. E., Wang, W., Tyler-Kabara, E. C., ... & Schwartz, A. B. (2013). High-performance neuroprosthetic control by an individual with tetraplegia. *Lancet, 381*, 557–564.

Collins, J. A., & Olson, I. R. (2014). Beyond the FFA: The role of the ventral anterior temporal lobes in face processing. *Neuropsychologia, 61*, 65–79.

Colman, R. J., Beasley, T. M., Kemnitz, J. W., Johnson, S. C., Weindruch, R., & Anderson, R. M. (2014). Caloric restriction reduces age-related and all-cause mortality in rhesus monkeys. *Nature Communications, 5*, 3557.

Colombo, M., & Broadbent, N. (2000). Is the avian hippocampus a functional homologue of the mammalian hippocampus? *Neuroscience and Biobehavioural Reviews, 24*, 465–484.

Colvin, M. K., Dunbar, K., & Grafman, J. (2001). The effects of frontal lobe lesions on goal achievement in the water jug task. *Journal of Cognitive Neuroscience, 13*, 1129–1147.

Colwell, C. S. (2011). Linking neural activity and molecular oscillations in the SCN. *Nature Reviews Neuroscience, 12*, 553–569.

Conforti, L., Adalbert, R., & Coleman, M. P. (2007). Neuronal death: Where does the end begin? *Trends in Neurosciences, 30*, 159–166.

Conners, B. W., & Long, M. A. (2004). Electrical synapses in the mammalian brain. *Annual Review of Neuroscience, 27*, 393–418.

Connor, S. A., & Wang, Y. T. (2015). A place at the table: LTD as a mediator of memory genesis. *Neuroscientist, 1073858415588498.*

Cook, R., Bird, G., Catmur, C., Press, C., & Heyes, C. (2014). Mirror neurons: From origin to function. *Behavioral and Brain Sciences, 37*, 177–241.

Cooper, J. A. (2013). Mechanisms of cell migration in the nervous system. *Journal of Cell Biology, 202*, 725–734.

Cooper, R. M., & Zubek, J. P. (1958). Effects of enriched and restricted early environments on the learning ability of bright and dull rats. *Canadian Journal of Psychology, 12*, 159–164.

Cooper, S. A., Joshi, A. C., Seenan, P. J., Hadley, D. M., ... & Metcalfe, R. A. (2012). Akinetopsia: Acute presentation and evidence for persisting defects in motion vision. *Journal of Neurology, Neurosurgery and Psychiatry, 83*, 229–230.

Corballis, M. C. (2015). What's left in language? Beyond the classical model. *Annals of the New York Academy of Sciences, 1359*, 14–29.

Corbetta, M., Miezin, F. M., Dobmeyer, S., Shulman, G. L., & Petersen, S. E. (1990). Attentional modulation of neural processing of shape, color, and velocity in humans. *Science, 248*, 1556–1559.

Corina, D. P., Loudermilk, B. C., Detwiler, L., Martin, R. F., Brinkley, J. F., & Ojemann, G. (2010). Analysis of naming errors during cortical stimulation mapping: Implications for models of language representation. *Brain and Language, 115*, 101–112.

Corina, D. P., Poizner, H., Bellugi, U., Feinberg, T., Dowd, D., & O'Grady-Batch, L. (1992). Dissociation between linguistic and nonlinguistic gestural systems: A case for compositionality. *Brain and Language, 43*, 414–447.

Corkin, S. (2002). What's new with the amnesic patient H.M.? *Nature Reviews Neuroscience, 3*, 153–160.

Corkin, S., Milner, B., & Rasmussen, R. (1970). Somatosensory thresholds. *Archives of Neurology, 23*, 41–59.

Corsi, P. I. (1991). *The enchanted loom: Chapters in the history of neuroscience.* New York, NY: Oxford University Press.

Costafreda, S. G., Brammer, M. J., David, A. S., & Fu, C. H. Y. (2008). Predictors of amygdala activation during the processing of emotional stimuli: A meta-analysis of 385 PET and fMRI studies. *Brain Research Reviews, 58*, 57–70.

Costanzo, E. Y., Villarreal, M., Drucaroff, L. J., Ortiz-Villafañe, M., Castro, M. N., ... & Guinjoan, S. M. (2015). Hemispheric specialization in affective responses, cerebral dominance for language, and handedness: Lateralization of emotion, language, and dexterity. *Behavioural Brain Research, 288*, 11–19.

Cotman, C. W., Berchtold, N. C., & Christie, L.-A. (2007). Exercise builds brain health: Key roles of growth factor cascades and inflammation. *Trends in Neurosciences, 30*, 464–472.

Courchesne, E., & Pierce, K. (2005). Why the frontal cortex in autism might be talking only to itself: Local over-connectivity but long-distance disconnection. *Current Opinion in Neurobiology, 15*, 225–230.

Couzin-Frankel, J. (2013). When mice mislead. *Science, 342*, 922–925.

Cowan, W. M. (1979, September). The development of the brain. *Scientific American, 241*, 113–133.

Cox, J. J., Reimann, F., Nicholas, A. K., Thornton, G., Roberts, E., Springell, K., ... & Woods, C. G. (2006). An SCN9A channelopathy causes congenital inability to experience pain. *Nature, 444*, 894–898.

Craig, L. A., Hong, N. S., & McDonald, R. J. (2011). Revisiting the cholinergic hypothesis in the development of Alzheimer's disease. *Neuroscience and Biobehavioral Reviews, 35*, 1397–1409.

Crane, B. R. (2012). Nature's intricate clockwork. *Science, 337*, 165–166.

Crane, J. M., Murphy, P., Burrage, L., & Hutchens, D. (2013). Maternal and perinatal outcomes of extreme obesity in pregnancy. *Journal of Obstetrics and Gynaecology Canada, 35*, 606–611.

Crane, N. A., Schuster, R. M., Fusar-Poli, P., & Gonzalez, R. (2013). Effects of cannabis on neurocognitive functioning: Recent advances, neurodevelopment influences, and sex differences. *Neuropsychology Review, 23*, 117–137.

Creese, I., Burt, D. R., & Snyder, S. H. (1976). Dopamine receptor binding predicts clinical and pharmacological potencies of anti-schizophrenic drugs. *Science, 192*, 481–483.

Crepaldi, D., Berlingeri, M., Cattinelli, L., Borghese, N. A., Luzzatti, C., & Paulesu, E. (2013). Clustering the lexicon in the brain: A meta-analysis of the neurofunctional evidence on noun and verb processing. *Frontiers in Human Neuroscience, 7*, 303.

Crespo, C. S., Cachero, A. P., Jiménez, L. P., Barrios, V., & Ferreiro, E. A. (2014). Peptides and food intake. *Frontiers in Endocrinology, 5*, 58.

Cressey, D. (2015). The cannabis experiment. *Nature, 524*, 280–283.

Crisp, A. H. (1983). Some aspects of the psychopathology of anorexia nervosa. In P. L. Darby, P. E. Garfinkel, D. M. Garner, & D. V. Coscina (Eds.), *Anorexia nervosa: Recent developments in research* (pp. 15–28). New York, NY: Alan R. Liss.

Crisp, J., & Ralph, M. A. L. (2006). Unlocking the nature of the phonological-deep dyslexia continuum: The keys to reading aloud are in phonology and semantics. *Journal of Cognitive Neuroscience, 18*, 348–362.

Crone, E. A., & Dahl, R. E. (2012). Understanding adolescence as a period of social-affective engagement and goal flexibility. *Nature Reviews Neuroscience, 13*, 636–650.

Crossley, N. A., Constante, M., McGuire, P., & Power, P. (2010). Efficacy of atypical v. typical antipsychotics in the treatment of early psychosis: Meta-analysis. *British Journal of Psychiatry, 196*, 434–439.

Crowell, C. R., Hinson, R. E., & Siegel, S. (1981). The role of conditional drug responses in tolerance to the hypothermic effects of ethanol. *Psychopharmacology, 73*, 51–54.

Culbertson, F. M. (1997). Depression and gender. *American Psychologist, 52*, 25–31.

Culham, J. C., & Kanwisher, N. G. (2001). Neuroimaging of cognitive functions in human parietal cortex. *Current Opinion in Neurobiology, 11*, 157–163.

Curcio, G., Ferrara, M., & De Gennaro, L. (2006). Sleep loss, learning capacity and academic performance. *Sleep Medicine Reviews, 10*, 323–337.

Curry, A. (2009). Evolution: Creationist beliefs persist in Europe. *Science, 323*, 1159.

Curtin, K., Fleckenstein, A. E., Robison, R. J., Crookston, M. J., Smith, K. R., & Hanson, G. R. (2015). Methamphetamine/amphetamine abuse and risk of Parkinson's disease in Utah: A population-based assessment. *Drug and Alcohol Dependence, 146*, 30–38.

Curtiss, S. (1977). *Genie: A psycholinguistic study of a modern-day "wild child."* New York, NY: Academic Press.

Custers, R., & Aarts, H. (2010). The unconscious will: How the pursuit of goals operates outside of conscious awareness. *Science, 329*, 47–50.

Czeisler, C. A., Duffy, J. F., Shanahan, T. L., Brown, E. N., Mitchell, J. F., Rimmer, D. W., ... & Kronauer, R. E. (1999). Stability, precision, and near-24-hour period of the human circadian pacemaker. *Science, 284*, 2177–2181.

Czyz, W., Morahan, J. M., Ebers, G. C., & Ramagopalan, S. V. (2012). Genetic, environmental and stochastic factors in monozygotic twin discordance with a focus on epigenetic differences. *BMC Medicine, 10*, 1.

D'Ausilio, A., Maffongelli, L., Bartoli, E., Campanella, M., Ferrari, E., ... & Fadiga, L. (2014). Listening to speech recruits specific tongue motor synergies as revealed by transcranial magnetic stimulation and tissue-Doppler ultrasound imaging. *Philosophical Transactions of the Royal Society of London. Series B, Biological Sciences, 369*, 20130418.

D'Esposito, M., & Postle, B. R. (2015). The cognitive neuroscience of working memory. *Annual Review of Psychology, 66*, 115–142.

D'Souza, D., Cole, V., Farran, E. K., Brown, J. H., Humphreys, K., ... & Karmiloff-Smith, A. (2015). Face processing in Williams syndrome is already atypical in infancy. *Frontiers in Psychology, 6*, 760.

Daan, S., Honma, S., & Honma, K. (2013). Body temperature predicts the direction of internal desynchronization in humans isolated from time cues. *Journal of Biological Rhythms, 28*, 403–411.

Dalton, R. P., & Lomvardas, S. (2015). Chemosensory receptor specificity and regulation. *Annual Review of Neuroscience, 38*, 331–349.

Dalva, M. B., McClelland, A. C., & Kayser, M. S. (2007). Cell adhesion molecules: Signalling functions at the synapse. *Nature Reviews Neuroscience, 8*, 206–220.

Daly, M., & Wilson, M. (1983). *Sex, evolution, and behavior.* Boston, MA: Allard Grant Press.

Damasio, H. (1989). Neuroimaging contributions to the understanding of aphasia. In F. Boller &

J. Grafman (Eds.), *Handbook of neuropsychology* (Vol. 2, pp. 3–46). New York, NY: Elsevier.

Damasio, H., Grabowski, T. J., Tranel, D., Hichwa, R. D., & Damasio, A. R. (1996). A neural basis for lexical retrieval. *Nature, 380,* 499–505.

Damasio, H., Grabowski, T., Frank, R., Galaburda, A. M., & Damasio, A. R. (1994). The return of Phineas Gage: Clues about the brain from the skull of a famous patient. *Science, 264,* 1102–1105.

Dampney, R. A. (2015). Central mechanisms regulating coordinated cardiovascular and respiratory function during stress and arousal. *American Journal of Physiology-Regulatory, Integrative and Comparative Physiology, 309,* R429–R443.

Dance, A. (2015). Neuroscience: Connectomes make the map. *Nature, 526,* 147–149.

Dando, R., & Roper, S. D. (2009). Cell-to-cell communication in intact taste buds through ATP signalling from pannexin 1 gap junction hemichannels. *Journal of Physiology, 587,* 5899–5906.

Danna, J., & Velay, J. L. (2015). Basic and supplementary sensory feedback in handwriting. *Frontiers in Psychology, 6,* 169.

Darke, S., Duflou, J., & Torok, M. (2010). The comparative toxicology and major organ pathology of fatal methadone and heroin toxicity cases. *Drug and Alcohol Dependence, 106,* 1–6.

Darlison, M. G., & Richter, D. (1999). Multiple genes for neuropeptides and their receptors: Co-evolution and physiology. *Trends in Neurosciences, 22,* 81–88.

Daubert, E. A., & Condron, B. G. (2010). Serotonin: A regulator of neuronal morphology and circuitry. *Trends in Neurosciences, 33,* 424–434.

Dauvilliers, Y., Siegel, J. M., Lopez, R., Torontali, Z. A., & Peever, J. H. (2014). Cataplexy—clinical aspects, pathophysiology and management strategy. *Nature Reviews Neurology, 10,* 386–395.

Davare, M., Kraskov, A., Rothwell, J. C., & Lemon, R. N. (2011). Interactions between areas of the cortical grasping network. *Current Opinion in Neurobiology, 21,* 565–570.

Davidson, A. G., Chan, V., O'Dell, R., & Schieber, M. H. (2007). Rapid changes in throughput from single motor cortex neurons to muscle activity. *Science, 318,* 1934–1937.

Davidson, J. M. (1980). Hormones and sexual behavior in the male. In D. T. Krieger & J. C. Hughes (Eds.), *Neuroendocrinology* (pp. 232–238). Sunderland, MA: Sinauer Associates.

Davis, S. R., & Braunstein, G. D. (2012). Efficacy and safety of testosterone in the management of hypoactive sexual desire disorder in postmenopausal women. *Journal of Sexual Medicine, 9,* 1134–1148.

Davis, S. R., Davison, S. L., Donath, S., & Bell, R. J. (2005). Circulating androgen levels and self-reported sexual function in women. *Journal of the American Medical Association, 294,* 91–96.

Dawson, M., Soulières, I., Gernsbacher, M. A., & Mottron, L. (2007). The level and nature of autistic intelligence. *Psychological Science, 18,* 657–662.

de Araujo, I. E., & Simon, S. A. (2009). The gustatory cortex and multisensory integration. *International Journal of Obesity, 33,* S34–S43.

De Butte-Smith, M., Gulinello, M., Zukin, R. S., & Etgen, A. M. (2009). Chronic estradiol treatment increases CA1 cell survival but does not improve visual or spatial recognition memory after global ischemia in middle-aged female rats. *Hormones and Behavior, 55,* 442–453.

De Deyn, P. P. (2015). Dementia: Cerebrospinal fluid biomarkers in dementias. *Nature Reviews Neurology, 11,* 549–550.

De Feo, D., Merlini, A., Laterza, C., & Martino, G. (2012). Neural stem cell transplantation in central nervous system disorders: From cell replacement to neuroprotection. *Current Opinion in Neurobiology, 25,* 322–333.

de Gelder, B. (2010). Uncanny sight in the blind. *Scientific American, 302,* 60–65.

De Gennaro, L., Ferrara, M., & Bertini, M. (2000). Muscle twitch activity during REM sleep: Effect of sleep deprivation and relation with rapid eye movement activity. *Psychobiology, 28,* 432–436.

De Groof, G., Poirier, C., George, I., Hausberger, M., & Van der Linden, A. (2013). Functional changes between seasons in the male songbird auditory forebrain. *Frontiers in Behavioral Neuroscience, 7,* 196.

de Haan, E. H. F., & Cowey, A. (2011). On the usefulness of 'what' and 'where' pathways in vision. *Trends in Cognitive Sciences, 15,* 460–466.

de Haan, M., Mishkin, M., Baldeweg, T., & Vargha-Khadem, F. (2006). Human memory development and its dysfunction after early hippocampal injury. *Trends in Neurosciences, 29,* 374–380.

de Hemptinne, C., Swann, N. C., Ostrem, J. L., Ryapolova-Webb, E. S., San Luciano, M., Galifianakis, N. B., & Starr, P. A. (2015). Therapeutic deep brain stimulation reduces cortical phase-amplitude coupling in Parkinson's disease. *Nature Neuroscience, 18,* 779–786.

de Kloet, E. R., Joëls, M., & Holsboer, F. (2005). Stress and the brain: From adaptation to disease. *Nature Reviews Neuroscience, 6,* 463–475.

de Knijff, P. (2014). How carrion and hooded crows defeat Linnaeus's curse. *Science, 344,* 1345.

de Kruif, P. (1945). *The male hormone.* New York, NY: Harcourt, Brace.

De Mees, C., Bakker, J., Szpirer, J., & Szpirer, C. (2006). Alpha-fetoprotein: From a diagnostic biomarker to a key role in female fertility. *Biomarker Insights, 1,* 82–85.

De Nardo, D. (2015). Toll-like receptors: Activation, signalling, and transcriptional modulation. *Cytokine, 74,* 181–189.

De Nicola, A. F., Brocca, M. E., Pietranera, L., & Garcia-Segura, L. M. (2012). Neuroprotection and sex steroids: Evidence of estradiol-mediated protection in hypertensive encephalopathy. *Mini Reviews in Medicinal Chemistry, 12,* 1081–1089.

De Renzi, E. (1997). Visuospatial and constructional disorders. In T. E. Feinberg & M. J. Farah (Eds.), *Behavioral neurology and neuropsychology* (pp. 297–308). New York, NY: McGraw-Hill.

De Valois, R. L., Cottaris, N. P., Elfar, S. D., Mahon, L. E., & Wilson, J. A. (2000). Some transformations of color information from lateral geniculate nucleus to striate cortex. *Proceedings of the National Academy of Science, USA, 97,* 4997–5002.

de Waal, F. B. M. (1999, December). The end of nature versus nurture. *Scientific American, 281,* 94–99.

De Zeeuw, C. I., & Ten Brinke, M. M. (2015). Motor learning and the cerebellum. *Cold Spring Harbor Perspectives in Biology, 7,* a021683.

Deadwyler, S. A., Hayashizaki, S., Cheer, J., & Hampson, R. E. (2004). Reward, memory and substance abuse: Functional neuronal circuits in the nucleus accumbens. *Neuroscience and Biobehavioural Reviews, 27,* 703–711.

Dean, C., & Dresbach, T. (2006). Neuroligins and neurexins: Linking cell adhesion, synapse formation and cognitive function. *Trends in Neurosciences, 29,* 21–29.

Debanne, D. (2004). Information processing in the axon. *Nature Reviews Neuroscience, 5,* 304–316.

Degenhardt, L., & Hall, W. (2012). Extent of illicit drug use and dependence, and their contribution to the global burden of disease. *The Lancet, 379,* 55–70.

DeGutis, J. M., Chiu, C., Grosso, M. E., & Cohan, S. (2014). Face processing improvements in prosopagnosia: Successes and failures over the last 50 years. *Frontiers in Human Neuroscience, 8,* 561.

Deisseroth, K. (2015). Optogenetics: 10 years of microbial opsins in neuroscience. *Nature Neuroscience, 18,* 1213–1225.

Dekker, A. D., Strydom, A., Coppus, A. M. W., Nizetic, D., Vermeiren, Y., … & De Deyn, P. P. (2015). Behavioral and psychological symptoms of dementia in Down syndrome: Early indicators of clinical Alzheimer's disease? *Cortex, 73,* 36–61.

Dekkers, M. P., & Barde, Y. A. (2013). Programmed cell death in neuronal development. *Science, 340,* 39–41.

Deliagina, T. G., Zelenin, P. V., & Orlovsky, G. N. (2012). Physiological and circuit mechanisms of postural control. *Current Opinion in Neurobiology, 22,* 646–652.

Dell, L. A., Karlsson, K. A., Patzke, N., Spocter, M. A., Siegel, J. M., & Manger, P. R. (2016a). Organization of the sleep related neural systems in the brain of the Minke whale (*Balaenoptera acutorostrata*). *Journal of Comparative Neurology, 524,* 2018–2035.

Dell, L. A., Patzke, N., Spocter, M. A., Siegel, J. M., & Manger, P. R. (2016b). Organization of the sleep related neural systems in the brain of the harbour porpoise (*Phocoena phocoena*). *Journal of Comparative Neurology, 524,* 1999–2017.

Delmas, P., Hao, J., & Rodat-Despoix, L. (2011). Molecular mechanisms of mechanotransduction in mammalian sensory neurons. *Nature Reviews Neuroscience, 12,* 139–152.

Demas, G. E., Cooper, M. A., Albers, H. E., & Soma, K. K. (2005). Novel mechanisms underlying neuroendocrine regulation of aggression: A synthesis of rodent, avian, and primate studies. In J. D. Blaustein (Ed.), *Behavioral neurochemistry and neuroendocrinology* (pp. 2–25). New York, NY: Kluwer Press.

Dement, W. C. (1978). *Some must watch while some must sleep.* New York, NY: Norton.

Dement, W. C., & Kleitman, N. (1957). The relation of eye movement during sleep to dream activity: An objective method for the study of dreaming. *Journal of Experimental Psychology, 53,* 339–346.

Dement, W. C., & Wolpert, E. A. (1958). The relation of eye movements, body motility and external stimuli to dream content. *Journal of Experimental Psychology, 55,* 543–553.

Demjaha, A., MacCabe, J. H., & Murray, R. M. (2012). How genes and environmental factors determine the different neurodevelopmental trajectories of schizophrenia and bipolar disorder. *Schizophrenia Bulletin, 38,* 209–214.

Deng, W., Aimone, J. B., & Gage, F. H. (2010). New neurons and new memories: How does adult hippocampal neurogenesis affect learning and memory? *Nature Reviews Neuroscience, 11,* 339–350.

Dennis, E. L., & Thompson, P. M. (2013). Typical and atypical brain development: A review of neuroimaging studies. *Dialogues in Clinical Neuroscience, 15,* 359–384.

Deppmann, C. D., Mihalas, S., Shama, N., Lonze, B. E., Niebur, E., & Ginty, D. D. (2008). A model for neuronal competition during development. *Science, 320,* 369–373.

Derdikman, D., & Moser, E. I. (2010). A manifold of spatial maps in the brain. *Trends in Cognitive Sciences, 14,* 561–569.

Deshmukh, V. A., Tardiff, V., Lyssiotis, C. A., Green, C. C., Kerman, B., … & Lairson, L. L. (2013). A regenerative approach to the treatment of multiple sclerosis. *Nature, 502,* 327–332.

Desmurget, M., & Sirigu, A. (2012). Conscious motor intention emerges in the inferior parietal lobule. *Current Opinion in Neurobiology, 22,* 1004–1011.

Desmurget, M., Reilly, K. T., Richard, N., Szathmari, A., Mottolese, C., & Sirigu, A. (2009). Movement intention after parietal cortex stimulation in humans. *Science, 324,* 811–813.

Dess, N. K., & Chapman, C. D. (1998). "Humans and animals"? On saying what we mean. *Psychological Science, 9*(2), 156–157.

Desseilles, M., Dang-Vu, T. T., Sterpenich, V., & Schwartz, S. (2011). Cognitive and emotional processes during dreaming: A neuroimaging view. *Consciousness and Cognition, 20,* 998–1008.

Deuschl, G., & Agid, Y. (2013). Subthalamic neurostimulation for Parkinson's disease with early fluctuations: Balancing the risks and benefits. *The Lancet Neurology, 12,* 1025–1034.

Devinsky, O., Vezzani, A., Najjar, S., De Lanerolle, N. C., & Rogawski, M. A. (2013). Glia and epilepsy: Excitability and inflammation. *Trends in Neurosciences, 36,* 174–184.

Devreotes, P., & Horwitz, A. R. (2015). Signaling networks that regulate cell migration. *Cold Spring Harbor Perspectives in Biology, 7,* a005959.

Deweerdt, S. (2014). A complicated relationship status. *Nature, 508,* S61–S63.

Dewsbury, D. A. (1988). The comparative psychology of monogamy. In D. W. Leger (Ed.), *Comparative perspectives in modern psychology: Nebraska Symposium on Motivation* (Vol. 35, pp. 1–50). Lincoln: University of Nebraska Press.

Dewsbury, D. A. (1991). Psychobiology. *American Psychologist, 46,* 198–205.

Dhabhar, F. S. (2014). Effects of stress on immune function: The good, the bad, and the beautiful. *Immunologic Research, 58,* 193–210.

Dhindsa, R. S., & Goldstein, D. B. (2016). Schizophrenia: From genetics to physiology at last. *Nature, 530,* 162–163.

Dhurandhar, E. J., Kaiser, K. A., Dawson, J. A., Alcorn, A. S., Keating, K. D., & Allison, D. B. (2015). Predicting adult weight change in the real world: A systematic review and meta-analysis accounting for compensatory changes in energy intake or expenditure. *International Journal of Obesity, 39,* 1181–1187.

Di Franza, J. R. (2008, May). Hooked from the first cigarette. *Scientific American, 298,* 82–87.

Di Giacomo, A. M., & Margolin, K. (2015). Immune checkpoint blockade in patients with melanoma metastatic to the brain. *Seminars in Oncology, 42,* 459–465.

Di Lollo, V. (2012). The feature-binding problem is an ill-posed problem. *Trends in Cognitive Sciences, 16,* 317–321.

Di Marzo, V., Stella, N., & Zimmer, A. (2015). Endocannabinoid signalling and the deteriorating brain. *Nature Reviews Neuroscience, 16,* 30–42.

Diamond, A. (1985). Development of the ability to use recall to guide action, as indicated by infants' performance on AB. *Child Development, 56,* 868–883.

Diamond, A. (1991). Neuropsychological insights into the meaning of object concept development. In S. Carey & R. Gelman (Eds.), *The epigenesis of mind: Essays on biology and cognition* (pp. 67–110). Hillsdale, NJ: Lawrence Erlbaum.

Diamond, J. (2004). The astonishing micropygmies. *Science, 306,* 2047–2048.

Diamond, M., & Sigmundson, H. K. (1997). Sex reassignment at birth: Long-term review and clinical implications. *Archives of Pediatric and Adolescent Medicine, 151,* 298–304.

Dias, B. G., & Ressler, K. J. (2014). Parental olfactory experience influences behavior and neural structure in subsequent generations. *Nature Neuroscience, 17,* 89–96.

Dias, B. G., Banerjee, S. B., Goodman, J. V., & Ressler, K. J. (2013). *Current Opinion in Neurobiology, 23,* 346–352.

Dias, B. G., Maddox, S. A., Klengel, T., & Ressler, K. J. (2015). Epigenetic mechanisms underlying learning and the inheritance of learned behaviors. *Trends in Neurosciences, 38,* 96–107.

DiCicco-Bloom, E. (2006). Neuron, know thy neighbor. *Science, 311,* 1560–1562.

Diekelmann, S., & Born, J. (2010). The memory function of sleep. *Nature Reviews Neuroscience, 11,* 114–126.

Diekhof, E. K., Kaps, L., Falkai, P., & Gruber, O. (2012). The role of the human ventral striatum and the medial orbitofrontal cortex in the representation of reward magnitude—an activation likelihood estimation meta-analysis of neuro-

imaging studies of passive reward expectancy and outcome processing. *Neuropsychologia, 50,* 1252–1266.

Deisseroth, K. (2011). Optogenetics. *Nature Methods, 8,* 26–29.

Dick, A. S., Bernal, B., & Tremblay, P. (2014). The language connectome new pathways, new concepts. *The Neuroscientist, 20,* 453–467.

Dieterich, D. C. (2010). Chemical reporters for the illumination of protein and cell dynamics. *Current Opinion in Neurobiology, 20,* 623–630.

Dietrich, M. O., & Horvath, T. L. (2013). Hypothalamic control of energy balance: Insights into the role of synaptic plasticity. *Trends in Neurosciences, 36,* 65–73.

Dietz, M. J., Friston, K. J., Mattingley, J. B., Roepstorff, A., & Garrido, M. I. (2014). Effective connectivity reveals right-hemisphere dominance in audiospatial perception: Implications for models of spatial neglect. *Journal of Neuroscience, 34,* 5003–5011.

DiMaggio, E. N., Campisano, C. J., Rowan, J., Dupont-Nivet, G., Deino, A. L., Bibi, F., . . . & Reed, K. E. (2015). Late Pliocene fossiliferous sedimentary record and the environmental context of early *Homo* from Afar, Ethiopia. *Science, 347,* 1355–1359.

Dimou, L., & Götz, M. (2014). Glial cells as progenitors and stem cells: New roles in the healthy and diseased brain. *Physiological Reviews, 94,* 709–737.

Dinges, D. F., Pack, F., Williams, K., Gillen, K. A., Powell, J. W., Ott, G. E., et al. (1997). Cumulative sleepiness, mood disturbance, and psychomotor vigilance performance decrements during a week of sleep restricted to 4–5 hours per night. *Sleep, 20,* 267–277.

Do-Monte, F. H., Quiñones-Laracuente, K., & Quirk, G. J. (2015). A temporal shift in the circuits mediating retrieval of fear memory. *Nature, 519,* 460–463.

Dobelle, W. H., Mladejovsky, M. G., & Girvin, J. P. (1974). Artificial vision for the blind: Electrical stimulation of visual cortex offers hope for a functional prosthesis. *Science, 183,* 440–444.

Dockray, G. J. (2014). Gastrointestinal hormones and the dialogue between gut and brain. *Journal of Physiology, 592,* 2927–2941.

Doetsch, F. (2003). The glial identity of neural stem cells. *Nature Neuroscience, 6,* 1127–1134.

Doetsch, F., & Hen, R. (2005). Young and excitable: The function of new neurons in the adult mammalian brain. *Current Opinion in Neurobiology, 15,* 121–128.

Dolgin, E. (2015). The elaborate architecture of RNA. *Nature, 523,* 398–399.

Dominici, N., Ivanenko, Y. P., Cappellini, G., d'Avella, A., Mondì, V., Cicchese, M., Fabiano, A., Silei, T., Di Paolo, A., Giannini, C., Poppele, R. E., & Lacquaniti, F. (2011). Locomotor primitives in newborn babies and their development. *Science, 334,* 997–999.

Drachman, D. A., & Arbit, J. (1966). Memory and the hippocampal complex. *Archives of Neurology, 15,* 52–61.

Drenowatz, C. (2015). Reciprocal compensation to changes in dietary intake and energy expenditure within the concept of energy balance. *Advances in Nutrition, 6,* 592–599.

Drewnowski, A., Halmi, K. A., Pierce, B., Gibbs, J., & Smith, G. P. (1987). Taste and eating disorders. *American Journal of Clinical Nutrition, 46,* 442–450.

Driscoll, T. R., Grunstein, R. R., & Rogers, N. L. (2007). A systematic review of the neurobehavioural and physiological effects of shiftwork systems. *Sleep Medicine Reviews, 11,* 179–194.

Driver, H. S., & Taylor, S. R. (2000). Exercise and sleep. *Sleep Medicine Reviews, 4,* 387–402.

Drummey, A. B., & Newcombe, N. (1995). Remembering versus knowing the past: Children's explicit and implicit memories for pictures.

Journal of Experimental Child Psychology, 59, 540–565.

Drummond, E. M., & Gibney, E. R. (2013). Epigenetic regulation in obesity. *Current Opinion in Clinical Nutrition & Metabolic Care, 16,* 392–397.

Du, Y., He, Y., Arnott, S. R., Ross, B., Wu, X., Li, L., & Alain, C. (2015). Rapid tuning of auditory "what" and "where" pathways by training. *Cerebral Cortex, 25,* 496–506.

Du, Y., Kong, L., Wang, Q., Wu, X., & Li, L. (2011). Auditory frequency-following response: A neurophysiological measure for studying the "cocktail-party problem." *Neuroscience and Biobehavioral Reviews, 35,* 2046–2057.

Dubischar-Krivec, A. M., Bölte, S., Braun, C., Poustka, F., Birbaumer, N., & Neumann, N. (2014). Neural mechanisms of savant calendar calculating in autism: An MEG-study of few single cases. *Brain and Cognition, 90,* 157–164.

Duchaine, B. C., & Nakayama, K. (2006). Developmental prosopagnosia: A window to content-specific face processing. *Current Opinion in Neurobiology, 16,* 166–173.

Duchaine, B., & Nakayama, K. (2005). Dissociations of face and object recognition in developmental prosopagnosia. *Journal of Cognitive Neuroscience, 17,* 249–261.

Duchaine, B., Cosmides, L., & Tooby, J. (2001). Evolutionary psychology and the brain. *Current Opinion in Neurobiology, 11,* 225–230.

Dudai, Y., & Morris, R. G. M. (2013). Memorable trends. *Neuron, 80,* 742–750.

Dudai, Y., Karni, A., & Born, J. (2015). The consolidation and transformation of memory. *Neuron, 88,* 20–32.

Dudanova, I., & Klein, R. (2013). Integration of guidance cues: Parallel signaling and crosstalk. *Trends in Neurosciences, 36,* 295–304.

Dugan, P., & Devinsky, O. (2013). Guidelines on vagus nerve stimulation for epilepsy. *Nature Reviews Neurology, 9,* 611–612.

Dulac, C., & Kimchi, T. (2007). Neural mechanisms underlying sex-specific behaviors in vertebrates. *Current Opinion in Neurobiology, 17,* 675–683.

Dully, H., & Fleming, C. (2007). *My lobotomy: A memoir.* New York, NY: Crown.

Duman, R. S., & Aghajanian, G. K. (2012). Synaptic dysfunction in depression: Potential therapeutic targets. *Science, 338,* 68–72.

Dunnett, S. B., Björklund, A., & Lindvall, O. (2001). Cell therapy in Parkinson's disease—stop or go? *Nature Reviews Neuroscience, 2,* 365–368.

Dunsmoor, J. E., Murty, V. P., Davachi, L., & Phelps, E. A. (2015). Emotional learning selectively and retroactively strengthens memories for related events. *Nature, 520,* 345–348.

Dutra, L., Stathopoulou, G., Basden, S. L., Leyro, T. M., Powers, M. B., & Otto, M. W. (2008). A meta-analytic review of psychosocial interventions for substance use disorders. *American Journal of Psychiatry, 165,* 179–187.

Duva, C. A., Kornecook, T. J., & Pinel, J. P. J. (2000). Animal models of medial temporal lobe amnesia: The myth of the hippocampus. In M. Haug & R. E. Whalen (Eds.), *Animal models of human emotion and cognition* (pp. 197–214). Washington, DC: American Psychological Association.

Duvarci, S., & Pare, D. (2014). Amygdala microcircuits controlling learned fear. *Neuron, 82,* 966–980.

Dyken, M. E., Yamada, T., & Lin-Dyken, D. C. (2001). Abnormal behaviors in sleep. *Acta Neurologica Taiwanica, 10,* 241–247.

Eagleman, D. M. (2001). Visual illusions and neurobiology. *Nature Reviews Neuroscience, 2,* 920–926.

Ecker, A. S., Berens, P., Keliris, G. A., Bethge, M., Logothetis, N. K., & Tolias, A. S. (2010). Decorrelated neuronal firing in cortical microcircuits. *Science, 327,* 584–586.

Egan, J. F. (2004). Down syndrome births in the United States from 1989 to 2001. *American Journal of Obstetrics and Gynecology, 191,* 1044–1048.

Egeland, M., Zunszain, P. A., & Pariante, C. M. (2015). Molecular mechanisms in the regulation of adult neurogenesis during stress. *Nature Reviews Neuroscience, 16,* 189–200.

Eggermont, J. J., & Tass, P. A. (2015). Maladaptive neural synchrony in tinnitus: Origin and restoration. *Frontiers in Neurology, 6,* 29.

Ehrhardt, A. A., Meyer-Bahlburg, H. F. L., Rosen, L. R., Feldman, J. F., Veridiano, N. P., Zimmerman, I., & McEwen, B. S. (1985). Sexual orientation after prenatal exposure to exogenous estrogen. *Archives of Sexual Behavior, 14,* 57–77.

Ehrlich, I., Humeau, Y., Grenier, F., Ciocchi, S., Herry, C., & Lüthi, A. (2009). Amygdala inhibitory circuits and the control of fear memory. *Neuron, 62,* 757–771.

Eichenbaum, H. (2014). Time cells in the hippocampus: A new dimension for mapping memories. *Nature Reviews Neuroscience, 15,* 732–744.

Eichenbaum, H. (2015). The hippocampus as a cognitive map…of social space. *Neuron, 87,* 9–11.

Eichenbaum, H., & Cohen, N. J. (2014). Can we reconcile the declarative memory and spatial navigation views on hippocampal function? *Neuron, 83,* 764–770.

Eigsti, I. M., & Shapiro, T. (2004). A systems neuroscience approach to autism: Biological, cognitive, and clinical perspectives. *Mental Retardation and Developmental Disabilities Research Reviews, 9,* 205–215.

Eilam, D., Izhar, R., & Mort, J. (2011). Threat detection: Behavioral practices in animals and humans. *Neuroscience and Biobehavioral Reviews, 35,* 999–1006.

Eilat-Adar, S., Eldar, M., & Goldbourt, U. (2005). Association of intentional changes in body weight with coronary heart disease event rates in overweight subjects who have an additional coronary risk factor. *American Journal of Epidemiology, 161,* 352–358.

Einhäuser, W., & König, P. (2010). Getting real—sensory processing of natural stimuli. *Current Opinion in Neurobiology, 20,* 389–395.

Eisenegger, C., Haushofer, J., & Fehr, E. (2011). The role of testosterone in social interaction. *Trends in Cognitive Sciences, 15,* 263–271.

Ejaz, N., Hamada, M., & Diedrichsen, J. (2015). Hand use predicts the structure of representations in sensorimotor cortex. *Nature Neuroscience, 18,* 1034–1040.

Ekman, P. (1985). *Telling lies.* New York, NY: Norton.

Ekman, P. (2016). What scientists who study emotion agree about. *Perspectives on Psychological Science, 11,* 31–34.

Ekman, P., & Friesen, W. V. (1971). Constants across cultures in the face and emotion. *Journal of Personality and Social Psychology, 17,* 124–129.

Ekman, P., & Friesen, W. V. (1975). *Unmasking the face: A guide to recognizing emotions from facial clues.* Englewood Cliffs, NJ: Prentice-Hall.

Elbert, T., Pantev, C., Wienbruch, C., Rockstroh, B., & Taub, E. (1995). Increased cortical representation of the fingers of the left hand in string players. *Science, 270,* 305–307.

Elbert, T., Sterr, A., Rockstroh, B., Pantev, C., Müller, M. M., & Taub, E. (2002). Expansion of the tonotopic area in the auditory cortex of the blind. *Journal of Neuroscience, 22,* 9941–9944.

Elder, G. A., Gama Sosa, M. A., & De Gasperi, R. (2010). Transgenic mouse models of Alzheimer's disease. *Mount Sinai Journal of Medicine, 77,* 69–81.

Elemans, C. P. (2014). The singer and the song: The neuromechanics of avian sound production. *Current Opinion in Neurobiology, 28,* 172–178.

Elert, E. (2014). Aetiology: Searching for schizophrenia's roots. *Nature, 508,* S2–S3.

Elgoyhen, A. B., Langguth, B., De Ridder, D., & Vanneste, S. (2015). Tinnitus: Perspectives from human neuroimaging. *Nature Reviews Neuroscience, 16,* 632–642.

Eling, P., Derckx, K., & Maes, R. (2008). On the historical and conceptual background of the Wisconsin Card Sorting Test. *Brain and Cognition, 67,* 247–253.

Ellis, J. G., Gehrman, P., Espie, C. A., Riemann, D., & Perlis, M. L. (2012). Acute insomnia: Current conceptualizations and future directions. *Sleep Medicine Reviews, 16,* 5–14.

Ellis, J. G., Perlis, M. L., Neale, L. F., Espie, C. A., & Bastien, C. H. (2012). The natural history of insomnia: Focus on prevalence and incidence of acute insomnia. *Journal of Psychiatric Research, 46,* 1278–1285.

Ellis, L., & Ames, M. A. (1987). Neurohormonal functioning and sexual orientation: A theory of homosexuality-heterosexuality. *Psychological Bulletin, 101,* 233–258.

Elman, I., & Borsook, D. (2016). Common brain mechanisms of chronic pain and addiction. *Neuron, 89,* 11–36.

Elmenhorst, E.-M., Elmenhorst, D., Luks, N., Maass, H., Vejvoda, M., & Samel, A. (2008). Partial sleep deprivation: Impact on the architecture and quality of sleep. *Sleep Medicine, 9,* 840–850.

Elmer, S., Hänggi, J., Meyer, M., & Jäncke, L. (2013). Increased cortical surface area of the left planum temporale in musicians facilitates the categorization of phonetic and temporal speech sounds. *Cortex, 49,* 2812–2821.

Engel, S. A. (1999). Using neuroimaging to measure mental representations: Finding color-opponent neurons in visual cortex. *Current Directions in Psychological Science, 8,* 23–27.

Endo, T., Roth, C., Landolt, H. P., Werth, E., Aeschbach, D., Achermann, P., & Borbély, A. A. (1998). Selective REM sleep deprivation in humans: Effects on sleep and sleep EEG. *American Journal of Physiology-Regulatory, Integrative and Comparative Physiology, 274,* R1186–R1194.

Engle-Friedman, M. (2014). The effects of sleep loss on capacity and effort. *Sleep Science, 7,* 213–224.

Enoch, M-A. (2012). The influence of gene-environment interactions on the development of alcoholism and drug dependence. *Current Psychiatry Reports, 14,* 150–158.

Epstein, L. H., Temple, J. L., Neaderhiser, B. J., Salis, R. J., Erbe, R. W., & Leddy, J. J. (2007). Food reinforcement, the dopamine D_2 receptor genotype, and energy intake in obese and nonobese humans. *Behavioral Neuroscience, 121,* 877–886.

Eriksson, P. S., Perfilieva, E., Björk-Eriksson, T., Alborn, A., Nordberg, C., Peterson, D. A., & Gage, F. H. (1998). Neurogenesis in the adult human hippocampus. *Nature Medicine, 4,* 1313–1317.

Ernst, A., Alkass, K., Bernard, S., Salehpour, M., Perl, S.,…& Frisén, J. (2014). Neurogenesis in the striatum of the adult human brain. *Cell, 156,* 1072–1083.

Ersche, K. D., Jones, P. S., Williams, G. B., Turton, A. J., Robbins, T. W., & Bullmore, E. T. (2012). Abnormal brain structure implicated in stimulant drug addiction. *Science, 335,* 601–604.

Ersche, K. D., Williams, G. B., Robbins, T. W., & Bullmore, E. T. (2013). Meta-analysis of structural brain abnormalities associated with stimulant drug dependence and neuroimaging of addiction vulnerability and resilience. *Current Opinion in Neurobiology, 23,* 615–624.

Etkin, A., Büchel, C., & Gross, J. J. (2015). The neural bases of emotion regulation. *Nature Reviews Neuroscience, 16,* 693–700.

Etminan, N., & Rinkel, G. J. (2015). Cerebral aneurysms: Cerebral aneurysm guidelines—more guidance needed. *Nature Reviews Neurology, 11,* 490–491.

Euston, D. R., & Steenland, H. W. (2014). Memories—getting wired during sleep. *Science, 344,* 1087–1088.

Euston, D. R., Gruber, A. J., & McNaughton, B. L. (2012). The role of medial prefrontal cortex in memory and decision making. *Neuron, 76,* 1057–1070.

Everitt, B. J. (1990). Sexual motivation: A neural and behavioral analysis of the mechanisms underlying appetitive and copulatory responses of male rats. *Neuroscience and Biobehavioral Reviews, 14,* 217–232.

Everitt, B. J., & Herbert, J. (1972). Hormonal correlates of sexual behavior in sub-human primates. *Danish Medical Bulletin, 19,* 246–258.

Everitt, B. J., Dickinson, A., & Robbins, T. W. (2001). The neuropsychological basis of addictive behaviour. *Brain Research Reviews, 36,* 129–138.

Everitt, B. J., Herbert, J., & Hamer, J. D. (1971). Sexual receptivity of bilaterally adrenalectomized female rhesus monkeys. *Physiology & Behavior, 8,* 409–415.

Evsyukova, I., Plestant, C., & Anton, E. S. (2013). Integrative mechanisms of oriented neuronal migration in the developing brain. *Annual Review of Cell and Developmental Biology, 29,* 299–353.

Ewers, M., Frisoni, G. B., Teipel, S. J., Grinberg, L. T., Amaro, E., Heinsen, H.,…& Hampel, H. (2011). Staging Alzheimer's disease progression with multimodality neuroimaging. *Progress in Neurobiology, 95,* 535–546.

Fabri, M., Polonara, G., Del Pesce, M., Quattrini, A., Salvolini, U., & Manzoni, T. (2001). Posterior corpus callosum and interhemispheric transfer of somatosensory information: An fMRI and neuropsychological study of a partially callosotomized patient. *Journal of Cognitive Neuroscience, 13,* 1071–1079.

Fagerström, K. O., & Bridgman, K. (2014). Tobacco harm reduction: The need for new products that can compete with cigarettes. *Addictive Behaviors, 39,* 507–511.

Fagiolini, M., Jensen, C. L., & Champagne, F. A. (2009). Epigenetic influences on brain development and plasticity. *Current Opinion in Neurobiology, 19,* 207–212.

Falasconi, M., Gutierrez-Galvez, A., Leon, M., Johnson, B. A., & Marco, S. (2012). Cluster analysis of rat olfactory bulb responses to diverse odorants. *Chemical Senses, 37,* 639–653.

Fama, R., Pitel, A.-L., & Sullivan, E. V. (2012). Anterograde episodic memory in Korsakoff's syndrome. *Neuropsychology Review, 22,* 93–104.

Famulski, J. K., & Solecki, D. J. (2013). New spin on an old transition: Epithelial parallels in neuronal adhesion control. *Trends in Neurosciences, 36,* 163–173.

Farah, M. J. (1990). *Visual agnosia: Disorders of object recognition and what they tell us about normal vision.* Cambridge, MA: MIT Press.

Farah, M. J. (2015). The unknowns of cognitive enhancement. *Science, 350,* 379–380.

Farah, M. J., & Murphy, N. (2009). Neuroscience and the soul [Letter to editor]. *Science, 323,* 1168.

Fareri, D. S., & Delgado, M. R. (2014). Social rewards and social networks in the human brain. *Neuroscientist, 20,* 387–402.

Farmer, J., Zhao, X., Van Praag, H., Wodke, K., Gage, F. H., & Christie, B. R. (2004). Effects of voluntary exercise on synaptic plasticity and gene expression in the dentate gyrus of adult male Sprague-Dawley rats in vivo. *Neuroscience, 124,* 71–79.

Farooqi, I. S., Jebb, S. A., Langmack, G., Lawrence, E., Cheetham, C. H., Prentice, A. M.,…& O'Rahilly, S. (1999). Effects of recombinant leptin therapy in a child with congenital leptin deficiency. *New England Journal of Medicine, 341,* 879–884.

Farzampour, Z., & Huguenard, J. (2015). Seizing upon mechanisms for impaired consciousness. *Neuron, 85,* 453–455.

Fasano, A., Aquino, C. C., Krauss, J. K., Honey, C. R., & Bloem, B. R. (2015). Axial disability and deep brain stimulation in patients with Parkinson disease. *Nature Reviews Neurology, 11,* 98–110.

Fastenrath, M., Coynel, D., Spalek, K., Milnik, A., Gschwind, L., Roozendaal, B.,…& de Quervain, D. J. (2014). Dynamic modulation of amygdala–hippocampal connectivity by emotional arousal. *Journal of Neuroscience, 34,* 13935–13947.

Fava, G. A., Ruini, C., Rafanelli, C., Finos, L., Conti, S., & Grandi, S. (2004). Six-year outcome of cognitive behavior therapy for prevention of recurrent depression. *American Journal of Psychiatry, 161*, 1872–1876.

Favre, P., Baciu, M., Pichat, C., Bougerol, T., & Polosan, M. (2014). fMRI evidence for abnormal resting-state functional connectivity in euthymic bipolar patients. *Journal of Affective Disorders, 165*, 182–189.

Fedirko, V., Tramacere, I., Bagnardi, V., Rota, M., Scotti, L., Islami, F., Negri, E., Straif, K., Romieu, I., La Vecchia, C., Boffetta, P., & Jenab, M. (2011). Alcohol drinking and colorectal cancer risk: An overall and dose-response meta-analysis of published studies. *Annals of Oncology, 22*, 1958–1972.

Feil, R., & Fraga, M. F. (2012). Epigenetics and the environment: Emerging patterns and implications. *Nature Reviews Genetics, 13*, 97–109.

Feinberg, T. E., Vennen, A., & Simone, A. M. (2009). The neuroanatomy of asomatognosia and somatoparaphrenia. *Journal of Neurology, Neurosurgery and Psychiatry, 81*, 276–281.

Feinberg, T. E., Venneri, A., Simone, A. M., Fan, Y., & Northoff, G. (2010). The neuroanatomy of asomatognosia and somatoparaphrenia. *Journal of Neurology, Neurosurgery & Psychiatry, 81*, 276–281.

Feindel, W. (1986). Electrical stimulation of the brain during surgery for epilepsy—historical highlights. In G. P. Varkey (Ed.), *Anesthetic considerations for craniotomy in awake patients* (pp. 75–87). Boston, MA: Little, Brown.

Feinstein, J. S. (2013). Lesion studies of human emotion and feeling. *Current Opinion in Neurobiology, 23*, 304–309.

Feldman, J. (2013). The neural binding problem(s). *Cognitive Neurodynamics, 7*, 1–11.

Feliciano, D. M., & Bordey, A. (2013). Newborn cortical neurons: Only for neonates? *Trends in Neurosciences, 36*, 51–61.

Feller, M. B., & Scanziani, M. (2005). A precritical period for plasticity in visual cortex. *Current Opinion in Neurobiology, 15*, 94–100.

Felsen, G., & Dan, Y. (2005). A natural approach to studying vision. *Nature neuroscience, 8*, 1643–1646.

Felsen, G., & Dan, Y. (2006). A natural approach to studying vision. *Nature Neuroscience, 8*, 1643–1646.

Fentress, J. C. (1973). Development of grooming in mice with amputated forelimbs. *Science, 179*, 704–705.

Ferracioli-Oda, E., Qawasmi, A., & Bloch, M. H. (2013). Meta-analysis: Melatonin for the treatment of primary sleep disorders. *PLoS One, 8*, e637773.

Ferrara, M., De Gennaro, L., & Bertini, M. (1999). The effects of slow-wave sleep (SWS) deprivation and time of night on behavioral performance upon awakening. *Physiology & Behavior, 68*, 55–61.

Ferrari, P. F., & Rizzolatti, G. (2014). Mirror neuron research: The past and the future. *Philosophical Transactions of the Royal Society B, 369*, 20130169.

Ficca, G., Axelsson, J., Mollicone, D. J., Muto, V., & Vitiello, M. V. (2010). Naps, cognition and performance. *Sleep Medicine Reviews, 14*, 249–258.

Fichten, C. S., Libman, E., Creti, L., Bailes, S., & Sabourin, S. (2004). Long sleepers sleep more and short sleepers sleep less: A comparison of older adults who sleep well. *Behavioral Sleep Medicine, 2*, 2–23.

Field, L. L., Shumansky, K., Ryan, J., Truong, D., Swiergala, E., & Kaplan, B. J. (2013). Dense-map genome scan for dyslexia supports loci at 4q13, 16p12, 17q22; suggests novel locus at 7q36. *Genes, Brain, and Behavior, 12*, 56–69.

Fields, R. D. (2005, February). Making memories stick. *Scientific American, 292*, 75–80.

Fields, R. D., & Burnstock, G. (2006). Purinergic signalling in neuron-glia interactions. *Nature Reviews Neuroscience, 7*, 423–435.

Figueiredo, F. P., Parada, A. P., de Araujo, L. F., Silva Jr., W. A., & Del-Ben, C. M. (2015). The influence of genetic factors on peripartum depression: A systematic review. *Journal of Affective Disorders, 172*, 265–273.

Figueiredo, V. C., & Silva, P. R. (2014). Cosmetic doping—when anabolic-androgenic steroids are not enough. *Substance Use and Misuse, 49*, 1163–1167.

Fillion, T. J., & Blass, E. M. (1986). Infantile experience with suckling odors determines adult sexual behavior in male rats. *Science, 231*, 729–731.

Fillmore, K. M., Kerr, W. C., Stockwell, T., Chikritzhs, T., & Bostrom, A. (2006). Moderate alcohol use and reduced mortality risk: Systematic error in prospective studies. *Addiction Research and Therapy, 14*, 101–132.

Finberg, J. P., & Gillman, K. (2011). Selective inhibitors of monoamine oxidase type B and the "cheese effect." *International Review of Neurobiology, 100*, 169–190.

Finkelstein, E. A., Trogdon, J. G., Cohen, J. W., & Dietz, W. (2009). Annual medical spending attributable to obesity: Payer- and service-specific estimates. *Health Affairs, 28*, w822–w831.

Finn, R. (1991). Different minds. *Discover, 12*, 52–58.

FitzGerald, G. A. (2014). Temporal targets of drug action. *Science, 346*, 921–922.

Fitzpatrick, S. M., & Rothman, D. L. (2000). Meeting report: Transcranial magnetic stimulation and studies of human cognition. *Journal of Cognitive Neuroscience, 12*, 704–709.

Flegal, K. M., Kit, B. K., Orpana, H., & Graubard, B. I. (2013). Association of all-cause mortality with overweight and obesity using standard body mass index categories. *JAMA, 309*, 71–82.

Flight, M. H. (2014). The gut-microbiome-brain connection. *Nature Reviews Neuroscience, 15*, 65.

Flint, J., & Kendler, K. S. (2014). The genetics of major depression. *Neuron, 81*, 484–503.

Flint, J., & Munafò, M. (2014). Schizophrenia: Genesis of a complex disease. *Nature, 511*, 412–413.

Flor, H., Nikolajsen, L., & Jensen, T. S. (2006). Phantom limb pain: A case of maladaptive CNS plasticity? *Nature Reviews Neuroscience, 7*, 873–881.

Floresco, S. B. (2015). The nucleus accumbens: An interface between cognition, emotion, and action. *Annual Review of Psychology, 66*, 25–52.

Floresco, S. B., Seamans, J. K., & Phillips, A. G. (1997). Selective roles for hippocampal, prefrontal cortical, and ventral striatal circuits in radial-arm maze tasks with or without a delay. *Journal of Neuroscience, 17*(5), 1880–1890.

Fontana, L., & Partridge, L. (2015). Promoting health and longevity through diet: From model organisms to humans. *Cell, 161*, 106–118.

Fontana, X., Hristiva, M., Da Costa, C., Patodia, S., Thei, L., Makwana, M., Spencer-Dene, B., Latouche, M., Mirsky, R., Jessen, K. R., Klein, R., Raivich, G., & Behrens, A. (2012). c-Jun in Schwann cells promotes axonal regeneration and motoneuron survival via paracrine signaling. *Journal of Cell Biology, 198*, 127–141.

Fortier-Brochu, É., Beaulieu-Bonneau, S., Ivers, H., & Morin, C. M. (2012). Insomnia and daytime cognitive performance: A meta-analysis. *Sleep Medicine Reviews, 16*, 83–94.

Foster, D. H. (2011). Color constancy. *Vision Research, 51*, 674–700.

Fournier, J. C., DeRubeis, R. J., Hollon, S. D., Dimidjian, S., Amsterdam, J. D., Shelton, R. C., & Fawcett, J. (2010). Antidepressant drug effects and depression severity: A patient-level meta-analysis. *JAMA, 303*, 47–53.

Fox, K. C. R., Spreng, R. N., Ellamil, M., Andrews-Hanna, J. R., & Christoff, K. (2015). The wandering brain: Meta-analysis of functional neuroimaging studies of mind wandering and related spontaneous thought processes. *Neuro-Image, 111*, 611–621.

Fox, K., Glazewski, S., & Schulze, S. (2000). Plasticity and stability of somatosensory maps in thalamus and cortex. *Current Opinion in Neurobiology, 10*, 494–497.

Fox, S. H., & Brotchie, J. M. (2010). The MPTP-lesioned non-human primate models of Parkinson's disease. Past, present, and future. *Progress in Brain Research, 184*, 133–157.

Fraga, M. F., Ballestar, E., Paz, M. F., Ropero, S., Setien, F., Ballestar, M. L., Heine-Suñer, D., Cigudosa, J. C., Urioste, M., Benitez, J., Boix-Chornet, M., Sanchez-Aguilera, A., Ling, C., Carlsson, E., Poulsen, P., Vaag, A., Stephan, Z., Spector, T. D., Wu, Y. Z., Plass, C., & Esteller, M. (2005). Epigenetic differences arise during the lifetime of monozygotic twins. *Proceedings of the National Academy of Sciences USA, 102*, 10604–10609.

Francis, D. D., & Meaney, M. J. (1999). Maternal care and the development of stress responses. *Current Opinion in Neurobiology, 9*, 128–134.

Franco, S. J., & Müller, U. (2013). Shaping our minds: Stem and progenitor cell diversity in the mammalian neocortex. *Neuron, 77*, 19–34.

Franco, S. J., Gil-Sanz, C., Martinez-Garay, I., Espinosa, A., Harkins-Perry, S. R., Ramos, C., & Müller, U. (2012). Fate-restricted neural progenitors in the mammalian cerebral cortex. *Science, 337*, 746–749.

Franklin, T. B., & Mansuy, I. M. (2010). The prevalence of epigenetic mechanisms in the regulation of cognitive function and behaviour. *Current Opinion in Neurobiology, 20*, 441–449.

Frasnelli, E. (2013). Brain and behavioral lateralization in invertebrates. *Frontiers in Psychology, 4*, 939.

Frasnelli, E., Vallortigara, G., & Rogers, L. J. (2012). Left-right asymmetries of behaviour and nervous system in invertebrates. *Neuroscience and Biobehavioral Reviews, 36*, 1273–1291.

Frayer, D. W., Lozano, M., Bermúdez de Castro, J. M., Carbonell, E., Arsuaga, J. L., Radovčić, J., Fiore, I., & Bondioli, L. (2012). More than 500,000 years of right-handedness in Europe. *Laterality, 17*, 51–69.

Freedman, D. H. (2011). How to fix the obesity crisis. *Scientific American, 304*, 40–47.

Freeman, J. H. (2015). Cerebellar learning mechanisms. *Brain Research, 1621*, 260–269.

Freeman, M. R. (2010). Specification and morphogenesis of astrocytes. *Science, 330*, 774–778.

Freiwald, W. A., & Tsao, D. Y. (2010). Functional compartmentalization and viewpoint generalization within the macaque face-processing system. *Science, 330*, 845–851.

Freund, J., Brandmaier, A. M., Lewejohann, L., Kirste, I., Kritzler, M., … & Kempermann, G. (2013). Emergence of individuality in genetically identical mice. *Science, 340*, 756–758.

Friederici, A. D., & Gierhan, S. M. E. (2013). The language network. *Current Opinion in Neurobiology, 23*, 250–254.

Friederici, A. D., & Singer, W. (2015). Grounding language processing on basic neurophysiological principles. *Trends in Cognitive Sciences, 19*, 329–338.

Friedman, J., Globus, G., Huntley, A., Mullaney, D., Naitoh, P., & Johnson, L. (1977). Performance and mood during and after gradual sleep reduction. *Psychophysiology, 14*, 245–250.

Friedmann, P. D., Hendrickson, J. C., Gerstein, D. R., & Zhang, Z. (2004). The effect of matching comprehensive services to patients' needs on drug use improvement in addiction treatment. *Addiction, 99*, 962–972.

Friese, M. A., Schattling, B., & Fugger, L. (2014). Mechanisms of neurodegeneration and axonal dysfunction in multiple sclerosis. *Nature Reviews Neurology, 10*, 225–238.

Frigon, A., & Rossignol, S. (2008). Adaptive changes of the locomotor pattern and cutaneous reflexes during locomotion studied in the same cats before and after spinalization. *Journal of Physiology, 12,* 2927–2945.

Froemke, R. C., & Jones, B. J. (2011). Development of auditory cortical synaptic receptive fields. *Neuroscience and Biobehavioral Reviews, 35,* 2105–2113.

Fromer, M., Pocklington, A. J., Kavanagh, D. H., Williams, H. J., Dwyer, S., Gormley, P., ... & Carrera, N. (2014). De novo mutations in schizophrenia implicate synaptic networks. *Nature, 506,* 179–184.

Fryer, J. D., Yu, P., Kang, H., Mandel-Brehm, C., Carter, A. N., Crespo-Barreto, J., Gao, Y., Flora, A., Shaw, C., Orr, H. T., & Zoghbi, H. Y. (2011). Exercise and genetic rescue of SCA1 via the transcriptional repressor Capicua. *Science, 334,* 690–693.

Fuhrmann, D., Knoll, L. J., & Blakemore, S. J. (2015). Adolescence as a sensitive period of brain development. *Trends in Cognitive Sciences, 19,* 558–566.

Fujiwara, N., Imai, M., Nagamine, T., Mima, T., Oga, T., Takeshita, K., Toma, K., & Shibasaki, H. (2002). Second somatosensory area (SII) plays a role in selective somatosensory attention. *Cognitive Brain Research, 14,* 389–397.

Fullager, H. H. K., Skorski, S., Duffield, R., Hammes, D., Coutts, A. J., & Meyer, T. (2015). Sleep and athletic performance: The effects of sleep loss on exercise performance, and physiological and cognitive responses to exercise. *Sports Medicine, 45,* 161–186.

Fusar-Poli, P., Borgwardt, S., Crescini, A., Deste, G., Kempton, M. J., Lawrie, S., Mc Guire, P., & Sacchetti, E. (2011). Neuroanatomy of vulnerability to psychosis: A voxel-based meta-analysis. *Neuroscience and Biobehavioral Reviews, 35,* 1175–1185.

Fushimi, A., & Hayashi, M. (2008). Pattern of slow-wave sleep in afternoon naps. *Sleep and Biological Rhythms, 6,* 187–189.

Fuster, J. M. (2000). The prefrontal cortex of the primate: A synopsis. *Psychobiology, 28,* 125–131.

Gaffan, D. (1974). Recognition impaired and association intact in the memory of monkeys after transection of the fornix. *Journal of Comparative and Physiological Psychology, 86,* 1100–1109.

Gage, F. H., & Temple, S. (2013). Neural stem cells: Generating and regenerating the brain. *Neuron, 80,* 588–601.

Gaillard, A., & Jaber, M. (2011). Rewiring the brain with cell transplantation in Parkinson's disease. *Trends in Neurosciences, 34,* 124–133.

Galef, B. G. (1989). Laboratory studies of naturally-occurring feeding behaviors: Pitfalls, progress and problems in ethoexperimental analysis. In R. J. Blanchard, P. F. Brain, D. C. Blanchard, & S. Parmigiani (Eds.), *Ethoexperimental approaches to the study of behavior* (pp. 51–77). Dordrecht, Netherlands: Kluwer Academic.

Galef, B. G., Whiskin, E. E., & Bielavska, E. (1997). Interaction with demonstrator rats changes observer rats' affective responses to flavors. *Journal of Comparative Psychology, 111,* 393–398.

Gallagher, M., & Koh, M. T. (2011). Episodic memory on the path to Alzheimer's disease. *Current Opinion in Neurobiology, 21,* 929–934.

Gallup, G. G., Jr. (1983). Toward a comparative psychology of mind. In R. L. Mellgren (Ed.), *Animal cognition and behavior* (pp. 473–505). New York, NY: North-Holland.

Gambino, F., Pagès, S., Kehayas, V., Baptista, D., Tatti, R., Carleton, A., & Holtmaat, A. (2014). Sensory-evoked LTP driven by dendrtitic plateau potentials in vivo. *Nature, 515,* 116–119.

Gandhi, N. J., & Katnani, H. A. (2011). Motor functions of the superior colliculus. *Annual Review of Neuroscience, 34,* 205–231.

Ganel, T., Tanzer, M., & Goodale, M. A. (2008). A double dissociation between action and perception in the context of visual illusions. *Psychological Science, 19,* 221–225.

Gangestad, S. W., Thornhill, R., & Garver-Apgar, C. E. (2005). Adaptations to ovulation: Implications for sexual and social behavior. *Current Directions in Psychological Science, 14,* 312–316.

Gao, Q., & Horvath, T. L. (2007). Neurobiology of feeding and energy expenditure. *Annual Review of Neuroscience, 30,* 367–398.

Gao, Z., van Beugen, B. J., & De Zeeuw, C. I. (2012). Distributed synergistic plasticity and cerebellar learning. *Nature Reviews Neuroscience, 13,* 619–635.

Gao, Z., Zhu, Q., Zhang, Y., Zhao, Y., Cai, L., Shields, C. B., & Cai, J. (2013). Reciprocal modulation between microglia and astrocyte in reactive gliosis following the CNS injury. *Molecular Neurobiology, 48,* 690–701.

Garcia-Falgueras, A., & Swaab, D. F. (2010). Sexual hormones and the brain: An essential alliance for sexual identity and sexual orientation. *Endocrine Development, 17,* 22–35.

Garcia, J., & Koelling, R. A. (1966). Relation of cue to consequence in avoidance learning. *Psychonomic Science, 4,* 123–124.

Gardner, R. M., & Brown, D. L. (2014). Body size estimation in anorexia nervosa: A brief review of findings from 2003 through 2013. *Psychiatry Research, 219,* 407–410.

Garofalo, S., D'Alessandro, G., Chece, G., Brau, F., Maggi, L., ... & Limatola, C. (2015). Enriched environment reduces glioma growth through immune and non-immune mechanisms in mice. *Nature Communications, 6,* 6623.

Gawin, F. H. (1991). Cocaine addiction: Psychology and neurophysiology. *Science, 251,* 1580–1586.

Gaynes, B. N., Lloyd, S. W., Lux, L., Gartlehner, G., Hansen, R. A., Brode, S., ... & Lohr, K. N. (2014). Repetitive transcranial magnetic stimulation for treatment-resistant depression: A systematic review and meta-analysis. *Journal of Clinical Psychiatry, 75,* 1–478.

Gazzaniga, M. S. (1967, August). The split brain in man. *Scientific American, 217,* 24–29.

Gazzaniga, M. S. (2005). Forty-five years of split-brain research and still going strong. *Nature Reviews Neuroscience, 6,* 653–659.

Gazzaniga, M. S. (2010). Neuroscience and the correct level of explanation for understanding mind. *Trends in Cognitive Sciences, 14,* 291–292.

Gazzaniga, M. S. (2013). Shifting gears: Seeking new approaches for mind/brain mechanisms. *Annual Review of Psychology, 64,* 1–20.

Gazzaniga, M. S., & Sperry, R. W. (1967). Language after section of the cerebral commissure. *Brain, 90,* 131–148.

Geddes, J. R., & Miklowitz, D. J. (2013). Treatment of bipolar disorder. *Lancet, 381,* 1672–1682.

Geddes, J. R., Carney, S. M., Davies, C., Furukawa, T. A., Kupfer, D. J., Frank, E., & Goodwin, G. M. (2003). Relapse prevention with antidepressant drug treatment in depressive disorders: A systematic review. *The Lancet, 361,* 653–661.

Geerling, J. C., & Loewy, A. D. (2008). Central regulation of sodium appetite. *Experimental Physiology, 93,* 177–209.

Gegenfurtner, K. R., & Kiper, D. C. (2003). Color vision. *Annual Review of Neuroscience, 26,* 181–206.

Gehring, W. J. (2014). The evolution of vision. *WIREs Developmental Biology, 3,* 1–40.

Geiselman, P. J. (1987). Carbohydrates do not always produce satiety: An explanation of the appetite-and hunger-stimulating effects of hexoses. *Progress in Psychobiology and Physiological Psychology, 12,* 1–46.

Gejman, P. V., Sanders, A. R., & Kendler, K. S. (2011). Genetics of schizophrenia: New findings and challenges. *Annual Review of Genomics and Human Genetics, 12,* 121–144.

Geng, J. J., & Behrmann, M. (2002). Probability cuing of target location facilitates visual search implicitly in normal participants and patients with hemispatial neglect. *Psychological Science, 13,* 520–525.

Genné-Bacon, E. A. (2014). Thinking evolutionarily about obesity. *Yale Journal of Biology and Medicine, 87,* 99–112.

Genzel, L., Kroes, M. C. W., Dresler, M., & Battaglia, F. P. (2014). Light sleep versus slow wave sleep in memory consolidation: A question of global versus local processes? *Trends in Neurosciences, 37,* 10–19.

Geoffroy, C. G., & Zheng, B. (2014). Myelin-associated inhibitors in axonal growth after CNS injury. *Current Opinion in Neurobiology, 27,* 31–38.

George, O., & Koob, G. F. (2010). Individual differences in prefrontal cortex function and the transition from drug use to drug dependence. *Neuroscience and Biobehavioral Reviews, 35,* 232–247.

Georgiadis, J. R. (2012). Doing it...wild? On the role of the cerebral cortex in human sexual activity. *Socioaffective Neuroscience and Psychology, 2,* 17337.

Georgiadis, J. R., & Kringelbach, M. L. (2012). The human sexual response cycle: Brain imaging evidence linking sex to other pleasures. *Progress in Neurobiology, 98,* 49–81.

Georgiadis, J. R., Kringelbach, M. L., & Pfaus, J. G. (2012). Sex for fun: A synthesis of human and animal neurobiology. *Nature Reviews Urology, 9,* 486–498.

Georgopoulos, A. P. (1991). Higher order motor control. *Annual Review of Neuroscience, 14,* 361–377.

Georgopoulos, A. P., & Carpenter, A. F. (2015). Coding of movements in the motor cortex. *Current Opinion in Neurobiology, 33,* 34–39.

Geschwind, D. H., & Rakic, P. (2013). Cortical evolution: Judge the brain by its cover. *Neuron, 80,* 633–647.

Geschwind, N. (1970). The organization of language and the brain. *Science, 170,* 940–944.

Geschwind, N. (1979, September). Specializations of the human brain. *Scientific American, 241,* 180–199.

Gevins, A., Leong, H., Smith, M. E., Le, J., & Du, R. (1995). Mapping cognitive brain function with modern high-resolution electroencephalography. *Trends in Neurosciences, 18,* 429–436.

Ghazanfar, A. A., & Takahashi, D. Y. (2014). The evolution of speech: Vision, rhythm, cooperation. *Trends in Cognitive Sciences, 18,* 543–553.

Ghezzi, A., Krishna, H. R., Lew, L., Prado, F. J., Ong, D. S., & Atkinson, N. S. (2013). Alcohol-induced histone acetylation reveals a gene network involved in alcohol tolerance. *PLoS Genetics, 9,* e1003986.

Ghose, D., & Wallace, M. T. (2014). Heterogeneity in the spatial receptive field architecture of multisensory neurons of the superior colliculus and its effects on multisensory integration. *Neuroscience, 256,* 147–162.

Giacobini, E., & Gold, G. (2013). Alzheimer disease therapy—moving from amyloid-β to tau. *Nature Reviews Neurology, 9,* 677–686.

Giacomo, L. M. (2015). Imagine a journey through time and space. *Nature Neuroscience, 18,* 163–164.

Giardino, N. D., Friedman, S. D., & Dager, S. R. (2007). Anxiety, respiration, and cerebral blood flow: Implications for functional brain imaging. *Comprehensive Psychiatry, 48,* 103–112.

Gibbons, A. (2014). Neanderthals and moderns made imperfect mates. *Science, 343,* 471–472.

Gibbons, A. (2009). A new kind of ancestor: *Ardipithecus* unveiled. *Science, 326,* 36–43.

Gibbons, A. (2015a). New human species discovered. *Science, 349,* 1149–1150.

Gibbons, A. (2015b). First modern humans in China. *Science, 350,* 264–264.

Gibbs, J., Young, R. C., & Smith, G. P. (1973). Cholecystokinin decreases food intake in rats. *Journal of Comparative and Physiological Psychology, 84,* 488–495.

Giedd, J. N. (2015). The amazing teen brain. *Scientific American, 312,* 32–37.

Giese, M. A., & Rizzolatti, G. (2015). Neural and computational mechanisms of action processing: Interaction between visual and motor representations. *Neuron, 88,* 167–180.

Giesel, A. J., & Datta, S. R. (2014). Olfactory maps, circuits and computations. *Current Opinion in Neurobiology, 24,* 120–132.

Gilbert, C. D., & Li, W. (2013). Top-down influences on visual processing. *Nature Reviews Neuroscience, 14,* 350–363.

Gilbert, C. D., & Wiesel, T. N. (1992). Receptive field dynamics in adult primary visual cortex. *Nature, 356,* 150–152.

Gillebart, C. R., Mantini, D., Thijs, V., Sunaert, S., Dupont, P., & Vandenberghe, R. (2011). Lesion evidence for the critical role of the intraparietal sulcus in spatial attention. *Brain, 134,* 1694–1709.

Gillespie-Lynch, K., Greenfield, P. M., Lyn, H., & Savage-Rumbaugh, S. (2014). Gestural and symbolic development among apes and humans: Support for a multimodal theory of language development. *Frontiers in Psychology, 5,* 1228.

Gillies, G. E., & McArthur, S. (2010). Estrogen actions in the brain and the basis for differential action in men and women: A case for sex-specific medicines. *Pharmacological Reviews, 62,* 155–198.

Gilman, S. R., Chang, J., Xu, B., Bawa, T. S., Gogos, J. A., Karayiorgou, M., & Vitkup, D. (2012). Diverse types of genetic variation converge on functional gene networks involved in schizophrenia. *Nature Neuroscience, 15,* 1723–1728.

Gilmartin, M. R., Balderston, N. L., & Helmstetter, F. J. (2014). Prefrontal cortical regulation of fear learning. *Trends in Neurosciences, 37,* 455–464.

Gilmore, J. H., Shi, F., Woolson, S. L., Knickmeyer, R. C., Short, S. J., Lin, W., Zhu, H., Hamer, R. M., Styner, M., & Shen, D. (2012). Longitudinal development of cortical and subcortical gray matter from birth to 2 years. *Cerebral Cortex, 22,* 2478–2485.

Gingras, J., Smith, S., Matson, D. J., Johnson, D., Nye, K., ... & McDonough, S. I. (2014). Global Nav1.7 knockout mice recapitulate the phenotype of human congenital indifference to pain. *PLoS ONE, 9,* e105895.

Giraud, A.-L., & Ramus, F. (2013). Neurogenetics and auditory processing in developmental dyslexia. *Current Opinion in Neurobiology, 23,* 37–42.

Giszter, S. F. (2015). Motor primitives—new data and future questions. *Current Opinion in Neurobiology, 33,* 156–165.

Gitler, A. D. (2011). Another reason to exercise. *Science, 334,* 606–607.

Gittis, A. H., & Brasier, D. J. (2015). Astrocytes tell neurons when to listen up. *Science, 349,* 690–691.

Gittis, A. H., & Kreitzer, A. C. (2012). Striatal microcircuitry and movement disorders. *Trends in Neurosciences, 35,* 557–564.

Gittis, A. H., Berke, J. D., Bevan, M. D., Chan, C. S., Mallet, N., Morrow, M. M., & Schmidt, R. (2014). New roles for the external globus pallidus in basal ganglia circuits and behavior. *Journal of Neuroscience, 34,* 15178–15183.

Glaser, R., Rice, J., Sheridan, J., Fertel, R., Stout, J., Speicher, C., ... & Kiecolt-Glaser, J. (1987). Stress-related immune suppression: Health implications. *Brain, Behavior, and Immunity, 1,* 7–20.

Gliga, T., Jones, E. J. H., Bedford, R., Charman, T., & Johnson, M. H. (2014). From early markers to neuro-developmental mechanisms of autism. *Developmental Review, 34,* 189–207.

Goadsby, P. J. (2015). Decade in review—migraine: Incredible progress for an era of better migraine care. *Nature Reviews Neurology, 11,* 621–622.

Goddard, G. V., McIntyre, D. C., & Leech, C. K. (1969). A permanent change in brain function resulting from daily electrical stimulation. *Experimental Neurology, 25,* 295–330.

Godoy, M. D. C. L., Voegels, R. L., Pinna, F. D., Imamura, R., & Frafel, J. M. (2015). Olfaction in neurologic and neurodegenerative diseases: A literature review. *International Archives of Otorhinolaryngology, 19,* 176–179.

Godtfredsen, N. S., & Prescott, E. (2011). Benefits of smoking cessation with focus on cardiovascular and respiratory comorbidities. *Clinical Respiratory Journal, 5,* 187–194.

Goedert, M. (1993). Tau protein and the neurofibrillary pathology of Alzheimer's disease. *Trends in Neurosciences, 16,* 460–465.

Goedert, M. (2015). Alzheimer's and Parkinson's diseases: The prion concept in relation to assembled Aβ, tau, and α-synuclein. *Science, 349,* 1255555.

Goense, J. B. M., & Logothetis, N. K. (2008). Neurophysiology of the BOLD fMRI signal in awake monkeys. *Current Biology, 18,* 631–640.

Goetz, C. G. (2011). The history of Parkinson's disease: Early clinical descriptions and neurological therapies. *Cold Spring Harbor Perspectives in Medicine, 1,* a008862.

Goetz, C. G., & Pal, G. (2014). Initial management of Parkinson's disease. *BMJ, 349,* g6258.

Gogolla, N., Galimberti, I., & Caroni, P. (2007). Structural plasticity of axon terminals in the adult. *Current Opinion in Neurobiology, 17,* 516–524.

Gogtay, N., & Thompson, P. M. (2010). Mapping gray matter development: Implications for typical development and vulnerability to psychopathology. *Brain and Cognition, 72,* 6–15.

Gold, R. M., Jones, A. P., Sawchenko, P. E., & Kapatos, G. (1977). Paraventricular area: Critical focus of a longitudinal neurocircuitry mediating food intake. *Physiology & Behavior, 18,* 1111–1119.

Goldacre, B. (2013). *Bad pharma.* McClelland & Stewart: Toronto.

Goldberg, E. M., & Coulter, D. A. (2013). Mechanisms of epileptogenesis: A convergence on neural circuit dysfunction. *Nature Reviews Neuroscience, 14,* 337–348.

Goldman, D. (2015). America's cannabis experiment. *JAMA Psychiatry, 72,* 969–970.

Goldman, S. A., & Nottebohm, F. (1983). Neuronal production, migration, and differentiation in a vocal control nucleus of the adult female canary brain. *Proceedings of the National Academy of Sciences, USA, 80,* 2390–2394.

Goldstein, R. Z., & Volkow, N. D. (2011). Dysfunction of the prefrontal cortex in addiction: Neuroimaging findings and clinical implications. *Nature Reviews Neuroscience, 12,* 652–669.

Golinkoff, R. M., & Hirsh-Pasek, K. (2006). Baby wordsmith: From associationist to social sophisticate. *Current Directions in Psychological Science, 15,* 30–33.

Goll, Y., Atlan, G., & Citri, A. (2015). Attention: The claustrum. *Trends in Neurosciences, 38,* 486–495.

Gollin, E. S. (1960). Developmental studies of visual recognition of incomplete objects. *Perceptual Motor Skills, 11,* 289–298.

Gollnick, P. D., & Hodgson, D. R. (1986). The identification of fiber types in skeletal muscle: A continual dilemma. *Exercise and Sport Sciences Reviews, 14,* 81–104.

Golombek, D. A., Pandi-Perumal, S. R., Brown, G. M., & Cardinali, D. P. (2015). Some implications of melatonin use in chronopharmacology of insomnia. *European Journal of Pharmacology, 762,* 42–48.

Golub, M. D., Chase, S. M., Batista, A. P., & Byron, M. Y. (2016). Brain—computer interfaces for dissecting cognitive processes underlying sensorimotor control. *Current Opinion in Neurobiology, 37,* 53–58.

Gomez-Marin, A., & Mainen, Z. F. (2016). Expanding perspectives on cognition in humans, animals, and machines. *Current Opinion in Neurobiology, 37,* 85–91.

González-Reimers, E., Santolaria-Fernández, F., Martín-Gonzalaz, M. C., Fernández-Rodríguez, C. M., & Quintero-Platt, G. (2014). Alcoholism: A systemic proinflammatory condition. *World Journal of Gastroenterology, 20,* 14660–14671.

Goodale, M. A. (2004). Perceiving the world and grasping it: Dissociations between conscious and unconscious visual processing. In M. Gazzaniga (Ed.), *The cognitive neurosciences* (pp. 1159–1172). Cambridge, MA: MIT Press.

Goodale, M. A., & Milner, A. D. (1992). Separate visual pathways for perception and action. *Trends in Neurosciences, 15,* 20–25.

Goodale, M. A., & Milner, A. D. (2004). *Sight unseen: An exploration of conscious and unconscious perception.* Oxford, England: Oxford University Press.

Goodale, M. A., & Westwood, D. A. (2004). An evolving view of duplex vision: Separate but interacting cortical pathways for perception and action. *Current Opinion in Neurobiology, 14,* 203–211.

Goodenough, D. R., Shapiro, A., Holden, M., & Steinschriber, L. (1959). A comparison of "dreamers" and "nondreamers": Eye movements, electroencephalograms, and the recall of dreams. *Journal of Abnormal and Social Psychology, 59,* 295–303.

Goodhill, G. J. (2016). Can molecular gradients wire the brain? *Trends in Neurosciences, 39,* 202–211.

Gonzalez-Maeso, J., & Sealfon, S. C. (2009). Psychedelics and schizophrenia. *Trends in Neurosciences, 32,* 225–232.

Gorman, C., & Maron, D. F. (2014). The RNA revolution. *Scientific American, 310,* 52–59.

Gorski, R. A. (1980). Sexual differentiation in the brain. In D. T. Krieger & J. C. Hughes (Eds.), *Neuroendocrinology* (pp. 215–222). Sunderland, MA: Sinauer.

Gorski, R. A., Gordon, J. H., Shryne, J. E., & Southam, A. M. (1978). Evidence for a morphological sex difference within the medial preoptic area of the rat brain. *Brain Research, 148,* 333–346.

Goshen, I. (2014). The optogenetic revolution in memory research. *Trends in Neurosciences, 37,* 511–522.

Goswami, U. (2014). Sensory theories of developmental dyslexia: Three challenges for research. *Nature Reviews Neuroscience, 16,* 43–54.

Gottesman, I. I., & Hanson, D. R. (2005). Human development: Biological and genetic processes. *Annual Review of Psychology, 56,* 263–286.

Gottfried, J. A. (2010). Central mechanisms of odour object perception. *Nature Reviews Neuroscience, 11,* 628–640.

Goulas, A., Bastiani, M., Bezgin, G., Uylings, H. B. M., Roebroeck, A., & Stiers, P. (2014). Comparative analysis of the macroscale structural connectivity in the macaque and human brain. *PLoS Computational Biology, 10,* e1003529.

Goy, R. W., & McEwen, B. S. (1980). Sexual differentiation of the brain. Cambridge, MA: MIT Press.

Grady, K. L., Phoenix, C. H., & Young, W. C. (1965). Role of the developing rat testis in differentiation of the neural tissues mediating mating behavior. *Journal of Comparative and Physiological Psychology, 59,* 176–182.

Graham, S. A., & Fisher, S. E. (2013). Decoding the genetics of speech and language. *Current Opinion in Neurobiology, 23,* 43–51.

Grandner, M. A., & Drummond, S. P. A. (2007). Who are the long sleepers? Towards an understanding of the mortality relationship. *Sleep Medicine Reviews, 11,* 341–360.

Grant, P. R. (1991, October). Natural selection and Darwin's finches. *Scientific American, 265,* 82–87.

Gratwicke, J., Jahanshahi, M., & Foltynie, T. (2015). Parkinson's disease dementia: A neural networks perspective. *Brain, 138,* 1454–1476.

Grau, J. W. (2014). Learning from the spinal cord: How the study of spinal cord plasticity informs our view of learning. *Neurobiology of Learning and Memory, 108,* 155–171.

Graybiel, A. M., & Grafton, S. T. (2015). The striatum: Where skills and habits meet. *Cold Spring Harbor Perspectives in Biology, 7,* a021691.

Grayson, B. E., Seeley, R. J., & Sandoval, D. A. (2013). Wired on sugar: The role of the CNS in the regulation of glucose homeostasis. *Nature Reviews Neuroscience, 14,* 24–37.

Graziano, M. S. (2016). Ethological action maps: A paradigm shift for the motor cortex. *Trends in Cognitive Sciences, 20,* 121–132.

Graziano, M. S. A. (2009). *The intelligent movement machine: An ethological perspective on the primate motor system*. New York, NY: Oxford University Press.

Green, A. M., & Kalaska, J. F. (2010). Learning to move machines with the mind. *Trends in Neurosciences, 34*, 61–75.

Green, S. R., Kragel, P. A., Fecteau, M. E., & LaBar, K. S. (2014). Development and validation of an unsupervised scoring system (Autonomate) for skin conductance response analysis. *International Journal of Psychophysiology, 91*, 186–193.

Greenblatt, D. J., & Roth, T. (2012). Zolpidem for insomnia. *Expert Opinion on Pharmacotherapy, 13*, 879–893.

Greene, D. J., & Schlaggar, B. L. (2012). Insights for treatment in Tourette syndrome from fMRI. *Trends in Cognitive Sciences, 16*, 15–16.

Greene, N. D. E., & Copp, A. J. (2014). Neural tube defects. *Annual Review of Neuroscience, 37*, 221–242.

Greene, P. E., Fahn, S., Tsai, W. Y., Winfield, H., Dillon, S., Kao, R., et al. (1999). Double-blind controlled trial of human embryonic dopaminergic tissue transplants in advanced Parkinson's disease: Long-term unblinded follow-up phase. *Neurology, 52*(Suppl. 2).

Grefkes, C., & Fink, G. R. (2011). Reorganization of cerebral networks after stroke: New insights from neuroimaging with connectivity approaches. *Brain, 134*, 1264–1276.

Greig, L. C., Woodworth, M. B., Galazo, M. J., Padmanabhan, H., & Macklis, J. D. (2013). Molecular logic of neocortical projection neuron specification, development and diversity. *Nature Reviews Neuroscience, 14*, 755–769.

Grigg-Damberger, M. M. (2012). The AASM scoring manual four years later. *Journal of Clinical Sleep Medicine, 8*, 323–332.

Griggs, J., Sinnayah, P., & Mathai, M. L. (2015). Prader-Willi syndrome: From genetics to behaviour, with special focus on appetite treatments. *Neuroscience and Biobehavioral Reviews, 59*, 155–172.

Grillner, S. (1985). Neurobiological bases of rhythmic motor acts in vertebrates. *Science, 228*, 143–149.

Grillner, S. (2011). Human locomotor circuits conform. *Science, 334*, 912–913.

Grillner, S., & Dickinson, M. (2002). Motor systems. *Current Opinion in Neurobiology, 12*, 629–632.

Grillner, S., & Jessell, T. M. (2009). Measured motion: Searching for simplicity in spinal locomotor networks. *Current Opinion in Neurobiology, 19*, 572–586.

Grill-Spector, K., & Malach, R. (2004). The human visual cortex. *Annual Review of Neuroscience, 27*, 649–677.

Grippo, A. J., & Scotti, M.-A. L. (2013). Stress and neuroinflammation. In A. Halaris & B. E. Leonard (Eds.), *Inflammation in psychiatry* (pp. 20–32). Basel: Karger.

Grone, B. P., & Baraban, S. C. (2015). Animal models in epilepsy research: Legacies and new directions. *Nature Neuroscience, 18*, 339–343.

Grosche, A., & Reichenbach, A. (2013). Developmental refining of neuroglial signaling? *Science, 339*, 152–153.

Gross, C. G., Moore, T., & Rodman, H. R. (2004). Visually guided behavior after V1 lesions in young and adult monkeys and its relation to blindsight in humans. *Progress in Brain Research, 144*, 279–294.

Gruart, A., Leal-Campanario, R., López-Ramos, J. C., & Delgado-García, J. M. (2015). Functional basis of associative learning and their relationships with long-term potentiation evoked in the involved neural circuits: Lessons from studies in behaving mammals. *Neurobiology of Learning and Memory, 124*, 3–18.

Grubbe, M. S., & Thompson, I. D. (2004). The influence of early experience on the development of

sensory systems. *Current Opinion in Neurobiology, 14*, 503–512.

Gründer, G., Hippius, H., & Carlsson, A. (2009). The 'atypicality' of antipsychotics: A concept re-examined and re-defined. *Nature Reviews Drug Discovery, 8*, 197–202.

Grunt, J. A., & Young, W. C. (1952). Differential reactivity of individuals and the response of the male guinea pig to testosterone propionate. *Endocrinology, 51*, 237–248.

Gucci, F., & Goldman, D. (2012). The genetic basis of addictive disorders. *Psychiatric Clinics of North America, 35*, 495–519.

Guerrini, R., Dobyns, W. B., & Barkovich, A. J. (2008). Abnormal development of the human cerebral cortex: Genetics, functional consequences and treatment options. *Trends in Neurosciences, 31*, 154–162.

Guillamón, A., & Segovia, S. (1996). Sexual dimorphism in the CNS and the role of steroids. In T. W. Stone (Ed.), *CNS neurotransmitters and neuromodulators. Neuroactive steroids* (pp. 127–152). Boca Raton, FL: CRC Press.

Guillon, Q., Hadjikhani, N., Baduel, S., & Rogé, B. (2014). Visual social attention in autism spectrum disorder: Insights from eye tracking studies. *Neuroscience & Biobehavioral Reviews, 42*, 279–297.

Guo, Y., & Udin, S. B. (2000). The development of abnormal axon trajectories after rotation of one eye in *Xenopus. Journal of Neuroscience, 20*, 4189–4197.

Gupta, P., Albeanu, D. F., & Bhalla, U. S. (2015). Olfactory bulb coding of odors, mixtures and sniffs is a linear sum of odor time profiles. *Nature Neuroscience, 18*, 272–281.

Gustavsen, I., Bramness, J. G., Skurtveit, S., Engeland, A., Neutel, I., & Mørland, J. (2008). Road traffic accident risk related to prescriptions of the hypnotics zopiclone, zolpidem, flunitrazepam and nitrazepam. *Sleep Medicine, 9*, 818–822.

Gutchess, A. (2014). Plasticity of the aging brain: New directions in cognitive neuroscience. *Science, 346*, 579–582.

Gutfreund, Y., Zheng, W., & Knudsen, E. I. (2002). Gated visual input to the central auditory system. *Science, 297*, 1556–1559.

Guyenet, P. G. (2006). The sympathetic control of blood pressure. *Nature Reviews Neuroscience, 7*, 335–346.

Haelterman, N. A., Yoon, W. H., Sandoval, H., Jaiswal, M., Shulman, J. M., & Bellen, H. J. (2014). A mitocentric view of Parkinson's disease. *Annual Review of Neuroscience, 37*, 137–159.

Haffenden, A. M., & Goodale, M. A. (1998). The effect of pictorial illusion on prehension and perception. *Journal of Cognitive Neuroscience, 10*, 122–136.

Hagoort, P. (2014). Nodes and networks in the neural architecture for language: Broca's region and beyond. *Current Opinion in Neurobiology, 28*, 136–141.

Hahn, N., Foxe, J. J., & Molholm, S. (2014). Impairments of multisensory integration and cross-sensory learning as pathways to dyslexia. *Neuroscience & Biobehavioral Reviews, 47*, 384–392.

Hahnloser, R. H. R., & Kotowicz, A. (2010). Auditory representations and memory in birdsong learning. *Current Opinion in Neurobiology, 20*, 332–339.

Halford, J. C., & Blundell, J. E. (2000). Separate systems for serotonin and leptin in appetite control. *Annals of Medicine, 32*, 222–232.

Hall, S. S. (2010). Revolution postponed. *Scientific American, 303*(4), 60–67.

Hall, W., & Degenhardt, L. (2014). The adverse health effects of chronic cannabis use. *Drug Testing and Analysis, 6*, 39–45.

Hallett, M. (2015). Tourette syndrome: Update. *Brain and Development, 37*, 651–655.

Halpern, B., & Halpern, A. (2015). Safety assessment of FDA-approved (orlistat and lorcaserin)

anti-obesity medications. *Expert Opinion on Drug Safety, 14*, 305–315.

Hamann, S., Herman, R. A., Nolan, C. L., & Wallen, K. (2004). Men and women differ in amygdala response to visual sexual stimuli. *Nature Neuroscience, 7*, 411–416.

Hamann, S. (2005). Sex differences in the responses of the human amygdala. *The Neuroscientist, 11*, 288–293.

Hammer, M. F. (2013). Human hybrids. *Scientific American, 308*, 66–71.

Hammock, E. A. (2015). Developmental perspective on oxytocin and vasopressin. *Neuropsychopharmacology, 40*, 24–42.

Hammond, P. H., Merton, P. A., & Sutton, G. G. (1956). Nervous gradation of muscular contraction. *British Medical Bulletin, 12*, 214–218.

Handel, A. E., & Ramagoplan, S. V. (2010). Is Lamarckian evolution relevant to medicine? *BMC Medical Genetics, 11*, 73.

Hanford, L. C., Nazarov, A., Hall, G. B., & Sassi, R. B. (2016). Cortical thickness in bipolar disorder: A systematic review. *Bipolar Disorders, 18*, 4–18.

Hannan, A. J. (2014). Environmental enrichment and brain repair: Harnessing the therapeutic effects of cognitive stimulation and physical activity to enhance experience-dependent plasticity. *Neuropathology and Applied Neurobiology, 40*, 13–25.

Hannon, E., Spiers, H., Viana, J., Pidsley, R., Burrage, J., Murphy, T. M., … & Bray, N. J. (2016). Methylation QTLs in the developing brain and their enrichment in schizophrenia risk loci. *Nature Neuroscience, 19*, 48–54.

Haque, F. N., Gottesman, I. I., & Wong, A. H. C. (2009). Not really identical: Epigenetic differences in monozygotic twins and implications for twin studies in psychiatry. *American Journal of Medical Genetics, 151C*, 136–141.

Harden, K. P., Turkheimer, E., & Loehlin, J. C. (2007). Genotype by environment interaction in adolescents' cognitive aptitude. *Behavioral Genetics, 37*, 273–283.

Hardy, J., & Selkoe, D. J. (2002). The amyloid hypothesis of Alzheimer's disease: Progress and problems on the road to therapeutics. *Science, 297*, 353–356.

Hare, D. J., Arora, M., Jenkins, N. L., Finkelstein, D. I., Doble, P. A., & Bush, A. I. (2015). Is early-life iron exposure critical in neurodegeneration? *Nature Reviews Neurology, 11*, 536–544.

Hari, R., & Parkkonen, L. (2015). The brain timewise: How timing shapes and supports brain function. *Philosophical Transactions of the Royal Society B, 370*, 20140170.

Harmon, K. (2013). Shattered ancestry. *Scientific American, 308*, 42–49.

Harrar, V., Tammam, J., Pérez-Bellido, A., Pitt, A., Stein, J., & Spence, C. (2014). Multisensory integration and attention in developmental dyslexia. *Current Biology, 24*, 531–535.

Harris, G. W. (1955). *Neural control of the pituitary gland*. London, England: Edward Arnold.

Harris, L. J. (1978). Sex differences in spatial ability: Possible environmental, genetic, and neurological factors. In M. Kinsbourne (Ed.), *Asymmetrical function of the brain* (p. 463). Cambridge, England: Cambridge University Press.

Harris, L. J., Clay, J., Hargreaves, F. J., & Ward, A. (1933). Appetite and choice of diet: The ability of the vitamin B deficient rat to discriminate between diets containing and lacking the vitamin. *Proceedings of the Royal Society of London (B), 113*, 161–190.

Harrison, P. J. (2016). Molecular neurobiological clues to the pathogenesis of bipolar disorder. *Current Opinion in Neurobiology, 36*, 1–6.

Harrison, T. C., & Murphy, T. H. (2014). Motor maps and the cortical control of movement. *Current Opinion in Neurobiology, 24*, 88–94.

Hart, C. (2013). *High price*. New York: Harper Collins.

Hart, C. L., Marvin, C. B., Silver, R., & Smith, E. E. (2012). Is cognitive functioning impaired in methamphetamine users? A critical review. *Neuropsychopharmacology, 37*, 586–608.

Harvey, A. G., & Tang, N. K. Y. (2012). (Mis)perception of sleep in insomnia: A puzzle and a resolution. *Psychological Bulletin, 138*, 77–101.

Haslam, D., Sattar, N., & Lean, M. (2006). Obesity—time to wake up. *British Medical Journal, 333*, 640–642.

Haslinger, R., Pipa, G., Lima, B., Singer, W., Brown, E. N., & Neuenschwander, S. (2012). Context matters: The illusive simplicity of macaque V1 receptive fields. *PLoS ONE, 7*, e39699.

Hata, Y., & Stryker, M. P. (1994). Control of thalamocortical afferent rearrangement by postsynaptic activity in developing visual cortex. *Science, 265*, 1732–1735.

Hattar, S., Lucas, R. J., Mrosovsky, N., Thompson, S., Douglas, R. H., Hankins, M. W., . . . & Yau, K.-W. (2003). Melanopsin and rod-cone photoreceptive systems account for all major accessory visual functions in mice. *Nature, 424*, 75–81.

Hauser, M. (2009). Origin of the mind. *Scientific American, 301*(3), 44–51.

Hauser, M. D., Yang, C., Berwick, R. C., Tattersall, I., Ryan, M. J., . . . & Lewontin, R. C. (2014). The mystery of language evolution. *Frontiers in Psychology, 5*, 401.

Hauser, S. L., Chan, J. R., & Oksenberg, J. R. (2013). Multiple sclerosis: Prospects and promise. *Annals of Neurology, 74*, 317–327.

Haut, S. R., & Shinnar, S. (2008). Considerations in the treatment of a first unprovoked seizure. *Seminars in Neurology, 28*, 289–296.

Haxby, J. V. (2006). Fine structure in representations of faces and objects. *Nature Neuroscience, 9*, 1084–1085.

Hayashi, Y., Kashiwagi, M., Yasuda, K., Ando, R., Kanuka, M., Sakai, K., & Itohara, S. (2015). Cells of a common developmental origin regulate REM/non-REM sleep and wakefulness in mice. *Science, 350*, 957–961.

Haynes, J.-D., & Rees, G. (2006). Decoding mental states from brain activity in humans. *Nature Reviews Neuroscience, 7*, 523–534.

Hebb, D. O. (1949). *The organization of behavior.* New York, NY: Wiley.

Hécaen, H., & Angelergues, R. (1964). Localization of symptoms in aphasia. In A. V. S. de Reuck & M. O'Connor (Eds.), *CIBA foundation symposium on the disorders of language* (pp. 222–256). London: Churchill Press.

Hedlund, P. (2014). Cannabinoids and the endocannabinoid system in lower urinary tract function and dysfunction. *Neurourology and Urodynamics, 33*, 46–53.

Heffner, H. E., & Heffner, R. S. (2003). Audition. In S. Davis (Ed.), *Handbook of research methods in experimental psychology* (pp. 413–440). Oxford, England: Blackwell.

Helgen, K. M. (2011). The mammal family tree. *Science, 334*, 458–459.

Heller, A. C., Amar, A. P., Liu, C. Y., & Apuzzo, M. L. J. (2006). Surgery of the mind and mood: A mosaic of issues in time and evolution. *Neurosurgery, 59*(4), 720–739.

Heller, E. A., Cates, H. M., Peña, C. J., Sun, H., Shao, N., Feng, J., . . . & Ferguson, D. (2014). Locus-specific epigenetic remodeling controls addiction- and depression-related behaviors. *Nature Neuroscience, 17*, 1720–1727.

Helmer, W. J. (1986, February). The madman in the tower. *Texas Monthly.*

Heni, M., Kullmann, S., Preissl, H., Fritsche, A., & Häring, H. U. (2015). Impaired insulin action in the human brain: Causes and metabolic consequences. *Nature Reviews Endocrinology, 11*, 701–711.

Henke, K., Kroll, N. E. A., Behniea, H., Amaral, D. G., Miller, M. B., Rafal, R., & Gazzaniga, M. S. (1999). Memory lost and regained following bilateral hippocampal damage. *Journal of Cognitive Neuroscience, 11*, 682–697.

Henley, C. L., Nunez, A. A., & Clemens, L. G. (2011). Hormones of choice: The neuroendocrinology of partner preference in animals. *Frontiers in Neuroendocrinology, 32*, 146–154.

Hennessey, A. C., Camak, L., Gordon, F., & Edwards, D. A. (1990). Connections between the pontine central gray and the ventromedial hypothalamus are essential for lordosis in female rats. *Behavioral Neuroscience, 104*, 477–488.

Herculano-Houzel, S. (2013). Sleep it out. *Science, 342*, 316–317.

Herman, J. P., McKlveen, J. M., Solomon, M. B., Carvalho-Netto, E., & Myers, B. (2011). Neural regulation of the stress response: Glucocorticoid feedback mechanisms. *Brazilian Journal of Medical and Biological Research, 45*, 292–298.

Herman, J. P., McKlveen, J. M., Solomon, M. B., Carvalho-Netto, E., & Myers, B. (2012). Neural regulation of the stress response: Glucocorticoid feedback mechanisms. *Brazilian Journal of Medical and Biological Research, 45*, 292–298.

Herman, R., He, J., D'Luzansky, S., Willis, W., & Dilli, S. (2002). Spinal cord stimulation facilitates functional walking in a chronic, incomplete spinal cord injured. *Spinal Cord, 2*, 65–68.

Hernández-Fonseca, K., Massieu, L., de la Cadena, S. G., Guzmán, C., & Carnacho-Arroyo, I. (2012). Neuroprotective role of estradiol against neuronal death induced by glucose deprivation in cultured rat hippocampal neurons. *Neuroendocrinology, 96*, 41–50.

Hernandez, G., Hamdani, S., Rajabi, H., Conover, K., Stewart, J., Arvanitogiannis, A., & Shizgal, P. (2006). Prolonged rewarding stimulation of the rat medial forebrain bundle: Neurochemical and behavioral consequences. *Behavioral Neuroscience, 120*, 888–904.

Herrington, J. D., Heller, W., Mohanty, A., Engels, A. S., Banich, M. T., Webb, A. G., & Miller, G. A. (2010). Localization of asymmetric brain function in emotion and depression. *Psychophysiology, 47*, 442–454.

Herrup, K. (2015). The case for rejecting the amyloid cascade hypothesis. *Nature Neuroscience, 18*, 794–798.

Herry, C., & Johansen, J. P. (2013). Encoding of fear learning and memory in distributed neuronal circuits. *Nature Neuroscience, 17*, 1644–1654.

Herry, C., & Johansen, J. P. (2014). Encoding of fear learning and memory in distributed neuronal circuits. *Nature Neuroscience, 17*, 1644–1654.

Hertzog, C., Kramer, A. F., Wilson, R. S., & Lindenberger, U. (2008). Enrichment effects on adult cognitive development: Can the functional capacity of older adults be preserved or enhanced? *Psychological Science in the Public Interest, 9*, 1–65.

Hervé, P.-Y., Zago, L., Petit, L., Mazoyer, B., & Tzourio-Mazoyer, N. (2013). Revisiting human hemispheric specialization with neuroimaging. *Trends in Cognitive Sciences, 17*, 69–80.

Herzfeld, D. J., & Shadmehr, R. (2014). Cerebellum estimates the sensory state of the body. *Trends in Cognitive Sciences, 18*, 66–67.

Hestrin, S., & Galarreta, M. (2005). Electrical synapses define networks of neocortical GABAergic neurons. *Trends in Neurosciences, 28*, 304–309.

Hetherington, A. W., & Ranson, S. W. (1940). Hypothalamic lesions and adiposity in the rat. *Anatomical Record, 78*, 149–172.

Heuser, J. E., Reese, T. S., Dennis, M. J., Jan, Y., Jan, L., & Evans, L. (1979). Synaptic vesicle exocytosis captured by quick freezing and correlated with quantal transmitter release. *Journal of Cell Biology, 81*, 275–300.

Heyes, C. (2010). Where do mirror neurons come from? *Neuroscience and Biobehavioral Reviews, 34*, 575–583.

Heymsfield, S. B., Greenberg, A. S., Fujioka, K., Dixon, R. M., Kushner, R., Hunt, T., . . . & McCamish, M. (1999). Recombinant leptin for weight loss in obese and lean adults. *Journal of the American Medical Association, 282*, 1568–1575.

Heys, J. G., MacLeod, K. M., Moss, C. F., & Hasselmo, M. E. (2013). Bat and rat neurons differ in theta-frequency resonance despite similar coding of space. *Science, 340*, 363–367.

Hickok, G., & Poeppel, D. (2007). The cortical organization of speech processing. *Nature Reviews Neuroscience, 8*, 393–402.

Hickok, G., Houde, J., & Rong, F. (2011). Sensorimotor integration in speech processing: Computational basis and neural organization. *Neuron, 69*, 407–422.

Hickok, G., Okada, K., Barr, W., Pa, J., Rogalsky, C., Donnelly, K., . . . & Grant, A. (2008). Bilateral capacity for speech sound processing in auditory comprehension: Evidence from Wada procedures. *Brain and Language, 107*, 179–184.

Higgins, S. T., Heil, S. H., & Lussier, J. P. (2004). Clinical implications of reinforcement as a determinant of substance use disorders. *Annual Review of Psychology, 55*, 431–461.

Higgs, S., Williamson, A. C., Rotshtein, P., & Humphreys, G. W. (2008). Sensory-specific satiety is intact in amnesics who eat multiple meals. *Psychological Science, 19*, 623–628.

Hikosaka, O., Kim, H. F., Yasuda, M., & Yamamoto, S. (2014). Basal ganglia circuits for reward value-guided behavior. *Annual Review of Neuroscience, 37*, 289–306.

Hill, M. (2015). Perspective: Be clear about the real risks. *Nature, 525*, S14.

Hillman, E. M. C. (2014). Coupling mechanism and significance of the BOLD signal: A status report. *Annual Review of Neuroscience, 37*, 161–181.

Hills, A. P., Mokhtar, N., & Byrne, N. M. (2014). Assessment of physical activity and energy expenditure: An overview of objective measures. *Frontiers in Nutrition, 1*, 5.

Himmelbach, M., & Karnath, H.-O. (2005). Dorsal and ventral stream interaction: Contributions from optic ataxia. *Journal of Cognitive Neuroscience, 17*, 632–640.

Hines, M. (2010). Sex-related variation in human behavior and the brain. *Trends in Cognitive Sciences, 14*, 448–456.

Hines, M. (2011). Gender development and the human brain. *Annual Review of Neuroscience, 34*, 69–88.

Hinnebusch, A. G. (2015). Blocking stress response for better memory? *Science, 348*, 967–968.

Hirose, S. (2014). Mutant GABA(A) receptor subunits in genetic (idiopathic) epilepsy. *Progress in Brain Research, 213*, 55–85.

Hitti, F. L., & Siegelbaum, S. A. (2014). The hippocampal CA2 region is essential for social memory. *Nature, 508*, 88–92.

Hobson, J. A. (1989). *Sleep.* New York, NY: Scientific American Library.

Hobson, J. A., & Pace-Schott, E. F. (2002). The cognitive neuroscience of sleep: Neuronal systems, consciousness and learning. *Nature Reviews Neuroscience, 3*, 679–693.

Hochedlinger, K. (2010). Your inner healers. *Scientific American, 302*, 47–52.

Hoeft, F., Meyler, A., Hernandez, A., Juel, C., Taylor-Hill, H., Martindale, J. L., . . . & Deutsch, G. K. (2007). Functional and morphometric brain dissociation between dyslexia and reading ability. *Proceedings of the National Academy of Sciences, 104*, 4234–4239.

Hoeren, M., Kümmerer, D., Bormann, T., Beume, L., Ludwig, V. M., . . . & Weiller, C. (2014). Neural bases of imitation and pantomime in acute stroke patients: Distinct streams for praxis. *Brain, 137*, 2796–2810.

Hofer, S. B., Mrsic-Flogel, T. D., Bonhoeffer, T., & Hübener, M. (2005). Prior experience enhances plasticity in adult visual cortex. *Nature Neuroscience, 9*, 127–132.

Hofer, S. B., Mrsic-Flogel, T. D., Bonhoeffer, T., & Hübener, M. (2006). Lifelong learning: Ocular dominance plasticity in mouse visual cortex. *Current Opinion in Neurobiology, 16,* 451–459.

Hoffman, H., Peterson, K., & Garner, H. (2012). Field conditioning of sexual arousal in humans. *Socioaffective Neuroscience and Psychology, 2,* 17336.

Hoffman, Y., & Pilpel, Y. (2015). MicroRNAs silence the noisy genome. *Science, 348,* 41–42.

Hoffmann, S., & Beste, C. (2015). A perspective on neural and cognitive mechanisms of error commission. *Frontiers in Behavioral Neuroscience, 9,* 50.

Hofman, M. A. (2014). Evolution of the human brain: When bigger is better. *Frontiers in Neuroanatomy, 8,* 1–12.

Holland, L. Z. (2009). Chordate roots of the vertebrate nervous system: Expanding the molecular toolkit. *Nature Reviews Neuroscience, 10,* 736–746.

Hollands, G. J., Shemilt, I., Marteau, T. M., Jebb, S. A., Lewis, H. B., Wei, Y., Higgins, J. P., & Ogilvie, D. (2015). Portion, package or tableware size for changing selection and consumption of food, alcohol, and tobacco. *Cochrane Database of Systematic Reviews, 9,* CD011045.

Hollenbeck, P. J. (2001). Insight and hindsight into Tourette syndrome. In D. J. Cohen, C. G. Goetz, & J. Jankovic (Eds.), *Tourette syndrome* (pp. 363–367). Philadelphia, PA: Lippincott Williams & Wilkins.

Hollins, M. (2010). Somesthetic senses. *Annual Review of Psychology, 61,* 243–271.

Hollon, S. D., Thase, M. E., & Markowitz, J. C. (2002). Treatment and prevention of depression. *Psychological Science in the Public Interest, 3,* 39–77.

Holtmaat, A., & Svoboda, K. (2009). Experience-dependent structural synaptic plasticity in the mammalian brain. *Nature Reviews Neuroscience, 10,* 647–658.

Holtzheimer, P. E., Kelley, M. E., Gross, R. E., Filkowski, M. M., Garlow, S. J., Barrocas, A., Wint, D., Craighead, M. C., Kozarsky, J., Chismar, R., Moreines, J. L., Mewes, K., Posse, P. R., Gutman, D. A., & Mayberg, H. S. (2011). Subcallosal cingulate deep brain stimulation for treatment-resistant unipolar and bipolar depression. *JAMA Psychiatry, 70,* 373–382.

Holzman, P. S., & Matthyse, S. (1990). The genetics of schizophrenia: A review. *Current Directions in Psychological Science, 1,* 279–286.

Homberg, J. R., Molteni, R., Calabrese, F., & Riva, M. A. (2014). The serotonin–BDNF duo: Developmental implications for the vulnerability to psychopathology. *Neuroscience & Biobehavioral Reviews, 43,* 35–47.

Hoon, M., Okawa, H., Della Santina, L., & Wong, R. O. L. (2014). Functional architecture of the retina: Development and disease. *Progress in Retinal and Eye Research, 42,* 44–84.

Hopkins, W. D., & Cantalupo, C. (2008). Theoretical speculations on the evolutionary origins of hemispheric specialization. *Current Directions in Psychological Science, 17,* 233–237.

Hopkins, W. D., Russell, J. L., & Cantalupo, C. (2007). Neuroanatomical correlates of handedness for tool use in chimpanzees (*Pan troglodytes*). *Psychological Science, 18,* 971–977.

Horgan, J. (2005, October). The forgotten era of brain chips. *Scientific American, 293,* 166–173.

Horne, J. (2000). Neuroscience: Images of lost sleep. *Nature, 403,* 605–606.

Horne, J. (2009). REM sleep, energy balance and "optimal foraging." *Neuroscience and Biobehavioral Reviews, 33,* 466–474.

Horne, J. (2010). The end of sleep: 'Sleep debt' versus biological adaptation of human sleep to waking needs. *Biological Psychology, 87,* 1–14.

Horne, J. (2011). Sleepiness as a need for sleep: When is enough, enough? *Neuroscience and Biobehavioral Reviews, 34,* 108–118.

Horne, J. (2013). Why REM sleep? Clues beyond the laboratory in a more challenging world. *Biological Psychology, 92,* 152–168.

Horton, J. (2009). Akinetopsia from nefazodone toxicity. *American Journal of Ophthalmology, 128,* 530–531.

Horton, J. C., & Sincich, L. C. (2004). A new foundation for the visual cortical hierarchy. In M. Gazzaniga (Ed.), *The cognitive neurosciences* (pp. 233–244). Cambridge, MA: MIT Press.

Hoshi, E., & Tanji, J. (2007). Distinctions between dorsal and ventral premotor areas: anatomical connectivity and functional properties. *Current Opinion in Neurobiology, 17,* 234–242.

Hosking, R., & Zajicek, J. (2014). Cannabis in neurology—a potted review. *Nature Reviews Neurology, 10,* 429–430.

Hostinar, C. E., Sullivan, R. M., & Gunnar, M. R. (2014). Psychobiological mechanisms underlying the social buffering of the hypothalamic–pituitary–adrenocortical axis: A review of animal models and human studies across development. *Psychological Bulletin, 140,* 256.

Howald, C., Merla, G., Digilio, M. C., Amenta, S., Lyle, R., Deutsch, S., . . . & Reymond, A. (2006). Two high throughput technologies to detect segmental aneuploidies identify new Williams-Beuren syndrome patients with atypical deletions. *Journal of Medical Genetics, 43,* 266–273.

Howard-Jones, P. A. (2014). Neuroscience and education: myths and messages. *Nature Reviews Neuroscience, 15,* 817–824.

Howarth, C. (2014). The contribution of astrocytes to the regulation of cerebral blood flow. *Frontiers in Neuroscience, 8,* 103.

Howells, D. W., Sena, E. S., & MacLeod, M. R. (2014). Bringing rigour to translational medicine. *Nature Reviews Neurology, 10,* 37–43.

Hrabovszky, Z., & Hutson, J. M. (2002). Androgen imprinting of the brain in animal models and humans with intersex disorders: Review and recommendations. *The Journal of Urology, 168,* 2142–2148.

Hromádka, T., & Zador, A. M. (2009). Representations in auditory cortex. *Current Opinion in Neurobiology, 19,* 430–433.

Hsieh, J., & Schneider, J. W. (2013). Neural stem cells, excited. *Science, 339,* 1533–1534.

Hsieh, J. H., Stein, D. J., & Howells, F. M. (2014). The neurobiology of methamphetamine induced psychosis. *Frontiers in Human Neuroscience, 8,* 537.

Hoshi, E., & Tanji, J. (2007). Distinctions between dorsal and ventral premotor areas: anatomical connectivity and functional properties. *Current Opinion in Neurobiology, 17,* 234–242.

Hsu, C. T., Jacobs, A. M., Altmann, U., & Conrad, M. (2015). The magical activation of left amygdala when reading Harry Potter: An fMRI study on how descriptions of supra-natural events entertain and enchant. *PLoS One, 10,* e0118179.

Huang, N., Chelliah, Y., Shan, Y., Taylor, C. A., Yoo, S.-H., Partch, C., Green, C. B., Zhang, H., & Takahashi, J. S. (2012). Crystal structure of the heterodimeric CLOCK:BMAL1 transcriptional activator complex. *Science, 337,* 189–194.

Huang, Y., & Mucke, L. (2012). Alzheimer mechanisms and therapeutic strategies. *Cell, 148,* 1204–1222.

Hubel, D. H., & Wiesel, T. N. (1979, September). Brain mechanisms of vision. *Scientific American, 241,* 150–162.

Hubel, D. H., & Wiesel, T. N. (2004). *Brain and visual perception: The story of a 25-year collaboration.* New York: Oxford University Press.

Hubel, D. H., Wiesel, T. N., & LeVay, S. (1977). Plasticity of ocular dominance columns in the monkey striate cortex. *Philosophical Transactions of the Royal Society of London, 278,* 377–409.

Huber, D., Gutnisky, D. A., Peron, S., O'Connor, D. H., Wiegert, J. S., Tian, L., Oertner, T. G., Looger, L. L., & Svoboda, K. (2012). Multiple dynamic representations in the motor cortex during sensorimotor learning. *Nature, 484,* 473–478.

Huber, M. A., & Tantiwongkosi, B. (2014). Oral and oropharyngeal cancer. *Medical Clinics of North America, 6,* 1299–1321.

Hublin, J.-J., Neubauer, S., & Gunz, P. (2015). Brain ontogeny and life history in pleistocene hominins. *Philosophical Transactions of the Royal Society B, 370,* 20140062.

Hudson, J. I., Hiripi, E., Pope, H. G., & Kessler, R. C. (2007). The prevalence and correlates of eating disorders in the National Comorbidity Survey Replication. *Biological Psychiatry, 61,* 348–358.

Hudspeth, A. J. (2014). Integrating the active process of hair cells with cochlear function. *Nature Reviews Neuroscience, 15,* 600–614.

Huffman, K. M., Redman, L. M., Landerman, L. R., Pieper, C. F., Stevens, R. D., Muehlbauer, M. J., Wenner, B. R., Bain, J. R., Kraus, V. B., Newgard, C. B., Ravussin, E., & Kraus, W. E. (2012). Caloric restriction alters the metabolic response to a mixed-meal: Results from a randomized, controlled trial. *PLoS ONE, 7,* e28190.

Hughes, V. (2014). The sins of the father. *Nature, 507,* 22–24.

Hughes, V. (2014). A gut-wrenching question. *Nature, 511,* 282–284.

Hull, E. M., & Dominguez, J. M. (2007). Sexual behavior in male rodents. *Hormones and Behavior, 52,* 45–55.

Hull, E. M., Lorrain, D. S., Du, J., Matuszewich, L., Lumley, L. A., Putnam, S. K., & Moses, J. (1999). Hormone-neurotransmitter interaction in the control of sexual behavior. *Behavioural Brain Research, 105,* 105–116.

Hulme, S. R., Jones, O. D., & Abraham, W. C. (2013). Emerging role of metaplasticity in behaviour and disease. *Trends in Neurosciences, 36,* 353–362.

Humbert-Claude, M., Davenas, E., Gbahou, F., Vincent, L., & Arrang, J.-M. (2012). Involvement of histamine receptors in the atypical antipsychotic profile of clozapine: A reassessment in vitro and in vivo. *Psychopharmacology, 220,* 225–241.

Hume, K. I., & Mills, J. N. (1977). Rhythms of REM and slow wave sleep in subjects living on abnormal time schedules. *Waking and Sleeping, 1,* 291–296.

Hunter, G. (2011). Transient global amnesia. *Neurologic Clinics, 29,* 1045–1054.

Hurlbert, A. (2003). Colour vision: Primary visual cortex shows its influence. *Current Biology, 13,* 270–272.

Hurlemann, R., Wagner, M., Hawellek, B., Reich, H., Pieperhoff, P., Amunts, K., . . . & Dolan, R. J. (2007). Amygdala control of emotion-induced forgetting and remembering: Evidence from Urbach-Wiethe disease. *Neuropsychologia, 45,* 877–884.

Hussain, M., & Mehta, M. A. (2011). Cognitive enhancement by drugs in health and disease. *Trends in Cognitive Science, 15,* 28–36.

Hustvedt, B. E., & Løvø, A. (1972). Correlation between hyperinsulinemia and hyperphagia in rats with ventromedial hypothalamic lesions. *Acta Physiologica Scandinavica, 84,* 29–33.

Hutchinson, J. B., Uncapher, M. R., Weiner, K. S., Bressler, D. W., Silver, M. A., . . . & Wagner, A. D. (2014). Functional heterogeneity in posterior parietal cortex across attention and episodic memory retrieval. *Cerebral Cortex, 24,* 49–66.

Hwang, D. H., Kim, B. G., Kim, E. J., Lee, S. I., Joo, I. S., Suh-Kim, H., Sohn, S., & Kim, S. U. (2009). Transplantation of human neural stem cells transduced with Olig2 transcription factor improves locomotor recovery and enhances myelination in the white matter of rat spinal cord following contusive injury. *BMC Neuroscience, 10,* 117.

Hyde, J. S. (2005). The gender similarities hypothesis. *American Psychologist, 60,* 581–592.

Hyman, S. E., & Fenton, W. S. (2003). What are the right targets for psychopharmacology? *Science, 299,* 350–351.

Iacono, W. G., & Koenig, W. G. R. (1983). Features that distinguish the smooth-pursuit eye-tracking performance of schizophrenic, affective-disorder, and normal individuals. *Journal of Abnormal Psychology, 92,* 29–41.

Ibbotson, M., & Krekelberg, B. (2011). Visual perception and saccadic eye movements. *Current Opinion in Neurobiology, 21,* 553–558.

Iino, M., Goto, K., Kakegawa, W., Okado, H., Sudo, M., Ishiuchi, S.,…& Ozawa, S. (2001). Glia-synapse interaction through calcium-permeable AMPA receptors in Bergmann glia. *Science, 292,* 926–929.

Ikeda, H., & Hayashi, M. (2008). Electroencephalogram activity before self-awakening. *Sleep and Biological Rhythms, 6,* 256–259.

Illert, M., & Kümmel, H. (1999). Reflex pathways from large muscle spindle afferents and recurrent axon collaterals to motoneurones of wrist and digit muscles: A comparison in cats, monkeys and humans. *Experimental Brain Research, 128,* 13–19.

Inestrosa, N. C., & Arenas, E. (2010). Emerging roles of Wnts in the adult nervous system. *Nature Reviews Neuroscience, 11,* 77–86.

Ingalhalikar, M., Smith, A., Parker, D., Satterthwaite, T. D., Elliott, M. A.,…& Verma, R. (2014). Sex differences in the structural connectome of the human brain. *PNAS, 111,* 823–828.

Inglis, J., & Lawson, J. S. (1982). A meta-analysis of sex differences in the effects of unilateral brain damage on intelligence test results. *Canadian Journal of Psychology, 36,* 670–683.

Innocenti, G. M., & Price, D. J. (2005). Exuberance in the development of cortical networks. *Nature Reviews Neuroscience, 6,* 955–965.

Inostroza, M., & Born, J. (2013). Sleep for preserving and transforming episodic memory. *Annual Review of Neuroscience, 36,* 79–102.

Insel, T. R., & Cuthbert, B. N. (2015). Brain disorders? Precisely. *Science, 348,* 499–500.

Inta, D., Cameron, H. A., & Gass, P. (2015). New neurons in the adult striatum: From rodents to humans. *Trends in Neurosciences, 38,* 517–523.

Interlandi, J. (2013). Breaking the brain barrier. *Scientific American, 308,* 52–57.

Iqbal, K., Liu, F., & Gong, C. X. (2016). Tau and neurodegenerative disease: The story so far. *Nature Reviews Neurology, 12,* 15–27.

Iremonger, K. J., Wamsteeker Cusulin, J. I., & Bains, J. S. (2013). Changing the tune: Plasticity and adaptation of retrograde signals. *Trends in Neurosciences, 8,* 471–479.

Irwin, D. J., Lee, V. M.-Y., & Trojanowski, J. Q. (2013). Parkinson's disease dementia: Convergence of alpha-synuclein, tau and amyloid-beta pathologies. *Nature Reviews Neuroscience, 14,* 626–636.

Irwin, M. R., Olmstead, R., & Carroll, J. E. (2016). Sleep disturbance, sleep duration, and inflammation: A systematic review and meta-analysis of cohort studies and experimental sleep deprivation. *Biological Psychiatry, 80,* 40–52.

Ishikawa, A., Shimegi, S., Kida, H., & Sato, H. (2010). Temporal properties of spatial frequency tuning of surround suppression in the primary visual cortex and the lateral geniculate nucleus of the cat. *European Journal of Neuroscience, 31,* 2086–2100.

Isoda, M., & Noritake, A. (2013). What makes the dorsomedial frontal cortex active during reading the mental states of others? *Frontiers in Neuroscience, 7,* 232.

Ito, K., & Suda, T. (2014). Metabolic requirements for the maintenance of self-renewing stem cells. *Nature Reviews Molecular Cell Biology, 15,* 243–256.

Itoh, Y., Tyssowski, K., & Gotoh, Y. (2013). Transcriptional coupling of neuronal fate commitment and the onset of migration. *Current Opinion in Neurobiology, 23,* 957–964.

Iwaniuk, A. N., & Whishaw, I. Q. (2000). On the origin of skilled forelimb movements. *Trends in Neurosciences, 23,* 372–376.

Iyer, A., & Marson, A. (2014). Pharmacotherapy for focal epilepsy. *Expert Opinion on Pharmacotherapy, 15,* 1543–1551.

Izaurralde, E. (2015). Breakers and blockers—miRNAs at work. *Science, 349,* 380–382.

Jabr, F. (2013). Gambling on the brain. *Scientific American, 309,* 28–30.

Jack, C. R., & Holtzman, D. M. (2013). Biomarker modeling of Alzheimer's disease. *Neuron, 80,* 1347–1358.

Jack, R. E., Garrod, O. G., Yu, H., Caldara, R., & Schyns, P. G. (2012). Facial expressions of emotion are not culturally universal. *Proceedings of the National Academy of Sciences, 109,* 7241–7244.

Jackson, G. M., Draper, A., Dyke, K., Pépés, S. E., & Jackson, S. R. (2015). Inhibition, disinhibition, and the control of action in Tourette syndrome. *Trends in Cognitive Sciences, 19,* 655–665.

Jacobs, G. H., & Nathans, J. (2009, April). The evolution of primate color vision. *Scientific American, 300,* 56–63.

Jacobs, G. H., Williams, G. A., Cahill, H., & Nathans, J. (2007). Emergence of novel color vision in mice engineered to express a human cone photopigment. *Science, 315,* 1723–1725.

Jacobs, H. I. L., Boxtel, M. P. J., Jolles, J., Verhey, F. R. J., & Uylings, H. B. M. (2012). Parietal cortex matters in Alzheimer's disease: An overview of structural, functional and metabolic findings. *Neuroscience and Biobehavioral Reviews, 36,* 297–309.

Jacobs, J., Weidemann, C. T., Miller, J. F., Solway, A., Burke, J. F.,…& Kahana, M. J. (2013). *Nature Neuroscience, 16,* 1188–1190.

Jaeger, J.-J., & Marivaux, L. (2005). Shaking the earliest branches of anthropoid primate evolution. *Science, 310,* 244–245.

Jaffe, A. E., Gao, Y., Deep-Soboslay, A., Tao, R., Hyde, T. M., Weinberger, D. R., & Kleinman, J. E. (2016). Mapping DNA methylation across development, genotype and schizophrenia in the human frontal cortex. *Nature Neuroscience, 19,* 40–47.

Jaffee, S. R., Price, T. S., & Reyes, T. M. (2013). Behavior genetics: Past, present, and future. *Development and Psychopathology, 25,* 1225–1242.

Jameson, K. A., Highnote, S. M., & Wasserman, L. M. (2001). Richer color experience in observers with multiple photopigment opsin genes. *Psychonomic Bulletin & Review, 8*(2), 244–261.

Janak, P. H., & Tye, K. M. (2015). From circuits to behaviour in the amygdala. *Nature, 517,* 284–292.

Jann, M. W. (2014). Diagnosis and treatment of bipolar disorders in adults: A review of the evidence on pharmacologic treatments. *American Health & Drug Benefits, 7,* 489.

Januszko, P., Niemcewicz, S., Gajda, T., Wołyńczyk-Gmaj, D., Piotrowska, A. J.,…& Szelenberger, W. (2015). Sleepwalking episodes are preceded by arousal-related activation in the cingulate motor area: EEG current density imaging. *Clinical Neurophysiology, 127,* 530–536.

Järvinen, A., Korenberg, J. R., & Bellugi, U. (2013). The social phenotype of Williams syndrome. *Current Opinion in Neurobiology, 23,* 414–422.

Järvinen, A., Ng, R., Crivelli, D., Neumann, D., Arnold, A. J.,…& Bellugi, U. (2015). Social functioning and autonomic nervous system sensitivity across vocal and musical emotion in Williams syndrome and autism spectrum disorder. *Developmental Psychobiology, 58,* 17–26.

Jbabdi, S., Sotiropoulos, S. N., Haber, S. N., Van Essen, D. C., & Behrens, T. E. (2015). Measuring macroscopic brain connections in vivo. *Nature Neuroscience, 18,* 1546–1555.

Jeannerod, M., Arbib, M. A., Rizzolatti, G., & Sakarta, H. (1995). Grasping objects: The cortical mechanisms of visuomotor transformation. *Trends in Neurosciences, 18*(7), 314–327.

Jenkins, I. H., Brooks, D. J., Bixon, P. D., Frackowiak, R. S. J., & Passingham, R. E. (1994). Motor sequence learning: A study with positron emission tomography. *Journal of Neuroscience, 14*(6), 3775–3790.

Jennings, J. H., Rizzi, G., Stamatakis, A. M., Ung, R. L., & Stuber, G. D. (2013). The inhibitory circuit architecture of the lateral hypothalamus orchestrates feeding. *Science, 341,* 1517–1521.

Jensen, F. E. (2014). Progress across the spectrum of epilepsy research. *Nature Review Neurology, 10,* 63–64.

Jerath, R., & Crawford, M. W. (2014). Neural correlates of visuospatial consciousness in 3D default space: Insights from contralateral neglect syndrome. *Consciousness and Cognition, 28,* 81–93.

Jernigan, T. L., Baaré, W. F., Stiles, J., & Madsen, K. S. (2011). Postnatal brain development: Structural imaging of dynamic neurodevelopmental process. *Progress in Brain Research, 189,* 77–92.

Jin, J., & Maren, S. (2015). Prefrontal-hippocampal interactions in memory and emotion. *Frontiers in Systems Neuroscience, 9,* 170.

Jin, X., & Yamashita, T. (2016). Microglia in central nervous system repair after injury. *Journal of Biochemistry, 159,* 491–496.

Johansen, J. P., Cain, C. K., Ostroff, L. E., & LeDoux, J. E. (2011). Molecular mechanisms of fear learning and memory. *Cell, 147,* 509–524.

Johnson, A. W. (2013). Eating beyond metabolic need: How environmental cues influence feeding behavior. *Trends in Neurosciences, 36,* 101–109.

Johnson, P. L., Federici, L. M., & Shekhar, A. (2014). Etiology, triggers and neurochemical circuits associated with unexpected, expected, and laboratory-induced panic attacks. *Neuroscience & Biobehavioral Reviews, 46,* 429–454.

Johnson, W., Turkheimer, E., Gottesman, I. I., & Bouchard, T. J. (2009). Beyond heritability: Twin studies in behavioral research. *Current Directions in Psychological Science, 18,* 217–220.

Johnston, T. D. (1987). The persistence of dichotomies in the study of behavioral development. *Developmental Review, 7,* 149–182.

Joiner, W. M., Cavanaugh, J., FitzGibbon, E. J., & Wurtz, R. H. (2013). Corollary discharge contributes to perceived eye location in monkeys. *Journal of Neurophysiology, 110,* 2402–2413.

Jonas, J., Maillard, L., Frismand, S., Colnat-Coulbois, S., Vespignani, H., Rossion, B., & Vignal, J. P. (2014). Self-face hallucinations evoked by electrical stimulation of the human brain. *Neurology, 83,* 336–338.

Jones, H. S., & Oswald, I. (1966). Two cases of healthy insomnia. *Electroencephalography and Clinical Neurophysiology, 24,* 378–380.

Jones, H. W., & Park, I. J. (1971). A classification of special problems in sex differentiation. In D. Bergsma (Ed.), *The clinical delineation of birth defects. Part X: The endocrine system* (pp. 113–121). Baltimore, MD: Williams and Wilkins.

Jones, O. D. (2015). Astrocyte-mediated metaplasticity in the hippocampus: Help or hindrance? *Neuroscience, 309,* 113–124.

Jones, R. S., & Lynch, M. A. (2014). How dependent is synaptic plasticity on microglial phenotype? *Neuropharmacology, 96,* 3–10.

Jones, W., & Klin, A. (2014). Attention to eyes is present but in decline in 2–6-month-old infants later diagnosed with autism. *Nature, 504,* 427–431.

Jordan-Young, R. M. (2012). Hormones, context, and "brain gender": A review of evidence from congenital adrenal hyperplasia. *Social Science & Medicine, 74,* 1738–1744.

Jordan-Young, R., & Rumiati. R. I. (2012). Hardwired for sexism? Approaches to sex/gender in neuroscience. *Neuroethics, 5,* 305–315.

Joseph, R. (1988). Dual mental functioning in a split-brain patient. *Journal of Clinical Psychology, 44,* 771–779.

Joshua, M., Adler, A., & Bergman, H. (2009). The dynamics of dopamine in control of motor behavior. *Current Opinion in Neurobiology, 19,* 615–620.

Josselyn, S. A., Köhler, S., & Frankland, P. W. (2015). Finding the engram. *Nature Reviews Neuroscience, 16,* 521–534.

Jost, A. (1972). A new look at the mechanisms controlling sex differentiation in mammals. *Johns Hopkins Medical Journal, 130,* 38–53.

Jourdain, P., Bergersen, L. H., Bhaukaurally, K., Bezzi, P., Santello, M., Domercq, M.,...& Volterra, A. (2007). Glutamate exocytosis from astrocytes controls synaptic strength. *Nature Neuroscience, 10*, 331–339.

Julien, R. M. (1981). *A primer of drug action.* San Francisco, CA: W. H. Freeman.

Jun, H. J., Joshi, Y., Patil, Y., Noland, R. C., & Chang, J. S. (2014). NT-PGC-1 activation attenuates high-fat diet-induced obesity by enhancing brown fat thermogenesis and adipose tissue oxidative metabolism. *Diabetes, 63*, 3615–3625.

Kaas, J. H., & Collins, C. E. (2001). The organization of sensory cortex. *Current Opinion in Neurobiology, 11*, 498–504.

Kaas, J. H., Krubtzer, L. A., Chino, Y. M., Langston, A. L., Polley, E. H., & Blair, N. (1990). Reorganization of retinotopic cortical maps in adult mammals after lesions of the retina. *Science, 248*, 229–231.

Kagawa, Y. (1978). Impact of Westernization on the nutrition of Japanese: Changes in physique, cancer, longevity, and centenarians. *Preventive Medicine, 7*, 205–217.

Kaila, K., Price, T. J., Payne, J. A., Puskarjov, M., & Voipio, J. (2014). Cation-chloride cotransporters in neuronal development, plasticity and disease. *Nature Reviews Neuroscience, 15*, 637–654.

Kaila, K., Ruusuvuori, E., Seja, P., Voipio, J., & Puskarjov, M. (2014). GABA actions and ionic plasticity in epilepsy. *Current Opinion in Neurobiology, 26*, 34–41.

Kaiser, J. (2010). Cancer's circulation problem. *Science, 327*, 1072–1074.

Kalil, K., & Dent, E. W. (2005). Touch and go: Guidance cues signal to the growth cone cytoskeleton. *Current Opinion in Neurobiology, 15*, 521–526.

Kalivas, P. W. (2005). How do we determine which drug-induced neuroplastic changes are important? *Nature Neuroscience, 8*, 1440–1441.

Kaller, C. P., Rahm, B., Spreer, J., Weiller, C., & Unterrainer, J. M. (2011). Dissociable contributions of left and right dorsolateral prefrontal cortex in planning. *Cerebral Cortex, 21*, 307–317.

Kallman, F. J. (1946). The genetic theory of schizophrenia: An analysis of 691 schizophrenic twin index families. *American Journal of Psychiatry, 103*, 309–322.

Kalynchuk, L. E., Pinel, J. P. J., Treit, D., & Kippin, T. E. (1997). Changes in emotional behavior produced by long-term amygdala kindling in rats. *Biological Psychiatry, 41*, 438–451.

Kanai, R., & Rees, G. (2011). The structural basis of inter-individual differences in human behaviour and cognition. *Nature Reviews Neuroscience, 12*, 231–242.

Kanayama, G., Hudson, J. I., & Pope, H. G. (2008). Long-term psychiatric and medical consequences of anabolic–androgenic steroid abuse: A looming public health concern? *Drug and Alcohol Dependence, 98*, 1–12.

Kanayama, G., Hudson, J. I., & Pope, H. G. (2010). Illicit anabolic-androgenic steroid use. *Hormones and Behavior, 58*, 111–121.

Kandel, E. R., & Squire, L. R. (2000). Neuroscience: Breaking down barriers to the study of brain and mind. *Science, 290*, 1113–1120.

Kanekiyo, T., Xu, H., & Bu, G. (2014). ApoE and Aβ in Alzheimer's disease: Accidental encounters or partners? *Neuron, 81*, 740–754.

Kanold, P. O., & Luhmann, H. J. (2010). The subplate and early cortical circuits. *Annual Review of Neuroscience, 33*, 23–48.

Kantarci, O. H. (2008). Genetics and natural history of multiple sclerosis. *Seminars in Neurology, 28*, 7–16.

Kappeler, P. M. (2013). Why male mammals are monogamous. *Science, 341*, 469–470.

Kappers, A. M. L. (2011). Human perception of shape from touch. *Philosophical Transactions of the Royal Society B, 366*, 3106–3114.

Kapur, N. (1997). *Injured brains of medical minds.* Oxford, England: Oxford University Press.

Karacan, I., Goodenough, D. R., Shapiro, A., & Starker, S. (1966). Erection cycle during sleep in relation to dream anxiety. *Archives of General Psychiatry, 15*, 183–189.

Karanti, A., Kardell, M., Lundberg, U., & Landén, M. (2016). Changes in mood stabilizer prescription patterns in bipolar disorder. *Journal of Affective Disorders, 195*, 50–56.

Karch, C. M., Cruchaga, C., & Goate, A. M. (2014). Alzheimer's disease genetics: From the bench to the clinic. *Neuron, 83*, 11–26.

Karnath, H.-O. (2015). Spatial attention systems in spatial neglect. *Neuropsychologia, 75*, 61–73.

Karnath, H.-O., & Rorden, C. (2012). The anatomy of spatial neglect. *Neuropsychologia, 50*, 1010–1017.

Karran, E., Mercken, M., & De Strooper, B. (2011). The amyloid cascade hypothesis for Alzheimer's disease: An appraisal for the development of therapeutics. *Nature Reviews Drug Discovery, 10*, 698–712.

Kasai, H., Fukuda, M., Watanabe, S., Hayashi-Takagi, A., & Noguchi, J. (2010). Structural dynamics of dendritic spines in memory and cognition. *Trends in Neurosciences, 33*, 121–130.

Kasai, K., Fukuda, M., Yahata, N., Morita, K., & Fujii, N. (2015). The future of real-world neuroscience: Imaging techniques to assess active brains in social environments. *Neuroscience Research, 90*, 65–71.

Katona, I., & Freund, T. F. (2012). Multiple functions of endocannabinoid signaling in the brain. *Annual Review of Neuroscience, 35*, 529–558.

Katsumata, N., Kuroiwa, T., Ishibashi, S., Li, S., Endo, S., & Ohno, K. (2006). Heterogeneous hyperactivity and distribution of ischemic lesions after focal cerebral ischemia in Mongolian gerbils. *Neuropathology, 26*, 283–292.

Katz, J. L., Ackman, P., Rothwax, Y., Sachar, E. J., Weiner, H., Hellman, L., & Gallagher, T. F. (1970). Psychoendocrine aspects of cancer of the breast. *Psychosomatic Medicine, 32*, 1–18.

Katzner, S., & Weigelt, S. (2013). Visual cortical networks: Of mice and men. *Current Opinion in Neurobiology, 23*, 202–206.

Kawai, R., Markman, T., Poddar, R., Ko, R., Fantana, A. L., Dhawale, A. K.,...& Ölveczky, B. P. (2015). Motor cortex is required for learning but not for executing a motor skill. *Neuron, 86*, 800–812.

Kawasaki, H., Adolphs, R., Oya, H., Kovach, C., Damasio, H., Kaufman, O., & Howard, M. (2005). Analysis of single-unit responses to emotional scenes in human ventromedial prefrontal cortex. *Journal of Cognitive Neuroscience, 17*, 1509–1518.

Kaye, W. H., Bailer, U. F., Frank, G. K., Wagner, A., & Henry, S. E. (2005). Brain imaging of serotonin after recovery from anorexia and bulimia nervosa. *Physiology & Behavior, 86*, 15–17.

Kaye, W. H., Bulik, C. M., Thornton, L., Barbarich, N., Masters, K., & the Price Foundation Collaborative Group. (2004). Comorbidity of anxiety disorders with anorexia and bulimia nervosa. *American Journal of Psychiatry, 161*, 2215–2221.

Kaye, W. H., Wierenga, C. E., Bailer, U. F., Simmons, A. N., & Bischoff-Grethe, A. (2013). Nothing tastes as good as skinny feels: The neurobiology of anorexia nervosa. *Trends in Neurosciences, 36*, 110–120.

Kaye, W. H., Wierenga, C. E., Bailer, U. F., Simmons, A. N., Wagner, A., & Bischoff-Grethe, A. (2013). Does a shared neurobiology for foods and drugs of abuse contribute to extremes of food ingestion in anorexia and bulimia nervosa? *Biological Psychiatry, 73*, 836–842.

Kelsch, W., Sim, S., & Lois, C. (2010). Watching synaptogenesis in the adult brain. *Annual Review of Neuroscience, 33*, 131–149.

Keltner, D., Kring, A. M., & Bonanno, G. A. (1999). Fleeting signs of the course of life: Facial expression and personal adjustment. *Current Directions in Psychological Science, 8*, 18–22.

Kempermann, G. (2013). What the bomb said about the brain. *Science, 340*, 1180–1182.

Kempermann, G., & Gage, F. H. (1999, May). New nerve cells for the adult brain. *Scientific American, 282*, 48–53.

Kenakin, T. (2005, October). New bull's-eyes for drugs. *Scientific American, 293*, 51–57.

Kenrick, D. T. (2001). Evolutionary psychology, cognitive science, and dynamical systems: Building an integrative paradigm. *Current Directions in Psychological Science, 10*(1), 13–17.

Kerstein, P. C., Nichol, R. H., IV, & Gomez, T. M. (2015). Mechanochemical regulation of growth cone motility. *Frontiers in Cellular Neuroscience, 9*, 244.

Kessels, R. P. C., De Haan, E. H. F., Kappelle, L. J., & Postma, A. (2001). Varieties of human spatial memory: A meta-analysis on the effects of hippocampal lesions. *Brain Research Reviews, 35*, 295–303.

Keung, A. J., & Khalil, A. S. (2016). A unifying model of epigenetic regulation. *Science, 351*, 661–662.

Keys, A., Broz, J., Henschel, A., Mickelsen, O., & Taylor H. L. (1950). *The biology of human starvation.* Minneapolis: University of Minnesota Press.

Khadra, A., & Li, Y.-X. (2006). A model for the pulsatile secretion of gonadotropin-releasing hormone from synchronized hypothalamic neurons. *Biophysical Journal, 91*, 74–83.

Khakh, B. S., & Sofroniew, M. V. (2015). Diversity of astrocyte functions and phenotypes in neural circuits. *Nature Neuroscience, 18*, 942–952.

Khan, A., Faucett, J., Lichtenberg, P., Kirsch, I., & Brown, W. A. (2012). A systematic review of comparative efficacy of treatments and controls for depression. *PLoS ONE, 7*, e41778.

Khan, R., Khazaal, Y., Thorens, G., Zullino, D., & Uchtenhagen, A. (2014). Understanding Swiss drug policy change and the introduction of heroin maintenance treatment. *European Addiction Research, 20*, 200–207.

Khang, P., & Dhand, A. (2015). Teaching video neuroimages: Movement of a paralyzed arm with yawning. *Neurology, 84*, e118.

Kheirbek, M. A., & Hen, R. (2013). (Radio)active neurogenesis in the human hippocampus. *Cell, 153*, 1183–1184.

Khoury, J., & Doghramji, K. (2015). Primary sleep disorders. *Psychiatric Clinics of North America, 38*, 683–704.

Kiehl, K. A., Liddle, P. F., Smith, A. M., Mendrek, A., Forster, B. B., & Hare, R. D. (1999). Neural pathways involved in the processing of concrete and abstract words. *Human Brain Mapping, 7*, 225–233.

Kiehn, O. (2016). Decoding the organization of spinal circuits that control locomotion. *Nature Reviews Neuroscience, 17*, 224–238.

Kieker, C., & Lumsden, A. (2012). The role of organizers in patterning the nervous system. *Annual Review of Neuroscience, 35*, 347–367.

Kilteni, K., Maselli, A., Kording, K. P., & Slater, M. (2015). Over my fake body: Body ownership illusions for studying the multisensory basis of own-body perception. *Frontiers in Human Neuroscience, 9*, 141.

Kim, E. J., Horovitz, O., Pellman, B. A., Tan, L. M., Li, Q., Richter-Levin, G., & Kim, J. J. (2013). Dorsal periaqueductal gray-amygdala pathway conveys both innate and learned fear responses in rats. *Proceedings of the National Academy of Sciences, 110*, 14795–14800.

Kim, E. J., Pellman, B., & Kim, J. J. (2015). Stress effects on the hippocampus: A critical review. *Learning & Memory, 22*, 411–416.

Kim, J. D., Leyva, S., & Diano, S. (2014). Hormonal regulation of the hypothalamic melanocortin system. *Frontiers in Physiology, 5*, 480.

Kim, M.-S., Pinto, S. M., Getnet, D., Nirujogi, R. S., Manda, S. S., et al. (2014) A draft map of the human proteome. *Nature, 509*, 575–581.

Kim, M. J., & Whalen, P. J. (2009). The structural integrity of an amygdala-prefrontal pathway predicts trait anxiety. *Journal of Neuroscience, 29,* 11614–11618.

Kim, Y. S., & Leventhal, B. L. (2015). Genetic epidemiology and insights into interactive genetic and environmental effects in autism spectrum disorders. *Biological Psychiatry, 77,* 66–74.

Kimble, G. A. (1989). Psychology from the standpoint of a generalist. *American Psychologist, 44,* 491–499.

Kimura, D. (1964). Left-right differences in the perception of melodies. *Quarterly Journal of Experimental Psychology, 16,* 355–358.

Kimura, D. (1973, March). The asymmetry of the human brain. *Scientific American, 228,* 70–78.

Kimura, D. (1979). Neuromotor mechanisms in the evolution of human communication. In H. E. Steklis & M. J. Raleigh (Eds.), *Neurobiology of social communication in primates* (pp. 197–219). New York, NY: Academic Press.

Kimura, D. (2011). From ear to brain. *Brain and Cognition, 76,* 214–217.

Kingsley, D. M. (2009, January). From atoms to traits. *Scientific American, 300,* 52–59.

Kinnamon, S. C. (2012). Taste receptor signalling—from tongues to lungs. *Acta Physiologica, 204,* 158–168.

Kippin, T. E. (2014). Adaptations underlying the development of excessive alcohol intake in selectively bred mice. *Alcoholism: Clinical and Experimental Research, 38,* 36–39.

Kirsch, I., Deacon, B. J., Huedo-Medina, T. B., Scoboria, A., Moore, T. J., & Johnson, B. T. (2008). Initial severity and antidepressant benefits: A meta-analysis of data submitted to the Food and Drug Administration. *PLoS ONE Medicine, 5,* e45.

Kirszenblat, L., & van Swinderen, B. (2015). The yin and yang of sleep and attention. *Trends in Neurosciences, 38,* 776–786.

Klawans, H. L. (1990). *Newton's madness: Further tales of clinical neurology.* New York: Harper & Row.

Klein, D. A., & Walsh, T. B. (2004). Eating disorders: Clinical features and pathophysiology. *Physiology & Behavior, 81,* 359–374.

Klein, P., Tyrlikova, I., & Mathews, G. C. (2014). Dietary treatments in adults with refractory epilepsy: A review. *Neurology, 83,* 1978–1985.

Klein, R., & Kania, A. (2014). Ephrin signalling in the developing nervous system. *Current Opinion in Neurobiology, 27,* 16–24.

Kleiner-Fisman, G., Fisman, D. N., Sime, E., Saint-Cyr, J. A., Lozano, A. M., & Lang, A. E. (2003). Long-term follow up of bilateral deep brain stimulation of the subthalamic nucleus in patients with advanced Parkinson disease. *Journal of Neuroscience, 99,* 489–495.

Kleitman, N. (1963). *Sleep and wakefulness.* Chicago: University of Chicago Press.

Klemm, W. R. (2011). Why does REM sleep occur? A wake-up hypothesis. *Frontiers in Systems Neuroscience, 5,* 73.

Klengel, T., & Binder, E. B. (2013). Gene-environment interactions in major depressive disorder. *Canadian Journal of Psychiatry, 58,* 76.

Klengel, T., & Binder, E. B. (2015). Epigenetics of stress-related psychiatric disorders and gene × environment interactions. *Neuron, 86,* 1343–1357.

Klinesmith, J., Kasser, T., & McAndrew, F. T. (2006). Guns, testosterone, and aggression: An experimental test of a mediational hypothesis. *Psychological Science, 17,* 568–571.

Klingelhoefer, L., & Reichmann, H. (2015). Pathogenesis of Parkinson disease—the gut-brain axis and environmental factors. *Nature Reviews Neurology, 11,* 625–636.

Klingemann, H., Sobell, M. B., & Sobell, L. C. (2009). Continuities and changes in self-change research. *Addiction, 105,* 1510–1518.

Klivington, K. A. (Ed.). (1992). *Gehirn und Geist.* Heidelberg, Germany: Spektrum Akademischer Verlag.

Kluver, H., & Bucy, P. C. (1939). Preliminary analysis of the temporal lobes in monkeys. *Archives of Neurology and Psychiatry, 42,* 979–1000.

Knöchel, C., Stäblein, M., Storchak, H., Reinke, B., Jurcoane, A., Prvulovic, D.,…& Alves, G. (2014). Multimodal assessments of the hippocampal formation in schizophrenia and bipolar disorder: Evidences from neurobehavioral measures and functional and structural MRI. *NeuroImage: Clinical, 6,* 134–144.

Knowlton, B. J., Mangels, J. A., & Squire, L. R. (1996). A neostriatal habit learning system in humans. *Science, 273,* 1399–1402.

Knudsen, E. I., & Brainard, M. S. (1991). Visual instruction of the neural map of auditory space in the developing optic tectum. *Science, 253,* 85–87.

Ko, C.-H., Liu, G.-C., Yen, J.-Y., Yen, C.-F., Chen, C.-S., & Lin, W.-C. (2013). The brain activations for both cue-induced gaming urge and smoking craving among subjects comorbid with internet gaming addiction and nicotine dependence. *Journal of Psychiatric Research, 47,* 486–493.

Koebeie, S. V., & Bimonte-Nelson, H. A. (2015). Trajectories and phenotypes with estrogen exposures across the lifespan: What does Goldilocks have to do with it? *Hormones and Behavior, 74,* 86–104.

Koelsch, S., & Skouras, S. (2014). Functional centrality of amygdala, striatum and hypothalamus in a "small-world" network underlying joy: An fMRI study with music. *Human Brain Mapping, 35,* 3485–3498.

Kohwi, M., & Doe, C. Q. (2013). Temporal fate specification and neural progenitor competence during development. *Nature Reviews Neuroscience, 14,* 823–838.

Kokras, N., & Dalla, C. (2014). Sex differences in animal models of psychiatric disorders. *British Journal of Pharmacology, 171,* 4595–4619.

Kolb, B., & Whishaw, I. Q. (1990). *Fundamentals of human neuropsychology* (3rd ed.). New York, NY: Freeman.

Koleske, A. J. (2013). Molecular mechanisms of dendrite stability. *Nature Reviews Neuroscience, 14,* 536–550.

Kononenko, N. L., & Haucke, V. (2015). Molecular mechanisms of presynaptic membrane retrieval and synaptic vesicle reformation. *Neuron, 85,* 484–496.

Koolhaas, J. M., Coppens, C. M., de Boer, S. F., Buwalda, B., Meerlo, P., & Timmermans, P. J. (2013). The resident-intruder paradigm: A standardized test for aggression, violence, and social stress. *Journal of Visualized Experiments, 77,* e4367.

Koopmans, H. S. (1981). The role of the gastrointestinal tract in the satiation of hunger. In L. A. Cioffi, W. B. T. James, & T. B. Van Italie (Eds.), *The body weight regulatory system: Normal and disturbed mechanisms* (pp. 45–55). New York, NY: Raven Press.

Kopelman, P. G. (2000). Obesity as a medical problem. *Nature, 404,* 635–648.

Koppel, B. S., Brust, J. C., Fife, T., Bronstein, J., Youssof, S., Gronseth, G., & Gloss, D. (2014). Systematic review: Efficacy and safety of medical marijuana in selected neurologic disorders: Report of the Guideline Development Subcommittee of the American Academy of Neurology. *Neurology, 82,* 1556–1563.

Koren, G., Zelner, I., Nash, K., & Koren, G. (2014). Foetal alcohol spectrum disorder: Identifying the neurobehavioral phenotype and effective interventions. *Current Opinion in Psychiatry, 27,* 98–104.

Kornack, D. R., & Rakic, P. (1999). Continuation of neurogenesis in the hippocampus of the adult macaque monkey. *Proceedings of the National Academy of Sciences, USA, 96,* 5768–5773.

Kornell, N. (2009). Metacognition in humans and animals. *Current Directions in Psychological Science, 18,* 11–15.

Koropouli, E., & Kolodkin, A. L. (2014). Semaphorins and the dynamic regulation of synapse assembly, refinement, and function. *Current Opinion in Neurobiology, 27,* 1–7.

Kosslyn, S. M., & Andersen, R. A. (1992). *Frontiers in cognitive neuroscience.* Cambridge, MA: MIT Press.

Kotas, M. E., & Medzhitov, R. (2015). Homeostasis, inflammation, and disease susceptibility. *Cell, 160,* 816–827.

Kotlar, A. V., Mercer, K. B., Zwick, M. E., & Mulle, J. G. (2015). New discoveries in schizophrenia genetics reveal neurobiological pathways: A review of recent findings. *European Journal of Medical Genetics, 58,* 704–714.

Koziol, L. F., Budding, D., Andreasen, N., D'Arrigo, S., Bulgheroni, S.,…& Yamazaki, T. (2014). Consensus paper: The cerebellum's role in movement and cognition. *Cerebellum, 13,* 151–177.

Kral, A., & Sharma, A. (2012). Developmental neuroplasticity after cochlear implantation. *Trends in Neurosciences, 35,* 111–122.

Kramer, C. K., Zinman, B., & Retnakaran, R. (2013). Are metabolically healthy overweight and obesity benign conditions? *Annals of Internal Medicine, 159,* 758–769.

Krashes, M. J., Shah, B. P., Madara, J. C., Olson, D. P., Strochlic, D. E.,…& Lowell, B. B. (2014). An excitatory paraventricular nucleus to AgRP neuron circuit that drives hunger. *Nature, 507,* 238–242.

Kraus, N., & Banai, K. (2007) Auditory-processing malleability: Focus on language and music. *Current Directions on Psychological Science, 16,* 105–110.

Kraus, S. L., Emmert, S., Schön, M. P., & Haenssle, H. A. (2012). The dark side of beauty: Acne fulminans induced by anabolic steroids in a male bodybuilder. *Archives of Dermatology, 148,* 1210–1212.

Krauzlis, R. J., Lovejoy, L. P., & Zénon, A. (2013). Superior colliculus and visual spatial attention. *Annual Review of Neuroscience, 36,* 165–182.

Kravitz, D. J., Saleem, K. S., Baker, C. I., & Mishkin, M. (2011). A new neural framework for visuospatial processing. *Nature Reviews Neuroscience, 12,* 217–230.

Krebs, T. S., & Johansen, P-Ø. (2012). Methodological weaknesses in non-randomized studies of ecstasy (MDMA) use: A cautionary note to readers and reviewers. *Neuropsychopharmacology, 37,* 1070–1071.

Krebs, T. S., Johansen, P-Ø., Jerome, L., & Halpern, J. H. (2009). Importance of psychiatric confounding in non-randomized studies of heavy ecstasy users. *Psychological Medicine, 39,* 876–878.

Kreitewolf, J., Friederici, A. D., & von Kriegstein, K. (2014). Hemispheric lateralization of linguistic prosody recognition in comparison to speech and speaker recognition. *Neuroimage, 102,* 332–344.

Kreukels, B. P. C., & Cohen-Kettenis, P. T. (2012). Male gender identity and masculine behavior: The role of sex hormones in brain development. In M. Maggi (Ed.), *Hormonal therapy for male sexual dysfunction* (1st ed.). New York, NY: John Wiley & Sons.

Kriebig, S. D. (2010). Autonomic nervous system activity in emotion: A review. *Biological Psychology, 84,* 394–421.

Kriegeskorte, N. (2011). Pattern-information analysis: From stimulus decoding to computational-model testing. *Neuroimage, 56,* 411–421.

Kriegstein, A., & Alvarez-Buylla, A. (2009). The glial nature of embryonic and adult neural stem cells. *Annual Review of Neuroscience, 32,* 149–184.

Kril, J. J., & Harper, C. G. (2012). Neuroanatomy and neuropathology associated with Korsakoff's syndrome. *Neuropsychology Review, 22,* 72–80.

Kring, A. M. (1999). Emotion in schizophrenia: Old mystery, new understanding. *Current Directions in Psychological Science, 8,* 160–163.

Kringelbach, M. L., & Berridge, K. C. (2012). The joyful mind. *Scientific American, 307,* 40–45.

Kripke, D. F., Garfinkel, L., Wingard, D. L., Klauber, M. R., & Marler, M. R. (2002). Mortality associated with sleep duration and insomnia. *Archives of General Psychiatry, 59,* 131–136.

Krishnan, A., & Schiöth, H. B. (2015). The role of G protein-coupled receptors in the early evolution of neurotransmission and the nervous system. *Journal of Experimental Biology, 218,* 562–571.

Kristensson, K. (2011). Microbes' roadmap to neurons. *Nature Reviews Neuroscience, 12,* 345–357.

Kropf, E., Yang, S. M., & Schinder, A. F. (2015). Dynamic role of adult-born dentate granule cells in memory processing. *Current Opinion in Neurobiology, 35,* 21–26.

Krubitzer, L., & Stolzenberg, D. S. (2014). The evolutionary masquerade: Genetic and epigenetic contributions to the neocortex. *Current Opinion in Neurobiology, 24,* 157–165.

Krubitzer, L., & Stolzenberg, D. S. (2014). The evolutionary masquerade: Genetic and epigenetic contributions to the neocortex. *Current Opinion in Neurobiology, 24,* 157–165.

Krueger, D. D., Tuffy, L. P., Papadopoulos, T., & Brose, N. (2012). The role of neurexins and neuroligins in the formation, maturation, and function of vertebrate synapses. *Current Opinion in Neurobiology, 22,* 412–422.

Krupic, J., Bauza, M., Burton, S., Barry, C., & O'Keefe, J. (2015). Grid cell symmetry is shaped by environmental geometry. *Nature, 518,* 232–235.

Krystal, A. D. (2008). A compendium of placebo-controlled trials of the risks/benefits of pharmacological treatments for insomnia: The empirical basis for U.S. clinical practice. *Sleep Medicine Reviews, 13,* 265–274.

Krystal, A. D. (2015). Current, emerging, and newly available insomnia medications. *Journal of Clinical Psychiatry, 76,* e1045.

Kuang, S., Morel, P., & Gail, A. (2015). Planning movements in visual and physical space in monkey posterior parietal cortex. *Cerebral Cortex, 26,* 731–747.

Kuba, H., Adachi, R., & Ohmori, H. (2014). Activity-dependent and activity-independent development of the axon initial segment. *Journal of Neuroscience, 34,* 3443–3453.

Kubie, J. L., Fenton, A., Novikov, N., Touretzky, D., & Muller, R. U. (2007). Changes in goal selection induced by cue conflicts are in register with predictions from changes in place cell field locations. *Behavioral Neuroscience, 121,* 751–763.

Kunz, L., Schröder, T. N., Lee, H., Montag, C., Lachmann, B., Sariyska, R., ... & Fell, J. (2015). Reduced grid-cell–like representations in adults at genetic risk for Alzheimer's disease. *Science, 350,* 430–433.

Kupferschmidt, K. (2014). High hopes. *Science, 345,* 18–23.

Kupferschmidt, K. (2014). The dangerous professor. *Science, 343,* 478–481.

Kurbat, M. A., & Farah, M. J. (1998). Is the category-specific deficit for living things spurious? *Journal of Cognitive Neuroscience, 10,* 355–361.

Kwakkel, G., Veerbeek, J. M., van Wegen, E. E. H., & Wolf, S. L. (2015). Constraint-induced movement therapy after stroke. *The Lancet Neurology, 14,* 224–234.

Kyritsis, N., Kizil, C., Zocher, S., Kroehne, V., Kaslin, J., Freudenreich, D., Iltzsche, A., & Brand, M. (2012). Acute inflammation initiates the regenerative response in the adult zebrafish brain. *Science, 338,* 1353–1356.

Laeng, B., & Caviness, V. S. (2001). Prosopagnosia as a deficit in encoding curved surface. *Journal of Cognitive Neuroscience, 13,* 556–576.

LaFerla, F. M., & Green, K. N. (2012). Animal models of Alzheimer disease. *Cold Spring Harbor Perspectives in Medicine, 2,* a006320.

Lagerlöf, O., Slocomb, J. E., Hong, I., Aponte, Y., Blackshaw, S., Hart, G. W., & Huganir, R. L. (2016). The nutrient sensor OGT in PVN neurons regulates feeding. *Science, 351,* 1293–1296.

Lai,. T. W., Zhang, S., & Wang, Y. T. (2014). Excitotoxicity and stroke: Identifying novel targets for neuroprotection. *Progress in Neurobiology, 115,* 157–188.

Laine, M., Salmelin, R., Helenius, P., & Marttila, R. (2000). Brain activation during reading in deep dyslexia: An MEG study. *Journal of Cognitive Neuroscience, 12,* 622–634.

Lamb, T. D., Collin, S. P., & Pugh, E. N. (2007). Evolution of the vertebrate eye: Opsins, photoreceptors, retina and eye cup. *Nature Reviews Neuroscience, 8,* 960–975.

Lamichhaney, S., Berglund, J., Almén, M. S., Maqbool, K., Grabherr, M., Martinez-Barrio, A., ... & Grant, B. R. (2015). Evolution of Darwin's finches and their beaks revealed by genome sequencing. *Nature, 518,* 371–375.

Landgraf, M., & Heinen, F. (2014). Diagnosis of fetal alcohol spectrum disorders. *Neuropediatrics, 45,* fp041.

Land, E. H. (1977, April). The retinex theory of color vision. *Scientific American, 237,* 108–128.

Land, M. F. (2014). Do we have an internal model of the outside world? *Philosophical Transactions of the Royal Society B, 369,* 20130045.

Landgraf, M. N., Nothacker, M., & Heinen, F. (2013). Diagnosis of fetal alcohol syndrome (FAS): German guideline version 2013. *European Journal of Paediatric Neurology, 17,* 437–446.

Lang, D.-Y., Li, X., & Clark, J. D. (2013). Epigenetic regulation of opioid-induced hyperalgesia, dependence, and tolerance in mice. *The Journal of Pain, 14,* 36–47.

Lange, N., & McDougle, C. J. (2013). Help for the child with autism. *Scientific American, 309,* 72–77.

Langston, J. W. (1985). MPTP and Parkinson's disease. *Trends in Neurosciences, 8,* 79–83.

Langston, R. F., Ainge, J. A., Couey, J. J., Canto, C. B., Bjerknes, T. L., Witter, M. P., Moser, E. I., & Moser, M.-B. (2010). Development of the spatial representation system in the rat. *Science, 328,* 1576–1580.

Lappin, J. S. (2014). What is binocular disparity? *Frontiers in Psychology, 5,* 870.

Larson-Prior, L. J., Ju, Y.-E., & Galvin, J. E. (2014). Cortical-subcortical interactions in hypersomnia disorders: Mechanisms underlying cognitive and behavioral aspects of the sleep-wake cycle. *Frontiers in Neurology, 5,* 165.

Larson, G., Piperno, D. R., Allaby, R. G., Purugganan, M. D., Andersson, L., et al. (2014). Current perspectives and the future of domestication studies. *PNAS, 111,* 6139–6146.

Laruelle, M. (2013). The second revision of the dopamine theory of schizophrenia: Implications for treatment and drug development. *Biological Psychiatry, 74,* 80–81.

Laruelle, M. (2014). Schizophrenia: From dopaminergic to glutamatergic interventions. *Current Opinion in Pharmacology, 14,* 97–102.

LaSalle, J. M., Powell, W. T., & Yasui, D. H. (2013). Epigenetic layers and players underlying neurodevelopment. *Trends in Neurosciences, 36,* 460–470.

Lashley, K. S. (1941). Patterns of cerebral integration indicated by the scotomas of migraine. *Archives of Neurology and Psychiatry, 46,* 331–339.

Lashuel, H. A., Overk, C. R., Oueslati, A., & Masliah, E. (2013). The many faces of 24a-synuclein: From structure and toxicity to therapeutic target. *Nature Reviews Neuroscience, 14,* 38–48.

Lask, B., & Bryant-Waugh, R. (Eds.). (2000). *Anorexia nervosa and related eating disorders in childhood and adolescence.* Hove, England: Psychology Press.

Lau, B. K., & Vaughan, C. W. (2014). Descending modulation of pain: The GABA disinhibition hypothesis of analgesia. *Current Opinion in Neurobiology, 29,* 159–164.

Lau, B. K., & Werner, L. A. (2014). Perception of the pitch of unresolved harmonics by 3- and 7-month-old human infants. *Journal of the Acoustical Society of America, 136,* 760–767.

Lavie, P., Pratt, H., Scharf, B., Peled, R., & Brown, J. (1984). Localized pontine lesion: Nearly total absence of REM sleep. *Neurology, 34,* 1118–1120.

Laviolette, S. R., & van der Kooy, D. (2004). The neurobiology of nicotine addiction: Bridging the gap from molecules to behavior. *Nature Reviews Neuroscience, 5,* 55–65.

Lavrov, I., Courtine, G., Dy, C. J., van den Brand, R., Fong, A. J., ... & Edgerton, V. R. (2008). Facilitation of stepping with epidural stimulation in spinal rats: Role of sensory input. *Journal of Neuroscience, 28,* 7774–7780.

Law, S. W., & Levine, S. R. (2015). Stroke: Support for IV tPA in ischaemic stroke in elderly people. *Nature Reviews Neurology, 12,* 8–9.

Lawrence, D. G., & Kuypers, H. G. J. M. (1968a). The functional organization of the motor system in the monkey: I. The effects of bilateral pyramidal lesions. *Brain, 91,* 1–14.

Lawrence, D. G., & Kuypers, H. G. J. M. (1968b). The functional organization of the motor system in the monkey: II. The effects of lesions of the descending brain-stem pathways. *Brain, 91,* 15–36.

Learney, K., Van Wart, A., & Sur, M. (2009). Intrinsic patterning and experience-dependent mechanisms that generate eye-specific projections and binocular circuits in the visual pathway. *Current Opinion in Neurobiology, 19,* 181–187.

Ledford, H. (2015). Drug that boosts nerve signals offers hope for multiple sclerosis. *Nature, 520,* 417.

LeDoux, J. E. (2014). Coming to terms with fear. *Proceedings of the National Academy of Sciences, 111,* 2871–2878.

Lee, B. H., Smith, T., & Paciorkowski, A. R. (2015). Autism spectrum disorder and epilepsy: Disorders with a shared biology. *Epilepsy & Behavior, 47,* 191–201.

Lee, D., & Seo, H. (2016). Neural basis of strategic decision making. *Trends in Neurosciences, 39,* 40–48.

Lee, D., Seo, H., & Jung, M. W. (2012). Neural basis of reinforcement learning and decision making. *Annual Review of Neuroscience, 35,* 287–308.

Lee, H. S., Ghetti, A., Pinto-Duarte, A., Wang, X., Dziewczapolski, G., et al. (2014). Astrocytes contribute to gamma oscillations and recognition memory. *PNAS, 111,* e3343–e3352.

Lee, J., Kim, K., Chung, S., & Lee, C. (2013). Suppression of spontaneous activity before visual response in the primate V1 neurons during a visually guided saccade task. *Journal of Neuroscience, 33,* 3760–3764.

Lee, L. J., Hughes, T. R., & Frey, B. J. (2006). How many new genes are there? *Science, 3,* 1709.

Lee, S.-C., Patrick, S. L., Richardson, K. A., & Connors, B. W. (2014). Two functionally distinct networks of gap junction-coupled inhibitory neurons in the thalamic reticular nucleus. *Journal of Neuroscience, 34,* 13170–13182.

Lee, T.-S. (2008). Contextual influences in visual processing. In M. D. Binder, N. Hirokawa, & U. Windurst (Eds.), *Encyclopedia of Neuroscience* (pp. 867–871). Berlin: Springer.

Leech, R., & Saygin, A. P. (2011). Distributed processing and cortical specialization for speech and environmental sounds in human temporal cortex. *Brain and Language, 116,* 83–90.

Lehky, S. R., & Tanaka, K. (2016). Neural representation for object recognition in inferotemporal cortex. *Current Opinion in Neurobiology, 37,* 23–35.

Leibowitz, S. F., Hammer, N. J., & Chang, K. (1981). Hypothalamic paraventricular nucleus lesions produce overeating and obesity in the rat. *Physiology & Behavior, 27,* 1031–1040.

Lemmens, R., & Steinberg, G. K. (2013). Stem cell therapy for acute cerebral injury: What do we know and what will the future bring? *Current Opinion in Neurology, 26,* 617–625.

Lener, M. S., & Iosifescu, D. V. (2015). In pursuit of neuroimaging biomarkers to guide treatment selection in major depressive disorder: A review of the literature. *Annals of the New York Academy of Sciences, 1344,* 50–65.

Leng, T., Shi, Y., Xiong, Z.-G., & Sun, D. (2014). Proton-sensitive cation channels and ion exchangers in ischemic brain injury: New therapeutic targets for stroke? *Progress in Neurobiology, 115,* 189–209.

Lennoff, H. M., Wang, P. P., Greenberg, F., & Bellugi, U. (1997, December). Williams syndrome and the brain. *Scientific American, 279,* 68–73.

Lennox, W. G. (1960). *Epilepsy and related disorders.* Boston, MA: Little, Brown.

Lenoir, M., Serre, F., Cantin, L., & Ahmed, S. H. (2007). Intense sweetness surpasses cocaine reward. *PLoS ONE, 8,* e698.

Lenroot, R. K., & Giedd, J. N. (2006). Brain development in children and adolescents: Insights from anatomical magnetic resonance imaging. *Neuroscience and Biobehavioural Reviews, 30,* 718–729.

Lenroot, R. K., & Giedd, J. N. (2010). Sex differences in the adolescent brain. *Brain and Cognition, 72,* 46–55.

Lense, M. D., Key, A. P., & Dykens, E. M. (2011). Attentional disengagement in adults with William syndrome. *Brain and Cognition, 77,* 201–207.

Lent, R., Azevedo, F. A. C., Andrade-Moraes, C. H., & Pinto, A. V. O. (2012). How many neurons do you have? Some dogmas of quantitative neuroscience under revision. *European Journal of Neuroscience, 35,* 1–9.

Lentini, E., Kasahara, M., Arver, S., & Savic, I. (2012). Sex differences in the human brain and the impact of sex chromosomes and sex hormones. *Cerebral Cortex,* doi: 10.1093/cercor/bhs222

Lenz, K. M., & McCarthy, M. M. (2010). Organized for sex-steroid hormones and the developing hypothalamus. *European Journal of Neuroscience, 32,* 2096–2104.

Lenz, K. M., Nugent, B. M., & McCarthy, M. M. (2012). Sexual differentiation of the rodent brain: Dogma and beyond. *Frontiers in Neuroscience, 6,* 26.

Leopold, D. A. (2012). Primary visual cortex: Awareness and blindsight. *Annual Review of Neuroscience, 35,* 91–109.

Leshner, A. I. (1997). Addiction is a brain disease, and it matters. *Science, 278,* 45–46.

Lesku, J. A., Rattenborg, N. C., Valcu, M., Vyssotski, A. L., Kuhn, S., Kuemmeth, F., Heidrich, W., & Kempenaers, B. (2012). Adaptive sleep loss in polygynous pectoral sandpipers. *Science, 337,* 1652–1658.

Lester, G. L. L., & Gorzalka, B. B. (1988). Effect of novel and familiar mating partners on the duration of sexual receptivity in the female hamster. *Behavioral and Neural Biology, 49,* 398–405.

LeVay, S. (1991). A difference in hypothalamic structure between heterosexual and homosexual men. *Science, 253,* 1034–1037.

Levelt, C. N., & Hübener, M. (2012). Critical-period plasticity in the visual cortex. *Annual Review of Neuroscience, 35,* 309–330.

Levi-Montalcini, R. (1952). Effects of mouse motor transplantation on the nervous system. *Annals of the New York Academy of Sciences, 55,* 330–344.

Levi-Montalcini, R. (1975). NGF: An uncharted route. In F. G. Worden, J. P. Swazey, & G. Adelman (Eds.), *The neurosciences: Paths of discovery* (pp. 245–265). Cambridge, MA: MIT Press.

Levine, A. J., Lewallen, K. A., & Pfaff, S. L. (2012). Spatial organization of cortical and spinal neurons controlling motor behavior. *Current Opinion in Neuobiology, 22,* 812–821.

Levine, M. S., Cepeda, C., Hickey, M. A., Fleming, S. M., & Chesselet, M.-F. (2004). Genetic mouse models of Huntington's and Parkinson's diseases: Illuminating but imperfect. *Trends in Neurosciences, 27,* 691–697.

Levy, J. (1969). Possible basis for the evolution of lateral specialization of the human brain. *Nature, 224,* 614–615.

Levy, J., Trevarthen, C., & Sperry, R. W. (1972). Perception of bilateral chimeric figures following hemispheric deconnection. *Brain, 95,* 61–78.

Levy, R. G., Cooper, P. N., & Giri, P. (2012). Ketogenic diet and other dietary treatments for epilepsy. *Cochrane Database of Systematic Reviews, 3,* CD001903.

Lewis, D. A., Hashimoto, T., & Volk, D. W. (2005). Cortical inhibitory neurons and schizophrenia. *Nature Reviews Neuroscience, 6,* 312–324.

Lewis, S. (2015). Circadian rhythms: Remembering night and day. *Nature Reviews Neuroscience, 16,* 3.

Lewis, T. L., & Maurer, D. (2005). Multiple sensitive periods in human visual development: Evidence from visually deprived children. *Developmental Psychobiology, 46,* 163–183.

Lezak, M. D. (1997). Principles of neuropsychological assessment. In T. E. Feinberg & M. J. Farah (Eds.), *Behavioral neurology and neuropsychology* (pp. 43–54). New York, NY: McGraw-Hill.

Li, G., Lin, W., Gilmore, J. H., & Shen, D. (2015). Spatial patterns, longitudinal development, and hemispheric asymmetries of cortical thickness in infants from birth to 2 years of age. *Journal of Neuroscience, 35,* 9150–9162.

Li, J., Na, L., Ma, H., Zhang, Z., Li, T., Lin, L., … & Li, Y. (2015). Multigenerational effects of parental prenatal exposure to famine on adult offspring cognitive function. *Scientific Reports, 5,* 13792.

Li, K., & Malhotra, P. A. (2015). Spatial neglect. *Practical Neurology, 15,* 333–339.

Li, X., & Wolf, M. E. (2014). Multiple faces of BDNF in cocaine addiction. *Behavioural Brain Research, 279,* 240–254.

Liang, D. Y., Li, X., & Clark, J. D. (2013). Epigenetic regulation of opioid-induced hyperalgesia, dependence, and tolerance in mice. *The Journal of Pain, 14,* 36–47.

Liblau, R. S., Vassalli, A., Seifinejad, A., & Tafti, M. (2015). Hypocretin (orexin) biology and the pathophysiology of narcolepsy with cataplexy. *Lancet Neurology, 14,* 318–328.

Lichtman, J. W., & Denk, W. (2011). The big and the small: Challenges of imaging the brain's circuits. *Science, 334,* 618–623.

Lichtman, J. W., Pfister, H., & Shavit, N. (2014). The big data challenges of connectomics. *Nature Neuroscience, 11,* 1448–1454.

Lien, W.-H., Klezovitch, O., Fernandez, T. E., Delrow, J., & Vasioukhin, V. (2006). AlphaE-catenin controls cerebral cortical size by regulating the hedgehog signaling pathway. *Science, 311,* 1609–1612.

Lieu, C. A., & Subramanian, T. (2012). The interhemispheric connections of the striatum: Implications for Parkinson's disease and drug-induced dyskinesias. *Brain Research Bulletin, 87,* 1–9.

Lightman, S. L., & Conway-Campbell, B. L. (2010). The crucial role of pulsatile activity of the HPA axis for continuous dynamic equilibration. *Nature Reviews Neuroscience, 11,* 710–717.

Likhtik, E., & Paz, R. (2015). Amygdala-prefrontal interactions in (mal)adaptive learning. *Trends in Neurosciences, 38,* 158–166.

Lim, J., & Dinges, D. F. (2010). A meta-analysis of the impact of short-term sleep deprivation on cognitive variables. *Psychological Bulletin, 136,* 375–389.

Lim, S. J., Fiez, J. A., & Holt, L. L. (2014). How may the basal ganglia contribute to auditory categorization and speech perception. *Frontiers in Neuroscience, 8,* 230.

Liman, E. E., Zhang, Y. V., & Montell, C. (2014). Peripheral coding of taste. *Neuron, 81,* 984–1000.

Limanowski, J., & Blankenburg, F. (2015). That's not quite me: Limb ownership encoding in the brain. *Social Cognitive and Affective Neuroscience.* Advance online publication. doi: 10.1093/scan/nsv079.

Lin, J. Y., Arthurs, J., & Reilly, S. (2014). Conditioned taste aversion, drugs of abuse and palatability. *Neuroscience & Biobehavioral Reviews, 45,* 28–45.

Lin, L., Faraco, J., Li, R., Kadotani, H., Rogers, W., Lin, X., … & Mignot, E. (1999). The sleep disorder canine narcolepsy is caused by a mutation in the hypocretin (orexin) receptor 2 gene. *Cell, 98,* 365–376.

Linde, K., Kriston, L., Rücker, G., Jamil, S., Schumann, I., Meissner, K., … & Schneider, A. (2015). Efficacy and acceptability of pharmacological treatments for depressive disorders in primary care: Systematic review and network meta-analysis. *Annals of Family Medicine, 13,* 69–79.

Lindell, A. K. (2013). Continuities in emotion lateralization in human and non-human primates. *Frontiers in Human Neuroscience, 7,* 464.

Lindquist, K. A., & Barrett, L. F. (2012). A functional architecture of the human brain: Emerging insights from the science of emotion. *Trends in Cognitive Sciences, 16,* 533–540.

Lindquist, K. A., Wager, T. D., Kober, H., Bliss-Moreau, E., & Barrett, L. F. (2012). The brain basis of emotion: A meta-analytic review. *Behavioral and Brain Sciences, 35,* 121–143.

Lindsay, P. H., & Norman, D. A. (1977). *Human information processing* (2nd ed.). New York, NY: Academic Press.

Lindsey, D. B., Bowden, J., & Magoun, H. W. (1949). Effect upon the EEG of acute injury to the brain stem activating system. *Electroencephalography and Clinical Neurophysiology, 1,* 475–486.

Linster, C., & Fontanini, A. (2014). Functional neuromodulation of chemosensation in vertebrates. *Current Opinion in Neurobiology, 29,* 82–87.

Lisman, J. E., Raghavachari, S., & Tsien, R. W. (2007). The sequence of events that underlie quantal transmission at central glutamatergic synapses. *Nature Reviews Neuroscience, 8,* 597–609.

Lisman, J., Grace, A. A., & Duzel, E. (2011). A neoHebbian framework for episodic memory; role of dopamine-dependent late LTP. *Trends in Neurosciences, 34,* 534–546.

Lisman, J., Yasuda, R., & Raghavachari, S. (2012). Mechanisms of CMKII action in long-term potentiation. *Nature Reviews Neuroscience, 13,* 169–182.

Littleton, J. (2001). Receptor regulation as a unitary mechanism for drug tolerance and physical dependence—not quite as simple as it seemed! *Addiction, 96,* 87–101.

Liu, C., & Grigson, P. S. (2005). Brief access to sweets protect against relapse to cocaine-seeking. *Brain Research, 1049,* 128–131.

Liu, D., Dorio, J., Tannenbaum, B., Caldji, C., Francis, D., Freedman, A., … & Meaney, M. J. (1997). Maternal care, hippocampal glucocorticoid receptors, and hypothalamic-pituitary-adrenal responses to stress. *Science, 277,* 1659–1662.

Liu, K., Tedeschi, A., Park, K. K., & He, Z. (2011). Neuronal intrinsic mechanisms of axon regeneration. *Annual Review of Neuroscience, 34,* 131–152.

Liu, S., & Borgland, S. L. (2015). Regulation of the mesolimbic dopamine circuit by feeding peptides. *Neuroscience, 289,* 19–42.

Liu, X., Hairston, J., Schrier, M., & Fan, J. (2011). Common and distinct networks underlying reward valence and processing stages: A meta-analysis of functional neuroimaging studies. *Neuroscience and Biobehavioral Reviews, 35,* 1219–1236.

Livet, J., Weissman, T. A., Kang, H., Draft, R. W., Lu, J., Bennis, R. A., … & Lichtman, J. W. (2007). Transgenic strategies for combinatorial expression of fluorescent proteins in the nervous system. *Nature, 450,* 56–62.

Livingstone, M. S., & Hubel, D. H. (1984). Anatomy and physiology of a color system in the primate visual cortex. *Journal of Neuroscience, 4,* 309–356.

Livingstone, M. S., & Hubel, D. H. (1988). Segregation of form, color, movement, and depth: Anatomy, physiology, and perception. *Science, 240,* 740–749.

Livingstone, M. S., & Tsao, D. Y. (1999). Receptive fields of disparity-selective neurons in macaque striate cortex. *Nature Reviews Neuroscience, 2,* 825–832.

Locke, A. E., Kahali, B., Berndt, S. I., Justice, A. E., Pers, T. H.,… & Speliotes, E. K. (2015). Genetic studies of body mass index yield new insights for obesity biology. *Nature, 518,* 197–206.

Lodatto, S., Shetty, A. S., & Arlotta, P. (2015). Cerebral cortex assembly: Generating and reprogramming projection neuron diversity. *Trends in Neurosciences, 38,* 117–125.

Loehlin, J. C., Harden, K. P., & Turkheimer, E. (2009). The effect of assumptions about parental assortative mating and genotype-environment interaction in the national merit twin study. *Behavioral Genetics, 39,* 165–169.

Logan, R. W., & McClung, C. A. (2016). Animal models of bipolar mania: The past, present and future. *Neuroscience, 321,* 163–188.

Logothetis, N. K., & Sheinberg, D. L. (1996). Visual object recognition. *Annual Review of Neuroscience, 19,* 577–621.

Lohse, A., Kjaer, T. W., Sabers, A., & Wolf, P. (2015). Epileptic aura and perception of self-control. *Epilepsy & Behavior, 45,* 191–194.

Lolak, S., Suwannarat, P., & Lipsky, R. H. (2014). Epigenetics of depression. *Progress in Molecular Biology and Translational Science, 128,* 103.

London, A. J., Kimmelman, J., & Carlisle, B. (2012). Rethinking research ethics: The case of postmarketing trials. *Science, 336,* 544–545.

Long, M. A., & Lee, A. K. (2012). Intracellular recording in behaving animals. *Current Opinion in Neurobiology, 22,* 34–44.

Long, P., & Corfas, G. (2014). To learn is to myelinate. *Science, 346,* 298–299.

López-Hidalgo, M., & Schummers, J. (2014). Cortical maps: A role for astrocytes? *Current Opinion in Neurobiology, 24,* 176–189.

Lordkipanidze, D., de León, M. S. P., Margvelashvili, A., Rak, Y., Rightmire, G. P., Vekua, A., & Zollikofer, C. P. (2013). A complete skull from Dmanisi, Georgia, and the evolutionary biology of early *Homo. Science, 342,* 326–331.

Lowenstein, D. H. (2015). Decade in review—epilepsy: Edging toward breakthroughs in epilepsy diagnostics and care. *Nature Reviews Neurology, 11,* 616–617.

Lowrey, P. L., Shimomura, K., Antoch, M. P., Yamazaki, S., Zemenides, P. D., Ralph, M. R.,… & Takahashi, J. S. (2000). Positional syntenic cloning and functional characterization of the mammalian circadian mutation tau. *Science, 288,* 483–491.

Loyd, D. R., & Murphy, A. Z. (2014). The neuroanatomy of sexual dimorphism in opioid analgesia. *Experimental Neurology, 259,* 57–63.

Lozano, A. M., & Kalia, S. K. (2005, July). New movement in Parkinson's. *Scientific American, 293,* 68–75.

Lozano, A. M., & Mayberg, H. S. (2015). Treating depression at the source. *Scientific American, 312,* 68–73.

Lozano, A. M., Giacobbe, P., Hamani, C., Rizvi, S. J., Kennedy, S. H., Kolivakis, T. T., Debonnel, G., Sadikot, A. F., Lam, R. W., Howard, A. K., Ilcewicz-Klimek, M., Honey, C. R., & Mayberg, H. S. (2012). A multicenter pilot study of subcallosal cingulate area deep brain stimulation for treatment-resistant depression. *Journal of Neurosurgery, 116,* 315–322.

Lozano, A. M., Mayberg, H. S., Giacobbe, P., Hamani, C., Craddock, R. C., & Kennedy, S. H. (2008). Subcallosal cingulate gyrus deep brain stimulation for treatment-resistant depression. *Biological Psychiatry, 64,* 461–467.

Lu, L., Shepard, J. D., Scott Hall, F., & Shaham, Y. (2003). Effect of environmental stressors on opiate and psychostimulant reinforcement, reinstatement and discrimination in rats: A review. *Neuroscience and Biobehavioral Reviews, 27,* 457–491.

Lucchintti, C. F., Popescu, B. F. G., Bunyan, R. F., Moll, N. M., Roemer, S. F., Lassman, H., Brücke, W., Parisi, J. E., Scheithauer, B. W., Giannini, C., Weigand, S. D., Madrekar, J., & Ransohoff, R. M. (2011). Inflammatory cortical demyelination in early multiple sclerosis. *New England Journal of Medicine, 365,* 2188–2197.

Lucey, B. P., & Holtzman, D. M. (2015). How amyloid, sleep and memory connect. *Nature Neuroscience, 18,* 933–934.

Lucidi, F., Devoto, A., Violani, C., Mastracci, P., & Bertini, M. (1997). Effects of different sleep duration on delta sleep in recovery nights. *Psychophysiology, 34,* 227–233.

Lucio, R. A., Rodríguez-Piedracruz, V., Tlachi-López, J. L., García-Lorenzana, M., & Fernández-Guasti, A. (2014). Copulation without seminal expulsion: The consequence of sexual satiation and the Coolidge effect. *Andrology, 2,* 450–457.

Luck, S. J., Hillyard, S. A., Mangoun, G. R., & Gazzaniga, M. S. (1989). Independent hemispheric attentional systems mediate visual search in split-brain patients. *Nature, 343,* 543–545.

Lukas, D., & Clutton-Brock, T. H. (2013). The evolution of social monogamy in mammals. *Science, 341,* 526–530.

Lumpkin, E. A., & Caterina, M. (2007). Mechanisms of sensory transduction in the skin. *Nature, 445,* 858–865.

Luo, C., Kuner, T., & Kuner, R. (2014). Synaptic plasticity in pathological pain. *Trends in Neurosciences, 37,* 343–354.

Luo, T. Z., & Maunsell, J. H. (2015). Neuronal modulations in visual cortex are associated with only one of multiple components of attention. *Neuron, 86,* 1182–1188.

Luppi, P.-H., Clément, O., Sapin, E., Gervasoni, D., Peyron, C., Léger, L., Salvert, D., & Fort, P. (2011). The neuronal network responsible for paradoxical sleep and its dysfunctions causing narcolepsy and rapid eye movement (REM) behavior disorder. *Sleep Medicine Reviews, 15,* 153–163.

Lykken, D. T. (1959). The GSR in the detection of guilt. *Journal of Applied Psychology, 43,* 385–388.

Lyon, A. M., Taylor, V. G., & Tesmer, J. J. G. (2014). Strike a pose: G_q complexes at the membrane. *Trends in Pharmacological Sciences, 35,* 23–30.

M'charak, A. (2014). Development: YseX is a matter of concern rather than a matter of fact. *Science, 343,* 731–732.

Ma, W. J., Husain, M., & Bays, P. M. (2014). Changing concepts of working memory. *Nature Neuroscience, 17,* 347–356.

Maalouf, M., Rho, J. M., & Mattson, M. P. (2008). The neuroprotective properties of caloric restriction, the ketogenic diet, and ketone bodies. *Brain Research Reviews, 59,* 293–315.

Macaluso, E., & Doricchi, F. (2013). Attention and predictions: Control of spatial attention beyond the endogenous-exogenous dichotomy. *Frontiers in Human Neuroscience, 7,* 685.

Macchi, G. (1989). Anatomical substrate of emotional reactions. In F. Boller & J. Grafman (Eds.), *Handbook of neuropsychology* (Vol. 3, pp. 283–304). New York, NY: Elsevier.

Maceira, A. M., Ripoll, C., Cosin-Sales, J., Igual, B., Gavilan, M., Salazar, J.,… & Pennell, D. J. (2014). Long term effects of cocaine on the heart assessed by cardiovascular magnetic resonance at 3T. *Journal of Cardiovascular Magnetic Resonance, 16,* 26.

Machado, V. M., Morte, M. I., Carreira, B. P., Azevedo, M. M., Takano, J.,… & Araújo, I. M. (2015). Involvement of calpains in adult neurogenesis: Implications for stroke. *Frontiers in Cellular Neuroscience, 9,* 22.

MacLean, P. D. (1952). Some psychiatric implications of physiological studies on frontotemporal portion of limbic system (visceral brain). *Electroencephalography and Clinical Neurophysiology, 4,* 407–418.

MacNeilage, P. F., Rogers, L. J., & Vallortigara, G. (2009). Origins of the left & right brain. *Scientific American, 301,* 60–67.

Maddox, W. T., Aparicio, P., Marchant, N. L., & Ivry, R. B. (2005). Rule-based category learning is impaired in patients with Parkinson's disease but not in patients with cerebellar disorders. *Journal of Cognitive Neuroscience, 17,* 707–723.

Madras, B. K. (2013). History of the discovery of the antipsychotic dopamine D2 receptor: A basis for the dopamine hypothesis of schizophrenia. *Journal of the History of the Neurosciences, 22,* 62–78.

Maeda, N. (2015). Proteoglycans and neuronal migration in the cerebral cortex during development and disease. *Frontiers in Neuroscience, 9,* 98.

Maekawa, F., Tsukahara, S., Kawashima, T., Nohara, K., & Ohki-Hamazaki, H. (2014). The mechanisms underlying sexual differentiation of behavior and physiology in mammals and birds: Relative contributions of sex steroids and sex chromosomes. *Frontiers in Neuroscience, 8,* 242.

Maffei, A., Haley, M., & Fontanini, A. (2012). Neural processing of gustatory information in insular circuits. *Current Opinion in Neurobiology, 22,* 709–716.

Maggio, M., Colizzi, E., Fisichella, A., Valenti, G., Ceresini, G.,… & Ceda, G. P. (2013). Stress hormones, sleep deprivation and cognition in older adults. *Maturitas, 76,* 22–44.

Maguire, E. A., Frith, C. D., Burgess, N., Donnett, J. G., & O'Keefe, J. (1998). Knowing where things are: Parahippocampal involvement in encoding object locations in virtual large-scale space. *Journal of Cognitive Neuroscience, 19,* 61–76.

Mahan, A. L., & Ressler, K. J. (2012). Fear conditioning, synaptic plasticity and the amygdala: Implications for posttraumatic stress disorder. *Trends in Neurosciences, 35,* 24–34.

Mahar, I., Bambico, F. R., Mechawar, N., & Nobrega, J. N. (2014). Stress, serotonin, and hippocampal neurogenesis in relation to depression and antidepressant effects. *Neuroscience & Biobehavioral Reviews, 38,* 173–192.

Mahowald, M. W., & Schenck, C. H. (2005). Insights from studying human sleep disorders. *Nature, 437,* 1279–1285.

Mahowald, M. W., & Schenck, C. H. (2009). The REM sleep behavior disorder odyssey. *Sleep Medicine Reviews, 13,* 381–384.

Mainland, J. D., Lundström, J. N., Reisert, J., & Lowe, G. (2014). From molecule to mind: An integrative perspective on odor intensity. *Trends in Neurosciences, 37,* 443–454.

Mair, W., Goymer, P., Pletcher, S. D., & Partridge, L. (2003). Demography of dietary restriction and death in *Drosophila. Science, 301,* 1731–1733.

Maixner, F., Krause-Kyora, B., Turaev, D., Herbig, A., Hoopmann, M. R., Hallows, J. L.,… & O'Sullivan, N. (2016). The 5300-year-old *Helicobacter pylori* genome of the Iceman. *Science, 351,* 162–165.

Majdan, M., & Shatz, C. J. (2006). Effects of visual experience on activity-dependent gene regulation in cortex. *Nature Neuroscience, 9,* 650–659.

Majewska, A. K., & Sur, M. (2006). Plasticity and specificity of cortical processing networks. *Trends in Neurosciences, 29,* 323–329.

Mak-McCully, R. A., Deiss, S. R., Rosen, B. Q., Jung, K.-Y., Sejnowski, T. J.,… & Halgren, E. (2014). Synchronization of isolated downstates (k-complexes) may be caused by cortically-induced disruption of thalamic spindling. *PLoS Computational Biology, 10,* e1003855.

Makinodan, M., Rosen, K. M., Ito, S., & Corfas, G. (2012). A critical period for social experience-dependent oligodendrocyte maturation and myelination. *Science, 337,* 1357–1360.

Maletic, V., & Raison, C. (2014). Integrated neurobiology of bipolar disorder. *Frontiers in Psychiatry, 5,* 98.

Malhi, G. S., Lingford-Hughes, A. R., & Young, A. H. (2016). Antidepressant treatment response: "I want it all, and I want it now!" *British Journal of Psychiatry, 208,* 101–103.

Malki, K., Keers, R., Tosto, M. G., Lourdusamy, A., Carboni, L., Domenici, E.,… & Schalkwyk, L. C.

(2014). The endogenous and reactive depression subtypes revisited: Integrative animal and human studies implicate multiple distinct molecular mechanisms underlying major depressive disorder. *BMC Medicine, 12,* 1.

Mallet, J. (2010). Group selection and the development of the biological species concept. *Philosophical Transactions of the Royal Society B, 365,* 1853–1863.

Malsbury, C. W. (1971). Facilitation of male rat copulatory behavior by electrical stimulation of the medial preoptic area. *Physiology & Behavior, 7,* 797–805.

Man, K., Damasio, A., Meyer, K., & Kaplan, J. T. (2015). Convergent and invariant object representations for sight, sound, and touch. *Human Brain Mapping, 36,* 3629–3640.

Man, K., Kaplan, J., Damasio, H., & Damasio, A. (2013). Neural convergence and divergence in the mammalian cerebral cortex: From experimental neuroanatomy to functional neuroimaging. *Journal of Comparative Neurology, 521,* 4097–4111.

Mander, B. A., Marks, S. M., Vogel, J. W., Rao, V., Lu, B., Saletin, J. M.,…& Walker, M. P. (2015). Beta-amyloid disrupts human NREM slow waves and related hippocampus-dependent memory consolidation. *Nature Neuroscience, 18,* 1051–1057.

Manganotti, P., & Del Felice, A. (2013). New perspectives in transcranial magnetic stimulation: Epilepsy, consciousness and the perturbational approach. *Behavioral Neurology, 27,* 155–167.

Manger, P. R. (2013). Questioning the interpretations of behavioral observations of cetaceans: Is there really support for a special intellectual status for this mammalian order? *Neuroscience, 250,* 664–696.

Manglik, A., & Kobilka, B. (2014). The role of protein dynamics in GPCR function: Insights from the beta2AR and rhodopsin. *Current Opinion in Cell Biology, 27,* 136–143.

Manolio, T. A., Collins, F. S., Cox, N. J., Goldstein, D. B., Hindorff, L. A., Hunter, D. J., McCarthy, M. I., Ramos, E. M., Cardon, L. R., Chakravarti, A., Cho, J. H., Guttmacher, A. E., Kong A., Kruglyak, L., Mardis, E., Rotimi, C. N., Slatkin, M., Valle, D., Whittemore, A. S., Boehnke, M., Clark, A. G., Eichler, E. E., Gibson, G., Haines, J. L., Mackay, T. F., McCarroll, S. A., & Visscher, P. M. (2009). Finding the missing heritability of complex diseases. *Nature, 461,* 747–53.

Marchi, N., Granata, T., & Janigro, D. (2014). Inflammatory pathways of seizure disorders. *Trends in Neurosciences, 37,* 55–65.

Marczylo, E. L., Amoako, A. A., Konje, J. C., Gant, T. W., & Marczylo, T. H. (2012). Smoking induces differential miRNA expression in human spermatozoa: A potential transgenerational epigenetic concern? *Epigenetics, 7,* 432–439.

Maren, S. (2015). Out with the old and in with the new: Synaptic mechanisms of extinction in the amygdala. *Brain Research, 1621,* 231–238.

Maren, S., Phan, K. L., & Liberzan, I. (2013). The contextual brain: Implications for fear conditioning, extinction, and psychopathology. *Nature Reviews Neuroscience, 23,* 417–428.

Marin, O. (2012). Interneuron dysfunction in psychiatric disorders. *Nature Reviews Neuroscience, 13,* 107–120.

Markov, N. T., & Kennedy, H. (2013). The importance of being hierarchical. *Current Opinion in Neurobiology, 23,* 187–194.

Markram, H., Toledo-Rodriguez, M., Wang, Y., Gupta, A., Silberberg, G., & Wu, C. (2004). Interneurons of the neocortical inhibitory system. *Nature Reviews Neuroscience, 5,* 793–807.

Marlowe, W. B., Mancall, E. L., & Thomas, J. J. (1985). Complete Kluver-Bucy syndrome in man. *Cortex, 11,* 53–59.

Maroon, J. C., Winkelman, R., Bost, J., Amos, A., Mathyssek, C., & Miele, V. (2015). Chronic traumatic encephalopathy in contact sports: A systematic review of all reported pathological cases. *PloS One, 10,* e0117338.

Marquez de la Plata, M., Hart, T., Hammond, F. M., Frol, A. B., Hudak, A., Harper, C. R., O'Neill-Pirozzi, T. M., Whyte, J., Carlile, M., & Diaz-Arrastia, R. (2008). Impact of age on long-term recovery from traumatic brain injury. *Archives of Physical Medicine and Rehabilitation, 89,* 896–903.

Marshall, D. L., Milloy, M.-J., Wood, E., Montaner, J. S. G., & Kerr, T. (2011). Reduction in overdose mortality after the opening of North America's first medically supervised safer injecting facility: A retrospective population-based study. *Lancet, 377,* 1429–1437.

Marshall, J. F., & O'Dell, S. J. (2012). Methamphetamine influences on brain and behavior: Unsafe at any speed? *Trends in Neurosciences, 35,* 536–545.

Marshall, L. (2014). Two of a kind. *Scientific American, 311,* 22.

Martens, M. (2013). Developmental and cognitive troubles in Williams syndrome. *Handbook of Clinical Neurology, 111,* 291–293.

Martin, A., State, M., Koenig, K., Schultz, R., Dykens, E. M., Cassidy, S. B., & Leckman, J. F. (1998). Prader-Willi syndrome. *American Journal of Psychiatry, 155,* 1265–1272.

Martin, B. J. (1981). Effect of sleep deprivation on tolerance of prolonged exercise. *European Journal of Applied Physiology, 47,* 345–354.

Martin, D. D. O., Ladha, S., Ehrnhoefer, D. E., & Hayden, M. R. (2015). Autophagy in Huntington disease and huntingtin in autophagy. *Trends in Neurosciences, 38,* 26–35.

Martinez-Conde, S., Macknik, S. L., & Hubel, D. H. (2004). The role of fixational eye movements in visual perception. *Nature Reviews Neuroscience, 5,* 229–240.

Marx, V. (2014). A deep look at synaptic dynamics. *Nature, 515,* 293–297.

Mashour, G. A., Walker, E. E., & Martuza, R. L. (2005). Psychosurgery: Past, present, and future. *Brain Research Reviews, 48,* 409–419.

Mason, M. F., Norton, M. I., Van Horn, J. D., Wegner, D. M., Grafton, S. T., & Macrae, C. N. (2007). Wandering minds: The default network and stimulus-independent thought. *Science, 315,* 393–395.

Mason, P. (2012). Medullary circuits for nociceptive modulation. *Current Opinion in Neurobiology, 22,* 640–645.

Masoro, E. J. (1988). Food restriction in rodents: An evaluation of its role in the study of aging [Minireview]. *Journal of Gerontology, 43,* 59–64.

Masri, S., & Sassone-Corsi, P. (2013). The circadian clock: A framework linking metabolism, epigenetics and neuronal function. *Nature Reviews Neuroscience, 14,* 69–75.

Masters, R. K., Reither, E. N., Powers, D. A., Yang, Y. C., Burger, A. E., & Link, B. G. (2013). The impact of obesity on US mortality levels: The importance of age and cohort factors in population estimates. *American Journal of Public Health, 103,* 1895–1901.

Matsumoto, J., Urakawa, S., Hori, E., de Araujo, M. F. P., Sakuma, Y., Ono, T., & Nishijo, H. (2012). Neuronal responses in the nucleus accumbens shell during sexual behavior in male rats. *Journal of Neuroscience, 32,* 1672–1686.

Matsuzawa, T. (2013). Evolution of the brain and social behavior in chimpanzees. *Current Opinion in Neurobiology, 23,* 443–449.

Matthews, P. M. (2013). Decade in review—multiple sclerosis: New drugs and personalized medicine for multiple sclerosis. *Nature Reviews Neurology, 11,* 614–616.

Matthews, S., Strigo, I., Simmons, A., Yang, T., & Paulus, M. (2009). Decreased functional coupling of the amygdala and supragenual cingulate is related to increased depression in unmedicated individuals with current major depressive disorder. *Journal of Affective Disorders, 111,* 13–20.

Mattick, J. S., & Mehler, M. F. (2008). RNA editing, DNA recoding and the evolution of human cognition. *Trends in Neurosciences, 31,* 227–233.

Mattick, R. P., Breen, C., Kimber, J., & Davoli, M. (2014). Buprenorphine maintenance versus placebo or methadone maintenance for opioid dependence. *Cochrane Database of Systematic Reviews, 6,* CD002207.

Matyash, V., & Kettenmann, H. (2010). Heterogeneity in astrocyte morphology and physiology. *Brain Research Reviews, 63,* 2–10.

Matzinger, P. (2002). The danger model: A renewed sense of self. *Science, 296,* 301–305.

Maurano, M. T., Humbert, R., Rynes, E., Thurman, R. E., Haugen, E., Wang, H., Reynolds, A. P., Sandstrom, R., Qu, H., Brody, J., Shafer, A., Neri, F., Lee, K., Kutyavin, T., Stehling-Sun, S., Johnson, A. K., Canfield, T. K., Giste, E., Diegel, M., Bates, D., Hansen, R. S., Neph, S., Sabo, P. J., Heimfeld, S., Raubitschek, A., Ziegler, S., Cotsapas, C., Sotoodehnia, N., Glass, I., Sunyaev, S. R., Kaul, R., & Stamatoyannopoulos, J. A. (2012). Systematic localization of common disease-associated variation in regulatory DNA. *Science, 337,* 1190–1195.

Maurer, D., Ellenberg, D., & Lewis, T. L. (2006). Repeated measurements of contrast sensitivity reveal limits to visual plasticity after early binocular deprivation in humans. *Neuropsychologia, 44,* 2104–2112.

Mc Allister, E., Pacheco-Lopez, G., Woods, S. C., & Langhans, W. (2015). Inconsistencies in the hypophagic action of intracerebroventricular insulin in mice. *Physiology & Behavior, 151,* 623–628.

McCann, T. S. (1981). Aggression and sexual activity of male southern elephant seals, *Mirounga leonina. Journal of Zoology, 195,* 295–310.

McCarthy, M. M., & Arnold, A. P. (2011). Reframing sexual differentiation of the brain. *Nature Neuroscience, 14,* 677–683.

McCarthy, M. M., Arnold, A. P., Ball, G. F., Blaustein, J. D., & De Vries, G. J. (2012). Sex differences in the brain: The not so inconvenient truth. *Journal of Neuroscience, 32,* 2241–2247.

McCarthy, M. M., Auger, A. P., & Perrot-Sinal, T. S. (2002). Getting excited about GABA and sex differences in the brain. *Trends in Neurosciences, 25,* 307–313.

McClintock, M. K., & Herdt, G. (1996). Rethinking puberty: The development of sexual attraction. *Current Directions in Psychological Sciences, 5,* 178–183.

McCoy, P. A., Huang, H-S., & Philpot, B. D. (2009). Advances in understanding visual cortex plasticity. *Current Opinion in Neurobiology, 19,* 298–304.

McDermott, K. B., Watson, J. M., & Ojemann, J. G. (2005). Presurgical language mapping. *Current Directions in Psychological Science, 14,* 291–295.

McEwen, B. S. (1983). Gonadal steroid influences on brain development and sexual differentiation. In R. O. Greep (Ed.), *Reproductive physiology IV.* Baltimore: University Park Press.

McEwen, B. S., & Karatsoreos, I. N. (2015). Sleep deprivation and circadian disruption: Stress, allostasis, and allostatic load. *Sleep Medicine Clinics, 10,* 1–10.

McEwen, B. S., Gray, J. D., & Nasca, C. (2015). Recognizing resilience: Learning from the effects of stress on the brain. *Neurobiology of Stress, 1,* 1–11.

McEwen, B. S., Nasca, C., & Gray, J. D. (2016). Stress effects on neuronal structure: Hippocampus, amygdala, and prefrontal cortex. *Neuropsychopharmacology, 41*(1), 3–23.

McGaugh, J. L. (2015). Consolidating memories. *Annual Review of Psychology, 66,* 1–24.

McGirr, A., Berlim, M. T., Bond, D. J., Fleck, M. P., Yatham, L. N., & Lam, R. W. (2015). A systematic review and meta-analysis of randomized, double-blind, placebo-controlled trials of ketamine in the rapid treatment of major depressive episodes. *Psychological Medicine, 45*, 693–704.

McGlone, F., & Reilly, D. (2010). The cutaneous sensory system. *Neuroscience and Biobehavioral Reviews, 34*, 148–159.

McGlone, F., Wessberg, J., & Olausson, H. (2014). Discriminative and affective touch: Sensing and feeling. *Neuron, 82*, 737–755.

McGlone, J. (1977). Sex differences in the cerebral organization of verbal functions in patients with unilateral brain lesions. *Brain, 100*, 775–793.

McGlone, J. (1980). Sex differences in human brain asymmetry: A critical survey. *Behavioral and Brain Sciences, 3*, 215–263.

McKenzie, I. A., Ohayon, D., Li, H., de Faria, J. P., Emery, B., et al. (2014). Motor skill learning requires active central myelination. *Science, 346*, 318–322.

McKim, W. A. (1986). *Drugs and behavior: An introduction to behavioral pharmacology.* Englewood Cliffs, NJ: Prentice-Hall.

McKone, E., Crookes, K., Jeffery, L., & Dilks, D. D. (2012). A critical review of the development of face recognition: Experience is less important than previously believed. *Cognitive Neuropsychology, 29*, 174–212.

McLaughlin, T., Hindges, R., & O'Leary, D. D. M. (2003). Regulation of axial patterning of the retina and its topographic mapping in the brain. *Current Opinion in Neurobiology, 13*, 57–69.

McMahon, D. B. T., Russ, B. E., Elnaiem, H. D., Kurnikova, A. I., & Leopold, D. A. (2015). Single-unit activity during natural vision: Diversity, consistency, and spatial sensitivity among AF face patch neurons. *Journal of Neuroscience, 35*, 5537–5548.

McNamara, P., Johnson, P., McLaren, D., Harris, E., Beauharnais, C., & Auerbach, S. (2010). REM and NREM sleep mentation. *International Review of Neurobiology, 92*, 69–86.

McNaughton, N., & Zangrossi, H. H., Jr. (2008). Theoretical approaches to the modeling of anxiety in animals. In R. J. Blanchard, D. C. Blanchard, G. Griebel, & D. J. Nutt (Eds.), *Handbook of anxiety and fear* (Vol. 17, pp. 11–27). Oxford, England: Elsevier.

McPartland, J. M., Duncan, M., Di Marzo, V., & Pertwee, R. (2014). Are cannabidiol and delta-9-tetrahydrocannabivarin negative modulators of the endocannabinoid system? A systematic review. *British Journal of Pharmacology, 172*, 737–753.

Meaney, M. J., & Szyf, M. (2005). Maternal care as a model for experience-dependent chromatin plasticity? *Trends in Neurosciences, 28*, 456–463.

Mechoulam, R., & Parker, L. A. (2013). The endocannabinoid system and the brain. *Annual Review of Psychology, 64*, 21–47.

Meddis, R. (1977). *The sleep instinct.* London, England: Routledge & Kegan Paul.

Medzhitov, R., & Janeway, C. A., Jr. (2002). Decoding the patterns of self and nonself by the innate immune system. *Science, 296*, 298–301.

Meier, M. H., Caspi, A., Ambler, A., Harrington, H., Houts, R., Keefe, R. S. E., McDonald, K., Ward, A., Poulton, R., & Moffitt, T. E. (2012). Persistent cannabis users show neuropsychological decline from childhood to midlife. *PNAS, 109*, E2657–E2664.

Mel, B. W. (2002). What the synapse tells the neuron. *Science, 295*, 1845–1846.

Meletti, S., Cantalupo, G., Santoro, F., Benuzzi, F., Marliani, A. F., Tassinari, C. A., & Rubboli, G. (2014). Temporal lobe epilepsy and emotion recognition without amygdala: A case study of Urbach-Wiethe disease and review of the literature. *Epileptic Disorders, 16*, 518–527.

Mello, N. K., & Mendelson, J. H. (1972). Drinking patterns during work-contingent and noncontingent alcohol acquisition. *Psychosomatic Medicine, 34*, 139–165.

Mello, N. K., & Negus, S. S. (1996). Preclinical evaluation of pharmacotherapies for treatment

of cocaine and opioid abuse using drug self-administration procedures. *Neuropsychopharmacology, 14*, 375–424.

Melrose, S. (2015). Seasonal affective disorder: An overview of assessment and treatment approaches. *Depression Research and Treatment, 2015*, 178564.

Melzack, R. (1992, April). Phantom limbs. *Scientific American, 266*, 120–126.

Melzack, R., & Wall, P. D. (1982). *The challenge of pain.* London, England: Penguin.

Melzack, R., Israel, R., Lacroix, R., & Schultz, G. (1997). Phantom limbs in people with congenital limb deficiency or amputation in early childhood. *Brain, 120*, 1603–1620.

Melzer, N., Meuth, S. G., & Wiendl, H. (2012). Neuron-directed autoimmunity in the central nervous system: Entities, mechanisms, diagnostic clues, and therapeutic options. *Current Opinion in Neurology, 25*, 341–348.

Meney, I., Waterhouse, J., Atkinson, G., Reilly, T., & Davenne, D. (1998). The effect of one night's sleep deprivation on temperature, mood, and physical performance in subjects with different amounts of habitual physical activity. *Chronobiology International, 15*, 349–363.

Merabet, L. F., & Pascual-Leone, A. (2010). Neural reorganization following sensory loss: The opportunity of change. *Nature Reviews Neuroscience, 11*, 44–52.

Mercer, J. G., & Speakman, J. R. (2001). Hypothalamic neuropeptide mechanisms for regulating energy balance: From rodent models to human obesity. *Neuroscience and Biobehavioural Reviews, 25*, 101–116.

Meredith, R. W., Janecka, J. E., Gatesy, J., Ryder, O. A., Fisher, C. A., Teeling, E. C., Goodbla, A., Eizirik, E., Simão, T. L., Stadler, T., Rabosky, D. L., Honeycutt, R. L., Flynn, J. J., Ingram, C. M., Steiner, C., Williams, T. L., Robinson, T. J., Burk-Herrick, A., Westermann, M., Ayoub, N. A., Springer, M. S., Murphy, W. J. (2011). Impacts of the Cretaceous terrestrial revolution and KPg extinction on mammal diversification. *Science, 334*, 521–524.

Mering, S., & Jolkkonen, J. (2015). Proper housing conditions in experimental stroke studies—special emphasis on environmental enrichment. *Frontiers in Neuroscience, 9*, 106.

Meunier, H., Vauclair, J., & Fagard, J. (2012). Human infants and baboons show the same pattern of handedness for a communicative gesture. *PLoS ONE, 7*, e33959.

Meyer-Lindenberg, A., Mervis, C. B., & Berman, K. F. (2006). Neural mechanisms in Williams syndrome: A unique window to genetic influences on cognition and behaviour. *Nature Reviews Neuroscience, 7*, 380–393.

Meyer, K. D., & Morris, J. A. (2009). Disc1 regulates granule cell migration in the developing hippocampus. *Human Molecular Genetics, 18*, 3286–3297.

Meyer, R. G., & Salmon, P. (1988). *Abnormal psychology* (2nd ed.). Boston, MA: Allyn & Bacon.

Meyers, E. M., Borzello, M., Freiwald, W. A., & Tsao, D. (2015). Intelligent information loss: The coding of facial identity, head pose, and non-face information in the macaque face patch system. *Journal of Neuroscience, 35*, 7069–7081.

Meyhöfer, I., Steffens, M., Kasparbauer, A., Grant, P., Weber, B., & Ettinger, U. (2014). Neural mechanisms of smooth pursuit eye movements in schizotypy. *Human Brain Mapping, Sept 5.*

Mielke, M. M., Vemuri, P., & Rocca, W. A. (2014). Clinical epidemiology of Alzheimer's disease: Assessing sex and gender differences. *Clinical Epidemiology, 6*, 37–48.

Miendlarzewska, E. A., & Trost, W. J. (2014). How musical training affects cognitive development: Rhythm, reward and other modulating variables. *Frontiers in Neuroscience, 7*, 279.

Mignot, E. (2013). The perfect hypnotic? *Science, 340*, 36–38.

Miguel-Aliaga, I., & Thor, S. (2009). Programmed cell death in the nervous system—a programmed cell fate? *Current Opinion in Neurobiology, 19*, 127–133.

Miles, F. J., Everitt, B. J., Dalley, J. W., & Dickinson, A. (2004). Conditioned activity and instrumental reinforcement following long-term oral consumption of cocaine by rats. *Behavioral Neuroscience, 118*, 1331–1339.

Millan, M. J., Andrieux, A., Bartzokis, G., Cadenhead, K., Dazzan, P., Fusar-Poli, P., … & Kahn, R. (2016). Altering the course of schizophrenia: Progress and perspectives. *Nature Reviews Drug Discovery.*

Miller, B. R., & Hen, R. (2015). The current state of the neurogenic theory of depression and anxiety. *Current Opinion in Neurobiology, 30*, 51–58.

Miller, D. I., & Halpern, D. F. (2014). The new science of cognitive sex differences. *Trends in Cognitive Sciences, 18*, 37–45.

Miller, E. K., & Buschman, T. J. (2013). Cortical circuits for the control of attention. *Current Opinion in Neurobiology, 23*, 216–222.

Miller, G. (2012). Stopping Alzheimer's before it starts. *Science, 337*, 790–792.

Miller, G. E., & Chen, E. (2006). Life stress and diminished expression of genes encoding glucocorticoid receptor and β_2-adrenergic receptor in children with asthma. *Proceedings of the National Academy of Sciences, USA, 103*, 5496–5501.

Miller, G. L., & Knudsen, E. I. (1999). Early visual experience shapes the representation of auditory space in the forebrain gaze fields of the barn owl. *Journal of Neuroscience, 19*, 2326–2336.

Miller, J. F., Neufang, M., Solway, A., Brandt, A., Trippel, … & Schulze-Bonhage, A. (2013). Neural activity in human hippocampal formation reveals the spatial context of retrieved memories. *Science, 342*, 111–1120.

Miller, T. M., & Cleveland, D. W. (2005). Treating neurodegenerative diseases with antibiotics. *Science, 307*, 361–362.

Milner, A. D., & Goodale, M. A. (1993). Visual pathways to perception and action. *Progress in Brain Research, 95*, 317–337.

Milner, B. (1965). Memory disturbances after bilateral hippocampal lesions. In P. Milner & S. Glickman (Eds.), *Cognitive processes and the brain* (pp. 104–105). Princeton, NJ: D. Van Nostrand.

Milner, B. (1971). Interhemispheric differences in the localization of psychological processes in man. *British Medical Bulletin, 27*, 272–277.

Milner, B. (1974). Hemispheric specialization: Scope and limits. In F. O. Schmitt & F. G. Worden (Eds.), *The neurosciences: Third study program* (pp. 75–89). Cambridge, MA: MIT Press.

Milner, B., Corkin, S., & Teuber, H. L. (1968). Further analysis of the hippocampal amnesic syndrome: 14-year follow-up study of H.M. *Neuropsychologia, 6*, 317–338.

Milner, C. E., & Cote, K. A. (2008). A dose-response investigation of the benefits of napping in healthy young, middle-aged, and older adults. *Sleep and Biological Rhythms, 6*, 2–15.

Milner, P. M. (1993, January). The mind and Donald O. Hebb. *Scientific American, 268*, 124–129.

Milnerwood, A. J., & Raymond, L. A. (2010). Early synaptic pathophysiology in neurodegeneration: Insights from Huntinton's disease. *Trends in Neurosciences, 33*, 513–523.

Milton, A. L., & Everitt, B. J. (2012). The persistence of maladaptive memory: Addiction, drug memories and anti-relapse treatments. *Neuroscience and Biobehavioral Reviews, 36*, 1119–1139.

Mindell, D. P. (2009, January). Evolution in the everyday world. *Scientific American, 300*, 82–89.

Minger, S. L., Ekonomou, A., Carta, E. M., Chinoy, A., Perry, R. H., & Ballard, C. G. (2007). Endogenous neurogenesis in the human brain following cerebral infarction. *Regenerative Medicine, 2*, 69–74.

Minkel, J., Moreta, M., Muto, J., Htaik, O., Jones, C., … & Dinges, D. (2014). Sleep deprivation potentiates HPA axis stress reactivity in healthy adults. *Health Psychology, 33,* 1430–1434.

Mirakaj, V., Brown, S., Laucher, S., Steinl, C., Klein, G., Köhler, D., Skutella, T., Meisel, C., Brommer, B., Rosenberger, P., & Schwab, J. M. (2011). Repulsive guidance molecule-A (RGM-A) inhibits leukocyte migration and mitigates inflammation. *Proceedings of the National Academy of Sciences USA, 108,* 6555–6560.

Mishkin, M., & Delacour, J. (1975). An analysis of short-term visual memory in the monkey. *Journal of Experimental Psychology: Animal Behavior Processes, 1,* 326–334.

Mistlberger, R. E. (2011). Neurobiology of food anticipatory circadian rhythms. *Physiology & Behavior, 104,* 535–545.

Mistlberger, R. E., de Groot, M. H. M., Bossert, J. M., & Marchant, E. G. (1996). Discrimination of circadian phase in intact and suprachiasmatic nuclei-ablated rats. *Brain Research, 739,* 12–18.

Mitchell, D. G. V., & Greening, S. G. (2011). Conscious perception of emotional stimuli: Brain mechanisms. *The Neuroscientist, 18,* 386–398.

Mitchell, P. B., & Hadzi-Pavlovic, D. (2000). Lithium treatment for bipolar disorder. *Bulletin of the World Health Organization, 78,* 515–517.

Mitchell, R. L. C., & Phillips, L. H. (2015). The overlapping relationship between emotion perception and theory of mind. *Neuropsychologia, 70,* 1–10.

Mitra, P. P. (2014). The circuit architecture of whole brains at the mesoscopic scale. *Neuron, 83,* 1273–1283.

Miyashita, Y. (2004). Cognitive memory: Cellular and network machineries and their top-down control. *Science, 306,* 435–440.

Mizrahi, A., Shalev, A., & Nelken, I. (2014). Single neuron and population coding of natural sounds in auditory cortex. *Current Opinion in Neurobiology, 24,* 103–110.

Moerel, M., De Martino, F., & Formisano, E. (2014). An anatomical and functional topography of human auditory cortical areas. *Frontiers in Neuroscience, 8,* 225.

Mogil, J. S. (2012). Sex differentiation in pain and pain inhibition: Multiple explanations of a controversial phenomenon. *Nature Reviews Neuroscience, 13,* 859–866.

Mohawk, J. A., & Takahashi, J. S. (2011). Cell autonomy and synchrony of suprachiasmatic nucleus circadian oscillators. *Trends in Neurosciences, 34,* 349–358.

Mohr, J. P. (1976). Broca's area and Broca's aphasia. In H. Whitaker & H. A. Whitaker (Eds.), *Studies in neurolinguistics* (Vol. 1, pp. 201–235). New York, NY: Academic Press.

Moitra, E., Dyck, I., Beard, C., Bjornsson, A. S., Sibrava, N. J., Weisberg, R. B., & Keller, M. B. (2011). Impact of stressful life events on the course of panic disorder in adults. *Journal of Affective Disorders, 134,* 373–376.

Mokdad, A. H., Marks, J. S., Stroup, D. F., & Gerberding, J. L. (2004). Actual causes of death in the United States, 2000. *The Journal of the American Medical Association, 291,* 1238–1245.

Moldovan, A.-S., Groiss, S. J., Elben, S., Südmeyer, M., Schnitzler, A., & Wojtecki, L. (2015). The treatment of Parkinson's disease with deep brain stimulation: Current issues. *Neural Regeneration Research, 10,* 1018–1022.

Molenberghs, P., Cunnington, R., & Mattingley, J. B. (2012). Brain regions with mirror properties: A meta-analysis of 125 human fMRI studies. *Neuroscience and Biobehavioral Reviews, 36,* 341–349.

Money, J. (1975). Ablatio penis: Normal male infant sex-reassigned as a girl. *Archives of Sexual Behavior, 4*(1), 65–71.

Money, J., & Ehrhardt, A. A. (1972). *Man & woman, boy & girl.* Baltimore, MD: Johns Hopkins University Press.

Mongan, N. P., Tadokoro-Cuccaro, R., Bunch, T., & Hughes, I. A. (2015). Androgen insensitivity syndrome. *Best Practice & Research Clinical Endocrinology & Metabolism, 4,* 569–580.

Mongiat, L. A., & Schinder, A. F. (2014). A price to pay for adult neurogenesis. *Science, 344,* 594–595.

Monk, T. H., Buysse, D. J., Welsh, D. K., Kennedy, K. S., & Rose, L. R. (2001). A sleep diary and questionnaire study of naturally short sleepers. *Journal of Sleep Research, 10,* 173–179.

Monteggia, L. M., Malenka, R. C., & Deisseroth, K. (2014). Depression: The best way forward. *Nature, 515,* 200–201.

Montero, T. D., & Orellana, J. A. (2015). Hemichannels: New pathways for gliotransmitter release. *Neuroscience, 286,* 45–59.

Montoya, E. R., Terburg, D., Bos, P. A., & van Honk, J. (2012). Testosterone, cortisol, and serotonin as key regulators of social aggression: A review and theoretical perspective. *Motivation and Emotion, 36,* 65–73.

Moore, D. J., West, A. B., Dawson, V. L., & Dawson, T. M. (2005). Molecular pathophysiology of Parkinson's disease. *Annual Review of Neuroscience, 28,* 57–87.

Moore, T., & Zirnsak, M. (2015). The what and where of visual attention. *Neuron, 88,* 626–628.

Moran, J., & Desimone, R. (1985). Selective attention gates visual processing in the extrastriate cortex. *Science, 229,* 782–784.

Moran, Y., Barzilai, M. G., Liebeskind, B. J., & Zakon, H. H. (2015). Evolution of voltage-gated ion channels at the emergence of the Metazoa. *Journal of Experimental Biology, 218,* 515–525.

Morey, L., Santanach, A., & Di Croce, L. (2015). Pluripotency and epigenetic factors in mouse embyonic stem cell fate regulation. *Molecular and Cellular Biology, 35,* 2716–2728.

Morgan, T. H., Sturtevant, A. H., Muller, H. J., & Bridges, C. B. (1915). *The mechanism of Mendelian heredity.* New York, NY: Holt.

Morgenthaler, J., Wiesner, C. D., Hinze, K., Abels, L. C., Prehn-Kristensen, A., & Göder, R. (2014). Selective REM-sleep deprivation does not diminish emotional memory consolidation in young healthy subjects. *PLoS ONE, 9,* e89849.

Mori, K., & Sakano, H. (2011). How is the olfactory map formed and interpreted in the mammalian brain? *Annual Review of Neuroscience, 34,* 467–499.

Mori, M., Rikitake, Y., Mandai, K., & Takai, Y. (2014). Roles of nectins and nectin-like molecules in the nervous system. *Advances in Neurobiology, 8,* 91–116.

Morici, J. F., Bekinschtein, P., & Weisstaub, N. V. (2015). Medial prefrontal cortex in recognition memory in rodents. *Behavioural Brain Research, 292,* 241–251.

Morimoto, K., Fahnestock, M., & Racine, R. J. (2004). Kindling and status epilepticus models of epilepsy: Rewiring the brain. *Progress in Neurobiology, 73,* 1–60.

Morin, L. P., & Allen, C. N. (2006). The circadian visual system. *Brain Research Reviews, 51,* 1–61.

Morris, C. J., Aeschbach, D., & Scheer, F. A. J. L. (2012). Circadian system, sleep and endocrinology. *Molecular and Cellular Endocrinology, 349,* 91–104.

Morris, M. J., Beilharz, J. E., Maniam, J., Reichelt, A. C., & Westbrook, R. F. (2014). Why is obesity such a problem in the 21st century? The intersection of palatable food, cues and reward pathways, stress, and cognition. *Neuroscience and Biobehavioral Reviews, 58,* 36–45.

Morris, N. M., Udry, J. R., Khan-Dawood, F., & Dawood, M. Y. (1987). Marital sex frequency and midcycle female testosterone. *Archives of Sexual Behavior, 16,* 27–37.

Morris, R. G. M. (1981). Spatial localization does not require the presence of local cues. *Learning and Motivation, 12,* 239–260.

Mort, D. J., Malhotra, P., Mannan, S. K., Rorden, C., Pambakian, A., Kennard, C., & Husain, M. (2003). The anatomy of visual neglect. *Brain, 126,* 1986–1997.

Morton, G. J., Meek, T. H., & Schwartz, M. W. (2014). Neurobiology of food intake in health and disease. *Nature Reviews Neuroscience, 15,* 367–377.

Moruzzi, G., & Magoun, H. W. (1949). Brain stem reticular formation and activation of the EEG. *Electroencephalography and Clinical Neurophysiology, 1,* 455–473.

Moscati, A., Flint, J., & Kendler, K. S. (2015). Classification of anxiety disorders comorbid with major depression: Common or distinct influences on risk? *Depression and Anxiety, 33,* 120–127.

Moseley, G. L., Gallace, A., & Spence, C. (2012). Bodily illusions in health and disease: Physiological and clinical perspectives and the concept of a cortical 'body matrix.' *Neuroscience and Biobehavioral Reviews, 36,* 34–46.

Moseley, G. L., Zalucki, N., Birklein, F., Marinus, J., van Hilten, J. J., & Luomajoki, H. (2008). Thinking about movement hurts: The effect of motor imagery on pain and swelling in people with chronic arm pain. *Arthritis Care Research, 59,* 623–631.

Moser, E. I., & Moser, M.-B. (2013). Grid cells and neural coding in high-end cortices. *Neuron, 80,* 765–774.

Moser, E. I., Roudi, Y., Witter, M. P., Kentros, C., Bonhoeffer, T., & Moser, M.-B. (2014). Grid cells and cortical representation. *Nature Reviews Neuroscience, 15,* 466–481.

Moser, M. B., & Moser, E. I. (2016). Where am I? Where am I going? *Scientific American, 314,* 26–33.

Mottron, L., Duret, P., Mueller, S., Moore, R. D., d'Arc B. F., … Xiong, L. (2015). Sex differences in brain plasticity: A new hypothesis for sex ratio bias in autism. *Molecular Autism, 6,* 33.

Moyle, J. J., Fox, A. M., Arthur, M., Bynevelt, M., & Burnett, J. R. (2007). Meta-analysis of neuropsychological symptoms of adolescents and adults with PKU. *Neuropsychology Review, 17,* 91–101.

Mu, Y., Lee, S. W., & Gage, F. H. (2010). Signaling in adult neurogenesis. *Current Opinion in Neurobiology, 20,* 416–423.

Muckli, L., & Petro, L. S. (2013). Network interactions: Non-geniculate input to V1. *Current Opinion in Neurobiology, 23,* 195–201.

Mühlnickel, W., Elbert, T., Taub, E., & Flor, H. (1998). Reorganization of auditory cortex in tinnitus. *Proceedings of the National Academy of Sciences, USA, 95,* 10340–10343.

Mukamel, R., Ekstrom, A. D., Kaplan, J., Iacoboni, M., & Fried, I. (2010). Single neuron responses in humans during execution and observation of actions. *Current Biology, 20,* 750–756.

Mulette-Gillman, O. A., Cohen, Y. E., & Groh, J. M. (2005). Eye-centered, head-centered, and complex coding of visual and auditory targets in the intraparietal sulcus. *Journal of Neurophysiology, 94,* 2331–2352.

Mullaney, D. J., Johnson, L. C., Naitoh, P., Friedman, J. K., & Globus, G. G. (1977). Sleep during and after gradual sleep reduction. *Psychophysiology, 14,* 237–244.

Müller-Dahlhaus, F., & Ziemann, U. (2015). Metaplasticity in human cortex. *Neuroscientist, 21,* 185–202.

Müller, C. P., & Schumann, G. (2011). Drugs as instruments: A new framework for non-addictive psychoactive drug use. *Behavioral and Brain Sciences, 34,* 293–347.

Mullins, C., Fishell, G., & Tsien, R. W. (2016). Unifying views of autism spectrum disorders: A consideration of autoregulatory feedback loops. *Neuron, 89,* 1131–1156.

Mumby, D. G. (2001). Perspectives on object-recognition memory following hippocampal damage: Lessons from studies in rats. *Behavioural Brain Research, 14,* 159–181.

Mumby, D. G., & Pinel, J. P. J. (1994). Rhinal cortex lesions impair object recognition in rats. *Behavioral Neuroscience, 108,* 11–18.

Mumby, D. G., Cameli, L., & Glenn, M. J. (1999). Impaired allocentric spatial working memory and intact retrograde memory after thalamic damage caused by thiamine deficiency in rats. *Behavioral Neuroscience, 113,* 42–50.

Mumby, D. G., Pinel, J. P. J., & Wood, E. R. (1989). Nonrecurring items delayed nonmatching-to-sample in rats: A new paradigm for testing nonspatial working memory. *Psychobiology, 18,* 321–326.

Mumby, D. G., Wood, E. R., & Pinel, J. P. J. (1992). Object-recognition memory is only mildly impaired in rats with lesions of the hippocampus and amygdala. *Psychobiology, 20,* 18–27.

Mumby, D. G., Wood, E. R., Duva, C. A., Kornecook, T. J., Pinel, J. P. J., & Phillips, A. G. (1996). Ischemia-induced object-recognition deficits in rats are attenuated by hippocampal ablation before or soon after ischemia. *Behavioral Neuroscience, 110*(2), 266–281.

Münzberg, H., & Myers, M. G. (2005). Molecular and anatomical determinants of central leptin resistance. *Nature Neuroscience, 8,* 566–570.

Muoio, V., Persson, P. B., & Sendeski, M. M. (2014). The neurovascular unit—concept review. *Acta Physiologica, 210,* 790–798.

Murdoch, B. E. (2010). The cerebellum and language: Historical perspective and review. *Cortex, 46,* 858–868.

Murphy, M. R., & Schneider, G. E. (1970). Olfactory bulb removal eliminates mating behavior in the male golden hamster. *Science, 157,* 302–304.

Murray, D. R., & Schaller, M. (2016). The behavioral immune system: Implications for social cognition, social interaction, and social influence. *Advances in Experimental Social Psychology, 53,* 75–129.

Murray, G., Suto, M., Hole, R., Hale, S., Amari, E., & Michalak, E. E. (2011). Self-management strategies used by "high functioning" individuals with bipolar disorder: From research to clinical practice. *Clinical Psychology & Psychotherapy, 18,* 95–109.

Murray, M. M., & Herrmann, C. S. (2013). Illusory contours: A window onto the neurophysiology of constructing perception. *Trends in Cognitive Sciences, 17,* 471–481.

Murru, A., Popovic, D., Pacchiarotti, I., Hidalgo, D., León-Caballero, J., & Vieta, E. (2015). Management of adverse effects of mood stabilizers. *Current Psychiatry Reports, 17,* 1–10.

Murthy, V. N. (2011). Olfactory maps in the brain. *Annual Review of Neuroscience, 34,* 233–258.

Musiek, E. S., & Holtzman, D. M. (2015). Three dimensions of the amyloid hypothesis: Time, space and 'wingmen'. *Nature Neuroscience, 18,* 800–806.

Myers, R. E., & Sperry, R. W. (1953). Interocular transfer of a visual form discrimination habit in cats after section of the optic chiasma and corpus callosum. *Anatomical Record, 115,* 351–352.

Mysore, S. P., & Knudsen, E. I. (2014). Descending control of neural bias and selectivity in a spatial attention network: Rules and mechanisms. *Neuron, 84,* 214–226.

Nabavi, S., Fox, R., Proulx, C. D., Lin, J. Y., Tsien, R. Y., & Malinow, R. (2014). Engineering a memory with LTD and LTP. *Nature, 511,* 348–352.

Nachev, P., Kennard, C., & Husain, M. (2008). Functional role of the supplementary and pre-supplementary motor areas. *Nature Reviews Neuroscience, 9,* 856–869.

Nadeau, J. H. (2009). Transgenerational genetic effects on phenotypic variation and disease risk. *Human Molecular Genetics, 18*(R2), R202–R210.

Nader, K. (2015). Reconsolidation and the dynamic nature of memory. *Cold Spring Harbor Perspectives in Biology, 7,* a021782.

Nader, K., Schafe, G. E., & LeDoux, J. E. (2000). Fear memories require protein synthesis in the amygdala for reconsolidation after retrieval. *Nature, 406,* 722–726.

Nader, M. A., Czoty, P. W., Gould, R. W., & Riddick, N. V. (2008). Positron emission tomography imaging studies of dopamine receptors in primate models of addiction. *Philosophical Transactions of the Royal Society B, 363,* 3223–3232.

Naeser, M. A., Hayward, R. W., Laughlin, S. A., & Zatz, L. M. (1981). Quantitative CT scan studies in aphasia. *Brain and Language, 12,* 140–164.

Nagai, C., Inui, T., & Iwata, M. (2011). Fading-figure tracing in William syndrome. *Brain and Cognition, 75,* 10–17.

Nagy, J. I., Dudek, F. E., & Rash, J. E. (2004). Update on connexins and gap junctions in neurons and glia in the mammalian nervous system. *Brain Research Reviews, 47,* 191–215.

Nahorski, M. S., Chen, Y. C., & Woods, C. G. (2015). New Mendelian disorders of painlessness. *Trends in Neurosciences, 38,* 712–724.

Naimi, T. S., Brown, D. W., Brewer, R. D., Giles, W. H., Mensah, G., Serdula, M. K., Mokdad, A. H., Hungerford, D. W., Lando, J., Naimi, S., & Stroup, D. F. (2005). Cardiovascular risk factors and confounders among nondrinking and moderate-drinking U.S. adults. *American Journal of Preventive Medicine, 28,* 369–373.

Nambu, A. (2008). Seven problems on the basal ganglia. *Current Opinion in Neurobiology, 18,* 595–604.

Nasrallah, I., & Dubroff, J. (2013). An overview of PET neuroimaging. *Seminars in Nuclear Medicine, 43,* 449–461.

National Commission on Marijuana and Drug Abuse. (1972). *Marijuana: A signal of misunderstanding.* New York, NY: New American Library.

Navarrete, M., & Araque, A. (2014). The Cajal school and the physiological role of astrocytes: A way of thinking. *Frontiers in Neuroanatomy, 8,* 33.

Nave, K-A. (2010). Myelination and the trophic support of long axons. *Nature Reviews Neuroscience, 11,* 275–283.

Nave, K.-A., & Werner, H. B. (2014). Myelination of the nervous system: Mechanisms and functions. *Annual Review of Cell and Developmental Biology, 30,* 503–533.

Navratilova, E., & Porreca, F. (2014). Reward and motivation in pain and pain relief. *Nature Neuroscience, 17,* 1304–1312.

Navratilova, Z., & Battaglia, F. P. (2015). CA2: It's about time—and episodes. *Neuron, 85,* 8–10.

Naya, Y., & Suzuki, W. A. (2011). Integrating what and when across the primate medial temporal lobe. *Science, 333,* 773–775.

Naya, Y., Yoshida, M., & Miyashita, Y. (2001). Backward spreading of memory-retrieval signal in the primate temporal cortex. *Science, 291,* 661–664.

Neary, J. T., & Zimmerman, H. (2009). Trophic functions of nucleotides in the central nervous system. *Trends in Neurosciences, 32,* 189–198.

Neavyn, M. J., Blohm, E., Babu, K. M., & Bird, S. B. (2014). Medical marijuana and driving: A review. *Journal of Medical Toxicology, 10,* 269–279.

Nedergaard, M., & Goldman, S. A. (2016). Brain Drain. *Scientific American, 314,* 44–49.

Nees, F. (2014). The nicotinic cholinergic system function in the human brain. *Neuropharmacology, 96,* 289–301.

Negrón-Oyarzo, I., Lara-Vásquez, A., Palacios-García, I., Fuentealba, P., & Aboitiz, F. (2016). Schizophrenia and reelin: A model based on prenatal stress to study epigenetics, brain development and behavior. *Biological Research, 49,* 1.

Neikrug, A. B., Avanzino, J. A., Liu, L., Maglione, J. E., Natarajan, L.,…& Ancoli-Israel, S. (2014). Parkinson's disease and REM sleep behavior disorder result in increased non-motor symptoms. *Sleep Medicine, 15,* 959–966.

Nelson, A. B., & Kreitzer, A. C. (2014). Reassessing models of basal ganglia function and dysfunction. *Annual Review of Neuroscience, 37,* 117–135.

Nelson, V. R., Nadeau, J. H. (2010). Transgenerational genetic effects. *Epigenomics, 2,* 797–800.

Nestler, E. J. (2005). Is there a common molecular pathway for addiction? *Nature neuroscience, 8,* 1445–1449.

Nestler, E. J. (2011). Hidden switches in the mind. *Scientific American, 305*(6), 76–83.

Nestler, E. J. (2014). Epigenetic mechanisms of depression. *JAMA Psychiatry, 71,* 454–456.

Nestler, E. J., Barrot, M., DiLeone, R. J., Eisch, A. J., Gold, S. J., & Monteggia, L. M. (2002). Neurobiology of depression. *Neuron, 34,* 13–25.

Netter, F. H. (1962). *The CIBA collection of medical illustrations. Vol. 1, The nervous system.* New York, NY: CIBA.

Neubauer, D. N. (2014). New and emerging pharmacotherapeutic approaches for insomnia. *International Review of Psychiatry, 26,* 214–224.

Neukomm, L. J., & Freeman, M. R. (2014). Diverse cellular and molecular modes of axon degeneration. *Trends in Cell Biology, 24,* 515–523.

Neumann, D., Keiski, M. A., McDonald, B. C., & Wang, Y. (2014). Neuroimaging and facial affect processing: Implications for traumatic brain injury. *Brain Imaging and Behavior, 8,* 460–473.

Neves, S. R., Ram, P. T., & Iyengar, R. (2002). G protein pathways. *Science, 296,* 1636–1639.

Newcombe, N. S., Drummey, A. B., Fox, N. A., Lie, E., & Ottinger Alberts, W. (2000). Remembering early childhood: How much, how, and why (or why not). *Current Directions in Psychological Science, 9,* 55–58.

Newcombe, N., & Fox, N. (1994). Infantile amnesia: Through a glass darkly. *Child Development, 65,* 31–40.

Newman, E. A. (2003). New roles for astrocytes: Regulation of synaptic transmission. *Trends in Neurosciences, 26,* 536–542.

Ngun, T. C., Ghahramani, N., S´nchez, F. J., Bocklandt, S., & Vilain, E. (2011). The genetics of sex differences in brain and behavior. *Frontiers in Neuroendocrinology, 32,* 227–246.

Nguyen, B. M., Kim, D., Bricker, S., Bongard, F., Neville, A., Putnam, B., Smith, J., & Plurad, D. (2014). Effect of marijuana use on outcomes in traumatic brain injury. *The American Surgeon, 80,* 979–983.

Niciu, M. J., Henter, I. D., Luckenbaugh, D. A., Zarate, C. A., Jr., & Charney, D. S. (2014). Glutamate receptor antagonists as fast-acting therapeutic alternatives for the treatment of depression: Ketamine and other compounds. *Annual Review of Pharmacology and Toxicology, 54,* 119–139.

Nicolaides, N. C., Kyratzi, E., Lamprokostopoulou, A., Chrousos, G. P., & Charmandari, E. (2014). Stress, the stress system and the role of glucocorticoids. *Neuroimmunomodulation, 22,* 6–19.

Nicolesis, M. A. L., & Chapin, J. K. (October, 2002). People with nerve or limb injuries may one day be able to command wheelchairs, prosthetics and even paralyzed arms and legs by "thinking them through" the motions. *Scientific American, 287,* 47–53.

Nicoll, R. A., & Alger, B. E. (2004). The brain's own marijuana. *Scientific American, 291,* 68–75.

Niculescu, D., & Lohmann, C. (2014). Gap junctions in developing thalamic and neocortical networks. *Cerebral Cortex, 24,* 3097–3106.

Niessen, E., Fink, G. R., & Weiss, P. H. (2014). Apraxia, pantomime and the parietal cortex. *Neuroimage: Clinical, 5,* 42–52.

Nigro, S. C., Luon, D., & Baker, W. L. (2013). Lorcaserin: A novel serotonin 2c agonist for the treatment of obesity. *Current Medical Research and Opinion, 29,* 839–848.

Nikić, I., Merkler, D., Sorbara, C., Brinkoetter, M., Kreutzfeld, M., Bareyre, F. M., Brück, W., Bishop, D., Misgeld, T., & Kerschensteiner, M. (2011). A reversible form of axon damage in experimental autoimmune encephalomyelitis and multiple sclerosis. *Nature Medicine, 17,* 495–499.

Nilsson, J. P., Söderström, M., Karlsson, A. U., Lekander, M., Åkerstedt, T., Lindroth, N. E., & Axelsson, J. (2005). Less effective executive functioning after one night's sleep deprivation. *Journal of Sleep Research, 14,* 1–6.

Nimmerjahn, A., & Bergles, D. E. (2015). Large-scale recording of astrocyte activity. *Current Opinion in Neurobiology, 32,* 95–106.

Nir, Y., & Tononi, G. (2010). Dreaming and the brain: From phenomenology to neurophysiology. *Trends in Cognitive Sciences, 14,* 88–100.

Nisbett, R. E., Aronson, J., Blair, C., Dickens, W., Flynn, J., Halpern, D. F., & Turkheimer, E. (2012). Intelligence: New findings and theoretical developments. *American Psychologist, 67,* 130–159.

Nishino, S., & Kanbayashi, T. (2005). Symptomatic narcolepsy, cataplexy and hypersomnia, and their implications in the hypothalamic hypocretin/orexin system. *Sleep Medicine Reviews, 9,* 269–310.

Nitschke, J. B., Sarinopoulos, I., Oathes, D. J., Johnstone, T., Whalen, P. J., Davidson, R. J., & Kalin, N. H. (2009). Anticipatory activation in the amygdala and anterior cingulate in generalized anxiety disorder and prediction of treatment response. *American Journal of Psychiatry, 166,* 302–310.

Nitz, D. (2015). A place for motion in mapping. *Nature Neuroscience, 18,* 6–7.

Noebels, J. (2015). Pathway-driven discovery of epilepsy genes. *Nature Neuroscience, 18,* 344–350.

Nomi, J. S., & Uddin, L. Q. (2015). Face processing in autism spectrum disorders: From brain regions to brain networks. *Neuropsychologia, 71,* 201–216.

Noonan, D. (2015). Marijuana's medical future. *Scientific American, 312,* 32–34.

Nordberg, A., (2015). Towards early diagnosis in Alzheimer disease. *Nature Reviews Neurology, 11,* 69–70.

Noreña, A. J., & Farley, B. J. (2013). Tinnitus-related neural activity: Theories of generation, propagation and centralization. *Hearing Research, 295,* 161–171.

Normand, E. A., & Rasband, M. N. (2015). Subcellular patterning: Axonal domains with specialized structure and function. *Developmental Cell, 32,* 459–468.

Normile, D. (2014). Faulty drug trials tarnish Japan's clinical research. *Science, 345,* 17.

Northoff, G. (2013). Gene, brains, and environment—genetic neuroimaging of depression. *Current Opinion in Neurobiology, 23,* 133–142.

Norton, E. S., Beach, S. D., & Gabrieli, J. D. E. (2015). Neurobiology of dyslexia. *Current Opinion in Neurobiology, 30,* 73–78.

Nosyk, B., Guh, D. P., Bansback, N. J., Oviedo-Joekes, E., Brissette, S., Marsh, D. C., Meikleham, E., Schecter, M. T., & Anis, A. H. (2012). Cost-effectiveness of diacetylmorphine versus methadone for chronic opioid dependence refractory to treatment. *CMAJ, 184,* E317–E328.

Noudoost, B., Chang, M. H., Steinmetz, N. A., & Moore, T. (2010). Top-down control of visual attention. *Current Opinion in Neurobiology, 20,* 183–190.

Nowak, M. A. (2012). Why we help: Far from being a nagging exception to the rule of evolution, cooperation has been one of its primary architects. *Scientific American, 307,* 34–39.

Nudo, R. J., Jenkins, W. M., & Merzenich, M. M. (1996). Repetitive microstimulation alters the cortical representation of movements in adult rats. *Somatosensory Motor Research, 7,* 463–483.

Nusser, Z. (2009). Variability in the subcellular distribution of ion channels increases neuronal diversity. *Trends in Neurosciences, 32,* 267–274.

Nutt, D. J. (2015). Consideration on the role of buprenorphine in recovery from heroin addiction from a UK perspective. *Journal of Psychopharmacology, 29,* 43–49.

Nutt, D. J., King, L. A., & Nichols, D. E. (2013). Effects of Schedule I drug laws on neuroscience research and treatment innovation. *Nature Reviews Neuroscience, 14,* 577–585.

Nutt, D. J., Lingford-Hughes, A., Erritzoe, D., & Stokes, P. R. (2015). The dopamine theory of addiction: 40 years of highs and lows. *Nature Reviews Neuroscience, 16,* 305–312.

Nykamp, K., Rosenthal, L., Folkerts, M., Roehrs, T., Guido, P., & Roth, T. (1998). The effects of REM sleep deprivation on the level of sleepiness/alertness. *Sleep, 21,* 609–614.

O'Brien, B. A., Wolf, M., & Lovett, M. W. (2012). A taxometric investigation of developmental dyslexia subtypes. *Dyslexia, 18,* 16–39.

O'Brien, J. (2014). The ever-changing electrical synapse. *Current Opinion in Neurobiology, 29,* 64–72.

O'Brien, R. J., & Wong, P. C. (2011). Amyloid precursor protein processing and Alzheimer's disease. *Annual Review of Neuroscience, 34,* 185–204.

O'Connor, E. C., Chapman, K., Butler, P., & Mead, A. N. (2011). The predictive validity of the rat self-administration model for abuse liability. *Neuroscience and Biobehavioral Reviews, 35,* 912–938.

O'Leary, C. M. (2004). Fetal alcohol syndrome: Diagnosis, epidemiology, and developmental outcomes. *Journal of Paediatrics and Child Health, 40,* 2–7.

O'Reilly, R. C. (2010). The *what* and *how* of prefrontal cortical organization. *Trends in Neurosciences, 33,* 355–361.

O'Tousa, D., & Grahame, N. (2014). Habit formation: Implications for alcoholism research. *Alcohol, 48,* 327–335.

Ocampo, B., & Kritikos, A. (2011). Interpreting actions: The goal behind mirror neuron function. *Brain Research Reviews, 67,* 260–267.

Oesch, N. W., Kothmann, W. W., & Diamond, J. S. (2011). Illuminating synapses and circuitry in the retina. *Current Opinion in Neurobiology, 21,* 238–244.

Ogden, C. L., Carroll, M. D., Kit, B. K., & Flegal, K. M. (2014). Prevalence of childhood and adult obesity in the United States, 2011–2012. *JAMA, 311,* 806–814.

Oh, J., & O'Connor, P. W. (2015). Progress in MS—classification, mechanisms and treatment. *Nature Reviews Neurology, 11,* 76–78.

Oh, S. W., Harris, J. A., Ng, L., Winslow, B., Cain, N., Mihalas, S.,...& Mortrud, M. T. (2014). A mesoscale connectome of the mouse brain. *Nature, 508,* 207–214.

Ohno-Shosaku, T., & Kano, M. (2014). Endocannabinoid-mediated retrograde modulation of synaptic transmission. *Current Opinion in Neurobiology, 29,* 1–8.

Ohshima, T. (2015). Neuronal migration and protein kinases. *Frontiers in Neuroscience, 8,* 458.

Ohzawa, I. (1998). Mechanisms of stereoscopic vision: The disparity energy model. *Current Opinion in Neurobiology, 8,* 509–515.

Oitzl, M. S., Champagne, D. L., van der Veen, R., & de Kloet, E. R. (2010). Brain development under stress: Hypotheses of glucocorticoid actions revisited. *Neuroscience and Biobehavioral Reviews, 34,* 853–866.

Ojemann, G. A. (1979). Individual variability in cortical localization of language. *Journal of Neurosurgery, 50,* 164–169.

Ojemann, G. A. (1983). Brain organization for language from the perspective of electrical stimulation mapping. *Behavioral and Brain Sciences, 2,* 189–230.

Oken, B. S., Chamine, I., & Wakeland, W. (2015). A systems approach to stress, stressors and resilience in humans. *Behavioural Brain Research, 282,* 144–154.

Okon-Singer, H., Hendler, T., Pessoa, L., & Shackman, A. J. (2015). The neurobiology of emotion–cognition interactions: Fundamental questions and strategies for future research. *Frontiers in Human Neuroscience, 9,* 58.

Oldenburg, I. A., & Sabatini, B. L. (2015). Antagonistic but not symmetric regulation of primary motor cortex by basal ganglia direct and indirect pathways. *Neuron, 86,* 1174–1181.

Olds, J., & Milner, P. (1954). Positive reinforcement produced by electrical stimulation of septal area and other regions of rat brain. *Journal of Comparative and Physiological Psychology, 47,* 419–427.

Oller, D. K., & Griebel, U. (2014). On quantitative comparative research in communication and language evolution. *Biological Theory, 9,* 296–308.

Olshansky, M. P., Bar, R. J., Fogarty, M., & DeSouza, J. F. (2015). Supplementary motor area and primary auditory cortex activation in an expert break-dancer during kinesthetic motor imagery of dance to music. *Neurocase, 21,* 607–617.

Olshansky, S. J. (2005). Projecting the future of US health and longevity. *Health Affairs, 24,* W5R86.

Olson, I. R., McCoy, D., Klobusicky, E., & Ross, L. A. (2013). Social cognition and the anterior temporal lobes: A review and theoretical framework. *Social Cognitive and Affective Neuroscience, 8,* 123–133.

Olson, S. D., Pollock, K., Kambal, A., Cary, W., Mitchell, G.-M., Tempkin, J., Stewart, H., McGee, J., Bauer, G., Kim, H. S., Tempkin, T., Wheelock, V., Annett, G., Dunbar, G., & Nolta, J. A. (2012). Genetically engineered mesenchymal stem cells as a proposed therapeutic for Huntington's disease. *Molecular Neurobiology, 45,* 87–98.

Olton, D. S., & Samuelson, R. J. (1976). Remembrance of places: Spatial memory in rats. *Journal of Experimental Psychology: Animal Behavior Processes, 2,* 97–116.

Oniani, T., & Lortkipanidze, N. (2003). Effect of paradoxical sleep deprivation on the learning and memory. *Neurobiology of Sleep-Wakefulness Cycle, 3,* 9–43.

Onishi, K., Hollis, E., & Zou, Y. (2014). Axon guidance and injury—lessons from Wnts and Wnt signaling. *Current Opinion in Neurobiology, 27,* 232–240.

Orban, G. A., & Caruana, F. (2014). The neural basis of human tool use. *Frontiers in Psychology, 5,* 1–12.

Oren, D. A., Koziorowski, M., & Desan, P. H. (2013). SAD and the not-so-single photoreceptors. *American Journal of Psychiatry, 170,* 1403–1412.

Orser, B. A. (2007, June). Lifting the fog around anesthesia. *Scientific American, 296,* 54–61.

Oruch, R., Elderbi, M. A., Khattab, H. A., Pryme, I. F., & Lund, A. (2014). Lithium: A review of pharmacology, clinical uses, and toxicity. *European Journal of Pharmacology, 740,* 464–473.

Osaki, H., Naito, T., Sadakane, O., Okamoto, M., & Sato, H. (2011). Surround suppression by high spatial frequency stimuli in the cat primary visual cortex. *European Journal of Neuroscience, 33,* 923–932.

Ostry, D. J., & Gribble, P. L. (2016). Sensory plasticity in human motor learning. *Trends in Neurosciences, 39,* 114–123.

Otten, M., & Meeter, M. (2015). Hippocampal structure and function in individuals with bipolar disorder: A systematic review. *Journal of Affective Disorders, 174,* 113–125.

Ou, C.-Y., & Shen, K. (2010). Setting up presynaptic structures at specific positions. *Current Opinion in Neurobiology, 20,* 489–493.

Oudiette, D., Dealberto, M.-J., Uguccioni, G., Golmard, J.-L., Milagros, M.-L., Tafti, M., Garma, L., Schwartz, S., & Arnulf, I. (2012). Dreaming without REM sleep. *Consciousness and Cognition, 21,* 1129–1140.

Oudman, E., Van der Stigchel, S., Wester, A. J., Kessels, R. P. C., & Postma, A. (2011). Intact memory for implicit contextual information in Korsakoff's amnesia. *Neuropsychologia, 49,* 2848–2855.

Overmier, J. B., & Murison, R. (1997). Animal models reveal the "psych" in the psychosomatics of peptic ulcers. *Current Directions in Psychological Science, 6,* 180–184.

Owen, A. M. (2014). Is anybody in there? *Scientific American, 310,* 52–57.

Owen, M. J., Sawa, A., & Mortensen, P. B. (2016). Schizophrenia. *Lancet.* Advance online publication. doi:10.1016/S0140-6736(15)01121-6.

Owens, D. M., & Lumpkin, E. A. (2014). Diversification and specialization of touch receptors in skin. *Cold Spring Harbor Perspectives in Medicine, 4*, a013656.

Padro, C. J., & Sanders, V. M. (2014). Neuroendocrine regulation of inflammation. *Seminars in Immunology, 26*, 357–368.

Pagliaccio, D., Barch, D. M., Bogdan, R., Wood, P. K., Lynskey, M. T.,…& Agrawal, A. (2015). Shared predisposition in the association between cannabis use and subcortical brain structure. *JAMA Psychiatry, 72*, 994–1001.

Paintner, A., Williams, A. D., & Burd, L. (2012). Fetal alcohol spectrum disorders—implications for child neurology, part I: Prenatal exposure and dosimetry. *Journal of Child Neurology, 27*, 258–263.

Paixão, S., & Klein, R. (2010). Neuron-astrocyte communication and synaptic plasticity. *Current Opinion in Neurobiology, 20*, 466–473.

Palagini, L., & Rosenlicht, N. (2011). Sleep, dreaming, and mental health: A review of historical and neurobiological perspectives. *Sleep Medicine Reviews, 15*, 179–186.

Palmer, B. F., & Clegg, D. J. (2015). The sexual dimorphism of obesity. *Molecular and Cellular Endocrinology, 402*, 113–119.

Palmer, L. M., & Stuart, G. J. (2006). Site of action potential initiation in layer 5 pyramidal neurons. *Journal of Neuroscience, 26*, 1854–1863.

Palmiter, R. D. (2007). Is dopamine a physiologically relevant mediator of feeding behavior? *Trends in Neurosciences, 30*, 375–381.

Pan, D., Caruthers, S. D., Senpan, A., Schmieder, A. H., Wickline, S. A., & Lanza, G. M. (2011). Revisiting an old friend: Manganese-based MRI contrast agents. *Wiley Interdisciplinary Reviews: Nanomedicine and Nanobiotechnology, 3*, 162–173.

Panksepp, J. (2011). Cross-species affective neuroscience decoding of the primal affective experiences of humans and related animals. *PLoS ONE, 6*, e21236.

Panksepp, J., & Trowill, J. A. (1967). Intraoral self-injection: II. The simulation of self-stimulation phenomena with a conventional reward. *Psychonomic Science, 9*, 407–408.

Pannasch, U., & Rouach, N. (2013). Emerging role for astroglial networks in information processing: From synapse to behavior. *Trends in Neurosciences, 36*, 405–417.

Paparelli, A., Di Forti, M., Morrison, P. D., & Murray, R. M. (2011). Drug-induced psychosis: How to avoid star gazing in schizophrenia research by looking at more obvious sources of light. *Frontiers in Behavioral Neuroscience, 5*, 1–9.

Papke, R. L. (2014). Merging old and new perspectives on nicotinic acetylcholine receptors. *Biochemical Pharmacology, 89*, 1–11.

Parikh, S. V., LeBlanc, S. R., & Ovanessian, M. M. (2010). Advancing bipolar disorder: Key lessons from the Systematic Treatment Enhancement Program for Bipolar Disorder (STEP-BD). *Canadian Journal of Psychiatry, 55*, 136–143.

Park, C. H., Chang, W. H., Lee, M., Kwon, G. H., Kim, L.,…& Kim, Y. H. (2015). Which motor cortical region best predicts imagined movement? *Neuroimage, 113*, 101–110.

Park, H.-J., & Friston, K. (2013). Structural and functional brain networks: From connectomics to cognition. *Science, 342*, 579–584.

Park, H., & Poo, M. (2013). Neurotrophin regulation of neural circuit development and function. *Nature Reviews Neuroscience, 14*, 7–23.

Park, T. J., Brand, A., Koch, U., Ikebuchi, M., & Grothe, B. (2008). Dynamic changes in level influence spatial coding in the lateral superior olive. *Hearing Research, 238*, 58–67.

Parker, G. A., & Birkhead, T. R. (2013). Polyandry: The history of a revolution. *Philosophical Transactions of the Royal Society B, 368*, 20120335.

Parker, S. T., Mitchell, R. W., & Boccia, M. L. (1994). *Self-awareness in animals and humans: Developmental perspectives.* New York, NY: Cambridge University Press.

Parkhurst, C. N., Yang, G., Ninan, I., Savas, J. N., Yates, J. R. 3rd, et al. (2013). Microglia promote learning-dependent synapse formation through brain-derived neurotrophic factor. *Cell, 155*, 1596–1609.

Parrott, A. C. (2013). Human psychobiology of MDMA or "Ecstasy": An overview of 25 years of empirical research. *Human Psychopharmacology, 28*, 289–307.

Parsons, L. H., & Hurd, Y. L. (2015). Endocannabinoid signalling in reward and addiction. *Nature Reviews Neuroscience, 16*, 579–594.

Parsons, M. P., & Raymond, L. A. (2014). Extrasynaptic NMDA receptor involvement in central nervous system disorders. *Neuron, 82*, 279–293.

Partridge, B. J., Bell, S. K., Lucke, J. C., Yeates, S., & Hall, W. D. (2012). Smart drugs "as common as coffee": Media hype about neuroenhancement. *PLoS One, 6*, e28416.

Pascalis, O., & Kelly, D. J. (2009). The origins of face processing in humans. *Perspectives on Psychological Science, 4*, 200–209.

Pascual-Leone, A., Amedi, A., Fregni, F., & Merabet, L. B. (2005). The plastic human brain cortex. *Annual Review of Neuroscience, 28*, 377–401.

Pascual-Leone, A., Walsh, V., & Rothwell, J. (2000). Transcranial magnetic stimulation in cognitive neuroscience—virtual lesion, chronometry, and functional connectivity. *Current Opinion in Neurobiology, 10*, 232–237.

Pasterkamp, R. J. (2012). Getting neural circuits into shape with semaphorins. *Nature Reviews Neuroscience, 13*, 605–618.

Pasterski, V., Geffner, M. E., Brain, C., Hindmarsh, P., Brook, C., & Hines, M. (2011). Prenatal hormones and childhood sex-segregation: Playmate and play style preferences in girls with congenital adrenal hyperplasia. *Hormones & Behavior, 59*, 549–555.

Patel, G. H., Kaplan, D. M., & Snyder, L. H. (2014). Topographic organization in the brain: Searching for general principles. *Trends in Cognitive Sciences, 18*, 351–363.

Patel, S. R., Ayas, N. T., White, D. P., Speizer, F. E., Stampfer, M. J., & Hu, F. B. (2003). A prospective study of sleep duration and mortality risk in women. *Sleep, 26*, A184.

Patin, A., & Pause, B. M. (2015). Human amygdala activations during nasal chemoreception. *Neuropsychologia, 78*, 171–194.

Patrick M. E., & Maggs, J. L. (2009). Does drinking lead to sex? Daily alcohol-sex behaviors and expectancies among college students. *Psychology of Addictive Behaviors, 23*, 472–481.

Patterson, K., & Ralph, M. A. L. (1999). Selective disorders of reading? *Current Opinion in Neurobiology, 9*, 235–239.

Patterson, K., Vargha-Khadem, F., & Polkey, C. E. (1989). Reading with one hemisphere. *Brain, 112*, 39–63.

Patzke, N., Olaleye, O., Haagensen, M., Hof, P. R., Ihunwo, A. O., & Manger, P. R. (2014). Organization and chemical neuroanatomy of the African elephant *(Loxodonta africana)* hippocampus. *Brain Structure and Function, 219*, 1587–1601.

Paulesu, E., Démonet, J.-F., Fazio, F., McCrory, E., Chanoine, V., Brunswick, N.,…& Frith, U. (2001). Dyslexia: Cultural diversity and biological unity. *Science, 291*, 2165–2167.

Paulesu, E., McCrory, E., Fazio, F., Menoncello, L., Brunswick, N., Cappa, S. F.,…& Frith, U. (2000). A cultural effect on brain function. *Nature Neuroscience, 3*, 91–96.

Paus, T. (2010). Growth of white matter in the adolescent brain: Myelin or axon? *Brain and Cognition, 72*, 26–35.

Paz, R., & Pare, D. (2013). Physiological basis for emotional modulation of memory circuits by the amygdala. *Current Opinion in Neurobiology, 23*, 381–386.

Pearce, T. M., & Moran, D. W. (2012). Strategy-dependent encoding of planned arm movements in the dorsal premotor cortex. *Science, 337*, 984–988.

Peelen, M. V., & Kastner, S. (2014). Attention in the real world: Toward understanding its neural basis. *Trends in Cognitive Sciences, 18*, 242–250.

Peever, J., Luppi, P.-H., & Montplaisir, J. (2014). Breakdown in REM sleep circuitry underlies REM sleep behavior disorder. *Trends in Neurosciences, 37*, 279–288.

Pellis, S. M., O'Brien, D. P., Pellis, V. C., Teitelbaum, P., Wolgin, D. L., & Kennedy, S. (1988). Escalation of feline predation along a gradient from avoidance through "play" to killing. *Behavioral Neuroscience, 102*, 760–777.

Pellow, S., Chopin, P., File, S. E., & Briley, M. (1985). Validation of open:closed arm entries in an elevated plus-maze as a measure of anxiety in the rat. *Journal of Neuroscience Methods, 14*, 149–167.

Pena, J. L., & Gutfreund, Y. (2014). New perspectives on the owl's map of auditory space. *Current Opinion in Neurobiology, 24*, 55–62.

Penfield, W., & Boldrey, E. (1937). Somatic motor and sensory representations in cerebral cortex of man as studied by electrical stimulation. *Brain, 60*, 389–443.

Penfield, W., & Evans, J. (1935). The frontal lobe in man: A clinical study of maximum removals. *Brain, 58*, 115–133.

Penfield, W., & Rasmussen, T. (1950). *The cerebral cortex of man: A clinical study of the localization of function.* New York, NY: Macmillan.

Penfield, W., & Roberts, L. (1959). *Speech and brain mechanisms.* Princeton, NJ: Princeton University Press.

Peng, Y., Gillis-Smith, S., Jin, H., Tränkner, D., Ryba, N. J., & Zuker, C. S. (2015). Sweet and bitter taste in the brain of awake behaving animals. *Nature, 527*, 512–515.

Pennisi, E. (2014). Lengthy RNAs earn respect as cellular players. *Science, 344*, 1072.

Pennisi, E. (2014). Genetics may foster bugs that keep you thin. *Science, 346*, 687.

Perea, G., Sur, M., & Araque, A. (2014). Neuron-glia networks: Integral gear of brain function. *Frontiers in Cellular Neuroscience, 8*, 378.

Pereda, A. E. (2014). Electrical synapses and their functional interactions with chemical synapses. *Nature Reviews Neuroscience, 15*, 250–263.

Perry, E. C. (2014). Inpatient management of acute alcohol withdrawal syndrome. *CNS Drugs, 28*, 401–410.

Persico, A. M., & Bourgeron, T. (2006). Searching for ways out of the autism maze: Genetic, epigenetic and environmental clues. *Trends in Neurosciences, 29*, 349–358.

Pertwee, R. G. (2012). Targeting the endocannabinoid system with cannabinoid receptor agonists: Pharmacological strategies and therapeutic possibilities. *Philosophical Transactions of the Royal Society of London B: Biological Sciences, 367*, 3353–3363.

Petersen, S. E., & Posner, M. I. (2012). The attention system of the human brain: 20 years after. *Annual Review of Neuroscience, 35*, 73–89.

Petersen, S. E., Fox, P. T., Posner, M. I., Mintun, M., & Raichle, M. E. (1988). Positron emission tomographic studies of the cortical anatomy of single-word processing. *Nature, 331*, 585–589.

Petronis, A. (2010). Epigenetics as a unifying principle in the aetiology of complex traits and diseases. *Nature, 465*, 721–727.

Petrovska, S., Dejanova, B., & Jurisic, V. (2012). Estrogens: Mechanisms of neuroprotective effects. *Journal of Physiology and Biochemistry, 68*, 455–460.

Peyrin, C., Lallier, M., Démonet, J. F., Pernet, C., Baciu, M., Le Bas, J. F., & Valdois, S. (2012). Neural dissociation of phonological and visual attention span disorders in developmental dyslexia: FMRI evidence from two case reports. *Brain and Language, 120*, 381–394.

Pezawas, L., Meyer-Lindenberg, A., Drabant, E. M., Verchinski, B. A., Munoz, K. E., Kolachana,

B. S.,...& Weinberger, D. R. (2005). 5-HTTLPR polymorphism impacts human cingulate-amygdala interactions: A genetic susceptibility mechanism for depression. *Nature Neuroscience, 8,* 828–834.

Pezzulo, G., van der Meer, M. A. A., Lansink, C. S., & Pennartz, C. M. A. (2014). Internally generated sequences in learning and executing goal-directed behavior. *Trends in Cognitive Sciences, 18,* 647–657.

Pfaus, J. G., Kippin, T. E., Coria-Avila, G. A., Gelez, H., Afonso, V. M., Ismail, N., & Parada, M. (2012). Who, what, where, when (and maybe even why)? How the experience of sexual reward connects sexual desire, preference, and performance. *Archives of Sexual Behavior, 41,* 31–62.

Pfeiffer, C. A. (1936). Sexual differences of the hypophyses and their determination by the gonads. *American Journal of Anatomy, 58,* 195–225.

Pfenning, A. R., Hara, E., Whitney, O., Rivas, M. V., Wang, R., Roulhac, P. L.,...& Mountcastle, J. (2014). Convergent transcriptional specializations in the brains of humans and song-learning birds. *Science, 346,* 1256846.

Pfrieger, F. W. (2010). Role of glial cells in the formation and maintenance of synapses. *Brain Research Reviews, 63,* 39–46.

Phelps, E. A. (2006). Emotion and cognition: Insights from studies of the human amygdala. *Annual Review of Psychology, 57,* 27–53.

Phelps, E. A., Lempert, K. M., & Sokol-Hessner, P. (2014). Emotion and decision making: Multiple modulatory neural circuits. *Annual Review of Neuroscience, 37,* 263–287.

Phelps, M. E., & Mazziotta, J. (1985). Positron tomography: Human brain function and biochemistry. *Science, 228,* 804.

Philip, R. C. M., Dauvermann, M. R., Whalley, H. C., Baynham, K., Lawrie, S. M., & Stanfield, A. C. (2012). A systematic review and meta-analysis of the fMRI investigation of autism spectrum disorders. *Neuroscience and Biobehavioral Reviews, 36,* 901–942.

Phillips, A. G., Coury, A., Fiorino, D., LePiane, F. G., Brown, E., & Fibiger, H. C. (1992). Self-stimulation of the ventral tegmental area enhances dopamine release in the nucleus accumbens: A microdialysis study. *Annals of the New York Academy of Sciences, 654,* 199–206.

Phillips, D. R., Quinlan, C. K., & Dingle, R. N. (2012). Stability of central binaural sound localization mechanisms in mammals, and the Heffner hypothesis. *Neuroscience and Biobehavioral Reviews, 36,* 889–900.

Phillips, M. L., & Kupfer, D. J. (2013). Bipolar disorder diagnosis: Challenges and future directions. *Lancet, 381,* 1663–1671.

Phoenix, C. H., Goy, R. W., Gerall, A. A., & Young, W. C. (1959). Organizing action of prenatally administered testosterone proprionate on the tissues mediating mating behavior in the female guinea pig. *Endocrinology, 65,* 369–382.

Piaggio, L. A. (2014). Congenital adrenal hyperplasia: Review from a surgeon's perspective in the beginning of the twenty-first century. *Frontiers in Pediatrics, 1,* 50.

Pickens, C. L., Airavaara, M., Theberge, F., Fanous, S., Hope, B. T., & Shaham, Y. (2011). Neurobiology of the incubation of drug craving. *Trends in Neurosciences, 34,* 411–420.

Pickering, R., Dirks, P. H. G. M., Jinnah, Z., de Ruiter, D. J., Churchil, S. E., Herries, A. I. R., Woodhead, J. D., & Hellstrom, J. C., & Berger, L. R. (2011). *Australopethicus sediba* at 1.977 Ma and implications for the origins of the genus *Homo. Science, 333,* 1421–1423.

Pierce, R. C., & Kumaresan, V. (2006). The mesolimbic dopamine system: The final common pathway for the reinforcing effect of drugs of abuse? *Neuroscience and Biobehavioural Reviews, 30,* 215–238.

Pierce, R. C., & Vanderschuren, L. J. M. J. (2010). Kicking the habit: The neural basis of ingrained behaviors in cocaine addiction. *Neuroscience and Biobehavioral Reviews, 35,* 212–219.

Pierce, S. E., Clack, J. A., & Hutchinson, J. R. (2012). Three-dimensional limb joint motility in the tetrapod *Ichthyostega. Nature.* doi:10.1038/nature11124.

Pierce, S. E., Hutchinson, J. R., & Clack, J. A. (2013). Historical perspectives on the evolution of tetrapodomorph movement. *Integrative and Comparative Biology, 53,* 209–223.

Pinel, J. P. J. (1969). A short gradient of ECS-produced amnesia in a one-trial appetitive learning situation. *Journal of Comparative and Physiological Psychology, 68,* 650–655.

Pinel, J. P. J., & Mana, M. J. (1989). Adaptive interactions of rats with dangerous inanimate objects: Support for a cognitive theory of defensive behavior. In R. J. Blanchard, P. F. Brain, D. C. Blanchard, & S. Parmigiani (Eds.), *Ethoexperimental approaches to the study of behavior* (pp. 137–150). Dordrecht, Netherlands: Kluwer Academic Publishers.

Pinel, J. P. J., & Treit, D. (1978). Burying as a defensive response in rats. *Journal of Comparative and Physiological Psychology, 92,* 708–712.

Pinel, J. P. J., Assanand, S., & Lehman, D. R. (2000). Hunger, eating, and ill health. *American Psychologist, 55,* 1105–1116.

Pinel, J. P. J., Mana, M. J., & Kim, C. K. (1989). Effect-dependent tolerance to ethanol's anticonvulsant effect on kindled seizures. In R. J. Porter, R. H. Mattson, J. A. Cramer, & I. Diamond (Eds.), *Alcohol and seizures: Basic mechanisms and clinical implications* (pp. 115–125). Philadelphia, PA: F. A. Davis.

Piomelli, D. (2014). More surprises lying ahead. The endocannabinoids keep us guessing. *Neuropharmacology, 76,* 228–234.

Pistillo, F., Clementi, F., Zoli, M., & Gotti, C. (2014). Nicotinic, glutamatergic, and dopaminergic synaptic transmission and plasticity in the mesocorticolimbic system: Focus on nicotine effects. *Progress in Neurobiology, 124,* 1–27.

Pistoia, F., Carolei, A., Sacco, S., Conson, M., Pistarini, C.,...& Sarà, M. (2015). Contribution of interoceptive information to emotional processing: Evidence from individuals with spinal cord injury. *Journal of Neurotrauma, 32,* 1981–1986.

Pitchers, K. K., Frohmader, K. S., Vialou, V., Mouzon, E., Nestler, E. J., Lehman, M. N., & Coolen, L. M. (2010). ΔFosB in the nucleus accumbens is critical for reinforcing effects of sexual reward. *Genes, Brain, and Behavior, 9,* 831–840.

Plant, T. M. (2015). 60 years of neuroendocrinology: The hypothalamo-pituitary-gonadal axis. *Journal of Endocrinology, 226,* T41–T54.

Platel, J.-C., Stamboulian, S., Nguyen, I., & Bordey, A. (2010). Neurotransmitter signaling in postnatal neurogenesis: The first leg. *Brain Research, 63,* 60–71.

Plesnila, N. (2016). The immune system in traumatic brain injury. *Current Opinion in Pharmacology, 26,* 110–117.

Ploegh, H. L. (1998). Viral strategies of immune evasion. *Science, 280,* 248–252.

Plomin, R., & McGuffin, P. (2005). Psychopathology in the postgenomic era. *Annual Review of Psychology, 54,* 205–228.

Plomin, R., DeFries, J. C., McGuffin, P., & Craig, I. W. (2002). *Behavioral genetics in the postgenomic era.* Washington, DC: American Psychological Association.

Poels, E. M. P., Kegeles, L. S., Kantrowitz, J. T., Slifstein, M., Javitt, D. C., Lieberman, J. A.,...& Girgis, R. R. (2014). Imaging glutamate in schizophrenia: Review of findings and implications for drug discovery. *Molecular Psychiatry, 19,* 20–29.

Poeppel, D. (2014). The neuroanatomic and neurophysiological infrastructure for speech and language. *Current Opinion in Neurobiology, 28,* 142–149.

Poeppel, D., Emmorey, K., Hickock, G., & Pylkkänen, L. (2012). Towards a new neurobiology of language. *Journal of Neuroscience, 32,* 14125–14131.

Poeppel, D., & Monahan, P. J. (2008). Speech perception: Cognitive foundations and cortical implementation. *Current Directions in Psychological Science, 17,* 80–85.

Poldrack, R. A., & Farah, M. J. (2015). Progress and challenges in probing the human brain. *Nature, 526,* 371–379.

Pollack, G. D. (2012). Circuits for processing dynamic interaural intensity disparities in the inferior colliculus. *Hearing Research, 288,* 47–57.

Pollick, A. S., & De Waal, F. B. (2007). Ape gestures and language evolution. *Proceedings of the National Academy of Sciences, 104,* 8184–8189.

Polyakova, M., Stuke, K., Schuemberg, K., Mueller, K., Schoenknecht, P., & Schroeter, M. L. (2015). BDNF as a biomarker for successful treatment of mood disorders: A systematic & quantitative meta-analysis. *Journal of Affective Disorders, 174,* 432–440.

Pons, T. P., Garraghty, P. E., Ommaya, A. K., Kaas, J. H., Taub, E., & Mishkin, M. (1991). Massive cortical reorganization after sensory deafferentation in adult macaques. *Science, 252,* 1857–1860.

Porkka-Heiskanen, T. (2013). Sleep homeostasis. *Current Opinion in Neurobiology, 23,* 799–805.

Porras, G., Li, Q., & Bezard, E. (2012). Modeling Parkinson's disease in primates: The MPTP model. *Cold Spring Harbor Perspectives in Medicine, 2,* a009308.

Porter, R., & Lemon, R. N. (1993). Corticospinal function and voluntary movement. *Monographs of the Physiological Society, No. 45.* Oxford, England: Oxford University Press.

Posner, M. I., & Raichle, M. E. (1994). *Images of the mind.* New York, NY: Scientific American Library.

Post, R. M. (2016). Treatment of bipolar depression: Evolving recommendations. *Psychiatric Clinics of North America, 39,* 11–33.

Post, R. M., Fleming, J., & Kapczinski, F. (2012). Neurobiological correlates of illness progression in the recurrent affective disorders. *Journal of Psychiatric Research, 46,* 561–573.

Postle, B. R., Corkin, S., & Growdon, J. H. (1996). Intact implicit memory for novel patterns in Alzheimer's disease. *Learning & Memory, 3,* 305–312.

Potenza, M. (2015). Perspective: Behavioural addictions matter. *Nature, 522,* S62.

Poucet, B., & Save, E. (2005). Attractors in memory. *Science, 308,* 799–800.

Powley, T. L., Opsahl, C. A., Cox, J. E., & Weingarten, H. P. (1980). The role of the hypothalamus in energy homeostasis. In P. J. Morgane & J. Panksepp (Eds.), *Handbook of the hypothalamus, 3A: Behavioral studies of the hypothalamus* (pp. 211–298). New York, NY: Marcel Dekker.

Prabhakaran, S., Ruff, I., & Bernstein, R. A. (2015). Acute stroke intervention. *JAMA, 313,* 1451–1462.

Prabhavalkar, K. S., Poovanpallil, N. B., & Bhatt, L. K. (2015). Management of bipolar depression with lamotrigine: An antiepileptic mood stabilizer. *Frontiers in Pharmacology, 6,* 242.

Prather, A. A., Janicki-Deverts, D., Hall, M. H., & Cohen, S. (2015). Behaviorally assessed sleep and susceptibility to the common cold. *Sleep, 38,* 1353–1359.

Prather, J. F. (2013). Auditory signal processing in communication: Perception and performance of vocal sounds. *Hearing Research, 305,* 144–155.

Pratt, L. A., Brody, D. J., & Gi, Q. (2012). Antidepressant use in persons aged 12 and over: United States, 2005–2008. *NCHS Data Brief. No. 76.* October 2011.

Prete, G., D'Ascenzo, S., Laeng, B., Fabri, M., Foschi, N., & Tommasi, L. (2015). Conscious and unconscious processing of facial expressions:

Evidence from two split-brain patients. *Journal of Neuropsychology, 9*, 45–63.

Preti, A. (2007). New developments in the pharmacotherapy of cocaine abuse. *Addiction Biology, 12*, 133–151.

Price, C. J. (2012). A review and synthesis of the first 20 years of PET and fMRI studies of heard speech, spoken language and reading. *Neuroimage, 62*, 816–847.

Price, C. J., Howard, D., Patterson, K., Warburton, E. A., Friston, K. J., & Frackowiak, R. S. J. (1998). A functional neuroimaging description of two deep dyslexic patients. *Journal of Cognitive Neuroscience, 10*, 303–315.

Primakoff, P., & Myles, D. G. (2002). Penetration, adhesion, and fusion in mammalian sperm-egg interaction. *Science, 296*, 2183–2185.

Pringle, H. (2013). Long live the humans. *Scientific American, 309*, 48–55.

Pringle, H. (2013). The origins of creativity. *Scientific American, 308*, 36–43.

Pringsheim, T., Jette, N., Frolkis, A., & Steeves, T. D. (2014). The prevalence of Parkinson's disease: A systematic review and meta-analysis. *Movement Disorders, 29*, 1583–1590.

Pritchard, J. K. (2010). How we are evolving. *Scientific American, 303*(4), 41–47.

Pritchett, D. L., & Carey, M. R. (2014). A matter of trial and error for motor learning. *Trends in Neurosciences, 37*, 465–466.

Pruszynski, J. A., & Diedrichsen, J. (2015). Reading the mind to move the body. *Science, 348*, 860–861.

Puelles, L., Harrison, M., Paxinos, G., & Watson, C. (2013). A developmental ontology for the mammalian brain based on the prosomeric model. *Trends in Neurosciences, 36*, 570–578.

Puhl, M. D., Blum, J. S., Acosta-Torres, S., & Grigson, P. S. (2012). Environmental enrichment protects against the acquisition of cocaine self-administration in adult male rate, but does not eliminate avoidance of a drug-associated saccharin cue. *Behavioural Pharmacology, 23*, 43–53.

Purger, D., Gibson, E. M., & Monje, M. (2015). Myelin plasticity in the central nervous system. *Neuropharmacology*. Advance online publication. doi:10.1016/j.neuropharm.2015.08.001.

Purves, D., Augustine, G. J., Fitzpatrick, D., Hall, W. C., LaMantia, A-S., McNamara, J. O., & Williams, S. M. (2004). *Neuroscience* (3rd ed.). Sunderland, MA: Sinauer Associates.

Pusey, A. E., & Schroepfer-Walker, K. (2013). Female competition in chimpanzees. *Philosophical Transactions of the Royal Society B, 368*, 20130077.

Pusey, A., Williams, J., & Goodall, J. (1997). The influence of dominance rank on the reproductive success of female chimpanzees. *Science, 277*, 828–830.

Puts, D. A., Jordan, C. L., & Breedlove, S. M. (2006). O brother, where art thou? The fraternal birth-order effect on male sexual orientation. *Proceedings of the National Academy of Sciences, USA, 103*, 10531–10532.

Pytka, K., Dziubina, A., Młyniec, K., Dziedziczak, A., Żmudzka, E., Furgała, A., … & Filipek, B. (2016). The role of glutamatergic, GABA-ergic, and cholinergic receptors in depression and antidepressant-like effect. *Pharmacological Reports, 68*, 443–450.

Quammen, D. (2004, May). Was Darwin wrong? No. The evidence for evolution is overwhelming. *National Geographic, 206*, 2–35.

Quick, S. L., Pyszczynski, A. D., Colston, K. A., & Shahan, T. A. (2011). Loss of alternative non-drug reinforcement induces relapse of cocaine-seeking in rats: Role of dopamine D(1) receptors. *Neuropsychopharmacology, 36*, 1015–1020.

Quigley, K. S., & Barrett, L. F. (2014). Is there consistency and specificity of autonomic changes during emotional episodes? Guidance from the conceptual act theory and psychophysiology. *Biological Psychology, 98*, 82–94.

Quinsey, V. L. (2003). The etiology of anomalous sexual preferences in men. *Annals of the New York Academy of Sciences, 989*, 105–117.

Quiroga, R. Q. (2012). Concept cells: The building blocks of declarative memory functions. *Nature Reviews Neuroscience, 13*, 587–597.

Quiroga, R. Q., Fried, I., & Koch, C. (2013). Brain cells for grandmother. *Scientific American, 308*, 30–35.

Quiroga, R. Q., Kraskov, A., Mormann, F., Fried, I., & Koch, C. (2014). Single-cell responses to face adaptation in the human medial temporal lobe. *Neuron, 84*, 363–369.

Qureshi, I. A., & Mehler, M. F. (2012). Emerging roles of non-coding RNAs in brain evolution, development, plasticity and disease. *Nature Reviews Neuroscience, 13*, 528–541.

Radhakrishnan, R., Wilkinson, S. T., & D'Souza, D. C. (2014). Gone to pot —a review of the association between cannabis and psychosis. *Frontiers in Psychiatry, 5*, 54.

Raichle, M. E. (2008). A brief history of human brain mapping. *Trends in Neurosciences, 32*, 118–126.

Raichle, M. E. (2010, March). The brain's dark energy. *Scientific American, 302*, 44–49.

Raichlen, D. A., Gordon, A. D., Harcourt-Smith, W. E. H., Foster, A. D., & Haas, Jr., W. R. (2010). Laetoli footprints preserve earliest direct evidence of human-like bipedal biomechanics. *PLoS One, 5*, e9769.

Raineki, C., Lucion, A. B., & Weinberg, J. (2014). Neonatal handling: An overview of the positive and negative effects. *Developmental Psychobiology, 56*(8), 1613–1625.

Rainville, P. (2002). Brain mechanisms of pain affect and pain modulation. *Current Opinion in Neurobiology, 12*, 195–204.

Raisman, G. (2015). 60 years of neuroendocrinology: Memoir: Geoffrey Harris and my brush with his unit. *Journal of Endocrinology, 226*, T1–T11.

Rakic, P. (1979). Genetic and epigenetic determinants of local neuronal circuits in the mammalian central nervous system. In F. O. Schmitt & F. G. Worden (Eds.), *The neurosciences: Fourth study program*. Cambridge, MA: MIT Press.

Rakic, P. (2009). Evolution of the neocortex: A perspective from developmental biology. *Nature Reviews Neuroscience, 10*, 724–735.

Ralph, M. R., & Menaker, M. (1988). A mutation of the circadian system in golden hamsters. *Science, 241*, 1225–1227.

Ralph, M. R., Foster, T. G., Davis, F. C., & Menaker, M. (1990). Transplanted suprachiasmatic nucleus determines circadian period. *Science, 247*, 975–978.

Ramachandran, V. S., & Blakeslee, S. (1998). *Phantoms in the brain*. New York, NY: Morrow.

Ramachandran, V. S., & Rogers-Ramachandran, D. (2000). Phantom limbs and neuronal plasticity. *Archives of Neurology, 57*, 317–320.

Ramagopalan, S. V., Dyment, D. A., & Ebers, G. C. (2008). Genetic epidemiology: The use of old and new tools for multiple sclerosis. *Trends in Neurosciences, 31*, 645–652.

Ramirez, S., Liu, X., MacDonald, C. J., Moffa, A., Zhou, J., … & Tonegawa, S. (2015). Activating positive memory engrams suppresses depression-like behaviour. *Nature, 522*, 335–339.

Ramsay, D. S., & Woods, S. C. (1997). Biological consequences of drug administration: Implications for acute and chronic tolerance. *Psychological Review, 104*(1), 170–193.

Ramsay, D. S., & Woods, S. C. (2014). Clarifying the roles of homeostasis and allostasis in physiological regulation. *Psychological Review, 121*, 225–247.

Ramus, F., Marshall, C. R., Rosen, S., & van der Lely, H. K. J. (2013). Phonological deficits in specific language impairment and developmental dyslexia: Towards a multidimensional model. *Brain, 136*, 630–645.

Rana, A., & Dolmetsch, R. E. (2010). Using light to control signaling cascades in live neurons. *Current Opinion in Neurobiology, 20*, 617–622.

Rangarajan, V., Hermes, D., Foster, B. L., Weiner, K. S., Jacques, C., Grill-Spector, K., & Parvizi, J. (2014). Electrical stimulation of the left and right human fusiform gyrus causes different effects in conscious face perception. *Journal of Neuroscience, 34*, 12828–12836.

Ransahoff, R. M., Hafler, D. A., & Lucchinetti, C. F. (2015). Multiple sclerosis—a quiet revolution. *Nature Reviews Neurology, 11*, 134–142.

Rao, S. C., Rainer, G., & Miller, E. K. (1997). Integration of what and where in the primate prefrontal cortex. *Science, 276*, 821–824.

Rapoport, S. I. (2014). Lithium and the other mood stabilizers effective in bipolar disorder target the rat brain arachidonic acid cascade. *ACS Chemical Neuroscience, 5*, 459–467.

Rapport, R. (2005). *Nerve endings: The discovery of the synapse*. New York, NY: Norton.

Rasch, B., Büchel, C., Gais, S., & Born, J. (2007). Odor cues during slow-wave sleep prompt declarative memory consolidation. *Science, 315*, 1426–1429.

Rasch, B., Pommer, J., Diekelmann, S., & Born, J. (2008). Pharmacological REM sleep suppression paradoxically improves rather than impairs skill memory. *Nature Neuroscience, 12*, 396–397.

Rasmussen, T., & Milner, B. (1975). Clinical and surgical studies of the cerebral speech areas in man. In K. J. Zulch, O. Creutzfeldt, & G. C. Galbraith (Eds.), *Cerebral localization* (pp. 238–257). New York, NY: Springer-Verlag.

Rassnick, S., Stinus, L., & Koob, G. F. (1993). The effects of 6-hydroxydopamine lesions of the nucleus accumbens and the mesolimbic dopamine system on oral self-administration of ethanol in the rat. *Brain Research, 623*, 16–24.

Ratliff, F. (1972, June). Contour and contrast. *Scientific American, 226*, 90–101.

Rattenborg, N. C., Martinez-Gonzales, D., & Lesku, J. A. (2009). Avian sleep homeostasis: Convergent evolution of complex brains, cognition and sleep functions in mammals and birds. *Neuroscience and Biobehavioral Reviews, 33*, 253–270.

Raushchecker, J. P. (2015). Auditory and visual cortex of primates: A comparison of two sensory systems. *European Journal of Neuroscience, 41*, 579–585.

Ravindran, L. N., & Stein, M. B. (2010). The pharmacologic treatment of anxiety disorders: A review of progress. *Journal of Clinical Psychiatry, 71*, 839–854.

Ravussin, E., Redman, L. M., Rochon, J., Das, S. K., Fontana, L., … & Roberts, S. B. (2015). A 2-year randomized controlled trial of human caloric restriction: Feasibility and effects of predictors of health span and longevity. *Journals of Gerontology. Series A, Biological Sciences and Medical Sciences, 70*, 1097–1104.

Raynor, H. A., & Epstein, L. H. (2001). Dietary variety, energy regulation, and obesity. *Psychological Bulletin, 127*, 325–341.

Raz, S., & Berger, B. D. (2010). Social isolation increases morphine intake: Behavioral and psychopharmacological aspects. *Behavioural Pharmacology, 21*, 39–46.

Reardon, S. (2014). Gene-hunt gain for mental health. *Nature, 511*, 393.

Reardon, S. (2014). Gut-brain link grabs neuroscientists. *Nature, 515*, 175–177.

Reardon, S. (2015). Alzheimer's drugs show progress. *Nature, 523*, 509–510.

Reardon, S. (2016). A mouse's house may ruin experiments. *Nature, 530*, 264.

Reber, P. J. (2013). The neural basis of implicit learning and memory: A review of neuropsychological and neuroimaging research. *Neuropsychologia, 51*, 2026–2042.

Reber, P. J., Knowlton, B. J., & Squire, L. R. (1996). Dissociable properties of memory system:

Differences in the flexibility of declarative and nondeclarative knowledge. *Behavioral Neuroscience, 110*(5), 861–871.

Recanzone, G. H. (2004). Acoustic stimulus processing and multimodal interactions in primates. In M. S. Gazzaniga (Ed.), *The cognitive neurosciences* (pp. 359–368). Cambridge, MA: MIT Press.

Recanzone, G. H., & Sutter, M. L. (2008). The biological basis of audition. *Annual Review of Psychology, 59*, 119–142.

Rechtschaffen, A., & Bergmann, B. M. (1995). Sleep deprivation in the rat by the disk-over-water method. *Behavioural Brain Research, 69*, 55–63.

Rechtschaffen, A., Gilliland, M. A., Bergmann, B. M., & Winter, J. B. (1983). Physiological correlates of prolonged sleep deprivation in rats. *Science, 221*, 182–184.

Reddy, L., & Kanwisher, N. (2006). Coding of visual objects in the ventral stream. *Current Opinion in Neurobiology, 16*, 408–414.

Reddy, L., & Thorpe, S. J. (2014). Concept cells through associative learning of high-level representations. *Neuron, 84*, 248–251.

Redondo, R. L., Kim, J., Arons, A. L., Ramirez, S., & Tonegawa, S. (2014). Bidirectional switch of the valence associated with a hippocampal contextual memory engram. *Nature, 513*, 426–430.

Rees, G., Kreiman, G., & Koch, C. (2002). Neural correlates of consciousness in humans. *Nature Reviews Neuroscience, 3*, 261–270.

Regan, P. C. (1996). Rhythms of desire: The association between menstrual cycle phases and female sexual desire. *Canadian Journal of Human Sexuality, 5*(3), 145–156.

Rehme, A. K., Fink, G. R., von Cramon, D. Y., & Grefkes, C. (2011). The role of the contralesional motor cortex for motor recovery in the early days after stroke assessed with longitudinal fMRI. *Cerebral Cortex, 21*, 756–768.

Reichenbach, A., Derouiche, A., & Kirchhoff, F. (2010). Morphology and dynamics of perisynaptic glia. *Brain Research Reviews, 63*, 11–25.

Reid, K. J., & Abbott, S. M. (2015). Jet lag and shift work disorder. *Sleep Medicine Clinics, 10*, 523–535.

Reinarman, C., Cohen, P. D., & Kaal, H. L. (2004). The limited relevance of drug policy: Cannabis in Amsterdam and San Francisco. *American Journal of Public Health, 94*, 836–842.

Reiner, W. (1997). To be male or female—that is the question. *Archives of Pediatrics and Adolescent Medicine, 151*, 224–225.

Rektor, I., Bočková, M., Chrastina, J., Rektorová, I., & Baláz, M. (2015). The modulatory role of subthalamic nucleus in cognitive functions—a viewpoint. *Clinical Neurophysiology, 126*, 653–658.

Renard, J., Krebs, M.-O., Le Pen, G., & Jay, T. M. (2014). Long-term consequences of adolescent cannabinoid exposure in adult psychopathology. *Frontiers in Neuroscience, 8*, 361.

Rengaraj, D., Kwon, W.-S., & Pang, M.-G. (2015). Bioinformatics annotation of human y chromosome-encoded protein pathways and interactions. *Journal of Proteome Research, 14*, 3503–3518.

Renna, J. M., Chellappa, D. K., Ross, C. L., Stabio, M. E., & Berson, D. M. (2015). Melanopsin ganglion cells extend dendrites into the outer retina during early postnatal development. *Developmental Neurobiology, 75*, 935–946.

Rensberger, B. (2000). The nature of evidence. *Science, 289*, 61.

Represa, A., & Ben-Ari, Y. (2006). Trophic actions of GABA on neuronal development. *Trends in Neurosciences, 28*, 279–283.

Revusky, S. H., & Garcia, J. (1970). Learned associations over long delays. In G. H. Bower & J. T. Spence (Eds.), *The psychology of learning and motivation* (Vol. 4, pp. 1–85). New York, NY: Academic Press.

Reyes-Centeno, H., Ghirotto, S., Détroit, F., Grimaud-Hervé, D., Barbujani, G., & Harvati, K. (2014). Genomic and cranial phenotype data support multiple modern human dispersals from Africa and a southern route into Asia. *PNAS, 111*, 7248–7253.

Reynolds, D. V. (1969). Surgery in the rat during electrical analgesia induced by focal brain stimulation. *Science, 164*, 444–445.

Rezvani, A. H., & Levin, E. D. (2001). Cognitive effects of nicotine. *Biological Psychiatry, 49*, 258–267.

Rheims, S., & Ryvlin, P. (2014). Pharmacotherapy for tonic-clonic seizures. *Expert Opinion on Pharmacotherapy, 15*, 1417–1426.

Rhodes, G., Byatt, G., Michie, P. T., & Puce, A. (2004). Is the fusiform face area specialized for faces, individuation, or expert individuation? *Journal of Cognitive Neuroscience, 16*, 189–203.

Rhodes, S. M., Riby, D. M., Fraser, E., & Campbell, L. E. (2011). The extent of working memory deficits associated with Williams syndrome: Exploration of verbal and spatial domains and executively controlled processes. *Brain and Cognition, 77*, 208–214.

Rial, R. V., Nicolau, M. C., Gamundi, A., Akaârir, M., Aparicio, S., Garau, C.,…& Esteban, S. (2007). The trivial function of sleep. *Sleep Medicine Reviews, 11*, 311–325.

Riccio, A. (2010). Dynamic epigenetic regulation in neurons: Enzymes, stimuli and signaling pathways. *Nature Neuroscience, 11*, 1330–1337.

Rich, P. D., Liaw, H.-P., & Lee, A. K. (2014). Large environments reveal the statistical structure governing hippocampal representations. *Science, 345*, 814–817.

Richards, W. (1971, May). The fortification illusions of migraines. *Scientific American, 224*, 89–97.

Richter, C. P. (1967). Sleep and activity: Their relation to the 24-hour clock. *Proceedings of the Association for Research on Nervous and Mental Disorders, 45*, 8–27.

Richter, C. P. (1971). Inborn nature of the rat's 24-hour clock. *Journal of Comparative and Physiological Psychology, 75*, 1–14.

Richter, C., Woods, I. G., & Schier, A. F. (2014). Neuropeptidergic control of sleep and wakefulness. *Annual Review of Neuroscience, 37*, 503–531.

Ridaura, V. K., Faith, J. J., Rey, F. E., Cheng, J., Duncan, A. E.,…& Gordon, J. I. (2013). Gut microbiota from twins discordant for obesity modulate metabolism in mice. *Science, 341*, 1079–1089.

Ridley, N. J., Draper, B., & Withall, A. (2013). Alcohol-related dementia: An update of the evidence. *Alzheimer's Research and Therapy, 5*, 3.

Riekki, T., Lindeman, M., & Lipsanen, J. (2013). Conceptions about the mind-body problem and their relations to afterlife beliefs, paranormal beliefs, religiosity, and ontological confusions. *Advances in Cognitive Psychology, 9*, 112–120.

Rigato, J., Murakami, M., & Mainen, Z. (2014). Spontaneous decisions and free will: Empirical results and philosophical considerations. *Cold Spring Harbor Symposia on Quantitative Biology, 79*, 177–184.

Rigby, N., & Kulathinal, R. J. (2015). Genetic architecture of sexual dimorphism in humans. *Journal of Cellular Physiology, 230*, 2304–2310.

Rijntjes, M., Dettmers, C., Büchel, C., Kiebel, S., Frackowiak, R. S. J., & Weiller, C. (1999). A blueprint for movement: Functional and anatomical representations in the human motor system. *Journal of Neuroscience, 19*, 8043–8048.

Riley, D. O., Robbins, C. A., Cantu, R. C., & Stern, R. A. (2015). Chronic traumatic encephalopathy: Contributions from the Boston University Center for the Study of Traumatic Encephalopathy. *Brain Injury, 29*, 154–163.

Rilling, J. K. (2014). Comparative primate neuroimaging: Insights into human brain evolution. *Trends in Cognitive Sciences, 18*, 46–55.

Riou, M. È., Jomphe-Tremblay, S., Lamothe, G., Stacey, D., Szczotka, A., & Doucet, É. (2015). Predictors of energy compensation during exercise

interventions: A systematic review. *Nutrients, 7*, 3677–3704.

Ripke, S., Neale, B. M., Corvin, A., Walters, J. T., Farh, K. H., Holmans, P. A.,…& Pers, T. H. (2014). Biological insights from 108 schizophrenia-associated genetic loci. *Nature, 511*, 421.

Rizzolatti, G., & Fabbri-Destro, M. (2008). The mirror system and its role in social cognition. *Current Opinion in Neurobiology, 18*, 179–184.

Rizzolatti, G., & Fogassi, L. (2014). The mirror mechanism: Recent findings and perspectives. *Philosophical Transactions of the Royal Society B, 369*, 20130420.

Rizzolatti, G., & Sinigaglia, C. (2010). The functional role of the parieto-frontal mirror circuit: Interpretations and misinterpretations. *Nature Reviews Neuroscience, 11*, 264–274.

Rizzoli, S. O., & Betz, W. (2005). Synaptic vesicle pools. *Nature Reviews Neuroscience, 6*, 57–69.

Robbins, T. W. (2016). Illuminating anhedonia. *Science, 351*, 24–25.

Robbins, T. W., & Clark, L. (2015). Behavioural addictions. *Current Opinion in Neurobiology, 30*, 66–72.

Roberts, S. A., Davidson, A. J., McLean, L., Beynon, R. J., & Hurst, J. L. (2012). Pheromonal induction of spatial learning in mice. *Science, 338*, 1462–1465.

Robinson, T. E., & Berridge, K. C. (2008). The incentive sensitization theory of addiction: Some current issues. *Philosophical Transactions of the Royal Society B, 363*, 3137–3146.

Robson, P. J. (2014). Therapeutic potential of cannabinoid medicines. *Drug Testing and Analysis, 6*, 24–30.

Rocchetti, M., Crescini, A., Borgwardt, S., Caverzasi, E., Politi, P., Atakan, Z., & Fusar-Poli, P. (2013). Is cannabis neurotoxic for the healthy brain? A meta-analytical review of structural brain alterations in non-psychotic users. *Psychiatry and Clinical Neurosciences, 67*, 483–492.

Rodin, J. (1985). Insulin levels, hunger, and food intake: An example of feedback loops in body weight regulation. *Health Psychology, 4*, 1–24.

Rodríguez-Manzo, G., Pellicer, F., Larsson, K., & Fernández-Guasti, A. (2000). Stimulation of the medial preoptic area facilitates sexual behavior but does not reverse sexual satiation. *Behavioral Neuroscience, 114*, 553–560.

Rodriguez-Arias, M., Navarrete, F., Blanco-Gandia, M. C., Arenas, M. C., Bartoll-Andrés, A., Aguilar, M. A.,…& Manzanares, J. (2016). Social defeat in adolescent mice increases vulnerability to alcohol consumption. *Addiction Biology, 21*, 87–97.

Rodriguez, M., Llanos, C., Gonzalez, S., & Sabate, M. (2008). How similar are motor imagery and movement? *Behavioral Neuroscience, 122*, 910–916.

Roe, A. W., Pallas, S. L., Hahm, J.-O., & Sur, M. (1990). A map of visual space induced in primary auditory cortex. *Science, 250*, 818–820.

Roecklein, K. A., Wong, P. M., Miller, M. A., Donofry, S. D., Kamarck, M. L., & Brainard, G. C. (2013). Melanopsin, photosensitive ganglion cells, and seasonal affective disorder. *Neuroscience and Biobehavioral Reviews, 37*, 229–239.

Roefs, A., Werrij, M. Q., Smulders, F. T. Y., & Jansen, A. (2006). The value of indirect measures for assessing food preferences in abnormal eating. *Journal für Verbraucherschutz und Lebensmittelsicherheit, 1*, 180–186.

Roerecke, M., & Rehm, J. (2011). Ischemic heart disease mortality and morbidity rates in former drinkers: A meta-analysis. *American Journal of Epidemiology, 173*, 245–258.

Roest, A. M., de Jonge, P., Williams, C. D., de Vries, Y. A., Schoevers, R. A., & Turner, E. H. (2015). Reporting bias in clinical trials investigating the efficacy of second-generation antidepressants in the treatment of anxiety disorders: A report of 2 meta-analyses. *JAMA Psychiatry, 72*, 500–510.

Roesti, M., & Salzburger, W. (2014). Natural selection: It's a many-small world after all. *Current Biology, 24*, 959–960.

Rogalsky, C., Raphel, K., Tomkovicz, V., O'Grady, L., Damasio, H., . . . & Hickok, G. (2013). Neural basis of action understanding: Evidence from sign language aphasia. *Aphasiology, 27*, 1147–1158.

Rogers, J., & Gibbs, R. A. (2014). Comparative primate genomics: Emerging patterns of genome content and dynamics. *Nature Reviews Genetics, 15*, 347–359.

Rogers, P. J., & Blundell, J. E. (1980). Investigation of food selection and meal parameters during the development of dietary induced obesity. *Appetite, 1*, 85–88.

Rohde, C., Mütze, U., Schulz, S., Thiele, A. G., Ceglarek, U., et al. (2014). Unrestricted fruits and vegetables in the PKU diet: A 1-year follow-up. *European Journal of Clinical Nutrition, 68*, 401–403.

Rolls, B. J. (1986). Sensory-specific satiety. *Nutrition Reviews, 44*, 93–101.

Rolls, B. J. (1990). The role of sensory-specific satiety in food intake and food selection. In E. D. Capaldi & T. L. Powley (Eds.), *Taste, experience, and feeding* (pp. 28–42). Washington, DC: American Psychological Association.

Rolls, B. J., Rolls, E. T., Rowe, E. A., & Sweeney, K. (1981). Sensory specific satiety in man. *Physiology & Behavior, 27*, 137–142.

Rolls, E. T. (1981). Central nervous mechanisms related to feeding and appetite. *British Medical Bulletin, 37*, 131–134.

Rolls, E. T. (2008). Top—down control of visual perception: Attention in natural vision. *Perception, 37*, 333–354.

Rolls, E. T. (2015). Limbic systems for emotion and for memory, but no single limbic system. *Cortex, 62*, 119–157.

Rolls, E. T., Critchley, H. D., Verhagen, J. V., & Kadohisa, M. (2010). The representation of information about taste and odor in the orbitofrontal cortex. *Chemosensory Perception, 3*, 16–33.

Romano, J. G., & Sacco, R. L. (2015). Decade in review-stroke: Progress in acute ischaemic stroke treatment and prevention. *Nature Reviews Neurology, 11*, 619–621.

Romanski, L. M., & Averbeck, B. B. (2009). The primate cortical auditory system and neural representation of conspecific vocalizations. *Annual Review of Neuroscience, 32*, 315–346.

Roney, J. R., & Simmons, Z. L. (2013). Hormonal predictors of sexual motivation in natural menstrual cycles. *Hormones and Behavior, 63*, 636–645.

Rorden, C., & Karnath, H.-O. (2004). Using human brain lesions to infer function: A relic from a past era in the fMRI age? *Nature Reviews Neuroscience, 5*, 813–819.

Rosa, M. G. P., Tweedale, R., & Elston, G. N. (2000). Visual responses of neurons in the middle temporal area of New World monkeys after lesions of striate cortex. *Journal of Neuroscience, 20*, 5552–5563.

Rosa, R. R., Bonnet, M. H., & Warm, J. S. (2007). Recovery of performance during sleep following sleep deprivation. *Psychophysiology, 20*, 152–159.

Rosenblum, L. D. (2013). A confederacy of senses. *Scientific American, 308*, 72–75.

Rosenheck, R. (2008). Fast food consumption and increased caloric intake: A systematic review of a trajectory towards weight gain and obesity risk. *Obesity Reviews, 9*, 535–547.

Rosenwasser, A. M., & Turek, F. W. (2015). Neurobiology of circadian rhythm regulation. *Sleep Medicine Clinics, 10*, 403–412.

Rossignol, S., & Frigon, A. (2011). Recovery of locomotion after spinal cord injury: Some facts and mechanisms. *Annual Review of Neuroscience, 34*, 413–440.

Rossini, P. M., Burke, D., Chen, R., Cohen, L. G., Daskalakis, Z., Di Iorio, R., . . . & Hallett, M. (2015). Non-invasive electrical and magnetic stimulation of the brain, spinal cord, roots and peripheral nerves: basic principles and procedures for routine clinical and research application. An updated report from an IFCN Committee. *Clinical Neurophysiology, 126*, 1071–1107.

Rossini, P. M., Martino, G., Narici, L., Pasquarelli, A., Peresson, M., Pizzella, V., . . . & Romani, G. L. (1994). Short-term brain "plasticity" in humans: Transient finger representation changes in sensory cortex somatotopy following ischemic anesthesia. *Brain Research, 642*, 169–177.

Roth, M. M., Dahmen, J. C., Muir, D. R., Imhof, F., Martini, F. J., & Hofer, S. B. (2016). Thalamic nuclei convey diverse contextual information to layer 1 of visual cortex. *Nature Neuroscience, 19*, 299–307.

Rothwell, J. C., Traub, M. M., Day, B. L., Obeso, J. A., Thomas, P. K., & Marsden, C. D. (1982). Manual motor performance in a deafferented man. *Brain, 105*, 515–542.

Rothwell, N. J., & Stock, M. J. (1982). Energy expenditure derived from measurements of oxygen consumption and energy balance in hyperphagic, "cafeteria"-fed rats. *Journal of Physiology, 324*, 59–60.

Rowe, J. B., Toni, I., Josephs, O., Frackowiak, R. S., & Pasingham, R. E. (2000). The prefrontal cortex: Response selection or maintenance within working memory? *Science, 288*, 1656–1660.

Rowland, D. C., & Moser, M-B. (2014). From cortical modules to memories. *Current Opinion in Neurobiology, 24*, 22–27.

Rowland, D. C., & Moser, M.-B. (2015). A three-dimensional neural compass. *Nature, 517*, 156–157.

Roy, D. S., Arons, A., Mitchell, T. I., Pignatelli, M., Ryan, T. J., & Tonegawa, S. (2016). Memory retrieval by activating engram cells in mouse models of early Alzheimer's disease. *Nature, 531*, 508–512.

Rozin, P., Dow, S., Moscovitch, M., & Rajaram, S. (1998). What causes humans to begin and end a meal? A role for memory for what has been eaten, as evidenced by a study of multiple meal eating in amnesic patients. *Psychological Science, 9*, 392–396.

Ruby, N. F., Brennan, T. J., Xie, X., Cao, V., Franken, P., Heller, H. C., & O'Hara, B. F. (2002). Role of melanopsin in circadian responses to light. *Science, 298*, 2211–2213.

Rudy, J. W., & Sutherland, R. J. (1992). Configural and elemental associations and the memory coherence problem. *Journal of Cognitive Neuroscience, 4*, 208–216.

Ruff, C. C. (2013). Sensory processing: Who's in (top-down) control? *Annals of the New York Academy of Sciences, 1296*, 88–107.

Rugg, M. D., & Vilberg, K. L. (2013). Brain networks underlying memory retrieval. *Current Opinion in Neurobiology, 23*, 255–260.

Ruigrok, A. N. V., Salimi-Khorshidi, G., Lai, M.-C., Baron-Cohen, S., Lombardo, M. V., . . . & Suckling, J. (2014). A meta-analysis of sex differences in human brain structure. *Neuroscience and Biobehavioral Review, 39*, 34–50.

Rumble, M. E., White, K. H., & Benca, R. M. (2015). Sleep disturbances in mood disorders. *Psychiatric Clinics of North America, 38*, 743–759.

Rupp, H. A., & Wallen, K. (2008). Sex differences in response to visual sexual stimuli: A review. *Archives of Sexual Behavior, 37*, 206–218.

Rusakov, D. A., Bard, L., Stewart, M. G., & Henneberger, C. (2014). Diversity of astroglial functions alludes to subcellular specialisation. *Trends in Neurosciences, 37*, 228–242.

Rushworth, M. F. S., Mars, R. B., & Sallet, J. (2013). Are there specialized circuits for social cognition and are they unique to humans? *Current Opinion in Neurobiology, 23*, 436–442.

Russell, J. A., Bachorowski, J.-A., & Fernandez-Dols, J.-M. (2003). Facial and vocal expressions of emotion. *Annual Review of Psychology, 54*, 329–349.

Russell, M., Breggia, A., Mendes, N., Klibanski, A., & Misra, M. (2011). Growth hormone is positively associated with surrogate markers of bone turnover during puberty. *Clinical Endocrinology, 75*, 482–488.

Russell, W. R., & Espir, M. I. E. (1961). *Traumatic aphasia—a study of aphasia in war wounds of the brain.* London, England: Oxford University Press.

Russo, S. J., & Nestler, E. J. (2013). The brain reward circuitry in mood disorders. *Nature Reviews Neuroscience, 14*, 609–625.

Ruthazer, E. S., & Aizenman, C. D. (2010). Learning to see: Patterned visual activity and the development of visual function. *Trends in Neurosciences, 33*, 183–192.

Rutherford, B. R., & Roose, S. P. (2013). A model of placebo response in antidepressant clinical trials. *American Journal of Psychiatry, 170*, 723–733.

Rutledge, L. L., & Hupka, R. B. (1985). The facial feedback hypothesis: Methodological concerns and new supporting evidence. *Motivation and Emotion, 9*, 219–240.

Rutter, M. L. (1997). Nature-nurture integration: The example of antisocial behavior. *American Psychologist, 52*, 390–398.

Ryan, M. M., Guévremont, D., Luxmanan, C., Abraham, W. C., & WIlliams, J. M. (2015). Aging alters long-term potentiation-related gene networks and impairs synaptic protein synthesis in the rat hippocampus. *Neurobiology of Aging, 36*, 1868–1880.

Ryan, T. J., Roy, D. S., Pignatelli, M., Arons, A., & Tonegawa, S. (2015). Engram cells retain memory under retrograde amnesia. *Science, 348*, 1007–1013.

Rymer, R. (1993). *Genie.* New York, NY: HarperCollins

Sacchetti, E., Scassellati, C., Minelli, A., Valsecchi, P., Bonvicini, C., Pasqualetti, P., Galluzzo, A., Pioli, R., & Gennarelli, M. (2013). Schizophrenia susceptibility and NMDA-receptor mediated signalling: An association study involving 32 tagSNPs of DAO, DAOA, PPP3CC, and DTNBP1 genes. *BMC Biomedical Genetics, 14*, 33.

Sachser, N., Kaiser, S., & Hennessy, M. B. (2013). Behavioural profiles are shaped by social experience: When, how, and why. *Philosophical Transactions of the Royal Society of London. Series B, Biological Sciences, 368*, 20120344.

Sack, A. T. (2006). Transcranial magnetic stimulation, causal structure–function mapping and networks of functional relevance. *Current Opinion in Neurobiology, 16*, 593–599.

Sack, R. L. (2010). Jet lag. *New England Journal of Medicine, 362*, 440–447.

Sacks, O. (1985). *The man who mistook his wife for a hat and other clinical tales.* New York, NY: Summit Books.

Saenz, M., & Langers, D. R. M. (2014). Tonotopic mapping of human auditory cortex. *Hearing Research, 307*, 42–52.

Sagoe, D., Molde, H., Andreassen, C. S., Torsheim, T., & Pallesen, S. (2014). The global epidemiology of anabolic-androgenic steroid use: A meta-analysis and meta-regression analysis. *Annals of Epidemiology, 24*, 383–398.

Sakamoto, M., Kageyama, R., & Imayoshi, I. (2015). The functional significance of newly born neurons integrated into olfactory bulb circuits. *Frontiers in Neuroscience, 8*, 121.

Sakuma, Y., & Pfaff, D. W. (1979). Mesencephalic mechanisms for the integration of female reproductive behavior in the rat. *American Journal of Physiology, 237*, 285–290.

Samuels, B. A., Anacker, C., Hu, A., Levinstein, M. R., Pickenhagen, A., Tsetsenis, T., . . . & Gross, C. T. (2015). 5-HT1A receptors on mature dentate gyrus granule cells are critical for the antidepressant response. *Nature Neuroscience, 18*, 1606–1616.

Sanders, D., & Bancroft, J. (1982). Hormones and the sexuality of women—the menstrual cycle. *Clinics in Endocrinology and Metabolism, 11*, 639–659.

Sanders, H., Rennó-Costa, C., Idiart, M., & Lisman, J. (2015). Grid cells and place cells: An integrated view of their navigational and memory function. *Trends in Neurosciences, 38,* 763–775.

Sandi, C., & Haller, J. (2015). Stress and the social brain: Behavioural effects and neurobiological mechanisms. *Nature Reviews Neuroscience, 16,* 290–304.

Sandrini, M., Cohen, L. G., & Censor, N. (2015). Modulating reconsolidation: A link to causal systems-level dynamics of human memories. *Trends in Cognitive Sciences, 19,* 475–482.

Sanes, D. H., & Bao, S. (2009). Tuning up the developing auditory CNS. *Current Opinion in Neurobiology, 19,* 188–199.

Sanes, J. N. (2003). Neocortical mechanisms in motor learning. *Current Opinion in Neurobiology, 13,* 225–231.

Sanes, J. N., Donoghue, J. P., Thangaraj, V., Edelman, R. R., & Warach, S. (1995). Shared neural substrates controlling hand movements in human motor cortex. *Science, 268,* 1775–1777.

Sanes, J. N., Suner, S., & Donoghue, J. P. (1990). Dynamic organization of primary motor cortex output to target muscles in adult rats. I. Long-term patterns of reorganization following motor or mixed peripheral nerve lesions. *Experimental Brain Research, 79,* 479–491.

Sapède, D., & Cau, E. (2013). The pineal gland from development to function. *Current Topics in Developmental Biology, 106,* 171–215.

Saper, C. B. (2013). The central circadian timing system. *Current Opinion in Neurobiology, 23,* 747–751.

Saper, C. B., Scammell, T. E., & Lu, J. (2005). Hypothalamic regulation of sleep and circadian rhythms. *Nature, 437,* 1257–1263.

Saupe, K., Schröger, E., Andersen, S. K., & Müller, M. M. (2009). Neural mechanisms of intermodal sustained selective attention with concurrently presented auditory and visual stimuli. *Frontiers in Human Neuroscience, 3,* 1–13.

Savage, L. M., Hall, J. M., & Resende, L. S. (2012). Translational rodent models of Korsakoff syndrome reveal the critical neuroanatomical substrates of memory dysfunction and recovery. *Neuropsychology Review, 22,* 195–209.

Savitz, J. B., Price, J. L., & Drevets, W. C. (2014). Neuropathological and neuromorphometric abnormalities in bipolar disorder: View from the medial prefrontal cortical network. *Neuroscience & Biobehavioral Reviews, 42,* 132–147.

Sawle, G. V., & Myers, R. (1993) The role of positron emission tomography in the assessment of human neurotransplantation. *Trends in Neurosciences, 16,* 172–176.

Sbragia, G. (1992). Leonardo da Vinci and ultrashort sleep: Personal experience of an eclectic artist. In C. Stampi (Ed.), *Why we nap: Evolution, chronobiology, and functions of polyphasic and ultra-short sleep.* Boston, MA: Birkhäuser.

Scammell, T. E. (2015). Narcolepsy. *New England Journal of Medicine, 373,* 2654–2662.

Schaefer, M., Flor, H., Heinze, H.-J., & Rotte, M. (2007). Morphing the body: Illusory feeling of an elongated arm affects somatosensory homunculus. *Neuroimage, 36,* 700–705.

Schaefer, M., Heinze, H.-J., & Rotte, M. (2009). My third arm: Shifts in topography of the somatosensory homunculus predict feeling of an artificial supernumerary arm. *Human Brain Mapping, 30,* 1413–1420.

Schaller, M., Miller, G. E., Gervais, W. M., Yager, S., & Chen, E. (2010). Mere visual perception of other people's disease symptoms facilitates a more aggressive immune response. *Psychological Science, 21,* 649–652.

Schally, A. V., Kastin, A. J., & Arimura, A. (1971). Hypothalamic follicle-stimulating hormone (FSH) and luteinizing hormone (LH)–regulating hormone: Structure, physiology, and clinical studies. *Fertility and Sterility, 22,* 703–721.

Scharfman, H. E. (2015). Metabolic control of epilepsy. *Science, 347,* 1312–1313.

Schärli, H., Harman, A. M., & Hogben, J. H. (1999a). Blindsight in subjects with homonymous visual field defects. *Journal of Cognitive Neuroscience, 11,* 52–66.

Schärli, H., Harman, A. M., & Hogben, J. H. (1999b). Residual vision in a subject with damaged visual cortex. *Journal of Cognitive Neuroscience, 11,* 502–510.

Scheiber, M. H. (1999). Somatotopic gradients in the distributed organization of the human primary motor cortex hand area: Evidence from small infarcts. *Experimental Brain Research, 128,* 139–148.

Scheiber, M. H., & Poliakov, A. V. (1998). Partial inactivation of the primary motor cortex hand area: Effects on individuated finger movements. *Journal of Neuroscience, 18,* 9038–9054.

Scheltens, P., & Goos, J. D. C. (2012). Microbleeds in dementia—singing about ARIA. *Nature Reviews Neurology, 8,* 68–70.

Schenck, C. H., Bundlie, S. R., Ettinger, M. G., & Mahowald, M. W. (1986). Chronic behavioral disorders of human REM sleep: A new category of parasomnia. *Sleep, 9,* 293–308.

Schenck, C. H., Montplaisir, J. Y., Frauscher, B., Hogl, B., Gagnon, J. F., . . . & Oertel, W. (2013). Rapid eye movement sleep behavior disorder: Devising controlled active treatment studies for symptomatic and neuroprotective therapy—a consensus statement from the international rapid eye movement sleep behavior disorder study group. *Sleep Medicine, 14,* 795–806.

Schendel, K., & Robertson, L. C. (2004). Reaching out to see: Arm position can attenuate human visual loss. *Journal of Cognitive Neuroscience, 16,* 935–943.

Schienle, A., Schäfer, A., Walter, B., Stark, R., & Vaitl, D. (2005). Brain activation of spider phobics towards disorder-relevant, generally disgust- and fear-inducing pictures. *Neuroscience Letters, 388,* 1–6.

Schlaggar, B. L., Brown, T. T., Lugar, H. M., Visscher, K. M., Miezin, F. M., & Petersen, S. E. (2002). Functional neuroanatomical differences between adults and school-age children in the processing of single words. *Science, 296,* 1476–1479.

Schlaug, G., Jäncke, L., Huang, Y., & Steinmetz, H. (1995). In vivo evidence of structural brain asymmetry in musicians. *Science, 267,* 699–701.

Schloesser, R. J., Martinowich, K., & Manji, H. K. (2012). Mood-stabilizing drugs: Mechanisms of action. *Trends in Neurosciences, 35,* 36–46.

Schmid, M. C., & Maier, A. (2015). To see or not to see—Thalamo-cortical networks during blindsight and perceptual suppression. *Progress in Neurobiology, 126,* 36–48.

Schmidt-Kastner, R. (2015). Genomic approach to selective vulnerability of the hippocampus in brain ischemia-hypoxia. *Neuroscience, 309,* 259–279.

Schmiedel, J. M., Klemm, S. L., Zheng, Y., Sahay, A., Blüthgen, N., Marks, D. S., & van Oudenaarden, A. (2015). MicroRNA control of protein expression noise. *Science, 348,* 128–132.

Schmithorst, V. J., & Yuan, W. (2010). White matter development during adolescence as shown by diffusion MRI. *Brain and Cognition, 72,* 16–25.

Schmitt, A., Malchow, B., Hasan, A., & Falkai, P. (2014). The impact of environmental factors in severe psychiatric disorders. *Frontiers in Neuroscience, 8,* 19.

Schneggenburger, R., & Neher, E. (2005). Presynaptic calcium and control of vesicle fusion. *Current Opinion in Neurobiology, 15,* 266–274.

Schnell, M. J., McGettigan, J. P., Wirblich, C., & Papaneri, A. (2010). The cell biology of rabies virus: Using stealth to reach the brain. *Nature Reviews Microbiology, 8,* 51–61.

Schoenfeld, M. A., Neuer, G., Tempelmann, C., Schüßler, K., Noesselt, T., Hopf, J.-M., &

Heinze, H.-J. (2004). Functional magnetic resonance tomography correlates of taste perception in the human primary taste cortex. *Neuroscience, 127,* 347–353.

Schomers, M. R., Kirilina, E., Weigand, A., Bajbouj, M., & Pulvermüller, F. (2015). Causal influence of articulatory motor cortex on comprehending single spoken words: TMS evidence. *Cerebral Cortex, 25,* 3894–3902.

Schoppa, N. E. (2009). Making scents out of how olfactory neurons are ordered in space. *Nature Neuroscience, 12,* 103–104.

Schreiner, C. E., & Polley, D. B. (2014). Auditory map plasticity: Diversity in causes and consequences. *Current Opinion in Neurobiology, 24,* 143–156.

Schroeder, L., Roseman, C. C., Cheverud, J. M., & Ackerman, R. R. (2014). Characterizing the evolutionary path(s) to early homo. *PLoS One, 9,* e114307.

Schübeler, D. (2012). Epigenetic islands in a genetic ocean. *Science, 338,* 756–757.

Schuch, J. J., Roest, A. M., Nolen, W. A., Penninx, B. W., & de Jonge, P. (2014). Gender differences in major depressive disorder: Results from the Netherlands study of depression and anxiety. *Journal of Affective Disorders, 156,* 156–163.

Schultz, C., & Engelhardt, M. (2014). Anatomy of the hippocampal formation. In K. Szabo, & M. G. Hennerici (Eds.), *The hippocampus in clinical neuroscience* (6–17). Basel: Karger AG.

Schultz, M. D., He, Y., Whitaker, J. W., Hariharan, M., Mukamel, E. A., Leung, D., . . . & Lin, S. (2015). Human body epigenome maps reveal noncanonical DNA methylation variation. *Nature, 523,* 212–216.

Schultz, W. (2002). Getting formal with dopamine and reward. *Neuron, 36,* 241–263.

Schwartz, A. B. (2004). Cortical neural prosthetics. *Annual Review of Neuroscience, 27,* 487–507.

Schwartz, G. J. (2016). A satiating signal. *Science, 351,* 1268–1269.

Schwartz, J. H., & Tattersall, I. (2015). Defining the genus *Homo. Science, 349,* 931–932.

Schwartz, M. D., & Kilduff, T. S. (2015). The neurobiology of sleep and wakefulness. *Psychiatric Clinics of North America, 38,* 615–644.

Schwartz, M. W. (2000). Staying slim with insulin in mind. *Science, 289,* 2066–2067.

Schweinsburg, A. D., Brown, S. A., & Tapert, S. F. (2008). The influence of marijuana use on neurocognitive functioning in adolescents. *Current Drug Abuse Reviews, 1,* 99–111.

Schweizer, F. E., & Ryan, T. A. (2006). The synaptic vesicle: Cycle of exocytosis and endocytosis. *Current Opinion in Neurobiology, 16,* 298–304.

Scott, K. M. (2014). Depression, anxiety, and incident cardiometabolic diseases. *Current Opinion in Psychiatry, 27,* 289–293.

Scott, S. K. (2005). Auditory processing—speech, space and auditory objects. *Current Opinion in Neurobiology, 15,* 197–201.

Scott, S. K., McGettigan, C., & Eisner, F. (2009). A little more conversation, a little less action—candidate roles for the motor cortex in speech perception. *Nature Reviews Neuroscience, 10,* 295–302.

Scoville, W. B., & Milner, B. (1957). Loss of recent memory after bilateral hippocampal lesions. *Journal of Neurology, Neurosurgery and Psychiatry, 20,* 11–21.

Scully, T. (2014). Society at large. *Nature, 508,* S50–S51.

Searle, L. V. (1949). The organization of hereditary maze-brightness and maze-dullness. *Genetic Psychology Monographs, 39,* 279–325.

Seeley, R. J., van Dijk, G., Campfield, L. A., Smith, F. J., Nelligan, J. A., Bell, S. M., et al. (1996). The effect of intraventricular administration of leptin (Ob protein) on food intake and body weight in the rat. *Hormone and Metabolic Research, 28,* 664–668.

Seeley, R. J., & Woods, S. C. (2003). Monitoring of stored and available fuel by the CNS: Implications for obesity. *Nature Reviews Neuroscience, 4,* 901–909.

Segerstrom, S. C., & Miller, G. E. (2004). Psychological stress and the human immune system: A meta-analytic study of 30 years of inquiry. *Psychological Bulletin, 130,* 601–630.

Segovia, S., Guillamón, A., del Cerro, M. C. R., Ortega, E., Pérez-Laso, C., Rodriguez-Zafra, M., & Beyer, C. (1999). The development of brain sex differences: A multisignaling process. *Behavioural Brain Research, 105,* 69–80.

Sekar, A., Bialas, A. R., de Rivera, H., Davis, A., Hammond, T. R., Kamitaki, N.,...& Genovese, G. (2016). Schizophrenia risk from complex variation of complement component 4. *Nature, 530,* 177–183.

Sekido, R. (2014). The potential role of SRY in epigenetic gene regulation during brain sexual differentiation in mammals. *Advances in Genetics, 86,* 135–165.

Sekido, R., & Lovell-Badge, R. (2013). Genetic control of testis development. *Sexual Development, 7,* 21–32.

Selkoe, D. J. (1991, November). Amyloid protein and Alzheimer's. *Scientific American, 265,* 68–78.

Selkoe, D. J. (2012). Preventing Alzheimer's disease. *Science, 337,* 1488–1494.

Sellayah, D., Cagampang, F. R., & Cox, R. D. (2014). On the evolutionary origins of obesity: A new hypothesis. *Endocrinology, 155,* 1573–1588.

Senkowski, D., Höfle, M., & Engel, A. K. (2014). Crossmodal shaping of pain: A multisensory approach to nociception. *Trends in Cognitive Sciences, 18,* 319–327.

Serajee, F. J., & Huq, A. M. (2015). Advances in Tourette syndrome: Diagnoses and treatment. *Pediatric Clinics of North America, 62,* 687–701.

Serati, M., Redaelli, M., Buoli, M., & Altamura, A. C. (2016). Perinatal major depression biomarkers: A systematic review. *Journal of Affective Disorders, 193,* 391–404.

Sereno, M. I., & Huang, R. S. (2014). Multisensory maps in parietal cortex. *Current Opinion in Neurobiology, 24,* 39–46.

Servos, P., Engel, S. A., Gati, J., & Menon, R. (1999). fMRI evidence for an inverted face representation in human somatosensory cortex. *NeuroReport, 10*(7), 1393–1395.

Seung, H. S., & Sümbül, U. (2014). Neuronal cell types and connectivity: Lessons from the retina. *Neuron, 83,* 1262–1272.

Seyfarth, R. M., & Cheney, D. L. (2014). The evolution of language from social cognition. *Current Opinion in Neurobiology, 28,* 5–9.

Shackman, A. J., Salomons, T. V., Slagter, H. A., Fox, A. S., Winter, J. J., & Davidson, R. J. (2011). The integration of negative affect, pain and cognitive control in the cingulate cortex. *Nature Reviews Neuroscience, 12,* 154–167.

Shamma, S. A., Elhilali, M., & Micheyl, C. (2011). Temporal coherence and attention in auditory scene analysis. *Trends in Neurosciences, 34,* 114–122.

Shan, L., Dauvilliers, Y., & Siegel, J. M. (2015). Interactions of the histamine and hypocretin systems in CNS disorders. *Nature Reviews Neurology, 11,* 401–413.

Shapely, R., & Hawken, M. (2002). Neural mechanisms for color perception in the primary visual cortex. *Current Opinion in Neurobiology, 12,* 426–432.

Shapiro, B., & Hofreiter, M. (2014). A paleogenomic perspective on evolution and gene function: New insights from ancient DNA. *Science, 343,* 1236573.

Shapiro, B. H., Levine, D. C., & Adler, N. T. (1980). The testicular feminized rat: A naturally occurring model of androgen independent brain masculinization. *Science, 209,* 418–420.

Sharp, A. J., & Akbarian, S. (2016). Back to the past in schizophrenia genomics. *Nature Neuroscience, 19,* 1–2.

Sharpee, T. (2014). Toward functional classification of neuronal types. *Neuron, 83,* 1329–1334.

Sharpee, T. O., Atencio, C. A., & Schreiner, C. E. (2011). Hierarchical representations in the auditory cortex. *Current Opinion in Neurobiology, 21,* 761–767.

Sharpless, B. A., & Barber, J. P. (2011). Lifetime prevalence rates of sleep paralysis: A systematic review. *Sleep Medicine Reviews, 15,* 311–315.

Shaw, P., Bramham, J., Lawrence, E. J., Morris, R., Baron-Cohen, S., & David, A. S. (2005). Differential effects of lesions of the amygdala and prefrontal cortex on recognizing facial expressions of complex emotions. *Journal of Cognitive Neuroscience, 17,* 1410–1419.

Sheffer-Collins, S. I., & Dalva, M. B. (2012). EphBs: An integral link between synaptic function and synaptopathies. *Trends in Neurosciences, 35,* 293–304.

Shelton, J. F., Tancredi, D. J., & Hertz-Picciotto, I. (2010). Independent and dependent contributions of advanced maternal and paternal ages to autism risk. *Autism Research, 3,* 30–39.

Shen, H. (2014). Tuning the brain. *Nature, 507,* 290–292.

Shen, H. (2015). Neuron encyclopaedia fires up to reveal brain secrets. *Nature, 520,* 13–14.

Shen, H. (2015). The hard science of oxytocin. *Nature, 522,* 410–412.

Shen, S., Lang, B., Nakamoto, C., Zhang, F., Pu, J., Kuan, S.-L.,...& St. Clair, D. (2008). Schizophrenia-related neural and behavioral phenotypes in transgenic mice expressing truncated Disc1. *Journal of Neuroscience, 28,* 10893–10904.

Shepherd, R. K., Shivdasani, M. N., Nayagam, D. A. X., Williams, C. E., & Blamey, P. J. (2013). *Trends in biotechnology, 31,* 562–570.

Sherman, D. L., & Brophy, P. J. (2005). Mechanisms of axon ensheathment and myelin growth. *Nature Reviews Neuroscience, 6,* 683–690.

Sherman, M. (2007). The thalamus is more than just a relay. *Current Opinion in Neurobiology, 17,* 417–422.

Sherry, D. F., & Vaccarino, A. L. (1989). Hippocampus and memory for food caches in black-capped chickadees. *Behavioral Neuroscience, 103,* 308–318.

Sheth, D. N., Bhagwate, M. R., & Sharma, N. (2005). Curious clicks—Sigmund Freud. *Journal of Postgraduate Medicine, 51,* 240–241.

Shevell, S. K., & Kingdom, F. A. A. (2008). Color in complex scenes. *Annual Review of Psychology, 59,* 143–166.

Shibata, M., Gulden, F. O., & Sestan, N. (2015). From trans to cis: Transcriptional regulatory networks in neocortical development. *Trends in Genetics, 31,* 77–87.

Shimada-Sugimoto, M., Otowa, T., & Hettema, J. M. (2015). Genetics of anxiety disorders: Genetic epidemiological and molecular studies in humans. *Psychiatry and Clinical Neurosciences, 69,* 388–401.

Shimomura, O., Johnson, F., & Saiga, Y. (1962). Extraction, purification and properties of aequorin, a bioluminescent protein from the luminous hydromedusan, *Aequorea. Journal of Cellular and Comparative Physiology, 59,* 223–239.

Shimura, T., & Shimokochi, M. (1990). Involvement of the lateral mesencephalic tegmentum in copulatory behavior of male rats: Neuron activity in freely moving animals. *Neuroscience Research, 9,* 173–183.

Shin, O.-H. (2014). Exocytosis and synaptic vesicle function. *Comprehensive Physiology, 4,* 149–175.

Shirazi, S. N., Friedman, A. R., Kaufer, D., & Sakhai, S. A. (2015). Glucocorticoids and the brain: Neural mechanisms regulating the stress response in glucocorticoid signaling. *Advances in Experimental Medicine and Biology, 872,* 235–252.

Shirazi, S. N., Friedman, A. R., Kaufer, D., & Sakhai, S. A. (2015). Glucocorticoids and the brain: Neu-ral mechanisms regulating the stress response. In *Glucocorticoid signaling* (pp. 235–252). New York: Springer.

Shohamy, D. (2011). Learning and motivation in the human striatum. *Current Opinion in Neurobiology, 21,* 408–414.

Short, S. D., & Hawley, P. H. (2015). The effects of evolution education: Examining attitudes toward and knowledge of evolution in college courses. *Evolutionary Psychology, 13,* 67–88.

Shrestha, P., & Klann, E. (2016). Alzheimer's disease: Lost memories found. *Nature, 531,* 450–451.

Shubin, N. H. (2009, January). This old body. *Scientific American, 300,* 64–67.

Siclari, F., LaRocque, J. J., Postle, B. R., & Tononi, G. (2013). Assessing sleep consciousness within subjects using a serial awakening paradigm. *Frontiers in Psychology, 4,* 542.

Siegel, J. M. (2005). Clues to the functions of mammalian sleep. *Nature 437,* 1264–1271.

Siegel, J. M. (2008). Do all animals sleep? *Trends in Neurosciences, 31,* 208–213.

Siegel, J. M. (2009). Sleep viewed as a state of adaptive inactivity. *Nature Reviews Neuroscience, 10,* 747–752.

Siegel, J. M. (2011). REM sleep: A biological and psychological paradox. *Sleep Medicine Review, 15,* 139–142.

Siegel, J. M. (2012). Suppression of sleep for mating. *Science, 337,* 1610–1611.

Siegel, M., Buschman, T. J., & Miller, E. K. (2015). Cortical information flow during flexible sensorimotor decisions. *Science, 348,* 1352–1355.

Siegel, S. (2011). The Four-Loko effect. *Perspectives on Psychological Science, 6,* 357–362.

Siegel, S., Hinson, R. E., Krank, M. D., & McCully, J. (1982). Heroin "overdose" death: Contribution of drug-associated environmental cues. *Science, 216,* 436–437.

Siegenthaler, J. A., Sohet, F., & Daneman, R. (2013). 'Sealing off the CNS': Cellular and molecular regulation of blood-brain barriergenesis. *Current Opinion in Neurobiology, 23,* 1057–1064.

Siffrin, V., Vogt, J., Radbruch, H., Nitsch, R., & Zipp, F. (2010). Multiple sclerosis—candidate mechanisms underlying CNS atrophy. *Trends in Neurosciences, 33,* 202–210.

Silbereis, J. C., Pochareddy, S., Zhu, Y., Li, M., & Sestan, N. (2016). The cellular and molecular landscapes of the developing human central nervous system. *Neuron, 89,* 248–268.

Silva, D., Feng, T., & Foster, D. J. (2015). Trajectory events across hippocampal place cells require previous experience. *Nature Neuroscience, 18,* 1772–1779.

Silva, S., Martins, Y., Matias, A., & Blickstein, I. (2011). Why are monozygotic twins different? *Journal of Perinatal Medicine, 39,* 195–202.

Silvanto, J. (2014). Is primary visual cortex necessary for visual awareness? *Trends in Neurosciences, 37,* 618–619.

Silveira, C., Marques-Teixeira, J., & de Bastos-Leite, A. J. (2012). More than one century of schizophrenia: An evolving perspective. *The Journal of Nervous and Mental Disease, 200,* 1054–1057.

Simms, B. A., & Zamponi, G. W. (2014). Neuronal voltage-gated calcium channels: Structure, function, and dysfunction. *Neuron, 82,* 24–45.

Simon, E., Schwarz, M., Roos, J., Dragano, N., Geraedts, M., Siegrist, J., Kamp, G., & Wendel, U. (2008). *Health and life outcomes, 6,* 25.

Simon, N. W., Wood, J., & Moghaddam, B. (2015). Action-outcome relationships are represented differently by medial prefrontal and orbitofrontal cortex neurons during action execution. *Journal of Neurophysiology, 114,* 3374–3385.

Simonds, S. E., & Cowley, M. A. (2013). Hypertension in obesity: Is leptin the culprit? *Trends in Neurosciences, 36,* 121–132.

Simons, D. J., & Rensink, R. A. (2005). Change blindness: Past, present, and future. *Trends in Cognitive Science, 9,* 16–20.

Sinclair, S. V., & Mistlberger, R. E. (1997). Scheduled activity reorganizes circadian phase of Syrian hamsters under full and skeleton photoperiods. *Behavioural Brain Research, 87*, 127–137.

Singer, B. F., Neugebauer, N. M., Forneris, J., Rodvelt, K. R., Li, D., Bubula, N., & Vezina, P. (2014). Locomotor conditioning by amphetamine requires cyclin-dependent kinase 5 signaling in the nucleus accumbens. *Neuropharmacology, 85*, 243–252.

Singer, J. J. (1968). Hypothalamic control of male and female sexual behavior in female rats. *Journal of Comparative and Physiological Psychology, 66*, 738–742.

Singh, J., Hallmayer, J., & Illes, J. (2007). Interacting and paradoxical forces in neuroscience and society. *Nature Reviews Neuroscience, 8*, 153–160.

Singh, S., Kumar, A., Agarwal, S., Phadke, S. R., & Jaiswal, Y. (2014). Genetic insight of schizophrenia: Past and future perspectives. *Gene, 535*, 97–100

Sisk, C. L., & Zehr, J. L. (2005). Pubertal hormones organize the adolescent brain and behavior. *Frontiers in Neuroendocrinology, 26*, 163–174.

Sitte, H. H., & Freissmuth, M. (2015). Amphetamines, new psychoactive drugs, and the monoamine transporter cycle. *Trends in Pharmacological Sciences, 36*, 41–50.

Skinner, M. M., Stephens, N. B., Tsegai, Z. J., Foote, A. C., Nguyen, N. H., et al. (2015). Human-like hand use in *Australopithecus africanus. Science, 347*, 395–399.

Sladek, J. R., Jr., Redmond, D. E., Jr., Collier, T. J., Haber, S. N., Elsworth, J. D., Deutch, A. Y., & Roth, R. H. (1987). Transplantation of fetal dopamine neurons in primate brain reverses MPTP induced Parkinsonism. In F. J. Seil, E. Herbert, & B. M. Carlson (Eds.), *Progress in brain research* (Vol. 71, pp. 309–323). New York, NY: Elsevier.

Sloan, S. A., & Barres, B. A. (2014). Looks can be deceiving: Reconsidering the evidence for gliotransmission. *Neuron, 84*, 1112–1115.

Slocombe, K. E., Kaller, T., Call, J., & Zuberbühler, K. (2010). Chimpanzees extract social information from agonistic screams. *PLoS One, 5*, e11473.

Sluder, G., & McCollum, D. (2000). The mad ways of meiosis. *Science, 289*, 254–255.

Smalle, E. H., Rogers, J., & Möttönen, R. (2015). Dissociating contributions of the motor cortex to speech perception and response bias by using transcranial magnetic stimulation. *Cerebral Cortex, 25*, 3690–3698.

Smith, A. M., & Dragunow, M. (2014). The human side of microglia. *Trends in Neurosciences, 37*, 125–135.

Smith, E. S., Junger, J., Derntl, B., & Habel, U. (2015). The transsexual brain—A review of findings on the neural basis of transsexualism. *Neuroscience & Biobehavioral Reviews, 59*, 251–266.

Smith, F. W., & Goodale, M. A. (2015). Decoding visual object categories in early somatosensory cortex. *Cerebral Cortex, 25*, 1020–1031.

Smith, H., Fox, J. R., & Trayner, P. (2015). The lived experiences of individuals with Tourette syndrome or tic disorders: A meta-synthesis of qualitative studies. *British Journal of Psychology, 106*, 609–634.

Smith, P. A. (2015). Brain, meet gut. *Nature, 526*, 312–314.

Smith, S. M., Vidaurre, D., Beckmann, C. F., Glasser, M. F., Jenkinson, M.,...& Van Essen, D. C. (2013). Functional connectomics from resting-state fMRI. *Trends in Cognitive Sciences, 17*, 666–682.

Sneed, A. (2014). Why babies forget. *Scientific American, 311*, 28.

Snyder, S. H. (1978). Neuroleptic drugs and neurotransmitter receptors. *Journal of Clinical and Experimental Psychiatry, 133*, 21–31.

Sobolewski, M. E., Brown, J. L., & Mitani, J. C. (2013). Female parity, male aggression, and the challenge hypothesis in wild chimpanzees. *Primates, 54*, 81–88.

Sofroniew, M. V. (2009). Molecular dissection of reactive astrogliosis and glial scar formation. *Trends in Neurosciences, 32*, 638–647.

Sohn, J.-W., Elmquist, J. K., & Williams, K. W. (2013). Neuronal circuits that regulate feeding behavior and metabolism. *Trends in Neurosciences, 36*, 504–512.

Solinas, M., Thiriet, N., Chauvet, C., & Jaber, M. (2010). Prevention and treatment of drug addiction by environmental enrichment. *Progress in Neurobiology, 92*, 572–592.

Sollars, P. J., & Pickard, G. E. (2015). The neurobiology of circadian rhythms. *Psychiatric Clinics of North America, 38*, 645–665.

Soloman, S. M., & Kirby, D. F. (1990). The refeeding syndrome: A review. *Journal of Parenteral and Enteral Nutrition, 14*, 90–97.

Soma, K. K. (2006). Testosterone and aggression: Berthold, birds and beyond. *Journal of Neuroendocrinology, 18*, 543–551.

Somers, J. M., Goldner, E. M., Waraich, P., & Hsu, L. (2006). Prevalence and incidence studies of anxiety disorders: A systematic review of the literature. *Canadian Journal of Psychiatry, 51*, 100–112.

Sommer, E. C., Aleman, A., Bouma, A., & Kahn, R. S. (2004). Do women really have more bilateral language representation than men? A meta-analysis of functional imaging studies. *Brain, 127*, 1845–1852.

Song, C., Luchtman, D., Kang, Z., Tam, E. M., Yatham, L. N., Su, K. P., & Lam, R. W. (2015). Enhanced inflammatory and T-helper-1 type responses but suppressed lymphocyte proliferation in patients with seasonal affective disorder and treated by light therapy. *Journal of Affective Disorders, 185*, 90–96.

Sotres-Bayon, F., & Quirk, G. J. (2010). Prefrontal control of fear: More than just extinction. *Current Opinion in Neurobiology, 20*, 231–235.

Soucy, E. R., Albeanu, D. F., Fantana, A. L., Murthy, V. N., & Meister, M. (2009). Precision and diversity in an odor map on the olfactory bulb. *Nature Neuroscience, 12*, 210–220.

Sousa-Ferreira, L., de Almeida, L. P., & Cavadas, C. (2014). Role of hypothalamic neurogenesis in feeding regulation. *Trends in Endocrinology and Metabolism, 25*, 80–88.

Sowa, J., Bobula, B., Glombik, K., Slusarczyk, J., Basta-Kaim, A., & Hess, G. (2015). Prenatal stress enhances excitatory synaptic transmission and impairs long-term potentiation in the frontal cortex of adult offspring rats. *PLoS One, 10*, e0119407.

Spadoni, A. D., McGee, C. L., Fryer, S. L., & Riley, E. P. (2007). Neuroimaging and fetal alcohol spectrum disorders. *Neuroscience and Biobehavioral Reviews, 31*, 239–245.

Spalding, K. L., Bergmann, O., Alkass, K., Bernard, S., Salehpour, M.,...& Frisén, J. (2013). Dynamics of hippocampal neurogenesis in adult humans. *Cell, 153*, 1219–1227.

Speakman, J. R. (2013). Evolutionary perspectives on the obesity epidemic: Adaptive, maladaptive, and neutral viewpoints. *Annual Review of Nutrition, 33*, 289–317.

Spering, M., & Carrasco, M. (2015). Acting without seeing: Eye movements reveal visual processing without awareness. *Trends in Neurosciences, 38*, 247–258.

Sperling, R., Mormino, E., & Johnson, K. (2014). The evolution of preclinical Alzheimer's disease: Implications for prevention trials. *Neuron, 84*, 608–622.

Sperry, R. W. (1963). Chemoaffinity in the orderly growth of nerve fiber patterns and connections. *Proceedings of the National Academy of Sciences, USA, 50*, 703–710.

Sperry, R. W. (1964, January). The great cerebral commissure. *Scientific American, 210*, 42–52.

Sperry, R. W., Zaidel, E., & Zaidel, D. (1979). Self recognition and social awareness in the deconnected minor hemisphere. *Neuropsychologia, 17*, 153–166.

Spiga, F., Walker, J. J., Terry, J. R., & Lightman, S. L. (2014). HPA axis-rhythms. *Comprehensive Physiology, 4*, 1273–1298.

Spinney, L. (2014). The forgetting gene. *Nature, 510*, 26–27.

Spires-Jones, T. L., & Hyman, B. T. (2014). The intersection of amyloid beta and tau at synapses in Alzheimer's disease. *Neuron, 82*, 756–771.

Spitzer, R. L., Skodol, A. E., Gibbon, M., & Williams, J. B. W. (1983). *Psychopathology: A case book.* New York, NY: McGraw-Hill.

Sprague, T. C., Saproo, S., & Serences, J. T. (2015). Visual attention mitigates information loss in small- and large-scale neural codes. *Trends in Cognitive Sciences, 19*, 215–226.

Squarzoni, P., Thion, M. S., & Garel, S. (2015). Neuronal and microglial regulators of cortical wiring: Usual and novel guideposts. *Frontiers in Neuroscience, 9*, 248.

Squire, L. R. (1987). *Memory and brain.* New York, NY: Oxford University Press.

Squire, L. R. & Zola-Morgan, S. (1991). The medial temporal lobe memory system. *Science, 253*, 1380–1386.

Squire, L. R., & Dede, A. J. O. (2015). Conscious and unconscious memory systems. *Cold Spring Harbor Perspectives in Biology, 7*, a021667.

Squire, L. R., & Zola-Morgan, S. (1985). The neuropsychology of memory: New links between humans and experimental animals. *Annals of the New York Academy of Sciences, 444*, 137–149.

Squire, L. R., Amaral, D. G., Zola-Morgan, S., Kritchevsky, M., & Press, G. (1989). Description of brain injury in the amnesic patient N.A. based on magnetic resonance imaging. *Experimental Neurology, 105*, 23–35.

Squire, L. R., Genzel, L., Wixted, J. T., & Morris, R. G. (2015). Memory consolidation. *Cold Spring Harbor Perspectives in Biology, 7*, a021766.

Squire, L. R., Slater, P. C., & Chace, P. M. (1975). Retrograde amnesia: Temporal gradient in very long term memory following electroconvulsive therapy. *Science, 187*, 77–79.

Squire, R. F., Noudoost, B., Schafer, R. J., & Moore, T. (2013). Prefrontal contributions to visual selective attention. *Annual Review of Neuroscience, 36*, 451–466.

St. George-Hyslop, P. H. (2000, December). Piecing together Alzheimer's. *Scientific American, 283*, 76–83.

Stamatakis, K. A., & Punjabi, N. M. (2007). Long sleep duration: A risk to health or a marker of risk? *Sleep Medicine Reviews, 11*, 337–339.

Stampi, C. (Ed.). (1992). *Why we nap: Evolution, chronobiology, and functions of polyphasic and ultrashort sleep.* Boston, MA: Birkhäuser.

Stankowski, R. V., Kloner, R. A., & Rezkalla, S. H. (2015). Cardiovascular consequences of cocaine use. *Trends in Cardiovascular Medicine, 25*, 517–526.

Stasenko, A., Bonn, C., Teghipco, A., Garcea, F. E., Sweet, C.,...& Mahon, B. Z. (2015). A causal test of the motor theory of speech perception: A case of impaired speech production and spared speech perception. *Cognitive Neuropsychology, 32*, 38–57.

Stasenko, A., Garcea, F. E., & Mahon, B. Z. (2013). What happens to the motor theory of perception when the motor system is damaged? *Language and Cognition, 5*, 225–238.

State, M. W., & Levitt, P. (2011). The conundrums of understanding genetic risks for autism spectrum disorders. *Nature Neuroscience, 14*, 1499–1506.

Steen, R. G., Mull, C., McClure, R., Hamer, R. M., & Lieberman, J. A. (2006). Brain volume in first-episode schizophrenia: Systematic review and meta-analysis of magnetic resonance imaging studies. *British Journal of Psychiatry, 188,* 510–518.

Steimer, T. (2011). Animal models of anxiety disorders in rats and mice: Some conceptual issues. *Dialogues in Clinical Neuroscience, 13,* 495–506.

Stein, D. J., Lund, C., & Nesse, R. M. (2013). Classification systems in psychiatry: Diagnosis and global mental health in the era of DSM-5 and ICD-11. *Current Opinion in Psychiatry, 26,* 493.

Steinbeck, J. A., & Studer, L. (2015). Moving stem cells to the clinic: Potential and limitations for brain repair. *Neuron, 86,* 187–206.

Steinberg, E. E., Christoffel, D. J., Deisseroth, K., & Malenka, R. C. (2015). Illuminating circuitry relevant to psychiatric disorders with optogenetics. *Current Opinion in Neurobiology, 30,* 9–16.

Steketee, J. D., & Kalivas, P. W. (2011). Drug wanting: Behavioral sensitization and relapse to drug seeking behavior. *Pharmacological Reviews, 63,* 348–365.

Stella, N. (2012). Inflammation to rebuild a brain. *Science, 338,* 1303–1304.

Stensola, T., Stensola, H., Moser, M.-B., & Moser, E. I. (2015). Shearing-induced asymmetry in entorhinal grid cells. *Nature, 518,* 207–212.

Stephan, B. C. M., & Caine, D. (2009). Aberrant pattern of scanning in prosopagnosia reflects impaired face processing. *Brain and Cognition, 69,* 262–268.

Stern, D. L. (2013). The genetic causes of convergent evolution. *Nature Reviews Genetics, 14,* 751–764.

Sternson, S. M., Betley, J. N., & Cao, Z. F. H. (2013). Neural circuits and motivational processes for hunger. *Current Opinion in Neurobiology, 23,* 353–360.

Stevens, C., & Bavelier, D. (2012). The role of selective attention on academic foundations: A cognitive neuroscience perspective. *Developmental Cognitive Neuroscience, 25,* S30–S48.

Stevens, M. S. (2015). Restless leg syndrome/Willis-Ekbom disease morbidity: Burden, quality of life, cardiovascular aspects, and sleep. *Sleep Medicine Clinics, 10,* 369–373.

Stevenson, R. J. (2012). The role of attention in flavour perception. *Flavour, 1,* 2.

Stickgold, R. (2005). Sleep-dependent memory consolidation. *Nature, 437,* 1272–1278.

Stickgold, R., & Walker, M. P. (2005). Memory consolidation and reconsolidation: What is the role of sleep? *Trends in Neurosciences, 28,* 408–415.

Stickgold, R., & Walker, M. P. (2013). Sleep-dependent memory triage: Evolving generalization through selective processing. *Nature Neuroscience, 16,* 139–145.

Stillman, P. E., Van Bavel, J. J., & Cunningham, W. A. (2015). Valence asymmetries in the human amygdala: Task relevance modulates amygdala responses to positive more than negative affective cues. *Journal of Cognitive Neuroscience, 27,* 842–851.

Stix, G. (2009). Turbocharging the brain. *Scientific American, 301,* 52–55.

Stockwell, T. (2012). Commentary on Roerecke & Rehm (2012): The state of the science on moderate drinking and health—a case of heterogeneity in and heterogeneity out? *Addiction, 107,* 1261–1262.

Stockwell, T., Zhao, J., Panwar, S., Roemer, A., Naimi, T., & Chikritzhs, T. (2016). Do "moderate" drinkers have reduced mortality risk? A systematic review and meta-analysis of alcohol consumption and all-cause mortality. *Journal of Studies on Alcohol and Drugs, 77,* 185–198.

Stoléru, S., Fonteille, V., Cornélis, C., Joyal, C., & Moulier, V. (2012). Functional neuroimaging studies of sexual arousal and orgasm in healthy men and women: A review and meta-analysis. *Neuroscience and Biobehavioral Reviews, 36,* 1481–1509.

Stone, W. L., Krishnan, K., Campbell, S. E., & Palau, V. E. (2014). The role of antioxidants and pro-oxidants in colon cancer. *World Journal of Gastrointestinal Oncology, 6,* 55–66.

Stoodley, C. J., & Stein, J. F. (2013). Cerebellar function in developmental dyslexia. *Cerebellum, 12,* 267–276.

Stowers, L., & Kuo, T.-H. (2015). Mammalian pheromones: Emerging properties and mechanisms of detection. *Current Opinion in Neurobiology, 34,* 103–109.

Stranahan, A. M., & Mattson, M. P. (2012). Recruiting adaptive cellular stress responses for successful brain ageing. *Nature Reviews Neuroscience, 13,* 209–216.

Strathdee, S. A., & Pollini, R. A. (2007). A 21st-century Lazarus: The role of safer injection sites in harm reduction and recovery. *Addiction, 102,* 848–849.

Stringer, C. (2014). Human evolution: Small remains still pose big problems. *Nature, 514,* 427–429.

Strisciuglio, P., & Concolino, D. (2014). New strategies for the treatment of phenylketonuria (PKU). *Metabolites, 4,* 1007–1017.

Strub, R. L., & Black, F. W. (1997). The mental status exam. In T. E. Feinberg & M. J. Farah (Eds.), *Behavioral neurology and neuropsychology* (pp. 25–42). New York, NY: McGraw-Hill.

Strubbe, J. H., & Steffens, A. B. (1977). Blood glucose levels in portal and peripheral circulation and their relation to food intake in the rat. *Physiology & Behavior, 19,* 303–307.

Stuchlik, A. (2014). Dynamic learning and memory, synaptic plasticity and neurogenesis: An update. *Frontiers in Behavioral Neuroscience, 8,* 108.

Stumvoli, M., Goldstein, B. J., & van Haeften, T. W. (2005). Type 2 diabetes: Principles of pathogenesis and therapy. *The Lancet, 365,* 1333–1346.

Stuss, D. T., & Alexander, M. P. (2005). Does damage to the frontal lobes produce impairment in memory? *Current Directions in Psychological Science, 14,* 84–88.

Su, P., Zhang, J., Wang, D., Zhao, F., Cao, Z., Aschner, M., & Luo, W. (2016). The role of autophagy in modulation of neuroinflammation in microglia. *Neuroscience, 319,* 155–167.

Suwa, G., Asfaw, B., Kono, R. T., Kubo, D., Lovejoy, C. O., & White, T. D. (2009). The Ardipithecus ramidus skull and its implications for hominid origins. *Science, 326,* 68.

Substance Abuse and Mental Health Services Administration. (2012). Results from the 2011 National Survey on Drug Use and Health: Summary of National Findings, NSDUH Series H-44, HHS Publication No. (SMA) 12-4713. Rockville, MD: Substance Abuse and Mental Health Services Administration.

Suchowersky, O. (2015). Decade in review—movement disorders: Tracking the pathogenesis of movement disorders. *Nature Reviews Neurology, 11,* 618–619.

Südhof, T. C. (2013). Neurotransmitter release: The last millisecond in the life of a synaptic vesicle. *Neuron, 80,* 675–690.

Sugita, M., & Shipa, Y. (2005). Genetic tracing shows segregation of taste neuronal circuitries for bitter and sweet. *Science, 309,* 781–785.

Sullivan, P. F. (2015). Genetics of disease: Associations with depression. *Nature, 523,* 539–540.

Sulzer, D. (2007). Multiple hit hypotheses for dopamine neuron loss in Parkinson's disease. *Trends in Neurosciences, 30,* 244–250.

Sun, D. (2015). Endogenous neurogenic cell response in the mature mammalian brain following traumatic injury. *Experimental Neurology, 275,* 405–410.

Sun, F., & He, Z. (2010). Neuronal intrinsic barriers for axon regeneration in the adult CNS. *Current Opinion in Neurobiology, 20,* 510–518.

Sun, Y., & Hevner, R. F. (2014). Growth and folding of the mammalian cerebral cortex: From molecules to malformations. *Nature Reviews Neuroscience, 15,* 217–232.

Sun, W., McConnell, E., Pare, J.-F., Xu, Q., Chen, M., Peng, W., Lovatt, D., Han, X., Smith, Y., & Nedergard, M. (2013). Glutamate-dependent neuroglial calcium signaling differs between young and adult brain. *Science, 339,* 197–200.

Sunday, S. R., & Halmi, K. A. (1990). Taste perceptions and hedonics in eating disorders. *Physiology & Behavior, 48,* 587–594.

Sung, Y. J., Simino, J., Kume, R., Basson, J., Schwander, K., & Rao, D. C. (2014). Comparison of two methods for analysis of gene-environment interactions in longitudinal family data: The Framingham heart study. *Frontiers in Genetics, 5,* 9.

Sur, M., & Rubenstein, J. L. R. (2005). Patterning and plasticity of the cerebral cortex. *Science, 310,* 805–810.

Surmeier, D. J., Graves, S. M., & Shen, W. (2014). Dopaminergic modulation of striatal networks in health and Parkinson's disease. *Current Opinion in Neurobiology, 29,* 109–117.

Surmeier, D. J., Mercer, J. N., & Chan, C. S. (2005). Autonomous pacemakers in the basal ganglia: Who needs excitatory synapses anyway? *Current Opinion in Neurobiology, 15,* 312–318.

Surmeier, D. J., Plotkin, J., & Shen, W. (2009). Dopamine and synaptic plasticity in dorsal striatal circuits controlling action selection. *Current Opinion in Neurobiology, 19,* 621–628.

Susilo, T., & Duchaine, B. (2013). Advances in developmental prosopagnosia research. *Current Opinion in Neurobiology, 23,* 423–429.

Sutcliffe, P. A., Dixon, S., Akehurst, R. L., Wilinson, A., Shippam, A., . . . & Caddy, C. M. (2009). Evaluation of surgical procedures for sex reassignment: A systematic review. *Journal of Plastic, Reconstructive & Aesthetic Surgery, 62,* 294–306.

Suwa, G., Kono, R. T., Simpson, S. W., Asfaw, B., Lovejoy, C. O., & White, T. D. (2011). Paleobiological implications of the *Ardipithecus ramidus* dentition. *Science, 326,* 94–99.

Suwanwela, N., & Koroshetz, W. J. (2007). Acute ischemic stroke: Overview of recent therapeutic developments. *Annual Review of Medicine, 58,* 89–106.

Suzuki, W. A. (2010). Untangling memory from perception in the medial temporal lobe. *Trends in Cognitive Sciences, 14,* 195–200.

Suzuki, W. A., & Naya, Y. (2014). The perirhinal cortex. *Annual Review of Neuroscience, 37,* 39–53.

Swaab, D. F. (2004). Sexual differentiation of the human brain: Relevance for gender identity, transsexualism and sexual orientation. *Gynecological Endocrinology, 19,* 301–312.

Swanson, L. W. (2000). What is the brain? *Trends in Neurosciences, 23,* 519–527.

Swanson, S. A., Crow, S. J., Le Grange, D., Swendsen, J., & Merikangas, K. R. (2011). Prevalence and correlates of eating disorders in adolescents: Results from the national comorbidity survey replication adolescent supplement. *Archives of General Psychiatry, 68,* 714–723.

Sweatt, J. D. (2013). The emerging field of neuroepigenetics. *Neuron, 80,* 624–632.

Swinnen, S. P. (2002). Intermanual coordination: From behavioral principles to neural-network interactions. *Nature Reviews Neuroscience, 3,* 350–361.

Syntichaki, P., & Tavernarakis, N. (2003). The biochemistry of neuronal necrosis: Rogue biology? *Nature Reviews Neuroscience, 4,* 672–684.

Szyf, M. (2014). Lamarck revisited: Epigenetic inheritance of ancestral odor fear conditioning. *Nature Neuroscience, 17,* 2–4.

Szyf, M. (2014). Nongenetic inheritance and transgenerational epigenetics. *Trends in Molecular Medicine, 21,* 134–144.

Tabri, N., Murray, H. B., Thomas, J. J., Franko, D. L., Herzog, D. B., & Eddy, K. T. (2015). Overvaluation of body shape/weight and engagement in non-compensatory weight-control behaviors in eating disorders: Is there a reciprocal relationship? *Psychological Medicine, 45,* 2951–2958.

Takahashi, K., Tanabe, K., Ohnuki, M., Narita, M., Ichisaka, T., Tomoda, K., & Yamanaka, S. (2007).

Induction of pluripotent stem cells from adult human fibroblasts by defined factors. *Cell, 131,* 861–872.

Takahashi, Y., Sipp, D., & Enomoto, H. (2013). Tissue interactions in neural crest cell development and disease. *Science, 341,* 860–863.

Takeichi, M. (2007). The cadherin superfamily in neuronal connections and interactions. *Nature Reviews Neuroscience, 8,* 11–20.

Takeuchi, T., & Morris, R. G. M. (2014). Shedding light on a change of mind. *Nature, 513,* 323–324.

Tamakoshi, A., & Ohno, Y. (2004). Self-reported sleep duration as a predictor of all-cause mortality: Results from the JACC study, Japan. *Sleep, 27,* 51–54.

Tamariz, E., & Varela-Echavarría, A. (2015). The discovery of the growth cone and its influence on the study of axon guidance. *Frontiers in Neuroanatomy, 9,* 51.

Tan, Q., Frost, M., Heijmans, B. T., von Bornemann Hjelmborg, J., Tobi, E. W., Christensen, K., & Christiansen, L. (2014). Epigenetic signature of birth weight discordance in adult twins. *BMC Genomics, 15,* 1.

Tanji, J., & Hoshi, E. (2001). Behavioral planning in the prefrontal cortex. *Current Opinion in Neurobiology, 11,* 164–170.

Tank, D. W., Sugimori, M., Connoer, J. A., & Llinás, R. R. (1998). Spatially resolved calcium dynamics of mammalian Purkinje cells in cerebellar slice. *Science, 242,* 7733–7777.

Tanzi, R. E. (2012). The genetics of Alzheimer disease. *Cold Spring Harbor Perspectives in Medicine, 2,* a006296.

Tattersall, I., & Matternes, J. H. (2000, January). Once we were not alone. *Scientific American, 282,* 56–62.

Tauber, M., Diene, G., Mimoun, E., Çabal-Berthoumieu, S., Mantoulan, C.,…& Salles, J. P. (2014). Prader-Willi syndrome as a model of human hyperphagia. *Frontiers of Hormone Research, 42,* 93–106.

Tavares, R. M., Mendelsohn, A., Grossman, Y., Williams, C. H., Shapiro, M., Trope, Y., & Schiller, D. (2015). A map for social navigation in the human brain. *Neuron, 87,* 231–243.

Taylor, D., Sparshatt, A., Varma, S., & Olofinjana, O. (2014). Antidepressant efficacy of agomelatine: Meta-analysis of published and unpublished studies. *British Medical Journal, 348,* g1888.

Teitelbaum, P. (1961). Disturbances in feeding and drinking behavior after hypothalamic lesions. In M. R. Jones (Ed.), *Nebraska symposium on motivation* (pp. 39–69). Lincoln: University of Nebraska Press.

Teitelbaum, P., & Epstein, A. N. (1962). The lateral hypothalamic syndrome: Recovery of feeding and drinking after lateral hypothalamic lesions. *Psychological Review, 69,* 74–90.

Teixeira, S., Machado, S., Velasques, B., Sanfim, A., Minc, D.,…& Silva, J. G. (2014). Integrative parietal cortex processes: Neurological and psychiatric aspects. *Journal of Neurological Sciences, 338,* 12–22.

ter Horst, J. P., de Kloet, E. R., Schächinger, H., & Oitzl, M. S. (2012). Relevance of stress and female sex hormones for emotion and cognition. *Cellular and Molecular Neurobiology, 32,* 725–735.

Testerman, T. L., & Morris, J. (2014). Beyond the stomach: An updated view of *Helicobacter pylori* pathogenesis, diagnosis, and treatment. *World Journal of Gastroenterology, 20,* 12781–12808.

Teuber, H.-L. (1975). Recovery of function after brain injury in man. In *Outcomes of severe damage to the nervous system.* CIBA Foundation Symposium 34. Amsterdam, Netherlands: Elsevier North-Holland.

Teuber, H.-L., Battersby, W. S., & Bender, M. B. (1960). Recovery of function after brain injury in man. In *Outcomes of severe damage to the nervous system.* CIBA Foundation Symposium 34.

Amsterdam, Netherlands: Elsevier North-Holland.

Teuber, H.-L., Milner, B., & Vaughan, H. G., Jr. (1968). Persistent anterograde amnesia after stab wound of the basal brain. *Neuropsychologia, 6,* 267–282.

Thach, W. T., & Bastian, A. J. (2004). Role of the cerebellum in the control and adaptation of gait in health and disease. *Progress in Brain Research, 143,* 353–366.

Theunissen, F. E., & Elie, J. E. (2014). Neural processing of natural sounds. *Nature Reviews Neuroscience, 15,* 355–366.

Theys, T., Romero, M. C., van Loon, J., & Janssen, P. (2015). Shape representation in the primate dorsal visual stream. *Frontiers in Computational Neuroscience, 9,* 43.

Thissen, S., Vos, I. G., Schreuder, T. H., Schreurs, W. M. J., Postma, L. A., & Koehler, P. J. (2014). Persistent migraine aura: New cases, a literature review, and ideas about pathophysiology. *Headache, 54,* 1290–1309.

Thomas, R. H., & Berkovic, S. F. (2014). The hidden genetics of epilepsy—a clinically important new paradigm. *Nature Reviews Neurology, 10,* 283–292.

Thomas, R., & Cavanna, A. E. (2013). The pharmacology of Tourette syndrome. *Journal of Neural Transmission, 120,* 689–694.

Thompson, P. M., Vidal, C., Giedd, J. N., Gochman, P., Blumenthal, J., Nicolson, R.,…& Rapoport, J. L. (2001). Mapping adolescent brain change reveals dynamic wave of accelerated gray matter loss in very early-onset schizophrenia. *Proceedings of the National Academy of Sciences, USA, 98,* 11650–11655.

Thompson, R. F. (2005). In search of memory traces. *Annual Review of Psychology, 56,* 1–23.

Tian, C., Wang, K., Ke, W., Guo, H., & Shu, Y. (2014). Molecular identity of axonal sodium channels in human cortical pyramidal cells. *Frontiers in Cellular Neuroscience, 8,* 297.

Tikidji-Hamburyan, A., Reinhard, K., Seitter, H., Hovhannisyan, A., Procyk, C. A.,…& Münch, T. A., (2015). Retinal output changes qualitatively with every change in ambient luminance. *Nature Neuroscience, 18,* 66–74.

Tison, F., Meissner, W. G. (2014). Diagnosing and treating PD—the earlier the better? *Nature Reviews Neurology, 10,* 65–66.

Tlachi-López, J. L., Eguibar, J. R., Fernández-Guasti, A., & Lucio, R. A. (2012). Copulation and ejaculation in male rats under sexual satiety and the Coolidge effect. *Physiology & Behavior, 106,* 626–630.

Toates, F. M. (1981). The control of ingestive behaviour by internal and external stimuli—a theoretical review. *Appetite, 2,* 35–50.

Toga, A. W., & Thompson, P. M. (2005). Genetics of brain structure and intelligence. *Annual Review of Neuroscience, 28,* 1–23.

Toga, A. W., Thompson, P. M., & Sowell, E. R. (2006). Mapping brain maturation. *Trends in Neurosciences, 29,* 148–159.

Toledano, R., & Gil-Nagel, A. (2008). Adverse effects of antiepileptic drugs. *Seminars in Neurology, 28,* 317–327.

Tomlinson, D. R., & Gardiner, N. J. (2008). Glucose neurotoxicity. *Nature Reviews Neuroscience, 9,* 36–45.

Tompa, T., & Sáry, G. (2010). A review on the inferior temporal cortex of the macaque. *Brain Research Reviews, 62,* 165–182.

Tong, F. (2003). Primary visual cortex and visual awareness. *Nature Reviews Neuroscience, 4,* 219–229.

Toni, N., Laplagne, D. A., Zhao, C., Lombardi, G., Ribak, C. E., Gage, F. H., & Schinder, A. F. (2008). Neurons born in the adult dentate gyrus form functional synapses with target cells. *Nature Neuroscience, 11,* 901–907.

Tononi, G., & Cirelli, C. (2013). Perchance to prune. *Scientific American, 309,* 34–39.

Tootell, R. B. H., Dale, A. M., Sereno, M. I., & Malach, R. (1996). New images from human visual cortex. *Trends in Neurosciences, 19,* 481–489.

Toppi, J., Astolfi, L., Poudel, G. R., Innes, C. R. H., Babiloni, F., & Jones, R. D. (2016). Time-varying effective connectivity of the cortical neuro-electric activity associated with behavioural microsleeps. *NeuroImage, 124,* 421–432.

Tordjman, S., Somogyi, E., Coulon, N., Kermarrec, S., Cohen, D.,…& Xavier, J. (2014). Gene x environment interactions in autism spectrum disorders: Role of epigenetic mechanisms. *Frontiers in Psychiatry, 5,* 53.

Tovote, P., Fadok, J. P., & Lüthi, A. (2015). Neuronal circuits for fear and anxiety. *Nature Reviews Neuroscience, 16,* 317–331.

Tracy, J. L., & Robins, R. W. (2007). The psychological structure of pride: A tale of two facets. *Journal of Personality and Social Psychology, 92,* 506–525.

Tragante, V., Moore, J. H., & Asselbergs, F. W. (2014). The ENCODE project and perspectives on pathways. *Genetics and Epidemiology, 38,* 275–280.

Tramontin, A. D., & Brenowitz, E. A. (2000). Seasonal plasticity in the adult brain. *Trends in Neurosciences, 23*(6), 251–258.

Tranel, D., & Damasio, A. R. (1985). Knowledge without awareness: An autonomic index of facial recognition by prosopagnosics. *Science, 228,* 1453–1454.

Trauer, J. M., Qian, M. Y., Doyle, J. S., Rajaratnam, S. M. W., & Cunnington, D. (2015). Cognitive behavioral therapy for chronic insomnia: A systematic review and meta-analysis. *Annals of Internal Medicine, 163,* 191–204.

Treadway, M. T., & Zald, D. H. (2011). Reconsidering anhedonia in depression: Lessons from translational neuroscience. *Neuroscience and Biobehavioral Reviews, 35,* 537–555.

Treffert, D. A. (2014a). Savant syndrome: Realities, myths and misconceptions. *Journal of Autism and Developmental Disorders, 44,* 564–571.

Treffert, D. A. (2014b). Accidental genius. *Scientific American, 311,* 52–57.

Treistman, S. N., & Martin, G. E. (2009). BK channels: Mediators and models for alcohol tolerance. *Trends in Neurosciences, 32,* 629–636.

Treit, D., Robinson, A., Rotzinger, S., & Pesold, C. (1993). Anxiolytic effects of serotonergic interventions in the shock-probe burying test and the elevated plus-maze test. *Behavioural Brain Research, 54,* 23–34.

Tremblay, A., Royer, M. M., Chaput, J. P., & Doucet, E. (2013). Adaptive thermogenesis can make a difference in the ability of obese individuals to lose body weight. *International Journal of Obesity, 37,* 759–764.

Tresch, M. C., Saltiel, P., d'Avella, A., & Bizzi, E. (2002). Coordination and localization in spinal motor systems. *Brain Research Reviews, 40,* 66–79.

Tribl, G. G., Wetter, T. C., & Schredl, M. (2013). Dreaming under antidepressants: A systematic review on evidence in depressive patients and healthy volunteers. *Sleep Medicine Reviews, 17,* 133–142.

Triplett, J. W. (2014). Molecular guidance of retinotopic map development in the midbrain. *Current Opinion in Neurobiology, 24,* 7–12.

Trivedi, B. P. (2012). Gustatory system: The finer points of taste. *Nature, 486,* S2–S3.

Trivedi, B. P. (2014). Dissecting appetite. *Nature, 508,* S64–S65.

Trivers, R. L. (1972). Parental investment and sexual selection. In B. Campbell (Ed.), *Sexual selection and the descent of man* (pp. 136–179). Chicago, IL: Aldine.

Trottier, G., Srivastava, L., & Walker, C. D. (1999). Etiology of infantile autism: A review of recent advances in genetic and neurobiological research. *Journal of Psychiatry and Neuroscience, 24,* 103–115.

Trounson, A., Thakar, R. G., Lomax, G., & Gibbons, D. (2011). Clinical trials for stem cell therapies. BMC *Medicine, 9,* 1.

Tryon, R. C. (1934). Individual differences. In F. A. Moss (Ed.), *Comparative psychology* (pp. 409–448). New York, NY: Prentice-Hall.

Tsai, H.-H., Li, H., Fuentealba, L. C., Molofsky, A. V., Taveira-Marques, R., Zhuang, H., Tenney, A., Murnen, A. T., Fancy, S. P. J., Merkle, F., Kessaris, N., Alvarez-Buylla, A., Richardson, W. D., & Rowitch, D. H. (2012). Regional astrocyte allocation regulates CNS synaptogenesis and repair. *Science, 337*, 358–362.

Tsai, L., & Barnea, G. (2014). A critical period defined by axon-targeting mechanisms in the murine olfactory bulb. *Science, 344*, 197–200.

Tsakiris, M., Hesse, M. D., Boy, C., Haggard, P., & Fink, G. R. (2007). Neural signatures of body ownership: A sensory network for bodily self-consciousness. *Cerebral Cortex, 17*, 2235–2244.

Tsao, D. Y., & Livingstone, M. S. (2008). Mechanisms of face perception. *Annual Review of Neuroscience, 31*, 411–437.

Tschida, K., & Mooney, R. (2012). The role of auditory feedback in vocal learning and maintenance. *Current Opinion in Neurobiology, 22*, 320–327.

Tse, M. T. (2012). Auditory system: Auditory thalamus is dysfunctional in dyslexia. *Nature Reviews Neuroscience, 13*, 667.

Tsetsos, K., Wyart, V., Shorkey, S. P., & Summerfield, C. (2014). Neural mechanisms of economic commitment in the human medial prefrontal cortex. *eLife, 3*, e03701.

Tshala-Katumbay, D., Mwanza, J. C., Rohlman, D. S., Maestre, G., & Oriá, R. B. (2015). A global perspective on the influence of environmental exposures on the nervous system. *Nature, 527*, S187–S192.

Tsien, J. Z., Li, M., Osan, R., Chen, G., Lin, L.,…& Kuang, H. (2013). On initial brain activity mapping of episodic and semantic memory code in the hippocampus. *Neurobiology of Learning and Memory, 105*, 200–210.

Tsien, R. (1998). The green fluorescent protein. *Annual Review of Biochemistry, 67*, 509–544.

Tsuda, M., & Inoue, K. (2016). Neuron-microglia interaction by purinergic signaling in neuropathic pain following neurodegeneration. *Neuropharmacology, 104*, 76–81.

Tsuda, M., Beggs, S., Salter, M. W., & Inoue, K. (2013). Microglia and intractable chronic pain. *Glia, 61*, 55–61.

Tsunozaki, M., & Bautista, D. M. (2009). Mammalian somatosensory mechanotransduction. *Current Opinion in Neurobiology, 19*, 362–369.

Tucker-Drob, E. M., Rhemtulla, M., Harden, K. P., Turkheimer, E., & Fask, D. (2011). Emergence of a gene x socioeconomic status interaction on infant mental ability between 10 months and 2 years. *Psychological Science, 22*, 125–133.

Tulving, E. (2002). Episodic memory: From mind to brain. *Annual Review of Neuroscience, 53*, 1–25.

Turcu, A. F., & Auchus, R. J. (2015). Adrenal steroidogenesis and congenital adrenal hyperplasia. *Endocrinology and Metabolism Clinics of North America, 44*, 275–296.

Turella, L., & Lingnau, A. (2014). Neural correlates of grasping. *Frontiers in Human Neuroscience, 8*, 686.

Turkheimer, E. (2000). Three laws of behavior genetics and what they mean. *Current Directions in Psychological Science, 9*(5), 160–164.

Turkheimer, E., Haley, A., Waldron, M., D'Onofrio, B., & Gottesman, I. (2003). Socioeconomic status modifies heritability of IQ in young children. *Psychological Science, 14*(6), 623–628.

Turkheimer, E., Pettersson, E., & Horn, E. E. (2014). A phenotypic null hypothesis for the genetics of personality. *Annual Review of Psychology, 65*, 515–540.

Turner, B. O., Marinsek, N., Ryhal, E., & Miller, M. B. (2015). Hemispheric lateralization in reasoning. *Annals of the New York Academy of Sciences, 1359*, 47–64.

Turner, R. S., & Desmurget, M. (2010). Basal ganglia contributions to motor control: A vigorous tutor. *Current Opinion in Neurobiology, 20*, 704–716.

Tylš, F., Páleníček, T., & Horáček, J. (2014). Psilocybin—summary of knowledge and new perspectives. *European Neuropsychopharmacology, 24*, 342–356.

Tymianski, M. (2014). Disappointments and advances in acute stroke intervention. *Nature Neuroscience, 10*, 66–68.

U.S. Department of Health and Human Services, Substance Abuse and Mental Health Services Administration. (2006). *2006 National Survey on Drug Use and Health.* Retrieved from http://www.oas.samhsa.gov/nsduhLatest.htm

U.S. Department of Health and Human Services. Substance Abuse and Mental Health Services Administration. Center for Behavioral Health Statistics and Quality. (2010). National survey on drug use and health. ICPSR32722-v3. Ann Arbor, MI: Interuniversity Consortium for Political and Social Research.

Uchida, N., Poo, C., & Haddad, R. (2014). Coding and transformations in the olfactory system. *Annual Review of Neuroscience, 37*, 363–385.

Uchtenhagen, A. (2010). Heroin-assisted treatment in Switzerland: A case study in policy change. *Addiction, 105*, 29–37.

Uddin, L. Q. (2011). Brain connectivity and the self: The case of cerebral disconnection. *Consciousness and Cognition, 20*, 94–98.

Ueno, M., & Yamashita, T. (2014). Bidirectional tuning of microglia in the developing brain: From neurogenesis to neural circuit formation. *Current Opinion in Neurobiology, 27*, 8–15.

Uher, R. (2014). Gene-environment interactions in severe mental illness. *Frontiers in Psychiatry, 5*, 48.

Ulrich, R. E. (1991). Commentary: Animal rights, animal wrongs and the question of balance. *Psychological Science, 2*, 197–201.

UN Global ATS Assessment. (2011). *Amphetamines and ecstasy.* United Nations Office on Drug and Crime.

Underwood, E. (2013). Why do so many neurons commit suicide during brain development? *Science, 340*, 1157–1158.

Underwood, E. (2014). Brain's GPS finds top honor. *Science, 346*, 149–149.

Underwood, E. (2015). The brain's identity crisis. *Science, 349*, 575–577.

Underwood, E. (2015a). Neuroscience: Seeking tests for a contested brain disease. *Science, 348*, 378–379.

Underwood, E. (2015b). Neuroscience: Brain implant trials raise ethical concerns. *Science, 348*, 1186–1187.

Underwood, E. (2015c). Alzheimer's amyloid theory gets modest boost. *Science, 349*, 464.

Ungerleider, L. G., & Haxby, J. V. (1994). "What" and "where" in the human brain. *Current Opinion in Neurobiology, 4*, 157–165.

Ungerleider, L. G., & Mishkin, M. (1982). Two cortical visual systems. In D. J. Ingle, M. A. Goodale, & R. J. W. Mansfield (Eds.), *Analysis of visual behavior* (pp. 549–586). Cambridge, MA: MIT Press.

Uzzi, B., Mukherjee, S., Stringer, M., & Jones, B. (2013). Atypical combinations and scientific impact. *Science, 342*, 468–472.

Valeeva, G., Valiullina, F., & Khazipov, R. (2013). Excitatory actions of GABA in the intact neonatal rodent hippocampus in vitro. *Frontiers in Cellular Neuroscience, 7*, 20.

Valenstein, E. S. (1973). *Brain control.* New York, NY: John Wiley & Sons.

Valenzuela, C. F., Morton, R. A., Diaz, M. R., & Topper, L. (2012). Does moderate drinking harm the fetal brain? Insights from animal models. *Trends in Neurosciences, 35*, 284–292.

Van Acker, G. M., Amundsen, S. L., Messamore, W. G., Zhang, H. Y., Luchies, C. W., & Cheney, P. D. (2014). Equilibrium-based movement endpoints elicited from primary motor cortex using repetitive microstimulation. *Journal of Neuroscience, 34*, 15722–15734.

van Amsterdam, J., Opperhuizen, A., & Hartgens, F. (2010). Adverse health effects of anabolic-androgenic steroids. *Regulatory Toxicology and Pharmacology, 57*, 117–123.

van den Heuvel, M. P., & Sporns, O. (2013). Network hubs in the human brain. *Trends in Cognitive Sciences, 17*, 683–696.

van den Hurk, J., Pegado, F., Martens, F., & de Beeck, H. P. O. (2015). The search for the face of the visual homunculus. *Trends in Cognitive Sciences, 19*, 638–641.

van den Pol, A. N. (2009). Viral infections leading to brain dysfunction: More prevalent than appreciated? *Neuron, 64*, 17–20.

van Erp, T. G. M., Hibar, D. P., Rasmussen, J. M., Glahn, D. C., Pearlson, G. D., Andreassen, O. A.,…& Melle, I. (2016). Subcortical brain volume abnormalities in 2028 individuals with schizophrenia and 2540 healthy controls via the ENIGMA consortium. *Molecular Psychiatry, 21*, 547–553.

Van Goozen, S. H. M., Slabbekoorn, D., Gooren, L. J. G., Sanders, G., & Cohen-Kettenis, P. T. (2002). Organizing and activating effects of sex hormones in homosexual transsexuals. *Behavioral Neuroscience, 116*, 982–988.

van Groen, T., Puurunen, K., Mäki, H.-M., Sivenius, J., & Jolkkonen, J. (2005). Transformation of diffuse β-amyloid precursor protein and β-amyloid deposits to plaques in the thalamus after transient occlusion of the middle cerebral artery in rats. *Stroke, 36*, 1551.

Van Herwegen, J. (2015). Williams syndrome and its cognitive profile: The importance of eye movements. *Psychology Research and Behavior Management, 8*, 143–151.

van Opstal, E. J., & Bordenstein, S. R. (2015). Rethinking heritability of the microbiome. *Science, 349*, 1172–1173.

Van Praag, H., Christie, B. R., Sejnowski, T. J., & Gage, F. H. (1999). Running enhances neurogenesis, learning, and long-term potentiation in mice. *Proceedings of the National Academy of Sciences, USA, 19*, 13427–13431.

Van Praag, H., Schinder, A. F., Christie, B. R., Toni, N., Palmer, T. D., & Gage, F. H. (2002). Functional neurogenesis in the adult hippocampus. *Nature, 415*, 1030–1034.

Van Praag, H., Shubert, T., Zhao, C., & Gage, F. H. (2005). Exercise enhances learning and hippocampal neurogenesis in aged mice. *Journal of Neuroscience, 25*, 8680–8685.

Van Tilborg, I. A. D. A., Kessels, R. P. C., Krujit, P., Wester, A. J., & Hulstijn, W. (2011). Spatial and nonspatial implicit motor learning in Korsakoff's amnesia: Evidence for selective deficits. *Experimental Brain Research, 214*, 427–435.

Van Vleet, T. M., & Robertson, L. C. (2006). Cross-modal interactions in time and space: Auditory influence on visual attention in hemispatial neglect. *Journal of Cognitive Neuroscience, 18*, 1368–1379.

Van Wagenen, W. P., & Herren, R. Y. (1940). Surgical division of commissural pathways in the corpus callosum: Relation to spread of an epileptic attack. *Archives of Neurology and Psychiatry, 44*, 740–759.

Vargas, C., López-Jaramillo, C., & Vieta, E. (2013). A systematic literature review of resting state network—functional MRI in bipolar disorder. *Journal of Affective Disorders, 150*, 727–735.

Vargha-Khadem, F., Gadian, D. G., Watkins, K. E., Connelly, A., van Paesschen, W., & Mishkin, M. (1997). Differential effects of early hippocampal pathology on episodic and semantic memory. *Science, 277*, 376–380.

Vassoler, F. M., & Sadri-Vakili, G. (2014). Mechanisms of transgenerational inheritance of addictive-like behaviours. *Neuroscience, 264*, 198–206.

Vassoler, F. M., Byrnes, E. M., & Pierce, R. C. (2014). The impact of exposure to addictive drugs on future generations: Physiological and behavioural effects. *Neuropharmacology, 76,* 269–275.

Vaupel, J. W., Carey, J. R., & Christensen, K. (2003). It's never too late. *Science, 301,* 1679–1681.

Vázquez, G. H., Baldessarini, R. J., & Tondo, L. (2014). Co-occurrence of anxiety and bipolar disorders: Clinical and therapeutic overview. *Depression and Anxiety, 31,* 196–206.

Vecchia, D., & Pietrobon, D. (2012). Migraine: A disorder of brain excitatory-inhibitory balance? *Trends in Neurosciences, 35,* 507–520.

Veldhuizen, M. G., & Small, D. M. (2011). Modality-specific neural effects of selective attention to taste and odor. *Chemical Senses, 36,* 747–760.

Veldhuizen, M. G., Gitelman, D. R., & Small, D. M. (2012). An fMRI study of the interactions between the attention and the gustatory networks. *Chemosensory Perception, 5,* 117–127.

Verkhratsky, A., Parpura, V., & Rodríguez, J. J. (2010). Where the thought dwells: The physiology of neuronal-glial "diffuse neural net." *Brain Research Reviews, 66,* 133–151.

Verleger, R., Binkofski, F., Friedrich, M., Sedlmeier, P., & Kömpf, D. (2011). Anarchic-hand syndrome: ERP reflections of lost control over the right hemisphere. *Brain and Cognition, 77,* 138–150.

Verstraeten, A., Theuns, J., & Van Broeckhoven, C. (2015). Progress in unraveling the genetic etiology of Parkinson's disease in a genomic era. *Trends in Genetics, 31,* 140–149.

Vertes, R. P., & Eastman, K. E. (2000). The case against memory consolidation in REM sleep. *Behavioral and Brain Sciences, 23,* 867–876.

Vertes, R. P., & Seigel, J. M. (2005). Time for the sleep community to take a critical look at the purported role of sleep in memory processing. *Sleep, 28,* 1228–1231.

Vetter, P., Grosbras, M.-H., & Muckli, L. (2015). TMS over V5 disrupts motion prediction. *Cerebral Cortex, 25,* 1052–1059.

Videnovic, A., Noble, C., Reid, K. J., Peng, J., Turek, F. W., ... & Zee, P. C. (2014). Circadian melatonin rhythm and excessive daytime sleepiness in Parkinson disease. *JAMA Neurology, 71,* 463–469.

Vidyasagar, T. R., & Eysel, U. T. (2015). Origins of feature selectivities and maps in the mammalian primary visual cortex. *Trends in Neurosciences, 38,* 475–485.

Vigneau, M., Beaucousin, V., Hervé, P.-Y., Jobard, G., Petit, G., Crivello, F., Mellet, E., Zago, L., Mazoyer, B., & Tzourio-Mazoyer, N. (2011). What is right-hemisphere contribution to phonological, lexico-semantic, and sentence processing? *Neuroimage, 54,* 577–593.

Vigneswaran, K., Neill, S., & Hadjipanayis, C. G. (2015). Beyond the world health organization grading of infiltrating gliomas: Advances in the molecular genetics of glioma classification. *Annals of Translational Medicine, 3,* 95.

Villablanca, P. A., Alegria, J. R., Mookadam, F., Holmes D. R., Wright, R. S., & Levine, J. A. (2015). Nonexercise activity thermogenesis in obesity management. *Mayo Clinic Proceedings, 90,* 509–519.

Villmoare, B., Kimbel, W. H., Seyoum, C., Campisano, C. J., DiMaggio, E. N., Rowan, J., ... & Reed, K. E. (2015). Early *Homo* at 2.8 Ma from Ledi-Geraru, Afar, Ethiopia. *Science, 347,* 1352–1355.

Viscomi, M. T., & Molinari, M. (2014). Remote neurodegeneration: Multiple actors at play. *Molecular Neurobiology, 50,* 368–389.

Vita, A., De Peri, L., Silenzi, C., & Dieci, M. (2006). Brain morphology in first-episode schizophrenia: A meta-analysis of quantitative magnetic resonance imaging studies. *Schizophrenia Research, 82,* 75–88.

Vlahov, D., Galea, S., Ahem, J., Resnick, H., Boscarino, J. A., ... & Kilpatrick, D. (2004). Consumption of cigarettes, alcohol, and marijuana among New York City residents six months after the September 11 terrorist attacks. *American Journal of Drug and Alcohol Abuse, 30,* 385–407.

Vo, N. K., Cambronne, X. A., & Goodman, R. H. (2010). MicroRNA pathways in neural development and plasticity. *Current Opinion in Neurobiology, 20,* 457–465.

Voigt, J.-P., & Fink, H. (2015). Serotonin controlling feeding and satiety. *Behavioural Brain Research, 277,* 14–31.

Voineskos, A. N., Felsky, D., Kovacevic, N., Tiwari, A. K., Zai, C., Chakravarty, M. M., Lobaugh, N. J., Shenton, M. E., Rajji, T. K., Miranda, D., Pollock, B. G., Mulsant, B. H., McIntosh, A. R., & Kennedy, J. L. (2012). Oligodendrocyte genes, white matter tract integrity, and cognition in schizophrenia. *Cerebral Cortex.* doi:10.1093/cercor/bhs188

Volkman, F. R., & McPartland, J. C. (2014). From Kanner to DSM-5: Autism as an evolving diagnostic concept. *Annual Review of Clinical Psychology, 10,* 193–212.

Volkmar, F. R., & McPartland, J. C. (2014). From Kanner to DSM-5: Autism as an evolving diagnostic concept. *Annual Review of Clinical Psychology, 10,* 193–212.

Volkow, N. D., & Baler, R. D. (2012). To stop or not to stop? *Science, 335,* 546–548.

Volkow, N. D., & Warren, K. R. (2011). The science of addiction; untangling complex systems. *Nature Reviews Neuroscience, 12,* 620.

Volkow, N. D., Wang, G.-J., Tomasi, D., & Baler, R. D. (2013). Unbalanced neuronal circuits in addiction. *Current Opinion in Neurobiology, 23,* 639–648.

Vollenweider, F. X., & Kometer, M. (2010). The neurobiology of psychedelic drugs: Implications for the treatment of mood disorders. *Nature Reviews Neuroscience, 11,* 642–651.

Vonck, K., Raedt, R., Naulaerts, J., De Vogelaere, F., Thiery, E., ... & Boon, P. (2014). Vagus nerve stimulation…25 years later! What do we know about the effects on cognition? *Neuroscience and Biobehavioral Reviews, 45,* 63–71.

Vonderschen, K., & Wagner, H. (2014). Detecting interaural time differences and remodeling their representation. *Trends in Neurosciences, 37,* 289–300.

Voss, M. W., Vivar, C., Kramer, A. F., & van Praag, H. (2013). Bridging animal and human models of exercise-induced brain plasticity. *Trends in Cognitive Sciences, 17,* 525–544.

Vuilleumier, P., Schwartz, S., Clarke, K., Husain, M., & Driver, J. (2002). Testing memory for unseen visual stimuli in patients with extinction and spatial neglect. *Journal of Cognitive Neuroscience, 14,* 875–886.

Vyazovskiy, V. V. (2015). Mapping the birth of the sleep connectome. *Science, 350,* 909–910.

Wada, J. A. (1949). A new method for the determination of the side of cerebral speech dominance. *Igaku to Seibutsugaku, 14,* 221–222.

Wager, T. D., & Atlas, L. Y. (2015). The neuroscience of placebo effects: Connecting context, learning and health. *Nature Reviews Neuroscience, 16,* 403–418.

Wager, T. D., Phan, K. L., Liberzon, I., & Taylor, S. F. (2003). Valence, gender, and lateralization of functional brain anatomy in emotion: A meta-analysis of findings from neuroimaging. *Neuroimage, 19,* 513–531.

Wake, H., Moorhouse, A. J., Miyamoto, A., & Nabekura, J. (2013). Microglia: Actively surveying and shaping neuronal circuit structure and function. *Trends in Neurosciences, 36,* 209–217.

Wald, G. (1964). The receptors of human color vision. *Science, 145,* 1007–1016.

Walker, A. W., & Parkhill, J. (2013). Fighting obesity with bacteria. *Science, 341,* 1069–1070.

Walker, L. C., & Jucker, M. (2013). Seeds of dementia. *Scientific American, 308,* 52–57.

Wallen, K. (2005). Hormonal influences on sexually differentiated behavior in nonhuman primates. *Frontiers in Neuroendocrinology, 26,* 7–26.

Wallis, C. (2014). Gut reactions. *Scientific American, 310,* 30–33.

Walløe, S., Pakkenberg, B., & Fabricius, K. (2014). Stereological estimation of total cell numbers in the human cerebral and cerebellar cortex. *Frontiers in Human Neuroscience, 8,* 508.

Walsh, D. M., & Selkoe, D. J. (2016). A critical appraisal of the pathogenic protein spread hypothesis of neurodegeneration. *Nature Reviews Neuroscience, 17,* 251–260.

Walsh, P., Elsabbagh, M., Bolton, P., & Singh, I. (2011). In search of biomarkers for autism: Scientific, social and ethical challenges. *Nature Reviews Neuroscience, 12,* 603–612.

Wan, H., Aggleton, J. P., & Brown, M. W. (1999). Different contributions of the hippocampus and perirhinal cortex to recognition memory. *Journal of Neuroscience, 19,* 1142–1148.

Wandell, B. A., & Yeatman, J. D. (2013). Biological development of reading circuits. *Current Opinion in Neurobiology, 23,* 261–268.

Wander, J. D., & Rao, R. P. N. (2014). Brain-computer interfaces: A powerful tool for scientific inquiry. *Current Opinion in Neurobiology, 25,* 70–75.

Wang, F., Zhu, J., Zhu, H., Lin, Z., & Hu, H. (2011). Bidirectional control of social hierarchy by synaptic efficacy in medial prefrontal cortex. *Science, 334,* 693–697.

Wang, H., Xu, T., Jiang, Y., Xu, H., Yan, Y., Fu, D., & Chen, J. (2015). The challenges and the promise of molecular targeted therapy in malignant gliomas. *Neoplasia, 17,* 239–255.

Wang, J., Yang, Y., Fan. L., Xu, J., Li, C., ... & Jiang, T. (2015). Convergent functional architecture of the superior parietal lobule unraveled with multimodal neuroimaging approaches. *Human Brain Mapping, 36,* 238–257.

Wang, L., & Marquardt, T. (2013). What axons tell each other: Axon-axon signaling in nerve and circuit assembly. *Current Opinion in Neurobiology, 23,* 974–982.

Wang, L., Leonards, C. O., Sterzer, P., & Ebinger, M. (2014). White matter lesions and depression: A systematic review and meta-analysis. *Journal of Psychiatric Research, 56,* 56–64.

Wang, M., Alexanderson, K., Runeson, B., & Mittendorfer-Rutz, E. (2015). Sick-leave measures, socio-demographic factors and health care as risk indicators for suicidal behavior in patients with depressive disorders—a nationwide prospective cohort study in Sweden. *Journal of Affective Disorders, 173,* 201–210.

Wang, S. S.-H., Kloth, A. D., & Badura, A. (2014). The cerebellum, sensitive periods, and autism. *Neuron, 83,* 518–532.

Wang, Y., See, J., Phan, R. C., & Oh, Y. H. (2015). Efficient spatio-temporal local binary patterns for spontaneous facial micro-expression recognition. *PLoS One, 10,* e0124674.

Wang, Y., Zhang, D., Zou, F., Li, H., Luo, Y., Zhang, M., & Liu, Y. (2016). Gender differences in emotion experience perception under different facial muscle manipulations. *Consciousness and Cognition, 41,* 24–30.

Wang, Z., Sa, Y.-L., Ye, X.-X., Zhang, J., & Xu, Y.-M. (2014). Complete androgen insensitivity syndrome in juveniles and adults with female phenotypes. *Journal of Obstetrics and Gynaecology Research, 40,* 2044–2050.

Ware, J. C. (2008). Will sleeping pills ever wake us up? *Sleep Medicine, 9,* 811–812.

Warrier, C., Wong, P., Penhune, V., Zatorre, R., Parrish, T., Abrams, D., & Kraus, N. (2009). Relating structure to function: Heschl's gyrus and acoustic processing. *Journal of Neuroscience, 29,* 61–69.

Watanabe, M., Fukuda, A., & Nabekura, J. (2014). The role of GABA in the regulation of GnRH neurons. *Frontiers in Neuroscience, 8,* 387.

Watanabe, N., & Yamamoto, M. (2015). Neural mechanisms of social dominance. *Frontiers in Neuroscience, 9*, 154.

Watson, J. B. (1930). *Behaviorism*. New York, NY: Norton.

Webb, W. B., & Agnew, H. W. (1967). Sleep cycling within the twenty-four hour period. *Journal of Experimental Psychology, 74*, 167–169.

Webb, W. B., & Agnew, H. W. (1970). Sleep stage characteristics of long and short sleepers. *Science, 163*, 146–147.

Webb, W. B., & Agnew, H. W. (1974). The effects of a chronic limitation of sleep length. *Psychophysiology, 11*, 265–274.

Webb, W. B., & Agnew, H. W. (1975). The effects on subsequent sleep of an acute restriction of sleep length. *Psychophysiology, 12*, 367–370.

Weber, F., Chung, S., Beier, K. T., Xu, M., Luo, L., & Dan, Y. (2015). Control of REM sleep by ventral medulla GABAergic neurons. *Nature, 526*, 435–438.

Wehrl, H. F., Hossain, M., Lankes, K., Liu, C.-C., Bezrukov, I., . . . & Pichler, B. J. (2013). Simultaneous PET-MRI reveals brain function in activated and resting state on metabolic hemodynamic and multiple temporal scales. *Nature Medicine, 9*, 1184–1190.

Weibel, R., Reiss, D., Karchewski, L., Gardon, O., Matifas, A., Filliol, D., Becker, J. A. J., Wood, J. N., Kieffer, B. L., & Gaveriaux-Ruff, C. (2013). Mu opioid receptors on primary afferent Nav1.8 neurons contribute to opiate-induced analgesia: Insight from conditional knockout mice. *PLoS ONE, 8*, e74706.

Weigelt, S., Koldewyn, K., & Kanwisher, N. (2012). Face identity recognition in autism spectrum disorder: A review of behavioral studies. *Neuroscience and Biobehavioral Reviews, 36*, 1060–1084.

Weil, R. S., & Rees, G. (2011). A new taxonomy for perceptual filling-in. *Brain Research Reviews, 67*, 40–55.

Weiller, C., & Rijntjes, M. (1999). Learning, plasticity, and recovery in the central nervous system. *Experimental Brain Research, 128*, 134–138.

Weindruch, R., & Walford, R. L. (1988). *The retardation of aging and disease by dietary restriction*. Springfield, IL: Charles C Thomas.

Weindruch, R. (1996). The retardation of aging by caloric restriction: Studies in rodents and primates. Toxicologic Pathology, 24, 742–745.

Weingarten, H. P. (1983). Conditioned cues elicit feeding in sated rats: A role for learning in meal initiation. *Science, 220*, 431–433.

Weingarten, H. P. (1984). Meal initiation controlled by learned cues: Basic behavioral properties. *Appetite, 5*, 147–158.

Weingarten, H. P. (1985). Stimulus control of eating: Implications for a two-factor theory of hunger. *Appetite, 6*, 387–401.

Weingarten, H. P. (1990). Learning, homeostasis, and the control of feeding behavior. In E. D. Capaldi & T. L. Powley (Eds.), *Taste, experience, and feeding* (pp. 14–27). Washington, DC: American Psychological Association.

Weiskrantz, L., Warrington, E. K., Sanders, M. D., & Marshall, J. (1974). Visual capacity in the hemianopic field following a restricted occipital ablation. *Brain, 97*, 709–728.

Weissman, D. H., & Banich, M. T. (2000). The cerebral hemispheres cooperate to perform complex but not simple tasks. *Neuropsychology, 14*, 41–59.

Weissman, M. M., & Olfson, M. (1995). Depression in women: Implications for health care research. *Science, 269*, 799–801.

Wekerle, H., Flügel, L., Schett, G., & Serreze, D. (2012). Autoimmunity's next top models. *Nature Medicine, 18*, 66–70.

Welberg, L. (2014). Epigenetics: A lingering smell? *Nature Reviews Neuroscience, 15*, 1.

Welberg, L. (2014). Synaptic plasticity: A synaptic role for microglia. *Nature Reviews Neuroscience, 15*, 69.

Welberg, L. (2014a). Neurogenesis: A striatal supply of new neurons. *Nature Reviews Neuroscience, 15*, 203.

Welberg, L. (2014b). Learning and memory: Neurogenesis erases existing memories. *Nature Reviews Neuroscience, 15*, 428–429.

Welberg, L. (2014c). Glia: A critical mass of microglia? *Nature Reviews Neuroscience, 15*, 133.

Weledji, E. P., & Assob, J. C. (2014). The ubiquitous neural cell adhesion molecule (N-CAM). *Annals of Medicine and Surgery, 3*, 77–81.

Wen, P. Y., & Reardon, D. A. (2016). Neuro-oncology in 2015: Progress in glioma diagnosis, classification and treatment. *Nature Reviews Neurology, 12*, 69–70.

Westheimer, G. (2009). The third dimension in the primary visual cortex. *The Journal of Physiology, 587*, 2807–2816.

Westmoreland, P., Krantz, M. J., & Mehler, P. S. (2015). Medical complications of anorexia nervosa and bulimia. *American Journal of Medicine, 129*, 30–37.

Weth, F., Fiederling, F., Gebhardt, C., & Bastmeyer, M. (2014). Chemoaffinity in topographic mapping revisited—is it more about fiber-fiber than fiber-target interactions? *Seminars in Cell and Developmental Biology, 35*, 126–135.

Wever, R. A. (1979). *The circadian system of man*. Seewiesen-Andechs, Germany: Max-Planck-Institut für Verhaltensphysiologie.

Whalen, P. J., Raila, H., Bennett, R., Mattek, A., Brown, A., Taylor, J., van Tieghem, M., Tanner, A., Miner, M., & Palmer, A. (2013). Neuroscience and facial expressions of emotion: The role of the amygdala-prefrontal interactions. *Emotion Review, 5*, 78–83.

Whalen, P. J., Raila, H., Bennett, R., Mattek, A., Brown, A., Taylor, J., . . . & Palmer, A. (2013). Neuroscience and facial expressions of emotion: The role of amygdala–prefrontal interactions. *Emotion Review, 5*, 78–83.

Whalley, K. (2014). Neurodegenerative disease: Propagating pathology. *Nature Reviews Neuroscience, 15*, 565.

Whalley, K. (2014). Psychiatric disorders: A feat of epigenetic engineering. *Nature Reviews Neuroscience, 15*, 768–769.

White, T. D., Asfaw, B., Beyene, Y., Haile-Selassie, Y., Lovejoy, C. O., Suwa, G., & WoldeGabriel, G. (2009). Ardipithecus ramidus and the paleobiology of early hominids. *Science, 326*, 64–86.

Whiten, A., & Boesch, C. (2001, January). The cultures of chimpanzees. *Scientific American, 284*, 61–67.

Wichterle, H., Gifford, D., & Mazzoni, E. (2013). Mapping neuronal diversity one cell at a time. *Science, 341*, 726–727.

Wickelgren, W. A. (1968). Sparing of short-term memory in an amnesic patient: Implications for strength theory of memory. *Neuropsychologia, 6*, 31–45.

Wiedemann, K. (2014). Where we came from. *Scientific American, 311*, 40–41.

Wiegert, J. S., & Oertner, T. G. (2015). Neighborly synapses help each other out. *Nature Neuroscience, 18*, 326–327.

Wiesner, C. D., Pulst, J., Krause, F., Elsner, M., Baving, L., . . . & Göder, R. (2015). The effect of selective REM-sleep deprivation on the consolidation and affective evaluation of emotional memories. *Neurobiology of Learning and Memory, 122*, 131–141.

Wilber, A. A., Clark, B. J., Forster, T. C., Tatsuno, M., & McNaughton, B. L. (2014). Interaction of egocentric and world-centered reference frames in the rat posterior parietal cortex. *Journal of Neuroscience, 34*, 5431–5446.

Will, R. G., Hull, E. M., & Dominguez, J. M. (2014). Influences of dopamine and glutamate in the medial preoptic area on male sexual behavior. *Pharmacology, Biochemistry, and Behavior, 121*, 115–123.

Willems, R. M., Peelen, M. V., & Hagoort, P. (2010). Cerebral lateralization of face-selective and body-selective visual areas depends on handedness. *Cerebral Cortex, 20*, 1719–1725.

Williams, M. (1970). *Brain damage and the mind*. Baltimore, MD: Penguin Books.

Williams, S. R., & Stuart, G. J. (2002). Dependence of EPSP efficacy on synapse location in neocortical pyramidal neurons. *Science, 295*, 1907–1910.

Williams, S. R., & Stuart, G. J. (2003). Role of dendritic synapse location in the control of action potential output. *Trends in Neurosciences, 26*(3), 147–154.

Williams, Z. M. (2015). Good vibrations with deep brain stimulation. *Nature neuroscience, 18*, 618–619.

Willment, K. C., & Golby, A. (2013). Hemispheric lateralization interrupted: Material-specific memory deficits in temporal lobe epilepsy. *Frontiers in Human Neuroscience, 7*, 546.

Willner, P., Scheel-Krüger, J., & Belzung, C. (2013). The neurobiology of depression and antidepressant action. *Neuroscience & Biobehavioral Reviews, 37*, 2331–2371.

Wills, T. A., Vaccaro, D., & McNamara, G. (1994). Novelty seeking, risk taking, and related constructs as predictors of adolescent substance use: An application of Cloninger's theory. *Journal of Substance Abuse, 6*, 1–20.

Wills, T. J., & Cacucci, F. (2014). The development of the hippocampal neural representation. *Current Opinion in Neurobiology, 24*, 111–119.

Wills, T. J., Lever, C., Cacucci, F., Burgess, N., & O'Keefe, J. (2005). Attractor dynamics in the hippocampal representation of the local environment. *Science, 308*, 873–876.

Willsey, A. J., & State, M. W. (2015). Autism spectrum disorders: From genes to neurobiology. *Current Opinion in Neurobiology, 30*, 92–99.

Willyard, C. (2014). Heritability: The family roots of obesity. *Nature, 508*. S58–S60.

Wilson, C. R. E., Gaffan, D., Browning, P. G. F., & Baxter, M. G. (2010). Functional localization within the prefrontal cortex: Missing the forest for the trees? *Trends in Neurosciences, 33*, 533–540.

Wilson, M. E., Moore, C. J., Ethun, K. F., & Johnson, Z. P. (2014). Understanding the control of ingestive behavior in primates. *Hormones and Behavior, 66*, 86–94.

Wilson, R. I., & Mainen, Z. F. (2006). Early events in olfactory processing. *Annual Review of Neuroscience, 29*, 163–201.

Wiltstein, S. (1995, October 26). Quarry KO'd by dementia. *Vancouver Sun*, p. 135.

Wilusz, J. E., & Sharp, P. A. (2013). A circuitous route to noncoding RNA. *Science, 340*, 440–441.

Wingfield, A., Tun, P. A., & McCoy, S. L. (2005). Hearing loss in older adulthood: What it is and how it interacts with cognitive performance. *American Psychological Society, 14*, 144–148.

Winter, S. S., Clark, B. J., & Taube, J. S. (2015). Disruption of the head direction cell network impairs the parahippocampal grid cell signal. *Science, 347*, 870–874.

Wirths, O., & Bayer, T. A. (2010). Neuron loss in transgenic mouse models of Alzheimer's disease. *International Journal of Alzheimer's Disease, 2010*, article 723782.

Wiseman, F. K., Al-Janabi, T., Hardy, J., Karmiloff-Smith, A., Nizetic, D., Tybulewicz, V. L., . . . & Strydom, A. (2015). A genetic cause of Alzheimer disease: Mechanistic insights from Down syndrome. *Nature Reviews Neuroscience, 16*, 564–574.

Witte, A. V., Fobker, M., Gellner, R., Knecht, S., & Flöel, A. (2009). Caloric restriction improves memory in elderly humans. *Proceedings of the National Academy of Sciences, USA, 106*, 1255–1260.

Wolf, J. M., Walker, D. A., Cochrane, K. L., & Chen, E. (2007, May). *Parental perceived stress influences inflammatory markers in children with asthma*. Paper delivered at the Western Psychological Association Convention, Vancouver, BC.

Wolgin, D. L., & Jakubow, J. J. (2003). Tolerance to amphetamine hypophagia: A microstructural analysis of licking behavior in the rat. *Behavioral Neuroscience, 117*, 95–104.

Wolpaw, J. R., & Tennissen, A. (2001). Activity-dependent spinal cord plasticity in health and disease. *Annual Review of Neuroscience, 24*, 807–843.

Wolstenholme, J. T., Rissman, E. F., & Bekiranov, S. (2013). Sexual differentiation in the developing mouse brain: Contributions of sex chromosome genes. *Genes, Brain and Behavior, 12*, 166–180.

Wommelsdorf, T., Anton-Erxleben, K., Pieper, F., & Treue, S. (2006). Dynamic shifts of visual receptive fields in cortical area MT by spatial attention. *Nature Neuroscience, 9*, 1156–1160.

Wong, A. C. Y., & Ryan, A. F. (2015). Mechanisms of sensorineural cell damage, death and survival in the cochlea. *Frontiers in Aging Neuroscience, 7*, 58.

Wong, C. C. Y., Caspi, A., Williams, B., Craig, I. W., Houts, R., Ambler, A., Moffitt, T. E., & Mill, J. (2010). A longitudinal study of epigenetic variation in twins. *Epigenetics, 5*, 1–11.

Wong, K. (Feb 2015). Neandertal minds. *Scientific American, 312*, 36–43.

Wong, K. (2005a, February). The littlest human. *Scientific American, 292*, 56–65.

Wong, K. (2005b, June). The morning of the modern mind. *Scientific American, 292*, 86–95.

Wong, K. (2012). First of our kind. Sensational fossils from South Africa spark debate over how we came to be human. *Scientific American, 306*(4), 30–39.

Wong, W. T., & Wong, R. O. L. (2000). Rapid dendritic movements during synapse formation and rearrangement. *Current Opinion in Neurobiology, 10*, 118–124.

Wood, A., Rychlowska, M., Korb, S., & Niedenthal, P. (2016). Fashioning the face: Sensorimotor simulation contributes to facial expression recognition. *Trends in Cognitive Sciences, 20*, 227–240.

Wood, B. (2010). Reconstructing human evolution: Achievements, challenges, and opportunities. *PNAS, 107*, 8902–8909.

Wood, B. (2011). Did early *Homo* migrate "out of" or "in to" Africa? *PNAS, 108*, 10375–10376.

Wood, B. (2014). Welcome to the family. *Scientific American, 311*, 42–47.

Wood, E. R., Mumby, D. G., Pinel, J. P. J., & Phillips, A. G. (1993). Impaired object recognition memory in rats following ischemia-induced damage to the hippocampus. *Behavioral Neuroscience, 107*, 51–62.

Woodruff-Pak, D. S. (1993). Eyeblink classical conditioning in H.M.: Delay and trace paradigms. *Behavioral Neuroscience, 107*, 911–925.

Woods, S. C. (2004). Lessons in the interactions of hormones and ingestive behavior. *Physiology & Behavior, 82*(1), 187–190.

Woods, S. C. (2013). Metabolic signals and food intake. Forty years of progress. *Appetite, 71*, 440–444.

Woods, S. C., & Begg, D. P. (2015). Food for thought: Revisiting the complexity of food intake. *Cell Metabolism, 22*, 348–351.

Woods, S. C., & Begg, D. P. (2016). Regulation of the motivation to eat. *Current Topics in Behavioural Neuroscience, 27*, 15–34.

Woods, S. C., Lotter, E. C., McKay, L. D., & Porte, D., Jr. (1979). Chronic intracerebroventricular infusion of insulin reduces food intake and body weight of baboons. *Nature, 282*, 503–505.

Woods, S. C., Schwartz, M. W., Baskin, D. G., & Seeley, R. J. (2000). Food intake and the regulation of body weight. *Annual Review of Neuroscience, 51*, 255–277.

Woodson, J. C., & Gorski, R. A. (2000). Structural sex differences in the mammalian brain: Reconsidering the male/female dichotomy. In A. Matsumoto (Ed.), *Sexual differentiation of the brain* (pp. 229–255). Boca Raton, FL: CRC Press.

Woolf, S. H. (2008). The meaning of translational research and why it matters. *JAMA, 299*, 211–213.

World Health Organization. (2015, March). Deafness and hearing loss. Retrieved from http://www.who.int/mediacentre/factsheets/fs300/en/

Worth, P. F. (2013). How to treat Parkinson's disease in 2013. *Clinical Medicine, 13*, 93–96.

Wu, M. V., & Shah, N. M. (2011). Control of masculinization of the brain and behavior. *Current Opinion in Neurobiology, 21*, 116–123.

Wu, N., Yu, A.-B., Zhu, H.-B., & Lin, X-K. (2012). Effective silencing of Sry gene with RNA interference in developing mouse embryos resulted in feminization of XY gonad. *Journal of Biomedicine and Biotechnology, 2012*, 343891.

Wurtz, R. H., McAlonan, K., Cavanaugh, J., & Berman, R. A. (2011). Thalamic pathways for active vision. *Trends in Cognitive Sciences, 15*, 177–184.

Wüst, S., Kasten, E., & Sabel, S. A. (2002). Blindsight after optic nerve injury indicates functionality of spared fibers. *Journal of Cognitive Neuroscience, 14*, 243–253.

Wylie, K., Rees, M., Hackett, G., Anderson, R., Bouloux, P.-M., . . . & Wu, F. (2010). Androgens, health and sexuality in women and men. *Maturitas, 67*, 275–289.

Xie, L., Kang, H., Xu, Q., Chen, M. J., Liao, Y., . . . & Nedergard, M. (2013). Sleep drives metabolite clearance from the adult brain. *Science, 342*, 373–377.

Xu, D., Bureau, Y., McIntyre, D. C., Nicholson, D. W., Liston, P., Zhu, Y., . . . & Robertson, G. S. (1999). Attenuation of ischemia-induced cellular and behavioral deficits by X chromosome–linked inhibitor of apoptosis protein overexpression in the rat hippocampus. *Journal of Neuroscience, 19*, 5026–5033.

Yager, J. Y., Wright, S., Armstrong, E. A., Jahraus, C. M., & Saucier, D. M. (2006). The influence of aging on recovery following ischemic brain damage. *Behavioural Brain Research, 173*, 171–180.

Yamamoto, T., Nakayama, K., Hirano, H., Tomonagai, T., Ishihama, Y., Yamada, T., . . . & Goshima, N. (2013). Integrated view of the human x-centric proteome project. *Journal of Proteome Research, 12*, 58–61.

Yang, C. F., & Shah, N. M. (2014). Representing sex in the brain, one module at a time. *Neuron, 82*, 261–278.

Yang, S. H., Liu, R., Wu, S. S., & Simpkins, J. W. (2003). The use of estrogens and related compounds in the treatment of damage from cerebral ischemia. *Annals of the New York Academy of Sciences, 1007*, 101–107.

Yap, Q. J., Teh, I., Fusar-Poli, P., Sum, M. Y., Kuswanto, C. & Sim, K. (2013). Tracking cerebral white matter changes across the lifespan: Insights from diffusion tensor imaging studies. *Journal of Neural Transmission, 120*, 1369–1395.

Yarmolinsky, D. A., Zuker, C. S., & Ryba, N. J. P. (2009). Common sense about taste: From mammals to insects. *Cell, 139*, 234–244.

Yartsev, M. M., & Ulanovsky, N. (2013). *Science, 340*, 367–372.

Yasuda, A., Tsuji, O., Shibata, S., Nori, S., Takano, M., Kobayashi, Y., Takahashi, Y., Fujiyoshi, K., Hara, C. M., Miyawaki, A., Okano, H. J., Nakamura, M., & Okano, H. (2011). Significance of remyelination by neural stem/progenitor cells transplanted into the injured spinal cord. *Stem Cells, 29*, 1983–1994.

Yau, J. M., Connor, C. E., & Hsiao, S. S. (2013). Representation of tactile curvature in macaque somatosensory area 2. *Journal of Neurophysiology, 109*, 2999–3012.

Yavari, A. (2009). Abuse of anabolic androgenic steroids. *Journal of Stress Physiology and Biochemistry, 5*, 22–32.

Yesalis, C. E., & Bahrke, M. S. (2005). Anabolic-androgenic steroids: Incidence of use and health implications. *President's Council on Physical Fitness and Sports Research Digest, 5*, 1–6.

Yetish, G., Kaplan, H., Gurven, M., Wood, B., Pontzer, H., . . . & Siegel, J. M. (2015). Natural sleep and its seasonal variations in three pre-industrial societies. *Current Biology, 25*, 2862–2868.

Yildiz, A., Vieta, E., Leucht, S., & Baldessarini, R. J. (2011). Efficacy of antimanic treatments: Meta-analysis of randomized, controlled trials. *Neuropsychopharmacology, 36*, 375–389.

Yonelinas, A. P., & Ritchey, M. (2015). The slow forgetting of emotional episodic memories: An emotional binding account. *Trends in Cognitive Sciences, 19*, 259–267.

Yoon, B.-E., & Lee, C. J. (2014). GABA as a rising gliotransmitter. *Frontiers in Neural Circuits, 8*, 141.

Yoon, J. M. D., & Vouloumanos, A. (2014). When and how does autism begin? *Trends in Cognitive Sciences, 18*, 272–273.

Youngstedt, S. D., & Kline, C. E. (2006). Epidemiology of exercise and sleep. *Sleep and Biological Rhythms, 4*, 215–221.

Youngstedt, S. D., & Kripke, D. F. (2004). Long sleep and mortality: Rationale for sleep restriction. *Sleep Medicine Reviews, 8*, 159–174.

Yournagov, G., Smith, K. G., Fridriksson, J., & Rorden, C. (2015). Predicting aphasia type from brain damage measured with structural MRI. *Cortex, 73*, 203–215.

Yu, J.-T., Tan, L., & Hardy, J. (2014). Apolipoprotein E in Alzheimer's disease: An update. *Annual Review of Neuroscience, 37*, 79–100.

Yücel, M., Solowij, N., Respondek, C., Whittle, S., Fornito, A., Pantelis, C., & Lubman, D. I. (2008). Regional brain abnormalities associated with long-term heavy cannabis use. *Archives of General Psychiatry, 65*, 694–701.

Yuste, R., & Church, G. M. (2014). The new century of the brain. *Scientific American, 310*, 38–45.

Zachariou, V., Klatzky, R., & Behrmann, M. (2014). Ventral and dorsal visual stream contributions to the perception of object shape and object location. *Journal of Cognitive Neuroscience, 26*, 189–209.

Zahr, N. M., Kaufman, K. L., & Harper, C. G. (2011). Clinical and pathological features of alcohol-related brain damage. *Nature Reviews Neurology, 7*, 284–294.

Zahs, K. R., & Ashe, K. H. (2010). "Too much good news"—are Alzheimer mouse models trying to tell us how to prevent, not cure, Alzheimer's disease? *Trends in Neurosciences, 33*, 381–389.

Zaidel, D. W. (2013). Split-brain, the right hemisphere, and art: Fact and fiction. *Progress in Brain Research, 204*, 3–17.

Zaidel, E. (1975). A technique for presenting lateralized visual input with prolonged exposure. *Vision Research, 15*, 283–289.

Zaidi, Z. F. (2010). Gender differences in human brain: A review. *The Open Anatomy Journal, 2*, 37–55.

Zangwill, O. L. (1975). Excision of Broca's area without persistent aphasia. In K. J. Zulch, O. Creutzfeldt, & G. C. Galbraith (Eds.), *Cerebral localization* (pp. 258–263). New York, NY: Springer-Verlag.

Zatorre, R. J., Fields, R. D., & Johansen-Berg, H. (2012). Plasticity in gray and white: Neuroimaging changes in brain structure during learning. *Nature Neuroscience, 15*, 528–536.

Zeidán-Chuliá, F., Salmina, A. B., Malinovskaya, N. A., Noda, M., Verkhratsky, A., & Moreira, J. C. F. (2014). The glial perspective of autism spectrum disorders. *Neuroscience and Biobehavioral Reviews, 38*, 160–172.

Zeigler, T. E. (2007). Female sexual motivation during non-fertile periods: A primate phenomenon. *Hormones and Behavior, 51*, 1–2.

Zeki, S. (2015). Area V5—a microcosm of the visual brain. *Frontiers in Integrative Neuroscience, 9*, 21.

Zeki, S. M. (1993a). *A vision of the brain*. Oxford, England: Blackwell Scientific.

Zelinski, E. L., Deibel, S.-J., & McDonald, R. J. (2014). The trouble with circadian clock dysfunction: Multiple deleterious effects on the brain and body. *Neuroscience & Biobehavioral Reviews, 40*, 80–101.

Zembrzycki, A., Chou, S.-J., Ashery-Padan, R., Stoykova, A., & O'Leary, D. D. M. (2013). Sensory cortex limits cortical maps and drives top-down plasticity in thalamocortical circuits. *Nature Neuroscience, 8*, 1060–1068.

Zhang, D., & Raichle, M. E. (2010). Disease and the brain's dark energy. *Nature Reviews Neurology, 6*, 15–28.

Zhang, D., Xia, H., Xu, L., Zhang, C., Yao, W., Wang, Y., Ren, J., Wu, J., Tian, Y., Liu, W., & Wang, X. (2012). Neuroprotective effects of 17beta-estradiol associate with KATP in rat brain. *Neuroreport, 23*, 952–957.

Zhang, J., Aggarwal, M., & Mori, S. (2012). Structural insights into the rodent CNS via diffusion tensor imaging. *Trends in Neurosciences, 35*, 412–421.

Zhang, N., Yacoub, E., Zhu, X.-H., Ugurbil, K., & Chen, W. (2009). Linearity of blood-oxygenation-level dependent signal at microvasculature. *NeuroImage, 48*, 313–318.

Zhang, T.-Y., & Meaney, M. J. (2010). Epigenetics and the environmental regulation of the genome and its function. *Annual Review of Psychology, 61*, 439–466.

Zhang, T. Y., Labonté, B., Wen, X. L., Turecki, G., & Meaney, M. J. (2013). Epigenetic mechanisms for the early environmental regulation of hippocampal glucocorticoid receptor gene expression in rodents and humans. *Neuropsychopharmacology, 38*(1), 111–123.

Zhang, Y., Cudmore, R. H., Lin, D. T., Linden, D. J., & Huganir, R. L. (2015). Visualization of NMDA receptor-dependent AMPA receptor synaptic plasticity in vivo. *Nature Neuroscience, 18*, 402–407.

Zhao, D., Hopkins, W. D., & Li, B. (2012). Handedness in nature: First evidence on manual laterality on bimanual coordinated tube task in wild primates. *American Journal of Physical Anthropology, 148*, 36–44.

Zhao, L., Woody, S. K., & Chhibber, A. (2015). Estrogen receptor β in Alzheimer's disease: From mechanisms to therapeutics. *Ageing Research Reviews, 24*, 178–190.

Zhou, W., & Yuan, J. (2014). Necroptosis in health and diseases. *Seminars in Cell and Developmental Biology, 35*, 14–23.

Zhu, J. M., Zhao, Y. Y., Chen, S. D., Zhang, W. H., Lou, L., & Jin, X. (2011). Functional recovery after transplantation of neural stem cells modified by brain-derived neurotrophic factor in rats with cerebral ischaemia. *Journal of International Medical Research, 39*, 488–498.

Zhuo, M. (2008). Cortical excitation and chronic pain. *Trends in Neurosciences, 31*, 199–207.

Ziauddeen, H., Farooqi, I. S., & Fletcher, P. C. (2012). Obesity and the brain: How convincing is the addiction model? *Nature Reviews Neuroscience, 13*, 279–286.

Zilles, K., & Amunts, K. (2010). Centenary of Brodmann's map—conception and fate. *Nature Reviews Neuroscience, 11*, 139–145.

Zilles, K., Palermo-Gallagher, N., & Amunts, K. (2013). Development of cortical folding during evolution and ontogeny. *Trends in Neurosciences, 36*, 275–284.

Zimmer, C. (2011). 100 trillion connections. *Scientific American, 304*(1), 58–63.

Zimmerman, A., Bai, L., & Ginty, D. D. (2014). The gentle touch receptors of mammalian skin. *Science, 346*, 950–954.

Zimmerman, J. E., Naidoo, N., Raizen, D. M., & Pack, A. I. (2008). Conservation of sleep: Insights from non-mammalian model systems. *Trends in Neurosciences, 31*, 371–376.

Zimmerman, J. L. (2012). Cocaine intoxication. *Critical Care Clinics, 28*, 517–526.

Zirnsak, M., & Moore, T. (2014). Saccades and shifting receptive fields: Anticipating consequences or selecting targets? *Trends in Cognitive Sciences, 18*, 621–628.

Zivin, J. A. (2000). Understanding clinical trials. *Scientific American, 282*, 69–75.

Zlokovic, B. V. (2011). Neurovascular pathways to neurodegeneration in Alzheimer's disease and other disorders. *Nature Reviews Neuroscience, 12*, 723–738.

Zoghbi, H. Y. (2003). Postnatal neurodevelopmental disorders: Meeting at the synapse? *Science, 302*, 826–830.

Zola-Morgan, S., Squire, L. R., & Amaral, D. G. (1986). Human amnesia and the medial temporal region: Enduring memory impairment following a bilateral lesion limited to field CA1 of the hippocampus. *Journal of Neuroscience, 6*, 2950–2967.

Zola-Morgan, S., Squire, L. R., & Mishkin, M. (1982). The neuroanatomy of amnesia: Amygdala-hippocampus versus temporal stem. *Science, 218*, 1337–1339.

Zola-Morgan, S., Squire, L. R., Rempel, N. L., Clower, R. P., & Amaral, D. G. (1992). Enduring memory impairment in monkeys after ischemic damage to the hippocampus. *Journal of Neuroscience, 12*, 2582–2596.

Zong, C., Lu, S., Chapman, A. R., & Xie, X. S. (2012). Genome-wide detection of single-nucleotide and copy-number variations of a single human cell. *Science, 338*, 1622–1626.

Zou, Y. (2004). Wnt signaling in axon guidance. *Trends in Neurosciences, 27*, 529–532.

Zuloaga, D. G., Puts, D. A., Jordan, C. L., & Breedlove, S. M. (2008). The role of androgen receptors in the masculinization of brain and behavior: What we've learned from the testicular feminization mutation. *Hormones and Behavior, 53*, 613–626.

Zwar, N. A., Mendelsohn, C. P., & Richmond, R. L. (2014). Supporting smoking cessation. *British Medical Journal, 348*, f7535.

Credits

Text Credits

Page 27: Based on "The Case of Jimmie G., the Man Frozen in Time," Simon & Schuster, Inc. and Pan Macmillan, London from The Man Who Mistook His Wife for a Hat and Other Clinical Tales by Oliver Sacks. Copyright © 1970, 1981, 1983, 1984, 1986 by Oliver Sacks.; **p. 29:** Pearson Education; **p. 30:** Ulrich, R. E. (1991). Commentary: Animal rights, animal wrongs and the question of balance. Psychological Science, 2, 197–201.; **p. 32:** Lester, G. L. L., & Gorzalka, B. B. (1988). Effect of novel and familiar mating partners on the duration of sexual receptivity in the female hamster. Behavioral and Neural Biology, 49, 398–405.; **p. 34-35:** Based on The Case of Mr. R., the Brain-Damaged Student Who Switched to Architecture" from Fundamentals of Human Neuropsychology, 3/e, by Bryan Kolb and Ian Q. Whishaw.; **p. 35:** UHB Trust/Getty Images; **p. 36:** Dewsbury, D. A. (1991). Psychobiology. American Psychologist, 46, 198–205.; **p. 40-41:** Valenstein, E. S. (1973). Brain control. New York, NY: John Wiley & Sons. ; **p. 46:** Watson, 1930, pp. 127–128.; **p. 46:** Source P.I. Corsi. Oxford University Press. 1991; **p. 47:** Based on "The Case of the Man Who Fell Out of Bed," Simon & Schuster, Inc. and Pan Macmillan, London from The Man Who Mistook His Wife for a Hat and Other Clinical Tales by Oliver Sacks. Copyright © 1970, 1981, 1983, 1984, 1986 by Oliver Sacks.; **p. 47:** "Toward a Comparative Psychology of Mind" by G. G. Gallup, Jr., American Journal of Primatology 2:237–248, 1983. Copyright © 1983 John Wiley & Sons, Inc.; **p. 50:** Quammen, D. (2004, May). Was Darwin wrong? No. The evidence for evolution is overwhelming. National Geographic, 206, 2–35.; **p. 51:** Based on McCann, T. S. (1981). Aggression and sexual activity of male southern elephant seals, Mirounga leonina. Journal of Zoology, 195, 295–310; **p. 59:** Based on Buss, D. M. (1992). Mate preference mechanisms: Consequences for partner choice and intrasexual competition. In J. M. Barkow, L. Cosmides, & J. Tooby (Eds.), The adapted mind (pp. 273–289). New York, NY: Oxford University Press; **p. 69:** Data from Cooper, R. M., & Zubek, J. P. (1958). Effects of enriched and restricted early environments on the learning ability of bright and dull rats. Canadian Journal of Psychology, 12, 159–164; **p. 69:** Data from Cooper, R. M., & Zubek, J. P. (1958). Effects of enriched and restricted early environments on the learning ability of bright and dull rats. Canadian Journal of Psychology, 12, 159–164.; **p. 96:** Based on Rakic, P. (1979). Genetic and epigenetic determinants of local neuronal circuits in the mammalian central nervous system. In F. O. Schmitt & F. G. Worden (Eds.), The neurosciences: Fourth study program. Cambridge, MA: MIT Press.; **p. 102:** Based on NEWTON'S MADNESS by Harold Klawans (Harper & Row 1990). Reprinted by permission of Jet Literary Associates, Inc; **p. 143:** Jeff Lichtman, MD,PhD, Jeremy R. Knowles, Professor of Molecular and Cellular Biology and Santiago Ramon y Cajal, Professor of Arts and Sciences, Harvard University; **p. 160:** Based on Lamb, Collin, & Pugh, 2007.; **p. 165:** Based on Lindsay & Norman, 1977; **p. 169:** Based on Netter, 1962; **p. 171:** Based on Ratliff, 1972; **p. 181:** Based on Teuber, H.-L., Battersby, W. S., & Bender, M. B. (1960). Recovery of function after brain injury in man. In Outcomes of severe damage to the nervous system. CIBA Foundation Symposium 34. Amsterdam, Netherlands: Elsevier North-Holland.; **p. 181:** Lashley, 1941, p. 362; **p. 182:** Weiskrantz, L., Warrington, E. K., Sanders, M. D., & Marshall, J. (1974). Visual capacity in the hemianopic field following a restricted occipital ablation. Brain, 97, 709–728.; **p. 184:** Goodale, M. A. (2004). Perceiving the world and grasping it: Dissociations between conscious and unconscious visual processing. In M. Gazzaniga (Ed.), The cognitive neurosciences (pp. 1183–1196). Cambridge, MA: MIT Press.; **p. 191:** Williams, M. (1970). Brain damage and the mind. Baltimore, MD: Penguin Books.; **p. 192:** * Based on The Man Who Mistook His Wife for a Hat and Other Clinical Tales by Oliver Sacks. Copyright © 1970, 1981, 1983, 1984, 1986 by Oliver Sacks.; **p. 204:** Based on Servos et al., 1999; **p. 205:** Based on NEWTON'S MADNESS by Harold Klawans (Harper & Row 1990).; **p. 215:** Dr. James T. Enns; **p. 221:** Rothwell, J. C., Traub, M. M., Day, B. L., Obeso, J. A., Thomas, P. K., & Marsden, C. D. (1982). Manual motor performance in a deafferented man. Brain, 105, 515–542.; **p. 227:** Based on Penfield & Rasmussen, 1950.; **p. 242:** Based on Jenkins et al., 1994; **p. 246-247:** (c) Pearson; **p. 249:** Based on Cowan, 1979.; **p. 257:** Based on Antonini & Stryker, 1993; **p. 263:** Finn.

"Different Minds", Discover. June 1991.; **p. 272:** Junior Seau: An Illustrative Case of Chronic Traumatic Encephalopathy and Update on Chronic Sports-Related Head Injury. Tej D. Azad, Amy Li, Arjun V. Pendharkar, Anand Veeravagu, Gerald A. Gran. World Neuroscience. February 2016 Volume 86, Pages 539.e11–515.e16. Elsevier.; **p. 275:** Lennox, W. G. (1960). Epilepsy and related disorders. Boston, MA: Little, Brown.; **p. 279:** Goedert, M. (1993). Tau protein and the neurofibrillary pathology of Alzheimer's disease. Trends in Neurosciences, 16, 460–465. and Selkoe, D. J. (1991, November). Amyloid protein and Alzheimer's. Scientific American, 265, 68–78.; **p. 282:** Langston, J. W. (1985). MPTP and Parkinson's disease. Trends in Neurosciences, 8, 79–83.; **p. 286:** Based on Sanes et al., 1990; **p. 289:** Klawans, H. L. (1990). Newton's madness: Further tales of clinical neurology. New York: Harper & Row.; **p. 292:** Based on Ramachandran & Blakeslee, 1998; **p. 292:** Based on Ramachandran & Blakeslee, 1998.; **p. 295:** Marc Grimberg/Getty Images; **p. 299:** Milner, B. (1965). Memory disturbances after bilateral hippocampal lesions. In P. Milner & S. Glickman (Eds.), Cognitive processes and the brain (pp. 128–129). Princeton, NJ: D. Van Nostrand.; **p. 301:** Tulving, E. (2002). Episodic memory: From mind to brain. Annual Review of Neuroscience, 53, 1–25.; **p. 302:** Zola-Morgan, S., Squire, L. R., & Amaral, D. G. (1986). Human amnesia and the medial temporal region: Enduring memory impairment following a bilateral lesion limited to field CA1 of the hippocampus. Journal of Neuroscience, 6, 2950–2967.; **p. 303:** Teuber, H.-L., Milner, B., & Vaughan, H. G., Jr. (1968). Persistent anterograde amnesia after stab wound of the basal brain. Neuropsychologia, 6, 267–282; **p. 306:** Squire, L. R., Slater, P. C., & Chace, P. M. (1975). Retrograde amnesia: Temporal gradient in very long term memory following electroconvulsive therapy. Science, 187, 77–79; **p. 307:** Based on Squire & Zola-Morgan, 1991; **p. 311:** Based on Zola-Morgan, S., Squire, L. R., & Amaral, D. G. (1986). Human amnesia and the medial temporal region: Enduring memory impairment following a bilateral lesion limited to field CA1 of the hippocampus. Journal of Neuroscience, 6, 2950–2967; Mumby, Pinel, & Wood, 1989 (rats).; **p. 320:** Traces courtesy of Michael Corcoran, Department of Psychology, University of Saskatchewan; **p. 328:** Rozin, P., Dow, S., Moscovitch, M., & Rajaram, S. (1998). What causes humans to begin and end a meal? A role for memory for what has been eaten, as evidenced by a study of multiple meal eating in amnesic patients. Psychological Science, 9, 392–396.; **p. 338:** Based on Teitelbaum, P. (1961). Disturbances in feeding and drinking behavior after hypothalamic lesions. In M. R. Jones (Ed.), Nebraska symposium on motivation (pp. 63–93). Lincoln: University of Nebraska Press.; **p. 341:** Martin, A., State, M., Koenig, K., Schultz, R., Dykens, E. M., Cassidy, S. B., & Leckman, J. F. (1998). Prader-Willi syndrome. American Journal of Psychiatry, 155, 1265–1272.; **p. 350:** Farooqi, I. S., Jebb, S. A., Langmack, G., Lawrence, E., Cheetham, C. H., Prentice, A. M., O'Rahilly, S. (1999). Effects of recombinant leptin therapy in a child with congenital leptin deficiency. New England Journal of Medicine, 341, 879–884.; **p. 352:** Keys, A., Broz, J., Henschel, A., Mickelsen, O., & Taylor H. L. (1950). The biology of human starvation. Minneapolis: University of Minnesota Press.; **p. 370:** Money, J., & Ehrhardt, A. A. (1972). Man & woman, boy & girl. Baltimore, MD: Johns Hopkins University Press.; **p. 373:** de Kruif, P. (1945). The male hormone. New York, NY: Harcourt, Brace.; **p. 374:** Based on Grunt, J. A., & Young, W. C. (1952). Differential reactivity of individuals and the response of the male guinea pig to testosterone propionate. Endocrinology, 51, 237–248; **p. 388:** Dement, W. C., & Wolpert, E. A. (1958). The relation of eye movements, body motility and external stimuli to dream content. Journal of Experimental Psychology, 55, 543–553.; **p. 391:** Kleitman N. Sleep and Wakefulness. Chicago, IL: University of Chicago Press; 1963.; **p. 391:** Dement, W. C. (1978). Some must watch while some must sleep. New York, NY: Norton.; **p. 393:** Based on Rechtschaffen, A., Gilliland, M. A., Bergmann, B. M., & Winter, J. B. (1983). Physiological correlates of prolonged sleep deprivation in rats. Science, 221, 182–184.; **p. 397:** (Based on Wever, R. A. (1979). The circadian system of man. SeewiesenAndechs, Germany: Max-Planck-Institut für Verhaltensphysiologie.); **p. 400:** Saper, C. B., Scammell, T. E., & Lu, J. (2005). Hypothalamic regulation of sleep and circadian rhythms. Nature, 437, 1257–1263.; **p. 402:** Vertes, R. P. (1983). Brainstem control of the events of REM sleep. Progress in Neurobiology, 22, 241–288; **p. 405:** Dement, W. C. (1978). Some must watch while some must sleep. New York, NY: Norton.; **p. 407:** Schenck, C. H., Bundlie, S. R., Ettinger, M. G., & Mahowald, M. W. (1986). Chronic behavioral disorders of human REM sleep: A new category of parasomnia. Sleep, 9, 293–308; **p. 410:** (Vertes, R. P. (1983). Brainstem control of the events of REM sleep. Progress in Neurobiology, 22, 241–288.; **p. 418:** Based on Pinel, J. P. J., Mana, M. J., & Kim, C. K. (1989). Effect-dependent tolerance to ethanol's anticonvulsant effect on kindled seizures. In R. J. Porter, R. H. Mattson, J. A. Cramer, & I. Diamond (Eds.), Alcohol and seizures: Basic mechanisms and clinical implications (pp. 139–149). Philadelphia, PA: F. A. Davis.; **p. 419:** Based on Crowell, C. R., Hinson, R. E., & Siegel, S. (1981). The role of conditional drug responses in tolerance to the hypothermic effects of ethanol. Psychopharmacology, 73, 51–54.; **p. 421:** Brecher, E. M. (1972). Licit and illicit drugs. Boston, MA: Little, Brown.; **p. 424:** The Schafer Commision, FKA, National Commission on Marijuana and Drug Abuse, 1972, p. 92; **p. 427:** McKim, W. A. (1986). Drugs and behavior: An introduction to behavioral pharmacology. Englewood Cliffs, NJ: Prentice-Hall.; **p. 428:** McKim, W. A. (1986). Drugs and behavior: An introduction to behavioral pharmacology. Englewood Cliffs, NJ: Prentice-Hall.; **p. 429:** Based on the National Survey on Drug Use and Health, 2011. US Department of Health and Human Services; **p. 429:** Student Excerpt. Anonymous; **p. 430:** Julien, R. M. (1981). A primer of drug action. San Francisco, CA: W. H. Freeman.; **p. 432:** Based on Klivington, K. A. (Ed.). (1992). Gehirn und Geist. Heidelberg, Germany: Spektrum Akademischer Verlag.; **p. 436:** Data redrawn from Pickens et al. (2011).; **p. 451:** Joseph, R. (1988). Dual mental functioning in a split-brain patient. Journal of Clinical Psychology, 44, 771–779.; **p. 456:** Based on Schlaug, G., Jäncke, L., Huang, Y., & Steinmetz, H. (1995). In vivo evidence of structural brain asymmetry in musicians. Science, 267, 699–701; **p. 457:** Corina, D. P., Poizner, H., Bellugi, U., Feinberg, T., Dowd, D., & O'Grady-Batch, L. (1992). Dissociation between linguistic and non-linguistic gestural systems: A case for compositionality. Brain and Language, 43, 414–447.; **p. 463:** Based on Mohr, J. P. (1976). Broca's area and Broca's aphasia. In H. Whitaker & H. A. Whitaker (Eds.), Studies in neurolinguistics (Vol. 1, pp. 225–259). New York, NY: Academic Press; **p. 464:** Based on Penfield, W., & Roberts, L. (1959). Speech and brain mechanisms. Princeton, NJ: Princeton University Press.; **p. 465, 466:** Based on Penfield & Roberts,, Speech and Brain Mechanisms 1959. Princeton University Press.; **p. 471:** Patterson, Vargha-Khadem, & Polkey, 1989 Reading with one hemisphere. Brain, A Journal of Neurology. 112, 39-63; **p. 475:** Based on Damasio, H., Grabowski, T., Frank, R., Galaburda, A. M., & Damasio, A. R. (1994). The return of Phineas Gage: Clues about the brain from the skull of a famous patient. Science, 264, 1102–1105; **p. 480:** Generously supplied by Kyung Jae Lee and Stephen DiPaola of the iViz-Lab, Simon Fraser University. The expressions were created in video game character style using FaceFx 3D software, which allows DiPaola and Lee to create and control facial expressions of emotion in stills and animated sequences; see ivizlab.sfu.ca; **p. 480:** Based on Rutledge, L. L., & Hupka, R. B. (1985). The facial feedback hypothesis: Methodological concerns and new supporting evidence. Motivation and Emotion, 9, 219–240; **p. 499:** Meyer, R. G., & Salmon, P. (1988). Abnormal psychology (2nd ed.). Boston, MA: Allyn & Bacon.; **p. 503:** Based on Snyder, S. H. (1978). Neuroleptic drugs and neurotransmitter receptors. Journal of Clinical and Experimental Psychiatry, 133, 21–31.; **p. 517:** Based on Himle, M.B., & Woods, D.W., 2005 An Experimental Evaluation of Tic Suppression and the Tic Rebound Effect. Behaviour Research and Therapy, 43, 1443-1451.; **p. 518:** Hollenbeck, PJ. Insight and hindsight into Tourette syndrome; Advances in Neurology, 2001;85:363-7 New York, Raven Press.; **p. 519:** Based on Zivin, J. A. (2000, April). Understanding clinical trials. Scientific American, 282, 69–75.

Photo Credits

Page 25: Photobac/Shutterstock; **p. 26:** UHB Trust/Getty Images; **p. 31:** Bettmann/Getty Images; **p. 36:** Todd C. Handy; **p. 44:** Corbis/SuperStock; **p. 48:** The Povinelli Group LLC; **p. 51:** Francois Gohier/Science Source; **p. 52:** Beth Rooney; **p. 53:** Kevin Schafer/Photolibrary/Getty Images; **p. 53:** Vladimir Sazonov/Shutterstock; **p. 53:** Anatoliy Lukich/Shutterstock; **p. 53:** Michael Krabs/Alamy; **p. 53:** Daniel Frauchiger, Switzerland/Flickr/Getty Images; **p. 54:** Lealisa Westerhoff/AFP/Getty Images; **p. 55:** John Reader/Science Source; **p. 58:** Nature Picture Library/Alamy Stock Photo; **p. 51:** David M. Phillips/Science Source; **p. 71:** Arturo Alvarez-Buylla; **p. 74:** David Blackman/Everett Collection; **p. 76:** Braxton Bruce Photography/Getty Images; **p. 86:** T. Chan Ling; **p. 87:** Martin M. Rotker/Science source; **p. 87:** Dr. Brian Christie; **p. 87:** OMIKRON/Science Source; **p. 99:** National Institute of Mental Health; **p. 99:** doc-stock/Alamy; **p. 101:** KTSDesign/Science Photo Library/Getty Images; **p. 114:** Don W. Fawcett/Science Source; **p. 119:** Dr. David Jacobowitz/Science Photo Library/Getty Images; **p. 121:** Image Source/Corbis; **p. 124:** Wallace George/Corbis; **p. 126:** The Photolibrary Wales/Alamy Stock Photo; **p. 129:** CNRI/Science Source; **p. 130:** Science Source; **p. 131:** Scott Camazine/Science Source; **p. 131:** Simon Fraser/Science Source; **p. 132:** Kent Kiehl and Peter Liddle, University of British Columbia; **p. 132:** Simon Fraser/Science Source; **p. 138:** Courtesy of Richard Mooney, Dept. of Neurosciences, University of Toledo College of Medicine; **p. 141:** Rod Cooper, University of Calgary; **p. 141:** Courtesy of Mark Klitenick and Chris Fibiger, Department of Psychiatry, University of British Columbia; **p. 142:** Chris Fibiger/University of British Columbia ; **p. 143:** Photo of *Caenorhabditis elegans* from the cover of Science Vol. 263, no. 5148, 11 February 1994. Photo: Martin Chalfie. Reprinted with permission from AAAS.; **p. 145:** PET scans courtesy of Marcus Raichle, Mallinckrodt Institute of Radiology, Washington University Medical Center; **p. 153:** Dr. John Pinel; **p. 153:** Dr. John Pinel; **p. 153:** Dr. John Pinel; **p. 153:** Dr. John Pinel; **p. 156:** IndiaPicture/Alamy; **p. 160:** Amana Images inc./Alamy; **p. 161:** Hemis/Alamy Stock Photo; **p. 161:** Duncan Shaw/Science Source; **p. 161:** C.K. Lorenz/Science Source; **p. 161:** Nigel J. Dennis/Science Source; **p. 161:** Cyril Laubscher/DK Images; **p. 161:** Colin Varndell/Nature Picture Library; **p. 163:** Ralph Eagle/Science Source; **p. 164:** Ralph C. Eagle, Jr./Science Source; **p. 189:** Fuse /Getty Images; **p. 199:** AJPhoto/Science Source; **p. 199:** Gene J. Puskar/AP Images; **p. 204:** Kateland Photo; **p. 207:** Rex Features/AP Images; **p. 211:** OMIKRON/Photo Researchers, Inc./Science Source; **p. 215:** Dr. James T. Enns; **p. 218:** Sean Sprague/The Image Works; **p. 234:** CNRI/Photo Researchers/Science Source; **p. 245:** Exactostock/Superstock; **p. 246:** Doug Goodman/Science Source; **p. 251:** Courtesy of Naweed I. Syed, Ph.D., Departments of Anatomy and Medical Physiology, the University of Calgary; **p. 252:** Tom Wang/Shutterstock; **p. 259:** Dr. Brian Christie; **p. 266:** PHANIE AGENCY/Science Source; **p. 268:** NEIL BORDEN/Living Art Enterprises/Science Source; **p. 269:** SMC Images/Getty Images; **p. 269:** Dr. John Pinel; **p. 270:** Science Photo Library/Alamy Stock Photo; **p. 272:** Scott Camazine/Alamy; **p. 272:** epa european pressphoto agency b.v./Alamy Stock Photo; **p. 288:** Dr. Brian Christie; **p. 291:** Carolyn A. McKeone/Science Source; **p. 305:** Craig Durling/ZUMA Wire/Alamy Live News; **p. 314:** Alex Fieldhouse/Alamy Stock Photo; **p. 315:** WARNER BROS. PICTURES /Album/Newscom; **p. 326:** Shutterstock /g-stockstudio; **p. 336:** Thomas Barwick /Getty Images; **p. 336:** Tooga/Getty Images; **p. 336:** photographer and designer /Getty Images; **p. 349:** The Jackson Laboratory, Bar Harbor, Maine; **p. 383:** xPACIFICA/Getty Images; **p. 386:** Photo Researchers, Inc.; **p. 388:** Radius/SuperStock; **p. 389:** paul prescott /Shutterstock; **p. 390:** iStockphoto/ThinkStock/Getty; **p. 391:** Reuters; **p. 406:** tab62/Fotolia; **p. 413:** Exactostock/SuperStock; **p. 420:** Angela Hampton Picture Library/Alamy Stock Photo; **p. 422:** Marcos Mesa Sam Wordley /Shutterstock; **p. 425:** Jan Mika /model released people collection /Alamy; **p. 426:** ejwhite/Shutterstock; **p. 440:** Shutterstock /adriaticfoto; **p. 450:** EDHAR/Shutterstock; **p. 450:** Jason Stitt/Shutterstock; **p. 451:** eranicle/Fotolia; **p. 456:** Stanimir G.Stoev /Shutterstock; **p.458:** Shutterstock; **p.473:** Mike Powell/Getty Images; **p. 475:** Patrick Landmann /Science Source; **p. 481:** Reproduced with permission of Jessica Tracy, Department of Psychology, University of British Columbia; **p. 486:** From Carr et al., 2003, Neural Mechanisms of Empathy, 100, pgs. 5497-5502. Figure 1 on page 574. Copyright (2003) National Academy of Sciences, U.S.A.; **p. 487:** Iowa Neurological Patient Registry at the University of Iowa; **p. 489:** (Right-hand image from ScienceSource/Getty Images.); **p. 489:** 17.12 Leonardo da Vinci, "Mona Lisa"; **p. 492:** Eye of Science /Science Source; **p. 497:** Matthieu Spohn/ès/Corbis; **p. 504:** National Institute of Mental Health; **p. 505:** From Thompson et al., 2001, National Academy of Sciences, 98, pgs. 11650-11655. Figure 1 on page 11675. Copyright (2001) National Academy of Sciences, U.S.A.; **p. 509:** Pearson Education; **p. 511:** St. Jude Medical, Inc.; **p. 517:** Shaun Clark/Getty Images

Name Index

Porras, G., 283
Porreca, F., 206, 207
Porter, R. J., 231, 418
Posner, M. I., 28, 149, 215
Post, R. M., 512
Postle, B. R., 222, 304, 317
Potenza, M., 435
Potts, R., 53
Poucet, B., 313
Powell, W. T., 66
Prabhakaran, S., 269
Prabhavalkar, K. S., 512, 513
Prat, A., 86
Prather, J. F., 71
Prescott, E., 421
Price, C. J., 467, 470
Price, J. L., 513
Price, T. S., 36
Pringle, H., 54, 491
Pringsheim, T., 276
Pritchard, J. K., 50
Pritchett, D. L., 230
Pruszynski, J. A., 229
Puhl, M. D., 434
Punjabi, N. M., 410
Purger, D., 255
Purkinje, J., 166
Pusey, A. E., 51
Puts, D. A., 379
Pytka, K., 509

Q
Qawasmi, A., 404
Quammen, D., 50
Quick, S. L., 436
Quigley, K. S., 478
Quinlan, C. K., 196
Quiñones-Laracuente, K., 317
Quinsey, V. L., 379
Quirk, G. J., 317, 488
Quiroga, R. Q., 314, 315

R
Rabinstein, A. A., 303
Racine, R. J., 282
Radhakrishnan, R., 424
Raghavachari, S., 111, 322
Raichle, M. E., 35, 149, 174
Raineki, C., 494
Rainer, G., 224
Rainville, P., 207
Raisman, G., 359
Raison, C., 512, 513
Rakic, P., 57, 95, 96, 258
Ralph, M. A. L., 470
Ralph, M. R., 398, 399
Ramachandran, V. S., 262, 292
Ramagopalan, S. V., 67, 278
Ramirez, S., 315
Ramsay, D. S., 332
Ramus, F., 469
Rangarajan, V., 186
Ransohoff, R. M., 278

Rao, S. C., 224, 509
Rapoport, S. I., 512
Rapport, R., 86
Rasmussen, T., 204, 205, 463
Ratliff, F., 171
Rattenborg, N. C., 389
Rauschecker, J. P., 192
Ravindran, L. N., 515
Ravussin, E., 342, 343
Raymond, L. A., 270
Raynor, H. A., 336
Raz, S., 434, 437
Reardon, D. A., 269
Reardon, S., 37, 280, 347, 500, 504
Reber, P. J., 300
Rebsam, A., 256
Recanzone, G. H., 196
Rechtschaffen, A., 393
Reddy, L., 183, 315
Redondo, R. L., 315
Rees, G., 150, 163, 191
Rehm, J., 423
Rehme, A. K., 287
Reichenbach, A., 86, 118
Reichmann, H., 276
Reid, K. J., 397
Reilly, D., 203
Reilly, K. T., 201
Reilly, S., 152
Reimer, D., 371–372
Reiner, W., 372
Rektor, I., 230
Renard, J., 424
Rengaraj, D., 358
Renna, J. M., 398
Rensberger, B., 40
Rensink, R. A., 214
Reschke, E., 87
Resende, L. S., 303
Ressler, K. J., 67, 513–514
Retnakaran, R., 346
Revusky, S. H., 152
Reyes, T. M., 36
Reyes-Centeno, H., 54
Reynolds, D. V., 207
Rezkalla, S. H., 425–426
Rezvani, A. H., 435
Rheims, S., 276
Rho, J. M., 343
Rhodes, S. M., 263
Rial, R. V., 393
Riccio, A., 67
Rich, P. D., 313
Richards, W., 158
Richardson, R., 323
Richmond, R. L., 421
Richter, C., 407
Richter, C. G., 193
Richter, C. P., 396
Ridaura, V. K., 347
Rigato, J., 225
Rigby, N., 368
Rijntjes, M., 240, 290

Riley, E. P., 271, 423
Rilling, J. K., 457
Rinkel, G. J., 270
Riou, M. E., 348
Ripke, S., 500, 504
Rissman, E. F., 367
Ritchey, M., 317
Rizzolatti, G., 226–227
Robbins, T. W., 418, 431, 435, 435–436
Roberts, L., 444, 463, 465
Roberts, S. A., 209
Robertson, L. C., 205, 223
Robins, R. W., 481
Robinson, T. E., 420, 435
Rocca, W. A., 278
Rochetti, M., 424
Rodat-Despoix, L., 201
Rodin, J., 347
Rodman, H. R., 182
Rodríguez, J. J., 86
Rodriguez, M., 227
Rodriguez-Arias, M., 490
Rodriguez-Manzo, G., 377
Roe, A. W., 257
Roecklein, K. A., 398
Roefs, A., 352
Roerecke, M., 423
Roest, A. M., 521
Roesti, M., 51
Rogalsky, C., 457
Rogers, J., 53, 459
Rogers, L. J., 457
Rogers, N. L., 397
Rogers, P. J., 335
Rohde, C., 70
Rolls, B. J., 333, 336
Rolls, E. T., 209, 213, 377
Romano, J. G., 270
Romanski, L. M., 197
Roney, J. R., 374
Rong, F., 459
Roose, S. P., 521
Roper, S. D., 209, 211
Rosa, M. G. P., 182, 392
Rosenblum, L. D., 205
Rosenheck, R., 346
Rosenlicht, N., 388
Rosenwasser, A. M., 398
Rossignol, S., 287
Rossini, P. M., 133
Roth, M. M., 176, 403
Rothstein, M. A., 36
Rothwell, N. J., 221, 343
Rotte, M., 206
Rouach, N., 117, 118
Rowe, J. B., 225
Rowland, D. C., 95, 313
Roy, D. S., 315
Rozin, P., 328
Ruby, N. F., 142
Ruff, C. C., 192, 269
Rugg, M. D., 301
Ruigrok, A. N. V., 366

Rumble, M. E., 405
Rumiati, R. I., 357
Rupp, H. A., 378
Rusakov, D. A., 117, 118
Russell, J. L., 457
Russell, W. R., 444
Russo, S. J., 509
Ruthazer, E. S., 258
Rutherford, B. R., 521
Rutledge, L. L., 479–480
Rutter, M. L., 48
Ruvulo, P., 489
Ryan, A. F., 199
Ryan, T. J., 315, 322
Ryba, N. J. P., 209
Rymer, R., 246
Ryvlin, P., 276

S
Sabatini, B. L., 113, 230
Sabel, A., 182
Sacchetti, E., 504
Sacco, R. L., 270
Sachser, N., 482
Sack, A. T., 132
Sacks, O., 27, 47, 192, 223, 262
Saenz, M., 197
Sagoe, D., 375
Saiga, Y., 142–143
Sakamoto, M., 260
Saksida, L. M., 311, 316
Sakuma, Y., 377
Sale, A., 256
Salmon, P., 499
Salter, M. W., 208
Salzburger, W., 51
Samuels, B. A., 510
Samuelson, R. J., 152
Sanders, A. R., 500
Sanders, C. J., 490
Sanders, H., 313
Sandi, C., 495
Sandoval, D. A., 337
Sandrini, M., 305
Sanes, J. N., 228, 241, 286
Santanach, A., 248
Sapède, D., 404
Saper, C. B., 398, 400
Saproo, S., 214
Sarvaiya, N., 506
Sáry, G., 183
Sassone-Corsi, P., 396, 399
Satpute, A. B., 488
Sattar, N., 346
Sauerbier, A., 276
Saupe, K., 215
Save, E., 313
Savitz, J. B., 513
Sawa, A., 501
Sawle, G. V., 289
Sawtell, N. B., 230
Saygin, A. P., 468
Sbragia, G., 409
Scammell, T. E., 400

Surmeier, D. J., 230, 276
Susilo, T., 185
Sutcliffe, P. A., 380
Sutter, M. L., 196
Sutton, G. G., 39
Suwa, G., 53
Suwannarat, P., 506
Suzuki, W. A., 210, 316
Swaab, D. F., 381
Swanson, S. A., 328
Swapna, I., 258
Sweatt, J. D., 67
Swinnen, S. P., 240
Syed, N. I., 251
Szyf, M., 67

T

Tabri, N., 352
Takahashi, D. Y., 458
Takahashi, J. A., 398
Takahashi, K., 290
Takahashi, Y., 250
Takeuchi, T., 315
Tamakoshi, A., 409–410
Tamariz, E., 252
Tan, Q., 74, 280
Tanaka, K., 316, 317
Tancredi, D. J., 261
Tang, N. K. Y., 405
Tanji, J., 225, 226
Tantiwongkosi, B., 422
Tanzer, M., 241
Tass, P. A., 199
Tattersall, I., 54
Taube, J. S., 313
Tauber, M., 341
Tavares, R. M., 314
Taylor, D., 507
Taylor, V. G., 115–116, 508
Teitelbaum, P., 338
Teixeira, S., 222
Temple, S., 249
Ten Brinke, M. M., 317
Tennissen, A., 291
ter Horst, J. P., 369
Tesmer, J. J. G., 115–116
Testerman, T. L., 491
Teuber, H. L., 181, 287, 303
Thach, W. T., 230
Thase, M. E., 508
Theunissen, F. E., 197
Theuns, J., 276
Theys, T., 185
Thion, M. S., 252
Thissen, S., 158
Thomas, R., 518
Thomas, R. H., 274
Thompson, P. M., 264, 304, 505
Thompson, R. F., 37
Thor, S., 253
Thornhill, R., 374
Thorpe, S. J., 315
Tikidji-Hamburyan, A., 176
Tison, F., 277

Tlachi-López, J. L., 31
Toates, F. M., 333
Todorov, A., 481
Toga, A. W., 264
Tomlinson, D. R., 349
Tompa, T., 183
Tondo, L., 515
Toni, N., 260
Tononi, G., 388, 394
Tooby, J., 36, 59–60
Toppi, J., 392
Torok, M., 428
Tovote, P., 485
Tracy, J. L., 481
Tranel, D., 186
Trayner, P., 517
Treffert, D. A., 262
Treistman, S. N., 416
Treit, D., 153
Tremblay, A., 343
Tresch, M. C., 240
Trevarthen, C., 450
Tribl, G. G., 394
Triplett, J. W., 252
Trivedi, B. P., 211, 341
Trivers, R. L., 58
Trojanowski, J. Q., 276
Trope, Y., 481
Trost, W. J., 257
Tryon, R. C., 68–69
Tsai, H. H., 253
Tsai, L., 210
Tsakiris, M., 47, 206
Tsao, D. Y., 175, 186
Tschida, K., 70
Tse, M. T., 469
Tsetsos, K., 488
Tshala-Katumbay, D., 273
Tsien, J. Z., 139
Tsien, R. W., 111, 116, 262
Tsien, R. Y., 143
Tsou, B. H., 177
Tsuda, M., 208
Tsunozaki, M., 201
Tucker-Drob, E. M., 74
Tulving, E., 301
Tun, P. A., 199
Turcu, A. F., 371
Turek, F. W., 398
Turella, L., 222, 223
Turkheimer, E., 72, 74
Turner, B. O., 454
Turner, R. S., 230
Twain, M., 48
Tweedale, R., 182
Tye, K. M., 484, 485, 516
Tylš, F., 504
Tymianski, M., 270
Tyrlikova, I., 276
Tyssowski, K., 248

U

Uchida, N., 209
Uchtenhagen, A., 428

Uddin, L. Q., 263, 447
Udin, S. B., 251
Ueno, M., 254
Uher, R., 49, 499, 500
Ulanovsky, N., 313
Underwood, E., 81, 253, 271, 277, 280, 313
Ungerleider, L. G., 183, 184, 215

V

Vaccarino, A. L., 313–314
Vaccaro, D., 434
Valeeva, G., 119
Valenstein, E. S., 40–41
Valentino, R. J., 506
Valenzuela, C. F., 423
Valiullina, F., 119
Val-Laillet, D., 333
Vallortigara, G., 457
Van Acker, G. M., 228
van Amsterdam, J., 375
Van Balkom, A. J. L. M., 515
Van Bavel, J. J., 487
van Beugen, B. J., 317
Van Broeckhoven, C., 276
van den Heuvel, M. P., 132
van den Hurk, J., 186
van den Pol, A. N., 273
Van der Haegen, L., 250, 454
van Erp, T. G. M., 505
Van Goozen, S. H. M., 381
van Groen, T., 312
Van Herwegen, J., 263
van Opstal, E. J., 347
Van Praag, H., 259
Van Tilborg, I. A. D. A., 303
Van Vleet, T. M., 223
Van Wagenen, W. P., 447
Varela-Echavarría, A., 252
Vargas, C., 513
Vargha-Khadem, F., 301
Vassoler, F. M., 423
Vauclair, J., 459
Vaughan, C. W., 207
Vaughan, H. G., 303
Vaupel, J. W., 343
Vázquez, G. H., 515
Velay, J. L., 221
Veldhuizen, M. G., 215
Vemuri, P., 278
Verkhratsky, A., 86
Verstraetan, A., 276
Vertes, R. P., 394
Vetter, P., 187
Videnovic, A., 404
Vidyasagar, T. R., 174
Vieta, E., 513
Vigneau, M., 444
Vigneswaran, K., 269
Vilberg, K. L., 301
Villmoare, B., 53
Viscomi, M. T., 274

Vita, A., 505
Vlahov, D., 436
Vo, N. K., 258
Vogel, J. W., 447
Voigt, J. P., 341, 350
Volkmar, F. R., 261
Volkow, N. D., 435
Vollenweider, F. X., 504
Vonck, K., 276
Vonderschen, K., 196
von Economo, B. C., 400
von Kriegstein, K., 454
Voss, M. W., 291
Vouloumanos, A., 262
Vuilleumier, P., 224
Vyazivskiy, V. V., 394

W

Wada, J. A., 147, 443
Wager, T. D., 488, 521
Wagner, H., 196
Wake, H., 86
Wakeland, W., 490
Wald, G., 177
Walford, R. L., 342
Walker, A. W., 347
Walker, L. C., 281
Walker, M. P., 42, 394
Wall, P. D., 206
Wallace, M. T., 196
Wallen, K., 368, 374, 378
Wallis, C., 347
Walløe, S., 26
Walsh, D. M., 281
Wamsteeker Cusulin, J. I., 120
Wandell, B. A., 132
Wang, F., 289
Wang, H., 222, 269
Wang, L., 252
Wang, M., 506, 508
Wang, S., 197, 198
Wang, S. S. H., 262
Wang, Y., 480, 487
Wang, Y. T., 270, 322
Wang, Z., 370
Ware, J. C., 403
Warm, J. S., 392
Warren, K. R., 435
Warrier, C., 455
Washburn, A. L., 339–340
Washington, G., 424
Wasserman, L. M., 177
Watanabe, M., 119
Watanabe, N., 255
Waters, D., 457
Watson, J. B., 46
Watson, J. M., 466
Webb, W. B., 393, 395, 408
Weber, F., 401
Webster, M. M., 152
Wehrl, H. F., 130
Weigelt, S., 30, 262
Weil, R. S., 163
Weiller, C., 290

Subject Index